Endorsements

'This book does a remarkable job providing the first in-depth analysis of global shareholder stewardship. The skill, diversity, and creativity of its contributors – combined with its thoughtful curation and insightful comparative theories – is why this book is destined to be the leading authority in the field. It is a must read for anyone interested in the regulation of financial markets, institutional investors, or corporate governance.'

Marco Becht, Professor of Finance and the Goldschmidt Professor of Corporate Governance, Solvay Brussels School; Executive Director, European Corporate Governance Institute (ECGI)

'This book is a goldmine of information on, and insights into, one of the most important phenomena of contemporary corporate governance: shareholder stewardship. It combines an impressive number of chapters reporting about stewardship and the related soft (and, increasingly, hard) law in individual jurisdictions with a variety of sharp and profound theoretical and comparative analyses of responsible ownership and its implications for listed companies, investors and other stakeholders.'

Luca Enriques, Professor of Corporate Law, Faculty of Law, University of Oxford

'Institutional investors face growing pressure to assume "stewardship" responsibilities through engagement with portfolio companies; "stewardship codes" have proliferated. This superbly imagined and edited volume demonstrates that the contours of "stewardship" vary widely throughout the world, depending on the persistence of controlling owners and different government efforts to deploy "stewardship" in pursuit of various economic and political objectives. The book is essential reading for those seeking to understand the evolving pattern of global corporate governance.'

Jeffrey N. Gordon, Richard Paul Richman Professor of Law, Columbia Law School

'*Global Shareholder Stewardship* is a must-read for institutional investors with international portfolios. Its systematic analysis of stewardship code regulation in major capital markets will be of great value for practitioners. It also tackles critical questions such as the role of index funds and stewardship enforcement, and suggests ways to optimize the impact of stewardship. This is one of the books that will have a place on my desk.'

Dr. Hans Christoph Hirt, Executive Director, Head of EOS, Federated Hermes

'An amazing book fully canvassing global shareholder stewardship. The forty-two authors go well beyond the twenty excellent country reports. They analyse the foundations – the UK Stewardship Code being the international model – and present thorough comparative essays covering topics such as corporate governance, sustainable finance, shareholder stewardship enforcement and ESG, as well as convergence and strong remaining path dependencies. A wealth of economic and legal information, to be bought and read!'

Klaus Hopt, Emeritus Professor, Max Planck Institute of Comparative and International Private Law

'The first comprehensive and sophisticated attempt to examine the proliferation of stewardship codes in recent years, this book elucidates principal issues concerning shareholder stewardship, and at the same time reveals the subtle interaction between local corporate governance factors and the codes of individual jurisdictions. Those who aspire to achieve a mature understanding of this significant global phenomenon will find this admirable outcome of a large-scale international joint endeavour an indispensable source of reference.'

Kon Sik Kim, Professor and Dean Emeritus, Seoul National University School of Law

'Dionysia Katelouzou and Dan Puchniak have orchestrated a masterful study, covering a sample of countries from every inhabited continent, to which they add insightful conceptual analyses. Against a backdrop of genuine urgency in addressing global-scale social challenges, from environmental degradation to climate change, coupled with the emergence of mammoth-size institutional investors, this volume provides an invaluable resource for assessing whether these investors could play a role in addressing such challenges.'

Amir Licht, Professor of Law, Harry Radzymer Law School, Reichman University

'What if shareholders around the world are called to save companies, economies and the planet? In *Global Shareholder Stewardship*, an outstanding group of experts from a wide array of jurisdictions join forces to examine the spread of stewardship codes worldwide as the latest corporate governance trend. Refusing to take global diffusion at face value, the book digs into local manifestations of the phenomenon, unveiling remarkable diversity. A tour de force of comparative scholarship, it offers invaluable lessons for scholars and practitioners in corporate governance and transnational policymaking about the challenges and promises of adapting international developments to different national contexts.'

Mariana Pargendler, Professor of Law at Fundação Getulio Vargas School of Law in São Paulo

'*Global Shareholder Stewardship* is an excellent compendium of codes around the world today. The 2003 ICGN Statement on Institutional Shareholder Responsibilities clarified the important role of investors in holding companies to account for preserving and enhancing long-term sustainable value, ultimately contributing to strong economic growth, prosperous societies and a healthy environment. Nearly two decades later, this book confirms that stewardship is now mainstream and vital in global capital markets to mitigate risk, while also creating long-term sustainable value.'

Kerrie Waring, Chief Executive Officer, International Corporate Governance Network (ICGN)

GLOBAL SHAREHOLDER STEWARDSHIP

This is the first in-depth comparative and empirical analysis of shareholder stewardship, revealing the previously unknown complexities of this global movement. It highlights the role of institutional investors and other shareholders, examining how they use their formal and informal power to influence companies. The book includes an in-depth chapter on every jurisdiction which has adopted a stewardship code and analyzes stewardship in the world's two largest economies without codes. Several comparative chapters draw on the rich body of jurisdiction-specific knowledge, to analyze stewardship comparatively from multiple interdisciplinary perspectives. Ultimately, this book provides a cutting-edge and comprehensive understanding of shareholder stewardship, which challenges existing theories and informs many of the most important debates in comparative corporate law and governance.

Dionysia Katelouzou is Reader at the Dickson Poon School of Law, King's College London and a Research Associate at the Centre of Business Research at the University of Cambridge. Dionysia writes and teaches comparative and transnational corporate law and governance and the regulation of financial institutions. She has earned a reputation for her interdisciplinary legal research, has been involved in policy-related projects and is the recipient of multiple teaching awards and research grants.

Dan W. Puchniak is Associate Professor at the National University of Singapore Faculty of Law and a Research Member of the European Corporate Governance Institute. Dan is an internationally recognized scholar in the field of comparative corporate law and governance in Asia. He has received numerous domestic and international awards for his academic research and teaching.

Global Shareholder Stewardship

Edited by

DIONYSIA KATELOUZOU

King's College London

DAN W. PUCHNIAK

National University of Singapore

CAMBRIDGE UNIVERSITY PRESS

CAMBRIDGE
UNIVERSITY PRESS

University Printing House, Cambridge CB2 8BS, United Kingdom

One Liberty Plaza, 20th Floor, New York, NY 10006, USA

477 Williamstown Road, Port Melbourne, VIC 3207, Australia

314–321, 3rd Floor, Plot 3, Splendor Forum, Jasola District Centre,
New Delhi – 110025, India

103 Penang Road, #05–06/07, Visioncrest Commercial, Singapore 238467

Cambridge University Press is part of the University of Cambridge.

It furthers the University's mission by disseminating knowledge in the pursuit of education, learning, and research at the highest international levels of excellence.

www.cambridge.org
Information on this title: www.cambridge.org/9781108843102
DOI: 10.1017/9781108914819

© Cambridge University Press 2022

This publication is in copyright. Subject to statutory exception
and to the provisions of relevant collective licensing agreements,
no reproduction of any part may take place without the written
permission of Cambridge University Press.

First published 2022

A catalogue record for this publication is available from the British Library.

Library of Congress Cataloging-in-Publication Data
NAMES: Global Shareholder Stewardship Conference (2019 : King's College London) | Katelouzou, Dionysia, editor. | Puchniak, Dan W., 1976– editor.
TITLE: Global shareholder stewardship / edited by Dionysia Katelouzou, King's College London; Dan W. Puchniak, National University of Singapore.
DESCRIPTION: Cambridge, United Kingdom ; New York, NY : Cambridge University Press, 2022. | Includes bibliographical references and index.
IDENTIFIERS: LCCN 2021044800 (print) | LCCN 2021044801 (ebook) | ISBN 9781108843102 (hardback) | ISBN 9781108914819 (ebook)
SUBJECTS: LCSH: Corporate governance – Law and legislation – Congresses. | Stockholders – Legal status, laws, etc. – Congresses. | Social responsibility of business – Law and legislation – Congresses. | LCGFT: Conference papers and proceedings.
CLASSIFICATION: LCC K1327.A6 G56 2019 (print) | LCC K1327.A6 (ebook) | DDC 346/.0664–dc23/eng/20220202
LC record available at https://lccn.loc.gov/2021044800
LC ebook record available at https://lccn.loc.gov/2021044801

ISBN 978-1-108-84310-2 Hardback

Cambridge University Press has no responsibility for the persistence or accuracy of URLs for external or third-party internet websites referred to in this publication and does not guarantee that any content on such websites is, or will remain, accurate or appropriate.

DK
To my family, past and present
DWP
To my wife Norah and son Malakai

Contents

List of Figures		*page* xii
List of Tables		xiv
List of Contributors		xvi
Foreword by Brian R. Cheffins		xix
Acknowledgements		xxii
List of Abbreviations		xxiv

PART I FOUNDATIONS

1. Global Shareholder Stewardship: Complexities, Challenges and Possibilities — 3
   Dionysia Katelouzou and Dan W. Puchniak

2. The UK Stewardship Code 2010–2020: From Saving the Company to Saving the Planet? — 44
   Paul Davies

3. The Market for Stewardship and the Role of the Government — 67
   Dionysia Katelouzou and Eva Micheler

PART II JURISDICTIONS

4. Shareholder Stewardship in the Netherlands: The Role of Institutional Investors in a Stakeholder-Oriented Jurisdiction — 91
   Christoph Van der Elst and Anne Lafarre

5. Capitalist Stakeholders: Shareholder Stewardship in Switzerland — 111
   Daniel Daeniker and Gérard Hertig

6. Institutional Investor Stewardship in Italian Corporate Governance — 130
   Giovanni Strampelli

7. The Danish Stewardship Code: The Past, the Present and the Future — 150
   Hanne S. Birkmose and Marina B. Madsen

8	Stewardship Norwegian-Style: Fragmented and State-Dominated (but Not without Potential?) Jukka Mähönen, Beate Sjåfjell and Monica Mee	174
9	Stewardship and Shareholder Engagement in Germany Wolf-Georg Ringe	192
10	The Japanese Stewardship Code: Its Resemblance and Non-resemblance to the UK Code Gen Goto	222
11	Korea's Stewardship Code and the Rise of Shareholder Activism: Agency Problems and Government Stewardship Revealed Sang Yop Kang and Kyung-Hoon Chun	239
12	The Assessment of Taiwan's Shareholder Stewardship Codes: From International Stewardship Principle to Alternative Good Stewardship Andrew Jen-Guang Lin	261
13	Stewardship in the Hong Kong International Financial Centre: Adding 'Responsible Owners' to an Entrepreneurial Market David C. Donald	284
14	Singapore's Embrace of Shareholder Stewardship: A Puzzling Success Dan W. Puchniak and Samantha S. Tang	297
15	Institutional Investor Stewardship in Malaysia: Code, Context and Challenges Petrina Tan Tjin Yi	316
16	The Thai Institutional Investors Stewardship Code and Its Implementation Patanaporn Kowpatanakit and Piyabutr Bunaramrueang	335
17	Shareholder Stewardship in India: The Desiderata Umakanth Varottil	360
18	Institutional Investors in China: An Autochthonous Mechanism Unrelated to UK-cum-Global Stewardship Dan W. Puchniak and Lin Lin	379
19	Stewardship and Collective Action: The Australian Experience Tim Bowley and Jennifer G. Hill	417
20	Stewardship Principles in Canada Cynthia A. Williams	437
21	The Uncertain Stewardship Potential of Index Funds Jill Fisch	454

22	Encouraging Sustainable Investment in South Africa: CRISA and Beyond Natania Locke	471
23	Stewardship in Kenya: Just a Code or Something More? Austin Ouko	490
24	The Brazilian Stewardship Framework Bruno Bastos Becker, Rafael Andrade and Viviane Muller Prado	507

PART III   COMPARISONS

25	Investment Management, Stewardship and Corporate Governance Roles Roger M. Barker and Iris H.-Y. Chiu	529
26	Sustainable Finance and Stewardship: Unlocking Stewardship's Sustainability Potential Dionysia Katelouzou and Alice Klettner	549
27	Shareholder Stewardship Enforcement Dionysia Katelouzou and Konstantinos Sergakis	572
28	Can a Global Legal Misfit Be Fixed? Shareholder Stewardship in a Controlling Shareholder and ESG World Ernest Lim and Dan W. Puchniak	599
29	Shareholder Stewardship in Asia: Functional Diversity within Superficial Formal Convergence Alan K. Koh, Dan W. Puchniak and Gen Goto	613
30	The Global Diffusion of Stewardship Codes Dionysia Katelouzou and Mathias Siems	631

Index 663

Figures

4.1	Participation rates at Dutch AGMs (%)	page 100
4.2	Mean approval rates for different agenda items (%)	102
4.3	Average number of approving institutional investors for different agenda items (%)	103
4.4	Average number of approving Eumedion members for different agenda items (%)	104
7.1	Comparison of the Danish and UK stewardship principles	155
7.2	Result of the consultation on the individual principles	157
7.3	Result of the consultation on the individual principles (excluding consultation responses with no specific response)	157
7.4	Position towards the individual principles	164
9.1	European AuM by geographical breakdown at end 2017 (in EUR billion and %)	207
9.2	Largest investment funds invested in DAX firms in 2018 (USD million)	209
9.3	Market share of the insurance industry in EU countries as part of the OECD total (2018)	219
9.4	AuM by type of client and country at the end of 2017	219
9.5	Domestic and foreign clients at the end of 2017	220
10.1	Share-ownership structure of Japanese listed companies	226
16.1	Average scores for the five criteria of the OECD Corporate Governance Principles	338
16.2	Signatories to the Thai Code as of 2018	341
16.3	Net purchases by investor groups (million THB/year) on the Thailand SET Index	342
16.4	The largest shareholding and types of investor of SET100	345
16.5	The largest shareholding proportion and types of investor of SET100	345
16.6	Types of investor with the largest shareholding of SET100 and ESG classification	346
16.7	Vote castings of all asset management companies as reported in 2018	353
16.8	Vote castings of twenty-two asset management companies as reported in 2018	353
16.9	Institutional investors and issues they voted for abstention on as reported in 2018	354
16.10	Institutional investors and issues they voted in opposition on as reported in 2018	354
18.1	A-share investors based on market capitalization (2003–18)	384

18.2	A-share institutional investors as a percentage of the free-float market (2003–18)	385
18.3	A taxonomy of institutional investors in China's A-shares market	387
18.4	Network of influence over institutional investors in China	414
30.1	The evolution of stewardship codes	639
30.2	Network showing all >6 per cent overlaps of pairs of codes	645
30.3	Hierarchical cluster of current codes	647
30.4	Relative frequencies of seven stewardship principles	650

Tables

1.1	The seven core principles in the UK Code 2010/2012	page 10
1.2	Percentage of codes that adopted the UK Code 2010/2012's seven principles	13
1.3	Enforcement of stewardship codes	22
1.4	Shareholding statistics in jurisdictions that have adopted stewardship codes	26
1.5	Stewardship codes around the world after 2010	38
4.1	All shareholders', all institutional investors' and Eumedion members' approval rates (%)	108
4.2	Voting items companies with concentrated ownership (%)	108
5.1	Comparison of the UK Code and the Swiss Guidelines	127
7.1	Development in institutional investors' stewardship reporting 2017/18	165
7.2	Engagement by institutional investors	166
7.3	Comprehensiveness of the minutes 2018/19	167
9.1	Top fifteen investors in DAX firms (2018)	208
9.2	Number of pension funds and their assets under management (2018)	218
10.1	Comparison of the Japanese Code 2014 and the UK Code 2012	230
10.2	Signatories to the Japanese Code as of 27 December 2019	232
11.1	Summary of the comparable principles of the Korean Code 2016 and the UK Code 2012	246
13.1	Comparison of the UK Code and the Hong Kong Principles	290
16.1	Summary of the letter of intent, stewardship policy and annual stewardship report (2018)	347
17.1	Shareholding pattern of Indian companies	364
17.2	Specific instances of institutional shareholder activism	365
17.3	Comparison of the stewardship codes of the IDRAI, the PFRDA and SEBI	368
23.1	Trends in investor holdings at the NSE (2009–19)	493
24.1	Reporting by signatories of the AMEC Code	514
24.2	Reporting by foreign signatories of the AMEC Code	515
26.1	ESG consideration in stewardship codes around the world	562
27.1	A broad enforcement taxonomy	576
27.2	Setting and enforcing shareholder stewardship codes around the world	581
27.3	The enforcement taxonomy applied to shareholder stewardship	587
29.1	Percentages of the latest version of jurisdiction-specific codes containing each of the seven principles in the UK Code 2010/12	620
30.1	Stewardship codes around the world	633

30.2	Most similar pairs of codes by common strings	643
30.3	'Marker' words for the principles of the UK Code 2012	649
30.4	Possible explanatory categories	653
30.5	Tests of group differences between post-2012 codes	655
30.6	Coverage of principles at a level equivalent to the UK Code 2012	656
30.7	Ranked similarity to the UK Code 2012 (with 'over-compliance' disregarded)	657
30.8	Length of stewardship codes	660
30.9	Coding of explanatory categories for diffusion	661

Contributors

Rafael Andrade, Guest Professor, Fundação Getulio Vargas Direito

Roger M. Barker, Director of Policy and Governance, The Institute of Directors

Bruno Bastos Becker, Professor, Fundação Getulio Vargas Direito São Paulo

Hanne S. Birkmose, Professor, University of Southern Denmark, Department of Law

Tim Bowley, Sessional Lecturer, Monash University, Faculty of Law

Piyabutr Bunaramrueang, Professor of Law, Chulalongkorn University

Iris H.-Y. Chiu, Professor of Company Law and Financial Regulation, UCL, Faculty of Law

Kyung-Hoon Chun, Professor, Seoul National University, School of Law

Daniel Daeniker, Senior Partner, Homburger AG

Paul Davies, Senior Research Fellow, University of Oxford, Harris Manchester College

David C. Donald, Emeritus Professor, The Chinese University of Hong Kong, Faculty of Law

Jill Fisch, Saul A. Fox Distinguished Professor of Business Law; Co-Director, Institute for Law and Economics, University of Pennsylvania, Carey Law School

Gen Goto, Professor of Law, The University of Tokyo, Graduate Schools for Law and Politics

Gérard Hertig, Professor, Singapore-ETH Centre

Jennifer G. Hill, Chair in Corporate and Commercial Law; Director of the Centre for Commercial Law and Regulatory Studies, Monash University, Faculty of Law

Sang Yop Kang, Professor of Law, Peking University, School of Transnational Law; Research Member, ECGI (European Corporate Governance Institute)

Dionysia Katelouzou, Senior Lecturer (Associate Professor), King's College London, The Dickson Poon School of Law

Alice Klettner, Senior Lecturer, University of Technology Sydney

Alan K. Koh, Assistant Professor of Law, Nanyang Technological University, Nanyang Business School

Patanaporn Kowpatanakit, Professor of Law, Chulalongkorn University

Anne Lafarre, Assistant Professor, Tilburg University, Law School

Ernest Lim, Associate Professor, National University of Singapore, Faculty of Law

Andrew Jen-Guang Lin, Professor, Taiwan National University, College of Law

Lin Lin, Associate Professor, National University of Singapore, Faculty of Law

Natania Locke, Associate Professor in Law, Swinburne University of Technology

Marina B. Madsen, Legal advisor, ph.d., FSR - Danish Auditors

Jukka Mähönen, Professor, University of Oslo, Faculty of Law; Professor, University of Oslo, Faculty of Law

Monica Mee, Director Governance and Finance, NORCAP, Norwegian Refugee Council

Eva Micheler, Associate Professor in Law, London School of Economics

Austin Ouko, General Manager, National Social Security Fund Kenya

Viviane Muller Prado, Professor, Fundação Getulio Vargas Direito São Paulo

Dan W. Puchniak, Associate Professor, National University of Singapore, Faculty of Law and ECGI Research Member

Wolf-Georg Ringe, Director of the Institute of Law and Economics, University of Hamburg; Visiting Professor, University of Oxford, Faculty of Law

Konstantinos Sergakis, Professor of Capital Markets Law and Corporate Governance, University of Glasgow

Mathias Siems, Professor of Private Law and Market Regulation, European University Institute

Beate Sjåfjell, Professor, University of Oslo, Faculty of Law; Adjunct Professor, Norwegian University of Science and Technology

Giovanni Strampelli, Professor of Business Law, Bocconi University

Petrina Tan Tjin Yi, PhD Candidate National University of Singapore, Faculty of Law

Samantha S. Tang, Sheridan Fellow, National University of Singapore, Faculty of Law

Christoph Van der Elst, Professor, Tilburg University, Law School

Umakanth Varottil, Associate Professor, National University of Singapore, Faculty of Law

Cynthia A. Williams, Professor, York University, Osgoode Hall Law School

Foreword

The adage that one should 'never make predictions, especially about the future' has been credited variously to the famous physicist Niels Bohr and baseball legends Yogi Berra and Casey Stengall.[1] Like moths to a flame, however, academics often act as amateur prognosticators. I succumbed to temptation with early work in what is now an extensive literature on stewardship, arguing that the initial UK Stewardship Code, issued in 2010, was unlikely to foster substantially greater shareholder involvement in corporate governance.[2] This prediction has been largely borne out, with respect to both the original UK Code and a modestly revised version issued in 2012.[3]

A second prediction logically followed on from a forecast that the UK Code would be a shareholder activism bust, namely that the UK Code – the world's first[4] – would fail to be influential internationally. Indifference elsewhere would have been a departure from past trends. The Cadbury Corporate Governance Code, issued in 1992, served as a model for the development of corporate governance codes around the world.[5] The UK also was a 'say on pay' pioneer, becoming in 2002 the first of numerous jurisdictions to vest shareholders with a vote on remuneration of their executives.[6] Surely, though, if the UK Code was destined to be a shareholder activism non-event, the UK Code would barely cause a ripple outside Britain.

When I attended the Global Shareholder Stewardship Conference organized by Dionysia Katelouzou and Dan Puchniak in September 2019, it was immediately obvious that I had dodged an academic bullet by failing to commit publicly to this second prediction. At the conference, which would serve as the departure point for *Global Shareholder Stewardship*, speakers from more than twenty countries gave papers discussing stewardship initiatives in their jurisdictions. A recurrent theme was the influence that the UK Code had had on such initiatives. Against the odds, then, yet another British corporate governance innovation had had a meaningful global impact.

In addition to reaffirming the UK's ongoing outsized influence on cross-border corporate governance trends, the present volume is an exemplar of well-executed multi-participant comparative legal scholarship. *Global Shareholder Stewardship* contains twenty-two jurisdiction-specific chapters that offer detailed analysis of stewardship developments 'on the ground',

---

[1] Brian R Cheffins, *The Public Company Transformed* (OUP 2018) 344.
[2] Brian R Cheffins, 'The Stewardship Code's Achilles' Heel' (2010) 73 *Modern Law Review* 1004.
[3] Davies, The UK Stewardship Code 2010–2020, Chapter 2.
[4] Katelouzou and Puchniak, Global Shareholder Stewardship, Chapter 1.
[5] Brian R Cheffins, 'Corporate Governance Reform: Britain as an Exporter' (2000) 8 *Hume Papers on Public Policy* 10, 12–14.
[6] Randall S Thomas and Christoph Van der Elst, 'Say on Pay Around the World' (2015) 92 *Washington University Law Review* 653, 655.

oriented around thoughtful guidance that Katelouzou and Puchniak have provided as editors. There are also eight insightful chapters dealing with key general stewardship themes, one of which is an excellent introductory overview chapter that the editors have co-written.

In their introductory chapter, Katelouzou and Puchniak go well beyond offering a capable roadmap for what follows. For instance, having informed the reader that 'stewardship is far more complex than originally understood', they identify an intellectual upside to this potentially disappointing news, maintaining that 'understanding the drivers and consequences of the complexity is where valuable insights are gained'.[7] Katelouzou and Puchniak then draw skilfully on the findings from the reports from individual jurisdictions that comprise the bulk of *Global Shareholder Stewardship* to offer various such insights. The tone thus is set perfectly for the illuminating chapters which follow.

One topic that Katelouzou and Puchniak handle deftly in their introductory chapter is the seemingly paradoxical combination of the UK Code underperforming domestically while being influential globally. Katelouzou and Puchniak argue that while superficially the UK Code has done much to shape stewardship initiatives elsewhere, there is in fact 'a mirage of global uniformity based on the UK Model of stewardship',[8] with stewardship initiatives elsewhere being weak in comparison. They point out, for instance, that nearly half of the stewardship codes that *Global Shareholder Stewardship* canvasses were generated by fully private organizations rather than being promulgated by a governmental body or a quasi-governmental regulator such as the UK's Financial Reporting Council. Moreover, most stewardship codes around the world are ultimately fully voluntary, lacking a mechanism equivalent to a Financial Conduct Authority Handbook provision that puts UK asset managers under an onus to disclose their approach to stewardship.[9]

Why has the ostensible mimicking of the UK stewardship model resembled a 'mirage'? Katelouzou and Puchniak argue that a desire to convey a commitment to global norms of good corporate governance 'without significantly changing how [a] jurisdiction's corporate governance actually works in practice' has played an important role.[10] They correspondingly reason pessimistically that stewardship has emerged as 'a malleable, inexpensive tool, co-opted by institutional investors and governments to serve their own self-interests'.[11]

The generally gloomy assessment that Katelouzou and Puchniak offer of the stewardship enterprise seemingly does not auger well for a major recent stewardship trend, this being a strong focus on environmental, social and governance (ESG) factors. If stewardship designed to prompt shareholder activism has underwhelmed, the ESG variant seemingly is destined to suffer the same fate. Katelouzou and Puchniak shy away, however, from offering a pessimistic verdict, saying that 'ESG-focused stewardship may comport with the business models of an increasingly large portion of institutional investors'.[12] Perhaps. One has to wonder, though, what stewardship codes will really add to the ESG mix when such codes apparently have done little to prompt increased activism by institutional investors well aware of the theoretical governance case in favour of shareholder-oriented stewardship.

The foregoing quibble regarding ESG and stewardship does not detract in any way from a major academic accomplishment. For those largely unfamiliar with the corporate governance

---

[7] Katelouzou and Puchniak, Global Shareholder Stewardship, Chapter 1.
[8] ibid.
[9] COBS 2.2.3R (06/12/2010).
[10] Katelouzou and Puchniak, Global Shareholder Stewardship, Chapter 1.
[11] ibid.
[12] ibid.

version of stewardship, *Global Shareholder Stewardship* provides an excellent multi-jurisdictional introduction. Those already well versed in the stewardship literature will learn valuable lessons from the richly detailed chapters on individual jurisdictions and from the perceptive chapters that provide stewardship context. *Global Shareholder Stewardship*, in sum, is an outstanding example of comparative corporate governance/corporate law scholarship. Enjoy.

Brian R. Cheffins
SJ Berwin Professor of Corporate Law, Faculty of Law, University of Cambridge

Acknowledgements

What started off in 2018 as a small academic dream has materialized into an exciting intellectual odyssey that reveals what this book coins 'Global Shareholder Stewardship'. This book project shatters the narrow, myopic, and inaccurate prior understanding of UK-centric shareholder stewardship. The result is a multi-jurisdictional, pluralistic, and truly global understanding that illuminates the complexities, challenges, and possibilities of one of the most intriguing corporate governance and financial regulatory mechanisms of our time.

To state the obvious, such a global intellectual odyssey could not have been achieved without global collaborations. The foundations of this book were built on a unique gathering – the Global Shareholder Stewardship Conference – held at King's College London (KLC) in 2019 which, for the first time, brought together corporate law experts, regulators, and practitioners from each of the twenty jurisdictions with a stewardship code – and other major economies without a code – to undertake an in-depth contextual, comparative and empirical analysis of shareholder stewardship. Global Shareholder Stewardship would not have come to be properly understood without the participants of the conference and, most importantly, each of the authors in this book. The books authors – a remarkable group of intellectual leaders which we have had the honor of working together with – are the source of all the ideas that are in the exciting pages that follow. At this point we can only say two words to the authors: Thank you!

However, intellectuals cannot live on ideas alone and books do not emerge out of thin air. We are grateful to the British Academy's Partnership with the Department for Business, Energy, and Industrial Strategy, the European (SRG1819\190891), the Social Research Council (ESRC) Social Science Impact Fund, the Dickson Poon School of Law (KCL) and the Transnational Law Institute (KCL) for funding the inaugural Global Shareholder Stewardship Conference. We are also grateful to the National University of Singapore Faculty of Law (NUS Law) – particularly the Centre for Asian Legal Studies (CALS) and the EW Barker Centre for Law and Business (EWBCLB) for generously supporting this book project as well as the King's Undergraduate Research Fellowship scheme (2020–21). Our sincere thanks also go to the European Corporate Governance Institute (ECGI) which supported the inaugural Global Shareholder Stewardship Conference and highlighted the research in our project. As in most academic projects, research assistants were invaluable in producing this book – and we were particularly blessed with magnificent ones. We acknowledge and sincerely thank Jordan Ng Qi Le from NUS Law for his exceptional work as the lead research assistant throughout this project – which exceeded our highest expectations and was at the core of the book's production. In addition, we are grateful to Ivan Tan Ren Yi from NUS Law for his exceptional research assistant work on the China, Asia, and comparative chapters. Further, we are grateful to Jean Ang, Koh

Kai Jie, and Chen Ching Kuang from NUS Law who also skilfully assisted as research assistants with early draft chapters in this book as well as Gabriella Gropper and Zuraiha Binti Yusof, two students at KCL, who have been essential in getting the book wrapped up for submission to the publisher. We are thankful to Cambridge University Press for being a remarkable publisher, with the skill, knowhow, and experience to bring out the best in academic scholarship.

Last, but not least, we thank you for taking the time to read this book. We hope that you enjoy reading it as much as we enjoyed working on it.

Dionysia Katelouzou, London, March 2022
Dan W Puchniak, Singapore, March 2022

Abbreviations

1MDB	1Malaysia Development Berhad
ABRAPP	National Association of Pension Funds (Brazil)
ACSI	Australian Council of Superannuation Investors
AEX	Euronext Amsterdam
AFC	1997 Asian Financial Crisis
AFM	Dutch Financial Supervisory Authority
AGM	annual general meeting
AIF	alternative investment fund
AIFM	alternative investment fund managers
AIFMD	Alternative Investment Fund Managers Directive
AIMC	Association of Investment Management Companies
AIMG	Australian Investment Managers Group
AMEC	Association of Capital Markets Investors (Brazil)
AMNT	Association of Member Nominated Trustees
AMX	Amsterdam Midkap Exchange
ANBIMA	Financial and Capital Markets Association (Brazil)
APIMEC	Association of Capital Markets Analysts and Investment Professionals (Brazil)
ARUG II	*Aktionärs-Richtlinie-Umsetzungs-Gesetz* (Second Shareholders' Rights Directive)
ASEAN	Association of South East Asian Nations
ASIC	Australian Securities and Investments Commission
ASISA	Association for Saving and Investment South Africa
Assodire	Association of Responsible Investors (Italy)
ASX	Australian Securities Exchange
ATP	*Arbejdsmarkedets Tillidspension* (Labour Market Supplementary Pension)
AuM	assets under management
BaFin	Federal Financial Supervisory Authority (Germany)
BATSETA	Principal Officers Association
BEA	Bank of East Asia
BEIS	Department for Business, Energy and Industrial Strategy (UK)
BNDES	Brazilian Development Bank
BNDESPAR	BNDES Participações S.A.
BTS	Bangkok Mass Transit System
BVI	Bundesverband Investment und Asset Management e.V. (German Investment Funds Association)

CAD	Canadian dollar
CBCA	Canada Business Corporations Act
CBIRC	China Banking and Insurance Regulatory Commission
CCGG	Canadian Coalition for Good Governance
CCP	Chinese Communist Party
CEO	chief executive officer
CGC	Corporate Governance Code (UK)
CIRC	China Insurance Regulatory Commission
CMA	Competition and Markets Authority (UK) *or* Capital Markets Authority (Kenya)
CMN	*Conselho Monetário Nacional* (Brazil)
CMRA	Capital Markets Regulatory Authority
CONSOB	Financial Markets Supervisory Authority (Italy)
Covid-19	Coronavirus disease 2019
CP	Canadian Pacific
CRISA	Code for Responsible Investing in South Africa
CSA	Canadian Securities Administrators
CSR	corporate social responsibility
CSRC	China Securities Regulatory Commission
CVM	Securities and Exchange Commission (Brazil)
DAX	*Deutscher Aktienindex* (German stock index)
DC	defined contribution
DCC	Dutch Civil Code
DCGC	Dutch Corporate Governance Code
DIA	Dow Jones Industrial Average
DLT	distributed ledger technology
DNV	decision not to vote
DOL	Department of Labor (US)
DRRR	Directors' Remuneration Report Regulations (2002)
DVFA	German Association of Investment Professionals
DWP	Department for Work and Pensions (UK)
EFAMA	European Fund and Asset Management Association
EGCO	Electricity Generating Public Company Limited
EGM	extraordinary general meeting
EPS	earnings per share
ERISA	Employee Retirement Income Security Act
ESG	environmental, social and governance
ETF	exchange traded fund
EU	European Union
EUR	euro
EY	Ernst & Young Global Limited
FB77	Family Business Campaign
FCA	Financial Conduct Authority
FKI	Federation of Korean Industries
FRC	Financial Reporting Council
FSA	Financial Services Agency (Japan)

FSC	Financial Services Commission (South Korea) *or* Financial Services Council (Australia)
FSCA	Financial Sector Conduct Authority
FSDC	Financial Stability and Development Council (India)
FSMA	Financial Services and Markets Authority (Belgium)
FSS	Financial Supervisory Services (South Korea)
G20	Group of Twenty
GCGC	German Corporate Governance Code
GDP	gross domestic product
GEPF	Government Employees Pension Fund
GFC	2008 Global Financial Crisis
GLC	government-linked company
GLIC	government-linked investment company
GPF	Government Pension Fund (Thailand)
GPIF	Government Pension Investment Fund
GRI	Global Reporting Initiative
GSIA	Global Sustainable Investment Alliance
GTSM	Gre Tai Securities Market
HDFC	Housing Development Finance Corporation
HLEG	High-Level Expert Group on Sustainable Finance
IBGC	Institute of Corporate Governance (Brazil)
ICGN	International Corporate Governance Network
IDC	Investment Decision Committee
IFC	International Financial Centre
II Council	Institutional Investors Council Malaysia
IIFA	International Investment Funds Association
ILO	International Labour Organization
IMF	International Monetary Fund
IOD	Institution of Directors Association (Thailand)
IoDSA	Institute of Directors in Southern Africa
IOSCO	International Organization of Securities Commissions
IPO	initial public offering
IRDAI	Insurance Regulatory and Development Authority of India
ISA	individual savings account
ISC	Institutional Shareholders' Committee (UK)
ISG	Investor Stewardship Group
ISS	Institutional Shareholder Services Inc.
JSE	Johannesburg Stock Exchange
KAG	*Kapitalanlagegesellschaft* (investment fund management companies)
KCC	Korean Commercial Code
KCGS	Korea Corporate Governance Service
KCMI	Korea Capital Market Institute
KDB	Korea Development Bank
KEPCO	Korea Electric Power Corporation
KLCA	Korea Listed Companies Association
KLP	*Kommunal Landspensjonskasse Gjensidig Forsikringsselskap* (mutual insurance company in Norway)

KOFIA	Korea Financial Investment Association
KOSDAQ	Korean Securities Dealers Automated Quotations
KOSDAQA	Korean Securities Dealers Automated Quotations Listed Companies Association
KRW	Korean won
LD	*Lønmodtagernes Dyrtidsfond* (The Cost-of-Living Allowance Fund, Denmark)
LSE	London Stock Exchange
M&A	mergers and acquisitions
MiFID I	Market in Financial Instruments Directive (2007)
MiFID II	Market in Financial Instruments Directive (2018)
MOF	Ministry of Finance (China)
MSWG	Minority Shareholder Watchdog Group
NAV	net asset value
NBIM	Norges Bank Investment Management
NCAs	National Competent Authorities
NCGB	Norwegian Corporate Governance Board
NED	non-executive director
NEST	National Employment Savings Trust (UK)
NGO	non-governmental organization
NPO	non-profit organization
NPS	National Pension Service (Korea)
NSE	Nairobi Securities Exchange
NSSF	National Social Security Fund
NT$	new Taiwan dollar
OECD	Organisation for Economic Co-operation and Development
OSC	Ontario Securities Commission
PBOC	People's Bank of China
PFRDA	Pension Fund Regulatory and Development Authority (India)
PIC	Public Investment Corporation
POE	private-owned enterprise
POII	private-owned institutional investor
PREVIC	National Pension Funds Authority (Brazil)
PRI	UN Principles of Responsible Investment
QFII	qualified foreign institutional investor
REIT	real estate investment trust
RG 128	Regulatory Guide 128: Collective Action by Investors
RMB	Chinese renminbi
ROE	return on equity
RPTs	related party transactions
RQFII	Renminbi qualified foreign institutional investor
SAC	Securities Association of China
SAFE	State Administration of Foreign Exchange
SASAC	State-owned Assets Supervision and Administration Commission of the State Council
SCBP	Swiss Code of Best Practice for Corporate Governance
SDGs	Sustainable Development Goals
SDX	Shareholder-Director Exchange
SEBI	Securities and Exchange Board of India

SEC	Securities and Exchange Commission
SEHK	Stock Exchange of Hong Kong
SET	Stock Exchange of Thailand
SFC	Securities and Futures Commission (Hong Kong)
SFIPA	Securities Investor and Futures Trader Protection Act
SFIPC	Securities and Futures Investors Protection Center (Taiwan)
SGX	Singapore Exchange
ShareSoc	Shareholders Society (UK)
SID	senior independent director
SIF	securities investment fund
SITCA	Securities Investment Trust and Consulting Association of the ROC
SME	small and medium-sized enterprise
SOCSO	Social Security Organization (also known as PERKESO)
SOE	state-owned enterprise
SOII	state-owned institutional investor
SRD I	Shareholder Rights Directive
SRD II	Revised Shareholder Rights Directive
SRI	socially responsible investment
SSF	Social Security Fund (Thailand)
SSO	Social Security Office (Thailand)
SWF	sovereign wealth fund
TCFD	Task Force on Climate-related Financial Disclosures
THB	Thai baht
TIA	Thai Investors Association
TPEx	Taipei Exchange
TPR	The Pensions Regulator (UK)
TSEA	Taiwan Securities and Exchange Act (2006)
TSMC	Taiwan Semiconductor Corporation
TSX	Toronto Stock Exchange
TSXV	TSX Venture Exchange
TWSE	Taiwan Stock Exchange
UCITS	Undertakings for the Collective Investment in Transferable Securities
UK	United Kingdom
UK Code	UK Stewardship Code
UKSA	UK Shareholders Association
UKSIF	UK Sustainable Investment and Finance Association
UN	United Nations
UNCTAD	United Nations Conference on Trade and Development
UNEP FI	United Nations Environment Programme Finance Initiative
UNGP	UN Guiding Principles on Business and Human Rights
UNPRI	United Nations Principles for Responsible Investment
US	United States
USD	United States dollar
VFF	Fund and Asset Manager Association (Norway)
WVR	weighted voting rights
ZAR	South African rand

PART I

Foundations

1

Global Shareholder Stewardship

Complexities, Challenges and Possibilities

Dionysia Katelouzou and Dan W. Puchniak[*]

1.1 INTRODUCTION

In 2019, when we started this research project, the world was a very different place. Not only could we never have anticipated that, as this book went to press, facemasks would be a ubiquitous accessory, but it was beyond our wildest imaginations how much our understanding of *shareholder stewardship* would expand and evolve. As the excitement of research lies in discovering the unknown, the pages that follow in this book are full of excitement as they reveal many important discoveries.

Upon reflection, perhaps from the outset, we should have been more sanguine about the prospects for this research project. In 2010, the United Kingdom hastily released the world's first stewardship code (UK Code 2010) in response to the 2008 Global Financial Crisis (GFC).[1] The UK Code 2010 was designed to cure what was perceived to be the UK's primary corporate governance malady: rationally passive institutional investors in a country characterized by a dispersed ownership structure. It sought to achieve this by using a 'soft'[2] law code to incentivize institutional investors – who own most of the shares in UK listed companies[3] – to become actively engaged shareholder 'stewards'.

In the 2010s, this bespoke solution to the UK's 'ownerless corporations' problem went global. UK-style stewardship codes (in the broad sense) now exist in twenty jurisdictions, on six

---

[*] The authors would like to thank the Centre for Asian Legal Studies at the National University of Singapore Faculty of Law for funding the research assistance for the chapter and Jordan Ng for his exceptional work as a research assistant. Any errors remain our own.

[1] Financial Reporting Council, *The UK Stewardship Code* (July 2010) www.frc.org.uk/getattachment/e223e152-5515-4cdc-a951-da33e093eb28/UK-Stewardship-Code-July-2010.pdf accessed 25 May 2021 [hereinafter UK Code 2010].

[2] 'Soft', non-binding and more often non-statist rules in corporate governance – as opposed to 'hard', legally binding and statist rules – have a long history back to the exponential rise of corporate governance codes in the 1990s. While this binary distinction between soft and hard law rules is important in heuristic terms, it is important to recognize that in practice there are overlaps between the two and soft corporate governance norms often bear a high degree of coerciveness. See e.g. Gregory C Shaffer and Mark A Pollack, 'Hard vs. Soft Law: Alternatives, Complements, and Antagonists in International Governance' (2010) 94 *Minnesota Law Review* 706, 716 (examining the relationship between hard and soft law and noting that 'hard and soft law are best seen not as binary categories but rather as choices arrayed along a continuum'). For a more recent discussion in the area of corporate governance rules, see Dionysia Katelouzou and Peer Zumbansen, 'The New Geographies of Corporate Governance' (2020) 42 *University of Pennsylvania Journal of International Law* 51, 114–20.

[3] The latest data from the Office of National Statistics reveal that 80.4% of UK public equity as of 2018 is in the hands of institutional investors, but the majority of them (54.9%) are foreign (non-UK) investors. See Office for National Statistics, 'Ownership of UK Quoted Shares: 2018' (14 January 2020) www.ons.gov.uk/releases/ownershipofukquotedshares2018 accessed 4 February 2022.

continents, and are embedded in a panoply of legal systems, shareholder markets and corporate cultures.[4] In addition, stewardship codes have been developed at international and regional levels,[5] making shareholder stewardship an international corporate law phenomenon.[6] The appearance of UK-style stewardship codes and similar initiatives in such diverse and foreign environments should have alerted us to the fact that there was still much to be explored – but the existing Anglo-American-centric scholarship was blinding.[7]

To the best of our knowledge, before this project, never before had corporate law experts from each of the twenty jurisdictions with a stewardship code been brought together to undertake an in-depth contextual, comparative and empirical analysis of shareholder stewardship.[8] The result of this undertaking – which also includes analyses of stewardship in the world's two largest economies without stewardship codes (China and Germany) – is the revelation that stewardship

---

[4] Appendix (Table 1.5) and Table 1.2. We adopt the broadest definition of stewardship codes as including 'preliminary stewardship initiatives'. As such, we have included Norway in the appendix of stewardship codes in this chapter (see Appendix, Table 1.5) and included a chapter on Norway in this book for comparative purposes. For the definitional distinction between stewardship codes and preliminary stewardship initiatives on the basis of three criteria (drafting style, content and scope), see Katelouzou and Siems, The Global Diffusion of Stewardship Codes, Chapter 30. See also Mähönen, Sjåfjell and Mee, Stewardship Norwegian-Style, Chapter 8 (noting that Norway does not have a stewardship code in the conventional sense but a 'preliminary stewardship initiative').

[5] The most important transnational stewardship codes include the ones developed by the European Fund and Asset Management Association (EFAMA) and the International Corporate Governance Network (ICGN). The revised EU Shareholder Rights Directive (Directive (EU) 2017/828 of the European Parliament and of the Council of 17 May 2017 amending Directive 2007/36/EC as regards the encouragement of long-term shareholder engagement [2017] OJ L132/1 (SRD II)) also incorporates aspects of shareholder stewardship usually found in stewardship codes in its articles 3g (engagement policy), 3h (investment strategy of institutional investors and arrangements with asset managers) and 3i (transparency of asset managers), but it is excluded from the Appendix (Table 1.5) because of its legal nature as a directive rather than a code. Further on the stewardship provisions of the SRD II, see Iris H-Y Chiu and Dionysia Katelouzou, 'From Shareholder Stewardship to Shareholder Duties: Is the Time Ripe?' in Hanne S Birkmose (ed), *Shareholders' Duties* (Kluwer Law International 2017) 131–52 and Dionysia Katelouzou and Konstantinos Sergakis, 'When Harmonization Is Not Enough: Shareholder Stewardship in the European Union' (2021) 22 *European Business Organization Law Review* 203.

[6] The role of international organizations as key standard-setters of corporate law today is illuminated in the recent work by Pargendler, who highlights that, in the area of stewardship, the IMF and the World Bank have also supported the diffusion of norms through their ROSC (Report on the Observance of Standards and Codes) assessments. See Mariana Pargendler, 'The Rise of International Corporate Law' (2021) 98 *Washington University Law Review* 1765.

[7] Gen Goto, Alan K Koh and Dan W Puchniak, 'Diversity of Shareholder Stewardship in Asia: Faux Convergence' (2020) 53 *Vanderbilt Journal of Transnational Law* 829. See also Koh, Puchniak and Goto, Shareholder Stewardship in Asia, Chapter 29. It should be noted that Jennifer Hill's article (Jennifer G Hill, 'Good Activist/Bad Activist: The Rise of International Stewardship Codes' (2018) 41 *Seattle University Law Review* 497) stands out as a piece of research that preceded this project in undertaking a comparative analysis of stewardship. However, as noted in Chapter 29, '[a]lthough Hill correctly identifies the difference in policy objectives between [codes,] she does not go so far as to consider the alternative possibility that stewardship itself means different things in [different jurisdictions]'. In a subsequent article, Hill summarized recent developments in Asia as follows: 'Japan adopted its own Stewardship Code, based on the U.K. model, in 2014, and many other Asian jurisdictions have now followed suit.' See Jennifer G Hill, 'The Trajectory of American Corporate Governance: Shareholder Empowerment and Private Ordering Combat' [2019] *University of Illinois Law Review* 507, 516.

[8] The following chapters all contain empirical evidence: Van der Elst and Lafarre, Shareholder Stewardship in the Netherlands, Chapter 4; Birkmose and Madsen, The Danish Stewardship Code, Chapter 7; Ringe, Stewardship and Shareholder Engagement in Germany, Chapter 9; Kang and Chun, Korea's Stewardship Code and the Rise of Shareholder Activism, Chapter 11; Lin, The Assessment of Taiwan's Shareholder Stewardship Codes, Chapter 12; Donald, Stewardship in the Hong Kong International Financial Centre, Chapter 13; Tan, Institutional Investor Stewardship in Malaysia, Chapter 15; Kowpatanakit and Bunaramrueang, Thai Institutional Investors Stewardship Code and Its Implementation, Chapter 16; Varottil, Shareholder Stewardship in India, Chapter 17; Puchniak and Lin, Institutional Investors in China, Chapter 18; Ouko, Stewardship Code in Kenya, Chapter 23; Katelouzou and Klettner, Sustainable Finance and Stewardship, Chapter 26; Katelouzou and Sergakis, Shareholder Stewardship Enforcement, Chapter 27; Katelouzou and Siems, The Global Diffusion of Stewardship Codes, Chapter 30.

is far more complex than originally understood. However, merely revealing that something is complex is of marginal benefit – understanding the drivers and consequences of the complexity is where valuable insights are gained.

Against this backdrop, the goal of this chapter is to explain why shareholder stewardship around the world – *global shareholder stewardship* – is far more complex than the existing literature suggests, and how this complexity impacts current theories and existing practices. To explain complexity, this chapter provides a loose taxonomy of global shareholder stewardship by categorizing stewardship along three dimensions. The first dimension illuminates how stewardship can be *conceived* in a variety of ways – which makes the intellectual exercise of understanding stewardship complex and presents a challenge for policymakers to implement an idea with multiple conceptions. The second dimension compares the *formal design* and the *content* of stewardship codes globally and reveals that they have largely been modelled after the first version of the UK Code (2010/2012) – creating a mirage of global uniformity based on the UK model of stewardship. The third dimension demonstrates how the different origins of the codes (government codes versus institutional investor codes), a variety of mechanisms for enforcing (or not enforcing) codes, and jurisdiction-specific corporate governance factors that impact how the codes *function*, result in stewardship serving a variety of functions which would have never been anticipated by the original drafters of the UK Code. This complexity, which has largely been overlooked in the literature, creates *distinct varieties of stewardship*. Based on the distinct varieties of stewardship in jurisdictions around the world, this chapter concludes by illuminating the *challenges* and *possibilities* of global shareholder stewardship. The taxonomy also serves as a useful lens for observing the common themes and points of intersection that make the whole of this book greater than the sum of its individual chapters.

1.2 MULTIPLE CONCEPTIONS OF SHAREHOLDER STEWARDSHIP: INTELLECTUAL COMPLEXITY REVEALED

The starting point for any comparative analysis is to identify the subject of comparison. At the outset of this project, we (incorrectly) assumed that this would be relatively simple as the project was focused on a global comparison of 'shareholder stewardship'. What we quickly realized, however, was that 'shareholder stewardship' is an ambiguous term which has come to mean different things, at different times, in different places.

From our review of the chapters in this book, there are at least five conceptions of what the term 'shareholder stewardship' means. The first conception is that institutional investors will *actively engage* as 'stewards' in the *corporate governance* of companies in which they are shareholders. This concept of stewardship fits with the idea behind the original UK Code 2010 and its revised 2012 version:[9] to incentivize passive institutional investors to become active shareholder stewards by using a 'comply or explain' code.[10] In theory, this concept of stewardship made sense in the UK context as institutional investors own a majority of shares in listed companies and, therefore, collectively have the legal right to steward them *if* they have the incentive to do so. Although, in theory, the concept was sound, in practice, after a decade, the

---

[9] Financial Reporting Council, *The UK Stewardship Code* (September 2012) <www.frc.org.uk/getattachment/d67933f9-ca38-4233-b603-3d24b2f62c5f/UK-Stewardship-Code-(September-2012).pdf> accessed 25 May 2021 [hereinafter UK Code 2012].

[10] The overall aim of shareholder stewardship in the original UK codes was to promote long-term shareholder value in alignment with the principle of enlightened shareholder value which is mandated under the Companies Act 2006, s 172. See Dionysia Katelouzou, *The Path to Enlightened Shareholder Stewardship* (CUP) (forthcoming).

consensus is that the UK Codes 2010 and 2012 (which are fundamentally the same)[11] failed to incentivize institutional investors to become actively engaged shareholder stewards.[12] Surprisingly, despite this domestic failure, this original, corporate governance–focused concept of stewardship appears in the overwhelming majority of the jurisdictions in the world that have adopted a stewardship code (a curiosity that we will examine in detail).

However, despite its global ubiquity, this original, corporate governance–focused concept of stewardship is a *misfit* in all the jurisdictions that have adopted a code, with the notable exceptions of the UK and the US.[13] This is because, outside of the UK and the US, institutional investors rarely own a majority of shares in listed companies.[14] Therefore, even if the code succeeds in transforming institutional investors into actively engaged shareholders, they will not have the collective legal power to 'steward' listed companies in most of the jurisdictions around the world. This is reinforced by the fact that, outside of the UK and the US, and a handful of other jurisdictions, a substantial portion of companies have a rationally active *controlling-block shareholder* who has both the legal rights and the economic incentive to steward the company.[15] In these jurisdictions, 'ownerless companies' are virtually non-existent and passive institutional investors – who own only a minority of shares in listed companies – are more akin to 'absentee tenants' than 'absentee landlords'.[16] Thus, in practice, outside of the UK and the US, the original corporate governance–focused conception of stewardship on the part of institutional investors theoretically should have a completely different target.

This is how the second conception of stewardship emerged. While in the UK and the US the direct target of shareholder stewardship is corporate (mis)management, in jurisdictions with increased concentration of equity ownership, shareholder stewardship arguably should be conceived to transform institutional investors into actively engaged shareholders to monitor controlling shareholders and reduce 'tunnelling'.[17] Using the economic jargon, while the first conception of shareholder stewardship aims to minimize the agency problems between corporate managers and shareholders, the second conception aims to solve the agency problems between majority and controlling shareholders.[18] Although controlling shareholders, rather than management, should be the key target of corporate governance–focused shareholder stewardship where concentrated ownership structures prevail, there is surprisingly no stewardship code which has explicitly adopted this second conception of stewardship. Rather, as will be explained, almost all stewardship codes have been modelled on the UK Code 2010/2012, and there are only passing references to the need for engagement by institutional investor-stewards with controlling shareholders in two jurisdictional-specific codes, those of

---

[11] See also Davies, The UK Stewardship Code 2010–2020, Chapter 2, and Katelouzou (n 10) (referring to them together as the 'first version' or 'first generation' of the UK Code, respectively).

[12] For an early critique, see Brian R Cheffins, 'The Stewardship Code's Achilles' Heel' (2010) 73 *Modern Law Review* 1004. More recently, see John Kingman, 'Independent Review of the Financial Reporting Council' (Department for Business, Energy and Industrial Strategy, December 2018) https://assets.publishing.service.gov.uk/government/uploads/system/uploads/attachment_data/file/767387/frc-independent-review-final-report.pdf accessed 4 February 2022 [hereinafter Kingman Review]; Edward Rock, 'Institutional Investors in Corporate Governance' in Jeffrey Gordon and Wolf-Georg Ringe (eds), *The Oxford Handbook of Corporate Law and Governance* (OUP 2018) 16–28.

[13] Dan W Puchniak, 'The False Hope of Stewardship in the Context of Controlling Shareholders: Making Sense Out of the Global Transplant of a Legal Misfit' *The American Journal of Comparative Law* (forthcoming).

[14] Puchniak (n 13); see also Lim and Puchniak, Can a Global Legal Misfit Be Fixed?, Chapter 28.

[15] Puchniak (n 13). For a detailed discussion, see this chapter, Section 1.4.

[16] Puchniak (n 13); see also Lim and Puchniak, Can a Global Legal Misfit Be Fixed?, Chapter 28.

[17] Puchniak (n 13). See also Lim and Puchniak, Can a Global Legal Misfit Be Fixed?, Chapter 28; Koh, Puchniak and Goto, Shareholder Stewardship in Asia, Chapter 29; Goto, Koh and Puchniak (n 7).

[18] For a seminal analysis of the various legal strategies to mitigate these agency problems, see Reinier Kraakman and others (eds), *The Anatomy of Corporate Law: A Comparative and Functional Approach* (3rd edn, OUP 2017).

Canada and Kenya.[19] The International Corporate Governance Network (ICGN) model code also provides that, '[i]n the case of controlled companies, investor engagement may also extend to meeting with controlling shareholders'.[20] But these passing references to controlling shareholders in the current stewardship codes fall short of focusing on the potential of institutional shareholder-driven stewardship to act as a check on controlling shareholder power.[21]

The third conception of stewardship identifies the corporate governance actor who has actual control over the company and creates a code to try to encourage that actor to steward the company in a way that maximizes the benefits for all stakeholders. The most prominent example of this is the 'Stewardship Principles for Family Businesses' in Singapore (Singapore Family Code).[22] The concept at the core of the Singapore Family Code is to use soft law to incentivize family controllers to use their controlling power to benefit all corporate stakeholders and society. This concept of stewardship arguably makes sense in the Singaporean context as a majority of listed companies are family firms with controlling shareholders who have both the legal right and the economic incentive to steward the company.[23] Stewardship Asia, which is based in Singapore and released the Singapore Family Code, has been promoting it throughout Asia where family firms make up a significant portion of listed companies in many jurisdictions.[24] While the Family Code has not yet gained traction in other jurisdictions, conceiving of controlling shareholders, such as family controllers or the state, as stewards is not alien to the way in which shareholder stewardship is, in reality, already practised in many jurisdictions with concentrated ownership structures.[25] Private benefits of control may jeopardize the effectiveness and efficiency of this type of stewardship,[26] but what becomes clear is that current stewardship

---

[19] See Principle 4 of the Canadian Code (Canadian Coalition for Good Governance, 'Stewardship Principles' (May 2020) <https://ccgg.ca/wp-content/uploads/2020/05/2020-Stewardship-Principles-CCGG-new-branding.pdf> accessed 25 May 2021) and paragraph 2 of the application section of the Kenyan Code (Stewardship Code for Institutional Investors 2017 (9 May 2017), enacted by the Capital Markets Authority vide Kenya Gazette Notice No. 6016 dated 23 June 2017), respectively. It is also notable that the Securities and Futures Commission in its consultation preceding the adoption of the Hong Kong code noted that '[i]n a market dominated by controlling shareholders, there is evidence to support the view that investors will often find it more productive to engage directly with the controlling shareholder rather than seek to engage with the board of directors as a whole through the usual voting channels'. See Securities and Futures Commission, 'Consultation Paper on the Principles of Responsible Ownership' (2015) 6, para 25 <www.sfc.hk/edistributionWeb/gateway/EN/consultation/openFile?refNo=15CP2> accessed 29 May 2021. But this different target of stewardship was not incorporated in the final Hong Kong code: see Koh, Puchniak and Goto, Shareholder Stewardship in Asia, Chapter 29. See also Goto, Koh and Puchniak (n 7).

[20] International Corporate Governance Network, ICGN Global Governance Principles (2016) 17, Principle 4.4 <http://icgn.flpbks.com/icgn-global-stewardship-principles/files/extfile/DownloadURL.pdf> accessed 25 May 2021. For a discussion of this point, see Goto, Koh and Puchniak (n 7).

[21] It is noteworthy that the 2018 Chinese Corporate Governance Code appears to adopt the second concept of stewardship in its attempt to incentivize institutional investors to engagement in the corporate governance of their investee companies to act as a check on controlling shareholders. However, as explained in Puchniak and Lin, Institutional Investors in China, Chapter 18, this use of institutional investors as a check on controlling shareholder power has a long history in China and must be understood on its own terms. To label it as 'stewardship' would be to incorrectly impose an Anglo-American understanding on an autochthon Chinese corporate governance mechanism.

[22] Stewardship Asia Centre, Stewardship Principles for Family Businesses (2018) <www.stewardshipasia.com.sg/sites/default/files/2020-09/SPFB-brochure-0913.pdf> accessed 25 May 2021 [hereinafter Singapore Family Code]. Puchniak and Tang, Singapore's Embrace of Shareholder Stewardship, Chapter 14.

[23] Puchniak and Tang, Singapore's Embrace of Shareholder Stewardship, Chapter 14. See Lim and Puchniak, Can a Global Legal Misfit Be Fixed?, Chapter 28 for a critique of the Singapore Family Code (n 22) as a mechanism for mitigating the majority/minority agency problem that is prominent in jurisdictions dominated by controlling shareholders.

[24] Puchniak and Tang, Singapore's Embrace of Shareholder Stewardship, Chapter 14.

[25] Puchniak (n 13). See also Puchniak and Tang, Singapore's Embrace of Shareholder Stewardship, Chapter 14; Lim and Puchniak, Can a Global Legal Misfit Be Fixed?, Chapter 28; Koh, Puchniak and Goto, Shareholder Stewardship in Asia, Chapter 29.

[26] Lim and Puchniak, Can a Global Legal Misfit Be Fixed?, Chapter 28.

practices are indicative of the conventional boundaries between the different stewards – 'institutional investor stewards' versus 'non-institutional investor stewards' – already being blurred in most non-UK/US jurisdictions, as they tend to have an abundance of controlling shareholders.

A fourth conception of stewardship – which only recently began to increase in prominence – is institutional investor–driven stewardship with the aim of advancing the environmental, social and governance (ESG) movement. This conception of stewardship differs from the previous ones in two respects. First, the primary target of stewardship is not to solve any specific agency problem but rather to incentivize the companies in which institutional investors invest to adopt an ESG agenda.[27] Second, it aims to provide the ultimate beneficiaries of institutional investors with the information and means to channel their funds towards ESG investments. Although this concept of stewardship was non-existent in the UK Code 2010 and received only a fleeting reference in the UK Code 2012, it is at the core of the latest version of the UK Code (UK Code 2020).[28] This recent shift in the focus of stewardship in the UK has been described by a pre-eminent UK corporate law academic as a movement 'from saving the company to saving the planet'.[29] It is also noteworthy that, over the last decade, this ESG concept of stewardship has found its way into stewardship codes around the world. Empirical evidence based on a review of the text of the latest versions of stewardship codes reveals that 84 per cent of the codes now refer 'at least once to ESG factors' and that only four current codes (i.e., Danish Code 2016, Korean Code 2016, Swiss Code 2013 and US Code 2017) do not mention ESG factors at all.[30]

The fifth – and final – conception of stewardship is about what stewardship means 'inwards' for the institutional investors themselves. This conception is focused on the 'investment management' side of stewardship, that is, the relationship between the institutional investor – an investment intermediary – and their ultimate beneficiaries/clients. Most investors are organized on the basis of what has been described as a 'separation of funds and managers'.[31] This means that the investors' assets and liabilities are placed into one entity, the fund, whereas the fund's assets are managed by a separate entity, the management company.[32] The primary goal of this conception of stewardship is to reconcile a constructive stewardship role with the investors' own internal business models. The inaugural UK Code 2010/2012 incorporated good investment management practices within the notion of shareholder stewardship, such as managing conflicts of interest (between funds, between managers and fund investors, and between investors) in discharging stewardship and promoting transparency across the investment chain. These

[27] There is a portion of ESG stewardship which may fall under the agency problem between the company and society, which is explained as the third type of agency problem that corporate law may address: Kraakman and others (n 18) 36. However, ESG is more than preventing companies from producing 'negative externalities'; it also includes incentivizing companies to be agents of positive change to solve societal problems that they themselves may not have created.

[28] Financial Reporting Council, *The UK Stewardship Code 2020* (2019) <www.frc.org.uk/getattachment/5aae591d-d9d3-4cf4-814a-d14e156a1d87/Stewardship-Code_Dec-19-Final-Corrected.pdf> accessed 4 February 2022 [hereinafter UK Code 2020].

[29] Davies, The UK Stewardship Code 2010–2020, Chapter 2. See also Katelouzou (n 10) for a thorough analysis of this 'enlightened' conception of stewardship.

[30] Katelouzou and Klettner, Sustainable Finance and Stewardship, Chapter 26. This change in the focus of shareholder stewardship from corporate governance problems to societal problems needs to be understood within the increasing shift of 'corporate purpose' away from a sole focus on shareholder primacy. The debate is currently taking prominence in the US and the UK, the two countries where the original corporate governance–focused conception of stewards found fertile ground. For a good overview of the relevant literature, see Edward Rock, 'For Whom Is the Corporation Managed in 2020? The Debate Over Corporate Purpose' (2021) 76 *The Business Lawyer* 363.

[31] John Morley, 'The Separation of Funds and Managers: A Theory of Investment Fund Structure and Regulation' (2014) 123 *Yale Law Journal* 1228, 1232.

[32] The resulting separation of funds and managers alienates the owners of record and the beneficial owners and results in what has been defined as 'the agency costs of agency capitalism'. See Ronald Gilson and Jeffrey Gordon, 'The Agency Costs of Agency Capitalism: Activist Investors and the Revaluation of Governance Rights' (2013) 113 *Columbia Law Review* 863.

principles travelled well around the world,[33] but, even though the corporate governance and investment management sides of stewardship are intertwined,[34] the investment management side of stewardship has remained at the periphery of the academic and policy debates.[35] One explanation may be that the original UK Code did not make it clear whether institutional investors, by discharging their stewardship obligations as shareholders in their investee companies (i.e., the 'corporate governance side' of stewardship), were concurrently discharging their duties to their clients and ultimate beneficiaries (i.e., the 'investment management side' of stewardship). The failure to explicitly identify the difference between the corporate governance and investment management sides of stewardship, and how they interrelate, has often resulted in the importance of the investment management side of stewardship being overlooked.[36]

Against a largely monolithic literature and practice with a narrow focus on the first conception of shareholder stewardship as good corporate governance by institutional investors in dispersed-owned companies – and more recently on ESG – our taxonomy adds significant value in capturing a variety of stewards (institutional investors and various controlling shareholders) and targets (corporate governance, ESG, and investment management) which all contribute to how shareholder stewardship is *conceived*. Indeed, without all five conceptions it is impossible to accurately understand the past or anticipate the future of global shareholder stewardship. By recognizing the existence of and the problems and possibilities raised by the five conceptions of global shareholder stewardship and their overlap, this book adds significant insight and detail to what we know of stewardship around the world.

Finally, before moving on, two important points concerning the terminology used for this comparative and contextual analysis must be explained. We chose to use the term 'shareholder stewardship' over the term 'investor stewardship' for two reasons: first, we do not solely focus on 'institutional investor stewards' but also consider 'non-institutional investor stewards' (e.g. different types of controlling shareholders); and second, our focus is on the roles of these stewards as shareholders of public companies and does not take into account stewardship in other assets beyond equities. We also prefer the term 'shareholder stewardship' over merely the term 'stewardship', which is too broad to be analytically useful.

1.3 HOW THE SEVEN PRINCIPLES OF THE UK CODE WENT GLOBAL

1.3.1 *The Historical Roots of the UK-cum-Global Stewardship Code Model*

In 1991, the Institutional Shareholders' Committee (ISC), a private body composed of four prominent UK institutional investors and fund managers, released a statement entitled 'The

---

[33] See Section 1.3.
[34] For a thorough analysis of the links between the two sides of stewardship in the UK, see Roger M Barker and Iris H-Y Chiu, *Corporate Governance and Investment Management: The Promises and Limitations of the New Financial Economy* (Edward Elgar 2017) 4 (calling this 'the "governance nexus" between the fund management sector and the corporate sector'). It is also important to note here that the investment management side of stewardship is interrelated to all the other conceptions of stewardship except for the third one, which views controlling shareholders as the potential stewards. For all the other conceptions of stewardship, investment management sets the means, limits and possibilities for the institutional investors' stewardship abilities and capacities.
[35] For an exception, see Barker and Chiu, Investment Management, Stewardship and Corporate Governance Roles, Chapter 25. On the incentives and abilities of index funds to pursue stewardship, see Fisch, The Uncertain Stewardship Potential of Index Funds, Chapter 21.
[36] This gap was filled by the UK Code 2020 (n 28) which clarifies that shareholder engagement is part of good investment management and emphasizes on the governance of stewardship and its integration with investment management. See, further, Katelouzou (n 10).

TABLE 1.1 *The seven core principles in the UK Code 2010/2012*

Principle 1	Publicly disclose their policies on how they will discharge stewardship responsibility
Principle 2	Have a robust policy on managing conflicts of interest
Principle 3	Monitor investee companies
Principle 4	Establish clear guidelines on when and how to escalate stewardship activities
Principle 5	[Be] willing to work collectively with other investors
Principle 6	Have a clear policy on voting and disclosure of voting activity
Principle 7	Report periodically on stewardship and voting activities to their clients/beneficiaries

Responsibilities of Institutional Shareholders in the UK'.[37] This statement, which was only three pages long and included nine principles of good practice, can be seen as the genesis of the first corporate governance–focused conception of shareholder stewardship – despite the intriguing absence of the word 'stewardship' from its text. It was revised three times, in 2002, 2005 and 2007, until in 2009 it was reformulated into seven principles – 'The ISC Code on the Responsibilities of Institutional Investors' – which formed the basis for the UK Code in 2010.[38]

Although the ISC Code can be seen as the genesis of shareholder stewardship codes, the UK Code 2010 is often referred to as the world's first stewardship code. This is largely because the UK Code 2010 was released by the Financial Reporting Council (FRC), a quasi-government body, which gave it the imprimatur of the UK government. By 2010, the UK had established itself as a global corporate governance leader by creating the world's first corporate governance code, which had by then been transplanted around the world. In this context, the UK Code 2010 seemed like an encore by the UK to reaffirm its status as a global corporate governance leader – but this time by focusing on shareholder stewardship.[39] The position of the UK Code as the global 'gold standard' has been reinforced by European and international bodies (both public and private ones)[40] adopting to a large extent the UK Code 2010/2012 model of the seven principles – part of a larger movement which has recently been coined 'international corporate governance'.[41] Several chapters in this book analyze the seven principles of the UK Code 2010/2012 so the details will not be repeated here. Table 1.1 provides a snapshot of the seven core principles of the UK Code 2010, which were transferred almost completely into the revised UK Code 2012.

The UK Code 2010/2012 has had a significant impact globally. Before the publication of the UK Code in 2010, the only trace of shareholder stewardship outside the UK was in the 2005 Canadian Coalition for Good Governance statement on shareholder involvement by a group of Canadian institutional investors.[42] Internationally, some early stewardship traces can be found in the ICGN 'Statement on Institutional Shareholder Responsibilities' published in

---

[37] See Katelouzou and Zumbansen (n 2) 91–92 (elaborating the synthesis of the ISC and the evolution of its principles).

[38] In its consultation preceding the introduction of the UK Code, the FRC recognized the ISC 2009 Code as a 'good starting code' for the UK Code and included it in its Appendix B. See Financial Reporting Council, 'Consultation on a Stewardship Code for Institutional Investors' (19 January 2010) <www.frc.org.uk/consultation-list/2010/consult ation-on-a-stewardship-code-for-institution> accessed 4 February 2022. For a comprehensive analysis of the history of the UK Code, see Katelouzou (n 10).

[39] Recommendation 17 of the Walker Review recommended FRC to 'ratify' the ISC Code. See David Walker, 'A Review of Corporate Governance in UK Banks and Other Financial Industry Entities. Final Recommendations' (26 November 2009) <https://ecgi.global/sites/default/files/codes/documents/walker_review_261109.pdf> accessed 25 May 2021 [hereinafter Walker Review]. See further Katelouzou (n 10).

[40] See text accompanying n 6.

[41] Pargendler (n 6).

[42] Williams, Stewardship Principles in Canada, Chapter 20.

2003.[43] However, these two pre-2010 stewardship initiatives bear little resemblance to the stewardship codes that proliferated after 2010 based on the UK Code 2010/2012.[44]

Following the publication of the UK Code in 2010, stewardship codes have been issued in twenty jurisdictions on six continents (eight in Asia, six in Europe, two in Africa, two in North America, one in Australia and one in South America).[45] In three jurisdictions, more than one type of stewardship code has been issued to deal with either different types of institutional investor (Australia/India) or different types of shareholder (Singapore).[46] In addition, in several jurisdictions (Canada, India, Italy, Japan, the Netherlands, Norway and the UK) a subsequent amended version(s) of the inaugural stewardship code has been issued – resulting in a total of thirty-five codes having been issued in twenty jurisdictions.[47] To this impressive list one should add the European Fund and Asset Management Association (EFAMA) and ICGN codes which were issued by regional and international bodies respectively – resulting in a total of thirty-nine stewardship codes being issued after 2010.

1.3.2 *Evidence from the Formal Design and Content of Non-UK Stewardship Codes*

1.3.2.1 The Core Principles of the UK Code Have Been Transplanted Around the World

Prior to this book project, it was often assumed that UK-style stewardship had been transplanted around the world.[48] However, this claim had never been tested. This assumption likely arose for good reasons. First, the UK Code 2010 has widely come to be considered the world's first stewardship code and stewardship codes began to appear around the world following its release. Second, over the previous two decades, UK-style corporate governance codes had been adopted in ninety jurisdictions around the world and stewardship codes were seen to likely follow the same path.[49] Third, and perhaps most importantly, in jurisdictions that adopted codes, leading academics, government officials and/or the text of the code itself explicitly recognize the influence of the UK Code 2010/2012.[50] Indeed, in the main conference which brought together leading corporate governance scholars and policymakers from all the jurisdictions with codes for

---

[43] International Corporate Governance Network, 'ICGN Statement on Institutional Shareholder Responsibilities' (2003) <www.icgn.org/sites/default/files/2003%20Statement%20on%20Shareholder%20Responsibilities.pdf> accessed 25 May 2021.

[44] For empirical evidence, see Katelouzou and Siems, The Global Diffusion of Stewardship Codes, Chapter 30.

[45] See the Appendix to this chapter (Table 1.5) for the full list of stewardship codes. We adopt a broad definition of stewardship codes as including 'preliminary stewardship initiatives', like the one in Norway. For the definitional details, see Katelouzou and Siems, The Global Diffusion of Stewardship Codes, Chapter 30, Section 30.3.1.

[46] See the Appendix (Table 1.5) for details.

[47] ibid.

[48] Koh, Puchniak and Goto, Shareholder Stewardship in Asia, Chapter 29.

[49] However, despite comparisons between the global spread of UK-style corporate governance codes and that of UK-style stewardship codes, the proliferation of the former has been far greater: corporate governance codes now exist in almost ninety jurisdictions and have made independent directors globally ubiquitous. See Puchniak (n 13).

[50] Australian Council of Superannuation Investors, 'Australian Asset Owner Stewardship Code' (May 2018) 1 <https://acsi.org.au/wp-content/uploads/2020/01/AAOSC_-The_Code.pdf> accessed 25 May 2021 [hereinafter Australian (ACSI) Code 2018]; Financial Services Council, 'FSC Standard 23: Principles of Internal Governance and Asset Stewardship' (July 2017) 7 <www.fsc.org.au/web-page-resources/fsc-standards/1522-23s-internal-governance-and-asset-stewardship> accessed 25 May 2021 [hereinafter Australian (FSC) Code 2017]; Associação de Investidores no Mercado de Capitais (AMEC), 'Código AMEC de Princípios e Deveres dos Investidores Institucionais: Stewardship [AMEC Code of Principles and Duties of Institutional Investors: Stewardship]' (27 October 2016) 6 <www.amecbrasil.org.br/wp-content/uploads/2016/06/CODIGOAMECSTEWARDSHIPMinutaparaConsultaPublica.pdf> accessed 9 February 2022 [hereinafter Brazil Code 2016];Williams, Stewardship Principles in Canada, Chapter 20; The Committee on Corporate Governance, 'Stewardship Code' (November 2016) 3 <https://corporategovernance.dk/sites/default/files/180116_stewardship_code.pdf> accessed 25 May 2021 [hereinafter Danish Code 2016]; Donald,

this book project, perhaps the most common theme was that jurisdictions had modelled their codes on the UK Code 2010/2012. This theme was based primarily on repeated references to stewardship codes around the world being modelled on the seven core principles contained in the UK Code 2010/2012[51] – which, over the course of the conference, were coined the 'UK's Seven Magic Principles'.[52]

It is one thing for academics and policymakers to say that their jurisdiction intended to use the UK Code 2010/2012 as the model and another to verify whether this general impression was put into practice. To determine this, it makes sense to analyze the *formal design* of non-UK stewardship codes along three dimensions: their (1) core concept, (2) primary content and (3) text/language.[53] As explained, the *core concept* of the UK Code 2010/2012 was to incentivize passive institutional investors to become active shareholder stewards by using a 'comply or explain' code. An examination of all thirty-six jurisdictional and inter-jurisdictional non-UK codes published after 2010 reveals that the only code that does not conceptualize institutional investors as being the focus of stewardship is the Singapore Family Code.[54] In addition, in the thirty-five stewardship codes that see institutional investors as the 'stewards', twenty-nine out of thirty-five are designed overwhelmingly around the first conception of stewardship, that is, that institutional investors will *actively engage* as 'stewards' in the *corporate governance* of companies in which they are shareholders; the small minority of other codes (six out of thirty-five) see institutional investors as playing more of a role promoting ESG or focus more on the investment management conception of stewardship.[55]

In this sense, it is clear that the core concept of the UK Code 2010/2012 has served as a model which has shaped the primary target of stewardship around the world: institutional investors.

Stewardship in the Hong Kong International Financial Centre, Chapter 13; Varottil, Shareholder Stewardship in India, Chapter 17; Strampelli, Institutional Investor Stewardship in Italian Corporate Governance, Chapter 6; Goto, Japanese Stewardship Code, Chapter 10; Ouko, Stewardship Code in Kenya, Chapter 23; Kang and Chun, Korea's Stewardship Code and the Rise of Shareholder Activism, Chapter 11; Minority Shareholder Watchdog Group (MSWG) and Securities Commission Malaysia (SC), 'Malaysian Code for Institutional Investors' (June 2014) 18 <https://www.sc.com.my/api/documentms/download.ashx?id=9f4e32d3-cb97-4ff5-852a-6cb168a9f936> accessed 25 May 2021 [hereinafter Malaysian Code 2014]; Eumedion, 'Best Practices for Engaged Share-Ownership Intended for Eumedion Participants' (30 June 2011) 2 <www.eumedion.nl/en/public/knowledgenetwork/best-practices/best_practices-engaged-share-ownership.pdf> accessed 25 May 2021 [hereinafter Dutch Code 2011]; Eumedion, 'Dutch Stewardship Code' (20 June 2018) 2 <www.eumedion.nl/en/public/knowledgenetwork/best-practices/2018-07-dutch-stewardship-code-final-version.pdf> accessed 25 May 2021 [hereinafter Dutch Code 2018]; Puchniak and Tang, Singapore's Embrace of Shareholder Stewardship, Chapter 14; Institute of Directors in Southern Africa, 'Code for Responsible Investing in South Africa 2011' (2011) 12 <https://cdn.ymaws.com/www.iodsa.co.za/resource/collection/79874DB1-8300-49EB-AE0D-993809CAAA6C/CRISA_Code_for_Responsible_Investing_in_South_Africa.pdf> accessed 25 May 2021 [hereinafter South African Code 2011]; Association Suisse des Institutions de Prévoyance (ASIP), 'Guidelines for Institutional Investors Governing the Exercising of Participation Rights in Public Limited Companies' (21 January 2013) 3 <https://ecgi.global/code/guidelines-institutional-investors-governing-exercising-participation-rights-public-limited> accessed 25 May 2021 [hereinafter Swiss Code 2013]; Lin, The Assessment of Taiwan's Shareholder Stewardship Codes, Chapter 12; Securities and Exchange Commission, 'Investment Governance Code for Institutional Investors' (2017) 32 <https://www.sec.or.th/cgthailand/EN/Documents/ICode/ICodeBookEN.pdf> accessed 25 May 2021 [hereinafter Thai Code 2017]; Fisch, The Uncertain Stewardship Potential of Index Funds, Chapter 21.

[51] See Table 1.1.
[52] Dionysia Katelouzou and Henning Jacobsen, 'Global Shareholder Stewardship: A Conference Report' (2020) 24 <https://ssrn.com/abstract=3610792> accessed 25 May 2021 ('[w]hat all the jurisdictional panels have demonstrated is that ostensibly "seven" is the "magic number" in terms of stewardship principles').
[53] This approach was first developed and undertaken in Puchniak (n 13), but here we take into account both jurisdiction-specific and inter-jurisdictional codes and the use of the language of 'stewardship'.
[54] It is noteworthy that Singapore has a second code that focuses on institutional investors. As such, every jurisdiction that has adopted a stewardship code has at least one code that focuses on institutional investors: Puchniak and Tang, Singapore's Embrace of Shareholder Stewardship, Chapter 14.
[55] See the Appendix (Table 1.5). See also Section 1.3.2.2 for a discussion of the codes that incorporate other conceptions such as ESG and investment management.

This finding is significant because this concept of stewardship does not appear to fit into jurisdictions with controlling shareholders which, as will be explained in detail,[56] is the shareholder landscape in all the non-UK jurisdictions that have adopted stewardship codes (with the notable exception of the US). It has also meant that the ESG and investment management conceptions of stewardship have not been the primary focus in the vast majority of non-UK jurisdictions – but, as will also be explained,[57] this may change in the near future with the UK Code 2020 adding ESG as one of its primary focal points.

In terms of the *primary content*, the vast majority of non-UK codes around the world adopted all, or almost all, of the seven principles in the UK Code (see Table 1.2).[58] If we consider all thirty-five non-UK stewardship codes (i.e., jurisdiction-specific, regional and international codes) that focus on institutional investors, 74.29% have adopted all seven principles – with 91.43% of the codes adopting five or more principles. Thus, it is clear that the primary content of the UK Code 2010/2012 has been significantly embraced by stewardship codes globally – definitive evidence of a *UK-cum-global stewardship code model*. This evidence is even more overwhelming if one considers the latest versions of all non-UK codes focused on institutional investors, with 83.3% adopting all seven UK principles and 95.8% adopting five or more principles. Definitively, 100% of the regional and international codes have adopted the seven UK principles. This reaffirms how the seven principles served as the model for the primary content of codes globally as these non-jurisdiction specific codes were intended to promote the dissemination of stewardship around the world – which empirical evidence in Chapter 30 proves was indeed the case.

In terms of the *text* of non-UK codes, an automated textual analysis of the specific wording used in non-UK codes in Chapter 30 confirms that much of the text of non-UK codes has been copied from the UK Code 2012. The UK Code 2012 is found to be the most influential text in a sample of forty-one UK and non-UK stewardship codes – particularly among Asian common law jurisdictions.[59] However, the same chapter confirms that diffusion of stewardship norms is

TABLE 1.2 *Percentage of codes that adopted the UK Code 2010/2012's seven principles*[60]

Types of code	Number of codes	Percentage that adopted all 7 principles	Percentage that adopted 5 or more principles
All Stewardship Codes	36	72.2%	88.89%
Latest Versions of All Stewardship Codes	25	80%	92%
All Institutional Investor Focused Codes	35	74.29%	91.43%
Latest Version of Institutional Investor Focused Codes	24	83.3%	95.8%
All Interjurisdictional Codes	4	100%	100%
Latest Interjurisdictional Codes	2	100%	100%
All Jurisdiction Specific Codes	32	68.75%	87.5%
Latest Jurisdiction Specific Codes	23	78.26%	91.3%

---

[56] Section 1.4.3.
[57] Section 1.4.5.
[58] Katelouzou and Siems, The Global Diffusion of Stewardship Codes, Chapter 30; Puchniak (n 13).
[59] Katelouzou and Siems, The Global Diffusion of Stewardship Codes, Chapter 30; Puchniak (n 13).
[60] The preamble, principles and guidance of the latest versions of codes in every jurisdiction that has adopted a stewardship code for institutional investors were examined to determine whether each of the seven core principles contained in the UK Code 2010/2012 had an equivalent provision in each jurisdictions code. See the Appendix (Table 1.5) for more details.

multidimensional with the intra-jurisdictional codes of EFAMA and ICGN playing an influential role in the travelling of stewardship principles and with regional clusters, such as the one between Korea and Japan, also explaining jurisdictional variety in stewardship codes.[61] While studying the text of stewardship codes with computational tools revealed more complicated patterns of stewardship diffusion than a unidimensional transfer from the UK Code 2010/2012, it is admitted that a textual analysis may underestimate the extent to which core concepts or principles have been transplanted from the UK Code 2010/2012 to other codes because the same concepts are sometimes described using different words or are lost in translation when expressed in non-English languages – suggesting that the influence of the text of the UK Code 2010/2012 on codes globally may be even greater than the automated textual analysis suggests.[62]

Another point is that the linguistic choices for the titles of the codes add further evidence of the influence of the UK Code 2010/2012 as the model for stewardship codes around the world. Out of the thirty-six jurisdictional-specific codes, twenty-five include the word 'stewardship' in their title. This demonstrates how the term 'stewardship', which was coined in the title of the UK Code 2010, has been disseminated around the world. It is interesting that policymakers and academics from the jurisdictions that did not include the word 'stewardship' in the title of their codes still tend to colloquially, and in their chapters in this book, refer to their codes as 'stewardship' codes – demonstrating that the UK Code 2010/2012 made 'stewardship' the lingua franca for describing these codes around the world.

1.3.2.2 Outliers and Deviations from the UK Model

Despite the strong evidence that the UK Code 2010/2012 has served as the model for stewardship codes around the world, there are interesting observations that can be drawn from jurisdictions which have chosen to deviate from the UK model in terms of the core concept, primary content or text of their codes.

In terms of the *core concept*, as highlighted already and explained in detail in Chapter 14, the Singapore Family Code is the only stewardship code that does not mention institutional investors.[63] Instead, it focuses on family controllers, which fits Singapore's corporate governance context as family-controlled companies comprise the vast majority of companies on the Singapore Exchange.[64] As most non-UK jurisdictions have shareholder landscapes dominated by controlling shareholders (and not institutional investors), an interesting question is why other jurisdictions have not taken such an approach and whether other jurisdictions will follow the Singapore Family Code model in the future – which has been promoted for export by Stewardship Asia.[65] Also, it is noteworthy that from the thirty-five non-UK codes treating institutional investors as 'stewards', six do not focus on the corporate governance–oriented core concept of the UK Code 2010/2012.[66] The Norwegian Codes, the Swiss Code 2013, the

---

[61] Katelouzou and Siems, The Global Diffusion of Stewardship Codes, Chapter 30.
[62] For instance, the Malaysian Code 2014 (n 50) does not mention even once the term 'escalat-e/ion' but in substantive terms has an equivalent principle on intervention which resembles too closely Principle 4 of the UK Code 2010/2012. Similarly, the Canadian Code (n 19) does not make any reference to the word 'collect-ive' but it includes a principle on collaborative action which draws heavily on Principle 5 of the UK Code 2010/2012. The use of different words to express similar content may be attributed to differences in translation of English words but may also suggest that the principles have been 'softened' to account for different market, legal and cultural environments.
[63] Section 1.2. Also Puchniak and Tang, Singapore's Embrace of Shareholder Stewardship, Chapter 14.
[64] ibid.
[65] Puchniak and Tang, Singapore's Embrace of Shareholder Stewardship, Chapter 14.
[66] See the Appendix (Table 1.5).

Australian (FSC) Code 2017 and the ICGN Code 2013 appear to place more of an emphasis on the investment management conception of stewardship than other codes, raising the question of whether this conception of stewardship will be stressed more in other codes in the future. Finally, the South African Code, which was released in 2011, adopts ESG – instead of the corporate governance of investee companies – as its core concept to be advanced by institutional investors.[67] As already mentioned, the UK Code 2020 added ESG as a major focal point, in addition to its original core concept on transforming institutional investors into actively engaged shareholder stewards. At the same time, the UK Code 2020 is much more focused on the investment management side of stewardship compared to its predecessors.[68] This, combined with the rise of the ESG movement, raises another interesting question, which we discuss in Section 1.5: will ESG become the core concept of stewardship codes in the future and, if so, will the UK Code 2020 serve as the new model for this movement?[69]

In terms of the *primary content*, in the small minority of non-UK codes that have not adopted all seven principles, two principles are most often the 'missing principles': (1) escalating monitoring activities in investee companies (Principle 4 of the UK Code 2010/2012); and (2) collective action and collaboration among institutional investors (Principle 5 of the UK Code 2010/2012).[70] This may be because the codes which lack these principles are in jurisdictions where institutional investors collectively are minority shareholders – which, as explained by Puchniak elsewhere, makes the concepts of escalation and collective action less meaningful.[71] It is also likely that because escalating activities and collective action are closely associated with shareholder activism, these principles are not well-perceived by local market and governmental actors with more stakeholder or 'communitarian' views of the firm, which in turn may explain the absence of such principles from stewardship codes in jurisdictions like Japan.[72] It is also noteworthy that two early non-UK codes (Canadian Code 2010 and Italian Code 2013) did not include an equivalent of the conflicts of interests principle (Principle 2 of the UK Code 2010/2012) and two (Canadian Code 2010 and Norwegian Code 2012) did not include an equivalent to Principle 7 of the UK Code 2010/2012, which refers to periodic reporting of the stewardship activities to ultimate beneficiaries of institutional investors.[73] Both Principles 2 and 7 are part of the investment management aspect of stewardship and their absence in earlier versions may be attributed to the fact that codes have generally de-emphasized the investment management conception of stewardship. However, all three codes have now been amended to include equivalents of Principles 2 and 7 – suggesting that, although investment management is not the core concept of any code, it is still an important aspect of stewardship (the reasons for which are explained in detail later in this book).[74] Finally, it is important to note that twenty-three out of the thirty-six non-UK codes (63.9%) have adopted principles that are not included in the UK Code 2010/2012.[75] Among these non-UK originated principles is a principle on ESG investing which is

---

[67] Locke, Encouraging Sustainable Investment in South Africa, Chapter 22.
[68] Appendix (Table 1.5). See also Katelouzou (n 10).
[69] Section 1.4.5.
[70] This is also confirmed by automated textual analysis: Katelouzou and Siems, The Global Diffusion of Stewardship Codes, Chapter 30.
[71] Puchniak (n 13).
[72] See Katelouzou and Siems, The Global Diffusion of Stewardship Codes, Chapter 30.
[73] See the Appendix (Table 1.5) for details.
[74] Barker and Chiu, Investment Management, Stewardship and Corporate Governance Roles, Chapter 25.
[75] Of course, here one needs to include the Singapore Family Code (n 22) which includes a completely different set of principles addressed to family owners, compared to the institutional investor–targeted UK model.

found in ten stewardship codes including the UK Code 2020 – suggesting the importance of ESG in the future of stewardship.[76]

In terms of the *text*, while Chapter 30 provides clear evidence of the diffusion of the text of the UK Code 2012 around the world (especially among Asian common law countries but also through diffusion to the EFAMA Code 2011 and Japanese Code 2017), there are interesting observations that can be drawn from codes that significantly deviate from the text used in the UK Code 2012. Four codes are found to be textually detached from the UK Code 2012 even though they all include the seven UK principles: the Australian (FSC) Code 2017, the Australian (ACSI) Code 2018, the South African Code 2011 and the Taiwanese Code 2018.[77] There are three reasons for these – perhaps surprising at first – linguistic deviations. First, textual differences may be attributed to the manner in which the seven UK principles are expressed in each code, which tends to differ significantly – in that some principles are combined together in a single 'combine principle' and others are split up into several smaller parts.[78] Second, that a non-UK code may have all seven UK principles does not necessarily mean that it has only these seven principles. Rather, the majority of non-UK codes also include principles that are *not* included in the UK Code 2010/2012. For instance, the Australian (ACSI) Code 2018 includes a principle addressed to policymakers with the aim of encouraging them to 'better align the operation of the financial system and regulatory policy with the interests of long-term investors'.[79] Finally, as we have seen, the Australian (FSC) 2017 Code and the South African Code 2011 differ from the UK Code 2010/2012 in terms of their core concept, which explains why, despite adopting the seven UK principles, these codes also have many additional principles which reflect their different core concepts, investment management and ESG.

Another important observation is that while textual differences, when the primary content of non-UK codes is similar to the UK 2010/2012 model, do not challenge the basic proposition that the UK Code 2010/2012 served as the global stewardship model, there are a few codes that are different from the UK model in terms of both text and primary content. Two non-UK codes stand out here: the Brazil Code 2016 and the Swiss Code 2013. They are both found to be textually dissimilar to the UK model.[80] And they both differ from the UK model in terms of their primary content.[81] The Brazil Code 2016 has a principle with no direct correspondence with the UK model; its Principle 3 urges institutional investors to take into account ESG factors.[82] The Swiss Code 2013 is the code that lacks most of the UK principles (it has only four out of seven) which may be attributed to the fact that the code has a different core concept: it focuses on the investment management side of stewardship and aims to minimize the agency costs between asset managers and their clients when the former exercising their shareholder rights, rather than turning institutional investors into active monitors of investee companies.[83]

---

[76] Non-UK codes that include ESG-related principles are: Brazil Code 2016 (n 50); Canadian Code 2017/2020 (n 19); Japanese Code 2020 (n 50); Kenya Code 2017 (n 50); Malaysian Code 2014 (n 50); Dutch Code 2011/2018 (n 50); South African Code 2011 (n 50).
[77] Katelouzou and Siems, The Global Diffusion of Stewardship Codes, Chapter 30.
[78] There is, therefore, a great variety in the number of principles among non-UK codes, with the Australian (FSC) Code 2017 (n 50) and the Taiwanese Code 2018 (n 50), for instance, having three and six generic principles, respectively.
[79] The Australian (FSC) Code 2017 (n 50) and the South African Code 2011 (n 50) also include principles that are not included in the UK Code 2010/2012. See Section 1.4.1.
[80] Katelouzou and Siems, The Global Diffusion of Stewardship Codes, Chapter 30.
[81] See Appendix (Table 1.5).
[82] Becker, Andrade and Prado, The Brazilian Stewardship Framework, Chapter 24.
[83] See also Daeniker and Hertig, Capitalist Stakeholders, Chapter 5.

1.4 VARIETIES OF GLOBAL SHAREHOLDER STEWARDSHIP: COMPLEXITY REVEALED

It has been more than two decades since the legal origins theory captivated comparative corporate law scholarship based purely on a comparison of 'corporate law on the books' – without any examination into how the corporate law provisions that were being compared across jurisdictions were enforced and actually functioned in practice.[84] Although the original legal origins research is heavily cited and its progeny spawned an index currently (mis)used by the World Bank,[85] its validity and ability to accurately explain the reality of how corporate law functions in different jurisdictions have been persuasively debunked.[86] In the wake of the legal origins debacle, a primary lesson learned is that examining how the law is enforced and analyzing other jurisdiction-specific factors that influence how the law functions in practice are critical for any meaningful comparative corporate law analysis. Based on our review of the chapters in this book, the case of stewardship codes is no exception.

From our analysis in Section 1.3, it is clear that the UK Code 2010/2012 has served as the model for the proliferation of stewardship codes around the world. Outliers and deviations may have been revealed, but this does not alter the fact that the UK-cum-global stewardship model has been adopted in an overwhelming majority of jurisdictions with codes and has significantly influenced the form and/or content of virtually every stewardship code in the world. This finding is important as it confirms that the UK Code 2010 was the genesis of the global stewardship movement. It also suggests why, prior to this book project, the conventional wisdom was that UK-style stewardship had proliferated around the world. However, to stop our analysis here would be to repeat the fundamental flaw in the legal origins scholarship: merely because the UK Code 2010/2012 served as a model for the design of stewardship codes globally does *not* mean that these codes were adopted for similar reasons, and/or have performed a similar function, as in the UK.

Indeed, as explained in this section, and elaborated upon in several chapters in this book, the opposite is often the case. Most jurisdictions have formally adopted the seven principles of the UK Code 2010/2012 and the UK's institutional investor, corporate governance–focused, conception of stewardship. However, shareholder stewardship in jurisdictions around the world has often functioned in a way that is different from – and in some cases diametrically opposed to – shareholder stewardship in the UK. This is a core reason for why understanding shareholder stewardship globally appears simple but is, in fact, teeming with complexity. We now turn to an examination of the forces that have driven stewardship to function in a variety of ways around the world.

1.4.1 *The Origins of Stewardship Codes: A Bifurcated World*

Although stewardship codes globally have overwhelmingly adopted the formal design and content of the UK Code 2010/2012, the ostensible simplicity of this global legal transplant is only skin-deep. If we drill down a bit by examining the origins of the codes, the largely unified

---

[84] Rafael La Porta, Florencio Lopez-de-Silanes, Andrei Shleifer and Robert W Vishny, 'Law and Finance' (1998) 106 *Journal of Political Economy* 1113; Holger Spamann, 'The "Antidirector Rights Index" Revisited' (2010) 23 *Review of Financial Studies* 467.

[85] Dan W Puchniak and Umakanth Varottil, 'Related Party Transactions in Commonwealth Asia: Complicating the Comparative Paradigm' (2020) 17 Berkeley Business Law Journal 1; Jedidiah Kroncke, 'Intransigent Indices and the Laments of Comparative Law: Why Legal Origins Won't Die' (*JOTWELL*, 19 November 2020) <https://intl.jotwell.com/intransigent-indices-and-the-laments-of-comparative-law-why-legal-origins-wont-die/> accessed 25 May 2021.

[86] Spamann (n 84); Puchniak and Varottil (n 85); Dionysia Katelouzou and Mathias Siems, 'Disappearing Paradigms in Shareholder Protection: Leximetric Evidence for 30 Countries, 1990–2013' (2015) 15 Journal of Corporate Law Studies 127; Jeffrey Gordon, 'Convergence and Persistence in Corporate Law and Governance' in Jeffrey Gordon and Wolf-Georg Ringe (eds), The Oxford Handbook of Corporate Law and Governance (OUP 2018) 34.

global rise of stewardship becomes bifurcated into two worlds: (1) there have been nineteen codes in eleven jurisdictions issued by government or quasi-government bodies (public or governmental codes); and (2) there have been sixteen codes in nine jurisdictions issued by private organizations composed of, or supported by, mainly institutional investors (private or institutional investor codes). In addition, the four inter-jurisdictional codes are all private in nature.[87]

The motives for adopting a stewardship code and the mechanisms available to enforce a code may differ significantly between public (governmental or quasi-governmental) bodies and private institutional investor organizations. Governments may be driven by a desire to demonstrate that they are acting in response to an economic crisis and/or to signal that their jurisdiction is at the cutting-edge of global norms of good corporate governance.[88] Governments can survey their jurisdictions' corporate governance landscape and tailor the stewardship code to the stakeholder that has de facto or actual control of most listed companies.[89] Governments can use the coercive power of the state to bind institutional investors – or another type of steward – in their jurisdiction to the code.[90] Governments may create codes to advance their own political agenda, using a stewardship code as a form of policy-channelling that may have little to do with any of the conceptions of stewardship, and everything to do with politics.[91]

In contrast, the motives for institutional investor organizations to come together to create a code appear to be narrower as they will naturally be focused on promoting the interests of institutional investors.[92] Institutional investors will only draft codes that consider institutional investors to be the 'stewards' regardless of the shareholder landscape of a jurisdiction.[93] Institutional investor organizations can only create codes that use the coercive power of membership in the organization to enforce their codes.[94] Institutional investors may be driven by a desire to create a code to promote self-regulation and avoid being regulated by the government.[95] Institutional investors may create codes to serve as vehicles for overcoming the collective action problems that they tend to face as small minority shareholders.

In this context, the fact that fifteen out of the twenty codes adopted by institutional investors include all seven UK principles is unsurprising.[96] As the UK Code 2010/2012 was designed with institutional investors at its core, it fits well with the agenda of institutional investor organizations. Also, as the UK Code 2010/2012 has gained the status of being the 'gold standard' for stewardship codes globally, adopting this gold standard sends a signal that institutional investors

---

[87] See Appendix (Table 1.5).
[88] Koh, Puchniak and Goto, Shareholder Stewardship in Asia, Chapter 29; Goto, Japanese Stewardship Code, Chapter 10; Lin, The Assessment of Taiwan's Shareholder Stewardship Codes, Chapter 12; Donald, Stewardship in the Hong Kong International Financial Centre, Chapter 13; Puchniak and Tang, Singapore's Embrace of Shareholder Stewardship, Chapter 14; Kowpatanakit and Bunaramrueang, Thai Institutional Investors Stewardship Code and Its Implementation, Chapter 16.
[89] Puchniak and Tang, Singapore's Embrace of Shareholder Stewardship, Chapter 14.
[90] Davies, The UK Stewardship Code 2010–2020, Chapter 2; Varottil, Shareholder Stewardship in India, Chapter 17.
[91] The term 'policy channeling' was first coined by Milhaupt and Pargendler in their research on related party transactions in SOEs. Curtis J Milhaupt and Mariana Pargendler, 'Related Party Transactions in State-Owned Enterprises' in Luca Enriques and Tobias Troger (eds), *The Law and Finance of Related Party Transactions* (CUP 2019) 245–46. In this chapter, we extend the use of the term 'policy channeling' to global shareholder stewardship. In this context, 'policy channeling' refers to governments using stewardship codes to advance their political agendas – as opposed to using them to improve corporate governance or shareholder stewardship more specifically. See also Koh, Puchniak and Goto, Shareholder Stewardship in Asia, Chapter 29; Puchniak (n 13).
[92] Puchniak (n 13).
[93] ibid.
[94] ibid. See also Katelouzou and Sergakis, Shareholder Stewardship Enforcement, Chapter 27.
[95] See e.g. Katelouzou (n 10) (explaining the development of the pre-2010 UK codes to the lobbying power of UK institutional investors).
[96] See Appendix (Table 1.5).

in a jurisdiction are taking stewardship seriously – an effective method for promoting self-regulation and pre-empting the government issuing a code. Indeed, there is no non-UK jurisdiction in which institutional investors have adopted a UK-style stewardship code where the government has subsequently attempted to issue a public code – suggesting that this pre-emptive strategy has been effective so far.

Another notable observation is that institutional investors are more likely to adapt the original UK model to their specific needs by adding 'additional principles':[97] from the twenty-three codes with additional principles, fifteen are issued by a private drafter. In addition to principles on ESG and long-termism, which are included in many non-UK Codes, it is not surprising that several non-governmental codes address the investment management side of stewardship, including specific principles on internal governance and organization. For instance, this is the case with all four of the jurisdictional codes focusing on the investment management conception of stewardship, that is, the Australian (FSC) Code 2017, the two Norwegian Codes and the Swiss Code 2013. Other additional principles included in private codes reflect the stakeholder orientation of some jurisdictions and ask institutional investors to communicate with stakeholders and exercise their shareholder rights, including the right to request a special meeting (e.g. the Dutch Code and the Swiss Code), which may allow institutional investors to demonstrate their understanding of trends within a jurisdiction and to expand their client base in this manner. Finally, some non-governmental codes ask institutional investors to work with policymakers and regulators (e.g. Canadian Codes), perhaps in an attempt to co-regulate and pre-empt future governmental regulation.

While the adoption of private codes closely resembling the UK model is unsurprising, from a narrow corporate governance perspective, the widespread transplantation of the UK Code 2010/2012 by government or quasi-government bodies is, at first blush, more puzzling. This is because, when viewed through a narrow corporate governance lens, one would expect that governments would create stewardship codes to fit the corporate governance context in their respective jurisdictions. As institutional investors collectively do not comprise a majority of shareholders in any non-UK jurisdiction with a government code – and most non-UK jurisdictions with government codes are dominated by controlling-block shareholders who have the incentive and the voting rights to steward most listed companies – one may expect that governments would adapt codes to be targeted towards controlling shareholders (rather than institutional investors) as the natural stewards of companies.

However, as noted earlier, the Singapore Family Code is the only stewardship code that has taken such an approach.[98] Rather, as explained in several chapters in this book and confirmed in our hand-compiled data, the overwhelming majority of public codes (eleven out of sixteen) have adopted all seven UK principles. The extensive adoption of the UK model by government or quasi-government bodies is also confirmed by the fact that all sixteen of the government codes adopt the core corporate governance–focused concept of the UK model to transform institutional investors into active shareholder stewards. This is paradoxical because, as will be explained in detail, stewardship has functioned in a wide variety of ways in these jurisdictions owing to the influence of jurisdiction-specific factors.[99]

Before moving on, it is noteworthy that there is a stark geographic divide in terms of governmental codes versus institutional investor codes.[100] All the Asian codes (fourteen codes in eight jurisdictions) are governmental codes, while outside of Asia only two non-UK jurisdictions – Denmark and

---

[97] Outside the UK 2010/2012 model.
[98] Section 1.2. Also Puchniak and Tang, Singapore's Embrace of Shareholder Stewardship, Chapter 14.
[99] Section 1.4.4.
[100] See Puchniak (n 13) as the only other place we are aware of that makes this observation.

Kenya – have governmental codes. In this respect, Asia has adhered more closely to the design of the UK model of a governmental code than other parts of the world – a finding that has been entirely overlooked. There are three reasons why this geographic divide may have arisen. First, in non-Asian jurisdictions, institutional investors tend to have a larger ownership stake in listed companies,[101] which may provide institutional investors with greater incentives to create a code. Second, governments and public regulation tend to play a larger role in Asian economies and corporate governance than in many Western jurisdictions. Third, there is less of a history of shareholder activism by private institutional investors in most of Asia than in the West.[102] The centrality of governments in Asian corporate governance systems – combined with the general weakness of institutional investors throughout most of Asia – may explain why all the codes in Asia have been issued by government entities or entities supported by the government.[103] This contrasts with a litany of institutional investor organizations outside of Asia, which have developed from the ground up, without any government involvement, and have produced stewardship codes driven by free-market forces.[104]

1.4.2 Stewardship in a World of Lax Enforcement: The UK as a Global Outlier

Surprisingly, although an overwhelming majority of jurisdictions with stewardship codes adopted the seven principles of the UK Code 2010/2012, *none* of them have adopted the UK's model for enforcing their stewardship codes. In the UK, since December 2010, all asset managers authorized by the Financial Conduct Authority (FCA) have been required to publicly disclose their commitment to the UK Code, or explain where they do not commit.[105] As most UK authorized asset managers are 'domestic' investors,[106] this has effectively meant that all domestic asset managers in the UK are bound to commit to the principles and reporting obligations in the UK Code.

In stark contrast, seventeen out of the nineteen jurisdictions that have adopted UK-style stewardship codes have made them *entirely voluntary* in scope – with one of the codes in Australia[107] and all four Indian codes being the only non-UK codes that are non-voluntary for a certain portion of institutional investors in their respective jurisdictions.[108] The implications of almost all the world's stewardship codes being entirely voluntary in scope – that is, with institutional investors free to decide whether or not to be signatories of the code – are difficult to overstate. It makes stewardship entirely optional for institutional investors – or family controllers in the case of the Singapore Family Code. As discussed in Chapter 27, this

---

[101] See Table 1.4.
[102] Yu-Hsin Lin, 'When Activists Meet Controlling Shareholders in the Shadow of the Law: A Case Study of Hong Kong' (2019) 14 Asian Journal of Comparative Law 1. We note that Japan is an exception – but activism targeting Japanese companies has been mainly brought by US hedge funds and has to do with the fact that Japan has few controlling shareholders and is the most dispersed jurisdiction in Asia. See e.g. John Buchanan, Dominic Heesang Chai and Simon Deakin, Hedge Fund Activism in Japan: The Limits of Shareholder Primacy (CUP 2012); Dan W Puchniak, 'Multiple Faces of Shareholder Power in Asia: Complexity Revealed' in Jennifer G Hill and Randall S Thomas (eds), Research Handbook on Shareholder Power (Edward Elgar 2015) 511; Dan W Puchniak and Masafumi Nakahigashi, 'The Enigma of Hostile Takeovers in Japan: Bidder Beware' (2018) 15 Berkeley Business Law Journal 4.
[103] Koh, Puchniak and Goto, Shareholder Stewardship in Asia, Chapter 29; Puchniak (n 13).
[104] Appendix (Table 1.5). See e.g. Australian (FSC) Code 2017, Australian (ACSI) Code 2018, Brazil Code 2016, Canadian Codes, Italian Codes, Dutch Codes, Norwegian Codes, South African Code 2011, Swiss Code 2013, and US Code.
[105] COBS 2.2.3R (06/12/2010).
[106] Although UK authorized asset managers are usually 'domestic' investors, international asset managers can be authorized by the FCA. See Financial Conduct Authority, 'Our Approach to International Firms' (February 2021) <www.fca.org.uk/publication/corporate/approach-to-international-firms.pdf> accessed 25 May 2021.
[107] Australian (FSC) Code 2017 (n 50).
[108] See Appendix (Table 1.5).

distinguishes stewardship codes from corporate governance codes – almost all of which are linked to a stock exchange or other mandatory regulations which do not allow listed companies to ignore corporate governance codes even if they would prefer to.[109]

The most extreme example of the deleterious impact that the voluntary scope of stewardship codes can have on translating a code into practice comes from Kenya. Since the Kenya Code was issued in 2017, not a single institutional investor has volunteered to be bound by it.[110] As such, Kenya has a stewardship code that applies to no one – the archetypal example of a code that formally creates shareholder stewardship, with no functional effect in practice. Interestingly, the Kenya Code is a government issued code, which raises the question of why a government, which has the coercive power of the state, would issue a code that binds no one. Although the Kenya Code 2017 is highlighted as the only voluntary code to which no one has agreed to be bound, its voluntary scope is typical of non-UK governmental codes – and also institutional investor codes – which are almost all entirely voluntary. For institutional investor codes, their voluntary scope makes sense as the private organizations that issue the codes lack the coercive power of the state, and membership in the private organizations themselves is almost always voluntary. However, the failure of governments to use their coercive power – distinct from what most have done in the case of corporate governance codes – to make codes binding on a certain constituency of shareholders is a puzzling development in the evolution of global shareholder stewardship that has gone largely unrecognized and which we address here.

The outlier status of the UK's enforcement model becomes even starker when the increasingly onerous *obligations* that institutional investors have under the UK Code are compared with the surprisingly lax, and even non-existent, obligations under most other non-UK codes. The UK Code 2010/2012 employed a 'comply or explain' *mode* of enforcement – which allows institutional investors who are bound by the code (whether because they fall within its scope or because they voluntarily signed up) to deviate from it if they provide an explanation for doing so. However, as the quality of commitment and that of disclosure in the UK were seen as lacking, in 2016 the FRC introduced a public tiering system of the signatories to the UK Code 2012, dividing institutional investors into tiers based on the quality of their disclosure.[111] Most recently, the UK Code 2020 adopted an 'apply and explain' principle which suggests more strongly that those who are bound by the code should apply it.[112]

In sum, the story of the UK enforcement regime has three key components. First, domestic institutional investors are legally bound to commit to the code or explain otherwise (i.e., it is non-voluntary for domestic asset managers). Second, the obligation to 'comply or explain' is evaluated and explicitly subjected to market pressure, previously by the public tiering exercise conducted by

---

[109] See, further, Katelouzou and Sergakis, Shareholder Stewardship Enforcement, Chapter 27 (developing a simple enforcement taxonomy based on three dimensions: (i) the nature of the norm-enforcer (self-enforcement and third-party enforcement), (ii) the nature of the enforcement mechanism (formal and informal) and (iii) the temporal scope of enforcement).

[110] Ouko, Stewardship Code in Kenya, Chapter 23.

[111] Further on the tiering exercise as a 'formal' (but not judicial) enforcement mechanism, see Katelouzou and Sergakis, Shareholder Stewardship Enforcement, Chapter 27. The tiering exercise of the signatories to the UK Code 2012 has now been discontinued. See <www.frc.org.uk/investors/uk-stewardship-code/origins-of-the-uk-stewardship-code> accessed 10 February 2022.

[112] On the new stewardship reporting system, see Financial Reporting Council, Effective Stewardship Reporting (November 2021), <www.frc.org.uk/getattachment/42122e31-bc04-47ca-ad8c-23157e56c9a5/FRC-Effective-Stewardship-Reporting-Review_November-2021.pdf> It should be noted that an outcomes-based enforcement approach was also adopted by the South African Code 2011 (n 50) which operates on an 'apply or explain' basis. See Locke, Encouraging Sustainable Investment in South Africa, Chapter 22. However, it did not gain traction in any other jurisdiction until the UK adopted an 'apply and explain' mode in 2020.

the FRC and currently with the outcomes-focused reporting approach of the UK Code 2020. Third, recently the 'comply or explain' obligations have been replaced with 'apply and explain' obligations which move the obligation to conform to the principles in the UK Code a step closer to becoming mandatory rules.[113]

In stark contrast, as reported in Table 1.3, ten codes in seven non-UK jurisdictions with stewardship codes and three inter-jurisdictional codes provide that those who voluntarily agree to be 'bound' by the code have *no obligations* under it.[114] It is shocking that in a significant portion of jurisdictions that have adopted UK-style stewardship codes, those who have agreed to be 'bound' by the code are required *to do nothing at all* – a game-changing reality of global shareholder stewardship that has been completely overlooked.[115] These codes are merely suggested principles issued to those who voluntarily sign up; they do not require the signatories to comply, explain or do anything at all. This mode of enforcement – which more correctly should be called a mode of 'non-enforcement' – makes such codes more like statements of best suggested practices. These 'no-obligations' codes, which are drafted by both governmental (as in Singapore) and private issuers (as in the US), are perhaps the most deceptive codes – and the most difficult to understand – as signing up to something which requires nothing from one seems like an exercise in futility. However, our examination of jurisdiction-specific factors illuminates some possible rationales for this ostensibly futile exercise.[116] There is also some evidence of 'hardening'[117] in terms of the mode of enforcement as the latest versions of the Italian and Canadian codes moved from a no-obligations mode to a comply-or-explain one.[118]

In fact, Table 1.3 confirms that, outside the UK, only the Australian (FSC) Code 2017 and the Indian (IRDAI) Code 2017 adopt the original enforcement model of the UK Code 2010/2012, that is, non-voluntary scope and the comply-or-explain mode. In seventeen non-UK codes, institutional investors who are bound by the code are required to comply or explain with the principles in the code.[119] At first blush, these jurisdictions may be seen to have adopted the UK-style

TABLE 1.3 *Enforcement of stewardship codes*[120]

	Degree of coerciveness	SCOPE Voluntary	Non-voluntary (for some)	Total
MODE	No obligations	13 (7)	0 (0)	13 (7)
	Comply or explain	17 (13)	4 (2)	21 (15)
	Apply and explain	1 (1)	1 (1)	2 (2)
	Mandatory	0 (0)	3 (3)	3 (3)
	Total	31 (21)	8 (6)	39 (27)

[113] Katelouzou (n 10).
[114] It is also notable that from the ten jurisdiction-specific codes, six are the latest versions (that is: Australian (ACSI) Code 2018 (n 50), Malaysian Code 2014 (n 50), Norway Code 2019, Singapore Code 2016, Singapore Family Code (n 22), US Code 2017).
[115] Puchniak and Tang, Singapore's Embrace of Shareholder Stewardship, Chapter 14 raises this most forcefully.
[116] Section 1.4.4.
[117] On hardening of stewardship rules, see Chiu and Katelouzou (n 5) 131–52.
[118] See Appendix (Table 1.5) for further details.
[119] These include sixteen jurisdictional-specific codes in twelve non-UK jurisdictions and the EFAMA Code 2018. For further details, see Appendix (Table 1.5).
[120] Table 1.3 takes into account all intra- and inter-jurisdictional codes. The numbers in brackets relate to the latest versions of the codes.

comply-or-explain enforcement regime. However, upon closer examination, the enforcement regimes in these comply-or-explain jurisdictions differ significantly from UK-style enforcement. To start with, as all the codes which adopt the comply-or-explain enforcement mode – except for the Australian (FSC) Code 2017 and the Indian (IRDAI) Code 2017 – are voluntary, those institutional investors who do not want to comply or explain can simply decide that they no longer want to be bound by the code – which is not an option for domestic institutional investors in the UK.

The UK's experience with *foreign* institutional investors, for which the UK Code is voluntary, demonstrates how institutional investors opting out of a voluntary code when it suits their self-interest is a real risk. After the UK adopted its public tiering exercise of the signatories to the UK Code 2012, a significant number of foreign institutional investors (some of which were foreign) who wanted to avoid the embarrassment of being placed in the bottom tier simply opted to no longer be bound by the UK Code.[121] As one of the UK's most prominent corporate law scholars has persuasively argued, the fact that the UK Code is voluntary for foreign institutional investors has rendered it virtually nugatory for this important class of institutional investors in the UK.[122] However, what has gone almost entirely unnoticed prior to this book project is that, with two exceptions (Australian (FSC) Code 2017 and Indian (IRDAI) Code 2017), globally all the jurisdictions that have adopted the UK's comply-or-explain standard have done so in the context of codes which are voluntary codes for all (*both* domestic and foreign) institutional investors – while all other codes, aside from the three latest Indian codes (Indian (PFRDA) Code, Indian (SEBI) Code and Indian (IRDAI) Code 2020), are no-obligations codes which require nothing at all from those who volunteer to be 'bound' by them.

As if the UK enforcement system was not already enough of an outlier, there is not a single non-UK jurisdiction that has adopted anything in its enforcement regime that even comes close to approximating the UK's public tiering exercise. This suggests that the UK stands alone as having the only enforcement system which evaluates the quality of commitment to and disclosure of the principles in its stewardship code, with a market mechanism to explicitly sanction poor performers.[123] Moreover, the UK's recent adoption of its stricter 'apply and explain' standard, which has not yet been followed by any other jurisdiction, and its emphasis in the UK Code 2020 on stewardship outcomes rather than mere policies further accentuate its outlier status as having an enforcement regime that places considerably more pressure on institutional investors (or other shareholders bound by a code) to take stewardship seriously. This is somewhat ironic because the UK Code has faced harsh criticism for its 'soft law' approach – but, when viewed through a comparative lens, the UK's shareholder stewardship regime is the 'hardest' in the world.[124]

This observation is important because the global ubiquity of stewardship codes with the UK's seven principles has resulted in the widespread misunderstanding that UK-style stewardship has been transplanted around the world. Indeed, a recent prominent article on 'The Agency Problems of Institutional Investors' lumps the UK Code together with non-UK codes as being 'nonbinding stewardship codes which various institutional investors have pledged to follow'.[125] An important insight from this prominent article is that most often institutional investors lack the economic incentives to properly invest in stewardship. While we agree with this general

---

[121] See Katelouzou (n 10) for data.
[122] Cheffins (n 12).
[123] Further on market mechanisms, see Katelouzou and Sergakis, Shareholder Stewardship Enforcement, Chapter 27.
[124] The three latest Indian codes, PFRDA 2018, SEBI 2019 and IRDAI 2020, are mandatory in terms of the mode of enforcement, but there is no active monitoring of the quality of compliance as in the UK: Varottil, Shareholder Stewardship in India, Chapter 17. This is why the UK code is perceived as the 'hardest' code in terms of enforcement.
[125] Lucian A Bebchuk, Alma Cohen and Scott Hirst, 'The Agency Problems of Institutional Investors' (2017) 31 Journal of Economic Perspectives 89.

observation, the variety in enforcement regimes that we have identified suggests that a finer grained analysis – which differentiates among the different types of enforcement regime in different jurisdictions with stewardship codes – is required.

Given the extremely lax and non-existent enforcement regimes in almost all non-UK jurisdictions, there is an acute risk that UK-style stewardship codes in these jurisdictions will be ineffective in motivating institutional investors to adequately invest in corporate governance. However, in the UK, where the regime is binding on domestic institutional investors and places real obligations on all institutional investors bound by the code, the analysis is different. In the UK, the success of corporate governance–focused stewardship will depend on whether this regulatory nudge will be enough to change the economics of investing in stewardship for institutional investors in the UK. The widespread consensus is that the regulatory nudge under the UK Code 2010/2012 was insufficient. However, it is important to recognize that, different from non-UK jurisdictions, the UK has developed an enforcement regime that provides a stronger regulatory nudge than in almost any other jurisdiction and that it has recently been strengthened further by replacing the comply-or-explain with the apply-and-explain standard. Moreover, as will be discussed, the economic incentive problem preventing institutional investors from investing in stewardship may be less acute when the focus of stewardship is ESG rather than corporate governance.[126] This, combined with the UK Code's new stricter apply-and-explain standard, may provide a glimmer of hope for the new ESG-focused UK Code 2020.

Finally, a clear question that arises from the totality of this comparative analysis of stewardship enforcement regimes around the world is: Why have almost all jurisdictions departed from the UK's enforcement model? There are at least five reasons that may explain this development. First, the original conception of stewardship, which focuses on transforming institutional investors into actively engaged shareholders, is contrary to the business models of several types of institutional investor – which makes a voluntary code more tenable as those institutional investors which have a business model that suits the code can choose to join (and, perhaps more importantly, those with incongruent business models are not bound). Second, from a corporate law perspective, shareholders normally have no obligation to be actively engaged in corporate governance and, therefore, making codes voluntary avoids stewardship conflicting with a fundamental tenet of corporate law. Third, the ambiguity of what stewardship is – which, as described earlier, has five different conceptions[127] – is more conducive to a voluntary regime as ambiguous principles are hard to strictly enforce. Fourth, with the UK Code 2020 making ESG obligations a central component of stewardship, some jurisdictions may be hesitant to require institutional investors to follow these principles when their corporate law may still be centred on a narrower conception of corporations focusing on maximizing shareholder value.[128] Fifth, a UK-style stewardship code may not fit with the shareholder environment in jurisdictions that are dominated by controlling shareholders – a voluntary code may allow such jurisdictions to formally adopt the code to signal compliance with a global standard of 'good corporate governance', without it having much impact in practice. It is to this critical aspect of global shareholder stewardship – the transplantation of UK-style codes to a world in which institutional investors are normally collectively minority shareholders and controlling-block shareholders are normally predominant – to which we now turn.

---

[126] Sections 1.4.5 and 1.5. See also Katelouzou (n 10).
[127] Section 1.2.
[128] For example, jurisdictions such as the US: Lucian Bebchuk and Roberto Tallarita, 'The Illusory Promise of Stakeholder Governance' (2020) 106 Cornell Law Review 91, 106, 128; and Rock (n 30) 19.

1.4.3 UK-Style Codes: Misfits in a World of Minority Institutional Investors and Controlling Shareholders

It is now time to play a thought experiment. Assume that non-UK stewardship codes around the world were not hobbled by the lax and non-existent enforcement problems just highlighted. In fact, let us go one step further. Assume that institutional investors around the world followed the principles in their UK-style stewardship codes to a tee. At first blush, one may expect that this would produce similar results around the world as almost all codes have adopted the UK's seven principles and enforcement would be moot. However, in reality, the opposite would be the truth – the corporate governance effect in the UK would be dramatically different from that in most non-UK jurisdictions.

This is because, as explained in detail by Puchniak elsewhere and elaborated on in Chapter 28 of this book, for the UK Code to have its intended corporate governance effect, a jurisdiction's shareholder landscape must have two foundational features: (1) institutional investors collectively have the legal rights to control most listed companies; and (2) a single or small group of block shareholders does not have the voting rights to control most listed companies.[129] As will be explained, the UK and the US are virtually the only two jurisdictions in the world in which these two features exist. As such, they are the only two jurisdictions where *if* a stewardship code succeeds in incentivizing institutional investors to become actively engaged shareholders, those institutional investors will be able to 'steward' most listed companies.

For decades, it has been well-known and widely accepted that *if* institutional investors act collectively they have the legal rights to control the corporate governance in most UK listed companies.[130] As a result, this assumption was the intellectual starting point for the idea to create a stewardship code in the UK and has been at the core of the UK's stewardship regime ever since.[131] This assumption was embedded in the design of the UK Code 2010, which assumes that if institutional investors act collectively they normally have the legal rights to intervene in a company's corporate governance by taking measures such as replacing the board of directors.[132] The UK Code 2020 also assumes that if institutional investors act collectively they have the ability to control a wide-enough swath of UK listed companies to 'respond to market-wide and systemic risks to promote a well-functioning financial system'.[133] In fact, the entire idea of making institutional investors – rather than another corporate stakeholder – the focus of the UK Code is predicated on the fact that if institutional investors act collectively they have the legal right to steward most UK listed companies.

However, the fact that collectively institutional investors have the legal right to control most listed companies makes the UK exceptional and cannot be assumed to be the case in almost any other jurisdiction. With the notable exception of the US, institutional investors

---

[129] Puchniak (n 13).

[130] ibid; Paul Myners, 'Institutional Investment in the United Kingdom: A Review' (HM Treasury 2001) 27 <https://uksif.org/wp-content/uploads/2012/12/MYNERS-P.-2001.-Institutional-Investment-in-the-United-Kingdom-A-Review.pdf> accessed 25 May 2021 [hereinafter Myners Review].

[131] Puchniak (n13); Myners Review (n 130) 1; John Kay, 'The Kay Review of UK Equity Markets and Long-Term Decision Making' (Department for Business, Innovation and Skills, July 2012) 50 https://assets.publishing.service.gov.uk/government/uploads/system/uploads/attachment_data/file/253454/bis-12-917-kay-review-of-equity-markets-final-report.pdf accessed 4 February 2022 [hereinafter Kay Review]; Walker Review (n 39) 87; Financial Conduct Authority/Financial Reporting Council, 'Building a Regulatory Framework for Effective Stewardship' (Discussion Paper, January 2019) 14 www.fca.org.uk/publication/discussion/dp19-01.pdf accessed 25 May 2021.

[132] UK Code 2010 (n 1) 8 (Principle 5); Davies, The UK Stewardship Code 2010–2020, Chapter 2, Sections 2.3.3 and 2.4.1.

[133] UK Code 2020 (n 28) 11 (Principle 4). For a detailed analysis see Puchniak (n 13).

TABLE 1.4 *Shareholding statistics in jurisdictions that have adopted stewardship codes*

Region	Jurisdiction	Percent of shares owned by institutional investors	Percent of listed companies with 3 largest owners controlling majority of shares	Institutional ownership Mean for region	Institutional ownership Median for region	3 largest owners as controllers Mean for region	3 largest owners as controllers Median for region
Asia	Japan	31%	15%	15%	13%	56%	66%
	Korea	13%	45%				
	India	19%	66%				
	Hong Kong	12%	75%				
	Thailand	8%	51%				
	Malaysia	11%	72%				
	Singapore	6%	70%				
	Taiwan	18%	N.A.				
Europe	UK	68%	12%	38%	38%	37%	33%
	Netherlands	39%	31%				
	Norway	26%	35%				
	Italy	16%	71%				
	Denmark	33%	N.A.				
	Switzerland	23%	N.A.				
North America	US	80%	4%	62%	62%	10%	10%
	Canada	43%	15%				
Africa	South Africa	33%	38%	33%	33%	38%	38%
	Kenya	N.A.	N.A.				
South America	Brazil	22%	72%	22%	22%	72%	72%
Australia	Australia	29%	N.A.	29%	29%	N.A.	N.A.
All jurisdictions				29%	25%	45%	45%
All jurisdictions (excl. UK/US)				23%	23%	50%	51%
Jurisdictions with public codes (excl. UK)				17%	13%	56%	66%
Jurisdictions with private codes				37%	31%	38%	35%

do not own a majority of the shares in listed companies in any other major economy.[134] To the contrary, based on the hand-calculated data in Table 1.4, at the end of 2017 the mean share ownership of institutional investors in the jurisdictions that have adopted a stewardship code, excluding the UK and the US, was 23% – a stark contrast to 68% in the UK and 80% in the US. In Asian jurisdictions, where UK-style stewardship codes have proliferated, at the end of 2017 the mean shareholder ownership of institutional investors was just 15%. Thus, the global corporate governance reality is the opposite of that in the UK: in most jurisdictions, institutional investors collectively hold a minority of shares in most listed companies and do not have the legal rights to control them. In short, the assumption embedded in the UK Code's design – that institutional investors collectively have the legal rights to act as stewards in most listed companies – does not fit the global corporate governance reality.

---

[134] Adriana De La Cruz, Alejandra Medina and Yung Tang, 'Owners of the World's Listed Companies' (OECD Capital Market Series, 17 October 2019) 18, figure 8 <www.oecd.org/corporate/owners-of-the-worlds-listed-companies.htm> accessed 25 May 2021. See also Puchniak (n 13).

As would be expected, there is some variation in the level of institutional shareholder ownership across jurisdictions and there are a handful of jurisdictions in which institutional investors collectively own a sizable *minority* of shares in listed companies. For instance, as reported in Table 1.4, in Canada and Australia the mean share ownership of institutional investors is 43% and 29%, respectively, while block holders are fading. It is, therefore, likely that in these jurisdictions institutional investors may, in some cases, possibly be able to make use of company law rights to block corporate actions pursued by controlling shareholders.[135] However, in jurisdictions where the collective shareholder ownership of institutional investors is in the small single digits, the company law remedies available to block actions pursued by the controlling shareholders and the benefits of acting collectively will be considerably more limited.

While the variation in the size of the minority share ownership stake of institutional investors is meaningful, it should not obscure the reality that institutional investors acting primarily as minority shareholders does not fit the assumption embedded in the UK Code or its ambitious goals. It does not provide institutional investors with the legal rights to steward companies if they act collectively – let alone to be 'guardians of market integrity' who 'respond to market-wide and systemic risks', as contemplated in the UK Code 2020.[136] Nor does institutional shareholders collectively acting as minority shareholders fit with the goal of solving the systemic problems of excessive risk taking and short-termism revealed by the GFC in UK listed companies – which was the impetus behind the UK Code 2010's goal of transforming rationally passive institutional investors into actively engaged shareholder stewards.[137] However, in the UK's corporate governance reality, where institutional investors collectively own a sizable majority of shares, the UK Code's aim of transforming institutional investors into the solution for the UK's core corporate governance – or even societal – problems makes sense.

The rationale for transplanting a UK-style stewardship code to other countries appears even more curious considering the game-changing fact that in most countries, with the notable exception of the UK/US, a single or small group of block-shareholders, who are *not* institutional investors, controls the voting rights in most listed companies. These controlling shareholders – who are often wealthy families or individuals, the state, or other corporations – have the voting rights and the economic incentive to control the corporate governance in their respective listed companies.[138] As 'stewardship' has become a global buzzword to signify good corporate governance, some of these rationally active, non-institutional, controlling-block shareholders have begun to label themselves as 'good stewards' of the companies they control – giving life to the third conception of stewardship explained earlier.[139] However, nothing in the history, policy

---

[135] However, even in these jurisdictions the ability of institutional investors to have an impact on corporate governance may be limited. As noted in Williams, Stewardship Principles in Canada, Chapter 20, there is a significant portion of Canadian companies where the UK Code's concept of institutional investor stewardship does not fit owing to its 'predominance of public companies with controlling shareholders who are by definition exercising stewardship' (Section 20.1). For a summary of shareholder rights that can be exercised by minority shareholders, see Luca Enriques, Henry Hansmann, Reinier Kraakman and Mariana Pargendler, 'The Basic Governance Structure: Minority Shareholders and Non-Shareholder Constituencies' in Reinier Kraakman and others (eds), The Anatomy of Corporate Law: A Comparative and Functional Approach (3rd edn, OUP 2017) 84. See also Williams, Stewardship Principles in Canada, Chapter 20, this present volume, highlighting the extensive shareholder rights provided by statute in Canada.
[136] UK Code 2020 (n 28) 4.
[137] Davies, The UK Stewardship Code 2010–2020, Chapter 2, Section 2.2; UK Code 2010 (n 1) 7.
[138] Lim and Puchniak, Can a Global Legal Misfit Be Fixed?, Chapter 28; Puchniak (n 13).
[139] Section 1.2. Temasek is an example; see Dan W Puchniak and Samantha Tang, 'Singapore's Puzzling Embrace of Shareholder Stewardship: A Successful Secret' (2020) 53 Vanderbilt Journal of Transnational Law 989; Temasek, 'A Trusted Steward' <www.temasekreview.com.sg/steward/a-trusted-steward.html> accessed 25 May 2021 (on its website, Temasek calls itself a 'trusted steward' and an investor with an institutional conscience and a duty towards present and future generations).

rationale or content of the UK Code suggests that it was ever intended to apply to such controlling shareholders.[140]

Nevertheless, as is clear from Table 1.4, listed companies are dominated by non-institutional controlling shareholders in most non-UK jurisdictions that have UK-style stewardship codes: in 50% of companies outside the UK/US the three largest shareholders control a majority of shares, whereas in the UK and the US it is 12% and 4%, respectively. Moreover, if one considers smaller block shareholders and the mechanisms they use to maintain control, outside of the UK/US, in most jurisdictions most listed companies are controlled by controlling shareholders.[141] Therefore, UK-style codes in jurisdictions with controlling shareholders are legal misfits as they target institutional shareholders (the original conception of stewardship), rather than non-institutional controlling shareholders (the third conception of stewardship), as the stewards of listed companies – which fits the corporate governance realities in the UK/US, but not in almost any other jurisdiction with a stewardship code.

A final important observation relates to the origin of stewardship codes. As we have seen,[142] stewardship codes have been issued either by government or quasi-government bodies (public or governmental codes) or by private organizations composed of, or supported by, mainly institutional investors (private or institutional investor codes). It is clear from Table 1.4 that private codes – as opposed to public codes – have tended to arise in non-UK jurisdictions in which institutional investors control a greater percentage of the stock market and controlling-block holders are less pronounced.

The average percentage of stock market capitalization owned by institutional investor ownership in non-UK jurisdictions with private codes is 37% – compared to 17% in non-UK jurisdictions that have public codes – while the average percentages of block-holders in the two camps are 38% and 56%, respectively.[143] This makes sense because in jurisdictions where institutional investors have a greater ownership stake, they will have a greater incentive to act collectively as they may be able to use their collective power to form a significant minority block of shares which may give them access to important veto rights. In addition, in jurisdictions in which institutional shareholders have a larger presence, they may have a greater ability to organize and to pre-empt government regulation by creating a self-regulatory stewardship regime. This is not surprising: institutional investors have the incentives to adopt a code as a pre-emptive device in order to maintain self-regulation.[144] In the absence of controlling shareholders, institutional investors have not only the incentives, but also the abilities, to adopt such a code and formalize collective engagement.

In sum, a game-changing fact, which was entirely overlooked prior to this book project, is that UK-style stewardship codes have been largely transplanted into jurisdictions in which institutional investors are collectively minority shareholders and controlling shareholders predominate,

---

[140] Puchniak (n 13). See also Katelouzou and Siems, The Global Diffusion of Stewardship Codes, Chapter 30 (explaining that UK-style stewardship codes aim to address the agency problem caused by the rise of institutional investors).

[141] In contrast, 'the vast majority [of jurisdictions in the world] have corporations with controlling shareholders as the dominant characteristic'. See OECD, 'OECD Corporate Governance Factbook 2019' (2019) 17–18 <www.oecd.org/corporate/corporate-governance-factbook.pdf> accessed 25 May 2021; see also Puchniak (n 13).

[142] Section 1.4.1.

[143] However, two jurisdictions stand out as an exception here: Japan and Italy. In the former, public/governmental codes have been adopted despite the relatively high institutional ownership and the lack of controlling block-holders, whereas in the latter, private codes have been adopted despite the low institutional ownership and the high percentage of block-holder ownership. For jurisdiction-specific factors that may explain this apparent disparity, see Goto, Japanese Stewardship Code, Chapter 10 and Strampelli, Institutional Investor Stewardship in Italian Corporate Governance, Chapter 6.

[144] Section 1.4.1.

making them 'legal misfits'.[145] What is more, this legal misfit has been mainly driven by government or quasi-government bodies rather than by private actors. This fact, however, has not rendered the impact of the global proliferation of UK-style stewardship codes nugatory. To the contrary, as we explain in Section 1.4.4, these misfitted UK-style stewardship codes have served diverse, often jurisdictionally contingent functions – many of which would have been beyond the wildest imaginations of the original drafters of the UK Code. Understanding these functions, which prior to this book project were entirely overlooked, is necessary to have an accurate picture of the global proliferation of shareholder stewardship. It is to this that we now turn.

1.4.4 Jurisdictional-Contingent Drivers of Global Shareholder Stewardship

1.4.4.1 Politics as an Important Driver of Public Stewardship Codes

In the binary world of private versus public codes, one may have to look for jurisdictional-contingent factors to explain the observed paradox of the proliferation of UK-style stewardship codes in terms of formal design and content but not in terms of enforcement. One such factor in the case of the adoption of UK-style codes by governmental and quasi-governmental bodies has been political motives. Several chapters in this book provide rich examples of the role of politics as a driver of the adoption of public stewardship codes, especially in Asia where, as we have seen,[146] all stewardship codes have been issued by governmental or quasi-governmental bodies. Sometimes governments appear to implement a UK-style code as it is considered the gold standard of stewardship, to signal that their jurisdiction complies with *global standards* of good corporate governance. Sometimes adopting a UK-style code demonstrates the government's responsiveness to an *economic crisis* or a scandal by adopting a corporate governance mechanism which almost universally has been seen as an indicium of good corporate governance. Sometimes a UK-style code allows the government to promote its own political agenda, with the code serving as a cover for *policy channelling*.

First, contributions in this book reveal that in some Asian jurisdictions the adoption of UK-style codes by governmental or quasi-governmental bodies has been driven by the government's motive to signal that their jurisdiction embraces cutting-edge global norms of 'good' corporate governance. The rationale behind such government action is to attract foreign investment by bolstering the jurisdiction's image and to strengthen the local investment market, without significantly changing how the jurisdiction's corporate governance actually works in practice – a corporate governance reform strategy which is described in Chapter 14 as 'halo signalling'.[147] As halo signalling does not involve the corporate governance mechanism effecting actual change, importance is placed on the jurisdiction's formal adoption of a mechanism that is considered to be the global gold standard of 'good' corporate governance.

As we have explained, where stewardship is concerned, the gold international standard is the UK Code 2010/2012.[148] The fact that the UK Code 2010/2012 is a poor fit in jurisdictions with controlling shareholders is irrelevant for the public drafters of stewardship codes, as the impetus for adopting a code is to signal formal compliance with the gold standard, and not to effect actual

---

[145] Puchniak (n 13).
[146] Section 1.4.1.
[147] Puchniak and Tang, Singapore's Embrace of Shareholder Stewardship, Chapter 14. See also Koh, Puchniak and Goto, Shareholder Stewardship in Asia, Chapter 29. The concept of 'halo signalling' was coined by Puchniak and Lan in their comparative research on Independent directors in Singapore: Dan W Puchniak and Luh Luh Lan, 'Independent Directors in Singapore: Puzzling Compliance Requiring Explanation' (2017) 65 *The American Journal of Comparative Law* 265.
[148] Section 1.4.1.

change. That public stewardship codes follow the UK model only as far as the formal design and content are concerned but deviate in terms of enforcement is a further indicator of signalling. Adopting the UK stewardship model only as far as its formal content is concerned, while turning its scope and compliance to voluntary standards and sometimes no obligations at all, makes it easy for governments to signal compliance while they limit their code's bite.

As this book shows, the two jurisdictions where signalling appears to have played the most significant role as a driver in the adoption of UK-style public stewardship codes are Hong Kong and Singapore.[149] Both jurisdictions adopted a code that mirrors the core concept, primary content and text of the UK Code 2010/2012, but they significantly deviated from the UK model of enforcement.[150] In both jurisdictions, for reasons explained elsewhere,[151] the codes served well the purpose of halo signalling. But that is not to say that signalling is a phenomenon unique to Asian 'International Financial Centres'.[152] Rather, there is some evidence that, in other jurisdictions with public codes, adopting the UK model was at least in part driven by an attempt to signal compliance with global corporate governance standards. For instance, the introduction of the Taiwanese Code by governmental bodies appears to be an attempt to signal conformance with Anglo-American-cum-global norms of 'good' corporate governance.[153] A similar force could be at play in Thailand where General Prayut Chan-o-cha's military junta, which took power in a coup d'état a few years earlier, issued a UK-style code in 2017 to send a message to the world that Thailand was at the cutting-edge of global trends in 'good' corporate governance.[154] Outside Asia, the introduction of a public stewardship code in Kenya has also been described as a political attempt to align with global best practices.[155]

Second, beyond halo signalling, another significant driver for the adoption of a UK-style public code is the political desire of the government to indicate its responsiveness to an economic crisis or scandals by adopting a corporate governance mechanism which almost universally has been seen as an indicium of good corporate governance.[156] The Japanese Code stands out here. As is thoughtfully explained in Chapter 10 of this book, the Japanese Code was adopted as a key part of the Abenomics strategy to reinvigorate the Japanese economy with the aim of transforming Japanese institutional investors into active stewards in close ties with their overseas counterparts. But serving these political desires via the medium of a UK-style code appears to promote, or at least incentivize, a more short-termist culture among Japanese investors which is antithetical to the original corporate governance–oriented conception of long-term active monitors which is at the heart of the UK Code 2010/2012.[157]

Third, the adoption of a UK-style code by a public body can serve as a cover for *policy channelling*. Chapter 11 insightfully illuminates that the Korean Code may have been adopted

---

[149] Donald, Stewardship in the Hong Kong International Financial Centre, Chapter 29; Puchniak and Tang, Singapore's Embrace of Shareholder Stewardship, Chapter 14; Koh, Puchniak and Goto, Shareholder Stewardship in Asia, Chapter 29.
[150] Section 1.4.2.
[151] Puchniak (n 13). See also Koh, Puchniak and Goto, Shareholder Stewardship in Asia, Chapter 29.
[152] For an insightful analysis of Singapore and Hong Kong as International Financial Centres, see Donald, Stewardship in the Hong Kong International Financial Centre, Chapter 13.
[153] Lin, The Assessment of Taiwan's Shareholder Stewardship Codes, Chapter 12.
[154] Puchniak (n 13). See also Kowpatanakit and Bunaramrueang, The Thai Institutional Investors Stewardship Code and Its Implementation, Chapter 16.
[155] Ouko, Stewardship Code in Kenya, Chapter 23.
[156] Responding to a scandal can be the motivation behind the introduction of a private code too. See Becker, Andrade and Prado, The Brazilian Stewardship Framework, Chapter 24, Section 24.2.1.
[157] Goto, Japanese Stewardship Code, Chapter 10.

by Korean financial regulators to exert their political agenda and power over private industry. As the authors explain, there is reason to believe that the government has used its influence over the Korean National Pension Service (NPS) – which is the largest institutional investor in Korea and the third-largest public pension fund in the world – to execute a strategy which has been labelled by its critics as 'pension-fund socialism' under the guise of stewardship.[158] Malaysia's embrace of a UK-style stewardship code may have also been motivated by concerns to cover policy channelling. As illuminated in Chapter 15, the Malaysian government's position as the controlling shareholder in many of the country's most powerful investment companies and listed companies has inextricably linked stewardship and the state. As it is explained, there is a real risk that Malaysia's government is using a UK-style code to achieve its political agenda, such that it is unclear 'whether the interests of the state are aligned with those of the asset owners, the asset managers and, more importantly, those of the ultimate beneficiaries or clients which are at the end of the investment chain'.[159]

These examples illustrate how the adoption of UK-style stewardship codes by public bodies may have more to do with a government's desire to execute its political agenda than corporate governance – making the fit of the UK-style code with the jurisdiction's corporate governance context a subsidiary concern. Beyond politics, however, it appears there are other significant drivers for the adoption of UK-style stewardship codes by both public and private bodies, which will now be explored.

1.4.4.2 Legal Forces as an Important Driver of Stewardship Codes: Complements, Substitutes and Accents

Legal forces have always been an important driver for the adoption (or non-adoption) of soft corporate governance standards. Central to a legal pluralist perspective of corporate governance is the observation of how mandatory and soft laws may operate in complementary or substitute fashion and how corporate governance norms today contain elements of both hard and soft law, or mandatory and voluntary rules.[160] As Katelouzou (forthcoming) has thoroughly explained elsewhere, rules relating to shareholder stewardship are mixed in nature: some rules are laid down in soft-law stewardship or corporate governance codes, but others (including rules about investment management and shareholder rights) are laid down in statutory instruments.[161] Stewardship codes, therefore, are part and parcel of a broader, multi-layer regulatory framework of mandatory and soft rules relating to corporate governance and investment management, described as 'stewardship ecology'.[162] The adoption of UK-style stewardship codes both by public bodies and by private actors appears to be – at least in part – driven by these legal forces.

Sometimes stewardship codes may be introduced to *complement* mandatory rules or other soft-law standards. Sometimes stewardship codes – especially when they emanate from private actors – may be introduced to fill existing gaps in mandatory rules and *substitute* for 'harder' state-emanated regulation. But, at the same time, mandatory rules may substitute the need for stewardship codes. Sometimes stewardship codes may reinforce and *accent* distinctive legal features.

---

[158] Kang and Chun, Korea's Stewardship Code and the Rise of Shareholder Activism, Chapter 11, Section 11.4.4.
[159] Tan, Institutional Investor Stewardship in Malaysia, Chapter 15, Section 15.1.
[160] Katelouzou and Zumbansen (n 2).
[161] Katelouzou (n 10).
[162] ibid.

First, it appears that the adoption of UK-style stewardship codes has been largely motivated by a desire to *complement* the jurisdiction's existing corporate governance code.[163] The origins of this complementarity can be found in the UK Code 2010/2012 itself. The Preamble of the UK Code makes it clear that one of its aims is to establish a framework of 'effective stewardship' for institutional investors which works in parallel with the principles of the UK Corporate Governance Code that underlie 'an effective board' and thereby support (in place at the time) the comply-or-explain system.[164] In addition, under Principle 3 of the UK Code 2010/2012, monitoring companies includes, among other things, evaluating whether companies' boards adhere to the UK Corporate Governance Code and thus supporting the conformity with good corporate governance standards.[165] In other words, institutional investors are expected to assess the company's displayed compliance with the UK Corporate Governance Code as part of their stewardship obligations and give effect to the (then existing) comply-or-explain enforcement model. This need to complement good corporate governance principles – which are mainly aimed at increasing the effectiveness of the board of directors by transforming institutional investors into 'good stewards' to be a catalyst for the comply-or-explain regulatory model – can be found in many non-UK codes.

For example, the Danish Code, which was introduced by the same governmental body that adopted the Danish Corporate Governance Code – the Danish Committee on Corporate Governance – works in a 'parallel' fashion to and supports its corporate governance counterpart.[166] The Dutch Code explicitly acknowledges its complementarity to the Dutch Corporate Governance Code. The Guidance to Principle 1 of the original Dutch Code 2011 recommends to investors belonging to Eumedion – the institutional investor association that introduced the Dutch Code – to 'make a thorough assessment of the reasons provided by the company for any non-compliance with the best practice provisions of the Dutch corporate governance code'.[167] In a similar vein, the Dutch Code 2018 highlights that the 'Code should be read in conjunction with the Dutch Corporate Governance Code'.[168]

Outside Europe, this complementarity is recognized by the Kenyan Code which aims, among other things, to reinforce the implementation of the 'apply-or-explain' system of the Kenyan corporate governance code.[169] South Africa is also a prime example of this complementarity. As Chapter 22 skilfully highlights, the South Africa Code 2011 interacts very closely with the King IV report. In Asia, the Thai Code, in a fashion similar to the UK model, provides that, as part of monitoring, institutional investors should ensure that the board of directors and the subcommittees of their investee companies conform to the Thai Corporate Governance Code.[170] In a less direct way, the Japanese Code 2014 recognizes in its Preamble that 'the function of the board and that of institutional investors as defined in the Code are complementary and both form essential elements of high-quality corporate governance'.[171]

---

[163] For the complementarity between the two types of code, see Katelouzou (n 10).
[164] UK Code 2012 (n 9) 1. Further on the changes in the enforcement mode between the two versions of the UK Code, see Katelouzou (n 10).
[165] UK Code 2012 (n 9) 7. On the complementarity between the two codes, see Katelouzou (n 10).
[166] Birkmose and Madsen, The Danish Stewardship Code, Chapter 7, Section 7.3.1.
[167] Dutch Code 2011 (n 50) 5.
[168] Dutch Code 2018 (n 50) 2.
[169] Kenya Code (n 19) Schedule, para 5; Ouko, Stewardship Code in Kenya, Chapter 23, Section 23.2.4.
[170] Thai Code 2017 (n 50) 42, Principle 3.2.
[171] The Council of Experts Concerning the Japanese Version of the Stewardship Code, 'Principles for Responsible Institutional Investors "Japan's Stewardship Code" – To Promote Sustainable Growth of Companies through Investment and Dialogue' (26 February 2014) 2 <www.fsa.go.jp/en/refer/councils/stewardship/20140407/01.pdf> accessed 25 May 2021.

It seems, therefore, that the adoption of UK-style stewardship codes by both public bodies and private actors has been – at least in part – driven by the perceived need to complement and support the implementation of the jurisdiction's corporate governance code and give effect to the comply-or-explain system. Beyond that, complementarity runs on other levels too. For instance, non-UK stewardship codes have been adopted to complement various soft and hard law stewardship-related rules, as in the case of the Brazil Code 2016, or investment management rules, as in the case of the South African Code 2011.[172]

Within the EU, another legal factor that appears to impact the adoption – but also the rejection – of the UK stewardship model is the introduction of the amended Shareholder Rights Directive (SRD II) in 2017.[173] As Chiu and Katelouzou explain elsewhere, the SRD II has largely followed the steps of the UK Code 2010/2012 in introducing an engagement policy for all institutions and a form of disclosure-based regulation of institutions' investment policies and strategies, their arrangements with asset managers, and the accountability of asset managers to institutions.[174] Despite the fact that the SRD II does not adopt the term stewardship and refers, rather, to 'shareholder engagement', the European notion of shareholder engagement includes monitoring, collaborative activities, conducting dialogue with companies and exercising voting rights and is thereby consonant with the UK-style stewardship.[175] The SRD II was adopted in 2017, but its first version started to be negotiated in 2014 – long before the spike in the evolution of stewardship codes which Chapter 30 dates as being between the years 2016 and 2017.[176] Katelouzou and Sergakis have elsewhere illuminated that the stewardship provisions of the SRD II were transposed in a literal and minimalistic fashion despite divergent national specifications.[177] This was attributed in part to the more apt soft, flexible and mostly bottom-up stewardship codes contained in private stewardship codes in the EU.[178]

Whereas it is plausible that the direction of causality runs from earlier soft stewardship codes to the mandatorily transposed SRD II rules, one cannot exclude the possibility that the relationship between the SRD II and national stewardship codes is not unidirectional and can go both ways. The case of the Netherlands is indicative here. Previous literature suggests that because of the pre-existing Dutch Code 2011, the SRD II was transposed in the Netherlands in a literal and minimalistic fashion.[179] But, at the same time, the revised Dutch Code 2019 can be viewed as the direct result of the implementation of the SRD II in the Netherlands.[180] Of course, this two-way exchange of stewardship norms is more difficult to be found in other EU member states with stewardship codes introduced by investor associations with less lobbying power than the Dutch Eumedion.[181] For instance, in Italy, although the SRD II was transposed in a literal and minimalistic way,[182] this transposition took place separately from the revisions of the Italian Code, which itself was introduced by an association of asset managers (Assogestioni), and

---

[172] See Locke, Encouraging Sustainable Investment in South Africa, Chapter 22 and Becker, Andrade and Prado, The Brazilian Stewardship Framework, Chapter 24.
[173] SRD II (n 5).
[174] Chiu and Katelouzou (n 5).
[175] SRD II (n 5) art 3h para 2.
[176] Katelouzou and Siems, The Global Diffusion of Stewardship Codes, Chapter 30, Section 30.3.1.
[177] Katelouzou and Sergakis (n 5).
[178] ibid.
[179] ibid.
[180] Van der Elst and Lafarre, Shareholder Stewardship in the Netherlands, Chapter 4, Section 4.2.2.
[181] On the lobbying of Eumedion on the transposition of the SRD II in the Netherlands, see Van der Elst and Lafarre, Shareholder Stewardship in the Netherlands, Chapter 4, Section 4.1.
[182] Katelouzou and Sergakis (n 5).

Chapter 6 claims that the SRD II transposed rules do not seem to have a positive impact 'in enhancing the relevance' of the Italy Code (2016).[183]

The impact of the SRD II on the appetite of EU member states with no stewardship code, like Germany, to introduce a code is even more questionable. Chapter 9 argues that the SRD II may act as a *substitute* and thereby make the introduction of a domestic code nugatory. A substituting impact upon domestic codes may also be found in Denmark. Chapter 7 contends that, as a consequence of the implementation of the SRD II engagement provisions, which are very similar to the Danish Code, the Danish Committee on Corporate Governance – the drafter of the Danish Code – made tentative steps to phase out the Code and weaken its enforcement mode.[184] That the jurisdiction of origin of the global stewardship model (the UK) – which has provided the yardstick and the bedrock of the SRD II – is no longer part of the EU may further negatively impact the future diffusion of the UK model in the EU.[185]

Finally, the adoption of a UK-style code may be motivated by and *accent* distinctive legal rules. Italy serves as a prime example in this regard. We have already highlighted the paradox of the origins of the Italian code as a private code introduced by an Italian investment management association despite the low presence of institutional investors in Italian public forms and the predominance of controlling shareholders.[186] Chapter 6 skilfully explains this paradox by reference to the so-called slate (or list) voting system which enables minority shareholders to appoint at least one director on the management and statutory auditor boards. Data show that a significant number of minority-appointed directors has, in recent years, been appointed by institutional investors co-ordinated by Assogestioni, the drafter of the Italian Code.[187] This suggests that a UK-style code can still fit in a jurisdiction with controlling shareholders if there are other distinctive legal forces that can foster the role of minority institutional investors.

While it is too early to reach a conclusion about the symbiosis of stewardship rules and principles, what our analysis makes clear is that the shareholder stewardship landscape is complex and multilevel and that legal forces can highly influence the adoption and sometimes rejection of UK-style stewardship codes.

1.4.5 ESG Movement: Enriching the UK Model

In addition to jurisdiction-specific factors, a driver which more recently appears to motivate the adoption of both public and private codes is a focus on ESG considerations in investment management. For public codes, the increased focus on ESG increasingly garners political support in many jurisdictions. The increased focus on ESG in private codes also makes sense as ESG is now an important part of the business model for an increasing number of institutional investors in response to the increasing demand by clients.[188]

---

[183] Strampelli, Institutional Investor Stewardship in Italian Corporate Governance, Chapter 6, Section 6.6.

[184] Birkmose and Madsen, The Danish Stewardship Code, Chapter 7, Section 7.6 (noting that the Committee announced that the Code's signatories are not expected to report on their compliance following the transposition of the SRD II). But no final steps have been taken by the Committee as this book goes to press: Committee on Corporate Governance, 'Udfasning af Anbefalinger for aktivt Ejerskab [Phasing Out Recommendations on Active Ownership]' (28 January 2020) <https://corporategovernance.dk/udfasning-af-anbefalinger-aktivt-ejerskab> accessed 25 May 2021.

[185] For a more positive view on the future diffusion of soft stewardship codes, see Katelouzou and Sergakis (n 5).

[186] See text accompanying n 146.

[187] Strampelli, Institutional Investor Stewardship in Italian Corporate Governance, Chapter 6, Section 6.5.1.

[188] Puchniak (n 13). Further on the demand side of the market for stewardship, see Katelouzou and Micheler, The Market for Stewardship and the Role of the Government, Chapter 3.

1 Global Shareholder Stewardship 35

Indeed, the rise of ESG as a factor mentioned in the latest versions of stewardship codes globally is striking. The original UK Code 2010/2012 hardly mentions ESG, and the South African Code 2011 was an outlier among first generation non-UK codes with the core focus on ESG.[189] Building on the UN Principles for Responsible Investing, the South African Code 2011 includes five principles aimed at incorporating sustainability and ESG into investment management.[190] But the South African Code – despite deviating from the UK model along all three of the dimensions identified earlier (i.e., core concept, primary content and text/language)[191] – did not manage to establish itself as a global stewardship leader.

Nevertheless, Chapter 26 reveals that 84% of the latest versions of stewardship codes now refer 'at least once to ESG factors' and that only four current codes (i.e., Danish Code 2016, Korean Code 2016, Swiss Code 2013 and US Code 2017) do not mention ESG factors at all.[192] This comports with our hand-collected data showing that ten non-UK codes include at least one principle on ESG.[193] Chapter 26 also, however, highlights that several of these codes mention ESG only in a cursory manner for reasons that have more to do with politics and attracting foreign investment than a genuine commitment to ESG.[194] This is reinforced by the fact that only a minority of codes link the goal of implementing ESG with fiduciary duties. As Chapter 26 notes, 'from the nineteen codes that explicitly link stewardship practices to the fulfilment of investors' legal duties, only four codes ... clearly regard the consideration of ESG factors as part of institutional investors' fiduciary responsibility'.[195] These four codes are three jurisdictional codes – the Brazil Code 2016, the Kenyan Code 2017 and the Thai Code 2017 – and the latest version of the intra-jurisdictional ICGN Code 2016.[196]

The UK Code 2020, which has itself manifested an expanded, 'enlightened' vision of stewardship with its pivot to ESG, makes no mention of fiduciary duties.[197] This point is important because investor or beneficiary welfare is still the goal of stewardship in the second version of the UK Code.[198] We will discuss the potential of ESG as a catalyst for stewardship and whether the UK Code 2020 will serve as a new model in this regard, but what is clear is that the rise of the ESG movement provides another possible rationale for the global proliferation of UK-style codes. Public and private codes enriched with references to ESG – sometimes passing but other times more extended – find it easier to adopt the UK-model.

1.5 THE FUTURE OF GLOBAL SHAREHOLDER STEWARDSHIP: CHALLENGES AND POSSIBILITIES REVEALED

As illuminated in this chapter and detailed in this book, although formally UK-style stewardship codes have been transplanted around the world, the jurisdiction-specific reasons which have driven their adoption, the way in which they have been enforced and the local corporate governance and legal environments in which they exist have combined to produce varieties of stewardship that perform diverse functions – which would have been beyond the wildest

---

[189] Katelouzou and Siems, The Global Diffusion of Stewardship Codes, Chapter 30.
[190] Locke, Encouraging Sustainable Investment in South Africa, Chapter 22, Sections 22.2 and 23.3.
[191] ibid, Section 22.3.2.
[192] Katelouzou and Klettner, Sustainable Finance and Stewardship, Chapter 26, Section 26.3.3.
[193] See Section 1.3.2.2.
[194] Katelouzou and Klettner, Sustainable Finance and Stewardship, Chapter 26, Section 26.3.3.
[195] ibid.
[196] ibid.
[197] Katelouzou (n 10) for the term 'enlightened stewardship'.
[198] ibid.

imaginations of the original drafters of the UK Code. By revealing these varieties of stewardship, this chapter and this book not only illuminate the untold complexity of global shareholder stewardship but also reveal the diverse roles that it plays – or, perhaps more importantly, does not play – in different jurisdictions around the world.

Despite this diversity and complexity, if we take a step back, there are two features of shareholder stewardship that appear to present serious challenges to its utility globally: (1) lax enforcement regimes designed to change the behaviour of institutional investors in ways that are often contrary to their business models; and (2) a regulatory design that is premised on institutional investors collectively holding a majority of shares in most listed companies when, in fact, they most often are collectively minority shareholders. These two ubiquitous features suggest that the future of shareholder stewardship is bleak as they appear to seriously undercut its ability to solve most firm-specific or systematic corporate governance problems in most jurisdictions around the world.[199] However, the rise of ESG as a recent focal point of stewardship appears to present a hopeful possibility for its future. This is because it presents a way to overcome the two main challenges to shareholder stewardship and to be part of the burgeoning ESG movement, which may become a mega-trend in the foreseeable future. Providing a more detailed explanation of these two serious challenges and ESG as the possible future of stewardship is what we will now do.

In terms of the first challenge, since the inaugural UK code was released in 2010, the most widely cited feature for its ineffectiveness has been the lax nature of its enforcement regime. This critique was widely discussed and well-known among academics and pundits within the UK prior to this book project. Indeed, as explained earlier, this critique drove UK regulators to make several amendments to the UK's enforcement regime, moving it towards a more mandatory approach, which now borders on hard law.[200]

This chapter and book project, however, reveal that the enforcement regimes for stewardship codes globally are substantially laxer than the UK's regime – with the vast majority being entirely voluntary in scope and a significant portion requiring institutional investors to do nothing at all. This revelation is critical as there is convincing theoretical and empirical evidence that it is contrary to the business models of most institutional investors to actively engage in shareholder stewardship[201] – which formally, based on the text of codes, is the stated mission of most stewardship codes globally. The revelation that although almost all jurisdictions adopted the UK's seven principles – but none have adopted the UK's stricter enforcement regime – strongly suggests that the UK's failure to change the behaviour of rationally passive institutional investors will be repeated, in an even more definitive way, globally.

The second primary challenge to shareholder stewardship globally is that even if it succeeds in transforming institutional investors into actively engaged shareholders, this will not result in institutional investors acting as the stewards of most listed companies in most jurisdictions globally. As explained in this chapter and this book, this is because in all major economies, aside from those of the UK and the US, institutional investors are collectively minority shareholders. Moreover, in most jurisdictions globally, most listed companies have a controlling shareholder who is a rationally active steward in most listed companies. As such, in the unlikely scenario where stewardship codes transform institutional investors into actively engaged shareholders, they will most often serve as active minority shareholders – but not shareholder stewards.

---

[199] Jeffrey Gordon, 'Systemic Stewardship' (2021) ECGI Law Working Paper No 566/2021 <https://ssrn.com/abstract=3782814> accessed 25 May 2021.
[200] Section 1.4.2.
[201] Bebchuk, Cohen and Hirst (n 125).

This reality – that the UK's shareholder stewardship model is a 'global legal misfit' – was entirely unknown prior to this book project.[202] It also may be the nail in the coffin for institutional shareholder–driven stewardship globally – as it demonstrates why it is currently impossible for institutional shareholders to steward most listed companies outside of the UK/US.

However, before resigning this book to being a detailed autopsy documenting the demise of global shareholder stewardship, the transformation of shareholder stewardship into a mechanism to promote ESG may spark its resurrection. As explained in this book, ESG-focused stewardship may not be hobbled by the economic incentive problems inherent in institutional shareholder–driven stewardship focused on improving corporate governance. This is because ESG-focused stewardship may comport with the business models of an increasingly large portion of institutional investors – nudging in the same direction as their business models (rather than being a mechanism reliant on changing their business models). In addition, institutional investors acting as minority shareholders may be able to effectively give voice to the ESG movement and pressure controlling shareholders into becoming part of the movement. This may make the fact that institutional investors normally are not collectively majority shareholders less relevant. However, as Chapter 28 also highlights, there is the possibility that institutional investors and corporate controllers may all signal a concern for ESG without making any changes in practice. If this occurs, it may continue the widespread trend, revealed in this book, of stewardship being a malleable, inexpensive tool co-opted by institutional investors and governments to serve their own self-interests.

Finally, it is possible, but at present unlikely, that the evolution of global shareholder stewardship may surprise us by adopting one of the other conceptions of stewardship, described at the outset of this chapter, as its main focal point. Rather than being a global legal misfit, jurisdictions may start to realize that an important role for stewardship in most jurisdictions is to serve as a check on controlling shareholder abuse, and amend their codes to focus on the role of institutional investors as collective minorities – but there is no evidence that this is occurring in stewardship codes. However, the analyses of China (Chapter 18) and Germany (Chapter 9) suggest that regulators may be inserting provisions into corporate governance codes to incentivize institutional investors to act as checks on controlling shareholders – bringing some life to this conception of stewardship. Another possibility is that jurisdictions in Asia may follow Singapore and draft codes that make controlling shareholders, rather than institutional investors, a focal point of stewardship – which would be more theoretically sound, but which has its own challenges, as highlighted in Chapter 28. Finally, the investment management conception of stewardship may become more prominent if institutional investors drive the future proliferation of shareholder stewardship globally – which does appear to be the trend that is occurring outside of Asia.

If this book project has taught us one thing, it is to keep an open mind and be humble. Indeed, when we started this project, we never anticipated how much about global shareholder stewardship we would discover – particularly how pervasively it would diverge in practice from the original UK model and how many varieties of shareholder stewardship would emerge. This suggests that the future will likely hold some more surprises that we have not anticipated – it is indeed likely the beginning of history for shareholder stewardship.

---

[202] For a detailed explanation of this point, see Puchniak (n 13).

APPENDIX

TABLE 1.5 *Stewardship codes around the world after 2010*

Jurisdiction	Year	Title	Drafter(s)	Type	Enforcement Scope	Enforcement Mode	No of principles (form)	Core concept (CG, IM, ESG, CS)	P1	P2	P3	P4	P5	P6	P7	Additional (non-UK 2010/2012) principles
Jurisdiction-Specific																
Australia	2017	FSC Standard 23: Principles of Internal Governance and Asset Stewardship	Financial Services Council (FSC)	private	non-voluntary for members	comply-or-explain	3	IM	Yes	Yes	Yes	Yes	Yes	Yes	Yes	Yes
	2018	Australian Asset Owner Stewardship Code	Australian Council of Superannuation Investors (ACSI)	private	voluntary	no-obligations	6	CG	Yes	Yes	Yes	Yes	Yes	Yes	Yes	Yes
Brazil	2016	AMEC Stewardship Code	AMEC	private	voluntary	comply-or-explain	7	CG	Yes	Yes	Yes	No	Yes	Yes	Yes	Yes
Canada	2010	Principles for Governance Monitoring, Voting and Shareholder Engagement	Canadian Coalition for Good Governance (CCCG)	private	voluntary	no-obligations	7	CG	Yes	No	Yes	No	Yes	Yes	No	Yes
	2017	CCGC Stewardship Principles	Canadian Coalition for Good Governance (CCCG)	private	voluntary	no-obligations	7	CG	Yes	Yes	Yes	Yes	Yes	Yes	Yes	Yes
	2020	CCGC Stewardship Principles	Canadian Coalition for Good Governance (CCCG)	private	voluntary	comply-or-explain	7	CG	Yes	Yes	Yes	Yes	Yes	Yes	Yes	Yes

Country	Year	Code	Issuer	Public/Private	Voluntary	Comply-or-explain	Principles	CG					
Denmark	2016	Stewardship Code	The Committee on Corporate Governance	public	voluntary	comply-or-explain	7	CG	Yes	Yes	Yes	Yes	Yes	No
Hong Kong	2016	Principles of Responsible Ownership	Securities and Futures Commission	public	voluntary	comply-or-explain	7	CG	Yes	Yes	Yes	Yes	Yes	No
India	2017	Guidelines on Stewardship Code for Insurers	IRDAI	public	non-voluntary for members	comply-or-explain	7	CG	Yes	Yes	Yes	Yes	Yes	No
	2018	Common Stewardship Code	PFRDA	public	non-voluntary for members	mandatory	6	CG	Yes	Yes	Yes	Yes	Yes	No
	2019	Stewardship Code	SEBI	public	non-voluntary for members	mandatory	6	CG	Yes	Yes	Yes	Yes	Yes	No
	2020	Guidelines on Stewardship Code for Insurers	IRDAI	public	non-voluntary for members	mandatory	7	CG	Yes	Yes	Yes	Yes	Yes	No
Italy	2013	Italian Stewardship Principles for the exercise of administrative and voting rights in listed companies	Assogestioni	private	voluntary	no-obligations	6	CG	Yes	No	Yes	Yes	Yes	No
	2015	Italian Stewardship Principles for the exercise of administrative and voting rights in listed companies	Assogestioni	private	voluntary	comply-or-explain	6	CG	Yes	Yes	Yes	Yes	Yes	No
	2016	Italian Stewardship Principles for the exercise of	Assogestioni	private	voluntary	comply-or-explain	6	CG	Yes	Yes	Yes	Yes	Yes	No

TABLE 1.5 *(continued)*

Jurisdiction	Year	Title	Drafter(s)	Type	Enforcement Scope	Enforcement Mode	No of principles (form)	Core concept (CG, IM, ESG, CS)	UK Code 2010/2012 principles (substance) P1	P2	P3	P4	P5	P6	P7	Additional (non-UK 2010/2012) principles
		administrative and voting rights in listed companies														
Japan	2014	Principles for Responsible Institutional Investors <<Japan's Stewardship Code>>	Council of Experts Concerning the Japanese Version of the Stewardship Code	public	voluntary	comply-or-explain	7	CG	Yes	Yes	Yes	No	No	Yes	Yes	Yes
	2017	Principles for Responsible Institutional Investors <<Japan's Stewardship Code>>	Council of Experts Concerning the Japanese Version of the Stewardship Code	public	voluntary	comply-or-explain	7	CG	Yes	Yes	Yes	No	Yes	Yes	Yes	Yes
	2020	Principles for Responsible Institutional Investors <<Japan's Stewardship Code>>	Council of Experts Concerning the Japanese Version of the Stewardship Code	public	voluntary	comply-or-explain	8	CG	Yes	Yes	Yes	No	Yes	Yes	Yes	Yes
Kenya	2017	Stewardship Code for Institutional Investors	Capital Markets Authority	public	voluntary	comply-or-explain	7	CG	Yes	Yes	Yes	Yes	Yes	Yes	Yes	Yes
Korea	2016	Principles on the Stewardship Responsibilities of Institutional Investors	Korea Stewardship Code Council	public	voluntary	comply-or-explain	7	CG	Yes	Yes	Yes	No	No	Yes	Yes	Yes

Malaysia	2014	Malaysian Code for Institutional Investors	Minority Shareholder Watchdog Group	public	voluntary	no-obligations	6	CG	Yes	Yes	Yes	Yes	Yes	Yes
Netherlands	2011	Best Practices for Engaged Share-Ownership	Eumedion	private	voluntary	comply-or-explain	10	CG	Yes	Yes	Yes	Yes	Yes	Yes
	2018	Dutch Stewardship Code	Eumedion	private	voluntary	comply-or-explain	11	CG	Yes	Yes	Yes	Yes	Yes	Yes
Norway	2012	Industry Recommendation for the Members of the Norwegian Fund and Asset Management Association: Exercise of Ownership Rights	Norwegian Fund and Asset Management Association	private	voluntary	no-obligations	N.A.	IM	Yes	Yes	No	No	No	Yes
	2019	Industry Recommendation for the Members of the Norwegian Fund and Asset Management Association: Exercise of Ownership Rights	Norwegian Fund and Asset Management Association	private	voluntary	no-obligations	8	IM	Yes	Yes	Yes	Yes	Yes	Yes
Singapore	2016	Singapore Stewardship Principles for Responsible Investors	Stewardship Asia	public	voluntary	no-obligations	7	CG	Yes	Yes	Yes	Yes	Yes	No
	2018	Stewardship Principles for Family Businesses	Stewardship Asia	public	voluntary	no-obligations	7	CS	N.A.					N.A.

TABLE 1.5 (continued)

Jurisdiction	Year	Title	Drafter(s)	Type	Enforcement Scope	Enforcement Mode	No of principles (form)	Core concept (CG, IM, ESG, CS)	UK Code 2010/2012 principles (substance) P1	P2	P3	P4	P5	P6	P7	Additional (non-UK 2010/2012) principles
South Africa	2011	Code for Responsible Investing in South Africa	Institute of Directors Southern Africa	private	voluntary	apply-or-explain	5	ESG	Yes	Yes	Yes	Yes	Yes	Yes	Yes	Yes
Switzerland	2013	Guidelines for institutional investors governing the exercising of participation rights in public limited companies	ASIP, Swiss Federal Social Security Funds, economiesuisse, Ethos, Swiss Banking and SwissHoldings	private	voluntary	comply-or-explain	5	IM	No	Yes	Yes	No	No	No	Yes	Yes
Taiwan	2016	Stewardship Principles for Institutional Investors	Taiwan Stock Exchange	public	voluntary	comply-or-explain	7	CG	Yes	Yes	Yes	Yes	Yes	Yes	Yes	No
Thailand	2017	Investment Governance Code for Institutional Investors	Thai Securities and Exchange Commission	public	voluntary	comply-or-explain	7	CG	Yes	Yes	Yes	Yes	Yes	Yes	Yes	No
United Kingdom	2010	The UK Stewardship Code	Financial Reporting Council (FRC)	public	non-voluntary (for some)	comply-or-explain	7	CG	Yes	Yes	Yes	Yes	Yes	Yes	Yes	N.A.
	2012	The UK Stewardship Code	Financial Reporting Council (FRC)	public	non-voluntary (for some)	comply-or-explain	7	CG	Yes	Yes	Yes	Yes	Yes	Yes	Yes	N.A.
	2020	The UK Stewardship Code	Financial Reporting Council (FRC)	public	non-voluntary (for some)	apply-and-explain	12	CG/IM/ESG	Yes	Yes	Yes	Yes	Yes	Yes	Yes	Yes
US	2017	Stewardship Framework for Institutional Investors	Investor Stewardship Group	private	voluntary	no-obligations	6	CG	Yes	Yes	Yes	Yes	Yes	Yes	Yes	Yes

Inter-Jurisdictional											
EU	2011	EFAMA Code for external governance: Principles for the exercise of ownership rights in investee companies	European Fund and Asset Management Association (EFAMA)	private	voluntary	no-obligations	6	CG	Yes Yes Yes Yes Yes	Yes	No
	2018	EFAMA Code for external governance: Principles for the exercise of ownership rights in investee companies	European Fund and Asset Management Association (EFAMA)	private	voluntary	comply-or-explain	6	CG	Yes Yes Yes Yes Yes	Yes	No
International	2013	ICGN Statement of Principles on Institutional Shareholder Responsibilities	International Corporate Governance Network (ICGN)	private	voluntary	no-obligations	12	IM	Yes Yes Yes Yes Yes	Yes	Yes
	2016	ICGN Global Stewardship Principles	International Corporate Governance Network (ICGN)	private	voluntary	no-obligations	7	CG	Yes Yes Yes Yes Yes	Yes	Yes

2

The UK Stewardship Code 2010–2020

From Saving the Company to Saving the Planet?

Paul Davies

2.1 INTRODUCTION

The UK adopted a Stewardship Code (UK Code) in the wake of the 2008 Global Financial Crisis (GFC), as a result of a recommendation in the Walker Review.[1] The first version of the UK Code, which appeared in 2010,[2] was hastily put together by the Financial Reporting Council (FRC), the quasi-governmental agency which Walker recommended should take charge of the drafting and implementation of the UK Code. It was very substantially based on the 'statement of principles' which the representative body of the institutional shareholders itself had produced nearly twenty years earlier and had revised at various times subsequently.[3] The 2002 version of this statement had constituted a temporarily successful, but ultimately unavailing, manoeuvre on the part of the institutional shareholders to head off an earlier proposal for an official stewardship code made by the Myners Review.[4] Perhaps because of its origins, the UK Code 2010 was quickly revised in 2012, with substantial detail added, but in a way which did not alter its fundamental orientation.[5] These two iterations of the UK Code are referred to in this chapter cumulatively as 'the first version' of the UK Code.

There was no further version of the UK Code until the current 'second' version which came into force at the beginning of 2020.[6] Given that its companion but longer established UK Corporate Governance Code (CGC)[7] was revised from its 2012 version three times in the same period, the longevity of the first version of the UK Code is, perhaps, surprising. As we shall see, the FRC appears to have devoted its efforts during this period to an ultimately unsuccessful attempt to make the first version 'work'. In December 2018, the Kingman Review

---

[1] David Walker, 'A Review of Corporate Governance in UK Banks and Other Financial Industry Entities. Final Recommendations' (26 November 2009) <https://ecgi.global/sites/default/files/codes/documents/walker_review_261109.pdf> accessed 7 May 2020 [hereinafter Walker Review].

[2] Financial Reporting Council, *The UK Stewardship Code* (July 2010) <www.frc.org.uk/getattachment/e223e152-5515-4cdc-a951-da33e093eb28/UK-Stewardship-Code-July-2010.pdf> accessed 7 May 2020 [hereinafter UK Code 2010].

[3] Institutional Shareholders' Committee, 'Code on the Responsibilities of Institutional Shareholders' (November 2009) <https://web.archive.org/web/20120119184202/http://institutionalshareholderscommittee.org.uk/sitebuildercontent/sitebuilderfiles/ISCCode161109.pdf> archived 19 January 2012, accessed 7 May 2020. Originally published in 1991.

[4] Paul Myners, 'Institutional Investment in the United Kingdom: A Review' (HM Treasury 2001) <https://uksif.org/wp-content/uploads/2012/12/MYNERS-P.-2001.-Institutional-Investment-in-the-United-Kingdom-A-Review.pdf> accessed 7 May 2020 [hereinafter Myners Review].

[5] 'This edition of the Code does not change the spirit of the 2010 Code.' (Financial Reporting Council, *The UK Stewardship Code* (September 2012) 2 <www.frc.org.uk/getattachment/d67933f9-ca38-4233-b603-3d24b2f62c5f/UK-Stewardship-Code-(September-2012).pdf> accessed 7 May 2020 [hereinafter UK Code 2012]).

[6] Financial Reporting Council, *The UK Stewardship Code 2020* (2019) <www.frc.org.uk/getattachment/5aae591d-d9d3-4cf4-814a-d14e156a1d87/Stewardship-Code_Final2.pdf> accessed 7 May 2020 [hereinafter UK Code 2020].

[7] Financial Reporting Council, *The UK Corporate Governance Code* (July 2018) <www.frc.org.uk/getattachment/88bd8c45-50ea-4841-95b0-d2f4f48069a2/2018-UK-Corporate-Governance-Code-FINAL.pdf> accessed 7 May 2020.

of the FRC concluded that the Code was 'not effective in practice'.[8] The FRC was criticized for focusing its compliance efforts on assessing the quality of the stewardship policies, which signatories to the UK Code are required to produce, while passing lightly over the implementation of those policies by the asset owners and asset managers which signed up to the UK Code. It concluded that if a change of focus towards outcomes and effectiveness 'cannot be achieved, and [the UK Code] remains simply a driver of boilerplate reporting, serious consideration should be given to its abolition'.[9]

Given its reputational investment in the UK Code, it is perhaps not surprising that the FRC did not choose the abolition option. The second version of the UK Code gives full weight to the Kingman Review's criticism about effectiveness. The 'Guidance' which surrounded the Principles in the first version has been replaced by, often very detailed, 'Reporting Expectations', designed to reveal what signatories have done by way of stewardship. However, there is a more significant contrast between the first and second versions of the UK Code than the addition of outcomes to the FRC's assessment exercise. The second version contains a much broader concept of stewardship and of the techniques to be deployed to further it than does the first version. In effect, the FRC doubled down on its bets: it is now committed to producing a code which operates not only effectively but also over a much broader set of stewardship goals than previously. Given the acknowledged failure of the first version, the question that this chapter seeks to address is whether the second version is likely to fare better. However, it is necessary first to put some detail on the contrast between the goals of the first and second versions.

Section 2.2 elaborates upon the contrast between the goals of the first and second versions of the UK Code. Section 2.3 analyzes the reasons for the failure of the first version, focusing on the capacities and incentives for institutional investors to engage with portfolio companies and on the difficulties of collectivizing engagements. Section 2.4 considers the potential for reputational incentives to play a more significant role under the second version of the UK Code with its emphasis on climate change and environmental, social and governance (ESG) factors more generally. Section 2.5 concludes.

2.2 THE GOALS OF STEWARDSHIP IN THE TWO VERSIONS

The first version of the UK Code can be seen best as an adjunct to the CGC. Since its introduction in the wake of the Cadbury Committee Report of 1992,[10] the CGC had been based on the model of a 'monitoring' board, as shown by the increasing emphasis over the various versions of that code on the role and functions of independent non-executive directors (NEDs). Their role was to ensure the loyalty of the executive management of the company to the shareholders' interests, not only in the obvious sense of handling overt

---

[8] John Kingman, 'Independent Review of the Financial Reporting Council' (Department for Business, Energy and Industrial Strategy, December 2018) 7–8 <https://assets.publishing.service.gov.uk/government/uploads/system/uploads/attachment_data/file/767387/frc-independent-review-final-report.pdf> accessed 7 May 2020 [hereinafter Kingman Review]. The Kingman Review was critical of the FRC as a whole and proposed that it be replaced by a standard, statutory regulator, which is likely to happen in 2022. At the time of writing the FRC is still a hybrid, originally established by the accounting and auditing professions as a private body; the government now appoints its chair and deputy chair and its powers are largely derived from delegation to it by the government.
[9] ibid 10.
[10] Adrian Cadbury, *Report of the Committee on the Financial Aspects of Corporate Governance* (Financial Reporting Council, Gee Publishing 1992) <https://ecgi.global/code/cadbury-report-financial-aspects-corporate-governance> accessed 7 May 2020.

conflicts of interest but across the general management of the company.[11] However, the Walker Review concluded in 2009 that, in the run-up to the GFC, NEDs had failed. Their performance was assessed as 'seriously inadequate'. The Walker Review identified 'above all the failure of individuals or of NEDs as a group to challenge the executive'.[12] The implication of this analysis for shareholders was stated to be that 'the board and director shortcomings discussed in the previous chapter would have been tackled more effectively had there been more vigorous scrutiny and engagement by major investors acting as owners'.[13] For its concept of 'engagement' the Walker Review relied on the institutional investors' statement of principles. Engagement procedures would involve arrangements 'for monitoring investee companies, for meeting as appropriate with a company's chairman, SID [senior independent director] or senior management, a strategy for intervention where judged appropriate and policy on voting and voting disclosure'.[14] So, engagement was a strategy based on 'voice'; in fact, 'exit' was not thought to count as engagement. Selling shares might send a signal to management:[15]

> But in many cases such a signal may be disregarded or will be relatively ineffective as an influence. Even if it is seen as conveying a strongly negative message, it is more likely to be a blunt instrument than one targeted at a specific change in company leadership or direction ... [A] situation in which the influence of major shareholders in their companies is principally executed through market transactions in the stock cannot be regarded as a satisfactory ownership model.

The Walker Review was a review of the governance of financial institutions, but his recommendations were applied across the board, as he apparently expected, even though the evidence suggested that non-financial corporate governance had performed moderately well in the crisis.[16] Accepting this extension, it was not surprising that the engagement approach was carried through into the first version of the UK Code. The first sentence from the Preface of the UK Code 2010 stated: 'The Stewardship Code aims to enhance the *quality of engagement* between institutional investors and companies to help improve long-term returns to shareholders', while the second sentence defined engagement as 'pursuing purposeful dialogue on strategy, performance and the management of risk'.[17] The high expectations held of engagement were revealed especially in the Guidance to Principle 3 ('Institutional investors should monitor their investee companies') in the 2012 iteration of the first version: 'Institutional investors should endeavour to identify at an early stage issues that may result in a significant loss of investment value'.[18] Engagement was clearly expected to be more than a reaction to problems which were already well developed, and would require continuous, close monitoring of the company's development, at least at a high strategic level. The first version could as well have been called an

---

[11] ibid paras 4.4–4.6. 'Non-executive directors have two particularly important contributions to make to the governance process as a consequence of their independence from executive responsibility ... The first is in reviewing the performance of the board and of the executive ... The second is in taking the lead where potential conflicts of interest arise.'
[12] Walker Review (n 1) paras 4.1, 4.3.
[13] ibid para 5.11. There were many board-centred reform recommendations as well, most of which found their way into the CGC.
[14] ibid para 5.14.
[15] ibid paras 5.6–5.7.
[16] Brian R Cheffins, 'Did Corporate Governance "Fail" during the 2008 Stock Market Meltdown? The Case of the S&P 500' (2009) 65 *The Business Lawyer* 1.
[17] UK Code 2010 (n 2) 1 (emphasis added).
[18] UK Code 2012 (n 5) 7.

engagement code as a stewardship code, as is recognized in the Directive amending the Shareholder Rights Directive (SRD II),[19] which was heavily influenced in the stewardship area by the first version. SRD II uses the term 'stewardship' only once (in a recital) whereas the words 'engage' or 'engagement' appear eighteen times in the recitals and eleven times in the body of SRD II.

The second version of the UK Code clearly moves away from an almost exclusive focus on engagement as the recommended version of stewardship. A glance at the structure of the UK Code 2020 (as it applies to asset owners and asset managers)[20] shows a significant development. The second version has four sections, of which only one is labelled 'Engagement' (Principles 9–11). There are two substantial new segments labelled 'Purpose and Governance' (Principles 1–5) and 'Investment Approach' (Principles 6–8). Even if we throw the fourth section ('Exercising Rights and Responsibilities' with a single Principle 12) in with the Engagement section, on the grounds that for asset managers and owners it principally involves voting, which was covered in the first version of the UK Code, non-engagement principles now outweigh the engagement principles by eight to four. Something is clearly going on beyond the initial concept of stewardship as engagement.

The techniques of stewardship are now defined in a more expansive way, so that, although engagement is still given emphasis, it is only one among a number of available techniques: 'Stewardship activities include investment decision-making, monitoring assets and service providers, engaging with issuers and holding them to account on material issues, collaborating with others, and exercising rights and responsibilities'.[21] In particular, buy and sell decisions ('investment decisions') are given apparently equal weight with engagement, so that monitoring may be done as much for this purpose as for engagement. The same point emerges from the very first sentence in the UK Code 2020: 'Stewardship is the responsible allocation, management and oversight of capital …'.[22] If engagement is one technique for responsible management and oversight of capital, entrance and exit decisions are another, while allocation seems to refer primarily to entrance and exit decisions.

Equally significant is a shift of focus so as to embrace not just the fortunes of individual investee companies but the share market as a whole. 'The Code also recognises that asset owners and asset managers play an important role as guardians of market integrity and in working to minimise systemic risks as well as being stewards of the investments in their portfolios.'[23] Principle 4 puts this introductory statement in normative form: 'Signatories identify and respond to market-wide and systemic risks to promote a well-functioning financial system'.[24]

It is suggested that what is driving these developments is the heavy emphasis placed on ESG factors, especially climate change, in the second version as compared with the first version.[25] The UK Code 2012 contained a fleeting reference to ESG factors, but most people would probably

---

[19] Directive (EU) 2017/828 of the European Parliament and of the Council of 17 May 2017 amending Directive 2007/36/EC as regards the encouragement of long-term shareholder engagement [2017] OJ L132/1 (SRD II). On the other hand, it is perhaps equally disingenuous to place these shareholder obligations in a Shareholder *Rights* Directive.

[20] The UK Code 2020 (n 6) now has a separate, and shorter, set of principles for 'service providers' (e.g. proxy advisers and investment consultants), which I ignore in this chapter. It also now covers investments in 'fixed income, bonds, real estate and infrastructure'. I shall ignore this extension also.

[21] UK Code 2020 (n 6) 7.

[22] UK Code 2020 (n 6) 4.

[23] ibid.

[24] UK Code 2020 (n 6) 11. Though, following modern fashion, the UK Code uses the indicative rather than the imperative mood.

[25] On the broader trend of incorporating ESG factors in stewardship codes, see Katelouzou and Klettner, Sustainable Finance and Stewardship, Chapter 26.

have missed it.[26] By contrast, the second version insists that '[s]ignatories systematically integrate stewardship and investment, including material environmental, social and governance issues, and climate change, to fulfil their responsibilities', and that '[s]ignatories should explain how information gathered through stewardship has informed acquisition, monitoring and exit decisions...'.[27] The aim is clearly to mainstream ESG factors into stewardship, not simply to present them as an add-on. The same can be seen in the definition of market-wide factors. The definitions attached to Principle 4 mention specifically that systemic risks include 'climate change'.[28]

The references to climate change are particularly important in explaining the development of the second version. Achieving climate change goals is likely to require a concerted effort by businesses across the economy, so that co-opting institutional investors to support market-wide standards is likely to be as important as a focus on individual companies. Of course, the businesses of some types of companies are likely to be particularly threatening from an environmental perspective, but engagement may not be the optimum strategy for moderating that threat. The result may simply be to reduce the financial attractiveness of those businesses. From the point of view of those entrusting their savings to asset owners and asset managers, it is not ideal to encourage investment in those companies in order to bring about their full or partial demise. Not investing, by contrast, may put pressure on those companies by raising their cost of capital, without involving financial sacrifice of the hard-earned savings of potential or actual pensioners. Contrary to what the Walker Review thought in relation to engagement, capital allocation decisions may turn out to be a more acceptable way forward for all the parties on the investment side.

2.3 THE FAILURE OF THE FIRST VERSION OF THE UK CODE

What underlay the Kingman Review's assessment of the ineffectiveness of the first version was the view that the level of engagement on the part of institutional investors with portfolio companies had not significantly increased since 2010. This view was widely shared among those knowledgeable in the field,[29] though it has to be said that the Kingman Review carried out no empirical studies which might have tested the truth of the underlying proposition. What it focused on instead was the FRC's inability to demonstrate that levels of engagement had increased since 2010, because it focused its assessments on signatories' engagement policies rather than their reports of the outcomes of engagement. Given the lack of FRC assessment, these reports were characterized as 'boilerplate'.[30] In defence of the FRC, it has to be said that assessment of outcomes is a less straightforward task than the Kingman Review presented it to be. The Walker Review itself stated:[31] 'It is not the role of institutional shareholders to micromanage or "second guess" the managements of their companies. Indeed, the dispersed ownership model relies on the appointment and performance of high quality directors who enjoy substantial

---

[26] It was to be found at the end of the final sentence of the first paragraph of guidance to Principle 4 (UK Code 2012 (n 5) 8).
[27] UK Code 2020 (n 6) 15, Principle 7 and Reporting Expectation – Outcome.
[28] UK Code 2020 (n 6) 11.
[29] Arad Reisberg, 'The UK Stewardship Code: On the Road to Nowhere?' (2015) 15 *Journal of Corporate Law Studies* 217.
[30] Kingman Review (n 8) 51.
[31] Walker Review (n 1) para 5.30. See also the marvellously incomplete analysis in the UK Code 2012 (n 5) 1: 'In publicly listed companies responsibility for stewardship is shared. The primary responsibility rests with the board of the company, which oversees the actions of its management. Investors in the company also play an important role in holding the board to account for the fulfilment of its responsibilities'.

autonomy in discharge of their obligations without need for detailed oversight by dispersed owners, at any rate in "normal" situations'.

It is perhaps too much to expect Walker, the FRC and Kingman to solve one of the most debated issues in corporate law, namely, the appropriate balance between autonomy and accountability for the board, but it might have been sensible for them to recognize that their views on the issue were opaque and so the implications of the UK Code for the optimal level of engagement by institutional investors was uncertain. Asset owners and managers could well conclude that they had a large measure of discretion under the UK Code as to when they should engage.

Given the widespread, and probably correct, view that levels of engagement had not significantly increased over the decade: how might this be explained?[32] It has to be said at the outset that what the UK Code was seeking to achieve was more demanding than what the CGC aimed at, contrary to the view of the Myners Review.[33] The CGC contained a set of structural recommendations for the board and its committees, emphasizing in particular the role of NEDs and the chair of the board. It was, therefore, fairly straightforward for companies to work out how to implement the recommendations and for investors to see whether those recommendations had been complied with. Certainly, compliance with the recommendations was expected to alter corporate behaviour (and the extent to which this has happened has been a controversial topic for research ever since), but, at the level of applying the CGC, this issue did not concern either investors or companies, except perhaps where the company advanced an argument for non-compliance with the CGC's recommendations.

By contrast, the UK Code was concerned with changing behaviour directly, not via structural changes in the governance system. It aimed at both the behaviour of institutional investors as against investee companies and the behaviour of investee companies, for example in relation to their business strategies. However, the appropriate behavioural changes were inherently firm-specific and fact-dependent, since the business models and environments of investee companies were many and various. Certainly, Principle 4 of the UK Code 2012 listed the tools available for engagement, for example voting on resolutions put forward by management at shareholder meetings, participating in private meetings with corporate management or the chair of the board, or proposing shareholder motions at general meetings to change policy or remove directors, and it required a commitment from shareholders and asset managers to use these tools, as and when appropriate.[34] But the UK Code had little to say about the identification of the 'as and when'. The appropriate occasions and the appropriate tools for particular occasions were not, and could not be, identified *ex ante* in the UK Code itself. The UK Code contained only high-level engagement recommendations, not specific ones equivalent to the structural recommendations of the CGC.

Somewhat disingenuously, the UK Code tried to push the formation of *ex ante* engagement rules onto the institutions themselves, through the obligation to establish a stewardship policy, as Principle 1 of the first version required. Under Principle 4, if the board proved unresponsive to initial approaches, '[i]nstitutional investors should establish clear guidelines on when and how

---

[32] I will take for granted that neither the lack of legal powers for shareholders nor the co-ordination costs of institutional investors play a significant role in the explanation. On both these points, see Paul Davies, 'Shareholders in the United Kingdom' in Jennifer G Hill and Randall S Thomas (eds), *Research Handbook on Shareholder Power* (Edward Elgar 2015). See Reisberg (n 29) for an earlier and penetrating assessment of the first version of the UK Code.

[33] Myners Review (n 4) 3. It argued that, since the UK CGC had been 'on any reasonable analysis' a success, a comply-or-explain stewardship code could be expected to be as well.

[34] UK Code 2012 (n 5) 8.

they will escalate their stewardship activities'.[35] However, institutional investors with a diversified portfolio of investee companies are hardly in a better position to work out, *ex ante*, when and how they would or should intervene, in comparison to the drafters of the UK Code. The correct response is still highly fact- and case-specific, and incapable of *ex ante* generalization, whether it is a regulator or an investor seeking to develop a portfolio-wide policy. The policies developed by investors turned out, not surprisingly, to consist only of generalities, just like the UK Code itself. For example, M&G, a long-established and well-respected fund manager, stated in the 2020 version of its policy: 'As a general policy, we are supportive of the management of the companies in which we invest. However, when companies consistently fail to meet our reasonable expectations, we will actively promote changes. These changes might range from the formulation of a new strategy to the appointment of new directors'.[36] This embodied eminent good sense but did not convey any information which probably would not have been found on M&G's website, even if the UK Code had never been adopted.

In a behavioural setting where firm guidance is lacking, the issues of capacity and the incentives for institutional investors to engage move centre-stage. These issues provide two plausible explanations why the expectations generated in some quarters by the Walker Review and the first version of the UK Code failed to materialize. Did institutional shareholders possess the capacity to devise effective engagements, even if they had the legal capacity to engage and could overcome their co-ordination issues? Did asset owners and asset managers lack the incentives to engage in the desired way, even if they have both the legal and the factual capacity to do so? We will look at each question in turn.

2.3.1 *Shareholders' Functional Capacities*

The first question is whether and in what circumstances institutional shareholders (and asset managers acting on their behalf)[37] have the knowledge and understanding to improve the quality of corporate decisions. Is more engagement by them likely to produce worse corporate decisions, rather than the better ones anticipated by the Walker Review? The view that shareholders' engagement should be kept at a low level in the interests of good decision-making (even at the level of choosing strategy) is not implausible, was partially accepted by the Walker Review[38] and is advocated by some academics.[39] However, even jurisdictions which are protective of management as against shareholders, for example Germany and, traditionally, Delaware, follow the general approach of corporate law around the world, and accept the proposition that for some corporate decisions, shareholder involvement is mandatory.[40] In these cases, at least, the involvement of the

---

[35] ibid.
[36] M&G Investments, 'M&G Equities' Approach to Responsible Investment' (February 2020) <https://global.mandg.com/~/media/Files/M/MandG-Plc/documents/responsible-investing/MG%20Equities%20approach%20to%20responsible%20investment-03-20.pdf> accessed 7 May 2020.
[37] It is conventional, and helpful, to distinguish between 'asset owners' and 'asset managers', provided one remembers that a single entity may perform both functions. Thus, a large pension fund (asset owner) may manage a large part of its investments (thus acting as asset manager as well) while a smaller fund may contract out most or all of the management function to a fund manager. Equally, a mutual fund (unit trust, investment trust, exchange traded fund, UCITS) may manage its funds as well as gather in contributions and deal with redemptions, but it may contract out the management function to a third party.
[38] Text to n 31 (Walker Review (n 1) para 5.30).
[39] Stephen Bainbridge, 'Director Primacy and Shareholder Disempowerment' (2006) 119 *Harvard Law Review* 1735 <https://ssrn.com/abstract=808584> accessed 7 May 2020.
[40] See Edward Rock and others, 'Fundamental Changes' in Reinier Kraakman and others (eds), *The Anatomy of Corporate Law: A Comparative and Functional Approach* (3rd edn, OUP 2017).

shareholders must be thought likely to improve the quality of corporate decisions. The question, then, is whether, beyond this limited, mandatory list of decisions, shareholders should be permitted and encouraged to insert themselves into the management of the company, and whether such engagement is likely to be fruitful.

When exploring this issue, it is useful to keep in mind that the answers to the question may differ according to the investment strategy followed by the asset owner or manager and the level or type of engagement which is contemplated. There are two principal types of investment strategy – index tracking and stock picking – though some hybrids exist and the stock picking strategy obviously covers a wide range of investment philosophies. However, at least as a first cut, one can say that an index tracker makes no decision as to which shares to invest in or about the weight of the investment in any particular stock. Once the tracker has chosen the index it will track, the buy and sell decisions then follow automatically. What the index tracker offers is diversification at a lower price than a stock picker will charge, and it must be capable of tracking the chosen index with only a very small 'error' factor.

Functional capacity to engage also varies from engagement strategy to engagement strategy. For example, voting on a proposal put forward by management (or an activist hedge fund) for consideration by the shareholders requires less in the way of knowledge and insight on the part of the shareholders than does participating in an initiative to change the company's business strategy against the wishes of the incumbent management. Even with a significant managerial resolution, for example, a proposal to dispose of or acquire a substantial business, index investors may be as well placed as anyone else to evaluate its impact upon firm value. Management will have devoted substantial time and resources to developing the proposal and will be obliged to disclose most, if not all, of their rationale for the proposal because the rules surrounding shareholder meetings require it and because the management will wish to do so to maintain or increase the market price of the company's equity. Naturally, management disclosures will stress the advantages of their proposal, but, in the case of large publicly traded companies, analysts who follow the company will provide an assessment from an external viewpoint and that assessment will become known to the shareholders, indirectly (via its impact on the share price) or directly (e.g. because the analyst releases the assessment publicly or the financial press picks it up). So, a lot of the work (and cost) of gathering information and analyzing it is taken out of the hands of the shareholders in this case and even index trackers, who will have good market intelligence, will be well placed to respond to it.

In the case of management or hedge fund proposals, therefore, the functional capacity of institutional shareholders, even index funds, to engage appears not to be a serious cause for concern. However, this is not the type of engagement which the first version of the UK Code appeared to advocate most strongly. Over the past thirty years, levels of institutional voting on resolutions put before them, typically by management, have been on the increase.[41] Since this type of institutional engagement was already in place, the UK Code's contribution to promoting stewardship must be assessed by reference to engagement beyond 'reactive' voting. What is the functional capacity of shareholders in respect of these more demanding forms of engagement?

As far as index managers are concerned, it is unlikely that their capacity is high. Their business model does not call for them to employ analysts to develop insights into the business potential of

---

[41] Myners Review (n 4) 91, fn 24, noted that in 1999 about half of shareholders voted on resolutions, the figure having been about 20% a decade earlier. By 2005 the figure was reported to be 58%: Chris Mallin, 'Trends in Levels of Voting and Voting Disclosure' (March 2006) 14 *Corporate Governance* 73. Given that retail shareholders show a lower propensity to vote, this implies a rather higher level of voting by institutional shareholders than the headline figures would suggest, especially, perhaps, on non-routine resolutions.

particular companies or to identify and correct strategic mistakes by management before damage is done. Their expertise lies in tracking an index with minimum error and minimum cost. Irrespective of their incentives to engage deeply with portfolio companies (which we discuss in Section 2.3.2), there is little reason to have confidence that business policy initiatives which index trackers might decide to take would be well chosen.

However, this is not to argue that all non-reactive voting by index funds is unreliable. When they vote on the application of market-wide codes (notably corporate governance codes) to investee companies, for example, their views are deserving of as much respect as those of stock-picking managers, since they are as likely as stock pickers to be in a position to observe which structural governance provisions are important and in which situations. However, in the core area for the UK Code, of shareholder-initiated fundamental change, the index funds do not appear as reliable initiators. While it may be clear to an index-tracking manager that a company is underperforming and while the tracker may respond by voting for the strict application of market-wide codes to that company or against particular executive directors (or their remuneration), that is not the high-level engagement response envisaged by the Walker Review. As Kahan and Rock have pointed out, 'to develop more precise measures, a more detailed analysis is required. Without such analysis, it is hard to pinpoint the cause for low performance and to recommend specific changes.'[42] This is the typical predicament of the index tracker. The implication of the analysis is that the UK Code is misguided to push for proactive engagement on the part of partly incompetent index-tracking funds to bring about changes in investee companies' business strategies, and that self-aware trackers are unlikely to want to participate in this form of engagement.[43]

By contrast, stock pickers appear better placed to engage in proactive engagement. Their business model requires them to acquire an understanding of a potential investee company's strategies and of their strengths and weaknesses. If an investment is made, the company's performance will be closely monitored and, if it is regarded as unsatisfactory, that understanding is available to inform proposals for change. This argument carries greatest conviction in the case of a fund whose strategy is to invest in only a small number of companies. Its focus on that small number is likely to generate a high level of understanding of the company's potential and capacities. By contrast, some funds present themselves as stock pickers (and charge the appropriate higher fees), but invest widely, while avoiding a commitment to any particular index. A generalist stock-picking fund may be in little better position than an index tracker to identify appropriate changes of policy within particular companies. Overall, the extent of the functional advantage of stock pickers over index funds turns on the nature of the stock picker's strategy and those strategies are, in principle, many and various. Nevertheless, it is reasonable to suppose that, overall, stock pickers are better

---

[42] Marcel Kahan and Edward Rock, 'Index Funds and Corporate Governance: Let Shareholders Be Shareholders' (October 2019) NYU Law and Economics Research Paper No. 18-39 <https://ssrn.com/abstract=3295098> accessed 7 May 2020. The focus of their highly sophisticated analysis is a rebuttal of the proposition that index funds should be deprived entirely of their voting rights. Their aim is thus to identify classes of case where index fund voting is reliable – or no less reliable than stock pickers' votes – rather than to identify types of engagement activity (beyond voting) where index funds might perform poorly. See also Fisch, The Uncertain Stewardship Potential of Index Funds, Chapter 21.

[43] More than 50 per cent of equities managed by UK fund managers are managed on a passive basis: The Investment Association, 'Asset Management in the UK 2017–2018' (September 2018) 50 <www.theia.org/sites/default/files/2019-04/20180913-fullsummary.pdf> accessed 7 May 2020.

placed to implement the engagement strategies promoted by the UK Code than are index funds.

2.3.2 Asset Owner and Asset Manager Incentives

Even if it were clear that institutional shareholders had the capacity to engage beyond reactive voting, there is a further question about the strength of their incentives to engage.[44] The analysis of incentives needs to distinguish carefully between: (i) financial incentives related to the immediate value of the fund, and the remuneration of asset managers; and (ii) reputational incentives for owners and managers to engage even in the absence of immediate financial benefit.

2.3.2.1 Financial Incentives of Asset Owners and Managers

It will be suggested in this section that, just as index tracking funds have limited capacity to engage, so also do they have limited financial incentives to do so. In fact, their capacity and their financial incentives seem to line up quite well. This is a desirable outcome, since an actor with strong incentives to intervene, but little capacity to judge which interventions will be successful, could bring about substantial wealth destruction. By contrast, stock pickers have greater capacity and incentives to engage, but, even then, those features are unlikely to apply uniformly across the whole of the investment portfolio.

The argument for the limited financial incentives of index trackers to engage is well established in the literature and does not need to be considered in detail.[45] Even assuming the engagement is successful in financial terms, the fund's attractiveness to investors is likely to be improved only marginally, if at all. The fund will still have achieved only the goal of tracking the chosen index and all its competitors will have done the same, so that intervening fund will not be comparatively better off. Few investors will notice that the level of the index has been affected in an upwards direction by the actions of the particular intervening fund. Even worse, since the benefit of the upward impact will accrue to all funds tracking the relevant index, the intervening fund will not be able to recoup from its investors the costs of intervention, which its competitors will not have borne, for fear of causing them (or new investors) to move to the competitors.

However, this does not mean that index trackers will not engage at all. They will have a financial incentive to do so if the engagement proposed is low cost and that cost will probably be covered (at least across a series of engagements) by the likely increase in remuneration for the fund. This will be so even when that remuneration is based on receiving only a modest percentage, for example less than 1 per cent, of the assets under management (AUM), especially if that increase in the value of the investee company is likely to continue into future years.[46] In this analysis, it is irrelevant that other, non-voting index trackers may reap the same monetary benefit. In fact, however, the incentives to engage in thoughtful, low-cost engagement will apply to competitors as well, so that fears of giving competitors a comparative advantage by voting when they do not are likely to be subdued. However, the typical form of engagement which this

---

[44] There is also the question of whether the investment management and governance models of asset owners and asset managers pose any challenges for engaged governance roles for institutional shareholders. On this, see Barker and Chiu, Investment Management, Stewardship and Corporate Governance Roles, Chapter 25.

[45] See Lucian Bebchuk and Scott Hirst, 'Index Funds and the Future of Corporate Governance: Theory, Evidence, and Policy' (December 2019) 119 *Columbia Law Review* 2029 <https://columbialawreview.org/wp-content/uploads/2019/12/Bebchuk-Hirst-Index_Funds_and_the_Future_of_Corporate_Governance.pdf> accessed 7 May 2020.

[46] These cases are discussed in some detail in Kahan and Rock (n 42).

argument promotes is, once again, voting on a resolution put forward by management or another shareholder, because voting is a low-cost (though not costless) activity. As already indicated, the UK Code is aimed at promoting proactive engagement by institutional shareholders on a much wider (and more expensive) basis than thoughtful voting on resolutions put forward by others. The view that index trackers have limited incentives to initiate high-cost engagement to change management strategy remains untouched by the arguments about their reactive voting incentives.

It is sometimes argued that index funds are incentivized to engage because they are locked into the index they have chosen to track. This is a non sequitur. The fact that one is trapped in some particular situation does not answer the question of whether it is worth one's while to try to change it, or some feature of it, as Shakespeare recognized.[47] The answer depends on the costs and benefits of the change which is contemplated, which brings us back to the capacity and incentive analysis above.

Does the matter stand differently in relation to stock-pickers? In some cases it is likely that it does. Although some funds are closet index trackers, as noted, whose incentives are not much different from those of transparent trackers, genuine stock pickers may choose to be overweight in a particular stock and see benefits from engagement (beyond voting), even if there are (non-overweight) competitors present on the same share register. The asset manager will benefit directly from the AUM formula, while out-performance on the part of the fund will attract new investors, thus increasing AUM again. But there are constraints on the amount that even an overweight fund will devote to engagement (beyond voting). The return to high-level engagement must provide (on a probabilistic basis) a higher return to the fund than alternative courses of action, such as doing nothing or divesting and investing the proceeds elsewhere. When assessing the probabilities, engagement beyond voting starts with a handicap, since its likely costs (firm-specific investigation and firm-specific activism) will be higher than those of the alternatives, while its returns may be uncertain, though potentially large.

This argument does not mean that stock pickers will not participate in routine interactions with investee companies. Analysts employed by fund managers inevitably meet with investee companies on a regular basis because they hope to gain insights relevant to trading decisions, and corporate governance teams, generally less well-resourced and meeting less frequently, do so as well. However, both sets of meetings tend to concentrate on the short term – short-term financial projections in the former case, the up-coming annual general meeting in the latter. Strategic issues, likely to be relevant to the UK Code, very much take a second place in both types of meeting, especially in meetings with corporate governance teams.[48]

Even when the corporate governance team flags up a set of concerns, an enhanced level of engagement with the investee company appears not to be the exclusive response on the part of the fund manager. There is a recent study, admittedly of a single fund manager,[49] Standard Life Aberdeen, which shows that adverse reports by the governance team trigger not only increased

---

[47] 'To die, to sleep, / To sleep, perchance to Dream; ay, there's the rub, / For in that sleep of death, what dreams may come, / When we have shuffled off this mortal coil, / Must give us pause' (*Hamlet*, Act 3, Scene 1).

[48] Jonathan Atack, 'The Four Dialogues: The Need to Improve How Investors and Companies Engage on Governance' (*The Investor Forum*, April 2019) 16 <www.investorforum.org.uk/wp-content/uploads/securepdfs/2019/07/The-Four-Dialogues-Governance-engagement-Full-report.pdf> accessed 7 May 2020.

[49] Marco Becht, Julian Franks and Hannes Wagner, 'Corporate Governance through Voice and Exit' (2019) ECGI Finance Working Paper No 633/2019 <https://ssrn.com/abstract=3456626> accessed 7 May 2020. For the operation of this strategy in relation to a particular investee company, see Business, Energy and Industrial Strategy and Work and Pensions Committees, 'Carillion' (HC 769, May 2018) 49 <https://publications.parliament.uk/pa/cm201719/cmselect/cmworpen/769/769.pdf> accessed 7 May 2020 [hereinafter Carillion Report] (available at <https://publications.parliament.uk/pa/cm201719/cmselect/cmworpen/769/76906.htm#_idTextAnchor099> accessed 7 May 2020).

interventions with the management of the company but also sale decisions by the investment team. This suggests that the fund manager was hedging its bets with problem companies, devoting some resources to engagement but also reducing the fund's exposure to that particular company. If this is a general approach on the part of funds, it will reduce the incentive to expend resources on deep engagement.

Overall, genuine stock pickers are likely to have greater incentives than index trackers to engage at a high level and, as we saw in Section 2.3.1, their capacity to engage is likely to be greater than in the case of index funds. Nevertheless, that incentive is not without limits related to the costs of intervention nor is it likely to operate across the whole of the stock picker's portfolio, for example where the stock picker has an underweight holding in a particular company.

2.3.2.2 Reputational Incentives

Consequently, the picture that emerges is one in which both index funds and stock pickers have only limited financial incentives to engage beyond voting or the enforcement of market-wide best practice. Do reputational incentives change the picture? There is some evidence that reputational incentives are at work in this area to encourage adherence to the UK Code. The Kingman Review found that in 2018 the UK Code had 278 signatories, of whom some 100, mainly asset owners, were (at that time) under no obligation to adhere to it.[50] Equally, to encourage higher levels of commitment to the UK Code, the FRC introduced a public tiering system, based on an assessment of the quality of the signatories' engagement policies.[51] There were no overt sanctions for an institution which failed to achieve the top tier, but many did. The obvious incentive operating here was to avoid governmental action which might turn a comply-or-explain code into more intrusive regulation.

There is also some evidence that reputational incentives have influenced institutions' voting patterns. Thus, in relation to executive remuneration – a long-standing headache for government – recent research has shown that institutions voted against the company's pay proposals in 8 per cent of cases (the average across all management proposals being just over 2 per cent) and pay votes showed the lowest similarity with the recommendations of the two largest proxy advisers.[52] Both facts suggest thoughtful voting on remuneration on the part of the institutions and their asset managers. However, there appears to be no evidence that, in relation to the first version of the UK Code, reputational incentives encouraged engagement activity beyond voting.

2.3.3 *Collectivizing Engagement*

The incentive problems just discussed could be addressed by collectivizing engagement. Collectivization would spread the costs of engagement, thus facilitating some of the high-cost versions of this activity and reducing the free-rider problem. It might also serve to reduce the capacity issues, for example, where the collective body employed its own specialists. Following

---

[50] Kingman Review (n 8) paras 2.80–2.83. At that time only asset managers were required under Financial Conduct Authority (FCA) rules (COBS 2.2.3R) to disclose whether they were committed to the UK Code and the extent of that commitment. After the enactment of SRD II (n 14), a similar requirement was extended by the FCA to pension funds and insurance companies.

[51] Further on shareholder stewardship enforcement, see Katelouzou and Sergakis, Shareholder Stewardship Enforcement, Chapter 27.

[52] Suren Gomtsian, 'Voting Engagement by Large Institutional Investors' (2020) 45 *Journal of Corporation Law* 659, 694–95, figure 8.

the Kay Review,[53] an initiative was undertaken in this direction. The Investor Forum, funded by its institutional members, provides a mechanism to facilitate engagement by those members who wish to take an issue forward. However, over its first five years, the Forum initiated only a modest number of engagements (thirty-two). Two aspects of its functioning suggest that it has not fully overcome the collective action problems of the institutions. First, an almost equal number of engagements was proposed by members (twenty-five), but these proposals were not taken forward because of their failure to attract support from a sufficient number of other members. Second, engagement is defined by the Forum as the robust presentation of investor views to the board about the problems the company faces, but it equally stresses discretion. It therefore operates in private, though its interventions are reported once concluded. It appears never to have conducted a public battle with an intransigent board. In addition, robust presentation of investor views does not typically extend to the formulation of strategies for dealing with the problems raised. This is justified on the basis that it is not the role of the investors to devise solutions; that is for the company.[54]

An alternative, market solution to the collectivization issue is the activist hedge-fund. As we have seen, the incentives to engagement on the part of institutional investors are low mainly because of their cost and the difficulty of spreading those costs over all competing institutions, while capacity constraints derive from the fact that their business models do not reliably capture all the relevant firm-specific information and understanding necessary for successful engagement. An activist hedge fund presents a solution to both those problems, by reducing the required engagement on the part of traditional institutional shareholders to thoughtful voting or other low-cost expressions of support for or opposition to the activist.[55] The activist hedge fund has itself deployed the resources necessary to work out whether a change of strategy and/or management on the part of the company would improve its value, so that this task no longer falls on the institutions.

The hedge fund is able to discharge this function because its business model is different from that of the 'long-only' institutions, whether index trackers or stock pickers. Even for stock pickers, a company which requires high-level engagement represents a failure: the investment choice is made on the basis that the company already has a good strategy and management team in place, and is in a position to adapt successfully to changes in the business environment. By contrast, a hedge fund operates on an investment model which requires it to have the capacity and the financing to seek out companies where a change in strategy or management is likely to bring about an increase in its share price. Typically, these are companies whose performance prior to the intervention has fallen below that of others in the same market segment. However, provided

---

[53] John Kay, 'The Kay Review of UK Equity Markets and Long-Term Decision Making' (Department for Business, Innovation and Skills, July 2012) <https://assets.publishing.service.gov.uk/government/uploads/system/uploads/attachment_data/file/253454/bis-12-917-kay-review-of-equity-markets-final-report.pdf> accessed 7 May 2020.

[54] The analysis in this paragraph is derived from The Investor Forum, 'Review 2018' (January 2019) <www.investorforum.org.uk/wp-content/uploads/2019/01/Annual_Review_2018.pdf> accessed 7 May 2020; The Investor Forum, 'Review 2019' (January 2020) <www.investorforum.org.uk/wp-content/uploads/securepdfs/2020/01/The-Investor-Forum-Annual-Review-2019-Final-Version.pdf> accessed 7 May 2020. Many of its engagements are driven by concerns arising under the CGC rather than the UK Code. On the potential for third-party facilitators of this type, see Gaia Balp and Giovanni Strampelli, 'Institutional Investor Collective Engagements: Non-Activist Cooperation vs Activist Wolf Packs' (2020) 14 *Ohio State Business Law Journal* 135. The Investor Forum is in many ways a recreation of the 'case committees' run by the trade associations of the institutional investors in the 1970s to 1990s, which eventually faded for lack of enthusiasm on the part of the members: GP Stapledon, *Institutional Investors and Corporate Governance* (Clarendon Press 1996) 135–38.

[55] See Balp and Strampelli (n 54); Ronald Gilson and Jeffrey Gordon, 'The Agency Costs of Agency Capitalism: Activist Investors and the Revaluation of Governance Rights' (March 2013) 113 *Columbia Law Review* 863.

change is likely to improve the share price, an activist hedge fund may intervene to produce change even in a successful company. For example, a successful company may become more so if merged with a competitor, a step which the incumbent management may resist if it means a complete or partial loss of control to the merger partner. Having made a substantial, but non-controlling, investment in the company's shares, the activist agitates for the proposed changes, attempts to secure other investors' support for its proposals, and moves on once the changes have been implemented and the share price increased.

The value or otherwise of the changes brought about by activist hedge funds is one of the most hotly debated topics in current corporate law. It is not necessary to comment on that debate here, except to make two points. First, activist hedge funds do not rely on the UK Code for their effectiveness, except perhaps to give themselves some marginal ideological support. What the hedge fund relies on is its capacity to (threaten to) put pressure on management when it has the support of other major investors. This means that the corporate governance rights of shareholders (rather than their duties) are central to their strategy. These are generally to be found in corporate law (e.g. the right to easily remove members of the board and rules facilitating inter-shareholder communication) though soft law may sometimes be helpful (e.g. the presence of a senior independent director as a channel for shareholder communication).

Thus, if activist hedge funds are the answer to the engagement problem, there is no need for the UK Code to provide it and the FRC can devote its resources to something else. Second, it is clear, however, that the Walker Review did not think activist hedge funds were the answer because it took the view that their goals were short-term while the purpose of the UK Code was to promote the long-term value of companies. As the Walker Review put it:[56]

> Differentiation is needed between the motivation behind the proposals ... for enhancing dialogue and longer-term engagement between investors and boards and increased shareholder pressure on boards to perform in the short term. Before the recent crisis phase, such short-term pressure involved analyst and activist investor argument for specific short-term initiatives such as increased leverage, spin-offs, acquisitions or share buybacks, with the result in some cases of a stronger stock price and higher short-term earnings. ... The focus in what follows is on dialogue and engagement between investors and companies where the investors are likely to be relatively long-term holders for whom divestment in potential problem situations comes to be seen as a last rather than first resort.

On this analysis, the UK Code recovers its role but cannot rely on activist hedge funds to rescue it from ineffectiveness. On either analysis of hedge funds, the first version of the UK Code is open to a futility assessment: it is either unnecessary or impotent.

2.4 THE SECOND VERSION OF THE UK CODE

2.4.1 *Engagement*

It seems unlikely that engagement, as envisaged by the Walker Review, will occur on a more significant level under the second version of the UK Code than under the first. This prediction is made on the basis that the capacity and the incentive problems identified here have not been addressed in the second version.[57] As noted, the second version addresses the Kingman Review's

---

[56] Walker Review (n 1) para 5.27. For scepticism on this point, see Anna Christie, 'The New Hedge Fund Activism: Activist Directors and the Market for Corporate Quasi-control' (2019) 19 *Journal of Corporate Law Studies* 1.

[57] Below I take a more optimistic view about ESG engagement and it is possible that there will be some spillover from ESG engagement to Walker-style engagement.

ineffectiveness critique by enhancing the reporting requirements for the UK Code signatories in relation to their engagement outcomes. In relation to Engagement (Principles 9–11), besides disclosing their engagement strategy (including its escalation if the initial engagement is unsuccessful), the UK Code 2020 requires signatories to disclose 'the outcomes of engagement that is ongoing or has concluded in the preceding 12 months',[58] including the outcomes of any collaborative engagement or escalated engagement. Although the annual[59] reporting requirement is an obvious way of keeping up the pressure on signatories to the UK Code, it is not clear that it is an appropriate one. Of course, many institutions already produce annual reports on their stewardship activities of a fairly general kind, for example indicating, anonymously, concerns raised with some investee managements. It seems that the UK Code 2020 is designed to generate more detailed reporting than this. The question is whether detailed annual reporting of engagement outcomes will undermine the UK Code's commitment to the improvement of the long-term value of companies. The risk with a detailed annual reporting requirement is that it will generate activity, which may or may not enhance the long-term value of investee companies, but will certainly generate reportable events. It would be an ironic outcome if the revised reporting requirements reduced the timescale for engagement pay-offs.[60]

Ironically, signatories may perform better on the traditional engagement metric under the second version than the first, not because they engage more but because the UK Code's expectations of engagement (now only one part of the UK Code, as we have seen) have been reduced. This argument is somewhat speculative, but there are hints to this effect in the second version. First, the Guidance attached to Principle 3 of the UK Code 2012 encouraging 'early intervention' by institutional investors to avoid loss of value[61] is not repeated in the second version. Second, escalation of engagement, where management is initially resistant to the initial (and usually private) approaches of investors, is perhaps the acid test of commitment to engagement. The first version set out the techniques of escalation, including various public actions, such as making a public statement in advance of general meetings of shareholders, submitting resolutions and speaking at general meetings, and requisitioning a meeting, in some cases proposing to change board membership.[62] Under the second version, escalation still merits a separate Principle (11) but the techniques of escalation are no longer laid out, perhaps suggesting that the limited form of escalation practised by The Investor Forum is acceptable.[63] Third, with the expansion of stewardship techniques to give equal weight to buy/sell decisions and engagement, an institution could improve its stewardship score without a higher level of engagement. Thus, the 'outcome' to be reported under Principle 7 (the first Principle in the 'Investment Approach' section of the UK Code 2020) is defined as follows: 'Signatories should explain how information gathered through stewardship has informed *acquisition*, monitoring *and exit* decisions.'[64]

---

[58] UK Code 2020 (n 6) 18.
[59] Curiously, the UK Code 2020 (n 6) does not explicitly require a report to be made annually, though it seems that this is the FRC's expectation. See n 86 (Financial Reporting Council, 'UK Stewardship Code' <www.frc.org.uk/investors/uk-stewardship-code> accessed 7 May 2020).
[60] It is recognized that outcomes may take more than a year to achieve, but, even then, 'progress' during the year is required to be reported (UK Code 2020 (n 6) 6). This risk is heightened because the assumption that the long term is easy to identify is misplaced: see John Kay and Mervyn King, *Radical Uncertainty: Decision-Making Beyond the Numbers* (WW Norton & Company 2020).
[61] UK Code 2012 (n 5) 7.
[62] UK Code 2012 (n 5) 8, Guidance to Principle 4.
[63] Discussed in Section 2.3.3.
[64] UK Code 2020 (n 6) 15 (emphasis added).

Against this, the requirement under Principle 4 to address market risks includes in this category 'the failure of a business or group of businesses', which suggests a renewed emphasis on engagement, though this statement is not to be found in the Engagement section of the UK Code. What might be required of institutional investors in this context is not clear. In the recent collapse of Carillion plc, most of the public blame was apportioned to the board and the company's auditors. The institutional investors, holding some third of the companies' equity, had not gone beyond private meetings with the board (and in some cases votes against the remuneration policy) but had steadily sold down their shareholdings in the period before the collapse. The parliamentary investigation put the blame for this low level of engagement squarely on the board since '[e]ffective stewardship by investors depends in large part on the availability of trustworthy financial reporting and on honest engagement with board members in response to the raising of concerns'. In this case, where these features were lacking, 'investors were left with little option other than to divest'.[65] Nevertheless, the prospect of public scrutiny of collapsed companies may induce some greater commitment to engagement on the part of asset owners and managers in relation to potentially failing companies.

2.4.2 Social and Environmental Issues

As noted in Section 2.2, the stewardship goals of the second version are defined more broadly than in the first version. Intervention to reduce overly risky business strategies, as with the pre-GFC banks or Carillion plc, or to modify strategies that are failing in market terms, no longer captures the range of the second version's ambitions for stewardship. Systemic risks are expected to be addressed by institutional investors and climate change is expressly included within that category (Principle 4). Principle 7 requires systematic integration of ESG factors into institutional investors' acquisition, monitoring and exit decisions. Are these provisions likely to be more successful than the engagement model of the first version? It will be suggested here that reputational incentives may in fact operate more effectively in relation to ESG factors, including climate change, under the second version of the code than they did in relation to the first version. However, before turning to that argument, it is necessary to look at the force of the argument that companies with high ESG scores perform better than companies with lower ones. If this is the case, then the case for ESG investing will fit easily with the standard business models of both index-tracking and stock-picking funds, without the need to identify reputational incentives to add to the business model incentives.

2.4.2.1 Performance

It is often argued that the financial performance of firms which adopt strong ESG policies is superior to those which do not.[66] This is the classic 'doing well by doing right'. Unfortunately, the empirical evidence for the proposition is at best mixed. There is evidence that the volatility of the share prices of companies with high ESG disclosures is less than

---

[65] Carillion Report (n 49) paras 111, 113. There was no adverse comment on BlackRock, holding nearly 9% of the equity at one stage, whose shareholdings reduced automatically as Carillion sank in the relevant index and which engaged with the company apparently only over its remuneration proposals.

[66] See e.g. Mark Carney, 'TCFD: Strengthening the Foundations of Sustainable Finance' (Bank of England, TCFD Summit 2019, Tokyo, 8 October 2019) <www.bankofengland.co.uk/-/media/boe/files/speech/2019/tcfd-strengthening-the-foundations-of-sustainable-finance-speech-by-mark-carney.pdf?la=en&hash=D28F6D67BC4B97DD CCDE91AF8111283A39950563> accessed 7 May 2020.

that of companies which are not in this category. This is probably because a higher level of ESG disclosure gives analysts and thus investors more information about the company, so that its share price is less often subject to correction as unexpected information emerges. So, the purchase of such shares is, along this dimension, less risky. But it is difficult to find a statistically significant link between ESG disclosures and firm performance, adjusted for risk, except in the US, where ESG disclosure is not mandatory and so voluntary disclosure may act as a proxy for superior performance.[67]

The point is important because investor or beneficiary welfare is still the goal of stewardship in the second version of the UK Code. Asset owners and managers are not expected to push for the adoption of ESG policies by investee companies where the financial interests of beneficiaries will suffer. The draft of the second version suggested differently, that is, that it aimed to promote benefit to society at least in some cases independently of the benefit of those who provide the funds for investment, with the implication that in some cases sustainable benefit for society might come at the expense of beneficiaries' financial returns. Thus, the draft stated: 'Stewardship is the responsible allocation and management of capital across the institutional investment community to create sustainable value for beneficiaries, the economy and society.'[68] There was push-back from some asset owners and managers against this proposal, and in the adopted version a more conventional statement appears: 'Stewardship is the responsible allocation, management and oversight of capital to create long-term value for clients and beneficiaries *leading to* sustainable benefits for the economy, the environment and society.'[69] Thus, it would seem, the benefits to the economy, the environment and society are expected to flow from the creation of long-term value for investors, not independently of investor value.

The revised approach aligns the normative structure for investment intermediaries under the UK Code with that for directors under section 172 of the Companies Act 2006. More influential was probably the work done by the Law Commission on the application of fiduciary law to pension fund trustees,[70] later adopted by the relevant government department, the Department for Work and Pensions (DWP),[71] and referred to in an Annex to the UK Code 2020.[72] The DWP/Law Commission work endorses, not surprisingly, the view that pension fund trustees may,

---

[67] Florencio Lopez-de-Silanes, Joseph McCahery and Paul Pudschedl, 'ESG Performance and Disclosure: A Cross-Country Analysis' (2019) ECGI Law Working Paper No 481/2019 <https://ssrn.com/abstract=3506084> accessed 7 May 2020. See also Katelouzou and Micheler, The Market for Stewardship and the Role of the Government, Chapter 3.

[68] Financial Reporting Council, 'Proposed Revision to the UK Stewardship Code: Annex A – Revised UK Stewardship Code' (January 2019) 1 <www.frc.org.uk/getattachment/bf27581f-c443-4365-ae0a-1487f1388a1b/Annex-A-Stewardship-Code-Jan-2019.pdf> accessed 7 May 2020.

[69] UK Code 2020 (n 6) 4, 8 (emphasis added). Some sense of the push-back is provided in Financial Conduct Authority, 'Building a Regulatory Framework for Effective Stewardship, Feedback to DP 19/1' (Feedback Statement, October 2019) paras 3.7ff <www.fca.org.uk/publication/feedback/fs19-7.pdf> accessed 7 May 2020.

[70] Law Commission, *Fiduciary Duties of Investment Intermediaries* (Law Com No 350, 2014) https://s3-eu-west-2.amazonaws.com/lawcom-prod-storage-11jsxou24uy7q/uploads/2017/06/Final-report-Pension-funds-and-socia....pdf accessed 7 February 2022; Law Commission, *Pension Funds and Social Investment* (Law Com No 374, 2017)<https://s3-eu-west-2.amazonaws.com/lawcom-prod-storage-11jsxou24uy7q/uploads/2017/06/Final-report-Pension-funds-and-socia....pdf> accessed 7 May 2020. Some trust lawyers regard the Law Commission's approach as too lax in its permitted departures from purely financial benefit. See e.g. Philip Bennett, 'Must an Occupational Pension Scheme Take into Account ESG Factors Even If There Is a Risk of Financial Detriment to the Pension Fund?' (2019) 32 *Trust Law International* 239.

[71] Department for Work and Pensions, 'Consultation on Clarifying and Strengthening Trustees' Investment Duties' (June 2018) <https://assets.publishing.service.gov.uk/government/uploads/system/uploads/attachment_data/file/716949/consultation-clarifying-and-strengthening-trustees-investment-duties.pdf> accessed 7 May 2020; The Pension Protection Fund (Pensionable Service) and Occupational Pension Schemes (Investment and Disclosure) (Amendment and Modification) Regulations 2018, SI 2018/988.

[72] UK Code 2020 (n 6) 32.

indeed must, take ESG factors into account when they are relevant to the value of a proposed investment, and engage with investee companies on the same basis. Those factors may have positive or negative implications for investment. Taking climate change as an example, it is likely to render investment in a vineyard in Southern England more attractive than previously, while consumer or governmental reaction to climate change is likely to do the same thing for investment in the manufacture of some component vital for electrically propelled cars. On the other hand, ESG considerations are likely to render investment in a petrol distribution business less attractive. This is entirely straightforward, and one would expect such assessments to be carried out by corporate boards and asset managers, whether there was a hard- or soft-law requirement for it or not.

Where the ESG factor is not financially relevant, the Law Commission's analysis is permissive, not mandatory, and the permission is subject to significant caveats. Trustees may take into account members' views which favour financially disadvantageous investments, but are not bound to do so. Crucially, that permission is subject to the conditions: (i) that the weight of those views is in favour of a particular policy – a condition, it is said, not likely to be met in the case of controversial policies;[73] and (ii) that, even then, the financial disadvantage to the fund should not be significant.[74] Although the Law Commission's work was the result of its analysis of what trust law requires and not all contributor/institution relationships are based on trust law, its more general influence on the UK Code is probably explained by the consideration that the UK Code could hardly advocate a version of stewardship which was unlawful for one significant sub-group of asset owners.[75]

The bite of the Law Commission's binary analysis depends heavily upon the determination of which limb is applicable. Under the first limb, taking ESG factors into account is mandatory; under the second, it is permitted but subject to tight constraints. Given the uncertainties surrounding the empirical data, it is likely that pension fund trustees (and other asset owners subject to similar duties) will have a significant discretion in this area, provided that they act in good faith and remain within conventional views about the financial value of pursuing ESG policies. This is not an issue, it may be noted, on which the UK Code itself gives any fine-grained guidance.

The determination of the applicable limb is likely to be sensitive to the timescale of the investment. For example, the benefits of carbon emission reduction, and the costs of not reducing them, are likely to show over a period of decades. On this basis it is sometimes suggested that pension funds and other retirement-based savings mechanisms should be more open to ESG factors than, say, a mutual fund where the average holding period by investors in the fund is less than five years. However, even this rule of thumb is not as obvious as it seems. The position of a new entrant to a pension scheme, contemplating retirement in forty years, may indeed fit this analysis, but a person near retirement or with a pension in payment will have a stronger financial interest in the fund having enough cash to meet its payment obligations over a much shorter period.

Overall, it seems likely that asset owners (and their investment advisers) will have significant leeway in determining the extent to which they will take into account ESG factors, while still remaining within the applicable legal rules. Thus, we come back to the question of their incentives to take a broad or a narrow view of their powers in relation to ESG factors.

---

[73] 'These proposals are not intended to give any support to activist groups for boycotts or disinvestment from certain assets' (Department for Work and Pensions (n 71) 11, para 26).
[74] Department for Work and Pensions (n 71) 10–11, paras 24–25.
[75] Similar, if less easily definable, issues arise in relation to contract-based investment in any event: Law Commission, *Fiduciary Duties of Investment Intermediaries* (n 70) ch 8. On the interrelationship between hard and soft law in this area, see Dionysia Katelouzou, *The Path to Enlightened Shareholder Stewardship* (CUP) (forthcoming).

2.4.2.2 Incentives

The preceding argument suggests that one can identify one significant continuity between the first and second versions of the UK Code, despite the expanded scope of the latter. The UK Code still seeks to change the behaviour of asset owners and asset managers, but without precise guidance as to what should be done in any particular case. So, the issue of the incentives remains central for how owners and managers are likely to react to the second version of the UK Code. The difference between the first and second versions is the possibility that the incentive structure is significantly different in the two versions, because reputational incentives will operate more strongly in relation to the second version of the UK Code.

Reputational incentives here are conceptualized as the incentive to maintain a good name with somebody who has the capacity to inflict harm on you, if you lose that good name, or to promote your interests, as long as the good name is maintained. This is not the same as the warm glow a person may experience from knowing that others think well of him or her – though the creation of that warm glow could operate in some contexts as an incentive. Asset owners' and managers' stance on ESG matters is required to be disclosed under the UK Code, not only as a result of reporting under Principles 4 and 7, discussed earlier, but also from reporting under Principle 1. This requires reporting of 'signatories' purpose, investment beliefs, strategy, and culture' and how, via long-term value for beneficiaries, they lead to 'sustainable benefits for the economy'.[76] Thus, asset owners and managers which pay little attention to ESG matters cannot hope that this fact will remain hidden.

The most obvious wielder of reputational sanctions in the ESG context is the government, through its control of the legislative and regulatory framework through which the asset management industry operates. This is no theoretical possibility. In the run-up to the second version, the Financial Conduct Authority (FCA) (the rule-maker for companies listed on the Main Market of the London Stock Exchange (LSE)) and the FRC issued a joint discussion paper on the balance between regulation and soft law in promoting stewardship.[77] In its feedback on the responses, the FCA concluded that, given the imminent arrival of the UK Code 2020, it should not introduce additional regulatory requirements at this stage, but it added: 'We will consider the need for any further actions as the new Code takes effect, so that the regulatory framework continues to support effective stewardship.'[78] As The Investor Forum politely put it in its 2019 Report,[79] referring to the recently revised CGC and the UK Code, '[i]f market participants step up to deliver and demonstrate effective outcomes ... regulators and supervisors can focus on incentivising positive behaviour rather than enforcing prescribed rules'.

The government, via the FCA, has thus shown general support for the UK Code. Within that general support, there is particular emphasis on climate change.[80] The UK government, as a signatory to the Paris climate change accords, is committed to policies of carbon dioxide emission reduction and, in particular, to achieve a net zero carbon economy by 2050 (though this is a

---

[76] UK Code 2020 (n 6) 8.
[77] Financial Conduct Authority/Financial Reporting Council, 'Building a Regulatory Framework for Effective Stewardship' (Discussion Paper, January 2019) <www.fca.org.uk/publication/discussion/dp19-01.pdf> accessed 7 May 2020.
[78] FCA FS19/7 (n 69) para 1.9.
[79] The Investor Forum, 'Review 2019' (n 54) 10.
[80] A similar story could be told about the proportion of women on the boards of publicly traded companies, where the official policy, developed outside the FRC, is for one-third of board members of FTSE 350 companies to be women by 2020. This policy has more relevance to the CGC, which stresses diversity at board level, than the UK Code. Some asset managers have expressly taken up this point in their governance interactions with companies. LGIM, a large UK index tracker, has a policy of voting against the board chair where female directors do not constitute one-quarter of the board (the original target) (Gomtsian (n 52) 5).

timetable which is too slow for some). Some important steps towards this goal are achievable by regulation outside corporate law, such as the phasing out of coal-fired power stations, or the prohibition of the sale of new non-electrically propelled cars, or environmental standards for new housing. However, fine-grained carbon reduction activity by individual businesses (and, indeed, non-businesses) is thought to be necessary for the goal to be achieved, and this activity is not susceptible to *ex ante* specification across the board through regulatory rules. Thus, it is necessary, in the government's eyes, to co-opt corporate managers and those in a position to influence them in the pursuit of environmental targets. The FRC, a quasi-regulator, is one obvious channel towards this co-option, and the UK Code one obvious instrument available to it.

Two examples, relevant to investor incentives, can be given of government interest in carbon reduction initiatives. First, the DWP, despite its formal adherence to the Law Commission's guidelines, gives pension fund trustees a heavy steer that climate change considerations should be given significant weight when assessing both the financial returns to an investment or engagement action, and the views of the scheme's members.[81] The resulting regulations include ESG factors within the definition of factors which trustees must take into account under their statement of investment policy when they consider them financially material, but only climate change is specifically mentioned as an ESG item.[82] The DWP is clearly unwilling to leave an important government policy in the entirely unfettered hands of the trustees. Second, the FCA, while eschewing general stewardship regulation in the immediate aftermath of the introduction of the second version of the UK Code, as we have seen, nevertheless does propose to introduce rules requiring regulated asset managers and life insurers to enhance their disclosure of matters relevant to climate change.[83] In this case, therefore, the regulator of the capital markets is not prepared to leave disclosure wholly in the hands of those who have signed up to the UK Code.

These indications of the government view of the importance of climate change for investment decisions underline the reputational risk for signatories of the UK Code if they do not respond fully to the UK Code's climate-change provisions, which, as we have seen, identify the issue as a 'systemic' risk. Signs are already emerging that asset owners and managers can see the writing on the wall. The Investor Forum's Report for 2019 states that '[a]sset managers are re-designing investment approaches to meet client interest in ESG factors',[84] while individual asset owners, especially those holding assets acquired from outside the private sector, have publicly announced a change of focus towards more emphasis on climate change.[85] A fuller picture will emerge when the first reports from signatories to the new UK Code become available, as

---

[81] 'The UK's commitment to the Paris Agreement on Climate Change demonstrates the Government's view that climate change represents a significant concern' (Department for Work and Pensions (n 71) 18–19, para 17); 'Trustees may therefore use knowledge of broad public opinion or ratification of relevant treaties by the UK Government to draw conclusions about members' views' (Department for Work and Pensions (n 71) 21, para 28).

[82] The Occupational Pension Schemes (Investment) Regulations 2005, SI 2005/3378, reg 2(3)(b)(vi) and (4) (as amended).

[83] FCA FS19/7 (n 69) para 4.41.

[84] The Investor Forum, 'Review 2019' (n 54) 4.

[85] For example, the *Financial Times* reporting that '[t]he Church of England Pension Board, overseer of the £n retirement savings pot for the Anglican clergy, will on Thursday launch a passive index aligned with the Paris climate goals on the London Stock Exchange' (Peter Smith, 'Church of England Joins Passive Push with Climate Index' Financial Times (London, 30 January 2020) <www.ft.com/content/b1f8b262-41ae-11ea-a047-eae9bd51ceba> accessed 7 May 2020) and reporting that '[o]ne of Britain's largest pension schemes has given its 130 asset managers a two-year deadline to reduce their exposure to climate change or risk being fired' (Owen Walker, 'Top UK Pension Scheme Threatens Managers over Climate Risk' Financial Times (FTfm, 27 January 2020) <www.ft.com/content/988b5378-7dd8-4902-82e6-a7dcc96e2524> accessed 7 May 2020).

from the spring of 2021.[86] The FRC has already announced that it will pay particular attention to climate change when assessing these first reports.[87]

We argued earlier that index trackers had very limited incentives to take robust action under the first version of the UK Code. By contrast, index funds may be more open to reputational incentives, driven by fear of adverse governmental action, than stock pickers. First, the adverse financial consequences for beneficiaries of ESG investing (in so far as they exist) are not a major competitive concern for index funds, since they will exist also for their competitors who track the same index. Of course, index trackers need an ESG index to track and it may be that ESG indexes will fare worse than non-ESG indexes.[88] However, index trackers can hedge against this risk by offering both types of fund and seeing what choices investors make. Stock pickers, by contrast, may be unwilling to abandon particularly profitable investments on ESG grounds, unless they have a captive set of investors, as some pension funds do.[89] But stock pickers as well could hedge the risk by offering both types of fund. Hedging of both types can be identified in a recent strategic change by BlackRock, which will both increase the number of ESG index-tracking funds on offer and enable clients to remove certain types of company from their active funds, though there will also be an apparently across-the-board removal of their investments in companies which derive more than 25 per cent of their revenues from thermal coal production.[90] Here, therefore, there is scope for reputational incentives to be supported by changes in investor preferences. If beneficiaries change their preferences in favour of ESG, then the institutions' self-interest will push them in the same direction.[91] If they do not, the institutions can deflect governmental criticism by pointing to investor choice.

As to capacity to pursue ESG goals and climate change targets in particular, the second version of the UK Code appears less likely to require asset managers to expend resources on acquiring in-depth firm-specific knowledge than the first. As we have noted, the second version gives equal weight to capital allocation and engagement as ways of pursuing stewardship, capital allocation being an inherent function of asset management. It appears to be open to stock pickers to rely mainly on buy or sell decisions to implement ESG policies and deploy engagement only where it appears appropriate to them to do so. Moreover, moves are underway to improve the climate change reporting by companies, in terms of both detail and commonality across companies.[92] To the extent that these

---

[86] FRC (n 59).

> Organisations wanting to become signatories to the Code will be required to produce an annual Stewardship Report explaining how they have applied the Code in the previous 12 months. The FRC will evaluate Reports against our assessment framework, and those that meet the reporting expectations will be listed as signatories to the Code. To be included in the first list of signatories, organisations must submit a final report to the FRC by 31 March 2021.

[87] Financial Reporting Council, 'FRC Assesses Company and Auditor Responses to Climate Change' (20 February 2020) <www.frc.org.uk/news/february-2020-(1)/frc-assesses-company-and-auditor-responses-to-clim> accessed 7 May 2020.

[88] It is also an open question how far ESG indexes (or the exclusion of particular types of company from active funds) encourage investee companies to change their policies so as to secure inclusion. See Paul Brest, Ronald Gilson and Mark Wolfson, 'How Investors Can (and Can't) Create Social Value' (2018) ECGI Law Working Paper No 394/2018 <https://ssrn.com/abstract=3150347> accessed 7 May 2020.

[89] See n 85.

[90] BlackRock, 'Sustainability as BlackRock's New Standard for Investing' (2020) <www.blackrock.com/corporate/investor-relations/blackrock-client-letter> accessed 7 May 2020.

[91] See Katelouzou and Micheler, The Market for Stewardship and the Role of the Government, Chapter 3.

[92] See FCA, *Proposals to Enhance Climate Related Disclosures by Listed Issuers*, cp 20/3, March 2020; Sabrina Bruno, "Climate Corporate Governance: Europe vs. USA?" (2019) 16 *European Company and Financial Law Review* 687.

moves are successful, they will reduce analysts' costs in the same way that mandatory, uniform financial reporting has long done, especially if the information revealed is aggregated by service providers. In this way the costs of making allocation decisions which are responsive to climate change factors are reduced, and such reporting may also reduce the costs of engagement by owners and managers on climate-related issues.

2.5 CONCLUSION

The UK Code can be said to have had a remarkable escape from its condemnation as ineffective in the Kingman Review. None of the plausible reasons to explain the reluctance of asset owners and asset managers under the first version of the UK Code to engage with investee companies have been addressed in the second (2020) version. Instead, the focus of the UK Code has pivoted away from the performance of individual companies towards the impact of companies on society. Obviously, the two are connected, but there has been a change of emphasis from a narrow conception of stewardship as engagement (first version) to a broader concept of stewardship (second version) or, as Peter Montagnon has put,[93] a shift from a purely inward approach to stewardship to one which puts as much, if not more, emphasis on the outward impact of companies on society.

Will the second version of the UK Code be more successful than the first? It has been argued in this chapter that it is possible to construct a plausible argument in favour of a positive answer to this question, despite the bolder goals contained in the second version. This argument turns on the identification of a new and more forceful set of incentives for asset owners and managers to comply with the second version, together with a greater capacity to do so. The first version failed because engagement was not well aligned with the financial incentives and capacities generated by the business models of asset managers and asset owners. The second version, in addition to placing capital allocation decisions on par with engagement, creates a new set of incentives for compliance with the UK Code. Asset owners and managers, it is argued, will want to keep regulation at bay in order to protect their business models, and that will require doing enough in relation to ESG considerations to keep the government happy. Whether asset owners and managers, individually, are on the side of Extinction Rebellion or of President Trump and the Prime Minister of Australia does not really matter because they are likely to share a common concern to keep government regulation of investment intermediation to a minimum.

The argument developed here is thus based on the idea of soft law operating in the shadow of regulation, much as, in its early days, the non-statutory UK Takeover Code secured the support of the investment banks, in order to discourage the government from legislating on takeovers. This prediction that the second version will have a significant impact does depend, therefore, on the shadow of regulation continuing to loom over asset owners and managers in this area. This does seem a reasonable prediction in relation to climate change, given the UK government's commitment to achieving a carbon-neutral economy over the next thirty years. In relation to other ESG elements, especially the social elements, it is less clear how strong and sustained the government's policy commitments will turn out to be.

---

[93] See also Peter Montagnon, 'Stewardship in a Stakeholder World' (Corporate Governance Forum, Stockholm, 3 June 2019) <http://kabstiftelse.se/wp-content/uploads/2019/07/Montagnon-CORPORATE-GOVERNANCE-AND-STEWARDSHIP-IN-A-STAKEHOLDER-WORLD_.pdf> accessed 7 May 2020, welcoming the 'outward facing' qualities of the second version, but regretting its more prescriptive approach. This was his final public address before his untimely death.

However, the incentive argument can be refined here in terms of a more general incentive to reduce the threat of regulation. It is widely accepted that since the 2008 GFC, public confidence in the private sector of the economy has fallen significantly and not just in the financial sector. Big companies and their investors thus have an interest in restoring the legitimacy of capitalist organizations, so as to ward off public support for measures such as the nationalization of industries or the compulsory transfer of shares to state or employee funds.[94] Thus, the second version of the UK Code can claim to be aligned with broader concerns in UK society in a way that the first was not.

It is also significant that climate change and restoration of the legitimacy of big business are not parochial UK concerns. Climate change and business legitimacy are pressing issues across the developed world. Thus, BlackRock has made a major change on ESG investment, as we have seen, and other non-UK managers have voiced similar concerns. The chief executives of Fidelity International (a US global asset manager) and Allianz Global Investors (a German global asset manager) have recently called for more focus on sustainability, even suggesting that economic growth and investor returns need to be sacrificed to this end.[95] Although different jurisdictions will deal with ESG and climate-change issues in different ways, a broadly shared view of the underlying problems is an important element in the potential support of the UK Code in a world in which equity investment takes place across borders. It appears that the UK Code requires signatory asset owners and managers to report on stewardship activities in relation to foreign equities which they own as well as in relation to domestic equities.[96] Equally, cross-border ESG concerns may encourage foreign investment managers based in the UK to sign up to the UK Code and those based outside the UK to follow at least some parts of the UK Code in relation to their UK equity holdings.[97] In this respect, the salience of climate change and other ESG issues among North American and European investors will be most significant for the UK Code. Some 55 per cent of UK listed equities are held beneficially by investors based outside the UK, but just over half of this category is held by investors from North America, about a quarter by European investors and only about 15 per cent by Asian investors for whom (as yet) these issues may be less salient.[98]

Whatever one may think of the value of ESG developments within corporate law to society as a whole, they probably represent good news for the second version of the UK Code, since they suggest that the new UK Code is cutting with, not across, the grain of more general, if incipient, changes in society. It is not too hard to discern a symbiosis between the UK Code and these broader changes. It may be that the UK Code will be more a reflection, or consolidation, than a driver of social change, but that is perhaps the role which all sets of rules most comfortably fulfil. Conditional upon these changes continuing and receiving political backing, the second version of the UK Code may turn out to be an unlikely success story. We shall see.

---

[94] Both items appeared in the manifesto of the Labour Party for the 2019 general election: Labour Party, *It's Time for Real Change* (2019) <https://labour.org.uk/wp-content/uploads/2019/11/Real-Change-Labour-Manifesto-2019.pdf> accessed 7 May 2020.

[95] Patrick Jenkins, 'City Fund Managers Call for Rethink of Capitalism' *Financial Times* (London, 15 November 2019) <www.ft.com/content/1999422c-057a-11ea-9afa-d9e2401fa7ca> accessed 7 May 2020.

[96] For example, under Principle 7, signatories are asked to report 'how integration of stewardship and investment has differed for funds, asset classes and *geographies*' (emphasis added) (UK Code 2020 (n 6) 15).

[97] Contrast Cheffins's view that the foreign holdings were the Achilles' heel of the first version of the UK Code because of its parochial focus: Brian R Cheffins, 'The Stewardship Code's Achilles' Heel' (2010) 73 *Modern Law Review* 1004.

[98] Office for National Statistics, 'Ownership of UK Quoted Shares: 2018' (14 January 2020) figure 9 <www.ons.gov.uk/economy/investmentspensionsandtrusts/bulletins/ownershipofukquotedshares/2018> accessed 7 May 2020. Even these statistics overestimate the potential difficulties for the Code since a proportion of the overseas holdings are managed by fund managers based in the UK. On this point, see Paul Davies (n 32) 375–76.

3

The Market for Stewardship and the Role of the Government

Dionysia Katelouzou and Eva Micheler

3.1 INTRODUCTION

In this chapter, we focus on the market for stewardship, as it has been developing in the UK. We observe that the UK Code 2020, more clearly than previous stewardship codes (both in the UK and elsewhere), articulates the concept of a *market for stewardship*.[1] The UK Code 2020 now more openly than before takes into account the position of end-investors and beneficiaries.[2] The hope is that stewardship will be delivered because those whose money is invested ask for it. We agree that stewardship does start with those who contribute the funds invested in the market. The focus on end-investors and beneficiaries is, however, not enough. As this chapter explains, by limiting the analysis to these groups, the UK government overlooks the fact that it is itself a financial contributor to the market. A study commissioned by the Competition and Markets Authority (CMA) finds, for example, that 90 per cent of the revenue of investment consultants and fiduciary managers derives from pensions.[3] The government contributes to pension investments through the provision of tax credit. It is a significant financial investor in the market. Tax credit also deprives end-investors and beneficiaries of a financial incentive to oversee asset owners, asset managers and other service providers.[4] We therefore suggest that the UK government should act as a steward in relation to its own investment and tailor tax credit to investments that are stewardship active.

The chapter proceeds as follows. Section 3.2 introduces the market for stewardship and explains its development out of the preceding and complementary market for corporate governance. We then focus on the demand side of the market for stewardship and argue that there are two reasons why contributors to financial markets would request stewardship activity from asset owners, asset managers and other service providers.[5] The first reason is financial return. The second reason motivating demand for stewardship is altruism. We analyze both motives in Section 3.3.

In Section 3.4 we take a closer look at the current structure of the market for stewardship. We create a taxonomy of market participants and examine their respective perspectives. We distinguish between beneficiaries of workplace and personal pensions, small portfolio end-investors and large portfolio end-investors. We also examine the role of pension trustees and members of

---

[1] Dionysia Katelouzou, *The Path to Enlightened Shareholder Stewardship* (CUP) (forthcoming).
[2] As defined in Sections 3.4.1–3.4.3.
[3] Competition and Markets Authority, 'Investment Consultants Market Investigation: Final Report' (12 December 2018) 29, para 1.14 <https://assets.publishing.service.gov.uk/media/5c0fee5740f0b60c8d6019a6/ICMI_Final_Report.pdf> accessed 3 December 2020.
[4] As defined in Sections 3.4.4 and 3.4.5.
[5] ibid.

independent governance committees and the position of investment consultants and fiduciary managers. We conclude that demand for stewardship can most realistically emerge from large scale portfolio end-investors who are prepared to be guided by altruistic motives. It is also possible that younger individuals will be prepared to forgo financial return to support good causes when they start making investment decisions. These investors benefit from the UK Code 2020. Their market share is, however, not large enough yet to make a significant difference.

We then examine in Section 3.5 the role of the UK government and argue that the government acts as a regulator of the industry ensuring that end-investors and beneficiaries give informed consent and that the contractual promises made to them are kept. It does, however, fall short of appreciating that it is a financial contributor. The government heavily subsidizes pension investments. The cost of tax relief of registered pension schemes in 2017–18 (the most recent available data) is £37.8 billion.[6] In that capacity, the government should act as a steward in the same way it expects everybody else to.[7] Tax credit should be available only for stewardship active investments. Section 3.6 concludes.

3.2 STEWARDSHIP AS A MARKET-DRIVEN CONCEPT

3.2.1 A Market for Corporate Governance and a Market for Stewardship

The UK approach to corporate governance and stewardship is to encourage the market to deliver good corporate governance through stewardship. The UK government is generally reluctant to legislate in the area of corporate law and governance.[8] The preferred approach is to develop standards in cooperation with market participants. These standards then set an example of best practice which the government hopes will be adopted. Shareholders and institutional investors perform a key role in this context.

The 1992 Cadbury Code, for example, was designed as a ready-made agenda enabling institutions and individual shareholders to make representations to boards.[9] The Cadbury Committee explicitly and primarily looked to market-based enforcement for the nineteen principles of its Code of Best Practice.[10] The expectation was that the development of best practice standards would encourage pressure from shareholders to hasten a widespread adoption of these standards.[11] The Cadbury Report also states that institutional investors 'now own the

---

[6] HM Revenue and Customs, 'Personal Pensions: Contribution and Tax Relief Statistics' (2019) <www.gov.uk/government/collections/personal-pensions-statistics#national-statistics> assessed 3 December 2020.

[7] This chapter draws a distinction between the government acting as a regulator and the government acting as a financial contributor to the market. When the government acts as a regulator, the rules apply to all investors. In this chapter, we propose that as far as the government subsidizes certain investments such as pensions through preferential tax treatment, it is an investor in its own right and should thus act as a steward.

[8] On the traditionally self-regulatory approach to financial market regulation in the UK, see e.g. Marc T Moore, *Corporate Governance in the Shadow of the State* (Hart 2013) 167–74.

[9] Adrian Cadbury, *Report of the Committee on the Financial Aspects of Corporate Governance* (Financial Reporting Council, Gee Publishing 1992) <https://ecgi.global/code/cadbury-report-financial-aspects-corporate-governance> accessed 3 December 2020 [hereinafter Cadbury Report]; para 6.16: '[t]he obligation on companies to state how far they comply with the Code provides institutional and individual shareholders with a ready-made agenda for their representations to boards'.

[10] Cadbury Report (n 9), para 6.16 ('[it] is up to them [the shareholders] to put it [the Code] to good use. The Committee is primarily looking to such market-based regulation to turn its proposals into action) and para 1.10 ('We believe that our approach, based on compliance with a voluntary code coupled with disclosure, will prove more effective than a statutory code. It is directed at establishing best practice, at encouraging pressure from shareholders to hasten its widespread adoption, and at allowing some flexibility in implementation.').

[11] Cadbury Report (n 9) 11 (para 1.10), 51 (para 6.16), 18 (para 3.14) and 53 (para 4).

majority of the shares in quoted companies'.[12] It observes that the readiness of institutional investors to make good use of their voting power turns on the degree to which they see their engagement 'as ... in the interest of those whose money they are investing'.[13] It recommends that institutional investors disclose the policies on the use of their voting rights and warmly welcomes the 1991 statement by the Institutional Shareholders' Committee (ISC) on the Responsibilities of Institutional Shareholders in the UK.[14] That statement encourages pension funds, insurance companies and investment trusts and other collective investment vehicles to involve themselves actively in the governance of investee companies. It also makes the point that this engagement forms part of the fulfilment of their obligations to end-beneficiaries.[15]

The combination of a ready-made Corporate Governance Code with a set of industry-led guidelines for institutional investors which evolved into an ISC 'Code on the Responsibilities of Institutional Investors' in 2009 did, however, not produce the desired effect.[16] In the post-mortem of the 2008 financial crises, the Walker Review criticized the passivity and widespread acquiescence to (or even encouragement of) excessive risk-taking by some banks and other financial institutions.[17] The remedy to the problem was to take the development of stewardship principles out of the hands of the industry. The Financial Reporting Council (FRC) was given the responsibility to develop and encourage stewardship principles for institutional investors and asset managers. The hope was that this would attract and promote more adherence to best practice in stewardship as a matter of public interest and would facilitate informed decisions by beneficiaries, trustees and other end-investors.[18]

Stewardship was promoted by the FRC as an activity that has benefits for end-investors and beneficiaries.[19] The preface to the UK Code 2010 states that stewardship helps to 'improve the long-term returns to shareholders and the efficient exercise of governance responsibilities'.[20]

[12] Cadbury Report (n 9) 49, para 6.9. For more recent data on the institutionalization of the UK public equity, see Office for National Statistics, 'Ownership of UK Quoted Shares: 2018' (14 January 2020) <www.ons.gov.uk/economy/investmentspensionsandtrusts/bulletins/ownershipofukquotedshares/2018> assessed 3 December 2020.

[13] Cadbury Report (n 9) 49, para 6.10. Subsequent reports have also emphasized the corporate governance role of institutional shareholders, highlighting at the same time the responsibility of investors to their clients. See Committee on Corporate Governance, *Final Report* (Gee Publishing 1998) 40–41 <https://ecgi.global/code/hampel-report-final> accessed 3 December 2020; Paul Myners, 'Institutional Investment in the United Kingdom: A Review' (HM Treasury 2001) <https://uksif.org/wp-content/uploads/2012/12/MYNERS-P.-2001.-Institutional-Investment-in-the-United-Kingdom-A-Review.pdf> accessed 3 December 2020; Derek Higgs, 'Review of the Role and Effectiveness of Non-executive Directors' (UK Department of Trade and Industry, January 2003) para 15.21 <https://ecgi.global/code/higgs-report-review-role-and-effectiveness-non-executive-directors> accessed 3 December 2020.

[14] Cadbury Report (n 9) 49 (paras 6.11–6.12), 55 (para 16) and 56 (para 19).

[15] Memorandum of the Institutional Shareholder Committee, 'The Responsibilities of Institutional Shareholders and Agents – Statement of Principles' (2003) <https://publications.parliament.uk/pa/cm200203/cmselect/cmtrdind/439/439ap09.htm> assessed 3 December 2020.

[16] The current corporate governance code in the UK (effective for accounting periods commencing or on after 1 January 2019) is the UK Corporate Governance Code 2018. This was evolved out of the Combined Code 2010 and the earlier Cadbury Code of Best Practice. For a recent assessment of the effectiveness of the comply-or-explain approach in the UK, see Bobby V Reddy, 'Thinking Outside the Box – Eliminating the Perniciousness of Box-Ticking in the New Corporate Governance Code' (2019) 82 *Modern Law Review* 692.

[17] David Walker, 'A Review of Corporate Governance in UK Banks and Other Financial Industry Entities. Final Recommendations' (26 November 2009) 17, 71–73 <https://ecgi.global/sites/default/files/codes/documents/walker_review_261109.pdf> accessed 3 December 2020 [hereinafter Walker Review].

[18] Walker Review (n 17) para 5.9.

[19] For a Polanyian-influenced analysis of stewardship which connects the interests of the beneficiaries and end investors with the public interest, see Dionysia Katelouzou, 'Shareholder Stewardship: A Case of (Re)Embedding Institutional Investors and the Corporation?' in Beate Sjåfjell and Christopher M Bruner (eds), *Cambridge Handbook of Corporate Law, Corporate Governance and Sustainability* (CUP 2019) 581–95.

[20] Financial Reporting Council, *The UK Stewardship Code* (July 2010) 1 <www.frc.org.uk/getattachment/e223e152-5515-4cdc-a951-da33e093eb28/UK-Stewardship-Code-July-2010.pdf> accessed 3 December 2020 [hereinafter UK Code

Along similar lines, the 2012 revision of the UK Stewardship Code contends that stewardship 'aims to promote the long term [sic] success of companies in such a way that the ultimate providers of capital also prosper'.[21]

A parallel assertion has always been that good corporate governance and stewardship is good for the economy. The Cadbury Report opens with the claim that '[t]he country's economy depends on the drive and efficiency of its companies'.[22] The UK Code 2010 stresses the importance of stewardship in enforcing good standards of corporate governance.[23] The UK Code 2012 states that 'effective stewardship benefits companies, investors and the economy as a whole'.[24]

However, neither the 2010 nor the 2012 UK Code has achieved its goals. The Kingman Review concluded in December 2018 that '[t]he Stewardship Code, whilst a major and well-intentioned intervention, is not effective in practice'.[25] The FRC directly responded to the criticisms made by the Kingman review and revised the UK Code 2012 with a focus on outcomes. The 2020 version of the UK Code is different from its precedent code in many ways. In addition to the focus on outcomes rather than policies, it adopts a broader concept of stewardship and an emphasis on environmental, social and governance (ESG) factors, especially climate change.[26]

From our perspective, the UK Code 2020 continues to stress that stewardship creates 'long-term value' for investors' clients and beneficiaries.[27] In addition, it embeds this assumption into a market framework of its own right. A key aim of the 2020 revisions is the creation of 'a *market for stewardship* driven by a demand from asset owners and beneficiaries for better quality information about how asset managers and service providers fulfil their responsibilities'.[28]

This constitutes a transformation of the idea that 'stewardship is good for beneficiaries and end-investors' into 'beneficiaries and end-investors should be able to ask for stewardship because it is good for them'. Traces of this notion of a 'market for stewardship' can be found in the Kay Review which preceded the UK Code 2012 and emphasized the promotion of trust and

---

2010]. See also Davies, The UK Stewardship Code 2010–2020, Chapter 2 (characterizing the UK Code 2010 as an 'Engagement Code').

[21] Financial Reporting Council, *The UK Stewardship Code* (September 2012) 1 <www.frc.org.uk/getattachment/d67933f9-ca38-4233-b603-3d24b2f62c5f/UK-Stewardship-Code-(September-2012).pdf> accessed 3 December 2020 [hereinafter UK Code 2012]. See also John Kay, 'The Kay Review of UK Equity Markets and Long-Term Decision Making' (Department for Business, Innovation and Skills, July 2012) 65 <https://assets.publishing.service.gov.uk/government/uploads/system/uploads/attachment_data/file/253454/bis-12-917-kay-review-of-equity-markets-final-report.pdf> accessed 3 December 2020 [hereinafter Kay Review]: 'The equity investment chain will best serve the interests of savers and companies if relationships along it are based on the concept of stewardship.'

[22] Cadbury Report (n 9) 10, para 1.1.

[23] UK Code 2010 (n 20) 1.

[24] UK Code 2012 (n 21) 1. Further on the evolution of the notion of stewardship, see Katelouzou (n 1).

[25] John Kingman, 'Independent Review of the Financial Reporting Council' (Department for Business, Energy and Industrial Strategy, December 2018) 8 <https://assets.publishing.service.gov.uk/government/uploads/system/uploads/attachment_data/file/767387/frc-independent-review-final-report.pdf> accessed 3 December 2020 [hereinafter Kingman Review].

[26] Further on the differences between the two stewardship codes, see Davies, The UK Stewardship Code 2010–2020, Chapter 2.

[27] Financial Reporting Council, *The UK Stewardship Code 2020* (2019) 4 <www.frc.org.uk/getattachment/5aae591d-d9d3-4cf4-814a-d14e156a1d87/Stewardship-Code_Dec-19-Final-Corrected.pdf> accessed 3 December 2020 [hereinafter UK Code 2020].

[28] Financial Reporting Council, 'Proposed Revision to the UK Stewardship Code' (January 2019) 1 <www.frc.org.uk/getattachment/8caa0e9c-58bb-41b2-923e-296223755174/Consultation-on-Proposed-Revisions-to-the-UK-Stewardship-Code-Jan-2019.pdf> accessed 3 December 2020 [emphasis added]; Financial Conduct Authority/Financial Reporting Council, 'Building a Regulatory Framework for Effective Stewardship' (Discussion Paper, January 2019) <www.fca.org.uk/publication/discussion/dp19-01.pdf> accessed 3 December 2020.

confidence along the investment chain.[29] The FRC's tiering exercise introduced in 2016 also aimed at developing such a market by providing a reputational incentive on signatories to join the top tier.[30] But, as Section 3.2.2 will show, with the UK Code 2020 the aspiration for a market for stewardship is taking more distinctive shape.[31]

3.2.2 The Role of the UK Code 2020

The UK Code 2020 more clearly than its predecessors articulates the idea of a market for stewardship that starts with end-investors and beneficiaries. It aims to support such a market by encouraging standardized disclosure. This is designed to help market participants to make informed choices. Signatories are thus required to explain their organization's purpose, strategy and culture and how these enable them to practise effective stewardship.[32] They are also expected to show that they are demonstrating this commitment through appropriate governance, workforce, resourcing and incentives.[33]

Compared to the previous two versions, the UK Code 2020 defines its scope of application in a more targeted way. The aim is to better capture the different roles performed by the different participants in the investment industry.[34] The Code distinguishes between asset owners, asset managers and other service providers. Asset owners are, for example, trustees of occupational pension schemes, trustees of defined contribution pension schemes, insurers and reinsurers. Asset managers are instructed by asset owners to take investment decisions. Other service providers serve either asset owners or asset managers, for example in the form of consultancy or proxy advice.

The UK Code 2020 sets out twelve principles for asset owners and asset managers. These principles are supported by reporting expectations. The Code acknowledges that some reporting expectations may be more relevant for asset owners while others will be more relevant to asset managers.[35] In addition, there are six separate principles for service providers which are also supported by reporting expectations.[36]

Moreover, the UK Code 2020 aims to 'help align the approach of the whole community in the interest of end-investors and beneficiaries'.[37] To this end, Principle 3 encourages signatories to 'put the best interests of clients and beneficiaries first'.[38] Principle 6 states that 'signatories take account of client and beneficiary needs and communicate the activities'. These suggest a concern for the immediate clients of signatories but also for the interests of end-investors and beneficiaries who may not have a direct relationship with a signatory.

---

[29] Kay Review (n 21) para 13.18 (highlighting the need to recreate 'an equity investment chain that meets the needs of users and that is based on trust, respect, confidence and cooperation').

[30] More information on the tiering exercise can be found here: Financial Reporting Council, 'Tiering of Signatories to the Stewardship Code' (14 November 2016) <www.frc.org.uk/news/november-2016/tiering-of-signatories-to-the-stewardship-code> accessed 3 December 2020. For a criticism, see Kingman Review (n 25) 46 (highlighting that 'the existing tiering approach focuses predominantly on checking the content of stewardship statements, not on actual effectiveness or outcomes'). Generally on the role of market enforcement in the context of shareholder stewardship, see Katelouzou and Sergakis, Shareholder Stewardship Enforcement, Chapter 27.

[31] On a detailed analysis of the supply and demand side of this market for stewardship, see Katelouzou (n 1).

[32] UK Code 2020 (n 27) Principle 1.

[33] UK Code 2020 (n 27) Principle 2.

[34] Financial Reporting Council, 'Consulting on a Revised UK Stewardship Code' (Feedback Statement, October 2019) 1 <www.frc.org.uk/getattachment/2912476c-d183-46bd-a86e-dfb024f694ad/191023-Feedback-Statement-Consultation-on-revised-Stewardship-Code-FINAL.pdf> accessed 3 December 2020.

[35] UK Code 2020 (n 27) 5.

[36] UK Code 2020 (n 27) 23–29.

[37] FRC, Feedback Statement (n 34) 1.

[38] UK Code 2020 (n 27) Principle 3. For service providers, see UK Code 2020 (n 27) 26, Principle 3.

The UK Code 2020 is also broader in scope than its predecessors. Both the 2010 and the 2012 versions applied to shares only. The 2020 version is designed to apply across all asset classes including but not limited to listed and private equity, fixed income, real estate and infrastructure, and investments outside the UK.

Sustainability also features prominently in the new Code. In addition to focusing on governance, the UK Code 2020 now also refers to environmental and social factors, particularly climate change.[39] Principle 7 requires that 'signatories systematically integrate stewardship and investment, including material environmental, social and governance issues, and climate change, to fulfil their responsibilities'.[40]

Unlike its predecessors and the UK Corporate Governance Code, which all adopted the 'comply or explain' model, the UK Code 2020 applies on an 'apply and explain' basis.[41] Market participants who have adopted the UK Code are referred to as signatories.[42] Signatories have to report annually on stewardship activity and its outcomes in a Stewardship Report.[43] The focus on reporting on 'activity and outcome' is new. The previous two stewardship codes focused solely on policy statements.[44] Under the UK Code 2020, signatories are expected to apply the principles and make a clear statement to explain which activities they have carried out in the previous year and what the outcome has been. Boilerplate reporting is actively discouraged. Reports should be engaging, succinct and in plain English. They should be as specific and as transparent as possible, giving a clear picture of how the organization has applied the Code. Reporting should acknowledge setbacks experienced and lessons learnt as well as successes.[45] To smooth the transition to the new Code and encourage good reporting the FRC assessed the Stewardship Reports from the first round of applications in November 2021 and set expectations for the 2022 applications, but it did not identify subscribers to the UK Code 2022 as either Tier 1 or Tier 2 participants, at least for the first year of reporting.[46]

From the perspective of the market for stewardship, the new rendition of the UK 2020 Code puts the ball more clearly into the court of beneficiaries and end-investors. It also leans more specifically on asset owners, such as pension trustees and insurance companies offering pensions, by setting higher standards as to how they integrate stewardship responsibilities into their investment decision-making and mandates and promoting outcomes-focused stewardship to meet their information needs.[47]

In addition, the UK Code 2020 takes the 'public good' component of stewardship further than its predecessors to what Katelouzou terms 'enlightened stewardship'.[48] In the 2020

---

[39] UK Code 2020 (n 27) 4. Further on sustainability and stewardship, see Katelouzou and Klettner, Sustainable Finance and Stewardship, Chapter 26.
[40] UK Code 2020 (n 27) 15.
[41] UK Code 2020 (n 27) 4. Further on the coerciveness of this approach, see Dionysia Katelouzou and Peer Zumbansen, 'The New Geographies of Corporate Governance' (2020) 42 *University of Pennsylvania Journal of International Law* 51.
[42] The current signatory list to the UK Code 2020 is available here: <www.frc.org.uk/investors/uk-stewardship-code/uk-stewardship-code-signatories> accessed 4 February 2022. Information on the signatories to the UK Code 2012 as of September 2021 is available here: <https://www.frc.org.uk/document-library/corporate-governance/stewardship-statements/stewardship-code-2012-signatory-list> accessed 4 February 2022.
[43] UK Code 2020 (n 27) 5.
[44] Cf. Financial Reporting Council, 'Proposed Revision to the UK Stewardship Code: Annex A – Revised UK Stewardship Code' (January 2019) 3 <www.frc.org.uk/getattachment/bf27581f-c443-4365-ae0a-1487f1388a1b/Annex-A-Stewardship-Code-Jan-2019.pdf> accessed 3 December 2020, proposing two different disclosures: a Policy and Practice Statement and an annual Activities and Outcomes Report.
[45] UK Code 2020 (n 27) 6.
[46] FRC, Feedback Statement (n 34) 12; Financial Reporting Council, 'Effective Stewardship Reporting: Examples from 2021 and expectations for 2022' (November 2021) <www.frc.org.uk/getattachment/42122e31-bc04-47ca-ad8c-23157e56c9a5/FRC-Effective-Stewardship-Reporting-Review_November-2021.pdf> accessed 4 February 2022.
[47] See e.g. UK Code 2020 (n 27) 16 (differentiating the reporting expectations to Principle 8 for asset managers and asset owners).
[48] Katelouzou (n 1).

version of the Code, stewardship is defined more broadly than in previous versions as creating long-term value 'for ... the economy, the environment and society'.[49] The UK Code 2020 expresses that 'asset owners and asset managers play an important role as guardians of market integrity and in working to minimize systemic risks as well as being stewards of the investments in their portfolios'.[50]

The authors of the UK Code 2020 hope that beneficiaries and end-investors will encourage those acting for them to be stewardship active. The government itself role-models the attitude that it would like to encourage. To facilitate automatic enrolment (introduced in 2012), it has set up a workplace pension scheme referred to as NEST. The promotional video for NEST uses the following statement: 'We believe in investing all your contributions responsibly including with companies who we encourage to meet high standards of environmental, social and corporate governance, not only because it's the right thing to do, but because it's been shown to give you better returns over time.'[51]

Growing the demand for responsible investment and stewardship presents a great opportunity, but also a great challenge, a subject to which we turn in Section 3.3.

3.3 DEMAND FOR STEWARDSHIP: MOTIVATING FACTORS

As the preceding discussion explains, the UK Code 2020 aims to stimulate 'demand' for stewardship. It is therefore important to take a comprehensive view examining how to best generate demand for stewardship and where such demand can come from. In this section we examine two motivating factors that can give rise to demand for stewardship: the promise of financial return and altruism.

3.3.1 *Financial Return*

The statement that stewardship benefits end-investors and beneficiaries contains an empirical claim. Whether or not 'stewardship as such' contributes to financial returns has yet to become the subject of a vibrant academic debate, but there exists an extensive empirical literature analyzing the impact of ESG activism by investors and the returns of socially responsible investment (SRI). While neither ESG activism nor SRI is always synonymous with stewardship,[52] this empirical literature is the closest kin to stewardship, especially after the heavy emphasis of the UK Code 2020 on ESG.[53] Contributors have analyzed the effect of ESG activism and SRI from three perspectives: financial return for investors, the financial well-being of issuers and the economy as a whole.

3.3.1.1 Financial Return for Investors

The literature examining the relationship between ESG activism and engagement, on the one hand, and financial return for investors, on the other, unfortunately does not support a general claim that ESG activism leads to better returns for investors over time. The evidence is mixed.

---

[49] UK Code 2020 (n 27) 4, 8, Principle 1.
[50] UK Code 2020 (n 27) 4. See also Financial Conduct Authority, 'Building a Regulatory Framework for Effective Stewardship, Feedback to DP 19/1' (Feedback Statement, October 2019) 8 <www.fca.org.uk/publication/feedback/fs19-7.pdf> accessed 3 December 2020.
[51] NEST, 'Welcome to NEST' (2020) <www.nestpensions.org.uk/schemeweb/nest/aboutnest/welcome-to-NEST.html> accessed 3 December 2020.
[52] For a comprehensive analysis of stewardship, see Katelouzou (n 1).
[53] UK Code 2020 (n 27) Principles 5 and 7.

On the one hand, some studies conclude that ESG activism is associated with financial benefit for investors. For example, a 2015 study on corporate social responsibility (CSR) engagements focused on a single investment firm in the US finds positive abnormal returns but only for successful engagements.[54] Another recent study concludes that co-ordinated engagements targeting environmental or social issues are value-enhancing (in the sense of significant abnormal stock returns), especially when they are headed by a lead investor and are successful.[55] On the other hand, another recent study examines 847 engagements around the globe and finds that ESG activism comes only with modest financial returns during the engagement period from the perspective of the activist fund.[56] For index funds, in particular, academic contributors increasingly question whether engagement and stewardship are cost-effective and meaningful from the perspective of beneficiaries.[57]

Another body of the empirical literature compares the performance of funds that invest in SRI funds with their conventional competitors. The conclusions on the whole are that both types achieve similar returns and that there are at best negligible gains for SRI funds.[58] There is some evidence that responsible investing acts as a 'risk mitigation' tool.[59] But the overall conclusion from the empirical literature seems to be that, 'at the worst case, investors in ESG mutual funds can expect to lose nothing compared to conventional fund investments'.[60]

More generally, the UK CMA has recently investigated the market for investment consultants and concluded that it is not possible to claim that, once fees have been taken into account, managed funds do better than index trackers.[61]

This creates a situation where there seems to be no clear evidence that ESG activism and responsible investment more broadly are good for investors, but where there also is no clear evidence that they are bad for them. From the perspective of the market for stewardship, the evidence currently available cannot sufficiently incentivize end-investors and beneficiaries to demand stewardship. But it also means that overall ESG activism and responsible investment do not obviously expose them to harm. We argue in this chapter that this can explain why beneficiaries and end-investors are generally passive. We will show that the government is

---

[54] Elroy Dimson, Oğuzhan Karakaş and Xi Li, 'Active Ownership' (2015) 28 *Review of Financial Studies* 3225.
[55] Elroy Dimson, Oğuzhan Karakaş and Xi Li, 'Coordinated Engagements' (29 October 2019) <https://ssrn.com/abstract=3209072> accessed 3 December 2020.
[56] Tamás Barkó, Martijn Cremers and Luc Renneboog, 'Shareholder Engagement on Environmental, Social, and Governance Performance' (2018) <https://ssrn.com/abstract=2977219> accessed 3 December 2020.
[57] Fisch, The Uncertain Stewardship Potential of Index Funds, Chapter 21.
[58] For comprehensive literature reviews, see Joshua D Margolis, Hillary Anger Elfenbein and James P Walsh, 'Does It Pay to Be Good . . . And Does It Matter? A Meta-analysis of the Relationship between Corporate Social and Financial Performance' (2009) <https://ssrn.com/abstract=1866371> accessed 3 December 2020; Tamás Barkó and Luc Renneboog 'Mutual Funds: Management Styles, Social Responsibility, Performance and Efficiency' in H Kent Baker, Greg Filbeck and Halil Kiymaz (eds), *Mutual Funds and Exchange-Traded Funds: Building Blocks to Wealth* (OUP 2016) 268–90; see also Samuel M Hartzmark and Abigail B Sussman, 'Do Investors Value Sustainability? A Natural Experiment Examining Raking and Fund Flows' (2019) ECGI Finance Working Paper No 565/2018 <https://ssrn.com/abstract=3016092> accessed 3 December 2020.
[59] See Rajna Gibson and others, 'Responsible Institutional Investing Around the World' (2019) Swiss Finance Institute Research Paper No 20-13 <https://ssrn.com/abstract=3525530> accessed 3 December 2020. For earlier evidence focusing on the US market, see Rajna Gibson, Philipp Krueger and Shema Mitali, 'The Sustainability Footprint of Institutional Investors' (2018) Swiss Finance Institute Research Paper No 17-05 <https://ssrn.com/abstract=2918926> accessed 3 December 2020.
[60] Gunnar Friede, Timo Busch and Alexander Bassen, 'ESG and Financial Performance: Aggregated Evidence from More Than 2000 Empirical Studies' (2015) 5 *Journal of Sustainable Finance & Investment* 210, 226.
[61] Competition and Markets Authority (n 3) 16, para 50.

a financial contributor to pension investments. It therefore should connect its own contribution to pension investments with a requirement for stewardship.

3.3.1.2 Financial Return for Issuers

Another section of the literature examines whether ESG activism is good for the financial performance of issuers. Here, too, the results are mixed. The FRC and the FCA cite academic contributions showing that 'deep engagement' by asset managers with investee companies can make it more likely that these companies pursue innovative strategies,[62] have reduced 'downside risk' (especially when target firms respond with material actions to the activists' requests),[63] and are less likely to become entrenched and engage in value-destroying mergers and acquisitions (M&A) activity.[64] However, a recent paper reviews the breadth of the empirical literature analyzing the relationship between ESG activism and firm value and concludes that the results are mixed.[65] Results are also mixed for the relationship between ESG activity and firm performance measured in accounting terms.[66] It is therefore not possible to assert that ESG activity on the whole enhances firm value. But, again, there is no evidence that ESG activity is generally harmful to issuers.[67]

3.3.1.3 Benefits for the Economy

The joint FRC–FCA discussion paper preceding the introduction of the UK Code 2020 references an article in which the authors conclude that a high-quality financial market has a strong positive impact on macro-economic performance and supports sustainable economic growth over the long term, which reduces the risk of financial crises and thereby improves economic performance.[68] This is a positive outcome from the perspective of the UK government, but it does not directly translate into positive financial return for investors. The argument does not suggest that end-investors and beneficiaries do better by demanding stewardship activity. They may well be financially better off in the long term by having their service providers act strategically agile in the short term.

---

[62] FCA/FRC (n 28) 11–12, para 3.7 citing Philippe Aghion, John Van Reenen and Luigi Zingales, 'Innovation and Institutional Ownership' (2013) 103 *American Economic Review* 277.

[63] FCA/FRC (n 28) 11–12, para 3.7 citing Andreas Hoepner and others, 'ESG Shareholder Engagement and Downside Risk' (AFA 2018 conference paper, August 2019) <https://ssrn.com/abstract=2874252> accessed 3 December 2020; Jędrzej Białkowski and Laura T Starks, 'SRI Funds: Investor Demand, Exogenous Shocks and ESG Profiles' (2016) Working Papers in Economics 16/11, University of Canterbury, Department of Economics and Finance <https://ideas.repec.org/p/cbt/econwp/16-11.html> accessed 3 December 2020.

[64] FCA/FRC (n 28) 11–12, para 3.8 citing Cornelius Schmidt and Rüdiger Fahlenbrach, 'Do Exogenous Changes in Passive Institutional Ownership Affect Corporate Governance and Firm Value?' (2017) 124 *Journal of Financial Economics* 285.

[65] Hans B Christensen, Luzi Hail and Christian Leuz, 'Adoption of SCR and Sustainability Reporting Standards: Economic Analysis and Review' (2019) ECGI Finance Working Paper 623/2019, 33 <https://ssrn.com/abstract=3427748> accessed 3 December 2020; for a recent theoretical analysis on when mutual funds should vote, see Sean J Griffith, 'Opt-In Stewardship: Toward an Optimal Delegation of Mutual Fund Voting Authority' (2020) 98 *Texas Law Review* 983.

[66] Christensen, Hail and Leuz (n 65) 33.

[67] But see Daniel Ferreira, David Kershaw, Tom Kirchmaier and Edmund-Philipp Schuster, 'Measuring Management Insulation from Shareholder Pressure' (13 June 2016) LSE Legal Studies Working Paper No 01/2016 <https://ssrn.com/abstract=2170392> accessed 3 December 2020. They argue that banks with actively engaged shareholders were more likely to need a bailout during the financial crisis.

[68] FCA/FRC (n 28) 11, para 3.5.

3.3.1.4 Conclusion

To conclude, our read of the empirical literature is that there is no such thing as evidence supporting claims along the lines of 'end-investors and beneficiaries will benefit in the long term' from stewardship activities translated to ESG and SRI investments. What is good for the return of beneficiaries depends on their respective circumstances. Overall, there appears to be no harm in stewardship either, but that is not enough to justify end-investors and beneficiaries spending their own resources to become stewardship active.

3.3.2 Altruism

The UK Code 2020, in its introduction, defines stewardship as the 'responsible allocation, management and oversight of capital … leading to sustainable benefits for the economy, the environment and society'.[69] This suggests that stewardship is 'the right thing to do' irrespective of financial returns. By asking for stewardship, end-investors and beneficiaries can make a contribution to the common good. They are encouraged to take investment decisions with a view to creating a better world. We show here that there exists a group of suppliers of 'responsible' investment products who believe that their market will grow in the future. They are encouraged by the fact that younger pension beneficiaries and retail individuals say in surveys that they are interested in using their investment to further the common good. For the time being, that investment market is, however, relatively small.[70] In addition, there exists a group of investors with large portfolios who actively pursue altruistic aims.[71]

3.4 THE MARKET PARTICIPANTS

In this section, the market for stewardship in the UK is analyzed from the perspective of its respective participants. A distinction is drawn among beneficiaries of workplace and personal pensions, small portfolio end-investors and large portfolio end-investors. We also analyze the perspective of pension trustees and members of independent governance committees as well as the role of investment consultants and fiduciary managers.

3.4.1 Beneficiaries of Workplace and Personal Pensions

Beneficiaries of pension schemes are a significant group of investors. In the UK they make up 90 per cent of the revenues of investment consultants and fiduciary managers.[72] In terms of motivation, they focus mainly on financial return and tax benefits. For instance, the Law Commission cites a study carried out by Ignition House for the FCA. The respondents to this study report that they interact with pension providers to enquire what their fund is currently worth, to find out whether they could access tax-free cash, and to let the providers know they wanted access to their pension money owing to a change in circumstances such as redundancy or health issues.[73]

---

[69] UK Code 2020 (n 27) 4.
[70] See Sections 3.4.1 and 3.4.2.
[71] See Section 3.4.3.
[72] Competition and Markets Authority (n 3) 29, para 1.14.
[73] Ignition House, 'Exploring Consumer Decision Making and Behaviour in the At-Retirement Landscape' (prepared by Ignition House for the Financial Conduct Authority, December 2014) 40 <www.fca.org.uk/publication/research/rims-ignition-house.pdf> accessed 3 December 2020.

The purpose of a pension scheme is to accumulate money for retirement, so it is not a surprise that financial value, including employer contribution levels, investment returns and tax allowance, is a dominant factor for beneficiaries. When asked to describe what they were thinking about when they were making retirement plans, the most common unprompted consideration was how much tax-free cash they can have and what the maximum level of income was that they can generate with the rest. Beyond this, respondents needed to be prompted to consider factors such as longevity, health and inflation.[74]

We have seen that the empirical evidence as to whether ESG activism and SRI enhance the financial performance of funds is mixed.[75] It is therefore no surprise that pension beneficiaries in the UK revert to default investment choices. This default option bias is well documented across many countries.[76] In addition, pension beneficiaries reported being 'uncertain about their ability to make equity-based investments'.[77] They also felt that they received too much narrative information that was difficult to navigate and full of jargon.[78]

The Law Commission observes further that members of pension schemes view pension decisions as 'complex, unpleasant, boring, time consuming and something to be put off indefinitely'.[79] In addition, most pension savers do not appear to know how much of their pension is invested ethically.[80] This suggests that most beneficiaries of pensions are not likely to view their pension investment as a means through which they actively contribute to the common good.

There exists industry-funded empirical research showing that only a small proportion of investors are prepared to sacrifice return with a view to ensuring that their savings support a good cause.[81] As a result, altruism does not seem to be the main contributing factor for stimulating demand for stewardship. Younger respondents (eighteen to twenty-four-year-olds), however, express a greater interest in investing in a stewardship active way than older individuals.[82] It remains to be seen if this interest translates into decisions that prioritize stewardship over returns once the members of this group begin to make investment decisions in relation to pension. It is nevertheless encouraging that the investment industry has identified stewardship-active investment as a market with growth potential.

From the perspective of this chapter, we need to conclude that the beneficiaries of workplace and personal pensions, while collectively very significant, are currently unlikely to be a source for demand for stewardship activity. The UK Code 2020 does not change this. This is a shame

---

[74] Ignition House (n 73) 45.
[75] See Section 3.3.1.
[76] For Singapore, see e.g. Joelle H Fong 'Taking Control: Active Investment Choice in Singapore's National Defined Contribution Scheme' (2020) 17 *Journal of the Economics of Ageing* 1.
[77] Ignition House (n 73) 16.
[78] ibid 40.
[79] Law Commission, *Pension Funds and Social Investment* (Law Com No 374, 2017) paras 1.41 and 9.7.
[80] Madeleine Davies, 'Savers Blind to How Pensions Are Invested' *Church Times* (28 September 2018) <www.churchtimes.co.uk/articles/2018/28-september/news/uk/savers-blind-to-how-pensions-invested> accessed 3 December 2020.
[81] Movement Research, 'Identifying New Ways to Engage with Savers in Defined Contribution Pensions' (Defined Contribution Investment Forum, 2013) <www.dcif.co.uk/wp-content/uploads/2017/06/identifying-new-ways-to-engage-with-savers-in-defined-contribution-pensions-.pdf> accessed 3 December 2020.
[82] 'New Good Money Week/YouGov Poll Results Announced' (*Good Money Week*, 2016) <www.goodmoneyweek.com/media/press-releases/new-good-money-weekyougov-poll-results-announced> accessed 3 December 2020; Davies (n 80); Franklin Templeton and Adoreboard, 'The Power of Emotions: Responsible Investment as a Motivator for Generation DC' (2019) <www.franklintempleton.co.uk/download/en-gb/common/ko3xuf49> accessed 3 December 2020; there also exists experimental evidence that investors value sustainability: Hartzmark and Sussman (n 58).

because they are the major source for the assets invested through investment consultants and fiduciary managers.

It is worth noting, however, that, for this group, tax is a critical factor. We argue in Section 3.5 that, through tax credit, the government is an investor in its own right. At present the government makes pension credit available irrespective of how the money is invested. We take the view that a good way of achieving better stewardship is to design pension credit in a way that favours stewardship-active investment.

3.4.2 Small Portfolio End-Investors

Small portfolio end-investors are individuals who hold financial investments. In 2016, the BIS conducted a study on the intermediated shareholding model.[83] It found that 76 per cent of individual investors had a low interest in voting or attending AGMs, although there were equity investors who valued their shareholder rights.[84] There exists, however, a group of investors who belong to shareholder representative organizations such as the Shareholders Society (ShareSoc) and the UK Shareholders Association (UKSA). For this group, shareholder rights are important. They frequently describe their investment as a 'hobby' suggesting that they do not expect the time spent in researching companies and engaging with them to be compensated by returns.[85] Such investors articulate demand for stewardship.[86] The study commissioned by the BIS focused on engagement for governance purposes. It did not ask questions about ecological and social motives for engagement.

The market for stewardship-active retail investment appears to be currently relatively small. There exists research examining the attitude of retail investors towards altruistic investment strategies. A study making recommendations on how to encourage social impact investing, for example, found that only 13 per cent of respondents have previously invested in impact investments and that only 18 per cent of respondents were more than moderately interested in such investments.[87] A number of suppliers of what can loosely be termed 'responsible investment products' have conducted empirical research predicting substantial future growth in the market for responsible investing. Younger respondents appear to be more willing than older individuals to forgo financial return in favour of positive social or environmental outcomes.[88] It is

---

[83] Department for Business, Innovation & Skills, 'Exploring the Intermediated Shareholding Model' (January 2016) BIS Research Paper Number 261 <www.uksa.org.uk/sites/default/files/BIS_RP261.pdf> accessed 3 December 2020.
[84] ibid 16.
[85] ibid.
[86] For an analysis of the impact of shareholder sponsored proposals, see Nickolay Gantchev and Mariassunta Giannetti, 'The Costs and Benefits of Shareholder Democracy' (August 2020) ECGI Finance Working Paper Series 586/2018 <https://ecgi.global/sites/default/files/working_papers/documents/gantchevgiannettifinal_0.pdf> accessed 3 December 2020.
[87] Greg B Davies and Centapse, 'SII Attitudinal and Behavioural Research' (2017) 6 <https://assets.publishing.service.gov.uk/government/uploads/system/uploads/attachment_data/file/659060/Social_Impact_Investment_Attitudinal_and_Behavioural_Research__Centapse.pdf> accessed 3 December 2020.
[88] IFF Research (Ethex), 'Understanding the Positive Investor 2017' (2017) <www.ethex.org.uk/understanding-the-positive-investor-2017_1923.html> accessed 3 December 2020; Triodos Bank, 'Socially Responsible Investing Market on the Cusp of Momentous Growth (173%)' (5 September 2018) <www.triodos.co.uk/press-releases/2018/socially-responsible-investing-market-on-cusp-of-momentus-growth> accessed 3 December 2020; Barclays, 'Investor Motivations for Impact: A Behavioural Examination' (July 2018) <www.barclays.co.uk/content/dam/documents/wealth-management/investments/impact-investing-product/investor-motivations-for-impact.pdf> accessed 3 December 2020; AXA Investment Managers UK, 'Voices: Listening to the Savers and Investors of Today and Tomorrow' (2018) <https://adviser.axa-im.co.uk/documents/26049/7590708/Brochure+Retail+Survey_EN-low.pdf/dd1c0c17-22f7-d6d0-b2ad-c2cd307f84c3> accessed 3 December 2020; Newton Investment Management, 'Social Investment: Matching Strategies to Investors' Goals' (16 April 2019) <www.newtonim.com/uk-lgps/insights/articles/social-investment-matching-strategies-to-investors-goals-uk/> accessed 3 December 2020.

encouraging that there exists a group of suppliers of stewardship-active investment products who envisage a robust future for their market. If this demand materializes, the UK Code 2020 will have a role to play in supporting the provision of disclosure.

3.4.3 Large Portfolio End-Investors

There exists a group of end-investors who have portfolios that are sufficiently large for them to be able to stimulate demand for stewardship. Examples are endowment funds and sovereign wealth funds (SWFs). These are potential candidates from which demand for stewardship can emerge.

Empirical evidence systematically surveying the attitudes of these investors in relation to stewardship is, however, scarce.[89] The Schroder 2019 survey among institutional investors (pension funds, insurance companies, foundations, endowments and SWFs) confirms that sustainable investing gains traction globally. Of the respondents, 50% state that they have increased their sustainable investments over the last five years, while 75% believe that 'sustainability will play a more important role in the next five years'. But performance concerns and a lack of transparency are reported as institutional investors' biggest sustainability challenges. In fact, 49% of the respondents (up from 34% in 2018) consider performance to be the most important driver for future adoption of sustainable investing.[90] While this survey is not limited to endowment funds and SWFs, it suggests that the extent to which large portfolio end-investors engage in stewardship depends on their respective investment strategy. If their focus is on generating a financial return, they will take a view on how this is best achieved. This may lead to engagement in stewardship.[91] It may, however, also lead to the conclusion that their financial goals are best served by adopting an agile short-term strategy. Either way, the fact that there is no clear evidence that ESG and sustainable investing leads to better financial results means that financial return is hardly going to be a motivator encouraging this group to embark on stewardship activities.

There are, of course, some large portfolio beneficiaries who pursue investment strategies that, in addition to financial return, are also influenced by wider aims. The Norwegian Government Pension Fund Global, the world's largest sovereign wealth fund, is a key example of an early adopter of sustainable investing practices.[92] But while there is some evidence that the Norwegian SWF can effect changes in the corporate governance policies of its portfolio firms,[93] there are academic voices that warn that sustainability and stewardship are not given any priority at the expense of financial returns.[94]

---

[89] There is, of course, a body of literature analyzing family-controlled businesses, but these are not the focus of this chapter.

[90] Schroders, 'Institutional Investor Study: Sustainability 2019' (2019) <www.schroders.com/en/sysglobalassets/digital/institutional-investor-study/sustainability/pdf/Schroder2019_SIIS_Sustainabilityv2.pdf> accessed 3 December 2020.

[91] There is evidence that SWFs do take climate change and sustainability seriously. See, for instance, the One Planet Sovereign Wealth Funds, <https://oneplanetswfs.org/> accessed 3 December 2020.

[92] For the investment approach adopted by the Norwegian government, see Norges Bank Investment Management, 'About the Fund' <www.nbim.no/en/the-fund/about-the-fund/> accessed 3 December 2020. For how stewardship is exercised in Norway, see generally Mähönen, Sjåfjell and Mee, Stewardship Norwegian-Style, Chapter 8.

[93] Ruth V Aguilera, Vicente J Bermejo, Javier Capapé and Vicente Cuñat, 'The Systemic Governance Influence of Universal Owners' (2020) European Corporate Governance Institute – Finance Working Paper No 625/2019 <https://ssrn.com/abstract=3411566> accessed 3 December 2020.

[94] For a critical view, see Beate Sjåfjell, Heidi R Nilsen and Benjamin J Richardson, 'Investing in Sustainability or Feeding on Stranded Assets? The Norwegian Government Pension Fund Global' (2017) 52 *Wake Forest Law Review* 949.

Charitable organizations with a large investment portfolio also fall in this category.[95] A survey including seventy-five non-profits in the US finds that, while sustainable investing strategies are gaining traction (38% invest in sustainability and a further 12% plan to do so in 2019), 60% of the respondents cite 'concerns about performance' as the key factor preventing them from investing in sustainable investments.[96] Some of them receive scrutiny from the public. In the UK the Church of England falls in this category.[97] Another UK example is the Duchy of Cornwall, which funds the public, charitable and private activities of the Prince of Wales and his family. Investments held by the Duchy of Cornwall have been publicly scrutinized against the values promoted by the current holder of the title.[98]

Some large portfolio end-investors are therefore motivated to generate demand for stewardship. It is worth noting, however, that the focus of the public interest in this context is on environmental and social factors. There is less public scrutiny in relation to the level of engagement in the area of governance. The public interest in governance tends to scrutinize issuers rather than investors.

For end-investors with large portfolios, we can assume that, given the empirical evidence, financial return is likely to be a weak factor motivating demand for stewardship. Some in this group are nevertheless motivated to exercise and deliver demand for stewardship for altruistic reasons. They will benefit from better disclosure of stewardship activity. They also have the bargaining power to carry out negotiations with their respective service providers. It is doubtful, however, how far their efforts on their own can go to generate the desired demand for stewardship.

3.4.4 *The Role of Pension Trustees and Members of Independent Governance Committees*

Most workplace pension schemes are overseen by trustees.[99] There are also pension schemes which operate on the basis of a contract rather than a trust. The providers of personal pensions are overseen by the FCA, which has imposed a requirement for an independent governance committee. The committee has the duty to scrutinize the value for money of the provider's pension schemes taking into account transaction costs. They must act solely in the interests of the relevant scheme members and independently of the provider.[100]

Both pension trustees and members of governance committees are appointed to ensure that pensions are adequately managed. They have the mandate to protect the interests of beneficiaries. Pension trustees identify the service providers who manage pension assets. They rely on advice

---

[95] Based on recommendations by the Law Commission, the duties of charitable trustees in relation to social investment have recently been clarified (Law Commission, 'Social Investment by Charities, The Law Commission's Recommendations' (September 2014) <www.lawcom.gov.uk/document/social-investment-by-charities-report/> accessed 3 December 2020; The Charities (Protection and Social Investment) Act 2016, 2016 c 4).
[96] SEI, 'Institutional Investors Sustainable Investment Survey 2018' (2018) <https://seic.com/sites/default/files/inline-files/SEI%20Sustainable%20Investing%20Survey%202018.pdf> accessed 3 December 2020.
[97] For the approach adopted by the Church of England, see the Church of England, 'Church Commissioners for England Achieve a Positive Return of 1.8% for 2018 and Forecast Further Volatility' (2019) <www.churchofengland.org/more/media-centre/news/finance-news/church-commissioners-england-achieve-positive-return-18-2018> accessed 3 December 2020. On social shareholder engagement by religious organizations in general, see Jennifer Goodman 'Religious Organizations as Shareholders: Salience and Empowerment' in Maria Goranova and Lori V Ryan (eds), *Shareholder Empowerment: A New Era in Corporate Governance* (Palgrave 2015) 201.
[98] Hilary Osborne, 'Prince Charles's Estate Made Big Profit on Stake in Friend's Offshore Firm' *The Guardian* (7 November 2017) <www.theguardian.com/news/2017/nov/07/prince-charles-profit-best-friend-hugh-van-cutsem-offshore-firm-paradise-papers> accessed 3 December 2020.
[99] Pensions Act 1985, ss 16–21; Pensions Act 2004, ss 241–243.
[100] FCA, COBS 19.5.

from investment consultants in taking these decisions. They also appoint and oversee fiduciary management services.

Pension trustees and committee members are bound by the terms on which they have been appointed. Invariably, the core focus of their mandate is the generation of financial return. They have to consider ESG factors when these are financially material.[101] The law is sufficiently flexible to permit pension trustees to make investment decisions that are based on non-financial factors (such as environmental and social concerns) provided that they have a good reason to think that the scheme members share the concern, and that there is no risk of significant financial detriment to the fund.[102] Investment by a default fund therefore should not provide a significantly lower return than one available elsewhere.[103]

From the perspective of generating demand for stewardship, trustees and committee members are likely to tread carefully.[104] Financial materiality is an overriding factor and there is no evidence that ESG activity leads to generally better financial returns. Even if pension trustees have good reasons to think that beneficiaries hold values that favour investments with a certain impact, they cannot risk significant financial detriment. Trustees are therefore able to integrate ESG only in their assessment of financial risk. They are likely to be more acutely aware of short-term risk factors. These are easier to identify and require a timely response. Medium- or long-term risk factors are more difficult to integrate into decision-making. They are harder to predict. Moreover, it is for the trustees' discretion to evaluate which risks are material and how to take them into account.[105] From the perspective of financial return, engaging with issuers may not be the best strategy to address medium- to long-term risk. The better strategy may be to avoid exposure to issuers associated with these risks. The Church of England has, for example, recently announced that it will withdraw from investing in carbon intensive industries.[106]

From 1 October 2019, trust-based defined contribution (DC) pension schemes are required to set out in their Statement of Investment Principles (SIP) how they take into account financial material considerations, including those arising from ESG, and their policies in relation to stewardship, including the exercise of voting rights and other engagement and monitoring activities.[107] A survey by the UK Sustainable Investment and Finance Association (UKSIF) finds that two-thirds of trustees have not complied with the new requirement to publish their policies by mid-November 2019. Among those who have published their SIPs, policies are mostly vague and they have all given their investment manager full discretion for managing financially

---

[101] *Penson Funds and Social Investment* (n 79) 2, 5 (para 1.25) and 130 (para 1.20); Law Commission, *Fiduciary Duties of Investment Intermediaries* (Law Com No 350, 2014) paras 6.99–6.102; there exists, for example, empirical evidence that climate risk is a factor that institutional investors, including pensions funds, incorporate into their decision-making (Philip Krueger, Zacharias Sautner and Laura T Starks, 'The Importance of Climate Risks for Institutional Investors' (2019) European Corporate Governance Institute – Finance Working Paper No 610/2019 <https://ssrn.com/abstract=3235190> accessed 3 December 2020).

[102] *Penson Funds and Social Investment* (n 79) 2, 5 (para 1.26).

[103] ibid 5, para 1.26.

[104] Barriers, for instance, are posed by the 'interpretative pluralism' of the concept of fiduciary duties. See Anna Tilba and Arad Reisberg 'Fiduciary Duty under the Microscope: Stewardship and the Spectrum of Pension Fund Engagement' (2019) 82 *Modern Law Review* 456.

[105] *Penson Funds and Social Investment* (n 79) 130, para 1.20.

[106] Josh Gabbatiss, 'Church of England Votes to Withdraw Funds from Companies That Contribute to Climate Change' *The Independent* (9 July 2018) <www.independent.co.uk/news/uk/home-news/church-of-england-climate-change-investment-withdraw-paris-agreement-fossil-fuels-a8437781.html> accessed 3 December 2020.

[107] See the Occupational Pension Schemes (Investment) Regulations 2005, 2(3)(b)(vi) and 2(3)(c) for financially material ESG considerations and stewardship, respectively. On the relationship between these new rules and the UK Code 2020, see Katelouzou (n 1).

material ESG risks and stewardship. The survey concludes that 'building a market in stewardship will require a step change in trustees' approaches'.[108]

The UK Code 2020 does not substantially change the approaches adopted by trustees. As we have seen, stewardship is defined as the responsible allocation, management and oversight of capital to create 'long-term value' for clients and beneficiaries 'leading to sustainable benefits for the economy, the environment and society'.[109] Along similar lines, Principle 1 states that signatories' purpose, investment beliefs, strategy and culture enable stewardship that creates long-term value for clients and beneficiaries 'leading to sustainable benefits for the economy, the environment and society'. Neither the phrase 'leading to sustainable benefits for the economy, the environment and society' nor the phrase 'long-term value' is intended to modify the mandates governing the decision-making of trustees. Trustees would not be able to bind themselves to the Code if it required them to act in breach of duty. The UK Code 2020 itself acknowledges that trustees need to act in the best interests of clients and beneficiaries. Principe 6 states that signatories take account of client and beneficiary needs and communicate the activities and outcomes of their stewardship and investment to them.[110] They are encouraged to disclose the length of the investment time horizon they have considered appropriate to deliver to the needs of clients and beneficiaries.[111]

Moreover, the government has expressly stated that it does not intend to direct the investment decisions or strategies of trustees of pension schemes. They 'will never exhort or direct private sector schemes to invest in a particular way. Trustees have absolute primacy in this area.'[112] Notwithstanding the work that went into the clarification of the duties of trustees and the updating of the UK Code, financial materiality continues to be the overriding factor. In addition, there exists a structural problem. The CMA finds that trustees of small schemes and trustees of defined contribution schemes are less engaged.[113] Less engaged trustees, for example, do not set objectives against which the quality of their investment consultants can be judged.[114] This observation that engagement and stewardship are difficult for small scheme trustees and trustees for DC schemes seems to still exist notwithstanding the 2019 regulatory changes.[115]

Small schemes are likely to suffer from the fact that they do not have sufficient resources. DC schemes suffer from the limited oversight by their beneficiaries. In DC schemes, the beneficiaries are the individual members and we have already seen that they do not take great interest in their pensions. In defined benefit (DB) schemes, members receive retirement income depending on the years worked and depending on their final salary. The employer thus bears the risk of poor investment outcomes.[116] It is possible that trustees of such schemes benefit from greater

---

[108] UK Sustainable Investment and Finance Association (UKSIF), 'Changing Course? How Pensions Are Approaching Climate Change and ESG Issues Following Recent UK Reforms' (February 2020) <www.responsible-investor.com/reports/uksif-or-changing-course-how-pensions-are-approaching-climate-change-and-esg-issues-following-recent-uk-reforms> accessed 3 December 2020.

[109] UK Code 2020 (n 27) 4.

[110] See also UK Code 2020 (n 27) 8, second bullet point under the heading 'Outcome'.

[111] UK Code 2020 (n 27) 13, second bullet point under the heading 'Context'.

[112] Department for Work & Pensions, 'Clarifying and Strengthening Trustees' Investment Duties: Government Response' (September 2018) 3 <https://assets.publishing.service.gov.uk/government/uploads/system/uploads/attachment_data/file/739331/response-clarifying-and-strengthening-trustees-investment-duties.pdf> accessed 3 December 2020.

[113] Competition and Markets Authority (n 3) 13, para 32.

[114] ibid 11 (para 24) and 15 (para 48).

[115] *Penson Funds and Social Investment* (n 79).

[116] Competition and Markets Authority (n 3) 17, paras 58–59; for an analysis of decisions taken by pension trustees acting for defined benefit schemes, see João F Cocco and Paolo Volpin, 'The Corporate Governance of Defined Benefit Pension Plans: Evidence from the United Kingdom' (2005) ECGI – Finance Working Paper No 76/2005 <https://ssrn.com/abstract=670685> accessed 3 December 2020.

engagement by employers. The CMA has made recommendations addressing the lack of engagement by trustees.[117] These, however, do not modify the mandate of trustees to prioritize in the financial interest of their beneficiaries.

From the perspective of this chapter, we therefore need to conclude that the financial materiality requirement presents a barrier to the ability of trustees to make a stewardship contribution for the benefit of the public good and to prioritize altruism over financial return.

3.4.5 Investment Consultants and Fiduciary Managers

Investment consultants provide advice in relation to strategic asset allocation, manager selection and fiduciary management. Fiduciary managers (using the CMA terminology) make and implement investment decisions including but not limited to the responsibility for asset allocation and fund/manager selection.[118] These service providers are able to supply stewardship. Service providers who operate as consultants can incorporate stewardship into their advice. Service providers who are in a position to exercise shareholder rights can integrate stewardship ensuring that they make appropriate use of the rights with which they have been entrusted.

The conclusion of the previous sections has been that these providers are receiving limited demand for stewardship.[119] Beneficiaries of workplace and personal pensions contribute 90 per cent to the revenue of these providers.[120] But their focus is on financial return and there is no equivocal evidence that responsible investment increases the return of investors. Small portfolio end-investors who care about stewardship are unlikely to use the services of investment consultants or fiduciary managers. They are more likely to put together their own portfolios and hold securities directly as well as holding savings accounts and/or ISAs.[121] There is a hope that the market for stewardship will grow in the future when younger individuals who have expressed an interest in stewardship-active investment products come into money. Some large portfolio end-investors care about stewardship and exercise demand, but while their efforts can serve as role-models, their market share is too small to bring about a market for stewardship. On the whole, therefore, the terms on which investment consultants and fiduciary managers are appointed are very likely to focus on the generation of financial return without substantially integrating stewardship factors.

In addition, the CMA has identified problems with competition. The CMA observes that customers do not have sufficient information to judge the quality of their provider. There is also limited information for prospective customers to compare investment consultants' fees and quality of service. It is very difficult for prospective customers to assess the quality of different providers. For example, the different ways used by investment consultants and fiduciary management providers to show the performance of their recommended asset management products

---

[117] Competition and Markets Authority (n 3) 7.
[118] Competition and Markets Authority (n 3) 8, para 3.
[119] For previous literature highlighting the lack of incentives to engage in stewardship arising from the perspective of the internal governance and business structures of funds, see Roger M Barker and Iris H-Y Chiu, *Corporate Governance and Investment Management: The Promises and Limitations of the New Financial Economy* (Edward Elgar 2017). Davies, The UK Stewardship Code 2010–2020, Chapter 2 and Fisch, The Uncertain Stewardship Potential of Index Funds, Chapter 21 also highlight the limited ability of institutional investors and index funds (respectively) to deliver stewardship activity.
[120] Competition and Markets Authority (n 3) 29, para 1.14.
[121] See e.g. Ethex (n 88) (finding that most of the UK population are most interested in less sophisticated savings and investment products (44% interested in savings accounts, 43% in current accounts and 40% in a positive ISA) as the method of making a positive investment).

make this information difficult to compare.[122] Investment performance is often reported on a gross of fee basis which does not reflect the real outcome for the pension scheme.[123] Moreover, there are concerns about investment consultants using their position to steer clients into their own fiduciary management services.[124]

There is also a concentration occurring in the market for fiduciary management services.[125] In the US, funds managed by BlackRock, Vanguard and State Street have become the largest investors in capital markets. They now have significant influence over issuers.[126] While this means that they have the bargaining power to be actively engaged with issuers, it unfortunately also means that they are becoming increasingly immune to pressures from their clients.

There is also evidence that asset managers in particular are reluctant to respond to demand from trustees in relation to stewardship. The Association of Member Nominated Trustees (AMNT) has been active in engaging with asset managers in relation to stewardship and voting. They have developed a model policy for shareholder engagement.[127] The AMNT has published a report reviewing the voting policies and practices of fund managers in 22 May 2019.[128] They found that the efforts of their members to engage with service providers on stewardship had not been welcomed by them. Trustees were told that they should leave stewardship to fund managers as they have the resources and expertise to develop voting policies. They were also told that if clients do not like their fund manager's approach to stewardship, they should take their business elsewhere.[129]

The AMNT expressed the view that the use of ambiguous and seemingly boilerplate language, coupled with the small number of fund managers disclosing a voting guideline on this, leaves trustees with little information with which to ascertain the degree of seriousness the fund managers apply to the issue.[130] This fits with views expressed by pension beneficiaries in the survey conducted for the FCA. They mentioned that they received too much narrative information that was difficult to navigate and full of jargon.[131]

Another example pointing towards low levels of motivation for stewardship engagement on the part of asset managers is the Investor Form. It was set up following a recommendation by the Kay Review to facilitate co-operation across the industry, but has generated a small amount of collective activity. Its website reports that in four (!) years it conducted twenty-three engagements at board level with individual issuers, conducted eight major stewardship projects and twelve full stewardship and strategy fora.[132]

We have already seen that the UK Code 2020 is trying to address the problem of boilerplate reporting by requiring reports to set out activities and analyze outcomes. This should inspire

---

[122] Competition and Markets Authority (n 3) 10–11, paras 24–29.
[123] ibid 12, para 27.
[124] ibid 13, paras 36 and 39.
[125] ibid 17, para 56.
[126] Marcel Kahan and Edward Rock, 'Index Funds and Corporate Governance: Let Shareholders Be Shareholders' (October 2019) NYU Law and Economics Research Paper No 18–39 <https://ssrn.com/abstract=3295098> accessed 3 December 2020.
[127] Red Line Voting <http://redlinevoting.org> accessed 3 December 2020.
[128] Association of Member Nominated Trustees, 'AMNT Review into Fund Managers' Voting Policies and Practices' (May 2019) <https://amnt.org/wp-content/uploads/2019/05/AMNT-final-review-for-FCA-22-May-2019.pdf> accessed 3 December 2020.
[129] ibid 5.
[130] ibid 8.
[131] Ignition House (n 73) 40.
[132] The Investor Forum, 'Review 2018' (January 2019) 3 <www.investorforum.org.uk/wp-content/uploads/2019/01/Annual_Review_2018.pdf> accessed 3 December 2020.

signatories to improve the quality of their reporting. On its own, however, this is not sufficient to bring about a market for stewardship.

3.5 THE ROLE OF THE GOVERNMENT

We argue in this section that the UK government falls short of fully appreciating its role in relation to stewardship. It commits substantial resources to overseeing the market, but does not give sufficient weight to the fact that it makes a significant financial contribution by subsidizing the provision of pensions through the tax system. We will first show how the government currently oversees the market and then suggest that the government is an investor in its own right. It should do what it expects of other market participants and insist on stewardship active investment.

3.5.1 *The Government as a Facilitator and Supervisor of the Market*

The UK government defines its role as facilitating a market for stewardship and also as overseeing financial services providers, ensuring that they live up to the commitments they have made to their clients. This puts beneficiaries and end-investors at the centre stage of the market for stewardship.

The immediate responsibility for the Stewardship Code lies with the FRC/ARGA.[133] But this is only the tip of the iceberg. Several departments and government bodies have active workstreams in the area, addressing the topic from their respective responsibilities. The entities that are involved in addition to the FRC are the FCA, the Treasury, the Department for Business, Energy and Industrial Strategy (BEIS), the Department for Work and Pensions (DWP) and the Pensions Regulator (tPR).

The FCA oversees financial services providers. It has expressed a strong interest in effective stewardship. It takes the position that high stewardship standards will contribute to the FCA's strategic objective to ensure that markets function well, including its three operational objectives: market integrity, consumer protection and effective competition.[134] The FCA believes that stewardship enhances the quality of markets and the effectiveness of capital allocation.[135] It aims to ensure that regulated financial services firms such as asset managers and life insurers deliver good outcomes for their customers.[136] It also believes that it has a role in setting standards for the interaction between issuer companies and their investors.[137] The FCA will consider the extent to which a firm that claims to engage in stewardship is doing it appropriately, and will also review how stewardship contributes to the fulfilment of a firm's stated purpose.[138]

Neither the FRC nor the FCA, however, can and should modify the contractual terms that operate between clients and their service providers. The FCA does take the view that '[f]or many firms, the exercise of stewardship will be integral to the effective delivery of their services to clients and beneficiaries, for example, when an asset manager invests on behalf of asset owners

---

[133] On the transition of the FRC to the new Audit, Reporting and Governance Authority (ARGA), see Financial Reporting Council, 'The FRC Sets Out Its Transition Pathway' (23 May 2019) <www.frc.org.uk/news/may-2019/the-frc-sets-out-its-transition-pathway> accessed 3 December 2020.
[134] FCA/FRC (n 28) 4, paras 1.13–1.14
[135] ibid 4–5 (para 1.15) and 8 (para 2.9).
[136] ibid 4, para 1.14.
[137] ibid 4–5 (para 1.15) and 8.
[138] ibid 5, para 1.16.

over the long term'.[139] But the FRC and the FCA also concede that, '[i]n other cases, stewardship may not be integral to a firm's acting effectively as the agent for its clients'.[140]

The Treasury has conducted work with a view to ensuring that UK-based firms have access to long-term (patient) finance allowing them to scale up.[141] One of the aims is to encourage the pension industry and in particular those responsible for the growing pot of money held in DC schemes to invest in innovative high-growth firms.[142] The Treasury was also responsible for adopting the Proxy Advisors (Shareholders' Rights) Regulation 2019.[143] None of these efforts, however, override what is agreed contractually between market participants.

The BEIS is responsible for company law. It has also published research on the Intermediated Shareholder Model. The aim of the paper was to identify operational barriers to the exercise of voting rights by shareholders.[144] The BEIS was also responsible for the implementation into UK law of the sections relating to the remuneration of Shareholder Rights Directive 2017.[145] It has no powers to cause end-investors and beneficiaries to adopt a particular approach towards investment.

The Department for Work and Pensions is responsible for legislation for private occupational pensions.[146] The Pension Regulator oversees pension trustees and employers. We have seen already that the Pension Regulator's work operates within the framework of financial materiality.

It would be possible to impose a regulatory duty on service providers to exercise stewardship.[147] That would solve the problem that they are currently not receiving sufficient demand from end-investors and beneficiaries to be ESG active. Such a regulatory strategy would, however, be a significant intervention imposing an investment strategy across the market.

The UK government is fully committed to bringing about stewardship. It has invested a significant amount of effort into reviewing the duties of trustees and developing a stewardship code. These efforts have, however, fallen short of appreciating the full range of factors influencing demand for stewardship. While it is right to integrate the interests of end-investors and beneficiaries into the analysis, it is wrong to stop there. It is important that the government should take into account that it is a financial contributor to the market for stewardship in its own right.

---

[139] ibid 4, para 1.14.
[140] ibid 4, para 1.14.
[141] HM Treasury, *Financing Growth in Innovative Firms: One Year On* (October 2018) 2 <https://assets.publishing.service.gov.uk/government/uploads/system/uploads/attachment_data/file/769428/Financing_growth_in_innovative_firms_one-year_on.pdf> accessed 3 December 2020.
[142] ibid 2.
[143] The Proxy Advisors (Shareholders' Rights) Regulations 2019, SI 2019/926; the FCA is currently in the process of bringing its rulebook in line with the 2019 Regulation: Financial Conduct Authority, 'PS19/28: Proxy Advisors (Shareholders' Rights) Regulations Implementation (DEPP and EG)' (2019) <www.fca.org.uk/publications/consultation-papers/cp19-21-proxy-advisors-shareholders-rights-regulation-depp-and-eg> accessed 3 December 2020.
[144] Department for Business, Innovation & Skills (n 83) 14.
[145] Directive (EU) 2017/828 of the European Parliament and of the Council of 17 May 2017 amending Directive 2007/36/EC as regards the encouragement of long-term shareholder engagement [2017] OJ L132/1 (SRD II) and Commission Implementing Regulation (EU) 2018/1212 of 3 September 2018 laying down minimum requirements implementing the provisions of Directive 2007/36/EC of the European Parliament and of the Council as regards shareholder identification, the transmission of information and the facilitation of the exercise of shareholders rights [2018] OJ L223/1; the sections relating to proxy advisers were implemented by the Treasury.
[146] Department for Work and Pensions (n 112).
[147] See, further, Iris H–Y Chiu and Dionysia Katelouzou, 'Making a Case for Regulating Institutional Shareholders' Corporate Governance Roles' [2018] *Journal of Business Law* 67; Iris H–Y Chiu, 'Is the Time Ripe to Subject Asset Management to More Regulatory Governance?' (2019) 40 *Company Lawyer* 205–7.

3.5.2 As a Financial Advisor

The government is a significant financial contributor to the financial services industry and thus a financial stakeholder in the market for stewardship. It has already been mentioned that the CMA concluded that pension schemes represent 90 per cent of the revenues of investment consultants and fiduciary managers.[148]

The current prominence of pension schemes is not a spontaneous market-driven phenomenon. The government makes a significant contribution to the monies invested through pensions. It contributes through tax relief. Pension tax relief is available only for financial assets. Non-financial assets such as residential property do not qualify for pension tax relief.[149] This has channelled money into financial investments and generated demand for the provision of investment consultancy and fiduciary management services.

By giving tax-favourable treatment to certain types of investment, the government has helped to create a market that has not previously existed. Fifty years ago, most shares in UK companies were owned by individuals. They dealt through brokers.[150] From the 1960s the coverage of occupational pension schemes among UK employees was greatly extended.[151] Auto-enrolment has recently further widened the scope of occupational pensions.

In so far as the government makes a financial contribution to investments, it is entitled to involve itself in how investment decisions for pensions are taken. It also has a responsibility to engage. Like all other beneficiaries of and contributors to the market, the government should act as a steward in relation to its own investment.

Moreover, through its tax contribution, the government skews the market. Beneficiaries of pensions make their return through tax savings. This discourages them from paying close attention to the returns generated by their investment portfolios. This in turn deprives the investment consultancy and fiduciary management industry of oversight and thus creates a problem in its own right.

While there is no direct evidence on how tax relief affects the demand of stewardship, when it comes to sustainability investing, it seems that tax relief on the investment is not considered to be a key factor when selecting an investment that supports a social or environmental cause. Transparency on where the funds are going, the expected financial risks and the likely returns on the investment are considered more important. But the same survey reports that for younger, higher-income, investment-savvy and educated city-dwellers (impact-maximizers), tax relief is an important aspect in trading off financial for social outcomes.[152]

The government is also a financial stakeholder as a residual loss bearer. When the financial system collapsed in 2008, the government bore the financial burden of the rescue. The government is likely to feel obliged to intervene if the pension system experiences a shock.

The problem that there is not sufficient demand for stewardship could be solved through a regulatory duty imposed on service providers to be stewardship active.[153] Such a duty would, however, cover all investments, in particular those to which the government has not made a financial contribution. For these, the government has no right to insist om any particular investment strategy. An indiscriminate regulatory duty also does not resolve the problem that the government is currently distorting the market.

---

[148] Competition and Markets Authority (n 3) 29, para 1.14.
[149] Only commercial real estate does.
[150] Kay Review (n 21) para 3.1.
[151] ibid para 3.2.
[152] Davies and Centapse (n 87).
[153] See Chiu and Katelouzou (n 147).

In our view, the government's decision to invest, by granting tax breaks, its own money into the pension sector without insisting on ESG engagement is a significant contributor to the problems that the UK Stewardship Code is trying to solve. In addition to providing sets of principles that asset owners and asset managers as well as service providers are encouraged to adopt and that end-investors and beneficiaries are encouraged to demand, the government should acknowledge that it is an investor in the industry. In that capacity, the government has its own stewardship responsibilities. It should take these seriously and ensure that its own money is responsibly invested and in line with the stewardship principles it has set for all other market participants. We propose that pension reliefs are attached to conditions that funds invested through these schemes be invested responsibly in a way that promotes stewardship. Reforming pension tax reliefs is already the subject of intense debate in the UK.[154] But no attention has been given so far to the potential social value of tax reliefs.[155] Utilizing tax reliefs to increase the flow of stewardship-active capital can place the tax system at the wider service of promoting the sustainability of the financial system and stimulating the demand side of the stewardship market.[156] Such tax reliefs will not only have a direct impact on the investment strategies of pension schemes but also meet the increasing demand – especially for millennials – for social investments.

3.6 CONCLUSION

The UK government believes that stewardship has benefits for investors, issuers and the economy as a whole. The UK Code 2020 is built on this premise. Asset owners, asset managers and other service providers work for the benefit of those who contribute the funds that they invest. They do what they are told to do by their clients. The government is therefore right to conclude that stewardship can be brought about by encouraging those whose money is invested to demand stewardship activity from asset owners, asset managers and other service providers. The government is, however, wrong to limit its encouragement to end-investors and beneficiaries. While some demand for stewardship may grow in the future from younger individuals interested in stewardship-active investment or some large portfolio end-investors, their market share is too small on the whole to bring about a market for stewardship.

For a market for stewardship to materialize, the UK government should put its own money where its mouth is. The government contributes substantial funds to the market for financial investments. The government makes its contribution through the provision of tax credit. A whopping 90 per cent of the revenue of investment consultants and fiduciary managers derives from pensions. In 2017–18, tax credit for registered pension schemes cost £37.8 billion. This chapter critically argues that, as a sponsor of pensions and other forms of savings, the government has a significant financial stake in the vast majority of financial investments. It should therefore act in the same way it expects beneficiaries and end-investors to act, and demand stewardship. Tax credit relief should change and be available only for stewardship-active forms of financial investment.

---

[154] Djuna Thurley and Richard Cracknell, 'Reform of Pension Tax Relief' (Briefing Paper, House of Commons, 7 February 2020) <https://commonslibrary.parliament.uk/research-briefings/cbp-7505/> accessed 3 December 2020.

[155] Note that the social value of tax relief in the UK has been already utilized in relation to community investment and the aim to develop a 'social impact investment market'. See e.g. Jay Wiggan, 'Policy Boosting the Social Impact Investment Market in the UK' (2018) 47 Journal of Social Policy 721.

[156] For similar tax proposals in the UK and the US connecting tax reliefs to the mitigation of climate change, see Andrew Baker and Richard Murphy 'Modern Monetary Theory and the Changing Role of Tax in Society' (2020) 19 Social Policy & Society 454, 465.

PART II

Jurisdictions

4

Shareholder Stewardship in the Netherlands

The Role of Institutional Investors in a Stakeholder-Oriented Jurisdiction

Christoph Van der Elst and Anne Lafarre

4.1 INTRODUCTION

Following regulatory, market and societal demands, companies need to be aware of their impact beyond their relationships with contractual counterparties more than ever before. In recent years, corporate law has been used to address the internal governance of business corporations to tackle broader social and economic problems.[1] An example includes the European non-financial disclosure obligations related to 'environmental, social and employee matters, respect for human rights, anti-corruption and bribery matters'.[2] Academics have questioned the shareholder value model and the related corporate objective function that was largely influenced by Friedman's 1970 article for a long time.[3] For instance, Hart and Zingales argue that the corporate goal should be maximizing not market value but shareholder welfare, which can be different if shareholders also have ethical and social concerns.[4] Additionally, practice and academic research tell us that many shareholders indeed have concerns other than (short-term) market value. In particular, various investors use negative (positive) screening to exclude (include) companies with poor (good) sustainability performance, influencing sustainability performance with this behaviour.[5] Others use their control rights to actively engage with their investees on environmental, social and governance (ESG) matters.[6] Shareholder engagement takes a central role in corporate governance and is the focal point of many (soft) regulatory initiatives to stimulate long-term value creation, which is now the first principle of the Dutch Corporate Governance Code (DCGC).[7] Institutional investors are targeted particularly, as these investors can have a huge impact on market-wide corporate governance best practices with their large investment portfolios.[8]

---

[1] Reinier Kraakman and others (eds), *The Anatomy of Corporate Law: A Comparative and Functional Approach* (3rd edn, OUP 2017) 93.

[2] Directive 2014/95/EU of the European Parliament and of the Council of 22 October 2014 amending Directive 2013/34/EU as regards disclosure of non-financial and diversity information by certain large undertakings and groups [2014] OJ L330/1.

[3] See, for instance, Oliver Hart and Luigi Zingales, 'Companies Should Maximize Shareholder Welfare Not Market Value' (2017) 2 *Journal of Law, Finance and Accounting* 247.

[4] Hart and Zingales (n 3). See also Colin Mayer, *Prosperity: Better Business Makes the Greater Good* (OUP 2019).

[5] Alexander Dyck, Karl V Lins, Lukas Roth and Hannes F Wagner, 'Do Institutional Investors Drive Corporate Social Responsibility? International Evidence' (2019) 131 *Journal of Financial Economics* 693; Elroy Dimson, Oğuzhan Karakaş and Xi Li, 'Active Ownership' (2015) 28 *Review of Financial Studies* 3225. See also Patrick Bolton, Tao Li, Enrichetta Ravina and Howard Rosenthal, 'Investor Ideology' (2020) 137 *Journal of Financial Economics* 320.

[6] Dimson, Karakaş and Li (n 5); Bolton, Li, Ravina and Rosenthal (n 5).

[7] The English version of the current Dutch Corporate Governance Code can be found here: Corporate Governance Code Monitoring Committee, 'The Revised Dutch Corporate Governance Code 2016' (2016) <www.mccg.nl/?page=4738> accessed 6 July 2020 [hereinafter DCGC 2016].

[8] For instance, Marcel Kahan and Edward Rock, 'Index Funds and Corporate Governance: Let Shareholders Be Shareholders' (October 2019) NYU Law and Economics Research Paper No 18–39 <https://ssrn.com/abstract=3295098> accessed 6 July 2020.

In Europe, more than a decade ago, the first Shareholder Rights Directive (SRD I) already emphasized that 'effective shareholder control is a prerequisite to sound corporate governance and should, therefore, be facilitated and encouraged'.[9] The Revised Shareholder Rights Directive (SRD II) added to this kind of shareholder control, the role of institutional investors in fostering sustainable companies in particular, and, inter alia, requires them to disclose an engagement policy.[10] In the Netherlands, the implementation of the SRD II was approved in November 2019.[11] Also, the Dutch Stewardship Code,[12] developed by institutional investor platform Eumedion and several institutional investors, came into force in January 2019, emphasizing engagement and the responsibilities of institutional investors in Dutch listed companies. Exemplifying Eumedion's key role in Dutch corporate governance is its lobbying during the implementation of the SRD II under Dutch law. This led to the adoption of a qualified majority requirement of 75 per cent for remuneration policy resolutions in the new article 2:135a(2) Dutch Civil Code (DCC),[13] providing institutional investors with a stronger tool with which to address pay issues in Dutch listed companies.

However, whereas the role of institutional investors and their responsibilities are considered important now in corporate governance in the Netherlands, Dutch corporate law can be characterized by an *institutional approach* that puts the interests of the company and not the shareholders at the centre.[14] Particularly, Dutch landmark cases highlight that the interests of shareholders do not take priority over the interests of other stakeholders.[15] This institutional vision was also confirmed by the DCGC 2016, which takes a clear stakeholder approach.[16] The corporate board plays a central role in Dutch corporate law: under the supervision of the supervisory board (or non-executive directors, see Section 4.2), the management board independently determines the strategy and policies of the corporation.[17] This board autonomy (in Dutch: *'bestuursautonomie'*) is widely established in Dutch case law.[18]

---

[9] Directive 2007/36/EC of the European Parliament and of the Council of 11 July 2007 on the exercise of certain rights of shareholders in listed companies [2007] OJ L184/17 (SRD I) preamble (3).

[10] Directive (EU) 2017/828 of the European Parliament and of the Council of 17 May 2017 amending Directive 2007/36/EC as regards the encouragement of long-term shareholder engagement [2017] OJ L132/1 (SRD II).

[11] 'Wetsvoorstel implementatie EU richtlijn bevordering aandeelhoudersbetrokkenheid [Bill on the implementation of the EU directive on the promotion of shareholder involvement]' <https://wetgevingskalender.overheid.nl/Regeling/WGK008744> accessed 6 July 2020.

[12] The Dutch Stewardship Code can be found at Eumedion's website: Eumedion, 'Dutch Stewardship Code' (20 June 2018) <www.eumedion.nl/en/public/knowledgenetwork/best-practices/2018-07-dutch-stewardship-code-final-version.pdf> accessed 6 July 2020 [hereinafter Dutch Stewardship Code]. Eumedion is the Dutch Corporate Governance Forum that 'represents institutional investors' interests in the field of corporate governance and related sustainability performance' (Eumedion, 'Over Eumedion [About Eumedion]' <www.eumedion.nl/en/abouteumedion> accessed 6 July 2020).

[13] SRD II (n 10) preamble 55.

[14] See Section 4.2.1.

[15] Enterprise Chamber of the Amsterdam Court of Appeal 29 May 2017, JOR 2017, 261 (Akzo Nobel). See Section 4.2.2.

[16] For example, DCGC 2016 (n 7) 13, Principle 1.1 on long-term value creation states: 'The management board is responsible for the continuity of the company and its affiliated enterprise. The management board focuses on long-term value creation for the company and its affiliated enterprise, and takes into account the stakeholder interests that are relevant in this context. The supervisory board monitors the management board in this.'

[17] Dutch Civil Code, art 2:129: 'the Board of Directors is charged with the governance (management) of the Corporation'. As regards board duties, Dutch Civil Code, art 2:9, stipulates the duty of care which is directed towards the company. Art 2:129(5) includes the duty of loyalty. The famous Dutch Forumbank-case (1955) determined that the AGM cannot provide the board binding instructions with regard to the powers that the board has under the law and the articles of association. HR 21 January 1955, ECLI:NL:PHR:1955:AG2033, NJ 1959/43 m.nt. Hijmans van den Bergh (Forumbank).

[18] See also HR Forumbank, n 17.

This chapter sheds fresh light on the engagement and stewardship of institutional investors in the Netherlands and their position in Dutch corporate law. The commonly used definition of shareholder engagement – or, perhaps more aggressively, shareholder activism – describes the attempts to 'change the status quo through "voice", without a change in control of the firm'.[19] This chapter discusses the use of voice by institutional investors in the Netherlands in theory and practice, focusing on shareholder voting in particular. After a brief introduction to the Dutch corporate law framework in Section 4.2, we outline and discuss the shareholder stewardship (regulatory) initiatives. Next, in Section 4.3 we outline our empirical framework for the practical assessment of shareholder stewardship engagements in the Netherlands. Here, we investigate the use of voting rights by institutional investors in the shareholder meetings, for which Section 4.4 provides some statistical analyses. Section 4.5 provides concluding remarks.

4.2 THE DUTCH FRAMEWORK OF SHAREHOLDER STEWARDSHIP

4.2.1 Statutory Shareholder Rights and Duties

Although the annual general meeting (AGM) does not have the 'highest powers' in the Dutch corporate law framework, it traditionally has an important position as it receives the residual powers of control.[20] Besides the appointment and removal of board members, shareholders are granted several other statutory rights. The right to request information is incorporated in article 2:107(2) DCC. This provision states that the management board and the supervisory board must provide the AGM with all requested information, unless such information would run contrary to a substantial company interest. In contrast with article 9(1) SRD I that includes the European shareholder question right, article 2:107(2) DCC does not limit the scope of the questions to the items on the agenda of the AGM, and thus individual shareholders also have the right to request information about matters other than agenda items under Dutch law. In addition to the right to request information, all shareholders have the right to speak during shareholder meetings.[21] The AGM has a large number of formal decision-making rights, including, inter alia, the adoption of the annual accounts,[22] the appointment of board members[23] and the external auditor,[24] say-on-pay resolutions and the approval of mergers and takeovers.[25] Shareholders may add their proposals to the general meeting's agenda since 2004.[26] Thereto, a shareholder has to hold 3 per cent of the issued capital or the lower threshold as provided in the articles of association. In addition to adding shareholder proposals to the meeting's agenda,

---

[19] Stuart L Gillan and Laura T Starks 'A Survey of Shareholder Activism: Motivation and Empirical Evidence' (1998) 2 *Contemporary Finance Digest* 10.
[20] Dutch Civil Code, art 2:107(1) states that 'the general meeting, within the limits set by law and the articles of association, has all powers that are not assigned to the board or to others' (translation by the authors).
[21] Dutch Civil Code, art 2:117.
[22] Dutch Civil Code, art 2:101(3).
[23] Depending on the board structure, shareholders appoint the executive and non-executive directors, or the supervisory board members. Most Dutch listed companies voluntarily apply the *structuurregime* [structure regime] (Dutch Civil Code, arts 2:132, 2:142, 2:144 and 2:162).
[24] The AGM provides the external auditor with the instruction to control the annual account (Dutch Civil Code, art 2:393(2)).
[25] Many of these decision-making rules stem from the European regulatory framework (Dutch Civil Code, arts 2:135 and 145).
[26] Dutch Civil Code, art 2:114a.

shareholders are also able to request the convening of a shareholder meeting in court with a 10 per cent capital stake.[27] Lastly, shareholders are able to initiate private litigation.[28]

Next, it is well-established in Dutch case law and legal scholarship that shareholders may act in their own interest, but need to take into account the boundaries of article 2:8 DCC as regards reasonableness and fairness.[29] A recent Dutch phenomenon consists of the 'testing' of the division of powers between the corporate board and the shareholders, taking place in the courtroom, in which particularly Anglo-Saxon hedge funds are involved.[30] A recent landmark case involves Dutch listed company AkzoNobel and hedge fund Elliott Management Corp ('Elliott').[31] AkzoNobel received three unsolicited friendly offers from the American Fortune 500 company PPG Industries in 2017, which the AkzoNobel's board all rejected, inter alia, arguing that these bids do not reflect the value of the company and PPG does not make any serious commitments to AkzoNobel's stakeholders. However, after the rejection of the second bid, Elliott requested to call a general meeting to remove AkzoNobel's chairman. Although the 10 per cent threshold required under Dutch law was met, the request was rejected by AkzoNobel,[32] and after the rejection of the third bid, Elliott started a legal action using the Dutch inquiry procedure (in Dutch: '*enquêteprocedure*') before the Enterprise Chamber,[33] to investigate the decision-making concerning the rejection of PPG's offers, and filed for immediate measures (in Dutch: '*onmiddellijke voorzieningen*'), including calling for a general meeting to vote on the ousting of AkzoNobel's chairman. The Enterprise Chamber rejected the request for these immediate measures and held that there were no serious grounds on which to question the proper management of the company, confirming the earlier stakeholder model ruling in the ABN AMRO[34] case.

While the Dutch corporate governance landscape is characterized by certain landmark feuds between hedge funds and the corporate board in the past, nowadays we more commonly observe increased engagement by institutional investors. Institutional investors became the shareholder class with the largest holdings in a vast majority of Dutch companies. Recent research found that around 87 per cent of the shares of Dutch large cap companies were owned by (mostly) foreign institutional investors in 2014.[35] While these investors usually engage behind the scenes, some regulatory initiatives make their role in corporate governance more visible, in particular through disclosure requirements. Article 5:86 of the Dutch Financial Supervision Act (Wft) requires institutional investors to publicly disclose how they are accountable for those DCGC provisions applicable to them.[36] The Dutch Financial Supervisory Authority (AFM) can fine any violation of this disclosure requirement.[37] As a result, the provisions in the DCGC addressing institutional investors' and shareholders' duties seem

---

[27] Dutch Civil Code, art 2:110.
[28] Typically, shareholder litigation in the Netherlands takes place before the Enterprise Chamber. Often, shareholders use their right to order an inquiry into the policy of the company.
[29] Dutch Civil Code, art 2:8.
[30] Prominent examples include the ABN AMRO, Stork and ASMI cases 17 January 2007, LJN AZ 6440 (Stork). See n 18 for ABN AMRO and ASMI. Other examples are JANA Capital's pressure on the board of TNT NV. For instance, see Matt Steinglass, 'TNT Express Feud with Shareholders Widens' *Financial Times* (Amsterdam, 6 February 2012) <www.ft.com/content/1d2de1e6-50af-11e1-8cdb-00144feabdc0> accessed 6 July 2020.
[31] Akzo Nobel (n 15).
[32] Shareholders also need to have a 'reasonable interest' (in Dutch: '*redelijk belang*') in order to request the convening of a general meeting ex Dutch Civil Code, art 2:111(1). The supervisory board argued that this reasonable interest was lacking.
[33] This is a specialized chamber of the Amsterdam Court of Appeal.
[34] ABN AMRO (n 18).
[35] Rients Abma, Diana van Kleef, Niels Lemmers and Mieke Olaerts, *De algemene vergadering van Nederlandse beursvennootschappen [The General Meeting of Dutch Listed Companies]* (Kluwer 2017).
[36] These provisions include provision 4.3.5 on the 'Publication of institutional investors' voting policy' and provision 4.3.6 on the 'Report on the implementation of institutional investors' voting policy' (DCGC 2016 (n 7) 38).
[37] Besluit bestuurlijke boetes financiële sector [Decree on Administrative Fines in the Financial Sector], art 10.

to be an important driver behind the engagement practices of institutional investors in the Netherlands.[38] More recently, with the implementation of SRD II, institutional investors must, among other things, include in their engagement policy information on how they exercise their voting rights and other rights attached to their shares (new article 5:87 c Wft). Regarding this policy, the Dutch parliamentary explanatory statement clarifies:[39]

> The engagement policy deals with the way in which [institutional investors] monitor (a) the relevant matters of the companies invested in, (b) conducting a dialogue with these companies, (c) exercising their voting rights, (d) with other shareholders collaborate and (e) communicate with relevant stakeholders of these companies, such as the works council. Relevant matters (a) include the strategy, the financial and non-financial performance and risks, the capital structure, the social and environmental effects and corporate governance of their investees.

4.2.2 Soft-Law Stewardship Requirements

In addition to mandatory, statutory corporate law,[40] the Dutch corporate governance system for listed companies is governed by the DCGC. In accordance with the European Directive 2006/46/EC,[41] the DCGC was endorsed by the Dutch legislator as a mandatory comply or explain regime. The DCGC 2003,[42] introduced in the aftermath of corporate governance scandals like Enron and Ahold, was the first code following a binding 'comply-or-explain' principle.[43] It further developed the role of shareholders by stating that 'good corporate governance requires the fully-fledged participation of shareholders in the decision-making in the general meeting of shareholders'.[44] Moreover, the general meeting should be able to exert such influence on the corporate policy that it plays a fully-fledged role in the system of checks and balances.[45] Institutional investors need to act responsibly for their beneficiaries, by making careful decisions to exercise their shareholder rights and entering into dialogue with the company in situations where the company is non-compliant with the DCGC 2003 in an unacceptable manner.[46] The DCGC 2003 recommended

---

[38] See Section 4.2.2 in which the Dutch Corporate Governance Code is discussed.
[39] Kamerstukken II (Chamber Documents II) 2018–2019, 35058 n 3, 62, translated by the authors.
[40] In addition, the Dutch Pension Act (in Dutch: *Pensioenwet*) is applicable to pension funds. Under article 135(4) of the Dutch Pension Act, pension funds must state in their management report how their investment policy takes account of the environment, climate issues, human rights and social matters. Following the implementation of the IORP II Directive (Directive (EU) 2016/2341 of the European Parliament and of the Council of 14 December 2016 on the activities and supervision of institutions for occupational retirement provision [2016] OJ L354/37), in the Netherlands, ESG matters are further included in, inter alia, the Dutch Pension Act and in the Wft.
[41] Directive 2006/46/EC of the European Parliament and of the Council of 14 June 2006 amending Council Directives 78/660/EEC on the annual accounts of certain types of companies, 83/349/EEC on consolidated accounts, 86/635/EEC on the annual accounts and consolidated accounts of banks and other financial institutions and 91/674/EEC on the annual accounts and consolidated accounts of insurance undertakings [2006] OJ L224/1.
[42] An English version of the DCGC 2003 ('*de Code Tabaksblad*') is available at Corporate Governance Code Monitoring Committee, 'The Dutch Corporate Governance Code Principles of Good Corporate Governance and Best Practice Provisions' (9 December 2003) <www.mccg.nl/publicaties/codes/2003/12/9/corporate-governance-code-2003> accessed 9 February 2022 [hereinafter DCGC 2003].
[43] Dutch Civil Code, art 2:391. The first DCGC was published in 1997 and did not follow the mandatory comply-or-explain principle. One of its guidelines requested shareholder involvement in the critical assessment of strategy, risks, activities and financial results. Yet, the code acknowledged that the company should be allowed to curb the influence of shareholders, in particular in takeover situations, indicating that 'the quality of the input by shareholders sometimes leaves much to be desired'. See Peters Commission, 'Corporate Governance in Nederland – De Veertig Aanbevelingen [Corporate Governance in the Netherlands – Forty Recommendations]' (25 June 1997) <www.mccg.nl/publicaties/publicaties/1997/6/25/aanbevelingen-commissie-peters> accessed 11 February 2022.
[44] DCGC 2003 (n 42) 25, Principle IV.1.
[45] ibid.
[46] DCGC 2003 (n 42) 30, Principle IV.4.

that institutional investors develop a voting policy with annual reporting about this policy, and reporting at least every quarter of the year about it and how shares are voted.[47]

Shortly after the introduction of the DCGC 2003, short-termism of hedge funds and other active investors became an influential Dutch corporate governance feature.[48] Correspondingly, in the new DCGC that was published in December 2008, the responsibilities of shareholders vis-à-vis their investees were further developed. In addition to the provisions regarding the stewardship role allocated to institutional investors as already contained in the DCGC 2003,[49] a responsibility for all shareholders was added.[50] The DCGC 2008 also expects the shareholders, when using their legal right to put an item on the agenda of the general meeting, to consult the management board prior to the meeting. The shareholder must also explain its proposal during the general meeting, requiring the shareholder to attend the meeting in person or by proxy.[51]

In December 2016, the DCGC was again revised,[52] emphasizing 'long-term value creation' in its very first provision. The DCGC 2016 strengthened the existing requirements for institutional investors, stating in particular the following:[53]

> 4.3.5 Publication of institutional investors' voting policy: Institutional investors (pension funds, insurers, investment institutions and asset managers) should post annually, in any event on their website, their policy on the exercise of the voting rights for shares they hold in listed companies.
>
> 4.3.6 Report on the implementation of institutional investors' voting policy: Institutional investors should report annually, on their website and/or in their management report, on how they implemented their policy on the exercise of the voting rights in the relevant financial year. In addition, they should report on their website at least once per quarter on whether and, if so, how they have voted as shareholders at general meetings. This report will be posted on the website of the institutional investor.

Before the introduction of the DCGC 2016, the Dutch Monitoring Committee already indicated that with a future review of the DCGC it would be recommended to evaluate the possibility of including the shareholder duties in a separate Dutch Stewardship Code. However, given the pending SRD II at the time, the Committee indicated that it was too early to make substantial amendments to the DCGC as regards the relationship of the company with the (general meeting of) shareholders.[54]

---

[47] DCGC 2003 (n 42) 30, Best Practice Provisions IV.4.3.
[48] See e.g. ABN AMRO (n 18) and Stork (n 30).
[49] An English version of the 2008 DCGC ('*de Code Frijns*') is available at Corporate Governance Code Monitoring Committee, 'The Dutch Corporate Governance Code 2008' (2008) 33, Principle IV.4 <www.mccg.nl/publicaties/codes/2008/12/1/corporate-governance-code-2008-en> accessed 9 February 2022 [hereinafter DCGC 2008].
[50] 'Shareholders shall act in relation to the company, the organs of the company and their fellow shareholders in keeping with the principle of reasonableness and fairness. This includes the willingness to engage in a dialogue with the company and their fellow shareholders' (ibid).
[51] DCGC 2008 (n 49) 34, Best Practice Provision IV.4.4. and IV.4.6.
[52] DCGC 2016 (n 7).
[53] DCGC 2016 (n 7) 38, Best Practice Provisions 4.3.5 and 4.3.6. In addition, Provision 4.2.2 adds that companies should formulate an outline policy on bilateral contacts with the shareholders and should post this policy on their websites (DCGC 2016 (n 7) 37). From the 2018 report of the Corporate Governance Code Monitoring Committee, it follows that about 85% of the Dutch listed companies comply with this provision. The report is available at Corporate Governance Code Monitoring Committee, 'Rapport Monitoring Boekjaar 2018 [Monitoring Report 2018]' (2019) <www.mccg.nl/publicaties/rapporten/2019/12/13/rapport-monitoring-boekjaar-2018> accessed 9 February 2022.
[54] Corporate Governance Code Monitoring Committee, 'Voorstel voor herziening van de Code [Proposal for Revision of the Code]' (2016) <www.mccg.nl/publicaties/codes/2016/2/11/voorstel-voor-herziening> accessed 9 February 2022. However, the Monitoring Committee indicated that, given the developments at the time (the SRD II was not yet adopted at the European level), significant changes to the DCGC in 2016 regarding the provisions on shareholder duties and stewardship were not suitable.

Partly as a result of the introduction of SRD II, the Dutch Stewardship Code that entered into force on 1 January 2019, was introduced by Eumedion and its institutional members.[55] In 2011, Eumedion already issued ten Best (stewardship) Practices,[56] including the requirement to develop a policy concerning situations when there are remaining different opinions between the corporate board and the institutional investor.[57]

The Dutch Stewardship Code contains eleven principles and also provides – like the UK Code 2012 – guidance principles.[58] The principles include the 2011 Best Practices and provide further guidance as to the requirements set forth in the DCGC 2016.[59] All institutional investors that hold shares in Dutch listed companies are expected to report about their compliance with the principles in the Dutch Stewardship Code starting from the financial year 2019 (Preamble 5) on a comply-or-explain basis. However, unlike the DCGC, the Dutch Stewardship Code is not included in the Dutch statutory corporate law framework. Despite its lagging legal basis and the fact that this code is written by Eumedion members only, Eumedion expects that *all* institutional members follow the Dutch Stewardship Code.[60] The 'service document' of Eumedion and the *Pensioenfederatie (Pension Federation)* provide guidance on how the principles in the Dutch Stewardship Code should be addressed by institutional investors.[61] We outline the Dutch stewardship principles next.

The Dutch Stewardship Code states that 'engagement is conducting a meaningful dialogue with listed companies on these aspects as well as on issues that are the subject of votes at general meetings'.[62] Principle 2 explains the issues that should be monitored by institutional investors: 'Material issues, including, but not limited to, the company's business model for creating long-term value, the company's strategy, performance and risks and opportunities, the capital structure, social and environmental impact, corporate governance and corporate actions such as mergers and acquisitions.'[63]

Principles 3, 4 and 5 consider dialogue, co-operation and communication with stakeholders as important facets of stewardship:[64]

---

[55] Dutch Stewardship Code (n 12).
[56] Eumedion, 'Best Practices for Engaged Share-Ownership Intended for Eumedion Participants' (30 June 2011) <www.eumedion.nl/en/public/knowledgenetwork/best-practices/best_practices-engaged-share-ownership.pdf> accessed 6 July 2020.
[57] ibid 5, Best Practice 3.
[58] Dutch Stewardship Code (n 12); Financial Reporting Council, *The UK Stewardship Code* (September 2012) 4, 'Comply or Explain' <www.frc.org.uk/getattachment/d67933f9-ca38-4233-b603-3d24b2f62c5f/UK-Stewardship-Code-(September-2012).pdf> accessed 6 July 2020.
[59] Preamble 3 of the Dutch Stewardship Code (n 12) outlines that it incorporates the stewardship obligations for asset owners and asset managers from the SRD II and the relevant provisions in the DCGC 2016 (n 7) and Preamble 8 mentions that the secretariat of Eumedion will annually monitor the compliance of its members and those other asset owners and asset managers that requested to be included, based on the disclosed information on the websites and in the annual reports.
[60] Manon Cremers and Sandra Rietveld, 'Aandeelhoudersbetrokkenheid van institutionele beleggers bij Nederlandse beursvennootschappen en de Nederlandse Stewardship Code [Shareholder Involvement of Institutional Investors in Dutch Listed Companies and the Dutch Stewardship Code]' (2019) 4 *Tijdschrift voor de Ondernemingsrechtpraktijk* 36.
[61] See Eumedion, 'Verantwoord en betrokken aandeelhouderschap [Responsible and Committed Shareholding]' (2019) <www.eumedion.nl/nl/public/kennisbank/best-practices/2018-12-servicedocument-nederlandse-stewardship-code.pdf> accessed 6 July 2020.
[62] Dutch Stewardship Code (n 12) 1–2, Preamble 2.
[63] Dutch Stewardship Code (n 12) 5. Principle 2 adds that 'material issues are those matters that are likely to significantly affect the company's ability to create long-term value'.
[64] The Dutch Stewardship Code (n 12) mentions stakeholders seven times.

Principle 3 – Asset owners and asset managers are prepared to enter into dialogue with the executive and/or supervisory directors of their Dutch listed investee companies and are prepared to escalate their stewardship activities in case issues remain unresolved, where appropriate and at their discretion.

Principle 4 – Asset owners and asset managers cooperate with other shareholders in exercising stewardship activities towards Dutch listed investee companies, where appropriate and at their discretion.

Principle 5 – Asset owners and asset managers communicate with relevant stakeholders of Dutch listed investee companies, where appropriate and at their discretion.

As in other jurisdictions including the UK, in the Netherlands shareholder engagement involves more than just voting. Yet, voting is considered an important aspect of shareholder stewardship, and hence Principle 7 stipulates that institutional investors should exercise their voting rights in an informed manner, and publicly disclose (i) at least every three months how they voted their shares 'at an individual company level and per voting item' and (ii) at least annually a general description of their voting behaviour and an explanation 'of the most significant votes'. Following Preamble 18 of the SRD II, votes can be 'significant' owing to the subject matter of the vote or the size of the holding in the company (Guidance Principle 7).[65] As regards the subject matter, Guidance Principle 11 explains that this includes a resolution that is (i) of economic or strategic importance, (ii) which voting outcome is anticipated to be close or controversial, or (iii) where the asset owner or asset manager disagrees with the recommendation of the company's board.[66] It is important to note that it is Eumedion's policy to issue an alert to its members when there is a controversial voting item on the agenda of Dutch AGMs.[67]

Late December 2019, Eumedion published the Implementation Progress Report 2019 of the Dutch Stewardship Code.[68] Eumedion finds that about half of its investigated members[69] mention the Dutch Stewardship Code in their disclosures, and that a vast majority of Eumedion members provide 'high levels of transparency on their voting behaviour'.[70] As regards the 'significant votes', Eumedion uses its own alerts service to establish a sample of significant voting items in order to investigate compliance by institutional investors.[71] The results show that about half of the members in the sample reported on the alerted voting items. With respect to continuous dialogue between institutional investors and companies, Eumedion finds that about 96% of the participating institutional

---

[65] In the Dutch parliamentary proceedings about the implementation of the SRD II, 'significant votes' (in Dutch: *belangrijkste stemmingen*) are also addressed. It is stated that 'significant votes' in any case include votes on matters receiving a lot of media attention and matters that have been considered to be spearheaded by institutional investors and asset managers prior to the general meeting. Kamerstukken II (Chamber Documents II) 2018–2019, 35058 n 3, 34 (translated by the authors).

[66] Dutch Stewardship Code (n 12) 6, Principle 7 adds that when institutional investors vote against a particular management resolution, or withhold their votes, the reasons for such a request should be explained at least at the request of the company. In addition, Principle 8 states that those asset owners and asset managers that use proxy advisers and other voting services need to ensure that their votes are cast in line with their own voting policy.

[67] However, Eumedion abstains from providing any voting recommendation. See Eumedion, 'Beleidsplan 2020: Invloedrijk op goed bestuur en duurzaamheid [Policy Plan 2020: Influence on Good Governance and Sustainability]' (2019) 17 <www.eumedion.nl/clientdata/215/media/clientimages/Beleidsplan-2020.pdf?v=191223123841> accessed 6 July 2020.

[68] See Eumedion, 'Dutch Stewardship Code Implementation Progress Report 2019' (2019) <www.eumedion.nl/clientdata/215/media/clientimages/Dutch-Stewardship-Code-Implementation-Progress-Report-2019.pdf?v=191220152455> accessed 6 July 2020.

[69] The report investigates a sample of twenty-seven asset owners and asset managers, about half of its members, which is considered a representative sample according to ibid 3–4.

[70] ibid 7–8.

[71] ibid 8.

investors engage with their companies, whereas only 44% disclose engagement goals and 19% report on the consequences of engagements.[72]

Since voting can be considered an important aspect of shareholder stewardship, based on a categorization of significant voting items, we empirically investigate the voting behaviour of institutional investors and Eumedion members in particular, in the next sections. Since stewardship in the Netherlands is understood as a continuous dialogue of which voting constitutes only one element, we also consider the open shareholder dialogues that take place during Dutch AGMs.

4.3 EMPIRICAL FINDINGS

4.3.1 *Methodology*

We constructed a sample of twenty-nine Dutch AEX (large-cap) and AMX (mid-cap) companies.[73] Thomson Reuters Eikon data show that the average aggregate ownership share of institutional investors in these companies is 42.3 per cent.[74] However, it is highly likely that these ownership shares are underestimating institutional ownership in the Netherlands. For instance, Wolters Kluwer announces in its 2018 Annual Report that the institutional ownership is approximately 85%,[75] whereas the institutional ownership data from Thomson Reuters Eikon show only a 63.3% stake.[76] Also, as stated above, previous research found that 87% of the shares in Dutch companies is owned by (foreign) institutional investors.[77]

Next, using the Proxy Insight database, information on institutional investors' voting behaviour and rationale is retrieved for all AGMs and extraordinary general meetings (EGMs)[78] of those twenty-nine Dutch listed companies for a five-year period (2015–19). We removed all agenda items that contained only discussion items from the sample and considered only those resolutions that are recorded as voting items in the Proxy Insight database. The total number of institutional investor funds' voting decisions in the sample is 633,976, including yes and no-votes, abstentions, voting splits and occasionally the decision not to vote (DNV).[79] In addition to data from the Proxy Insight database, we used hand-collected turnout (or participation) rate[80] data and AGM transcripts of the same sample of twenty-nine Dutch listed companies. It is common practice for Dutch companies to disclose the transcripts of their general meetings on the corporate websites for compliance with Principle 4.1.10 of the

---

[72] ibid 12.
[73] Since part of the empirical research contains an analysis of the AGM transcripts for these companies, the sample was established based on the requirement that the AGM transcripts were available for five years (2015–19). The list of companies is available from the authors upon request.
[74] Data retrieved on 20 October 2019 from Thomson Reuters Eikon. Note that Gemalto NV was acquired at the time that the authors conducted this analysis, and is therefore excluded from this sample.
[75] Wolters Kluwer, 'Annual Report 2018' (2019) 28 <www.wolterskluwer.com/en/news/wolters-kluwer-publishes-its-2018-annual-report> accessed 6 July 2020.
[76] Also see Anastasiia Tupitcyna, 'Committed Shareholders: Institutional Ownership Report' (2018) <www.rsm.nl/fileadmin/Images_NEW/Erasmus_Platform_for_Sustainable_Value_Creation/Committed_shareholders_01.pdf> accessed 6 July 2020.
[77] Abma, Kleef, Lemmers and Olaerts (n 35) 8.
[78] The sample retrieved from the Proxy Insight database (<www.proxyinsight.com/> accessed 6 July 2020) also contains EGMs. Especially amendments to articles of association (one of the four voting item categories we focus on in Sections 4.3.3 and 4.3.4) are often voted on by shareholders during these extraordinary general meetings. The AGM turnout analysis (Section 4.3.2) only contains AGMs.
[79] Note that the empirical analyses in this chapter are carried out at the fund level.
[80] Turnout (or participation) rates are based on the disclosed voting results by the Dutch listed companies and calculated as the total number of votes cast divided by the total number of votes outstanding times 100%.

DCGC. These transcripts are relevant for research on institutional investor engagement practices, as shareholders in the Netherlands are able to ask questions and make remarks in Dutch general meetings.[81] Since it is common practice for different shareholder types to ask questions in Dutch AGMs,[82] the AGM transcripts offer valuable insights into institutional investor engagement practices. Finally, we also hand-collected the voting results of those voting items that were missing from the Proxy Insight database.[83]

4.3.2 AGM Participation

Figure 4.1 shows that overall turnout rates of Dutch AGMs stabilized at around 70 per cent over the last years.[84]

Figure 4.1 shows that shareholders of Dutch listed companies have a relatively high willingness to vote compared to many other jurisdictions in continental Europe, which is likely owing to the relatively high level of institutional investors' share-ownership.[85] Figure 4.1 shows that more than 75% of the AGMs were visited by more than 65% of the shareholders and 25% of the AGMs experienced a turnout rate of more than 80%. The high maximum is owing to a specific Dutch system that some companies make use of – *depository receipts*.[86] Shares are deposited in

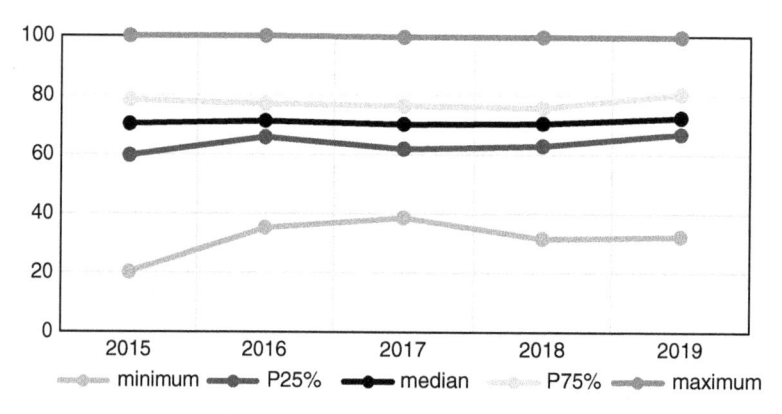

FIGURE 4.1 Participation rates at Dutch AGMs (%)[87]

---

[81] Dutch Civil Code, arts 2.107(2) 2:117. Also in accordance with SRD I (n 9). See Section 4.2.1.
[82] See Anne Lafarre and Christoph Van der Elst, 'Corporate Sustainability and Shareholder Activism in the Netherlands' in Beate Sjåfjell and Christopher M Bruner (eds), *Cambridge Handbook of Corporate Law, Corporate Governance and Sustainability* (CUP 2019).
[83] For the four voting item categories discussed in Sections 4.3.3–4.3.4, about 10% of the voting results were missing. In addition, a close analysis of the voting decisions contained in the Proxy Insight database showed us that several voting items were withdrawn before the general meeting. These voting items are excluded from all analyses in Sections 4.3.3–4.3.4.
[84] An earlier study of Eumedion shows that since 2014 the increase in participation almost stopped, while in the ten-year period before that, the attendance at Dutch AGMs doubled. See Eumedion, 'Groot aantal bestuursvoorstellen door aandeelhouders verworpen of ingetrokken: Eumedion publiceert evaluatierapport aandeelhoudersvergaderingen 2019 [Large Number of Management Proposals Rejected or Withdrawn By Shareholders: Eumedion Publishes Evaluation Report For Shareholder Meetings 2019]' (5 July 2019) <www.eumedion.nl/nl/public/kennisbank/persberichten/2019-07-persbericht-evaluatie-ava-seizoen-2019.pdf> accessed 6 July 2020.
[85] Abma, Kleef, Lemmers and Olaerts (n 35) 8. Also see Christoph Van der Elst, 'Shareholder Engagement Duties: The European Move Beyond Stewardship' in Hanne S Birkmose and Konstantinos Sergakis (eds), *Enforcing Shareholders' Duties* (Edward Elgar 2019) 66.
[86] For more information, see Anne Lafarre, *The AGM in Europe: Theory and Practice of Shareholder Behaviour* (Emerald 2017) 122.
[87] Figure 4.1 shows the turnout rates for the twenty-nine companies in the research sample (own data).

a trust office and the trust issues non-voting share certificates, thus separating capital rights from voting rights. The owners of these share certificates, however, may submit a request to receive proxies for voting.[88] The trust office votes the remaining shares that the depository receipts holders did not vote for.

4.3.3 Overall Approval Rates

Next, we consider the approval rates for important voting items by all shareholders and institutional investors in particular, in line with the emphasis on 'significant votes' in the Dutch Stewardship Code (see Section 4.2.2 for an explanation of these 'significant votes'). The agenda items that we consider containing significant votes are:

1. approval of amendments to articles of association;
2. approval of board elections;
3. approval of discharging board members; and
4. approval of remuneration proposals.

First, the articles of association (or the corporate charter) can be considered as the constitution of the company, and any amendment to these articles can therefore be denoted as a fundamental change.[89] The second voting item category contains all proposals to (re-)elect board members, since this shareholder right can be considered a key strategy for controlling the enterprise in corporate governance.[90] In Dutch listed companies with a two-tier board structure, shareholders are generally able to elect only the supervisory board members.[91] The third category contains all discharge resolutions. Shareholders in the Netherlands are asked to vote on the discharge of board members.[92] In general, discharge is an act of the general meeting that bindingly declares not to hold the directors liable for conduct in the financial year they are discharged for. The decision to discharge, however, limits only internal liability for the conduct that was known upon approval of the annual accounts. Hence, discharge protects the board members against liability claims and, perhaps more important for practice, signals the shareholders' satisfaction with the course of action of the board.

Lastly, shareholders have a binding say on the remuneration policy since 2004, long before the SRD II introduced this shareholder right at the European level.[93] Article 2:135(1) DCC stipulates that the general meeting is the only corporate body that can adopt the remuneration policy as well as any (major) amendments to the remuneration policy.[94] The approval of (an amendment of) the remuneration policy is a key feature of Dutch corporate governance. It is known that boards intensively discuss the remuneration

---

[88] Dutch Civil Code, art 2:118a.
[89] Also see Kraakman and others (n 1) 175ff.
[90] ibid 37.
[91] Under the *structuurregime* [structure regime], the supervisory board has the authority to (re-)elect and dismiss members of the management board ex Dutch Civil Code, art 2:162. Dutch listed companies generally follow the *structuurregime* [structure regime] requirements.
[92] Supervisory and management board members or non-executive and executive directors, Dutch Civil Code, art 2:121.
[93] Wet van 9 juli 2004 tot wijziging van boek 2 van het Burgerlijk Wetboek in verband met aanpassing van de structuurregeling, Staatsblad (Stb.) 2004, 370 <https://zoek.officielebekendmakingen.nl/stb-2004-370.html> accessed 6 July 2020.
[94] Derived from Kamerstukken II [Chamber Documents II] (2009–10) 31877, nr 5 (Nota naar aanleiding van het verslag) [Note following the report], p 25.

policy with the shareholders[95] and sometimes the company even withdraws the proposal to change the policy when a shareholder signals before the meeting that the new policy is unacceptable.[96] Contrary to the remuneration policy, the approval of compensation packages for individual board members can be delegated to another corporate body in the articles of association,[97] which is usually the supervisory board.[98] However, even in this case, article 2:135(5) DCC requires shareholder approval on pay schemes in the form of shares and options. The remuneration of the supervisory board also requires shareholder approval.[99]

Figure 4.2 summarizes the overall mean approval rates by all shareholders for these four agenda item categories.

Figure 4.2 shows that, generally, shareholders overwhelmingly support all these voting items. The high means, however, hide some resolutions that shareholders significantly opposed for all categories. This is illustrated by the 2018 sample mean of 90.8% of the votes in favour for remuneration proposals. If only remuneration policy proposals are considered, the mean approval rate drops to 83.3% in 2018. Since the remuneration policy requires a vote only if it is amended, the total number of observations is limited to five in 2018, of which two remuneration policy proposals received approximately 30% opposition, owing to specific company-related performance issues. As regards the articles of association, only four companies changed their articles in 2015, and at one company a significant number of the shareholders opposed the changes (with 55.7% in favour[100]), resulting in a mean approval rate of 87.2% for this voting item category in 2015. Nonetheless,

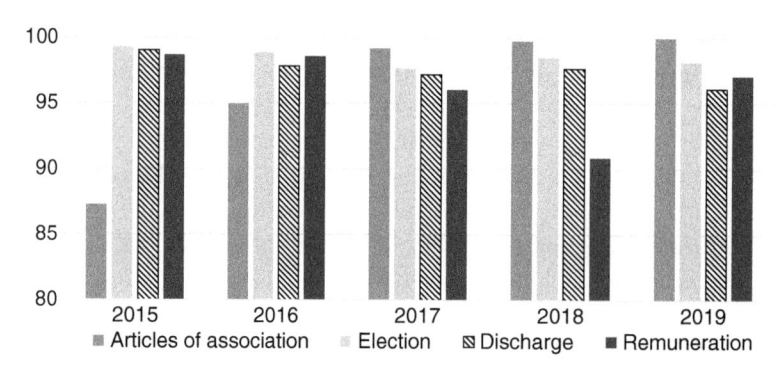

FIGURE 4.2 Mean approval rates for different agenda items (%)[101]

---

[95] Eumedion (n 84).
[96] Christoph Van der Elst and Anne Lafarre, 'Shareholder Voice on Executive Pay: A Decade of Dutch Say on Pay' (2017) 18 *European Business Organization Law Review* 51.
[97] Dutch Civil Code, art 2:135(4).
[98] Christoph Van der Elst and Anne Lafarre, 'Executive Pay and Say-on-Pay in the Netherlands' in Christoph Van der Elst (ed), *Executive Directors' Remuneration in Comparative Corporate Perspective* (Kluwer Law International 2015).
[99] Dutch Civil Code, art 2:145.
[100] In the Netherlands, the articles of association can be modified with a simple majority of the votes if more than half of the capital is represented at the meeting.
[101] Figure 4.2 contains all the voting items included in the Proxy Insight database for the twenty-nine Dutch listed companies in the 2015–19 research period for which voting results were available. We identified 28 agenda items concerning the articles of association, 445 agenda items related to director elections, 291 related to discharge and 96 concerning remuneration.

generally, changes of the articles of association are usually well-prepared and shareholders approve the changes with an overwhelming majority of the votes, as illustrated by the years after 2016.

4.3.4 Institutional Voting Behaviour

In this section, we consider institutional investors' voting behaviour and compare their votes to the overall voting outcome as discussed in Section 4.3.3. Since Eumedion plays an active role in the establishment of the Dutch shareholder stewardship framework and the Dutch Stewardship Code in particular, we also research the engagement of Eumedion's institutional members.[102]

We included the 'for', 'against', and 'abstain' voting decisions of institutional investors at the fund level as reported by the Proxy Insight database for the 2015–2019 period.[103] In almost 97% of the cases, institutional investors voted in favour of a resolution. In 2.75%, institutional investors voted against, and in 0.3% they abstained. Whereas Eumedion members also vote in favour in almost 97% of the cases, they slightly more often vote against with 3% of the total votes cast. The approval rates of institutional investors provided in the sections that follow are calculated as: for / (for + against) * 100%. Hence, similar to the calculation of voting results, abstentions are not taken into account in the voting outcomes shown in this section.[104]

Figures 4.3 and 4.4 provide the findings regarding the voting behaviour of respectively all institutional investors and the Eumedion members for the aforementioned four voting item

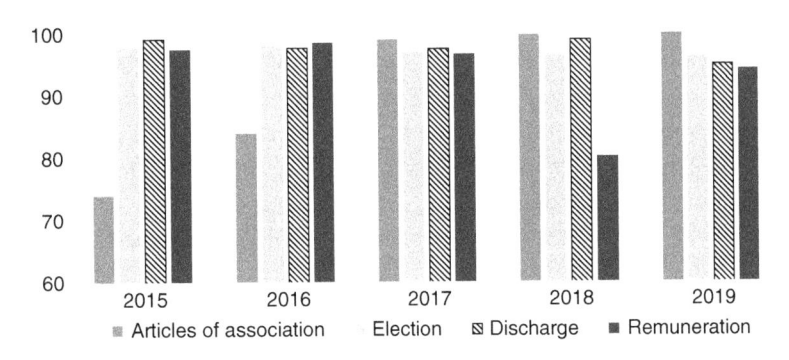

FIGURE 4.3 Average number of approving institutional investors for different agenda items (%)[105]

---

[102] An overview of Eumedion members can be found at: Eumedion, 'Deelnemers [Members]' <www.eumedion.nl/Over-Eumedion/deelnemers.html> accessed 6 July 2020.
[103] We excluded other voting options reported in the Proxy Insight database, including voting splits and did not vote ('DNV') decisions
[104] However, one should note that the data presented in the following sections (including in Figures 4.3 and 4.4 and Tables 4.1–4.3) regarding the aggregate voting results for institutional investors and Eumedion members are calculated equally weighting each institutional investor's voting decision. In other words, the voting stakes of the institutional investors are not taken into account, as this information is not available for all institutional investors.
[105] Figure 4.3 contains the mean approval rates of institutional investors (equally weighted) for the voting items included in the Proxy Insight database for the twenty-nine Dutch listed companies in the 2015–19 research period for which voting results were available. We identified 28 agenda items concerning the articles of association, 445 agenda items related to director elections, 291 related to discharge and 96 concerning remuneration.

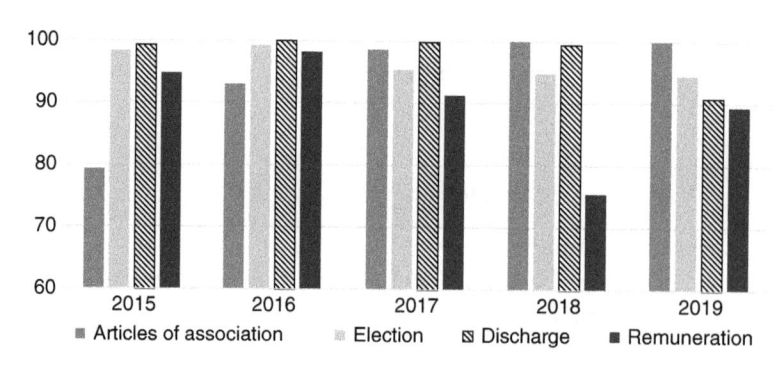

FIGURE 4.4 Average number of approving Eumedion members for different agenda items (%)[106]

categories. Generally, these results are quite comparable to the overall approval rates presented in Figure 4.2.

With respect to the voting category 'Articles of Association', most voting items received (large) support from the institutional investors (and the Eumedion members) with an average approval rate of 93.1% from all institutional investors and 95.4% from the Eumedion members. However, occasionally, voting items receive very high opposition rates, which is also shown by the average approval rates falling below 80% in 2015. As mentioned in Section 4.3.3, during one of the AGMs only 55.7% of the votes were in favour of the proposed amendment of the articles of association. When considering institutional investors only for this particular resolution, only *8.8% of the thirty-four institutional investors* recorded in the Proxy Insights database voted in favour of this resolution (and 20% of the Eumedion members). In this particular situation, the articles of association were modified in several ways and involved, inter alia, an increase of the dividend of the preferential shares and an increase of the required threshold to call a general meeting. A large majority of the (institutional investors') proxy votes voted against these changes. This is more than likely owing to the increase in the threshold to call a general meeting,[107] which is considered a strong limitation of shareholder rights. The board of directors withdrew this modification of the articles and the attending shareholders approved the other modifications. As most institutional investors usually vote by proxy prior to the general meeting, the dissatisfaction with the withdrawn amendment was still reflected in the voting result.[108]

The average approval rates presented in Figures 4.3 and 4.4 for 'Elections' show that director elections receive significant support with average approval rates of 97.2% and 96.4% for all investors and Eumedion members, respectively, and we observed only minor deviations in the average approval rates over the years. Only in particular situations did institutional investors vote against *en masse*. An example of this institutional investor revolt was the re-election of a supervisory

---

[106] Figure 4.4 contains the mean approval rates of Eumedion members (equally weighted) for the voting items included in the Proxy Insight database for the twenty-nine Dutch listed companies in the 2015–19 research period for which voting results were available. We identified 28 agenda items concerning the articles of association, 445 agenda items related to director elections, 291 related to discharge and 96 concerning remuneration.
[107] Which was also part of the changes to the articles of association.
[108] The voting rationales available in the Proxy Insight database reflect this. For instance, Acadian Asset Management LLC declared:

> A vote AGAINST is warranted because: The company proposes to amend the article that refers to the minimum requirement to place an item on the agenda. Instead of requiring a minimum threshold of 1 percent, management proposes to refer to the statutory minimum, which is increased to 3 percent. Such development is not favourable for minority shareholders. It is proposed to increase the preferred dividend on preference shares in order to finance an antitakeover instrument, which is considered not in the best interests of shareholders.

board member during the 2017 AGM of Heineken. Heineken has a concentrated ownership structure with a controlling shareholder: the Heineken family is the ultimate owner controlling via a pyramid structure an indirect stake of 50.005% in Heineken. Next, its second largest shareholder FEMSA is an allied shareholder of the Heineken family that holds an indirect stake of 8.6% in Heineken.[109] Although the opposition was 'only' 4.85% against the re-election of the supervisory board member, given the concentrated ownership structure, this rate includes a significantly lower 77.7% approval rate of all institutional investors and only 26.2% approval – hence, disapproval – by Eumedion members. The representative of institutional investors (including some Eumedion members) present during Heineken's 2017 AGM[110] declared their vote to be against the re-election of the supervisory board member, based on the (lack of) independency of this supervisory board member as the chair of the remuneration committee and the exceeding of the terms of his appointment.[111] Some institutional investors based their vote against on other rationales. PGGM and Allianz Global Investors' voting rationale sounded like this:[112]

> PGGM: The proposed candidate is considered to be a non-independent director and is becoming the chairman of the remuneration committee. This is not in line with PGGM guidelines and PGGM will therefore oppose this resolution.
>
> Allianz Global Investors: It believes that the board's Nomination committee should be at least majority independent and comprise directors who have qualifications, experience, skills and capacity to effectively contribute to the committee's work.[113]

During Heineken's 2019 AGM, another supervisory board member was re-elected to the supervisory board with an overall approval rate of 92.6%, hiding the fierce opposition rates of institutional investors of 32.5% and even 92.5% from Eumedion members only. The voting rationales of these investors show similar arguments to those in the 2017 resolution.

Overall, the approval rates by institutional investors for the voting item category 'Discharge' are high (97.7% for all institutional investors and 97.7% for Eumedion). However, some discharge proposals received fierce investor criticism. During the 2019 AGM of ING NV, the proposals to discharge both the management and the supervisory board members were rejected by all shareholders with an approval rate of only about 37%. It is noteworthy that the institutional investors massively rejected these ING 2019 AGM proposals with approval rates of only 19.6% and 18.7% for the management board members and the supervisory board members respectively.[114] Particularly, from the disclosed institutional investors' voting rationales, it follows that ING's (supervisory) board members were criticized by their shareholders for the money laundering affair that led to a fine of EUR 775 million in 2018.[115] The representative of PGGM

---

[109] Data are retrieved from Heineken, 'Annual Report 2017' (2018) <www.theheinekencompany.com/sites/theheinekencompany/files/Investors/financial-information/results-reports-presentations/Heineken-NV-Annual-Report-2017_1.PDF> accessed 6 July 2020.

[110] Representing a large group of institutional investors, including Triodos Investment Management, Achmea Investment Management, Menzis and Aegon Investment Management BV.

[111] This supervisory board member is, since 1994, a member of the supervisory board of Heineken.

[112] These voting statements are retrieved from the Proxy Insight database.

[113] Note that the supervisory board member that is reappointed is also a member of the Selection and Appointment board committee of Heineken.

[114] Remarkably, we find that Eumedion members dismissed the discharge of the board members with a 30% approval rate but that of the supervisory board members with a 6.67% approval rate as recorded by Proxy Insight. This may indicate that Eumedion members consider the supervisory board particularly responsible for the course of affairs.

[115] See, for instance, Toby Sterling and Bart H Meijer, 'Dutch Bank ING Fined $900 Million for Failing to Spot Money Laundering' *Reuters* (Amsterdam, 4 September 2018)<www.reuters.com/article/us-ing-groep-settlement-money-laundering/dutch-bank-ing-fined-900-million-for-failing-to-spot-money-laundering-idUSKCN1LK0PE> accessed 6 July 2020.

Investments critically stated the following during the 2019 AGM of ING, according to the AGM transcripts:[116]

> Ms [X] referred to PGGM's obligation to its members to take responsibility for how it voted on the policy implemented by and supervision at companies in which it invests. She believed that the principal duty of the Executive Board of a systemically important bank, under the supervision of the Supervisory Board, was to safeguard the reputation of the bank and public confidence in it. In respect of ING she listed the two main issues from 2018, the CEO's remuneration and the settlement agreement with the Dutch Public Prosecution Service, which she believed had been detrimental to ING's reputation and had led to adverse public sentiment towards the bank. These two issues were reasons why PGGM would not support the proposal to grant discharge to the members and former members of the Executive Board and the Supervisory Board in respect of their duties performed during 2018.[117]

The average approval rates for remuneration-related proposals are lower than for the other three voting item categories in our sample, with average approval levels of 94.9% for all institutional investors, and 91.0% for Eumedion members. Some companies, including Unilever, experienced heavy opposition from their shareholders for this voting item. In particular for the year 2018, we can find lower average approval rates of 80.2% from all institutional investors and only 75.4% from Eumedion members. For instance, during Unilever's 2018 AGMs, the remuneration policy proposal received significant shareholder opposition. Unilever is a Dutch listed company that is also incorporated in the UK; thus, it organizes two AGMs each year, one in the UK and one in the Netherlands. The total dissent rates on the new remuneration policy proposal at these two AGMs were more than 35% and more than 26% for the UK and the Dutch AGMs for this dually listed company, respectively. When we exclude the Unilever Trust Office from the voting results, 43% of the shareholders voted against.[118] For the institutional investors, we find *approval rates* of only 48.1% (all institutional investors) and 36.4% (Eumedion members). Although Eumedion does not disclose its issued voting alerts (cf. Section 4.2.4), from its 2018 annual report we can deduce that it issued an alert for this 2018 Unilever remuneration item to its members and thus considered this voting item controversial, as shown by the significant dissent rate of its members.[119] The representative of seven institutional investors[120] voiced his opinion about the new Unilever remuneration policy, making the following statement:[121]

> We would like to thank you for discussing this policy with us prior to the AGM. There are good aspects, for example the simplification. . . . In addition, you have also listened to the shareholders by including that 75% discretionary cap. But we also have a few points of criticism, because . . . the fact remains that the short-term bonus in the new program is rising faster than the long-term bonus component. We think that's a shame. In addition, there is an observation that the salary can rise sharply in maximum terms: by 21%. In addition, there is still a transition-forward option with a buy-out

---

[116] Ms. [X] speaks on behalf of PGGM Investments and on behalf of its clients and shareholders.
[117] ING Groep, 'Minutes of the Annual General Meeting of ING Groep N.V.' (23 April 2019) 15 <www.ing.com/web/file?uuid=9be45076-849b-4fdd-87af-00af7dbb55d2&owner=b03bc017-e0db-4b5d-abbf-003b12934429&contentid=48136&elementid=2101798> accessed 6 July 2020. The authors removed the speaker's name.
[118] Also see Eumedion, 'Wetsvoorstel ter implementatie van de richtlijn langetermijnbetrokkenheid aandeelhouders [Bill to Implement the Long-Term Involvement of Shareholders Directive]' (Kamerstukken II 2018/19, 35 058, nr 1 e. v.)' (21 November 2018) <www.eumedion.nl/nl/public/kennisbank/wet-en-regelgeving/2018/2018-11-commentaar-wetsvoorstel-implementatie-richtlijn-aandeelhoudersbetrokkenheid.pdf> accessed 6 July 2020.
[119] See Eumedion, 'Jaarverslag 2018 [Annual Report 2018]' (2019) 22 <www.eumedion.nl/clientdata/215/media/clientimages/jaarverslag-2018.pdf?v=191223123841> accessed 6 July 2020.
[120] The represented institutional investors are also members of Eumedion: MN Services, Achmea, Menzis, NN Investment Partners, Robeco, Double Dividend and PGGM.
[121] Translated by the authors.

award without a formal upper limit. There you can find yourself in a situation where the board or the future director from outside may be in a strong negotiating position. Every investor, I speak on behalf of several investors, but everyone ultimately makes their own assessment of whether they will vote for or against the remuneration policy. I would at least like to inform you that MN [Services] will vote against, in particular because of the possible welcome bonus for a new external director.

Hence, although there were some good elements in the amended remuneration policy, the institutional investors clearly voiced their discontentment during the 2018 Dutch AGM of Unilever. In addition, the first sentence of this statement also directly refers to another engagement tool that is commonly used by institutional investors: private conversations with the corporate management prior to the AGM.

On the other hand, both the average approval rates in Figures 4.2–4.4 and the Unilever 2018 AGM example show that institutional investors may more heavily criticize remuneration proposals compared to the entire shareholder base, although this is not always the case. A textbook example can be found during the SBM Offshore 2018 AGM: when more than 30% of the shareholders voted against,[122] the representative of the institutional investors[123] at the AGM stated their support for the proposed remuneration policy, 'since it is easier to understand and more transparent for shareholders'.[124]

4.4 STATISTICAL ANALYSES

4.4.1 *Overall Analysis*

In this section, we further analyze the descriptive results in Sections 4.3.2–4.3.4. In particular, we measure whether institutional investors and Eumedion members make statistically significant different voting decisions. Table 4.1 shows the results.

Table 4.1 shows that institutional investors are more critical than the aggregate shareholder base for most of the voting items. In particular, for approval of amendments to the articles of association, institutional investors show higher dissent rates than all shareholders (with a statistically significant difference of −3.9%; see column 4 of Table 4.1). Also, for remuneration proposals, institutional investors, and in particular Eumedion members, more often do not agree with the corporate management: column 5 of Table 4.1 shows that the difference in approval rates between all shareholders and Eumedion members is almost 6% (statistically significant at the 1% level). For these proposals, we see that Eumedion members are also more critical than all institutional investors: the difference is almost 4% (statistically significant at the 1% level).

4.4.2 *Ownership Concentration*

The data in Section 4.3 show that several companies in the Netherlands have a rather concentrated ownership structure. Using the data from Thomson Reuters Eikon, we analyze the statistically significant differences among approval rates of all shareholders, all institutional investors and Eumedion members for these concentrated ownership companies. We divide the companies in our sample in two panels: panel 1 contains all companies with 80% or less of the outstanding share capital in free float (hence, all companies with an ownership concentration of at least 20%, that is,

---

[122] Calculated as: votes against / (votes against + votes in favour) * 100%.
[123] MN Services and Menzis.
[124] SBM Offshore, 'Minutes of the General Meeting of SBM Offshore N.V.' (11 April 2018) 9 <www.sbmoffshore.com/sites/sbm-offshore/files/sbm-offshore/investors/shareholders-meetings/2018/minutes-of-the-agm-of-sbm-offshore-nv-2018-04-11.pdf> accessed 9 February 2022.

TABLE 4.1 *All shareholders', all institutional investors' and Eumedion members' approval rates (%)*[125]

Voting items	All shareholders	All institutional investors	Eumedion members	Difference (all shareholders – all institutional)	Difference (all shareholders – Eumedion members)	Difference (all institutional – Eumedion members)
Articles of Association (n=28)	96.99	93.12	95.43	−3.90* (−1.60)	−1.56 (−1.15)	2.31* (1.54)
Elections (n=445)	98.48	97.17	96.39	−1.31*** (−6.24)	−2.09*** (−4.10)	−0.78** (−1.81)
Discharge (n=291)	97.58	97.73	97.91	0.15 (0.51)	−0.33 (−0.49)	0.18 (0.28)
Remuneration (n=96)	96.75	94.91	91.04	−1.84** (−1.80)	−5.71*** (−3.72)	−3.87*** (−4.19)

TABLE 4.2 *Voting items companies with concentrated ownership (%)*[126]

Ownership structure	All shareholders	All institutional investors	Eumedion members	Difference (all shareholders – Institutional investors)	Difference (all shareholders – Eumedion members)	Difference (all institutional – Eumedion members)
All categories						
Ownership top 5 (n=146)	99.26	96.31	93.86	−2.95*** (−4.98)	−5.40*** (−4.11)	−2.45*** (−2.70)
Ownership 20% (n=255)	98.92	96.15	94.85	−2.77*** (−5.73)	−4.06*** (−4.76)	−1.30** (−2.08)
Remuneration						
Ownership top 5 (n=18)	98.33	92.39	85.95	−5.94** (−1.79)	−12.38** (−2.39)	−6.44*** (−2.77)
Ownership 20% (n=32)	97.78	93.35	88.80	−4.44** (−1.93)	−8.98*** (−2.59)	−4.54*** (-3.14)

nine companies) and panel 2 contains the five companies in our sample with the highest ownership concentration (all companies have about 50% or less of their shares in free float).[127] Since Table 4.1 has shown that particularly resolutions in the 'Remuneration' category receive higher dissent rates from institutional investors than all shareholders, we also provide separate analyses of the remuneration proposals for these concentrated ownership companies. Table 4.2 shows the results.

---

[125] *, ** and *** indicate statistical significance at the 10%, 5% and 1% levels, respectively; t-values are reported in parentheses.

[126] *, ** and *** indicate statistical significance at the 10%, 5% and 1% levels, respectively; t-values are reported in parentheses.

[127] This threshold of 20% is in line with the earlier work of La Porta and others. See, for instance, Rafael La Porta, Florencio Lopez-De-Silanes and Andrei Shleifer, 'Corporate Ownership around the World' (1999) 54 *Journal of Finance* 471.

Table 4.2 shows that the difference in approval rates between institutional investors, and Eumedion members in particular, and the entire shareholder base is even more prominent when ownership concentration is taken into account. When we only consider the five companies with the highest ownership concentration, we see that the difference in approval rates is almost 3% for all institutional investors, and even about 5.5% for Eumedion members. Table 4.1 shows that remuneration proposals are generally most critically evaluated by Eumedion members: when we consider these proposals for concentrated ownership companies, we see that the difference in approval rates between all shareholders and Eumedion members even exceeds 12% for the top five companies with the highest ownership concentration.

4.4.3 Withdrawn Resolutions

In the Proxy Insight database, we found eight voting items related to one of the four resolution categories that were withdrawn prior to the general meeting, for which the institutional investors, however, disclosed their voting behaviour.[128] The average approval rate for these resolutions is 56.73% for all institutional investors and 63.0% for Eumedion members (with a standard deviation of respectively 37.0% and 38.0%). These average approval rates show high dissent rates. The highest dissent rate could be found for resolution 5 of the 2016 Ahold NV EGM, concerning a proposed amendment of the articles of association regarding an option right to *Stichting Ahold Continuïteit* (the Ahold trust office), with an approval rate of 13.5% from all institutional investors in the Proxy Insight database and of only 8.1% from Eumedion members. Another voting item was also withdrawn from the agenda prior to this Ahold meeting, concerning a proposed amendment to the remuneration policy (resolution 8): this voting item received approval rates of institutional investors and Eumedion members of, respectively, 42.6% and 62.2%.

4.5 A SERIOUS STEWARDSHIP ROLE IN A STAKEHOLDER ENVIRONMENT

In the Netherlands, the corporate legal system embraces the stakeholder approach, which is widely recognized by Dutch scholarship, case law and the DCGC with its focus on long-term value creation. Nonetheless, investor stewardship is gaining importance in the Dutch context. The recent implementation of SRD II and the introduction of the Dutch Stewardship Code further emphasized this corporate governance feature.

Currently, (foreign) institutional investors hold a large part of the shares in Dutch listed companies. These foreign institutional investors are encouraged to take into account the Dutch stakeholder model when deciding to act as a steward in their Dutch investee companies, as the Dutch model differs substantially from the more shareholder-oriented models in the US and the UK. With its significant influence on the Dutch corporate governance landscape and the introduction of the Dutch Stewardship Code that recognizes the involvement of stakeholders, Eumedion can play a pivotal role spreading good stewardship practices.

The Dutch turnout rates that are among the highest in Europe[129] and the observed opposition against controversial voting items show that many institutional investors take their engagement

---

[128] These voting items are not included in the previous analyses (see Section 4.3.1).
[129] This can be explained by the combination of high levels of institutional ownership in many Dutch listed companies and high ownership concentration in many other companies, since both types of shareholder (institutional investors and block-holders) actively make use of their voting rights.

role seriously. Institutional investors critically consider (non-)current voting items which could negatively affect shareholder rights, like some of the amendments of the articles of association as well as remuneration packages of directors that contain insufficient or inappropriate incentives. Compared to other investors, institutional investors show significantly higher opposition rates regarding these voting items. Particularly, Eumedion members show even higher opposition rates than institutional investors in general for the different voting items addressed in this research. However, there may be room for a stronger focus on the activities and outcomes of stewardship, including changing the behaviour of companies, and not just policy statements.[130] This is also shown by the Eumedion finding that fewer than 20% of the institutional investors currently report on the consequences of engagements.[131]

We have also shown that the high ownership concentration in some Dutch companies has a major impact on voting outcomes. In these situations, voting can be insufficient to initiate a change in the behaviour of the investee companies. While institutional investors and Eumedion members sometimes heavily oppose agenda items, with up to 90 per cent of those investors voting against, large and in particular controlling shareholders align with management and the board and generally approve all the proposals. This raises questions as to whether the current system of voting based solely on the number of voting rights is appropriately balancing the powers between controlling shareholders on the one side and the board, co-operative shareholders and other shareholders on the other. Alternatively, other voting systems, like the majority of minority rule, could enhance the effects of stewardship of, in particular, institutional investors. Meanwhile, institutional investors may seek further co-operation with other shareholders in exercising stewardship activities and engage with other stakeholders of their Dutch listed investee companies as Principles 4 and 5 of the Dutch Stewardship Code suggest. We will have to wait a few more years to find out whether the Dutch Stewardship Code efforts complementary to the DCGC indeed further encourage interaction between Dutch companies and their (institutional) shareholders.

---

[130] See Davies, The UK Stewardship Code 2010–2020, Chapter 2 and Katelouzou and Micheler, The Market for Stewardship and the Role of the Government, Chapter 3 on the UK, as this change was incorporated in the UK Code 2020.

[131] Katelouzou and Micheler, The Market for Stewardship and the Role of the Government, Chapter 3, Section 3.2.2.

5

Capitalist Stakeholders

Shareholder Stewardship in Switzerland

Daniel Daeniker and Gérard Hertig[*]

5.1 INTRODUCTION

To understand shareholder stewardship in Switzerland, it is important to note the idiosyncrasies of the country. First, Switzerland is a *grassroots society*. This is evidenced, in the political context, by a tradition of devolving authority to the lowest possible level – and in the economy by the historical prevalence of 'co-operatives', business associations based on mutual self-help. Second, Swiss corporate law and practice have always emphasized and protected *stakeholder interests* over the principle of maximizing shareholder value. Third, the blueprint for Swiss corporations large and small has been the *family-controlled* business enterprise, with shareholders taking the long view and being prone to exercise their rights responsibly. Shareholder stewardship – the notion that shareholders should engage with investee companies in order to create long-term corporate performance that is also sustainable for other beneficiaries – should, as far as Switzerland is concerned, be understood within this triangle.

Nowadays, co-operatives are rare in the realm of large Swiss business enterprises and non-existent in the listed company space. In this modern environment, corporations with a stated profit-making purpose are the norm. Even so, the Swiss corporate modus operandi continues to be based on two assumptions. To begin with, firms' business is sustainable in the long term only if it is run in a way that is profitable from the perspective of both stakeholders and shareholders. Moreover, Swiss boards of directors must conduct business in the best interests of the firm, and this does *not* mean putting shareholder interests ahead of everything else. Depending on the firm, other goals such as employee interests, the interests of society as a whole and environmental, social and governance (ESG) considerations may be equally important. This approach already reflects a stewardship model – understood as responsible conduct of business – on the corporate level. It is endorsed by Swiss court practice and part of the political consensus as to how Swiss companies should operate.

The Swiss stewardship orientation on a corporate level also has to do with most Swiss corporations being or having at some time been controlled by families. Family shareholders think in generations rather than calendar quarters. They also tend to embrace the interests of employees or the communities in which the company operates, rather than focusing only on profit-making. Admittedly, in the listed company space, family control is becoming less and less important, but, as will be shown later, the blueprint remains. Also, a more recent sequel of family

---

[*] The authors would like to thank Daniel Häusermann, Christoph Heinimann, Jasmin Künzle and Patric Brand for their valuable comments on earlier drafts of this chapter, and Mirjam Staub-Bisang, Peter Böckli, Adam O. Emmerich and Martin Lipton for their endorsement of the theories expounded in this chapter.

control in Swiss medium-sized listed companies is the rise of 'anchor' shareholders, investors with sizeable stakes and a stated long-term investment horizon.

Shareholder stewardship implies that shareholders of Swiss corporations act as 'enlightened' owners and take responsibility in exercising their property rights, an exception to the stated legal rule, in Switzerland and elsewhere, that a shareholder owes no duty to the corporation. Sometimes shareholders exercise their ownership rights responsibly on a purely voluntary basis, owing to their long-term investment focus, especially in controlled companies; sometimes, these considerations are caused by self-regulatory initiatives or investor pressure. Either way, responsible ownership in Switzerland has little to do with legislative efforts.

Clearly, the approach just outlined is sustainable only if shareholders re-elect board members who endorse the responsible ownership model. Here, the position of institutional investors (whose ownership stakes have recently become significant) is particularly relevant. So far, they show little appetite for the stewardship approach: many institutional investors simply follow the recommendations of proxy advisers. However, there is evidence that major financial institutions are starting to assume the stewardship role traditionally played by controlling and anchor shareholders.

Most, if not all, other jurisdictions adopt a more neutral approach. For example, Germany is following a rather hands-off policy when it comes to fostering stewardship obligations.[1] Similarly, while Singapore encourages family firms to be good stewards, institutional investors are merely asked to state clearly the model they follow.[2] To be sure, the 2008 Global Financial Crisis (GFC) prompted various jurisdictions, in particular the United Kingdom, to take a more proactive approach to stewardship; however, compliance with the resulting reforms remains an issue.

Our analysis is structured as follows. First, we provide a background of Swiss corporate law in the context of the Continental European legal tradition (Section 5.2). We then document the Swiss ownership regime and its implications in terms of corporate control and shareholder engagement (Section 5.3). Next, we provide evidence of the presence of an enlightened stewardship model, under which shareholders more directly take into account stakeholder interests (Section 5.4). We conclude in Section 5.5 that the Swiss system is likely to continue to operate effectively in the twenty-first century.

5.2 SWISS CORPORATE LAW IN CONTEXT

5.2.1 *Historical Background*

Switzerland is the epitome of a grassroots society. While democratic structures were not universal until the mid-nineteenth century, many Swiss communities traditionally had a strong penchant for self-reliance and mutual assistance.[3] In the rural set-up, especially in mountainous areas, this was visible through the prevalence of commons, the use and maintenance of which was determined by mutual agreement to avoid over-exploitation.[4] Owing to this social structure, the proverbial 'Tragedy of the Commons'[5] is largely unknown in Switzerland.

---

[1] Ringe, Stewardship and Shareholder Engagement in Germany, Chapter 9, Section 9.3.2.
[2] Puchniak and Tang, Singapore's Embrace of Shareholder Stewardship, Chapter 14, Section 14.3.1.
[3] Adolf Gasser, *Gemeindefreiheit als Rettung Europas [Community Autonomy, a Saviour of Europe]* (Bücherfreunde 1943); Wolfgang Wartburg, *Geschichte der Schweiz [History of Switzerland]* (Oldenbourg 1951).
[4] The Canton of Valais provides a telling example: local rules allocate riparian rights to the users of irrigation channels and stipulate the obligations to participate in the upkeep of these channels. See Jean-Henry Papilloud, *Die Suonen des Wallis [The Irrigation Channels of Valais]* (Editions Monographic 1999).
[5] Garrett Hardin, 'The Tragedy of the Commons' (1968) 162 *Science* 1243.

When it comes to business associations, the grassroots element is corroborated by the abundance of co-operatives, business associations based on mutual self-help.[6] Prototypical examples are agricultural and similar co-operatives in rural communities; consumer co-operatives in towns and cities, out of which the two biggest Swiss retailers (Migros and Coop) have grown over time; insurance co-operatives, in the areas of both life assurance (Swiss Life) and property and casualty insurance (Schweizerische Mobiliar); and the Raiffeisen banking co-operatives outside of the urban sprawl.

Even where business associations are operating as profit-oriented enterprises, there is a strong tradition of being stakeholder-oriented. From that perspective, it is not surprising that social differences have generally been smaller in Switzerland than in other countries. For example, Switzerland is one of the few countries where the GINI coefficient has remained broadly stable, highlighting the fact that inequality has not increased over the past forty years.[7]

This state of affairs goes hand-in-hand with the democratic structures formalized by the 1848 Constitution.[8] It was inspired by the US model,[9] with particular regard to the vertical separation of powers between the Confederation and the Cantons (member states). This division of roles at the territorial level supplemented the horizontal separation of powers among the legislative, executive and judicial branches of government. Today, political power in Switzerland continues to be divided between the Confederation, the Cantons and (to a certain degree) the communities.[10] In particular, each of these three territorial subdivisions has its own taxing authority, so that – unlike in many other countries – Cantons and communities are not wholly dependent on handouts from the central government.

Finally, in the Swiss version of direct democracy, the electorate is regularly asked to vote on questions of substance.[11] Some pundits argue that direct democracy never really works, pointing to California and other jurisdictions as examples.[12] Nevertheless, direct democracy works in Switzerland, possibly owing to the grassroots component being pervasive in society.

This observation is also relevant for business law. Direct democracy naturally fosters stakeholder – and more recently stewardship – considerations in Swiss corporate practice, often caused by environmental and social concerns or societal discomfort with governance issues such

---

[6] 'A cooperative is a corporate entity consisting of an unlimited number of persons or commercial enterprises who join together for the primary purpose of promoting or safeguarding the specific economic interests of the society's members by way of collective self-help.' See *Obligationenrecht* [Swiss Code of Obligations], first enacted 30 March 1911, last revised 6 November 2019, SR 220, art 828, para 1.

[7] Ursina Kuhn and Christian Suter, 'Die Entwicklung der Einkommensungleichheit in der Schweiz [The Development of Income Inequality in Switzerland]' (2015) *Social Change in Switzerland No 2* <www.socialchangeswitzerland.ch/?p=574> accessed 14 June 2020; Ruchir Sharma, 'The Happy, Healthy Capitalists of Switzerland' *The New York Times* (2 November 2019) <www.nytimes.com/2019/11/02/opinion/sunday/switzerland-capitalism-wealth.html> accessed 14 June 2020.

[8] Switzerland is the only country in which the liberal revolution of 1848 permanently changed the political system. Neither Germany nor France achieved this, while England was not part of the mid-nineteenth-century European upheaval.

[9] See e.g. James H Hutson, *The Sister Republics: Switzerland and the United States from 1776 to the Present* (Library of Congress 1991) 24–31.

[10] See e.g. Presence Switzerland, 'Federalism' (*admin.ch*, 27 November 2017)<www.eda.admin.ch/aboutswitzerland/en/home/politik-geschichte/politisches-system/foederalismus.html> accessed 9 February 2022.

[11] As an example, the Swiss variant of say-on-pay rules was enacted as a result of a popular initiative (see n 153). On the topic more generally, see Presence Switzerland, 'Direct Democracy' (*admin.ch*, 20 August 2019) <www.eda.admin.ch/aboutswitzerland/en/home/politik-geschichte/politisches-system/direkte-demokratie.html> accessed 9 February 2022.

[12] Andreas Kluth, 'The People's Will' *The Economist* (Special Report, 23 April 2011) <www.economist.com/sites/default/files/special-reports-pdfs/democracy_in_california.pdf> accessed 14 June 2020; Michael Ignatieff, 'Can a Country Ever Recover from a Rough Referendum?' *The Economist* (17 January 2019) <www.economist.com/open-future/2019/01/17/can-a-country-ever-recover-from-a-rough-referendum> accessed 14 June 2020.

as excessive management compensation. A hundred thousand Swiss voters can request a vote on constitutional amendments via popular initiative.[13] If accepted, such initiatives will result in prompt and significant corporate law adjustments.[14] Business circles, courts and the legislative process are therefore prone to pre-empt the likelihood of constitutional amendments by taking into account stakeholder and stewardship considerations already when adopting self-regulatory measures, adjudicating major cases and enacting new legislation. It is thus evident that grassroots considerations have influenced and will continue to influence Swiss corporate law and practice.

5.2.2 Swiss Corporate Law Codifications

Swiss corporate law was first codified in 1881. At the time, lawmakers were inspired by the *laissez-faire* approach of the late nineteenth century.[15] A series of post–World War I corporate crises led to an overhaul of the legislative framework. The 1936 law gave the board of directors significant discretion in managing corporate affairs in difficult situations; in essence, survival of the enterprise replaced providing returns to shareholders as the key goal.[16]

Significant adjustments have occurred since the 1990s via legislative efforts, self-regulatory initiatives and voluntary compliance by Swiss listed corporations with international standards and expectations of large institutional investors.[17] Even so, today's Swiss corporate system remains embedded in the Continental European 'controlling owners' tradition.[18] The focus is still on the long-term well-being of the corporation, with owners generally remaining free to choose the capital structure and to regulate internal affairs.

5.2.3 Board System and Shareholder Rights

When it comes to the board system, Swiss corporations generally have a choice between the UK/US-style unitary model and the German-style two-tier system; a two-tier board is mandatory only for regulated financial institutions.[19] Even where one-tier boards are permitted, corporate practice largely tracks the German model. In 2013, only 33% of the twenty largest Swiss listed companies had one or more members of executive management on the board of directors; in 2017, the figure was even lower, at 20%.[20]

---

[13] *Bundesverfassung (Bundesverfassung der Schweizerischen Eidgenossenschaft)* [Federal Constitution], first enacted 18 April 1999, AS 1999, S 2556, last revised 13 March 2019, SR 101, art 139, para 1.

[14] See Section 5.4.4.

[15] Peter Forstmoser, Arthur Meier-Hayoz and Peter Nobel, *Schweizerisches Aktienrecht [Swiss Corporation Law]* (Stämpfli 1996) s 4, fn 39; Raouf Boucekkine and others, 'Contract Rules in Codes and Statutes: Easing Business Across the Cleavages of Legal Origins' in Michèle Schmiegelow and Henrik Schmiegelow (eds), *Institutional Competition between Common Law and Civil Law: Theory and Policy* (Springer 2014) 59.

[16] Daniel Daeniker, 'Der "Geheimbericht Gautschi" zum Aktienrecht [The "Gautschi Secret Report" on Corporation Law]' (2015) 111 *Schweizerische Juristen-Zeitung* 593, 594.

[17] Hans Caspar von der Crone and Daniel Daeniker, 'Aktienrecht und Finanzmarktregulierung [Corporation Law and Financial Services Regulation]' (2016) 112 *Schweizerische Juristen-Zeitung* 457, 462.

[18] Daniel Daeniker and Daniel Hasler, 'M&A und Governance bei Familiengesellschaften [M&A and Governance in Family-Controlled Companies]' in Rudolf Tschäni (ed), *Mergers & Acquisitions XIX* (Schulthess Verlag 2017) 105–6.

[19] Bankenverordnung (Verordnung über die Banken und Sparkassen) [Banking Ordinance], first enacted 20 April 2014, last revised 6 November 2019, SR 952.02, art 11, para 2; Aufsichtsverordnung (Verordnung über die Beaufsichtigung von privaten Versicherungsunternehmen) [Insurance Supervision Ordinance], first enacted 9 November 2005, last revised 25 November 2015, SR 961.011, art 13, para 1.

[20] Spencer Stuart, 'Switzerland Board Index 2017' (2017) 10 <www.spencerstuart.com/-/media/pdf%20files/research%20and%20insight%20pdfs/biswitzerland_17.pdf> accessed 14 June 2020.

The board of directors of a Swiss corporation has the authority to delegate corporate powers to an executive management team under its control. The relevant statutory provision is strikingly similar to Delaware's equivalent provision.[21] Unlike Delaware law, however, Swiss law provides a list of inalienable and non-delegable powers.[22] Swiss corporate law thereby enables the board of directors to act as the corporation's strategy-setting body, while management's role – at least in theory – is confined to the day-to-day execution of the board's strategy. This sets the Swiss two-tier board system apart from the German equivalent,[23] where the supervisory board (*Aufsichtsrat*) has only a monitoring role,[24] while the management board (*Vorstand*) assumes sole responsibility for leading the company.[25] But the difference between the Swiss and German systems should not be overestimated: like their German counterparts, Swiss non-executive directors are involved in corporate affairs only on a part-time basis – and thus often follow the lead of more involved and better-informed executive managers.

Shareholder rights in Switzerland are similar to those provided in other continental European jurisdictions. Shareholders have a say when it comes to fundamental issues such as the appointment and removal of directors[26] and the approval of board compensation.[27] Shareholders also approve the payment of dividends,[28] executive compensation[29] (while the appointment and removal of executives remains an inalienable board matter),[30] the issuance of new shares[31] and the authorization of equity capital for later issuance by the board of directors.[32]

Fundamental decisions concerning the set-up of a corporation are subject to a shareholder vote with a two-thirds supermajority, such as a change in the corporate purpose, the introduction of dual-class common stock, certain issuances of new shares, the creation of restrictions on the transferability of registered shares, and the change of place of incorporation.[33] The two-third supermajority also applies to mergers and statutory demergers.[34]

---

[21] Compare Swiss Code of Obligations (n 6) art 716, para 2: 'The board of directors manages the business of the company, unless responsibility for such management has been delegated' with Delaware General Corporation Law 1899, last revised 1 January, 2020, Delaware Code, Title 8, ch 1, s 141(a): 'The business and affairs of every corporation organised under this chapter shall be managed by or under the direction of a board of directors ....'

[22] Reserved powers include, among other things, the ultimate direction of the firm; determination of the firm's organization; organization of accounting, financial control and planning systems; appointment, supervision and dismissal of executive management; preparation of the annual report and shareholders' meetings; implementation of shareholders' resolutions; notifying courts in case of insolvency (Swiss Code of Obligations (n 6) art 716a, para 1).

[23] It is notable that the Dutch system follows Germany. See Van der Elst and Lafarre, Shareholder Stewardship in the Netherlands, Chapter 4, Section 4.2.

[24] German *Aktiengesetz* [Stock Corporation Act], first enacted 6 September 1965, last revised 12 December 2019, BGBl. I, 1089, ss 105 and 111, para 4.

[25] German *Aktiengesetz* (n 24) s 76, para 1.

[26] Swiss Code of Obligations (n 6) art 698, para 2(2). In listed companies, directors are elected and re-elected to one-year terms only; see *Verordnung gegen übermässige Vergütungen bei börsenkotierten Aktiengesellschaften* [Ordinance against Excessive Compensation in Listed Companies], enacted 20 November 2013, SR 221.331, art 3, para 2.

[27] Ordinance against Excessive Compensation in Listed Companies (n 26), art 18, para 1; see Section 5.4.4 of this chapter.

[28] Swiss Code of Obligations (n 6) art 698, para 2(4).

[29] Ordinance against Excessive Compensation in Listed Companies (n 26) art 18, para 1; see Section 5.4.4 of this chapter.

[30] Swiss Code of Obligations (n 6) art 716a, para 1(4).

[31] Swiss Code of Obligations (n 6) art 650, para 1.

[32] Authorized capital, which can be issued by the board of directors for other purposes, is limited to 50% of outstanding share capital (Swiss Code of Obligations (n 6) art 651, para 2). Conditional capital, reserved for employee share ownership plans, convertible bonds and similar capital market instruments, is limited to a further 50%, (Swiss Code of Obligations (n 6) art 653a, para 1).

[33] Swiss Code of Obligations (n 6) art 704, para 1.

[34] *Fusionsgesetz* (*Bundesgesetz über Fusion, Spaltung, Umwandlung und Vermögensübertragung*) [Merger Act], first enacted 3 October 2003, last revised 23 December 2011, SR 221.301, art 18, para 1, lit a and art 43, para 2.

Shareholders individually or collectively holding at least 10 per cent of voting rights can request to call an extraordinary shareholders meeting.[35] The 10 per cent threshold also applies to (generally unsuccessful) requests for courts to order a special audit into the affairs of a corporation[36] or the winding-up of the corporation for significant reasons.[37]

Any shareholder may challenge shareholders' resolutions – but generally not board resolutions – that violate the law or the articles of association.[38] In addition, shareholders may take directors and officers to court for breaches of statutory duties.[39] However, Swiss procedural rules do not favour shareholder lawsuits: litigation is governed by the 'loser pays' principle,[40] and plaintiffs are generally requested to post a bond at the suit filing stage.[41] In the Swiss context, these rules effectively deter spurious lawsuits of the kind seen in the US and Germany, with the practical side-effect of protecting incumbent boards of directors.

5.2.4 *Majority Control*

Swiss law has historically favoured majority control. Decisions taken by a majority of shareholders are generally protected by the courts unless there are egregious circumstances indicating an abuse of power.[42] As a result, Swiss corporate law generally benefits incumbent boards. The majority principle is further reinforced by the statutory rules described later in the chapter.[43]

The articles of association may include limitations on voting rights. Listed companies can thus limit shareholder voting, for example when an acquirer refuses to confirm that he or she acquired the shares for their own account, or more generally when the articles of association impose a percentage limitation on the exercise of voting rights.[44] The restriction can be abolished by a shareholders' vote with a supermajority,[45] which often happens in the context of public takeover offers.

In terms of board representation, Swiss law does not recognize class rights or similar minority protection mechanisms.[46] Therefore, the composition of the board of directors can be determined in its entirety by shareholders representing 50 per cent plus one share, regardless of whether a sizeable minority shareholder group wishes otherwise. In addition, co-ordination among shareholders is made difficult owing to the share register being non-public and not available to shareholders.[47] It thus follows that the representation of minorities and the designation of independent directors on Swiss boards of directors are purely voluntary. Notwithstanding this voluntary nature, such representation is recommended by the Swiss Code of Best Practice

---

[35] Swiss Code of Obligations (n 6) art 699, para 3.
[36] Swiss Code of Obligations (n 6) art 697b, para 1.
[37] Swiss Code of Obligations (n 6) art 736(4).
[38] Swiss Code of Obligations (n 6) art 706.
[39] Swiss Code of Obligations (n 6) art 754.
[40] *Zivilprozessordnung* [Civil Procedure Code], first enacted 12 September 1950, last revised 6 November 2019, SR 272, art 106.
[41] Civil Procedure Code (n 40) arts 98 and 99.
[42] Decisions of the Swiss Federal Supreme Court, BGE 99 II 62 (1973) and 136 III 279 (2010).
[43] In contrast, Italy stands out as a champion of the minority shareholder; see Strampelli, Institutional Investor Stewardship in Italian Corporate Governance, Chapter 6, Sections 6.3 and 6.5.
[44] Listed companies sometimes provide for grandfathering provisions in favour of pre-IPO shareholders.
[45] Two-thirds of the shareholder votes represented at the meeting must vote in favour as implied in the Swiss Code of Obligations (n 6) art 704, para 1(3). The articles of association can impose a higher threshold.
[46] Italy appears to be more minority-friendly; see Strampelli, Institutional Investor Stewardship in Italian Corporate Governance, Chapter 6, Section 6.5.
[47] Peter Böckli, *Schweizer Aktienrecht [Swiss Corporation Law]* (4th edn, Schulthess Verlag 2009) s 6, fn 371.

(SCBP)[48] and considered good corporate practice throughout the Swiss listed company universe, even in companies with controlling shareholders.[49]

Proxy materials are drafted by the board of directors acting alone. Thus, minority shareholders who table a proposal have no influence on the wording of proxy statements. In this respect, the US is more shareholder-friendly: SEC Rule 14a-8[50] mandates registered issuers to integrate proposals from eligible shareholders in their proxy materials.[51] Similarly, where US shareholders only need to own shares worth USD 2,000 to file a proposal,[52] the threshold for Swiss shareholders can be as high as 10 per cent of the share capital,[53] soon to be lowered to 0.5 per cent for listed companies.[54]

5.2.5 Shareholder Value and Stakeholder Interests

Swiss corporate law is rather unspecific about the interests that a Swiss board should serve. It essentially states that directors and managers must safeguard the interests of the company,[55] without referring to any particular constituency. This open-ended approach generated the Swiss equivalent of the 1930s debate between US scholars Adolf Berle and Merrick Dodd.[56]

In the US, Berle argued that the corporate purpose was to advance the interests of the owners, predominantly to increase their wealth; if corporate managers were allowed to consider the interests of all constituencies without being legally bound by any, there would be a lack of accountability.[57] Dodd challenged this view by suggesting that not only does a business have responsibilities to the community but corporate managers should – voluntarily and without waiting for legal requirement – also manage it in a way that fulfils those responsibilities.[58] Later iterations of the debate include Milton Friedman's famous quip 'the business of businesses is business',[59] countered by a flurry of proposals advocating the interests of alternative constituencies[60] and most recently a shift in business opinion.[61]

---

[48] On the SCBP, see n 71 and Section 5.4.3 of this chapter.
[49] All of the controlled companies referred to in (n 78) provide for representation by directors who are affiliated neither with the executive management nor with the controlling shareholder(s). In Roche, LafargeHolcim and Swatch, the unaffiliated directors even form a majority of the board.
[50] 17 CFR § 240.14a-8, available online at US Securities and Exchange Commission, 'Amendments to Regulation A: A Small Entity Compliance Guide' (4 February 2019) <www.sec.gov/info/smallbus/secg/regulation-a-amendments-secg.shtml> accessed 14 June 2020.
[51] There are, however, concerns underlying this rule; see Fisch, The Uncertain Stewardship Potential of Index Funds, Chapter 21, this volume.
[52] Securities Exchange Act of 1934, General Rules and Regulations, 17 CFR Part 240, SEC Rule 14a-8(b)(1).
[53] Swiss Code of Obligations (n 6) art 699, para 3. Note that the articles of association may provide for a lower threshold: for example, the threshold at Nestlé S.A. is 0.15% (which still means shares worth around USD 450m).
[54] Swiss Code of Obligations (n 6), new art 699b, para 1(1), expected to enter into effect on 1 January 2022.
[55] Swiss Code of Obligations (n 6) art 717.
[56] On this debate, see Fisch, The Uncertain Stewardship Potential of Index Funds, Chapter 21, Section 21.4.
[57] Adolf A Berle, 'Corporate Powers as Powers in Trust' (1931) 44 *Harvard Law Review* 1049; Adolf A Berle, 'For Whom Corporate Managers Are Trustees: A Note' (1932) 45 *Harvard Law Review* 1365, 1367.
[58] E Merrick Dodd Jr, 'For Whom Are Corporate Managers Trustees?' (1932) 45 *Harvard Law Review* 1145.
[59] Milton Friedman, 'The Social Responsibility of Business Is to Increase Its Profit' The New York Times Magazine (New York, 13 September 1970).
[60] William T Allen, 'Our Schizophrenic Conception of the Corporation' (1992) 14 *Cardozo Law Review* 261, 264–65; Henry J Smith, 'The Shareholders vs. Stakeholders Debate' (2003) 44 *MIT Sloan Management Review* 85.
[61] The US Business Roundtable recently changed its statement on 'the purpose of a corporation' to say that corporate leaders should take into account all stakeholders; see David Benoit, 'Move Over, Shareholders: Top CEOs Say Companies Have Obligations to Society' *The* Wall Street Journal (New York, 19 August 2019) <www.wsj.com/articles/business-roundtable-steps-back-from-milton-friedman-theory-11566205200> accessed 14 June 2020.

But, to date, Friedman's view continues to dominate the line of reasoning in Delaware courts.[62]

The Swiss controversy took place three decades after the Berle–Dodd debate. In 1959, Walter Schluep, the most prominent corporate law scholar of his time, summarized the prevalent view in Swiss legal writing and court practice as follows: the role of a corporation is to serve the interests of the enterprise, understood as a long-term profit-making entity operating to benefit shareholders, employees, creditors and society alike.[63] This approach presaged the modern definition of the stakeholder principle; yet, Schluep's view was probably more inspired by the cartelistic structure of the Swiss economy at the time of writing than by considerations of social justice and concern for the environment.

In the early 1960s, various scholars challenged Schluep's view, contending that shareholders expected and deserved nothing more than investment returns.[64] Nevertheless, the Swiss courts have sided with Schluep, consistently taking stakeholder interests into account when adjudicating shareholder lawsuits.[65] Also, if ever the Swiss Federal Supreme Court endorses shareholder interests, the focus is always on long-term profitability.[66] In financial services regulation, shareholders' interests generally take a back seat against the interests of depositors or the stability of the financial system – especially after the GFC.[67]

This is not to say that the shareholder value theory was never fashionable in Switzerland; the theory gained some popularity in the late 1980s, but quickly lost ground in the early 2000s, when the Dotcom bubble burst and corporate scandals such as WorldCom, Enron, Parmalat and Satyam cast doubt on the shareholder-centric model. The GFC further increased scepticism towards the shareholder value proposition.[68] It thus comes as no surprise that the stakeholder principle continues to pervade Swiss corporate law and practice.[69] In particular, the 2014 revision of the SCBP[70] emphasizes the responsibility of a Swiss corporate board for the sustainable

[62] Leo E Strine Jr, 'The Dangers of Denial: The Need for a Clear-Eyed Understanding of the Power and Accountability Structure Established by the Delaware General Corporation Law' (2015) 50 *Wake Forest Law Review* 761.
[63] Walter Schluep, 'Schutz des Aktionärs auf neuen Wegen? [New Ways for Shareholder Protection?]' (1961) 33 *Die Schweizerische Aktiengesellschaft* [SAG] 137, 170 and 188.
[64] Rolf Bär, 'Grundprobleme des Minderheitenschutzes in der Aktiengesellschaft [Fundamental Issues Concerning Minority Protection in the Corporation]' (1959) 95 *Zeitschrift des Bernischen Juristenvereins* [ZBJV] 369; Georg Gautschi, *Bericht und Vorschläge zu einer Revision des schweizerischen Aktienrechts von 1936* [Report and Proposals on an Amendment of the 1936 Corporation Law] (Unpublished Report, Archives Fédérales Suisses, E 4110 (b) 1989/197, vol 37, 1966) 232.
[65] Decisions of the Federal Supreme Court, BGE 95 II 164 (1969) 104 II 35 (1978) 105 II 128 (1979) and 138 III 298 (2012). One of the few judgments explicitly favouring shareholders over alternative constituencies was rendered in BGE 126 III 268 (2000), though subsequent cases demonstrate that the Federal Supreme Court continues to weigh stakeholder interests against those of the shareholders; see BGE 136 III 280 (2010).
[66] Decisions of the Federal Supreme Court, BGE 100 II 393 (1974) and 136 III 282 (2010).
[67] This now appears to be a universal view; see Klaus J Hopt, 'Comparative Company Law' in Mathias Reimann and Reinhard Zimmermann (eds), *The Oxford Handbook of Comparative Law* (2nd edn, OUP 2019) 1137.
[68] Peter Forstmoser, 'Profit – Das Mass aller Dinge? [Profits – The Measure of All Things?]' in Roger Zäch and others (eds), *Individuum und Verband: Festgabe zum schweizerischen Juristentag* [Commemorative Publication of the Swiss Lawyers' Day] (Schulthess Verlag 2006) 71–72; Arhur Meier-Hayoz, Peter Forstmoser and Rolf Sethe, *Schweizerisches Gesellschaftsrecht* [Swiss Corporate Law] (12th edn, Stämpfli 2018) 328–43. One of us continues to endorse the shareholder value theory, arguing along the lines of Berle; see Daniel Daeniker, 'Wer kontrolliert die Aktiengesellschaft? [Who Controls the Corporation?]' [2016] *Schweizerische Zeitschrift für Wirtschafts- und Finanzmarktrecht* [SZW] 434, 436.
[69] Peter Böckli, 'Corporate Boards in Switzerland' in Paul Davies, Klaus Hopt, Richard Nowak and Gerard van Solinge (eds), *Corporate Boards in Law and Practice: A Comparative Analysis in Europe* (OUP 2013) 660 points out that Swiss discourse tends to focus less on such fundamental questions but, rather, as is explored in this chapter, strives to address more concrete problems like shareholders' rights, minority protection and, especially, excessive executive pay.
[70] On the SCBP, see Section 5.4.3 of this chapter.

development of enterprises[71] and – unlike its 2002 predecessor[72] – downplays shareholder value considerations.

Major Swiss corporations, for their part, endorse broader entrepreneurial goals in their articles of association. For example, the articles of Nestlé S.A., one of the world's largest food and beverage manufacturers and Europe's most capitalized company,[73] expressly state that the company 'shall, in pursuing its business purpose, aim for long-term, sustainable value creation'.[74]

Even so, the Swiss variant of the stakeholder principle is not as far-reaching as other Continental European jurisdictions. Employee relations provide a good example: Swiss corporate practice has always emphasized their importance, as evidenced by a conspicuous absence of strikes and collective bargaining disputes. However, while employee interests are included in the Swiss stakeholder principle,[75] Swiss law fails to give employees a formal voice in corporate decision-making: unlike in Germany and many other EU jurisdictions, co-determination of employees never took hold in Swiss legislation or practice.[76]

5.3 OWNERSHIP REGIME IN SWISS CORPORATIONS

5.3.1 *The Role of Long-Term Shareholders*

The blueprint for Swiss listed as well as unlisted companies has been the *family-controlled business enterprise*, with outside capital provided by non-management family members or, at a more mature stage, outside investors.[77] By nature, family companies take the long-term view, thinking in generations rather than calendar quarters. As a result, family shareholders have often embraced the interests of other constituencies, including those of the company's employees, its customers and the community in which a given company operates.

As part of the family company blueprint, some of the largest Swiss corporations, including Nestlé and Roche, still bear the names of their founders. More significantly, among the twenty highest capitalized Swiss companies – all worldwide leaders in their field – five still feature significant or even controlling family shareholders.[78]

---

[71] economiesuisse, 'Swiss Code of Best Practice for Corporate Governance' (2016) 9 <www.economiesuisse.ch/sites/default/files/publications/economiesuisse_swisscode_e_web.pdf> accessed 14 June 2020. The approach is similar to the Dutch emphasis on 'long-term value creation'; seeVan der Elst and Lafarre, Shareholder Stewardship in the Netherlands, Chapter 4, Section 4.2.

[72] See economiesuisse, 'Swiss Code of Best Practice for Corporate Governance' (2002) 2.2 <www.ecgi.org/codes/documents/swisscodeofbestpractice_english.pdf> accessed 22 February 2022.

[73] 'Nestlé Now Europe's Most Valuable Company' *Le News* (10 January 2019) <https://lenews.ch/2019/01/10/nestle-now-europes-most-valuable-company/> accessed 11 February 2022.

[74] Nestlé, 'Articles of Association of Nestlé S.A.' (11 April 2019) art 2, para 3 <www.nestle.com/sites/default/files/asset-library/documents/library/documents/corporate_governance/articles-of-association-of-nestle-en.pdf> accessed 14 June 2020.

[75] See text accompanying n 63.

[76] Forstmoser, Meier-Hayoz and Nobel (n 15) s 3, fn 73.

[77] See also Lim and Puchniak, Can a Global Legal Misfit Be Fixed?, Chapter 28 on controlling shareholders and stewardship.

[78] These companies are Roche (pharmaceuticals), Richemont (luxury goods), Schindler (elevators and escalators), Swatch Group (watches) and LafargeHolcim (cement); in four of these five companies (Roche, Richemont, Schindler and Swatch), the founding families continue to have voting control. Some continental European jurisdictions such as Italy feature even more concentrated ownership; see Strampelli, Institutional Investor Stewardship in Italian Corporate Governance, Chapter 6, Section 6.2.

In listed companies without controlling shareholders, a similar responsible ownership perspective is sometimes taken by so-called anchor shareholders, investors with a clearly stated long-term investment horizon.[79] Sometimes, listed companies try to enlist the support of anchor shareholders via control arrangements allowing for representation on the board of directors.[80] While anchor shareholders may not think in generations as families do, they invest well beyond the short term. In that vein, anchor shareholders are merely the most recent avatar of the family shareholder model.

The Swiss statutory regime enables controlling shareholder structures by allowing the issuance of *dual-class common stock*, whereby the statute sets maximum voting leverage at ten to one.[81] The number of listed corporations that adopt such weighted voting rights (WVR) structures is getting smaller from year to year.[82] This evolution is sometimes attributed to a widely publicized dispute involving Sika. In that case, the family who controlled a Swiss listed building materials company transferred its voting control – based on merely 16 per cent of the share capital – to a French rival, without arranging for a public takeover offer to minority shareholders or even involving the board of directors. The move alienated the public shareholders, who had provided more than 80 per cent of the company's capital, and resulted in years of litigation followed by a settlement.[83] In our view, however, the Sika case is an outlier; the use of WVR structures remains broadly undisputed and is not expected to change in the context of the current Swiss corporate law reform proposals.[84]

In today's Swiss corporate landscape, even though family-controlled listed companies are diminishing in number, the Swiss blueprint for shareholder engagement has not fundamentally changed. The long-term view remains the norm in most Swiss companies.[85] In addition, Swiss corporate boards are increasingly engaged in a dialogue with their key institutional shareholders.[86] While this dialogue may lead to a cacophony of views, its purpose is the same as it was under the controlling shareholders regime: allowing managers – agents of a corporation's owners – better to understand what their principals really want.

5.3.2 *Costs and Benefits of Corporate Control*

As discussed,[87] Swiss corporate law generally favours majority control, protects legacy shareholder groups and gives incumbent corporate boards significant discretion. Moreover, the Swiss

---

[79] Rolf Watter and Dieter Dubs, 'Anchor Shareholders und Grossaktionäre [Anchor Shareholders and Large Shareholders]' in Rudolf Tschäni (ed), *Mergers & Acquisitions XII* (Schulthess Verlag 2010) 3.
[80] Watter and Dubs (n 79) 14.
[81] Swiss Code of Obligations (n 6) art 693, para 2.
[82] Daniel Daeniker, 'One Share, One Vote – Bedeutung der Debatte für die M&A-Praxis [One Share, One Vote – The Debate's Meaning for M&A-Practice]' in Rudolf Tschäni (ed), *Mergers & Acquisitions XV* (Schulthess Verlag 2013) 149.
[83] Daniel Imwinkelried, 'Ein Kompromiss zur allseitigen Gesichtswahrung beendet den Sika-Zwist [A Compromise for Universal Face-Saving Ends the Sika Brawl]' *Neue Zürcher Zeitung* (Zurich, 11 May 2018) <www.nzz.ch/wirtschaft/ein-kompromiss-zur-allseitigen-gesichtswahrung-ld.1384990> accessed 14 June 2020; see also Daniel Daeniker, 'Understanding Sika: Who Controls a Public Company?' (*Spencer Stuart*, 2015) 5–6 <www.homburger.ch/en/publications/understanding-sika-controls-swiss-public-company> accessed 9 February 2022.
[84] Federal Council, 'Botschaft des Bundesrates zur Änderung des Obligationenrechts' [Dispatch on the Amendment Swiss Code of Obligations] [2017] Bundesblatt [BBl] 399, 461.
[85] Contrary to, for example, France, Switzerland has never seen a need for measures to encourage long-term shareholding (Böckli, 'Corporate Boards in Switzerland' (n 69) 689).
[86] See text accompanying n 133.
[87] See Section 5.2.4.

litigation system deters rather than encourages shareholder lawsuits owing to the 'loser pays' rule.[88]

Does this mean that minority shareholders are subject to abuses of majority power, with controlling shareholders reaping the *private benefits of control* or even engaging in corporate looting?[89] Empirically, corporate scandals involving fraud or majority shareholder enrichment are few and far between; the most spectacular failures usually involved listed companies with a dispersed shareholder base rather than those with concentrated ownership.[90]

That said, controlling or anchor shareholders seem to have a sobering effect on management and foster a stewardship state of mind.[91] The claim sometimes made by private equity investors – that direct control is superior to public ownership in terms of monitoring management[92] – also seems to apply to Swiss listed firms. Moreover, dominant shareholders often bear the *private costs of control*.[93] When their reputation and entrepreneurial track record are good, other investors can even take a free ride on their efforts.

The historical evidence is inconclusive on whether controlled companies perform better or worse than companies with dispersed share ownership.[94] Recent research suggests that the family business model provides superior returns: according to a Credit Suisse 2018 study conducted over more than a decade,[95] Swiss family-owned companies outperformed Swiss non-controlled companies by 9 per cent per year.[96]

---

[88] See Section 5.2.5.
[89] On corporate looting generally, see Frank H Easterbrook and Daniel R Fischel, *The Economic Structure of Corporate Law* (Harvard University Press 1991) 129–30; Ronald Gilson and Jeffrey Gordon, 'Controlling Controlling Shareholders' (2003) 152 *University of Pennsylvania Law Review* 785; Luca Enriques, Henry Hansmann, Reinier Kraakman and Mariana Pargendler, 'The Basic Governance Structure: Minority Shareholders and Non-shareholder Constituencies' in Reinier Kraakman and others (eds), *The Anatomy of Corporate Law: A Comparative and Functional Approach* (3rd edn, OUP 2017) 79. By contrast, for a discussion on minority shareholder protection in Switzerland and how American notions of majority shareholding may (unintentionally) undermine it, see Peter Böckli, 'Stimmenmehrheit unter Verdacht: Wege und Irrwege im aktienrechtlichen Minderheitenschutz [Majority Voting Under Suspicion: Ways and Errors in Minority Protection under Corporate Law]' [2016] SZW 444, 447.
[90] The grounding and subsequent insolvency of Switzerland's flag carrier Swissair in 2001, the losses of UBS in the GFC and governance failures in the Raiffeisen banking group uncovered in 2018 all arose in companies without controlling shareholders. A counter-example involved family-controlled Bank Vontobel in 2001, but that scandal related to a series of compliance breaches by executive management rather than corporate looting.
[91] Ringe, Stewardship and Shareholder Engagement in Germany, Chapter 9, Section 9.3.2.2 critically reflects on this theory in the context of controlling shareholders in Germany. Puchniak and Tang, Singapore's Embrace of Shareholder Stewardship, Chapter 14 provides an antithesis hereto with the Singaporean model of state majority shareholding.
[92] Felix Barber and Michael Goold, 'The Strategic Secret of Private Equity' *Harvard Business Review* (September 2007) <https://hbr.org/2007/09/the-strategic-secret-of-private-equity> accessed 14 June 2020.
[93] Karl Hofstetter, 'One Size Does Not Fit All: Corporate Governance for "Controlled Companies"' (2006) 31 *North Carolina Journal of International Law and Commercial Regulation* 597, 619; Daniel Daeniker, 'Angebotspflicht und Kontrollprämie – die Schweiz gegen den Rest der Welt? [Mandatory Bid Obligation and Control Premium – Switzerland against the Rest of the World?]' in Rudolf Tschäni (ed), *Mergers & Acquisitions XIII* (Schulthess Verlag 2010) 95, 101.
[94] Hofstetter (n 93) 608–14.
[95] Eugene Klerk, Maria Bhatti, Richard Kersley and Brandon Vair, 'The Swiss Family Business Model' (Credit Suisse Research Institute, September 2017) <www.credit-suisse.com/media/assets/corporate/docs/about-us/research/publications/the-swiss-family-business-model.pdf> accessed 14 June 2020; Eugene Klerk, Maria Bhatti, Richard Kersley and Brandon Vair, 'The CS Family 1000 in 2018' (Credit Suisse Research Institute, September 2018) <www.credit-suisse.com/media/assets/corporate/docs/about-us/research/publications/the-cs-family-1000-in-2018.pdf> accessed 14 June 2020.
[96] Klerk, Bhatti, Kersley and Vair, 'The CS Family 1000 in 2018' (n 95) 6, 9. This study also shows that, on a worldwide basis, family-owned companies outperformed companies with dispersed shareholdings by 4% year on year (Klerk, Bhatti, Kersley and Vair, 'The CS Family 1000 in 2018' (n 95) 7). This is not as spectacular as in Switzerland, but is still quite respectable.

5.3.3 *Institutional Share Ownership and Voting Behaviour*

Public equity markets around the world are increasingly dominated by large institutional investors, with commentators detecting a rising influence of the 'Giant Three' – BlackRock, State Street and Vanguard.[97] In the US, funds advised or managed by the 'Giant Three' own around 20 per cent of S&P 500 shares, but control around 25 per cent of the votes because they are more likely to cast their votes than other investors.[98]

In Switzerland, institutional share ownership is generally increasing,[99] but the concentration of voting rights is much less pronounced than in the US. Based on public reporting for positions at or above 3% of voting rights,[100] BlackRock at year-end 2018 held significant positions in seventeen of the top twenty Swiss listed corporations and in twenty-one of the next thirty; its median shareholding was still below 5%.[101] State Street, for its part, disclosed one position above 3%, whereas Vanguard reported none.[102] In other words, even assuming that each of the 'Giant Three' holds sizeable positions below 3% in every large and mid-cap Swiss listed corporation, their combined shareholdings would remain in the single digits, as compared to 20% in the US.

In addition, the two largest Swiss asset managers, UBS and Credit Suisse, as of year-end 2018 reported positions above 3 per cent only in eight and five, respectively, of the top fifty Swiss listed corporations.[103] One may, therefore, conclude that no single institutional investor dominates the Swiss corporate landscape.[104] That said, the collective influence of institutional investors as a class is sizeable: among those Swiss corporations that voluntarily disclose the aggregate number of shares held by private and by institutional shareholders,[105] the latter's collective holdings range between 50 per cent and 82 per cent.[106]

More importantly, voting participation in Swiss shareholders' meetings has increased substantially, from 50% in 2011 to 66% in 2017.[107] The increase is even more significant in companies without dominant shareholders – from 34% in 2012 to 61% in 2016.[108] Recent surveys suggest that increased shareholder participation is coupled with a marked improvement in shareholder engagement, that is, an increasing dialogue between institutional investors and Swiss corporate

---

[97] For the US, see Lucian Bebchuk and Scott Hirst, 'The Specter of the Giant Three' (2019) 99 *Boston University Law Review* 721; Fisch, The Uncertain Stewardship Potential of Index Funds, Chapter 21, Section 21.3, this volume.

[98] Bebchuk and Hirst (n 97) 724, 736.

[99] To take an example, Nestlé S.A. reported an increase in institutional (as opposed to private) share ownership from 70% to 80% between 2002 and 2018.

[100] Pursuant to the Swiss Finanzmarktinfrastrukturgesetz (Bundesgesetz über die Finanzmarktinfrastrukturen und das Marktverhalten im Effekten- und Derivatehandel) [Financial Market Infrastructures Act], first enacted 19 June 2015, last revised 6 November 2019, SR 958.1, art 120, para 1, shareholders must report acquisitions of 3% or more of a Swiss listed company's voting rights.

[101] Source: proprietary research compiled on the basis of public record information.

[102] Source: proprietary research compiled on the basis of public record information.

[103] Source: proprietary research.

[104] This is in drastic contrast to the corporate landscape in Singapore, where the state acts as a dominant shareholder-behemoth (see Puchniak and Tang, Singapore's Embrace of Shareholder Stewardship, Chapter 14, Section 14.2).

[105] Eight of the top fifty Swiss corporations (Nestlé, Swiss Re, Credit Suisse, Swisscom, Adecco, Swiss Prime Site, PSP Swiss Property, and Georg Fischer, in order of market capitalization) disclose the aggregate shareholdings of institutional investors.

[106] Source: proprietary research.

[107] Yola Biedermann, Fanny Ebener, Christian Richoz, Valérie Roethlisberger, Sébastien Dubas and Romain Perruchoud, 'Ethos Studie 2017: Generalversammlung, Vergütungen, Corporate Governance [Ethos Study 2017: Shareholders' Meetings, Compensation, Governance]' (Ethos, August 2017) 8 <www.ethosfund.ch/sites/default/files/2017-08/EtudeAG17_DE_FINAL.pdf> accessed 14 June 2020.

[108] Alexander Wagner and Christoph W Bernasconi, 'Corporate Governance: Beyond Best Practice' (Swiss Finance Institute White Paper, December 2016) 19 <www.sfi.ch/system/tdf/WP_CorporateGovernance_BeyondBestPractice_WEB.pdf?file=1> accessed 14 June 2020.

boards.[109] Foreign institutional investors appear to be more active than Swiss asset managers and pension funds who are more likely to rely on the services of proxy advisory firms.[110]

Proxy advisers control around 30 per cent of the 'free float' shareholder votes in most Swiss listed companies.[111] ISS is by far the most influential, followed by Glass Lewis.[112] By contrast, Ethos, the most prominent Swiss player in the field, generally moves less than 5 per cent of shareholder votes. However, domestic proxy advisers are more relevant when it comes to relations with the Swiss financial press. There is also anecdotal evidence of proxy adviser influence decreasing with the contentious nature of a shareholder vote.[113] One may consider this to be efficient behaviour: when faced with controversy, boards are forced to do a better job in explaining the merits of a proposal, which in turn allows for informed voting by shareholders at large.

5.4 FROM STAKEHOLDER INTERESTS TO SHAREHOLDER STEWARDSHIP

5.4.1 *What Drives Shareholder Stewardship in Switzerland?*

The shareholder stewardship approach assumes that investors exercise their property rights responsibly.[114] This concept can be seen as an exception to the rule enshrined in Swiss law[115] that a shareholder owes no duty to the corporation.[116] While Swiss law subjects large stakeholders to reporting obligations for substantial shareholdings[117] and to public takeover offer obligations for control transactions,[118] it does not impose a duty on any shareholders to exercise their voting rights responsibly.[119]

This absence of statutory duties seems to leave the door open for abuses by dominant shareholders. However, Swiss courts have provided a counterbalance: Swiss corporate boards – whose members are subject to fiduciary duties – are protected against the demands of shareholders with no such duties by the stakeholder principle.[120]

The stakeholder principle is not the sole contributor to stewardship. Responsible behaviour also occurs where shareholders are willing to take the long-term view. Various factors can

---

[109] Daniel Daeniker, 'Was ist "wirtschaftsverträgliches" Aktienrecht? [What Is "Business-Friendly" Corporation Law?]' [2019] *Schweizerische Zeitschrift für Wirtschafts- und Finanzmarktrecht* 438, 448.
[110] Wagner and Bernasconi (n 108) 20; see also n 129.
[111] Mariel Hoch, 'Proxy Advisory' [2016] *Schweizerische Zeitschrift für Wirtschafts- und Finanzmarktrecht* 487, 488. Wagner and Bernasconi put the number at 20%, see Wagner and Bernasconi (n 108) 21.
[112] See James R Copland, David F Larcker and Brian Tayan, 'The Big Thumb on the Scale: An Overview of the Proxy Advisory Industry' (2018) Stanford University Graduate School of Business Research Paper No 18-27 <https://ssrn.com/abstract=3188174> accessed 14 June 2020.
[113] Specifically, in a contested shareholder vote on Credit Suisse's executive compensation in 2017, the influence of proxy advisers on the outcome of the vote was lower than anticipated (Daniel Daeniker and Joy Malka, 'Salärgovernance: Zwischenbilanz und Lehren für die Aktienrechtsrevision [Salary Governance: Taking Stock and Learnings for the Corporation Law Reform]' [2017] *Schweizerische Zeitschrift für Wirtschafts- und Finanzmarktrecht* 564, 568, fn 31).
[114] See the comments in Section 5.1 of this chapter.
[115] Swiss Code of Obligations (n 6) art 680, para 1.
[116] This rule is in stark contrast to the Swiss law rule governing partnerships, which emphasizes the duty of loyalty of each partner towards the business venture (Swiss Code of Obligations (n 6) art 536).
[117] See n 100.
[118] Swiss Financial Market Infrastructures Act (n 100) art 135.
[119] The situation is different where an individual shareholder also sits on the board of directors of the company in question; here the fiduciary duties placed upon a board member may well also have an impact on the way the shareholder exercises ownership rights.
[120] See Section 5.2.5.

contribute to shareholders switching to stewardship mode. One is pressure from large institutional investors, who themselves pursue a stewardship agenda.[121] Another is the ability of Swiss voters to launch popular initiatives,[122] thanks to which significant shifts in public opinion have a direct and immediate impact on corporate law and practice. They can be seen as an attempt to press large institutional shareholders to exercise the same function of *responsible and enlightened shareholding* that controlling family members have traditionally assumed.[123]

5.4.2 Do Institutional Shareholders Assume a Stewardship Role?

International institutional investors are starting to play a more engaged role globally. They often do so without formally subscribing to stewardship principles, even though some prominent players have published their own stewardship standards.[124] International institutional investors appear to be more convinced than their Swiss counterparts of the positive effects of exercising voting rights.[125] By implication, they are more willing to incur the costs of making an informed decision when casting their votes, again moving towards what controlling family shareholders have always done.[126]

Swiss-based collective investment schemes[127] and pension funds[128] are legally bound to exercise their voting rights in listed companies, but there are no laws, self-regulatory instruments or industry guidelines detailing how these voting rights should be exercised. For Swiss-based asset managers, no rules exist at all. Given their lack of motivation when it comes to making informed decisions, it comes as no surprise that Swiss institutional investors are unlikely to engage with corporate boards.[129] They are more prone to follow the recommendations of proxy advisers, thus applying an unhelpful 'one-size-fits-all' approach when exercising their voting rights. Going forward, however, we expect Swiss institutional investors eventually to follow their international brethren in assuming responsible and enlightened share ownership.[130]

Even activist investors, often criticized for their short-term approach to governance, nowadays engage in some degree of oversight. Clearly, a constructive contribution to corporate decision-making is a function of their ability to present convincing ideas to management or shareholders.[131] Whether activists follow principles of responsible ownership or are simply out

---

[121] BlackRock principles on investment stewardship (BlackRock, 'Investment Stewardship' <www.blackrock.com/corporate/about-us/investment-stewardship> accessed 14 June 2020); Vanguard Investment Stewardship Commentary (Vanguard Group, 'What We Do. How We Do It. Why It Matters' (*Vanguard*, April 2019) <https://global.vanguard.com/documents/vg-investment-stewardship-why-it-matters.pdf> accessed 12 February 2022.

[122] See Section 5.2.1.

[123] See Section 5.3.1.

[124] See n 121.

[125] SWIPRA, 'Market Discipline and Regulation: A Survey by SWIPRA' (2015) 19 <www.swipra.ch/uploads/news/SWIPRA_Survey2015_Results_web_V2.pdf> accessed 14 June 2020; SWIPRA, 'Corporate Governance between Globalization, Shareholder Activism and Proxy Advisors: A Survey by SWIPRA' (2016) 10 <www.swipra.ch/uploads/news/SWIPRA_Survey2016_Results_web.pdf> accessed 14 June 2020.

[126] See text accompanying n 93.

[127] *Kollektivanlagegesetz (Bundesgesetz über die kollektiven Kapitalanlagen)* [Collective Investment Schemes Act], first enacted 23 June 2006, last revised 6 November 2019, SR 951.31, art 23, para 1.

[128] Ordinance against Excessive Compensation in Listed Companies (n 26) art 22.

[129] A survey taken in 2016 among Swiss and foreign institutional investors indicates a 100% engagement level for foreign investors against merely 42% for Swiss asset managers and a paltry 24% for Swiss pension funds; see SWIPRA (n 125) 12.

[130] On how institutional investors adopt enlightened stewardship in the UK, see Dionysia Katelouzou, *The Path to Enlightened Shareholder Stewardship* (CUP) (forthcoming).

[131] Ronald Gilson and Jeffrey Gordon, 'The Agency Costs of Agency Capitalism: Activist Investors and the Revaluation of Governance Rights' (2013) 113 *Columbia Law Review* 863.

for the short-term gain remains open to debate.[132] But even an activist with short-term goals may ultimately end up protecting long-term shareholder and stakeholder interests (e.g. by rooting out management failures that are detrimental to all constituencies).

In any event, Swiss corporate boards will be forced to engage more actively with their shareholders to ensure that their motions carry the day. Clearly, the decision-making process is more cumbersome when a listed company board has to engage with twenty or thirty sizeable shareholders rather than with one person or family only. Nevertheless, there is evidence of an increased interest in stewardship engagement on both sides: corporate boards are increasingly willing to listen, and more and more investors are willing to assume the private costs of intervention.[133]

5.4.3 Evolving Self-Regulatory Instruments

Two self-regulatory instruments are of interest when it comes to responsible shareholding: the SCBP,[134] a self-regulatory instrument applicable to all Swiss listed companies, and the *Guidelines for Institutional Investors Governing the Exercising of Participation Rights in Public Limited Companies* (Swiss Guidelines). The SCBP was published by economiesuisse, a Swiss non-governmental organization (NGO) representing the interests of the Swiss business community.[135] The Swiss Guidelines were a joint effort of economiesuisse and all relevant interest groups.[136]

The SCBP was first promulgated in 2002 and revised in 2014. It is relatively similar to codes adopted elsewhere, in particular the UK.[137] Its scope addresses the *governance of companies* rather than shareholder conduct. Nevertheless, it had the practical effect of significantly increasing shareholder rights and shareholder engagement by improving transparency and corporate processes.

The SCBP only provides recommendations. It is governed by the 'comply or explain' principle, under which a company must explain if and why it does not follow a specific recommendation.[138] Despite its soft-law character, the SCBP has proven to be remarkably effective in Swiss corporate practice, especially with regards to facilitating the exercise of shareholder rights,[139] board independence and diversity,[140] and transparency of governance

---

[132] Bebchuk and others argue that short-termism is a myth and that activist interventions demonstrably have a long-term effect on shareholder value (Lucian Bebchuk, Alon Brav and Wei Jiang, 'The Long-Term Effects of Hedge Fund Activism' (2015) 115 *Columbia Law Review* 1085; Institutional Shareholder Services (ISS), 'The IRR of "No"' (22 October 2014) <https://pcg.law.harvard.edu/wp-content/uploads/2016/02/Hostile-Bids-The-IRR-of-No.pdf> accessed 14 June 2020). A contrary view is taken by Martin Lipton and others, 'The Long-Term Value of the Poison Pill' (*Harvard Law School Forum on Corporate Governance*, 18 December 2015) <https://corpgov.law.harvard.edu/2015/12/18/the-long-term-value-of-the-poison-pill/> accessed 14 June 2020.

[133] Daeniker, 'Was ist "wirtschaftsverträgliches" Aktienrecht?' (n 109) 448.

[134] See n 71.

[135] ibid.

[136] economiesuisse joined forces with the government (Swiss Federal Office for Social Security, responsible for the oversight of Switzerland's statutory old-age pension system), industry groups including the Association of Swiss Pension Fund Providers and the Swiss Bankers Association, as well as Ethos, the Swiss Foundation for Sustainable Development.

[137] Böckli, *Schweizer Aktienrecht* (n 47) s 14, fn 220.

[138] The SIX Swiss Exchange requires Swiss listed companies to discuss their compliance with the SCBP as part of their annual reporting; see *Richtlinie Corporate Governance (Richtlinie betr. Informationen zur Corporate Governance)* [Corporate Governance Directive], first enacted 17 April 2002, revised 20 June 2019, art 7. The UK applies a more rigorous standard; see Katelouzou and Micheler, The Market for Stewardship and the Role of the Government, Chapter 3, Section 3.3, this volume.

[139] The SCBP, among other things, nudged Swiss public companies to reduce the threshold level for shareholder proposals; economiesuisse (n 71) 7 and text accompanying n 57.

[140] economiesuisse (n 71) 10–11.

processes in general.[141] This development is partly driven by disclosure requirements imposed by the SIX Swiss Exchange,[142] partly by a desire of Swiss corporations to be seen as good corporate citizens,[143] and finally – to the extent that the SCBP mirrors international trends – by pressure exerted by institutional investors and proxy advisers.[144]

Looking at the SCBP from the stewardship angle, the 2002 version was first and foremost an initiative to increase shareholder engagement, while its 2014 version added an element of responsible business conduct. The SCBP 2002 referred to the pursuit of shareholder interests, while the 2014 version focuses on the *sustainable development* of enterprises.[145] This evolution reflects the shareholder-stakeholder shift discussed earlier.[146] Moreover, as the explanatory report to the 2014 SCBP[147] states, corporate value creation presupposes that companies are equally serious about corporate social responsibility. Market dynamics, held before the GFC to be the holy grail of all economic activity, are mentioned only in the context of market failures – a clear paradigm shift.[148]

The Swiss Guidelines, for their part, address the *conduct of shareholders* rather than the inner workings of a corporate venture. They were promulgated in 2013 and constitute a somewhat watered-down version of the UK Code 2012.[149] In particular, as is made clear in the comparison in Table 5.1, the UK Code repeatedly refers to stewardship when addressing institutional investor obligations; by contrast, the corresponding provisions of the Swiss Guidelines do not use the term at all. This is owing to the Swiss Guidelines focusing on the presumed interests of the clients of Swiss asset managers – the ultimate beneficiaries of investment funds, pension funds and the like. In other words, the Swiss Guidelines address the principal-agent problem of asset managers[150] rather than concerns relating to responsible shareholding. The approach is similar to the one taken by the EU Shareholder Rights Directive II,[151] which holds that a medium- to long-term approach in share ownership is a key enabler of *responsible stewardship* of assets,[152] but does not promulgate any obligations on shareholders to this effect.

The Swiss Guidelines are *voluntary*. So far, only a few institutional investors, all of them Swiss, have formally subscribed to their principles. Their impact on the Swiss governance landscape is therefore much less tangible than for the SCBP.

---

[141] Böckli, 'Corporate Boards in Switzerland' (n 69) 707, notes the success of the SCBP as a complement to the Corporate Governance Directive, with Swiss listed companies only rarely deviating from their respective recommendations.

[142] See n 137.

[143] Daniel Daeniker, 'Good Governance bei M&A-Transaktionen [Good Governance in M&A Transactions]' in Rudolf Tschäni (ed), *Mergers & Acquisitions XX* (Schulthess Verlag 2018) 75, 85.

[144] 'Comply or explain' does not work equally well in all legal systems; see Varottil, Shareholder Stewardship in India, Chapter 17, Section 17.5 and Ouko, Stewardship Code in Kenya, Chapter 23, Section 23.4.

[145] economiesuisse (n 71) 9. The interests of a corporation's owners are mentioned only in passing when it comes to aligning executive compensation with the interests of long-term committed shareholders; see economiesuisse (n 71) 19.

[146] See text accompanying nn 68–71.

[147] Karl Hofstetter, 'Swiss Code of Best Practice for Corporate Governance 2014: Grundlagenbericht zur Revision [Swiss Code of Best Practice for Corporate Governance 2014, Fundamental Report on the Revision]' (*economiesuisse*, 2014) 4 <www.economiesuisse.ch/sites/default/files/publications/swiss-code-best-practice-basic-report-de.pdf> accessed 14 June 2020.

[148] Peter Nobel, *Das Aktienrecht: Systematische Darstellung [Corporation Law: Systematic Description]* (Stämpfli 2017) 586.

[149] For a critical review, see Katelouzou and Micheler, The Market for Stewardship and the Role of the Government, Chapter 3, Sections 3.3 and 3.4.

[150] Gilson and Gordon (n 131); Daeniker, 'Wer kontrolliert die Aktiengesellschaft?' (n 68) 442–43.

[151] Directive (EU) 2017/828 of the European Parliament and of the Council of 17 May 2017 amending Directive 2007/36/ EC as regards the encouragement of long-term shareholder engagement [2017] OJ L132/1.

[152] ibid 19, preamble.

TABLE 5.1 *Comparison of the UK Code and the Swiss Guidelines*

UK Stewardship Code	Swiss Guidelines
Institutional investors should:	Institutional investors assume certain responsibilities in the exercising of their participation rights.
1 Publicly disclose their policy on how they will discharge their stewardship responsibilities.	1 No direct equivalent.
2 Have a robust policy on managing conflicts of interest in relation to stewardship which should be publicly disclosed.	2 Institutional investors shall take due account of the interests of their clients when exercising their participation rights.
3 Monitor their investee companies.	3 Institutional investors are to exercise their participation rights insofar as this is deemed appropriate and feasible in the interests of their clients.
4 Establish clear guidelines on when and how they will escalate their stewardship activities.	4 Institutional investors shall assume responsibility for exercising the participation rights to which they are entitled.
5 Be willing to act collectively with other investors where appropriate.	5 No direct equivalent.
6 Have a clear policy on voting and disclosure of voting activity.	6 Institutional investors shall communicate the principles and processes involved in exercising their participation rights to their clients.
7 Report periodically on their stewardship and voting activities.	7 Once a year, institutional investors shall disclose the manner in which they have exercised their participation rights.

5.4.4 *Statutory Reform*

In recent years, the considerations of responsible shareholding or responsible corporate behaviour have made their way into various Swiss statutory initiatives. Their impact on stewardship is sometimes indirect (as seen in the 'say-on-pay' initiative) but may end up being quite significant (as seen in the group responsibility initiative).

Switzerland has been one of the first countries to impose a mandatory 'say-on-pay' regime under which a shareholder vote on compensation is binding rather than just consultative.[153] This new regime came into force following the March 2013 acceptance of a popular initiative by almost 68 per cent of the Swiss electorate – one of the highest initiative approval rates ever.[154] Today, shareholders of listed companies approve the compensation of both the board of directors and the executive management in a binding vote.[155] In addition, individual director compensation, compensation for the highest-paid executive and aggregate compensation of top-level management are disclosed in the annual report.[156]

The results of this 'say-on-pay' initiative are mixed. It provides investors with more detailed numbers and key performance indicators for executive compensation. These rules had

---

[153] See for a general overview Wikipedia, 'Say on Pay' <https://en.wikipedia.org/wiki/Say_on_pay> accessed 14 June 2020.

[154] A chronology of Swiss popular initiatives is available: Bundeskanzlei BK, 'Chronologie Volksabstimmungen [Chronology of Referendums]' <www.bk.admin.ch/ch/d/pore/va/vab_2_2_4_1.html> accessed 14 June 2020; Marc Brupbacher, 'Die Demokratie explodiert [Democracy Explodes]' *Tages-Anzeiger* (3 March 2013).

[155] Ordinance against Excessive Compensation in Listed Companies (n 26) art 18.

[156] Ordinance against Excessive Compensation in Listed Companies (n 26) art 14.

a sobering effect in terms of transparency, shareholder engagement and shareholder decision-making,[157] but did not curb the absolute amount of executive pay.[158] This is largely owing to the fact that foreign (mainly American) institutional investors take a more relaxed view towards executive pay than the Swiss electorate and the Swiss financial press.

A popular initiative on worldwide responsible business conduct of Swiss-based groups of companies[159] was narrowly voted down in November 2020. While a slim majority of the Swiss electorate voted in favour of the initiative, only a minority of the Cantons voted yes. Accordingly, the initiative did not meet the double majority required to amend the Swiss Constitution. Had the initiative been accepted, it would have required Swiss parent companies, their overseas subsidiaries and arguably even some of their suppliers to comply with international standards for the protection of human rights and the environment in all their business activities.

If in violation of these standards, the Swiss parent company would have been liable for any damage caused by the overseas companies and even suppliers under their control, contrary to the general principle of limited liability within groups of companies.[160] The initiative further provided for a place of jurisdiction in Switzerland even if no lawsuit had been filed in the country of incorporation of the relevant subsidiary or supplier. The burden of proof would have laid with the defendant Swiss corporation; it would have been held liable unless it could either prove having taken due care to avoid a damage or demonstrate that the damage would have occurred even if all due care had been taken. Clearly, these rules would have been promulgated to promote responsible behaviour of *companies* rather than shareholders; but the thrust of the legislative effort – ensuring better consideration of ESG standards – is quite the same as in shareholder stewardship initiatives, albeit considerably more far-reaching in both scope and effect.

In view of significant resistance by business circles, the Swiss Parliament crafted a counter-proposal that narrows down the scope of the initiative and addresses the issue below the constitutional level.[161] Together with the rejection of the initiative, the Swiss electorate accepted the counter-proposal, which is expected to take effect as of 1 January 2022. The counter-proposal follows EU-style reporting obligations, specifically Directive 2014/95/EU on the disclosure of non-financial and diversity information (known as the Non-financial Reporting Directive or NFRD) rather than imposing liability on the Swiss parent companies for the actions and omissions of their overseas subsidiaries.[162] Even so, the debate is far from over: trends in international corporate practice favour both broader due diligence obligations in relation to

---

[157] Meanwhile, a lack of such transparency has led some shareholders in Germany to actively turn on executive boards, as described in Ringe, Stewardship and Shareholder Engagement in Germany, Chapter 9, Section 9.3.1.

[158] Von der Crone and Daeniker (n 17) 460.

[159] The text of the initiative can be found in the Federal Reporter ([2015] BBl 3245). An English translation is available online at Swiss Coalition for Corporate Justice, 'About the Initiative' <https://corporatejustice.ch/about-the-initiative/> accessed 14 June 2020.

[160] The concept of liability of parent undertakings for the wrongdoings of their subsidiaries can also be observed in antitrust enforcement; see e.g. Case C-724/17 *Vantaan kaupunki v Skanska Industrial Solutions Oy u. a.* [2019] ECLI:EU:C:2019:204.

[161] Bundesversammlung, 'Parlament will Gegenvorschlag zu Konzernverantwortungsinitiative [Parliament Wants Counter-Proposal to Group Responsibility Initiative]' (9 June 2020) <www.parlament.ch/de/services/news/Seiten/2020/20200609090519598194158159041_bsd048.aspx> accessed 22 July 2020.

[162] Thomas Schürpf, 'Das Parlament einigt sich auf den weniger weit gehenden Gegenvorschlag zur Konzernverantwortsinitiative [Parliament Agrees on the Less Far-Reaching Counter-Proposal to the Corporate Responsibility Initiative]' *Neue Zürcher Zeitung* (Zurich, 8 June 2020) <www.nzz.ch/wirtschaft/die-konzerninitiative-steht-vor-dem-showdown-ld.1560143#subtitle-was-schl-gt-der-st-nderat-vor-second> accessed 7 July 2020.

human rights and environmental standards, and a stricter liability regime for corporate groups in ESG matters is before the courts in many countries.[163]

5.5 CONCLUSION: STAKEHOLDER-ORIENTED CAPITALISTS

There is no question that Switzerland embraces capitalism and has a market-oriented economy. At the same time, a grassroots-oriented political system has allowed for the emergence of a uniquely Swiss stakeholder-oriented business regime.

Hence, Swiss corporate law generally embraces the stakeholder principle to a larger degree than the shareholder-oriented Anglo-Saxon world. Stakeholder interests are given significant weight by the courts and this, in turn, lays the foundation for responsible shareholder behaviour, in family companies and otherwise. However, shareholder stewardship initiatives have yet to gain traction in Switzerland. Responsible conduct in the business environment also remains a concern for public opinion, a good example being that Switzerland has become an experimental field for a variety of stewardship-related popular initiatives.

All in all, the legal framework and societal fabric for Swiss multinational companies are fit for purpose, and Switzerland punches well above its weight. While the country's population amounts to only 2 per cent of the EU member states, the number of large listed companies is much higher – Switzerland accounts for more than 12 per cent of the 400 issuers included in the MSCI Europe Index.[164] This may not be a direct consequence of Swiss corporate law, but it is a clear indication that the Swiss legal set-up is sufficiently flexible to allow its multinational companies to prosper in the international arena for now.

---

[163] See e.g. the 2019 UK Supreme Court case *Vedanta Resources PLC and another v Lungowe and Others* [2019] UKSC 20 or the ongoing litigation in the Netherlands relating to Shell (*Milieudefensie et al v Royal Dutch Shell* [ECLI:NL:RBDHA:2021:5337]).

[164] Daniel Daeniker, 'Zur Rolle des Verwaltungsrates in schweizerischen Publikumsgesellschaften [On the Role of the Board of Directors in Swiss Listed Companies]' [2018] *Schweizerische Zeitschrift für Wirtschafts- und Finanzmarktrecht* 317, 327.

6

Institutional Investor Stewardship in Italian Corporate Governance

Giovanni Strampelli

6.1 INTRODUCTION

Despite the limited size of the national equity market,[1] Italy is one of the countries in which institutional investors, both national and foreign, are on the rise and are playing an increasingly active role in the governance of their investee companies. There is no doubt that this increasing role of institutional investors has been favoured to a large extent by the influence of the global stewardship movement. Indeed, Italy is one of the continuously increasing number of jurisdictions where a stewardship code or similar initiative exists.[2] In 2013, Assogestioni[3] (the non-profit Investment Management Association representing most Italian and foreign asset managers operating in Italy) published the first version of the Italian Stewardship Principles.[4]

Nevertheless, leaving aside the significant influence of the international and European stewardship movement, the Italian regulatory system has some distinctive features, which make it unique and help to promote active institutional ownership. In particular, as is widely recognized,[5] one distinct characteristic of the Italian corporate governance system is the so-called slate (or list) voting system, which enables minority shareholders to appoint at least one board member. In addition, the implementation of the Shareholder Rights Directive[6] and, specifically, the record date system for participating in and voting at general meetings has contributed significantly in turning institutional investors into major players in the corporate governance arena. Moreover, this favourable regulatory context is coupled with a particularly effective form of collective engagement by institutional investors promoted by Assogestioni, which seeks to facilitate the appointment of a minority of the members of the management and the statutory auditors' boards through the slate voting system.

---

[1] See e.g. OECD, 'OECD Corporate Governance Factbook 2019' (2019) 20–24 <www.oecd.org/corporate/corporate-governance-factbook.htm> accessed 8 July 2020.

[2] For an overview of the countries where a stewardship code exists, see Katelouzou and Puchniak, Global Shareholder Stewardship, Chapter 1; Katelouzou and Siems, The Global Diffusion of Stewardship Codes, Chapter 30; Bhakti Mirchandani, 'Model Stewardship Code for Long-Term Behavior' (*Harvard Law School Forum on Corporate Governance*, 9 July 2019) <https://corpgov.law.harvard.edu/2019/07/09/model-stewardship-code-for-long-term-behavior/> accessed 8 July 2020.

[3] For a brief description of the history and activities of Assogestioni, see International Corporate Governance Network, 'Assogestioni' <www.icgn.org/partners/assogestioni> accessed 8 July 2020.

[4] Assogestioni, 'Italian Stewardship Principles' (2016) 11 <www.assogestioni.it/sites/default/files/docs/principi_ita_stewardship072019.pdf> accessed 8 July 2020 [hereinafter Italian Stewardship Principles]

[5] See e.g. Giovanni Strampelli, 'How to Enhance Directors' Independence at Controlled Companies' (2018) 44 *Journal of Corporation Law* 103, 133.

[6] Directive 2007/36/EC of the European Parliament and of the Council of 11 July 2007 on the exercise of certain rights of shareholders in listed companies [2007] OJ L184/17 (SRD I).

Against this backdrop, and with a view to providing a comprehensive analysis of institutional investors' stewardship in Italy, this chapter will proceed as follows. Section 6.2 will illustrate the rise of institutional investors in Italy by analyzing available evidence on ownership patterns of listed companies and statistics concerning institutional investors' voting behaviour. Section 6.3 will provide an overview of the relevant statutory provisions and the Italian Corporate Governance Code recommendations that are relevant for institutional investors' stewardship. Section 6.4 will provide an in-depth analysis of the Italian Stewardship Principles. Section 6.5 will illustrate the specific characteristics of the Italian Stewardship regime, in particular the slate voting system and the institutional investor-driven appointment of independent directors. Section 6.6 will discuss some concerns that have been raised owing to the absence of effective enforcement of the Italian Stewardship Principles and analyze some solutions that could help to enhance its role. Section 6.7 will then conclude by considering future developments.

6.2 INSTITUTIONAL OWNERSHIP IN ITALY

International corporate governance surveys usually label Italy a concentrated-ownership country, where most publicly listed companies are controlled by a single shareholder or a group made up of a limited number of shareholders. For example, statistics recently provided by the Organisation for Economic Co-operation and Development (OECD) confirm this view by showing that Italian companies display the most concentrated ownership when compared to other EU member states including France, Germany and Spain, with the largest single, largest three and largest five shareholders holding an average of 38%, 50% and 54% of the share capital, respectively.[7]

Accordingly, the Italian Financial Markets Supervisory Authority (CONSOB) found that, at the end of 2018, 203 out of 231 companies listed on the Italian Stock Exchange (representing 86% of the total number of companies) were controlled, in about 77% of the cases, by a single shareholder holding either more than half of the capital (123 companies) or a lower stake (57 companies).[8] CONSOB also reported that '[t]he ultimate controlling agent is the family in 152 listed firms, accounting for the 33% of the market capitalization; the State (and other local authorities) in 23 large companies (37.8% of the market capitalization); a financial entity in 11 cases (mainly small firms)'.[9] Against this background, the number of non-controlled, widely held companies is still limited, although it grew from eleven in 2010 to thirteen in 2018.[10]

Despite the predominance of controlled companies, institutional investors are still relevant shareholders in a significant number of Italian listed companies. They hold relevant stakes, averaging 7.6%, in sixty-two listed companies, accounting for 26.8% of the market.[11] Interestingly, while Italian institutional investors are relevant shareholders[12] in only thirteen companies, foreign institutional investors hold relevant stakes in fifty-one companies.[13]

---

[7] OECD, 'Capital Market Review of Italy 2018: Mapping Report' (2018) 55 <www.oecd.org/corporate/OECD-Capital-Market-Review-Italy-Mapping-Report-2018.pdf> accessed 8 July 2020.
[8] CONSOB, *Report on Corporate Governance of Italian Listed Companies* (2019) 13 <www.consob.it/documents/46180/46181/rcg2019.pdf/941e4e4e-60db-4f89-afb3-32bddb8488e0> accessed 8 July 2020.
[9] ibid 16.
[10] ibid.
[11] ibid 18.
[12] For the purposes of CONSOB's statistics, major institutional investors are defined as investment funds, banks and insurance companies subject to reporting obligations according to CONSOB rules and whose shareholdings are lower than 10%.
[13] CONSOB (n 8) 18.

The increasing weight of institutional investors within the shareholder base of Italian listed companies has been accompanied by a tendency for investors to be more active in exercising their voting rights. In 2018, the annual general meeting season registered record highs for both the share capital represented at meetings (72 % on average) and participation by institutional investors (around 21% of the company's capital).[14] From 2012 to 2018, attendance rates for institutional investors grew significantly in terms of both the investors attending as well as the percentage of share capital represented.[15] Significantly, foreign institutional investors attended meetings for all 100 of the largest Italian companies since 2015 and, in 2018, cast on average around 29% of the votes.[16] Namely, for the 2018 proxy season, institutional investors collectively held a majority of the votes cast at the general meetings of one-third of the thirty-five most capitalized Italian listed companies.[17]

As far as voting by institutional investors is concerned, available evidence regarding votes on remuneration policies shows that institutional investors mostly tend to side with directors, although dissent is increasing significantly and is far higher than other shareholders.[18] Abstentions and against-votes by institutional investors have increased over the last year to about 8% of the share capital and 41% of the total number of shares held by them.[19] Interestingly, since 2017, dissent has grown markedly in Italian blue chips, reversing the decreasing trend for Ftse Mib[20] companies from 2012 to 2016.

That said, it must be pointed out that this evidence does not tell the full story. First, it must be considered that stewardship involves not only exercising votes at general meetings but also engaging with investee companies, through monitoring and interacting with these companies, which usually takes place behind the scenes. Indeed, the still limited empirical analyses show that private discussions with directors have become one of the most popular forms of shareholder engagement by institutional investors.[21] However, as they are generally conducted behind closed doors, the actual relevance of such engagement between investors and investee companies cannot be reliably estimated.[22]

In addition, in order to better understand the actual influence exerted by institutional investors over Italian listed companies, it must also be considered that, over the last few years,

---

[14] ibid 39.
[15] ibid 40.
[16] ibid.
[17] Antonella Olivieri, 'L'avanzata dei fondi: in Borsa comandano in una blue chip su tre [The Rise of Mutual Funds: They Control One-Third of Blue Chips]' *Il sole24ore* (Milan, 4 August 2019) 8.
[18] CONSOB (n 8) 39.
[19] ibid 39, noting that institutional investors' dissent appears to be lower in widely held companies and when institutional investors hold a major stake.
[20] The FTSE MIB is the primary benchmark Index for the Italian equity markets including the forty most capitalized companies and capturing approximately 80% of the domestic market capitalization.
[21] Elroy Dimson, Oğuzhan Karakaş and Xi Li, 'Active Ownership' (2015) 28 *Review of Financial Studies* 3225, 3226; Joseph McCahery, Zacharias Sautner and Laura Starks, 'Behind the Scenes: The Corporate Governance Preferences of Institutional Investors' (2016) 71 *The Journal of Finance* 2905, 2911–12; David Solomon and Eugene Soltes, 'What Are We Meeting For? The Consequences of Private Meetings with Investors' (2015) 58 *The Journal of Law & Economics* 325, 326–28.
[22] See Lucian A Bebchuk and Michael S Weisbach, 'The State of Corporate Governance Research' (2010) 23 *The Review of Financial Studies* 939, 942. In Italy, Assogestioni provides some data on the engagement activities of institutional investors. However, the relevance of such statistics is rather limited since they consider only a restricted number of Italian institutional investors. See Assogestioni, 'Monitoraggio sullo stato di applicazione dei Principi Italiani di Stewardship per l'esercizio dei diritti amministrativi e di voto nelle Società quotate [Monitoring the Application of the Italian Stewardship Principles for the Exercise of Administrative and Voting Rights in Listed Companies]' (2017) 15–16 <www.assogestioni.it/sites/default/files/docs/stewardship_report_2017.pdf> accessed 8 July 2020.

the population of institutional investors has been undergoing significant change. In particular, the role of activist investors and the number of interventions by them are growing. Although comprehensive data on shareholder activism in Italy are lacking,[23] a recent study by Becht, Franks, Grant and Wagner found, for the period of 2000 to 2010, that, '[w]hile the United States and the United Kingdom have the largest number of engagements, in relative terms, activism is less frequent after adjusting for the number of listed companies than in Italy or Germany'.[24] Impressively, according to this study, Italy is the country where activism is most frequent in relative terms, after the US.[25]

6.3 THE ITALIAN REGULATORY FRAMEWORK FOR INSTITUTIONAL INVESTOR STEWARDSHIP

The conventional wisdom that Italy is a country where minority shareholders and, in particular, institutional investors are inadequately protected is outdated in many respects. In fact, the current legal environment seems to be – at least in terms of the 'law in the books' – minority shareholder-friendly and favourable to institutional investor stewardship. As regards the exercise of voting rights, a number of rules seek to promote active conduct by institutional investors.

Article 35-decies 1(e) of the Consolidated Law on Finance (*Testo Unico della Finanza*) states that asset management companies 'must provide, in the investors' interests, for the exercise of the voting rights associated with the financial instruments of the collective investment schemes managed, unless required otherwise by law'.[26] Despite the wording used within the legislation ('must provide'), the prevailing view is that Article 35-decies does not establish an obligation for asset management companies to exercise their voting rights under all circumstances.[27] In keeping with their general duty to 'operate diligently, correctly and with transparency in the best interests of the collective investment schemes managed, the relevant investors and the integrity of the market',[28] asset management companies are expected to vote only when it is in the interest of the ultimate beneficiaries of the funds managed.[29] In addition, Article 124-quinquies – implementing Article 3 g SRD II[30] – requires institutional investors and asset managers to adopt an engagement policy that, inter alia, illustrates the ways in which they exercise voting rights and other rights associated with shares.[31] Similarly, institutional investors and asset managers must publicly disclose each year how their engagement policy has been

---

[23] For an overview of the available anecdotal evidence, see Simone Alvaro, Marco Maugeri and Giovanni Strampelli, 'Institutional Investors, Corporate Governance and Stewardship Codes: Problems and Perspectives' (2019) CONSOB Legal Research Papers No 19, 28 <https://ssrn.com/abstract=3393780> accessed 8 July 2020.

[24] Marco Becht, Julian Franks, Jeremy Grant and Hannes Wagner, 'Returns to Hedge Fund Activism: An International Study' (2017) 30 *The Review of Financial Studies* 2933, 2940. See also Massimo Belcredi and Luca Enriques, 'Institutional Investor Activism in a Context of Concentrated Ownership and High Private Benefits of Control: the Case of Italy' (2014) ECGI Law Working Paper No 225/2013, 13–15 <https://papers.ssrn.com/sol3/papers.cfm?abstract_id=2325421> accessed 8 February 2022.

[25] Becht, Franks, Grant and Wagner (n 24) 2941.

[26] Testo Unico della Finanza [Consolidated Law on Finance], Legislative Decree 24 February 1998, n 58, updated on 10 May 2019, Legislative Decree no 49, art 35-decies 1(e).

[27] Renzo Costi, 'Risparmio gestito e governo societario [Asset Management and Corporate Governance]' [1988] *Giurisprudenza Commerciale* 322; Renzo Costi and Luca Enriques, 'Il mercato mobiliare [Financial Market]' in Gastone Cottino (ed), *Trattato di diritto commerciale* [Treaty on Commercial Law], vol VIII (Cedam 2004) 420.

[28] Consolidated Law on Finance (n 26) art 35-decies 1(a).

[29] Mario Stella Richter Jr, 'L'esercizio del voto con gli strumenti finanziari gestiti [Asset Managers' Voting]' in Enrico Gabrielli and Raffaele Lener (eds), *I contratti del mercato finanziario* [Financial Market Contracts] (2nd edn, UTET 2011) 800.

[30] On the SRD II, see Katelouzou and Sergakis, Shareholder Stewardship Enforcement, Chapter 27.

[31] Consolidated Law on Finance (n 26) art 124-quinquies.

implemented and provide a general description of voting behaviour, including an explanation of the most significant votes and the use of the services of proxy advisers.

In recognition of the importance of institutional investors' voting and in keeping with the goal of incentivizing their active conduct, minority shareholders holding a minimum shareholding threshold, that is, usually institutional investors,[32] are also vested with additional powers. First, as far as the procedural aspects of the general meeting are concerned, shareholders holding at least 5 per cent of the share capital, either individually or collectively, have the right to call a general meeting.[33] In addition, shareholders holding at least 2.5 per cent of the share capital, either individually or collectively, may ask for additional matters to be placed on the agenda of the general meeting and table new proposed resolutions for a vote.[34] Moreover, Article 127-ter grants all voting shareholders the right to submit questions in advance of the shareholders' meeting.[35] In addition, in order to promote participation by minority shareholders, the proxy voting and proxy solicitation systems were deregulated and simplified in 2010.[36]

Second, the list of issues falling within the remit of a general meeting has broadened over time.[37] For example, defensive tactics against hostile takeovers (unless the company has opted out of the so-called board neutrality rule) need to be authorized by a shareholders' meeting.[38] Moreover, after introducing a non-binding 'say on pay' vote on the company's compensation policy in 2012, the current version of Article 123-ter of the Consolidated Law on Finance[39] makes the 'say on pay' vote binding.[40] Similarly, the requirement of a supermajority of two-thirds of the share capital represented at the meeting in order to approve any amendments to the articles of association is clearly aimed at incentivizing attendance by minority shareholders.

Third, as will be illustrated in depth, the most peculiar feature of the Italian corporate governance framework is the power granted to minority shareholders to appoint at least one member of each of the management and supervisory boards. In particular, the Consolidated Law on Finance introduced the slate voting system for elections to the boards of statutory auditors in all listed firms in 1998.[41] In the wake of the Parmalat financial scandal, slate voting was then extended to elections of management board members.[42]

However, none of these provisions have proven to be decisive in actually stimulating participation by institutional investors. While they do empower minority shareholders, the provisions illustrated here are unable to effectively incentivize attendance and voting by minority shareholders by reducing the attendant costs. In fact, the blocking requirement imposed on their shares for up to two days prior to the meeting amounted to a significant impediment on

---

[32] Stella Richter (n 29).
[33] See Codice Civile [Civil Code] RD 16 March 1942, no. 262, art 2367.
[34] Consolidated Law on Finance (n 26) art 126-bis. Both the right to call a special meeting and that to put items on the agenda cannot be exercised for items in relation to which, under Italian law, shareholders may be called to resolve on draft resolutions that have to be submitted or drafted by directors.
[35] Consolidated Law on Finance (n 26) art 127-ter.
[36] See Consolidated Law on Finance (n 26) arts 136–144.
[37] Belcredi and Enriques (n 24) 7–8.
[38] See Consolidated Law on Finance (n 26) art 104.
[39] As amended by Legislative Decree no 49 of 10 May 2019 implementing Article 9a SRD II.
[40] Consolidated Law on Finance (n 26) art 123-ter.
[41] Massimo Belcredi, Stefano Bozzi and Carmine Di Noia, 'Board Elections and Shareholder Activism: The Italian Experiment' in Massimo Belcredi and Guido Ferrarini (eds), *Boards and Shareholders in European Listed Companies: Facts, Context and Post-Crisis Reforms* (CUP 2013) 367.
[42] ibid.

institutional investor attendance at general meetings, as it seriously restricted the ability of investors to freely trade their portfolio of shares for a significant number of days.[43]

Thus, as the evidence available clearly demonstrates,[44] the introduction of the record date system[45] in 2010 (upon the implementation of SRD I) has proven to be key in promoting institutional investor participation in the general meetings of their investee companies. Unsurprisingly, the introduction of the record date system has greatly reduced transaction costs associated with participation in the general meeting and has proven to be important, especially for foreign institutional investors.[46]

While various actions have been taken in order to stimulate institutional investor participation and voting at shareholders' meetings, other forms of engagement that usually take place outside the general meeting remain substantially unregulated, despite their increasing relevance within the practice of engagement.[47]

Article 124-quinquies, which requires only that the engagement policy must be published annually by institutional investors, illustrates, among other things, the ways in which 'investors monitor investee companies on important issues, including strategy, financial and non-financial results as well as risks, capital structure, social and environmental impact and corporate governance, interact with investee companies, … cooperate with other shareholders, and communicate with the relevant stakeholders of the investee companies'.[48]

Similarly, while recognizing that the board 'shall endeavour to pursue a continuous dialogue with the shareholders based on the understanding of their reciprocal roles', the current version of the Italian Corporate Governance Code (unlike other codes) does not provide any specific guidance as to how such dialogue should be conducted.[49]

Hence, against this background, the Italian Stewardship Principles fill an important gap within the Italian regulatory framework, as they provide detailed guidance on how investors should monitor investee companies and engage with them, and explicitly aim to promote discussion and co-operation between institutional investors and the listed companies in which they invest.[50]

---

[43] B Espen Eckbo and Giulia Paone, 'Reforming Share-Voting Systems: The Case of Italy' (2011) Tuck School of Business Working Paper No 2011-93, 7–8 <https://ssrn.com/abstract=1822287> accessed 8 July 2020.
[44] See Section 6.2.
[45] According to the Consolidated Law on Finance (n 26) art 83-sexies, shareholders of Italian listed companies are allowed to attend shareholders' meetings by means of a notice of share ownership issued by their financial intermediary to the issuer, based on the intermediary's records at the close of business on the seventh trading day prior to the date of the meeting ('record date'). Therefore, shareholders may attend a meeting and exercise voting rights even if they transfer their shares after the record date.
[46] Belcredi and Enriques (n 24) 21.
[47] See Section 6.2.
[48] Consolidated Law on Finance (n 26) art 124-quinquies.
[49] Luca Enriques, 'The Role of Italian Companies' Boards in the Age of Disruptive Innovation' (*Oxford Business Law Blog*, 6 December 2016) <www.law.ox.ac.uk/business-law-blog/blog/2016/12/role-italian-companies%E2%80%99-boards-age-disruptive-innovation> accessed 8 July 2020. A slightly more detailed recommendation is provided by the new version of the Italian Corporate Governance Code adopted in December 2019 and applicable starting from the first financial year that begins after 31 December 2020. According to the new Code, '[t]he board of directors promotes dialogue with shareholders and other stakeholders which are relevant for the company, in the most appropriate way' and to this end 'the board of directors adopts and describes in the corporate governance report a policy for managing dialogue with the generality of shareholders, taking into account the engagement policies adopted by institutional investors and asset managers'. See Italian Corporate Governance Committee, 'Corporate Governance Code' (2020) 5–6 <www.borsaitaliana.it/comitato-corporate-governance/codice/2020eng.en.pdf> accessed 8 July 2020.
[50] Italian Stewardship Principles (n 4).

6.4 THE ITALIAN STEWARDSHIP PRINCIPLES

The Italian Stewardship Principles, adopted by Assogestioni, were first published in 2013, and subsequently revised in 2015 and 2016.[51] They largely follow the model of the EFAMA Code for External Governance[52] (currently known as the EFAMA Stewardship Code following the 2018 revision[53]) adopted by the European Fund and Asset Management Association (of which Assogestioni is a member), which in turn shares many common features with the UK Code 2012.[54] In line with the EFAMA model, the Italian Stewardship Code consists of six brief, general principles and related recommendations which provide detailed guidance on the principles' implementation.[55] According to Principle 1, asset managers should have a documented policy available to the public on whether, and if so how, they exercise their ownership responsibilities.[56] The policy should illustrate, inter alia, how investee companies are monitored and how conflicts of interest are managed. Principle 2 generally recommends that asset managers should monitor their investee companies, while Principle 3 provides more detailed guidance on how asset managers should engage with the investee companies and, if necessary, escalate stewardship activities, also involving other institutional investors according to Principle 4.[57] Principle 5 recommends that asset managers should exercise their voting rights in a considered way.[58] Finally, Principle 6 deals with the report on their exercise of ownership rights and voting activities and highlights the importance of having a policy on external governance disclosure.[59]

While their structure closely resembles that of the EFAMA Code 2011, the Italian Stewardship Principles include some recommendations that are strictly related to the national regulatory framework and, especially, to the slate voting system for the election of the management and supervisory boards as well as dialogues, usually taking place behind closed doors, between the board of directors and major shareholders. Therefore, the following analysis will mainly focus on Principles 3, 4 and 5, including the recommendations that are more closely related to the Italian regulatory framework.

---

[51] Italy is among the jurisdictions where stewardship codes are adopted by institutional investors themselves. See Jennifer G Hill, 'Good Activist/Bad Activist: The Rise of International Stewardship Codes' (2018) 41 *Seattle University Law Review* 497, 506–13, advancing a taxonomy of the stewardship codes based on the type of bodies issuing stewardship principles (regulators or quasi-regulators on behalf of the government, private industry participants, investors).

[52] European Fund and Asset Management Association, 'EFAMA Code for External Governance: Principles for the Exercise of Ownership Rights in Investee Companies' (6 April 2011) 6 <www.efama.org/newsroom/news/efama-code-external-governance-principles-exercise-ownership-rights-investee> accessed 8 February 2022 [hereinafter EFAMA Code 2011].

[53] European Fund and Asset Management Association, 'EFAMA Stewardship Code: Principles for Asset Managers' Monitoring of, Voting in, Engagement with Investee Companies' (2018) <www.efama.org/newsroom/news/efama-stewardship-code-principles-asset-managers-monitoring-voting-engagement> accessed 8 February 2022 [hereinafter EFAMA Code 2018]. For an overview of the EFAMA Code 2018, see Dionysia Katelouzou and Konstantinos Sergakis, 'When Harmonization Is Not Enough: Shareholder Stewardship in the European Union' (2021) 22 *European Business Organization Law Review* 203.

[54] On the UK Stewardship Code, see Davies, The UK Stewardship Code 2010–2020, Chapter 2 and Katelouzou and Micheler, The Market for Stewardship and the Role of the Government, Chapter 3.

[55] For an overview of the textual similarities between the EFAMA Code and the Italian Stewardship Principles (n 4), see Katelouzou and Siems, The Global Diffusion of Stewardship Codes, Chapter 30.

[56] Italian Stewardship Principles (n 4) 15.

[57] ibid 15–18.

[58] ibid 18.

[59] ibid 18–19.

6.4.1 *Voting*

The Italian Stewardship Principles are no doubt based on the fundamental assumption that, in order to enhance the value of their portfolio and to create added value for their clients, institutional investors should monitor investee companies by exercising voting rights and engaging with them.[60]

As regards the exercise of voting rights, institutional investors are required to vote in a considered manner, by defining 'an effective and adequate strategy for exercising the participation and voting rights'.[61] In order to ensure that, and to keep with Article 35-decies 1(e) of the Consolidated Law on Finance,[62] voting rights are exercised by institutional investors solely in the interest of their clients. The voting strategy should establish procedures and measures for ensuring that the exercise of voting rights complies with the objectives and investment policies of each fund managed, and for preventing or adequately managing potential conflicts of interest resulting from the exercise of voting rights.[63]

Where institutional investors decide to exercise voting rights in an investee company, Principle 5 recommends that they should, if possible, vote in a uniform manner for all shares held. However, this statement is not entirely convincing as it is inconsistent with the Italian Stewardship Principles' purpose of 'prevent[ing] or manag[ing] any conflicts of interest deriving from the exercise of voting rights'.[64] While it may be the case that leading institutional investors usually adopt standardized voting policies, which they tend to apply quite strictly to all portfolio companies listed in the same market or located within a given geographic area,[65] adherence to a uniform voting policy irrespective of individual fund objectives and characteristics may be detrimental for some beneficiaries.[66]

Interestingly, Vanguard – the world's second largest asset manager – announced that it will no longer adopt centralized proxy voting across all of its funds; instead, its externally managed funds – including almost all active funds managed by Vanguard – will adopt their own proxy voting policies.[67] Although this move may have been prompted by different regulatory concerns,[68] there is no doubt that it also aims to limit any potential conflicts of interest among different fund categories that might be brought about by the application of uniform voting policies across the whole portfolio.[69] In addition, it is also worth mentioning that neither the EFAMA Code 2011 – which largely inspired the Italian Stewardship Principles – nor the current EFAMA Code 2018 recommends that institutional investors vote in a uniform manner for all the

---

[60] ibid 12 recognizes that the interaction between institutional investors and investee companies aims to ensure that governance and investment processes are closely linked.
[61] Italian Stewardship Principles (n 4) 18, Principle 5.
[62] Consolidated Law on Finance (n 26) art 35-decies 1(e).
[63] Italian Stewardship Principles (n 4) 18, Principle 5.
[64] ibid.
[65] For example, BlackRock adopts global engagement principles – defining the general framework and purposes of engagement – and regional proxy guidelines that apply to specific markets (e.g. the US, the UK, other European countries).
[66] Sean J Griffith and Dorothy S Lund, 'Conflicted Mutual Fund Voting in Corporate Law' (2019) 99 *Boston University Law Review* 1151, 1182–86; Ann M Lipton, 'Family Loyalty: Mutual Fund Voting and Fiduciary Obligation' (2017) 19 *Transactions: The Tennessee Journal of Business Law* 175.
[67] Vanguard, 'Vanguard Funds Plan to Grant Proxy Voting Responsibilities to External Managers' (2019) <www.vanguardeurope.com/documents/proxy-voting-to-external-managers.pdf> accessed 8 February 2022; Ann Lipton, 'Vanguard's Votes' (*Business Law Prof Blog*, 11 May 2019) <https://lawprofessors.typepad.com/business_law/2019/05/vanguards-votes.html> accessed 8 July 2020.
[68] Ann Lipton (n 67).
[69] ibid.

shares held. Instead, the EFAMA Code 2018 states only that applicants should seek to vote for all shares held.[70]

6.4.2 Engagement

Although the exercise of voting rights is recognized as an important element of investor stewardship, the Italian Stewardship Principles mainly focus on engagement, which is the interaction with investee companies and their boards taking place on a regular basis, usually in private meetings held separately from the shareholders' meeting. In fact, in defining the purposes of the Italian Stewardship Principles, particular emphasis is placed on the interaction between institutional investors and investee companies and the quality of that communication.[71] Moreover, according to Principle 5, before voting against management proposed resolutions that could have a significant effect on the company, institutional investors are advised to consider engaging with the investee company. Therefore, in line with the aim of promoting co-operation between investors and listed companies, casting a vote against the management is regarded as a last resort, to be used only when interaction with investee companies, and in particular with board members, does not lead to the expected result.

Thus, Principle 3, which states that institutional investors 'should establish clear guidelines on when and how they will intervene in investee companies to protect and enhance value',[72] lies at the heart of the engagement framework designed by the Italian Stewardship Principles. This principle in fact sets the tone for investors' conduct insofar as it recommends that institutional investors establish clear guidelines on when and how they will escalate their stewardship activities.[73]

In particular, according to Principle 3, institutional investors should determine whether and how to communicate any issue or problem arising in relation to their monitoring of the investee company.[74] Institutional investors are expected to be keen to engage with investee companies with regards to corporate governance or the approach to environmental and social issues, or when, for example, they have significant concerns regarding strategy and performance.

In keeping with the pro–co-operation purpose underlying the Italian Stewardship Principles,[75] according to Principle 3 engagement should start with collaborative contact with the investee companies.[76] Recommendations on the escalation of engagement make it clear that private meetings between institutional investors and investee companies, and in particular their board members, are the key element within the engagement process. It is only if the board fails to react constructively that institutional investors must decide whether and how to escalate their action, considering too the possibility of involving other institutional investors pursuant to Principle 4.[77] Initiatives aimed at increasing pressure on the company include, inter alia, releasing a public declaration before or during the annual or any extraordinary shareholders' meeting, submitting resolutions at shareholders' meetings, calling a shareholders' meeting or

---

[70] EFAMA Code 2018 (n 53) 8.
[71] Italian Stewardship Principles (n 4) 12.
[72] ibid 18.
[73] See Hill (n 51) 520–21, noting that some stewardship codes (e.g. the UK Stewardship Code) envisage a more confrontational model of stewardship than that accepted by other codes (e.g. the Japanese Code).
[74] Italian Stewardship Principles (n 4) 16.
[75] ibid 12.
[76] ibid 16.
[77] ibid 17, Principle 4 states that 'cooperation with other investors may be the most effective method of engagement. It may be appropriate to carry out collective engagement, for example in the case of significant corporate events or issues of public interest (such as serious economic or sectoral crises).'

asking for additional matters to be placed on the agenda of a shareholders' meeting that has already been called in order to propose specific initiatives to the shareholders (e.g. making changes to the companies' boards).

In line with international best practice,[78] Principle 3 recognizes that not only the chairperson of the board of directors but also other non-executive directors may be involved in private meetings with institutional investors.[79] Also, depending on the allocation of functions within the board and the topics under discussion, the executive directors, the lead independent director, the chairperson of the board of statutory auditors, the chairperson of an internal committee or other independent directors, including minority-appointed board members, may attend meetings with institutional investors.[80]

6.5 UNIQUE FEATURE OF ITALIAN STEWARDSHIP: MINORITY-APPOINTED DIRECTORS

As mentioned in Section 6.3, the most distinctive characteristic of the Italian corporate governance regulatory framework is the so-called slate system for the election of members of the management and statutory auditor boards. Under this system, minority shareholders can appoint at least one director and one member of the supervisory board. Article 147-ter of the Consolidated Law on Finance states that shareholders holding a minimum threshold of shares – set by the CONSOB and currently varying between 0.5% and 4.5%[81] – can present lists of candidates for election to the management board and the board of statutory auditors. At least one member must be elected from the minority-submitted slate, having obtained the largest number of votes,[82] and the shareholders who submit the minority slate must not be related in any way, either directly or indirectly, to the shareholders who voted on the list that received the largest number of votes.[83] According to Article 148 of the Consolidated Law on Finance, the slate voting system also applies to the election of members of the board of statutory auditors, and the chair of the board must be selected from the statutory auditors elected from the minority slate.[84] In line with these provisions, the Italian Stewardship Principles state that '[t]he presentation of candidates for election as independent minority members of boards of investee companies, also

---

[78] Giovanni Strampelli, 'Knocking at the Boardroom Door: A Transatlantic Overview of Director-Institutional Investor Engagement in Law and Practice' (2018) 12 *Virginia Law & Business Review* 187, 231–7.
[79] Italian Stewardship Principles (n 4) 16.
[80] See Section 6.5.2.
[81] CONSOB, Regulation no 11971 of May 14, 1999 (Regulation implementing Italian Legislative Decree No 58 of 24 February 1998, concerning the discipline of issuers) (Regulation no 11971) art 144-quater. The minimum threshold of shares set by the CONSOB varies according to the company's capitalization. The CONSOB Regulation does not prevent shareholders from establishing a lower shareholding threshold.
[82] Consolidated Law on Finance (n 26) art 147-ter (3). In companies organized under the one-tier system, the member elected from the minority slate must satisfy the integrity, experience and independence requirements established pursuant to articles 148(3) and 148(4). Failure to satisfy the requirements shall result in disqualification from the position. See generally Guido Ferrarini, Gian Giacomo Peruzzo and Marta Roberti, 'Corporate Boards in Italy' in Paul Davies, Klaus Hopt, Richard Nowak and Gerard van Solinge (eds), *Corporate Boards in Law and Practice: A Comparative Analysis in Europe* (OUP 2013) 367, 392–93.
[83] CONSOB Regulation no 11971 (n 81) art 144(6) clearly states:

> A shareholder may not submit or vote for more than one list, including through nominees or trust companies. Shareholders belonging to the same group and shareholders participating in a shareholder agreement involving the shares of the issuer may not submit or vote for more than one list, including through nominees or trust companies. A candidate may only be present in one list, under penalty of ineligibility.

See Belcredi and Enriques (n 24) 8–9; Belcredi, Bozzi and Di Noia (n 41) 378–83.
[84] Consolidated Law on Finance (n 26) art 148.

through the [Assogestioni's] Investment Managers' Committee, represents a continuous and constructive method of engaging with investee companies'.[85] This recommendation is key to the Italian stewardship framework, since the presentation of candidates at elections of board members is becoming an increasingly significant stewardship tool in Italy.

6.5.1 Collective Engagement and the Election of Minority-Appointed Board Members

Even though the slate voting system was introduced some years before,[86] until 2010 institutional investors were only able to appoint directors and statutory auditors within a small group of listed companies.[87] Since 2010, owing to the introduction of a record date system for participating in and voting at general meetings,[88] participation by institutional investors in voting at board elections has increased significantly and, over the years, growing numbers of directors and statutory auditors have been elected by institutional investors.[89] Currently, 100 out of 232 listed companies' boards include at least 1 minority-appointed director.[90] Minority-appointed directors represent, on average, 17 per cent of the members of the boards where they are present.[91] Moreover, the boards of statutory auditors in 112 listed companies include at least 1 minority-appointed member.[92]

A significant proportion of the minority-supported members of these boards have been appointed by institutional investors under the co-ordination of Assogestioni. In 2019, Assogestioni presented sixty-four slates and appointed seventy-six candidates in forty-nine listed companies.[93] Although the shareholdings of the Italian institutional investors that formally present the lists usually do not exceed, on average, 3.5 per cent of the votes cast, the lists promoted by Assogestioni are able to attract the votes of a sizable number of other Italian and foreign institutional investors, and frequently receive more than 30 per cent – and sometimes around 50 per cent – of the votes cast.[94] Given the decreasing weight of Italian mutual funds in the Italian stock market, the support of foreign institutional investors has proven to be essential in this respect.[95] This is also owing to the support of proxy advisory firms, which usually prefer lists submitted by institutional investors over those presented by the controlling shareholders.

In light of such outcomes, collective engagement promoted by Assogestioni with a view to appointing board members is deemed to be a fairly effective tool for monitoring investee companies. The presence of independent directors appointed by institutional investors can

---

[85] Italian Stewardship Principles (n 4) 17.
[86] See Section 6.3.
[87] Belcredi and Enriques (n 24) 19–20.
[88] See Section 6.3.
[89] Belcredi and Enriques (n 24) 21.
[90] Assonime, 'La Corporate Governance in Italia: Autodisciplina, Remunerazioni e Comply-or-Explain [Corporate Governance in Italy: Soft Law, Remunerations and Comply-or-Explain]' (2019) 37 <www.assonime.it/attivita-editoriale/studi/Pagine/note-e-studi-1-2019.aspx> accessed 8 July 2020; CONSOB (n 8) 17.
[91] CONSOB (n 8) 17.
[92] ibid.
[93] Assogestioni, 'Stagione Assembleare 2019 [2019 Proxy Season Review]' (2019) 10 <www.comitatogestori.it/articolo/stagione-assembleare-2019> accessed 8 July 2020.
[94] ibid.
[95] As far as the role of foreign institutional investors is concerned, it is worth noting that, while it can reduce the costs associated with participating in, and voting at, shareholder meetings, the introduction of the record date system does not lower the costs associated with selecting director nominees and submitting the slate. Nevertheless, such costs do not represent an effective hurdle as costs associated with candidates' selection are borne by Assogestioni.

favour some form of monitoring within the board itself, by enhancing board disclosure, given the fact that such directors are primarily expected to protect minority interests.[96]

The Investment Managers' Committee operating under the auspices of Assogestioni[97] plays a central role in selecting candidates for boards and submitting minority slates to be voted on. In particular, candidates are selected in accordance with the 'Principles for the Selection of Candidates for Corporate Bodies of Listed Companies' drawn up by the Assogestioni Corporate Governance Committee, which is composed of members of the Association's Board and representatives of member investors.[98] Candidates for election as minority representatives to the corporate bodies of investee listed issuers are selected by the Investment Managers' Committee with the assistance of an independent adviser, who is in charge of both maintaining a database of possible candidates and submitting to the Investment Managers' Committee a shortlist of those that appear to best meet the requirements for each corporate appointment.[99]

Furthermore, the selection principles drawn up by the Assogestioni Corporate Governance Committee require that candidates must have adequate professionalism, integrity and independence.[100] Specifically, in order to avoid possible conflicts of interest and to foster the candidates' independence from the institutional investors supporting the candidacy, legal representatives of investment management companies cannot be selected as candidates for corporate boards.[101] In addition, any person who has served in a senior management or executive role at an investment management company may not be selected as a candidate until at least a year has elapsed since the relevant appointment was relinquished.[102]

The selection principles drawn up by the Assogestioni Corporate Governance Committee also aim to promote the candidates' independence from the company for which they are nominated. In particular, 'members of governing or supervisory bodies and senior managers of institutions and companies that have significant business ties with the company for which they are nominated may be selected as candidates provided that at least one year has elapsed since the end of these appointments'.[103]

Furthermore, if elected, candidates are requested to refrain from accepting any senior management position or corporate appointment at the same company or at any other company from the same group for at least one year after the end of their term, unless they are nominated again as candidates by the Investment Managers' Committee.[104]

---

[96] Finding a positive relationship between the proportion of independent minority directors and firm value, see e.g. Nicola Moscariello, Michele Pizzo, Dmytro Govorun and Alexander Kostyuk, 'Independent Minority Directors and Firm Value in a Principal–Principal Agency Setting: Evidence from Italy' (2019) 23 *Journal of Management and Governance* 165; finding that minority-appointed directors are more likely to dissent than directors appointed with a majority of the votes, see Piergaetano Marchetti, Gianfranco Siciliano and Marco Ventoruzzo, 'Dissenting Directors' (2017) 18 *European Business Organization Law Review* 659.

[97] The Investment Managers' Committee is composed solely of representatives of the member investment management companies or other Italian or foreign institutional investors. They communicate their interest in participating in the presentation of the individual lists for the election or cooptation of minority candidates for the corporate bodies of Italian investee listed issuers to the Committee's secretariat each time. See Assogestioni, 'Protocol of Duties and Responsibilities of the Corporate Governance Committee and the Investment Managers' Committee' (2017) 22 <www.comitatogestori.it/sites/comitatogestori.it/files/protocollo_compiti_e_funzioni_ccg_e_cg.pdf> accessed 8 July 2020.

[98] ibid 20–21.
[99] ibid 24–25.
[100] ibid 26.
[101] ibid 29.
[102] ibid 28–29.
[103] ibid 27.
[104] ibid 28.

That said, it is also worth noting that the engagement strategy adopted by Assogestioni and affiliated institutional investors is quite different from that usually adopted by activist hedge funds.[105] Assogestioni seeks to achieve less confrontational engagement with the management of portfolio companies,[106] and focuses almost exclusively on the election of directors, through the presentation of minority lists comprising a number of candidates representing less than half of the positions to which appointments are to be made.[107] This clearly shows that the institutional investor engagement promoted by Assogestioni is primarily aimed at minimizing 'the agency costs arising from the presence of a controlling shareholder by sharing management decisions, and thus, by exercising closer monitoring.'[108] Unlike the usual approach of hedge funds, the aim is not to force major changes in corporate strategy or to replace management.

Thus, the Italian institutional investor-driven approach to engagement seems to represent an alternative to activist-driven engagement. First, the co-ordination role performed by Assogestioni – or a similar co-ordinating entity – could help overcome collective action and resource-related problems underlying the stewardship passivity of institutional investors by favouring the sharing of stewardship-related benefits and costs among investors.[109] Second, institutional investor-driven engagement also covers companies that raise potential agency problems posed by controlling shareholders but are not targeted by activist hedge funds. For example, while larger controlled firms are generally less likely to be targeted by hedge funds, experience in Italy shows that institutional investors co-ordinated by Assogestioni have been successful in appointing minority directors at major Italian listed companies with controlling shareholders. Third, the criteria for selecting independent directors adopted by Assogestioni imply a strict assessment of the candidates' skills and independence, and seek to ensure that there are no ties either with the institutional shareholders who nominate them or with the company for which they are nominated.[110]

For all of the above reasons, the Italian system suggests that slate voting, coupled with the co-ordination role performed by a co-ordinating entity, can foster the involvement of institutional investors in the appointment of some independent directors and make these directors useful in reducing the agency costs affecting listed companies.

Moreover, the institutional investor-driven approach fostered by the Italian Stewardship Principles and the co-ordinating role played by Assogestioni do not aim to replace the activist-driven

---

[105] Matteo Erede, 'Governing Corporations with Concentrated Ownership Structure: An Empirical Analysis of Hedge Fund Activism in Italy and Germany, and Its Evolution' (2013) 10 *European Company and Financial Law Review* 328, 370.
[106] ibid.
[107] Assogestioni, 'Protocol of Duties and Responsibilities of the Corporate Governance Committee and the Investment Managers' Committee' (n 97) 25.
[108] Erede (n 105) 371. See also Belcredi, Bozzi and Di Noia (n 41) 414; Luigi Zingales, 'Italy Leads in Protecting Minority Investors' *Financial Times* (13 April 2008) <www.ft.com/content/357c40c4-094d-11dd-81bf-0000779fd2ac> accessed 8 July 2020, observing that a vote for a minority list sponsored by Assogestioni is not 'a vote against the management but a vote to ensure truly independent board members and avoid the representation of other opportunistic minority shareholders, who might have other goals in mind'.
[109] Gaia Balp and Giovanni Strampelli, 'Institutional Investor Collective Engagements: Non-activist Cooperation vs Activist Wolf Packs' (2020) 14 *Ohio State Business Law Journal* 135.
[110] The selection process adopted by Assogestioni significantly differs from that of activist investors. As is widely recognized, activist investors usually do not seek independent directors and quite frequently appoint their employees as directors. See e.g. Lazard, '2018 Review of Shareholder Activism' (2019) 8 <www.lazard.com/media/450805/lazards-2018-review-of-shareholder-activism.pdf> accessed 8 July 2020, showing that, in 2018, 22% of directors appointed by activist investors were their employees; John C Coffee Jr, Robert J Jackson Jr, Joshua R Mitts and Robert E Bishop, 'Activist Directors and Agency Costs: What Happens When an Activist Director Goes on the Board' (2019) 104 *Cornell Law Review* 381, 382, finding that approximately 70% of hedge fund–nominated director slates include a hedge fund employee.

approach.[111] For example, institutional investors might avoid intervening directly, preferring to support hedge fund campaigns and proxy fights when they believe that the hedge funds' strategy can improve the governance of targeted companies and enhance their value. Since the success of activist campaigns frequently depends on support from institutional investors,[112] institutional investors could discipline activist hedge funds by making them more inclined to adopt good corporate governance practices and to select directors who are actually independent.[113] Therefore, the ability to play a more active role in the election of independent directors could help mainstream institutional investors exert a disciplining effect on hedge funds, even where institutional investors refrain from presenting their own candidates.[114]

Nevertheless, in light of the ownership patterns of Italian listed companies illustrated here, the slate voting system can lead to some unexpected and, to some extent, counter-intuitive consequences. In particular, in so-called de facto controlled companies, where the controlling shareholder holds less than half of the share capital, institutional investors can collectively own the majority of the share capital or a stake larger than that of the controlling shareholders.[115] Therefore, it is increasingly the case that the list submitted by the institutional investors under the co-ordination of Assogestioni receives more votes, sometimes even an absolute majority of the votes, than the list submitted by the de facto controlling shareholders.[116] This is especially the case in larger corporations where the de facto controlling shareholder holds a relatively small stake.[117] Hence, given that institutional investors present only minority lists, this means that the majority of the shareholders appoint a minority of directors, whilst the minority (the de facto controlling shareholder) appoints a majority.

This result, whilst paradoxical, is not surprising as it is consistent with the objectives pursued by institutional investors. Indeed, institutional investors submit only a short list of director nominees since they do not want to appoint a majority of directors and take control of the company.[118] This approach is in line with the Italian Stewardship Principles,

---

[111] See Dionysia Katelouzou, 'The Rhetoric of Activist Shareholder Stewards' (2022) (working paper) 32–39 and 61–73.
[112] See Section 6.7.
[113] Attracta Mooney, 'Activists Become Wolves in Sheep's Clothing' *Financial Times* (21 July 2019) <www.ft.com/content/bf1e6037-bbdd-3465-ab0c-d111e301624c> accessed 8 July 2020.
[114] It is worth mentioning that, in theory, the co-ordination role played by a non-profit organization representing institutional investors might also favour more 'proactive' institutional investors' initiatives against potential value-disrupting activists' campaigns. For example, it seems that such an approach – by facilitating investors' co-ordination and sharing of costs – might favour the implementation of an intriguing proposal set forth by Coffee. He suggests that institutional investors who fear that they are being disenfranchised by hedge funds' private settlements could form 'a steering committee and assemble a team of outside directors (who were not their employees) that they could seek to place on corporate boards in the event of an activist attack. This would take some advance preparation, but the effort and expense could be shared among the dozen (or more) institutions participating in such a committee. This committee could contact the corporation at the outset of an activist campaign to suggest either its own nominees or its desire to be involved in the settlement process.' See John C Coffee, 'The Agency Costs of Activism: Information Leakage, Thwarted Majorities, and the Public Morality' (2017) ECGI Law Working Paper No 373/2017, 26–27 <https://ssrn.com/abstract=3058319> accessed 8 July 2020.
[115] OECD (n 7) 53–54.
[116] Mario Stella Richter Jr and Federico Ferdinandi, 'The Evolving Role of the Board: Board Nomination and the Management of Dissenting Opinions' (2018) 4 *The Italian Law Journal* 611, 613.
[117] ibid.
[118] See Assogestioni, 'Protocol of Duties and Responsibilities of the Corporate Governance Committee and the Investment Managers' Committee' (n 97) 23. Interestingly, as noted by Coffee and Palia, this is true also for the hedge funds that most often take advantage of short-slate rules. Indeed, the submission of a short slate can encourage 'hedge funds to seek board representation with the possible objective of putting the company up for sale, but without

according to which the appointment of some independent directors only 'serve[s] as a method of monitoring'.[119]

In addition, the support provided to the minority list assembled by the Investment Managers' Committee generally does not result in the formation of a group that can be considered to exercise control.[120] In line with the ESMA guidelines,[121] CONSOB has clarified that any co-operation between shareholders in relation to the submission of lists of candidates for elections to corporate bodies pursuant to Articles 147-ter and 148 of the Consolidated Law on Finance will not be classified as concerted action, 'provided that said lists include a number of candidates that is less than half of the members to be elected or are by design predetermined for the election of representatives of minority interests'.[122] Moreover, in order to avoid the regulatory risks associated with concerted action, the protocol adopted by Assogestioni states:[123]

> The Investment Managers' Committee shall not under any circumstances pass any resolutions concerning the exercise of voting rights in the general meetings of investees that are listed issuers, and the Committee members shall have no requirement to consult in relation to the exercise of this right. Even when minority lists are presented for elections to corporate bodies, the Committee members shall not undertake any obligation regarding the exercise of voting rights during general meetings.

6.5.2 Interactions between Institutional Investors and Minority-Appointed Directors

The appointment of independent minority-supported directors through slate voting raises some regulatory issues and the question as to whether directors drawn from the minority slate are allowed to make direct contact with the minority shareholders who elected them. In particular, since minority slates are frequently supported by institutional investors, some practitioners have raised concerns about the potential threat for board collegiality and the risk of market abuse infringements posed by the fact that the establishment of a direct channel of communication with minority-elected directors would grant institutional investors direct and permanent access to the board.[124]

---

themselves acquiring control. Because hedge funds are not typically strategic bidders and traditionally did not want control (which carried some risk of liability), this rule well served their needs'. See John C Coffee Jr and Darius Palia, 'The Wolf at the Door: The Impact of Hedge Fund Activism on Corporate Governance' (2016) 41 *Journal of Corporation Law* 545, 560.

[119] Italian Stewardship Principles (n 4) 16; Coffee and Palia (n 118) 560, noting that '[t]he goal of the short slate rule also was to encourage "constructive engagement" through minority board representation without a confrontational battle between activists and the issuer'.

[120] Therefore, in this respect, talking about minorities that become majorities could be partially misleading.

[121] European Securities and Markets Authority, 'Information on Shareholder Cooperation and Acting in Concert under the Takeover Bids Directive' (20 June 2014) 6–7 <www.esma.europa.eu/document/information-shareholder-cooperation-and-acting-in-concert-under-takeover-bids-directive-0> accessed 8 February 2022, stating that, when determining whether or not shareholder co-operation in relation to board appointments will lead to the shareholders being regarded as persons acting in concert, a number of factors must be considered, including 'the number of proposed board members being voted for pursuant to a shareholders' voting agreement'; 'whether the shareholders have cooperated in relation to the appointment of board members on more than one occasion'; and 'whether the appointment of the proposed board member(s) will lead to a shift in the balance of power on the board'.

[122] CONSOB Regulation no. 11971 (n 81) art 44-quarter 2(b).

[123] Assogestioni, 'Protocol of Duties and Responsibilities of the Corporate Governance Committee and the Investment Managers' Committee' (n 97) 23.

[124] Strampelli (n 78) 234–37.

Further, in light of such concerns, guidance provided by the Italian Stewardship Principles concerning the role of minority-appointed directors engaging in dialogue with shareholders was significantly overhauled in 2016.[125]

Under the 2015 version of Principle 3, any institutional investors that had significant concerns regarding the strategy and performance of investee listed issuers were encouraged to intervene by requesting a meeting with the management and/or board members, including non-executive directors elected by institutional investors themselves.[126] More specifically, according to the 2015 version of Principle 3, engaging in discussions with independent minority board members was viewed as a permissible way for institutional investors to intervene, enabling them to communicate actively. However, this was subject to the following provisos: that it was carried out in accordance with an organized and collective procedure; and that it occurred at the request of minority members of the board, or on the initiative of institutional investors, provided in the latter instance that a meeting had previously been held with the chairperson, the executive directors or the lead independent director of the investee issuer.[127]

The previous version of Principle 3 raised concerns among issuers, who considered it to be not fully in line with international practice and were concerned that its application could lead to information asymmetries within the board.[128] According to critics, the Italian Stewardship Principles allowed minority members of the board to engage in dialogue directly with the institutional investors who had elected them, without requiring the participation of other board members, the auditing body or other managers, and without any consideration as to the allocation of functions within the management and the statutory auditors' boards.[129]

Following these criticisms, Italian Stewardship Principle 3 was revised in 2016. Presently, the revised version of Principle 3 recommends that institutional investors meet with the board members, including minority-appointed members, taking the allocation of functions within corporate bodies into account.[130] Furthermore, the principle makes it clear that dialogue between directors and institutional investors should be conducted according to an organized and collective procedure. In particular, this procedure seeks to ensure compliance with the general principle of freedom from any mandate and independence vis-à-vis the shareholders who proposed or voted for the candidate.[131] The revised version of Principle 3 seems capable of overcoming the criticisms levelled against the previous version. In line with international best practices, the selection of the board's minority members involved in dialogue is no longer dependent only on the nominating shareholders; it now also depends on the role played by a given director within the board (e.g. the lead independent director or the chair of a board's

---

[125] Assogestioni, 'Monitoraggio sullo stato di applicazione dei Principi Italiani di Stewardship per l'esercizio dei diritti amministrativi e di voto nelle società quotate [Monitoring the Application of the Italian Stewardship Principles for the Exercise of Administrative and Voting Rights in ListedcCompanies]' (2016) 3 <www.assogestioni.it/sites/default/files/docs/stewardship-report_20171009_0.pdf> accessed 8 July 2020.

[126] Assogestioni, 'Italian Stewardship Principles' (2015) 11 <https://ecgi.global/sites/default/files/codes/documents/principi_it_stewardship_settembre2015_en.pdf> accessed 8 July 2020 [hereinafter Italian Stewardship Principles 2015].

[127] ibid.

[128] Gabriele Galateri, 'Lavorare nell'interesse di tutti gli azionisti [Working in the Interest of All Shareholders]' *Il Sole24ore* (Milan, 30 March 2016) <www.intermediachannel.it/lavorare-nellinteresse-di-tutti-gli-azionisti> accessed 8 July 2020. But see Luigi Zingales, 'I consiglieri di maggioranza e il loro ruolo nel board [Majority-Appointed Directors: Their Role within the Board]' *Il Sole24ore* (Milan, 27 March 2016) <www.ilsole24ore.com/art/commenti-e-idee/2016-03-27/i-consiglieri-maggioranza-e-loro-ruolo-board-081206.shtml?uuid=ACDwMYvC> accessed 8 July 2020.

[129] Italian Stewardship Principles 2015 (n 126) 17.

[130] Italian Stewardship Principles (n 4) 16.

[131] ibid 17.

committee).¹³² In addition, Principle 3 stresses that the organized and collective procedure regulating dialogue aims to prevent board members from disclosing any information that could compromise the investors' ability to trade the company's shares without the prior consent of their counterparties.¹³³

That being said, it is important to note that the significance of the compliance risks associated with dialogue between certain board members and institutional investors largely depends on the way in which such exchanges are conducted.¹³⁴ According to the distinction drawn by the EFAMA Code 2018, board/shareholders dialogues 'can consist in unilateral communication from asset managers to board members (one-way engagement), or in bilateral dialogue (bi-engagement)'.¹³⁵ Therefore, while bi-engagement dialogue entails the mutual exchange of information, institutional investors in one-way engagements are usually willing to communicate their concerns about specific aspects of the company's governance and strategies to directors, without, however, receiving any information in return from the directors.¹³⁶

Hence, as legal risks are obviously higher in two-way dialogues, participants in such dialogue are advised to adopt specific procedures in order to avoid the disclosure of non-public material information. For example, in the US, the SDX Protocol¹³⁷ recommends that investee companies select two or more individuals to represent them in engagements, in order to ensure regulatory compliance, mitigate risks of misunderstanding, and improve communication after the engagement.¹³⁸ Moreover, as far as topics to be discussed are concerned, the SDX Protocol states that 'it is inappropriate for shareholder-director engagement to include discussion of general business operations, current and projected financial results, strategic execution, and other operational and performance issues for which company management is directly responsible'.¹³⁹

By contrast, as they do not imply any exchange of information, a more flexible approach to the selection of the directors who are to be involved in the meetings, or of the relevant topics, can be accepted in relation to one-way contacts. Therefore, institutional investors could be allowed to ask for a meeting with a single director who, depending on the role played by him or her within the board, may also be a minority-appointed director.

However, the possibility for an individual board member to engage in direct dialogue with the shareholders who proposed or approved his or her election can impede the board's cohesiveness and undermine trust among directors. Clearly, risks for board cohesiveness are much less significant within one-way dialogues with a limited number of shareholders who are willing to communicate their concerns and opinions to directors, without receiving any information from

---

[132] According to the Shareholder-Director Exchange (SDX) protocol – a set of guidelines to provide a framework for shareholder-director engagements adopted by a working group of leading US independent directors and representatives from some of the largest and most influential long-term institutional investors – '[t]he company will specify participating directors based on the specific topic(s) to be discussed. Participants will be chosen based on experience, expertise, board role, and past relationship with the investor. The independent non-executive chairman, lead director, or relevant board committee chair will be one of the attendees.' See e.g. the Shareholder-Director Exchange (SDX), 'Introduction and Protocol' (2014) 14 <www.sdxprotocol.com/download-pdf> accessed 8 July 2020.
[133] Italian Stewardship Principles (n 4) 17.
[134] The relevance of compliance risks associated with the presence of minority-appointed directors may also depend on the type of appointing institutional investor. See e.g. Coffee, Jackson, Mitts and Bishop (n 110) 422, showing that 'information leakage increases with the intervention of hedge fund activists in a way that differs meaningfully from interventions by other investors'.
[135] EFAMA Code 2018 (n 53) 7.
[136] ibid.
[137] SDX (n 132) 13.
[138] ibid 14.
[139] ibid 13.

them in return. Nevertheless, in order to prevent information asymmetries within the board, any director who is contacted by the shareholders has a duty to share the information received with the entire board. In addition, to limit the risk of inadvertent disclosure of inside information, it would be preferable for the selected director to meet the shareholders accompanied by another director, a company manager (the person usually responsible for investor relations) or the board secretary.

6.6 THE ENFORCING GAP OF THE ITALIAN STEWARDSHIP PRINCIPLES

Like most stewardship codes adopted around the world, the Italian Stewardship Principles are applied on a 'comply or explain' basis.[140] Therefore, signatories to the Principles are free to not apply some of the recommendations, provided that they explain the reasons for doing so.[141] In order to enhance transparency and incentivize the application of the Stewardship Principles, it is recommended that institutional investors publicly declare their intention to adhere to the Stewardship Principles (e.g. on their website or in their annual financial statements). Moreover, signatories should commit to publishing an annual report containing easily understandable information about the methods used to apply the Principles.[142]

Nevertheless, as Assogestioni has no power to enforce compliance with the Italian Stewardship Principles, there remains the question of whether the lack of adequate enforcement mechanisms will limit the relevance of the Italian Stewardship Principles.[143]

The disclosure obligation concerning the engagement policy imposed by Article 124-quinquies of the Consolidated Law on Finance – implementing Article 3 g SRD II – does not seem to be sufficient in enhancing the relevance of the Italian Stewardship Principles. Indeed, Article 124-quinquies does not require disclosure of whether, and, if so, how, institutional investors adhere to a set of stewardship principles, and can only indirectly incentivize actual compliance with the Italian Stewardship Principles.

Other measures should therefore be considered in order to promote more effective compliance with Italian Stewardship Principles. As Simone Alvaro, Marco Maugeri and I have noted,[144] a tiering system similar to that adopted by the FRC,[145] or, preferably, a legal obligation to state within the engagement policy regulated by Article 124-quinquies of the Consolidated Law on Finance, whether and how stewardship principles have been adopted, could help in this regard.[146] In addition, as a stronger incentive, the legislator could explicitly state that the actual

---

[140] See Katelouzou and Sergakis, Shareholder Stewardship Enforcement, Chapter 27, providing an overview of the enforcement mode across all the stewardship codes.
[141] Italian Stewardship Principles (n 4) 11.
[142] ibid.
[143] As far as the UK Stewardship Code is concerned, see John Kingman, 'Independent Review of the Financial Reporting Council' (Department for Business, Energy and Industrial Strategy December 2018) 42 <https://assets.publishing.service.gov.uk/government/uploads/system/uploads/attachment_data/file/767387/frc-independent-review-final-report.pdf> accessed 8 February 2022.
[144] Alvaro, Maugeri and Strampelli (n 23) 58–62. See also John Coates, 'The Future of Corporate Governance Part 1: The Problem of Twelve' (2018) Harvard Public Law Working Paper No. 19-07, 20-21 <https://ssrn.com/abstract=3247337> accessed 8 July 2020, suggesting, as a tougher form of regulation, to turn the contents of the stewardship codes into affirmative legal obligations, with some form of public enforcement or auditing.
[145] In 2016, the FRC categorized signatories to the Stewardship Code into tiers based on the quality of their Code statements. Nevertheless, the efficacy of such a tiering exercise remains controversial. See Alvaro, Maugeri and Strampelli (n 23) 60.
[146] As, currently, compliance with Italian Stewardship Principles (n 4) is voluntary and based on a comply-or-explain principle, non-adhering issuers are not required to provide any disclosure. In addition, the Italian Stewardship Principles do not set out an obligation to illustrate in detail how they comply with the principles. See Katelouzou and Sergakis, Shareholder Stewardship Enforcement, Chapter 27.

adoption of the Stewardship Principles provides a relevant indication of compliance with the general duty of institutional investors to operate diligently, correctly and with transparency in the best interests of their beneficiaries, as required under Article 35-decies 1(a) of the Consolidated Law on Finance.[147]

6.7 CONCLUSION

The analysis set out in this chapter has shown that the Italian regulatory framework adequately supports institutional investor stewardship. However, given also the economic disincentives towards investing appropriate resources into engagement activities,[148] some potential developments that could affect the actual ability of the Italian Stewardship Principles to promote active ownership by institutional investors remain. For example, evidence shows that institutional investors submit lists of director nominees in only a fairly limited number of publicly listed companies, and, in fact, almost exclusively at larger investee companies.[149] Moreover, the future of the slate voting system seems uncertain as there have been calls for it to be revised or for alternative solutions to be used, such as the presentation of a unitary list of candidates by the incumbent board.[150]

That said, it must also be considered that the actual relevance of the Italian Stewardship Principles depends on developments affecting financial market actors and the principles themselves. As mentioned, the increase in the presence of activist investors in the Italian capital markets could influence the role played by institutional investors in Italy and lessen the relevance of stewardship codes. Indeed, given their different incentive structures, activist investors are more willing than mainstream institutional investors to take costly initiatives with a view to changing the target company's policies or management. Therefore, even institutional investors who adhere to the Italian Stewardship Principles might decide to support activist initiatives, which usually feature a more confrontational approach that largely diverges from that characteristic of stewardship principles. For example, the recent battle for control of Telecom Italia between Vivendi and Elliott Advisors has shown that this form of 'co-operation' between activist and mainstream institutional investors could enhance the relevance of activist-driven initiatives and lead to a more confrontational model of engagement in Italy. In the Telecom Italia case, the majority of mainstream institutional investors decided to side with Elliott Advisors and the co-operation between activist and non-activist institutional investors helped Elliott Advisors to appoint ten out of fifteen members of the Telecom Italia board.[151]

It is also worth recalling that the Italian Stewardship Principles are currently undergoing a review and that a revised version of the principles is expected to be released in the near future. Should Assogestioni decide to follow the approach adopted by the FRC for the review of the UK Stewardship Code, the relevance of the Stewardship principles could be significantly affected.

---

[147] For a similar proposal in the UK context, see Iris H–Y Chiu and Dionysia Katelouzou, 'Making a Case for Regulating Institutional Shareholders' Corporate Governance Roles' (2018) *Journal of Business Law* 67.

[148] Alvaro, Maugeri and Strampelli (n 23) 32–44.

[149] Assogestioni, '2019 Proxy Season Review' (n 93) 10.

[150] See e.g. Stella Richter and Ferdinandi (n 116) 613–14.

[151] Whether the diffusion of such initiatives can be beneficial for the Italian capital markets is difficult to predict as the potential effects of increased shareholder activism also depend, to a certain extent, on the ownership structure of target companies. See Gaia Balp, 'Activist Shareholders at De Facto Controlled Companies' (2019) 13 *Brooklyn Journal of Corporate, Financial & Commercial Law* 341, 348 noting that, as far as de facto controlled companies are concerned, 'an activist's power to exert substantial influence over the company's management premised on a small equity stake, coupled with the presence of a much larger, but (theoretically) disempowered, blockholder is likely to cause instability at the corporate-governance level'.

Although no information as to which path Assogestioni intends to follow is available yet, it can be reasonably assumed that the explicit incorporation of environmental, social and governance (ESG) factors into the stewardship framework could in some sense alter the role of the Italian Stewardship Principles and, to some extent, broaden their role, especially if guidance will be provided as to how ESG factors should be incorporated into stewardship activities.[152] There is, in fact, a growing consensus throughout the investment industry as to the importance of incorporating ESG factors into the investment process.

---

[152] Dionysia Katelouzou, 'Shareholder Stewardship: A Case of (Re)Embedding Institutional Investors and the Corporation?' in Beate Sjåfjell and Christopher M Bruner (eds), *Cambridge Handbook of Corporate Law, Corporate Governance and Sustainability* (CUP 2019); Iris H–Y Chiu and Dionysia Katelouzou, 'In Need of a Revised Stewardship Code for "Shareholder Stewardship" as a Matter of Corporate Governance Relations in UK Listed Equity' (Financial Reporting Council 2019) 1 <www.frc.org.uk/getattachment/201c2704-302f-4fdd-a4d9-f1eb71b9539d/Chiu,-Dr-(University-College-London)-Katelouzou,;.aspx> accessed 8 July 2020.

7

The Danish Stewardship Code

The Past, the Present and the Future

Hanne S. Birkmose and Marina B. Madsen

7.1 INTRODUCTION

Along with companies all over Europe, Danish companies suffered during the global financial crisis (GFC) from 2008 onwards. However, contrary to other member states, notably the UK, Denmark's post-crisis discussions on who and what caused the crisis had only a very limited focus on the role of shareholders. This was pronounced for the public debate, but also for the Danish Committee on Corporate Governance, where the development of the stewardship code in the UK (UK Code) and the later amendment of the Shareholder Rights Directive (SRD II)[1] was a side issue at first. However, in 2016, following a public consultation, the Danish Committee on Corporate Governance adopted a stewardship code (Danish Code).[2] The Danish Code is heavily inspired by the original version of the UK Code,[3] and it consists of seven principles.[4] The aim of the Danish Code is to promote long-term value creation in Danish listed companies and thereby contribute to maximizing long-term return for investors.[5] In this respect, the Danish Code shares a mutual purpose with the Danish 'Recommendations on Corporate Governance',[6] which seek to 'support value creation and accountable management, thus strengthening the long-term competitiveness of the companies'.[7] The Danish Code does not intend to establish a uniform approach for the exercise of stewardship activities by institutional investors. Rather, it aims to increase transparency as to how the individual investor chooses to exercise stewardship activities. This is emphasized by the application of the comply-or-explain principle, which is based on voluntariness and leaves it to the individual investor to determine the extent to which the principles are complied with.[8]

---

[1] Directive (EU) 2017/828 of the European Parliament and of the Council of 17 May 2017 amending Directive 2007/36/EC as regards the encouragement of long-term shareholder engagement [2017] OJ L132/1 (SRD II). SRD II is transposed by Act no 369 of 9 April 2019.

[2] Committee on Corporate Governance, 'Stewardship Code' (November 2016) <https://corporategovernance.dk/sites/default/files/180116_stewardship_code.pdf> accessed 25 July 2020 [hereinafter Danish Code].

[3] Financial Reporting Council, *The UK Stewardship Code* (September 2012) <www.frc.org.uk/getattachment/d67933f9-ca38-4233-b603-3d24b2f62c5f/UK-Stewardship-Code-(September-2012).pdf> accessed 13 July 2020 [hereinafter UK Code 2012].

[4] Danish Code (n 2) 3. It is mentioned in the preface that 'the Committee has sought to ensure that the Code is in line with leading foreign stewardship principles, notably including The UK Stewardship Code'.

[5] ibid.

[6] Committee on Corporate Governance, 'Recommendations on Corporate Governance' (August 2019) <https://corporategovernance.dk/sites/default/files/190911_recommendations_version_260819.pdf> accessed 25 July 2020 [hereinafter Recommendations on Corporate Governance]. See Danish Code (n 2) 3.

[7] Recommendations on Corporate Governance (n 6) 3.

[8] On the somehow more coercive approach adopted by the UK Stewardship Code, see Dionysia Katelouzou and Peer Zumbansen, 'The New Geographies of Corporate Governance' (2020) 42 *University of Pennsylvania Journal of International Law* 51.

On the face of it, the Danish Code is not significantly different from the UK Code. However, as already stated, the rationale behind the Danish Code is mainly linked to the listed companies' value creation for the good of investors. The stewardship element that is an embedded part of the UK Code,[9] and which builds on fiduciary relations between institutional investors and their beneficiaries, is seemingly missing from the Danish Code.[10] Consequently, the Danish Code appears to serve as a parallel to the Recommendations on Corporate Governance aimed at the board of directors of listed companies.[11]

The effect of stewardship in Denmark depends mainly on two factors. The first is the regulatory framework, which allows shareholders, in particular institutional investors and asset managers, to contribute to establishing and maintaining good corporate governance in listed companies. We discuss the legal framework for stewardship in Section 7.2 and argue that, in particular, the Companies Act grants shareholders very extensive rights in relation to their influence at general meetings and thereby sets the scene for stewardship activities. However, experience shows that engagement by institutional investors and asset managers may be a long haul, and this is further complicated by stewardship in Denmark being a recent development that is closely related to the introduction of the Danish Code. Thus, we continue our contribution with a presentation of the Danish Code: not only the Code as it stands (Section 7.3) but also its genesis and the experience with compliance so far (Section 7.4). Institutional investors and asset managers that have signed up for the Danish Code were required to submit their first report on stewardship in 2018. Given the very limited lifespan of the Danish Code, it is difficult to make any conclusions regarding the development of stewardship in Denmark. However, the past AGM seasons do not leave us with much optimism regarding the effect of the Danish Code, and the emerging question is whether this is likely to change with the implementation of the amended SRD II in Danish law (Section 7.5). However, because the transposition of SRD II has resulted in the Danish Code being phased out[12] and because the two frameworks share many similarities, this development does not leave us with much optimism either. The future of Danish stewardship is the theme of the final part of this chapter (Section 7.6). We argue that new initiatives may be required as the implementation of SRD II may be insufficient to secure a strong stewardship regime in Denmark. In this respect, we discuss whether the Recommendations on Corporate Governance can serve as a catalyst for further and better engagement by institutional investors through the establishment of a stronger interplay between the Recommendations and the Danish Code.

---

[9] See among others Iris H-Y Chiu, 'Turning Institutional Investors into "Stewards": Exploring the Meaning and Objectives of "Stewardship"' (2013) 66 *Current Legal Problems* 443, 460 ff.; Dionysia Katelouzou, 'Reflections on the Nature of the Public Corporation in an Era of Shareholder Activism and Stewardship' in Barnali Choudhury and Martin Petrin (eds), *Understanding the Company: Corporate Governance and Theory* (CUP 2017); and Arad Reisberg, 'The Notion of Stewardship from a Company Law Perspective: Re-defined and Re-assessed in Light of the Recent Financial Crisis?' (2011) 18 *Journal of Financial Crime* 126, 135.

[10] See Marina B Madsen, 'Anbefalinger for aktivt Ejerskab – corporate governance eller stewardship? [Recommendations on Active Ownership: Corporate Governance or Stewardship?]' [2017] *Nordisk Tidsskrift for Selskabsret [Nordic Journal on Company Law]* 36. One could argue that 'stewardship' may not be the right term in that case. However, the Committee's translation of the Danish Code (in Danish it is labelled 'Recommendations on Active Ownership') is 'Stewardship Code', and we therefore apply the term in our contribution.

[11] Recommendations on Corporate Governance (n 6).

[12] This was announced on 28 January 2020 by the Committee on Corporate Governance: Committee on Corporate Governance, 'Udfasning af Anbefalinger for aktivt Ejerskab [Phasing Out Recommendations on Active Ownership]' (28 January 2020) <https://corporategovernance.dk/udfasning-af-anbefalinger-aktivt-ejerskab> accessed 25 July 2020.

7.2 THE STEWARDSHIP LANDSCAPE

7.2.1 *The Legal Framework*

The influence of institutional investors and asset managers on the corporate governance affairs of listed companies depends partly on their formal rights at the general meeting. Thus, stewardship in Denmark may have a potentially significant effect as Danish company law grants shareholders very extensive rights in relation to the general meeting. These rights have been an essential part of the Danish governance framework since the first Company Act in 1917,[13] and they give shareholders broad powers to influence the direction of the company at the general meeting. The general meeting can decide on any matter concerning the company where such power is not given, by law, to either the board of directors or the management. Thus, the annual general meeting is considered omnipotent.[14]

Although the idea of shareholder democracy is deeply rooted in the Danish governance framework and most fundamental shareholder rights were statutorily enshrined in the Companies Act even before the 2007 Shareholder Rights Directive,[15] the rules on the registration of shareholders in some situations appear to be an impediment to active ownership by institutional shareholders in particular. Institutional investors often hold shares through nominee accounts. As a consequence, it is the nominee that is registered by name in the share register of the company. However, current Danish practice is such that the registration of a named nominee is not sufficient in terms of the nominee being entitled to exercise the rights attached to the shares (except for the economic rights).[16] Thus, the nominee is not able to vote at general meetings unless the de facto shareholder has at least given notice of his acquisition of the shares to the company, established good title to them, and has provided the nominee with a valid proxy. This practice often results in a large number of voting instructions (around 30 per cent) being dismissed for non-compliance owing to the fact that the nominee has not been given a valid proxy by the de facto shareholder.[17] While this shortcoming in the Danish governance framework is not being changed with the implementation of SRD II, the amendment may still improve the de facto shareholders' position as it increases the possibility of listed companies being able to communicate directly with the de facto shareholders.[18]

Aside from the Companies Act, existing regulations on financial institutions, including mutual funds, alternative investment funds and pension funds, shape the stewardship

---

[13] Today, lov 2009-06-12 nr. 470 om aktie- og anpartsselskaber (selskabsloven) (Act no 470 2009 on Public and Private Limited Companies (the Companies Act)). For an English translation, see Danish Business Authority, 'Danish Act on Public and Private Limited Companies (the Danish Companies Act)' <https://danishbusinessauthority.dk/sites/default/files/danish_companies_act.pdf> accessed 25 July 2020 (please note that there is no translated version which is updated with the latest amendments).

[14] See Hanne Birkmose and Therese Strand, 'Institutional Investors: Active Ownership through Nomination Committees' in Stephen Gates and Suzanne Young (eds), *Institutional Investors' Power to Change Corporate Behavior: International Perspectives*, vol 5 (Emerald 2013) 206; Jesper Lau Hansen, *Nordic Company Law: The Regulation of Public Companies in Denmark, Finland, Iceland, Norway and Sweden* (DJØF Forlag 2003) 81 ff; Paul Krüger Andersen and Evelyne JB Sørensen, *The Danish Companies Act: A Modern and Competitive European Law* (DJØF Publishing 2012) 162.

[15] Directive 2007/36/EC of the European Parliament and of the Council of 11 July 2007 on the exercise of certain rights of shareholders in listed companies [2007] OJ L184/17.

[16] Lars Bunch and Søren Corfixsen Whitt, *Selskabsloven med kommentarer [Commented Companies Act]* (Karnov Group 2018) § 52.

[17] See VP Securities, 'Memorandum: The Possibility of Simplifying the Proxy Voting Process in Denmark' (22 February 2018) 2 <www.vp.dk/News-and-Insights/News-List/2018/2/Memorandum-The-possibility-of-simplifying-the-proxy-voting-process-in-Denmark> accessed 25 July 2020.

[18] SRD II (n 1) art 3a is transposed into the Companies Act, s 49(a).

framework. However, such regulation of financial institutions is largely built on EU legislation. A key issue here relating to the stewardship framework is the identification and handling of conflicts of interest so as to ensure that financial institutions do not act in a way which may be harmful to their clients.[19] Another relevant aspect is that this regulatory framework – though limited – is intended to guide the financial institutions' investment practices.[20] In this respect, the Danish framework does not seem to go beyond the original EU legislative documents and therefore does not add anything of particular interest to the Danish stewardship debate.

While Danish shareholder democracy grants shareholders with great powers that enable them not only to monitor and control corporate governance arrangements but also to shape the rules governing the extensive powers of shareholders, shareholder engagement at the general meeting has traditionally been low.[21] Neither the reason for this observation nor the consequences for value creation in Danish companies have been explored in a Danish context. It seems likely that a game changer is needed to increase engagement and support value creation in listed companies, and this is the reason why the stewardship development is welcomed.

7.2.2 *The Shareholder Landscape*

In general, the Nordic markets are characterized by a high degree of ownership concentration.[22] This is also the case in Denmark. At the end of 2019, 60% of all companies listed at the Nasdaq OMX Copenhagen had at least one shareholder controlling more than 20% of the capital, and in addition to this, 24% had at least one shareholder controlling more than 50% of the capital.[23]

It is very difficult to find data on the composition of shareholders in Danish listed companies. Companies are only required to disclose information on shareholders holding more than 5 per cent of either the share capital or the votes.[24] However, as in many other European countries, retail investors hold a declining number of the shares, while institutional investors increase their share of the listed shares. In recent years, in particular foreign institutional investors have increased their ownership.[25] Still, even though foreign investors, presumably

---

[19] Among others, lovbekendtgørelse 2019-09-06 nr. 937 om finansiel virksomhed section 101 (Financial Business Act), lovbekendtgørelse 2019-10-14 nr. 1046 om investeringsforeninger m.v. section 51 (1)(5) (Investment Associations, etc. Act) and lovbekendtgørelse 2019-10-14 nr. 1047 om forvaltere af alternative investeringsfonde m.v. section 18 (1)(5) (Alternative Investment Fund Managers Act).

[20] See, among others, Dionysia Katelouzou, 'Shareholder Stewardship: A Case of (Re)Embedding Institutional Investors and the Corporation?' in Beate Sjåfjell and Christopher M Bruner (eds), *Cambridge Handbook of Corporate Law, Corporate Governance and Sustainability* (CUP 2019); and Hanne S Birkmose and Florian Möslein, 'Mapping Shareholders' Duties for Corporate Sustainability' in Alfonso Martínez-Echevarría (ed), *Interés social y gobierno corporativo sostenible: deberes de los administradores y deberes de los accionistas* [*Social Interest and Sustainable Corporate Governance: Duties of Administrators and Duties of Shareholders*] (Thomson Reuters 2019) s 4.1.

[21] See Birkmose and Strand (n 14) 217ff; and Therese Strand, 'Bolagsstämmor i praktiken – preliminära slutsatser från Sverige och Danmark [Shareholder Voting in Practice – Preliminary Conclusions from Sweden and Denmark]' (2008) 10 *Nordisk Tidsskrift for Selskabsret* [Nordic Journal on Company Law] 80, 90 ff. However, the reasons behind this observation do not seem to have been explored.

[22] Per Lekvall (ed), *The Nordic Corporate Governance Model* (SNS Förlag 2014) 48ff.

[23] Hand-collected data from the Orbis database. In 2013, 57% of all companies listed at the Nasdaq OMX Copenhagen had at least one shareholder controlling more than 20% of the votes of the company, and 28% had at least one shareholder controlling more than 50% of the votes of the company. Lekvall (n 22) 283 ff.

[24] The Companies Act, s 55.

[25] Jesper Lau Hansen and Carsten Lønfeldt, 'Corporate Governance in Denmark' in Per Lekvall (ed), *The Nordic Corporate Governance Model* (SNS Förlag 2014) 117 f. The percentage has increased from 24% in 2006 to 56% in 2016. See Klaus Søgaard, Michael Brichmann and Louise Celia Korpela Martiny, Generalforsamlinger i børsnoterede selskaber – Udvalgte emner og problemstillinger (del 2) [Annual Meetings in Listed Companies – Selected Topics and Problems (Part 2)] (2017) 1 *Revision & Regnskabsvæsen* [*Auditing & Accounting*] 14.

mainly institutional investors, held 54 per cent of the total capital listed in 2018,[26] they own only small shares of each listed company. The same is the case for Danish institutional investors.[27] Thus, despite the institutionalization of the capital market, the majority shareholders are not found among the institutional investors; rather, Danish industrial foundations play an important role as majority owners in a number of the largest Danish listed companies.[28]

7.3 THE DANISH STEWARDSHIP CODE

7.3.1 *The Scope and Target Group of the Danish Code*

In January 2016, the Minister of Business and Growth requested the Danish Committee on Corporate Governance to draft a stewardship code directed at Danish institutional investors based on the 'comply or explain' principle. Earlier in June 2014, the Committee had approached the Minister to draw his attention to the increasing focus on shareholder engagement in listed companies, and that other countries had by then adopted codes to promote shareholder engagement.[29] Thus, the initiating steps of the Danish Code were taken by the Committee on Corporate Governance, and it was then supported by the Minister, who highlighted the way in which shareholder engagement by institutional investors can benefit the competitive position of Danish companies.[30] In the Code's preface, the Committee stated the increased focus on the role of institutional investors in listed companies as one of the reasons behind the development of the Danish Code. The intended aim is 'to promote the companies' long-term value creation and thereby contribute to maximising long-term return for investors'.[31] The aim of the Danish Code is similar to that of the Recommendations on Corporate Governance,[32] and they are therefore mutually reinforcing.

The decision to adopt codes with mutually reinforcing aims can be explained by the fact that, in Denmark, the Danish Committee on Corporate Governance publishes both the Recommendations on Corporate Governance[33] and the Danish Code.[34] The Committee serves

---

[26] See VP Securities, 'AGM Analysis 2018' (June 2018) (on file with the authors). Regarding 2019, data from the Danish National Bank showed that 57% of the twenty-five largest listed companies (the so-called C25 index) was owned by foreign investors, see Danmarks Nationalbank, 'Værdistigninger øger udlandets ejerandel af C25-aktier [Increases in Value Increase the Foreign Ownership of C25 Shares]' (7 January 2020) <https://www.nationalbanken.dk/da/statistik/find_statistik/Sider/2019/Vaerdipapirer-20200107.aspx> accessed 29 January 2021.

[27] Holdings are below the 5% disclosure threshold, and that is the reason why more specific data on the size of the holdings are not available.

[28] Steen Thomsen, *The Danish Industrial Foundations* (DJØF Publishing 2017) 13. In 2011, some 68% of the total market capitalization of the Nasdaq OMX Copenhagen was held by industrial foundations. From 1980 until 2011, the number of listed companies owned by industrial foundations was stable at around sixteen to twenty companies, ibid 112f. Today, the number is within the same range; cf. hand-collected data from the database Orbis.

[29] Letter to the Minister of Business and Growth from the Danish Committee on Corporate Governance (10 June 2014) (on file with the authors).

[30] See Ministry of Industry, Business and Financial Affairs, 'Aktivt ejerskab skal understøtte en sund udvikling i danske virksomheder [Active Ownership is to Support a Healthy Development in Danish businesses]' (25 January 2016) <https://em.dk/nyhedsarkiv/2016/januar/aktivt-ejerskab-skal-understoette-en-sund-udvikling-i-danske-virksomheder/> accessed 25 July 2020.

[31] Danish Code (n 2) 3.

[32] Recommendations on Corporate Governance (n 6) 3, the aim of the Recommendations on Corporate Governance is 'to support value creation and accountable management, thus strengthening the long-term competitiveness of the companies'.

[33] ibid.

[34] Danish Code (n 2).

as an independent body under the Danish Business Authority. The members are all appointed by the Danish Minister of Business based on nominations by the Committee, and they represent the business community. Furthermore, it follows, from the Committee's articles of association, that the Committee should, at any point in time, collectively possess significant knowledge of and practical experience with: (i) management of listed companies; (ii) capital injections to listed companies; (iii) asset management as an institutional investor with either its own or an external management; and (iv) counselling of listed companies.[35] Strong ties between the two codes and the business community are therefore apparent.

The Danish Code is directed at 'Danish institutional investors, who invest in shares of companies that are publicly listed in Denmark. The Code is directed at shareholders and asset managers, as well as investors who perform both roles and directly or indirectly manage third party funds.'[36] As no uniform definition of an institutional investor exists, the Committee has clarified its target group by stating that the Danish Code is relevant primarily to 'investment funds, insurance companies, investment firms, pension funds and financial institutions'. During the consultation period leading up to the publication of the Danish Code, this broad definition of the target group gave rise to several remarks, which will be discussed.[37]

The Danish Code consists of seven principles and the Committee's explanatory comments to the individual principles. These comments can be used as a guideline and source of inspiration in the investors' work with the principles.[38] The themes covered by the seven principles are similar to those in the UK Code.[39]

The obligation of institutional investors to manage the funds on behalf of their beneficiaries derives from the management's general duties and good practice within the field of activity.[40] In the Danish context, these duties are of a contractual origin rather than of a fiduciary origin.

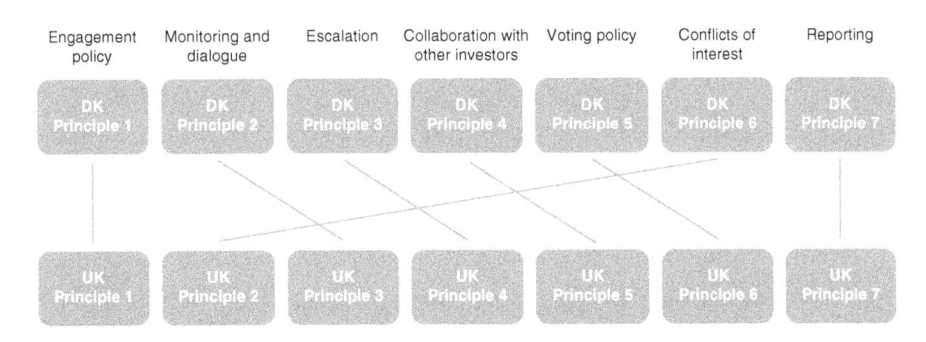

FIGURE 7.1 Comparison of the Danish and UK stewardship principles

---

[35] Committee on Corporate Governance, 'Vedtægter for Komitéen for god Selskabsledelse [Articles of Association of the Committee on Corporate Governance]' (2017) <https://corporategovernance.dk/sites/default/files/vedtaegter_for_komitten_for_god_selskabsledelse_-_januar_2017.pdf> accessed 25 July 2020. All four categories are to be present in the Committee at any point in time. However, there must an overrepresentation in the Committee of persons with knowledge of and practical experience with management of listed companies.
[36] Danish Code (n 2) 4. Thus, the code is limited to *Danish* institutional investors' *domestic* investments.
[37] See Section 7.4.2.
[38] Danish Code (n 2) 5.
[39] Figure 7.1. Despite the seemingly identical content, the wording of the two codes differs. On the textual differences between these codes, see Katelouzou and Siems, The Global Diffusion of Stewardship Codes, Chapter 30.
[40] See as an example the Danish Financial Business Act, s 43(1).

Consequently, the Danish Code does not support such duties,[41] which is contrary to the UK stewardship framework.[42]

Taking the above into account along with the wording of the concordant purposes and the genesis of the Danish Code, we argue that the Danish Code originates from a corporate governance context and thus serves as a parallel to the Recommendations on Corporate Governance.

7.3.2 Consultation Leading to the Danish Code

To understand both the Danish Code and the preliminary experiences with its application, it is relevant to refer to the consultation leading up to the publication of the Code. Prior to publication, the Committee issued a consultation period in the autumn of 2016. The Committee sent the draft Code to sixteen different respondents and issued an open consultation.[43] The Committee received fifteen consultation responses from fourteen respondents.[44] The respondents represented institutional investors, retail investors, interest groups, the business community and the Danish Financial Supervisory Authority.[45] The limited number of consultation invitations suggests that the discussion from the outset was intended for a small pre-selected group, but the few responses received also point towards a limited interest in discussing stewardship in Denmark outside of a narrow community. However, as many of the respondents were associations and interest groups, we should assume that they represent the opinions of their members, and that the implicit reach of the consultation was wider than merely fourteen respondents.

A review of the consultation responses generally showed a positive attitude towards the Danish Code's soft law approach in the form of the 'comply or explain' principle, which leaves room for the needs of individual investors and for investment strategies. However, some critical remarks appeared during the process. These remarks concern the scope of the Danish Code in terms of a national focus (investments of Danish investors in Danish listed companies) and the established target group. The former was deemed too narrow and the latter too imprecise.

Figures 7.2 and 7.3 show a graphical depiction of the consultation responses.[46]

As the figures show, the respondents mainly had objections to Principles 5 and 6 on voting policy and conflicts of interest, respectively. The position towards these particular principles was also reflected later on in the institutional investors' stewardship reporting.[47] Furthermore, some

---

[41] See Madsen (n 10) 36–56.
[42] See LS Sealy, 'Fiduciary Relationships' (1962) 20 *The Cambridge Law Journal* 69; Deborah A DeMott, 'Beyond Metaphor: An Analysis of Fiduciary Obligation' [1988] *Duke Law Journal* 879; Iris H-Y Chiu and Dionysia Katelouzou, 'From Shareholder Stewardship to Shareholder Duties: Is the Time Ripe?' in Hanne S Birkmose (ed), *Shareholders' Duties* (Kluwer Law International 2017). On the symbiosis of different layers of stewardship rules (hard, semi-hard and soft), see Dionysia Katelouzou, *The Path to Enlightened Shareholder Stewardship* (CUP) (forthcoming).
[43] The list of consultation invitations can be found here: Committee on Corporate Governance, 'Nye Anbefalinger for aktivt Ejerskab sendt i høring [New Recommendations on Active Ownership Submitted For Consultation]' (1 September 2016) <https://corporategovernance.dk/nye-anbefalinger-aktivt-ejerskab-sendt-i-hoering> accessed 25 July 2020.
[44] One respondent gave both a primary and a supplementary consultation response.
[45] A list of the respondents can be found here: Committee on Corporate Governance, 'Liste over afgivne høringssvar [List of Respondents to the Consultation]' <https://corporategovernance.dk/sites/default/files/media/document/hoeringsnotat_med_links_-_anbefalinger_for_aktivt_ejerskab.pdf> accessed 25 July 2020.
[46] Some respondents responded only to the proposed Code on an aggregate level and not to the individual principles, causing data material to be limited.
[47] See Section 7.5.1.

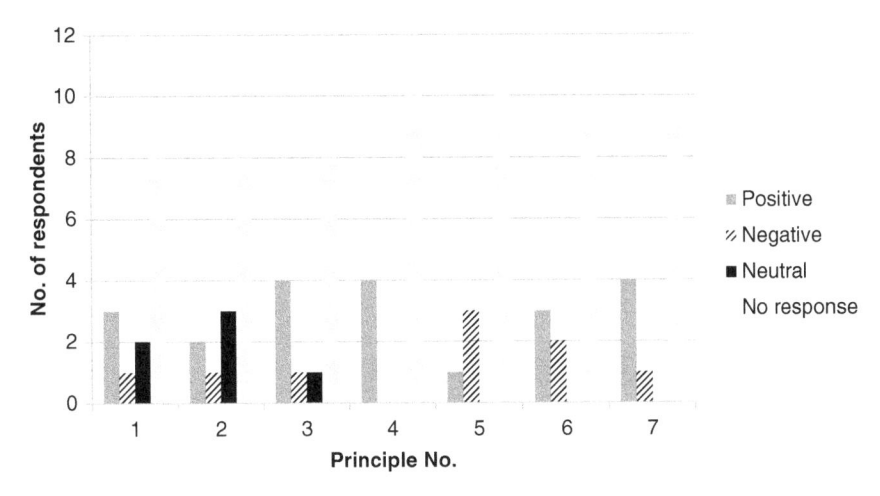

FIGURE 7.2 Result of the consultation on the individual principles

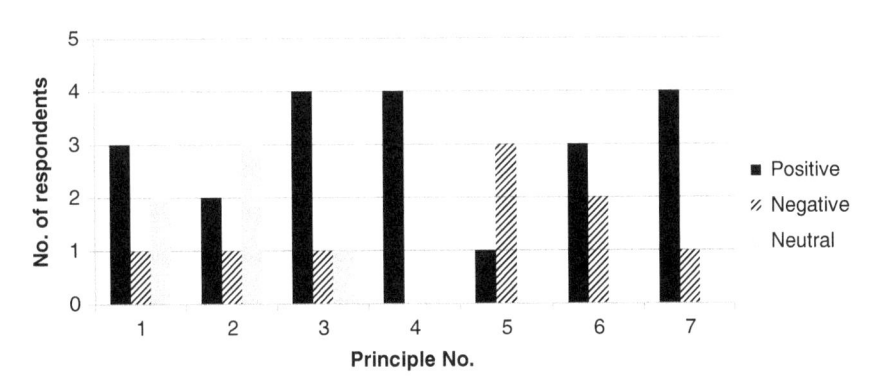

FIGURE 7.3 Result of the consultation on the individual principles (excluding consultation responses with no specific response)

responses to the consultation noted that the 'timing' of the Danish Code should perhaps have been considered more carefully given the (at that time) ongoing negotiations in the EU regarding the future amendment of the Shareholder Rights Directive.[48]

Following the consultation period, the Committee on Corporate Governance made some (non-material) changes to the code,[49] after which the Danish Code was published on 29 November 2016.

7.3.3 *The Content of the Code*

7.3.3.1 The Principle of Proportionality

As stated, the themes and the content of the principles are similar to those in the UK Code and, consequently, also in line with leading foreign stewardship principles.[50] By issuing a Danish

---

[48] See Section 7.6.
[49] For example, the Committee elaborated on the principle of proportionality, clarified ambiguities in comments on the principles and made a number of rephrases.
[50] Danish Code (n 2) 3.

Code, the Danish Committee on Corporate Governance addresses points of criticism, for example shareholder passivity, raised by the European Commission during and after the GFC.[51]

Despite the similarity in relation to the themes of the two codes, the Danish Code holds a principle of proportionality which is not explicitly found in the UK Code.[52] According to the Danish Code, '[t]he scope and the exercise of stewardship activities should be considered in light of a principle of proportionality, which takes into account portfolio allocation, the number of shares held in the particular company and an assessment of the need to seek influence on company operations and/or strategy on the basis of good corporate governance'.[53] As a consequence, three factors may influence the given investor's stewardship activities: the number of companies in the investor's portfolio (a highly diversified portfolio may prove it difficult for the investor to engage fully in all companies); the investor's influence in the given company measured by the number of shares held; and a case-by-case assessment of the severity of the particular issue and, hence, the need for the investor to engage. These three factors may result in increased or decreased stewardship activity from a given investor. While these three factors may influence the kind and extent of activity,

> [t]he principle of proportionality must also be considered in light of the particular investment strategy (e.g. active versus passive) and investment method (e.g. direct versus synthetic exposures[54]). In this context, it should be emphasized that a passive/index-based investment strategy does not exempt investors from exercising stewardship activities.[55]

As seen in the first part of the quote, the Committee acknowledges that shareholder engagement is not a natural part of the strategy of some investors, and that, consequently, they cannot be expected to perform such activities.[56] This is central to the Danish investor environment as shareholder engagement is not without cost.[57] However, the final part of the quote stresses that a passive investment strategy does not per se exempt an investor from engagement.

Applying a principle of proportionality in a stewardship code necessarily entails that the Committee is of the opinion that shareholder engagement might not always be a rational choice

---

[51] European Commission, 'Action Plan: European Company Law and Corporate Governance – A Modern Legal Framework for More Engaged Shareholders and Sustainable Companies' COM (2012) 744 final, 8:

> Effective, sustainable shareholder engagement is one of the cornerstones of listed companies' corporate governance model, which depends inter alia on checks and balances between the different organs and different stakeholders. If, for instance, the majority of shareholders remain passive, do not seek interaction with the company, and do not vote, the functioning of the current corporate governance system is less effective.

[52] Even though the UK Stewardship Code does not explicitly hold considerations on proportionality, one may argue that the 'comply or explain' principle in itself carries an element of proportionality; cf. also the wording of the UK Code 2012 (n 3) 4: 'smaller institutions may judge that some of its principles and guidance are disproportionate in their case. In these circumstances, they should take advantage of the 'comply or explain' approach and set out why this is the case.'

[53] Danish Code (n 2) 3.

[54] See Regulation (EU) No 575/2013 of the European Parliament and of the Council of 26 June 2013 on prudential requirements for credit institutions and investment firms and amending Regulation (EU) No 648/2012 [2013] OJ L176/1, art 4(1), point 126.

[55] Danish Code (n 2) 7.

[56] See Marina B Madsen, 'A New Approach to Shareholder Heterogeneity' in Hanne S Birkmose (ed), *Shareholders' Duties* (Kluwer Law International 2017). This has especially been accentuated in relation to index investments; see Giovanni Strampelli, 'Are Passive Index Funds Active Owners? Corporate Governance Consequences of Passive Investing' (2018) 55 *San Diego Law Review* 803.

[57] Michael C Jensen and William H Meckling, 'Theory of the Firm: Managerial Behavior, Agency Costs and Ownership Structure' (1976) 3 *Journal of Financial Economics* 305; Ronald Gilson and Jeffrey Gordon, 'The Agency Costs of Agency Capitalism: Activist Investors and the Revaluation of Governance Rights' (2013) 113 *Columbia Law Review* 863.

for institutional investors or a natural part of their investment activities.[58] This is also in line with previous remarks on the Danish Code about not holding a fiduciary element.[59] Furthermore, as the Committee has made its remarks on the principle of proportionality in the preface of the Danish Code, it implies that all principles in the Danish Code are to be read in light of the principle of proportionality.[60] However, the significance of the principle should be more apparent in relation to Principle 1 on the engagement policy as it sets the frame for all stewardship activities.

While the principle of proportionality may affect investors' and asset managers' overall approach to stewardship, it does not affect the reporting requirement according to Principle 7.[61] Consequently, if an institutional investor employs a passive investment strategy (which is part of the factors mentioned earlier), an application of the principle of proportionality may cause the investor to perform any stewardship activities not at all or to only a limited extent. Institutional investors and asset managers that have signed up to the Code are in any case expected to report annually on their stewardship based on the 'comply or explain' principle in relation to the individual principles.

Regardless of the interpretation of the 'comply and explain' principle and the principle of proportionality, it is clear that the Committee, in applying the principles, safeguards the interests of institutional investors. Had the Danish Code been built upon fiduciary relations, we would have expected a greater emphasis on the institutional investors' beneficiaries in the Code.[62]

7.3.3.2 Engagement Policy and Reporting

The first principle of the Danish Code recommends that Danish institutional investors should publicly disclose an engagement policy with respect to investments in shares in companies that are publicly listed in Denmark.[63] It is one of the most central principles in the Danish Code as it forms the basis of the investors' stewardship activities. In disclosing an engagement policy and at least an annual reporting hereof,[64] the institutional investors are held responsible for their stewardship activities. Hence, the first principle concretizes the expectations for institutional investors, and, in consideration of the 'comply or explain' principle, institutional investors are expected to 'explain *to which extent and, if necessary, how* the investor exercises stewardship activities and how stewardship activities fit into the broader investment process'.[65] With such wording, the Committee emphasizes that shareholder engagement is not a requirement.[66]

In its comments to the principle, the Committee emphasizes that the ultimate responsibility for the exercise of stewardship activities remains with the investor regardless of the investor's

---

[58] See Lars Nordén and Therese Strand, 'Shareholder Activism among Portfolio Managers: Rational Decisions or 15 Minutes of Fame?' (2011) 15 *Journal of Management & Governance* 375.
[59] See Section 7.4.1.
[60] During the consultation period, some respondents requested the Committee to be more specific in its definition of the principle of proportionality, especially with regard to the question of whether a higher degree of engagement is expected from an institutional investor that is the only large shareholder in a company.
[61] Danish Code (n 2) 11.
[62] The only reference made to the institutional investors' beneficiaries is in the comments to Principle 6 on conflicts of interest, 'in order to safeguard the interests of the customers/clients/beneficiaries of the institutional investor' (Danish Code (n 2) 10).
[63] Danish Code (n 2) 6.
[64] ibid 11.
[65] ibid 6 (emphasis added).
[66] Cf. also Section 7.3.3.1 on the principle of proportionality

potential outsourcing of certain investment activities. If the investors have outsourced activities or made use of service providers, the investors should explain how they ensure that the activities are carried out in accordance with the adopted investment policy.[67]

Principle 7 recommends that institutional investors report on their stewardship activities – including voting activity – at least annually. An important element of stewardship lies in transparency by institutional investors regarding the performed stewardship activities. To secure transparency, it is important that the investors disclose this information. In its comments, the Committee on Corporate Governance stated that the report 'should give a clear impression of how the investor's engagement policy was implemented over the course of the year'.[68] The report should be based on the investor's engagement policy and mention any deviation from it. Furthermore, it follows from the comments that institutional investors should make use of both quantitative and qualitative information to report on the activities performed without disclosing any confidential information. Consequently, unless institutional investors report comprehensively to the Code, the 'explain' component of the 'comply or explain' principle may serve as an indirect impediment to transparency.

Lastly, to spare institutional investors from double reporting if an institutional investor reports on stewardship activities in accordance with international guidelines or standards, for example another stewardship code, reference can be made to that report.

7.3.3.3 Stewardship Activities and Conflicts of Interest

Principles 2–6 concern the stewardship activities that Danish institutional investors are encouraged to perform, for example monitoring and dialogue, escalation, collaboration with other investors and voting, as well as identification and management of conflicts of interest.

The second principle recommends that institutional investors should monitor and engage in dialogue with the companies in which they invest, taking due account of their investment strategy and the principle of proportionality.[69] The second principle of the Danish Code is a natural continuation of the first principle on engagement policy. With this principle, the Committee accentuates two activities in particular that were called for by the European Commission during and after the GFC.[70]

While monitoring and dialogue are important elements of stewardship, they are also potentially very cost-intensive activities for institutional investors. Similar to the other principles, this principle is subject to the principle of proportionality, except that in this case the principle of proportionality is explicitly mentioned in the text of the principle and not in the comments. However, one must presume that this difference does not have a material significance as the Committee has accounted for the general application of the principle in the preface.

In its comments, the Committee stated that important topics for dialogue may include 'strategy, performance, risk, capital structure, corporate governance, corporate culture, management remuneration and corporate social responsibility, cf. Section 99 a–b of the Financial

---

[67] Danish Code (n 2) 6.
[68] ibid 11.
[69] ibid 7.
[70] European Commission, 'Corporate Governance in Financial Institutions and Remuneration Policies' (Green Paper) COM (2010) 284 final, 8 <https://publications.europa.eu/en/publication-detail/-/publication/1788e830-b050-447c-8214-77ed51b13241> accessed 25 July 2020; European Commission, 'The EU Corporate Governance Framework' (Green Paper) COM (2011) 164 final, 10–11 <https://publications.europa.eu/en/publication-detail/-/publication/3eed7997-d40b-4984-8080-31d7c4e91fb2/language-en> accessed 25 July 2020; European Commission, 'Action Plan' (n 51) 8.

Statements Act'. Despite the recommendation to engage in dialogue on important aspects of the company, it is important to note that the dialogue should not result in disclosure of information that may potentially affect the investors' ability to trade. However, investors who are willing to be given insider status should indicate it in their engagement policy.[71]

Principles 3 and 4 recommend that institutional investors should, as part of their engagement policy, determine how they may escalate their stewardship activities beyond regular monitoring and dialogue, and how they will act collectively with other investors in order to achieve greater effect and impact. While Principle 2 on monitoring and dialogue is concerned with the institutional investor's continuous stewardship activities, Principles 3 and 4 are, on the other hand, brought into play if an investor has misgivings regarding the investee company or its economic and/or corporate governance direction.

Principles 3 and 4 address one of the weightiest concerns stemming from the GFC, which is that boards of directors took excessive risks, and that the institutional investors remained passive or even encouraged excessive risk-taking.[72] The Danish approach is that institutional investors are recommended to determine how they may escalate their stewardship activities beyond regular monitoring and dialogue, and how they will co-operate with other investors in order to achieve greater effect and impact.

Principle 3 contains a list of potential escalation activities.[73] These are, inter alia, additional meetings specifically to discuss the investor's concerns, escalating stewardship activities in collaboration with other investors, making public statements (e.g. in advance of general meetings), requesting a general meeting to be convened, proposing to change board membership or choose a completely new board, and selling the shares.

These activities naturally continue on to Principle 4, according to which the Committee states that it can be effective for institutional investors to collaborate in relation to escalation.[74] With the word 'effective', the Committee may be referring either to a potentially greater impact if the shareholders co-operate or to the costs associated with shareholder engagement. The European Commission has acknowledged that the costs which institutional investors would face can dissuade them from engagement.[75] With co-operation, the institutional investors can share the costs between them and potentially make shareholder engagement an economically rational choice.

Despite the benefits of shareholder co-operation, the Committee emphasized that investors must be careful that their co-operation does not cause them to be subject to the mandatory bid rule in the Takeover Bids Directive.[76]

According to Principle 5, institutional investors are recommended to adopt a voting policy and to be willing to publicly disclose whether and how they have voted. Voting at the general meeting is tangible evidence of an investor's willingness to engage with the investee company, and the Committee recommends that institutional investors should vote at all general meetings. Attending the general meeting is an essential part of Danish shareholder democracy.[77]

Institutional investors are recommended to adopt a voting policy and be willing to be transparent regarding their voting practices. One of the principles that drew critical remarks from the respondents to the consultation was Principle 5.[78] In particular, the value of disclosure

---

[71] Danish Code (n 2) 7.
[72] European Commission, 'Corporate Governance in Financial Institutions and Remuneration Policies' (n 70) 8.
[73] Danish Code (n 2) 8.
[74] ibid 8–9.
[75] European Commission, 'Corporate Governance in Financial Institutions and Remuneration Policies' (n 70) 8.
[76] Danish Code (n 2) 8–9.
[77] See Section 7.2.
[78] See Section 7.4.2.

of investors' votes cast was questioned. As one respondent remarked, casting of votes usually takes place in confidence in Denmark.[79]

In its comments, the Committee noted that the starting point for many investors is typically to support the board of directors. However, it added that 'this ought not to be investors' default position'. The Committee further stated:[80]

> If the investor is unable to achieve a satisfactory outcome through dialogue, the investor should consider its options for voting at a general meeting. In cases where the investor intends to abstain from voting or to vote against the recommendations of the board of directors, the investor should consider informing the board of directors in advance of its intentions and its reasons for doing so.

This phrase emphasizes the Committee's intent to safeguard the good relations between institutional investors and the company. By informing the board of directors in advance, the board of directors will be provided with an opportunity to respond to the investor's critique in advance of a general meeting. Thus, the intended escalation by the investor may benefit the company as a whole. On the other hand, such information could also prompt the board of directors to collect proxies from the other shareholders who might not be aware of the critique raised by the institutional investor.[81] In such a situation, informing the board of directors could be strategically disadvantageous.

As stated in Section 7.3.1, the Danish Code is primarily relevant to investment funds, insurance companies, investment firms, pension funds and financial institutions.[82] Many of these are already subject to sector-specific regulations on conflicts of interest (e.g. the Danish Financial Business Act, s 71(1) and the Investment Associations, etc. Act, s 51(1)).[83] Still, Principle 6 recommends that the engagement policy should contain a description of how conflicts of interest in relation to stewardship are identified and managed. It follows from the Code's preface that sector-specific regulation takes precedence over the Code. If a description on how the investor identifies and manages conflicts of interest in relation to its stewardship activities has already been made publicly available, a reference to the description in the investor's engagement policy would suffice. Investors not subject to such regulation are recommended to establish 'procedures for the identification and management of potential conflicts of interest in order to safeguard the interests of the customers/clients/beneficiaries of the institutional investor'.[84]

7.3.4 Soft Law and Accountability

Historically, corporate governance initiatives have primarily been regulated using soft law tools,[85] and the Danish Code is no exception. The Danish Committee on Corporate

---

[79] Consultation response from Danske Advokater (Association of Danish Law Firms).
[80] Danish Code (n 2) 9.
[81] It is common in Danish companies that the board represents a majority of the votes at the general meeting; see Hanne S Birkmose and Karsten Engsig, 'Shareholder Activism in Danish Listed Companies' in Christoph Van der Elst, Anne Lafarre, Harpreet Kaur and Chao Xi (eds), Cambridge Handbook of Comparative Shareholding Engagement and Voting in Major Markets (CUP) (forthcoming).
[82] Danish Code (n 2) 4; see also Section 7.3.1.
[83] See n 19.
[84] Danish Code (n 2) 10.
[85] This is explained by two facts: first, the first initiatives were taken without the participation of regulating authorities; and second, heavy objections have been raised in the EU towards an potential application of hard law instruments to harmonize member states' corporate governance systems; cf. European Commission, *Acts of the Conference on Company Law and the Single Market* (1997) 18 <https://op.europa.eu/en/publication-detail/-/publication/dbe5cfdb-dd81-4054-974c-65616e0eae8c> accessed 25 July 2020; and José Engrácia Antunes and others, 'Report of the Reflection Group on the Future of EU Company Law' (5 April 2011) 11 <https://papers.ssrn.com/sol3/papers.cfm?abstract_id=1851654> accessed 29 January 2021.

Governance stated that self-regulation in the form of soft law is the best solution as soft law is more dynamic than traditional hard-law instruments. The principles in the Danish Code are easier to adjust to societal developments and are thus easier to keep up to date.[86] Still, the Recommendations on Corporate Governance and the Danish Code are subject to a consultation period, which prolongs the process and makes it more cumbersome for the parties involved.

As the Danish Code is based on soft law and voluntariness, it is only natural that it is supplemented with the 'comply or explain' principle. It is, thus, up to the individual investor to decide to what extent it wishes to adhere to the principles. Similar to the approach taken by the UK Financial Reporting Council, the Danish Committee has published a list of signatories (*positivliste*) that is a list of institutional investors who have declared to the Committee that they intend to respond to the Danish Code.[87] However, the Committee does not perform a 'tiering' of the published reports based on their quality. Consequently, there is poor transparency with respect to the quality of the published reports from the signatories. Stakeholders are therefore left to review the reports themselves or to read the general remarks in the Committee's annual report.[88] Consequently, it also relies on the stakeholders to respond to the published reports.[89]

The lack of formal sanctions in case of non-compliance with the 'comply or explain' principle or for reports of poor quality[90] is different from the Danish Recommendations on Corporate Governance, where the 'comply or explain' principle is incorporated in the Danish Financial Statement Act.[91] Accordingly, these recommendations have gained a status of 'semi-hard law'.[92]

---

[86] Danish Code (n 2) 4.

[87] See Committee on Corporate Governance, 'Positivliste over investorer, der vil forholde sig til Anbefalingerne for aktivt Ejerskab [List of Signatories to the Danish Code]' (7 October 2019) <https://corporategovernance.dk/sites/default/files/191007_positivliste_aktivt_ejerskab_071019f25667161156671152.pdf> accessed 25 July 2020. But it is important to note that, unlike the UK Code whose apply-and-explain approach is mandatory for FCA-authorized asset managers, the Danish code is completely voluntary. Further on the enforcement of stewardship codes, see Katelouzou and Sergakis, Shareholder Stewardship Enforcement, Chapter 27.

[88] The latest report can be found here: Committee on Corporate Governance, 'Årsberetning 2018–2019 [Annual Report 2018–2019]' (September 2019) <https://corporategovernance.dk/sites/default/files/media/aarsberetning_2018-2019_kommiteen-for-god-selskabsledelse.pdf> accessed 25 July 2020.

[89] To the authors' knowledge, no empirical evidence has been collected in Denmark to uncover whether institutional investors experience bottom-up pressure from beneficiaries to engage in stewardship activities. Further on the demand for stewardship, see Katelouzou and Micheler, The Market for Stewardship and the Role of the Government, Chapter 3.

[90] The tiered list in the UK thereby entails a form of 'naming and shaming' or 'reputational shaming'. See regarding these enforcement strategies: Judith van Erp, 'Reputational Sanctions in Private and Public Regulation' (2008) 1 *Erasmus Law Review* 145, esp. 147 and 155; John Armour, 'Enforcement Strategies in UK Corporate Governance: A Roadmap and Empirical Assessment' in Alessio M Pacces (ed), *The Law and Economics of Corporate Governance: Changing Perspectives* (Edward Elgar 2010) 216; Konstantinos Sergakis, 'Legal vs Social Enforcement of Shareholder Duties' in Hanne S Birkmose and Konstantinos Sergakis (eds), *Enforcing Shareholders' Duties* (Edward Elgar 2019) 141; and Katelouzou and Sergakis, Shareholder Stewardship Enforcement, Chapter 27, this volume. See, however, Section 7.6.

[91] According to the Danish Financial Statements Act, s 164, non-compliance with s 107b, which mandates listed companies to 'comply or explain' with the recommendations, is punishable by a fine. Furthermore, the recommendations are part of the Nasdaq OMX's Rules for Issuers of Shares. If an issuer violates the Rules for Issuers of Shares, the Exchange may among other things give the issuer a reprimand or a fine. The rules are available at Nasdaq, 'Rules for Issuers of Shares' (2016) <www.nasdaq.com/docs/Nasdaq-Copenhagen-Rules-for-Issuers-of-Shares_EN_upcoming_version.pdf> accessed 25 July 2020.

[92] Further on the coerciveness of corporate governance norms, see Katelouzou and Zumbansen (n 8).

7.4 EXPERIENCES WITH THE APPLICATION OF THE DANISH STEWARDSHIP CODE

7.4.1 *Danish Institutional Investors' Stewardship Reports*

The Danish Code came into effect for financial years starting on 1 January 2017 or thereafter.[93] Consequently, the first reports were published in the spring of 2018, concerning stewardship activities carried out in 2017. This implies that, at the time of writing, Danish institutional investors have published two reports. We will first look at the recent reports and then turn to a comparison of the two successive years.

As of 27 July 2019, thirty-four Danish institutional investors had signed up for the Danish Code.[94] Their compliance with the individual principles is depicted in Figure 7.4.

Overall, the reports show a high degree of compliance with the principles, with the strongest reticence observed regarding Principles 5 and 6 on voting policy and conflicts of interest.[95] This is not surprising considering the result of the consultation process.[96] If we compare the reports of 2017 to the recent reports of 2018, the following appears.

The overall trend is that more institutional investors are complying with the principles in 2018 than in 2017. Across the seven principles, only positive developments were detected regarding investors that comply in full. However, as Table 7.1 shows, there was an interesting development regarding Principle 6 on conflicts of interest. In one year, there was a 9.7 percentage point decrease in investors who comply in part. This development is shared between a positive development in 'Complies', but also a 5.8 percentage point increase in 'Does not comply'. As revealed in the consultation, Principle 6 was one of the principles that faced a large number of critical remarks.[97] A reading of the 2018 reports shows that some 'Does not comply' investors address conflicts of interest in their internal guidelines or in employee manuals, and others refer to prevalent sector-specific law and do not mention conflicts of interest in their engagement policy as recommended by the Committee on Corporate Governance.

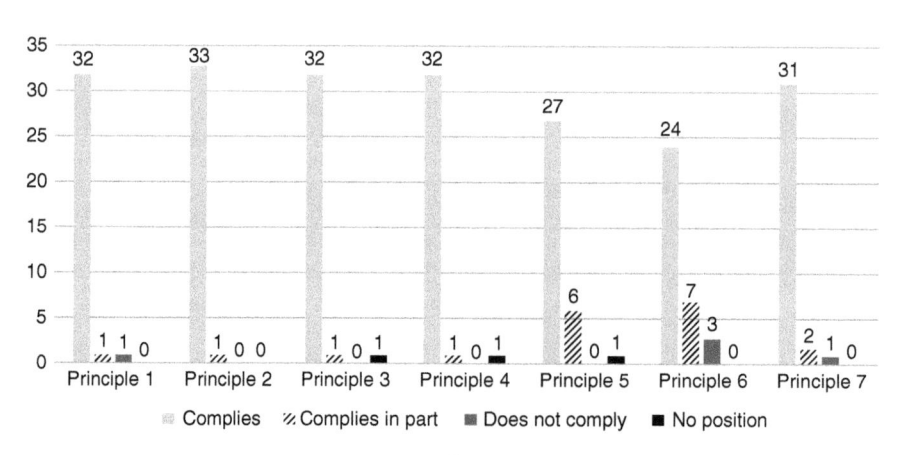

FIGURE 7.4 Position towards the individual principles

---

[93] Danish Code (n 2) 3.
[94] This is an increase of one investor in a year.
[95] Where an investor chooses to comply in part or not to comply, an explanation should be provided by the investor in the report. The majority of investors do so.
[96] See Section 7.4.2.
[97] ibid.

TABLE 7.1 *Development in institutional investors' stewardship reporting 2017/18*

	Principle 1		Principle 2		Principle 3		Principle 4		Principle 5		Principle 6		Principle 7	
	2017	2018	2017	2018	2017	2018	2017	2018	2017	2018	2017	2018	2017	2018
Complies	90,9%	94,1%	97,0%	97,1%	90,9%	94,1%	93,9%	94,1%	69,7%	79,4%	66,7%	70,6%	75,8%	91,2%
Development		⬅		⬅		⬅		⬅		⬅		⬅		⬅
Complies in part	6,1%	2,9%	3,0%	2,9%	6,1%	2,9%	3,0%	2,9%	27,3%	17,6%	30,3%	20,6%	24,2%	5,9%
Development		⬇		⬇		⬇		⬇		⬇		⬇		⬇
Does not comply	3,0%	2,9%	0,0%	0,0%	0,0%	0,0%	0,0%	0,0%	0,0%	0,0%	3,0%	8,8%	0,0%	2,9%
Development		⬇		⬆		⬆		⬆		⬆		⬆		⬅
No position	0,0%	0,0%	0,0%	2,9%	3,0%	2,9%	3,0%	2,9%	3,0%	2,9%	0,0%	0,0%	0,0%	0,0%
Development		⬆		⬆		⬇		⬇		⬇		⬆		⬆

Another interesting – and positive – development is found in Principle 5 on voting policies. During the consultation, this principle also received many critical responses. However, from 2017 to 2018, the number of investors who comply in part decreased from 27.3% to 17.6%, and none of the investors chose not to comply. Given the somewhat negative attitude in the consultation and in the first reports, this is a surprising, yet positive, development.

Generally, Danish institutional investors have responded positively to the Danish Code. Unfortunately, it is not possible to cross-check with actual voting behaviour as Danish companies are not required to publish details on voting results at the general meeting.[98] However, it is relevant to investigate whether an increase in shareholder engagement can be detected at the companies' general meeting following the adoption of the Danish Code.

7.4.2 *The Past GM Season*

Section 7.4.1 showed an overall positive perception of Danish stewardship. In this section, we will compare data from the general meetings of the 'GM season' 2017/2018 to 2018/2019 to see if there has been an increase in engagement from institutional investors. Despite the fact that an increase cannot necessarily be ascribed to the Danish Code, it is interesting to investigate the actual activity because the aim is, in all cases, to ensure that institutional investors contribute to companies' long-term value creation through shareholder engagement.

The data comprises agendas and minutes of annual general meetings and extraordinary general meetings (held between May 2017 and May 2019) from Danish companies listed on the 'Large cap' index.[99] The data show that, in the GM season 2018/2019, shareholders put an item on the agenda 31 times, only once did a shareholder propose an amendment to an item on the agenda, 130 addresses to the general meeting were made and 137 questions were asked of the management. The findings are summarized in Table 7.2, which also shows that the Danish institutional investors' share (in the table denoted 'By II') in the shareholder engagement, visible at the general meeting in the season 2018/2019, is limited;[100] institutional investors made 14% of the addresses and asked 4% of the questions. However, in relation to both, institutional investors increased their engagement compared to 2017/2018.

TABLE 7.2 *Engagement by institutional investors*

	2018/2019 Total	2018/2019 By II	2017/2018 Total	2017/2018 By II	Change Total	Change By II
Items on the agenda	31	0	4	0	675%	–
Amendments to items on the agenda	1	0	2	0	–50%	–
Addresses to the general meeting	130	18	66	13	97%	38%
Questions to management	137	5	111	4	23%	25%

[98] Only the voting results have to be published for listed companies unless a shareholder requires a complete account of the vote; cf. the Danish Companies Act, s 101(5) and (6). These provisions transpose the SRD II (n 1) art 14(1) and (2).

[99] These are the largest companies with the most liquid shares in Denmark. Usually, the AGM takes place in the spring, as listed companies with financial year from 1 January to 31 December are required to submit their annual report (approved by the AGM) to the Danish Business Authority within four months after the end of the financial year; cf. the Danish Financial Statements Act, s 138.

[100] None of the minutes revealed engagement from non-Danish institutional investors.

TABLE 7.3 *Comprehensiveness of the minutes 2018/19*

	No.	%
Extensive protocol	19	49%
Record of decisions	14	36%
Minutes in between the two above	6	15%

While engagement from Danish institutional investors is limited, our hand-collected data show that non-institutional investors have dramatically increased their engagement. For instance, there has been a 675% increase in the number of items put on the agenda and a 111% increase in the addresses made to the general meeting by non-institutional investors.[101]

A methodological challenge in conducting a review based on publicly available data from the companies lies in the fact that no uniform approach exists. Some companies publish only a record of decisions, whereas others publish an extensive protocol. Therefore, the aggregate level of shareholder engagement at the general meetings may be higher than the figures in Table 7.2 show. Table 7.3 shows the comprehensiveness of the 2018/19 minutes. Also, the data collected are only an expression of the formal shareholder engagement that takes place at general meetings. The informal shareholder engagement that takes place outside general meetings might be the type of engagement that the institutional investors primarily exert.[102]

7.5 IMPLEMENTATION OF THE SRD II IN DANISH LAW

The SRD II was transposed to Danish law in June 2019.[103] However, a several of the provisions did not come into force until later.[104] This approach was chosen to give the affected parties more time to adjust to the new legal framework. The provisions on transparency of institutional investors and asset managers have been transposed as amendments to several existing acts,[105] including the Financial Business Act and the Alternative Investment Fund Managers Act.[106] The Act transposing SRD II is

---

[101] This is partly owing to a number of individuals who have been very active. They represent either themselves or an interest group, e.g. the Danish Shareholders' Association, which is a non-profit organization with the objective of supporting the members in their capacity as shareholders, investors and pension savers and to improve their conditions; Dansk Aktionærforening, 'Dansk Aktionærforenings vedtægter [Articles of Association of the Danish Shareholders' Association]' (22 November 2014) <www.shareholders.dk/dansk-aktionaerforening/102096/dansk-aktionaerforenings-vedtaegter> accessed 25 July 2020. See also Strampelli, Institutional Investor Stewardship in Italian Corporate Governance, Chapter 6.

[102] Brian L Connelly, Robert E Hoskisson, Laszlo Tihanyi and S Trevis Certo, 'Ownership as a Form of Corporate Governance' (2010) 47 *Journal of Management Studies* 1561; and Joseph McCahery, Zacharias Sautner and Laura Starks, 'Behind the Scenes: The Corporate Governance Preferences of Institutional Investors' (2016) 71 *Journal of Finance* 2905. See also Section 7.4.1 on the Danish institutional investors' high degree of compliance with the Stewardship Code.

[103] Lov 2019-04-09 nr. 369 om ændring af selskabsloven, lov om kapitalmarkeder, lov om finansiel virksomhed og forskellige andre love (Gennemførelse af ændringer i aktionærrettighedsdirektivet om tilskyndelse til langsigtet aktivt ejerskab) (Act No 369 of 9 April 2019 on the amendment of the Company Act, the Capital Markets Act, the Financial Business Act and different other acts (Transposition of Changes in the Shareholder Rights Directive on the Encouragement of Long-Term Active Ownership)) (our translation).

[104] The provisions on transparency of institutional investors and asset managers came into force for financial years starting on 1 January 2020. Consequently, the first reporting took place in 2021. The provisions on identification of shareholders came into force on 3 September 2020.

[105] SRD II (n 1) ch 1b also includes provisions on transparency of proxy advisers. These, however, are out of the scope of this chapter.

[106] Consolidating Act No 937 of 6 September 2019 and Consolidating Act No 1047 of 14 October 2019.

structured such that section 1 contains the different provisions to be implemented in the Companies Act, section 2 contains the provisions to be implemented in the Capital Markets Act, and so on. Therefore, the provisions transposing articles 3g–3i of the SRD II are found in several sections. More precisely, they are found in section 3, no. 3 (aimed at asset managers) and no. 4 (insurance companies), section 4, no. 3 (asset managers regulated by the AIFM Directive), section 5, no. 2 (Undertakings for Collective Investment of Transferable Securities (UCITS) funds which have not delegated the management to an investment management company), section 6, no. 2 (pension funds), section 7, no. 1 (ATP) and section 8, no. 1 (LD). The transposition is in general true to the wording of the SRD II, which is why provisions found in the different acts are comparable.

Danish acts did not use the term 'institutional investor' anywhere prior to the transpositions, despite it being an established term. Owing to the regulatory approach, the term is still not a part of the transposition of the SRD II. Rather, the different provisions found in the different acts use sector-specific terms that are natural to the specific acts that transpose Directive 2009/138/EC[107] and Directive (EU) 2016/2341[108] as these make up the SRD II's 'institutional investor' scope.[109] Therefore, even though the transposing acts do not use the term 'institutional investors', the scope is the same as in the Directive. However, it was stated in the preparatory document that it is important to the Danish regulators that national undertakings which are naturally seen as institutional investors should be included as well.[110] Consequently, the scope is widened as compared to the SRD II as the so-called Arbejdsmarkedets Tillidspension (ATP) and Lønmodtagernes Dyrtidsfond (LD)[111] are given the same duties as SRD II's institutional investors. The term 'asset manager' was also not found in any Danish act prior to the implementation of the SRD II. However, rather than using established terms, this term is now defined in the relevant acts; including the Financial Business Act, section 3(1)(70) and the Alternative Investment Fund Managers Act, section 3(1)(54). The definitions follow the definition found in the SRD II, article 1(2)(b).

According to the Danish provisions (which transpose the SRD II), institutional investors and asset managers must develop and publicly disclose a policy for active ownership in listed companies. The requirements relating to the content of the policy closely follow the wording of the SRD II, and institutional investors must publish an engagement policy independent of whether or not investments are made through an asset manager.

Moreover, institutional investors as well as asset managers have to disclose, on an annual basis, how their engagement policy has been implemented, along with a general description of their voting behaviour, a statement of the most significant votes, and a statement on the use of the services of proxy advisers. Institutional investors and asset managers also must disclose how they cast votes at the general meeting of companies in which they hold shares. Such disclosure, however, may exclude votes that are insignificant owing to the subject matter of the vote or the size of the holding in the company. This option follows from SRD II Article 1(3). Recital 18 of the preamble states that '[s]uch insignificant votes may include votes cast on purely procedural matters or votes cast in companies where the investor has a very minor stake compared to the investor's holdings in other investee companies'. This understanding of 'insignificant votes' is peculiar in relation to the latter because, offhand, it seems more relevant to

---

[107] Directive 2009/138/EC of the European Parliament and of the Council of 25 November 2009 on the taking-up and pursuit of the business of Insurance and Reinsurance [2009] OJ L335/1 (Solvency II).

[108] Directive (EU) 2016/2341 of the European Parliament and of the Council of 14 December 2016 on the activities and supervision of institutions for occupational retirement provision [2016] OJ L354/37.

[109] Institutional investors are defined in SRD II (n 1) art 2(b)(d).

[110] Proposal no. 157 of 6 February 2019 for the Act on the amendment of the Companies Act, the Capital Markets Act, the Financial Business Act and different other acts (Transposition of Changes in the Shareholder Rights Directive on the Encouragement of Long-Term Active Ownership) (our translation) s 2.2.3.

[111] ATP and LD are both Danish labour market supplementary pension funds.

look at the investor's stake of the shares of a given company relative to the full share capital of the specific company and therefore the investor's potential influence in the said company. Despite this, the same wording is found in the Danish preparatory document.[112] Recital 18 also states that '[i]nvestors should set their own criteria regarding which votes are insignificant on the basis of the subject matter of the vote or the size of the holding in the company, and apply them consistently'. This is also repeated in the Danish preparatory document,[113] and no further guidance is given on the matter. Disclosure of how the votes have been cast does not have to be made on an annual basis. Neither the SRD II nor the Danish provisions specify the frequency with which such information has to be disclosed.[114] However, in order to ensure the relevance and timeliness of such information, it is to be expected that such information must be disclosed at least on a yearly basis. This could be done in connection with the publication of the policy and the implementation of the policy.

The transparency provisions that transpose article 3g of the SRD II are subject to the 'comply or explain' principle. According to section 344 of the Danish Financial Business Act, the Danish Financial Supervisory Authority shall supervise compliance with the provisions of the Financial Business Act and therefore also compliance with the 'comply or explain' provisions.[115] Sanctions in cases of non-compliance with the 'comply or explain' approach include reprimands and orders, but not pecuniary sanctions. There are no formal requirements laid down for disclosure.[116] However, as the information has to be made freely available to the public on the institutional investor's or the asset manager's website, this form of media is expected to be the preferred form for the required disclosure.

The relationship between institutional investors and asset managers is generally of interest to the institutional investors' beneficiaries, investee companies and other stakeholders. Consequently, the SRD II includes provisions that ensure transparency regardless of whether an institutional investor engages with investee companies or appoints an asset manager.[117] This includes public disclosure of information on the contents of the arrangement with the asset manager.[118] Moreover, to ensure that institutional investors monitor the activities of the asset manager, the SRD II requires that asset managers disclose information on their investment strategy and implementation thereof to show how it complies with their arrangement with the institutional investor.[119] While this disclosure is not public, it has to be done on an annual basis to the institutional investors with whom the asset manager has an arrangement to invest on their behalf. In these matters, the transposition of articles 3g(2) and 3h in Danish law follows the wording of SRD II.[120]

7.6 THE FUTURE OF DANISH STEWARDSHIP

As mentioned, the timing for the publication of the Danish Code was questioned as work on SRD II was at an advanced stage at that time,[121] and the content of the Danish Code was very similar to what was expected to be part of the forthcoming Directive. Therefore,

---

[112] n 110, explanatory notes for section 3, no 4 and section 4, no 3.
[113] ibid.
[114] SRD II (n 1) art 3g (1)(b).
[115] Similar supervisory provisions apply for other types of institutional investor.
[116] Further on the transposition of Article 3g of the SRD II and the enforcement trends across member states; see Katelouzou and Sergakis, Shareholder Stewardship Enforcement, Chapter 27.
[117] This requirement follows from SRD II (n 1) arts 3g(2) and 3h. See among others Chiu and Katelouzou (n 42) 143–44.
[118] SRD II (n 1) art 3h(2).
[119] SRD II (n 1) art 3i(1).
[120] Supra (n 103) section 3, no 4; section 4, no 3; section 5, no 2; section 6, no 2; section 7, no 1; and section 8, no 1.
[121] Marina B Madsen, 'Nye Anbefalinger for Aktivt Ejerskab for danske institutionelle investorer [New Recommendations on Active Ownership for Danish Institutional Investors]' [2017] *Nordisk Tidsskrift for Selskabsret* [Nordic Journal for Company Law] 30, 42–43.

commentators foresaw that the implementation of SRD II would overlap with the suggested stewardship framework.[122] This prediction turned out to be correct as this chapter so far has shown. The differences between the Danish Code and the Danish provisions implementing SRD II are very small, and, as a consequence, the Danish Code is being phased out.[123] The Committee on Corporate Governance has explained that this decision has been made to avoid an overlap between hard-law regulation and the Danish Code. Therefore, the Committee will report on the compliance with the Danish Code for the last time in its annual report for 2019/20.

7.6.1 *Impact of the SRD II on Danish Stewardship*

The Danish provisions transposing the Directive's chapter 1b on transparency become effective for financial years beginning 1 January 2020 or later.[124] Consequently, the institutional investors and asset managers must report on their stewardship in 2021. As mentioned, this approach has been chosen to give institutional investors and asset managers sufficient time to adjust to the 'comply or explain' provisions that are now found in hard-law provisions.[125] This transition period seems to be most relevant to institutional investors and asset managers that have not previously applied the Danish Code as it allows them to discuss whether to adjust their practices to comply with the stewardship provision either in whole or in part, or to explain why they do not comply in whole or in part.[126] Institutional investors and asset managers that are currently signed up to the Danish Code may continue their current practice while they prepare for the necessary amendments, such as the scope of the policy. This is because, from 2020, the policy should cover their entire portfolio and not only investments in Danish listed companies.

The targeted institutional investors and asset managers of the two frameworks are largely identical. The Danish Code is addressed to Danish institutional investors which invest in shares of companies that are publicly listed in Denmark. The term 'institutional investor' is not defined in the Danish Code, but, from the introduction to the Code, it is clear that the understanding of the term is very wide as it includes 'shareholders and asset managers, as well as investors who perform both roles and directly or indirectly manage third party funds'.[127] The transposed provisions on stewardship are also aimed at Danish institutional investors and asset managers, but the provisions apply regardless of whether they invest in Danish listed shares or foreign shares. Owing to the widening of the scope of the SRD II in Danish law,[128] institutional investors and asset managers that are covered by the transposed provisions on stewardship are more or less

---

[122] The Committee on Corporate Governance was also aware of the forthcoming amendment of the Shareholder Rights Directive. In the preface of the Danish Code (n 2) 3, it is said that '[t]he Committee is monitoring the proposal closely and will consider an update of the Code to the extent necessary'.

[123] See Committee on Corporate Governance, 'Udfasning af Anbefalinger for aktivt Ejerskab' (n 12).

[124] Lov 2019-04-09 nr. 369 (n 103) s 9.

[125] On the symbiosis of soft and semi-hard stewardship requirements in the EU, see Dionysia Katelouzou and Konstantinos Sergakis, 'When Harmonization Is Not Enough: Shareholder Stewardship in the European Union' (2021) 22 *European Business Organization Law Review* 203.

[126] The exact number of investors and asset managers that have not signed up to the code is unknown, partly because it is difficult to extract only those that invest in Danish listed companies from the Danish Financial Supervisory Authority's registers. However, the list of signatories shows a clear lack of asset managers, so the number is probably as high as a couple of hundred.

[127] Danish Code (n 2) 4.

[128] See Section 7.6.

similar to the institutional investors invited to sign up to the stewardship code, other than the scope of the former being marginally narrower.[129]

A review of the legal requirements in relation to the content of the policy on active ownership also reveals a great deal of overlap. This is not surprising as both frameworks were greatly inspired by the UK Code.[130] The only recommendation in the Danish Code which is not found in the transposed provisions on stewardship is Principle 3 on escalation.[131] However, it can be argued that escalation is an implicit part of shareholder engagement and therefore should be reflected in the institutional investors' and asset managers' policies on active ownership. Institutional investors and asset managers which engage with investee companies can be expected to escalate their approach if dialogue with the companies is unsuccessful. Therefore, escalation can be seen as an integrated part of the institutional investors' and asset managers' stance on dialogue as well as co-operation with other shareholders. In other words, the elements of the policy on active ownership can be said to make up an escalation in itself: from monitoring, to dialogue, to co-operation, to voicing out at the general meeting.

Consequently, there seemed to be little room for the Danish Code in the future stewardship framework; when the Committee on Corporate Governance announced that the Danish Code is being phased out, it came as no surprise.

7.6.2 A Possible Interplay between Directors' Duties and Shareholders' Engagement

The Danish decision to phase out the Danish Code rather than developing this soft law framework alongside the transposed hard-law framework[132] should not be seen as the culmination of Danish stewardship, though. The development of corporate governance practices in Europe and in Denmark (including stewardship) has been an ongoing process for years, and it hardly ends with the implementation of the SRD II. This is especially so because it is not obvious that the SRD II will radically change the stewardship environment in Denmark; further developments may be necessary to secure further and better engagement by institutional investors. The experiences with the Danish Code are few, arguably as a result of its voluntary opt-in regime, which arguably is insufficient to coerce an increase in stewardship by institutional investors and asset managers. Although the regulatory approach is hardened with the SRD II,[133] its real effect may continue to be limited owing to the comply-or-explain principle. Moreover, the enforcement mechanisms may be insufficient to ensure a positive change to shareholder engagement.[134]

Even though we argue that the Danish Code is a corporate governance measure,[135] the development of the Code was somewhat detached from the development of the Danish Recommendations on Corporate Governance. This is, for instance, illustrated by the fact that the previous mentions of active ownership in the Recommendations on Corporate Governance

---

[129] An example of an institutional investor not covered by the transposed provisions is the so-called group 2 insurance companies, *per contra* the wording of the Danish Financial Business Act, s 159.
[130] See explicitly the Danish Code (n 2) 3.
[131] Danish Code (n 2) 8.
[132] See Katelouzou and Sergakis (n 125).
[133] See Chiu and Katelouzou (n 42) 143.
[134] See the various contributions to Hanne S Birkmose and Konstantinos Sergakis (eds), *Enforcing Shareholders' Duties* (Edward Elgar 2019) and Katelouzou and Sergakis, Shareholder Stewardship Enforcement, Chapter 27, this volume.
[135] But see Katelouzou and Puchniak, Global Shareholder Stewardship, Chapter 1 and Katelouzou (n 42) for a thorough analysis of the investment management aspects of stewardship.

were removed at the same time that the Danish Code was introduced.[136] Thus, the Danish corporate governance framework is made up by the Recommendations on Corporate Governance aimed at the board of directors of listed companies and the Danish Code aimed at institutional investors and asset managers.

One possible way to strengthen the role of institutional investors and asset managers in corporate governance could be to reverse this approach and approximate the duties of the boards of directors in listed companies, and of institutional investors and asset managers.[137] Inspiration can be found in jurisdictions such as Belgium, the Netherlands and the UK, where the boards of directors are expected to react to the active ownership of their shareholders. When the board of directors is explicitly encouraged to consult with major investors or institutional investors before and after the general meeting, it is likely that dialogue between investors and the board and the accountability of both parties will improve. While the chosen approach is different in the mentioned member states, two features can be observed. First, the board of directors has to be active in encouraging and facilitating active ownership.[138] This includes a duty by the boards of directors not only to reach out to major shareholders to understand their views on the performance of the company but also to encourage these shareholders to engage with the company and to attend the general meeting. Second, the boards of directors have a duty to seek and understand the motivation behind the votes cast at the general meeting when a significant number of shareholders voted against a resolution.[139] This requires the board to approach the shareholders and initiate a dialogue on their motivation for their votes. However, it may also result in more dialogue *prior* to the general meeting as the duty to react occurs only when a significant number of shareholders vote against a resolution. If listed companies engage with major shareholders, including institutional investors, they may get a better understanding of shareholders' preferences and consequently avoid significant opposition to a resolution. Such increased dialogue will also support stewardship as dialogue is an important tool for institutional investors and asset managers.

7.7 CONCLUSION

In this chapter, we have argued that the Danish understanding of stewardship has close ties to the corporate governance framework. The Committee of Corporate Governance developed the Danish Code as a parallel to the Recommendations on Corporate Governance, and the two codes share a mutual purpose in their aim to support long-term value creation in listed

---

[136] The Corporate Governance Code did not include any recommendations aimed at the institutional investors; it was merely a mentioning of the responsibilities of the larger shareholders in relation to active ownership and the responsibility of the listed company to consider the investors' opinions. See Recommendations on Corporate Governance (n 6) 5–6, section 4 of the introduction.

[137] An alternative way would be to strengthen the duties of investors themselves via investment management law. On this, see Iris H–Y Chiu and Dionysia Katelouzou, 'Making a Case for Regulating Institutional Shareholders' Corporate Governance Roles' (2018) *Journal of Business Law* 67.

[138] See e.g. Corporate Governance Committee, 'The 2020 Belgian Code on Corporate Governance' (2019) 24, Principles 8.8–8.9 <www.corporategovernancecommittee.be/en/over-de-code-2020/2020-belgian-code-corporate-governance#:~:text=The%202020%20Code%20is%20the%20third%20Belgian%20Code,on%20or%20after%201%20January%202020%20%28%E2%80%98compulsory%20application%E2%80%99%29> accessed 29 January 2021 [hereinafter Belgian Corporate Governance Code]; and Financial Reporting Council, *The UK Corporate Governance Code* (July 2018) 4, Principle D <www.frc.org.uk/getattachment/88bd8c45-50ea-4841-95b0-d2f4f48069a2/2018-UK-Corporate-Governance-Code-FINAL.pdf> accessed 25 July 2020 [hereinafter UK Corporate Governance Code]. It is also observed in the Recommendations on Corporate Governance (n 6). However, it is less explicit here.

[139] See Belgian Corporate Governance Code (n 138) 24, Principles 8.8–8.9; UK Corporate Governance Code (n 138) 5, provision 4; and the Large and Medium-sized Companies and Groups (Accounts and Reports) (Amendment) Regulations 2013 (UK), Statutory Instruments 2013, No 1981.

companies. The 2016 Danish Code was the first of its kind in Denmark. Owing to its relatively short lifespan, we have limited knowledge of the Danish institutional investors' and asset managers' engagement with listed companies. The tentative conclusions suggest that Danish listed companies may not get the engagement from institutional investors and asset managers that is beneficial to their value creation. Anecdotal evidence suggests that there is a shift towards passive index funds and that engagement is outsourced to proxy advisers.[140] However, we do not believe that the transposition of the SRD II will serve as a catalyst for more and better engagement here and now. It may, however, bring about an enlightening process through which institutional investors, asset managers and their stakeholders may initiate discussions on the role of institutional investors and asset managers in corporate governance. These discussions may spark the development of a stronger stewardship framework in the future. In the meantime, other measures may be applied to kick-start the process. We believe that it is possible to seek closer integration of the duties of the institutional investors and asset managers and of the board of directors. Inspiration can be found in other EU member states, where the board of directors is given responsibilities that are interconnected with the engagement of institutional investors and asset managers. In this respect, we should take advantage of the fact that the development of both Codes has been assigned to the Committee of Corporate Governance. Thus, the Committee has the knowledge and experience to facilitate a development of the duties ascribed to the boards of directors that is parallel and interconnected to the duties of the institutional investors and asset managers in relation to active ownership.

---

[140] See VP Securities (n 26). On the way index funds engage in stewardship, see Fisch, The Uncertain Stewardship Potential of Index Funds, Chapter 21.

8

Stewardship Norwegian-Style

Fragmented and State-Dominated (but Not without Potential?)

Jukka Mähönen, Beate Sjåfjell and Monica Mee

8.1 INTRODUCTION

The perceived shift in corporate governance from the role of the board to the role of corporate shareholders[1] has emerged as principles 'to ensure long-term stability and social responsibility'.[2] This is partly owing to a change in controlling structures from dispersed shareholdings to more concentrated ones with institutional shareholders.[3] Institutional investors, the mainly profit-maximizing intermediaries that invest on behalf of their ultimate beneficiaries, foremostly mutual funds, pension funds and insurance companies, hold 41 per cent of the global market capitalization of listed companies.[4] For instance, the US domiciled institutional investors alone account for 65 per cent of global institutional investor holdings.[5] This major capital market shift, which Gilson and Gordon have labelled 'agency capitalism', has important implications for both investor 'activism' and regulation.[6]

An important part of the trend has been shareholder 'empowerment', a policy shift making corporate managers accountable to shareholders as perceived 'owners' of the company.[7] According to this policy thinking, corporate boards should be 'independent' (whatever that means) and focus on monitoring on behalf of the shareholders, rather than managing the company independently. Instead, shareholders should 'engage' with companies on issues

---

[1] Popularly denoted as 'stewardship', spearheaded by the UK Code 2010, see Financial Reporting Council, *The UK Stewardship Code* (July 2010) <www.frc.org.uk/getattachment/e223e152-5515-4cdc-a951-da33e093eb28/UK-Stewardship-Code-July-2010.pdf> accessed 17 June 2020.

[2] Dionysia Katelouzou, 'Shareholder Stewardship: A Case of (Re)Embedding Institutional Investors and the Corporation?' in Beate Sjåfjell and Christopher M Bruner (eds), *Cambridge Handbook of Corporate Law, Corporate Governance and Sustainability* (CUP 2019) 581.

[3] Jennifer G Hill, 'Good Activist/Bad Activist: The Rise of International Stewardship Codes' (2018) 41 *Seattle University Law Review* 497, 524, 499.

[4] Adriana De La Cruz, Alejandra Medina and Yung Tang, 'Owners of the World's Listed Companies' (OECD 2019) 5 <www.oecd.org/corporate/owners-of-the-worlds-listed-companies.htm> accessed 17 June 2020.

[5] De La Cruz, Medina and Tang (n 4) 9.

[6] Ronald J Gilson and Jeffrey N Gordon, 'Agency Capitalism: Further Implications of Equity Intermediation' in Jennifer G Hill and Randall S Thomas (eds), *Research Handbook on Shareholder Power* (Edward Elgar 2015) 32–33; Hill, 'Good Activist/Bad Activist' (n 3) 500.

[7] 'Owners' in quotation marks, as we do not know any jurisdiction in which the shareholders of a limited liability company are recognized as its owners under property law. Shareholders own shares, entitling their holders to rights and duties in a company. From a property rights perspective, a company owns its own assets and owes its own responsibilities. Beate Sjåfjell, Andrew Johnston, Linn Anker-Sørensen and David Millon, 'Shareholder Primacy: The Main Barrier to Sustainable Companies' in Beate Sjåfjell and Benjamin J Richardson (eds), *Company Law and Sustainability: Legal Barriers and Opportunities* (CUP 2015) 79–80.

ranging from strategy to corporate responsibility, issues that company law assigns to the board.[8]

This trend has been reflected in corporate governance regulation. Since the early 1990s these shareholder engagement and empowerment policies have become increasingly embedded in corporate governance codes, listing rules, company legislation, European Union directives and transnational regulatory standards.[9] As a response to the global financial crisis of 2008–09, in spite of doubts that it happened because of, rather than in spite of, the shareholder empowerment trend, the influence of the stewardship trend has become even stronger. We see this especially in the 2017 reform of the 2007 Shareholders' Rights Directive,[10] and a number of European jurisdictions have seen the emergence of specific stewardship codes. The 2017 amended Shareholders' Rights Directive (SRD II)[11] includes elements found in previous stewardship codes, such as a requirement for institutional investors to publicly disclose their policy for integrating shareholder engagement into their investment strategies or explain why they have chosen not to do so ('comply or explain').[12] According to the arguments behind the codes (and also in stewardship regulation per the EU Directive), encouraging shareholders to act as 'stewards' is a way forward not only towards better corporate governance in the mainstream, economics-focused sense but also towards more sustainable and responsible companies in light of the environmental and social challenges we, as a global community, face.

The stewardship concept is widely connected to institutional investors, referring to the actions that asset managers can take in order to enhance the value of the companies that they invest in on behalf of their own beneficiaries. However, as seen in this book, the nature of stewardship varies from jurisdiction to jurisdiction based on shareholder structures. In the Nordic region (similar to many Asian jurisdictions), the role of states, sovereign holding companies and wealth funds, other public market actors such as public pension funds, families, family-controlled investment companies and family-based foundations is significant compared to (other) national and international institutional investors.[13] For this reason, we understand 'stewardship' in this chapter in its wider meaning, governing all controlling structures, not only those dominated by institutional investors.[14]

In this chapter, we discuss the peculiarities of Nordic stewardship before concentrating on Norway and Norwegian stewardship, which is dominated by the state and the municipalities, but also to some extent by private investors. The structure of the chapter is as follows. In Section 8.2 we discuss the Nordic stewardship in light of international stewardship discussion, before concentrating on Norway and the current regulatory framework of stewardship there in Section 8.3. Norway is a particularly interesting case study for stewardship in the Nordic region,

---

[8] Simon Deakin, 'Against Shareholder Empowerment' in Janet Williamson, Ciaran Driver and Peter Kenway (eds), *Beyond Shareholder Value: The Reasons and Choices for Corporate Governance Reform* (Trades Union Congress 2014) 36.

[9] Deakin (n 8) 36.

[10] Directive 2007/36/EC of the European Parliament and of the Council of 11 July 2007 on the exercise of certain rights of shareholders in listed companies [2007] OJ L184/17.

[11] Directive (EU) 2017/828 of the European Parliament and of the Council of 17 May 2017 amending Directive 2007/36/EC as regards the encouragement of long-term shareholder engagement [2017] OJ L132/1 (SRD II).

[12] EY, 'Q&A on Stewardship Codes' (August 2017) 2 <www.ey.com/Publication/vwLUAssets/ey-stewardship-codes-august-2017/$FILE/ey-stewardship-codes-august-2017.pdf> accessed 17 June 2020.

[13] See Gen Goto, Alan K Koh and Dan W Puchniak, 'Diversity of Shareholder Stewardship in Asia: Faux Convergence' (2020) 53 *Vanderbilt Journal of Transnational Law* 829; Dan W Puchniak, 'The False Hope of Stewardship in the Context of Controlling Shareholders: Making Sense Out of the Global Transplant of a Legal Misfit' *The American Journal of Comparative Law* (forthcoming).

[14] On these 'multiple faces' of stewardship, see Katelouzou and Puchniak, Global Shareholder Stewardship, Chapter 1.

together with Denmark and its stewardship code.[15] In comparison, there is nothing that resembles a stewardship code in Finland, Iceland and Sweden. Norway has strong public, semi-public and private institutional investors, notably its sovereign wealth funds, the state as direct shareholder, public pension funds, private foundations and strong families. Further, the Norwegian version of a stewardship code consists in the peculiar principles of the Industry Recommendation of Use of Ownership (Norwegian Recommendation 2019),[16] issued by the board of the Norwegian Fund and Asset Manager Association (VFF).[17]

In Section 8.4, we reflect on the Norwegian choices on stewardship against global trends and especially jurisdictions in Asia with similar shareholder structures, with strong state and family shareholders. We also include comparisons with Denmark. Conclusions on why a stewardship code is not needed in Norway can be found at the end of Section 8.4.

8.2 STEWARDSHIP IN THE NORDIC REGION

In the Nordic region, including Denmark, Finland, Iceland, Norway and Sweden, the issue of 'stewardship' in its wider meaning is highly relevant as its shareholder structures in both non-listed and listed large companies are highly concentrated.[18] There is nothing strange in that as such; even at a global level, fully dispersed ownership is today a rather rare phenomenon: almost 85 per cent of the world's largest listed companies have a single shareholder holding more than 10 per cent of the company's capital, and the three largest shareholders hold more than 30 per cent of the capital in three-quarters of all listed companies and above 50 per cent of the capital in half of the listed companies worldwide. In only 1 per cent of the listed companies worldwide do the three largest shareholders hold less than 10 per cent of the company's equity capital.[19]

However, albeit the public sector is an important owner of shares in listed companies all over the world, reaching 14 per cent of market capitalization globally,[20] in the Nordic countries its role is even stronger, reaching its peak in Norway with 35 per cent.[21] Besides the public sector (Nordic states, sovereign wealth funds, and state, regional and municipal public pension funds), shareholdership is dominated not by institutional investors but by individual entrepreneurs and families, and private foundations.[22] Almost two-thirds of Nordic listed companies have only one dominant shareholder,[23] although the dominant shareholder varies from country to country and from company to company. However, what we see typically are bank-based business groups in Sweden, pension funds in Iceland,[24] state-controlled enterprises in Norway, institutional

---

[15] See Birkmose and Madsen, The Danish Stewardship Code, Chapter 7.
[16] Verdipapirfondenes Forening, 'Bransjeanbefaling for medlemmene i Verdipapirfondenes forening: Utøvelse av eierskap [Industry Recommendation for the Members of the Norwegian Fund and Asset Management Association: Exercise of Ownership Rights]' (1 January 2020) <https://vff.no/assets/Bransjeanbefaling-utøvelse-av-eierskap-januar-2020.pdf> accessed 17 June 2020 [hereinafter Norwegian Recommendation 2019].
[17] Verdipapirfondenes Forening, 'About the Norwegian Fund and Asset Management Association' <https://vff.no/about-the-norwegian-fund-and-asset-management-association> accessed 17 June 2020.
[18] Steen Thomsen, 'Nordic Corporate Governance Revisited' (2016) 65 Nordic Journal of Business 4; Per Lekvall (ed), The Nordic Corporate Governance Model, with Comment by Ronald J. Gilson (SNS Förlag 2014).
[19] De La Cruz, Medina and Tang (n 4) 17.
[20] ibid 9.
[21] ibid 39.
[22] ibid 9; Jeffrey Gordon, 'Convergence and Persistence in Corporate Law and Governance' in Jeffrey Gordon and Wolf-Georg Ringe (eds), The Oxford Handbook of Corporate Law and Governance (OUP 2018) 30.
[23] Thomsen (n 18) 6.
[24] Jón B Magnússon, 'Investment Stewardship of Institutional Investors in Iceland' (MSc thesis, Reykjavik University 2018) <https://skemman.is/bitstream/1946/31224/1/MS_thesis_0605804139.pdf> accessed 17 June 2020.

investors such as a Finnish occupational pension insurance company (a domestic type of institutional investor)[25] and civil law foundation share ownership in Denmark and Sweden. Generally, foundations controlling business companies are more common in the Nordic area than elsewhere in the world.[26] However, foreign ownership in Finnish listed companies is also quite high, at 43 per cent.[27] The institutional investors that own shares in Nordic listed companies are generally also mostly foreign. The exceptions are Iceland and Sweden. In Denmark, 25% of total market capitalization is foreign (19% domestic); in Finland 24% (11% domestic); and in Norway 19% (10% domestic). In Iceland, 55% of total market capitalization is in the hands of domestic institutional investors (compared to 6% foreign) and in Sweden 20% is domestic (18% foreign).[28]

Concentrated share ownership brings dominating shareholders to the forefront of Nordic corporate governance. This gives rise to the question of whether they are friends or foes of *sustainable governance*. We understand sustainable governance as governance that ensures the contribution of business to sustainability, to securing the social foundation for humanity now and in the future within planetary boundaries.[29] In the international discussion there are two dominant views of institutional investors' role. Hill describes these views as narratives of the 'bad activist' versus the 'good activist'.[30] The first is a negative perception of investors', asset managers' and proxy advisers' role in corporate governance as predatory, myopic and prone to destructive short-termism.[31] In many discussions, this view is culminated in the activist role of hedge funds and acquisitions in causing the financial crisis.[32]

The second is a positive perception, emphasizing the increased shareholder power and engagement in corporate governance as a solution to the financial crisis, not a cause of it. According to this analysis, the problem during the crisis was not too much shareholder pressure on management but too little.[33] Accordingly, shareholder power and engagement should be

---

[25] Owning totally 10% of market capitalization in Finland; see Ulf Jakobsson and Timo Korkeamäki, *Ownership and Governance of Large Finnish Firms* (Prime Minister's Office Reports 6/2014, 18 December 2014) 21 <https://julkaisut.valtioneuvosto.fi/handle/10024/79695> accessed 22 January 2022. On the other hand, the public sector holds still 14% of total capitalization; De La Cruz, Medina and Tang (n 4) 37.

[26] Thomsen (n 18) 7.

[27] Euroclear Finland, 'Foreign Ownership of Shares Issued' (31 December 2021) <https://www.euroclear.com/dam/EFi/Statistics/ForeignOwners/ForeignOwners20101/Foreign_ownership_20211231.pdf> accessed 26 January 2022.

[28] De La Cruz, Medina and Tang (n 4) 39.

[29] This is elaborated on in the H2020 Sustainable Market Actors for Responsible Trade (SMART) project; see SMART Report D2.4: Beate Sjåfjell, Jukka Mähönen, Andrew Johnston and Jay Cullen, 'Obstacles to Sustainable Global Business: Towards EU Policy Coherence for Sustainable Development' (2019) University of Oslo Faculty of Law Research Paper No 2019-02 <https://ssrn.com/abstract=3354401> accessed 17 June 2020. On planetary boundaries, see Johan Rockström and others, 'Planetary Boundaries: Exploring the Safe Operating Space for Humanity' (2009) 14 *Ecology and Society* <www.ecologyandsociety.org/vol14/iss2/art32/> accessed 17 June 2020; Will Steffen and others, 'Planetary Boundaries: Guiding Human Development on a Changing Planet' (2015) 347 *Science* 736. On securing the social foundation within planetary boundaries, see Melissa Leach, Kate Raworth and Johan Rockström, 'Between Social and Planetary Boundaries: Navigating Pathways in the Safe and Just Space for Humanity' in International Social Science Council and UNESCO, *World Social Science Report 2013: Changing Global Environments* (OECD Publishing 2013) 84–90. See also European Commission, *General Union Environment Action Programme to 2020: Living well, within the limits of our planet* (European Union 2014).

[30] Hill, 'Good Activist/Bad Activist' (n 3) 500.

[31] Jennifer G Hill, 'Images of the Shareholder – Shareholder Power and Shareholder Powerlessness' in Jennifer G Hill and Randall S Thomas (eds), *Research Handbook on Shareholder Power* (Edward Elgar 2015).

[32] Martin Lipton, 'Do Activist Hedge Funds Really Create Long Term Value?' (*Harvard Law School Forum on Corporate Governance*, 22 July 2014) <https://corpgov.law.harvard.edu/2014/07/22/do-activist-hedge-funds-really-create-long-term-value/> accessed 17 June 2020; Hill, 'Good Activist/Bad Activist' (n 3) 501.

[33] Hill, 'Good Activist/Bad Activist' (n 3) 503.

increased as they can do good.[34] For this reason, shareholders should be granted stronger rights, encouraged to make greater use of their existing powers to engage with the companies in which they invest, or both.[35]

The proponents of the negative perception emphasize the need to protect companies from shareholders.[36] They require more mandatory regulation, emphasizing a broader societal purpose of the enterprise and the need for strengthening the role of corporate boards and their independence from shareholders, with the duties of the board being to the company itself.[37] Some aspects of the European Commission Sustainable Finance Initiative reflect this perception,[38] while the belief in shareholders and notably institutional investors as potential drivers for sustainability is also reflected in the initiative. The positive perception is most clearly reflected in the stewardship codes, firstly the UK Stewardship Code, and the Organisation for Economic Co-operation and Development (OECD) Principles of Corporate Governance,[39] and also in SRD II and the earlier Dodd-Frank Act[40] in the US.[41]

8.3 STEWARDSHIP NORWEGIAN-STYLE

8.3.1 *No Stewardship Code*

The Norwegian Recommendation 2019 does not constitute a proper stewardship code and covers only fund and asset managers as a 'steward' type/group. In this section we will consider how the Norwegian Recommendation is developed further in practice, and contrast it with rules and guidelines on more important Norwegian shareholders, especially, on the one hand, the Norwegian state's own principles for responsible 'ownership' and, on the other, the principles, policies and fund management of one of the world's largest sovereign wealth funds, the Norwegian Government Pension Fund Global, managed by Norges Bank Investment Management (NBIM).[42]

8.3.2 *The Fragmented Regulatory Picture of Stewardship in Norway*

The lack of a Norwegian institutional investor stewardship code is natural as domestic institutional investors own only 10 per cent of shares in Norwegian listed companies, foreign institutional

---

[34] John Kay, 'The Kay Review of UK Equity Markets and Long-Term Decision Making' (Department for Business, Innovation and Skills, July 2012) <https://assets.publishing.service.gov.uk/government/uploads/system/uploads/attachment_data/file/253454/bis-12-917-kay-review-of-equity-markets-final-report.pdf> accessed 17 June 2020.
[35] Hill, 'Images of the Shareholder' (n 31).
[36] Hill, 'Good Activist/Bad Activist' (n 3) 500–503.
[37] Beate Sjåfjell and Mark B Taylor, 'A Clash of Norms: Shareholder Primacy vs. Sustainable Corporate Purpose' (2018) 13 *International and Comparative Corporate Law Journal* 40; Sjåfjell, Johnston, Anker-Sørensen and Millon (n 7).
[38] See European Commission, 'Sustainable Finance' <https://ec.europa.eu/info/business-economy-euro/banking-and-finance/sustainable-finance_en> accessed 17 June 2020; European Commission, 'Action Plan: Financing Sustainable Growth' COM (2018) 97 <https://ec.europa.eu/transparency/regdoc/rep/1/2018/EN/COM-2018-97-F1-EN-MAIN-PART-1.PDF> accessed 17 June 2020.
[39] OECD, *G20/OECD Principles of Corporate Governance* (2015) <www.oecd.org/daf/ca/Corporate-Governance-Principles-ENG.pdf> accessed 17 June 2020.
[40] An Act to promote the financial stability of the US by improving accountability and transparency in the financial system, to end 'too big to fail', to protect the American taxpayer by ending bailouts, to protect consumers from abusive financial services practices, and for other purposes (Dodd–Frank Wall Street Reform and Consumer Protection Act), Pub. L. No. 111–203, 124 Stat. 1376–2223.
[41] As an example, say-on-pay.
[42] Norges Bank Investment Management <www.nbim.no> accessed 17 June 2020.

investors following their own codes or recommendations owning 19 per cent.[43] Instead of institutional investors, the Norwegian investor scene is dominated by public actors, foremostly the Norwegian state, being a controlling shareholder in major Norwegian listed companies such as Equinor and Telenor.[44] The Norwegian Government Pension Fund Global, although not a part of the Norwegian investor scene as it does not invest in Norway, may be perceived as a standard-setter for other investors also in Norway. Additionally, there are other strong public investors such as Argentum Fondsinvesteringer AS, a Norwegian government investment vehicle for private equity fund investments, Norwegian sovereign wealth fund Folketrygdfondet investing in Norway and other Nordic countries, managing the assets of Government Pension Fund Norway, and Kommunal Landspensjonskasse Gjensidig Forsikringsselskap (KLP), a mutual insurance company responsible for the management of municipal and county pensions and insurances. As a private counterforce, there are strong private institutional investors such as Storebrand ASA, with, however, public investors as major shareholders.

In many ways the Norwegian shareholder structure resembles Asian economies, such as Singapore.[45] Yet, unlike Singapore, Norway may be said to have addressed the 'stewardship puzzle' by abandoning the idea of a stewardship code. The other uniquely Singaporean phenomenon, the Stewardship Principles for Family Businesses,[46] developed for family companies, can, however, be compared with Norwegian state guidelines for use of its shareholder rights in companies it controls, encouraging the state to be a good 'steward' of its companies.[47]

Typically, the Norwegian investors each follow their own sets of guidelines.[48] These guidelines emphasize elements of stewardship: active engagement, better corporate governance, requirements of sustainability and responsibility, and response to environmental and social challenges, albeit they do not mention the word stewardship.[49] The guidelines endorse the Norwegian Corporate Governance Board (NCGB) Code of Practice for Corporate Governance (Norwegian Corporate Governance Code)[50] and international standards such as the

---

[43] De La Cruz, Medina and Tang (n 4) 39.

[44] Norwegian Ministry of Trade, Industry and Fisheries, 'State Ownership Report 2020' (2020) <https://www.regjeringen.no/contentassets/ca3c0a55b6b041ff8be7d04cf6b0a3cd/state-ownership-report-202-v5.pdf> accessed 17 June 2020.

[45] Dan W Puchniak and Samantha Tang, 'Singapore's Puzzling Embrace of Shareholder Stewardship: A Successful Secret' (2020) 53 *Vanderbilt Journal of Transnational Law* 989; Puchniak and Tang, Singapore's Embrace of Shareholder Stewardship, Chapter 14.

[46] Stewardship Asia Centre, *Stewardship Principles for Family Businesses* (2018) <www.stewardshipasia.com.sg/sites/default/files/2020-09/SPFB-brochure-0913.pdf> accessed 19 May 2021.

[47] Norwegian Ministry of Trade, Industry and Fisheries, 'Diverse and Value-Creating Ownership' (White Paper, Meld. St. 27 (2013–2014), Report to the Storting) <www.regjeringen.no/contentassets/899ac257df2648d788942b78c6d59787/en-gb/pdfs/stm201320140027000engpdfs.pdf> accessed 17 June 2020 [hereinafter Norwegian State Guidelines].

[48] See Norges Bank Investment Management, 'Global Voting Guidelines' (2019) <www.nbim.no/contentassets/3dbdc33d893f4e82b63198025c2dde99/votingguidelines_web.pdf> accessed 17 June 2020 (Norwegian Government Pension Fund Global); Argentum, 'Samfunnsansvar [Social Responsibility]' <https://argentum.no/nb/samfunnsansvar/> accessed 17 June 2020 (in Norwegian only); Folketrygdfondet, 'Prinsipper for ansvarlig forvaltningsvirksomhet [Principles for Responsible Asset Management]' (24 April 2019) <www.folketrygdfondet.no/getfile.php/131895-1581944084/Dokumenter/V%C3%A5r%20forvaltning/prinsipper%20for%20ansvarlig%20forvaltningsvirksomhet%20240419.PDF> accessed 17 June 2020 (Government Pension Fund Norway); KLP, 'Guideline for KLP as Responsible Investor' (13 June 2019) <www.klp.no/en/english-pdf/Guidelines%20for%20KLP%20as%20a%20responsible%20investor.pdf> accessed 17 June 2020 (KLP); Storebrand Asset Management, 'Storebrand Sustainability Investment Policy' <https://www.storebrand.no/en/asset-management/sustainable-investments/exclusions/_/attachment/inline/89be61ce-5de9-4fa2-b0bf-2e86651a23f2:26d810d6642be32583f0b126a8fd1e123b756fa9/20210309_Storebrand_Sustainable_Investment_Policy.pdf> accessed 22 January 2022 (Storebrand).

[49] KLP mentions stewardship; Storebrand emphasizes its duty to be good long-term stewards of their clients' capital.

[50] Norwegian Corporate Governance Board (NCGB/NUES), *The Norwegian Code of Practice for Corporate Governance* (10th edn, 14 October 2021) <https://nues.no/wp-content/uploads/2021/10/2021-10-14-Den-norske-anbefalingen-om-eierstyring-og-selskapsledelse.pdf> accessed 22 January 2022.

G20/OECD Principles of Corporate Governance,[51] the OECD Guidelines for Multinational Enterprises,[52] the UN Guiding Principles on Business and Human Rights,[53] the UN Principles of Responsible Investment (PRI)[54] and the UN Global Compact.[55] They emphasize elements regarded as central to stewardship: the role of active shareholdership,[56] especially to reduce environmental, social and governance (ESG) associated financial risks,[57] boards' commitment to long-term shareholder value,[58] and shareholders' rights, including those concerning takeovers.

8.3.3 *The Norwegian Recommendation*

The board of the VFF issued in 2003 its 'industry recommendation' for its fund and asset manager members for 'use of ownership'.[59] The Norwegian Recommendation was revised in 2012 and again in 2019.[60] The Recommendation is only in Norwegian.

Unlike an ordinary VFF 'industry standard' that is adopted by the VFF general meeting with an obligation to be followed by VFF members, a recommendation is issued by the VFF board. It is non-binding guidance and advice for VFF members, and there is no 'comply or explain', either. In that sense it is more a type of 'preliminary stewardship initiative' than a 'stewardship code' proper,[61] although it is (somewhat misleadingly) internationally listed as such.[62]

The Norwegian Recommendation 2012 was intended as an implementation of the original 2011 EFAMA Stewardship Principles,[63] the VFF being a member of the European Fund and Asset Management Association (EFAMA).[64] The 2019 revision takes into consideration SRD II, and the 2018 revision of the EFAMA Stewardship Principles, the EFAMA Stewardship Code,[65]

---

[51] OECD (n 39).
[52] OECD, *OECD Guidelines for Multinational Enterprises* (2011) <www.oecd.org/daf/inv/mne/48004323.pdf> accessed 17 June 2020.
[53] United Nations, 'Guiding Principles on Business and Human Rights – Implementing the United Nations "Protect, Respect and Remedy" Framework' (2011) <www.ohchr.org/documents/publications/guidingprinciplesbusinesshr_en.pdf> accessed 17 June 2020.
[54] See PRI, 'Signatories' <www.unpri.org/searchresults?qkeyword=norway&PageSize=10&parametrics=WVSECTIONCODE%7C1018&cmd=GoToPage&val=4&SortOrder=2> accessed 17 June 2020.
[55] See UN Global Compact, 'Our Participants' <www.unglobalcompact.org/what-is-gc/participants/search?utf8=%E2%9C%93&search%5Bkeywords%5D=&search%5Bcountries%5D%5B%5D=231&search%5Bper_page%5D=10&search%5Bsort_field%5D=&search%5Bsort_direction%5D=asc> accessed 17 June 2020.
[56] See n 48 (Norwegian Government Pension Fund Global; Storebrand).
[57] See n 48 (Norwegian Government Pension Fund Global; Government Pension Fund Norway; KLP; Storebrand and SKAGEN).
[58] See n 48 (Norwegian Government Pension Fund Global; Government Pension Fund Norway; KLP).
[59] Verdipapirfondenes Forening, 'Bransjeanbefaling for medlemmene av Verdipapirfondenes forening: Utøvelse av eierskap [Industry Recommendation for the Members of the Norwegian Fund and Asset Management Association: Exercise of Ownership Rights]' (7 June 2012) <https://vff.no/assets/Bransjenormer/Bransjeanbefalinger/Bransjeanbefaling-utøvelse-av-eierskap.pdf> accessed 17 June 2020 [hereinafter Norwegian Recommendation 2012].
[60] See Norwegian Recommendation 2019 (n 16).
[61] See Katelouzou and Siems, The Global Diffusion of Stewardship Codes, Chapter 30.
[62] See International Corporate Governance Network, 'Global Stewardship Codes Network' <www.icgn.org/policy/global-stewardship-codes-network> accessed 17 June 2020.
[63] European Fund and Asset Management Association, 'EFAMA Code for External Governance: Principles for the Exercise of Ownership Rights in Investee Companies' (6 April 2011) <www.efama.org/Publications/Public/Corporate_Governance/11-4035%20EFAMA%20ECG_final_6%20April%202011%20v2.pdf> accessed 17 June 2020; see Norwegian Recommendation 2012 (n 59) para 1.
[64] European Fund and Asset Management Association, 'National Member Associations: Norway' <www.efama.org/about/SitePages/National_Associations.aspx#Norway> accessed 17 June 2020.
[65] European Fund and Asset Management Association, 'EFAMA Stewardship Code: Principles for Asset Managers' Monitoring of, Voting in, Engagement with Investee Companies' (2018) <www.efama.org/Publications/Public/Corporate_Governance/EFAMA%20Stewardship%20Code.pdf> accessed 17 June 2020.

itself revised based on SRD II. SRD II has not been implemented yet in Norway, but the Norwegian Recommendation 2019 takes into consideration the proposed amendments in the Norwegian Act on Securities Funds (the Securities Funds Act).[66]

The Norwegian Recommendation 2019 says that it is 'compatible' with the UK Code 2012 – but not its most recent revision, UK Code 2020 – though it does not follow it.[67] Unlike the EFAMA Stewardship Code, the Norwegian Recommendation 2019 emphasizes creditor rights in the investee companies. Additionally, the Recommendation follows the Norwegian Corporate Governance Code and is applied only to Norwegian companies.[68]

In addition to the Norwegian Recommendation 2019 being not a stewardship code but a preliminary stewardship initiative, it is also a hybrid between a list of references to Norwegian national law and a Norwegian language summary of the EFAMA Stewardship Code, with references to the 2011 EFAMA Principles as revised in 2017–18. Additionally, as it is only in Norwegian, it is excluded from the empirical textual comparison in this volume, which considers only stewardship codes that are available in English.[69]

The Norwegian Recommendation 2019 has two parts. The first part concentrates on referring to Norwegian law, mostly the Securities Funds Act[70] and the Securities Funds Regulation.[71] The provisions referred to in the Recommendation concern the rules of conduct for a securities fund management company (section 2-15 of the Act and section 2-24 of the Regulation), election of board and general manager in a securities fund management company (section 2-5 of the Act) and the management company's competence to make dispositions on the funds under management (section 2-14 of the Act). Further included are the proposed rules on active shareholding (then proposed and later in 2019 adopted, but not yet in force, section 8-8 of the Act,[72] to implement Article 3 g regarding engagement policy, as does the ESMA Stewardship Code), and rules on exercise of voting rights in the investee companies (section 2-24 of the Regulation). An important part of these rules is the board's duty to supervise, on behalf of the funds managed, the use of voting rights in the target companies. The board of VFF has given a separate Recommendation on board conduct in securities fund management companies, including the use of voting rights.[73]

---

[66] Lov om verdipapirfond, LOV-2011-11-25-44. Unofficial translation by the Financial Supervisory Authority of Norway, 'Act on Securities Funds (Securities Funds Act)' (2018) <www.finanstilsynet.no/globalassets/laws-and-regulations/laws/securities-funds-act.pdf> accessed 17 June 2020; Prop. 135 L (2018–2019), Endringer i aksjelovgivningen mv. (langsiktig eierskap i noterte selskaper mv.) [Amendments to the legislation on companies etc (long-term ownership in listed companies etc)].

[67] Norwegian Recommendation 2019 (n 16) 2. Further on the UK Code 2020, see Davies, The UK Stewardship Code 2010–2020, Chapter 2 and Katelouzou and Micheler, The Market for Stewardship and the Role of the Government, Chapter 3.

[68] Norwegian Recommendation 2019 (n 16) 2.

[69] Katelouzou and Siems, The Global Diffusion of Stewardship Codes, Chapter 30.

[70] Securities Funds Act (n 66).

[71] Forskrift til verdipapirfondloven, FOR-2011-12-21-1467 as amended by FOR-2018-11-16-1710. Unofficial translation by the Financial Supervisory Authority of Norway, 'Regulations of 21 December 2011 to the Securities Funds Act (Securities Funds Regulations)' (2018) <www.finanstilsynet.no/globalassets/laws-and-regulations/regulations/securities-funds-regulations.pdf> accessed 17 June 2020.

[72] Lov om endringer i aksjelovgivningen mv. (langsiktig eierskap i noterte selskaper mv.) [Act amending company legislation (long-term ownership in listed companies etc], LOV-2019-12-06-77.

[73] Verdipapirfondenes Forening, 'Bransjeanbefaling for medlemmene i Verdipapirfondenes forening: Styrearbeid i fondsforvaltningsselskap [Industry Recommendation for the Members of the Norwegian Fund and Asset Management Association: Board Conduct in Fund Management Companies]' (22 August 2019) especially para 9.2 <https://vff.no/bransjeanbefalinger#styrearbeid-i-fondsforvaltningsselskaper> accessed 17 June 2020 (available only in Norwegian).

The second part concentrates on referring to the EFAMA Stewardship Code, with summaries of the background, the scope and Principles 1–6 translated into Norwegian.[74] In addition, the Recommendation includes an endorsement to the management companies to ensure that the Norwegian Corporate Governance Code is followed in the companies in which they invest, and a recommendation on 'an industry practice beyond what is stated in current legal rules for active (discretionary) management'.[75]

The Norwegian Corporate Governance Code does not mention institutional investors, but the Norwegian Institutional Investor Forum is a member of the NCGB issuing the Norwegian Corporate Governance Code.[76] The members of the Institutional Investor Forum are Alfred Berg Kapitalforvaltning, DNB Kapitalforvaltning, Folketrygdfondet, Holberg Fondsforvaltning, KLP, Nordea Fondene, Odin Forvaltning, Oslo Pensjonsforsikring, the Ministry of Trade, Industry and Fisheries (Department of Ownership), Equinor Kapitalforvaltning and Storebrand. The heavy emphasis on the Norwegian Corporate Governance Code both in the Norwegian Recommendation 2019 and in the individual investors' guidelines shows how Norwegian stewardship is reflected strongly through corporate governance, confirming the complementarity between stewardship and the corporate governance codes, a relationship emphasized by the UK stewardship codes of 2010 and 2012, but not the UK Code 2020.[77]

Additionally, according to the Norwegian Recommendation 2019, in client agreements for active (discretionary) management, it should be stated whether it is the asset manager or the customer who exercises voting rights in connection with the client's managed funds.[78] Furthermore, it should be stated whether it is the manager or the customer who follows up on the need for, and possibly implements other forms of, 'ownership' influence in connection with the customer's managed funds.

All in all, the true scope of the Norwegian Recommendation 2019 is narrow as it concentrates on the investment side of stewardship only, the relationship between a securities fund and asset management company and the unit-holders in its funds, seen as passive end-investors, not as actively engaging participants in governance. According to Norwegian law referred to in the Recommendation, unit-holders have only a very limited effect on the voting on specific companies in a fund. Accordingly, the influence of unit-holders is even more distant from any ability to impact the companies in the fund they are invested in – which would be the true purpose of a stewardship code. Additionally, the Recommendation is applicable to fund and asset managers only, not to other institutional investors or direct shareholders as the public sector important to Norway, especially the Norwegian sovereign fund, the Government Pension Fund Global and the Norwegian state. However, KLP Kapitalforvaltning AS, a subsidiary of KLP, and Storebrand are members, and Folketrygdfondet is an 'associate member'.

This emphasis on the 'investment side' of stewardship, rather than on the corporate governance side, covered by references to the corporate governance code only and without an independent idea of governance, indicates a lack of anything in the direction of a full-fledged stewardship code. This is natural. First, Norwegian corporate governance relies on the Norwegian company law and the Norwegian Corporate Governance Code, so there is no need for a specific stewardship regulation besides the relationship between the investor and its customers. Second, the investors already follow their firm-specific guidelines, inspired often by

---

[74] Norwegian Recommendation 2019 (n 16) 4.
[75] Norwegian Recommendation 2019 (n 16) 6, para 5.8.
[76] Norwegian Corporate Governance Code (n 50) 4.
[77] See Dionysia Katelouzou, *The Path to Enlightened Shareholder Stewardship* (CUP) (forthcoming).
[78] Norwegian Recommendation 2019 (n 16) 6, para 5.8.

international standards and recommendations. In the following we discuss them, starting with NBIM, which governs the Norwegian Government Pension Fund Global.

8.3.4 The Principles for the Management of the Norwegian Government Pension Fund Global

The Norwegian Government Pension Fund Global is the Norwegian sovereign wealth fund, with EUR 1.03 trillion of assets under management.[79] According to NBIM, which manages the Fund, it[80]

> exists to help finance the Norwegian welfare state for future generations and must therefore have a long investment horizon. We want companies to be equipped to deal with long-term global challenges. We aim to promote good governance, increased profitability and responsible business practices. Our work on generating a long-term return is enhanced by investing in companies that act responsibly and create long-term value.

As a 'long-term and responsible' steward, NBIM has as its 'single objective' the 'highest possible return with a moderate risk',[81] which, according to the Fund's investment mandate,[82] is 'dependent on sustainable development in economical, environmental and social terms [and] well-functioning, legitimate and efficient markets'.[83] In fulfilling its objective, NBIM sees its role as promoter of principles and standards to the target companies for 'well-functioning markets and good corporate governance'.[84] From 2012, NBIM has set requirements on what the Fund expects from its global portfolio companies in terms of corporate governance practices. According to Aguilera, Bermejo, Aguilar and Cuñat, this caused improvements in the Fund's portfolio companies, adding influence to corporate practices to the traditional influence tools of 'exit' (divesting) and 'voice' (engagement).[85]

NBIM promotes the G20/OECD Principles of Corporate Governance, the OECD Guidelines for Multinational Enterprises, the UN Global Compact, the UN Guiding Principles on Business and Human Rights (UNGP) and the UN Conference on Trade and Development (UNCTAD) Principles on Promoting Responsible Sovereign Lending and Borrowing.[86] Global Compact and the OECD Principles and Guidelines are also mentioned in the NBIM investment mandate.[87] NBIM also promotes national corporate governance codes in the countries it invests in, especially in Africa and Asia as well as in Europe. Besides supporting the recent Japanese corporate governance and stewardship reforms,[88] the Japanese

---

[79] Norges Bank Investment Management, 'Market Value' (11 October 2019) <www.nbim.no/en/the-fund/market-value/> accessed 17 June 2020.
[80] Norges Bank Investment Management, 'Responsible Investment: Government Pension Fund Global' (2019) 11 <www.nbim.no/contentassets/aaa1c4c4557e4619bd8345db022e981e/spu_responsible-investments-2019_web.pdf> accessed 17 June 2020.
[81] ibid 7, 11.
[82] Norges Bank Investment Management, 'Investment Mandate Government Pension Fund Global' (29 April 2020) <www.nbim.no/en/organisation/governance-model/executive-board-documents/investment-mandate–government-pension-fund-global/> accessed 17 June 2020.
[83] ibid para 2.1.
[84] Norges Bank Investment Management, 'Responsible Investment' (n 80) 20.
[85] Ruth V Aguilera, Vicente J Bermejo, Javier Capapé Aguilar and Vicente Cuñat, 'Firms' Reaction to Changes in the Governance Preferences of Active Institutional Owners' (2019) ECGI Finance Working Paper No 625/2019 <https://ssrn.com/abstract=3411566> accessed 17 June 2020.
[86] Norges Bank Investment Management, 'Responsible Investment' (n 80) 20–21.
[87] Norges Bank Investment Management, 'Investment Mandate Government Pension Fund Global' (n 82) para 2.1.
[88] Goto, The Japanese Stewardship Code, Chapter 10.

government initiatives with the aim of reforming Japan's traditional lifetime-employee, risk-averse and stakeholder-oriented governance system towards a more shareholder-oriented, profit-maximizing and less risk-averse governance system,[89] NBIM has also supported the German and UK corporate governance reforms, emphasizing in both board independence, board diversity and long-termism in executive remuneration.[90]

Albeit endorsing international and national corporate governance codes, NBIM does not follow or endorse any *specific* stewardship code or codes. What is important, as NBIM invests only outside the Nordic countries, is that it cannot and does not endorse the Norwegian Corporate Governance Code. NBIM, however, sees the OECD Principles of Corporate Governance as part of its basis because they apply in many countries that the Fund invests in.[91]

For the same reasons, it cannot endorse the Norwegian Recommendation 2019. Additionally, NBIM is sceptical towards stewardship codes generally. In its letter to the OECD Corporate Governance Committee in 2014, it stated this scepticism, especially in relation to the stewardship codes' requirements for institutional investors to disclose their policies with respect to corporate governance. Although NBIM understood and supported the desire for relevant and predictable conduct by investors in their role as shareholders, it emphasized that for institutional investors to play an adequate role in corporate governance, they must have incentives and flexibility to do so. NBIM believed that authorities can most effectively strengthen the incentives by focusing on transparency, the practicality of shareholder rights, the mechanisms by which boards are accountable to shareholders, and the room that shareholders have in which to co-ordinate governance efforts with each other.[92] Codified stewardship encouragement can, according to NBIM, bring only limited results in lieu of effective corporate governance tools for investors. There may be a risk that the disclosure requirements for institutional investors will lead to more box-ticking, not less. In its 2016 letter to the Council of Experts concerning the Japanese stewardship code, NBIM makes clear that stewardship is best practice – but indicates a reticent attitude towards stewardship codes because one size does not fit all, and investors are different, in terms of size, strategies and portfolios.[93] NBIM has followed up in this line, with its 2016 report on responsible investment setting its own definition of stewardship,[94] which it then goes on to explain how it follows up, without reference to any stewardship codes. In comparison, the 2019 report on responsible investment does not mention 'stewardship' once.[95]

Although NBIM, in its independent role, is seen by many as a leading star in responsible investment, an in-depth analysis of its investment policies and results gives reason to question the efficacy of its approach. The positive results are too incremental, and its follow-up of the around

---

[89] Goto, Koh and Puchniak (n 13).
[90] Norges Bank Investment Management, 'Responsible Investment: Government Pension Fund Global' (2018) 25–26 <www.nbim.no/contentassets/e1632963319146bbb040024114ca65af/responsible-investment_2018.pdf> accessed 17 June 2020.
[91] Yngve Slyngstad and William Ambrose, 'OECD Principles of Corporate Governance' (Norges Bank Investment Management, 30 December 2014) <www.nbim.no/globalassets/documents/ownership/2014/2014-12-30-nbim-letter-to-oecd-on-principles-of-corporate-governance.pdf> accessed 17 June 2020.
[92] ibid.
[93] Gavin Grant and Runa Urheim, 'Response to FSA's Request for Comments on the Issues Concerning Constructive Dialogues Between Companies and Institutional Investors' (Norges Bank Investment Management, 21 June 2016) <www.nbim.no/contentassets/28a84003b1314f859bfea3286e6b2e26/nbim-comments-to-fsa-request-june-2016.pdf> accessed 17 June 2020.
[94] 'We define stewardship as the role and responsibility of an investor to oversee and safeguard the long-term value of the equity holdings in a portfolio' (Norges Bank Investment Management, 'Responsible Investment: Government Pension Fund Global' (2016) 43 <www.nbim.no/contentassets/2c3377d07c5a4c4fbd442b345e7cfd67/government-pension-fund-global–responsible-investment-2016.pdf> accessed 17 June 2020).
[95] Norges Bank Investment Management, 'Responsible Investment' (n 80).

9,000 companies it is invested in too superficial.[96] This is, however, not a result of lack of stewardship principles; rather, it is reflective of a general criticism, to which we return in the concluding Section 8.4.

8.3.5 *The Norwegian State and Its Principles for Responsible Investment*

In Norway the state is the only shareholder,[97] a controlling shareholder (more than 50 per cent of the voting rights) or a major shareholder (more than 33 per cent of the voting rights, which gives a veto right, for instance to amendments of articles, mergers and divisions) of some of the country's largest listed and non-listed companies, usually together with Folketrygdfondet (Norwegian Government Pension Fund Norway), itself a 100 per cent state-controlled company.[98] According to the Norwegian view, this gives the state an obligation to strive to be a role model when it comes to corporate governance.[99] The state's guidelines regarding governance are documented in 'Diverse and Value-Creating Ownership', a recommendation of the Ministry of Trade, Industry and Fisheries approved by the Council of State in 2014 (Norwegian State Guidelines).[100] The Norwegian State Guidelines cover both public and private enterprises with a state interest.

The Norwegian State Guidelines have a stewardship starting point, focusing on shareholder primacy as the ultimate goal: 'The main objective of the state's commercial ownership (companies in categories 1–3) is to achieve the highest possible return on invested capital over time. The return is made up of the sum total of the increase in market value of a company's equity and yield in the form of dividends and any share buybacks.'[101]

According to the Norwegian State Guidelines, the Norwegian government has both general and more specific expectations of companies in the field of 'corporate social responsibility' (CSR). Generally, the government 'expects all Norwegian companies should demonstrate CSR, whether under private-sector or public-sector ownership and regardless of whether their undertaking is located in Norway or abroad'.[102]

Besides this general obligation to all Norwegian undertakings, the government expects *companies in which the state has a holding* 'to work systematically on their CSR and to be exemplary in their respective fields'. The specific expectations relate to four thematic key areas: climate and environment, human rights, employee and worker rights, and anti-corruption. The government's expectations are informed by and based on national and international standards, conventions and reporting norms. Boards of the investee companies are responsible for assessing

---

[96] Beate Sjåfjell, Heidi R Nilsen and Benjamin J Richardson, 'Investing in Sustainability or Feeding on Stranded Assets? The Norwegian Government Pension Fund Global' (2017) 52 *Wake Forest Law Review* 949.

[97] For instance the energy company Statkraft, alcohol monopoly AS Vinmonopolet, Avinor AS running all the Norwegian airports, or railway transport monopoly Vygruppen AS, to just name a few.

[98] According to WorldAtlas, the largest companies by revenue are Equinor (67% state controlled), Telenor (54%), Norsk Hydro (34% state, 6.5% Folketrygdfondet), Yara International (36% state, 6.6% Folketrygdfondet) and DNB (34% state, 6% Folketrygdfondet): Sophy Owuor, 'Largest Companies in Norway' (*WorldAtlas*, 22 July 2019) <www.worldatlas.com/articles/largest-companies-in-norway.html> accessed 17 June 2020.

[99] Forum for Utvikling og Miljø [Forum for Development and Environment], 'Statlig eierskap og menneskerettigheter: Forslag til et mer ansvarlig statlig eierskap [State Ownership and Human Rights: A Proposal for a More Responsible State Ownership]' (April 2011) <www.forumfor.no/assets/docs/Statlig-eierskap_.pdf> accessed 17 June 2020.

[100] Norwegian State Guidelines (n 47).

[101] ibid 75 (para 8.3.1).

[102] ibid 74 (para 8.2.11).

how expectations from the state in its capacity as an owner may best be honoured and implemented effectively.[103]

As relevant standards, the Norwegian State Guidelines mention the UNGP, the International Labour Organization's (ILO) eight core conventions as the foundation for corporate activities, the Global Reporting Initiative (GRI), the UN Global Compact, the OECD Guidelines for Multinational Enterprises, the OECD guidelines on taxation, and the standards of the Global Forum on Transparency and Exchange of Information for Tax Purposes.[104] Specific attention is given to the UNGP, seen as an integrated part of the Global Compact and incorporated into the OECD Guidelines for Multinational Enterprises. The UNGP are perceived as a 'precautionary approach in risk identification and prevention'.[105] Besides that, the government emphasizes the investee companies' boards' responsibilities 'in respect of CSR'.[106]

In spite of the Norwegian state's strong position as shareholder, facilitating in theory an active engagement as a sustainability-oriented 'steward', there is no evidence of the Norwegian state as shareholder acting as such a steward. The Norwegian state is satisfied with making public its expectations of the companies, without being willing to follow these up actively in ways that are observable, notably in the general meetings.[107]

8.3.6 Reflections on Norwegian Stewardship in the Crossfire between Shareholder Primacy and Sustainable Corporate Governance

Norway, with one of the largest sovereign wealth funds in the world and other institutional shareholders such as the state and the public pension fund, seems to have coped well without a stewardship code. This gives rise to the question: Do we need a stewardship code? Like Germany, Norway has not joined the stewardship code club, in the same way that it has been reluctant to implement SRD II (albeit the national legislation has finally been given). The 'engagement' that has been the basis of the UK Code 2012 and SRD II has not been in the focus of Norwegian investors. The engagement level is even lower in Norway than in Germany, with average shareholder turnout in annual general meetings in Norway at 50.90%, compared to 64.86% in Germany (both in 2010–11).[108] The reason may very well be the concentrated control in both countries' listed companies.[109]

Norwegian company law, with its clear hierarchical structure,[110] gives room for a stronger role for active shareholders, even to the extent that the general meeting can, within certain limits, give direct instructions to the board. In this sense the controlling shareholder could perhaps be perceived as a 'good steward', but for the benefit of minority shareholders and contractual parties and not for the society as a whole or the environment.[111] This is not possible to that extent in

---

[103] ibid 80 (para 8.3.3).
[104] ibid 80–88.
[105] ibid 81.
[106] ibid 82–83.
[107] Indeed, not much has changed in this regard over the last decade; compare Beate Sjåfjell, 'Towards a Sustainable Development: Internalising Externalities in Norwegian Company Law' (2011) 8 *International and Comparative Corporate Law Journal* 103.
[108] Paul Hewitt, 'The Exercise of Shareholder Rights: Country Comparison of Turnout and Dissent' (2011) OECD Corporate Governance Working Papers No 3, 15 <http://dx.doi.org/10.1787/5kg54dol1lvf-en> accessed 17 June 2020.
[109] On Germany, see Ringe, Stewardship and Shareholder Engagement in Germany, Chapter 9.
[110] Lov om allmennaksjeselskaper [Norwegian Public Companies Act] § 5-1(1); see Beate Sjåfjell and Cecilie Kjelland, 'Norway: Corporate Governance on the Outskirts of the EU' in Andreas Fleckner and Klaus Hopt (eds), *Comparative Corporate Governance: A Functional and International Analysis* (CUP 2013).
[111] Beate Sjåfjell, 'Sustainable Companies: Possibilities and Barriers in Norwegian Company Law' (2015) 11 *International and Comparative Corporate Law Journal* 1; Jukka Mähönen and Guðrún Johnsen, 'Law, Culture

German company law, which emphasizes the autonomy of the management board[112] and therefore provides an incentive for 'engagement'. On the other hand, the principle of shareholder equality, which is held dear in both Norwegian[113] and German[114] law, requires a balance between engagement of the controlling shareholders and protection of the minority institutional investors and the creditors. Further, in Norwegian company law, protection of creditors and minority shareholders from the abuse of controlling shareholders is strongly emphasized, setting an obligation for the board to promote the interests of the company as a whole and not its shareholders.

There have been no proposals for a Norwegian stewardship code so far. To pursue the question of whether there is a need for a code in Norway, we first discuss the potential benefits continuing with the solution Norway has today, before considering the possible benefits from a code.

Firstly, Norway has (finally) implemented SRD II,[115] making a stewardship code at least partly superfluous. The amendments required by SRD II have been given,[116] but not all have entered into force.[117] Articles 3g and 3h of SRD II have been implemented in the Act on Financial Institutions and Financial Groups,[118] the Act Relating to the Management of Alternative Investment Fund,[119] the Securities Funds Act and the Act on Securities Trading,[120] including rules on guidance for active shareholdership and publication of investment strategy. Article 3i has been implemented in the Securities Funds Act, the Act Relating to the Management of Alternative Investment Funds and the Act on Securities Trading, including rules on information obligations of life insurance undertakings and pension undertakings.

As Birkmose and Madsen evaluate in Chapter 7 of this book, SRD II is unlikely to have much of an effect on Danish stewardship owing to the many parallels to the existing Stewardship Code.[121] The same would apply vice versa in Norway; there is no need for a code as the engagement rules have been implemented in the law. On the other hand, SRD II and a stewardship code might be seen as complementing each other, as noted by Van der Elst and Lafarre on the Dutch Stewardship Code in Chapter 4 of this book.[122] This might be achieved by

---

and Sustainability: Corporate Governance in the Nordic Countries' in Beate Sjåfjell and Christopher M Bruner (eds), *Cambridge Handbook of Corporate Law, Corporate Governance and Sustainability* (CUP 2019) 218.

[112] Aktiengesetz [German Stock Corporation Act] § 76(1); see Ringe, Stewardship and Shareholder Engagement in Germany, Chapter 9.

[113] Norwegian Public Companies Act § 5-21 and 6-28; see Sjåfjell and Kjelland (n 110).

[114] German Stock Corporation Act § 53(a); see Ringe, Stewardship and Shareholder Engagement in Germany, Chapter 9.

[115] Høring om ny lov om røystingsrådgjevarar og endringer i aksjelovgivningen mv. [Consultation on Act on Proxy Advisors and Amendments to the Company Legislation etc] (19 November 2019) <www.regjeringen.no/no/dokumenter/horing-om-ny-lov-om-roystingsradgjevarar-og-endringer-i-aksjelovgivningen-mv/id2678178/?expand=horingsnotater&fbclid=IwA R3D5_iqPAQjddThzQhKudi_PHbt25O2Zx5C3uweK-U7lkK3H7BgsVj5qUQ> accessed 17 June 2020.

[116] Lov om endringer i aksjelovgivningen mv. (langsiktig eierskap i noterte selskaper mv.) [Act Amending Company Legislation (Long-Term Ownership in Listed Companies Etc)], LOV-2019-12-06-77.

[117] Norway, as an EFTA member of the European Economic Area Agreement, has a somewhat delayed timeline in the implementation of EU rules.

[118] Lov om finansforetak og finanskonsern (finansforetaksloven) [Act on Financial Institutions and Financial Groups (Financial Institutions Act)], LOV-2015-04-10-17.

[119] Lov om forvaltning av alternative investeringsfond [Act on the Management of Alternative Investment Funds], LOV-2014-06-20-28.

[120] Lov om verdipapirhandel (verdipapirhandelloven) [Securities Trading Act], LOV-2007-06-29-75.

[121] Birkmose and Madsen, The Danish Stewardship Code, Chapter 7.

[122] Van der Elst and Lafarre, Shareholder Stewardship in the Netherlands, Chapter 4.

the new Norwegian Recommendation 2019 referring to the amended provisions in the Securities Funds Act, referred to earlier.

Secondly, an advantage to Norwegian investors of not having a code is the flexibility for them to adapt to the latest changes in international standards of conduct, without lagging behind with outdated and weak comply-or-explain-based stewardship codes such as those copying the UK Code 2012, now obsolete in the UK after the totally new apply-and-explain-based UK Code 2020.[123] An example is the adaptation of NBIM to the OECD Guidelines for Multinational Enterprises[124] and the UN Sustainable Development Goals.[125] This flexibility makes it possible for investors both to ensure good corporate governance and to adjust to changes in stewardship practices in a timely manner, which is essential for keeping up the pace in the transition to sustainability. Following the Norwegian Recommendation 2019 would not make this possible, as it is lagging behind international developments as illustrated in its reference to the now outdated UK Code 2012.

Thirdly, we see that most UN and EU initiatives increasingly become clearer in their expectations and calls for action from companies. This has been especially visible after the climate meeting in New York at the end of September 2019.[126] In addition, the EU is preparing proposals for harmonizing European law to ensure a higher speed towards sustainable investment, as is clear from the European Commission Sustainable Finance Initiative, emphasized further in the European Green Deal.[127] This ramping up is informed by the lack of progress through merely relying on voluntary standards and guidelines. In this respect, it could be argued that having the flexibility to adapt could be an even bigger advantage going forward for investors who wish to be frontrunners.

In many initiatives, such as the EU Commission Sustainable Finance Initiative[128] and the Commission Guidelines on non-financial reporting,[129] much trust is placed on the recommendations of the Task Force on Climate-related Financial Disclosures (TCFD) established

---

[123] On the progress of the stewardship codes, see Dionysia Katelouzou and Peer Zumbansen, 'The New Geographies of Corporate Governance' (2020) 42 *University of Pennsylvania Journal of International Law* 51.

[124] The adaptation started in 2013 when the Norwegian National Contact Point for the OECD Guidelines for Multinational Enterprises concluded that NBIM had violated the OECD Guidelines, first by refusing to cooperate with the Contact Point, a violation of the OECD Guidelines Procedural Guidance, and second by not having any strategy on how to identify and handle possible human rights violations in the companies it invests in, in that case relating to child labour: Norwegian National Contact Point for the OECD Guidelines for Multinational Enterprises, 'Final Statement: Complaint from Lok Shanti Abhiyan, Korean Transnational Corporations Watch, Fair Green and Global Alliance and Forum for Environment and Development vs POSCO (South Korea), ABP/APG (Netherlands) and NBIM (Norway)' (27 May 2013) <https://nettsteder.regjeringen.no/ansvarlignaringsliv2/files/2013/12/nbim_final.pdf> accessed 17 June 2020. NBIM breached human rights through its investment in the mining company POSCO, where NBIM owned 0.9% of voting rights. The case got a lot of attention, and NBIM had to adjust their interpretation and implementation of OECD Guidelines.

[125] Transforming Our World: The 2030 Agenda for Sustainable Development, United Nations General Assembly Res 70/1 (25 September 2015) UN Doc A/RES/70/1 <www.undocs.org/A/RES/70/1> accessed 17 June 2020.

[126] See e.g. Fiona Reynolds, 'Asset Owners Step Up to Take Unprecedented Action on Climate Change' (*UNPRI*, 24 September 2019) <www.unpri.org/pri-blog/asset-owners-step-up-to-take-unprecedented-action-on-climate-change/4900.article> accessed 17 June 2020; Peter Lacy and Jessica Long, 'UNGC – Accenture Strategy CEO Study on Sustainability' (*accenture*, 24 September 2019) <www.accenture.com/us-en/insights/strategy/ungcceostudy> accessed 17 June 2020.

[127] European Commission (n 38); European Commission, 'A European Green Deal' <https://ec.europa.eu/info/strategy/priorities-2019-2024/european-green-deal_en> accessed 17 June 2020; European Commission, 'Sustainable Europe Investment Plan – European Green Deal Investment Plan' COM (2020) 21 final <https://eur-lex.europa.eu/legal-content/EN/TXT/?uri=CELEX:52020DC0021> accessed 17 June 2020.

[128] European Commission (n 38).

[129] Communication from the Commission – Guidelines on Non-financial Reporting: Supplement on Reporting Climate-Related Information C/2019/4490 [2019] OJ C209/1.

by the G20's Financial Stability Board,[130] giving them the status of a benchmark of expectations towards companies regarding governance of sustainability strategy and risks (albeit limited to climate).[131] The recommendations set clear expectations and responsibilities for company boards regarding what actions to take and what information to disclose in their reporting. The recommendations have been embraced and incorporated in a number of UN standards and EU initiatives, in addition to several countries (Belgium, Canada, France, Sweden and the UK), and by investors representing USD 34 trillion asset under management as well as thirty-six central banks. The recommendations seem to have a bigger impact on the behaviour of investors and companies than stewardship codes.

As an example, the EU Commission Sustainable Finance Action Plan Action 7 proposes a clarification of institutional investors' and asset managers' duties in relation to sustainability. It does so by suggesting requiring them to integrate sustainability considerations over time in the investment decision-making process and to increase transparency towards end-investors on how they integrate such sustainability factors in their investment decisions, in particular as concerns their exposure to sustainability risks.[132] We find the first implementation of Action 7 in the EU Disclosure Regulation.[133]

As we see, Norway may not need a stewardship code. What Norway does need is a clear and mandatory regulation to ensure that Norwegian business and finance contribute to the transition to sustainability. A stewardship code would not be a sufficiently strong measure. Conversely, it could hold Norwegian business and finance back in the face of the rapid developments on EU and international level.

8.4 CONCLUDING REFLECTIONS

During the last decade there has been a perceived shift in the corporate governance role of major institutional shareholders in listed companies, popularly denoted as 'stewardship', leading to a flux of similar stewardship codes in various countries. At the same time, there has been a trend of voluntary guidelines from the UN, the OECD and the EU.

This gives rise to the question of whether shareholder stewardship is the best way to ensure the needed integration of sustainability into business? The Asian chapters in this book are illustrative. The Japanese government adopted a stewardship code with the aim of reforming its traditional lifetime-employee, risk-averse and stakeholder-oriented governance system towards a more shareholder-oriented, profit-maximizing and less risk-averse governance system.[134] The Singapore chapter shows that even in economies in which the role of institutional investors is minor compared to domestic public sector investors and private investors as families, stewardship has a marketing function, a form of 'halo signalling'. We see this in the Singapore Stewardship Code, introduced to demonstrate Singapore's 'commitment to the Anglo-American-cum-global norms of "good" corporate governance'.[135] 'Halo signalling' refers to the

---

[130] Task Force on Climate-Related Financial Disclosures <www.fsb-tcfd.org> accessed 17 June 2020.
[131] For a broader discussion of the financial risks of unsustainability, see Beate Sjåfjell and others, 'Securing the Future of European Business: SMART Reform Proposals' (2020) University of Oslo Faculty of Law Research Paper No 2020-11 <https://ssrn.com/abstract=3595048> accessed 17 June 2020.
[132] European Commission (n 38).
[133] Regulation (EU) 2019/2088 of the European Parliament and of the Council of 27 November 2019 on sustainability-related disclosures in the financial services sector [2019] OJ L317/1.
[134] Goto, Koh and Puchniak (n 13).
[135] Stewardship Asia Centre, *Singapore Stewardship Principles for Responsible Investors* (November 2016) <http://www.stewardshipasia.com.sg/sites/default/files/2020-09/Section%202%20-%20SSP%20%28Full%20Document%29.pdf> accessed 22 January 2022.

strategic adoption of regulation to attract foreign investment notwithstanding the apparent practical irrelevance of such regulation to the jurisdiction's corporate environment.[136] The Danish chapter shows that the Danish Stewardship Code, the only stewardship code proper in the Nordic countries, is parallel to the Danish Corporate Governance Code; the two codes share a mutual purpose in their aim to support listed companies' long-term value creation.[137]

Why is there then in Norway only an 'industry recommendation' for asset managers, not important enough to have even an English translation, not even for the most recent revision?

As Katelouzou and Siems show,[138] stewardship means different things for different types of company and investor. The existence and the content of stewardship regulation vary from jurisdiction to jurisdiction. There are separate codes for different kinds of investee company such as for family businesses in Singapore, and there is also investor-specific self-regulation such as the Santiago Principles for sovereign wealth funds by the International Forum of Sovereign Wealth Funds.[139] Interestingly, the major Norwegian Government Pension Fund Global is not a member of this Forum.[140]

The fundamental characteristic of Norwegian (and generally Nordic) company law is protection of creditors and minority shareholders from the abuse of controlling shareholders, a problem also pinpointed in Asian controlled shareholder systems.[141] The company law is in essence based on the idea of the controlling shareholder as a 'good steward' for the benefit of minority shareholders and contractual parties, albeit not for society as a whole or the environment.[142]

According to Norwegian and Nordic company law, the power to run the company is vested with the board.[143] As shareholders are heterogenous groups as far as their goals are concerned and therefore impossible to regulate through voluntary and flexible stewardship codes, we cannot make a definitive conclusion as to whether concentrated share ownership is a friend or a foe for sustainable governance. What does seem clear is that the responsibility for sustainability focus and conduct should be the duty of the boards, instead of relying on voluntary actions and guidelines. The focus on sustainable governance would be independent from the shareholders (whatever nationality, type, shape or size).[144] This resonates also with the EU Sustainable Finance Initiative's reference to the board in its Action 10.

Further, the most important Norwegian investor, the Norwegian Government Pension Fund Global, does not need a Norwegian stewardship code. Nor have the most important domestic Norwegian investors, the Norwegian state and Folketrygdfondet, demonstrated any interest in a Norwegian stewardship code. There is thus no demand for a Singapore-style signalling that Norway is part of the global shareholder stewardship movement.[145]

---

[136] Puchniak and Tang, Singapore's Embrace of Shareholder Stewardship, Chapter 14.
[137] Birkmose and Madsen, The Danish Stewardship Code, Chapter 7.
[138] Katelouzou and Siems, The Global Diffusion of Stewardship Codes, Chapter 30.
[139] International Forum of Sovereign Wealth Funds, 'Santiago Principles' <www.ifswf.org/santiago-principles> accessed 17 June 2020.
[140] International Forum of Sovereign Wealth Funds, 'Our Members' <www.ifswf.org/our-members> accessed 17 June 2020.
[141] Goto, Koh and Puchniak (n 13).
[142] Sjåfjell (n 111); Mähönen and Johnsen (n 111).
[143] Sjåfjell (n 111).
[144] See, for instance, the proposals of the Sustainable Market Actors for Responsible Trade (SMART) project: Beate Sjåfjell and others, 'Supporting the Transition to Sustainability: SMART Reform Proposals' (13 December 2019) University of Oslo Faculty of Law Research Paper No 2019-63 <https://ssrn.com/abstract=3503310> accessed 17 June 2020.
[145] Further on the demand for stewardship, see Katelouzou and Micheler, The Market for Stewardship and the Role of the Government, Chapter 3.

The question may also be raised that even if a stewardship code is needed, who would introduce it? The Norwegian regulatory framework is fragmented with many regulatory and private actors taking a more or less active interest in stewardship. The Norwegian legislation, even before full implementation of SRD II, includes stewardship-related rules. As in many other jurisdictions both in the EU and beyond,[146] legal rules cover the key concerns of shareholder engagement usually addressed by stewardship codes. As far as sustainability in investments is concerned, a regulatory approach as introduced in the European Sustainable Finance Initiative such as the Taxonomy Regulation and the Disclosure Regulation can be seen as a more efficient regulatory approach.[147] Unlike regulation, the codes do not include efficient enforcement mechanisms.[148]

Most importantly, voluntary stewardship seems not to be a strong enough management tool for handling an issue as important as that of securing the contribution of business to sustainability, in a world with increasingly rapid changes in its surroundings and greater uncertainty and volatility in the global markets.[149] To handle this, there is a need for a responsible body which can demonstrate fast decisions and ensure corporate flexibility. The boards of investee companies stand out as the right governance structure in which to place such responsibility, not the shareholders. The heterogeneity of investors and voluntary actions makes stewardship weak and uncertain. Additionally, the stewardship codes mainly focus on shareholder value. As a Nordic example, the Danish Stewardship Code, which is an integrated part of the corporate governance framework, has the aim to 'promote the companies' long-term value creation and thereby contribute to maximising long-term return for investors'.[150] As Birkmose and Madsen conclude in Chapter 7 of this book, instead of working with two parallel codes, it would be better to seek a closer integration of the duties of institutional investors and asset managers and of the boards of the investee companies themselves.[151]

In summary, stewardship must not be allowed to misdirect attention that instead should be focused on core company law issues, including the duties of the board, if the aim is to ensure the contribution of companies to the necessary transition to sustainability.

---

[146] Becker, Andrade and Prado, The Brazilian Stewardship Framework, Chapter 24.
[147] European Commission (n 38); European Commission, 'The European Green Deal' COM (2019) 640 final; European Commission, 'Sustainable Europe Investment Plan European Green Deal Investment Plan' COM (2020) 21 final; Regulation of the European Parliament and of the Council on the establishment of a framework to facilitate sustainable investment, and amending Regulation 2019/2088 on sustainability-related disclosures in the financial services sector [2020] OJ L198/13.
[148] Further on stewardship enforcement, see Katelouzou and Sergakis, Shareholder Stewardship Enforcement, Chapter 27.
[149] For a more optimistic stance on how stewardship can address sustainability, see Katelouzou and Klettner, Sustainable Finance and Stewardship, Chapter 26.
[150] The Committee on Corporate Governance, 'Stewardship Code' (November 2016) 3 <https://corporategovernance.dk/sites/default/files/180116_stewardship_code.pdf> accessed 26 January 2022. See Birkmose and Madsen, The Danish Stewardship Code, Chapter 7.
[151] See Birkmose and Madsen, The Danish Stewardship Code, Chapter 7.

9

Stewardship and Shareholder Engagement in Germany

Wolf-Georg Ringe[*]

9.1 INTRODUCTION

Shareholder engagement is one of the most significant issues in corporate governance today. Ever since regulators identified passive shareholders, or 'absent owners', as one of the key governance problems that contributed to excessive risk-taking leading up to the financial crisis, regulators have been busy designing ways to improve shareholder 'engagement'. The goal is to promote shareholder engagement with their investee companies, and to encourage more responsible and long-term–oriented value creation.[1]

The iconic 'Stewardship Code' in the UK is the most visible example of such activity. The UK Code sets forth a number of best-practice principles that institutional investors, asset managers and proxy advisers are expected to follow. It was originally adopted in 2010 by a body known as the Financial Reporting Council (FRC), and is directed at asset managers who hold voting rights in UK firms.[2] Most recently, the key concept of adopting best practices guidelines for institutional investors has found its way into EU legislation, in particular the revised Shareholder Rights Directive 2019 (SRD II).[3]

Yet the EU's largest economy remains surprisingly reluctant to join in the merry-go-round. Lawmakers and regulators in Germany have been sitting on the fence on the issue during the past several years, hesitating on what to do. Most saliently, Germany has refused to adopt an official stewardship code, and the SRD II reform is eyed with some suspicion. This chapter explores the role that stewardship and shareholder engagement play in the German context and investigates the reasons behind the reluctance of lawmakers to follow the international trend.

As we shall see, although shareholder engagement is awakening among German investors recently, regulators have refused to develop a code mandating stewardship or shareholder engagement. While many doctrinal or functional reasons are put forward to explain this, this chapter argues that the main political reason for this reluctance lies in the limited geographical reach of such a code, which would primarily apply to the (limited) domestic fund industry and

---

[*] I am very grateful to Maria Grigoropoulou for excellent research assistance. Thanks go to Alexander Bassen, Theodor Baums, Brian Cheffins, Dionysia Katelouzou, Karsten Paetzmann, Dan Puchniak, Henrik Schmidt, Michael Schmidt, Birgit Spießhofer and Christian Strenger, as well as workshop participants at the Global Stewardship conference at King's College London and at a Law & Finance conference at Goethe University Frankfurt for very valuable conversations and comments on an earlier draft of this chapter. An earlier version of this chapter was published in honour of Brigitte Haar in (2021) 22 *European Business Organization Review* 87.

[1] See, for example, Iris H-Y Chiu, 'Turning Institutional Investors into "Stewards": Exploring the Meaning and Objectives of "Stewardship"' (2013) 66 *Current Legal Problems* 443.

[2] See Davies, The UK Stewardship Code 2010–2020, Chapter 2.

[3] Directive (EU) 2017/828 of the European Parliament and of the Council of 17 May 2017 amending Directive 2007/36/EC as regards the encouragement of long-term shareholder engagement [2017] OJ L132/1 (SRD II).

would be unable to prescribe any meaningful principles to foreign-based asset managers. Still, I argue that the adoption of a code in the German context may make sense, for example to define expectations and to clarify the obligations of investee companies. Most importantly, it would benefit domestic investors that are typically 'home biased' and thereby frequently disproportionately invested in domestic funds.

This chapter is organized as follows: Section 9.2 discusses the emergence of 'stewardship' as a phenomenon and traces its development from being a post-crisis shareholder engagement remedy to the much broader, ESG-encompassing silver bullet of today's equity markets. Section 9.3 then turns to the question of why Germany has so far refused to give stewardship any regulatory backing. Section 9.4 discusses whether, despite the ostensible difficulties, the introduction of a stewardship code would still be desirable and concludes that an additional useful scope for it remains. Section 9.5 concludes.

9.2 STEWARDSHIP AND SHAREHOLDER ENGAGEMENT

9.2.1 *Encouraging Shareholders*

The roots of the current debate around increased shareholder engagement are to be found in the 2008 Global Financial Crisis (GFC). Policymakers and academics identified many reasons behind the disaster, and one of the reasons put forward was severe flaws in the system of corporate governance. In particular, shareholders frequently got the blame. Many saw a lack of critical oversight by shareholders as the key problem, and institutional investors in particular were criticized for their 'passivity'.[4] Crucially, the seminal *Walker Review of Corporate Governance in the UK Banking Industry*, led by Sir David Walker, found in 2009 that institutional investors 'appear to have been slow to act where issues of concern were identified … and of limited effectiveness in seeking to address them either individually or collaboratively'.[5] Further, the review stated that 'the board and director shortcomings … would have been tackled more effectively had there been more vigorous scrutiny and engagement by major investors acting as owners'.[6] This claim was picked up by public figures such as the former UK City Minister Lord Paul Myners, who accused institutional investors of being 'absentee landlords'.[7] The subsequent *Kay Review* considered improvements to the UK equity markets and to long-term decision-making, with a special focus on corporate and investor behaviour.[8]

It is against this background that the FRC was eventually charged with developing a specific instrument to improve shareholder engagement.[9] Following a consultation in early 2010,[10] the

---

[4] Brian R Cheffins, 'The Stewardship Code's Achilles' Heel' (2010) 73 *Modern Law Review* 1004, 1009–10; Arad Reisberg, 'The UK Stewardship Code: On the Road to Nowhere?' (2015) 15 *Journal of Corporate Law Studies* 217, 220–21.

[5] David Walker, 'A Review of Corporate Governance in UK Banks and Other Financial Industry Entities. Final Recommendations' (26 November 2009) para 5.10 <https://ecgi.global/sites/default/files/codes/documents/walker_review_261109.pdf> accessed 6 January 2020 [hereinafter Walker Review].

[6] ibid para 5.11.

[7] Paul Myners, 'Record of Speech Made to the Association of Investment Companies' (April 2009) para 38 <http://webarchive.nationalarchives.gov.uk/20091207163737/http://hm-treasury.gov.uk/speech_fsst_210409.htm> archived 4 December 2009, accessed 6 January 2020.

[8] John Kay, 'The Kay Review of UK Equity Markets and Long-Term Decision Making' (Department for Business, Innovation and Skills, July 2012) <https://assets.publishing.service.gov.uk/government/uploads/system/uploads/attachment_data/file/253454/bis-12-917-kay-review-of-equity-markets-final-report.pdf> accessed 6 January 2020.

[9] The Walker Review (n 5) had recommended that the FRC's remit should be extended in this way.

[10] See Financial Reporting Council, 'Consultation on a Stewardship Code for Institutional Investors' (19 January 2010) <www.frc.org.uk/consultation-list/2010/consultation-on-a-stewardship-code-for-institution> accessed 6 January 2020.

FRC was rather quick to publish the original UK Stewardship Code in July 2010[11] along with a separate report concerning its implementation.[12] The Code was revised in 2012[13] and again in 2019[14].

At the moment of its birth, the policy objective of stewardship was twofold. At an individual company level, stewardship was expected to help promote high standards of corporate governance and performance of the *investee company*. In other words, its role is a supportive one, to call upon corporate owners to fulfil their governance responsibilities. Here, stewardship is about enhancing long-term value creation. At the same time, stewardship should also operate on the *investor* level (i.e. between the investor and the asset manager).[15] Reinforcing the accountability of institutional investors and asset managers to their clients should also strengthen trust in the financial system more generally.[16]

Initially, the use of the UK Stewardship Code had just been recommended on a voluntary basis. However, with effect from 6 December 2010, the then Financial Services Authority[17] required that UK-approved asset management companies must disclose to what extent they comply with or derogate from its requirements.[18] For other institutional investors and foreign investors whose investment activity extends to companies in the United Kingdom, a non-binding recommendation for use remains without publicity.

A similar trend was soon picked up elsewhere. After the financial crisis, the European Commission also looked into corporate governance, resulting in a 2010 Green Paper.[19] In this context, the Commission argued that 'shareholders do not seem to have fulfilled their role of "responsible owners"'[20] and that they 'seem to show little interest in the long-term governance objectives of the businesses/financial institutions in which they invest'.[21] Former Commissioner Michel Barnier said in a 2010 speech that '[w]e have spoken for years about shareholder rights. It is time to also talk about shareholders' obligations.'[22] Following the

---

[11] See Financial Reporting Council, *The UK Stewardship Code* (July 2010) <www.frc.org.uk/getattachment/e223e152-5515-4cdc-a951-da33e093eb28/UK-Stewardship-Code-July-2010.pdf> accessed 6 January 2020 [hereinafter UK Code 2010].

[12] Financial Reporting Council, 'Implementation of the UK Stewardship Code' (July 2010) <www.frc.org.uk/getattachment/34d58dbd-5e54-412e-9cdb-cb30f21d5074/Implementation-of-Stewardship-Code-July-2010.pdf> accessed 6 January 2020.

[13] Financial Reporting Council, *The UK Stewardship Code* (September 2012) <www.frc.org.uk/getattachment/d67933f9-ca38-4233-b603-3d24b2f62c5f/UK-Stewardship-Code-(September-2012).pdf> accessed 6 January 2020 [hereinafter UK Code 2012].

[14] The most recent version of the UK Stewardship Code came into force on 1 January 2020. See Financial Reporting Council, *The UK Stewardship Code 2020* (2019) <www.frc.org.uk/getattachment/5aae591d-d9d3-4cf4-814a-d14e156a1d87/Stewardship-Code_Dec-19-Final-Corrected.pdf> accessed 18 August 2020 [hereinafter UK Code 2020]. Further on stewardship in the UK, see Davies, The UK Stewardship Code 2010–2020, Chapter 2 and Katelouzou and Micheler, The Market for Stewardship and the Role of the Government, Chapter 3.

[15] On these two sides of stewardship, see Dionysia Katelouzou, 'Shareholder Stewardship: A Case of (Re)Embedding Institutional Investors and the Corporation?' in Beate Sjåfjell and Christopher M Bruner (eds), *Cambridge Handbook of Corporate Law, Corporate Governance and Sustainability* (CUP 2019).

[16] FRC, 'Consultation on a Stewardship Code for Institutional Investors' (n 10) para 1.11.

[17] Now the Financial Conduct Authority (FCA).

[18] FCA Handbook, Conduct of Business Sourcebook (COBS) 2.2.3R (06/12/2010) and 2.2A.5R (03/01/2018).

[19] European Commission, 'Corporate Governance in Financial Institutions and Remuneration Policies' (Green Paper) COM (2010) 284 final <https://publications.europa.eu/en/publication-detail/-/publication/1788e830-b050-447c-8214-77ed51b13241> accessed 6 January 2020.

[20] European Commission, 'Corporate Governance in Financial Institutions: Lessons to Be Drawn from the Current Financial Crisis, Best Practices' (Commission Staff Working Document) SEC (2010) 669, s 4.1 <https://eur-lex.europa.eu/legal-content/EN/ALL/?uri=CELEX:52010SC0669> accessed 5 February 2020.

[21] European Commission, 'Corporate Governance in Financial Institutions and Remuneration Policies' (n 19) s 3.5.

[22] Michel Barnier, 'Re-establishing Responsibility and Accountability at the Heart of the Financial System' (Speech at the 1st Congress of the Alumni Solvay School, Brussels, 25 October 2010).

Green Paper consultation, the vast majority of respondents supported further legislative activity in this field.[23] This concerned, in particular, institutional investors' obligation to publish their voting policies and records. The hope was that public disclosure would improve investor awareness, optimize investment decisions by the ultimate investors, facilitate issuers' dialogue with investors, and encourage shareholder engagement.

The European Commission first analyzed these issues in the more specific context of corporate governance of banks and financial institutions, but has subsequently taken listed companies generally into consideration.[24] A 2011 Green Paper thus subsequently extended the framework to public companies more generally and identified short-termism as the main factor contributing to market inefficiency. The measures discussed were addressed to institutional investors and included the publication of their voting decisions, the identification and publication of any conflicts of interest, the disclosure of a remuneration policy for financial intermediaries, and an improvement in the level of information to investors about the risks associated with an investment. An academic 'Reflection Group' also considered whether an EU-wide best practice code would be a useful tool.[25]

At the end of 2012, the Commission then presented an Action Plan, which transferred the theoretical framework into specific regulatory objectives for the coming years.[26] The Action Plan was based on the three main areas of improving transparency between the company and its investors, strengthening the long-term commitment of shareholders, and improving the legal framework for the cross-border operation of firms.[27] This ultimately led to the revision of the original 2007 Shareholder Rights Directive to introduce elements of the stewardship idea.[28] It took, however, some time until this went ahead. The SRD II was adopted in May 2017, and member states were obliged to implement the new standards by June 2019.[29]

In the meantime, the trend has led to the adoption of codes on active ownership in many countries – not just in the EU but worldwide.[30] International bodies such as the International Corporate Governance Network (ICGN) have also published their own standards.[31] The Organisation for Economic Co-operation and Development (OECD) has also done work in this area[32] and has incorporated stewardship elements into its Corporate Governance

---

[23] European Commission, 'Summary of Responses to Commission Green Paper on Corporate Governance in Financial Institutions' (Feedback Statement) (2010).

[24] This resulted in another, broader green paper: European Commission, 'The EU Corporate Governance Framework' (Green Paper) COM (2011) 164 final <https://publications.europa.eu/en/publication-detail/-/publication/3eed7997-d40b-4984-8080-31d7c4e91fb2/language-en> accessed 6 January 2020.

[25] José Engrácia Antunes and others, 'Report of the Reflection Group on the Future of EU Company Law' (5 April 2011) s 3.1.4 <www.ilf-frankfurt.de/fileadmin/_migrated/content_uploads/ILF_WP_126.pdf> accessed 18 August 2020.

[26] European Commission, 'Action Plan: European Company Law and Corporate Governance – A Modern Legal Framework for More Engaged Shareholders and Sustainable Companies' (Communication) COM (2012) 744 final.

[27] European Commission, 'Action Plan' (n 26) 5.

[28] See Klaus J Hopt, 'Corporate Governance in Europe: A Critical Review of the European Commission's Initiatives on Corporate Law and Corporate Governance' (2015) 12 *New York University Journal of Law & Business* 139, 176ff.

[29] SRD II (n 3) art 2(1).

[30] For a list of all the stewardship codes, see Katelouzou and Puchniak, Global Shareholder Stewardship, Chapter 1 and Katelouzou and Siems, The Global Diffusion of Stewardship Codes, Chapter 30. For a good discussion, see Brenda Hannigan, 'The Rise of Stewardship – "Smoke and Mirrors" or Governance Realignment?' in Helmut Siekmann (ed), *Festschrift für Theodor Baums zum siebzigsten Geburtstag* (Mohr Siebeck 2017) 561.

[31] International Corporate Governance Network, *ICGN Global Governance Principles* (2016) <https://ecgi.global/code/icgn-global-governance-principles-2016?field_categories_tid%5B0%5D=9430&field_categories_tid%5B1%5D=9376&field_categories_tid%5B2%5D=9415> accessed 11 February 2022.

[32] OECD, *The Role of Institutional Investors in Promoting Good Corporate Governance* (2011) <www.oecd.org/daf/ca/49081553.pdf> accessed 6 January 2020.

Principles.[33] Industry bodies such as the European Fund and Asset Management Association (EFAMA) have also adopted their own stewardship rules.[34]

All these codes, best practice guidelines and also the SRD II share a number of common elements. Besides encouraging shareholder engagement, they typically require institutional investors to disclose their engagement policies and the results of their implementation. Moreover, these instruments also emphasize that shareholders should play a more active role in ensuring that companies are accountable not only to shareholders but also to society as a whole.

9.2.2 ESG Stewardship

So far, we have considered the genesis of stewardship as a shareholder-focused development, which was intended as a means to foster shareholder engagement and to monitor managerial excessive risk-taking. More recently, stewardship has morphed from this original purpose to cover a broader set of issues, which have become known as 'ESG' (environment, social and governance) policies. This is an umbrella term for investment policies that seek positive returns and long-term impact on society, the environment and the performance of the business. With some granularity, the ESG agenda bears a certain resemblance to the well-established trend of corporate social responsibility (CSR), which in turn has been rebranded and is now more commonly referred to as socially responsible investing (SRI).[35]

From an investment perspective, ESG factors are a subset of non-financial performance indicators which include sustainable, ethical and corporate governance issues such as managing a company's carbon footprint and ensuring that there are systems in place to guarantee accountability. They are factors incorporated into both investment decisions and risk-management processes.

The ESG movement was boosted with the adoption of the United Nations Principles for Responsible Investment (UNPRI), a UN-backed set of principles which aim at contributing to the development of a more sustainable global financial system.[36] The PRI, originally launched in April 2006, received increased interest following the GFC and a sharp rise in the number of signatories.[37] Further, the important proposal of an EU 'framework for sustainable investment' lists ten initiatives to strengthen financial stability through a stronger emphasis on ESG factors and to improve the contribution of the financial sector to sustainable growth.[38] This instrument seeks to integrate ESG factors into the decision-making processes of institutional investors and asset managers.[39]

---

[33] OECD, *G20/OECD Principles of Corporate Governance* (2015) <www.oecd.org/daf/ca/Corporate-Governance-Principles-ENG.pdf> accessed 6 January 2020. See in particular section III of the document, where an explicit reference to the stewardship idea is at 29–30.

[34] European Fund and Asset Management Association, 'EFAMA Stewardship Code: Principles for Asset Managers' Monitoring of, Voting in, Engagement with Investee Companies' (2018) <www.efama.org/Publications/Public/Corporate_Governance/EFAMA%20Stewardship%20Code.pdf> accessed 6 January 2020. The 2018 EFAMA Code is based on its predecessor, the 2011 EFAMA Code for External Governance.

[35] The EU adopted a 'CSR Directive' in 2014 to introduce so-called non-financial reporting. See Directive 2014/95/EU of the European Parliament and of the Council of 22 October 2014 amending Directive 2013/34/EU as regards disclosure of non-financial and diversity information by certain large undertakings and groups [2014] OJ L330/1.

[36] See <www.unpri.org/> accessed 6 January 2020.

[37] Mike Scott, 'Investors Urged to Track ESG Risks' *Financial Times* (20 February 2012) <www.ft.com/content/51378844-4e56-11e1-8670-00144feabdc0> accessed 18 August 2020.

[38] European Commission, 'Proposal for a Regulation of the European Parliament and of the Council on the Establishment of a Framework to Facilitate Sustainable Investment' COM (2018) 353 final.

[39] European Commission, 'Public Consultation on Institutional Investors' and Asset Managers' Duties Regarding Sustainability' (24 May 2018) <https://ec.europa.eu/info/sites/info/files/2017-investors-duties-sustainability-feedback-statement_en.pdf> accessed 6 January 2020.

Most recently, the ESG movement has found its way directly into stewardship principles. For example, the most recent version of the UK Stewardship Code, which came into force on 1 January 2020, recognizes the importance of ESG factors: 'The proposed Code now refers to environmental, social and governance (ESG) factors. Signatories are expected to take material ESG issues into account when fulfilling their stewardship responsibilities.'[40] In a similar vein, the ICGN is currently consulting on a revised version of its Global Stewardship Principles. Among the various changes that are proposed, one of the key features includes the use of ESG factors in investment decision-making, as well as in stewardship.[41]

Comparing this trend with the original policy objectives,[42] it appears that the purpose of stewardship is expanded yet again: as we saw, it originally sought to fulfil a corporate governance purpose (at the investee company level) and an informed investment decision-making purpose (at the investor/investment fund level). Now, the investment approach includes the consideration of wider ethical, environmental and social factors and the consideration of relevant systemic risks. In a broader context, stewardship is thus seen as enhancing not only sustainability and long-term economic growth but overall financial market stability.[43]

It is submitted that the move from a shareholder-oriented concept to an ESG programme changes the substance of stewardship considerably. Stewardship has always been hailed as the path to more sustainable investing and the path to a better world, but the inclusion of ESG standards gives the movement a quasi-religious authority. Seen in this light, adherence to ESG issues is frequently seen as the 'holy grail', with the potential of solving multiple problems of society at large. It is thus reminiscent of the development of corporate governance, which has turned into a means of addressing all different social and economic issues that were once predominantly the concern of government regulation.[44]

The success story of stewardship and ESG principles thereby takes the place of lawmakers' previous favourite governance feature: independent directors. As is well documented, many instances of corporate governance reform over the last several decades have seen an increased promotion of independence criteria and quotas.[45] This is even more surprising given that academic evidence of their financial performance is mixed at best.[46]

Perhaps the latest trend towards shareholder empowerment and engagement is evidence of a learning process: it may be understood as regulators accepting the limited benefits of outside directors as a monitoring tool, and now identifying shareholders as the better incentivized group to take up a governance role in the firm.

[40] UK Code 2020 (n 14). Financial Reporting Council, 'FRC Strengthens Stewardship Code' (30 January 2019) <www.frc.org.uk/news/january-2019-(1)/frc-strengthens-stewardship-code> accessed 6 January 2020.
[41] ICGN, 'ICGN Policy Priorities 2019/2020' (2019) <www.icgn.org/sites/default/files/ICGN%20Policy%20Priorities%202019-20.pdf> accessed 18 August 2020.
[42] See Section 9.2.1.
[43] ICGN (n 41) 2.
[44] See Marcel Kahan and Edward Rock, 'Symbolic Corporate Governance Politics' (2014) 94 Boston University Law Review 1997; see also Mariana Pargendler, 'The Corporate Governance Obsession' (2016) 42 Journal of Corporation Law 359.
[45] See e.g. Wolf-Georg Ringe, 'Independent Directors: After the Crisis' (2013) 14 European Business Organization Law Review 401. For an international comparison, see Dan W Puchniak, Harald Baum and Luke Nottage (eds), Independent Directors in Asia: A Historical, Contextual and Comparative Approach (CUP 2017).
[46] Sanjai Bhagat and Bernard Black, 'The Uncertain Relationship between Board Composition and Firm Performance' (1999) 54 Business Lawyer 921; Sanjai Bhagat and Bernard Black, 'The Non-correlation between Board Independence and Long-Term Firm Performance' (2002) 27 Journal of Corporation Law 232; Nuno Fernandes, 'EC: Board Compensation and Firm Performance: The Role of "Independent" Board Members' (2008) 18 Journal of Multinational Financial Management 30.

9.2.3 Index Funds and Stewardship

Most recently, stewardship is facing fresh challenges owing to market developments, notably the advent of index investing.[47] Index funds are generally considered as a nightmare for corporate governance since they do not take an interest in any strategic matters of their target firms; rather, they invest in a company only because the company's shares are part of an index. Despite these original fears, sceptical voices now see index funds in a more positive light. The reason is that index funds have no other option than to fix certain problems and to take measures that improve the performance of their portfolio companies, since exit is not a viable alternative for them.[48] Accordingly, they have lately changed their voting patterns, and are more willing to vote together with activists – they are both becoming active owners[49] and are particularly ESG-minded as their perspective is for the long run.

Exercising 'voice' instead of 'exit' creates a free-riding problem for the exercising investor.[50] More specifically, an index fund's performance is typically measured against the performance of rival index funds. If an index fund undertakes an investment in stewardship, this investment will increase the value of a particular portfolio company, but 'the increase will be shared with all other investors in the company, including rival index funds that replicate the same index'.[51] As a result, an index fund's stewardship engagement offers competitive advantages to its rivals that share in engagement's benefits without being subject to stewardship's costs. Regulatory authorities have acknowledged this free-riding problem.[52] The introduction of a regulatory initiative rendering stewardship a mandatory activity for all companies of the investment management industry can be perceived as eliminating the free-riding problem. However, such an introduction would face two challenges.

First, imposing an obligation to develop a stewardship activity is a dead letter if there are no guarantees about the quality of shareholder engagement.[53] This argument was among the main concerns of industry stakeholders before the adoption of the UK Stewardship Code,[54] and

---

[47] See Fisch, The Uncertain Stewardship Potential of Index Funds, Chapter 21.
[48] Jill E Fisch, Assaf Hamdani and Steven D Solomon, 'The New Titans of Wall Street: A Theoretical Framework for Passive Investors' (2019) 168 *University of Pennsylvania Law Review* 17, 37.
[49] Ian R Appel, Todd A Gormley and Donald B Keim, 'Passive Investors, Not Passive Owners' (2016) 121 *Journal of Financial Economics* 111.
[50] Paul Myners, 'Institutional Investment in the United Kingdom: A Review' (HM Treasury 2001) paras 5.34, 5.88 <https://uksif.org/wp-content/uploads/2012/12/MYNERS-P.-2001.-Institutional-Investment-in-the-United-Kingdom-A-Review.pdf> accessed 18 August 2020; Demetra Arsalidou, 'Shareholders and Corporate Scrutiny: The Role of the UK Stewardship Code' (2012) 9 *European Company and Financial Law Review* 342, 364; Reisberg (n 4) 231, 247; Vanda Heinen, *Die Rolle institutioneller Investoren und Stimmrechtsberater in der deutschen Corporate Governance [The Role of Institutional Investors and Proxy Advisors in German Corporate Governance]* (Springer Gabler 2019) 20, 27; Simone Alvaro, Marco Maugeri and Giovanni Strampelli, 'Institutional Investors, Corporate Governance and Stewardship Codes: Problems and Perspectives' CONSOB Legal Papers No 19/2019 <https://ssrn.com/abstract=3393780> accessed 6 January 2020.
[51] Lucian Bebchuk and Scott Hirst, 'Index Funds and the Future of Corporate Governance: Theory, Evidence, and Policy' (2019) 119 *Columbia Law Review* 2029, 2057.
[52] Walker Review (n 5) paras 5.9, 5.16; European Commission, 'Corporate Governance in Financial Institutions and Remuneration Policies' (n 19); Financial Conduct Authority/Financial Reporting Council, 'Building a Regulatory Framework for Effective Stewardship' (Discussion Paper, January 2019) paras 2.13, 5.6, 5.18 <www.fca.org.uk/publication/discussion/dp19-01.pdf> accessed 6 January 2020.
[53] Peter Böckli and others, 'Shareholder Engagement and Identification' (February 2015) <https://europeancompanylawexperts.wordpress.com/publications/shareholder-engagement-2015/> accessed 6 January 2020. The European Company Law Expert Group Response to the Public Consultation for Commission's Proposal for a Directive of the European Parliament and of the Council amending Directive 2007/36/EC as regards the encouragement of long-term shareholder engagement and Directive 2013/34/EU as regards certain elements of the corporate governance statement.
[54] Opinion Letters of Aberdeen Asset Management, CFA Institute, GC100, ICAEW, ICGN, JP Morgan Asset Management, NAPF to Consultation on a Stewardship Code for Institutional Investors 2010.

remains one of the main points of criticism against the effects of the Code.[55] Market participants[56] as well as regulatory authorities[57] argue that less qualitative reporting of stewardship activities is prompted by a regulatory framework consisting of prescriptive mandatory rules.[58] The need for more qualitative shareholder engagement explains the positive industry response to the introduction of an annual Activities and Outcomes Report besides the Policy and Practice Statement upon signing the Code.[59]

The second challenge has to do with the addressees of any regulatory initiative. Empirical evidence shows that even in jurisdictions where there is no regulatory initiative relating to stewardship, such as the US, asset managers integrate stewardship and ESG factors in their investment decision-making process. The most important fund managers are the 'Big Three', Black Rock, State Street Global Investors and Vanguard. Even though they do not have any legal obligation to perform stewardship, they do so on a voluntary basis. As such, the following question arises: What are the characteristics of these managers that incentivize them to invest in stewardship? The benefits they enjoy out of their stewardship activity must outweigh the costs they incur respectively.[60]

On the benefit side, the adoption of stewardship activities might have a positive impact on an institutional investor's reputation, which leads to an increase of demand from end-beneficiaries, provided that they have stewardship preferences and do select institutional investors based on these preferences. The same can be said for the selection of asset managers by institutional investors.[61] On the costs side, empirical evidence supports the argument that the 'Big Three' under-invest in stewardship given the size of their portfolio.[62] This under-investment in stewardship in combination with the economies of scale that are achieved through the increase of common ownership held by the dominant institutional investors[63] renders the undertaking of stewardship activities by them cost-effective.

The first insight that we gain from the cost–benefit analysis of the integration of stewardship in the Big Three's business model is that the economic incentive to undertake stewardship is associated with the size of the institutional investor or asset manager. This is confirmed by

---

[55] Arsalidou (n 50) 346, 356; OECD, *G20/OECD Principles of Corporate Governance* (n 33).

[56] Opinion Letters of Alex Edmans, Allianz Global Investors, Association of Member Nominated Trustees, CFA Society UK, GC100, Black Sun plc, Implementation Taskforce, M&G Investments, Merian Global Investors, Share Action and Smart Pension to Public Consultation for FRC's Proposed Revision to the UK Stewardship Code (Financial Reporting Council, 'Consulting on a Revised UK Stewardship Code' (30 January 2019) <www.frc.org.uk/consultation-list/2019/consulting-on-a-revised-uk-stewardship-code> accessed 18 August 2020).

[57] Financial Conduct Authority, 'Proposals to Promote Shareholder Engagement: Feedback to CP 19/7 and Final Rules' (Policy Statement, May 2019) para 2.20 <www.fca.org.uk/publication/policy/ps19-13.pdf> accessed 6 January 2020.

[58] Chiu, 'Turning Institutional Investors into "Stewards"' (n 1).

[59] Financial Reporting Council, 'Consulting on a Revised UK Stewardship Code' (Feedback Statement, October 2019) para 2.20 <www.frc.org.uk/getattachment/2912476c-d183-46bd-a86e-dfb024f694ad/191023-Feedback-Statement-Consultation-on-revised-Stewardship-Code-FINAL.pdf> accessed 6 January 2020.

[60] See Marcel Kahan and Edward Rock, 'Index Funds and Corporate Governance: Let Shareholders be Shareholders' (October 2019) NYU Law and Economics Research Paper No 18–39 <https://ssrn.com/abstract=3295098> accessed 18 August 2020.

[61] Paul Cox, Stephen Brammer and Andrew Millington, 'An Empirical Examination of Institutional Investor Preferences for Corporate Social Performance' (2004) 52 *Journal of Business Ethics* 27; Magnus Jansson and Anders Biel, 'Motives to Engage in Sustainable Investment: A Comparison between Institutional and Private Investors' (2011) 19 *Sustainable Development* 135; Rob Bauer, Tobias Ruof and Paul Smeets, 'Get Real! Individuals Prefer More Sustainable Investments' (2021) 34 *Review of Financial Studies* 3976.

[62] Bebchuk and Hirst, 'Index Funds and the Future of Corporate Governance' (n 51).

[63] James Hawley and Andrew Williams, 'Universal Owners: Challenges and Opportunities' (May 2007) 15 *Corporate Governance: An International Review* 415; Lucian Bebchuk and Scott Hirst, 'The Specter of the Giant Three' (2019) 99 *Boston University Law Review* 721.

current literature[64] and a qualitative analysis of market participants' responses to the FRC 2010 public consultation.[65] The differentiated cost-management between large and small institutional investors can transform stewardship into a regulatory barrier for small institutional investors and asset managers. For this reason, any regulatory initiative should be supplemented by initiatives that will create a level playing field in the investment management industry. Such an initiative can be, for example, the promotion of shared outside research services.[66]

9.3 A STEWARDSHIP CODE IN GERMANY?

Having explored the general context in which the idea has developed, this section now moves on to consider stewardship and investor engagement in the German context particularly.

9.3.1 *Corporate Engagement in Germany*

It is well documented that the German corporate ownership system has been undergoing profound changes over the past twenty years.[67] While Germany has long been seen as the paradigm example of an insider-dominated economy with strong networks across the country, the ownership of German firms has more recently opened up and given way to more outside holdings and more active engagement policies. Several studies[68] have identified a constant increase of equity shareholdings in German companies held by institutional investors. Among them, investment fund management companies (KAGs) and insurance companies have the largest ownership stake. In contrast, German pension funds are not as developed as in other countries, such as the UK.[69] The general increase can be attributed to legislative initiatives aiming to unwind cross-holdings in German companies, such as the changes in capital gains taxation in 2001, the higher capital requirements for banks, and the implementation of new insider trading laws.[70] The dissolution of cross-ownership has also been followed by a significant increase in the stake of foreign institutional investors in German companies.[71] The presence of foreign investors is even more salient in DAX companies; meaning the German companies with the largest market capitalization. Among the top fifteen DAX investors, the 'Big Three' have a very prominent position.[72]

---

[64] Riikka Sievänen, Hannu Rita and Bert Scholtens, 'The Drivers of Responsible Investment: The Case of European Pension Funds' (2012) 117 *Journal of Business Ethics* 137.
[65] FRC, 'Consultation on a Stewardship Code for Institutional Investors' (n 10).
[66] Bebchuk and Hirst, 'The Specter of the Giant Three' (n 63).
[67] Wolf-Georg Ringe, 'Changing Law and Ownership Patterns in Germany: Corporate Governance and the Erosion of Deutschland AG' (2015) 63 *The American Journal of Comparative Law* 493.
[68] For EU companies: Observatoire de l'Epargne Européenne and INSEAD OEE Data Services, *Who Owns the European Economy? Evolution of the Ownership of EU-Listed Companies between 1970 and 2012* (2013) <https://op.europa.eu/en/publication-detail/-/publication/db5b2604-e1d7-11e5-8a50-01aa75ed71a1/language-en> accessed 18 August 2020; for German companies: OECD, *The Role of Institutional Investors in Promoting Good Corporate Governance* (n 32) 115.
[69] See Section 9.3.2.4.
[70] OECD, *The Role of Institutional Investors in Promoting Good Corporate Governance* (n 32) 112; Steffen Rapp and Christian Strenger, 'Corporate Governance in Germany: Recent Developments and Challenges' (2015) 27 *Journal of Applied Corporate Finance* 16, 20–22.
[71] Şebnem Kalemli-Özcan, Volodymyr Korsun, Bent E Sørensen and Carolina Villegas-Sanchez, 'Who Owns Europe's Firms? Globalization and Foreign Investment in Europe' (November 2013) <https://editorialexpress.com/cgi-bin/conference/download.cgi?db_name=NAWM2015&paper_id=241> accessed 6 January 2020.
[72] IHS Markit/DIRK, 'Who Owns the German DAX?' (8th edition, 2021) <https://www.dirk.org/wp-content/uploads/2021/06/DAX-Study-2020-Investoren-der-Deutschland-AG-8_0.pdf> accessed 27 January 2022.

Institutional investors' corporate engagement activity is regulated by the German Stock Corporation Act (Aktiengesetz) and the Capital Investment Act (Kapitalanlagegesetzbuch).[73] The first Act determines the rights and obligations of institutional investors in their capacity as shareholders, while the second Act determines their fiduciary duties towards their clients. Shareholder engagement entails a broad range of formal and informal types of corporate governance intervention.[74] An example of formal shareholder engagement is the participation and the exercise of voting rights in Annual General Meetings (AGMs). Studies have shown that the average voting turnout rate in German companies fluctuates between 52% and 58%,[75] which is low in comparison to the UK and other countries of continental Europe, such as France.

Informal shareholder engagement, such as behind-the-scenes communication between shareholders and the supervisory board of directors, can substitute the comparatively low turnout rate. This has been the case with hedge funds initiating activist campaigns in Germany.[76] Hedge fund activists frequently employ informal means of communication with the board of directors before communicating their corporate governance concerns to the public.[77] This escalation of shareholder engagement activities has also been adopted as a principle of the UK Code 2020.[78]

All of this has led to more active engagement at companies' general meetings.[79] For example, many DAX executives and board members are likely to remember vividly the weak voting results at the 2016 and 2017 AGMs. After decades of approval rates beyond 90 percent, results with less than three-quarters of approval rate may be read not as an expression of fundamental mistrust but rather as a clearer articulation of shareholder interests.[80] This all culminated in the 2019 AGM of Bayer AG, where the shareholders, for the first time in German corporate history, refused to approve the management board (*Entlastung*).[81] The reasons for this shareholder 'revolt' are manifold. Non-transparent compensation structures for management board members, blank authorizations for capital increases, and doubts about the independence of supervisory board members are the most frequent criticisms by shareholders.

The good news is that some companies apparently are listening and responding to the concerns of investors. For example, software company SAP has responded to the vote at its

---

[73] The *Aktiengesetz* is available in English at Norton Rose Fulbright, 'German Stock Corporation Act (Aktiengesetz)' (10 May 2016) <www.nortonrosefulbright.com/-/media/files/nrf/nrfweb/imported/german-stock-corporation-act.pdf> accessed 18 August 2020.

[74] For the distinction between activism, engagement and stewardship, see Alvaro, Maugeri and Strampelli (n 50).

[75] For the period 1998–2010: Jose M Mendoza, Christoph Van der Elst and Erik P M Vermeulen, 'Entrepreneurship and Innovation: The Hidden Costs of Corporate Governance in Europe' (2010) 7 *South Carolina Journal of International Law and Business* 1; for the period 2010–2013: Anne Lafarre, 'Shareholder Activism at European AGMs: Voting Turnout and Behavior of (Small) Shareholders' (Master Thesis, Tilburg University 2014).

[76] Andreas Engert, 'Shareholder Activism in Germany' in Holger Fleischer, Hideki Kanda, Kon Sik Kim and Peter Mülbert (eds), *German and East Asian Perspectives on Corporate and Capital Market Law: Investors versus Companies* (Mohr Siebeck 2019); Amadeus Moeser, 'Shareholder Activism in Germany' (*Harvard Law School Forum on Corporate Governance*, 29 January 2019) <https://corpgov.law.harvard.edu/2019/01/29/shareholder-activism-in-germany-2/> accessed 6 January 2020.

[77] Nickolay Gantchev, 'The Costs of Shareholder Activism: Evidence from a Sequential Decision Model' (2013) 107 *Journal of Financial Economics* 610.

[78] UK Code 2020 (n 14).

[79] See Peter Köhler, Anke Rezmer, Michael Maisch and Bert Fröndhoff, 'Aufstand der Investoren: Das Kapital wagt die Revolte [Investor Rebellion: Capital Dares to Revolt]' *Handelsblatt* (17 May 2019) <www.handelsblatt.com/finanzen/anlagestrategie/trends/hauptversammlungen-aufstand-der-investoren-das-kapital-wagt-die-revolte/v_detail_tab_comments/24344364.html?ticket=ST-10476244-D0latNDe7Nf3mMAJc3lC-ap6> accessed 18 August 2020.

[80] Christoph Berger, 'Active Stewardship im deutschen Kapitalmarkt [Active Stewardship in the German Capital Market]' (2019) 72 *Zeitschrift für das gesamte Kreditwesen* 85.

[81] More than 55% of the shareholders voted in favour of a 'no-confidence' motion. See Guy Chazan, 'Bayer Execs Face Investor Heat after Rare No-Confidence Vote' *Financial Times* (Berlin, 28 April 2019) <www.ft.com/content/0a6cc01c-69a3-11e9-80c7-60ee53e6681d> accessed 18 August 2020.

2017 AGM and has made every effort to understand the scepticism of its shareholders in order to change the incentive structure and transparency of their compensation system.[82] It appears that institutional investors are especially concerned about executive compensation issues, which is why rejection rates are highest for these corporate decisions.[83] Other topics of concern include the capital structure, in particular the issuance of new shares or convertible bonds; there were doubts about the number of refusals in terms of independence of members of the supervisory board, and in particular members of the audit committee are subject to stringent requirements. Bayer was a special case: the public mistrust mostly stemmed from the disastrous performance of the share price since the firm had acquired US rival Monsanto, which resulted in mounting legal problems over glyphosate, a controversial weed-killer that may be causing cancer.[84] These no-confidence votes are not legally binding and do not trigger any direct legal consequence. Still, the reputational damage for the management may be enormous: no member of the management or supervisory board can permanently afford to act against the will and without the trust of the shareholders.

9.3.2 *A Stewardship Code for Germany?*

A number of explanations may be found that can contribute to shedding light on the reluctance of German lawmakers to adopt a stewardship code. I will explore this question from a range of different perspectives. Most prominently, some academic commentators put forward a range of doctrinal objections to the project, arguing that a stewardship code would sit at odds with some key principles of German corporate law. One may, however, also understand the German position in more functional terms: since ownership here is more concentrated than elsewhere, stewardship is not needed. A third account would rely on the presence of lobbying and interest group theory to explain objections against a stewardship code. Finally, and maybe most convincingly, there is a political dimension to the story. We shall explore these different explanations in turn.

9.3.2.1 Legal Objections

Academic commentators worldwide have long been critical towards the stewardship movement, citing many legal and doctrinal reasons why such a concept would be alien to the German system of corporate law.

For example, many commentators in German academia respond to the very idea of stronger shareholder engagement and stewardship with outright hostility.[85] They argue that increased shareholder engagement may interfere with the well-balanced system of checks and balances in German corporate governance.[86] For example, a perceived 'micro-management' of entrepreneurial decisions by investors would not be consistent with the management autonomy of the

---

[82] Berger (n 80) 86.
[83] For example, the voting behaviour of Allianz Global Investors in Germany – which is available on the website – over the twelve-month period from October 2017 to September 2018 shows that the highest rejection rate (out of a total of 50%) can be found in the agenda for executive board compensation.
[84] Chazan (n 81).
[85] See, in particular, Peter Hommelhoff, 'Aktuelle Impulse aus dem europäischen Unternehmensrecht: Eine Herausforderung für Deutschland [Current Impulses from European Corporate Law: A Challenge for Germany]' (2015) 18 *Neue Zeitschrift für Gesellschaftsrecht* 1329, 1332, 1335.
[86] Holger Fleischer and Christian Strothotte, 'Ein Stewardship Code für institutionelle Investoren: Wohlverhaltensregeln und Offenlegung der Abstimmungspolitik als Vorbild für Deutschland und Europa? [A Stewardship Code for Institutional Investors: Rules of Conduct and Disclosure of Voting Policy as a Model for Germany and Europe?]' (2011) 56 *Die Aktiengesellschaft* 221, 227.

management board.[87] In addition, they fear conflicts with the supervisory board's supervisory responsibility as it is the supervisory board's exclusive role to monitor management.[88] In consequence, monitoring by institutional investors must under no circumstances lead to the establishment of a de facto 'shadow supervisory board'.[89] Further, an increased engagement of institutional investors may undermine the concept of shareholder equality, which is held dear in German doctrine.[90] This principle demands equal treatment of shareholders with equal characteristics.[91] It is argued that the risk is that enhanced engagement leads to differentiated treatment of shareholders, for example by encouraging management to pass on confidential information only to certain (active) shareholders.[92] However, if it can be shown that (some) institutional investors have specific characteristics that legitimize their differentiated treatment in comparison with other shareholders, the principle of equivalent treatment may not be violated.

In a similar vein, some commentators argue that the stewardship movement may grant institutional investors certain idiosyncratic 'private benefits' at the detriment of other shareholders.[93] This may run against the well-established doctrine of fiduciary duties that shareholders are subject to, and may also be in conflict with German principles concerning corporate groups (the so-called *Konzernrecht*).[94]

Finally, a number of critics maintain that there is no good normative reason why passive investment strategies, owing to the 'comply or explain' mechanism, should bear the stigma of needing justification.[95] Aktiengesetz § 54(1) – the 'Magna Carta' of the shareholder – requires investors to pay only their financial contribution, and does not entail any other obligation; this is seen as significantly furthering the attractiveness of this form of investment.[96] This principle is associated with the classical perception of shareholders as capital providers who do not bear any duties towards other shareholders, stakeholders or the company per se.[97] In the extreme, the share is seen as a piece of property that may be handled by its owner as they may please.[98] This

---

[87] Aktiengesetz [German Stock Corporation Act], s 76(1)
[88] Aktiengesetz [German Stock Corporation Act], s 111(1). See Patrick Hell, 'Institutionelle Investoren, Stewardship und ESG [Institutional Investors, Stewardship and ESG]' (2019) 22 *Neue Zeitschrift für Gesellschaftsrecht* 338, 342.
[89] Holger Fleischer, 'Zukunftsfragen der Corporate Governance in Deutschland und Europa: Aufsichtsräte, institutionelle Investoren, Proxy Advisors und Whistleblowers [Future Issues of Corporate Governance in Germany and Europe: Supervisory Boards, Institutional Investors, Proxy Advisors and Whistleblowers]' (2011) 40 *Zeitschrift für Unternehmens-und Gesellschaftsrecht* 155, 166.
[90] Aktiengesetz [German Stock Corporation Act], s 53a.
[91] Fleischer and Strothotte (n 86) 228.
[92] ibid fn 69; see also Holger Fleischer, 'Investor Relations und informationelle Gleichbehandlung im Aktien-, Konzern- und Kapitalmarktrecht [Investor Relations and Informational Equal Treatment in the Law of Stock Corporations, Groups and Capital Markets]' (2009) 38 *Zeitschrift für Unternehmens- und Gesellschaftsrecht* 505, 524.
[93] Peter Forstmoser, 'Exit oder Voice? Das Dilemma institutioneller Investoren [Exit or Voice? The Dilemma of Institutional Investors]' in Eugen Bucher, Claus-Wilhelm Canaris, Heinrich Honsell and Thomas Koller (eds), *Norm und Wirkung. Festschrift für Wolfgang Wiegand zum 65. Geburtstag* (Stämpfli/Beck 2005) 785, 803.
[94] Fleischer and Strothotte (n 86) 227.
[95] Fleischer, 'Zukunftsfragen der Corporate Governance in Deutschland und Europa' (n 89) 167.
[96] Marcus Lutter, '§ 54' in Wolfgang Zöllner (ed), *Kölner Kommentar zum Aktiengesetz [Cologne Commentary on the Stock Corporation Act]* (2nd edn, Heymann 1988) § 54 para 2.
[97] Fleischer, 'Zukunftsfragen der Corporate Governance in Deutschland und Europa' (n 89) 167.
[98] This view has a rich tradition, interestingly, in UK company law. See from the seminal case law *Pender v Lushington* (1877) 6 ChD 70, 75; *North-West Transportation Co Ltd v Beatty* [1887] UKPC 39, (1887) 12 AppCas 589; *Burland v Earle* [1902] AC 83 (PC); *Carruth v Imperial Chemical Industries Ltd* [1937] AC 707 (HL); *Peter's American Delicacy Co Ltd Heath* [1939] HCA 2, (1939) 61 CLR 457, 504; *Northern Counties Securities Ltd v Jackson & Steeple Ltd* [1974] 1 WLR 1133, 1144. See in more detail Wolf-Georg Ringe, 'Das Beschlussmängelrecht in Großbritannien [Contesting Shareholder Resolutions under English Law]' (2017) 81 *Rabel Journal of Comparative and International Private Law (RabelsZ)* 249, 265–67.

view would be difficult to reconcile with the sudden imposition of shareholders' stewardship obligations. Still, it is widely accepted that the 'no obligations' rule in a pure form does not reflect reality. For example, it has been relaxed in favour of minority protection and market integrity.

More recently, in the context of the stewardship debate, the focus of attention has shifted to one particular aspect: the legal limits on a potential dialogue between institutional investors and the supervisory board.[99] Scholars have pointed out barriers to such dialogue that may result from both corporate law and capital markets law. Corporate law barriers root once more in the perception of the supervisory board as an internal organ of the corporation with no or very limited external authority, and the division of authority between the management board and the supervisory board. Capital markets law barriers may arise from the insider trading prohibition and the limitations on 'acting in concert'.[100] This controversial issue was partly addressed in a 2017 reform of the German Corporate Governance Code (GCGC), which now states in section 5.2 that the chairman of the supervisory board 'should be available – within reasonable limits – to discuss Supervisory Board-related issues with investors'.[101] This change goes back to proposals made by a working group composed of representatives of institutional investors, firms and academics, resulting in the adoption of guidelines for the dialogue between an investor and the supervisory board.[102]

9.3.2.2 Functional Story

In contrast to the doctrinal explanations sketched in Section 9.3.2.1, a better story for stewardship sceptics to tell might be that greater stewardship by institutional shareholders is not equally *necessary* in the German context, since the frequent presence of controlling shareholders (unlike in the UK) ensures that management is adequately monitored. This would be a *functional* argument: essentially, one could argue that the objective of the UK Code – to encourage greater investor engagement in the long term – is not anything that needs to (or even should) be

---

[99] See e.g. Hans-Christoph Hirt, Klaus J Hopt and Daniela Mattheus, 'Dialog zwischen dem Aufsichtsrat und Investoren: Rechtsvergleichende und rechtsdogmatische Überlegungen zur Investorenkommunikation in Deutschland [Dialogue between Supervisory Board and Investors: Comparative and Doctrinal Considerations on Investor Communication in Germany]' (2016) 61 *Die Aktiengesellschaft* 725; Eberhard Vetter, 'Shareholders' Communication – Wer spricht mit den institutionellen Investoren? [Shareholder Communication – Who Is Talking to the Institutional Investors?]' (2016) 61 *Die Aktiengesellschaft* 873; Gregor Bachmann, 'Dialog zwischen Investor und Aufsichtsrat [Dialogue between Investor and Supervisory Board]' in Gesellschaftsrechtliche Vereinigung (ed), *Gesellschaftsrecht in der Diskussion 2016 – Jahrestagung der gesellschaftsrechtlichen Vereinigung (VGR) [Corporate Law in Discussion 2016 – Annual Conference of the Association of Corporate Law (VGR)]* (Verlag Dr. Otto Schmidt 2017) 136; Klaus J Hopt, 'The Dialogue between the Chairman of the Board and Investors: The Practice in the UK, the Netherlands and Germany and the Future of the German Corporate Governance Code under the New Chairman' (2017) 9 *Revue Trimestrielle de Droit Financier* 97; Hauke Hein, *Die Stewardship-Verantwortung institutioneller Investoren: Plädoyer für einen aktienrechtkonformen Deutschen Stewardship Kodex [The Stewardship Responsibility of Institutional Investors: Plea for a German Stewardship Code That Complies with Corporate Law]* (Tectum Verlag 2018) 239–90.

[100] Uwe H Schneider, 'Abgestimmtes Verhalten durch institutionelle Anleger: Gute Corporate Governance oder rechtspolitische Herausforderung? [Co-ordinated Behavior between Institutional Investors: Good Corporate Governance or Legal Policy Challenge?]' (2012) 41 *Zeitschrift für Unternehmens- und Gesellschaftsrecht* 518, 530–31.

[101] Regierungskommission Deutscher Corporate Governance Kodex, *German Corporate Governance Code* (7 February 2017) <www.dcgk.de//files/dcgk/usercontent/en/download/code/170214_Code.pdf> accessed 6 January 2020 [hereinafter GCGC 2017].

[102] Alexander Bassen and others, *Leitsätze für den Dialog zwischen Investor und Aufsichtsrat [Guidelines for the Dialogue between Investor and Supervisory Board]* (July 2016) <www.bvi.de/fileadmin/user_upload/Regulierung/Branchenstandards/Dialog_zwischen_Investor_und_Aufsichtsrat/2016_07_11_Leits%C3%A4tze__f%C3%BCr_den_Dialog_zwischen_Investor_und_Aufsichtsrat.pdf> accessed 6 January 2020.

addressed in the German arena, given that the domestic nature of ownership concentration renders this objective superfluous.

This argument is, however, flawed on two grounds. First, the theoretical argument that a controlling shareholder may exercise close monitoring over corporate management has great appeal. After all, it has been argued that a controlling shareholder may police the management of public corporations effectively: because they hold a large equity stake, the argument runs, a controlling shareholder would be likely to have proper incentives either to monitor managers effectively or to manage the company itself and, because of proximity and lower information costs,[103] may be able to detect any problems earlier.[104] However, in reality, it has long been recognized that controlling shareholders bring their own problems with them. Controlling shareholders will frequently extract private benefits of control from the company, for example through a technique referred to as 'tunnelling', that is, through contractual dealings with the company, like transfer pricing, that favour the controlling shareholder.[105] This (and many other techniques) is said to raise intra-shareholder agency costs where controlling shareholders may exercise power to the detriment of any minority investors. It is therefore an illusion to believe that stewardship in the German context may not be necessary just because the monitoring of corporate management would be carried out by any controlling shareholders.

Second, even when assuming for a moment that the first argument was correct, it has been demonstrated that the presence of controlling shareholders in German firms is shrinking. Since the turn of the century, triggered not only by globalization forces but also by an idiosyncratic taxation reform in Germany, formerly large investors have started to divest of their equity holdings in domestic firms.[106] This has triggered a fundamental rethink of the role of corporate law and corporate governance in Germany where the recognition is growing that the legal system must partly be reconfigured to cater for firms in dispersed ownership rather than being controlled.[107]

In light of these two considerations, it becomes evident that we cannot reasonably rely on controlling shareholders to exercise the role of a serious policeman in the German corporate landscape.

9.3.2.3 Economic Rationale

It is of course possible that lawmakers in Germany are simply not convinced that a stewardship code would have a meaningful impact. After all, the effectiveness of such a code is very difficult to measure, and a number of commentators have argued that there is no tangible benefit.

For example, the UK, as the frontrunner in terms of stewardship, has long seen sceptical comments on the stewardship concept.[108] Many market participants are unconvinced that the British advance has actually resulted in increased shareholder engagement.[109] However, most

---

[103] Ruth V Aguilera and Rafel Crespi-Cladera, 'Global Corporate Governance: On the Relevance of Firms' Ownership Structure' (2016) 51 *Journal of World Business* 50.
[104] Ronald Gilson, 'Controlling Shareholders and Corporate Governance: Complicating the Comparative Taxonomy' (2006) 119 *Harvard Law Review* 1641, 1651.
[105] See e.g. Simon Johnson, Rafael La Porta, Florencio Lopez-de-Silanes and Andrei Shleifer, 'Tunneling' (May 2000) 90 *American Economic Review* 22.
[106] See Ringe, 'Changing Law and Ownership Patterns in Germany' (n 67).
[107] ibid 526ff.
[108] See e.g. Chiu, 'Turning Institutional Investors into "Stewards"' (n 1); Iris H-Y Chiu, 'Reviving Shareholder Stewardship: Critically Examining the Impact of Corporate Transparency Reforms in the UK' (2014) 38 *Delaware Journal of Corporate Law* 983; Hannigan (n 30).
[109] Pauline Skypala, 'Fund Managers Cannot Be Stewards' Financial Times (FTfm, London, 19 March 2012) <www.ft.com/content/9ec5594c-6f8f-11e1-b368-00144feab49a> accessed 18 August 2020.

critical commentators fall short of providing reliable evidence for their claims. The 2018 *Kingman Review* into the operation of the FRC voiced some serious criticisms of the UK Stewardship Code.[110] The Review recommended that a fundamental shift in approach would be needed to ensure that the Code more clearly differentiates excellence in stewardship. According to Kingman, the Code should focus on the 'outcomes and effectiveness' of the stewardship process, and not on the formal policy statements.[111]

Edward Rock, in a recent article, put forward a rather disillusionist experience report from a 2003 'mutual fund experiment' in the US.[112] A Securities and Exchange Commission (SEC) release from 2003 mandated US mutual funds to disclose proxy voting policies and proxy votes, and described 'best practices' for proxy voting guidelines. Rock describes that the industry responded by turning the requested activities into 'compliance function', a rather schematic box-ticking exercise, and that investors apparently do not care about the disclosures.[113]

It is, however, unlikely that lawmakers would be unaware of more positive findings in the academic literature. For example, a study by Hoepner, Oikonomou, Sautner, Starks and Zhou has revealed that stewardship and promoting of ESG issues can have a positive impact on firm value and may also create value for other stakeholders.[114] The authors conclude that companies with a completed ESG campaign have, on average, a significantly lower risk profile. Further, the authors were also able to show causation in a sense that the lower risk profiles result from successful stewardship activities, where a change was made to the respective company with regard to its ESG strategy. Another paper comes to a similar conclusion, showing that firms with a successful ESG engagement are followed by positive abnormal returns.[115]

Consistent with this perspective, other research has found that where institutional investors engage more deeply with their portfolio companies, these firms are more likely to pursue innovative strategies.[116] Similarly, a 2017 study concluded that without the discipline of active engagement by investors, a company's management is more likely to become entrenched and to engage in value-destroying mergers and acquisitions (M&A) activity.[117]

Finally, and more generally, a recent article finds that the overall quality of the capital market has a strong impact on economic performance, supporting long-term sustainable economic growth and reducing the risk of financial crises. In the authors' view, market quality may be improved by greater transparency requirements and by promoting more active investor engagement.[118]

---

[110] John Kingman, 'Independent Review of the Financial Reporting Council' (Department for Business, Energy and Industrial Strategy, December 2018) <https://assets.publishing.service.gov.uk/government/uploads/system/uploads/attachment_data/file/767387/frc-independent-review-final-report.pdf> accessed 6 January 2020.
[111] ibid 46 (recommendation 42).
[112] Edward Rock, 'Institutional Investors in Corporate Governance' in Jeffrey Gordon and Wolf-Georg Ringe (eds), *The Oxford Handbook of Corporate Law and Governance* (OUP 2018) 363, 375ff.
[113] ibid 379.
[114] Andreas Hoepner and others, 'ESG Shareholder Engagement and Downside Risk' ECGI Finance Working Paper No 671/2020 (April 2020), https://ecgi.global/sites/default/files/working_papers/documents/hoepneroikonomousautnerstarkszhoufinal.pdf accessed 18 December 2021.
[115] Elroy Dimson, Oğuzhan Karakaş and Xi Li, 'Active Ownership' (2015) 28 *Review of Financial Studies* 3225. See also Tamas Barko, Martijn Cremers and Luc Renneboog, 'Shareholder Engagement on Environmental, Social, and Governance Performance' Journal of Business Ethics (2021), <https://doi.org/10.1007/s10551-021-04850-z>.
[116] Philippe Aghion, John Van Reenen and Luigi Zingales, 'Innovation and Institutional Ownership' (2013) 103 *American Economic Review* 277.
[117] Cornelius Schmidt and Rüdiger Fahlenbrach, 'Do Exogenous Changes in Passive Institutional Ownership Affect Corporate Governance and Firm Value?' (2017) 124 *Journal of Financial Economics* 285.
[118] Kevin R James, Akshay Kotak and Dimitrios Tsomocos, 'Market Quality, Financial Crises, and TFP Growth in the US: 1840–2014' (Working Paper 2018).

Where does this leave us? To be sure, scepticism is widespread, but it may not always be founded on concrete evidence. There is, by contrast, growing academic literature that acknowledges and demonstrates the economic case for stewardship and shareholder engagement, especially with a focus on ESG policy. The argument that lawmakers ought to reject further stewardship initiatives with reference to their uncertain effects thus remains a hypothesis at best.

9.3.2.4 Political Perspective

Instead, probably the most convincing explanation for German lawmakers' reluctance to subscribe to the stewardship idea seems to be rooted in politics. At its core, the reason is simple: as the market share of Germany-based institutional investors is small in comparison to other jurisdictions, it would not be an optimal allocation of public resources to devote legislative energy to a project that would not improve shareholder engagement in any meaningful way.

A few figures may illustrate the point (see Figure 9.1). Germany is the third largest European asset management market measured by assets under management (AuM) (at EUR 2.161 bn). Nonetheless, its market share of 9.1% of the European market is far less than its economic power and its population size; in fact, it is comparatively significantly smaller than the respective market share of the two largest asset management markets, the UK (36.5% with EUR 8.670 bn AuM) and France (17.4% with EUR 4.142 bn AuM). Furthermore, assets under management in Germany constitute 66% of German gross domestic product (GDP), a ratio well below the UK (371%), French (181%) and European (140%) AuM/GDP ratios. One reason advanced is that

Country	AuM	Δ in 2017 [1]	Market Share	AuM / GDP
UK	8,670	7%	36.5%	371%
France	4,142	4%	17.4%	181%
Germany	2,161	3%	9.1%	66%
Switzerland	1,887	4%	7.9%	314%
Italy	1,294	5%	5.4%	75%
Netherlands	844	n.a.	3.6%	114%
Denmark	425	10%	1.8%	145%
Spain [3]	409	30%	1.7%	35%
Belgium	332	10%	1.4%	76%
Finland	223	n.a.	0.9%	100%
Austria [4]	141	7%	0.6%	38%
Portugal	82	11%	0.3%	42%
Hungary	30	8%	0.1%	24%
Turkey	26	29%	0.1%	3%
Greece	10	7%	<0.1%	6%
Romania	9	6%	<0.1%	5%
Croatia	4	n.a.	<0.1%	7%
Slovenia	3	9%	<0.1%	6%
Bulgaria	1	36%	<0.1%	1%
Other	3,058	n.a.	12.9%	n.a.
Europe	23,750	4%	100%	140%

FIGURE 9.1 European AuM by geographical breakdown at end 2017 (in EUR billion and %)
Source: efama, *Asset Management in Europe* (11th edition 2019) 11.

there are no tax benefits for long-term savings with mutual funds in Germany.[119] This argument is supported by literature that correlates the adoption of responsible investment with the size of the fund management industry.[120]

Given the ownership structure of the largest German companies, the following question arises: Is it feasible to introduce a German Stewardship Code in order to promote institutional investors' engagement with the governance of German investee companies? The answer to this question depends on the domicile of the institutional investors. That can set limits to the geographical scope of a German stewardship Code. Put differently, since many German firms are owned by institutional investors that are predominantly based abroad, any official German stewardship initiative would not have a significant effect on domestic shareholder engagement.

Recent figures show that institutional investors investing in German companies are by far mostly resident *outside* of Germany. Table 9.1 and Figure 9.2 show the top fifteen DAX investors and the twenty-five largest investment funds that have invested in German DAX companies. According to Table 9.1, only 10.8% out of the top 34% DAX share can be attributed to Germany-based institutional investors / asset managers. The same picture is illustrated in Figure 9.2; only two out of the top twenty-five funds are based in Germany, and they account for just 16.28% of the investment volume in year 2018. The German asset managers with the largest investment

TABLE 9.1 *Top fifteen investors in DAX firms (2018)*

Rank firm name	DAX value in $m Dec-18	% share DAX inst.	City
1 The Vanguard Group, Inc.	32,377.9	4.6%	USA – Malvern, PA
2 BlackRock Fund Advisors	28,026.8	4.0%	USA – San Francisco CA
3 Norges Bank Investment Management (Norway)	27,638.6	3.9%	NOR – Oslo
4 DWS Investment GmbH	24,104.8	3.4%	DEU – Frankfurt
5 Amundi Asset Management S.A.	18,524.6	2.6%	FRA – Paris
6 BlackRock Asset Management (Deutschland) AG	15,103.6	2.2%	DEU – Munich
7 Deka Investment GmbH	13,745.8	2.0%	DEU-Frankfurt
8 Allianz Global Investors GmbH	11,914.5	1.7%	DEU – Frankfurt
9 Harris Associates, L.P.	11,522.3	1.6%	USA – Chicago, IL
10 BlackRock Advisors (U.K.), LTD	11,147.8	1.6%	GBR – London
11 Union Investment Privatfonds GmbH	10,700.1	1.5%	DEU – Frankfurt
12 Fidelity Management & Research Company	10,527.2	1.5%	USA – Boston, MA
13 State Street Global Advisors, LTD	9,456.5	1.3%	GBR – London
14 Lyxor Asset Management SAS	8,806.1	1.3%	FRA – Paris
15 BNP Paribas Asset Management France	8,038.0	1.1%	FRA – Paris
Total	241,634.7	34.4%	

Source: adapted from IHS Markit and Deutscher Investor Relations Verband (DIRK), *Who Owns the German DAX?* (6th edn 2019) 11

[119] OECD, 'The Role of Institutional Investors in Promoting Good Corporate Governance' (OECD Peer Review April 2011) 106 <www.oecd.org/officialdocuments/publicdisplaydocumentpdf/?cote=DAF/CA/CG(2011)2/FINAL&docLanguage=En> accessed 6 January 2020.

[120] Bert Scholtens and Riika Sievänen, 'Drivers of Socially Responsible Investing: A Case Study of Four Nordic Countries' (2013) 115 *Journal of Business Ethics* 605.

Größte im DAX investierte Investmentfonds im Jahr 2018 (in Millionen US-Dollar)

Größte Investmentfonds im DAX nach investiertem Kapital 2018

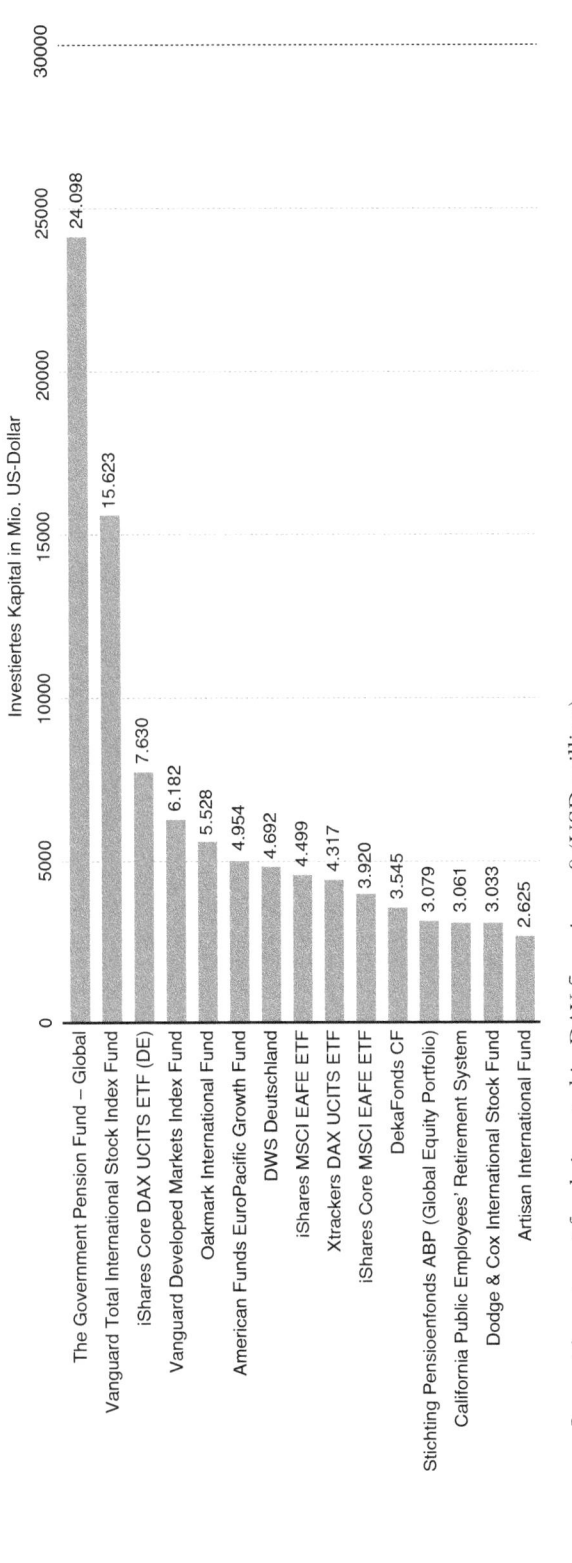

Fund	Investiertes Kapital in Mio. US-Dollar
The Government Pension Fund – Global	24.098
Vanguard Total International Stock Index Fund	15.623
iShares Core DAX UCITS ETF (DE)	7.630
Vanguard Developed Markets Index Fund	6.182
Oakmark International Fund	5.528
American Funds EuroPacific Growth Fund	4.954
DWS Deutschland	4.692
iShares MSCI EAFE ETF	4.499
Xtrackers DAX UCITS ETF	4.317
iShares Core MSCI EAFE ETF	3.920
DekaFonds CF	3.545
Stichting Pensioenfonds ABP (Global Equity Portfolio)	3.079
California Public Employees' Retirement System	3.061
Dodge & Cox International Stock Fund	3.033
Artisan International Fund	2.625

FIGURE 9.2 Largest investment funds invested in DAX firms in 2018 (USD million)
Source: Statista, *Investmentfonds im Überblick* (2019)

positions in German companies are DWS Investment GmbH, Deka Investment GmbH and Allianz Global Investors GmbH.[121] DWS is the asset management arm of Deutsche Bank;[122] DekaBank[123] is the investment fund manager for the German *Sparkassen* (savings banks), and Allianz Global Investors[124] is the asset management arm of Allianz SE. The other fund managers are based either in European countries, such as the Government Pension Fund of Norway, the French Amundi Asset Management SA and the Dutch National Civil Pension Fund, or in the US (Vanguard, Blackrock, Capital One, etc.).

Based on these figures, it becomes clear that any prospect of effectively regulating the activities of investment fund managers by defining a set of stewardship principles seems to be a challenging task for German policymakers since the overwhelming majority of the investment decisions in German firms *are made by foreign-based vehicles*. Certainly, Germany might adopt a voluntary code or a set of guiding principles, but the legislative underpinning of a 'comply or explain' rule would not be able to catch any foreign-based institutions. This argument is supported by the geographical scope of application of the existing stewardship codes.[125]

Consider the UK Code as the paradigm example. At the outset, the UK Code is addressed to 'institutional investors, by which is meant asset owners and asset managers with equity holdings in UK listed companies'.[126] That seems to include foreign institutions. It is, however, important to understand that the application of the UK Code to foreign investors is entirely voluntary. In contrast, the more constraining element of the UK stewardship regime, the 'comply or explain' rule,[127] applies only to domestic UK funds.[128] This is because the jurisdictional reach of the Financial Conduct Authority (FCA) does not extend to fund managers based outside the UK, who merely invest in shares of companies quoted on the London Stock Exchange, as this will not amount to the carrying out of a 'regulated activity' in the UK.[129] Correspondingly, the 'comply or explain' regime has a purely UK focus and cannot apply to foreign investors.[130] Therefore, the primary focus of the UK Code is on domestically based institutional investors.

The same would be true in Germany if German regulators chose to adopt a stewardship code. The regulatory authority of BaFin[131] as the main market watchdog applies to institutional

---

[121] One additional factor distinguishing the German asset management market from the UK one is the fact that almost half of the German asset managers are part of the banking groups, while 80% of the UK asset managers operate as stand-alone companies. See EFAMA, 'Asset Management in Europe' (11th edn, September 2019) 9 <www.efama.org/sites/default/files/publications/Asset%20Management%20Report%202019.pdf> accessed 11 February 2022.

[122] DWS is a signatory party to the UK Code and is categorized in Tier 1 of asset managers. It is also a signatory party to the UNPRI since 2008. DWS has published two Responsible Investment Statements (January 2017 and July 2018). In these statements DWS refers explicitly to stewardship as part of its 'active ownership' philosophy and expresses its 'aim to comply with and to assist (its) clients in complying with local stewardship codes given the increasing pace and scope of regulation'. See DWS, 'Responsible Investment Statement' (July 2018) paras 2, 4 <www.dws.com/contentassets/273435074d9d40208172096ba524b149/responsible-investment-statement.pdf> accessed 18 August 2020.

[123] Deka Investment GmbH is not a signatory party to the UK Code but it has adhered to the UNPRI since 2010.

[124] Allianz GI is a signatory party to both the UK Stewardship Code as a Tier 1 asset manager and the UNPRI since 2007. It has participated repeatedly in the FRC public consultation related to amendments of the UK Stewardship Code.

[125] Walker Review (n 5) para 6.4; Cheffins (n 4) 1004ff; Arsalidou (n 50) 355ff; Reisberg (n 4) 236–38.

[126] UK Code 2012 (n 13) 2.

[127] COBS 2.2.3R.

[128] See Financial Services and Markets Act 2000, s 418; PERG 2.4.5 (01/07/2005).

[129] Paul Davies, 'Shareholders in the United Kingdom' in Jennifer G Hill and Randall S Thomas (eds), *Research Handbook on Shareholder Power* (Edward Elgar Publishing 2015) 355, 376. See also Cheffins (n 4) 1015.

[130] Initially, the UK Code was introduced without a corresponding 'comply or explain' requirement. Instead, the FRC simply encouraged 'all institutional investors to report if and how they applied the Code' (FRC, 'Implementation of the UK Stewardship Code' (n 12) para 21). At the same time, however, the FRC stated that it 'hope(s) that investors outside the UK will commit to the Code' but recognizes 'that, in practice, local institutions usually take the lead in engagement' ((n 12) para 25).

[131] Bundesanstalt für Finanzdienstleistungsaufsicht [Federal Financial Supervisory Authority].

investors domiciled in Germany, and the acquisition of shares in German companies through a foreign investment vehicle does not trigger the application of the relevant investment legislation.[132] Any German 'comply or explain' mechanism that would require institutional investors to respond to stewardship principles could therefore apply only to Germany-based funds or fund managers. This is how the new provisions after the implementation of SRD II apply only to institutional investors and asset managers located in Germany.[133] The same is true, by the way, for the GCGC, where the 'comply or explain' principle is enshrined in Aktiengesetz § 161, and applies exclusively to companies incorporated under German law.

9.3.2.5 Conclusion

What might be the better alternative to promote the interests of investee companies, from the perspective of the German government? The obvious answer is to focus any regulatory effort on domestic (target) firms, and to seek improvements here in the form of traditional corporate governance. In other words, since the jurisdictional reach of government regulation over German firms is not a problem, it appears more effective to bundle any regulatory efforts on those. Improving the corporate governance of domestic firms is therefore the politically easier and more effective way of improving engagement, as seen from the perspective of German policymakers. It is in this spirit that the German Corporate Governance Commission has repeatedly revised and updated the GCGC over the past several years, the latest revision of which is from 2019.[134] It is noteworthy that its latest version, which came into force in 2020, focuses almost exclusively on the operation of both the management board and the supervisory board. Shareholders do not play an important role in corporate governance, German-style.

It is only in the preamble that the GCGC states that '[i]nstitutional investors are of particular importance to companies. They are expected to exercise their ownership rights actively and responsibly, in accordance with transparent principles that also respect the concept of sustainability.'[135] This statement was introduced in 2017 and clearly mirrors the stewardship idea, albeit in the context of a corporate governance code. In a similar vein, the explanatory notes to the 2019 GCGC version state:[136]

> Institutional investors – whether passively managed index funds, active investors or so-called activist investors – are showing increasing interest in corporate governance specifically implemented in the enterprises. Such investors recognise the benefit of standards for good and responsible corporate governance for the performance of their investments; they establish dedicated own ideas regarding corporate governance, and use these as the basis for their voting behaviour in the General Meeting.

---

[132] Most notably, the Kapitalanlagegesetzbuch (KAGB) [German Capital Investment Act].
[133] For a critical perspective, see Theodor Baums, 'Editorial' (2019) 183 *Zeitschrift für das gesamte Handelsrecht und Wirtschaftsrecht (ZHR)* 605, 608. See also Jens Koch, 'Der Kapitalanleger als Corporate Governance-Akteur im Rahmen der neuen §§ 134 a ff. AktG [The Investor as a Corporate Governance Actor within the Framework of the New §§ 134 a ff. AktG]' (2020) 20 *Zeitschrift für Bank- und Kapitalmarktrecht* 1, 3.
[134] The GCGC 2017 (n 101) is the version in force. The 2019 revision (Regierungskommission Deutscher Corporate Governance Kodex, 'German Corporate Governance Code 2019' (9 May 2019) <www.dcgk.de/en/code/code-2019.html> accessed 6 January 2020) will only come into force when the Act for Implementing the Second EU Shareholder Rights Directive has been adopted.
[135] GCGC 2017 (n 101) Foreword para 3.
[136] Regierungskommission Deutscher Corporate Governance Kodex, 'German Corporate Governance Code as Resolved by the Commission' (Code including rationale, 9 May 2019) <www.dcgk.de/files/dcgk/usercontent/en/Consultations/2019/Code%202019/190522%20GCGC%202019%20with%20rationale.pdf> accessed 6 January 2020.

Crucially, neither of these statements carries any serious obligation or other formal requirement; both are rather descriptive declarations that express a certain expectation. This follows the logic developed in this chapter: since Germany is virtually unable to regulate any dominant institutional investors, it is able to formulate only a number of non-binding statements for them. The substantial principles of the corporate governance code, the recommendations that are subject to the 'comply or explain' principle, in essence concern very different topics, mostly about the composition and the obligations of the supervisory board. This is consistent with the rationale developed earlier: the jurisdictional power of German policymakers fits much better to the domestic players, thus, in particular, the board members.

In summary, then, the rationale appears to be that a prudent deployment of government resources leads to public efforts focusing on domestic corporate governance instead of global stewardship.

9.4 WOULD A GERMAN CODE STILL MAKE SENSE?

The analysis so far has focused on the perspective of the government, and we have seen why policymakers have been so reluctant to adopt an official stewardship code. Still, this does not say anything about the question of whether a stewardship code in the German context would be desirable from a social welfare position.

9.4.1 *Voluntary Compliance*

At first, it is important to stress that several arguments speak against the adoption of a German code, thus supporting the German government's position. One point is that a high number of the (foreign) funds that are active in the German market already comply with a stewardship framework, mostly of foreign origin. There is empirical evidence that they adhere to (foreign) national stewardship codes as well as to international standards of best practice on a voluntary basis. For example, when looking at the top fifteen DAX investors, the vast majority of foreign investors (representing 14.1% of the DAX share) annually publish stewardship statements fulfilling their obligations as signatory parties to the UK Stewardship Code.[137] The high rate of adhering to responsible investment principles on a voluntary basis, despite the lack of a mandatory regulatory framework, has also attracted the interest of academics. Hoepner, Majoch and Zhou[138] examined the rates of adoption of the UNPRI by asset owners and managers from different jurisdictions. According to their findings, asset managers operating in jurisdictions characterized by soft law regulation[139] are more willing to (deliberately) adhere to the UNPRI than asset managers from jurisdictions with respective mandatory regulation. One factor that could justify the voluntary compliance is the perception that by signalling the ability of the financial industry to regulate itself on a voluntary basis, mandatory regulation by policymakers with their own understanding of responsibility can be avoided. In that way, code creation can be framed as 'the outcome of a tacit or implicit consensus of institutional actors involved in a self-interested behavioural process'.[140]

---

[137] A list of signatories of the UK Code is available (Financial Reporting Council, 'Tiering of 2012 Stewardship Code Signatories' <www.frc.org.uk/investors/uk-stewardship-code/uk-stewardship-code-statements> accessed 6 January 2020). See also nn 122, 123 and 124.

[138] Andreas Hoepner, Arleta Majoch and Xiao Zhou, 'Does an Asset Owner's Institutional Setting Influence Its Decision to Sign the Principles of Responsible Investment?' (2019) *Journal of Business Ethics* 1.

[139] ESG regulation has been used in their analysis as a proxy of the regulatory framework of responsible investment. Thus, the analysis has not taken into consideration any specific stewardship regulatory initiative.

[140] Ilir Haxhi, Hans van Ees and Arndt Sorge, 'A Political Perspective on Business Elites and Institutional Embeddedness in the UK Code-Issuing Process' (2013) 21 *Corporate Governance: An International Review* 535, 543.

UK regulatory authorities aim to achieve a high rate of compliance by foreign investors on a voluntary basis. That is why the 2010 and 2012 versions of the UK Code emphasized that '[o]verseas investors who follow other national or international codes that have similar objectives should not feel the application of the Code duplicates or confuses their responsibilities. Disclosures made in respect of those standards can also be used to demonstrate the extent to which they have complied with the Code.'[141] The same issue was addressed in the context of the public consultation for the 2010 Code. The FCA expects the UK Code 2020 to give foreign owners the proper incentives to sign up to the Code. However, some of the challenges that foreign investors may allegedly face are the different legal and regulatory requirements, different local market conditions, and the need to use local agents across the different jurisdictions.[142]

9.4.2 *Private Initiatives*

It is worth noting that, in the absence of any governmental scheme, there are a number of private initiatives, mostly from institutional investors, that push for the adoption of a code or even a set of industry principles.

Among them, the most noteworthy are the BVI Rules of Conduct,[143] a set of principles adopted by the German Investment Funds Association BVI.[144] BVI is the largest interest group representing the German fund industry, promoting issues of regulation of the fund business as well as business education and competition vis-à-vis policymakers and regulators. BVI's more than 100 members manage assets of some 3 trillion euros.

The BVI Rules of Conduct, first introduced in 2003, set out a range of voluntary standards and take account of the principle of trusteeship, which places particular obligations on asset managers vis-à-vis their investors.[145] The rules of conduct comprise five principles, namely that asset managers: (1) do not incur undue costs and fees, and do not undermine investor interests through unfair market practices; (2) observe clear execution principles for market-compliant settlement and fair investor treatment; (3) render information in a clear, comprehensive and understandable manner; (4) work towards good corporate governance within the asset management company; and (5) take on social responsibility in ESG.

These principles are subject to a self-defined 'comply or explain' rule: that is, the fund companies inform their investors whether, and to what extent, they comply with the rules of conduct. They may deviate from the principles, but they then have to disclose this annually and justify any deviations.[146] The adherence to the BVI's Rules of Conduct by German asset managers may be unsatisfactory because: (1) there is no legal obligation to disclose compliance or non-compliance with the Rules in contrast to UK asset managers' obligation to disclose commitment to FRC's Stewardship Code;[147] and (2) there is no monitoring mechanism, such as FRC's tiering system.

---

[141] UK Code 2012 (n 13) 3.
[142] Financial Conduct Authority, 'Building a Regulatory Framework for Effective Stewardship, Feedback to DP 19/1' (Feedback Statement, October 2019) para 3.32 <www.fca.org.uk/publication/feedback/fs19-7.pdf> accessed 6 January 2020.
[143] BVI, 'Wohlverhaltensregeln des BVI [BVI Rules of Conduct]' (English Version, 2019) <www.bvi.de/fileadmin/user_upload/Regulierung/2019_07_BVI_Rules_of_conduct.pdf> accessed 6 January 2020.
[144] Bundesverband Investment und Asset Management e.V. (BVI).
[145] The current version of the BVI Rules of Conduct has been in force since 1 July 2019.
[146] However, BVI states that 'to the extent that individual rules are not applicable in view of the respective investment strategy (such as benchmark-oriented investing or property investments), business activity or organisational structure, deviations do not need to be explained separately' (BVI (n 143) 2).
[147] COBS 2.2.3.

BVI was also among the German stakeholders that responded to the public consultation on the EU corporate governance framework. Based on this consultation, the Commission submitted the proposal for the amendment of the Directive 2007/36, which led to the adoption of SRD II. Even though BVI advocated for measures promoting long-termism, shareholders' communication, and proxy advisers' transparency, it had a negative position with regard to the regulation of the relationship between asset owners and asset managers. The main argument was the constraints imposed on the contractual freedom of the parties. According to BVI, institutional investors should have the freedom to choose their asset managers and agree with them on the contractual conditions. There is no need to take additional measures because institutional investors are already obliged to protect their clients' interests (then AIFM and MiFID I, now UCITS and MiFID II requirements respectively), and they have the means to supervise the affiliated asset managers.

In its comments on the draft ARUG II law[148] (which implemented the SRD II into German law), BVI welcomed the adoption of transparency requirements for asset managers, but drew attention to their scope of application. More specifically, it was opposed to the application of the ARUG II to Germany-based asset managers in case they undertake the management of assets issued abroad.[149]

The second important instrument to consider is the Code by the German Association of Investment Professionals (DVFA).[150] DVFA represents more than 1,400 financial analysts and asset managers in German financial and capital markets. DVFA supports the professionalization of the investment industry, develops a range of policy standards, and promotes young professionals in the sector. DVFA has recently published its new Stewardship Guidelines, setting out a similar set of issues as the BVI Code.[151]

What to make of such codes? Are they obviating the need for an official instrument? A careful analysis reveals that a fully-fledged and government-sponsored code such as the UK Stewardship Code is typically much more ambitious than industry self-regulation. That is not very surprising and emerges from several considerations. For example, some observers opine that industry codes are primarily designed to pre-empt any regulation. In other words, they are half-hearted attempts suggesting that self-regulation is in control but in reality (of course) omitting any requirements that bite.[152] Another, more charitable interpretation points to the genesis of such industry-sponsored codes. Industry-made codes often bear the handwriting of consensus: they are typically adopted by a trade association that needs to moderate frequently controversial

---

[148] Gesetz zur Umsetzung der zweiten Aktionärsrechterichtlinie (ARUG II) of 12 December 2019, Bundesgesetzblatt [Federal Gazette] 2019 I, 2637.

[149] BVI e.V., Stellungnahme zum Referentenentwurf eines Gesetzes zur Umsetzung der zweiten Aktionärsrichtlinie (ARUG II):

> Wir begrüßen, dass die Regelung als Anknüpfungspunkt für die Pflichten von Vermögensverwaltern deren Zulassung im Inland vorsieht (s.u. zu § 134c Abs. 4 AktG-E). Wir teilen jedoch nicht die Auffassung, dass die Pflichten auch Anwendung finden, soweit es sich um Aktien handelt, die im außereuropäischen Ausland notiert sind [We welcome the fact that the regulation provides for approval in Germany for the duties of asset managers to apply (see also section 134c(4) AktG-E). However, we do not share the view that the obligations also apply to shares that are listed outside of Europe].

See BVI, 'Stellungnahme des BVI zum Entwurf eines Gesetzes zur Umsetzung der zweiten Aktionärsrechterichtlinie (ARUG II)' (26 November 2018).

[150] Deutsche Vereinigung für Finanzanalyse und Asset Management e.V. (DVFA).

[151] DVFA, 'DVFA Stewardship Guidelines' (March 2020) <www.dvfa.de/fileadmin/downloads/Verband/Kommissionen/Governance_Stewardship/DVFA_Stewardship_Guidelines.pdf> accessed 20 August 2020.

[152] Haxhi, van Ees and Sorge (n 140). See also Puchniak and Tang, Singapore's Embrace of Shareholder Stewardship, Chapter 14, in which the authors coin the term 'pre-emptive corporate governance' for this.

discussion and thereby needs to take into account many different views and arguments. The result is typically a regulatory standard that is not too restrictive.

In that context, we may wonder why the fund industry is at all concerned with developing de facto regulatory standards, which, in the case of stewardship, are concerned with creating new *obligations* for (institutional) shareholders rather than defining shareholder entitlements or rights. The seemingly absurd and counterintuitive result is that institutional owners promote their own standards that prescribe costly stewardship activities, thus adding to their own regulatory burden. Apart from the political argument, according to which the industry seeks to fend off a more stringent and prescriptive government-sponsored code, there are at least three reasons that help explain this conundrum.

First, industry self-regulation helps to support market standardization. The higher the degree of market standardization, the lower the costs for institutional investors and asset managers to integrate any stewardship policies into their investment strategy. The different standards promoted are de facto replaced or supplemented with a common standard, which may also be more tailored towards the real needs of the industry.[153] In a similar vein, this may solve the current free-riding situation where some funds are performing engagement policies and thus produce a public good (of better market culture and higher performance) for those that are not.

Second, according to Hoepner, Majoch and Zhou, 'compliance with voluntary regulation has reputational and socially legitimizing benefits'.[154] The adoption of stewardship can function more efficiently as a differentiating factor among the compliant and non-compliant market participants when it is not perceived as compliance with the minimum legal requirements.

Third, having a regulatory framework setting standards of best practice can clarify the legitimacy of institutional investors' corporate actions. For example, institutional investors face uncertainty with regard to the breach of their fiduciary duties[155] when they take into consideration non-financial factors in their investment decision-making; or with regard to the breach of 'acting in concert' provisions[156] when they co-operate in corporate governance affairs. A national regulatory initiative backed up by a supervisory authority can give, especially to small-sized institutional investors, access to implementation support and know-how–sharing networks, raising barriers to entry.

9.4.3 *Substitutes*

When assessing the merits of adopting regulatory standards on stewardship and shareholder engagement, one must consider any pre-existing substitutes that may – even though in a different form or context – achieve very similar objectives in a different way. Ignoring such substitutes risks overburdening any legal system, and potentially duplicating legal obligations, with the result of dysfunctional rules.

First, it is straightforward and easily understandable that legal critics of any stewardship involvement, as discussed, will readily find a range of substitutes in the domestic legal

---

[153] Andreas Binder and Roman Gutzwiller, 'Soft Law für institutionelle Investoren [Soft Law for Institutional Investors]' (2013) 8 *Gesellschafts- und Kapitalmarktrecht* 84.
[154] Hoepner, Majoch and Zhou (n 138) 14.
[155] Carmen Juravle and Alan Lewis, 'Identifying Impediments to SRI in Europe: A Review of the Practitioner and Academic Literature' (July 2008) 17 *Business Ethics: A European Review* 285; Joakim Sandberg, 'Socially Responsible Investment and Fiduciary Duty: Putting the Freshfields Report into Perspective' (2010) 101 *Journal of Business Ethics* 143; Joakim Sandberg, '(Re-)Interpreting Fiduciary Duty to Justify Socially Responsible Investment for Pension Funds' (2013) 21 *Corporate Governance: An International Review* 436.
[156] Fleischer and Strothotte (n 86) 226.

system.[157] As we saw, these critics will thus argue that the German system of corporate governance, and in particular the supervisory board, is perfectly able to play the same monitoring role that would otherwise be attributed to institutional investors under a stewardship paradigm. With regard to promoting end-beneficiaries' interests, MiFID II and UCITS would thereby function as the appropriate regulatory framework for enhancing transparency between the parties of the investment chain. The existing regulatory framework for financial services providers imposes increased disclosure requirements. The CSR Directive[158] as well as the Commission's legislative proposals on sustainable finance promote the integration of long-term considerations in financial institutions' investment strategy.

SRD II is the most important recent legislative initiative with regard to stewardship because it constitutes mandatory provisions imposing similar disclosure obligations to all EU-based institutional investors and asset managers. Thus, this degree of harmonization may create a level playing field across member states.[159] The EU provisions are minimum legal requirements that can be supplemented by national legislation or codes of conduct.[160] It is obvious that the UK, as the pioneer in stewardship regulatory initiatives,[161] will have a competitive advantage against other jurisdictions that have to comply with SRD II but have not adopted any relative regulation, such as Germany. The German implementation of SRD II stays rather close to the text of the European Directive and does not develop these requirements into a workable framework for practical application.[162]

All these arguments would, however, rest on the implicit assumption that the German legal framework for shareholder engagement or corporate monitoring is de facto *effective* in curbing managerial slack. In other words, the argument that powerful substitutes exist in German law that justify the absence of a stewardship code is acceptable only if those substitutes are equally effective as a fully-fledged stewardship code would be. This, however, is very much an open question. The effectiveness of the monitoring procedures mandated by German law have long been questioned.[163] For example, it is unclear whether German supervisory boards are sufficiently independent to exercise an adequate review of managerial actions.[164] Equally, the shortcomings of German group law (*Konzernrecht*) have long been documented, and only very few other countries have followed this example.[165]

A second substitute may be found in the self-commitment by some institutional investors, in particular those who are members of either or both of the associations BVI and DVFA.[166] However, we saw already that these self-binding codes do not live up to the obligations of a sophisticated stewardship code, and do not come with a comparable legal force. In fact, such market initiatives will frequently be adopted with the specific objective of fending off any more stringent legal action.

---

[157] See Section 9.3.2.1.
[158] See n 35.
[159] European Commission, 'Proposal for a Directive of the European Parliament and of the Council amending Directive 2007/36/EC as regards the encouragement of long-term shareholder engagement and Directive 2013/34/EU as regards certain elements of the corporate governance statement' COM (2014) 213 final, 2014/0121 (COD) 6–7.
[160] FRC/FCA (n 52) paras 1.6, 6.9, 6.13; FCA FS19/7 (n 142) para 3.86.
[161] Juravle and Lewis (n 155).
[162] Koch (n 133).
[163] See e.g. OECD, *The Role of Institutional Investors in Promoting Good Corporate Governance* (n 32) 119.
[164] Theodor Baums and Kenneth E Scott, 'Taking Shareholder Protection Seriously? Corporate Governance in the United States and Germany' (2005) 53 *The American Journal of Comparative Law* 31; Heidrick & Struggles, 'Challenging Board Performance' (European Corporate Governance Report 2011) <www.essere-associes.com/media/2011-HeidrickStruggles-Challenging-board-performance.pdf> accessed 6 January 2020.
[165] Antunes and others (n 25) 59.
[166] See Section 9.4.2.

Institutional investors and asset managers can also self-commit to either national or international standards of best practice. Among the most prominent international standards are the ICGN Global Stewardship Principles and the UNPRI. The international scope of these principles makes the choice of complying with them superior to the choice of complying with national codes of conduct. This is especially the case for jurisdictions that have so far not developed a regulatory framework for stewardship. Based on this, the marginal benefits from introducing a stewardship code in Germany may be small, provided that there is a body of international principles with a broader base of signatory parties.[167]

We should also take into consideration that the introduction of stewardship regulation on the national level would require resources for the establishment of the necessary monitoring and enforcement infrastructure. The benefits expected from such an initiative would have to exceed the administrative cost of enforcement, and such an estimation should take into consideration the inefficiencies of the existing monitoring mechanisms.[168]

9.4.4 *Discussion*

Can the problems concerning the applicability of a national stewardship code to foreign owners and the existence of private initiatives as well as possible substitutes justify the constant refusal of the German government to follow the trend and to set up a UK-style stewardship code? There are several factors that would still give ample room for a German code to play a useful role in the German corporate landscape.

First, the sceptics' position would be understandable if the sole objective of a code was to promote the interests of the investee companies. However, as we saw earlier, it is among the primary objectives of any legislation, including the UK Code and SRD II, to also further the interests of end-beneficiaries. Their interests can be efficiently protected through achieving greater transparency among the parties of the investment chain, the asset managers–institutional investors and the institutional investors–end-beneficiaries.[169] Greater transparency is perceived as an important condition for making effective stewardship a differentiating factor across the firms of the investment management industry,[170] a market with strong anti-competitive forces.[171] An improvement of competition is in the interests of institutional investors' and asset managers' clients and, thus, beneficial for market quality and integrity.[172] Therefore, even if many institutional investors are not based in Germany, their activity affects German companies and German end-beneficiaries. With the aim of promoting the interests of the latter stakeholders, a German stewardship initiative would be both politically feasible and legitimate.

---

[167] A list of ICGN Global Stewardship Principles endorsers is available at ICGN, 'ICGN Global Stewardship Principles & Endorsers' <www.icgn.org/policy/icgn-global-stewardship-principles-endorsers> accessed 6 January 2020, and a list of UNPRI signatories is available at <https://d8g8t13e9vf20.cloudfront.net/Uploads/w/j/y/signatorydirectoryupdated112019_169996_778605_873356.xlsx> accessed 6 January 2020.

[168] Konstantinos Sergakis, 'Legal vs Social Enforcement of Shareholder Duties'; Iris H-Y Chiu, 'Private vs Public Enforcement of Shareholder Duties' in Hanne S Birkmose and Konstantinos Sergakis (eds), *Enforcing Shareholders' Duties* (Edward Elgar 2019). See also Katelouzou and Sergakis, Shareholder Stewardship Enforcement, Chapter 27.

[169] European Commission (n 159).

[170] Financial Conduct Authority, 'Consultation on Proposals to Improve Shareholder Engagement' (Consultation Paper, January 2019) paras 1.13–1.15 <www.fca.org.uk/publication/consultation/cp19-07.pdf> accessed 6 January 2020.

[171] Financial Conduct Authority, 'Asset Management Market Study – Further Remedies' (Policy Statement, February 2019) <www.fca.org.uk/publication/policy/ps19-04.pdf> accessed 6 January 2020.

[172] FCA FS19/7 (n 142) para 1.1.

TABLE 9.2 *Number of pension funds and their assets under management (2018)*

Country	Number of pension funds	Assets held by pension funds (billion EUR)	Number of members	Number of beneficiaries
Netherlands	260	1,360.15	5,646,763	13,046,483
UK	1,300	1,173.80	20,000,000	10,493,000
Switzerland	1,650	749.06	4,174,580	1,183,910
Germany	171	184.80	7,903,000	1,493,000
Ireland	71,340	147.60	437,711	750,000
Italy	252	111.81	4,034,220	116,282
Spain*	1,576	76.47	4,583,652	97,551
Sweden*	62	36.72	1,112,062	187,637
Norway	84	34.80	148,000	360,000
Iceland	24	28.47	264,902	126,222
Austria	10	22.70	928,000	99,000
Belgium	197	32.00	974,842	759,473
Portugal	189	18.43	166,530	131,831
France	25,489	15.90	2,400,000	n/k
Croatia	12	12.23	1,844,272	n/k
Romania	7	8.53	7,042,179	20,000
Bulgaria	18	5.97	3,965,174	n/k
Finland	47	4.33	166,530	48,796
Estonia	22	3.60	744,675	37,373
Luxembourg	13	1.55	16,466	n/k
Hungary	4	0.77	n/k	n/k
TOTAL	101,437	4028.21		

Source: PensionsEurope, Pension Funds Statistics and Trends (2018) 4, 7

Second, a stewardship initiative may be even more urgent in Germany than in other European jurisdictions. The reason is the clientele of German asset managers. In Germany, the pension funds industry is not as developed as in the UK or the Netherlands (see Table 9.2). This is also the case for the insurance industry, where the UK and France are the leading insurance markets (Figure 9.3). German asset managers' clients are split equally into institutional and retail investors, in contrast to the UK and France, where more than 75% of asset managers' clients are institutional investors (Figure 9.4).

Instead, retail clients usually invest in investment funds, while institutional investors delegate discretionary mandates to their asset managers. One of the main differences between the two investment practices is that, in the case of discretionary mandates, the investment strategy is agreed beforehand with each client, so that it is tailor-made to the specific investment goals of that individual investor.[173] In Germany, the main investment vehicle for both retail and institutional investors is the investment fund.[174] The investment strategy of the investment fund is predetermined, and clients can choose to either opt in or not invest in it at all. The fact that end-beneficiaries do not have a say in the investment strategy of the fund makes their support at the stage of selecting and monitoring the fund even more important. Enhanced transparency achieved by imposing disclosure requirements with regard to stewardship can support end-beneficiaries in making selection decisions and monitoring on an informed

[173] EFAMA (n 121) 3.
[174] ibid 6.

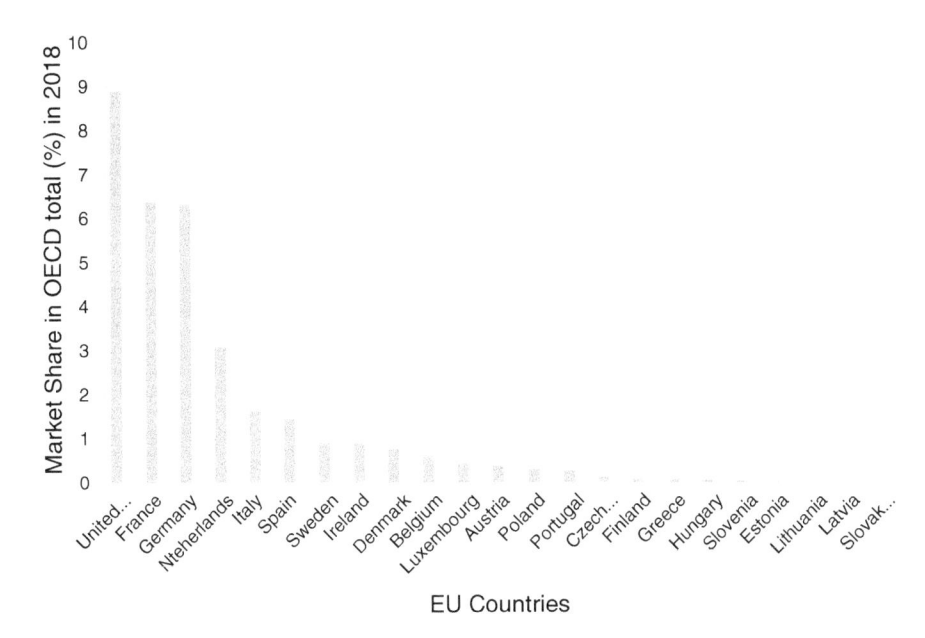

FIGURE 9.3 Market share of the insurance industry in EU countries as part of the OECD total (2018)
Source: OECD, https://stats.oecd.org/Index.aspx?DataSetCode=INSIND

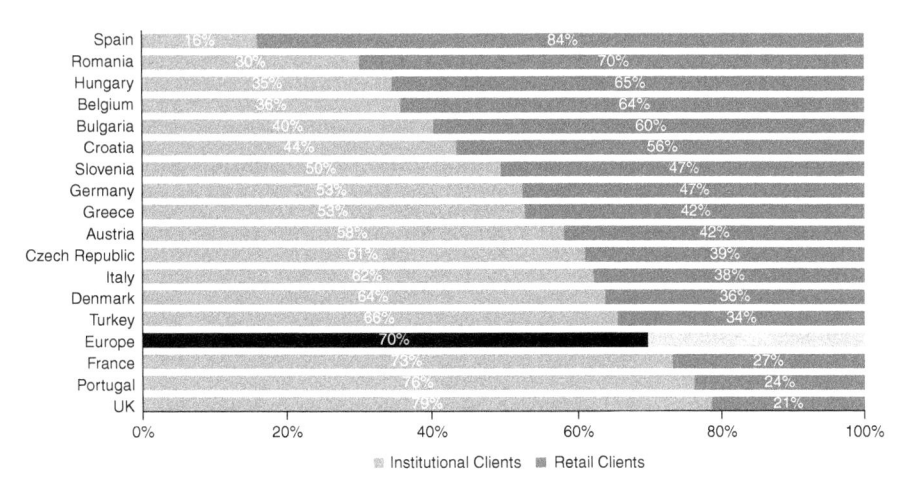

FIGURE 9.4 AuM by type of client and country at the end of 2017
Source: EFAMA, *Asset Management in Europe* (11th edn, 2019) 5.

basis.[175] End beneficiaries should then be able to evaluate whether a fund's strategy aligns with their investment preferences.[176]

True, the main problem concerning the possibility of regulating the activities of foreign institutional investors through German regulatory initiatives remains, but it is less salient with regard to end-beneficiaries than investee companies. The reason lies in the 'home bias' that is

---

[175] FairPensions, 'Submission to the Financial Reporting Council's Consultation on a Stewardship Code for Institutional Investors' (2010) (on file with the author).
[176] See text accompanying n 61.

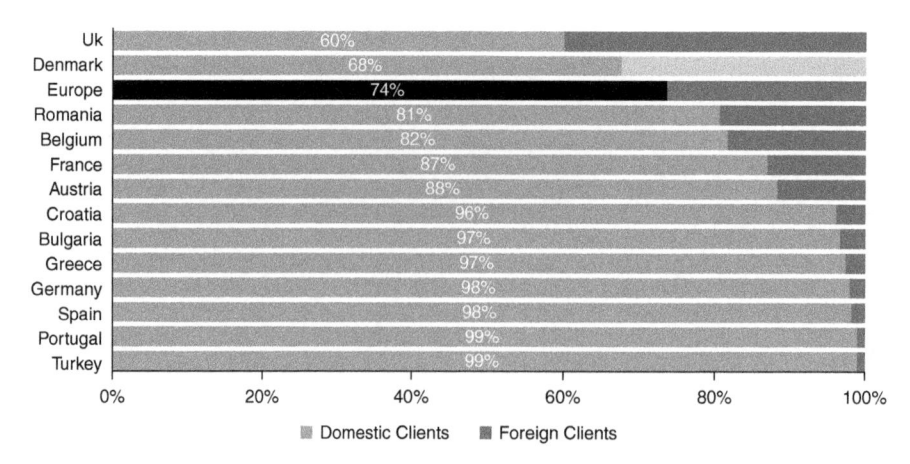

FIGURE 9.5 Domestic and foreign clients at the end of 2017
Source: EFAMA, *Asset Management in Europe* (11th edn, 2019) 6.

typically inherent in the process of selecting asset managers (see Figure 9.5). Based on this bias, German end-beneficiaries will tend to frequently select German funds to manage their assets, so that any legislative initiative that improves the activities of Germany-based funds will disproportionately benefit German institutional and retail investors.[177]

As we saw earlier, the largest investors in DAX companies, both foreign and German, already have adopted some type of a stewardship agenda in their investment strategy. This may be based on a foreign national code or on domestic or international standards of best practice, typically on a voluntary basis. Should any German stewardship initiative be forthcoming, it would naturally be more effective in addressing domestic small and medium-sized institutional investors.[178] A national regulatory framework for stewardship, even if it technically does not bind foreign investors, may still support domestic institutional investors or end-beneficiaries in their selection of domestic asset managers and institutional investors, respectively. If stewardship is compatible with end-beneficiaries' preferences, and if there is an efficient mechanism for monitoring stewardship activities, the adoption of stewardship regulation can give a competitive advantage to institutional investors and asset managers that adopt stewardship activities either on a mandatory or on a voluntary basis.[179]

Further benefits from a German code may be expected in less salient areas. For example, a German code may simply define expectations of what policymakers believe good stewards should do, even though enforcement powers may be limited. It would equally standardize market practices, which are currently, as we have seen, relying on a patchwork of foreign and international standards as well as domestic industry initiatives. It would clarify the obligations

[177] Rob Bauer, Gordon L Clark and Michael Viehs, 'The Geography of Shareholder Engagement: Evidence from a Large British Institutional Investor' (2013) <https://ssrn.com/abstract=2261649> accessed 6 January 2020.
[178] Qualitative analysis of the responses of UK stakeholders in the context of the public consultation for the UK Code 2010 has shown that medium- and small-sized asset managers were reluctant towards the introduction of the Code basically because of the costs to be borne with regard to the fulfilment of stewardship obligations. Some of these asset managers were F&C Investments, M&G Investments, Rathbone Investment Management, Rothschild Wealth Management (UK) Ltd, Royal London Asset Management, and South Yorkshire Pensions Authority. Most of the initially reluctant asset managers have since been categorized as Tier 1 asset managers.
[179] According to a survey by CREATE-Research/DWS, stewardship is a central competition factor for passive investment funds (Amin Rajan, 'Passive Investing 2019, The Rise of Stewardship' (CREATE-Research/DWS 2019) <www.dws.com/de-de/unser-profil/medien/medieninformationen/laut-einer-von-der-dws-gefoerderten-pensionskassenumfrage-ist-stewardship-ein-zentraler-wettbewerbsfaktor-fuer-passive-vermoegensverwalter/> accessed 6 January 2020).

and reporting requirements of investee companies and define legally acceptable practices, such as to what extent 'acting in concert' is permissible. In sum, a stewardship code would contribute to improving the market culture of the German capital market, essentially a public good that requires a neutral, government-led approach.[180]

9.5 CONCLUSION

This chapter has explored the role of shareholder engagement and stewardship in the German context. Although shareholders have taken a more assertive role as active investors recently, it is surprising to see the comparative reluctance of the German government towards promoting a stewardship code that would define and promote engagement practices. Thereby, Germany is swimming upstream by refusing to follow the international trend towards such a code of best practices.

While many doctrinal and functional arguments are advanced to explain this refusal, this chapter has argued that the main reason for Germany's reluctance may be rooted in politics: simply put, the comparatively small size of the German fund industry relative to the economy may explain why regulating it may not be the government's top priority. Instead, the German position is following traditional patterns of domestic corporate governance and law.

Still, I argue that a stewardship code would be a useful complementary instrument for the German market. It would standardize market practices, improve market culture, and clarify the obligations of investee companies. Most importantly, however, it would benefit domestic investors that are typically 'home biased' and thereby frequently disproportionately invested in domestic funds.

The implementation of SRD II into German law should therefore not be seen as the end of the debate. Rather, we should strive to continue our efforts towards strengthening engagement and accountability in the German market.

---

[180] For a similar conclusion, see Baums (n 133) 615.

10

The Japanese Stewardship Code

Its Resemblance and Non-resemblance to the UK Code

Gen Goto[*]

10.1 INTRODUCTION

In February 2014, the Council of Experts Concerning the Japanese Version of the Stewardship Code (Council of Experts), which had been established by the Financial Services Agency (FSA) of Japan the previous August, adopted the Japanese Stewardship Code,[1] making Japan one of the earliest followers of the UK. Since then, Japan has revised its Stewardship Code in 2017[2] and again in 2020.[3] This swiftness in adoption and keenness on revision suggest Japan's emphasis on, and high expectations of, stewardship codes.

The Japanese Stewardship Code, both in its original 2014 version (Japanese Code 2014) and in the 2017 revised version (Japanese Code 2017), consists of seven principles, each supplemented by more detailed guidance.[4] The structure of the Japanese Code strongly resembles that of the UK Stewardship Code in its original 2010 version (UK Code 2010) and the 2012 revised version (UK Code 2012).[5] Not only the structure but also the wording of the Japanese Codes, in their English

---

[*] This chapter has greatly benefited from a joint research project with Dan W. Puchniak and Alan K. Koh, assisted by Samantha S. Tang, and from valuable comments of the participants at the Kinyu-shohin-torihiki-ho Kenkyukai (Financial Instruments and Exchange Act Workshop) (10 September 2019, at Japan Securities Research Institute) and the Shoho Kenkyukai (Commercial Law Workshop) (24 January 2020, at Shojihomu). The author appreciates financial support by the Nomura Foundation.

[1] The Council of Experts Concerning the Japanese Version of the Stewardship Code, 'Principles for Responsible Institutional Investors «Japan's Stewardship Code» – To Promote Sustainable Growth of Companies through Investment and Dialogue' (26 February 2014) <www.fsa.go.jp/en/refer/councils/stewardship/20140407/01.pdf> accessed 13 July 2020 [hereinafter Japanese Code 2014].

[2] The Council of Experts on the Stewardship Code, 'Principles for Responsible Institutional Investors «Japan's Stewardship Code» – To Promote Sustainable Growth of Companies through Investment and Dialogue' (29 May 2017) <www.fsa.go.jp/en/refer/councils/stewardship/20170529/01.pdf> accessed 13 July 2020 [hereinafter Japanese Code 2017]. While the name of the council has been slightly modified from its original one, its composition remains substantially the same. See further Financial Services Agency, 'Finalization of Japan's Stewardship Code (Revised Version)' (29 May 2017) <www.fsa.go.jp/en/refer/councils/stewardship/20170529.html> accessed 13 July 2020.

[3] The Council of Experts on the Stewardship Code (FY2019), 'Principles for Responsible Institutional Investors «Japan's Stewardship Code» – To Promote Sustainable Growth of Companies through Investment and Dialogue' (24 March 2020) <www.fsa.go.jp/en/refer/councils/stewardship/20200324/01.pdf> accessed 13 July 2020 [hereinafter Japanese Code 2020]. See further Financial Services Agency, 'Finalization of Japan's Stewardship Code (Second Revised Version)' (24 March 2020) <www.fsa.go.jp/en/refer/councils/stewardship/20200324.html> accessed 13 July 2020.

[4] Japanese Code 2014 (n 1) 6–13; Japanese Code 2017 (n 2) 8–18.

[5] Financial Reporting Council, *The UK Stewardship Code* (July 2010) <www.frc.org.uk/getattachment/e223e152-5515-4cdc-a951-da33e093eb28/UK-Stewardship-Code-July-2010.pdf> accessed 13 July 2020; Financial Reporting Council, *The UK Stewardship Code* (September 2012) <www.frc.org.uk/getattachment/d67933f9-ca38-4233-b603-3d24b2f62c5f/UK-Stewardship-Code-(September-2012).pdf> accessed 13 July 2020 [hereinafter UK Code 2012]. See also Financial Reporting Council, 'Origins of the UK Stewardship Code' (2019) <www.frc.org.uk/investors/uk-stewardship-code/origins-of-the-uk-stewardship-code> accessed 13 July 2020.

versions, have a resemblance to that of the UK Code 2012.[6] This is actually not so surprising as the Council of Experts had based its consideration on the UK Code 2012, by first translating it into Japanese and then discussing the UK principles one by one to determine whether they required modification to fit the Japanese situation.[7] The addition in the 2020 revision of the Japanese Stewardship Code (Japanese Code 2020) of the eighth principle regarding providers of services to institutional investors[8] is also comparable to some extent to the introduction of a separate set of principles applicable to service providers in the 2020 version of the UK Stewardship Code (UK Code 2020),[9] which was also fully translated for discussion at the Council of Experts.[10]

Based on the textual resemblance and drafting process, one might think that the Japanese Stewardship Code is strongly influenced by the UK Stewardship Code and aims to achieve the same goal as the latter.[11] As the author has discussed elsewhere,[12] however, that is not the case.

To cut a long story short, while the goal of the UK Stewardship Code is to restrain excessive risk-taking and short-termism by making institutional investors more responsible to the public, the Japanese Stewardship Code intends to champion shareholders' interest by making domestic institutional investors more active shareholders who would exert pressure on entrenched management.[13] In the author's view, this nearly diametrical divergence of the goals of the two stewardship codes derives from the differences in the status quos of the corporate governance systems of the two countries: Japan has been long known for its stakeholder-oriented corporate governance, which stands in contrast with the Anglo-Saxon shareholder-centric corporate governance that the UK shares with the US.[14] Stewardship codes must be understood within the context of the corporate governance system of each respective jurisdiction, not just by a textual analysis of their principles in isolation.[15]

The remainder of this chapter will proceed as follows. Section 10.2 provides background and context by describing the state of Japanese corporate governance before and around the time of adoption of the Japanese Stewardship Code. Sections 10.3 and 10.4 analyze the goal of the Japanese Stewardship Code in light of its content and effect. Section 10.5 examines changes made in the 2020 revision to the Japanese Stewardship Code. Section 10.6 provides a brief conclusion, summarizing that the commonality between the Japanese Stewardship Code and the UK Stewardship Code lies in their intention to change the alleged status quo in each country, but not in the direction of the changes sought.

---

[6] Katelouzou and Siems, The Global Diffusion of Stewardship Codes, Chapter 30.

[7] See Financial Services Agency, 'Secretariat's Explanatory Material (Points to Consider in Formulating the Japanese Version of the Stewardship Code)' (18 October 2013) <www.fsa.go.jp/en/refer/councils/stewardship/material/20131018_1.pdf> accessed 13 July 2020.

[8] Japanese Code 2020 (n 3) 22.

[9] Financial Reporting Council, The UK Stewardship Code 2020 (2019) 23–29 <www.frc.org.uk/getattachment/5aae591d-d9d3-4cf4-814a-d14e156a1d87/Stewardship-Code_Dec-19-Final-Corrected.pdf> accessed 13 July 2020 [hereinafter UK Code 2020].

[10] 金融庁(Kinyucho) [Financial Services Agency], '英国スチュワードシップ・コード 2020 (仮訳) [UK Stewardship Code 2020 (Provisional Translation)]' (8 November 2019) <www.fsa.go.jp/singi/stewardship/siryou/20191108/07.pdf> accessed 13 July 2020.

[11] See e.g. Iris H–Y Chiu and Dionysia Katelouzou, 'From Shareholder Stewardship to Shareholder Duties: Is the Time Ripe?' in Hanne S Birkmose (ed), Shareholders' Duties (Kluwer Law International 2017) 131, 135.

[12] Gen Goto, 'The Logic and Limits of Stewardship Codes: The Case of Japan' (2018) 15 Berkeley Business Law Journal 365.

[13] ibid 396.

[14] David Larcker and Brian Tayan, Corporate Governance Matters: A Closer Look at Organizational Choices and Their Consequences (2nd edn, Pearson 2015) 32, 39.

[15] See Gen Goto, Alan K Koh and Dan W Puchniak, 'Diversity of Shareholder Stewardship in Asia: Faux Convergence' (2020) 53 Vanderbilt Journal of Transnational Law 829, 839–41.

10.2 BACKGROUND: JAPANESE CORPORATE GOVERNANCE BEFORE THE STEWARDSHIP CODE

10.2.1 *Traditional Japanese Corporate Governance System*

Japanese corporate law, which was originally drafted in the late nineteenth century with a strong German influence, has traditionally granted shareholders rights and powers that are much stronger than those enjoyed by shareholders of Delaware companies.[16] For example, shareholders in a general meeting have the power to decide the amount of dividends unless otherwise stipulated in the charter,[17] and a shareholder holding 300 or more voting rights can make a proposal, which will be binding when adopted, to increase dividends.[18] Also, directors can be dismissed by a simple majority at any shareholders' meeting,[19] and a shareholder holding 3 per cent or more of the company's voting rights can request to call a special meeting.[20] This means that, theoretically, shareholders can put strong pressure on the management of Japanese listed companies.

When the Japanese capital market was opened to foreign investors in 1964, the managements of Japanese listed companies were aware of the risk posed by these strong powers of shareholders. Accordingly, Japanese listed companies started holding each other's shares to protect themselves from foreign investors.[21] Eventually, Japanese companies formed a web of friendly shareholders ('stable shareholders' or *antei kabunushi*), which consisted of the company's banks and friendly business partners, leading to a phenomenon known as cross-shareholding (*kabushiki mochiai*). Since such shareholders have an incentive to support the management of the company in order to maintain good business relationships, this ownership structure has effectively insulated managers from shareholder pressure, and arguably enabled the management to focus on growth in the long term. It is also worth noting that, while the proportion of shares held by such 'stable shareholders' could be well above the majority, each of these 'stable shareholders' holds only a very small amount,[22] for example, 1 per cent of outstanding shares, meaning that there is also no single controlling shareholder to monitor management.

Based on such an ownership structure, Japanese companies after World War II established a unique system of corporate governance that worked quite well until the mid-1980s, supporting Japan's rapid economic recovery after World War II. This system is often referred to as the 'corporate community' or 'company as a family', as it focuses on the interests of employees and other stakeholders.[23] First, under the so-called lifetime employment system, Japanese companies refrained from lay-offs as much as possible, semi-guaranteeing employees jobs at the company until reaching their retirement age (which is usually sixty years old). Combined with seniority-based salaries and promotions, this system turned employees into quasi-residual

---

[16] See Gen Goto, 'Legally "Strong" Shareholders of Japan' (2014) 3 *Michigan Journal of Private Equity & Venture Capital Law* 125, 128–39.
[17] 会社法(*Kaishaho*) [Japanese Companies Act], Law No 86 of 2005, art 454, para 1.
[18] Japanese Companies Act, arts 304 and 305.
[19] Japanese Companies Act, art 341.
[20] ibid, art 297.
[21] Hideaki Miyajima and Fumiaki Kuroki, 'The Unwinding of Cross-Shareholding in Japan: Causes, Effects, and Implications' in Masahiko Aoki, Gregory Jackson and Hideaki Miyajima (eds), *Corporate Governance in Japan: Institutional Change and Organizational Diversity* (OUP 2007) 83–85.
[22] See Zenichi Shishido, 'Japanese Corporate Governance: The Hidden Problems of Corporate Law and Their Solutions' (2000) 25 *Delaware Journal of Corporate Law* 189, 210–11.
[23] For a more detailed description of the traditional Japanese corporate governance system, see Shishido (n 22) 201–14 and Gregory Jackson and Hideaki Miyajima, 'Introduction: The Diversity and Change of Corporate Governance in Japan' in Masahiko Aoki, Gregory Jackson and Hideaki Miyajima (eds), *Corporate Governance in Japan: Institutional Change and Organizational Diversity* (OUP 2007) 3–6.

claimants and incentivized them to make firm-specific human capital investments. Second, directors were predominantly selected from employees of the company as an extension of the internal promotion system. The number of directors was often large, sometimes more than thirty, to accommodate the promotion of many senior employees. Consequently, most of the directors were subordinates of the chief executive officer (CEO), and thus it was unrealistic to expect the board of directors to monitor the CEO. Third, companies were financed mostly by bank loans, and the main bank (i.e. the bank that lent the largest amount to a company) played an important role in the governance of that borrower.

10.2.2 Changes in Share-Ownership Structure in Japan

With the so-called burst of the Bubble Economy in 1991, however, Japan's high growth period finally came to an end, and some aspects of the traditional model were forced to change. The role of main banks both in funding and in governance of other companies weakened, as banks themselves were in financial distress, resulting from non-performing loans made during the Bubble Period.[24] Also, the government imposed a limit on banks' holding of shares of other companies to strengthen banks' financial stability.[25] As banks divested from other listed companies, domestic and foreign institutional investors increased their holdings. The result was unwinding of cross-shareholdings, as shown in Figure 10.1.[26]

While this unwinding of cross-shareholding was a significant change for Japanese capital market and listed companies, however, it was still unclear around the time of the adoption of the Japanese Code 2014 how much impact this would have on Japanese corporate governance for the following two reasons. First, as the unwinding took place mostly in large listed companies, cross-shareholdings were still intact in small and medium-sized listed companies.[27] Second, while foreign institutional investors that have no other business ties in Japan would not refrain from exerting pressure on the management of their investee companies, and would support hostile bidders or hedge fund activists if necessary, domestic institutional investors, in particular insurance companies and asset management companies, might be reluctant to do so as they often have business ties with their investee companies.[28]

10.2.3 Corporate Governance Reforms in 2010s

In the meantime, the Japanese economy has struggled in malaise since the Burst of the Bubble through the 1990s and the 2000s, the period which is often dubbed 'the lost two decades'.

---

[24] Jackson and Miyajima (n 23) 13.
[25] 銀行等の株式等の保有の制限に関する法律(Ginko to no kabushiki to no hoyu no seigen to ni kansuru horitsu) [Act on Restriction of Shareholdings by Banks], Law No 131 of 2001, art 3, para 1 (prohibiting banks from holding shares of other corporations in excess of the bank's capital).
[26] For details, see Goto, 'Legally "Strong" Shareholders of Japan' (n 16) 144–46.
[27] See Goto, 'Legally "Strong" Shareholders of Japan' (n 16) 145–46. See also 商事法務研究会 (Shoji-homu Kenkyukai) [Japan Institute of Business Law], '株主総会白書2013年版 (Kabunushi Sokai Hakusho 2013-nen-ban) [White Paper on Shareholders' Meetings 2013]' (2013) 2016 商事法務 (*Shojihomu*) [*Commercial Law Review*] 72 (reporting the result of an annual survey to Japanese listed companies in 2013, in which the ratio of shares held by stable shareholders as recognized by listed companies was higher as their size measured by their legal capital was smaller).
[28] For example, a life insurance company might sell group life insurance to its investee company's employees or be assigned from its investee company to manage its corporate pension fund. Also, an asset management company running mutual funds might be affiliated with a large financial conglomerate that has many business ties with investee companies of the mutual funds. It is worth noting that reluctance of domestic institutional investors owing to business ties with their investee companies may not be unique to Japan. See Lucian A Bebchuk, Alma Cohen and Scott Hirst, 'The Agency Problems of Institutional Investors' (2017) 31 *Journal of Economic Perspectives* 89, 102–103.

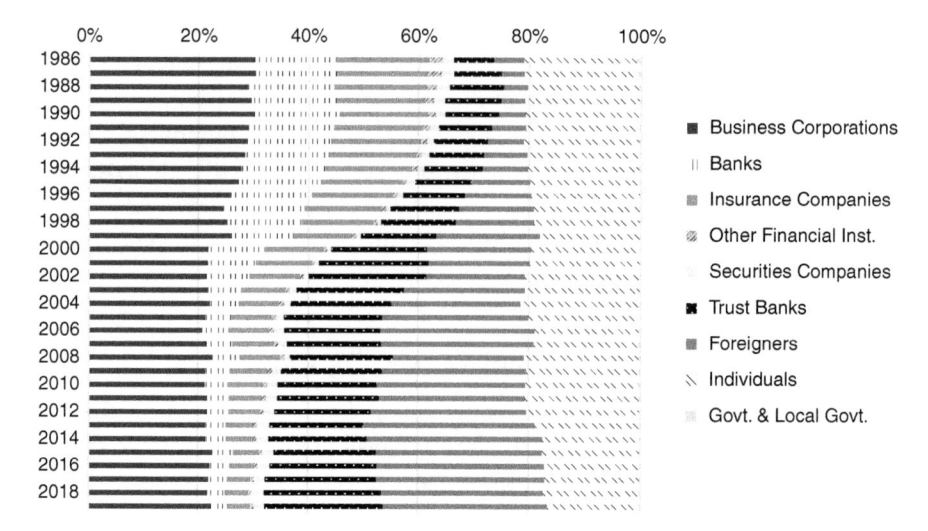

FIGURE 10.1 Share-ownership structure of Japanese listed companies
Source: Tokyo Stock Exchange, 2019 Shareownership Survey.

Prime Minister Shinzo Abe, who took office for his second time in December 2012, has been emphasizing corporate governance reform since 2013 as a key element of the third pillar of his signature economic policy to 'revitalize' the Japanese economy.[29] The basic idea is to introduce a shareholder-oriented viewpoint to the stakeholder-oriented management of Japanese companies to urge risk-taking for higher profitability.[30] The Japanese Corporate Governance Code, which was adopted in 2015 and later revised in 2018,[31] coins this idea as 'growth-oriented governance' and promotes the appointment of independent directors to represent the interests of shareholders in the boardroom and to function as a barrier insulating the management from

---

[29] See e.g. the speech by Prime Minister Shinzo Abe at the World Economic Forum 2014 (Shinzo Abe, 'A New Vision from a New Japan' (World Economic Forum 2014 Annual Meeting, Davos, 22 January 2014) <https://japan.kantei.go.jp/96_abe/statement/201401/22speech_e.html> accessed 13 July 2020). See also Curtis J Milhaupt, 'Evaluating Abe's Third Arrow: How Significant Are Japan's Recent Corporate Governance Reforms?' in Hiroshi Oda (ed), *Comparative Corporate Governance: The Case of Japan* (Journal of Japanese Law Special Issue 12, Carl Heymanns Verlag 2018) 67–70.

[30] A core economic policy document of the Abe administration states: 'What should be done to increase Japanese companies' earning power, in other words, medium to long-term profitability and productivity and to pass the fruits of such increase on to the people (households) evenly? First, it is important to strengthen the mechanism to enhance corporate governance and reform corporate managers' mindset so that they will make proactive business decisions to win in global competition for the purpose of attaining targets including globally-compatible level in return on equity. Particularly, companies that have achieved the highest earnings in several years should be encouraged to proactively use their earnings for new capital investment, bold business realignment, mergers and acquisitions, and other deals, instead of accumulating internal reserves.' Prime Minister's Office, 'Japan Revitalization Strategy Revised in 2014: Japan's Challenge for the Future' (24 June 2014) 5–6 <www.kantei.go.jp/jp/singi/keizaisaisei/pdf/honbunEN.pdf> accessed 13 July 2020.

[31] The Council of Experts Concerning the Corporate Governance Code, 'Japan's Corporate Governance Code [Final Proposal]: Seeking Sustainable Corporate Growth and Increased Corporate Value over the Mid- to Long-Term' (5 March 2015) <www.fsa.go.jp/en/refer/councils/corporategovernance/20150306-1/01.pdf> accessed 13 July 2020 [hereinafter Japanese Corporate Governance Code 2015]; Tokyo Stock Exchange, 'Japan's Corporate Governance Code: Seeking Sustainable Corporate Growth and Increased Corporate Value over the Mid- to Long-Term' (1 June 2018) <www.jpx.co.jp/english/news/1020/b5b4pj000000jvxr-att/20180601.pdf> accessed 13 July 2020 [hereinafter Japanese Corporate Governance Code 2018] (see also Japan Exchange Group, 'Publication of Revised Japan's Corporate Governance Code' (1 June 2018) <www.jpx.co.jp/english/news/1020/20180601.html> accessed 13 July 2020).

the interests of core employees,[32] while discouraging cross-shareholding that arguably leads to inefficiency and managerial slack via disclosure requirements.[33]

10.3 THE GOAL OF THE JAPANESE STEWARDSHIP CODE

10.3.1 *From the Context of Adoption*

The adoption of the Japanese Stewardship Code in February 2014 was the first measure of a series of corporate governance reforms implemented by the Abe administration, followed by the reform of the Companies Act in June. As such, the Japanese Stewardship Code must be understood together with other corporate governance reforms in the 2010s, in particular with the Japanese Corporate Governance Code, which is often cited together with the Japanese Stewardship Code as composing 'the two wheels of a cart'.[34]

Specifically, the Japanese Stewardship Code aims to change the reluctance of domestic institutional investors to take a tough stance against management owing to their business relationships with investee companies by emphasizing their stewardship obligations to their beneficiaries, with the broader objective of making Japanese listed companies more shareholder-oriented.[35] To put it differently, the Japanese Stewardship Code seeks to make domestic institutional investors act like foreign institutional investors to discipline the managements of their investee companies more effectively for the purpose of shareholders' interests. This can be seen from the existence of criticism against the Japanese Stewardship Code for not covering cross-shareholdings by banks and non-financial companies,[36] while foreign institutional investors are not considered the main target of the Japanese Stewardship Code as they are often viewed in Japan as being free from conflicts of interests and open to exerting pressure on the management of investee companies when necessary.[37]

---

[32] See Japanese Corporate Governance Code 2018 (n 31) 21–22, Principle 4.8 and Gen Goto, 'Recent Boardroom Reforms in Japan and the Roles of Outside/Independent Directors' in Hiroshi Oda (ed), *Comparative Corporate Governance: The Case of Japan* (Journal of Japanese Law Special Issue 12, Carl Heymanns Verlag 2018) 50–51. For details of the recent Japanese reforms on board independence, see also Gen Goto, Manabu Matsunaka and Souichirou Kozuka, 'Japan's Gradual Reception of Independent Directors: An Empirical and Political-Economic Analysis' in Dan W Puchniak, Harald Baum and Luke Nottage (eds), *Independent Directors in Asia: A Historical, Contextual and Comparative Approach* (CUP 2017) 135.

[33] The Japanese Corporate Governance Code 2015 (n 31) provides that Japanese listed companies shall disclose their policy on cross-shareholding, and provide an annual detailed explanation on the objective and rationale behind major cross-shareholdings after examining their mid- to long-term economic rationale (Principle 1.4). The Japanese Corporate Governance Code 2018 (n 31) further seeks to accelerate the reduction of cross-shareholdings by adding a supplementary principle calling on companies not to discourage their shareholders from divesting their shareholding by, for example, suggesting that such divestments would result in reduction of business transactions with them (Japanese Corporate Governance Code 2018 (n 31) 7, Supplementary Principle 1.4.1).

[34] For example, see Prime Minister's Office, 'Japan Revitalization Strategy Revised 2015' (30 June 2015) 4 <www.kantei.go.jp/jp/singi/keizaisaisei/pdf/dai2_3en.pdf> accessed 13 July 2020; Financial Services Agency, 'Secretariat's Explanatory Material' (24 September 2015) <www.fsa.go.jp/en/refer/councils/follow-up/material/20150924-3.pdf> accessed 13 July 2020.

[35] Goto, 'The Logic and Limits of Stewardship Codes' (n 12) 395–97.

[36] 大崎貞和 (Sadakazu Osaki), '日本版コード成功の条件(Nihon-ban kōdo seikō no jyōken) [The Japanese Code's Conditions for Success]' (2014) 66 企業会計(*Kigyō Kaikei*) [*Corporate Accounting*] 48, 51–52; Ryohei Nakagawa, 'Shareholding Characteristics and Imperfect Coverage of the Stewardship Code in Japan' (2017) 29 *Japan Forum* 338, 346.

[37] The criticism against the Japanese Stewardship Code cited here stands in good contrast with that by Professor Cheffins of the UK Stewardship Code based on its lack of effectiveness against foreign investors. Brian R Cheffins, 'The Stewardship Code's Achilles' Heel' (2010) 73 *Modern Law Review* 1004, 1018, 1023–24.

10.3.2 *From the Text of the Code*

The preface of the Japanese Stewardship Code defines 'stewardship responsibilities' as 'the responsibilities of institutional investors to enhance the medium- to long-term investment return for their clients and beneficiaries (including ultimate beneficiaries; ...) by improving and fostering the investee companies' corporate value and sustainable growth through constructive engagement, or purposeful dialogue, based on in-depth knowledge of the companies and their business environment'.[38]

The structure of this definition, with the use of the prepositions 'to' and 'by', prioritizes the interest of ultimate beneficiaries as the goal of stewardship responsibility and considers sustainable growth of investee companies a means to achieve this goal.[39] This emphasis on the interest of the ultimate beneficiaries coincides with the concern regarding the conflicts of interests of domestic institutional investors described earlier.

10.3.3 *Comparison with the UK Code*

In contrast to Japan, the UK adopted its Stewardship Code in the aftermath of the global financial crisis in 2010 with a view to making institutional investors more responsible to the general public and curtailing excessive risk-taking by the management of their investee companies.[40] Also, the UK Code 2012 placed emphasis on the long-term success of investee companies,[41] under the influence of the Kay Review,[42] which focused on combating short-termism.[43]

While the context of the adoption and revision of the UK Stewardship Code clearly differs from that of the Japanese Code,[44] it is noteworthy that the predecessor to the UK Code 2010, namely the Institutional Shareholders' Committee's Code on the Responsibilities of Institutional Investors (ISC Code),[45] took a stance similar to that of the Japanese Code as it declared in its preface that the 'duty of institutional investors is to their end-beneficiaries and/or

---

[38] Japanese Code 2014 (n 1) 1. The definition of stewardship responsibilities remains unchanged in the Japanese Code 2017 (n 2) 3.

[39] Goto, 'The Logic and Limits of Stewardship Codes' (n 12) 371–72.

[40] ibid 374–75, 377–78.

[41] The UK Code 2012 states that the aim of its stewardship is to 'promote the long-term success of companies in such a way that the ultimate providers of capital also prosper', noting that '(e)ffective stewardship benefits companies, investors and the economy as a whole' (UK Code 2012 (n 5) 1).

[42] John Kay, 'The Kay Review of UK Equity Markets and Long-Term Decision Making' (Department for Business, Innovation and Skills, July 2012) <https://assets.publishing.service.gov.uk/government/uploads/system/uploads/attachment_data/file/253454/bis-12-917-kay-review-of-equity-markets-final-report.pdf> accessed 13 July 2020.

[43] Goto, 'The Logic and Limits of Stewardship Codes' (n 12) 378–81.

[44] One might argue that the Japanese Stewardship Code also mentions the sustainable growth of investee companies in its definition of stewardship. However, the drafting history of the Japanese Stewardship Code, which the author has analyzed in detail elsewhere, suggests that the insertion of the phrase 'with the aim of promoting sustainable growth of companies' was not the driving force behind the Code but, rather, a compromise to appease those who resisted the trend towards a more shareholder-oriented system of corporate governance. See Goto, 'The Logic and Limits of Stewardship Codes' (n 12) 387–95.

[45] Institutional Shareholders' Committee, 'Code on the Responsibilities of Institutional Shareholders' (November 2009) <https://web.archive.org/web/20120119184202/http://institutionalshareholderscommittee.org.uk/sitebuildercontent/sitebuilderfiles/ISCCode16n09.pdf> archived 19 January 2012, accessed 13 July 2020 [hereinafter ISC Code]. The Institutional Shareholders' Committee was a private organization formed by trade associations of British institutional investors. The members of the ISC as of 2009 were the Association of British Insurers, the Association of Investment Trust Companies, the National Association of Pension Funds, and the Investment Management Association. ISC Code (n 45) 1 fn 1.

clients and not to the wider public'.[46] Although the Financial Reporting Council of the UK almost copied the ISC Code when adopting the UK Stewardship Code, this preface was unsurprisingly replaced.[47]

10.4 THE CONTENT OF THE JAPANESE STEWARDSHIP CODE

10.4.1 *Principles and Guidance*

10.4.1.1 The Principles of the 2014 Code

The Japanese Stewardship Code was an attempt to introduce the *practice* of stewardship and engagement by institutional investors in the UK as embodied in the UK Code, rather than the UK Code itself, to change the behaviour of domestic institutional investors in Japan. However, both listed companies and institutional investors resisted simply importing the UK practice, arguing that some parts of it do not fit the circumstances in Japan.[48] Accordingly, several modifications were made to the principles of the UK Code 2012 in a way that appear to apply less pressure on institutional investors in investee companies.[49]

The principles of the 2014 Japanese Code, which remained unchanged in the 2017 revision, are as shown in Table 10.1.[50]

While Principles 1, 2 and 6 of the Japanese Stewardship Code are substantially the same as Principles 1, 2 and 7 of the UK Code 2012, there are notable differences in the other principles.

First, the preamble to the Japanese principles puts sustainable growth of the investee company ahead of enhancement of the medium- and long-term investment return of clients and beneficiaries; the UK Code 2012 refers only to the interest of the ultimate beneficiaries. Second, while Principles 4 and 5 of the UK Code 2012 refer to the possibility of escalating stewardship activities when necessary, and recommend that institutional investors act collectively with other investors, no such reference can be found in the Japanese principles. Instead, Principle 4 of the Japanese Code 2014 expects that institutional investors shall arrive at a common understanding with investee companies, and work with them in solving problems. This might have an effect of giving Japanese companies room to argue that institutional investors requesting certain actions, such as an increase in pay-outs, are not making sufficient efforts to reach a common understanding. In a similar vein, Principle 7 calls on institutional investors to have in-depth knowledge of investee

---

[46] ISC Code (n 45) 2. The declaration in the text was made after stating that the amount of resources of institutional investors should be 'sufficient to allow them to fulfill their responsibilities effectively' but be 'commensurate with the benefits derived'.

[47] See Financial Reporting Council, 'Implementation of the UK Stewardship Code' (July 2010) 4, para 18 <www.frc.org.uk/getattachment/34d58dbd-5e54-412e-9cdb-cb30f21d5074/Implementation-of-Stewardship-Code-July-2010.pdf> accessed 13 July 2020.

[48] The Council of Experts Concerning the Japanese Version of the Stewardship Code, 'Minutes of the 1st Meeting' (6 August 2013) 6–7 (statements by Mr Ken Furuichi of Nippon Life Insurance and Mr Jyunichi Kawada of JX Holdings) <www.fsa.go.jp/en/refer/councils/stewardship/minutes/20130806.pdf> accessed 13 July 2020.

[49] The following paragraphs are based on the analysis of 田中亘 (Wataru Tanaka), '日本版スチュワードシップ・コードの検討 – 機関投資家の役割についてのアンビヴァレントな見方(Nihon-ban suchuwādoshippu kōdo no kento: Kikan-tōshika no yakuwari nitsuite no anbivarento na mikata) [An Analysis of the Japanese Stewardship Code: An Ambivalent View on the Role of Institutional Investors]' (July 2014) 629監査役 (*Kansayaku*) [*Statutory Auditors*] 66, 68–69. See also Goto, 'The Logic and Limits of Stewardship Codes' (n 12) 384–86.

[50] Japanese Code 2017 (n 2) 8 (the Principles of the Code). The principles remain unchanged from the original 2014 version. See the Japanese Code 2014 (n 1) 6.

TABLE 10.1 *Comparison of the Japanese Code 2014 and the UK Code 2012*

	Japanese Code 2014	UK Code 2012
Preamble	So as to promote sustainable growth of the investee company and enhance the medium- and long-term investment return of clients and beneficiaries,	So as to protect and enhance the value that accrues to the ultimate beneficiary,
Principle 1	Institutional investors should have a clear policy on how they fulfil their stewardship responsibilities, and publicly disclose it.	Institutional investors should publicly disclose their policy on how they will discharge their stewardship responsibilities.
Principle 2	Institutional investors should have a clear policy on how they manage conflicts of interest in fulfilling their stewardship responsibilities and publicly disclose it.	Institutional investors should have a robust policy on managing conflicts of interest in relation to stewardship which should be publicly disclosed.
Principle 3	Institutional investors should monitor investee companies so that they can appropriately fulfil their stewardship responsibilities with an orientation towards the sustainable growth of the companies.	Institutional investors should monitor their investee companies.
Principle 4	Institutional investors should seek to arrive at an understanding in common with investee companies and work to solve problems through constructive engagement with investee companies.	Institutional investors should establish clear guidelines on when and how they will escalate their stewardship activities.
Principle 5	Institutional investors should have a clear policy on voting and disclosure of voting activity. The policy on voting should not comprise only a mechanical checklist; it should be designed to contribute to the sustainable growth of investee companies.	Institutional investors should be willing to act collectively with other investors where appropriate.
Principle 6	Institutional investors in principle should report periodically on how they fulfil their stewardship responsibilities, including their voting responsibilities, to their clients and beneficiaries.	Institutional investors should have a clear policy on voting and disclosure of voting activity.
Principle 7	To contribute positively to the sustainable growth of investee companies, institutional investors should have in-depth knowledge of the investee companies and their business environment and the skills and resources needed to appropriately engage with the companies and make proper judgments in fulfilling their stewardship activities.	Institutional investors should report periodically on their stewardship and voting activities.

companies and their business environment, as well as developing skills and resources necessary for appropriate engagement.

Further, while Principle 3 of the English version of the Japanese Code is an exhortation to institutional investors to 'monitor' investee companies, similar to that of the UK Code 2012, the original Japanese document does not use the literal Japanese translation of the term 'monitor'; instead, what is meant is for investors to 'properly grasp the circumstances of investee companies'. Together with the reference to 'the sustainable growth of investee companies' in the same principle, the Japanese wording is more nuanced, and does not encourage institutional investors to take an aggressive stance against investee companies.

Overall, the Japanese principles can be described as being much friendlier to investee companies as compared to the UK principles. This divergence from the UK principles has been criticized by those who support the necessity of shareholders' pressure to discipline the management of listed companies effectively.[51]

10.4.1.2 The 2017 and 2020 Revisions

Partly in response to such criticisms, the 2017 revision and the 2020 revision have placed more emphasis on the pressure of institutional investors on investee companies by amending the guidance section.

For example, the 2017 revision added a paragraph on collective engagement, to which no reference was made in the original 2014 text, in the guidance section to Principle 4, stating that 'it would be beneficial for' institutional investors 'to engage with investee companies in collaboration with other institutional investors (collective engagement) as necessary'.[52]

To address conflicts of interest of asset managers who belong to financial conglomerates, the 2017 revision also requires institutional investors to disclose how they have voted on each agenda item at shareholders' meetings of individual investee companies.[53] The 2020 revision intends to further this policy by requiring institutional investors to disclose the reasons for their votes when there is an apparent conflict of interests between the institutional investor and its beneficiaries, or when an extra explanation is necessary as the vote deviates from the voting policy of the investor.[54]

In addition, the 2017 revision emphasizes the role of asset owners such as pension funds, to encourage them to be more active on stewardship.[55] It also urges institutional investors who follow a passive investment strategy to participate more actively in engagement and to vote with

---

[51] See e.g. 田中亘 (Wataru Tanaka), 'コーポレート・ガバナンスの観点から見た日本版スチュワードシップ・コード:英国コードとの差異に着目して(Kōporēto gabanansu no kanten kara mita nihonban suchuwādoshippu kōdo – Eikoku kōdo tono sa'i ni chakumoku shite) [The Japanese Stewardship Code from the Perspective of Corporate Governance: With Focus on the Differences between the UK Code]' (2014) 1 信託フォーラム (Shintaku Foramu) [Trust Forum] 35, 38 (criticizing the emphasis of the sustainable growth of investee companies in the principles of the Japanese Stewardship Code as such idea would sometimes contradict with the interest of clients and ultimate beneficiaries).

[52] Japanese Code 2017 (n 2) 13, Guidance 4-4.

[53] Japanese Code 2017 (n 2) 15, Guidance 5-3; 田原泰雅＝染谷浩史＝安井桂大 (Yasumasa Tahara, Hiroshi Someya and Keita Yasui), 'スチュワードシップコード改訂の解説 (Suchuwadoshippu codo kaitei no kaisetsu) [Commentaries on the Revision of the Stewardship Code]' (2017) 2138 商事法務(Shojihomu) [Commercial Law Review] 15, 21. This individual disclosure requirement was not included in the original 2014 version owing to the objections from the industry and some investors. 神作裕之 (Hiroyuki Kansaku), 'コーポレートガバナンス向上に向けた内外の動向:スチュワードシップ・コードを中心として(Koporeto gabanansu kojyo ni muketa naigai no doko – Suchuwadoshippu kodo wo chushin toshite) [Developments towards the Improvement of Corporate Governance in Japan and Other Countries: With Focus on Stewardship Codes]' (2014) 2030 商事法務 (Shojihomu) [Commercial Law Review] 11, 19. The Japanese Code 2017 also calls for effective control of conflicts of interest of asset managers, especially those belonging to financial conglomerates (Japanese Code 2017 (n 2) 11, Guidance 2-2, 2-3, 2-4).

[54] Japanese Code 2020 (n 3) 17, Guidance 5-3.

[55] Japanese Code 2017 (n 2) 9–10, Guidance 1-3, 1-4, 1-5. The 2020 revision has clarified that it does not intend to overburden asset owners with stewardship activities beyond their size and capacity (Japanese Code 2020 (n 3) 12, Guidance 1-3, 1-4, 1-5).

a mid-/long-term view as their options to sell shares are limited and thus they are more affected by the mid-/long-term growth of investee companies.[56]

10.4.2 *Enforcement*

10.4.2.1 List of Signatories

The Japanese Stewardship Code requests institutional investors that have accepted the Code to disclose their acceptance on their webpage and to explain how they comply with the principles and guidance of the Code (or why they do not comply with them).[57] It also requests such institutional investors to notify the FSA of their adoption of the Code, and the FSA to publicize the list of such institutional investors ('signatories' to the Code).[58] Table 10.2 shows the composition of these signatories as of 27 December 2019.[59]

Unlike the UK, where asset managers are required by the regulator to develop and publicly disclose an engagement policy, and also disclose the nature of their commitment to the UK Stewardship Code,[60] there is no formal obligation on any kind of institution to adopt the Japanese Stewardship Code. However, the signatories include most of Japan's major domestic trust banks, insurance companies and investment management companies, suggesting the existence of de facto pressure from the FSA, their regulator, to accept the Code.[61] It is also noteworthy that the Government Pension Investment Fund (GPIF), which is responsible for the management of Japan's national pension fund and is one of the largest institutional investors in the world, has been advocating for stewardship by including investment management companies' attitude on stewardship as one of the factors to consider in selecting asset managers, even for passive investments.[62]

TABLE 10.2 *Signatories to the Japanese Code as of 27 December 2019*

Type of signatory	Number of signatories
Trust banks	6
Investment managers (mutual funds and investment advisers)	188
Pension funds	49
Insurance companies	23
Other institutions (including proxy advisers)	7
Total	273

---

[56] Japanese Code 2017 (n 2) 13, Guidance 4-2.
[57] Japanese Code 2017 (n 2) 6–7, Preamble para 13.
[58] Japanese Code 2014 (n 1) 4 para 14 and Japanese Code 2017 (n 2) 6–7 para 13.
[59] Financial Services Agency, 'List of Institutional Investors Signing Up to "Principles for Responsible Institutional Investors" «Japan's Stewardship Code»' (5 April 2018) <www.fsa.go.jp/en/refer/councils/stewardship/20180405/en_list_01.pdf> accessed 13 July 2020.
[60] Financial Conduct Authority, Conduct of Business Sourcebook, 2.2B.5R (10/06/2019) and 2.2.3R (06/12/2010).
[61] 有吉尚哉 (Naoya Ariyoshi), 'スチュワードシップ・コード改訂への実務対応 (Suchuwadoshippu kodo kaitei heno jitsumu taio) [Practical Issues in Response to the Revision of the Stewardship Code]' (2017) 2141商事法務 (Shojihomu) [*Commercial Law Review*] 84, 91.
[62] Government Pension Investment Fund, 'Stewardship Activities Report 2018' (February 2019) 10–12, 28 <www.gpif.go.jp/en/investment/gpif_stewardship_activities_report_2018.pdf> accessed 13 July 2020.

On the other hand, adoption by private pension funds of Japanese companies is limited,[63] despite the effort of the 2017 revision to encourage stewardship activities by asset owners.[64] The reason for the low adoption rate by pension funds seems to be multi-fold. First, most of the private pension funds are small in size, holding less than 10 billion yen, and cannot afford to hire sufficient staff for stewardship activities.[65] Second, the beneficiaries of private pension funds are employees who are unlikely to monitor such funds effectively owing to collective action problems. Third, while the Defined-Benefit Corporate Pension Act stipulates that directors of a pension fund owe the duty of loyalty to the fund,[66] it does not provide that the beneficiaries of the fund can sue its directors for breach of their duty.[67] Fourth, unlike trust banks or investment managers, private pension funds are not supervised by the FSA and thus do not face regulatory pressure to sign up (except for those financial companies which are regulated by the Agency).[68] In this regard, the role of their regulator, the Ministry of Health, Labor and Welfare, would be crucial for active stewardship by private pension funds.[69]

Interestingly, 63 out of the 188 investment-manager (mutual funds and investment advisers) signatories are foreign institutions.[70] Among them are several activist hedge funds including Brandes Investment Partners, Dalton Investments, Effissimo Capital Management, Kohlberg Kravis Roberts & Co., Oasis Management Company, and Taiyo Pacific Partners. Some Japanese activists, such as SPARX Asset Management Co. and Strategic Capital, have also signed up.

---

[63] Tahara, Someya and Yasui (n 53) 18; 上田亮子 (Ryoko Ueda), '日本版スチュワードシップ・コードの改訂～機関投資家の役割と実効性の強化 (Nihonban suchuwadoshippu kodo no kaitei ~ Kikantoshika no yakuwari to jikkosei no kyoka) [The Revision of the Japanese Stewardship Code: The Role of Institutional Investors and Strengthening of Its Effectiveness]' (2017) 382 資本市場 (Shihon Shijyo) [Capital Market] 26, 30. Out of forty-nine pension-fund signatories as of 27 December 2019, thirteen are public pensions, three are foreign funds, four are association of private pension funds and twenty are pension funds of companies under the supervision of the FSA, such as banks and insurance companies. This leaves only 9 signatories that are pension funds of individual companies, out of a total of 762 private pension funds as of 1 January 2020. For total number of private pension funds, see 企業年金連合会(Kigyo Nenkin Rengokai) [Pension Fund Association], '企業年金に関する基本統計 (Kigyō nenkin ni kansuru kihon tōkei) [Basic Statistics on Corporate Pensions]' <www.pfa.or.jp/activity/tokei/nenkin/index.html> accessed 13 July 2020.

[64] Tahara, Someya and Yasui (n 53) 17–18.

[65] Ueda (n 63) 30. The 2018 revision of the Japanese Corporate Governance Code attempts to improve the situation by requesting listed companies to provide necessary human resources to their pension funds (Japanese Corporate Governance Code 2018 (n 31) 12, Principle 2.6).

[66] 確定給付企業年金法 (Kakutei Kyufu Kigyo-nenkin Ho) [Defined-Benefit Corporate Pension Act], Law No 50 of 2001, art 70, para 1.

[67] Ariyoshi (n 61) 91 suggests that fiduciary duties of directors of private pension funds would call for adequate stewardship activities, without mentioning how such duties should be enforced.

[68] Ariyoshi (n 61) 91.

[69] The Ministry of Health, Labor and Welfare, in collaboration with the Pension Fund Association (PFA), has issued a report to foster adoption of the Japanese Stewardship Code by private pension funds. スチュワードシップ検討会 (Suchuwadoshippu Kentokai) [The Study Group on Stewardship], '企業年金と日本版スチュワードシップ・コード (Kigyo nenkin to nihonban suchuwadoshippu kodo) [Corporate Pensions and the Japanese Stewardship Code]' (17 March 2017) <www.pfa.or.jp/kanyu/shiryo/stewardship/houkoku/files/all.pdf> accessed 13 July 2020. The PFA is an association of private pension funds and has been active in stewardship activities since early 2000s. See Bruce E Aronson, 'A Japanese CalPERS or a New Model for Institutional Investor Activism? Japan's Pension Fund Association and the Emergence of Shareholder Activism in Japan' (2011) 7 NYU Journal of Law & Business 571.

[70] The number of foreign investment managers is obtained by counting those without a corporate number that is assigned to legal persons established under Japanese law. Corporate numbers of signatories are only shown in the Japanese version of the list of signatories. See 金融庁 (Kinyucho) [Financial Services Agency], '『責任ある機関投資家の諸原則』≪日本版スチュワードシップ・コード≫～投資と対話を通じて企業の持続的成長を促すために ("Sekinin aru kikan tōshi-ka no sho gensoku"≪ nipponban suchuwādoshippu kōdo ≫~ tōshi to taiwa o tsūjite kigyō no jizoku-teki seichō o unagasu tame ni) ['List of Institutional Investors Signing Up to "Principles for Responsible Institutional Investors" «Japan's Stewardship Code»]' (5 April 2018) <www.fsa.go.jp/singi/stewardship/list/20180405/list_01.pdf> accessed 13 July 2020.

In addition, there are three foreign pension funds, namely, CalPERS, Fourth Swedish National Pension Fund, and the University of California. While the number of signatories itself does not guarantee the effectiveness of the Stewardship Code in improving the quality of institutional investors' engagement,[71] it is still noteworthy that foreign institutional investors, especially activist hedge funds, took the trouble of signing up to the Japanese Stewardship Code, which features rather investee company–friendly principles and guidance.[72] One possible reason for this move is that, by signing up, these investors are trying to portray themselves as long-term investors supportive of the 'sustainable growth of investee companies', and to dilute their image as hostile activists.[73] This tactic, however, may not be that effective as companies are unlikely to be so naïve as to believe in a declaration of this sort that is not supported by formal sanctions.

10.4.2.2 No Tiering System

To improve the quality of stewardship, in 2016 the Financial Reporting Council of the UK introduced the so-called tiering system, which classifies the signatories to the UK Stewardship Code into three tiers based on the quality of their disclosure on stewardship.[74]

Although the variance in the quality of disclosure was also one of the issues in Japan for the 2020 revision, the Council of Experts did not consider adoption of the tiering system as a solution.[75] Instead, the Council decided to request more specific disclosure, namely, of the reasons for the votes cast, to improve the quality of disclosure.[76] It might be the case that the FSA views its de facto pressure as being more effective than a tiering system, as the former seems to have played out quite well in persuading major domestic institutions that have signed up to the Japanese Stewardship Code to comply with the requirement on disclosure of voting records on individual agenda items, which was introduced in the 2017 revision.[77]

---

[71] Arad Reisberg, 'The UK Stewardship Code: On the Road to Nowhere?' (2015) 15 *Journal of Corporate Law Studies* 217, 224–26. See also Konstantinos Sergakis, 'The UK Stewardship Code: Bridging the Gap between Companies and Institutional Investors' (2013) 47 *Revue juridique Thémis de l'Université de Montreal* 109, 136.

[72] See Section 10.4.1.1.

[73] See Tanaka (n 51) 37–38 (suggesting that, if the Japanese Stewardship Code had taken more adversarial stance, Japanese domestic institutions would have been more reluctant to sign up to the Code).

[74] Financial Reporting Council, 'Tiering of 2012 Stewardship Code Signatories' <www.frc.org.uk/investors/uk-stewardship-code/uk-stewardship-code-statements> accessed 13 July 2020.

[75] The tiering system in the UK was introduced to the Council of Experts Concerning the Follow-Up of Japan's Stewardship Code and Japan's Corporate Governance Code, a body also established by the FSA, and recommends revision of the Japanese Stewardship Code to the Council of Experts on the Stewardship Code, together with its negative evaluation by the Kingman Review (John Kingman, 'Independent Review of the Financial Reporting Council' (Department for Business, Energy and Industrial Strategy, December 2018) <https://assets.publishing.service.gov.uk/government/uploads/system/uploads/attachment_data/file/767387/frc-independent-review-final-report.pdf> accessed 13 July 2020). See the Council of Experts Concerning the Follow-Up of Japan's Stewardship Code and Japan's Corporate Governance Code, 'Minutes of the 18th Meeting' (5 March 2019) <www.fsa.go.jp/en/refer/councils/follow-up/minutes/20190305.pdf> accessed 13 July 2020.

[76] Japanese Code 2020 (n 3) 17, Guidance 5-3.

[77] Despite strong opposition raised by some institutional investors and investee companies during the discussions at the Council of Experts, most major trust banks, insurance companies and investment advisers have quickly complied with the requirement on disclosure of voting records on individual agenda items, suggesting strong pressure from the FSA. For details, see Goto, 'The Logic and Limits of Stewardship Codes' (n 12) 401–403. Nippon Life Insurance, which was the only major player who had been resisting this requirement, finally started to disclose its individual voting records from September 2019. 日本生命保険相互会社 (Nihon Seimei Hoken Sogo Gaisha) [Nippon Life Insurance Mutual Company], 国内株式議決権行使結果の開示について (*Kokunai Kabushiki Giketsuken Koshi Kekka no Kaiji ni tsuite*) [On Disclosure of Voting Records of Domestic Stocks] (3 September 2019) <www.nissay.co.jp/news/2019/pdf/20190903.pdf> accessed 13 July 2020.

10.4.2.3 Effects of the Japanese Stewardship Code

Has the Japanese Stewardship Code been successful in changing the reluctance of domestic institutional investors to take a tough stance against management?

Although, to the best of the author's knowledge as of May 2020, there are few empirical studies analyzing the effect of the Japanese Code, in particular that of disclosure of votes for individual agenda items,[78] there is some anecdotal evidence suggesting that domestic institutional investors affiliated with large financial groups have changed their behaviour to avoid being criticized for conflict of interests as they are required to disclose how they voted for individual agenda items.[79] For example, Mitsubishi UFJ Trust Bank disclosed that it had voted against the re-election of directors of Mitsubishi Motors in December 2016, which was surprising as both companies belong to Mitsubishi group, one of the six largest *keiretsu* known for its strong group unity.[80] Also, in June 2017, Mizuho Trust Bank supported a shareholder's proposal that was opposed by the management of its parent company, Mizuho Financial Group.[81]

Moreover, the recent surge of hedge fund activism[82] and also the return of hostile takeovers in 2019[83] might be a result of higher expectations of activists and hostile bidders for support from domestic institutional investors.

---

[78] See 浜田宰 (Osamu Hamada), '議決権行使結果の個別開示をめぐる議論と機関投資家の対応状況 (Giketsuken koshi kekka no kobetsu kaiji wo meguru giron to kikan toshika no taio jyokyo) [Discussions on the Disclosure of Individual Voting Results and the Responses of Institutional Investors]' (2017) 2145 商事法務 (*Shojihomu*) [*Commercial Law Review*] 37, 40–41, 42, 43 fn 22 (citing a descriptive statistic reporting that at the shareholders' meetings of companies comprising the Nikkei 225 index in June 2017, the amount of decrease of the average ratio of votes supporting proposals made by the management, except for those on anti-takeover measures, was less than one percentage point). See also Yasutomo Tsukioka, 'The Impact of Japan's Stewardship Code on Shareholder Voting' (2020) 67 *International Review of Economics & Finance* 148 (studying the effects of the original Japanese Stewardship Code using data of investee companies from 2010 to 2016 on the ratio of shares held by institutional investors that adopted the Code and the ratio of votes for and against on the appointment of directors); and Yutaro Shiraishi, Naoshi Ikeda, Yasuhiro Arikawa and Kotaro Inoue, 'Stewardship Code, Institutional Investors, and Firm Value: International Evidence' (2019) RIETI Discussion Paper Series 19-E-077 <www.rieti.go.jp/jp/publications/dp/19e077.pdf> accessed 13 July 2020 (conducting a cross-country difference-in-differences analysis on the effects of the adoption of stewardship codes, reporting increases in the value of firms with high institutional ownership and mitigation of the free cash flow problem of the portfolio firms with low investment opportunities).

[79] Hamada (n 78) 41.

[80] 日本経済新聞 (Nihon Keizai Shinbun) [Japan Economics Newspaper], '三菱UFJ信託、三菱自動車の人事案に「NO」投資の論理前面に (Mitsubishi UFJ Shintaku, Mitsubishi Jidosha no jinjian ni "no" Toshi no ronri zenmenni) [Mitsubishi UFJ Trust Votes Against the Nomination of Directors in Mitsubishi Motors: The Logic of Investment Comes to the Fore]' (31 May 2017) <www.nikkei.com/article/DGXLASDC31H1Z_R30C17A5EE9000/> accessed 13 July 2020. While the shareholders' meeting in question was held before the 2017 revision of the Japanese Stewardship Code, disclosure of individual voting records had already been proposed by another council at the FSA on 30 November 2016. See The Council of Experts Concerning the Follow-Up of Japan's Stewardship Code and Japan's Corporate Governance Code, 'Effective Stewardship Activities of Institutional Investors – To Enhance Constructive Dialogue toward Sustainable Corporate Growth' (Opinion Statement No 3, 30 November 2016) 3–4 <www.fsa.go.jp/en/refer/councils/follow-up/statements_3.pdf> accessed 13 July 2020.

[81] 宮本岳則＝南雲ジェーダ (Takenori Miyamoto and Jeda Nagumo), '議決権行使で親会社に「反旗」アセマネOneなど (Giketsuken koshi de oyagaisha ni "hanki" Asemane Wan nado) [Rising in "Revolt" against the Parent Company in Voting of Shares: Asset Management One and Others]' 日本経済新聞 (*Nihon Keizai Shinbun*) (30 August 2017) <www.nikkei.com/article/DGXLASGD30H5H_Q7A830C1EE9000/> accessed 13 July 2020.

[82] Leo Lewis and Kana Inagaki, 'Funds Bullish as Japan Hums with Activism' *Financial Times* (Tokyo, 17 May 2019) <www.ft.com/content/7263a14e-77dc-11e9-bbad-7c18c0ea0201> accessed 13 July 2020.

[83] Min Jeong Lee, 'Shareholder Activism Rises in Japan as Firms Go Hostile and Investors Speak Out' *Japan Time* (16 December 2019) <www.japantimes.co.jp/news/2019/12/16/business/activist-shareholders-hostile-bids-japan/#.XluodZP7Qyk> accessed 13 July 2020.

10.5 THE 2020 REVISION OF THE JAPANESE STEWARDSHIP CODE

10.5.1 *ESG Issues*

The 2020 revision has attracted attention as it adds references to environmental, social and governance (ESG) issues in various places throughout the Code.[84] To start, the definition of stewardship responsibilities has been revised by adding at its end the phrase 'and their business environment and consideration of sustainability (medium- to long-term sustainability including ESG factors) corresponding to their investment management strategies'.[85] The same phrase, without the definition of sustainability in the parentheses, is also added to Principle 7 regarding the necessary skills and resources of institutional investors.[86] Moreover, institutional investors are required to disclose 'how they take the issues of sustainability into consideration in their policy, corresponding to their investment management strategies'.[87] Some might compare these changes to the UK Code 2020, which emphasized the importance of environmental and social issues including climate change.[88]

In the author's view, however, the 2020 revision does not alter the basic orientation of the Japanese Stewardship Code towards the interest of beneficiaries of institutional investors and shareholders of listed companies.[89] This is clear from the fact that the revised definition of stewardship responsibilities maintains its structure, placing enhancement of 'the medium- to long-term investment return for their clients and beneficiaries by improving and fostering the investee companies' corporate value and sustainable growth' as its goal.[90] Also, the 2020 revision inserts a new paragraph in the guidance section stating: 'Institutional investors, when they engage in the issues of sustainability, should be conscious to promote dialogue that is consistent with their investment management strategies and that leads to the medium- to long-term increase of corporate value and the sustainable growth of companies',[91] to meet the concern raised in the Council that over-emphasis on ESG issues in the Stewardship Code may lead to irresponsibility of management of investee companies at the expense of profitability and growth, which were the original goals of adopting the Stewardship Code.[92]

Nevertheless, an institutional investor is responsible to its beneficiaries to consider ESG issues in its stewardship activities if it advertises including ESG factors in its strategy. As ESG

---

[84] See e.g. Mari Ishibashi, 'Japanese Watchdog Wants Asset Managers to Focus on ESG' *Nikkei Asian Review* (Tokyo, 10 December 2019) <https://asia.nikkei.com/Business/Finance/Japanese-watchdog-wants-asset-managers-to-focus-on-ESG> accessed 13 July 2020.
[85] Japanese Code 2020 (n 3) 5.
[86] ibid 10.
[87] ibid 11, Guidance 1-2.
[88] UK Code 2020 (n 9) 5.
[89] It is also noteworthy that the Japanese Stewardship Code has been referring to social and environmental issues since the original 2014 Code as one of the risk factors of investee companies that institutional investors should monitor: Japanese Code 2014 (n 1) 9, Guidance 3-3.
[90] Japanese Code 2020 (n 3) 5.
[91] ibid 15, Guidance 4-2. Also, wherever a reference to consideration of sustainability is made, such reference is always qualified such that the consideration shall correspond to or be consistent with investment management strategies of institutional investors. See Japanese Code 2020 (n 3) 5 (definition of stewardship responsibilities), 10 (Principle 7), 11 (Guidance 1-1 and 1-2), 15 (Guidance 4-2), 20 (Guidance 7-1).
[92] The Council of Experts on the Stewardship Code (FY2019), 'Minutes of the 2nd Meeting' (8 November 2019) 35–38 (statement by Professor Wataru Tanaka) <www.fsa.go.jp/en/refer/councils/stewardship/minutes/20191108.pdf> accessed 13 July 2020. The stakeholder-oriented nature of the traditional Japanese corporate governance system suggests that Japanese listed companies have been rather enthusiastic on environmental and social issues. See Souichirou Kozuka, 'Corporate Governance Reform, Social Norms and Sustainability in Japanese Companies' in Beate Sjåfjell and Christopher M Bruner (eds), *Cambridge Handbook of Corporate Law, Corporate Governance and Sustainability* (CUP 2019) 446.

investment is gradually getting some traction in Japan,[93] the reference to ESG issues in the 2020 revision might turn out to have a substantial impact on stewardship in Japan.

10.5.2 Expanding the Scope of Assets

The Council of Experts also discussed whether Japan should follow the UK Code 2020, which expanded its scope to all classes of assets including fixed income bonds and real estate. While the responsibility of institutional investors to enhance investment returns for their clients and beneficiaries should apply regardless of the type of assets of their investment,[94] a concern was raised in the Council that the interest of creditors may sometimes conflict with that of shareholders.[95]

Accordingly, the 2020 revision maintains the current primary focus on Japanese listed shares, while admitting the applicability of the Stewardship Code 'to other asset classes as far as it contributes to fulfilling the stewardship responsibilities' as defined by the Code.[96] As such, the actual impact of this expansion of the scope may be limited.

10.5.3 Service Providers to Institutional Investors

The 2020 revision follows the UK Code 2020 in introducing a separate principle for providers of services to institutional investors, such as proxy advisers and investment consultants for pension funds.[97] While the issue of proxy advisers' responsibility is already covered by Guidance 5–5 introduced by the 2017 revision, the 2020 revision goes into more detail on three points. This was done in response to complaints from investee companies alleging that proxy advisers issue advice based on inaccurate understandings of circumstances in individual companies (while proxy advisers are becoming more influential as the ratio of passive funds grows).[98]

First, the 2020 revision requests proxy advisers to 'develop appropriate and sufficient human and operational resources' to provide 'proxy recommendations based on accurate information on individual companies', including 'setting up a business establishment in Japan'.[99] Second, it also requests proxy advisers not to rely only on the disclosed information of companies and to exchange views actively with companies as necessary.[100] Third, it recommends proxy advisers to provide listed companies an opportunity to confirm whether information upon which proxy

---

[93] A questionnaire by the Japan Investment Advisors Association to its members in Fall 2019 shows that 25.5% of their investments to Japanese stocks take ESG factors into consideration. 日本投資顧問業協会 (Nihon Toshikomongyo Kyokai) [Japan Investment Advisors Association], '日本版スチュワードシップ・コードへの対応等に関するアンケート(第6回)の結果について (2019 年 10 月実施分)' (*Nihon-ban Suchuwadoshippu Kodo heno Taio-to ni kansuru Anketo (dai-6-kai) no Kekka ni tsuite (2019-nen 10-gatsu Jissi-bun))* [*The Results of the 6th Questionnaire on the Japanese Stewardship Code (October 2019)*]' (October 2019) 1<www.jiaa.or.jp/osirase/pdf/steward_enq2019.pdf> accessed 13 July 2020.

[94] In particular, if the goal of the Japanese Stewardship Code were the promotion of the interests of Japanese ultimate beneficiaries, then it should target institutional investors funded by Japanese interests investing in non-Japanese listed shares as well.

[95] See The Council of Experts on the Stewardship Code (FY2019) (n 92) 16–17 (statement by Mr Yuichi Haruta of Japanese Trade Union Confederation) 31–32 (statement by Mr Tetsuya Yonehana of Mitsubishi UFJ Trust Bank).

[96] Japanese Code 2020 (n 3) 8 para 10.

[97] ibid 10, Principle 8.

[98] The Council of Experts on the Stewardship Code (FY2019) (n 92) 8–9 (statement by Mr Akihiro Matsuyama of Mitsubishi Electric Corporation) 20–21 (statement by Mr Jyoji Okada of Japan Audit and Supervisory Board Member Association).

[99] Japanese Code 2020 (n 3) 22, Guidance 8-2.

[100] Japanese Code 2020 (n 3) 22, Guidance 8-3.

advisers have relied is accurate and to provide their clients with the opinions of the companies together with their recommendation.[101]

10.6 CONCLUSION

After the so-called lost two decades, Japan has been trying in the 2010s to change its corporate governance system from its traditional stakeholder-oriented one to a more shareholder-oriented one. The adoption of the Japanese Stewardship Code was one of the measures to achieve this goal by urging domestic institutional investors to take a tough stance against the management of their investee companies when necessary. To this end, the Japanese Stewardship Code was modelled on the practice of stewardship and engagement by institutional investors in the UK, as embodied in the UK Stewardship Code – rather than the UK Code itself (which aims to restrain excessive risk-taking and short-termism of shareholders) – with some modifications to weaken institutional investors' pressure on management to meet the reality of Japanese corporate governance.

This, however, does not necessarily mean that the Japanese Stewardship Code and the UK Stewardship Code are aiming to achieve completely different results. The commonality between the Japanese Stewardship Code and the UK Stewardship Code is their intention to change the alleged status quo in each country (i.e. stakeholder-oriented corporate governance in Japan and shareholders' short-termism in the UK). The result of these two stewardship codes might be the corporate governance systems of the two countries meeting somewhere in the middle of the shareholder/stakeholder spectrum, starting from its two poles. Whether this happens remains to be seen.

---

[101] ibid. This third pillar seems to be taken from the SEC's draft regulation on proxy advisers proposed on 5 November 2019 (US Securities and Exchange Commission, 'SEC Proposes Rule Amendments to Improve Accuracy and Transparency of Proxy Voting Advice' (5 November 2019) <www.sec.gov/news/press-release/2019-231> accessed 13 July 2020).

11

Korea's Stewardship Code and the Rise of Shareholder Activism

Agency Problems and Government Stewardship Revealed

Sang Yop Kang and Kyung-Hoon Chun

11.1 INTRODUCTION

Institutional investors' stewardship is one of the most frequently discussed concepts and phenomena in recent corporate governance scholarship. The stewardship movement initially started in the UK as a response to the 2008 Global Financial Crisis (GFC), which revealed many corporate governance problems and led to a loss of investor confidence in the capital market. The UK established its Stewardship Code in 2010 (UK Code).[1] Later, the trend of stewardship gained momentum globally as many jurisdictions adopted stewardship codes.[2] Korea also joined in the movement by officially instating its stewardship code in 2016 (Korean Code).[3]

This chapter elucidates the features, impacts and implications of stewardship in Korea and its related shareholder activism. As will be discussed in Section 11.3, the Korean Code is remarkably similar to the UK Code in terms of the language it uses.[4] However, there are notable differences between these two countries as to the motivations and implications of stewardship and shareholder activism.

Above all, a significant difference lies between the motivations that propelled the adoption of the codes in both countries. A major concern behind the UK Code is the dormancy of institutional investors in 'ownerless corporations', a phenomenon found in a regime with widely-held shareholding.[5] On the contrary, the typical ownership structure of Korean corporations is characterized by the presence of strong controlling (family) shareholders. One of the primary purposes of stewardship in Korea is to keep such controlling shareholders in check, particularly by curbing 'tunnelling',[6] namely the transfer of wealth to controlling shareholders at the expense of non-controlling shareholders.

In relation to stewardship, another unique feature in Korea is the presence of the National Pension Service (NPS), which is the largest institutional investor in Korea and the third-largest

---

[1] Financial Reporting Council, *The UK Stewardship Code* (July 2010) <www.frc.org.uk/getattachment/e223e152-5515-4cdc-a951-da33e093eb28/UK-Stewardship-Code-July-2010.pdf> accessed 4 July 2020.
[2] For more explanation, see Katelouzou and Puchniak, Global Shareholder Stewardship, Chapter 1 and Katelouzou and Siems, The Global Diffusion of Stewardship Codes, Chapter 30.
[3] Korea Stewardship Code Council, '기관투자자의 수탁자책임에 관한 원칙 (gigwantujaja-ui sutakja-chaegim-e gwanhan wonchig) [Principles on the Stewardship Responsibilities of Institutional Investors]' (2016) <http://sc.cgs.or.kr/about/sc.jsp> accessed 4 July 2020 [hereinafter Korean Code]. The English version is available at <http://sc.cgs.or.kr/eng/about/sc.jsp> accessed 4 July 2020.
[4] See Section 11.3.
[5] See n 10 and its accompanying text.
[6] For a further explanation of tunnelling, see Simon Johnson, Rafael La Porta, Florencio Lopez-de-Silanes and Andrei Shleifer, 'Tunneling' (2000) 90 *American Economic Review* 22.

public pension fund in the world. The NPS became a participant of the Korean Code in 2018.[7] Even before the official participation in the Korean Code, however, the NPS was involved in shareholder activism more frequently than many other institutional investors. Regarding the NPS's role in stewardship and shareholder activism in Korea, there are two opposite assessments.

On the one hand, shareholder activism in Korea, which was almost non-existent in the past, is now emerging, if not fully developed. Reports show that, currently, institutional investors are involved in more active engagement with their investee companies.[8] It seems that this trend was triggered, at least partially, by the introduction of the Korean Code. The presence of the NPS – a significant investor in the domestic capital market and a powerful advocate of shareholder activism – acts as a catalyst in spreading stewardship and contributes to developing shareholder activism in Korea in a more effective and sophisticated manner.

On the other hand, since the NPS is a quasi-government agency, it is possible that the government, under the name of stewardship and shareholder activism, may intervene in the decision-making process of corporate policies and strategies even in private corporations. In essence, the autonomy of market players may be damaged. A related concern is that the government may use stewardship as a powerful policy tool to guide or, to put it more bluntly, to direct the private sector in a direction associated with a certain socio-political agenda which has less to do with the financial benefits of the NPS's beneficiaries. In other words, the NPS may create an agency problem and, in turn, injure the interest of its own ultimate beneficiaries.

Against this backdrop, the remainder of this chapter is organized as follows. Section 11.2 sketches out the motivation for introducing the Korean Code. Section 11.3 explains the contents and the enforcement mechanism of the Korean Code. Subsequently, Section 11.4 explores the impacts and implications of the Korean Code, and rigorously examines, in particular, the NPS's role associated with the Korean Code and shareholder activism. Finally, Section 11.5 summarizes and concludes the chapter.

11.2 THE MOTIVATION FOR INTRODUCING THE KOREAN CODE

11.2.1 *Overview: Different Motivations of Stewardship Codes*

The UK Code 2010, the first one of its kind, which became an exemplar for many other countries to follow, was intended to encourage the 'ownership mindset' of institutional investors in the absence of active owners in the investee companies.[9] Such motivation is apparent from various sources that preceded the code. For example, in the middle of the financial crisis, Paul Myners, the Financial Services Secretary to the Treasury of the UK, described the institutional investors as 'absentee landlords' and criticized that their inactivity resulted in 'ownerless corporations'.[10] The Walker Review of 2009, which prompted the FRC's adoption of the UK Code, argued that 'more vigorous scrutiny and engagement by major investors acting as owners' would have tackled

---

[7] Institutional investors who participated in the Korean Code are called 'participants' rather than 'signatories' to avoid any impression that the Code has binding effects like a signed contract.

[8] See Section 11.4.

[9] See e.g. Charles Cronin and John Mellor, 'An Investigation into Stewardship – Engagement between Investors and Public Companies: Impediments and Their Resolution' (Foundation for Governance Research and Education June 2011) 12 <www.foundationgre.com/Stewardship%20Report%20Final%20-%2022.6.11.pdf> accessed 4 July 2020 (stating that stewardship is 'synonymous with an ownership mindset').

[10] Lee Roach, 'The UK Stewardship Code' (2011) 11 *Journal of Corporate Law Studies* 463, 463.

the problems of the investee company.[11] The need to address problems of ownerless corporations, such as short-termism, motivated the adoption of the UK Code in the aftermath of the GFC.[12]

In Korea, the motivation was different. Unlike its UK counterpart that it was modelled on, the usual targets of the Korean Code were corporations that had strong controlling (family) shareholders. At the risk of oversimplifying, one may say that the Korean Code intended to address problems of strong but less-than-majority owners, while the UK Code intended to address problems of ownerless corporations. A brief look at corporate governance problems in Korea sheds light on this motivation.

11.2.2 Corporate Governance Problems in Korea

The well-known success of the Korean economy is heavily owed to the entrepreneurship of the founders of *chaebols* and their legendary growth.[13] *Chaebol* refers to a large group of related corporations engaged in diverse lines of business under highly concentrated family or individual control.[14] Large *chaebols* such as Samsung, Hyundai Motors, SK, LG, Lotte, GS, Hanwha, Hyundai Heavy Industry, Shinsegae, Doosan, and Hanjin have played crucial roles in Korea's economic development. Most of them started their businesses in the early or mid-twentieth century as small family-run enterprises and expanded rapidly throughout the late twentieth and early twenty-first century. They still represent a critical portion of the Korean economy in terms of revenue, exports, hiring, tax payment, patents and so forth.[15]

The governance structures of *chaebols* are diverse. Usually, only a few large flagship companies or holding companies at the top of the group structure are listed on the stock exchange, with many other affiliates being unlisted. The key person of the family typically holds a title such as Chair or Honorary Chair and exercises control over the management of the entire group, either as the CEO of the core company or as a de facto or shadow director who is not officially a member of the board. The controlling family members' shareholding ratio in the listed core company of each *chaebol* is mostly far less than 50 per cent and, in many cases, less than 10 per cent. However, circular shareholdings or pyramidal structures that tie together the member companies enable the controlling shareholders to exercise control over the entire group substantially greater than their cash flow rights – a typical problem of 'controlling minority shareholders' which often results in conflicts of interest between controlling shareholders and non-controlling shareholders.

Many corporate governance problems in Korea stem from this 'controlling minority shareholder' structure. Controlling families frequently engage in tunnelling by way of related party transactions, issuance of undervalued stocks, and unfair mergers to siphon off the value of group

---

[11] David Walker, 'A Review of Corporate Governance in UK Banks and Other Financial Industry Entities: Final Recommendations' (26 November 2009) <https://ecgi.global/sites/default/files/codes/documents/walker_review_261109.pdf> accessed 4 July 2020.

[12] See Davies, The UK Stewardship Code 2010–2020, Chapter 2.

[13] Korea ranks twelfth in terms of nominal gross domestic production (GDP) by the International Monetary Fund (2019) and the World Bank (2018). See e.g. World Bank, 'GDP Ranking' (1 July 2020) <https://datacatalog.worldbank.org/dataset/gdp-ranking> accessed 4 July 2020.

[14] Hwa-Jin Kim, 'Living with the IMF: A New Approach to Corporate Governance and Regulation of Financial Institutions in Korea' (1999) 17 *Berkeley Journal of International Law* 61, 63.

[15] For a further explanation of *chaebol*, see Sea-Jin Chang, *Financial Crisis and Transformation of Korean Business Groups: The Rise and Fall of Chaebols* (CUP 2003) 9–24; Ok-Rial Song, 'The Legacy of Controlling Minority Structure: A Kaleidoscope of Corporate Governance Reform in Korean Chaebol' (2002) 34 *Law & Policy in International Business* 183, 190–207.

companies.[16] Such practices have been regulated as 'undue support' by the Korea Fair Trade Commission, the authority in charge of policing *chaebols*, and are subject to both criminal and administrative penalties. Unfair related party transactions have often been prosecuted as criminal breach of trust (*baeim* in Korean), which is subject to criminal penalties up to life imprisonment.[17]

In sum, many Korean companies, in particular large *chaebol* companies, have been vulnerable to the opportunistic behaviours of their controlling family members. Domestic institutional investors have generally been too weak (or rationally inert) to effectively monitor the controlling shareholders, except for the NPS, which will be discussed in Section 11.4. The few cases of shareholder activism by foreign hedge funds and domestic non-government organizations were no more than anecdotal. Derivative actions have been rare,[18] and class actions are allowed only for a very narrow scope of securities claims.[19] Under these circumstances, criminal and administrative sanctions were virtually the only effective tools to regulate controlling families' tunnelling.[20]

The unrestrained power of controlling families raised both political and financial concerns. On the political dimension, anti-*chaebol* sentiment became salient among the general public. To address this concern (or to cater to this sentiment), in the 2012 presidential election, presidential candidate Geun-Hye Park asserted 'economic democratization' as the main campaign agenda. Its exact meaning is still (perhaps inherently) unclear, but it generally encompassed various 'progressive' agenda items such as stronger regulation of *chaebols*, greater distribution of market power, protection of minority shareholders, and support for small and medium-sized enterprises (SMEs).[21] In spite of its semantic vagueness, it seems that the catchphrase of 'economic democratization' contributed to her winning the presidency.

On the financial and economic dimension, it was alleged that the risk of tunnelling and inefficiency under family ownership,[22] and, more generally, the so-called owner risks,[23] exacerbated the systematic discount of the Korean stock market.[24] To address this concern, the regulators

---

[16] For a theoretical analysis of tunnelling, see Sang Yop Kang, '"Generous Thieves": The Puzzle of Controlling Shareholder Arrangements in Bad-Law Jurisdictions' (2015) 21 *Stanford Journal of Law, Business & Finance* 57, 85–96.

[17] For the substantive constraints on the related party transactions in Korea, see Kon Sik Kim, 'Related Party Transactions in East Asia' in Luca Enriques and Tobias Tröger (eds), *The Law and Finance of Related Party Transactions* (CUP 2019) 285, 307–309, 323.

[18] Since the enactment of the Korean Commercial Code in 1962, Korean courts have encountered around sixty derivative actions. Kyung-Hoon Chun, 'Multiple Derivative Actions: Debates in Korea and the Implication for a Comparative Study' (2019) 15 *Berkeley Business Law Journal* 306, 310.

[19] Hyeok-Joon Rho and Kon Sik Kim, 'Invigorating Shareholder Derivative Actions in South Korea' in Dan W Puchniak, Harald Baum and Michael Ewing-Chow (eds), *The Derivative Action in Asia: A Comparative and Functional Approach* (CUP 2012) 186, 191.

[20] Most derivative actions were 'follow-up suits' preceded by criminal prosecutions or bankruptcy proceedings; ibid 195.

[21] In the 2012 presidential election, note that Geun-Hye Park, who pre-empted and utilized this agenda, was the candidate of the conservative party.

[22] One example of such inefficiency is illustrated in Sang Yop Kang, '"Game of Thrones": Corporate Governance Issues of Children's Competition in Family Corporations' (2018) 15 *Berkeley Business Law Journal* 185 (in the course of the competition among the children of a parent-controller to take over the management of the firm, the children may have an incentive to take on suboptimal projects at the risk of shareholders and creditors).

[23] It refers to negative impacts on firm value or stock price caused by the family controller's illegal or unethical scandals, incompetence in management, or health problems.

[24] Such a general undervaluation is called the 'Korea discount' and is still witnessed to date. For example, as of 30 December 2019, the P/B ratio (price to book-value ratio) of the KOSPI 200 corporations was 0.93 (Korea Exchange, '80005 PBR Trend' <https://marketdata.krx.co.kr/mdi#document=13010104> accessed 4 July 2020) and their PER (price to earnings ratio) was 16.64 (Korea Exchange, '80004 PER Trend' <https://marketdata.krx.co.kr/mdi#document=13010103> accessed 4 July 2020). They were much lower than global benchmarks. As of 31 December 2019, the P/B Ratio of S&P 500 corporations was 3.65 (Standard & Poor's, 'S&P 500 Price to Book Value' <www.multpl.com

had to find a mechanism for sound monitoring of the controlling family members and proper intervention in the management. Since the reform of corporate law was the task of the Ministry of Justice,[25] financial regulators such as the Financial Services Commission (FSC) and the Financial Supervisory Services (FSS) had to focus on strengthening regulations on the capital market by either hard or soft law. At that juncture, the general idea of stewardship that had begun to gain popularity in the UK and Japan attracted the attention of the Korean financial regulators.

11.2.3 Adoption of the Korean Stewardship Code

The 'Plan to Revitalize Korea's Stock Market', issued by the FSC on 26 November 2014,[26] was the first official document prepared by the government that specifically mentioned the need to adopt a 'Korean version of the stewardship code'. In that document, the FSC identified the most severe problem of the Korean stock market as the 'lack of trust on the capital market among investors' and proposed, among others: (i) expanding the scope of financial products traded on the market; (ii) reinforcing the role of the institutional investors; and (iii) restoring the trust of investors by improving the public disclosure system.[27] Adopting a 'Korean version of the stewardship code' to 'encourage the exercise of voting rights by the institutional investors' was mentioned as a measure to reinforce the role of institutional investors in Korean corporate governance.[28]

In March 2015, the FSC took the lead in composing a committee for the adoption of a stewardship code (first committee). Out of nine committee members, two were from the FSC and one was from the FSS. The first committee released a draft of the code on 2 December 2015, based on the stewardship codes of the UK and Japan.

However, it faced strong opposition from the business community. For example, in May 2016, the Federation of Korean Industries (FKI), known as a powerful association of *chaebols*, released a 'joint suggestion' together with four other business associations, namely: Korea Listed Companies Association (KLCA); KOSDAQ Listed Companies Association (KOSDAQA); Federation of Middle Market Enterprises of Korea; and Korea Federation of SMEs.[29] They criticized and opposed the draft code for many reasons, including the following:

- the code would make the market less lively by increasing the burden on the companies and the market participants;
- the code would permit excessive interference in private companies, not only by the institutional investors but also by the government;
- it is unclear whether active voting by the institutional investors will enhance firm value;
- it is unrealistic for listed firms to engage in dialogues with each institutional investor;
- confidential information of listed firms may be leaked and abused by the institutional investors;
- fairness and transparency of the proxy advisers are questionable;

/s-p-500-price-to-book> accessed 4 July 2020) and their PER was 24.21 (Standard & Poor's, 'S&P 500 PE Ratio' <www.multpl.com/s-p-500-pe-ratio> accessed 4 July 2020).

[25] In Korea, corporate law is part of the Commercial Code (*sangbeob* in Korean). The Ministry of Justice is in charge of the amendment to the Commercial Code.
[26] Financial Services Commission, 'Plan to Revitalize Korea's Stock Market' (Press Release, 26 November 2014) <https://www.fsc.go.kr/eng/pr010101/22071> accessed 13 February 2022.
[27] ibid.
[28] ibid.
[29] Federation of Korean Industries, '스튜어드십 코드 도입에 대한 경제단체 공동건의 (seutyueodeusib kodeu doib-e daehan gyeongje-danche gongdong-geon-ui) [Joint Suggestions of Business Communities on the Introduction of the Stewardship Code]' (2016) <www.fki.or.kr/Common/Download.aspx?id=b4c408a0-87af-44a2-ac19-4c91632c9094> accessed 4 July 2020.

- fees paid to the proxy advisers would negatively affect the return of investors; and
- the experiences of the UK and Japan show that the effect of a stewardship code is unclear.

After the first committee was dissolved, the second committee was composed in August 2016, this time under the leadership of the Korea Corporate Governance Service (KCGS). The KCGS is a private non-profit organization founded in 2002 whose major founding members/sponsors were: the Korea Exchange;[30] the Korea Financial Investment Association (KOFIA); the KLCA; and the KOSDAQA.[31] The eleven members of the second committee were composed of: three from the KCGS;[32] three from the finance industry;[33] two from academia;[34] one from KOFIA; one from the Korea Capital Market Institute (KCMI); and one from a foreign institutional investor.

The second committee heard comments from various industries and associations in revising the first committee's draft. On 18 November 2016, it released a draft of the Korean Stewardship Code titled 'Principles on the Stewardship Responsibilities of Institutional Investors'. After another public hearing on 5 December 2016, the final version was released on 16 December 2016. This is the current version of the Korean Code.

The KCGS was not free from the suspicion or impression that it was also under government influence, since the Korea Exchange, the largest member/sponsor of the KCGS, was under the strict supervision of the government (the FSC and the FSS). Indeed, a few key members of the KCGS played crucial roles in both the first and the second committees. Drafts of the code released by both committees were similar in substance – both were voluntary norms composed of seven principles that took a comply-or-explain approach. Compared to the first committee, however, the second committee appeared less connected to the government because no committee member was a government official. Such a difference made the second committee less threatening to the business community and helped foster the adoption of the Korean Code.[35]

11.3 CONTENTS AND THE ENFORCEMENT MECHANISM OF THE KOREAN CODE

11.3.1 *Contents of the Korean Code*

11.3.1.1 Overview

The Korean Code sets forth detailed principles and guidelines for institutional investors to abide by while investing in listed companies in Korea. It is composed of five parts: (i) purposes and

---

[30] The Korea Exchange is the sole operator of the stock exchanges in Korea. It operates, among others, KOSPI market (which is for established firms) and KOSDAQ market (which is similar to NASDAQ in the US).
[31] Note that the KLCA and the KOSDAQA joined the FKI in opposing the stewardship code as discussed. It is no wonder that the KLCA and the KOSDAQA, as founding members, complained to the KCGS for taking the initiative in making a stewardship code. Here a delicate difference can be observed between Main Street (traditional industry represented by the FKI and KLCA) and Wall Street (financial industry represented by the KRX and the KOFIA) in a Korean setting.
[32] Out of three members from the KCGS, one of them is a finance professor at Korea University who was the non-standing chairperson of the KCGS in 2016. The other two members, PhDs in economics, were (and still are) standing researchers at the KCGS.
[33] Two officers of asset management firms and one CEO of an investment advisory company.
[34] One law professor at a law school and one finance professor at a business school.
[35] Stewardship codes can be categorized into three groups, namely (i) those issued by the regulators or quasi-regulators on behalf of the government, (ii) those initiated by various market participants, and (iii) those initiated by investors themselves. The Korean Stewardship Code was referred to as an interesting example of the second group in Jennifer G Hill, 'Good Activist/Bad Activist: The Rise of International Stewardship Codes' (2018) 41 *Seattle University Law Review* 497, 508. It is a fair statement, but a Korean observer may put the Korean Code between the first and the second group since the influence of the government in steering the draft into its adoption was not nil.

meanings of introducing the Code; (ii) application of the Code; (iii) principles; (iv) guidelines; and (v) recommendations.

One noteworthy point is the choice of Korean terminology. The Korean Code uses *sutakja* for steward and *sutakja-chaeg-im* for stewardship.[36] *Sutakja* is a well-established legal term that refers to a trustee under the Trust Act of Korea. Since *chaeg-im* refers to duty, responsibility or liability, *sutakja-chaeg-im* refers to the duty of a trustee or fiduciary duty. From this choice of words, a few questions may follow. Is a steward the same as a trustee and stewardship the same as fiduciary duty? If so, or at least if stewardship is similar to fiduciary duty, to whom does the institutional investor owe such a duty? Short answers to these fundamental questions under the Korean Code are that the concept of steward is not exactly the same as that of trustee, but that an institutional investor owes a 'stewardship responsibility' similar to a trustee's fiduciary duty towards its clients and beneficiaries, rather than towards the investee company.[37] The Korean Code clearly states that institutional investors have a duty to act in the best interests of their clients and beneficiaries.[38]

11.3.1.2 The Meaning and Purposes of the Korean Code

The Korean Code defines stewardship as the 'responsibility of an institutional investor, as a manager of other people's assets, to aim for mid- to long-term benefits for the clients and the beneficiaries by pursuing mid- to long-term value and sustainable growth of the investee companies'.[39] The definition is not neatly translatable into English, but it contains keywords such as long-term value, sustainable growth and benefits of the beneficiaries. It further states that institutional investors are 'responsible for constructive engagement such as monitoring, and, if necessary, having active dialogues with the board of directors of the investee companies'.[40] By doing so, 'institutional investors will not only help promote the investee companies' mid- to long-term growth and enhance investor returns, but also support the growth and development of the capital markets and the overall economy'.[41]

The Korean Code applies to 'domestic and overseas institutional investors (i.e., asset owners and asset managers) holding shares of listed companies in Korea' and 'domestic and overseas proxy advisers and investment advisors' who advise the institutional investors.[42] The Korean Code 'is not legally binding' and 'only applies to the institutional investors and advisors who have agreed to the Code and declared voluntary participation'.[43] Once the institutional investors and advisers 'declare participation', the Korean Code is applied on a comply-or-explain basis as discussed in Section 11.3.2.

---

[36] The 'stewardship' in the UK Code 2012 is referred to as *sutakja-chaeg-im* in the Korean Code. However, in the English translation of the Korean Code, *sutakja-chaeg-im* is often translated into 'stewardship responsibility' instead of just 'stewardship'. In other words, the feature of stewardship as duty/responsibility is clearly perceived by the drafters of the Korean Code, and when the Korean Code is again translated into English, such a feature is even amplified.

[37] Korea Corporate Governance Service, 'Korean Stewardship Code Guidebook Ver. 1' (June 2017) 3 <http://sc.cgs.or.kr/common/aboutdown.jsp?fp=agMgb5yRtiV6r6qmSXlBSw%3D%3D&fnm=vMu02gZ4f674KbsHF0i1YiMc3K0kM6wXBXlHQC1UuH3E5Mp%2FMyScIcEXmkC1%2FSOW> accessed 4 July 2020 [hereinafter Korean Stewardship Code Guidebook]. This is a publication by the KCGS that explains and supplements the Korean Code.

[38] Korean Code (n 3) 8.
[39] ibid 1.
[40] ibid.
[41] ibid.
[42] ibid 2.
[43] ibid.

11.3.1.3 Principles

The Korean Code provides seven principles which are basically similar to the principles of the UK Code 2012.[44] Table 11.1 compares the English summary of the principles of the Korean Code and the comparable principles of the UK Code 2012.

TABLE 11.1 *Summary of the comparable principles of the Korean Code 2016 and the UK Code 2012*

Korean Code 2016	UK Code 2012
1. Institutional investors should establish and publicly disclose a clear policy on how to perform their stewardship responsibilities.[45]	1. Institutional investors should publicly disclose their policy on how they will discharge their stewardship responsibilities.
2. Institutional investors should establish and publicly disclose an effective and clear policy on conflicts of interest in the course of their stewardship activities.[46]	2. Institutional investors should have a robust policy on managing conflicts of interest in relation to stewardship which should be publicly disclosed.
3. Institutional investors should regularly monitor investee companies in order to enhance investee companies' mid- to long-term value and thereby protect and raise their investment value.[47]	3. Institutional investors should monitor their investee companies.
4. While institutional investors should aim to form a consensus with investee companies, where necessary, they should establish internal guidelines on the timeline, procedures, and methods for stewardship activities.[48]	4. Institutional investors should establish clear guidelines on when and how they will escalate their stewardship activities.
N/A	5. Institutional investors should be willing to act collectively with other investors where appropriate.
5. Institutional investors should establish and publicly disclose a voting policy and publicly disclose voting records and the reasons for each vote so as to allow the verification of the appropriateness of their voting activities.[49]	6. Institutional investors should have a clear policy on voting and disclosure of voting activity.
6. Institutional investors should regularly report their voting and stewardship activities to their clients or beneficiaries.[50]	7. Institutional investors should report periodically on their stewardship and voting activities.
7. Institutional investors should have the capabilities and expertise required to implement stewardship responsibilities in an active and effective manner.[51]	N/A

---

[44] Financial Reporting Council, *The UK Stewardship Code* (September 2012) <www.frc.org.uk/getattachment/d67933f9-ca38-4233-b603-3d24b2f62c5f/UK-Stewardship-Code-(September-2012).pdf> accessed 4 July 2020. The 2010 and 2012 versions of the UK code are almost identical (see Davies, The UK Stewardship Code 2010–2020, Chapter 2), but our focus here is the 2012 version because the Korean Code was drafted after the publication of, and under the influence of, the 2012 version. It is consistent with the empirical finding of Katelouzou and Siems that the 2012 version was the key basis for the diffusion of stewardship norms (see Katelouzou and Siems, The Global Diffusion of Stewardship Codes, Chapter 30).
[45] Korean Code (n 3) 6.
[46] ibid 8.
[47] ibid 9.
[48] ibid 10.
[49] ibid 11.
[50] ibid 13.
[51] ibid 14.

The principles declared in the Korean Code are very similar to those of the UK Code 2012, other than on three points. First, the UK Code's fifth principle on the collective action with other investors is not in the Korean Code because many members of the business community were opposed to the idea of requiring collective action among investors.[52] In addition, investors' collective action may complicate the situation owing to a legal issue: under the Financial Investment Services and Capital Markets Act (article 147), such a collective action may constitute 'an act in concert' and be subject to a filing requirement that is triggered when the aggregate shareholding of those acting in concert reaches 5 per cent and increases by 1 per cent. Second, while the UK Code's fourth principle refers to 'escalation' of stewardship activities, the Korean Code is silent on that issue.[53] Third, the Korean Code's seventh principle requires institutional investors to enhance their capabilities and expertise. This is not in the UK Code 2012, but was instead influenced by the Japanese Code 2014.[54]

11.3.2 *Enforcement Mechanism*

The Korean Code itself declares that it takes a comply-or-explain approach.[55] More specifically, its Korean text reads that 'the participants should in principle comply with the Code, and explain the reasons for non-compliance when exceptionally it cannot comply with the Code'.[56] It is slightly different from the UK Code which does not, at least explicitly, indicate that compliance is the principle and explanation is allowed only under exceptional circumstances. In essence, however, both the Korean Code and the UK Code are similar to each other in this respect because the principle of comply-or-explain in the UK is also based on the understanding that one can explain rather than comply only in exceptional circumstances.[57]

The Korean Code requires participants to disclose and update certain information on their respective homepage: whether they participated in the Code, how they complied with the Code, guidelines and reasons for non-compliance, and whether the Code equally applies to each fund the participant is managing (and details of differences, if any).[58] The KCGS monitors the participants' performance of their responsibilities. The KCGS also discloses the list of participants and links to their websites on its own website to facilitate access to the information by the market participants. According to the KCGS website, as of 3 March 2020, there are 124 participants to the Code: 3 pension funds; 5 insurance companies; 43 asset managers; 37 private equity funds; 3 securities companies; 2 investment advisers; 4 proxy advisers; 2 commercial banks; and 25 others.[59] Most of them are domestic entities other than a few foreign asset managers, private equity fund managers and one foreign proxy adviser (Glass Lewis). In particular, the largest and the most powerful participants such as pension funds, insurance companies and commercial banks are all domestic entities.

---

[52] See e.g. Federation of Korean Industries (n 29) 3.
[53] However, the Korean Stewardship Code Guidebook published by the KCGS provides a list of 'additional shareholder activities' to be considered by the institutional investors which correspond to the 'escalated stewardship activities' under the UK Code. See Korean Stewardship Code Guidebook (n 37) 36.
[54] See Goto, Japanese Stewardship Code, Chapter 10. This diffusion of stewardship norms from Japan 2014 to Korea 2016 is confirmed in Katelouzou and Siems, The Global Diffusion of Stewardship Codes, Chapter 30.
[55] The phrase 'comply or explain' appears in English in the Korean text within a parenthesis.
[56] Korean Code (n 3) 3.
[57] Notably, this is no longer the case for the UK Code 2020, which is based on an 'apply and explain' approach (Davies, The UK Stewardship Code 2010–2020, Chapter 2).
[58] Korean Code (n 3).
[59] KCGS, 'Institutional Investors Participating in the Korea Stewardship Code' <http://sc.cgs.or.kr/eng/participation/investors.jsp> accessed 3 March 2020. Most of the entities that fall under the category of 'others' are venture capitalists.

The Korean Code contemplates not only the participants' active voting but also ongoing engagement and consultation with the board of directors of the investee companies. Stewardship activity 'is not limited to the exercise of voting rights' but extends to 'monitoring of the core management matters such as strategy, performance, risk management, and governance' and further to 'consultation with the board of directors, shareholder proposals, and participation in litigation'.[60] It also states that 'stewardship activity does not mean intervention in the daily operation of the investee companies' and that 'the institutional investors may consider selling the shares of the investee companies if it is the best alternative for the benefit of the clients and the beneficiaries'.[61]

More specifically, the Korean Stewardship Code Guidebook provides an illustrative list of 'additional shareholder activities', which generally correspond to the 'escalated stewardship activities' under the UK Code. They include: (i) requests for additional information and documents; (ii) delivery of a questionnaire to the company; (iii) conferences with the chair of a board or the management; (iv) delivery of an opinion letter; (v) active speech and discussion at a general meeting of shareholders; (vi) voting against the agenda and publicly disclosing it; (vii) submitting shareholder proposals or joining other shareholders' proposals; (viii) requesting the board to call an extraordinary general meeting of shareholders; (ix) distribution of a press release and public statements; and (x) filing or joining lawsuits.[62]

Regarding the final point (i.e., legal remedies), the Korean Commercial Code (KCC), the main statute that governs Korean companies, provides various tools: the right to remove directors; the right to convene a general meeting of shareholders; and the right to submit shareholder proposals. First, shareholders may remove directors by a special resolution of a general meeting of shareholders *without* cause at any time.[63] Second, shareholders holding a certain percentage of shares may request that the board call an extraordinary general meeting of shareholders.[64] If the board rejects such a request, the shareholders may bring the case to the court. Third, shareholders holding a certain percentage of shares are entitled to submit a proposal to be resolved at a general meeting of shareholders.[65] The board of directors must include the proposed item on the agenda unless the proposal violates the law or the articles of incorporation. The Korean Code neither excludes nor clearly mentions such legal remedies, but institutional investors may resort to such remedies if necessary to protect investment value.

11.4 IMPACTS AND IMPLICATIONS OF THE KOREAN CODE

11.4.1 *General Outcome of the Korean Code*

11.4.1.1 Weak Shareholders Before the Introductions of the Stewardship Code

In Korea, before the Korean Code was adopted, shareholder activism had long been weak except for a few incidents that aggressive foreign institutional investors (in particular, hedge

---

[60] Korean Code (n 3) 3.
[61] ibid 2.
[62] Korean Stewardship Code Guidebook (n 37) 36; UK Code 2012 (n 44) 8.
[63] Korean Commercial Code, art 385(1).
[64] At least 3% of the total issued shares (Korean Commercial Code, art 366(1)). For a listed firm, the shareholding threshold is lowered to 1% if the shares have been held at least for six months (Korean Commercial Code, art 542-6(1)).
[65] At least 3% of the total issued shares (Korean Commercial Code, art 363-2(1)). For a listed firm, the shareholding threshold is lowered to 1% or 0.5% (depending on the size of the firm) if the shares have been held at least for six months (Korean Commercial Code, art 542-6(2)).

funds) were involved in.⁶⁶ To explain this phenomenon, this section provides four possible accounts.

First, weak shareholder activism may be attributed to the highly conservative business culture in Korea. Under this deep-rooted culture, shareholder activism is not a well-adapted concept in the nation's capital market. Until recently, if investors wanted to engage actively in investee companies, they were treated as mavericks in the business circle. An investor's active engagement in an investee company was often portrayed as a greedy financial capitalist's unethical interference with the management.

Second, unlike jurisdictions with more sophisticated capital markets, in Korea, institutional investors have held a relatively small percentage of shareholding across investee companies in the capital market.⁶⁷ Compared to retail investors, institutional investors are more sophisticated; in addition, they are equipped with expertise and an economic incentive to monitor and engage with their investee companies. Accordingly, the phenomenon of significant shareholding by retail investors in Korea has led to relatively weak shareholder activism.

Third, *chaebols* wield substantial influence in various sectors of the Korean economy, including the capital market. If institutional investors were to engage in shareholder activism, they would be more interested in economically significant companies. Such companies, however, are mostly affiliated companies of *chaebols*. In the *chaebol*-dominated economy, it was (and perhaps still is, to some extent) difficult for institutional investors to carry out shareholder activism, which aims to revamp the business malpractices of *chaebols* and their controlling shareholders. Also, *chaebols* have securities brokerage firms as well as institutional investors such as asset management firms and insurance companies. A *chaebol*'s own institutional investor is not inclined to engage in shareholder activism against the affiliated companies of other *chaebols*. This practice of non-intervention has been, expressly or implicitly, complied with in the business community dominated by *chaebols*.

Fourth, owing to the 'collective action problem',⁶⁸ which takes place in any jurisdiction (not to mention Korea), shareholder activism often does not provide an adequate economic incentive to investors. Suppose that an institutional investor engaging in shareholder activism holds a 1 per cent share in an investee company and initiates shareholder activism against it. On the one hand, when shareholder activism fails, the institutional investor bears the costs associated with shareholder activism, while the other institutional investors which were inert and did not participate in shareholder activism do not bear any cost. On the other hand, when shareholder activism succeeds and, subsequently, the market value of the target company is enhanced, the institutional investor – even though it was the only investor that carried out shareholder activism – gains only 1 per cent of the improved corporate value of the target company.⁶⁹

---

⁶⁶ These incidents include activism occasions by Sovereign Asset Management in SK Group and Elliott Associates in Samsung Group. For a further explanation of the case of Sovereign Asset Management and SK Group, see Curtis J Milhaupt and Katharina Pistor, *Law & Capitalism: What Corporate Crises Reveal About Legal Systems and Economic Development Around the World* (University of Chicago Press 2008) ch 6.

⁶⁷ For instance, the portion of domestic institutional investors' investment in the Korean stock market was 12.4% in 2008. This portion became 17.1% in 2013. See Korea Financial Investment Association, '한미일 투자주체별 주식시장 비중 비교 (hanmiil tujajuchebyeol jusigsijang bijung bigyo) [Comparison of the Stock Market Shares by Each Category of Investors in Korea, the US and Japan]' (Press Release, 21 January 2015) <www.kofia.or.kr/npboard/m_18/view.do?nttId=108759&bbsId=BBSMSTR_000000000203> accessed 4 July 2020 (relying on the data from the Korea Exchange).

⁶⁸ For a brief explanation of the collective action problem in the context of corporate law, see William T Allen, Reinier H Kraakman and Guhan Subramanian, *Commentaries and Cases on the Law of Business Organization* (3rd edn, Aspen 2009) 366–67.

⁶⁹ For a similar view, see Lucian A Bebchuk, Alma Cohen and Scott Hirst, 'The Agency Problems of Institutional Investors' (2017) 31 *Journal of Economic Perspectives* 89, 96–97.

More precisely, the net benefit of the activist institutional investor is even less than 1 per cent of the improved corporate value since the institutional investor bears the costs associated with shareholder activism. In contrast, even if the other investors are apathetic about shareholder activism in the investee company, the net benefit to these inactive investors with the same 1 per cent shareholding is 1 per cent of the improved corporate value of the investee company.

In sum, under the collective action problem, regardless of whether shareholder activism succeeds or fails in investee companies, the optimal strategy of institutional investors would be to do nothing and free-ride when another institutional investor is involved in shareholder activism.[70]

11.4.1.2 Relatively Active Shareholders After the Introduction of the Stewardship Code

After the Korean Code was introduced, proponents of shareholder stewardship argue that institutional investors engaged more frequently in discussions with their investee companies. In the past, institutional investors tended not to exercise their voting rights vigorously in general meetings of shareholders in their investee companies. Since the inception of the Korean Code, however, the opposing rate of institutional investors, when they exercise their voting rights, has significantly increased. For instance, according to a study, the opposing rate of asset management firms that did not participate in the Korean Code before March 2018 did not change much over the previous year; however, during the same period, the opposing rate of asset management firms that participated in the Korean Code more than doubled.[71] As proponents of shareholder stewardship claim, perhaps the more aggressive shareholder activism of these institutional investors can be ascribed to the Korean Code, particularly Principle 6.[72]

Since the Korean Code was initiated, another newly observed phenomenon is that some institutional investors began to send opinion letters to the investee companies requesting to reform their corporate governance. For instance, KB Asset Management sent opinion letters to Kwangju Shinsegae, a company in the department store and distribution industry, suggesting to change the company's listing status, revamp the corporation's ownership structure and enhance its dividend payment level.[73] KB Asset Management explained that it aimed to communicate with its investee companies, improve the transparency of its investment and inform its clients of correspondences between KB Asset Management and its investee companies.[74] In terms of engagement with investee companies, KB Asset Management is considered one of the most active institutional investors in Korea. According to a report, during the period of its participation in the Korean Code from December 2017 to the end of July 2019, KB Asset Management disclosed twelve engagement activities with its eight investee companies.[75]

---

[70] As for plausible accounts of how the severe collective action problem can be attenuated, see Sections 11.4.1.2 and 11.4.3.

[71] KCGS, '스튜어드십 코드 도입 여부가 자산운용사 반대 의결권 행사에 미치는 영향 (seutyueodeusib kodeu doib yeobuga jasan-un-yongsa bandae uigyeolgwon haengsa-e michineun yeonghyang) [The Effects of the Introduction of the Stewardship Code on Asset Management Firms' Exercise of Voting Rights]' (7 June 2019) <www.cgs.or.kr/publish/report_view.jsp?tn=114&pp=3&spyear=&skey=&svalue=> accessed 4 July 2020.

[72] Korean Code (n 3). See e.g. an interview with Dr Min-Kyung Song, Senior Member of the KCGS in charge of stewardship (18 November 2019).

[73] KB Asset Management, '공시정보 (gongsijeongbo) [Disclosure Information]' <http://www.kbam.co.kr/announce/list> accessed 13 February 2022.

[74] ibid.

[75] Economic Reform Research Institute, '스튜어드십 코드 도입 자산운용사의 주주관여활동 현황 (2017 ~ 2019.7) (seutyueodeusib kodeu doib jasan-un-yongsa-ui jujugwan-yeohwaldong hyeonhwang (2017 ~ 2019.7)) [Shareholder Engagement Activities of Asset Management Companies That Adopted Stewardship Code (2017 ~ 2019.7)]' (27 August 2019) <www.erri.or.kr/bbs/board.php?bo_table=B12&wr_id=341&page=2> accessed 4 July 2020.

Shareholder stewardship, however, can still be ineffective if the pecuniary benefits from shareholder activism are not sufficient to cover its costs. In the case of KB Asset Management's activism, it is worth noting that KB Asset Management held 8.5 per cent shares of Kwangju Shinsegae. Owing to this significant stake in the investee company, KB Asset Management was not subject to a severe collective action problem.

Unlike the above case of KB Asset Management, however, institutional investors often encounter the situation where they hold a less significant portion (e.g. less than 1 per cent) of shareholding in their investee companies. Even if the inert shareholder activism culture in the business community is drastically changed, it is unlikely that these institutional investors holding small stakes in their investee companies can overcome the collective action problem inherent in shareholder activism. To these institutional investors who have insufficient financial incentives to carry out shareholder activism, the Korean Code would simply be a slogan that calls for reform in the corporate governance of investee companies. Despite the severe collective action problem and the lack of economic incentives to pursue shareholder activism, there are a few plausible reasons why institutional investors holding small stakes of investee companies may choose to pursue shareholder activism.

First, it is possible that, from the perspective of institutional investors in Korea, complying with the Korean Code is deemed to be a prevailing trend in the capital market. Under these circumstances, there is a concern by institutional investors that if they do not participate in the Korean Code, they may be considered to be business entities that do not follow a 'good' socio-economic movement or a 'global standard'.[76]

Second, institutional investors – whether they have economic incentives to be activists or not – may feel that the failure to comply with the Code may result in a variety of tangible and intangible disadvantages from the government. Officially, the Korean Code is a capital market reform movement led by the private sector. However, the perception among institutional investors is that the government initiated the process for adopting the Code and continues to support the stewardship activities.[77] Since the Korean government has broad regulatory power over the finance industry and wide discretion to use and allocate policy finance (which institutional investors are interested in managing), it is difficult for institutional investors (large ones in particular) to disregard the Code and the underlying policy of the government.

Third, some institutional investors may recognize the opportunity to create a new market related to shareholder stewardship. Accumulating track records of shareholder activism may broaden the new bases for clients who are enthusiastic about stewardship.[78] If institutional investors use stewardship as a marketing tool and are able to increase the assets under their management, the profitability of these institutional investors will improve owing to their enlarged asset size, which will generate a larger amount of fees. Put differently, even if an institutional investor holds a small stake in an investee company and its shareholder activism severely suffers from a collective action problem, it is possible that the financial benefits from pioneering the market for stewardship will more than cover the costs associated with shareholder activism.

---

[76] Whether the stewardship code is truly a global standard is another issue beyond the scope of this chapter.
[77] As discussed in Sections 11.2.2 and 11.2.3, in Korea, financial regulators introduced the stewardship movement.
[78] For instance, Dr Min-Kyung Song explained that an underlying incentive of KB Asset Management, which actively engages in its investee companies, is accumulating its track record to attract new clients (an interview with Dr Min-Kyung Song (18 November 2019)).

11.4.2 Shareholder Activism and the Korean Code: The Case of the NPS

11.4.2.1 The NPS and Its Significant Status in the Korean Capital Market

In the context of the Korean Code and shareholder activism in Korea, the NPS's role is critical. The NPS is a quasi-government agency in Korea, under the supervision of the Ministry of Health and Welfare. The NPS is the largest institutional investor in Korea and the third-largest pension fund in the world.[79] In July 2019, the amount of assets under the NPS's management exceeded 700 trillion Korean won (KRW).[80] In 2025, this is expected to grow up to KRW 1,000 trillion. As of the end of the third quarter in 2019, the NPS allocated 17.1 per cent of its assets under management, namely KRW 122.3 trillion, to investments in domestic stocks.[81] In the NPS's domestic stock investment, the NPS's direct investment in investee corporations accounts for 54.4 per cent (KRW 66.6 trillion) while the rest of the assets are invested by asset management firms, which the NPS selects and delegates investment decisions to.[82] According to the statistics in 2018, the NPS's equity investment in Korean companies accounts for approximately 7 per cent of the market capitalization of the domestic equity market.[83]

In the Korean capital market, which is relatively small compared to the US and China,[84] the NPS plays a crucial role as a significant investor in virtually all listed companies. In essence, the NPS is 'a whale in a well', and this feature marks the stark difference between the NPS and other active institutional investors overseas. With the introduction of the Korean Code and the NPS's adoption of the Code, the NPS has been making efforts to strengthen and exercise its rights in relation to shareholder voting. Since the NPS is a quasi-government agency, as will be discussed further in Section 11.4.4, the business community in Korea is concerned that the government, via the NPS's shareholder activism supported by the Korean Code, can and will intervene in the management of companies even in the private sector.

11.4.2.2 Shareholder Activism of the NPS

Prior to the adoption of the Korean Code, the NPS was subject to a few statutory and regulatory rules with respect to its voting rights in the investee companies. The National Finance Act, a basic statute that governs the financial matters of the Korean government, required (and still requires) the government-sponsored funds including the NPS to exercise their voting rights on the investee companies 'in good faith and for the benefit of the fund' and to make public

---

[79] See e.g. Eun-Young Jeong, 'Want to Oversee the World's Third-Largest Pension Fund? There's Just One Catch' *The Wall Street Journal* (11 September 2018) <www.wsj.com/articles/want-to-oversee-the-worlds-third-largest-pension-fund-theres-just-one-catch-1536677863> accessed 4 July 2020.

[80] Kyu-wook Yeon, '국민연금 적립금 700조 돌파 (gugmin-yeon-geum jeoglibgeum 700jo dolpa) [The NPS's Reserves Surpass 700 Trillion KRW]' *Maeil Business News* (8 July 2019) <www.mk.co.kr/news/economy/view/2019/07/499342/> accessed 4 July 2020. Roughly speaking, 700 trillion KRW is a little less than 700 billion USD. As of 21 December 2019, the exchange ratio between USD and KRW is 1: 1161. See e.g. Naver.Com, 'Exchange Ratio' <https://search.naver.com/search.naver?sm=tab_hty.top&where%20=nexearch&query=%ED%99%98%EC%9C%A8&oquery=%EB%A9%8B%EC%A0%81%EB%8B%A4&tqi=UQ3y2dp0JywssMnFtfossssth8-020898> accessed 21 December 2019.

[81] NPS Investment Management, '투자정보 (국내주식) (tujajeongbo (gugnaejusig)) [Investment Information (Domestic Stocks)]' (2019) <https://fund.nps.or.kr/jsppage/fund/mcs/mcs_04_01_01.jsp> accessed 4 July 2020.

[82] ibid.

[83] 108.9 trillion ÷ 1,572 trillion = 6.93%.

[84] As of 2018, the market capitalization of Korea was 1.41 trillion USD. The World Bank, 'Market Capitalization of Listed Domestic Companies (Current US$)' <https://data.worldbank.org/indicator/cm.mkt.lcap.cd> accessed 4 July 2020. As of 2018, the market capitalization of the US was 30.44 trillion USD, while that of China was 6.32 trillion USD (excluding 3.82 trillion USD in Hong Kong's capital markets).

disclosures on how they voted.[85] Pursuant to such a statutory mandate, the NPS prepared the 'Guidelines on the Exercise of Voting Rights' (Voting Guidelines) in 2005.[86] Its appendix contained a detailed list regarding how to vote on various agenda items at the investee companies' general meeting of shareholders. The NPS's internal 'Investment Committee' decided on how to exercise its voting rights and, for difficult cases, could request opinions from the 'Special Committee for the Exercise of Voting Rights' (Special Committee) composed of outside experts. Based on the Voting Guidelines, and sometimes pursuant to the Special Committee's recommendations, the NPS expressed opinions on and objected to the agenda items more actively than other domestic institutional investors, even before the adoption of the Korean Code.[87]

The NPS officially became a participant of the Korean Code in July 2018. Together with the participation, the NPS established 'Principles on the NPS's Stewardship' and 'Guidelines on the NPS's Stewardship Activities'. The latter, which stipulates the NPS's voting policy on investee companies, replaced the old Voting Guidelines. Also, in 2018, the newly established 'NPS Stewardship Special Committee' replaced the old Special Committee. This new committee, composed of nine (as of March 2020, three standing and six non-standing) members, has reviewed and decided upon the NPS's voting exercise since 2018.

The foregoing changes after the Korean Code are more than just renaming the existing committees and guidelines. The NPS is trying to redefine its shareholder activities by highlighting various 'engagement' activities such as private dialogues with the management, public announcements and shareholder proposals, beyond the mere exercise of voting rights. For that purpose, in December 2019 the NPS established 'Guidelines for Proactive Shareholder Activities' (Activities Guidelines), which provide the criteria for selecting targets of intensive shareholder activities and the procedures for escalating such activities (from a dialogue to a shareholder proposal).[88] The business community expressed great concerns and claimed that the Activities Guidelines, which are based on the Korean Code, are ambiguous to asset management firms (which are entrusted to manage part of the NPS's assets) as well as the NPS's investee companies (that are supposed to discuss with the NPS for its engagement). Indeed, owing to the open-ended features of the text in the Korean Code and the NPS's Guidelines, it is plausible that the discretionary power of the government and the NPS will be strengthened when they carry out shareholder stewardship in corporations and asset management firms.

The environmental, social and governance (ESG) aspects of stewardship, which are not clearly mentioned in the Korean Code, are also gaining attention from the NPS. Even before the Korean Code, there was a statutory ground for the NPS's interest in ESG issues. According to the National Pension Act, in principle, the Minister of Health and Welfare should manage the

---

[85] National Finance Act, art 64. This provision was introduced in 2005 as the Public Fund Management Basic Act, art 3-6, and moved to the current place in 2006.

[86] See Ministry of Health and Welfare, '국민연금, 주식 의결권행사 전문위원회 공식 출범 (gugmin-yeon-geum, jusig uigyeolgwonhaengsa jeonmunwiwonhoe gongsig chulbeom) [The NPS Officially Launched the Voting-Right Exercise Committee]' (Press Release, 13 March 2006) <www.mohw.go.kr/react/al/sal0301vw.jsp?PAR_MENU_ID=04&MENU_ID=0403&CONT_SEQ=37113&page=578> accessed 23 July 2020.

[87] Regarding the NPS's activism before the adoption of the Korean Code, see Kyung-Hoon Chun, 'Shareholder Activism in Korea: The Cases of PSPD and NPS' (30 April 2019) 16–23 <https://ssrn.com/abstract=3432126> accessed 4 July 2020.

[88] See Ministry of Health and Welfare, '국민연금, 기업가치 제고 및 투명하고 공정한 주주활동을 위한 '적극적 주주활동 가이드라인' 마련 (gugmin-yeon-geum, gieobgachi jego mich tumyeonghago gongjeonghan jujuhwaldong-eul wihan 'jeoggeugjeog jujuhwaldong gaideulain'malyeon) [The NPS Prepared "Guidelines for Proactive Shareholder Activities" for Corporate Value Enhancement and Transparent and Fair Shareholder Activities]' (Press Release 27 December 2019) <www.mohw.go.kr/react/al/sal0301vw.jsp?PAR_MENU_ID=04&MENU_ID=0403&CONT_SEQ=352083> accessed 4 July 2020.

fund to maximize its profitability.[89] To make long-term and stable profits, however, the NPS *can* – rather than *should* – take into account factors including ESG factors in relation to the investment target.[90] Accordingly, the NPS, as a significant shareholder, can engage and have conversations with its investee companies about ESG-related issues. In addition, the NPS Fund Management Guidelines confirm that ESG factors *can* be considered in the NPS's investment.[91] Based on the language in the NPS Act and Fund Management Guidelines, ESG investment is within the discretion of the NPS. After becoming a participant to the Korean Code, the NPS is showing more interest in ESG issues: for example, the Activities Guidelines specifically mention the results of ESG assessment as one of the criteria for selecting targets of intensive stewardship activities out of the hundreds of investee companies.[92]

A primary argument for the NPS's ESG investment is understood as follows: the NPS – the public pension fund that aims to enhance the welfare of all constituencies in Korea in the future as well as at present – should not demand only short-term-oriented performance from its investee companies. Instead, the NPS's investment activities should be aligned with the goal of 'long-term and stable revenue growth', which can be possibly nurtured by ESG investment. The ESG-related investment pays attention to the investee companies' non-financial factors as well as traditionally recognized financial benchmarks such as return on equity (ROE) and earnings per share (EPS). Accordingly, it is possible that the NPS uses its ESG investment as a device to reform corporate culture and policies, even in private companies.[93]

Since the NPS adopted the Korean Code, a few notable cases were known to the media as examples of the NPS's shareholder activism. In early 2019, the NPS called for higher dividend pay-outs by Namyang Dairy Products, where the NPS held 6.15 per cent of shares.[94] Namyang is a controlled corporation where the largest shareholder and related parties hold more than a majority of the corporation's shares.[95] Namyang declined to comply with the NPS's request, arguing that if the company were to adopt higher dividend pay-outs for its shareholders, the beneficiaries would be the controlling shareholder and related parties.[96]

In the general meeting of shareholders, the NPS's shareholder proposal about Namyang's dividend policy was not adopted.[97] This outcome was expected owing to the vast number of shares that the controlling shareholder and related parties held. Although the NPS's activism officially failed in Namyang, many of the NPS's investee companies perceived the Namyang case as a signal of the NPS's volition towards shareholder activism, in particular regarding dividend pay-out policies. Also, it is noteworthy that the NPS's shareholder activism targeting Namyang may be repeated on other occasions. Thus, Namyang's victory is merely a one-off.

---

[89] National Pension Act, art 102 (2).
[90] Ibid art 102 (4).
[91] NPS Fund Management Guidelines, art 17. See NPS Investment Management, '책임투자 현황 (chaeg-imtuja hyeonh-wang) [Current Status of Responsible Investment]' (2019) <https://fund.nps.or.kr/jsppage/fund/mcs/mcs_06_03.jsp> accessed 4 July 2020.
[92] Activities Guidelines (n 88).
[93] For a critical assessment of the NPS's ESG investment, see Section 11.4.4.2.
[94] Mi-jin Shin, '남양유업, 국민연금에 반기 … "고배당 시 오너 배불리기" (nam-yang-yueob, gugmin-yeon-geum-e bangi … "gobaedang si oneo baebulligi") [Namyang Dairy Is Against the NPS]' *Maeil Business News* (11 February 2019) <www.mk.co.kr/news/business/view/2019/02/82736/> accessed 4 July 2020.
[95] ibid.
[96] ibid.
[97] Min-gwan Shim, '남양유업, 국민연금 '배당 위원회 설치' 주주제안 부결 (nam-yang-yueob, gugmin-yeon-geum 'baedang wiwonhoe seolchi' jujujean bugyeol) [Namyang Dairy Rejected the NPS's Shareholder Proposal]' *ChosunBiz* (29 March 2019) <https://biz.chosun.com/site/data/html_dir/2019/03/29/2019032902191.html> accessed 4 July 2020.

A more dramatic example took place in Korean Air. In March 2019, Yang-Ho Cho, chairperson of Hanjin Group, was forced to resign from his directorship of Korean Air. At the annual general meeting of shareholders, 64.1 per cent of votes were cast in favour of his reappointment as a director, and 35.9 per cent of votes were cast in opposition.[98] Korean Air's articles of incorporation classified the appointment and dismissal of directors as a special resolution, which requires the consent of at least two-thirds of the shares represented at a general meeting of shareholders. Since the NPS was the second-largest shareholder of Korean Air (holding an 11.56 per cent stake), its voting against Mr Cho was crucial in his failure to be reappointed to his directorship. Soon after he stepped down from his directorship, in April 2019, Mr Cho suddenly died of a chronic illness.[99]

Regarding the NPS's activism in relation to Korean Air in 2019, three additional points are worth noting. First, from 2015 to 2018, the NPS had already voted against seven issues, including the appointment of Mr Cho as a director, at the general meetings of shareholders of Korean Air and Hanjin Kal, another core company of Hanjin Group that Mr Cho controlled.[100] In other words, based on its internal policies and Voting Guidelines, the NPS continued to vote against Mr Cho and Korean Air even before the NPS became a participant of the Korean Code. What made a different result in 2019 was the opposing votes of other shareholders including certain institutional investors, which may have been affected by the Korean Code. Second, given the special resolution situation in Korean Air (requiring approval by two-thirds of votes), veto power was practically awarded to a group of shareholders as long as their aggregate shares amounted to one-third of votes. As discussed, the success of the NPS's activism in Korean Air in 2019 was possible because of the 35.9 per cent opposition votes (including the NPS's own votes), slightly above the one-third threshold. Apart from the Korean Air case in 2019, however, in cases where a resolution requires only a majority of votes (which is the default rule under the KCC), the NPS could not have won a shareholder activism campaign against the corporation. Third, nonetheless, the NPS's victory concerning Mr Cho's directorship in 2019 – although the victory was achieved by a narrow margin and attributed largely to a special resolution requirement that is unique to Korean Air – caused a shock wave to the business community. It was virtually unprecedented for a controlling shareholder of a large corporate group to be ousted from a controlled corporation's board of directors.

11.4.3 Recent Reforms and Optimistic Expectations for the NPS's Activism

Since the NPS is a quasi-government agency, there is a concern that the exercise of shareholder rights by the NPS may be used to implement government policies and is subject to political bargaining or the collusive ties between politics and business. Many scholars and practitioners explain that the 2015 merger between Cheil Industries and Samsung C&T shows

---

[98] Bo-hyeong Kim, Ik-hwan Kim and Sang-yong Park, '대한항공 대표 갈아치운 국민연금 … 조양호 회장, 20년만에 '강제퇴진'' (daehanhang-gong daepyo gal-achiun gugmin-yeon-geum … joyangho hoejang, 20nyeonman-e 'gangjetoejin') [The NPS Made Chairman Yang-Ho Cho Step Down from Korean Air's Board]' *The Korea Economic Daily* (27 March 2019)<www.hankyung.com/economy/article/2019032725861> accessed 4 July 2020.

[99] Ji-won Cho, '조양호 한진그룹 회장 미국서 별세 … 향년 70세 (joyangho hanjingeulub hoejang migugseo byeolse … hyangnyeon 70se) [Chairman of Hanjin Group Dies in the US at the Age of 70]' *ChosunBiz* (8 April 2019) <https://biz.chosun.com/site/data/html_dir/2019/04/08/2019040800723.html> accessed 4 July 2020.

[100] Esther Lee, '국민연금, 대한항공·한진칼 주총서 4년간 7번 '반대표' 던졌지만 … (gugmin-yeon-geum, daehanhang-gong hanjinkal juchongseo 4nyeongan 7beon 'bandaepyo' deonjyeossjiman …) [The NPS Has Voted Against Seven Issues at General Meetings of Shareholders of Korean Air and Hanjin Kal for Four Years]' *JoongAng Ilbo* (28 January 2019) <https://news.joins.com/article/23326924> accessed 4 July 2020. In all these cases, the NPS did not win.

how politically sensitive the NPS was when exercising voting rights in its investee companies.[101]

Cheil Industries and Samsung C&T were affiliated companies of Samsung Group, the largest *chaebol* in Korea. It is generally explained that the main purpose of the merger was to reorganize the group's governance structure for the smooth succession of the corporate group's control from Kun-Hee Lee, the then controlling shareholder, to his son and heir-apparent, Jae-Yong Lee. The Lee family held 42 per cent and 1.4 per cent stakes of Cheil Industries and Samsung C&T, respectively.[102] It was alleged that, for the benefit of the Lee family, Samsung Group selected the timing of the merger and suppressed the stock price of Samsung C&T in order to arrange the merger ratio in favour of Cheil Industries and to the detriment of Samsung C&T (and its shareholders).

The NPS held 11.21 per cent and 4.84 per cent stakes of Samsung C&T and Cheil Industries, respectively.[103] Since the NPS held a higher stake in Samsung C&T than in Cheil Industries, if the merger ratio was unfavourable to Samsung C&T, the NPS had to, under ordinary circumstances, cast its votes against the merger at Samsung C&T's general meeting of shareholders. However, in arguing that the synergy created by the merger would ultimately enhance the investment value for the NPS and its beneficiaries, the NPS cast its votes in favour of the merger, which was eventually approved at Samsung C&T's general meeting of shareholders.[104] In relation to the merger, it is claimed that then-President Geun-Hye Park supported the family succession and abused the NPS's voting rights for the Lee family in exchange for financial aid by Samsung Group to establish foundations that Park and her close friend were involved in.

At the end of 2016, unprecedented political turmoil took place in Korea in relation to the impeachment of the president, and President Park was finally impeached in 2017. Part of the rationale for impeachment was grounded on Park's relationship with Samsung Group. After her impeachment, the NPS, under the new administration, continuously vowed that the NPS's previous political exercise of its shareholder franchise would not happen again. In accordance with this current stance, the NPS is seen as holding a firm, harsh policy against, in particular, *chaebols* and their controlling families.

After the NPS officially became a participant of the Korean Code, the NPS seemed to engage with its investee companies more actively. For instance, in 2019, the NPS unveiled, in advance, the direction for the exercise of its voting rights for ninety-six listed companies ahead of general meetings of shareholders.[105] Among these listed companies, forty-six faced opposition votes from the NPS.[106] It is noteworthy, however, that institutional investors often exercise shareholder activism in the form of a closed-door dialogue, which is supposed to be unknown to the media

---

[101] For a brief explanation of the merger within Samsung Group and its implications, see Sang Yop Kang, 'Rethinking Self-Dealing and the Fairness Standard: A Law and Economics Framework for Internal Transactions in Corporate Groups' (2016) 11 *Virginia Law & Business Review* 95.

[102] Jonathan Cheng, 'Elliott Associates Criticizes Proposed Takeover of Samsung C&T' *The Wall Street Journal* (Seoul, 3 June 2015) <www.wsj.com/articles/elliott-associates-buys-samsung-c-t-stake-1433378442> accessed 4 July 2020.

[103] Hyun-min Yoo, '국민연금 "삼성물산·제일모직 합병, 시너지 감안해 찬성"' (gugmin-yeon-geum "samseongmul-san·jeilmojig habbyeong, sineoji gam-anhae chanseong") [The NPS Approved Samsung C&T and Cheil Industries Merger for Synergy]' *Yonhap News* (23 November 2016) <www.yna.co.kr/view/AKR20161123126400008> accessed 4 July 2020.

[104] ibid.

[105] Jin-ho Yun, Jun-ho Yoo and Hyung-jun Lim, '대한항공 빼곤 … 국민연금 의결권 '빈손'' (daehanhang-gong ppaegon … gugmin-yeon-geum uigyeolgwon 'binson') [The NPS's Exercise of Voting Rights Is Futile Except Korean Air]' *Maeil Business News* (29 March 2019) <www.mk.co.kr/news/stock/view/2019/03/192375/> accessed 4 July 2020.

[106] ibid.

and the public. In effect, the scale of the NPS's shareholder activism is thus likely to be larger than is officially observed.

As explained, in terms of shareholding, the NPS is a significant investor with a substantial shareholding of virtually all major companies in the Korean capital market.[107] Under these circumstances, when an institutional investor finds corporate governance problems in a certain investee company and engages with the company, the institutional investor can expect a higher chance that the NPS will take a position in line with it. Accordingly, the expectation of the NPS's alliance in shareholder activism will further encourage institutional investors to initiate shareholder activism in the first place, since the costs of shareholder activism will be shared with the NPS and the chance of success in shareholder activism will rise. In short, the NPS's shareholder activism mitigates the collective action problem that other institutional investors were originally subject to. Also, if the NPS participates in engaging with a specific target corporation, the institutional investors may feel more comfortable about their shareholder activism in the target corporation because of the very involvement of the NPS. As such, an optimistic view is that the NPS-led shareholder activism will likely enhance the quality of corporate governance and provide solutions to at least the following problems: egregious corporate scandals; tunnelling; and other controversial transactions.

11.4.4 Concerns about the NPS's Activism

11.4.4.1 Pension Fund Socialism

Despite the optimistic view, there are some concerns regarding the massive influence of the NPS in the domestic capital market. Some people are worried about 'pension-fund socialism'. In the context of Korea, pension-fund socialism is understood as an ideology supporting the political-economic regime where large public pension funds led by the government deeply intervene in the management and operation of private companies. The government expects other institutional investors to join the Korean Code actively. Also, there is a political and social atmosphere that makes it difficult for institutional investors (large ones in particular) to turn down participation in shareholder stewardship. Under these circumstances, it can be argued that pension-fund socialism will be further strengthened such that politics may significantly hamper corporations' economic activities. In this light, it is possible that the political decision-making behaviour of the NPS – which, in the past, was exercised relatively intermittently – will be exercised in a more systematic manner.

11.4.4.2 ESG-Related Investment

In addition, the NPS's emphasis on ESG investment in its investee companies poses another concern. Note that the Korean Code does not explicitly mention ESG investment. Since ESG covers virtually every non-financial factor, it is possible that the government, through the NPS, can fulfil its policies, including those based on its political agenda, even in private companies. Further, among various ESG-related issues, the government may discretionally select only the issues that it would like to deal with and justify its policies based on the selected issues.

---

[107] In this respect, the NPS is a 'universal owner'. For further discussion of universal owners, see Dionysia Katelouzou, *The Path to Enlightened Shareholder Stewardship* (CUP) (forthcoming).

As for its ESG investment, the NPS pursues the long-term interest for the *welfare* of *society* rather than merely the short-term *financial* interest of an *investee company*. To accomplish this goal, ESG indices should be set adequately, logically and consistently. However, ESG indices are often subjective and less transparent, as well as inconsistent and even clumsily based on a rule of thumb. Besides, the NPS's messages about ESG investment could be rhetoric. For instance, compared to the *financial* performance of a *company* that is indicated by ROE and EPS, it is difficult to measure the level of the *welfare* of *society* and to recognize whether it is improved after a specific ESG investment has been adopted. Thus, following the welfare-of-society standard, the NPS may try to vindicate even failed investments as long as the NPS is able to find a positive effect on a certain constituency in society. In this light, there is a concern that the NPS functions as the government's apparatus in carrying out government policies in the name of ESG investing.

Also, owing to the *long-term* nature of ESG investment, it is possible that the NPS, even when the outcome of a specific ESG investment is clearly disappointing or devastating, can defend the investment by arguing that it will generate benefits in favour of the society *in the long run*. The time horizon of 'in the long run' is often ambiguous, and the NPS may therefore argue that 'in the long run' is not consummated yet until the ESG investment outcome turns out fine. Moreover, even if 'in the long run' is defined and consummated, it is possible that the very people in the NPS (and in the previous government) who carried out a suboptimal ESG policy would have already left the NPS (and the government). Under these circumstances, the NPS's accountability towards its ESG investment could be severely undermined.

11.4.4.3 Lack of Consistency in Shareholder Activism

Moreover, the NPS is seen to be exercising shareholder activism based on inconsistent standards. The underlying rationale for the NPS's shareholder activism and engagement (or intervention) in its investee companies, particularly in the private sector, is that the NPS, as a steward of all Korean citizens, should repair corporate governance problems of investee companies. The Korean Air case discussed in Section 11.4.2.2 vividly illustrates the NPS's active stewardship. Contrary to this rationale, however, the NPS now seems to overlook potential corporate governance problems associated with the incumbent government's policies. The case of Korea Electric Power Corporation (KEPCO) is an example of the inconsistency in the NPS's stewardship.

KEPCO is a monopoly producer in the electricity market in Korea. The major shareholders of KEPCO are the government, the Korea Development Bank (KDB) and the NPS, which hold 18.20%, 32.90%, and 7.23% stakes, respectively.[108] Since the KDB and the NPS are under the heavy influence of the government, the de facto controlling shareholder of KEPCO is the government. KEPCO also has a great number of minority shareholders, including foreign institutional investors.

For a long time, KEPCO was considered a blue-chip company with solid financial performance. In the midst of recent changes in macro-economic and energy-related policy factors, however, the management environment and performance indicators of KEPCO have worsened (e.g. huge operational losses were incurred). Some minority shareholders of KEPCO attribute the poor business state of the corporation to the incumbent government's nuclear

---

[108] See KEPCO, '자본금 및 주주현황 (jabongeum mich jujuhyeonhwang) [Capital and Shareholders]' (2020) <www.alio.go.kr/popReportTerm.do?apbaId=C0247&reportFormRootNo=31701> accessed 4 July 2020.

power phase-out policy and KEPCO's blind compliance with the policy.[109] In relation to the NPS's stewardship, what draws our attention is that KEPCO has a plan to found an education institute, tentatively named Korea Institute of Energy Technology (Kentech). Its establishment was a presidential election pledge of the incumbent president. Given KEPCO's massive operational losses, which are on a sharp increase, minority shareholders are discontented about KEPCO's plan to pour more than KRW 1.6 trillion into building a new education institute,[110] a move seen as politically driven.

Disgruntled minority shareholders have prepared to challenge KEPCO's management and board members.[111] With respect to corporate governance issues and potential political interference in KEPCO that may hurt shareholder wealth, there has thus far been no NPS activity related to shareholder involvement, activism or stewardship.[112] If the NPS remains silent on this issue, one may criticize it for its shareholder activism being inconsistent and politically biased – it depends on which corporation is a target of its shareholder stewardship and whether the specific engagement is in line with the current government's policy and stance.

11.5 CONCLUSION

This chapter delineates and analyzes stewardship, shareholder activism, and its impacts and implications in Korea. The Korean Code is similar to the UK Code in terms of their texts. Stewardship in Korea has, however, distinctive motivations of addressing the problems of controlling (family) shareholders. After the Korean Code was instated, shareholder activism, which was quiescent in the past, began to surface. Regarding stewardship and shareholder activism in Korea, the role of the NPS is markedly significant since it is the largest institutional investor in Korea and it exercises considerable influence on the Korean capital market in general.

It seems that shareholder activism in Korea, while still inchoate, was triggered and fostered at least partially by the introduction of the Code. So far, the expectations of stewardship and shareholder activism in Korea are mixed. The positive expectation is that active engagement by institutional investors will resolve the chronic tunnelling problem that *chaebols*' controlling shareholders are often involved in. Accordingly, the quality of corporate governance will improve, thereby enhancing the market capitalization of companies in the domestic capital market. This is favourable to beneficiaries of institutional investors. The negative expectation, among others, is that intervention by institutional investors will adversely affect the expertise of management in investee companies. Also, there is a concern that the government can intervene in the decision-making process of corporate policies and strategies in private companies via the NPS.

---

[109] The nuclear power phase-out policy has many corporate governance implications, but they are beyond this chapter's scope.

[110] Dong-A Ilbo, '한전, 공대 설립·운영비 13년간 1조6000억원 … 올해 법인 설립 (hanjeon, gongdae seollib-unyeongbi 13nyeongan 1jo6000eog-won … olhae beob-in seollib) [Establishment and Operation Costs for Kentech.: 1.6 Trillion KRW for 13 Years]' (5 September 2019) <www.donga.com/news/article/all/20190905/97290309/1> accessed 4 July 2020 (relying on KEPCO's estimate of the establishment and operation costs for Kentech).

[111] Sang-hee Ahn, '적자 투성이 한전, 공대 설립안 가결 … 소액주주 "대선 공약용" 반발 (jeogja tuseong-i hanjeon, gongdae seollib-an gagyeol … soaegjuju "daeseon gong-yag-yong" banbal) [KEPCO Approved a Plan to Establish Kentech, But Minority Shareholders Criticized the Plan for a Presidential Election's Pledge]' *ChosunBiz* (8 August 2019) <https://biz.chosun.com/site/data/html_dir/2019/08/08/2019080802689.html> accessed 4 July 2020.

[112] However, it is also possible that the NPS has already exercised shareholder activism in KEPCO through non-public engagement such as closed-door conversations.

Before we close this chapter, we briefly mention two additional points. First, as Professors Gen Goto, Alan Koh and Dan Puchniak explain, 'one of the many reasons for the popularity of stewardship codes in Asia is that they provide a convenient vehicle for local governments and/or market players to achieve their own particular interests through an inexpensive, non-binding, and malleable vehicle, the formal adoption of which sends a signal of "good corporate" governance'.[113] We agree with this view in general in relation to other major Asian economies, but expound that stewardship in Korea is more realistic than superficial because the business community genuinely perceives stewardship and shareholder activism as a formidable threat to its autonomy and economic interest.[114]

Second, to make stewardship in Korea more sophisticated, discussion on 'corporate governance of the NPS' is also vital. Under the current NPS system, the government's influence in the NPS's decision-making process and investment is enormous; the government acts as a de facto controller of the NPS. Accordingly, it is possible that the government can abuse the NPS as a means to carry out its policies, even though such policies may damage the interest of the NPS's beneficiaries. In this light, the next step forward for stewardship in Korea is to establish the independence of the NPS in its decision-making process and investment in investee companies, and thus, to resolve the agency problems in the NPS.

---

[113] Gen Goto, Alan K Koh and Dan W Puchniak, 'Diversity of Shareholder Stewardship in Asia: Faux Convergence' (2020) 53 *Vanderbilt Journal of Transnational Law* 829.

[114] More specifically, the business community is concerned about (i) the capital market's strengthened shareholder activism that further restrains the malpractice of *chaebols*, or (ii) excessive intervention by institutional investors and the government in investee companies, or (iii) both.

12

The Assessment of Taiwan's Shareholder Stewardship Codes

From International Stewardship Principle to Alternative Good Stewardship

Andrew Jen-Guang Lin

12.1 INTRODUCTION

After the 2008 Global Financial Crisis (GFC), the UK began the process of initiating the world's first stewardship code (UK Code), which requires institutional investors to play important roles as 'good stewards'. Nine years after, the Financial Reporting Council (FRC) announced the UK Code 2020, including environmental, social and governance factors (ESG) and emphasizing other sustainability reporting, as well as other recent amendments to the UK Corporate Governance Code.[1] After observing the international trends[2] and the development of shareholder stewardship regimes in jurisdictions like the UK, Hong Kong,[3] Japan[4] and Malaysia,[5] and the increasing market shares of institutional investors, Taiwan became the fifth country to adopt its own stewardship code on 30 June 2016 (Taiwan Code).[6] Taiwan's main motivation for launching its stewardship code is to further enhance corporate governance and to keep up with the international norm. Prior to the introduction of the Taiwan Code, Taiwan had already introduced the 'Corporate Social Responsibility Best Practice Principles for TWSE/GTSM Listed Companies' (CSR Code) in 2010, and asked listed companies to comply with the Global Reporting Initiative's (GRI) Sustainability Reporting Guidelines in 2015.[7] Corporate

---

[1] Financial Reporting Council, *The UK Stewardship Code 2020* (2019) <www.frc.org.uk/getattachment/5aae591d-d9d3-4cf4-814a-d14e156a1d87/Stewardship-Code_Dec-19-Final-Corrected.pdf> accessed 19 May 2021 [hereinafter UK Code 2020]; Dionysia Katelouzou, 'Shareholder Stewardship: A Case of (Re)Embedding Institutional Investors and the Corporation?' in Beate Sjåfjell and Christopher M Bruner (eds), *Cambridge Handbook of Corporate Law, Corporate Governance and Sustainability* (CUP 2019).

[2] Taiwan Stock Exchange, 'TWSE Launched the Stewardship Principles for Institutional Investors' (Press Release, 30 June 2016) <https://cgc.twse.com.tw/pressReleases/promoteNewsArticleEn/1207> accessed 22 May 2020.

[3] Securities and Futures Commission, 'Principles of Responsible Ownership' (7 March 2016) <www.sfc.hk/web/EN/rules-and-standards/principles-of-responsible-ownership.html> accessed 22 May 2020. See Donald, Stewardship in the Hong Kong International Financial Centre, Chapter 13.

[4] The Council of Experts Concerning the Japanese Version of the Stewardship Code, 'Principles for Responsible Institutional Investors «Japan's Stewardship Code» – To Promote Sustainable Growth of Companies through Investment and Dialogue' (26 February 2014) <www.fsa.go.jp/en/refer/councils/stewardship/20140407/01.pdf> accessed 22 May 2020. See Goto, Japanese Stewardship Code, Chapter 10.

[5] Securities Commission Malaysia and Minority Shareholders Watch Group, *Malaysian Code for Institutional Investors* (27 June 2014) <www.sc.com.my/api/documentms/download.ashx?id=9f4e32d3-cb97-4ff5-852a-6cb168a9f936> accessed 22 May 2020. See Tan, Institutional Investor Stewardship in Malaysia, Chapter 15.

[6] Taiwan Stock Exchange, 'Stewardship Principles for Institutional Investors' (30 June 2016) <https://cgc.twse.com.tw/static/stewardship_en.pdf> accessed 22 May 2020 [hereinafter Taiwan Code].

[7] Taiwan Stock Exchange Corporation Rules Governing the Preparation and Filing of Corporate Social Responsibility Reports by TWSE Listed Companies, s 3 (promulgated 26 November 2014) GRI Guidance was replaced with GRI Standard on 4 January 2019 amendment.

social responsibility (CSR) and ESG were driving forces behind the development and implementation of the Taiwan stewardship code.[8]

However, it is important to examine the shareholder structures of listed companies in order to assess the effectiveness of the Taiwan Code. The majority of listed companies (excluding foreign companies) in Taiwan have a more concentrated shareholding structure and are originally family-owned in most sectors.[9] In fact, many financial holding companies in Taiwan are examples of family-owned enterprises.[10] Domestic and foreign institutional investors have increased their shareholding of large listed companies in Taiwan. For example, as of May 2019, Taiwan Semiconductor Corporation (TSMC) had 338,926 shareholders, including 334,214 (or 98.6%) individual investors and 4,712 institutional investors.[11] Institutional investors held 23,797,291,831 shares (or 91.8%) of TSMC's outstanding shares.[12] Although 98.6% of shareholders were individual investors, institutional investors held more than 91% of TSMC's outstanding shares. There were 1,435 shareholders each holding more than one million TSMC shares, together holding 91.4% of TSMC's outstanding shares.[13] However, not every listed company can attract investment from institutional investors.

Two core pillars of corporate governance are the accountability of the board of directors and the enhancement of their monitoring functions. Taiwan's securities regulator and the Taiwan Stock Exchange (TWSE) have been devoted to promoting corporate governance since 2002. Shareholders' rights have also been emphasized through a shareholder proposal regime in Taiwan's Company Act in June 2005. Independent directors and audit committees were introduced in the 2006 Securities and Exchange Act amendment (TSEA).[14] The agenda for enhancing corporate governance in Taiwan has never been off the table. In other words, the announcement of the Taiwan Code by the TWSE in June 2016 is a further step to encourage institutional investors, including asset holders and managers, to exercise their expertise and power to enhance the corporate governance of investee companies and to pursue the long-term

---

[8] Taiwan Stock Exchange, 'Corporate Social Responsibility Best Practice Principles for TWSE/GTSM Listed Companies' (28 July 2016) <http://eng.selaw.com.tw/LawArticle.aspx?LawID=FL052368&ModifyDate=1050728> accessed 22 May 2020 [hereinafter CSR Code]. See discussion in Section 12.5.

[9] This phenomenon appears not only in Taiwan but also in many other Asian jurisdictions. See e.g. Dan W Puchniak and Samantha Tang, 'Singapore's Puzzling Embrace of Shareholder Stewardship: A Successful Secret' (2020) 53 *Vanderbilt Journal of Transnational Law* 989. See also Gen Goto, Alan K Koh and Dan W Puchniak, 'Diversity of Shareholder Stewardship in Asia: Faux Convergence' (2020) 53 *Vanderbilt Journal of Transnational Law* 829.

[10] It can easily be observed and publicly recognized that most financial holding companies, though publicly traded, are controlled by specific families. For example, both Cathay Financial Holdings and Fubon Financial Holdings are controlled by brothers of the Tsai family. Taishin Financial Holdings and Hsin Kong Financial Holdings are controlled by brothers of the Wu family.

[11] Information provided by TSMC (Market Observation Post System, TSMC code: 2330 <https://mops.twse.com.tw/mops/web/t16sn02> accessed 22 May 2020).

[12] As of May 2019, TSMC had 25,930,380,458 outstanding shares (ibid).

[13]

Number of shares held	Number of shareholders	Total number of shares held	% of outstanding shares
100,001-200,000	1,647	229,521,892	0.8851
200,001-400,000	1,059	297,217,087	1.1462
400,001-600,000	445	217,807,794	0.8400
600,001-800,000	291	202,310,823	0.7802
800,001-1000,000	192	172,937,054	0.6669
1000,001 and more	1,435	23,702,651,560	91.4088

[14] 證券交易法 (Zhèngquàn jiāoyì fǎ) [Securities and Exchange Act], amended 19 May 2020 [hereinafter TSEA].

interest of their clients and beneficiaries. As of 10 June 2020, 151 domestic and foreign institutional investors have filed with the TWSE Corporate Governance Center an 'Endorsement Statement' to prove their 'Public Endorsement'.[15] According to the list of signatories of the Taiwan Code published by the Corporate Governance Center of the TWSE, 32 institutional investors became signatories in 2016, 6 in 2017, 102 in 2018 and 9 in 2019.[16] Although most institutional investors have signed the declaration, the effectiveness of the Taiwan Code remains an open question.

In order to assess the effectiveness of the Taiwan Code, Section 12.2 will discuss the shareholding structure of listed companies. It will compare the shareholding of the institutional investors, particularly foreign investors. Section 12.3 of this chapter introduces the major contents of the Code and its connection to Taiwan's corporate governance regime. We will discuss whether there are enough incentives or other co-ordinated sets of measures available to accommodate and encourage institutional investors to actively play their role as good stewards in addition to signing the declaration. An analysis of the activities of institutional investors when they perform their stewardship functions will also be provided. In Section 12.4, we will introduce a unique investor protection institution, the Securities and Futures Investors Protection Center (SFIPC), which is a non-profit organization (NPO) and a non-governmental organization (NGO). The SFIPC uses the weapons authorized by the Securities Investor and Futures Trader Protection Act (SFIPA),[17] such as class actions, derivative suits and judicial removal of directors, to play the role of 'a good steward' in Taiwan. Section 12.5 discusses the Taiwan Code and its relationship with the evolution of the Taiwan corporate governance regime, including the most recent development of promoting ESG, responsible investment and sustainability. In Section 12.6, we provide analysis and comments on the Taiwan Code. Section 12.7 provides a conclusion that Taiwan should keep an eye on international developments and revise the Taiwan Code accordingly to make this regime more effective.

12.2 SHAREHOLDING STRUCTURE OF TAIWAN'S LISTED COMPANIES

International organizations and individual countries continuously amend and invent new regulatory strategies to enhance their corporate governance systems and improve their investment environments. After the announcement of the UK Code, Taiwan began to study and observe the global stewardship trend. The TWSE collaborated with Taiwan's Financial Services Roundtable, the Taiwan Depository and Clearing Corporation, and the ROC Securities Investment Trust and Consulting Association, to promulgate the *Stewardship Principles for Institutional Investors* on 30 June 2016.[18] On 19 September 2019, the TWSE held a half-day forum titled 'Enhancing Institutional Investor Stewardship and Listed Companies Investors Relation Forum', focusing on the discussion of implementing the stewardship policy and

---

[15] Taiwan Code (n 6) 3. Among the 151 signatories, 10 are foreign institutional investors, 13 are subsidiaries or joint ventures of foreign institutional investors, and the remaining 128 are Taiwan's local institutional investors. Taiwan Stock Exchange, '簽署名單 (Qiānshǔ míngdān) [List of Signatories of the Stewardship Code]' <https://cgc.twse.com.tw/stewardshipList/listCh> accessed 10 June 2020. English List available at <https://cgc.twse.com.tw/stewardshipList/listEn> accessed 10 June 2020.
[16] ibid.
[17] Securities Investor and Futures Trader Protection Act <https://law.moj.gov.tw/ENG/LawClass/LawAll.aspx?pcode=G0400038> accessed 10 June 2020.
[18] Taiwan Code (n 6). See Taiwan Stock Exchange, '證交所發布「機構投資人盡職治理守則」' (Zhèng jiāo suǒ fābù 'jīgòu tóuzī rén jìnzhí zhìlǐ shǒuzé') [The TWSE Promulgates Stewardship Principles for Institutional Investors]' (Press Release, 30 June 2016) <https://cgc.twse.com.tw/pressReleases/promoteNewsArticleCh/1206> accessed 22 May 2020.

promoting a better relationship between institutional investors and listed companies.[19] In this forum, in addition to the organizers, participants were mainly local and foreign institutional investors who were invited to share their experiences with stewardship activities.[20] These events demonstrated Taiwan's efforts in promoting the stewardship principles. Before we discuss Taiwan's shareholder stewardship regime, we will briefly introduce the shareholding structure of Taiwan's listed companies.

As of the end of December 2019, there were 1,717 listed companies, including 942 companies listed on the TWSE, 775 companies listed on the Taipei Exchange (TPEx) and 677 unlisted public companies.[21] There were 18,156,178 securities trading accounts at the end of December 2019, according to the Taiwan Depository and Clearing Corporation.[22] As of the end of March 2019, Taiwan's population was 23,589,195.[23] This shows that a large portion of Taiwanese are investing in public companies. In order to protect investors, the government has taken measures to ensure the safety and fairness of the stock market, and asked public companies to improve corporate governance. With regards to investment by foreigners in the Taiwan stock market, there were 932 approved cases from foreign institutional investors with inward remittances of USD 213.3 billion, and 51 approved cases from foreign individual investors.[24] The total accumulated net inward remittance in 2019 was USD 213.6 billion and roughly 38.34% of market value was held by foreign investors.[25]

12.2.1 Shareholding Structure of TWSE Listed Companies

The shareholding structure of public companies differs throughout the market. For example, TSMC is one of the largest companies in Taiwan in terms of issued capital and market capitalization.[26] According to the information retrieved from the Market Post Observation System, TSMC's corporate insiders, including directors, supervisors and managers, collectively held 1.742 billion shares or 6.72% of outstanding shares as of 13 September 2019.[27] In

---

[19] Taiwan Stock Exchange, '強化機構投資人盡職治理與上市公司投資人關係論壇, 共創雙方最大價值 (Qiánghuà jīgòu tóuzī rén jìnzhí zhìlǐ yǔ shàngshì gōngsī tóuzī rén guānxì lùntán, gòng chuàng shuāngfāng zuìdà jiàzhí) [Enhancing Institutional Investor Stewardship and Listed Companies Investors Relation Forum, Maximizing Value of Both Parties]' (Press Release, 24 September 2019) <https://cgc.twse.com.tw/pressReleases/promoteNewsArticleCh/3346> accessed 22 May 2020.

[20] Participants include BlackRock Investment Stewardship Team, BizLink Holding Inc., Ipreo by HIS Markit, Taiwan's TECO Electric & Machinery Co, and Bureau of Labor Funds (Taiwan Stock Exchange, 'The Strengthening Stewardship Principles for Institutional Investors and Listed Companies Investor Relations Forum Will Be Held on September 19' (Press Release, 16 September 2019) <https://cgc.twse.com.tw/pressReleases/promoteNewsArticleEn/3333> accessed 22 May 2020).

[21] Securities and Futures Bureau, '2019 December Catalog, Primary Market: Highlights of Equity Issuance by Public Companies' (15 January 2020) 2–3 <www.sfb.gov.tw/en/home.jsp?id=86&parentpath=0,7&mcustomize=important_view.jsp&dataserno=202001150002> accessed 22 May 2020.

[22] One person may have more than one securities trading account in different securities companies.

[23] Ministry of Interior Republic of China, *January-March 2019 Demography Quarterly Republic of China* (May 2019) 4 <www.ris.gov.tw/app/en/3912> accessed 22 May 2020.

[24] 2019 December Catalog (n 21) 43–44. Since 2 October 2003, foreign investors simply need to apply for an investment ID from the TWSE. The exchange rate used was USD 1 to NT$ 30.

[25] ibid.

[26] TSMC also issued American Depository Receipts traded on the New York Stock Exchange in the symbol TSM. TSMC's paid-in capital was NT$ 259.3 billion (USD 8.643 billion) as of September 2019 and its market capitalization was NT$ 68.066 trillion (USD 2.268 trillion). The market capitalization of TSM ADR was USD 222 billion as of 13 September 2019.

[27] Users can retrieve financial and other public disclosure information from the Market Post Observation System <https://mops.twse.com.tw/mops/web/t144sb09> accessed 22 May 2020.

the recent published corporate governance evaluation results, TSMC ranked in the top 5 per cent category.

If we look at the investor structure from the trading value on the TWSE market, institutional investors' trading value constituted roughly 40.2% in 2018.[28] Among them, foreign institutional investors traded around NT$ 16,891 billion or 26.3% of total trading value, whereas domestic institutional investors traded around NT$ 8,971 billion or 13.9% of the total trading value.[29] In 2019, 41.8% of trading value was created by institutional investors. Among them, NT$ 8,230 billion, or 14.2% of trading amount, was by domestic investors and NT$ 16,051 billion, or 27.6% of trading amount, was by foreign institutional investors.[30] In 2018, 59.8% of the total trading volume was contributed by individual investors,[31] including 59.7% by domestic individual investors and 0.1% by foreign individual investors. In 2019, NT$ 33,808 billion or 58.2% of total trading value was traded by domestic individual investors and only NT$2 2.35 billion or 0.1% was traded by foreign individual investors.[32] If we examine the ownership structure of TWSE listed companies as a whole, around 64% of the total market capitalization (USD 977 billion) was held by institutional investors as of the end of 2018 and 38% held by foreign investors.[33] We have also seen the growth trend of market capitalization held by institutional investors as well as the transaction value. These figures indicate that institutional investors can play an important role in listed companies. Because of the considerable amount of influence from institutional investors, listed companies hold investor conferences regularly, particularly to inform institutional investors.

12.2.2 *Shareholding Structure of TPEx Listed Companies*

Companies listed on the TPEx are either young companies or relatively small in terms of their paid-in capital. Therefore, institutional investors trade less on TPEx listed companies. In 2018, 23.1% of TPEx's trading value was contributed by institutional investors.[34] Among them, domestic institutional investors traded NT$ 2,028 billion or 11.7% while foreign institutional investors traded NT$ 1,976 or 11.4%.[35] TPEx listed companies are relatively smaller in capital size compared with those listed on the TWSE.

12.3 CONTENT OF THE TAIWAN STEWARDSHIP CODE

The Taiwan Code is primarily modelled after the UK Code. The Financial Supervisory Commission (FSC), the competent authority of the securities, banking and insurance industries, designated the TWSE to draft the Taiwan Code in the form of soft law similar to the Taiwan Corporate Governance Code (TWN CG Code) and the Taiwan Corporate Social

---

[28] 2019 December Catalog (n 21) 39.
[29] ibid. Among the domestic institutional investors, 6.7% (out of 13.9%) were traded by securities investment trust funds (1.2%) and dealers (5.5%). The remaining 7.2% were traded by other domestic institutional investors, such as insurance companies. 2019 December Catalog (n 21) 41.
[30] ibid.
[31] ibid 39.
[32] ibid.
[33] In 2018, the total inward remittance by foreign investors was USD 197.71 billion, in which USD 197.46 was by foreign institutional investors (ibid 43–44); 38.34% of total market value of Taiwan stock market was held by foreign investors (ibid).
[34] ibid 40.
[35] ibid.

Responsible Rules (TWN CSR Rules).[36] The TWSE took into consideration Taiwan's corporate governance regime and idiosyncratic local factors when drafting the Taiwan Code, through studying the UK Code and the experiences of other jurisdictions available.[37] The regulatory philosophy behind the Taiwan Code is to encourage institutional investors to play the role of good stewards and adopt the same approach of 'comply or explain' as was first made popular in the UK.[38] The Taiwan Code is the first code in Taiwan to adopt the 'comply or explain' approach. In contrast, in the TWN CG Code and TWN CSR Rules, the regulated institutions are either 'required to comply' or 'advised to follow'.[39] Although the authors of the Taiwan Code are self-regulators, the Code may still have some effect because this is a policy promoted by the FSC and many signatories are subject to supervision in other matters. Depending on how seriously the FSC and the TWSE would like to implement this policy, we can expect the Code to produce positive effects to some extent.

Under the Taiwan Code, institutional investors are expected to fulfil their fiduciary duties, make investments based on the long-term interest of fund providers, clients or beneficiaries, and monitor the investee companies by attending shareholders' meetings, exercising voting rights, engaging in appropriate dialogue and interacting with management.[40] However, would institutional investors still insist on the sustainable investment strategy had their clients directed them to do differently? The answer is obviously that the institutional investors would either discuss with their clients or respect the clients' decision. Therefore, whether the signatories have the freedom to adopt sustainable investment strategies while not violating their fiduciary duties remains controversial.

The Taiwan Code includes five chapters: (1) Institutional Investors and Their Duties; (2) Objectives of the Principles; (3) Endorsement and 'Comply or Explain'; (4) Stewardship Principles; and (5) Guidelines for Compliance with Principles. We will now introduce the major contents of the Taiwan Code.

12.3.1 *Duties of Institutional Investors under the Taiwan Code*

Chapter 1 of the Code defines institutional investors who may be subject to the Code and explains their 'duties'. The Code classifies institutional investors into (1) 'asset owners' that use their own funds or those of beneficiaries to invest, such as insurance companies and pension

---

[36] Instructed by the FSC, the Corporate Governance Center of the TWSE coordinates with the Taiwan Depository & Clearing Corporation, the Securities Investment Trust & Consulting Association and Taiwan Financial Services Roundtable, by reference to the international development experience and domestic practice, launched the "Stewardship Principles for Institutional Investors", aiming to leverage market mechanism, along with regulations and corporate self-improvement, to enhance corporate governance quality in Taiwan. (Taiwan Stock Exchange, 'Stewardship Principles Overview <https://cgc.twse.com.tw/frontEN/stewardship> accessed 22 May 2020)

[37] ibid.

[38] Taiwan Code (n 6) 3 (ch 3 'Endorsement and Comply or Explain') and Financial Reporting Council, *The UK Stewardship Code* (September 2012) 4, 'Comply or Explain' <www.frc.org.uk/getattachment/d67933f9-ca38-4233-b603-3d24b2f62c5f/UK-Stewardship-Code-(September-2012).pdf> accessed 22 May 2020. The UK Code 2020 no longer applies the comply or explain approach.

[39] See e.g. 'TWSE/GTSM listed companies are advised to follow the Corporate Governance Best Practice Principles for TWSE/GTSM Listed Companies, the Ethical Corporate Management Best Practice Principles for TWSE/GTSM Listed Companies, and the Code of Ethical Conduct for TWSE/GTSM Listed Companies to establish effective corporate governance frameworks and relevant ethical standards so as to enhance corporate governance' (CSR Code (n 8) art 6).

[40] The term 'fund provider' may include the institutional investor's clients, beneficiaries or shareholders. Taiwan Code (n 6) 1.

funds; and (2) 'asset managers' who provide investment management services to their clients, such as investment trust enterprises and investment advisers.[41] The Code covers these two types of domestic and foreign institutional investor that invest in Taiwan companies, regardless of whether the investee company is public or private, listed or non-listed.[42] Thus, the scope of institutional investors covered by the Taiwan Code is broader than that of the UK Code.

To fully understand the duties of institutional investors under the Taiwan Code, we must read chapter 1 together with the objectives and other parts of the Code so that we understand how this Code is implemented. In terms of institutional investors' duties, one may feel that the title of chapter 1, using the term 'duties', is too strong and may not properly reflect the comply-or-explain approach adopted in the Taiwan Code.[43] However, if we read through the Code, the term 'duties' is used to indicate institutional investors' duties to foster the long-term interest of the fund providers, including their clients, beneficiaries and shareholders. The duties of institutional investors to their fund providers are distinguished from the stewardship activities, such as dialogue with the investee companies and voting policies, suggested via stewardship principles and guidelines. In other words, the term 'duties' in the Taiwan Code refers to institutional investors' duties to their fund providers only – not to their stewardship role. While expecting institutional investors to be good stewards, the Code emphasizes the interest of investment institutions' clients or beneficiaries when conducting business.[44]

The Code does not specifically alter the fiduciary duty of institutional investors imposed by the Company Act and the Securities Investment Trust and Consulting Act. However, the Code emphasizes that the 'long-term interest' of clients, beneficiaries and shareholders should be the institutional investors' priority when investing and fulfilling their fiduciary duty.[45] Specifically, the Code expects institutional investors to monitor the operation status of their investee companies by attending shareholders' meetings, exercising voting rights, and conducting appropriate dialogue and interactions with the management team to improve corporate governance of the investee company.[46]

Taiwan Code expects that an institutional investor shall properly use its influence on the investee companies to improve the quality of corporate governance and promote the sustainable growth of investee companies.[47] There have been debates in other jurisdictions, such as in the UK and Europe, on the differences between shareholder activists and stewards, and whether they are to be considered short-term and long-term investors.[48] However, we have not seen such a debate in Taiwan, at least among legal scholars. In Taiwan, shareholder proposals are considered to be examples of shareholder activism. It was introduced into the Taiwan Company Act in 2005, and is considered to be a positive shareholder activism regime. Listed companies are required to publish information on shareholder proposals received before annual shareholders' meetings, including the content of shareholder proposals and whether they are

---

[41] Taiwan Code (n 6) 1.
[42] Taiwan Code (n 6) 2.
[43] Iris H-Y Chiu and Dionysia Katelouzou, 'From Shareholder Stewardship to Shareholder Duties: Is the Time Ripe?' in Hanne S Birkmose (ed), *Shareholders' Duties* (Kluwer Law International 2017) 131–52.
[44] Taiwan Code (n 6) 6, Guideline 2-1.
[45] Taiwan Code (n 6) 1.
[46] ibid.
[47] Taiwan Code (n 6) 2.
[48] See e.g. Dionysia Katelouzou, 'Reflections on the Nature of the Public Corporation in an Era of Shareholder Activism and Stewardship' in Barnali Choudhury and Martin Petrin (eds), *Understanding the Company: Corporate Governance and Theory* (CUP 2017).

included in the agenda of shareholders' meetings.[49] The Code also expects institutional investors to make shareholder proposals and to engage in dialogue with the investee companies regarding specific agendas of shareholders' meetings.[50]

Knowing that institutional investors may not be able to perform all activities by themselves, outsourcing part of the stewardship function to other professionals, such as proxy advisory firms or governance advisory firms who provide governance research services for institutional investors, is permitted by the Code.[51] However, the Code expressly emphasizes that the signatories shall bear the ultimate stewardship responsibilities to their clients and beneficiaries if they outsource the activities. Therefore, institutional investors shall monitor and maintain effective communication with the outsourced professional service providers to ensure the best interests of their clients and beneficiaries.

Another point that needs to be mentioned is that the Code does not clarify whether it applies to the professionals who perform the stewardship function for the signatories of the Code. Under the UK Code, those who perform the stewardship activities, disregarding the signatories themselves, their agents or trustees, shall comply with the Code.[52] We suggest that the Taiwan Code should reconsider this issue in future revisions and that the UK's approach may be worth considering.

12.3.2 Regulatory Philosophy: Voluntary Opt-In Model and Incentives

Although the Taiwan Code expects institutional investors to perform good stewardship functions, an institutional investor will not be subject to the Code unless it voluntarily opts in to become a signatory by making a public endorsement of the Taiwan Code and notifying the TWSE Corporate Governance Center.[53] The voluntary opt-in approach applies to both domestic and foreign institutional investors. In contrast, the UK Code applies to all FCA-authorized managers who have to comply or explain.[54]

As of 10 June 2020, 151 domestic and foreign institutional investors have voluntarily notified the TWSE Corporate Governance Center of their public endorsement of the Taiwan Code.[55] What is the legal effect of filing the Endorsement Statement? The Code expressly stipulates that signatories are not required to comply with the six stewardship principles. Instead, the Code adopts the regulatory philosophy of a 'comply or explain' approach, intended to provide flexibility to institutional investors while encouraging them to do as much as they can, as long

---

[49] The TWSE created a Corporate Governance Special Zone under the Market Observation Post System (<https://mops.twse.com.tw/mops/web/t144sb09> accessed 22 May 2020), allowing all listed companies to disclose the information of shareholder proposals so that everyone can access the information.
[50] Taiwan Code (n 6) 8–9, Guideline 4-2.
[51] Taiwan Code (n 6) 2.
[52] e.g. 'Proxy advisors are required under the Proxy Advisors (Shareholders' Rights) Regulations 2019 (PA Regulations), supervised by the FCA, to publicly disclose a code of conduct and explain how they have followed it. (UK Code 2020 (n 1) 31).
[53] Taiwan Code (n 6) 3.
[54] UK Code 2020 (n 1) 30–31. Occupational pension schemes are required 'to develop and explain how they have implemented policies for the exercise of the rights and engagement for all investments' and 'how their equity investment strategy is consistent with their liabilities and provide information on their arrangements with asset managers'. Insurers and reinsurers are required 'to develop and explain how they have implemented an engagement policy for their listed equity investments ... They will also be required to provide information on their arrangements with asset managers and explain how their equity investment strategy is consistent with their liabilities.' All asset managers are required to comply or explain.
[55] The signatories of endorsement of the Taiwan Stewardship Code can be found at TWSE Corporate Governance Center (Taiwan Stock Exchange, 'List of Signatories of the Stewardship Code' (n 15)).

as they stick to the principles of acting bona fide and with transparency when disclosing information.[56]

In the corporate governance regime, Taiwan's regulatory philosophy has been the escalation strategy (i.e. being soft and encouraging in the initial stage, using evaluation as a supplemental tool, and disclosing the information to the public). The competent authority or self-regulators may later expand the scope of application and add pressure. For example, when independent directors and audit committees were introduced in Taiwan in 2006, the TSEA on one hand gave public companies freedom to voluntarily appoint independent directors into the board and to establish audit committees to replace supervisors; on the other hand, the competent authority was authorized to designate what types of public company must have independent directors and an audit committee.[57] At the initial stage, the FSC designated financial institutions and listed companies with paid-in capital of NT$ 50 billion (USD 1.66 billion) and above as those that must have independent directors, but designated no company as being required to establish an audit committee.[58] After gradual broadening of the scope of application, all public companies have appointed independent directors since 2017.[59]

To encourage institutional investors to comply with the Taiwan Code, the TWSE provides a Taiwan Code Q&A to help signatories understand common questions.[60] So far, the TWSE has also issued two editions of Recommendations on Disclosure of Stewardship Information, which include examples from institutional investors' disclosures.[61] Moreover, the TWSE has issued evaluation criteria for evaluating the disclosure of signatories. The twenty-five criteria tell the signatories how they should disclose on each principle.[62]

Unlike the CSR report, which requires a listed company to follow the disclosure rules and the GRI standard, there is no specific rule regarding how a signatory discloses its stewardship report.[63] The evaluation criteria are only suggested disclosure guidelines. To encourage signatories to make better disclosure of their stewardship activities, the TWSE selected eight

---

[56] Taiwan Code (n 6) 4.
[57] TSEA, arts 14-2, 14-4.
[58] FSC Financial-Supervision-Securities-Issuance Order No 0950001616 (28 March 2006).
[59] The FSC issued an order granting a grace period for non-financial listed companies with paid-in capital less than NT $ 10 billion dollars to appoint independent directors in 2017. FSC Financial-Supervision-Securities-Issuance Order No 1020053112 (31 December 2013).
[60] Taiwan Stock Exchange, 'Q&A: Stewardship Principles for Institutional Investors' (15 February 2017) <https://cgc.twse.com.tw/static/20191203/8a828e176ecadafb016ecb01515b0000_0000000059fc1668015a3f90c0680014_Stewardship%20Principles%20for%20Institutional%20Investors-QA%2020170215.pdf> accessed 22 May 2020.
[61] Taiwan Stock Exchange, '機構投資人盡職治理活動揭露情形與揭露建議(Jīgòu tóuzī rén jìnzhí zhìlǐ huódòng jiēlù qíngxíng yǔ jiēlù jiànyì) [Review and Recommendations on Disclosure of Stewardship Information]' (April 2019) <https://cgc.twse.com.tw/stewardshipInfo/listEn> accessed 22 May 2020; Taiwan Stock Exchange, '機構投資人盡職治理資訊揭露建議 (Jīgòu tóuzī rén jìnzhí zhìlǐ zīxùn jiēlù jiànyì) [Recommendations on Disclosure of Stewardship Information]' (December 2019) <https://cgc.twse.com.tw/stewardshipInfo/listEn> accessed 22 May 2020.
[62] Taiwan Stock Exchange, '較佳實務遵循名單評比標準 (Jiào jiā shíwù zūnxún míngdān píngbǐ biāozhǔn) [Stewardship Evaluation Criteria]' (2019) <https://cgc.twse.com.tw/static/20191204/8a828e176ecfb3a8016ecfe8ac5a0000_較佳實務遵循名單評比標準.pdf> accessed 22 May 2020. English version available at <https://cgc.twse.com.tw/static/20200505/8a828e17718c42cd0171e39655b90010_Rating%20criteria%20for%20Signatories%20with%20better%20practices%20and%20compliances.pdf> accessed 22 May 2020.
[63] 'Where a listed company is under one of the following circumstances, it shall prepare and file a corporate social responsibility report ... according to these Rules.' Taiwan Stock Exchange Corporation Rules Governing the Preparation and Filing of Corporate Social Responsibility Reports by TWSE Listed Companies (2 January 2020) arts 2–3.

institutions and announced them as 'signatories with better practices and compliances' to the public on 30 December 2019.[64]

12.3.3 *Stewardship Principles and Guidance*

The Taiwan Code states its six stewardship principles in chapter 4 and provides guidelines for each in chapter 5.

Principle 1 asks the signatories to establish and disclose stewardship policies. To make appropriate stewardship policies, an institution must take into consideration its role in the investment chain, the nature of its business and the protection it offers its clients and beneficiaries.[65] Theoretically, an institution should monitor all of its investments and play the role of a 'good steward' in every investee company. However, for efficiency and cost concerns, an institution should be able to decide whether the focus of its stewardship activities, including outsourcing activities, targets certain types of investment in terms of investment amount or any other consideration.

Principle 2 asks the signatories to establish and disclose their policy for the management of conflicts of interest. Under the Company Act, there are several provisions regulating conflicts of interest. The purpose for establishing the policy for management of conflicts of interest is to protect the best interests of clients or beneficiaries of institutional investors.[66] In the policy, it shall disclose different types of conflict of interest and measurements for their management.[67] The Code further points out two types of conflict of interest. One is that the institutional investor makes harmful decisions or activities detrimental to its clients or beneficiaries because of its self-interest.[68] The other is that the institutional investor makes decisions that benefit specific clients or beneficiaries, but injures others.[69] In case of the occurrence of a significant conflict of interest, the institution must disclose and explain the matters to its clients or beneficiaries.[70]

Principle 3 asks signatories to regularly monitor the investee companies. As a professional institutional investor, it is its job to regularly monitor its investee companies. However, the Code emphasizes that the purpose of monitoring is to evaluate all relevant information regarding the investee companies, and the impact on the long-term interest of the clients or beneficiaries, to decide whether to make further dialogue and interaction with the investee companies to formulate future investment decisions.[71] Because there are so many aspects that need to be monitored, the Code suggests that an institutional investor may design a plan of monitoring after considering its investment purpose, cost and benefit.[72]

---

[64] The eight institutional investors that were selected as better compliers include five domestic signatories (Cathay Life Insurance, Cathay Century Insurance, Cathay Securities Investment Trust, Bureau of Labor Funds of the Ministry of Labor, and JP Morgan Securities Investment Trust (Taiwan subsidiary of JP Morgan Asset Management) and three foreign signatories (First State Investment, Hermes Investment Management Limited, and Robeco). Taiwan Stock Exchange, 'Signatories with Better Practices and Compliances' (30 December 2019) <https://cgc.twse.com.tw/stewardshipInfo/listEn> accessed 22 May 2020.
[65] Taiwan Code (n 6) 6, Guideline 1-1.
[66] Taiwan Code (n 6) 6, Guideline 2-1.
[67] Taiwan Code (n 6) 7, Guideline 2-2.
[68] Taiwan Code (n 6) 7, Guideline 2-3(1).
[69] Taiwan Code (n 6) 7, Guideline 2-3(2).
[70] Taiwan Code (n 6) 7, Guideline 2-5.
[71] Taiwan Code (n 6) 7–8, Guideline 3-1.
[72] Taiwan Code (n 6) 8, Guideline 3-2.

Principle 4 requires the signatories to conduct appropriate dialogue and interactions with the investee companies. This principle focuses on the corporate governance of the investee companies. The purpose and timing of such dialogue and interaction is to allow institutional investors to get more details of the important themes that investee companies are involved in, so that institutional investors may use their influence to improve the corporate governance of the investee companies.[73] In order to protect the interest of its clients or beneficiaries, an institutional investor is permitted to collaborate with other institutional investors to take necessary actions.[74] Collective action is permitted under Principle 4 of the Taiwan Code.

Compared with the UK Code, the Taiwan Code provides institutional investors with flexibility without much pressure. Principle 11 of the UK Code requires signatories to escalate stewardship activities to influence investee companies if necessary.[75] Signatories are required to explain how they set forth the expectations for escalating stewardship activities, how they select and prioritize the issues for escalation, and how escalation has differed for funds and assets.[76] Signatories also need to describe the outcome of escalation, whether the investee companies have taken any actions or made any changes and whether the outcome has affected the investment decisions.[77]

Principle 5 requires signatories to establish precise voting policies and disclose voting information. The voting policy and disclosure of voting information is probably one of the most important subjects of the Code. An institutional investor is expected to carefully evaluate the information and the impact on the long-term interest of its clients or beneficiaries before making voting decisions, even though it has obtained voting suggestions from proxy advisory firms.[78] The Code suggests that institutional investors retain their flexibility in deciding their voting policy. Institutional investors also have to disclose their voting policy regarding whether their general principle is to vote for or against the agenda proposed by the management, or whether there is any type of agenda that it will abstain from voting.[79] If a voting advisory report is obtained, the institutional investor needs to disclose the fact that it has obtained such a report and whether it will adopt the suggestion.[80] It is important to keep all the records, document all of the analysis and voting decisions, and disclose the voting information on a collective basis annually.[81]

Principle 6 requires signatories to periodically disclose to clients or beneficiaries the status of the fulfilment of stewardship responsibilities. In a recent announcement, Principle 6 was revised to 'Periodically Disclose to Clients or Beneficiaries about the Status of Fulfilment of Stewardship Responsibilities'.[82] The principle suggests that the disclosure should be accessible on the institutional investor's website or a website designated by the Taiwan Stock Exchange, and in its annual report.

---

[73] Taiwan Code (n 6) 8, Guideline 4-1.
[74] Taiwan Code (n 6) 9, Guideline 4-3.
[75] UK Code 2020 (n 1) 20.
[76] ibid.
[77] ibid.
[78] Taiwan Code (n 6) 9, Guideline 5-2.
[79] Taiwan Code (n 6) 10, Guideline 5-3(3).
[80] Taiwan Code (n 6) 10, Guideline 5-3(5).
[81] Taiwan Code (n 6) 10, Guideline 5-4.
[82] Taiwan Stock Exchange, Revision of Stewardship Principles for Institutional Investors <https://cgc.twse.com.tw/static/20200227/8a828e176fc2195a0170857b48d30008_Revision%20of%20Taiwan%20Stewardship%20Principles%20for%20Institutional%20Investors.pdf> accessed 10 June 2020.

12.4 INVESTOR PROTECTION CENTER'S ROLE AS AN ALTERNATIVE GOOD STEWARDSHIP MODEL

To ensure the fairness of securities markets and to prevent the occurrence of securities fraud, Taiwan enacted the SFIPA in July 2002 which came into force in January 2003. To help investors recover from their losses resulting from securities fraud, the securities regulator asked several institutions, according to the SFIPA, to found the SFIPC, a non-profit and non-governmental organization, to provide investor protection services such as bringing class actions against wrongdoers.[83] Investors do not have to pay the SFIPC to obtain their services. In class actions, if the SFIPC wins, after receiving the payments from the defendants, according to court judgments or settlements, the SFIPC distributes the money to investors after deducting court fees. If the SFIPC loses the case, investors owe nothing to the SFIPC. In the following subsections, we will briefly introduce the SFIPC's major functions, before discussing its role as a unique model of a good steward.

12.4.1 *Major Functions of the Securities and Futures Investors Protection Center*

The SFIPC was established in January 2003 under the SFIPA. The major investor protection services provided by the SFIPC include: (1) mediation; (2) class actions and class arbitration; (3) derivative actions; and (4) judicial removal of directors.

Mediation services can potentially reduce the burden on the courts, if disputes can be solved there. However, from past experience, most mediations do not end up solving disputes mainly because parties are unable to agree on a compensation amount.[84] For example, the SFIPC Mediation Committee handled forty-one mediation cases in 2018, but only four of them resulted in agreement that was approved by the court.[85] From the establishment of the SFIPC in 2003 to the end of 2018, there were 561 mediation cases, but only 51, or roughly 9 per cent, reached agreement.[86]

Whenever the SFIPC knows that potential cases[87] involve securities fraud, misleading prospectuses or financial reports, insider trading or market manipulation, it may execute a class action on behalf of qualified investors, who delegate their right against the wrongdoers to the SFIPC.[88] In 2018, the SFIPC, on behalf of more than 1,900 investors, brought 10 class

---

[83] '財團法人證券投資人及期貨交易人保護中心捐助章程' (Cáituán fǎrén zhèngquàn tóuzī rén jí qíhuò jiāoyì rén bǎohù zhōngxīn juānzhù zhāngchéng) [SFIPC Charter of Endowment], art 5 <www.selaw.com.tw/LawArticle.aspx?LawID=G0101801> accessed 22 May 2020.

[84] SFIPA, art 22:

> When a civil dispute occurs between a securities investor or a futures trader and an issuer, a securities firm, a securities service enterprise, a futures commission merchant, the Stock Exchange, the Taipei Exchange, a clearing institution or another interested party, where the dispute arises out of offerings, issuance, trading, futures transactions, or other securities-related matters, the securities investor or futures trader may apply to the protection institution for mediation.

[85] Securities and Futures Investors Protection Center, '2018 Annual Report' (2019) 19 <www.sfipc.org.tw/MainWeb/Article.aspx?L=2&SNO=cETUAHMWj7bwkiS59QXNww==> accessed 22 May 2020.

[86] ibid.

[87] The SFIPC begins to engage initial studies on cases that are either prosecuted or forwarded from the securities regulator, the TWSE or the TPEx, or based on reported news. Most cases brought by the SFIPC have been prosecuted by prosecutors because of evidence that is readily available.

[88] To bring a class action, there must be more than twenty qualified investors who delegate the right of litigation to the SFIPC. The SFIPC will conduct initial studies of the case. Subsequently, the Legal Service Division will make a proposal to the board of directors for approval before filing the suit with the court. After, the SFIPC will make a public announcement on potential class actions, and wait for qualified investors to sign the Form of Empowerment of Ligation Rights. SFIPA, art 28. Qualified investors are then selected by the SFIPC staff lawyers according to

actions for more than NT$ 1 billion (USD 32.25 million), which were the damages suffered by investors.[89] As of the end of 2018, there were 123 class actions pending in courts.[90] Separately, there have been 122 closed cases since 2003.[91] The SFIPC has won, fully or partially, forty-nine class actions since 2003.[92]

The SFIPA was amended on 20 May 2009 to add article 10-1, which grants the SFIPC a right to bring derivative actions against corporate directors who are found to have materially caused damages to the company, or violated the laws or the articles of incorporation in a significant manner.[93] Derivative action, regulated by articles 214 and 215 of the Company Act, has rarely been used, mainly because of the high threshold posed by the standing requirement and the lack of incentives for shareholders to bring such actions.[94] The SFIPC holds 1,000 shares of each public company.[95] Article 10-1 delegates the right to the SFIPC to bring derivative actions without imposing other shareholding requirements. From May 2009 to the end of 2018, the SFIPC has brought fifty-four derivative actions against directors and supervisors of public companies and has received NT$ 1.57 billion (US$ 50.64 million) in compensation or settlement payments from corporate and individual defendants.[96]

In the May 2009 addition, article 10-1 of the SFIPA also delegates a right to the SFIPC to request the court to remove a director or supervisor who, in the course of performing their duties, has caused material injury to the company or violated laws, regulations or the articles of incorporation in a significant manner.[97] Judicial removal of directors is regulated by article 200 of the Company Act. To request the court to remove a director, the plaintiff must hold more than 3 per cent of outstanding shares and a shareholders' meeting must have failed to remove such a director. Therefore, it has been very difficult to remove a director either by shareholders' meeting or by the court. According to article 10-1 of the SFIPA, the SFIPC can bring a case requesting the court to remove a director. Failure of a shareholders' meeting to pass a resolution to remove a director is not a prerequisite for the SFIPC to bring an action for the judicial removal of that director. From May 2009 to the end of 2018, the SFIPC brought fifty-three cases to court to have a director removed.[98] The SFIPC won sixteen cases and withdrew twenty because the defendant directors or supervisors resigned or would not be re-elected.[99]

When a corporate insider, director, supervisor or manager of a public company, buys and sells equity securities of the company within six months, the company is required to request such

---

relevant provisions of the TSEA, such as art 20-1 (civil liabilities for fraudulent financial reporting) and Art 32 (civil liabilities for fraudulent prospectuses) and the facts of each case, particularly the time of wrongdoing.

[89] Exchange rate: USD 1 = NT$ 31. Three of the ten class actions in 2018 related to making misleading financial statements, three related to market manipulation and four related to insider trading (SFIPC (n 85) 20).
[90] ibid.
[91] ibid.
[92] ibid.
[93] SFIPA, art 10-1, amended 10 June 2020.
[94] Before 1 November 2018, to bring a derivative action, the plaintiff must hold more than 3% of outstanding shares for more than one year. This threshold was lowered in August 2018 by an amendment to the Company Act (effective 1 November 2018) to holding 1% for more than six months. Taiwan Company Act, art 214. See also Wang R Tseng and Wallace WY Wang, 'Derivative Actions in Taiwan: Legal and Cultural Hurdles with a Glimmer of Hope for the Future' in Dan W Puchniak, Harald Baum and Michael Ewing-Chow (eds), *The Derivative Action in Asia: A Comparative and Functional Approach* (CUP 2012).
[95] The SFIPC can hold shares of listed companies according to the SFIPA. SFIPA, art 19; Regulations Governing the Securities Investor and Futures Trader Protection Institution, art 9.
[96] SFIPC (n 85) 21.
[97] SFIPA, art 10-1.
[98] SFIPC (n 85) 21.
[99] ibid.

a corporate insider to disgorge the short-swing profits to the company.[100] If the company does not make such a request, shareholders may request the company to exercise such a right in thirty days and may file an action with the court against the corporate insider for the disgorgement of short-swing trading profits if the company fails to exercise its right within thirty days of the request.[101] Currently, the SFIPC is the party that plays the role of requesting that the company exercise this right or that brings a derivative action for the disgorgement of short-swing profits.[102] The SFIPC brings short-swing disgorgement actions in accordance with the trading information provided by the TWSE and the TPEx where the surveillance system includes the account information of all corporate insiders of listed companies. From July 2017 to June 2018, the SFIPC brought 293 disgorgement cases, and a total of 7,886 cases were brought from 1994 to 2018.[103]

12.4.2 Role of the SFIPC as a Good Steward

Now that we have introduced the major functions of the SFIPC, we will discuss why it can play a role in 'good stewardship'.

12.4.2.1 Using Different Types of Litigation to Serve as a Good Steward

The SFIPA empowers the SFIPC to utilize certain weapons that enable it to become a good steward. Through the best use of these weapons, it deters public companies and corporate insiders from violating the law and the articles of incorporation.

The first type of weapon is using class actions against public companies and the wrongdoers who violate the TSEA. Though litigation is not expressly mentioned in the Taiwan Code, it does provide that a signatory may collaborate with other institutions to pursue the best interest of clients.[104] Among class actions brought by the SFIPC, three major types of litigation are directly relevant: (1) misleading prospectuses; (2) misleading financial statements; and (3) insider trading. Although class actions are an *ex post* mechanism, they have a deterrent function in that they educate public companies about the importance of legal compliance and corporate insiders about the need to exercise due diligence when performing their duties. Bringing class actions against wrongdoers sends a strong signal that the SFIPC will be responsible for private enforcement for the public interest and that wrongdoers should not take the chance that they will not be sued.

It is important to note that, unlike Principle 11 of the UK Code 2020, the Taiwan Code does not have an escalation requirement.[105] Although this is not a recognized form of good stewardship under the current Taiwan Code, and it may not be suitable for every institutional investor, the SFIPC has carefully and properly exercised its statutory power to act as a good steward in every listed company to enhance corporate governance and investor protection.

---

[100] TSEA, art 157.
[101] ibid.
[102] SFIPC Charter of Endowment (n 83) art 4.
[103] SFIPC (n 85) 22. Although the SFIPC was established in 2003, its predecessor, the Legal Service Division of the Securities and Futures Institute, began to perform this function in 1994.
[104] Taiwan Code (n 6) 8–9, Guideline 4-2. The sample endorsement statement provides that if the investee company has serious violations of corporate governance and harms the interest of the clients or beneficiaries, a signatory may 'act collectively with other investors to protect their interests'. Taiwan Code (n 6) 13, Appendix: Sample Statement on 'Stewardship Principles for Institutional Investors'.
[105] UK Code 2020 (n 1).

12.4.2.2 Attending Shareholders' Meetings to Serve as a Good Steward

Attending shareholders' meetings is a method identified in the Taiwan Code by which institutional investors can perform their duties of monitoring investee companies. As mentioned, the SFIPC holds 1,000 shares of each public company. Being a shareholder, the SFIPC has the right to attend the shareholders' meetings of every public company. The SFIPC dispatches staff to attend shareholders' meetings of select listed companies, based on the meeting agenda and whether it involves deciding on any material corporate affairs.[106] The SFIPC usually sends written inquiries to companies, and attends shareholders' meetings to monitor their progress. This forces companies to carefully take into consideration shareholders' interests. Moreover, the SFIPC continues to monitor how companies execute their resolutions. If it finds any violation of law or of the articles of incorporation, the SFIPC files an action with the court to invalidate the impugned resolution.

One may be sceptical about whether it is possible for the SFIPC to be a good steward with such a diversified portfolio. Moreover, the SFIPC is not considered to be an institutional investor according to the Taiwan Code and cannot become a signatory of the Code. So, how can the SFIPC be a good steward? The answer is that it may be difficult for a normal investor with a diversified portfolio to function as a good steward. In contrast, the SFIPC may act as a good steward while performing its statutory missions. Although the SFIPA does not require the SFIPC to attend shareholders' meetings, the SFIPC still actively acts as a good steward by participating in and observing meetings, and may undertake necessary actions such as seeking the invalidation of resolutions of shareholders' meetings if it finds any illegality in the procedure, voting or agenda contents.

12.4.2.3 Frequently Providing Investor Education Programmes as a Good Steward

Running investor education programmes for investors as well as listed companies is another type of good stewardship function, though it is not mentioned in the Taiwan Code as a suggested practice. The SFIPC performs good stewardship activities by providing frequent educational information via its website, TV and radio advertisements, and major newspapers. These programmes cover various themes focusing on promoting corporate governance and issues arising from real cases, such as the rights, liabilities and functions of independent directors, and how to prevent insider trading.[107] Providing class actions and mediation services is an *ex post* measure to help investors, while investor education is an *ex ante* measure that protects investors in advance. To be a good steward, it is equally important to provide protection before injuries occur.

12.5 FURTHER CONSIDERATIONS OF THE TAIWAN CODE: PROMOTING RESPONSIBLE INVESTMENT AND SUSTAINABILITY

International organizations and individual nations have been devoted to promoting good corporate governance. For example, the Organisation for Economic Co-operations and Development (OECD) adopted the first Principles of Corporate Governance in 1999, and has

---

[106] SFIPC (n 85) 5.
[107] See e.g. Ying-Qing Tsai, '提升獨立董事職能 強化公司治理 (Tíshēng dúlì dǒngshì zhínéng qiánghuà gōngsī zhìlǐ) [Elevating the Functions of Independent Directors and Enhancing Corporate Governance]' *Economic Daily* (11 July 2019) A12 (inviting scholars, regulators and practitioners to provide suggestions).

continued to modify them in response to and co-ordinated with the changes in business structures and environments.[108] The latest partnership with the G20 adopted the *G20/OECD Principles of Corporate Governance*.[109] The OECD emphasizes that '[g]ood corporate governance helps to build an environment of trust, transparency and accountability necessary for fostering long-term investment, financial stability and business integrity, thereby supporting stronger growth and more inclusive societies'.[110] At first, in some jurisdictions such as the US, shareholder protection, and protection of minority shareholders in particular, was the central focus of corporate governance.[111] This protection was gradually extended to cover the interests of other stakeholders or integrated with other corporate governance regimes that focus on protection of stakeholders.[112] More elements have been included into the scope of corporate governance, including more disclosures on the performance of CSR and ESG, particularly environmental issues.[113]

Reviewing the evolution of Taiwan's corporate governance regime shows that Taiwan has closely monitored and followed the international trend and norm in promoting good corporate governance. Although Taiwan was not hit by the 1997 Asian financial crisis, the government noticed the importance of corporate governance and included the promotion of corporate governance as one of its important government policies. The TWSE and the TPEx adopted the TWN CG Code on 4 October 2002.[114] In 2010, the TWN CSR Code was promulgated.[115] Listed companies are required to file CSR reports annually.[116] Additionally, the TWSE promulgated another rule, 'Ethical Corporate Management Best Practice Principles for TWSE/TPEx Listed Companies' (TWN Business Integrity Code), to promote business integrity.[117] Although

---

[108] After the 2008 global financial crisis, the OECD perceived the imperfectness of existing CG principles and developed a set of recommendations. The OECD Steering Group on Corporate Governance action plan engaged in three phases of studies and produced three reports: (1) Grant Kirkpatrick, *The Corporate Governance Lessons from the Financial Crisis* (OECD 2009) <www.oecd.org/finance/financial-markets/42229620.pdf> accessed 22 May 2020; (2) OECD, 'Corporate Governance and the Financial Crisis: Key Findings and Main Messages' (June 2009) <www.oecd.org/corporate/ca/corporategovernanceprinciples/43056196.pdf> accessed 22 May 2020 (the report was developed on the basis of the fact-finding study *The Corporate Governance Lessons from the Financial Crisis*, for the purpose of advancing the action plan on corporate governance and the financial crisis); and (3) OECD, 'Corporate Governance and the Financial Crisis: Conclusions and Emerging Good Practices to Enhance Implementation of the Principles' (24 February 2010) <www.oecd.org/daf/ca/corporategovernanceprinciples/44679170.pdf> accessed 22 May 2020.

[109] OECD, *G20/OECD Principles of Corporate Governance* (2015) <www.oecd.org/daf/ca/Corporate-Governance-Principles-ENG.pdf> accessed 22 May 2020.

[110] OECD, 'Corporate Governance' <www.oecd.org/corporate/> accessed 22 May 2020.

[111] The corporate governance can be defined as the 'rules and market practices which determine how companies, especially listed companies, make decisions, the transparency of their decision-making processes, the accountability of their directors, managers and employees, the information they disclose to investors, and the protection of minority shareholders.' Bernard S Black and others, 'Corporate Governance in Korea at the Millennium: Enhancing International Competitiveness (Final Report and Legal Reform Recommendations to the Ministry of Justice of the Republic of Korea)' (2001) 26 *Journal of Corporation Law* 546, 547–48.

[112] See Katharine V Jackson, 'Towards A Stakeholder-Shareholder Theory of Corporate Governance: A Comparative Analysis' (2011) 7 *Hastings Business Law Journal* 309, 311–12 (comparing different corporate governance models and their integration with each other, such as the 'shareholder-centric model' of the US and the 'stakeholder-oriented corporate governance systems' of Germany).

[113] See Davies, The UK Stewardship Code 2010–2020, Chapter 2 and Katelouzou and Klettner, Sustainable Finance and Stewardship, Chapter 26.

[114] Promulgated on 4 October 2002 per Public Announcement Ref. No. (91)-Taiwan-Stock-Shang-025298 of the Taiwan Stock Exchange Corporation.

[115] CSR Code (n 8).

[116] CSR Code (n 8) arts 28–29; Taiwan Stock Exchange Corporation Rules Governing the Preparation and Filing of Corporate Social Responsibility Reports by TWSE Listed Companies, art 3; Taipei Exchange Rules Governing the Preparation and Filing of Corporate Social Responsibility Reports by TPEx Listed Companies, art 3.

[117] Ethical Corporate Management Best Practice Principles for TWSE/GTSM Listed Companies, (promulgated 3 September 2010, last amended 23 May 2019) [hereinafter TWSE Business Integrity Code].

the TWN Business Integrity Code, similar to the TWN CG Code, contains best practice principles, which are considered soft law, it nevertheless promotes a responsible business culture. At a minimum, a company and its employees must comply with the relevant laws when conducting business.[118]

In order to comply with the GRI reporting requirement to fully disclose information regarding a company's contribution and compliance in CSR and ESG, the TWSE amended the 'Taiwan Stock Exchange Corporation Rules Governing the Preparation and Filing of Corporate Social Responsibility Reports by TWSE Listed Companies' (TWSE CSR Rules) in October 2015, requiring listed companies to prepare and file CSR reports in accordance with the GRI Sustainability Reporting Guidelines. In January 2019, the TWSE CSR Rules were further amended to require listed companies to comply with the GRI Sustainability Reporting Standards to support the Sustainable Development Goals promoted by the GRI.[119]

All these efforts are aimed at promoting corporate governance best practices and ensuring that the requirements are imposed on public companies. Yet, with all the current efforts on international and national levels, we still see problems occurring occasionally.[120] At this moment, we understand that merely imposing CSR and ESG responsibilities on companies and requiring them to file reports can produce some positive effects. However, asking institutional investors to act as good stewards to monitor these issues may produce more effective results.

12.6 COMMENTS AND RECOMMENDATIONS

The Taiwan Code, similar to its brothers and sisters in other countries, aims to encourage institutional investors to perform good stewardship functions. Although one of the objectives of the Code is to improve the corporate governance of investee companies, it works differently from the TWN CG Code which focuses on the corporate governance of listed companies. Another objective of the Code is to encourage institutional investors to perform fiduciary duties for their clients and beneficiaries. Could an institutional investor achieve the objectives of the Code? Would there be any potential conflicts that prevent an institutional investor from achieving these objectives? After the promulgation of the Code, are there any mechanisms available to monitor the performance of institutional investors? Is a 'comply or explain' approach a sufficient reason for not monitoring institutional investors while still ensuring that the objectives of the Code are achieved? Is reputation a sufficient incentive for institutional investors to comply with the Code? All these issues require greater explanation and discussion.

12.6.1 *Can the Taiwan Code Achieve Its Objectives?*

Under the Taiwan Code, an institutional investor is expected to ensure the long-term interest of its clients or beneficiaries on one hand, and to use its expertise and influence to improve the corporate governance of the investee companies on the other hand. These two objectives appear reasonable and not too difficult to achieve. However, one may be curious about how much effect

---

[118] TWSE Business Integrity Code, arts 4, 18.
[119] Taiwan Stock Exchange Corporation Rules Governing the Preparation and Filing of Corporate Social Responsibility Reports by TWSE Listed Companies, art 3.
[120] For example, in 2013, a listed company caused water pollution in its operations and was sued for violation of the Water Pollution Control Act. The Supreme Court dismissed the appeal in April 2019 and confirmed that the defendant company and its responsible persons were guilty. Taiwan Supreme Court 106 Tai-Shang 3470.

the Taiwan Code can have in reality. Close analysis of the Code Principles reveals a focus on the duties owed by institutional investors to their clients or beneficiaries. Compliance with the principles depends on the role of each individual institutional investor in the investment chain, whether it is the one making the investment decisions or one simply receiving instruction on making investments.

Institutional investors' duties are governed mainly by the contracts with their clients or beneficiaries and the relevant laws and regulations, such as the TSEA, the SITCA, the Insurance Act and their respective subsidiary legislation. Principle 2 regarding conflict of interest policies asks that institutional investors disclose any conflicts of interests that may occur between them and their clients or beneficiaries and how they intend to prevent or manage them. The purpose is to ensure that the signatories of the Code can pursue the long-term interest of their clients or beneficiaries when carrying out their business. However, one may wonder whether in practice an institution will really disclose all conflicts of interest between it and its clients, especially those that will benefit specific clients but harm the interests of other clients or beneficiaries. Conflicts of interest activities or transactions are usually in violation of the corporate, securities and other financial laws. Would institutional investors voluntarily disclose such information? Would the disclosure be in violation of the contracts between the institutional investors and their clients or beneficiaries? How about if there is a confidentiality clause preventing the institutional investors from making any disclosure? These are potential concerns that prevent Principle 2 from being effectively complied with. This chapter suggests that the idea and the direction of the Code are worth supporting. However, it also observes that the Code cannot transform every signatory institution into a perfect stewardship executor.

12.6.2 Who Is Monitoring the Stewards?

The Taiwan Code is a bit different from the TWN CG Code, although they were both prepared by the TWSE and are both soft law. The TWN CG Code has a greater impact on listed companies. This can be seen in several of its aspects. First, some contents of the TWN CG Code are binding because they are either already included in the Company Act or the TSEA, or have since been codified into the law. Second, a listed company must comply with the TWN CG Code if it was listed after its promulgation because, by signing the listing contract, the listed company agrees to comply with the law, regulations and rules of the TWSE or the TPEx. Third, the TWSE Corporate Governance Center together with the TPEx created the Corporate Governance Evaluation System and has begun to conduct evaluations since 2015.[121] The evaluation results divide the evaluated companies into seven categories (i.e. the top 5%, 6–20%, 21–35%, 36–50%, 51–65%, 66–80% and 81–100%).[122] This provides listed companies with pressure or incentives to comply with the Code and improve their corporate governance. In contrast, the UK companies' major pressure comes from the UK FRC, the independent competent authority who enacted the UK Corporate Governance Code, the UK Code and

---

[121] The evaluation of listed companies is implemented by the Securities and Futures Institute (SFI). The results of the evaluation are announced in April of each year, and the information is publicly accessible free of charge at the websites of the SFI (Securities and Futures Institute, '公司治理評鑑 (Gōngsī zhìlǐ píng jiàn) [Corporate Governance Evaluation]' <www.sfi.org.tw/cga/cga1> accessed 22 May 2020) and the TWSE Corporate Governance Center (Taiwan Stock Exchange, '公司治理評鑑 (Gōngsī zhìlǐ píng jiàn) [Corporate Governance Evaluation]' <https://cgc.twse.com.tw/evaluationCorp/listCh> accessed 22 May 2020).

[122] Taiwan Stock Exchange, 'Information Disclosure and Transparency Ranking System Overview' <https://cgc.twse.com.tw/frontEN/evaluationInfoOverview> accessed 22 May 2020, for an overview of the Information Disclosure and Transparency Ranking System.

the new principles of corporate governance for large private companies (the Wates Principles).[123] The FRC reviews the performance of regulated companies on corporate governance and stewardship matters.[124] The FRC in the Annual Review of the UK Corporate Governance Code indicated that many companies declared that they have fully complied with the UK Code, but, in reality, they failed to disclose in detail their policies and practices.[125]

In contrast, the Taiwan Code that was announced in June 2016 has not thus far had any further revision by the TWSE. Implementation of the Code is affected by several factors. First is whether the internal policy of the institutional investor supports its compliance with the Code; merely signing the compliance declaration does not ensure compliance with the Code in reality. Therefore, we must observe the stewardship reports disclosed by signatories to evaluate the quality of the disclosure. Second is whether the institutional investor is a listed company of the TWSE or the TPEx. Because most signatories of the Code are not listed companies, they are not subject to supervision by the TWSE or the TPEx. Therefore, compliance with the Code by non-TWSE or non-TPEx listed companies remains to be observed. It is hoped that, without any other mechanisms, reputation can be an effective incentive. Third is whether the institutional investor is a domestic financial institution but not a signatory. If so, the FSC may communicate with the specific financial institution on what should be improved because it is subject to the supervision of the FSC. We mentioned earlier that under the UK Code, all FCA-authorized managers are required to comply or explain. Interestingly, under the Taiwan Code, most financial institutions have become signatories. This is probably owing to the financial regulatory environment in Taiwan, in which financial institutions are usually supportive of, or at least not against, the regulatory policy of the competent authority.

Although the Code adopts the comply-or-explain approach, one may ask who is monitoring the performance of stewards to ensure that the Code's objectives are achieved? Unlike corporate governance, where there are many mechanisms to ensure that a company continues to comply and improve its corporate governance, is there any mechanism available to ensure that institutional investors comply with the Code after becoming a signatory? As discussed in Section 12.3.2, in 2019, the TWSE, on the one hand, issued the Recommendations on Disclosure of Stewardship Information hoping that signatories can do more and disclose information in more detail. On the other hand, the TWSE set forth the evaluation criteria and announced the list of 'signatories with better practices and compliances' in December 2019, hoping to encourage compliance and better disclosure to the public by signatories. Again, Taiwan's regulatory philosophy in the corporate governance and stewardship regime is relatively soft, using encouragement, incentives and evaluation. It is hoped that evaluation on the stewardship

---

[123] Financial Reporting Council, 'The Wates Corporate Governance Principles for Large Private Companies' (December 2018) <www.frc.org.uk/getattachment/31dfb844-6d4b-4093-9bfe-19cee2c29cda/Wates-Corporate-Governance-Principles-for-LPC-Dec-2018.pdf> accessed 12 June 2020.

[124] The FRC reports periodically 'to give an assessment of corporate governance and stewardship in the UK; to report on the quality of compliance with, and reporting against, the two Codes; to give our findings on the quality of engagement between companies and shareholders; and to indicate to the market where we would like to see changes in corporate governance behaviour or reporting.' Financial Reporting Council, 'Developments in Corporate Governance and Stewardship 2016' (January 2017) 6 <www.frc.org.uk/getattachment/ca1d9909-7e32-4894-b2a7-b971b4406130/Developments-in-Corporate-Governance-and-Stewardship-2016.pdf> accessed 22 May 2020.

[125] The FRC emphasizes that companies shall 'focus on the activities and outcomes of implementing the Principles of the 2018 Code, particularly on the board's effectiveness and decision-making, and how this has led to sustainable benefits for shareholders and wider stakeholders'. Financial Reporting Council, 'Annual Review of the UK Corporate Governance Code 2019' (January 2020) 1 <www.frc.org.uk/getattachment/53799a2d-824e-4e15-9325-33eb6a30f063/Annual-Review-of-the-UK-Corporate-Governance-Code,-Jan-2020_Final-Corrected.pdf> accessed 22 May 2020.

performance of signatories can be elevated to a scale similar to the evaluation of corporate governance in the future.

12.6.3 Will Sustainable Investment Become a Trend?

Will sustainable investment or responsible investment become a norm of investment in the future? We have seen that this trend has become more apparent since the GRI started promoting sustainability reporting and more advocacy activities were observed this year. For example, on 27 June 2019, the TWSE held the 'Global Trend of Responsible Investment and Corporate Governance Forum Taipei', inviting speakers and participants from institutional investors and listed companies.[126] We also see individual institutional investors holding forums promoting sustainable investment. For example, on 15 July 2019, Schroders Taiwan held a Thought Leadership Forum titled 'Sustainability: to Launch a New Investment Logic', inviting speakers from Schroders UK and Schroders Japan to share their thoughts and experience on sustainable investment, its impact and the regulatory environment.[127]

From the efforts of the GRI to promote CSR, ESG and sustainability reporting to the efforts of many institutional investors promoting sustainable and responsible investment, it is expected that sustainable and responsible investment will become a trend. Looking at the evolution of corporate governance up until the time when the Taiwan Code was prepared, all of the established regimes, including CSR and ESG, naturally became its content. From Principle 3, Guideline 3-2 and the appendix of the Taiwan Code to the thirty-item Index of Evaluation Criteria and the Stewardship Information Disclosure Recommendations, the TWSE encourages signatories to be good stewards and responsible investors.

In practice, although institutional investors may respond differently if their clients do not care about CSR and ESG, and focus only on investment return, we are hoping that, with the emphasis on and awareness of CSR and ESG, sustainable investment will become a trend. This chapter suggests that Taiwan's soft approach towards promoting corporate governance is suitable, although it may take a little bit longer to see results. The chapter also posits that we should recognize and accept the reality of the situation and try to come up with other mechanisms to accommodate the objectives of the Code. Based on the current practice of stewardship evaluation, we can expand the evaluation programme to give public recognition and awards to those institutional investors that perform extremely well, and maybe consider the gradual application of evaluation to all signatories in the next stage.[128] This may create more incentives for institutional investors to perform good stewardship.[129]

---

[126] The chairman of the FSC also attended the forum to show strong support for the theme of 'responsible investment'. Taiwan Stock Exchange, 'Global Trend of Responsible Investment and Corporate Governance Forum Taipei' (4 June 2019) <https://cgc.twse.com.tw/promoteEvent/promoteEventArticleEn/612> accessed 22 May 2020.

[127] ibid. Speakers include Jessica Ground (Global Head of Stewardship, Schroders UK), Taku Arai (CFA, Deputy Head of Japanese Equities, Schroders Japan), and Jordan Chen (Chief Investment Officer, Schroders Taiwan).

[128] The International Corporate Governance Network (ICGN), led by investors from more than fifty markets managing assets in excess of USD 34 trillion, launched the ICGN Global Stewardship Forum and Awards in 2018. This is another example of giving awards to institutional investors who perform excellent stewardship. The awards include 'Stewardship Champion Awards' and 'Stewardship Disclosure Awards' to assets owners and assets managers (International Corporate Governance Network, 'ICGN 2020 Global Stewardship Awards' (2020) <www.icgn.org/events/icgn-2020-global-stewardship-forum-awards> accessed 22 May 2020).

[129] See Katelouzou and Sergakis, Shareholder Stewardship Enforcement, Chapter 27 on the impact of informal enforcement.

Another approach worth considering is that employed by the UK FRC in 2016 (i.e. 'Tiering of 2012 Stewardship Code Signatories').[130] The FRC assesses the quality of the Code statements of signatories and distinguishes 'between signatories who report well and demonstrate their commitment to stewardship, and those where reporting improvements are necessary'.[131] The TWSE may similarly consider adopting a ranking of all signatories to the Taiwan Code. We believe that what the TWSE currently does (i.e. providing disclosure suggestions with excellent disclosure examples from signatories) may be useful for encouraging those who rank in the lower 50 per cent to improve.

12.6.4 Voting Methodology and Disclosure of Voting Results

So, how will representatives vote on the board and in a shareholders' meeting if there exist conflicts of interest? Since conflicts of interest are inevitable, an institutional investor can manage this issue as follows. First, the signatory needs to establish a special committee responsible for voting on the board and in the shareholders' meetings of the investee companies particularly when important issues are involved. The representative of the signatory serving as a director of the investee company may receive instruction from the special committee or exercise his or her own fiduciary duty to vote and report back to the signatory. Second, the representative and signatory shall comply with Principle 5 of the Taiwan Code to disclose their voting policy and result. They should also comply with Principle 2 to manage the conflicts of interest.

The disclosure of voting results is another important issue to be carefully considered because it seems to have had a significant impact for Japan.[132] In addition to the disclosure of voting policy and voting results suggested in Principle 5 of the Code, institutional investors need to comply with the laws and regulations that are applied to them. Depending on the type of institutional investor, a signatory of the Code may be subject to different regulations. For example, an insurance company is subject to the Insurance Act regarding the exercise of voting rights in investee companies. Although Principle 4 of the Code allows an institutional investor to collaborate with other institutional investors to have more influence on investee companies, the Insurance Act prohibits insurance companies from conducting exchanges of shares or transferring benefits by way of contract, mandates, authorizing or creating a trust and agreement with the investee company or a third person, and from harming the interest of the applicant, the insured and the beneficiary.[133]

Regarding keeping the record of voting decisions, an insurance company must conduct an analysis of the agendas of the shareholders' meetings of its investee companies, keep the evaluation records in writing and report to the board meeting of the insurance company after a shareholders' meeting.[134] Moreover, an insurance company is prohibited from conducting proxy contests itself or mandating others to conduct them.[135] An insurance company is also

---

[130] Financial Reporting Council, 'Tiering of signatories to the Stewardship Code' <www.frc.org.uk/news/november-2016/tiering-of-signatories-to-the-stewardship-code> accessed 12 February 2022.
[131] ibid.
[132] Japan amended its Stewardship Code in 2017 requiring institutional investors to disclose their votes on individual agenda items. The Council of Experts on the Stewardship Code, 'Principles for Responsible Institutional Investors «Japan's Stewardship Code» – To Promote Sustainable Growth of Companies through Investment and Dialogue' (29 May 2017) 15, Guidance 5-3 <www.fsa.go.jp/en/refer/councils/stewardship/20170529/01.pdf> accessed 14 May 2020. In a joint research, one of the impacts of this new disclosure rule on corporate governance is that it affects the passage of and objection against poison pills proposed by the company. Alan K Koh, Masafumi Nakahigashi and Dan W Puchniak, 'Land of the Falling "Poison" Pill: Understanding Defensive Measures in Japan on Their Own Terms' (2020) 41 *University of Pennsylvania Journal of International Law* 687.
[133] Taiwan Insurance Act, art 146-9.
[134] ibid.
[135] ibid.

prohibited from being elected as the director or supervisor of an investee company or voting on the election of other directors or supervisors, from participating in the management of an investee company and from managing the real estate investment trust fund of an investee company.[136] If the insurance company exercises its voting right in violation of these rules, the vote is void.[137] Some of the rules are different from the Code Principles. Therefore, an institutional investor must first comply with relevant laws and regulations, before it can comply with the Code. Currently, insurance companies comprise 40 signatories out of the 151.[138] In sum, signatories are subject to disclosure duties suggested by the Taiwan Code. However, because it is not compulsory and there are no penalties for non-compliance, non-compliance is permissible as long as the signatory provides an explanation in its statements. The signatories must pay attention to other disclosure obligations imposed by other laws and regulations, such as securities law, banking law and insurance law.

12.7 CONCLUSION

The creation of the Taiwan Code was a good decision by the TWSE. It is in line with the long-established policy in Taiwan to promote good corporate governance of public companies. The Taiwan Code takes a slightly different route focusing on the role of institutional investors in influencing and improving the corporate governance of their investee companies, which is different from the traditional TWN CG Code that focuses on the public company itself. The Taiwan Code aims to ensure the best interests of institutional investors' clients and beneficiaries. In addition to ensuring the long-term interest of their clients and beneficiaries, and to prevent conflicts of interest, institutional investors should make disclosures about how they comply with the Code or provide explanations as to why they cannot comply.

The current approach adopted by the Taiwan Code is to encourage institutional investors to voluntarily become signatories and to establish policies and disclose information as set forth in the six principles and the accompanying guidelines. This chapter supports the Code and hopes that institutional investors voluntarily comply with it in good faith after becoming signatories.

However, the chapter also recognizes the potential conflicts or factors that may hinder the functioning of the Code because of the different roles that signatories may serve simultaneously. First, the two major objectives of the Code expecting the institutional investor to act as a fiduciary to its clients and to simultaneously act as a good steward may potentially conflict with each other under some circumstances. For example, the long-term interest of the clients may not necessarily be beneficial to the corporate governance of the investee company. Also, the interest of one group of clients and beneficiaries may not be in line with that of other groups of clients and beneficiaries.

Second, currently the TWSE uses a soft mechanism to monitor the performance of the signatories and to encourage compliance with the Code Principles. For example, the TWSE provides examples and suggestions to signatories to improve compliance and disclosure. Those who comply best with the Code are also named. We suggest a more formal awards programme and the gradual establishment of a ranking system for all signatories.

Third, more incentives to encourage institutional investors to become signatories and to comply with the Code should be created. One suggestion is to adopt a stewardship evaluation system

---

[136] Taiwan Insurance Act, art 146-1.
[137] ibid.
[138] Taiwan Stock Exchange, 'List of Signatories of the Stewardship Code' (n 15).

similar to the corporate governance evaluation system. The TWSE may also adopt the UK FRC tiering system, to improve the quality of stewardship reporting through reputational pressure.

In addition, Taiwan has a unique institutional investor, the SFIPC, which performs good stewardship activities. The SFIPC, through carrying out its functions, can produce a deterrent effect, preventing public companies from wrongdoing and enhancing the corporate governance of investee companies. Although the SFIPC does not own many shares, it is effectively a shareholder of every public company in Taiwan. The SFIPC attends shareholders' meetings of public companies when it finds potential problems in the agenda or potential bad corporate governance practices. The SFIPC not only attends shareholders' meetings but acts to correct and improve the corporate governance of public companies. This is a special example of good stewardship worth promoting to the world.

Overall, Taiwan has taken a good step in creating the Taiwan Code. Since this is a developing regime and many jurisdictions have already announced revised versions of stewardship codes to improve their functions, Taiwan should continue to observe what happens in practice both domestically and internationally, then modify Taiwan's Code in time.

12.8 EPILOGUE

On 10 August 2020, shortly before this book went to press, the TWSE announced a new version of the Taiwan Code (2020 Taiwan Code).[139] The 2020 Taiwan Code maintains its six principles, but with a few noteworthy changes. First, the 2020 Taiwan Code inserted introductory paragraphs for chapter 5 – 'Guidelines for Compliance with the Principles' – which now expressly codify ESG. Second, previously chapter 1 'required' institutional investors to base their decisions on the 'long-term interests' of fund providers when making their investment decisions and carrying out their fiduciary duties – but now they are 'advised to' base their decisions on the 'overall interests' of the fund providers. Third, Principle 5 now requires disclosure by institutional investors of their voting policies and voting results – specifically with respect to important motions (which must now include their reasons for voting in favour of, against or abstaining). Fourth, institutional investors are now required to disclose the performance of stewardship activities to the public – rather than to the fund providers only. It should be noted that some of these revisions are contained in the 'Q&A: Stewardship Principles for Institutional Investors' and the sample statement on 'Stewardship Principles for Institutional Investors'.[140] It remains to be seen how the 2020 Taiwan Code will affect the stewardship performance of institutional investors. However, what is certain is that Taiwan will continue to pay careful attention to the development of stewardship regimes in foreign jurisdictions.

---

[139] Taiwan Stock Exchange, 'Revision of Stewardship Principles for Institutional Investors' (10 August 2020) <https://cgc.twse.com.tw/docs/Revision%20of%20Stewardship%20Principles%20for%20Institutional%20Investors-20200810.pdf> accessed 26 September 2020 [hereinafter 2020 Taiwan Code].

[140] Taiwan Stock Exchange, 'Q&A: Stewardship Principles for Institutional Investors' (15 February 2017) (n 60); Sample Statement on 'Stewardship Principles for Institutional Investors' (n 104).

13

Stewardship in the Hong Kong International Financial Centre

Adding 'Responsible Owners' to an Entrepreneurial Market

David C. Donald

13.1 INTRODUCTION

A complete understanding of shareholder stewardship rules in Hong Kong requires an examination of three intersecting and not fully settled issues: (i) the position of shareholders in listed companies and their normatively preferred role; (ii) the typical character of shareholding in Asian listed companies; and (iii) the forces that shape the regulatory choices of international financial centres (IFCs). Commentators on the first issue have seen shareholders as both dispersed victims and aggressive or indolent opportunists,[1] but each analysis will inevitably view issuing companies as participants in the financial – rather than the products or services – market. That is, the analysis centres on protecting share price and market stability rather than achieving successful creation of a product or service through good governance assisting successful management. Scholarship on the position of shareholders in listed companies has over time coined important terms that took on prominence in global discourse, like Berle and Mean's classic 'separation of ownership and control'[2] and Gilson and Gordon's newer and currently apt 'agency capitalism'.[3] A common feature bridging these studies – whether seeing shareholders as victims or aggressors that find themselves 'dispersed', in a 'minority' or 'intermediated' – is that the holdings are inevitably viewed as financial investments, and the analysis is thus centred on protecting share price, liquidity and the environment of investment. Whether passive or aggressive, short or long term, a financial investor focuses its attention on the value of a security, which has the sole purpose of generating return for that investor or, in the case of a fund, its own investors. Even the most diligent and responsible financial investor is ultimately unconcerned whether the issuer company produces this kind of widget or that, has factories based in this country or that, offers a world-changing technology, or makes its employees proud or unhappy, provided that profits are available for dividends now and within the horizon of the investment's expected duration.

Turning to Asia, it is common knowledge that such financial investors have been less prominent than in the US and the UK, as in Asia many of the largest companies are or have been family firms, state-owned enterprises (SOEs) or firms held through industrial cross-holdings.[4] This was also the case in much of Europe,[5] but is changing in connection with an EU programme launched in the

---

[1] An examination of shareholder stewardship's rise is presented in Jennifer G Hill, 'Good Activist/Bad Activist: The Rise of International Stewardship Codes' (2018) 41 *Seattle University Law Review* 497.
[2] Adolf A Berle and Gardiner C Means, *The Modern Corporation and Private Property* (Macmillan 1932) 6.
[3] Ronald Gilson and Jeffrey Gordon, 'The Agency Costs of Agency Capitalism: Activist Investors and the Revaluation of Governance Rights' (2013) 113 *Columbia Law Review* 863.
[4] An excellent overview and analysis of such shareholding is provided by Koh, Puchniak and Goto, Shareholder Stewardship in Asia, Chapter 29.
[5] See Fabrizio Barca and Marco Becht (eds), *The Control of Corporate Europe* (OUP 2002).

1990s to develop its financial markets and increase the volume of its listed securities in order to support a shift of pension systems towards these markets.[6] Europe has been moving away from its 'bad', 'bank-based' financial system to one based on the primary and secondary markets for securities.[7] The shift towards agency capitalism – if it will occur at all – is still early in Asia, and Asian shareholding structures have remained concentrated in entrepreneurs (family or otherwise) and the state.[8] This type of shareholder will seek profits from the company's participation in the markets for goods or services, and thus it has a horizon of interest that extends well beyond share price. Because the institutionally-centred type of securities ownership with a focus on market price and liquidity found in Western markets has, with notable exceptions,[9] served as a normative model for corporate law commentary, Asian shareholding structures have been viewed with suspicion and generally seen at best as a transitory stage of evolution[10] on their way to the higher, more Western form.

For purposes of signalling internationally that a jurisdictions accepts the dominant network of legal rules, it is therefore understandable that Asian markets would be willing to adopt Western-style takeover rules,[11] board structures[12] and 'stewardship codes',[13] despite the fact that the typical Asian holding structure might already reunite 'ownership and control' in the hands of investors with a long-term outlook for the company's operational success. However, for jurisdictions such as Hong Kong and Singapore there is an additional and very important motivation for such adoption. The issue of rules without apparent need arises because IFCs, including those in Asia, very often sell their services – regulatory framework among them – to internationally active financial institutions based in the US or the UK.[14] Thus, the introduction of Hong Kong's 'Principles of Responsible Ownership'[15] (Hong Kong Principles) is more indicative of the market for Anglo-American law, the world's leading network of concepts in which value is expressed and relationships are constituted,[16] than any need for governance change in Hong Kong. The irony of this process is that the Hong Kong Principles seek responsible ownership, which is essentially

---

[6] See e.g. Alexandre Lamfalussy and others, 'Final Report of the Committee of Wise Men on the Regulation of European Securities Markets' (15 February 2001) <www.spk.gov.tr/Sayfa/Dosya/114> accessed 29 June 2020.

[7] See the book-length study dedicated to the development of the financial system in Germany from bank-based to securities market–based, Jan P Krahnen and Reinhard H Schmidt (eds), *The German Financial System* (OUP 2004) specifically 513–15.

[8] See Dan W Puchniak, 'The False Hope of Stewardship in the Context of Controlling Shareholders: Making Sense Out of the Global Transplant of a Legal Misfit' *The American Journal of Comparative Law* (forthcoming) and Koh, Puchniak and Goto, Shareholder Stewardship in Asia, Chapter 29.

[9] See e.g. Michael E Porter, 'Capital Disadvantage: America's Failing Capital Investment System' *Harvard Business Review* (1992) <https://hbr.org/1992/09/capital-disadvantage-americas-failing-capital-investment-system> accessed 29 June 2020.

[10] See Dan W Puchniak, 'Multiple Faces of Shareholder Power in Asia: Complexity Revealed' in Jennifer G Hill and Randall S Thomas (eds), *Research Handbook on Shareholder Power* (Edward Elgar 2015) 513, 520.

[11] See e.g. Umakanth Varottil and Wai Yee Wan (eds), *Comparative Takeover Regulation: Global and Asian Perspectives* (CUP 2017).

[12] See Dan W Puchniak, Harald Baum and Luke Nottage (eds), *Independent Directors in Asia: A Historical, Contextual and Comparative Approach* (CUP 2017).

[13] Adoption of such codes is of course not restricted to Hong Kong; see Goto, Japanese Stewardship Code, Chapter 10 and Puchniak and Tang, Singapore's Embrace of Shareholder Stewardship, Chapter 14 for accounts of other Asian implementation.

[14] To a certain extent this also applies to financial centres that are not strictly IFCs but are not from the English-speaking world, either, such as Germany. See David C Donald, 'Endowment, Fundamentals and Fashion in the Market for Corporate Law' in Theodor Baums, Andreas Cahn and Helmut Siekmann (eds), *Festschrift für Theodore Baums* (Mohr Siebeck 2017).

[15] Securities and Futures Commission, 'Principles of Responsible Ownership' (7 March 2016) <www.sfc.hk/web/EN/rules-and-standards/principles-of-responsible-ownership.html> accessed 29 June 2020 [hereinafter Hong Kong Principles].

[16] On the concept of networked law, see David C Donald, 'Legal System Network Effects and Global Legal Development' (2020) 10 *Notre Dame Journal of International & Comparative Law* 267.

the aim of the 'entrepreneurial' block-holders strongly represented in the Hong Kong market. It is unlikely that the external mantle of a voluntary code can add anything more than a signalling function to the inherent interest that the dominant entrepreneurial shareholders already have in the long-term development of their companies.

This chapter will address the three interlocking issues briefly presented so far, and is arranged as follows. Section 13.2 will examine the role played by shareholders in contemporary listed companies and in this context present the Hong Kong Principles. It will also highlight the traditional analysis of shareholder behaviour, as seen from the perspective of financial market development against the background of a different analysis of shareholder behaviour from the perspective of the company as an integrated unit employing labour, capital and other resources to produce products or deliver services. Section 13.3 will review what we know about shareholders in Asia, with a focus on Hong Kong. Although a few Hong Kong banks are – like their Western counterparts – held by institutional investors, the remainder of the leading listed companies tend to be controlled outright by families, entrepreneur founders or a state holding company. Section 13.4 will examine the regulatory business of the IFC and its relationship with well-networked law created by leading jurisdictions. Given their business model, an IFC's adoption of governance rules substantially deviating from accepted global best practices (i.e. Western rules) would present the great risk of being considered barbaric, in the strict meaning of the word,[17] while offering very little benefit for an IFC economically dependent upon acceptance by the international community. Section 13.5 will conclude by explaining that, although the current goal of responsible shareholding is already achieved through entrepreneurial ownership in Hong Kong, the imposition of unnecessary ownership principles is not superfluous because signalling to bias-impaired world markets is just as important as substantial local reality for an IFC.

13.2 FROM VICTIMIZED TO RESPONSIBLE SHAREHOLDERS

The logic and progress of corporate law scholarship on shareholders in large companies have seen twists, turns and cases where the dominant script lagged behind both economic change and international facts, but has consistently focused on the needs of financial investors. While some assertions – such as those regarding weak and dispersed shareholders[18] – have lost relevance owing to economic change, others – such as the assertion that all corporations float freely without any owner[19] – can only be understood in their strategic context.[20]

---

[17] Barbarism is characteristic of persons foreign to the dominant network and not participating in its language and norms. See Encyclopædia Britannica, 'Barbarian' (13 November 2017) <www.britannica.com/topic/barbarian> accessed 29 June 2020 ('Barbarian, word derived from the Greek *bárbaros*, used among the early Greeks to describe all foreigners, including the Romans').

[18] Papers asserting the need to protect weak, dispersed shareholders from strong, concentrated management can still be found in the developing world, likely owing to lag time in learning and applying once-leading Western theories. The author was in 2019 asked by a prominent Asian university to act as examiner of a doctoral thesis applying the dispersed shareholder arguments common in the US in 1995 to a twenty-first-century Asian market.

[19] The idea here is essentially that shares of stock are securities just like bonds or debentures and are rapidly traded, so the co-operative property right they evidence, known as a 'chose in action' at common law, cannot be a property right because it does not give absolute control of the company or its assets in the way that an owner would achieve through fee simple in a plot of land. The author addresses this argument in depth in David C Donald, 'Shareholder Voice and Its Opponents' (2005) 5 *Journal of Corporate Law Studies* 305, 317–19.

[20] The laudable motivation for asserting that corporations have no owners was to weaken the financialized model of the corporation, often referred to as the 'shareholder value' paradigm. The logic of the argument ran that if shares of stock do not evidence property rights then it weakened the claim of shareholders that the corporation should exist to maximize profits for them as owners. See Lynn A Stout, 'Bad and Not-So-Bad Arguments for Shareholder Primacy' (2002) 75 *Southern California Law Review* 1189, 1191.

The modern shareholder rights journey begins with Berle and Means in 1932, who announced the 'separation of ownership and control'.[21] For the authors, this separation was relevant 'in terms of social organization', because they saw the modern corporation as 'a concentration of power in the economic field comparable to the concentration of religious power in the medieval church or of political power in the national state'.[22] A lack of control over such powerful social institutions left large corporations free to exercise irresponsible power:[23]

> Most fundamental of all, the position of ownership has changed from that of an active to that of a passive agent .... It has often been said that the owner of a horse is responsible. If the horse lives he must feed it. If the horse dies he must bury it. No such responsibility attaches to a share of stock. The owner is practically powerless through his own efforts to affect the underlying property. The spiritual values that formerly went with ownership have been separated from it.

The 'spiritual values' of ownership, as Berle and Means phrased it, might now be referred to as responsible stewardship, but when advising Franklin Delano Roosevelt, Berle advised the President to restore public control over what he saw as 'the despot of the twentieth century, on whom great masses of individuals relied for their safety and their livelihood, and whose irresponsibility and greed (if it were not controlled) would reduce them to starvation and penury'.[24] When the work of Berle and Means was rediscovered by corporate and financial scholars later in the twentieth century, however, the social mission remained largely undiscussed and the focus shifted to the capacity of financial shareholders to maximize investment return – rather than achieve a longer-term entrepreneurial goal.[25]

Dispersed shareholding proved to be a temporary phenomenon. In the 1960s, Eisenberg, as a pioneer in the new field of 'corporate governance', was one of the first to remark on the growth of institutional holdings.[26] With an eye on pension funds, Monks, in the early 1980s, as administrator of the Employee Retirement Income Security Act (ERISA) for the US Department of Labor (DOL), began advocating responsible ownership: 'casting a ballot ... with an eye toward one's banking relationships rather than to the intrinsic merits of the measure, clearly violates ERISA'.[27] Monks then established Institutional Shareholder Services Inc. (ISS) in 1984, which argued that institutional investors had been manipulated into casting votes to support portfolio company management in part because 'the current regulatory structure gives investment managers no incentives to vote independently'.[28] Four years later, the DOL issued its seminal 'Avon Letter', explaining that because 'the decision[s] as to how proxies should be voted ... are fiduciary acts of plan asset management', voting decisions fall under ERISA requirements 'that a fiduciary of a plan act prudently, solely in the interest of the plan's participants and beneficiaries, and for the exclusive purpose of providing benefits to

---

[21] Berle and Means (n 2) 6.
[22] ibid 309, discussed at length in Nicholas Lemann, *Transaction Man: The Rise of the Deal and the Decline of the American Dream* (Farrar, Straus and Giroux 2019) 38–42.
[23] Berle and Means (n 2) 64.
[24] Berle and Means (n 2) 47 (from a speech drafted by Berle and delivered by Roosevelt in 1932).
[25] See e.g. Bernard S Black, 'Agents Watching Agents: The Promise of Institutional Investor Voice' (1992) 39 *UCLA Law Review* 811, 813.
[26] 'The short of the matter is that at the present time one-third of the stock in corporations listed on the New York Stock Exchange is held by highly sophisticated investors': Melvin Eisenberg, 'The Legal Roles of Shareholders and Management in Modern Corporate Decisionmaking' (1969) 57 *California Law Review* 1, 53.
[27] This statement is attributed to Monks in James E Heard and Howard D Sherman, *Conflicts of Interest in the Proxy Voting System* (Investor Responsibility Research Center 1987) 32, 40–49. Also see Robert AG Monks, *The New Global Investors: How Shareowners Can Unlock Sustainable Prosperity Worldwide* (Capstone 2001) 132–34.
[28] Monks (n 27) 49.

participants and beneficiaries'.[29] In 1994, the DOL codified this duty for application also to include private pension funds subject to ERISA.[30] By the early 1990s, US legal scholars also began to bring the issue of institutional investor monitoring to the centre of the corporate governance literature,[31] where it has remained until today.

As Cheffins notes, a parallel development existed in the UK, from a mention of the importance of institutional investors in the 1992 Cadbury Report, to institutional engagement becoming a Principle in the Combined Code of 1998, and through the work of (Paul, now Lord) Myner and (Sir David) Walker, which eventually resulted in the UK Code 2012 as a result of perceived shareholder abdication of duty in the lead-up to the global financial crisis.[32] A related strand of this development began with the 1991 statement by the Institutional Shareholders' Committee on the Responsibilities of Institutional Shareholders in the UK.[33]

As framed in the original UK Stewardship Code,[34] the word 'stewardship' means that institutional investors should 'promote the long-term success of companies in such a way that the ultimate providers of capital also prosper', including through 'monitoring and engaging [in purposeful dialogue] with companies on matters such as strategy, performance, risk, capital structure, and corporate governance, including culture and remuneration'.[35] The aim of stewardship was broadened in the UK Code 2020 to require 'stewardship that creates long-term value for clients and beneficiaries leading to sustainable benefits for the economy, the environment and society'.[36] It should be noted that this broad mandate for invested capital to seek 'sustainable benefits for the economy, the environment and society' occurred in near simultaneity with a resounding defeat of the UK Labour Party in Parliament.[37] This appears to continue a four-decade trend away from regulatory control of capital through taxation and market restrictions that coincides with a move publicly to nudge market forces towards 'doing the right thing'.[38] While such statements do rise above a 'do no evil' platitude that might be included in a Davos press release, they have nothing of the robust strength found in article 14(2) of the German Basic Law: 'Property entails obligations. Its use shall also serve the public good.'[39]

---

[29] Labor Department Letter to Avon Products, Inc. on Proxy Voting by Plan Fiduciaries, 15 *Pension Reporter* (BNA) 391 n.4 (29 February 1988).

[30] DOL Interpretive bulletin relating to written statements of investment policy, including proxy voting policy or guidelines, 29 CFR § 2509.94-2 (2004).

[31] See e.g. John C Coffee Jr, 'Liquidity versus Control: The Institutional Investor as Corporate Monitor' (1991) 91 *Columbia Law Review* 1277; Edward B Rock, 'The Logic and (Uncertain) Significance of Institutional Shareholder Activism' (1991) 79 *Georgetown Law Journal* 445; Black (n 25).

[32] Brian R Cheffins, 'The Stewardship Code's Achilles' Heel' (2010) 73 *Modern Law Review* 1004, 1007–13.

[33] The chapter of this book addressing UK stewardship presents the history in some detail: Davies, The UK Stewardship Code 2010–2020, Chapter 2.

[34] ibid.

[35] Financial Reporting Council, *The UK Stewardship Code* (September 2012) <www.frc.org.uk/getattachment/d67933f9-ca38-4233-b603-3d24b2f62c5f/UK-Stewardship-Code-(September-2012).pdf> accessed 29 June 2020 [hereinafter UK Code 2012]. For more on the first version of the UK Stewardship Code (2010/12), see Davies, The UK Stewardship Code 2010–2020, Chapter 2.

[36] Financial Reporting Council, *The UK Stewardship Code 2020* (2019) <www.frc.org.uk/getattachment/5aae591d-d9d3-4cf4-814a-d14e156a1d87/Stewardship-Code_Dec-19-Final-Corrected.pdf> accessed 29 June 2020 [hereinafter UK Code 2020].

[37] Lewis Baston, 'This Defeat Leaves Labour Support Unrecognisable from 35 Years Ago' *The Guardian* (online only) (13 December 2019) <www.theguardian.com/commentisfree/2019/dec/13/defeat-labour-support-unrecognisable-30-years-michael-foot> accessed 29 June 2020.

[38] On trust in market efficiency and what it means for regulation, see David C Donald, 'Information, and the Regulation of *Inefficient* Markets' in Emilios Avgouleas and David C Donald (eds), *The Political Economy of Financial Regulation* (CUP 2019).

[39] 'Eigentum verpflichtet. Sein Gebrauch soll zugleich dem Wohle der Allgemeinheit dienen' (German Basic Law art 14(2)).

Thus, each version of the UK Code still refers to protecting the value of shares in the capital market, but moving from the millisecond value stability necessary for a high-frequency trader to a longer-term horizon – 'sustainable' investment.[40] It is doubtful whether the addendum that value should 'lead' to 'sustainable benefits' for 'the environment and society' will have any real bite, and even then, it appears questionable that causation could be established while disproving equally grave consequence from abandoning the alternative action. If the integration of 'material environmental, social and governance issues'[41] into the activity of stewardship were to be rigorously applied, it would bring the corporation in line with Berle's hope to use it as a tool for social good, like a church or government institution. Along these lines, it is notable that the UK codes in 2012 and 2020 have picked up the tendency of some corporate law scholars to avoid admitting that corporations are 'owned' by anyone. The UK Code 2012 refers to shareholders ('asset owners', i.e., securities owners) as 'providers of capital' and the UK Code 2020 refers to them as 'clients and beneficiaries'.[42] Removing ownership rights from shareholders, if it can be achieved without successful constitutional challenge, could greatly facilitate drafting the corporation into a general, socially relevant activity. Again, in a time when even income taxes come under increasing legal challenge, it is almost inconceivable that such a nationalization of private wealth could occur. More likely is that the assertion that corporations are free and unowned is not taken seriously outside of certain academic circles.

The duties of stewardship apply to all institutional investors on UK securities exchanges through the same voluntary-cum-reputational-force 'comply or explain' (now strengthened to 'apply and explain' in the UK Code 2020) mechanism developed in the UK in connection with the Cadbury Code.[43] Cheffins argues that because the holdings of UK institutions have dropped while those of foreign investors have risen in the UK, the Stewardship Code – which is aimed at domestic institutions – will have much less impact than hoped.[44]

Following the adoption of similar codes by so many jurisdictions that stewardship became a byword in corporate governance,[45] Hong Kong too adopted its own code in 2016.[46] The Hong Kong Principles closely track the original UK Code 2012, the only meaningful difference in the wording of the main principles being that disclosure of policies and activities must be publicized under the UK rules, but may be discreetly communicated to stakeholders under the rules issued in Hong Kong. Understanding the spread of the UK model like a new species of plant or bacteria throughout the global network ecosystem of corporate governance rules – modifying and supplanting chthonic institutions as it proceeds – is, in the author's opinion, one of the greatest contributions of this volume; Siems and Katelouzou provide a highly informative analysis of this process in Chapter 30.

Table 13.1 shows just how similar the sets of stewardship rules in the UK and Hong Kong are.

The Hong Kong Principles were drafted and issued by the primary market regulator, the Securities and Futures Commission (SFC), which has not changed the fact that the Principles are completely voluntary. As such, the failure to comply with them does not require any

---

[40] See e.g. Dionysia Katelouzou, 'Shareholder Stewardship: A Case of (Re)Embedding Institutional Investors and the Corporation?' in Beate Sjåfjell and Christopher M Bruner (eds), *Cambridge Handbook of Corporate Law, Corporate Governance and Sustainability* (CUP 2019).
[41] UK Code 2020 (n 36) 15, Principle 7.
[42] See UK Code 2012 (n 35) 1, Principle 1; UK Code 2020 (n 36) 8, Principle 1.
[43] See e.g. Andrew Keay, 'Comply or Explain in Corporate Governance Codes: In Need of Greater Regulatory Oversight?' (2014) 34 *Legal Studies* 279.
[44] Cheffins (n 32) 1024.
[45] An examination of shareholder stewardship's rise is presented in Hill (n 1) 507–10 and Katelouzou and Siems, The Global Diffusion of Stewardship Codes, Chapter 30.
[46] Hong Kong Principles (n 15).

TABLE 13.1 *Comparison of the UK Code and the Hong Kong Principles*

UK Stewardship Code (original numbering)	HK Principles (HK lettering in the UK order)
1. *publicly* disclose stewardship policy	(a) report to *stakeholders* ownership policies
2. have policy on managing conflicts of interest	(g) have policies on managing conflicts of interests
3. monitor investee companies	(b) monitor investee companies
4. establish clear guidelines on stewardship activities	(c) establish clear policies on engagement activities
5. be willing to act collectively with other investors	(e) be willing to act collectively with other investors
6. have a clear policy on voting and disclosure	(d) have clear policies on voting
7. report periodically on stewardship and voting activities	(f) report to *stakeholders* on discharge of ownership responsibilities

explanation. No record or register of persons applying the code is kept, so institutional investors have no central location at which to announce their acceptance of the Principles. It is also useful to note that the SFC has very little involvement with company law (tended in Hong Kong by the Registrar of Companies) or general corporate governance (tended by the Stock Exchange of Hong Kong).[47] This underlines the fact that the Principles are seen as a product directed to institutional investors in securities, which fall squarely within the SFC's regulatory purview.

When proposing adoption of the Hong Kong Principles, the SFC stated its belief, in line with those of other jurisdictions, that '[e]ffective engagement between shareholders and their investee company can aid the long-term success of the listed company thereby benefitting the ultimate providers of its capital'.[48] The Hong Kong Principles are designed to apply to 'those who invest money, or hold shares, on behalf of clients and other stakeholders and are accountable to such clients and other stakeholders', but not to 'those who are accountable only to themselves for their investments (or are accountable only to family members pursuant to a personal relationship, with no intention to create a client or business relationship)'.[49] The purpose and scope of the Principles thus track that of the UK Code – insuring responsible use of 'other people's money' – by applying to intermediaries even though, as will be explained in Section 13.3, the growing presence of such intermediaries, an event declared as necessitating the issuance of the Principles, never occurred in the Hong Kong market.

13.3 ENTREPRENEURIAL SHAREHOLDING IN LARGE ASIAN COMPANIES

When proposing the Principles for adoption, the Hong Kong SFC made the following argument which would ring true for many an observer of corporate governance scholarship since 2008: 'In the last couple of decades there has been a notable increase in institutional ownership of publicly listed companies, with these institutions increasingly demanding a voice in corporate

---

[47] For a presentation of Hong Kong's regulatory framework in corporate and securities matters, see David C Donald, *A Financial Centre for Two Empires: Hong Kong's Corporate, Securities and Tax Laws in Its Transition from Britain to China* (CUP 2014) 104–70.
[48] Securities and Futures Commission, 'Consultation Paper on the Principles of Responsible Ownership' (2015) 4 <www.sfc.hk/edistributionWeb/gateway/EN/consultation/openFile?refNo=15CP2> accessed 29 June 2020.
[49] ibid 10.

governance. In many instances, institutional investors exert rights traditionally held by individuals, families or bloc alliances.'[50]

This well-received, common-sense observation is, however, factually incorrect for Hong Kong. In a 2014 study of the key companies comprising the sub-indices of the Hong Kong Hang Seng Index, this author found that the block holdings of nearly every company examined had increased over the ten-year period from 2003 to 2013.[51] This contradicts the common-sense notion of companies evolving from the Neanderthals of private control to the sapiens of public dispersal. The largest companies listed on the Stock Exchange of Hong Kong (SEHK) are ultimately controlled either by the state holding company of the People's Republic of China (SASAC) or by families.[52] The SOE group contains every industry other than property development, which is clustered in about a dozen leading families. Smaller listed companies are often controlled by founders operating in a family or a quasi-partnership team.[53] The controlling shareholders in Hong Kong thus tend to be 'entrepreneurial', as the word is used in this chapter, in that they are more interested in conducting a viable business than achieving a high share price from quarter to quarter. The latter interest would be a main goal of institutional investors who are contract- and duty-bound to seek gains on shares for their clients.

Despite efforts by some law firms and investors to bring a more aggressive brand of financial shareholding to Hong Kong, it cannot be said that shorter-term investor activism has taken hold. Institutional investors have significant positions only in some of the financial firms that are not owned by SASAC.[54] While HSBC Hong Kong is wholly owned by its parent, HSBC plc,[55] the Bank of East Asia (BEA) has major shareholders that are Japanese, Spanish and Malaysian institutions – Sumitomo Mitsui Banking Corporation, Hong Leong Company (through its subsidiary Guoco Management Company) and Criteria Caixa S.A. Between 2013 and 2018, these institutions increased their combined holding in the Bank of East Asia from 40.22% to 50.46%.[56] In the context of the stewardship discussion, it is useful to note one lonely example of investor activism that occurred in 2015, when the hedge fund Elliott Capital took a 7.0% stake in BEA,[57] and then sued that bank to unwind holding agreements with those leading shareholders while arguing for the sale of the company.[58] The suit alleges unfair prejudice and has not yet

---

[50] ibid 4.
[51] Donald (n 47) 99–100. The only exception was one of the smallest major property developers.
[52] Donald (n 47) ch 2.
[53] The public float required by the SEHK is only 25% of issued shares (SEHK Listing Rule 8.08(1)(a)). Twelve times during the first seven months of 2019, the SFC issued 'high shareholding concentration announcements' to warn that a given listed company (these are inevitably small-cap companies) threatened to violate this rule by accumulating more than 75% of the company's voting rights in the hands of a single investor or small group of investors.
[54] It should be noted that Hong Kong's largest bank is HSBC, which is a UK company, and that HSBC is the sole shareholder of a substantial retail bank, Hang Seng. All of the largest internationally active banks in Hong Kong are subsidiaries of Chinese, US or British or other foreign banks.
[55] See HSBC, 'Annual Report and Accounts 2018' (2019) <www.hsbc.com/investors/results-and-announcements/all-reporting/group?page=1&take=20> accessed 13 February 2022.
[56] Bank of East Asia, 'Annual Report 2012' (2013) 112 <www.hkbea.com/html/en/bea-about-bea-investor-communication-annual-and-interim-reports.html> accessed 29 June 2020; Bank of East Asia, 'Annual Report 2018' (2019) 152 <www.hkbea.com/html/en/bea-about-bea-investor-communication-annual-and-interim-reports.html> accessed 29 June 2020.
[57] Bank of East Asia, 'Annual Report 2015' (2016) 136 <www.hkbea.com/html/en/bea-about-bea-investor-communication-annual-and-interim-reports.html> accessed 29 June 2020.
[58] As expressed in the most recent judicial decision on the matter, 'the claim advanced is that placements of shares to CriteriaCaixa ("Caixa") and SMBC (Sumitomo Mitsui Financial Group) were made for an improper purpose, namely to entrench the control of the Bank by Sir David Li and his Family'. *Elliott International LP v Bank of East Asia Ltd* [2018] HKEC 1897.

gone to trial. A review of all unfair prejudice actions recorded in Hong Kong[59] shows no previous Hong Kong or UK unfair prejudice action in which sale restrictions written into a pre-existing share purchase agreement are found unfairly to prejudice the interests of a shareholder entering the company after such agreement is in place.

While details differ among jurisdictions, the distinction between East and West as to how listed companies are owned is consistent enough that the category 'Asian' is meaningful when referring to ownership structure. Goto, Koh and Puchniak present a survey of shareholding in Asian markets in their chapter of this book,[60] and, elsewhere, Puchniak also remarks on the ironic twist found in Western thought on distributed and controlling shareholders:[61]

> The disempowerment of shareholders that axiomatically flows from being dispersed has been addressed in American corporate governance ... The 1990s saw the indisputable rise of the United States as the sole global economic superpower ... This development resulted in American corporate governance emerging as the *de facto* gold standard for "good" corporate governance around the world. In this context, somewhat ironically, the dispersed nature of shareholding in America's large public corporations came to be viewed as a primary reason for its economic success – not the bane of its existence as Berle and Means had suggested.

The peculiar logic that Puchniak observes is that the structure of the US economy led to governance problems connected with dispersed shareholding that the US addressed with certain remedies, and when US law came to set the global standard, the presence of those same remedies allowing a capital market to function in the face of dispersal became best practice, which led to thinking that dispersed shareholding is somehow a necessary characteristic of healthy market development. The corollary for Asia is that because its markets do not suffer from dispersed shareholding and the American remedies for dispersed holding have little use in those markets, the Asian markets must somehow be malformed or immature.

Living under the network effects of globally leading Western jurisdictions has been Asia's lot for centuries, as it received in transplant nearly all of its commercial law, and most of its home-grown institutions (if any remained) were seen as exotic through the lens of 'orientalism'.[62] Legal solutions from the US – and, to a lesser extent, the UK – have in recent decades taken on a value in the international governance discourse that approaches the transcendent perfection ascribed to natural law, so that a relative comparison between one jurisdiction and its solutions and another jurisdiction and its solutions is impossible. Instead, one asks, 'have they yet come up to Western standards?'.[63] The traditionally existing ethnocentrism among Western observers was strongly reinforced by the economic analysis of law from the 1970s, according to which some scholars found the best US laws and regulations to embody an economic perfection of transcendental value towards which other jurisdictions can only aspire to converge.[64]

[59] See David C Donald and Paul WH Cheuk, 'Hong Kong's Public Enforcement Model of Investor Protection' (2017) 4 *Asian Journal of Law and Society* 349, 371–72.
[60] Koh, Puchniak and Goto, Shareholder Stewardship in Asia, Chapter 29.
[61] Puchniak (n 10) 518.
[62] See e.g. Thomas Coendet, 'Critical Legal Orientalism: Rethinking the Comparative Discourse on Chinese Law' (2019) 67 *The American Journal of Comparative Law* 775.
[63] As Valcke argues, there can be no true comparison once the transcendental absolute of natural law is introduced as a value against which all laws are measured. Catherine Valcke, *Comparing Law: Comparative Law as Reconstruction of Collective Commitments* (CUP 2018) 73.
[64] In the field of corporate law, an excellent compendium of relatively intuitive economic essays that apply basic economic principles to settle once and for all the true and optimal shapes of limited liability, voting rights, fiduciary duties, tender offers, market abuse rules and transparency is Frank H Easterbrook and Daniel R Fischel, *The Economic Structure of Corporate Law* (Harvard University Press 1991). It is noteworthy that the ultimate truths there presented in no way depend on facts derived from any specific context.

In studying stewardship, which seeks shareholder behaviour geared towards the long-term prosperity of the company, the tendency of an Asian IFC to join the dominant regulatory network becomes very evident. The families and the holding companies controlling Hong Kong's major listed companies are both dedicated to the long-term operation of their firms and deeply engaged in management. Nevertheless, Hong Kong is expected to apply the same duty overlay seen as necessary to prevent short-term exploitation and lethargic index investment in the US and the UK. This, however, does not fully explain Hong Kong's attempt to corral its entrepreneurial shareholders with duties of 'responsible ownership', because Hong Kong is an IFC, and an IFC must sell its law to the world.

13.4 IFCS AND THE LEADING LAW

The Hong Kong economy consists mainly of port facilities and a financial centre shepherding goods and money into and out of China.[65] Since its founding in 2007, the Global Financial Centres Index has in most years placed Hong Kong at the third or fourth position (usually swapping places with Singapore on and off) among the world's financial centres.[66] In absolute value of funds raised from initial public offerings (IPOs) during six of the last ten years, Hong Kong led the world.[67] Hong Kong was ranked fourth globally in the World Bank's 2019 rankings for ease of doing business (the US, the UK and Germany ranked eighth, ninth and twenty-fourth, respectively).[68] In 2012, the World Economic Forum ranked Hong Kong first globally for financial development, while ranking the US, Germany and France, respectively, at positions two, eleven and fourteen.[69] Nevertheless, this success does not give Hong Kong freedom to innovate on securities regulation and corporate governance, or even indicate that it has regulation well-suited to its local problems, but rather shows just how well it provides what its customers (international banks) and the institutions rating its law (such as the World Economic Forum, Z/Yen and the Heritage Foundation) think valuable. Unlike the US (New York) or the UK (London), a small IFC like Hong Kong has little to fall back on if its foreign customers lose interest. This makes it very attentive to well-networked law seen as leading in the global financial economy.

Within the taxonomy developed by Dobbin, Simmons and Garret,[70] an IFC is a 'learning' economy engaging in a 'competitive' race to adopt regulation seen as best by the leading global financial players. Following the same taxonomy, Hong Kong initially received its law through 'coercive' transplantation directed by the UK colonial administration, but since 1997 has freely transformed its legal and regulatory system as necessary to meet the needs of the international financial community when dealing with China (Hong Kong's primary client jurisdiction). It has adopted a UK-style takeover code, although no hostile takeover has been launched in

---

[65] For a discussion of the economic relationship between Hong Kong and China, see David C Donald, 'Hong Kong's Roles in Supporting the Economic Development of China' (2017–2019) 6 *City University of Hong Kong Law Review* 1.

[66] Available at Long Finance, 'Recent Publications' <www.longfinance.net> accessed 29 June 2020.

[67] These data are available at the World Federation of Exchanges <www.world-exchanges.org/> accessed 29 June 2020.

[68] World Bank Group, 'Doing Business 2019: Training for Reform' (2019) 5 <www.doingbusiness.org/content/dam/doingBusiness/media/Annual-Reports/English/DB2019-report_web-version.pdf> accessed 29 June 2020.

[69] World Economic Forum, 'The Financial Development Report 2012' (2012) <www.weforum.org/reports/financial-development-report-2012> accessed 29 June 2020.

[70] Frank Dobbin, Beth Simmons and Geoffrey Garrett, 'The Global Diffusion of Public Policies: Social Construction, Coercion, Competition, or Learning?' (2007) 33 *Annual Review of Sociology* 449.

Hong Kong since that code's adoption in 1992;[71] it was among the first jurisdictions globally to promote shareholder derivative actions legislatively, although its lack of contingent fees means that it has seen an insignificant number of such actions since the law change;[72] and, when reorganizing its securities settlement system in 2019 in the face of ground-breaking progress in financial technology, it saw itself constrained to avoid innovation and adopt the US system first set up in New York in 1996 and of questionable efficacy.[73] Each of these regulatory 'gestures' shows that Hong Kong will adopt a global 'best practice' even if that particular practice is objectively unnecessary or outdated on its market.

This business model of the IFC explains why Hong Kong, albeit endowed with a market in which listed companies are dominated by entrepreneurial shareholders strongly committed to the long-term success of their companies, still adopts 'principles of responsible ownership' on a voluntary comply-or-explain basis. By limiting application to institutional investors with only a minor role in Hong Kong governance, the signalling function is evident. This layer of stewardship rules will in all probability not improve shareholder engagement in Hong Kong – where executive compensation is already low by international standards and market power usually translates into profitability – but it is also unlikely to deteriorate it. One possible side effect could be to supply institutional investors with an excuse to seek more collaboration with the entrepreneurial shareholders, which could have a positive or negative effect on market quality. Just after the Hong Kong Principles were published, Elliott Capital began its action against BEA and the agenda of aggressive investing has been actively promoted by at least one smaller law firm with an office in Hong Kong,[74] but this has not yet translated into any action in firms with controlling, entrepreneurial shareholders.

If the Hong Kong Principles were to accidentally provide leverage for institutional profit-seeking through increased share buybacks or extraordinary dividends, they could actually push Hong Kong shareholding towards a more financialized, short-term interest – precisely the opposite of what stewardship rules are meant to achieve. In some ways this would be the best of both worlds for financial investors, as it would allow them to advertise adherence to a code of 'responsible ownership' while giving them greater leverage to agitate for the type of cuts in research or myopic reorganizations that enable a financial investor to make a quick withdrawal of liquidity from a listed company through increases in dividends or share buybacks before divesting and moving on to another target.[75] From the point of view of a financial investor, an arrangement of this kind is excellent market regulation.

---

[71] See David C Donald, 'Evolutionary Development in Hong Kong of Transplanted UK-Origin Takeover Rules' in Umakanth Varottil and Wai Yee Wan (eds), *Comparative Takeover Regulation: Global and Asian Perspectives* (CUP 2017).

[72] See Donald and Cheuk (n 59).

[73] The model in question is the 'direct registration system' in which shares can be traded only if held in the name of a financial institution, but may be placed in the investor's name by pulling them out of the system and essentially making them illiquid. See Securities and Futures Commission/HKEX, 'Joint Consultation Paper on a Revised Operational Model for Implementing an Uncertificated Securities Market in Hong Kong' (January 2019) <www.hkex.com.hk/News/Market-Consultations/2016-to-Present/January-2019-USM?sc_lang=en> accessed 29 June 2020.

[74] A firm called ONC Lawyers has held a number of conferences (the latest on 25 October 2019) on 'Shareholder Engagement and Activism in Hong Kong' and the consultancy Finsbury in Hong Kong has published an op-ed: Finsbury, 'Activist Investors Turn Up the Heat on Asia' *South China Morning Post* (27 July 2015) <www.scmp.com/comment/insight-opinion/article/1844031/activist-investors-turn-heat-asia> accessed 29 June 2020. This attempt to kick-start a market has not borne tangible fruit, but political unrest and leverage from the Principles could work together to change this.

[75] The destruction of hundred-year-old Du Pont Nemur is a great example of how financial efficiency can be brought to a previously productive research-oriented company. See Leo E Strine Jr, 'Corporate Power Is Corporate Purpose I: Evidence from My Hometown' (2017) 33 *Oxford Review of Economic Policy* 176.

The special logic of the Hong Kong IFC's market regulation will also likely dissuade Hong Kong from seeking a family firm stewardship code of the sort issued by Singapore (absent broad acceptance of such a model). In their discussion of the Singapore Code, Puchniak and Tang explain that it contains solid advice tracking well-known aspects of the family firm, such as the dangers of succession and the tendency to be inward-looking. They conclude by arguing that the innovative family firm code shows 'Singapore's ambition of making Singapore the standard-bearer for a new Asian model of corporate governance'.[76] Hong Kong evidences no such aspiration, as its financial activity mainly serves fund flows between China and the world, and, to serve this function, it applies in rigorous fashion the most respected and accepted law and regulation, which is currently a mix of UK and US corporate and securities law. China, Hong Kong's major client state, seeks normality, not notoriety, when going to market with its firms and investment opportunities, and the Hong Kong regulatory model provides the blue-chip blandness that China requires.

The position of Hong Kong versus Singapore is not evidence of Hong Kong being dominated by the government of mainland China but rather of Hong Kong being structurally dominated by its dependence on the needs of a single client. Since its inception as an international financial centre with the creation of its SFC in 1989 while a Crown Colony, Hong Kong has never attempted to claim leadership, save perhaps for extending the unfair prejudice action to listed companies (while claiming that this was already the UK position),[77] applying criminal sanction to a failure to make shareholding notifications,[78] and imposing extremely burdensome annual disclosure requirements on even its unlisted companies.[79] The first can be understood as plugging a hole in Western regulation that did not really deal with powerful shareholders in listed companies, the second as a 'get tough' gesture to protect block-holders against creeping takeovers, and the third as a celebration of good transparency for investors that disregards the heavy burden placed on purely local, non-financial business operations. As the author has argued elsewhere, Hong Kong – unlike Singapore – made the seamless transition from British colony to Chinese region, always remaining integrated economically and logistically into a larger network that it serves,[80] even when it enjoyed a high degree of political autonomy.

13.5 CONCLUSION

Primarily following the needs of financial investors in the securities market, corporate governance has evolved over the last half-century from empowering dispersed minority shareholders to stabilizing the power of active institutional shareholders in listed companies. The most recent step, stewardship, seeks to nudge financial investors towards longer-term, sustainable engagement with listed firms. It is doubtful that the newest trends, which voluntarily assert that the stock corporation should 'do no evil', will turn investment towards broad social and environmental goals, when taxation and regulation to such ends are aggressively opposed by corporate lobbies.

At no time during its weaving history has the scholarship on shareholder power sought to direct such power towards improving the productive activity of the company – its entrepreneurial goal to provide a product or service. This is likely because the share of stock itself, with its open-ended

---

[76] Puchniak and Tang, Singapore's Embrace of Shareholder Stewardship, Chapter 14, Section 14.4.2.
[77] See *Luck Continent Ltd v Cheng Chee Tock Theodore* [2012] HKEC 567.
[78] See Hong Kong Securities and Futures Ordinance CAP 371, s 328.
[79] See Hong Kong Companies Ordinance, CAP 622, ss 388–391.
[80] See Donald (n 47).

upper value deriving from its proprietary character, creates incentives necessary to achieve that goal.

Asian markets, of which Hong Kong is one, tend to be populated with listed firms controlled by entrepreneurial shareholders, mainly SASAC and families in their second or third generation from the founders. The Hong Kong Principles of Responsible Ownership have the declared purpose of bringing institutional investors closer to this type of entrepreneurial goal, despite the fact that such institutional investors do not have anywhere near the type of power they exercise in Western markets. As such, the Principles are unlikely to have much practical impact on the bulk of governance in Hong Kong, or even be able to empower shorter-term shareholders to lower the long-term value of companies – but this does not make the Principles useless.

As an IFC, Hong Kong is obliged to adopt and implement norms and instruments found in the network of global best practices. Such global practices have for decades originated in the US and the UK. It is of little relevance whether those practices are well-adapted to the needs of the Hong Kong market. Given the type of shareholder controlling Hong Kong listed companies, it can be expected that responsible ownership will indeed be practised. This will not occur simply because of the Principles; however, the Principles will signal the type of expected stability without touching the substance of the market. IFC Hong Kong in this way buys into the network of leading Western law in order to protect its image, customer base and ranking, and the effect is real despite the fact that it lacks all substance.

14

Singapore's Embrace of Shareholder Stewardship

A Puzzling Success

Dan W. Puchniak and Samantha S. Tang[*]

14.1 INTRODUCTION

In 2010, the creation of the world's first stewardship code by the UK (UK Code) sparked global interest in stewardship.[1] Unsurprisingly, as an Asian corporate governance leader,[2] Singapore proposed its own version of a stewardship code in 2016. Stewardship Asia – a Singapore incorporated entity with the stated mission of promoting stewardship in Singapore and Asia – introduced the 'Stewardship Principles for Responsible Investors' (Singapore Stewardship Code),[3] which were ostensibly modelled on the UK Code.[4] This chapter critically analyzes Singapore's embrace of stewardship by presenting and solving three 'puzzles' that arise from its embrace of shareholder stewardship.

The first puzzle emanates from our observation that the UK concept of shareholder stewardship is not directly relevant to Singapore. Unlike the UK, most shares in Singapore's listed companies are owned not by institutional shareholders[5] but by controlling-block shareholders, who are able to directly monitor management or manage the company

---

[*] This chapter is an updated and condensed version of Dan W Puchniak and Samantha Tang, 'Singapore's Puzzling Embrace of Shareholder Stewardship: A Successful Secret' (2020) 53 Vanderbilt Journal of Transnational Law 989.

[1] Jennifer G Hill, 'Good Activist/Bad Activist: The Rise of International Stewardship Codes' (2018) 41 *Seattle University Law Review* 497, 506–13; Ernst & Young, 'Q&A on Stewardship Codes' (August 2017) <www.ey.com/Publication/vwLUAssets/ey-stewardship-codes-august-2017/$FILE/ey-stewardship-codes-august-2017.pdf> accessed 14 July 2020.

[2] See e.g. Dan W Puchniak and Umakanth Varottil, 'Related Party Transactions in Commonwealth Asia: Complicating the Comparative Paradigm' (2020) 17 *Berkeley Business Law Journal* 1; World Bank, 'Protecting Minority Investors' (May 2019) <www.doingbusiness.org/en/data/exploretopics/protecting-minority-investors> accessed 14 July 2020 (data extracted rank Singapore joint third in minority shareholder protection).

[3] Strictly speaking, the Singapore Institutional Investor Stewardship Code is a set of 'principles' rather than a 'code'. Stewardship Asia Centre, *Singapore Stewardship Principles for Responsible Investors* (November 2016) <www.stewardshipasia.com.sg/sites/default/files/2020-09/Section%202%20-%20SSP%20%28Full%20Document%29.pdf> accessed 13 February 2022 [hereinafter Singapore Stewardship Code].

[4] While the authors have not been able to locate any express statement from Stewardship Asia or contained in the Singapore Stewardship Code proper as to the relationship between the UK Code and the Singapore Stewardship Code, scholars have characterized the Singapore Stewardship Code as being 'inspired' by the UK Code. See e.g. Ernest Lim, *A Case for Shareholders' Fiduciary Duties in Common Law Asia* (CUP 2019) 280. See also Dan W Puchniak, 'The False Hope of Stewardship in the Context of Controlling Shareholders: Making Sense Out of the Global Transplant of a Legal Misfit' *The American Journal of Comparative Law* (forthcoming), finding that the Singapore Stewardship Code contains all seven core principles from the UK Code, and Katelouzou and Siems, The Global Diffusion of Stewardship Codes, Chapter 30, which finds that the text of the Singapore Stewardship Code is highly similar to the UK Code.

[5] Adriana De La Cruz, Alejandra Medina and Yung Tang, 'Owners of the World's Listed Companies' (OECD Capital Market Series, 17 October 2019) 12, 36, 37, 38 <www.oecd.org/corporate/owners-of-the-worlds-listed-companies.htm> accessed 14 July 2020 (average ownership by category of investor, end-2017 based on an analysis of 195 listed companies representing 83% of total market capitalization in Singapore, finding that institutional investors held 6% of listed companies shares on a non-market capitalization weighted basis and 12% of listed companies on a market capitalization weighted basis).

themselves.[6] A significant majority of its listed companies are family firms, whose corporate governance is dominated by family members through their shareholder voting rights.[7] Aside from family firms, the Singapore government – through its privately incorporated holding company Temasek Holdings Private Limited (Temasek) – controls the voting rights in most of Singapore's largest listed companies.[8] Institutional investors have played, and continue to play, only a minor role in Singapore corporate governance, especially when compared to state and family controlling shareholders.[9]

In this context, the primary concerns behind the creation of the UK Code in 2010 following the 2008 global financial crisis (GFC) – excessive risk-taking and short-termism by management left unmonitored because rationally apathetic institutional investors controlled the shareholder float[10] – are virtually absent in Singapore. Further, the very solution proposed by the UK Code to address institutional investor apathy – to incentivize institutional investors to take a more active role in corporate governance[11] – is less relevant in Singapore listed companies, where institutional investors are a comparatively powerless minority in the face of controlling shareholders. This raises the first puzzle: Why did Singapore adopt a stewardship code which was ostensibly modelled on the UK's, when it lacks the corporate governance problems that the UK Code was designed to address and the potential for the solution it aims to provide?

A closer examination of the Singapore Stewardship Code reveals the second puzzle: by comparison to the UK Code – and indeed many other stewardship codes – Singapore's Code is curiously toothless.[12] The very title of the Singapore Stewardship Code – 'Singapore Stewardship *Principles* for Institutional Investors' – demonstrates that the Singapore Stewardship Code is not actually a 'code' but a set of 'principles' intended to provide 'useful guidance' for institutional investors.[13] The Singapore Stewardship Code provides that all institutional investors (including domestic ones) are free to adopt the Singapore Stewardship Code in whole, in part or not at all; compliance is entirely voluntary.[14] Institutional investors who 'support'[15] the Code are not required to provide any evidence of

---

[6] Tan Cheng Han, Dan W Puchniak and Umakanth Varottil, 'State-Owned Enterprises in Singapore Model: Historical Insights into a Potential Model for Reform' (2015) 28 *Columbia Journal of Asian Law* 61, 91. However, state-controlled companies may rely on independent directors to perform monitoring functions: Dan W Puchniak and Luh Luh Lan, 'Independent Directors in Singapore: Puzzling Compliance Requiring Explanation' (2017) 65 *The American Journal of Comparative Law* 265, 315–16.

[7] Marleen Dieleman, Jungwook Shim and Muhammad Ibrahim, 'Success and Succession: A Study of SGX-Listed Family Firms' (Centre for Governance, Institutions and Organisations/DBS, May 2013) 8 <https://bschool.nus.edu.sg/cgio/wp-content/uploads/sites/7/2018/10/Success-and-Succession-2013.pdf> accessed 14 July 2020.

[8] Isabel Sim, Steen Thomsen and Gerard Yeong, 'The State as Shareholder: The Case of Singapore' (Centre for Governance, Institutions & Organisations/Chartered Institute of Management Accountants, June 2014) 6, 23–24 <https://bschool.nus.edu.sg/cgio/wp-content/uploads/sites/7/2018/10/SOE-The-State-as-Shareholder-2014.pdf> accessed 14 July 2020.

[9] De La Cruz, Medina and Tang (n 5).

[10] See e.g. Iris H–Y Chiu and Dionysia Katelouzou, 'From Shareholder Stewardship to Shareholder Duties: Is the Time Ripe?' in Hanne S Birkmose (ed), *Shareholders' Duties* (Kluwer Law International 2017) 131; Paul Davies, 'Shareholders in the United Kingdom' in Jennifer G Hill and Randall S Thomas (eds), *Research Handbook on Shareholder Power* (Edward Elgar 2015) 355, 373.

[11] Brian R Cheffins, 'The Stewardship Code's Achilles' Heel' (2010) 73 *Modern Law Review* 1004, 1014–15.

[12] Lim (n 4) 288–89.

[13] Singapore Stewardship Code (n 3) 5 (emphasis added).

[14] ibid 3; Stewardship Asia Centre, 'Stewardship for Singapore Investors: A Matter of Principles' (2 November 2016) <www.stewardshipasia.com.sg/sites/default/files/02Nov2016%20Press%20ReleaseSTEWARDSHIP%20FOR%20SINGAPORE%20INVESTORS-A%20MATTER%20OF%20PRINCIPLES_0.pdf> accessed 14 July 2020.

[15] It appears that Stewardship Asia has used the term 'supporters' rather than 'signatories' to demonstrate the relaxed nature of the commitment that is required by institutional investors.

compliance with it.[16] The impotence of Singapore's Code is accentuated by the fact that, unlike many existing codes,[17] it has no mechanism whatsoever to monitor whether 'supporters' have actually complied with it.[18] Moreover, the entity which spearheaded and promotes the Singapore Stewardship Code, Stewardship Asia, is a private entity that has no regulatory power to supervise the implementation of the Code or enforce it. The Singapore Stewardship Code does not even functionally provide a singular model for stewardship; it only encourages those who opt to follow it to 'take steps to *satisfy themselves* that they adhere to *their own* stewardship approach'.[19] For a jurisdiction that consistently tops Asian corporate governance rankings,[20] why did Singapore introduce a code that provides no singular model of stewardship, no method of determining who has opted to follow the Code, and no functional mechanism to significantly increase transparency or market pressure on institutional investors to act as 'good stewards'?

Having introduced an apparently impotent stewardship code for institutional investors, in late 2018 Stewardship Asia proceeded to introduce yet another stewardship code in Singapore directed at family companies. The 'Stewardship Principles for Family Businesses' (Family Stewardship Code)[21] is a version of the Singapore Stewardship Code developed for family companies, and is, to the best of our knowledge, the first (and, as of early 2022, the only) of its kind in the world. Stewardship Asia has been actively publicizing the Family Stewardship Code to jurisdictions in Asia to promote Singapore as a hub for corporate governance.[22] Directed at family controlling shareholders, the Family Stewardship Code encourages them to be good 'stewards' of their companies. It is noteworthy, however, that this Code does not contemplate divestment of control to non-family shareholders; rather, it promotes the entrenchment of family control.[23] It also does not appear to actively encourage or facilitate the involvement of institutional investors or shareholder activists in Singapore family companies. The vision of 'stewardship' at the heart of the Family Stewardship Code thus appears to be dramatically different from the concept of institutional investor 'stewardship' which is at the core of the UK Code.[24] This brings us to our third puzzle: why did Singapore introduce a second stewardship code addressed to family controlling shareholders – a constituency not contemplated by any other stewardship code?

Our solutions to these three puzzles, which we discuss in detail in this chapter, may be summarized as follows. For the first puzzle, notwithstanding the impotence of institutional

---

[16] Unlike the UK Code, there is no organizational equivalent to the Financial Reporting Council that monitors compliance with the Singapore Stewardship Code. Stewardship Asia has also explicitly stated: 'The SSP [Singapore Stewardship Principles] is not enforced or audited.' See Stewardship Asia Centre, 'Frequently Asked Questions' (2018) <www.stewardshipasia.com.sg/singapore-stewardship-principles-ssp#b108> accessed 14 July 2020.

[17] See e.g. Financial Services Agency, 'List of Institutional Investors Signing Up to "Principles for Responsible Institutional Investors" ≪Japan's Stewardship Code≫' (14 December 2018) <www.fsa.go.jp/en/refer/councils/stewardship/20181214/en_list_01.pdf> accessed 14 July 2020; Financial Reporting Council, 'Tiering of 2012 Stewardship Code Signatories' <www.frc.org.uk/news/november-2016/tiering-of-signatories-to-the-stewardship-code> accessed 13 February 2022.

[18] See generally Singapore Stewardship Code (n 3) 6.

[19] ibid (emphasis added).

[20] See e.g. World Bank, 'Doing Business 2019: Training for Reform' (16th edn, 31 October 2018) 5 <www.doingbusiness.org/content/dam/doingBusiness/media/Annual-Reports/English/DB2019-report_web-version.pdf> accessed 13 February 2022 (Singapore ranks second on the 'Ease of Doing Business' ranking).

[21] Stewardship Asia Centre, *Stewardship Principles for Family Businesses* (2018) <www.stewardshipasia.com.sg/sites/default/files/2020-09/SPFB-brochure-0913.pdf> accessed 19 May 2021 [hereinafter Family Stewardship Code].

[22] ibid.

[23] ibid.

[24] See Davies, The UK Stewardship Code 2010–2020, Chapter 2.

investors in Singapore, Singapore adopted a stewardship code ostensibly modelled after the UK Code as a form of 'halo signalling', demonstrating Singapore's commitment to Anglo-American-cum-global standards of good corporate governance.[25] The answer to the second puzzle – the comparatively 'toothless' Singapore Stewardship Code – appears to follow naturally from this. Since Singapore neither suffers from the problems nor possesses the ability to implement the solutions that the UK concept of stewardship prescribes, Singapore has no need for a stewardship code with actual 'bite'. It also has a strong incentive to create a code that allows institutional investors (and family firms) to comply with it effortlessly, which helps promote Singapore as a jurisdiction that is easy to do business in.

Diving deeper, an examination of the relationship between Singapore's state investment arm (Temasek), which is also the controlling shareholder of most of Singapore's largest listed companies, and Stewardship Asia reveals another driving force behind the Code. In this chapter, we provide the first analysis of the link between Stewardship Asia, the ostensibly private entity that designed and promotes the Code, and the Singapore state. This link is crucial because it explains how the entity writing the rules for how institutional investors should engage with controlling shareholders (i.e., Stewardship Asia) is itself an arm of Singapore's most powerful controlling shareholder: the Singapore government through its wholly owned holding company Temasek.[26]

In this context, it makes perfect sense that the Singapore Stewardship Code is not designed to disrupt the status quo for corporate controllers or promote powerful shareholder activism. Rather, the Code is designed to entrench the status quo for corporate controllers, namely the state and wealthy families in Singapore. Importantly, however, there is an institutional architecture in Singapore that serves as a functional substitute for shareholder activism in Singapore's state-owned enterprises (SOEs).[27] This prevents the type of wealth-reducing private benefits of control from being extracted by Temasek from Singapore's SOEs – something that may otherwise be expected in a market devoid of shareholder activists and in which the government is both the regulator and the most powerful shareholder.[28]

Further, by releasing the first stewardship code through Stewardship Asia, Singapore's state controlling shareholder effectively took control of this regulatory space and prevented 'bottom-up' free-market-based approaches to shareholder stewardship – which could have been unpredictable and potentially disruptive to Singapore's successful corporate governance model – from developing. This act of what we coin 'pre-emptive corporate governance' has allowed Singapore to maintain its existing corporate governance regime and its position as a global corporate governance leader by embracing the rising international trend of 'shareholder stewardship'.

The third puzzle represented by Singapore's Family Stewardship Code can be untangled with a close examination of the Code itself, and the importance and function of family-controlled companies in Singapore and Asia. We demonstrate that the Family Stewardship Code is a strategic effort by Stewardship Asia to put forward a version of stewardship adapted to Singapore's successful corporate environment, and to address the practical corporate

---

[25] Puchniak and Lan (n 6) 288.
[26] Temasek, 'Temasek Overview 2019' (2019) 38–39 <www.temasek.com.sg/content/dam/temasek-corporate/our-financials/investor-library/annual-review/en-tr-thumbnail-and-pdf/temasek-review-2019.pdf> accessed 13 February 2022.
[27] See generally Tan, Puchniak and Varottil (n 6) 67–69 (summarizing empirical studies on the performance of Singapore state-owned enterprises); Puchniak and Lan (n 6).
[28] Tan, Puchniak and Varottil (n 6); Puchniak and Lan (n 6).

governance issues faced by Asian jurisdictions, which are often distinct from those reflected in the Anglo-American paradigm. The concept of 'family stewardship' at the core of the Family Stewardship Code is entirely distinct from the concept, form and substance of 'stewardship' espoused in the UK Code. Interestingly, it also appears to propose a model of corporate governance distinct from the traditional Anglo-American model, and specifically tailored to Asia, with Singapore strategically positioned as the standard-bearer for Asia.

14.2 THE FIRST PUZZLE: WHY DID SINGAPORE ADOPT A STEWARDSHIP CODE WHEN IT LACKS THE UK'S GOVERNANCE PROBLEMS/SOLUTIONS?

14.2.1 *The Premise of Shareholder Stewardship*

The rise of institutional shareholders in the UK and the US has commanded scholarly attention because of the corporate governance challenges it poses. Most listed companies in the UK and the US are no longer examples of the archetypical Berle-Means company with atomized, dispersed shareholders; now, in most listed companies, a modest number of major institutional investors collectively hold a sufficient percentage of shares to exercise effective control.[29] This poses a seismic challenge to the Anglo-American corporate governance model founded on the shareholder-manager agency problem. While institutional investors can collectively exercise their voting power to minimize shareholder-manager agency costs and act as 'good stewards' of their investee companies, they have ordinarily no incentive to do so.[30] In fact, remaining passive is often their best option to maximize their profits.[31]

Following the GFC, institutional investors were criticized for failing to rein in the excessive managerial risk-taking and short-termism in listed companies, which has been identified as a key cause of the GFC.[32] In response, the UK issued the world's first stewardship code in 2010 to create incentives for institutional investors to act responsibly and engage with management.[33] Institutional investors were thus the problem addressed, and the solution supplied, by the UK Code.[34]

In a jurisdiction where institutional shareholders could potentially wield considerable influence over the internal affairs of listed companies by virtue of their collective substantial shareholding,[35] there is a certain logic in crafting a stewardship code premised on institutional investors being both the problem and the solution. This was the case with the UK Code. With

---

[29] Lucian A Bebchuk, Alma Cohen and Scott Hirst, 'The Agency Problems of Institutional Investors' (2017) 31 *Journal of Economic Perspectives* 89, 92–93; Cheffins (n 11) 1017–20.

[30] See Lucian Bebchuk and Scott Hirst, 'Index Funds and the Future of Corporate Governance: Theory, Evidence, and Policy' (2019) 119 *Columbia Law Review* 2029, but see Marcel Kahan and Edward Rock, 'Index Funds and Corporate Governance: Let Shareholders Be Shareholders' (October 2019) NYU Law and Economics Research Paper No 18–39, 33–34, 42–44 <https://ssrn.com/abstract=3295098> accessed 14 July 2020 (arguing that index fund managers have incentives to invest in acquiring company-specific information and engage in company-specific analysis).

[31] Bebchuk, Cohen and Hirst (n 29) 96–100.

[32] See e.g. Cheffins (n 11) 1005–1006.

[33] Prior to the GFC, the Institutional Shareholders' Committee had released a 'code' for institutional investors in 1991; the Stewardship Code released by the Financial Reporting Council in 2010 was substantially similar to this earlier code: Arad Reisberg, 'The UK Stewardship Code: On the Road to Nowhere?' (2015) 15 *Journal of Corporate Law Studies* 217, 221–22.

[34] Cheffins (n 11) 1014–15; see Davies, The UK Stewardship Code 2010–2020, Chapter 2 for the changes in the rationale underpinning the UK Code over the years.

[35] See Davies (n 10) 357–59. For the latest available figures, see Office for National Statistics, 'Ownership of UK Quoted Shares: 2016' (29 November 2017) <www.ons.gov.uk/economy/investmentspensionsandtrusts/bulletins/ownershipo fukquotedshares/2016> accessed 14 July 2020.

the corporate governance challenges posed by institutional shareholders well documented in the Anglo-American-dominated corporate governance discourse, it is tempting to assume that similar problems are shared by many other jurisdictions, and that stewardship codes would, barring obstacles, converge.[36] But is the underlying premise – that other jurisdictions' corporate governance landscapes and associated problems are on the whole similar – even valid to begin with?

Unlike the UK and the US, most listed companies in other jurisdictions are under the de facto (if not outright *de jure*) control of block shareholders that can be families, states or other corporations. Institutional shareholders control only a minority of the total voting power of listed companies, even if their shareholdings have generally increased with time.[37] Consequently, they have limited power to cause a change in corporate control or make a credible threat to do so. Instead of an absent steward, the principal corporate governance problem in these jurisdictions is an entrenched controlling shareholder who may use their power not to discharge the function of a steward but rather to extract private benefits of control at minority shareholders' expense.[38]

Singapore's listed companies are also dominated by block shareholders. In fact, Singapore turns the conventional wisdom about the superiority of the Anglo-American corporate governance model and the efficiency of dispersed shareholding on its head. As Singapore has risen from a developing, to a developed, and now one of the wealthiest economies in the world, its shareholder landscape has maintained – if not increased – its level of concentration.[39] Further, its state-controlled and family-controlled corporations have out-performed almost all others, dispelling the now anachronistic wisdom that state-controlled and family-controlled companies are pitstops on the path towards economic development.[40] In fact, the remarkable success of Singapore's state-controlled companies has itself become a model for developing countries – particularly China – to follow.[41] Most importantly from the perspective of the UK stewardship model, within the context of Singapore's shareholder landscape and corporate governance system, institutional investors have played a *de minimis* role. In this context, the introduction of a Singapore Stewardship Code, ostensibly modelled on the UK Code, is mystifying.

14.2.2 *Illuminating Singapore's Institutional Architecture and Shareholder Landscape*

Instead of institutional shareholders, the dominant players in Singapore's listed firms are controlling-block shareholders that possess sufficient control either to monitor management or, in the alternative, to intervene directly in the management of their investee companies personally.[42] Controlling shareholders may be divided primarily into two types. The first is family shareholders who collectively hold controlling blocks of voting rights in many of

---

[36] See Koh, Puchniak and Goto, Shareholder Stewardship in Asia, Chapter 29, Section 29.2.
[37] For detailed statistics and an analysis of this point, see Puchniak (n 4).
[38] See e.g. Dan W Puchniak, 'Multiple Faces of Shareholder Power in Asia: Complexity Revealed' in Jennifer G Hill and Randall S Thomas (eds), *Research Handbook on Shareholder Power* (Edward Elgar 2015) 511, 526–32.
[39] Puchniak and Lan (n 6) 268.
[40] Dieleman, Shim and Ibrahim (n 7) 2, 12.
[41] Tan, Puchniak and Varottil (n 6) 62–63; Li-Wen Lin and Curtis J Milhaupt, 'We Are the (National) Champions: Understanding the Mechanisms of State Capitalism in China' (2013) 65 *Stanford Law Review* 697, 754–55.
[42] See e.g. Tan, Puchniak and Varottil (n 6) 91; but see Puchniak and Lan (n 6) 315–16.

Singapore's listed companies. The second, which is the focus of this section, is the single largest player in Singapore's capital market: the state itself.

The state holds shares and voting rights through Temasek, which is a private incorporated company under Singapore's Companies Act.[43] The Singapore Minister for Finance – which is a body corporate[44] – is the sole shareholder of Temasek.[45] In turn, Temasek is the controlling shareholder of the companies in its portfolio of government-linked companies (GLCs).[46] These GLCs include twenty-three of Singapore's largest publicly listed companies, which comprise about 37 per cent of the total capitalization of the Singapore Exchange (SGX).[47] Moreover, Singapore's corporate landscape is dominated by controlling shareholders, rather than institutional shareholders, passive or otherwise. In fact, more than 90 per cent of Singapore's public listed companies have block shareholders who exercise controlling power.[48]

Singapore's state controlling shareholders perform distinct functions in Singapore's corporate environment. Notwithstanding Temasek's status as a wholly owned subsidiary of the Government of Singapore,[49] substantial constitutional safeguards[50] and an institutional architecture were put in place by the Singapore legislature to prevent the state from using its control over Temasek to tunnel wealth from GLCs or otherwise abuse its power.[51] What is perhaps most striking and significant is the fact that, on almost every available metric for corporate performance, Temasek and its GLCs have been highly successful. As Puchniak and Lan observe:[52]

> Temasek's initial portfolio of government-linked companies in 1974 was worth S$354 million, but today has grown to S$215 billion as of March 2013, with an astonishing average annual return since its inception of 16% – significantly outstripping the average performance of other large and mid-sized Singapore-listed companies. Likewise, empirical evidence suggests that government-linked companies on average are significantly more profitable, better governed, and receive much higher valuations than nongovernment-linked companies.

Further, although Temasek is an exempt private company – which under Singapore law is not required to disclose any financial information to the public[53] – it voluntarily publishes an annual group financial summary and portfolio of performance which has garnered it the highest possible ranking for transparency among sovereign wealth funds by the Linaburg-Maduell Transparency Index.[54]

---

[43] Puchniak and Lan (n 6) 316.
[44] Minister for Finance (Incorporation) Act 1959 (2020 Rev Ed Sing).
[45] Temasek Holdings, 'Investor Factsheet' (31 March 2021) <www.temasek.com.sg/content/dam/temasek-corporate/our-financials/investor-library/fact-sheet/tr21/Nov%202021%20Investor%20Factsheet_English.pdf> accessed 13 February 2022.
[46] Puchniak and Lan (n 6) 307.
[47] Sim, Thomsen and Yeong (n 8) 6, 23–24.
[48] Luh Luh Lan and Umakanth Varottil, 'Shareholder Empowerment in Controlled Companies: The Case of Singapore' in Jennifer G Hill and Randall S Thomas (eds), *Research Handbook on Shareholder Power* (Edward Elgar 2015) 572, 579.
[49] Puchniak and Lan (n 6) 307.
[50] Constitution of the Republic of Singapore (1985 Rev Ed, 1999 Reprint) arts 22C(3), 22D(5)–(6), Fifth Sch Pt II.
[51] Puchniak and Lan (n 6) 307–308.
[52] ibid 316.
[53] Companies (Filing of Documents) Regulations (Cap 50, Reg 7, 2005 Rev Ed), reg 6(1)(c)(i) (exempting solvent exempt private companies from filing documents in regulation 6(2)), reg 6(2) (requiring companies not otherwise exempt to file financial statements and auditors' report) (as amended by s 513/2018). The current version has been in force since 31 August 2018.
[54] Sovereign Wealth Fund Institute, 'Linaburg-Maduell Transparency Index (LMTI)' <www.swfinstitute.org/research/linaburg-maduell-transparency-index> accessed 14 July 2020 (giving Temasek Holdings the highest rating of ten based on a set of ten indicators).

Puchniak and Lan have compared Temasek's engagement with its GLCs as 'akin to an engaged pension fund, which actively votes its shares but does not become directly involved in the management of its portfolio companies'.[55] However, in exceptional cases, Temasek has actively intervened in the affairs of its investee companies when doing so was beneficial for the company's long-term performance. A clear example of this can be seen in a recent case where Temasek acted to defend one of its GLCs, Olam International, which was targeted by a short-selling campaign by Muddy Waters – an aggressive US activist hedge fund. When Muddy Waters released a spurious report alleging accounting malfeasance at Olam, Olam's share price suffered a serious fall. Olam's downward spiral was only gradually halted when one of Temasek's investment arms purchased sufficient shares to obtain a majority stake in Olam through an all cash offer, and Temasek had publicly announced its support for Olam. Market observers noted that Temasek's actions demonstrated that 'Temasek will back them to the hilt and shake out shorts (short-sellers) and doubters at the same time'.[56] Temasek's intervention in the Olam case demonstrates its commitment to long-term sustainable investment and judicious activism – while at the same time quelling the market for US-style activist shareholders and other long-term institutional investors. This government-centred form of corporate governance, which has proved extremely successful for decades, has made Singapore an attractive potential corporate governance model for China and many other jurisdictions.[57]

As with Temasek, Singapore's family controlling shareholders also have significant incentives – and have done so in practice – to actively monitor management of their companies with a long-term view towards promoting the company's success.[58] In short, Singapore's state and family controlling shareholders have acted as 'engaged stewards' seeking to promote the long-term interests of the companies even in the absence of the Singapore Stewardship Code.

By contrast, there is no evidence to show that institutional investors have played anything more than a minor role in the corporate governance of Singapore listed companies compared to state and family controlling shareholders. Based on a recent empirical study of 195 Singapore listed companies representing 83% of total market capitalization, institutional investors owned only 6% of shares in listed companies (12% on a market capitalization weighted ownership basis).[59] In addition, there is no evidence that institutional shareholders have used their limited shareholdings to play an active role in corporate governance. Indeed, the role of shareholder activists, and even proxy advisory firms, has been extremely limited in Singapore.[60] Private pension funds, which are major institutional investors in many developed economies, do not exist as such in Singapore. Instead, Singapore's state-run equivalent of a pension fund operates pursuant to a complex arrangement that reinforces the government's central role in corporate governance.[61] Without a body of institutional investors who collectively own a majority stake in

---

[55] Puchniak and Lan (n 6) 309.
[56] 'Temasek Offer Lifts Olam Clear of Muddy Waters' *Business Times* (Singapore, 15 March 2014) <www.businesstimes.com.sg/top-stories/temasek-offer-lifts-olam-clear-of-muddy-waters> accessed 14 July 2020; Christopher Langner and David Yong, 'Temasek Drags Olam from Muddy Waters to Winning $1 Billion Loan' (*Bloomberg*, 3 November 2015) <www.bloomberg.com/news/articles/2015-11-02/temasek-drags-olam-from-muddy-waters-to-winning-1-billion-loan> accessed 14 July 2020.
[57] Tan, Puchniak and Varottil (n 6) 62–63, 91; Lin and Milhaupt (n 41).
[58] See discussion at Section 14.4.
[59] De La Cruz, Medina and Tang (n 5).
[60] Lan and Varottil (n 48) 575–78.
[61] Singapore's pension fund equivalent is a compulsory savings plan operated by the Singapore government called the Central Provident Fund (CPF), to which all working Singaporeans and Permanent Residents are required to contribute; CPF funds are invested in Special Singapore Government Securities that are issued and guaranteed by the Singapore

listed companies, yet have remained rationally passive, Singapore clearly stands apart from the UK (and the US).

In sum, Singapore's corporate governance context features neither excessive risk-taking by listed companies dominated by management nor an absence of shareholder stewards leading to short-termism,[62] such that the concerns that drove the UK's adoption of the 2010 Stewardship Code are absent. Institutional investors do not dominate Singapore listed companies given that they have paltry voting rights in comparison to their UK counterparts;[63] rather, it is controlling shareholders that exercise effective control over Singapore listed companies. It would thus be unrealistic to expect the solutions that the UK Code proposes – for institutional investors to take an active role in corporate governance – to function in the same way in Singapore as they would in the UK. This brings us to our first puzzle: if none of the corporate governance problems or solutions that the UK Code was designed to address exist in Singapore, why did Singapore ostensibly adopt a UK-model stewardship code?

14.2.3 *Singapore's Stewardship Code: An Effective Signalling Device*

Given the practical impotence and limited irrelevance of institutional investors in Singapore, we argue that the Singapore Stewardship Code is a form of 'halo signalling' introduced to demonstrate Singapore's commitment to the Anglo-American-cum-global norms of 'good' corporate governance. Here, 'halo signalling' refers to the strategic adoption of regulation to attract foreign investment notwithstanding the apparent practical irrelevance of such regulation to the jurisdiction's corporate environment.

A previous example of Singapore's 'halo signalling' was its adoption of American-style independent directors in its Corporate Governance Code.[64] We believe that by adopting a UK-style stewardship code, Singapore is yet again engaging in a form of 'halo signalling'. We draw this conclusion based on the text of the Stewardship Code itself juxtaposed against the limited relevance of institutional investors themselves in Singapore and the reality of Singapore's shareholder landscape. In explaining the importance of the Singapore Stewardship Code, the preamble states: 'Many countries are seeing a trend towards fragmented ownership, especially in listed companies, with many shareholders each holding a small proportion of shares. Coupled with increasingly shorter shareholding tenure, the ownership mentality is arguably being eroded and replaced by a prevalent short-term view of investment and portfolio management. Hence, the emphasis on stewardship is relevant and timely.'[65]

While these corporate governance issues are relevant for jurisdictions with dispersed shareholding environments, they are not applicable to a jurisdiction with a controlling-block shareholder

---

government. The proceeds from these bonds are pooled with other funds from the Singapore government, and are ultimately converted to foreign assets and transferred to the Government of Singapore Investment Corporation (GIC), Singapore's sovereign wealth fund, to 'manage over a long investment horizon'. GIC invests the vast majority of its assets in listed companies outside of Singapore, especially in the US and Europe. See Central Provident Fund Board, 'CPF Overview' (2019) <www.cpf.gov.sg/member/cpf-overview> accessed 13 February 2022; Ministry of Finance, 'Section IV: Is Our CPF Money Safe? Can the Government Pay All Its Debt Obligations?' (2014) <www.mof.gov.sg/policies/reserves/is-our-cpf-money-safe-can-the-government-pay-all-its-debt-obligations> accessed 13 February 2022; GIC, 'Investments: Performance' (31 March 2019) <www.gic.com.sg/investments/performance/> accessed 14 July 2020.

[62] Lan and Varottil (n 48) 579–80.
[63] ibid. See Puchniak (n 4) for a detailed comparative analysis of institutional investors' power and controlling shareholders' power in the context of stewardship around the world.
[64] See generally Puchniak and Lan (n 6).
[65] Singapore Stewardship Code (n 3) 3.

environment, which has maintained or increased the concentration of its shareholder landscape over time, as is the case in Singapore.[66] The concerns articulated in the Code's preamble demonstrate a disconnect with the reality of Singapore's corporate environment, where controlling-block shareholders dominate listed companies.[67]

Further, the Code is also expressly addressed to 'institutional investors who are asset owners and asset managers',[68] and are 'most applicable to Singapore-based institutional investors with equity holdings in Singapore-listed companies'.[69] Yet, as explained earlier,[70] institutional investors play only a minor role in the corporate governance of Singapore listed companies as compared to state and family controlling shareholders. The purported concerns driving the introduction of the Code are clearly irrelevant to Singapore – and it is their very irrelevance that makes the case that the Code is being adopted for signalling reasons, rather than to address actual corporate governance problems in Singapore.

14.3 THE SECOND PUZZLE: WHY DID SINGAPORE ADOPT A 'TOOTHLESS' CODE?

14.3.1 *The 'Toothless' Nature of the Singapore Stewardship Code Revealed*

At first blush, a textual analysis of the seven broad principles in the Singapore Stewardship Code would lead one to conclude that it is similar to the UK Code. All seven principles articulated in the UK Code have broadly parallel principles in the Singapore Stewardship Code, with only a few minor differences in wording.[71] Thus, based on a superficial textual analysis of the seven principles in both codes, a reasonable conclusion might be made that the Singapore Stewardship Code addresses the same issues, and promotes the same responses to those issues, as the UK Code. However, as is often the case, the devil is in the details. A careful examination of the preamble of the Singapore Stewardship Code and a few subtle, but critical differences in wording in the Singapore Stewardship Code's principles reveal that the two codes are dramatically different – and that the Singapore Stewardship Code also departs from most other codes which claim to have been modelled on the UK Code.

First, the Singapore Stewardship Code does not articulate a singular model of stewardship with which investors should comply. The UK Code was specifically designed to set out clear and concise expectations for 'good stewardship' to encourage institutional investors to either adopt these practices or face market scrutiny if they decided to deviate from them, backed by a requirement that investors give reasons for their deviation.[72] Notwithstanding the Singapore Stewardship Code's apparent similarity to the text of the UK Code, the Guidance to Principle 1 of the Singapore Stewardship Code states that investors can '*satisfy themselves* that they adhere to their *own stewardship approach* in carrying out investment activities'.[73] The idea that each investor can develop their own view of stewardship, without benchmarking it against a single settled model or code, is significantly different from the UK Code. In other words, it is possible

---

[66] Tan, Puchniak and Varottil (n 6) 66–67.
[67] ibid.
[68] Singapore Stewardship Code (n 3) 3.
[69] ibid 4.
[70] See discussion at Section 14.2.2.
[71] For an analysis of the similarities between the UK Code 2010 and the Singapore Stewardship Code, see Katelouzou and Puchniak, Global Shareholder Stewardship, Chapter 1; Puchniak (n 4); Katelouzou and Siems, The Global Diffusion of Stewardship Codes, Chapter 30.
[72] Reisberg (n 33) 221–23; Cheffins (n 11) 1005–1006; Davies, The UK Stewardship Code 2010–2020, Chapter 2.
[73] Singapore Stewardship Code (n 3) 6 (emphasis added).

for each institutional investor to adopt a version of the Singapore Stewardship Code that is adapted to their own needs. Even if there is substantial variation among the versions of the Singapore Stewardship Code adopted by each individual investor, all of them can be considered to have adopted and complied with the Singapore Stewardship Code.

Second, flowing axiomatically from the fact that there is no single model, the Singapore Stewardship Code does not employ a 'comply or explain' approach. Rather, the preamble states that the 'level of commitment [to the principles] are matters that are left to each individual investor to adopt, on a wholly voluntary basis'.[74] This, combined with the aforementioned 'self-satisfaction standard', provides the Singapore Stewardship Code with neither benchmark nor venue for disclosure – elements that lie at the core of a typical 'comply or explain' regime. Without such a regime, the Singapore Stewardship Code is not designed to significantly increase market pressure on institutional investors to follow a singular model of 'good stewardship' – which is central to the UK Code and most other stewardship codes.[75] Pursuant to the UK Code, signatories promise to publish a statement of commitment to the Code, and the Financial Reporting Council (FRC) has a website with links to the individual pledges by the institutional investors.[76] The FRC also lists and tiers the institutional investors based on the quality of their disclosures under the UK Code – further enhancing transparency and market pressure to promote that Code's model of good stewardship.[77]

None of these features exists for the Singapore Stewardship Code. Stewardship Asia refers to institutional investors who have decided to adopt the Code as 'supporters' – as opposed to the 'signatories' referred to in the UK Code. The softer language of 'supporters' suggests that Stewardship Asia wants a more relaxed regime than the UK Code. Stewardship Asia's webpage explicitly states that the Singapore Stewardship Code 'is not enforced or audited at all'.[78] While Stewardship Asia has provided a list of such supporters on its website, there is no information as to the degree of their compliance with the Code.[79] There is thus no mechanism to determine whether institutional investors have complied with the Singapore Stewardship Code, or to enforce compliance where institutional investors fall short.

Third, it goes without saying that the Singapore Stewardship Code is entirely voluntary. This reinforces the idea that the Singapore Stewardship Code is not designed to significantly alter the status quo. Stewardship veterans would recall that the initial version of the UK Code was itself entirely voluntary; the fact that the UK Code is now mandatory for certain domestic institutional investors is unique to the UK,[80] and it is not a characteristic that is shared by other jurisdictions that developed stewardship codes explicitly or implicitly modelled on the initial UK Code. While the purely voluntary nature of the Singapore Stewardship Code distinguishes it from the UK Code, this is in fact a red herring: there is nothing to voluntarily submit to at all. While the preamble of the Singapore Stewardship Code states that the principles are '*not intended to be a "box-ticking" exercise*', the better question is whether there are, in fact, any boxes to tick at all.[81]

Fourth, there is no regulatory agency in Singapore that is responsible for the administration of the Singapore Stewardship Code. The UK Code was issued by the FRC, which also issued and

---

[74] ibid 3.
[75] On the enforcement mechanisms of stewardship codes, see Katelouzou and Sergakis, Shareholder Stewardship Enforcement, Chapter 27.
[76] Financial Reporting Council (n 17).
[77] ibid.
[78] See Stewardship Asia Centre (n 16).
[79] Stewardship Asia Centre, 'Organisations Expressing Support for the Singapore Stewardship Principles' (6 January 2022) <www.stewardshipasia.com.sg/sites/default/files/2022-01/SSP%20Expressions%20of%20Support_6%20Jan%202022.pdf> accessed 13 February 2022.
[80] COBS 2.2.3R (06/12/2010) <www.handbook.fca.org.uk/handbook/COBS/2/2.html> accessed 14 July 2020.
[81] Singapore Stewardship Code (n 3) 2–4 (emphasis added).

administers the UK Corporate Governance Code.[82] The FRC is a quasi-regulatory body with enforcement power against accountants and actuaries,[83] whereas financial market regulation is the preserve of the Financial Conduct Authority (FCA).[84] By contrast, Stewardship Asia is a private entity seemingly tasked only with promoting the Singapore Stewardship Code and the Family Stewardship Code to investors.[85] Stewardship Asia has no mandate to regulate or enforce compliance with the Singapore Stewardship Code. Notably, neither the Monetary Authority of Singapore[86] (Singapore's closest equivalent to the FCA) nor the Accounting and Corporate Regulatory Authority[87] (Singapore's closest equivalent to the FRC) was tasked with the administration of the Singapore Stewardship Code.

14.3.2 A Code Designed for Signalling, Not for Disruptive Change

From this analysis, one might be inclined to conclude that Singapore's Code is either the most toothless stewardship code in the world or, in fact, not even a 'code at all' but merely publicity. We argue that this misses the point altogether. Singapore's adoption of a stewardship code should be understood as an effort to send a signal of good corporate governance without fundamentally up-ending Singapore's effective corporate governance system.

Even without any stewardship code, Singapore already had 'good stewards' in the form of Temasek and family controlling shareholders – backed by an institutional architecture and public enforcement mechanisms – which effectively controlled the problem of systematic wealth-reducing private benefits of control.[88] Notwithstanding its apparent dissimilarity from the Anglo-American idea of an 'institutional investor', Temasek has branded itself a 'steward' of its investee companies in recent years.[89] Temasek's involvement in Singapore's Stewardship Code has also gone beyond what one might expect from an institutional investor. Our detailed examination of public company records, press statements and business journalism reveals that Temasek funds Stewardship Asia, that Stewardship Asia is part of the Temasek group and that Temasek had a hand in Stewardship Asia's early efforts at drafting and promoting the Singapore Stewardship Code.[90] Temasek indirectly funds Stewardship Asia through the Temasek Trust, Temasek's philanthropic arm.[91]

---

[82] Financial Reporting Council, 'UK Stewardship Code' <www.frc.org.uk/investors/uk-stewardship-code> accessed 14 July 2020.
[83] Financial Reporting Council, 'Professional Oversight' <www.frc.org.uk/auditors/professional-oversight> accessed 14 July 2020.
[84] Financial Conduct Authority, 'About the FCA' (5 May 2020) <www.fca.org.uk/about/the-fca> accessed 14 July 2020.
[85] Stewardship Asia Centre, 'About Us' (2018) <www.stewardshipasia.com.sg/about-us> accessed 14 July 2020.
[86] Monetary Authority of Singapore, 'Regulation' <www.mas.gov.sg/regulation> accessed 14 July 2020.
[87] Accounting and Corporate Regulatory Authority, 'Overview of ACRA' <www.acra.gov.sg/who-we-are/overview-of-acra> accessed 14 July 2020.
[88] See generally Puchniak and Lan (n 6).
[89] See e.g. Temasek, 'Our Purpose, Charters and Values' <www.temasek.com.sg/en/about-us/our-purpose-charter-values> accessed 13 February 2022: 'Our Temasek Charter guides our day-to-day decision-making ... Temasek is a trusted steward – we strive for the advancement of our communities across generations.'
[90] Stewardship Asia was founded in 2011 as the Stewardship and Corporate Governance Centre, which was a Temasek-led initiative. See Ho Ching, 'Transcript: Luncheon Remarks by Ho Ching at Stewardship Asia 2018 Roundtable' (*Temasek*, 4 June 2018) <www.temasek.com.sg/en/news-and-views/news-room/speeches/2018/luncheon-remarks-by-ho-ching-stewardship-asia-2018.html> accessed 14 July 2020; Ravi Menon, 'Corporate Governance – Going Beyond the Rules' (Speech at the Securities Investors Association (Singapore) 4th Asian Investors' Corporate Governance Conference, Singapore, 1 October 2012) <www.bis.org/review/r121002a.pdf> accessed 14 July 2020. See also Singapore Institute of Directors, 'Shareholder Stewardship Gets a Push in Singapore' (*Directors' Bulletin*, 2017) <www.sid.org.sg//images/PDFs/Publications/DirectorsBulletin/2017Q1/Shareholder%20stewardship%20gets%20a%20push%20in%20Singapore.pdf> accessed 14 July 2020.
[91] Temasek (n 26) 42–43.

The relationship between Temasek and Stewardship Asia sets Singapore apart from other leading jurisdictions which have adopted stewardship codes.[92] Unlike the Japanese or UK stewardship codes, Singapore's Code is not the result of a 'top-down' government-led initiative, as the Code was not developed by a government regulator or agency and Stewardship Asia discloses no clear legal relationship to the Singapore government. However, Temasek's involvement in Stewardship Asia suggests that the Code is linked, at least in part, to the efforts of a state *controlling shareholder* – making it distinctly different from the US example, which was driven by private institutional investors and devoid of government involvement. This could lead foreign observers to believe that Singapore's Code is ostensibly the product of a 'bottom-up' initiative similar to the US Code, insofar as Stewardship Asia may be deemed by those unfamiliar with Singapore's context to be representing the interests of institutional investors in Singapore generally.[93]

Thus, it was Temasek, through its close relationship with Stewardship Asia, that spearheaded the Singapore Stewardship Code as a form of 'halo signalling' with minimal disruption to the status quo. In influencing and promoting the Singapore Stewardship Code, Temasek indirectly took control of a nascent regulatory space and its future development. This allowed the state, as the most powerful controlling shareholder, to pre-empt market players from creating a more aggressive bottom-up code that might disrupt the status quo maintained by Singapore's controlling shareholders. This form of 'halo signalling', without effecting any substantive change to institutional investors, is arguably efficient since Singapore's corporate governance issues do not lie with institutional investors, and Singapore overall has demonstrated its commitment to strong corporate governance. This is not to say that Temasek is acting against the interests of minority shareholders, or corporate governance in general, by seizing this regulatory space. Rather, Singapore's controlling shareholders – including Temasek – have substantial incentives to function as 'stewards' of their companies, and have an exceptional long-term track record of doing so effectively.[94]

Further, the 'toothless' nature of Singapore's Code arguably facilitates compliance by major institutional investors seeking to comply with stewardship codes in multiple jurisdictions. Given the diverse approaches to stewardship taken in various jurisdictions,[95] institutional investors with operations in these jurisdictions may face considerable challenges in complying with materially different requirements imposed by various stewardship codes. The fact that the Singapore Stewardship Code does not unilaterally impose a single model of stewardship, coupled with the 'self-satisfaction standard' employed by the Code,[96] means that it can accommodate diverse approaches to stewardship. This practically eliminates any compliance challenges that institutional investors might face with regards to the Singapore Stewardship Code, and facilitates its passive adoption by institutional investors around the world.

14.3.3 Is the State Controlling Shareholder Writing the Rules of the Game for Engagement with Itself?

Given Temasek's close relationship with Stewardship Asia, a sceptical observer might wonder if Temasek's influence over Stewardship Asia creates a serious conflict of interest. It would appear

---

[92] See discussion in Katelouzou and Puchniak, Global Shareholder Stewardship, Chapter 1, Section 1.1.
[93] ibid.
[94] Tan, Puchniak and Varottil (n 6) 68–69, 94.
[95] Koh, Puchniak and Goto, Shareholder Stewardship in Asia, Chapter 29.
[96] Singapore Stewardship Code (n 3) 6.

that the entity writing the rules for how institutional investors should engage with controlling shareholders (i.e., Stewardship Asia) is itself an arm of Singapore's most powerful controlling shareholder: the Singapore government through its wholly owned holding company Temasek. One might conclude that it would be in Temasek's interests for the Singapore Stewardship Code to be designed in a way that would avoid disrupting management or promoting powerful shareholder activism. As one might expect if Jeff Bezos and Mark Zuckerberg had written the rules for how BlackRock, Fidelity, and State Street should engage with Amazon and Facebook, the Code is designed in such a way as not to disrupt the status quo for corporate controllers – which in Singapore are the state and wealthy families.

These assumptions are, however, erroneous in Singapore's context. Distinct from the US corporate governance environment, Temasek is located within an institutional architecture that serves as a functional substitute for shareholder activism. There are substantial legal constraints that prevent undue state influence from being exerted on Temasek's board or its subsidiary companies, and ensure that decisions made by Temasek's management are based on commercial and not political reasons.[97] Temasek has further committed itself to refrain from being directly involved in the management of its investee companies.[98] This prevents the type of wealth-reducing private benefits of control from being extracted by Temasek from Singapore's SOEs – which one may expect would be extracted from Amazon and Facebook if Bezos and Zuckerberg were themselves the regulators and the US corporate governance environment was devoid of shareholder activism. We may assume that Temasek is abiding – and will continue to abide – by the same constraints in relation to Stewardship Asia. There is thus far no evidence that Temasek has exerted, or intends to exert, any undue influence over Stewardship Asia and the Singapore Stewardship Code, or to use the Code to protect the status quo purely for selfish reasons that result in inefficient wealth tunnelling.

Rather, it seems that the real reason for the enactment of the Singapore Stewardship Code may be far more benign. By releasing the first stewardship code through Stewardship Asia, the Singapore state controlling shareholder took control of this regulatory space and prevented more bottom-up approaches of shareholder stewardship – which could have been more unpredictable and potentially disruptive to Singapore's successful corporate governance model – from developing. This form of 'pre-emptive corporate governance' has allowed Singapore to maintain the existing system of corporate governance and its position as a global corporate governance leader by embracing 'shareholder stewardship'.

14.4 THE THIRD PUZZLE: WHY HAVE A STEWARDSHIP CODE FOR FAMILY COMPANIES?

14.4.1 *Singapore's Family Stewardship Code*

In October 2018, Stewardship Asia released a second 'stewardship code' under the title 'Stewardship Principles for Family Businesses' (Family Stewardship Code). At first glance, this appears to be a version of the Singapore Stewardship Code developed for family companies to encourage family controlling shareholders to be good 'stewards' of their companies.[99] The Family Stewardship Code is, to the best of our knowledge, the first and only one of its kind in the world. Given the importance of family companies to Singapore, this development does not

---

[97] See discussion at Section 14.2.2.
[98] Puchniak and Lan (n 6) 307–10.
[99] Family Stewardship Code (n 21).

surprise: family companies play a central role in Singapore's economy, and up to 60.8 per cent of publicly listed companies can be classified as family firms.[100] This is in line with broader economic trends in Asia; family firms comprise a substantial segment of both small and medium-sized enterprises and large public listed firms in many Asian jurisdictions.[101] By introducing the world's first family stewardship code, Singapore has positioned itself as a corporate governance leader for Asia and its leading economies.

Turning to the substantive provisions of the Family Stewardship Code, it is notable that, as with the Singapore Stewardship Code, the Family Stewardship Code is not a 'code' per se but a set of seven principles. These principles aim to encapsulate a way of doing business representing 'the essence of responsible and meaningful value creation in a sustainable way to benefit stakeholders, as well as the larger community that [family businesses] are a part of'.[102]

Principle 1 reads: 'Driven by a sense of purpose, anchored by values'; it encourages a family business to articulate and clearly communicate the purpose of the family business, and to implement them in practice. Principle 1 appears to contemplate that the 'purpose' of a family business should account for considerations other than pure profit-maximization or mere commercial goals, in that it directs family shareholders to aim for 'responsible wealth creation'.[103] This principle appears to have some broad similarity with Principle 1 of the Singapore Stewardship Code, which exhorts investors to 'establish and articulate their policies on their stewardship responsibilities', in that they both have to do with disclosure of stewardship principles generally.[104] However, unlike institutional investors who are ordinarily corporate outsiders and who individually cannot control the company, family controlling shareholders are the quintessential corporate insiders who can, and do, individually intervene in the company's management. As compared to corporate outsiders – such as institutional investors in most US and UK listed companies – family controllers are far more intimately connected with management and are normally the best informed.[105]

More importantly, what seems to have escaped the global stewardship movement's attention is the fact that, when one considers the function of the Family Stewardship Code, it is starkly different from any other stewardship code we are aware of. Principles 2 to 7 of the Family Stewardship Code have no direct equivalent in the Singapore Stewardship Code, or indeed any stewardship code to date.

Principle 2 is to 'Cultivate an ownership mentality'. This principle encourages owners and employees to take responsibility for the business's long-term growth. In particular, it discourages family owners from using company resources to benefit themselves, and encourages family owners to 'embrace the responsibility for creating long-term social and economic value to a wider group of stakeholders, and not just myopically focusing on family wealth to foster ownership mentality amongst all those who play a role in the success of the business'.[106] In a similar vein, Principle 3 encourages family shareholders to 'Integrate short-term and long-term perspectives', by ensuring that short-term goals are consistent with long-term goals, and looking beyond short-term gains to focus on the preservation of 'intangible values such as kinship and

---

[100] Dieleman, Shim and Ibrahim (n 7) 8.
[101] See e.g. Gur Aminadav and Elias Papaioannou, 'Corporate Control Around the World' (2020) 75 *The Journal of Finance* 1191; Adrian Wooldridge, 'To Have and to Hold: Special Report on Family Companies' *The Economist* (London, 18 April 2019) 2 <www.economist.com/sites/default/files/20150418_family.pdf> accessed 14 July 2020.
[102] Family Stewardship Code (n 21) 1.
[103] ibid 4.
[104] Singapore Stewardship Code (n 3) 6.
[105] Puchniak and Lan (n 6) 298–300.
[106] Family Stewardship Code (n 21) 4.

loyalty'.[107] Although their focus on long-term value over short-term profit makes Principles 2 and 3 broadly consistent with the general thrust of stewardship codes around the world, maintaining values of kinship and loyalty suggests the continuing entrenchment of the family as the corporate controller, which has no equivalent elsewhere.[108]

Principle 4 states: 'Expect changes, nurture agility and strengthen resilience.' This principle encourages family businesses to develop skills to adapt to new challenges in a rapidly changing business environment.[109] This reinforces the idea of keeping the family business viable in the long run, which would ultimately preserve the future for the family as the corporate controller.

Principle 5 emphasizes the importance of non-family participants and stakeholders, and exhorts family shareholders to 'Embrace inclusiveness and build strong stakeholder relationships'. In particular, board diversity is singled out as a good practice for family businesses; this is significant because many Singapore family companies have traditionally operated according to traditional Asian family values that emphasize control by an autocratic patriarch, 'who enlists his children and siblings *(women usually excepted)* to assist in the family business'.[110] Despite this call for diversity, there is nothing to suggest that the family should divest its controlling stake in the company to external organizations or individuals. Rather, the focus is on nurturing a strong stakeholder culture to sustain family-controlled companies for the future.

Principle 6 appears to reflect environmental, social and governance (ESG) concerns;[111] it states: 'Do well, do good, do right; contributing to community.' This principle promotes the importance of 'non-economic wealth', such as 'social capital, communal ties, family reputation and core values'.[112] Again, it seems that the Code is developing a model for long-term family control where reputation rather than shareholder activism drives good corporate governance in family companies.

Principle 7 is arguably the most interesting provision in the Family Stewardship Code. It states simply: 'Be mindful of succession.'[113] This principle recognizes the importance of timely and planned succession to not only family successors, but also the utility of external expertise and professional assistance. This principle is crucial because it reveals that while the concept of 'stewardship' espoused in the Family Stewardship Code appears to be consistent with that articulated in other stewardship codes – especially the Code's focus on long-term investment and stakeholder considerations[114] – it differs in critical ways. First, unlike the version of 'stewardship' employed in the UK Code – which envisions institutional shareholders playing a more active role in the corporate governance of their investee companies – Singapore's Family Stewardship Code does not contemplate complete divestment of control to non-family shareholders; rather, it anticipates the continued participation of family successors groomed for the task. The Code does not appear to actively encourage or facilitate the involvement of institutional investors or shareholder activists in Singapore family companies; there is nothing in the Family Stewardship Code which contemplates any action – collective or otherwise – by institutional investors at all.

[107] ibid 5.
[108] ibid 4–5.
[109] ibid 5.
[110] Samantha S Tang, 'Corporate Divorce in Family Companies' [2018] *Lloyd's Maritime & Commercial Law Quarterly* 19, 24 (emphasis added).
[111] See Katelouzou and Klettner, Sustainable Finance and Stewardship, Chapter 26.
[112] Family Stewardship Code (n 21) 6.
[113] ibid 7.
[114] See further Dionysia Katelouzou, 'Shareholder Stewardship: A Case of (Re)Embedding Institutional Investors and the Corporation?' in Beate Sjåfjell and Christopher M Bruner (eds), *Cambridge Handbook of Corporate Law, Corporate Governance and Sustainability* (CUP 2019) 581–95.

Further, the Family Stewardship Code takes a substantially different approach to compliance from that taken in the UK Code – and many other stewardship codes. The Code provides guidance on how these principles may be put into practice, but does not rely on any form of 'comply or explain' or any other mechanism to place any market pressure on family controllers.[115] As with the Singapore Stewardship Code, the Family Stewardship Code neither demands evidence of compliance from supporters who voluntarily 'sign up' to the Code nor provides any mechanism for shareholders or external regulatory agencies to monitor compliance with the Code.

14.4.2 *Stewardship for Family Controllers: A Meaningful Approach for a Truly Asian Problem*

The salience of the Family Stewardship Code in Singapore is underscored by the significant incentive that family controlling shareholders have to act as 'stewards' of their companies by monitoring and directly intervening in the company's management to promote the long-term success of the family business. Singapore family firms have a strong culture that encourages family controllers to preserve and pass on the family business to future generations of the controlling family or families.[116] These cultural norms also link the family's reputation to the success of the family business,[117] giving controllers significant incentives to monitor or directly manage the family firm to promote its long-term success. While tunnelling in family firms may be a concern in other jurisdictions, previous research by one of the authors posited 'that Singaporean-Chinese family corporate culture provides at least a partial functional substitute for effective monitoring of family member controllers by truly independent directors in family firms in Singapore'.[118] There is also anecdotal evidence that family controllers are reluctant to engage in obvious wealth tunnelling for fear of being caught by Singapore's efficient public regulators.[119]

Beyond Singapore, family-controlled firms also play a central role in many Asian jurisdictions. Examples of leading family businesses in Asia include Samsung (South Korea),[120] Suntory Holdings (Japan),[121] CK Hutchinson Holdings (Hong Kong) and Far East Organisation (Singapore). Singapore's development of the Family Stewardship Code is both salient and timely, and positions Singapore as the first jurisdiction to develop a stewardship code specifically directed at a business model widely adopted in Asia that faces unique corporate governance challenges. The Family Stewardship Code's Asian focus is evident from the recent launch of its Family Business Campaign (FB77) in September 2018 to promote the Family Stewardship Code

---

[115] For the enforcement of stewardship codes, see Katelouzou and Sergakis, Shareholder Stewardship Enforcement, Chapter 27. As revealed in Katelouzou and Sergakis's review of twenty-five codes, only five codes have a mandatory element (including the UK Code). However, thirteen out of the twenty non-binding codes have adopted the comply-or-explain approach, but on a completely voluntary basis. See also Katelouzou and Puchniak, Global Shareholder Stewardship, Chapter 1 and Lim and Puchniak, Can a Global Legal Misfit Be Fixed?, Chapter 28.
[116] Wilson Ng and John Roberts, '"Helping the Family": The Mediating Role of Outside Directors in Ethnic Chinese Family Firms' (2007) 60 H*uman Relations* 285, 287, 306–307; Dieleman, Shim and Ibrahim (n 7) 29, 31; Puchniak and Lan (n 6) 302.
[117] Ng and Roberts (n 116) 306–307.
[118] Puchniak and Lan (n 6) 303.
[119] ibid 304.
[120] Kang and Chun, Korea's Stewardship Code and the Rise of Shareholder Activism, Chapter 11.
[121] Suntory Holdings Ltd, '2018年12月期 決算概況〔ＩＦＲＳ〕（連結) (2018-nen 12-gatsu-ki: Kessan Gaikyō (IFRS) (Renketsu)) [Financial Statements as of December 2018 (IFRS) (Consolidated)]' (15 February 2019) 8–9 <www.suntory.co.jp/news/article/mt_items/SBF0807.pdf> accessed 14 July 2020.

to Australia, China, Indonesia, Japan, the Philippines, Singapore and Thailand.[122] The Code and FB77 thus demonstrate Singapore's ambition of making Singapore the standard-bearer for a new Asian model of corporate governance.

Given the centrality of family businesses to Asia, the absence of family companies from stewardship codes in other leading jurisdictions is a significant omission. This could arise from an excessively narrow perception of the problems sought to be resolved by stewardship in such jurisdictions. Singapore's Family Stewardship Code thus represents a meaningful contribution to the growing global stewardship movement and an increased focus on corporate governance in Asia.

14.5 SINGAPORE-STYLE STEWARDSHIP: A SUCCESSFUL SECRET

Stewardship in Singapore is far more complex than it appears at first blush. Indeed, a superficial textual analysis of the seven principles in the Singapore Stewardship Code would reasonably lead one to believe that stewardship in Singapore is a near carbon-copy of the original UK Code. Foreign readers of academic and popular reports that appear to assume that the Singapore Stewardship Code is merely a transplant of the UK Code may come away with the mistaken impression that the UK model of stewardship has been transplanted to Singapore.[123] That foreign observers might reasonably conclude that Singapore has embraced the apparently UK-driven stewardship movement is not an accident; it is by design. Singapore has a strong incentive to maintain its position as a corporate governance leader by signalling that it has embraced the UK model, which has become an indicium of good corporate governance.

However, stewardship in Singapore turns the UK model on its head, and appears to be uniquely Singaporean. Singapore does not have the corporate governance problems that sparked the UK Code, and the impotence of institutional investors in Singapore means that the UK stewardship solution is similarly absent in Singapore. A closer examination of the Singapore Stewardship Code reveals that it does not contemplate a single model of stewardship; rather, it allows investors to develop their own understanding of stewardship. Both of Singapore's stewardship codes comprise merely flexible principles rather than strict regulatory requirements, and there is no easy way to determine which institutions have chosen to implement these principles because there is no central repository of information to facilitate a true 'comply or explain' approach – as such an approach has not been adopted in Singapore. Further, there is no body with any regulatory power whatsoever to disseminate or enforce the Singapore Stewardship Code. Thus, viewed through a UK lens, stewardship in Singapore may be seen as a sham or failure.

To the contrary, we suggest that both of Singapore's stewardship codes have been decidedly successful. Through its implementation of not one but two stewardship codes, Singapore has reinforced its position as a corporate governance leader that embraces global norms of good corporate governance. By developing the concept of 'family stewardship', Singapore has also positioned itself as a stewardship leader in a way that resonates with a seminal corporate governance problem and solution in Asia, which may allow it to become a leader in an emerging movement of Asian corporate governance. The timing of this development is significant as regionalism appears to be replacing globalism as a mega-trend – which may be accelerated in the post-Covid-19 world.

---

[122] Family Stewardship Code (n 21).
[123] See text to n 4.

Importantly, Singapore has been able to position itself as a leader in the global stewardship movement without disrupting its highly successful state- and family-controlled system of corporate governance. Counter-intuitively, Singapore's unique brand of stewardship seems to have reinforced it. It would have been beyond the wildest imaginations of the original architects of the UK Code that shareholder stewardship would be successfully used as a mechanism for entrenching state control and family control over corporate governance. Nevertheless, Singapore's unique approach to stewardship may very well be a secret to Singapore's continued market-leading corporate governance success.

15

Institutional Investor Stewardship in Malaysia

Code, Context and Challenges

Petrina Tan Tjin Yi[*]

15.1 INTRODUCTION

Global developments have seen a deepening interest in the role of institutional investors as stewards with the consequent introduction of stewardship codes. In this respect, Malaysia formulated the Malaysian Code for Institutional Investors (Malaysian Code) in 2014,[1] and then set up the Institutional Investors Council Malaysia (II Council) in 2016, an industry body tasked with the oversight of the Malaysian Code. The Malaysian Code builds on the provisions of the Malaysian Companies Act 2016 and acts as a complement to the Bursa Malaysia Listing Requirements[2] and the Malaysian Corporate Governance Code[3] within the broader corporate governance ecosystem.

The enshrinement of the responsibilities of institutional investors as stewards of their clients and ultimate beneficiaries in a written code, as well as the formalization of an industry association dedicated to the advocacy and promotion of stewardship, are positive steps forward in Malaysia's corporate governance journey. Nevertheless, questions arise as to the factors which affect the effectiveness of the Malaysian Code and the embedding of stewardship practices into the Malaysian corporate sector. In this regard, it is argued that, in the Malaysian context, the effectiveness of the Malaysian Code is dependent not only on its principles, which draw upon the 2012 version of the UK Stewardship Code (UK Code),[4] but also on broader contextual factors which have implications for the overall effectiveness of stewardship practices.

---

[*] This chapter draws on and develops materials contained in the journal article Petrina Tan Tjin Yi, 'Institutional Investor Stewardship in the UK and Malaysia: Functionally Similar, Contextually Challenged' (2019) 14 *Asian Journal of Comparative Law* 279. I am grateful to the National University of Singapore, Centre for Banking & Finance Law for their support during my tenure as adjunct research fellow of the Centre from January to August 2018, which enabled the writing of the aforementioned journal article and this chapter subsequently. The law and data cited in this chapter are as of 30 December 2019. All errors and omissions are my own.

[1] Minority Shareholder Watchdog Group and Securities Commission Malaysia, 'Malaysian Code for Institutional Investors' (June 2014) <www.iicm.org.my/wp-content/uploads/2018/05/MALAYSIAN-CODE-FOR-INSTITUTIONAL-INVESTORS-MCII.pdf> accessed 13 July 2020 [hereinafter Malaysian Code].

[2] Bursa Malaysia, 'Consolidated Listing Requirements' (1 June 2020) <www.bursamalaysia.com/regulation/listing_requirements/main_market/listing_requirements> accessed 13 July 2020.

[3] Securities Commission Malaysia, 'Malaysian Code on Corporate Governance' (April 2017) <www.sc.com.my/api/documentms/download.ashx?id=239e5ea1-a258-4db8-a9e2-41c215bdb776> accessed 9 February 2022 [hereinafter Malaysian Code on Corporate Governance 2017]. It is noted that the Malaysian Code draws upon the older Malaysian Code on Corporate Governance 2012 (Securities Commission Malaysia, 'Malaysian Code on Corporate Governance' (2012) <http://micg.org.my/upload/file/articles/11/CODE-CG-2012.pdf> accessed 13 July 2020) and as such, later developments in the updated Malaysian Code on Corporate Governance 2017 are not incorporated (Malaysian Code (n 1) 17).

[4] Financial Reporting Council, *The UK Stewardship Code* (September 2012) <www.frc.org.uk/getattachment/d67933f9-ca38-4233-b603-3d24b2f62c5f/UK-Stewardship-Code-(September-2012).pdf> accessed 13 July 2020 [hereinafter UK Code 2012].

As a corollary, it is observed that the development of the Malaysian Code had similar origins as that of the UK Code: through the evolution of industry-led guidelines. Nevertheless, as this chapter will demonstrate, the constitution of industry within the Malaysian context is inevitably linked to the state through the ownership and control of government-linked investment companies (GLICs) and government-linked companies (GLCs). It is also pertinent to note that these GLICs and GLCs are a prominent feature of Malaysia's corporate landscape. As such, the decisions, acts and performance of these companies are affected by their relationship with the state, giving rise to concerns about whether the interests of the state are aligned with those of the asset owners, the asset managers and, more importantly, the ultimate beneficiaries or clients who are at the end of the investment chain, as well as the possible implications for agency conflicts and the effective practice of stewardship in Malaysia.

This chapter will proceed as follows. Section 15.2 examines the history and background of institutional investor stewardship in Malaysia leading to the introduction of the Malaysian Code. Section 15.3 sets out an analysis of the principles and oversight of the Malaysian Code. Section 15.4 will appraise the stewardship journey in Malaysia thus far. Section 15.5 provides the broader economic and institutional context within which the institutional investors operate and Section 15.6 reflects on the challenges affecting stewardship arising from these contextual factors. This chapter concludes, in Section 15.7, with a few brief summary remarks.

15.2 HISTORY AND BACKGROUND OF INSTITUTIONAL INVESTOR STEWARDSHIP IN MALAYSIA

The early steps towards the Malaysian Code were taken in 2007 through the issuance of the 'Guide of Best Practices for Institutional Investors' by the Institutional Investor Committee and Minority Shareholder Watchdog Group (MSWG),[5] as recommended by the first Capital Market Masterplan,[6] to complement the Malaysian Corporate Governance Code and 'The Green Book: Enhancing Board Effectiveness'.[7] The aforementioned Guide of Best Practices sets out a framework for how institutional investors should discharge their responsibilities on behalf of their beneficiaries and other stakeholders to influence, guide and monitor investee companies in a responsible way. Further, in 2010, the Malaysian Employees Provident Fund released its Corporate Governance Principles and Voting Guidelines, focusing on the size and composition of the board, board committees, separation of power between chairman and chief executive officer (CEO), re-election of directors, related-party transactions and dividend policy.[8]

---

[5] The Minority Shareholder Watchdog Group is an independent research organization on corporate governance matters. It provides a platform and collective voice to both retail and institutional minority shareholders, and it advises on voting at general meetings of public listed companies. See Minority Shareholder Watchdog Group, 'Who We Are' <www.mswg.org.my/who-we-are> accessed 13 July 2020.

[6] Securities Commission Malaysia, *Capital Market Masterplan: Malaysia* (February 2001) 48 <www.sc.com.my/api/documentms/download.ashx?id=458216e4-2354-4f9e-bdfd-1dd5ec1d9acc> accessed 13 July 2020.

[7] Putrajaya Committee on GLC High Performance, 'The Green Book: Enhancing Board Effectiveness' (April 2006) <www.pcg.gov.my/media/1080/initiative-1-enhance-board-effectiveness.pdf> accessed 13 July 2020.

[8] Securities Commission Malaysia, *Corporate Governance Blueprint 2011: Towards Excellence in Corporate Governance* (July 2011) 14 <www.sc.com.my/api/documentms/download.ashx?id=0a494b24-2910-4b14-98e0-ac6b99916d87> accessed 13 July 2020; Employees Provident Fund, 'EPF's Corporate Governance Principles and Voting Guidelines' (2010) <www.kwsp.gov.my/documents/20126/142907/Corporate_Governance_Principles_And_Voting_Guidelines_2010_24052017.pdf /7e86c3c1-d5d0-1e5f-cb53-b47d4eb95aa6> accessed 13 July 2020.

Concurrent with these developments, the positive relationship between corporate governance and institutional investors in Malaysia was established in an empirical study published in 2008.[9] This study presented evidence that corporate governance influenced pressure-insensitive investors positively. Pressure-insensitive investors were defined in the study as institutional investors that did not have any business relationship with the firms they invested in.[10] However, this relationship became less positive after the 2001 reforms, which saw the incorporation of the Malaysian Corporate Governance Code into the (then) Kuala Lumpur Stock Exchange (now renamed Bursa Malaysia) Listing Rules and the establishment of the MSWG.[11] The findings of this study implied that the monitoring role of both corporate governance and institutional investors could arise simultaneously and endogenously,[12] which in turn suggests that these 2001 reforms were successful in catalyzing the role of institutional investors and the Malaysian Corporate Governance Code.[13]

As a form of preparatory groundwork for the drafting of the Malaysian Code in 2011, the Corporate Governance Blueprint (CG Blueprint) issued by the Malaysian Securities Commission referred to the existence of various international codes, guidelines and principles pertaining to the role of institutional investors.[14] It highlighted in particular the International Corporate Governance Network (ICGN) Statement of Principles on Institutional Shareholder Responsibilities and the UK Code as possible reference points for the intended Malaysian Code.

The CG Blueprint also set out a case for changes to the prevailing practices of institutional investors, focusing on the effective exercise of ownership rights which were to be manifested via the expected best practices under the proposed new code for institutional investors.[15] The document also mooted the creation of a network of institutional investors to represent the common interest of all institutional investors and be a platform to shape and influence a wider sphere of corporate governance culture.[16] Here, the CG Blueprint referred to the UK and Australian experience of institutional investor stewardship, and cited the Institutional Investor Committee in the UK as an example of an institutional investor representative group. In summary, the CG Blueprint recommended that institutional investors drive the formulation of a new code and publish their commitment to the new code for institutional investors and create an industry-driven umbrella body for institutional investors.[17]

Pursuant to the recommendations of the CG Blueprint, the MSWG was tasked with overseeing the formation of a Steering Committee comprising CEOs and key representatives of Malaysian institutional investors, which included both asset owners and asset managers as well as working, expert and observer groups. The MSWG then jointly published a public consultation paper on the proposed new code with the Securities Commission. The consultation paper received a total of nineteen responses from various parties, including asset owners, asset managers, service providers and academics.[18]

---

[9] Effiezal AA Wahab, Janice How and Peter Verhoeven, 'Corporate Governance and Institutional Investors: Evidence from Malaysia' (2008) 4 *Asian Academy of Management Journal of Accounting and Finance* 67, 68.
[10] ibid 74.
[11] ibid.
[12] ibid 67.
[13] ibid.
[14] Securities Commission Malaysia (n 8) 14.
[15] ibid.
[16] ibid.
[17] ibid.
[18] Minority Shareholder Watchdog Group and Securities Commission Malaysia, 'Public Response Paper: The Malaysian Code For Institutional Investors 2014' (26 June 2014) 5 <www.sc.com.my/api/documentms/download.ashx?id=79aed48d-a8ff-40db-925b-cecc8d6953aa> accessed 13 July 2020.

The Malaysian Code was launched in 2014 as one of the deliverables of the CG Blueprint after incorporating the comments received from the public consultation.[19] The Malaysian Code was intended to give institutional investors guidance on the effective exercise of stewardship responsibilities to ensure delivery of sustainable long-term value to their ultimate beneficiaries or clients. It is noted that the Malaysian Code substantially adopted the provisions of the UK Code 2012.[20] The UK Code has since been the subject of a high-level public consultation in 2017 and a detailed consultation in 2019,[21] resulting in rather substantial changes to its content, including the introduction of higher standards of stewardship, a new focus on service providers and asset classes other than public equity and the usage of an 'apply and explain' regulatory system. The newly revised UK Code 2020 has been launched and took effect on 1 January 2020.[22]

Based on the preceding discussion, the emergence of the Malaysian Code can be traced back to industry-sponsored guidelines, similar to the developmental trajectory of the UK Code 2012.[23] Indeed, the Malaysian Code's origins and its subsequent development were consciously tagged to industry and intended to be driven by the institutional investors themselves rather than by external regulators as mandated by the CG Blueprint. An essential consideration is the implications for stewardship that arise when the line between industry and the state is blurred, as is the case with Malaysia.

15.3 AN ANALYSIS OF THE MALAYSIAN CODE FOR INSTITUTIONAL INVESTORS

By way of introduction, the term 'stewardship' is defined in the Malaysian Code as follows:[24]

> Stewardship is investor stewardship from the perspective of a **long-term institutional investor** in particular **asset owners** such as pension funds. It includes the responsible management and oversight of assets for the benefit of the institutional investors' ultimate beneficiaries or clients. The discharge of effective stewardship responsibilities would include development of a set of principles/policies, application of the principles/policies, oversight of agents, communications of expectations and reporting to their clients or beneficiaries. These activities also include monitoring and engagement with the investee companies on matters relating to strategy, performance, risk management, voting, corporate governance or sustainability issues.

A point of observation is the emphasis on a long-term investment horizon, with the explicit statement that stewardship is for the benefit of the institutional investors' ultimate beneficiaries or clients. This indicates that they are the intended recipients of the positive effects from stewardship. It is also noted that the Malaysian Code is framed from the perspective of asset owners such as pension funds. In addition, the reference to the long-term investment horizon is consistent with the 2017 Malaysian Corporate Governance Code's statement that the board of

---

[19] The Editor, 'Institutional Investors Encouraged to Adopt 2014 M'sian Code' (*The Edge Markets*, 27 June 2014) <www.theedgemarkets.com/article/institutional-investors-encouraged-adopt-2014-msian-code> accessed 13 July 2020.

[20] See also Katelouzou and Siems, The Global Diffusion of Stewardship Codes, Chapter 30, which provides empirical evidence showing the substantial adoption of the text of the UK Code into the Malaysian Code.

[21] Financial Reporting Council, 'Proposed Revision to the UK Stewardship Code' (30 January 2019) <www.frc.org.uk/consultation-list/2019/consulting-on-a-revised-uk-stewardship-code> accessed 13 July 2020.

[22] Financial Reporting Council, *The UK Stewardship Code 2020* (2019) <www.frc.org.uk/getattachment/5aae591d-d9d3-4cf4-814a-d14e156a1d87/Stewardship-Code_Dec-19-Final-Corrected.pdf> accessed 13 July 2020 [hereinafter UK Code 2020]. See the latest developments in Davies, The UK Stewardship Code 2010–2020, Chapter 2.

[23] See Davies, The UK Stewardship Code 2010–2020, Chapter 2 for the UK Code's history. See also Dionysia Katelouzou and Peer Zumbansen, 'The New Geographies of Corporate Governance' (2020) 42 *University of Pennsylvania Journal of International Law* 51 on the authorship of stewardship codes.

[24] Malaysian Code (n 1) 2–3 (emphasis added).

directors is collectively responsible for the long-term success of a company,[25] although it must be noted that the previous 2012 version of the Corporate Governance Code which the Malaysian Code referred to during the time of its public consultation did not contain a similar statement to this effect.[26]

The specific focus on asset owners in the Malaysian Code's definition of stewardship is unusual given that the definition of institutional investors in the Malaysian Code refers to both asset owners and asset managers with equity holdings in corporations listed on Bursa Malaysia.[27] Be that as it may, a subsequent section of the Malaysian Code explains how asset owners may show their commitment to the Malaysian Code. They may apply the principles of the Code to their investee companies either directly or indirectly through mandates given to asset managers.[28] However, the Malaysian Code appears to have omitted specifying how asset managers may do this. In this regard, the Malaysian Code should consider clarifying the manner in which asset managers are to display their commitment to the Code, as provided for in the UK Code 2012 which states that an asset manager should disclose how it delivers stewardship responsibilities on behalf of its clients. The UK Code 2012 also encourages asset managers to have the policies in their stewardship statements independently verified.[29] This is critical as asset managers may choose to sign up to the Malaysian Code independently of asset owners; thus, it is important to ensure that the Malaysian Code is scoped appropriately to include the roles of both asset owner and asset manager in the investment intermediation chain vis-à-vis stewardship. Given that the most recent revision of the UK Code sets out separate principles for asset owners and asset managers as well as service providers,[30] it is conceivable that the Malaysian Code may be structured similarly in the future to ensure that each party in the investment intermediation chain is made aware of their particular responsibilities and how they relate to each other.

The Malaysian Code begins with the first principle which requires institutional investors to disclose the policies on their stewardship responsibilities, with this disclosure reflecting their stewardship activities along the investment chain and how they will discharge their responsibilities arising from these activities.[31] These policies should be accessible to investee companies, beneficiaries and clients and written in plain and understandable language.[32] The guidance to this principle also covers situations where stewardship activities are outsourced. In a further illustration of the Malaysian Code's emphasis on asset owners, this principle also requires them to disclose general guidelines on how they select asset managers and other service providers.[33] It is important to note that while stewardship activities may be outsourced, the ultimate responsibility for stewardship still lies with the signatory, which ensures that accountability flows back to the asset owner as signatory to the Malaysian Code.

The second principle of the Malaysian Code states that institutional investors should monitor their investee companies.[34] The monitoring process is to be conducted in an active manner, and includes quantitative factors such as the company's performance, value drivers

---

[25] Malaysian Code on Corporate Governance 2017 (n 3) 12.
[26] See n 3.
[27] Malaysian Code (n 1) 2.
[28] ibid 4.
[29] UK Code 2012 (n 4) 3.
[30] UK Code 2020 (n 22) 7, 23.
[31] Malaysian Code (n 1) 8.
[32] ibid.
[33] ibid.
[34] ibid 9.

and potential problems which may lead to a significant loss in investment value as well as qualitative factors, namely the quality of company reporting, management discussion and analysis as well as adherence to the Malaysian Corporate Governance Code. Monitoring is also taken to include attending general meetings where practicable[35] and exercising voting rights.[36] It is worth noting that this second principle seems to be geared towards investors with active investment strategies, rather than passive investment strategies such as index funds.

In addition, the Malaysian Code requires institutional investors to carefully consider explanations from investee companies for departures from the Code and to inform the investee company's board of directors in writing if it does not agree with the company's explanation or position together with its reasons.[37] The monitoring role of institutional investors is buttressed by the disclosure regime prescribed in Chapter 9 of the Bursa Malaysia Listing Requirements in which investee companies are required to provide timely and accurate disclosure of all material information to the public.[38] These disclosures are made via immediate announcements, circulars, quarterly reports and annual reports. They are a critical component of the means by which institutional investors keep watch over the actions and performance of their investee companies.

Apart from monitoring, institutional investors are also called upon to engage with investee companies as appropriate, as required in the third principle of the Malaysian Code. Here, engagement is defined as an extension of monitoring activities and arises when institutional investors have a close and full understanding of the specific circumstances of the investee company in terms of performance, governance or risk management.[39] The key focus in engagement is purposeful dialogue with investee companies in order to preserve or enhance value on behalf of the institutional investors' beneficiaries or clients.[40] However, the Malaysian Code is cognisant of the potential for insider trading and expressly mandates that institutional investors must respect market abuse rules and not seek a trading advantage through the possession of price-sensitive information.[41] An interesting point to note is Guidance 3.3 of this principle which states that initial discussions should be carried out on a confidential basis with a clear approach for escalation where the usual avenues of dialogues and communications are failing,[42] envisaging a hierarchy of possible interventions of increasing severity which the institutional investor may undertake.

In the fourth Malaysian Code principle, institutional investors should adopt a robust policy to manage conflicts of interest which should be publicly disclosed. The wording used in this principle suggests that the Malaysian Code tacitly accepts the presence of conflicts of interest situations, notwithstanding the limited requirement for institutional investors to communicate

---

[35] The Malaysian Companies Act 2016, s 313, also prescribes that shareholders have the right to call for a general meeting at the company's expense.
[36] See Malaysian Companies Act 2016, s 71(1), which provides that a share in a company confers, among others, the right to attend, participate in and speak at a meeting; the right to vote on a show of hands on any company resolution; and the right to one vote for each share on a poll on any company resolution.
[37] Malaysian Code (n 1) 9.
[38] See Bursa Malaysia (n 2) ch 9, paras 9.01(1)–(4).
[39] Malaysian Code (n 1) 10.
[40] See Charles Cronin and John Mellor, 'An Investigation into Stewardship – Engagement between Investors and Public Companies: Impediments, and Their Resolution' (Foundation for Governance Research and Education, June 2011) 11 <www.foundationgre.com/Stewardship%20Report%20Final%20-%2022.6.11.pdf> accessed 13 July 2020, which cites Adam Smith's description of stewardship as 'anxious vigilance' performed by a good owner and is related to becoming sufficiently knowledgeable about the operations of a company to exercise its ownership rights.
[41] Malaysian Code (n 1) 10.
[42] ibid. See also Hairul Annuar, 'Changes in Ownership Forms and Role of Institutional Investors in Governing Public Companies in Malaysia' (2015) 11 *Journal of Accounting & Organizational Change* 455, 463.

to their service providers on the need to disclose all known potential conflicts of interest and to explain how they are managed.[43] It is argued that a clearer, more explicit statement calling for the disclosure of potential conflicts of interest situations by institutional investors and methods of dealing with these situations would be more useful and significant to recipients of stewardship practice and would accordingly strengthen the impact of the Malaysian Code. Here, the 2011 Code for Responsible Investing in South Africa may be a useful reference point as its Principle 4 requires institutional investors to recognize circumstances and relationships which may hold potential conflicts of interest and to proactively manage them.[44] The adoption of this wording would suggest a more active attitude towards identifying possible conflicts of interest and addressing them, as compared to the current formulation of the Malaysian Code.

The fifth principle of the Malaysian Code requires institutional investors to incorporate corporate governance and sustainability considerations into the investment decision-making process. While the Malaysian Code broadly maps against the provisions of the UK Code 2012, it is noted that the UK Code 2012 did not contain a corresponding principle.[45] The public feedback to the Malaysian Code stated that emphasis should be placed on the importance of integrating environmental, social and governance (ESG) factors into stewardship activities and not just in the investment process.[46] However, this principle was retained as the MSWG and the Securities Commission were of the view that it should be a stand-alone principle to encourage incorporation of corporate governance and sustainability issues into the investment decision-making process for a start, which is part of the stewardship role of institutional investors.

The inclusion of this principle brings the Malaysian Code into alignment with the United Nations Principles for Responsible Investment (PRI), in which investors are asked to incorporate ESG issues into their investment analysis and decision-making processes,[47] and the South Africa Code.[48] The inclusion of this principle is in the interest of the ultimate beneficiaries in the longer term as part of the delivery of enhanced risk-adjusted returns on investment. It is also in sync with the requirement for listed issuers to issue a sustainability statement as part of their annual report (i.e. a narrative statement of their management of material economic, environmental and social risks and opportunities).[49] The sustainability statement of listed issuers must contain balanced, comparable and meaningful information as stated in the Bursa Malaysia Sustainability Reporting Guide[50] or the GRI Sustainability Reporting Guidelines.[51]

The sixth principle of the Malaysian Code requires institutional investors to publish a voting policy, identifying it as an element of engagement to be exercised with due care and diligence. The guidance provides that institutional investors should seek to reach a clear decision in voting for or against a resolution, with the reasons communicated to the investee company. It is

---

[43] Malaysian Code (n 1) 12.
[44] Institute of Directors in Southern Africa, 'Code for Responsible Investing in South Africa 2011' (2011) 11 <https://cdn.ymaws.com/www.iodsa.co.za/resource/resmgr/crisa/crisa_19_july_2011.pdf> accessed 13 July 2020. See also Locke, Encouraging Sustainable Investment in South Africa, Chapter 22.
[45] For the changes in the focus of the UK Code 2020 (n 22) from engagement to an ESG focus, see Davies, The UK Stewardship Code 2010–2020, Chapter 2. Further on how stewardship codes integrate sustainability, see Katelouzou and Klettner, Sustainable Finance and Stewardship, Chapter 26.
[46] Minority Shareholder Watchdog Group and Securities Commission Malaysia (n 18) 5.
[47] UN PRI, 'What Are the Principles for Responsible Investment?' <www.unpri.org/about-us/what-are-the-principles-for-responsible-investment> accessed 9 February 2022.
[48] Institute of Directors in Southern Africa (n 44) 10. See also Locke, Encouraging Sustainable Investment in South Africa, Chapter 22.
[49] Bursa Malaysia (n 2) ch 9, Appendix 9C, Part A, para 29.
[50] ibid Practice Note 9, para 6.2.
[51] ibid para 6.4.

proposed that institutional investors set a policy on the threshold for active voting (i.e. the exercise of active voting beyond a certain ownership threshold as determined by the institutional investor's own internal policy guidelines).[52] Further, institutional investors are encouraged to set out a summary of their voting activities to provide greater clarity to beneficiaries on how the votes are cast and to demonstrate that conflicts of interest are properly managed.[53] This principle may be useful in addressing the observed lack of participation in annual general meetings on the part of investors, including institutional investors, in which the questions posed are generally directed towards financial results and dividend payments rather than other corporate governance matters.[54]

It is worth noting that, in the public consultation for the Malaysian Code, the principle that institutional investors should consider acting collectively with other investors where appropriate was included as the seventh principle, which was similar to the UK Code. However, this principle was subsequently deleted and moved to the preamble of the finalized Malaysian Code as a result of issues highlighted pursuant to the consultation.[55] Among the concerns raised which made the proposed principle impracticable were that collective action with other investors could be deemed to be acting in concert to manipulate the market,[56] and the difficulty of establishing clear policies on collective engagement and competition law concerns.[57] In view of this feedback, the MSWG and the Securities Commission decided not to include collective action with other institutional investors as one of the principles in the Malaysian Code, but incorporated it as prefatory remarks to the Code instead.

The Malaysian Code is characterized as soft law, as contrasted against a statutory regulatory regime with penalties for non-compliance.[58] Indeed, the Malaysian Code itself expressly states that it is a voluntary code.[59] It further provides that institutional investor signatories should explain how they have applied the principles in the Malaysian Code, taking into account the guidance provided under each principle which is set out in the form of best practice recommendations. It further advocates the adoption of standards beyond the minimum prescribed by regulations and for institutional investors to explain how they have applied the principles of the Malaysian Code, taking into account the guidance provided for each principle.

Further, although the Malaysian Code recognizes that stewardship is not 'one-size-fits-all', it remains committed to signatories providing a clear and complete account of stewardship for the benefit of the institutional investor's ultimate beneficiaries or clients. In this connection, the Malaysian Code provides that smaller institutions which may find that some of the Malaysian Code principles and guidance are disproportionate may explain why their business model precludes adherence to certain principles.[60] This principle of proportionality is also found in the UK Code,[61] as well as the Danish Stewardship Code.[62] Beyond reflecting the characteristic

[52] Malaysian Code (n 1) 15.
[53] ibid.
[54] Annuar (n 42) 455.
[55] Minority Shareholder Watchdog Group and Securities Commission Malaysia (n 18) 16.
[56] The term 'acting in concert' is defined in the Malaysian Capital Markets and Services Act 2007, s 216. See also Part VI, Division 2 of the Malaysian Code on Take-Overs Mergers and Compulsory Acquisition.
[57] Minority Shareholder Watchdog Group and Securities Commission Malaysia (n 18) 16.
[58] Iris H–Y Chiu, 'Institutional Shareholders as Stewards: Toward a New Conception of Corporate Governance' (2012) 6 *Brooklyn Journal of Corporate, Financial & Commercial Law* 387. She describes the soft law on corporate governance in the UK as developing in order to boost institutional shareholder monitoring as a form of private order beneath the corporate structure.
[59] Malaysian Code (n 1) 4.
[60] Malaysian Code (n 1) 5.
[61] UK Code 2012 (n 4) 4. See also UK Code 2020 (n 22) 6; Katelouzou and Puchniak, Global Shareholder Stewardship, Chapter 1, and Lim and Puchniak, Can a Global Legal Misfit Be Fixed?, Chapter 28.
[62] Birkmose and Madsen, The Danish Stewardship Code, Chapter 7, Section 7.2.3.1.

flexibility which soft law codes present, this principle also illustrates a measure of formal convergence in stewardship practices across jurisdictions.[63]

In keeping with its voluntary nature, there is no specific provision mandating that all types of signatory provide an explanation for non-compliance with particular provisions of the Malaysian Code. In this connection, it may be useful to look at the 2017 version of the Malaysian Corporate Governance Code which utilizes the 'Comprehend, Apply, Report' approach in which companies are to internalize the spirit and intention behind the CG principles and practices, implement them in substance and provide fair and meaningful disclosure on the company's corporate governance practices.[64] This has been described as a shift to support the mindset and culture change required to move away from the box-ticking approach to corporate governance.[65] A similar approach may accordingly be applied in future iterations of the Malaysian Code for greater alignment of practices and improved quality of disclosures within the corporate governance and stewardship spheres which are co-related to each other, which would also be consistent with the UK Code 2020's call for signatories to 'apply and explain'.[66]

An emphasis on upholding the broadly conceived interest of the ultimate beneficiaries resonates throughout the Malaysian Code. While recognizing the centrality of corporate governance matters and economic considerations in the investment decision-making process, the Malaysian Code advocates that institutional investors consider equally the issue of sustainability and believes that this approach is expected to be in the interest of the ultimate beneficiaries in the longer term as part of the delivery of enhanced risk-adjusted returns on investment, which is indicative of the dual nature of stewardship.[67] The Malaysian Code also expressly precludes compliance as an invitation to manage the affairs of a company or a stand against selling a holding where the institutional investor considers it in the best interest of beneficiaries or clients.[68] In this manner, the Malaysian Code acknowledges that stewardship should not amount to outright interference with the management of the company.

Oversight of the effective adoption of the Malaysian Code is carried out through the II Council, reflecting its industry-driven character alluded to in Section 15.2. The II Council was formally established as a society pursuant to the Societies Act 1966 on 29 December 2017. The II Council comprises representatives from statutory bodies, GLICs, the MSWG, government-linked fund managers and a private fund manager. It replaces the MSWG, which was previously tasked with overseeing the implementation of the Malaysian Code. The II Council is structurally similar to the UK Institutional Shareholders' Committee (which no longer exists) and has a similarly limited scope of powers, suggesting that, in the future, any changes to the Malaysian Code to harden its soft law principles into regulatory obligations would be a challenging task,

---

[63] See generally Katelouzou and Puchniak, Global Shareholder Stewardship, Chapter 1; Lim and Puchniak, Can a Global Legal Misfit Be Fixed?, Chapter 28; Koh, Puchniak and Goto, Shareholder Stewardship in Asia, Chapter 29; and Dan W Puchniak, 'The False Hope of Stewardship in the Context of Controlling Shareholders: Making Sense Out of the Global Transplant of a Legal Misfit' *The American Journal of Comparative Law* (forthcoming).

[64] Malaysian Code on Corporate Governance 2017 (n 3) 4.

[65] Securities Commission Malaysia, 'Corporate Governance Strategic Priorities 2017–2020' (September 2018) 9 <www.sc.com.my/api/documentms/download.ashx?id=7373ce94-78e9-456b-9b8f-c7749f11c08c> accessed 13 July 2020. See also Malaysian Code on Corporate Governance 2017 (n 3).

[66] See generally UK Code 2020 (n 22) 4. On the general enforcement of stewardship codes, see Katelouzou and Sergakis, Shareholder Stewardship Enforcement, Chapter 27.

[67] See Dionysia Katelouzou, 'Shareholder Stewardship: A Case of (Re)Embedding Institutional Investors and the Corporation?' in Beate Sjåfjell and Christopher M Bruner (eds), *Cambridge Handbook of Corporate Law, Corporate Governance and Sustainability* (CUP 2019) 581–95.

[68] Malaysian Code (n 1) 4.

although it is open to debate whether taking such an approach is necessary for the further growth and development of stewardship in Malaysia.

15.4 EVALUATING MALAYSIA'S STEWARDSHIP JOURNEY

The II Council issued its report titled 'Investor Stewardship and Future Key Priorities'[69] (IICM Report) in 2016, its first significant publication since the launch of the Malaysian Code in 2014. The IICM Report is akin to the annual UK Financial Reporting Council (FRC) Report on Developments in Corporate Governance and Stewardship.[70] By way of introduction, the IICM Report stated that, as at 31 December 2015, the featured institutional investors in the IICM Report collectively managed a fund size of approximately RM 1,321 billion and the total fund size in domestic equities of the above institutions amounted to approximately RM 524 billion.[71] This represented 31 per cent of the total of Bursa Malaysia's market capitalization of RM 1.69 trillion as at end December 2015, reflecting the magnitude of these institutions in the Malaysian capital market.

The findings of the IICM Report were intended to provide an indication of the extent of the stewardship and engagement activities undertaken by the selected institutional investors as well as their observations on the corporate governance practices of their investee companies, based on a survey of seven member organizations of the II Council. The II Council evaluated the stewardship, engagement and resources for stewardship,[72] as well as the key areas which showed progress and areas for improvement identified by the member institutional investors.[73]

As a corollary to this, there are currently twenty-two signatories to the Malaysian Code, comprising five asset owners,[74] sixteen asset managers[75] and one service provider, Hermes Equity Ownership Services, as of December 2019.[76] In addition, four out of five of the asset owner signatories to the Malaysian Code are GLICs.[77] The remaining asset owner signatory, SOCSO, is not a GLIC, although it is a government body mandated with

---

[69] Institutional Investor Council Malaysia, *Investor Stewardship and Future Key Priorities 2016* (2016) <www.iicm.org.my/wp-content/uploads/2018/05/INVESTORS-STEWARDSHIP-AND-FUTUER-KEY-PRIORITIES-2016.pdf> accessed 13 July 2020.

[70] See Financial Reporting Council, 'Developments in Corporate Governance and Stewardship' <www.frc.org.uk/directors/corporate-governance-and-stewardship/developments-in-corporate-governance-and-stewardsh> accessed 13 July 2020.

[71] The featured institutional investors were the Employees Provident Fund Malaysia, Permodalan Nasional Berhad, Kumpulan Wang Persaraan (Diperbadankan), Lembaga Tabung Haji, Khazanah Nasional Berhad, the Social Security Organisation and Aberdeen Asset Management Sdn Bhd.

[72] Institutional Investor Council Malaysia, *Investor Stewardship and Future Key Priorities 2016* (n 69) 18–25.

[73] ibid 26–33.

[74] Kumpulan Wang Persaraaan (Diperbadankan), Khazanah Nasional Berhad, Permodalan Nasional Berhad, the Employees Provident Fund Malaysia and SOCSO.

[75] Aberdeen Standard Investments (Malaysia) Sdn Bhd, Affin Hwang Asset Management Berhad, AIIMAN Asset Management Sdn Bhd, BNP Paribas Asset Management Malaysia Sdn Bhd, BNP Paribas Asset Management Najmah Malaysia Sdn Bhd, Kenanga Investors Berhad, Kenanga Islamic Investors Berhad, Nomura Asset Management Malaysia Sdn Bhd, Nomura Islamic Asset Management Sdn Bhd, Principal Asset Management Berhad, Principal Islamic Asset Management Sdn Bhd, Singular Asset Management Sdn Bhd, Valuecap Sdn Bhd, VCAP Asset Managers Sdn Bhd, Hermes Fund Managers and Legal & General Investment Management.

[76] Institutional Investor Council Malaysia, 'List of Signatories' <www.iicm.org.my/list-of-signatories/> accessed 12 December 2019.

[77] Kumpulan Wang Persaraaan (Diperbadankan), Khazanah Nasional Berhad, Permodalan Nasional Berhad and the Employees Provident Fund.

enforcing social security laws.[78] The primacy of GLICs in the list of asset owner signatories is notable and its significance will be discussed later in this chapter.

With regard to the asset manager signatories, a discernible trend which may be observed is the existence of two types of signatory, namely, foreign fund managers[79] and domestic asset managers linked to or associated with GLICs.[80] The prominence of GLICs and entities associated with GLICs in the list of signatories amounts to 50 per cent of the total number of signatories, bringing into sharp relief the absence of signatories which are not aligned with or linked to the state. Nevertheless, this is also indicative of the prominent role which the state plays in corporate affairs in Malaysia, which brings with it both risks and benefits.

As at December 2019, there are eleven publicly available compliance statements accessible on the II Council website.[81] These have been issued by all five asset owner signatories and six of the asset manager signatories. It is hoped that the remaining compliance statements will eventually be made available on the II Council website.

A brief review of the published compliance statements indicates that a majority of the statements suffer from the same issues which were highlighted by the UK FRC and which were addressed through its tiering of stewardship statements based on the disclosures provided.[82] In the UK FRC classification, Tier 1 signatories were those which provided a good-quality and transparent description of their approach to stewardship and explanations of an alternative approach where necessary; Tier 2 described signatories which met many of the reporting expectations but reported less transparently on their approach to stewardship or did not provide explanations where they departed from provisions of the UK Code.[83] The distinctions in terms of reporting quality in the Malaysian stewardship statements followed similar lines as those observed by the UK Code in the usage of its tiering criteria in that the quality of the compliance statements could be similarly distinguished. At the time of writing, there are no plans to introduce tiering criteria for the Malaysian Code compliance statements.

With regard to the asset owner signatories, it is heartening to note that the Employees Provident Fund, *Kumpulan Wang Persaraan (Diperbadankan)*, SOSCO and *Permodalan Nasional Berhad* provide relatively detailed and transparent descriptions of their stewardship approaches, which bodes well for the subsequent development of stewardship in Malaysia. However, Khazanah's compliance statement is brief by comparison and is hopefully an indicator of its status as a work in progress. It may be observed that the Employees Provident Fund cross-refers to its Corporate Governance Principles and Voting Guidelines, which were the precursors of the Malaysian Code, as alluded to in Section 15.2.[84] This is a positive sign and is in line with a building block approach in institutional investor stewardship.

---

[78] Social Security Organisation, 'Profile' (2019) <www.perkeso.gov.my/en/about-us/corporate-information/profile.html> accessed 9 February 2022.

[79] Hermes Fund Managers, Aberdeen Standard Investments (Malaysia) Sdn Bhd, Legal & General Investment Management, BNP Paribas Asset Management Malaysia Sdn Bhd, BNP Paribas Asset Management Najmah Malaysia Sdn Bhd and Singular Asset Management Sdn Bhd.

[80] ValueCAP Sdn Bhd, VCap Asset Managers Sdn Bhd, Affin Hwang Asset Management Berhad, AIIMAN Asset Management Sdn Bhd, Principal Asset Management Berhad and Principal Islamic Asset Management Sdn Bhd.

[81] Institutional Investor Council Malaysia, 'Compliance Statements' <www.iicm.org.my/compliance-statements/> accessed 12 December 2019.

[82] Financial Reporting Council, 'Tiering of signatories to the Stewardship Code <www.frc.org.uk/news/november-2016/tiering-of-signatories-to-the-stewardship-code> accessed 9 February 2022.

[83] Davies, The UK Stewardship Code 2010–2020, Chapter 2, Section 2.3.2.2; on enforcement, see Katelouzou and Sergakis, Shareholder Stewardship Enforcement, Chapter 27.

[84] Employees Provident Fund (n 8).

As regards asset manager signatories, Nomura Asset Management and Nomura Islamic Asset Management have the same wording in their compliance statements since they belong to the same corporate group. It is also noted that they are the only signatories to cross-refer to the UN Principles of Responsible Investment and the Malaysian Code principles as fundamental to their investment practices. Similarly, the Legal & General Investment Management and Aberdeen Standard Investments compliance statements cross-refer to the UK Code and the Japanese Stewardship Code, among other global stewardship codes and principles. It may be further observed that the compliance statements issued by Nomura, Legal & General Investment, and Aberdeen Standard Investments are fairly detailed, as reflected in their position in the Tier 1 ranking of the UK Code stewardship reporting.[85] This carried through in their stewardship statement for the Malaysian Code as part of their global stewardship commitments. A curious omission from this list of Malaysian compliance statements seems to be Hermes Fund Managers, which is ranked in Tier 1 of the UK Code stewardship reporting.[86]

In relation to domestic asset manager signatories, thus far, only Affin Hwang Asset Management Berhad and AIIMAN Asset Management Sdn Bhd have issued compliance statements, with the remaining local asset managers yet to provide their compliance statements on the IIC website.[87] Provision of the complete list of compliance statements issued by the asset manager signatories would enable meaningful comparison and benchmarking to discern the quality of stewardship reporting among domestic asset managers and foreign asset managers.

15.5 THE BROADER INSTITUTIONAL AND ECONOMIC CONTEXT OF MALAYSIAN INSTITUTIONAL INVESTORS

It is submitted that evaluation of Malaysia's stewardship practices needs to be grounded in the country's institutional and economic context so as to better understand the forces driving the adoption of stewardship practices among institutional investors. In this connection, Malaysia may be characterized as an emerging economy[88] and a developmental state which prioritizes economic growth, productivity and technological competitiveness.[89] Under this model, the state has more autonomous political power and control over the economy, which frees it up to plan the economy and prioritize long-term national interests without disruption from the short-term interests of either the corporate or the working class.[90] In short, the state is significantly involved in business, resulting in a unique set of consequences, particularly relating to institutional investor stewardship.

A clear example of state involvement in business may be seen in the role played by GLICs. As a corollary, it is noted that the institutional investor sphere in Malaysia is dominated by GLICs,

---

[85] Financial Reporting Council, 'Asset Managers' <www.frc.org.uk/investors/uk-stewardship-code/uk-stewardship-code-statements/asset-managers> accessed 13 July 2020.
[86] ibid.
[87] Institutional Investor Council Malaysia, 'List of Signatories' (n 76).
[88] See generally Nor Zalina Mohamad Yusof, 'Context Matters: A Critique of Agency Theory in Corporate Governance Research in Emerging Countries' (2016) 6 *International Journal of Economics and Financial Issues* 154.
[89] Yin-Wah Chu, 'The Asian Developmental State: Ideas and Debates' in Yin-Wah Chu (ed), *The Asian Developmental State: Reexaminations and New Departures* (Palgrave Macmillan 2016) 1.
[90] Richard W Carney and Michael A Witt, 'The Role of the State in Asian Business Systems' in Michael A Witt and Gordon Redding (eds), *The Oxford Handbook of Asian Business Systems* (OUP 2014) 548. See also Dan W Puchniak, 'Multiple Faces of Shareholder Power in Asia: Complexity Revealed' in Jennifer G Hill and Randall S Thomas (eds), *Research Handbook on Shareholder Power* (Edward Elgar 2015); Stijn Claessens, Simeon Djankov and Larry HP Lang, 'The Separation of Ownership and Control in East Asian Corporations' (2000) 58 *Journal of Financial Economics* 81.

as evidenced by their ownership and control of the top 100 quoted companies on the stock exchange, 35 of which were identified as GLCs and which constituted 42 per cent of the total market capitalization of all listed companies in 2013.[91]

GLICs have been defined by the Organisation for Economic Co-operation and Development (OECD) as[92]

> investment companies in which the federal government has influence over the management by appointing and approving board members and senior management, who in turn report directly to the government. The government may also provide funds for operations or to guarantee capital (and some income) placed by unit holders. The Ministry of Finance or the Prime Minister's office are usually the government representatives on the board of GLICs and thereby play a role in the governance and investment decisions of these companies.

The Malaysian Ministry of Finance has classified seven entities as GLICs.[93] All seven GLICs also have an equity interest in a number of other publicly listed companies.[94] The prominence of GLICs encompasses diverse sectors such as finance, media, plantations and oil and gas, apart from the utilities sector traditionally associated with state ownership via GLCs.[95] In addition, GLICs play a significant role in carrying out government policies,[96] and they are tasked with an obligation to comply with these government policies apart from seeing to their investments in their investee companies.[97] More particularly, they play a critical role in national development and the promotion of 'Bumiputera' participation in the economy.[98] *Bumiputera*, which literally means 'sons of the soil', refers to Malaysian citizens who are Malays or from other indigenous tribes; they are given special privileges as set out in the Federal Constitution of Malaysia.[99] Given the essential function of GLICs, the state exerts control over them through a variety of mechanisms, including by appointing their boards (e.g. the Employees Provident Fund board is appointed by the Minster pursuant to section 4 of the Employees Provident Fund Act 1991).

It is argued that the Malaysian Code is a crystallization of the prevailing practices of Malaysian institutional investors in relation to monitoring and engaging with investee companies. A previous study in 2015, predating the Malaysian Code, evaluated the role of institutional investors in governing public companies in Malaysia and highlighted the non-homogeneity of Malaysian institutional investors, which consisted of government-linked institutional investors or GLICs and those financial intermediaries without links to the government (e.g. banks and insurance companies).[100] Government-linked institutional investors may be further divided into

---

[91] Edmund Terence Gomez and others, *Minister of Finance Incorporated – Ownership and Control of Corporate Malaysia* (Palgrave Macmillan 2018) 7.

[92] OECD, *Investment Policy Reviews: Malaysia* (2013) 70 <https://aanzfta.asean.org/uploads/2016/12/OECD_Investment_Policy_Reviews_-_Malaysia.pdf> accessed 13 July 2020.

[93] They are: the Minister of Finance Incorporated, Khazanah Nasional Berhad, Permodalan Nasional Berhad, Employees Provident Fund, Kumpulan Wang Persaraan Diperbadankan, Lembaga Tabung Haji and Lembaga Tabung Angkatan Tentera.

[94] Gomez and others (n 91) 7.

[95] ibid 40.

[96] See Economic Planning Unit, *Eleventh Malaysia Plan: 2016–2020* (2015) <www.epu.gov.my/en/economic-developments/development-plans/rmk/previous-plans> accessed 9 February 2022; and Economic Planning Unit, *Tenth Malaysia Plan: 2011–2015* (2010) <www.pmo.gov.my/dokumenattached/RMK/RMK10_Eds.pdf> accessed 13 July 2020.

[97] Putrajaya Committee on GLC High Performance, 'Catalysing GLC Transformation to Advance Malaysia's Development' (29 July 2005) 19–20, 29–31, 45 <www.pcg.gov.my/media/1036/policy-guideline.pdf> accessed 13 July 2020.

[98] ibid.

[99] Gomez and others (n 91) xiv fn 1.

[100] Annuar (n 42) 458.

two categories, namely those which are large and allocate some or all of their funds to GLCs and those which have smaller investments, comprising government-linked foundations and state corporations, among others.[101]

The study noted that extreme forms of shareholder activism (i.e. media complaints, legal action and co-operative actions against investee companies) were rarely utilized because the size of investment for GLICs is often large enough for them to handle pressing issues without the need to co-operate; they also have a tendency to initiate actions where issues have been raised.[102] Critically and in summary, it was concluded that only GLICs appeared to be the type of institution which performed a controlling role in agency conflicts with regard to the governance of the company, as compared to non-GLICs which were more likely to sell off their investments in the open market if any of their investment criteria, especially those concerning financial performance, were impinged,[103] an action which accords with the Hirschman exit and voice model.[104]

Based on the foregoing analysis, the primacy of GLICs in the corporate governance of investee companies indicates that they are a key driving force in the development of stewardship in Malaysia. Consistent with the findings of this earlier study, there is little visible support for the Malaysian Code among non-government-linked institutional asset owners such as banks and financial institutions as well as non-government-linked asset managers. It is noted that there are currently eighty licensed asset management companies in Malaysia, although most of these firms are understood to be small, and future consolidation of the industry players is likely.[105] Be that as it may, in the long run, the exclusion of non-state-linked entities in the stewardship agenda may be problematic as there will be an imbalance in the subsequent growth and development of stewardship across the breadth of institutional investors in Malaysia. Nevertheless, these constraints may also be attributable to structural issues within investment management itself, as will be elaborated upon.

The emergence of the Malaysian Code, then, can be traced back to industry-sponsored guidelines. Indeed, the Malaysian Code's origins and its subsequent development were consciously tagged to industry and intended to be driven by the institutional investors themselves rather than by external regulators. Further, it must be noted that, in the case of Malaysia, what constitutes industry is inextricably linked to the state by means of its ownership and control of these GLICs and GLCs. A possible rationale for the industry-driven character of the Malaysian Code could be the desire for more active stakeholder participation in shaping intermediation and corporate behaviour to promote a culture of integrity and to align business policies with social goals, as set out in the second Capital Market Masterplan,[106] building on the foundation laid in the first Capital Market Masterplan. It is argued that the decision to situate institutional investor stewardship under

---

[101] ibid.
[102] ibid. See Gomez and others (n 91) 95–56 for a complex ownership network map illustrating the corporate ownership links of the GLICs and highlighting their shareholdings of the 35 GLCs among Bursa Malaysia's top 100 firms through the use of business groups where much of Malaysia's equity-based wealth has been concentrated.
[103] Annuar (n 42).
[104] See generally Albert O Hirschman, *Exit, Voice, and Loyalty: Responses to Decline in Firms, Organizations, and States* (Harvard University Press 1970).
[105] Adeline Paul Raj, 'Newsbreak: Two New Players to Emerge in Malaysia's Asset Management Industry' (*The Edge Markets*, 21 October 2019) <www.theedgemarkets.com/article/newsbreak-two-new-players-emerge-malaysias-asset-management-industry> accessed 13 July 2020.
[106] Securities Commission Malaysia, *Capital Market Masterplan 2* (April 2011) 84 <www.sc.com.my/resources/publications-and-research/cmp2> accessed 13 July 2020. This ties in with the concept of a broader range of authors of corporate governance norms, which is canvassed in Dionysia Katelouzou and Peer C Zumbansen, 'Transnational Corporate Governance: The State of the Art and Twenty-First Century Challenges' in Peer C Zumbansen ed. *Oxford Handbook of Transnational Law* (OUP 2021) 615.

the purview of industry in Malaysia together with the contextual factors in operation has led to a markedly different outcome with respect to stewardship as compared to the UK.[107]

Therefore, with regard to Malaysia, the breadth and depth of state ownership and control in GLICs and GLCs as asset owners and asset managers are essential in evaluating the realization of institutional investor stewardship, which seeks to deliver sustainable long-term returns for clients and/or beneficiaries. This is primarily because the performance of the GLICs is not merely an outcome of business decisions; it also reflects their relationship with the state.[108] In this regard, state ownership and control of GLICs and GLCs represents a crucial lever which drives the decisions and actions of these entities.

The aforementioned relationship in turn raises a critical question as to whether the interests of the state are aligned with those of the asset owners, the asset managers and, more importantly, those of the ultimate beneficiaries or clients which are at the end of the investment chain. It is submitted that agency conflicts exist between these parties as contrasted with the typical conceptualization of agency conflicts between manager-shareholders and majority-minority shareholders in the extant literature. As such, it is argued that, apart from concerns about the quality of stewardship statements and ownership engagement of institutional investors, structural issues such as the prevalence of the state in the ownership and control of GLICs and GLCs represent embedded factors which significantly challenge the practice of effective stewardship in Malaysia.[109]

15.6 CHALLENGES AND REFLECTIONS ON INSTITUTIONAL INVESTOR STEWARDSHIP IN MALAYSIA

Institutional investor stewardship is currently at a conceptual and practical crossroads. Unlike corporate governance, which has developed a firm conceptual basis and a practical working application via specific corporate governance codes and its incorporation into listing requirements in many countries, stewardship is still very much at an evolutionary stage – especially taking into consideration the nascent development of stewardship in Malaysia as described earlier. Indeed, the concept of stewardship itself has been brought into question and criticized as 'dangerous and misguided' in its characterization of shareholders as blameless and passive in the global financial crisis.[110] This may be contrasted with the conception of a commitment-focused approach to ownership and universal ownership which encourages investors to engage with investee corporations and to look at the long term.[111]

Notwithstanding the broader debate about whether shareholders are a positive or negative force in relation to the corporate governance of their investee companies, this chapter views the concept of stewardship as one of limited effectiveness as it is unable to fully address the agency conflicts among asset owners, asset managers and the ultimate beneficiaries or

---

[107] See Petrina Tan, 'Institutional Investor Stewardship in the UK and Malaysia: Functionally Similar, Contextually Challenged' (2019) 14 *Asian Journal of Comparative Law* 279. See also Gen Goto, 'The Logic and Limits of Stewardship Codes: The Case of Japan' (2018) 15 *Berkeley Business Law Journal* 365.

[108] Gomez and others (n 91) 231.

[109] For a contrasting example which has had some success in addressing similar issues, see Puchniak and Tang, Singapore's Embrace of Shareholder Stewardship, Chapter 14.

[110] Alan Dignam, 'The Future of Shareholder Democracy in the Shadow of the Financial Crisis' (2013) 36 *Seattle University Law Review* 639; Christopher M Bruner, 'Corporate Governance Reform in a Time of Crisis' (2011) 36 *Journal of Corporation Law* 309.

[111] Terry McNulty and Donald Nordberg, 'Ownership, Activism and Engagement: Institutional Investors as Active Owners' (2016) 24 *Corporate Governance: An International Review* 346, 348.

clients.[112] At this point, it must be noted that the presence and impact of agency conflicts in concentrated ownership scenarios between the management and shareholders[113] in Malaysia[114] has been well canvassed in the literature, although agency conflicts within the investment management sphere have received relatively less attention.

In this regard, research in the US context may be instructive and shed light on the agency issues which constrain the adoption and successful implementation of stewardship on the part of asset managers. A study conducted by Bebchuk, Cohen and Hirst in 2017 showed that agency problems exist between investment managers and their beneficial investors, regardless of whether the investment managers were actively managed funds or passive index funds.[115] Among the sources of these agency problems is the fact that investment managers bear the costs of stewardship activities but capture only a small fraction of the benefits they create.[116] As, by law, investment managers are unable to charge personnel and other management expenses arising from stewardship matters directly to their portfolios, payments to cover such expenses have to be taken from fees received from investors while the benefits from stewardship flow to the portfolio.[117]

As a corollary to the above, it was found that the investment horizons of institutional investors in Malaysia were a mix of both short and long term, with equity investments divided into two portfolios (i.e. investment and trading or treasury portfolios).[118] Investment portfolios had a longer investment horizon and were directed more towards establishing regular income in terms of satisfactory annual dividends as well as building a buffer of unrealized gains over a longer period of time.[119] Trading portfolios consisted of revolving funds managed in such a way as to meet the institutional investor's liquidity requirements, if and when the need arises, as well as to speculate on share prices during an opportune time.[120] This distinction takes on increased importance because the institutional investors' involvement in corporate governance and, by extension, stewardship would be at their most effective only with regard to investee companies in their investment portfolio rather than those in their trading portfolio.[121]

Ultimately, the foregoing analysis suggests that there is a problem with the lack of incentives for institutional investors to spend on stewardship; as such, stewardship codes which put forward aspirations, principles or guidelines would be likely to have less of an impact than if investment managers had appropriate incentives.[122] Put another way, the manner in which investment management is structured is itself not conducive to encouraging stewardship activities and the existence of a code dedicated to this purpose does not in itself address the underlying issue of the expected cost on the part of institutional investors without the corresponding benefits. This

---

[112] Ronald Gilson and Jeffrey Gordon, 'The Agency Costs of Agency Capitalism: Activist Investors and the Revaluation of Governance Rights' (2013) 113 *Columbia Law Review* 863.

[113] Claessens, Djankov and Lang (n 90).

[114] Kamini Singam, 'Corporate Governance in Malaysia' (2003) 15 *Bond Law Review* 314; On Kit Tam and Monica Guo-Sze Tan, 'Ownership, Governance and Firm Performance in Malaysia' (2007) 15 *Corporate Governance: An International Review* 208,210.

[115] Lucian A Bebchuk, Alma Cohen and Scott Hirst, 'The Agency Problems of Institutional Investors' (2017) 31 *Journal of Economic Perspectives* 89.

[116] ibid 96.

[117] ibid.

[118] Annuar (n 42) 461.

[119] ibid 462.

[120] ibid.

[121] ibid 461.

[122] John Kay, 'The Kay Review of UK Equity Markets and Long-Term Decision Making' (Department for Business, Innovation and Skills, July 2012) <https://assets.publishing.service.gov.uk/government/uploads/system/uploads/attachment_data/file/253454/bis-12-917-kay-review-of-equity-markets-final-report.pdf> accessed 13 July 2020.

incentive problem is further exacerbated by a fundamental misalignment between the interest of beneficiaries in long-term absolute performance versus the short-term relative performance valued by asset managers and the basis on which they are monitored by asset owners and beneficiaries.[123]

Apart from the lack of incentivization within the investment management sphere, it is argued that the Malaysian Code is unable to address the agency conflicts between asset owners and the ultimate beneficiaries as a result of the institutional framework governing them. For example, oversight of the GLICs and GLCs by the Malaysian Ministry of Finance via the Minister of Finance Incorporated allows controlling shareholders to secure political and business benefits from the GLICs and GLCs.[124] The further lack of incentive to prioritize the interests of the ultimate beneficiaries or clients over those of controlling shareholders may also be attributable to the lack of security of tenure with regard to the managerial teams of GLICs and GLCs wherein the Minister of Finance has the prerogative to remove them at will.[125] Under these circumstances, it is highly likely that the interests of the controlling shareholders would supersede those of the ultimate beneficiaries or clients, thus weakening the impact of stewardship in ensuring that their interests are safeguarded.

A stunning example of this agency conflict and its extensive ramifications is the 1MDB scandal which saw 1MDB, a non-listed GLIC, implicated in gross financial misconduct to the tune of more than USD 4.5 billion,[126] the arrest of the former prime minister of Malaysia, Datuk Seri Najib Razak,[127] as well as the controversial purchase of Tun Razak Exchange by a GLIC, Lembaga Tabung Haji, which has been criticized as a bailout of 1MDB in view of its position as an underperforming asset.[128] While this particular scandal has been headline-grabbing owing to the sheer magnitude of the sums involved and the seniority of the personalities implicated, it is worth noting that such controversies are not foreign to Malaysia. From as long ago as the 1980s, Malaysian GLICs and GLCs have carried out various controversial corporate actions,[129] evidencing the existence of agency conflicts between GLIC asset owners and ultimate beneficiaries where the GLICs were driven by factors other than those of promoting the interests of the ultimate beneficiaries. This included taking RM 1.5 billion from the Employees Provident Fund to fund a housing scheme implemented by the Federal Territories Minister despite not consulting the Employees Provident Fund board of employees representative beforehand.[130]

It is noted that the arguments here have a decidedly state-centric slant, which may prompt questions about the position of non-state asset owners within this analytical framework. To this end, it is agreed that non-state asset owners may not be subject to the particular structural issues which affect the incentives of GLICs to act as stewards or otherwise. However, as indicated by the list of signatories to the Malaysian Code, the participation of non-state-linked entities has been comparatively scant. This observation is consistent with the intervention patterns of non-state-linked asset owners established in earlier research and points to a need to find ways to

---

[123] ibid 41.
[124] Gomez and others (n 91) 8.
[125] ibid 219.
[126] Heather Chen, Kevin Ponniah and Mayuri Mei Lin, '1MDB: The Playboys, PMs and Partygoers Around a Global Financial Scandal' (*BBC News*, 9 August 2019) <www.bbc.com/news/world-asia-46341603> accessed 13 July 2020.
[127] Shamim Adam, Laurence Arnold and Yudith Ho, 'How Malaysia's 1MDB Scandal Shook the Financial World' (*Bloomberg*, 18 February 2020) <www.bloomberg.com/news/articles/2019-01-09/how-malaysia-s-1mdb-scandal-shook-the-financial-world-quicktake> accessed 13 July 2020.
[128] Shannon Teoh, '"Malaysia's Pilgrims" Fund Scandal Strikes at Core of Malay Worries' *The Sunday Times* (16 December 2018) <www.straitstimes.com/asia/se-asia/malaysias-pilgrims-fund-scandal-strikes-at-core-of-malay-worries> accessed 13 July 2020.
[129] Gomez and others (n 91) 78–87.
[130] ibid 83.

encourage them to play a more active role in engaging with investee companies for the benefit of their beneficiaries or clients. Given that Malaysia has opted to adopt an industry-led approach rather than a regulatory-sanctioned one, it would thus fall on the II Council to influence practices among Malaysian institutional investors which may or may not have the same reach as a regulator-backed code underpinned by sanctions. It is worth noting however, that the II Council is itself intertwined with the government, as earlier discussion has shown. Even if Malaysia decides to adopt a tougher, rule-based stance, questions arise as to which body should be tasked with this responsibility and the appropriate sanctions for non-compliance, the common bedevilling details following from a decision to regulate a particular sector.

While policymaker and industry efforts in Malaysia have been commendable in seeking to systematize institutional investor engagement and advocacy via the introduction of the Malaysian Code and the establishment of the II Council, the structural issues referred to earlier still remain a major hurdle to meaningful and significant engagement on the part of institutional investors.[131] Therefore, it would bode well for the state and policymakers to evaluate and address these issues to create a fertile environment for the development of an institutional investor community which is both responsible and engaged. While the UK's struggles in the area of stewardship have led many to call for enforcement to have a greater bite and a strengthened regulatory backing,[132] Malaysia may not need to tread a similar path if structural reforms are undertaken in tandem with the II Council's initiatives and outreach.[133]

15.7 CONCLUSION

Based on the preceding discussion, institutional investor stewardship in Malaysia has had a promising start in keeping with the Malaysian Code's status as the first of its kind in the ASEAN region.[134] While there may be areas for improvement in the drafting and coverage of the Malaysian Code as it currently stands, the principles of the Malaysian Code are fairly comprehensive and represent an appropriate launchpad for the continued expansion of stewardship in Malaysia. Be that as it may, the introduction and adoption of the Malaysian Code may be insufficient in itself to address the underlying agency conflicts among asset owners, asset managers and ultimate beneficiaries or clients within the investment chain. In addition, a more detailed analysis of the composition and type of signatories to the Malaysian Code, as juxtaposed against the background of the institutional framework and embedded practices influenced by Malaysia's political economy, raises the issue of structural constraints affecting

---

[131] Although there has been much discussion on the reform of GLCs and other systemic weaknesses in Malaysia since the watershed 14th General Election on 9 May 2018 which saw the incumbent Barisan Nasional coalition lose to the opposition after an unbeaten reign of sixty years as well as the 1MDB scandal, this is expected to be a slow process with many hiccups along the way. For more recent commentary, see Vivien Chen, 'How Malaysian Corporate Laws Can Recover After Corruption' (*Impact*, 21 November 2018) <impact.monash.edu/corporate-regulation/how-malaysian-corporate-laws-can-recover-after-corruption/> accessed 9 February 2022; Vivien Chen, 'Enforcement of Directors' Duties in Malaysia and Australia: The Implications of Context' (2019) 19 *Oxford University Commonwealth Law Journal* 91. See also Terence Gomez, Lau Zheng Zhou and Yash Shewandas, 'GLC Monitor 2019: State of Play Since GE 14' (Brief Ideas No 18, Institute for Democracy and Economic Affairs, October 2019) <www.ideas.org.my/publications-item/brief-ideas-no-18-glc-monitor-2019-state-of-play-since-ge14/> accessed 9 February 2022.

[132] See e.g. Lee Roach, 'The UK Stewardship Code' (2011) 11 *Journal of Corporate Law Studies* 463; and Arad Reisberg, 'The UK Stewardship Code: On the Road to Nowhere?' (2015) 15 *Journal of Corporate Law Studies* 217, highlighting the shortcomings of the UK Code in terms of compliance, among other issues.

[133] See Puchniak and Tang, Singapore's Embrace of Shareholder Stewardship, Chapter 14 for examples on how this has been achieved in practice.

[134] Institutional Investor Council Malaysia, 'Annual Report 2018' (2019) 7 <www.iicm.org.my/wp-content/uploads/2019/09/IIC-Annual-Report-2018_final.pdf> accessed 13 July 2020.

stewardship in Malaysia. In this respect, it is essential that these structural issues are examined and addressed, even as stewardship and sustainable investing movements gain greater traction in the country. Ultimately, it is a case of addressing the broader but arguably more difficult reforms first, over the laudable but narrower stewardship initiative to ensure that significant and meaningful change really does occur.

From a macro-level standpoint, it is important to ensure that, apart from incentivizing the take up of stewardship codes (which are voluntary), a long-term and sustainable approach to investments is developed, put in place and embedded within the practices of asset owners and asset managers. Apart from a focus on the overarching structures governing asset owners and asset managers, structural support also includes addressing the role of the individual beneficiary or client in driving demand for better stewardship. In a world that is driven by numbers and financials, the push towards stewardship should emanate not only from the regulator and industry but also from beneficiaries and clients, which would create an impetus for change. In tandem with the growing democratization and empowerment of individual shareholders, perhaps the time has come for a deeper examination into the exercise of individual shareholder rights as a form of check and balance against the actions or omissions of institutional investors.

16

The Thai Institutional Investors Stewardship Code and Its Implementation

Patanaporn Kowpatanakit and Piyabutr Bunaramrueang

16.1 INTRODUCTION

The Securities and Exchange Commission (SEC) introduced the Investment Governance Code for Institutional Investors in 2017 (Thai Code) as an integral part of its corporate governance framework.[1] The Thai Code is expected to complement the Thai Corporate Governance Code (CG Code) by utilizing the power of institutional investors to set a higher standard for the boards of directors of listed companies.[2] For more than twenty years, the corporate governance performance of listed companies has developed substantially and is well-regarded internationally, especially in relation to the effectiveness of boards, corporate disclosure and transparency.[3] This success in reforming the Thai corporate governance system is largely owing to the active collaboration of all stakeholders following the 1997 Asian Financial Crisis (AFC). The SEC aims to continue this success with the Thai Code, but, as this chapter explains, this is unlikely.

We divide this chapter as follows. Section 16.2 introduces the CG Code and its success in Thailand, as background for understanding the Thai Code. Section 16.3 sheds light on the larger context of the Thai capital market, to demonstrate that institutional investors in Thailand have had a limited impact as stewards. The Thai capital market is dominated by local private companies – especially family businesses – which often assume the role of de facto 'stewards' in most Thai companies. Section 16.4 analyses how institutional investors, especially asset management companies, have implemented the Thai Code. Section 16.5 concludes by highlighting how an in-depth empirical and case study analysis is required to understand the complexity of how the Thai Code works in practice.

16.2 FROM THE CG CODE TO THE THAI CODE

In Thailand, the Securities and Exchange Commission Act (1992) set up the SEC as the regulator of the Thai capital market.[4] Similar to financial market regulators in other countries,

---

[1] Securities and Exchange Commission, 'Investment Governance Code for Institutional Investors' (2017) <www.sec.or.th/cgthailand/EN/Documents/ICode/ICodeBookEN.pdf> accessed 3 June 2020 [hereinafter Thai Code]; Securities and Exchange Commission, 'Corporate Governance Code for Listed Companies 2017' (2017) 69 <www.sec.or.th/cgthailand/TH/Documents/Regulation/CGCode.pdf> accessed 3 June 2020 [hereinafter CG Code].

[2] eFinanceThai, '"รพี สุจริตกุล" 4 ปี กับการวางรากฐานตลาดทุน เพื่อการเติบโตที่ยั่งยืน ("Rphī sucrit kul" 4 pī kạb kār wāng rākṭhān tlād thun pheụ̄x kār teibto thī̀ yạ̀ngyụ̄n) ["Rapee Sucharitakul" 4 Years in Capital Market Foundation for Sustainable Growth]' (5 February 2019) <www.efinancethai.com/spinterview/SpInterviewMain.aspx?name=i_seco1> accessed 3 June 2020.

[3] See Section 16.2.1.

[4] The Securities and Exchange Commission (SEC) consists of representatives of government offices such as the Permanent Secretary of the Ministry of Finance and the Permanent Secretary of the Ministry of Commerce. The

the SEC has primary responsibility for promoting, developing, monitoring and regulating the Thai capital market. The SEC is an independent regulator with policy mandates from the government. Its mission is to 'assure a conducive environment for a fair, efficient, dynamic, and inclusive capital market'.[5]

The SEC established the corporate governance framework for the Thai capital market through corporate governance amendments to the SEC Act, which helped pave the way for the enforcement of the CG Code.[6] The Principles of the CG Code also integrate the essence of the G20/OECD (Organisation for Economic Co-operation and Development) Principles of Corporate Governance.[7] This significant legislative initiative would not have occurred were it not for the economic pressures following the 1997 AFC, and later the 2008 Global Financial Crisis (GFC). To prevent future crises, the government and the private sector made a concerted effort to set and implement higher standards of corporate governance through the CG Code – which has largely been viewed as a success.[8] The success that Thailand has had with adopting and implementing the CG Code provided the impetus for the SEC to embrace the latest international corporate governance trend of stewardship, and so implement the Thai Code, which is based on a UK-style stewardship code.[9] However, as discussed in this chapter, it seems unlikely that the Thai Code will be as successful as the CG Code.

16.2.1 The Thai Corporate Governance Code

To put the Thai Code in context, it is important to understand how and why the CG Code has been a success in Thailand. In 1997, the AFC (locally known as the *Tom-Yum-Goong crisis*) forced government and regulators to place corporate governance on the national agenda.[10] The SEC and the Stock Exchange of Thailand (SET) acted to reform their laws and regulations to improve companies' practices, especially in the areas of accountability, responsibility, equitable treatment and transparency.[11] The government created the National Corporate Governance Committee, wherein the Bank of Thailand, the SEC, SET, as well as professional organizations played important roles in the implementation and enforcement of these corporate governance

---

chairperson is appointed by the Council of Ministers from the Ministry of Finance's nominations. Three commission members are ex officio from the government. Four to six expert members are appointed by the Minister of Finance. The SEC has been functioning for almost thirty years. It has gone through booms and busts for quite a while and has a mixed reception based on its performances.

[5] Securities and Exchange Commission, 'Our Roles' <www.sec.or.th/EN/Pages/AboutUs/Whatwedo.aspx> accessed 3 June 2020.

[6] Asian Development Bank, *ASEAN Corporate Governance Scorecard: Country Reports and Assessments 2014: Joint Initiative of the ASEAN Capital Markets Forum and the Asian Development Bank* (2016) 65 <www.adb.org/sites/default/files/publication/185624/asean-cgscorecard-2014.pdf> accessed 3 June 2020; Rapee Sucharitakul, 'Building Trust and Transparency in the Thai Capital Market' (Securities and Exchange Commission, 4 April 2018) <www.thai-iod.com/imgUpload/Khun%20Rapee%20%20Sucharitakul.pdf> accessed 3 June 2020.

[7] OECD, *G20/OECD Principles of Corporate Governance* (2015) <www.oecd.org/daf/ca/Corporate-Governance-Principles-ENG.pdf> accessed 3 June 2020; CG Code (n 1) 69.

[8] Thai Institute of Directors Association, 'Corporate Governance Report of Thai Listed Companies 2018' (2019) <www.thai-iod.com/en/publications-detail.asp?id=447> accessed 3 June 2020.

[9] Thai Code (n 1).

[10] Piman Limpaphayom and Thomas J Connelly, 'Corporate Governance in Thailand' (June 2004) <http://econ.tu.ac.th/class/archan/Rangsun/MB%20663/MB%20663%20Readings/%E0%B9%93.%20%E0%B8%9A%E0%B8%A3%E0%B8%A3%E0%B8%A9%E0%B8%B1%E0%B8%97%E0%B8%A0%E0%B8%B4%E0%B8%9A%E0%B8%B2%E0%B8%A5/Corporate%20Governance/Thailand/Corporate%20Governance%20in%20Thailand.pdf> accessed 3 June 2020.

[11] ibid.

reforms. In 2001, the SET launched '15 Principles of Good Corporate Governance for Listed Companies' which was subsequently revised in 2006, 2012 and, most recently, in 2017.[12]

Initially, all listed companies were required to have an audit committee to enhance their transparency and the quality of their financial reports.[13] SET was influenced by international organizations to revise its guidelines to be more comprehensive and comparable to the OECD Principles of Corporate Governance.[14] SET also joined a project held by the World Bank in Corporate Governance,[15] and updated the CG Code for Listed Companies in 2006, based on a 'comply or explain' approach.[16] In 2012, the CG Code was revised again to be compatible with the ASEAN Corporate Governance Scorecard (ASEAN CG Scorecard).[17] The latest version of the CG Code was launched by the SEC in 2017 with eight principles.[18] The 2017 CG Code is based on an 'apply or explain' approach, where the board is able to apply each principle to each company's business circumstances. Listed companies must also explain why they cannot apply any principle.

Beyond the revisions to the CG Code, the SEC has progressively revised laws and regulations to comply with corporate governance practices. The SEC proposed and led the amendment both to the Public Limited Company Act in 2008, in order to strengthen minority shareholders' rights and information disclosure requirements, and to the SEC Act, in order to provide a clear standard of conduct for company boards and executives.[19] Moreover, the SEC's regulations were revised to address issues concerning conflict of interest transactions. The SEC emphasized that trust alone is not enough.[20] A listed company is further required to ensure good business performance with a balanced relationship among stakeholders.[21]

Thailand's strategy to strengthen its corporate governance is based on three pillars: regulatory discipline; market discipline; and self-discipline. For more than twenty years, the corporate governance performance of listed companies has developed substantially and is now well-recognized internationally, especially in terms of board effectiveness, disclosure and transparency. This is demonstrated by the average scores for the five criteria of the OECD Corporate Governance Principles, as shown in Figure 16.1.

Thailand received higher scores than Asia's averages in every category. According to the CG Report of Thai Listed Compan[ies] 2018, conducted by the Thai Institution of Directors

---

[12] ibid.
[13] Notification of the Capital Market Supervisory Board No. Tor Jor. 39/2559, Re: Application for Approval and Granting of Approval for Offering of Newly Issued Shares, cl 17(3) <https://capital.sec.or.th/webapp/nrs/data/7079se.pdf> accessed 3 June 2020.
[14] OECD (n 7); since its inception, the CG Code has consistently been updated to track the developments of the G20/OECD *Principles of Corporate Governance*; see CG Code (n 1) 69; Stock Exchange of Thailand (SET), 'The Principles of Good Corporate Governance for Listed Companies 2012' (2012) 55 <https://ecgi.global/code/principles-good-corporate-governance-listed-companies-2012> accessed 11 February 2022.
[15] David Robinett, Ratchada Anantavrasilpa and Catherine Hickey, 'Report on the Observance of Standards and Codes (ROSC): Corporate Governance Country Assessment – Thailand' (World Bank, January 2013) <http://documents.worldbank.org/curated/en/598741468118443110/pdf/908230ROSC0Box0ailand0201300PUBLIC0.pdf> accessed 3 June 2020.
[16] Stock Exchange of Thailand, 'หลักการกำกับดูแลกิจการที่ดีสำหรับบริษัทจดทะเบียนป2549 (Hlạk kā rkạ̄ kạb dūlæ kickār thī̀ dī sảh̄rạb brișạth cd tha beīyn p2549) [The Principles of Good Corporate Governance for Listed Companies 2006]' (2006) <https://capital.sec.or.th/webapp/nrs/data/4216ao.pdf> accessed 3 June 2020.
[17] SET, 'The Principles of Good Corporate Governance for Listed Companies 2012' (n 14).
[18] CG Code (n 1).
[19] For example, ch 3/1 (Governance of Publicly Traded Company) of the Securities and Exchange Act, B.E.2535 (1992) and its amendments provide the standard for directors and executives.
[20] CG Code (n 1) 69.
[21] ibid.

Rights of Shareholders	Equitable Treament of Shareholders	Role of Shareholders	Disclosure and Transparency	Board Responsibilities
94% (2018)	92% (2018)	80% (2018)	85% (2018)	72% (2018)
93% (2017)	92% (2017)	78% (2017)	84% (2017)	71% (2017)
92% (2016)	92% (2016)	74% (2016)	82% (2016)	68% (2016)

FIGURE 16.1 Average scores for the five criteria of the OECD Corporate Governance Principles[22]

Association (IOD), the average CG score was exceptional and was marked as a historical high of 81 per cent.[23] This demonstrates that Thai listed companies have become more responsible to stakeholders while seeking to achieve sustainable growth. With five scoring criteria, developed with reference to the OECD Principles, average scores were higher than 80 per cent in four categories. As such, it appears that Thailand's capital market has consistently exceeded the international standards for corporate governance – at least when compared with other countries in Asia.

16.2.2 *Investment Governance Code for Institutional Investors*

The seven principles of the Thai Code[24] are that institutional investors should:

1. adopt a clear written investment governance policy;
2. properly prevent and manage conflicts of interest and prioritize advancing the best interest of clients;
3. make informed investment decisions and engage in active ongoing monitoring of investee companies;
4. apply enhanced monitoring of and engagement with the investee companies if monitoring pursuant to Principle 3 is considered insufficient;
5. have a clear policy on exercising voting rights and disclosure of voting results;
6. act collectively with other investors and stakeholders as appropriate;
7. regularly disclose the investment governance policy and compliance with the policy.

In addition to the CG Code, the SEC also drafted the Thai Code. The SEC based the Thai Code on the UK Stewardship Code 2012 (UK Code).[25] This is in accordance with the SEC's general approach to developing regulations which normally start with international standards – especially those articulated by the OECD.

Furthermore, the SEC set up a steering committee to collaborate with all relevant stakeholders to promote the successful implementation of the Thai Code. The committee is responsible for issuing the Thai Code's Implementation Policy, developing guidelines, setting up training programmes, supporting the compliance management of institutional investors, and monitoring the effectiveness of the implementation of the Thai Code. The

---

[22] Thai Institute of Directors Association (n 8).
[23] ibid.
[24] Thai Code (n 1).
[25] Financial Reporting Council, *The UK Stewardship Code* (September 2012) <www.frc.org.uk/getattachment/d67933f9-ca38-4233-b603-3d24b2f62c5f/UK-Stewardship-Code-(September-2012).pdf> accessed 3 June 2020 [hereinafter UK Code 2012].

committee is also responsible for revising the Thai Code from time to time. The SEC's secretary-general is the chairman and the SEC's Corporate Governance Department acts as the secretary to the committee. This committee consists of key representatives from institutional investors and relevant organizations such as the Office of Insurance Commission, the Government Pension Fund, the Social Security Office, the Federation of Thai Capital Market Organizations, the Association of Investment Management Companies, the Thai General Insurance Association, the Thai Life Assurance Association, and the Association of Provident Funds.[26]

While the CG Code emphasizes the role of the board of directors in leading organizations to create long-term sustainable value,[27] the Thai Code highlights the responsibilities of institutional investors.[28] It emphasizes two factors. First, institutional investors are held to be a key mechanism of escalating engagement.[29] In the event that the confidential engagement is unsuccessful, institutional investors should progressively escalate their actions and provide an effective exercise of investment duties and stewardship responsibilities to further the interests of their ultimate beneficiaries.[30] Moreover, they should operate as a market force to strengthen investment governance. For example, institutional investors should make informed investment decisions and engage in active monitoring of their investee companies.[31] In addition, they should enhance the monitoring of and engagement with the investee companies if it is found that their monitoring is insufficient.[32]

Second, institutional investors should take into account environmental, social and governance (ESG) factors in their business practices, and engage with the investee company to improve the company's ESG performance.[33] As the OECD and other international organizations have raised the importance of society and environment, ESG factors are admitted as a key to serving the long-term sustainable values of companies. This is consistent with the development of the CG Code where the focus has shifted from short-term financial success to long-term sustainable value creation. As institutional investors play an important role in supporting the sustainable value of investee companies, they are expected to act as stewards of the capital they invest and of the investee companies. Institutional investors are not only responsible for monitoring the company risk closely; they are also required to take ESG factors into account. They should invest in companies that integrate ESG factors in their business model or engage in improving the ESG performance of investee companies.

To encourage institutional investors to adopt the Thai Code, the SEC pointed out that adopting it would help to attract foreign institutional investors.[34] According to global stewardship standards, foreign institutional investors are required to request that institutional investors in Thailand disclose their policies. If institutional investors in Thailand fail to provide their policies, the CG Score of the Thai capital market could be penalized in the future,[35] owing to

---

[26] Thai Code (n 1) 35.
[27] CG Code (n 1) 69.
[28] Thai Code (n 1) 31; see also Dionysia Katelouzou, 'Reflections on the Nature of the Public Corporation in an Era of Shareholder Activism and Stewardship' in Barnali Choudhury and Martin Petrin (eds), *Understanding the Company: Corporate Governance and Theory* (CUP 2017).
[29] Thai Code (n 1) 31, 45, Principle 4.
[30] Thai Code (n 1) 46, Practice [sic] 4.4.
[31] Thai Code (n 1) 42, Principle 3.
[32] Thai Code (n 1) 45, Principle 4.
[33] Thai Code (n 1) 31.
[34] Securities and Exchange Commission, 'เอกสารรับฟังความคิดเห็น เลขที่ อสภ.39/2559 เรื่อง หลักธรรมาภิบาลการลงทุน ส หรับผู้ลงทุนสถาบัน (Xeksār rạb fạng khwām khidh̄ĕn lek̄h thī̀ xs̄ph.39/2559 Reụ̄̀xng h̄lạk ṭhrrmāp̣hibāl kār lngthun s̄ ā h̄rạb p̄hū̂ lngthun s̄t̄hābạn) [Consultation Paper Or Sor Por 39/2559 Re: Investment Governance Code: I Code]' (29 August 2016) <https://capital.sec.or.th/webapp/phs/upload/phs1472460659hearing_39_2559.pdf> accessed 3 June 2020.
[35] ibid.

the importance of Principle 2 of the Thailand CG Code. After conducting two public hearings on the draft of the Thai Code, the SEC received positive responses from institutional investors. Most agreed with the principles.[36] Therefore, the SEC launched the Thai Code, which was developed with reference to the UK Code 2012.[37]

The Thai Code is voluntary and applies to institutional investors who have agreed to be signatories. While there is a broad definition of institutional investors, the Thai Code classifies institutional investors into three categories: asset managers; asset owners; and related service providers.[38]

In implementing the Thai Code, an institutional investor must first provide a self-assessment using the principles and propose the adoption of the code for the board of directors' approval. By filing a letter of intent signed by the chairman of the board of directors with the SEC, they become a signatory. According to the SEC's disclosure regulation,[39] effective from 1 September 2017, an asset management company is required to disclose on its website whether it is a signatory to the Thai Code. Signatories should annually disclose their investment governance policy on the engagement and exercise of voting rights, management of conflicts of interest, and actions according to their policy, on their website or in their annual report. They should also provide implementation reports on a 'comply or explain' basis.[40] In cases where one or more principles have not been applied, they should provide explanations or alternative measures adopted in compliance with their stewardship responsibilities.

16.2.3 Signatories to the Thai Code

As a signatory, each institutional investor is expected to provide three things: a letter of intent; its stewardship policy; and annual stewardship reports.[41] However, a letter of intent is completely voluntary. Once the code is adopted, the institutional investor must provide a stewardship policy on a 'comply or explain' basis. In terms of stewardship reports, signatories are expected to annually report their level of compliance with the Thai Code for each principle. The SEC has encouraged all asset managers, asset owners, and related service providers to be signatories by running roadshows and seminars.

As of 2018, there were fifty-seven institutional investors (both domestic and foreign) who had declared that they were signatories to the Thai Code (see Figure 16.2). In January 2018, the SEC announced that the signatories managed assets of THB 9.3 trillion, which accounted for 64 per cent of gross domestic product (GDP) in 2017.[42] They include government funds such as the Social Security Office (SSO) and GPF, and all twenty-six asset management companies. The fact that all twenty-six asset management companies are signatories is largely because they are SEC-licensed asset management companies. As mentioned earlier, the SEC required them to disclose

---

[36] Securities and Exchange Commission, 'ผลการรับฟังความคิดเห็นจากผู้เกี่ยวข้อง (hearing) เรื่องหลักการและร่างประกาศเกี่ยวกับการเปิดเผย การปฏิบัติ ตามหลักธรรมาภิบาลการลงทุนส หรับผู้ลงทุนสถาบัน (Phl kār ṛab fạng khwām khidh̄ĕn cāk p̄hū̂ keī̀ywk̄ĥxng (hearing) reụ̄̀xng h̄lạkkār læa r̀āng prakāṣ̄ keī̀yw kạb kār peidp̄hey kār pt̩ibạti tām h̄lạk ṭhr rmāp̣hi bāl kār lng thun s̄ ār̆h̄ rạb p̄hū̂ lngthun s̄t̄hābạn) [Results of Online Public Hearing Re: Investment Governance Code for Institutional Investors 21 June–21 July 2017]' (2017) <https://capital.sec.or.th/webapp/phs/upload/sum_hearing_18_2560.pdf> accessed 3 June 2020.

[37] See Katelouzou and Siems, The Global Diffusion of Stewardship Codes, Chapter 30, this volume.

[38] Thai Code (n 1) 32.

[39] SEC Notification Sor Nor 41/2560 on Disclosure in accordance with the Investment Governance Code for Institutional Investors <https://capital.sec.or.th/webapp/nrs/data/7418s.pdf> accessed 3 June 2020 [hereinafter SEC Disclosure Requirements].

[40] See Katelouzou and Sergakis, Shareholder Stewardship Enforcement, Chapter 27, this volume.

[41] SEC Disclosure Requirements (n 39).

[42] Rapee Sucharitakul, 'Responsible Investment' (FC Seminar No 1/2561, 28 June 2018) <www.sec.or.th/cgthailand/TH/Documents/Activities/บรรยายให้คกก%20PVD-CG-28June2018.pdf> accessed 3 June 2020.

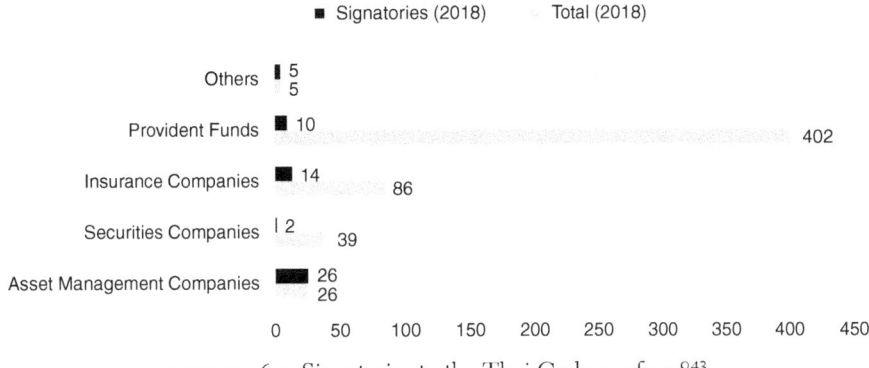

FIGURE 16.2 Signatories to the Thai Code as of 2018[43]

Category	Signatories (2018)	Total (2018)
Others	5	5
Provident Funds	10	402
Insurance Companies	14	86
Securities Companies	2	39
Asset Management Companies	26	26

whether they accepted becoming a signatory or provide reasons for not accepting. As expected, asset management firms (both foreign and domestic) followed the SEC's regulations.[44]

According to two 2015 reports from the Office of Insurance Commission, there are eighty-six insurance companies.[45] Their total investments in the capital market are about THB 220 billion, or 16.88% of the total assets of non-life insurance companies and 5.53% of life insurance companies.[46] Only fourteen out of the eighty-six insurance companies are signatories. This strongly suggests that insurance companies were not under the same pressure as asset management companies to become signatories, perhaps because the Insurance Commission does not have a similar stewardship policy even though it is a member of the Thai Code's steering committee. Furthermore, these fourteen insurance companies are just signatories on paper – they have yet to provide a single stewardship policy.

In addition, there are 402 provident funds[47] in the market, with investments in listed companies of approximately THB 192 billion.[48] Only ten of them, which are all state enterprises, have agreed to be signatories. But only one out of the ten has provided a stewardship policy and reports which is the provident fund of the Office of SEC. It has been noted that 15 asset management companies manage most of the 402 funds as asset managers.[49] Since the funds themselves are asset owners under the code, they feel no pressure to accept the code.

---

[43] Securities and Exchange Commission, 'List of Code Signatories' <www.sec.or.th/cgthailand/EN/Pages/RulesRegulation/ICodeLists.aspx> accessed 3 June 2020.

[44] SEC, 'List of Code Signatories' (n 42).

[45] Office of Insurance Commission, 'สถิติธุรกิจประกันวินาศภัยรายปี (S̄t̄hiti ṭhurkic prakạnwināṣ̄phạy rāy pī) [Annual General Insurance Business Statistics (Annual Report)]' (2015) <www.oic.or.th/en/industry/statistic/data/40/2> accessed 3 June 2020; Office of Insurance Commission, 'สถิติธุรกิจประกันชีวิต รายปี (S̄t̄hiti ṭhurkic prakạnchīwit rāy pī) [Annual Life Insurance Business Statistics (Annual Report)]' (2015) <www.oic.or.th/en/industry/statistic/data/32/2> accessed 3 June 2020.

[46] ibid.

[47] A provident fund is a fund set up voluntarily between employers and employees. Assets of the fund consist of money contributed by both employer and employees, meaning that not only are employees saving for their retirement but the employer is helping them by contributing to the fund. The contribution to be made by the employer shall always equal or supersede the rate of the employee's savings. Therefore, setting up a provident fund can be regarded as a kind of benefit so as to motivate employees to work with the employer; see Provident Fund Act B.E.2530 (1987).

[48] Association of Investment Management Companies, 'การจัดสรร เงิน ลงทุน ของกอง ทุนสำรอง เลี้ยง ชีพ รายปี (Kār cạds̄rr ngein lngthun k̄hxngkxng thuns̄ảrxng lēı̂yng chīph rāy pī) [Annual Fund Allocation of Provident Funds]' (22 January 2020) <http://oldweb.aimc.or.th/23_overview_detail.php?nid=30&subid=0&ntype=4> accessed 3 June 2020 [hereinafter AIMC Provident Funds].

[49] There are a total of sixteen investment management companies, including fifteen asset management companies who manage provident funds; see Association of Investment Management Companies, 'Company Members' <http://oldweb.aimc.or.th/en/14_about_member_index.php> accessed 3 June 2020.

There are also securities companies who may act as asset managers for their private funds and who, therefore, one would expect as asset managers to become signatories to the code. However, only two out of thirty-nine securities companies signed in 2018.[50] This is largely because the SEC's regulation of 1 September 2017 only applied to asset management companies, not securities companies.[51]

16.3 PROPORTION AND SIGNIFICANCE OF INSTITUTIONAL INVESTORS

In order to appreciate the impact of the Thai Code, despite only some institutional investors adopting it, we must first look at the larger picture of all Thai institutional investors which include asset management companies, government funds, securities companies, insurance companies and provident funds.

16.3.1 *Investment Proportion of Institutional Investors in the Thai Capital Market*

Since the 1997 AFC, the SET market capitalization has increased significantly. In August 2019, the capitalization was about THB 17,000 billion (USD 560 billion).[52] Foreign investments have been underweight in the SET for quite some time. As can be seen from Figure 16.3, foreign investors have been negative net purchasers, especially since 2008. It is estimated that the proportion of foreign investors is now about 22% of the SET, and so local investors contribute about 78%. Domestic institutional investors hold around

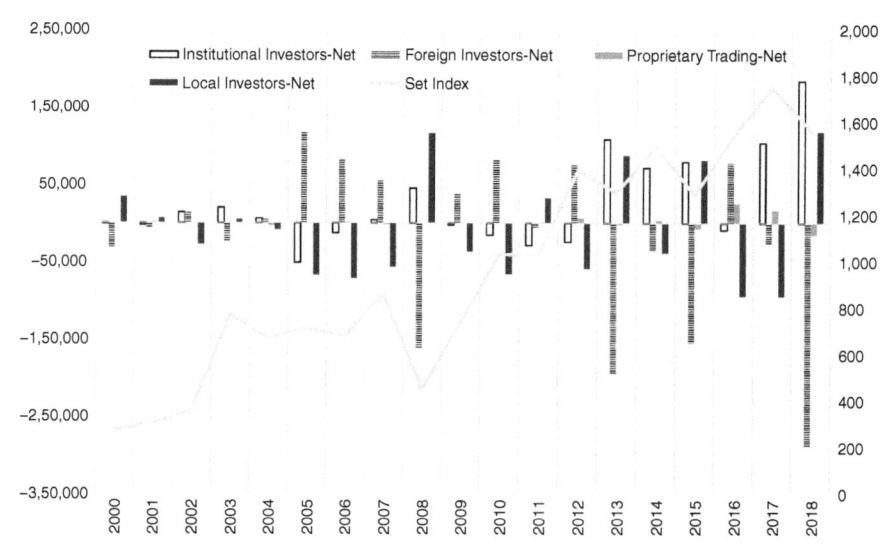

FIGURE 16.3 Net purchases by investor groups (million THB/year) on the Thailand SET Index[53]

---

[50] SEC, 'List of Code Signatories' (n 42); Stock Exchange of Thailand, 'Member of SET' <www.set.or.th/set/memberlist.do?language=en&country=US> accessed 3 June 2020.
[51] SEC Disclosure Requirements (n 39).
[52] The Stock Exchange of Thailand, 'Market Capitalization (Sep 1988 to Present)' <www.set.or.th/static/mktstat/Table_MKTCap.xls> accessed 3 June 2020.
[53] efinanceThai, 'Trading by Investor Types 2000–2018' <www.efinancethai.com/stockfocus/customertype.aspx?from=01/01/00&to=31/12/18&by=2&type=SET&tfexfuture=-1> accessed 3 June 2020.

14% of local investment.[54] So local investors are now the driving force in the market. Institutional investors have generated positive net purchases for the past six years (2013–18). The small proportion of domestic institutional investors suggests that they make only a limited impact on stewardship behaviour, and thus lack the ability to control most listed companies through the Thai Code.

As mentioned, institutional investors' assets are estimated to be about 14% of SET's market capitalization (THB 17,000 billion) which is about 14.6% of Thailand's GDP (THB 16,300 billion).[55] Apart from asset managers, asset owners like SSF, GPF, mutual funds and provident funds are also significant in the Thai capital market. SSF is a governmental fund managed by SSO. It is the largest, with a net asset value (NAV) of THB 1.999 trillion (USD 60.5 billion) or about 12.25% of Thailand's GDP.[56] However, SSF is limited by regulation and cannot invest in assets with a high level of risk (i.e. greater than 40% of total assets). At the moment, SSF has invested in listed companies with only 14.88% of its NAV, which amounts to about THB 297 billion.[57] Although it is the largest fund in Thailand, it invests minimally in listed companies owing to legal limitations.[58] GPF is also a governmental fund with a NAV of THB 881 billion. Its investments are about THB 382 billion, of which only THB 3.28 billion are invested in listed companies.[59] Again, this government fund is limited to investing only in equity securities amounting to not more than 40% of its total assets and not more than 30% in foreign equity securities.[60] Both SSF and GPF lack the ability to control listed companies owing to their small ownership stakes.

On the other hand, there are 402 provident funds managed by 15 asset management companies with NAV of about THB 1.12 trillion.[61] Their investments in securities are about 87% of their total NAV. They have invested in listed companies for about 17% of their total NAV, which is about THB 192 billion. Other investments include 29% for debentures, 28% for government bonds and 13% for warrants and other investment units.[62] It seems that provident funds can contribute significantly to the investment governance of the Thai capital market. However, as of 2018, only 10 out of 402 were signatories to the Thai Code.[63]

A similar trend can be seen in mutual funds. There are more than 1,700 mutual funds managed by 23 asset management companies with a total NAV of about THB 5 trillion, which accounts for about 30.98% of Thailand's GDP.[64] It has been reported that they have invested in

---

[54] Wattanapong Jaiwat, 'มาทำความเข้าใจ โครงสร้างตลาดหุ้นไทย กองทุน หรือ ต่างชาติ ที่เป็นคนผลักดัน SET Index (Mā thảkhwām k̄hêācı khorngs̄r̂āng tlādh̄ûn thịy kxngthun h̄rụ̄x t̀āng chāti thī̀ pĕn khn p̄hlạk dạn SET Index) [Understanding the Structure of the SET Index: Funds or Foreigners Driving the Index]' (*Brand Inside*, 4 February 2019) <https://brandinside.asia/anatomy-of-thai-stock-exchange-from-hsbc-research/> accessed 3 June 2020, which cites data from HSBC.

[55] SET, 'Market Statistics' (n 52).

[56] Social Security Office, 'รายงานประจำปี 2561 (สำนักงานประกันสังคม) (Rāyngān pracả pī 2561 (s̄ảnạkngān prakạn s̄ạngkhm)) 43 [Annual Report 2018 (Social Security Office)]' <www.sso.go.th/wpr/assets/upload/files_storage/sso_th/f4dabf6d2e90ebe9015c5c72a50a6ff5.pdf> accessed 3 June 2020.

[57] ibid 46.

[58] Social Securities Commission Rule on Investment of Social Securities Fund (2016) art 6.

[59] Government Pension Fund, 'Investment Portfolio' (December 2018) <www3.gpf.or.th/thai2013/invest/ratio.asp> accessed 3 June 2020.

[60] Ministerial Regulation on Rules and Procedures for Investment of Government Pension Fund (No 2) 2016, art 6 in accordance with the Government Pension Fund Act B.E.2539 (1996) s 70.

[61] AIMC Provident Funds (n 48); AIMC, 'Company Members' (n 49).

[62] ibid.

[63] SEC, 'List of Code Signatories' (n 42).

[64] Association of Investment Management Companies, 'มูลค่าทรัพย์สินสุทธิกองทุนรวมเทียบ GDP และเงินฝาก ปี 2535–2561 (Mūlkh̀ā thrạphy̒s̄in s̄uthṭhi kxngthun rwm thẹ̄yb GDP læa ngein f̄āk pī 2535–2561) [Proportion of Mutual Fund Net Asset Value per GDP and Deposit, Year 1992-2018]' (18 February 2019) <http://oldweb.aimc.or.th/21_overview_detail.php?nid=8&subid=0&ntype=2> accessed 3 June 2020 [hereinafter AIMC Mutual Funds].

only about half of all listed companies (more than 600 by the end of 2016).[65] Almost all of their capital is allocated to about 33% of all the stocks they invest in, most of which are large-cap growth stocks.[66] As of July 2019, it is estimated that the total NAV of equity funds is about THB 1,500 billion, not including those equity in mutual funds and other investments.[67] Similarly, mutual funds should contribute significantly to the investment governance of the Thai capital market owing to their holding a large proportion of the market. All twenty-three asset management companies have already adopted the Thai Code. However, it has not been as much as expected owing to their small proportion of holdings in investee companies.

16.3.2 *Domination of Family Business*

In Asia, the prevalence of family businesses in listed companies is widespread. In many jurisdictions in Asia, institutional investors constitute only a small minority of listed companies, and so lack any real power compared with family-controlling shareholders.[68] In the context of Singapore, Puchniak and Tang explain how family controllers have been viewed as stewards and, owing to their large controlling-block shareholdings, wield significantly more power over listed companies than institutional investors.[69] In the context of Thailand, we examine the prevalence of family controlled firms among SET100 companies.[70]

Based on our hand-collected data, it appears that the SET100 is dominated by family-controlled companies. Figure 16.4 shows that Thai family members are the largest shareholders in 41% of SET100 companies. In addition, in 39% of SET100 companies, private companies are the largest shareholders – with 72% of these private companies being closely related to the family members who have effective control over these companies. Institutional investors are not the largest shareholders in any SET100 companies. As such, it appears that family controllers are the dominant shareholders and de facto stewards in most of Thailand's largest listed companies.

Figure 16.5 provides a picture of the level of shareholder concentration in Thailand's largest listed companies. Based on our hand-collected data, in the SET100, in ninety-five out of ninety-eight companies there is a shareholder who holds more than 10 per cent of the shares; in eighty-nine companies a shareholder who holds more than 20 per cent; and in thirty-four companies a shareholder who holds more than 50 per cent. As explained already, family controllers are dominant in these large block shareholders. Conversely, institutional shareholders generally hold only a small minority stake in most SET100 companies.

---

[65] Roongkiat Ratanabanchuen and Kanis Saengchote, 'Institutional Capital Allocation and Equity Returns: Evidence from Thai Mutual Funds' Holdings' (2020) 32 *Finance Research Letters* 101085.
[66] ibid.
[67] AIMC Mutual Funds (n 64).
[68] Gen Goto, Alan K Koh and Dan W Puchniak, 'Diversity of Shareholder Stewardship in Asia: Faux Convergence' (2020) 53 *Vanderbilt Journal of Transnational Law* 829; Luh Luh Lan and Umakanth Varottil, 'Shareholder Empowerment in Controlled Companies: The Case of Singapore' in Jennifer G Hill and Randall S Thomas (eds), *Research Handbook on Shareholder Power* (Edward Elgar 2015).
[69] See Dan W Puchniak and Samantha Tang, 'Singapore's Puzzling Embrace of Shareholder Stewardship: A Successful Secret' (2020) 53 *Vanderbilt Journal of Transnational Law* 989.
[70] The SET100 index is calculated 'to represent the performance of the top 100 large market capitalization which consist[s in] coverage of and high correlation with [the] Thai market'. See calculation methodology at the Stock Exchange of Thailand, 'SET50 and SET100 Indices Rule' (January 2013) <www.set.or.th/en/products/index/files/2013-01-SET50-100-IndexRule-EN.pdf> accessed 3 June 2020.

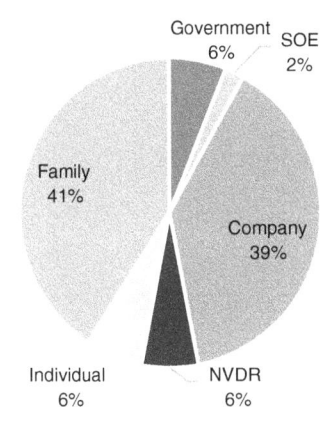

FIGURE 16.4 The largest shareholding and types of investor of SET100[71]

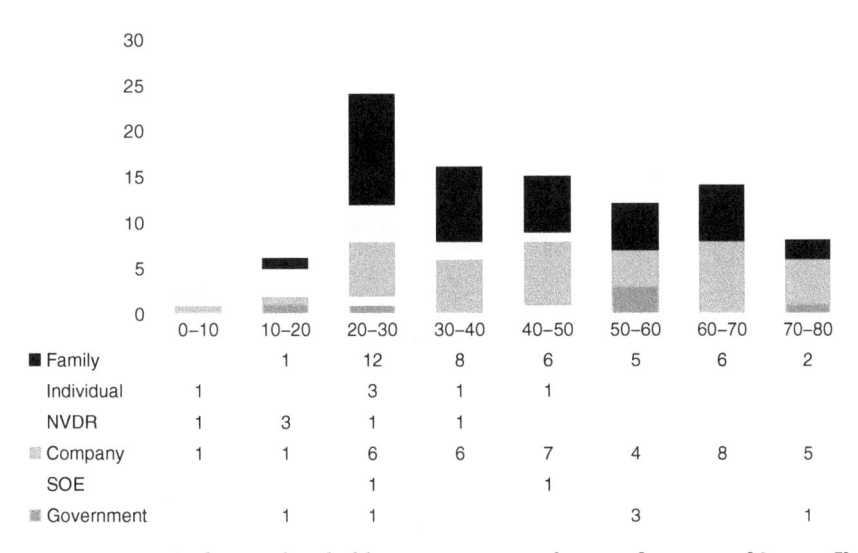

FIGURE 16.5 The largest shareholding proportion and types of investor of SET100[72]

Figure 16.6 shows the number of SET100 companies that are defined as ESG and non-ESG,[73] and the proportion of the largest shareholders in the companies. From ninety-eight SET100 companies, thirty-four are defined as ESG and sixty-four as non-ESG. As mentioned earlier, ESG is an investment factor of the Thai Code.[74] Figure 16.6 shows that institutional investors like NVDR, SOE and government funds under stewardship responsibilities are investing more

---

[71] This information was prepared based on the publicly available information on companies/securities published by the Stock Exchange of Thailand, which was accessed online during August 2019. Moreover, additional searches were done to gather information about THSI (Thailand Sustainability Investment), the sustainability awards that SET grants to listed companies (Stock Exchange of Thailand, 'Thailand Sustainability Investment (THSI)' <www.setsustainability.com/page/thsi-thailand-sustainability-investment> accessed 3 June 2020). Patanaporn Kowpatanakit and Piyabutr Bunaramrueang, Family Business Data (August 2019) (unpublished data) (on file with authors).
[72] Kowpatanakit and Bunaramrueang (n 71).
[73] For the methodology and definition of ESG, see SET, 'Thailand Sustainability Investment (THSI)' (n 71); SET, 'รายชื่อ Thailand Sustainability Investment (THSI) ปีล่าสุด (Rāy chụ̄̀x Thailand Sustainability Investment (THSI) pī lāsud) [List of THSI Companies Latest Year]' <www.setsustainability.com/libraries/710/item/thailand-sustainability-investment-lists> accessed 3 June 2020.
[74] Thai Code (n 1) 31.

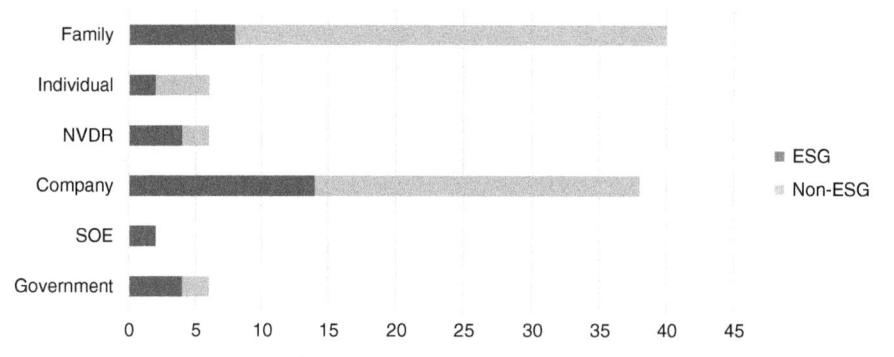

FIGURE 16.6 Types of investor with the largest shareholding of SET100 and ESG classification[75]

in ESG businesses. On the contrary, individuals, family businesses and private companies are investing more in non-ESG businesses.

Overall, a large number of listed companies in Thailand are family-owned firms. Even though the 1997 AFC wiped out some large family business groups, most of them survived by restructuring and obtaining the financial resources necessary from financial institutions and the capital market. Institutional investors in Thailand are subject to several code requirements such as ESG and stewardship. As a result, they tend to own minority stakes in listed companies and so, in general, they are unable to play any significant role in influencing company activities and management.

16.4 INSTITUTIONAL INVESTORS AND THEIR IMPLEMENTATION OF THE THAI CODE

The adoption of the Thai Code has been rather smooth for asset management companies. They adopted the code promptly owing to the SEC Disclosure Requirement. Not a single company refused to adopt the code. In part, this was because the code was not new to them. They all had been implementing some form of CG policies, especially proxy voting policies and anti-corruption policies. Principle 5 of the Thai Code encourages institutional investors to be transparent in their proxy voting and engagement guidelines and to align them with the Code.[76] Similar to Principle 6 of the UK Code 2012, institutional investors need to participate in shareholder meetings and report what they do as shareholders.[77] Before adopting the Thai Code, twenty-four out of all twenty-six asset management companies had already implemented their own proxy voting policies as a result of an initiative by the Association of Investment Management Companies (AIMC).[78] In addition, the Thai Code encourages anti-corruption measures for both the institutional investor and investee

[75] Kowpatanakit and Bunaramrueang (n 71).
[76] Thai Code (n 1) 48, Principle 5.
[77] UK Code 2012 (n 25) 9.
[78] On 10 May 1994, AIMC was registered and licensed as an association relating to and representing the investment management industry by the Office of the Securities and Exchange Commission (SEC). AIMC is a non-profit organization supported by its members, which are securities companies licensed to run asset management businesses. To promote SET's 'Principles of Good Corporate Governance for Listed Companies 2012' (n 14), AIMC worked out in 2014 the voting guidelines and practices for asset management companies; see Association of Investment Management Companies, 'Proxy Voting' (2014) <http://oldweb.aimc.or.th/en/71_proxyvote_guidelines.php> accessed 3 June 2020. At present, AIMC members are asset management companies in three business groups comprising mutual fund business, private fund business, and provident fund business. See the examples of voting policies published on their websites at SCB Asset Management (SCBAM), 'Fund Supervisory Policy' <www.scbam.com/en/about/about-conflict/> accessed 3 June 2020; TISCO, 'Funds' Voting Rights' <www.tiscoasset.com/th/asset/html/funds-voting-rights.jsp> accessed 3 June 2020.

companies.[79] However, since 2013, all of these companies already had anti-bribery and corruption policies in place.[80] The five major institutional investors, including GPF, SSO and AIMC, have joined forces to announce the intention to set up the Ethical Investment Framework.[81] The existence of similar policies on CG would be a reason why it has not been difficult for asset management companies to adopt the code.

As all signatories are expected to provide a stewardship letter of intent, even though the Thai Code is based on a 'comply or explain' basis, all the fifty-seven signatories have agreed to apply all the principles. In fact, each of them provided a one-page letter of intent (mostly all in Thai), which conveyed their compliance with all seven principles.[82] As noted earlier, as asset management companies are SEC-regulated businesses, the intention to comply with the code appears to be merely a box-ticking exercise. Only twenty-five SEC-licensed asset management companies and one SEC-owned provident fund have complied with all three disclosure requirements of the Thai Code and provided a letter of intent, stewardship policy and stewardship report. As will be explained in detail, many of the signatories are not implementing the principles.

According to Principle 1 of the Thai Code, an institutional investor should adopt a clear written stewardship policy. The policy should set out their organizational structure which complies with and considers their roles and responsibilities for the best interest of their beneficiaries. As mentioned, all signatories have adopted all principles of the Thai Code. Moreover, the stewardship policy integrates several factors provided by the Thai Code, such as anti-bribery and corruption, and ESG.[83] Table 16.1 shows that four out of five government

TABLE 16.1 *Summary of the letter of intent, stewardship policy and annual stewardship report (2018)*[84]

	Total	Letter of intent	Stewardship policy	Annual stewardship report (2018)
Government agencies, associations and other institutions	5	5	4	0
Asset management companies	26	26	26	25
Securities companies	39	2	0	0
Insurance companies	86	14	1	0
Provident funds (as asset owners)	402	10	2	1
Total	558	57	33	26

---

[79] Thai Code (n 1) 39, Principle 1.3.2.
[80] The SEC encouraged listed companies, securities companies and asset management companies to join the Private Sector Collective Action Coalition Against Corruption (CAC) to enhance integrity and transparency in the Thai capital market and be a role model for non-listed companies and other business organizations when it comes to building capital market confidence and promoting robust economic growth. The SEC also encouraged listed companies to establish and implement anti-corruption measures and requires them to disclose such policy and performance in the annual report, the annual registration statement (Form 56-1) and the registration statement for offering of securities (Form 69-1).
[81] Securities and Exchange Commission, 'Anti-Corruption' (21 June 2018) <www.sec.or.th/cgthailand/EN/Pages/corruption.aspx> accessed 3 June 2020.
[82] SEC, 'List of Code Signatories' (n 42).
[83] Thai Code (n 1) 31, 39, Principle 1.3.2.
[84] This information was prepared based on publicly available information provided on asset management companies' websites which were accessed online during December 2019. Moreover, additional internet searches were done to gather information relating to their stewardship policies and annual reports. Patanaporn Kowpatanakit and Piyabutr Bunaramrueang, Stewardship Policies and Annual Reports (December 2019) (unpublished data) (on file with authors).

funds and all asset management companies have adopted stewardship policies with board of directors' approval. But of all the signatories, only about half of them have provided stewardship policies. Moreover, only twenty-five asset management companies and one provident fund have provided annual stewardship reports – which is less than half of the total number of signatories.

According to Principle 7 of the Thai Code, starting in 2018, asset management companies were required to provide an annual report disclosing their implementation of the code. At first blush, it appears that all asset management companies have complied. However, there are still differences in policies and reports which makes it difficult to understand them and, in turn, to assess their actual stewardship performance. In the remainder of this section, we attempt to make a substantive assessment of the implementation of Principles 2 to 6. When evaluating whether an institutional investor has discharged its stewardship responsibilities, both the outcomes achieved and the process followed are of critical importance.[85] We examine actual compliance with each of the stewardship principles next.

16.4.1 Stewardship Responsibilities of Institutional Investors in Thailand

An institutional investor is charged with the care of an asset that belongs to their customers. As asset owners or asset managers, they are expected to engage and actively participate in the operation and governance of their investee companies to improve and increase the governance of these companies and foster sustainable performance. It is important to note that stewardship responsibilities adopt a soft-law approach and are not the same as legal fiduciary duties.[86]

To ensure that an institutional investor discharges its stewardship responsibilities, the SEC regulations provide that a signatory, upon adopting its stewardship policy, is required to file a report annually to the SEC that discloses its level of compliance with each principle of the Thai Code.[87] This is limited to asset management companies under SEC regulations which have adopted the code voluntarily – which is different from the UK Code 2012, which makes it mandatory for all UK-authorized asset managers to 'comply or explain' with the UK Code.[88] The report, according to the Thai Code, should also be disclosed on its website for its customers and other stakeholders to access.[89] There are various tasks an institution should implement to ensure delivery of sustainable long-term value for its customers in accordance with its stewardship responsibilities in compliance with the Thai Code.

16.4.1.1 Responsibility to Prevent and Manage Conflicts of Interest

A fiduciary has a duty to act in the best interest of its beneficiaries. An institutional investor, in the same vein, owes a primary duty to its customers' interest, and is prevented from entering into a transaction when its own interest conflicts with its customers' interest. In conducting the business of the company, Principle 2 of the Thai Code provides that institutional investors

---

[85] Valeria Piani, Kris Douma and Anna Georgieva, 'A Practical Guide to Active Ownership in Listed Equity' (*UNPRI*, 2018) 16 <www.unpri.org/download?ac=4151> accessed 3 June 2020.

[86] For the hardening of the law of shareholder stewardship, see Iris H–Y Chiu and Dionysia Katelouzou, 'From Shareholder Stewardship to Shareholder Duties: Is the Time Ripe?' in Hanne S Birkmose (ed), *Shareholders' Duties* (Kluwer Law International 2017).

[87] SEC Disclosure Requirements (n 39).

[88] UK Code 2012 (n 25).

[89] SEC Disclosure Requirements (n 39); Thai Code (n 1) 34.

should prevent and manage conflicts of interest, and prioritize the advancement of their clients' best interests. This is in accordance with section 124/1 of the SEC Act which provides:[90]

> For the management of a mutual fund, a securities company shall proceed with honesty and care to preserve the interests of all unitholders, using knowledge and competence as a professional. The securities company shall have a policy on prevention of conflicts of interest in managing a mutual fund and shall monitor and oversee acts that may cause a conflict of interest to the unitholders and any acts that may have an unfair characteristic toward the unitholders or may cause the unitholders to lose interest that should be received. In this regard, the securities company shall comply with the rules, conditions and procedures as specified in the notification of the Capital Market Supervisory Board.

This is a new provision added in 2019, which built upon the AIMC Proxy Voting Guidelines (2014) and the Thai Code.[91] In effect, all asset management companies now have a duty under the law and the Thai Code to closely monitor transactions by connected persons. Asset management companies should also have in place appropriate measures to prevent their employees from using inside information for personal benefit.

All asset management companies have issued their own stewardship policies to oversee conflicts of interest, which include conflicts arising between itself, its related parties, employees, and its clients, or among clients themselves.[92] Nevertheless, there is already a duty to manage conflicts of interest under section 124/1 of the SEC Act; asset management companies are able to implement their stewardship policies with no difficulty. For example, MFC Asset Management, an asset management company, clearly reported its vote for abstention in the shareholder meeting of its own company in its proxy voting report referred by its stewardship report, where it possessed two conflicted interests of the unit-holders and of the company itself.[93] SCB Asset Management, an asset management company, reported its vote for approval in the shareholder meeting of its parent company (SCB Bank) in a separate sheet under its proxy voting report to indicate its conflict of interests.[94]

16.4.1.2 Responsibility to Engage in and Active Ongoing Monitoring of Investee Companies

The Public Limited Company Act B.E.2535 (1992) recognizes a shareholder's right to inspect books and records where they hold no less than 5 per cent of the shareholdings.[95] It also recognizes a shareholder's right to protect their interests under derivative suits for one or more shareholders who hold an aggregate number of shares of not less than 5 per cent.[96] In order to be able to exercise those rights, shareholders must be able to engage and monitor the operations of

---

[90] Securities and Exchange Act B.E.2535 (1992) s 124/1.
[91] AIMC, 'Proxy Voting' (n 78); Thai Code (n 1).
[92] For examples, see MFC Asset Management, 'Investment Governance Policy' (2018) <www.mfcfund.com/web/Portals/0/cu/Invest_Gov_Policy.pdf> accessed 3 June 2020; BBL Asset Management, 'Investment Governance Policy: I-Code' (2018) <www.bblam.co.th/application/files/7215/4469/2325/Investment_Governance_Policy.pdf> accessed 3 June 2020.
[93] MFC Asset Management, 'รายละเอียดการใช้สิทธิออกเสียง 2018 (Rāy laxeīyd kār chı̂ s̄ithṭhi xxks̄eīyng) [Proxy Voting Report (2018)]' <www.mfcfund.com/web/Portals/0/cu/CONFLICT.pdf> accessed 3 June 2020.
[94] SCB Asset Management, 'รายงานสรุปเกี่ยวกับการใช้สิทธิออกเสียงประชุมผู้ถือหุ้น ประจำปี 2561 (Rāyngān s̄rup keīy wkạb kār chı̂ s̄ithṭhi xxks̄eīyng pra chum p̄hū̂ t̄hụ̄x ĥû̱ n pra čả pī 2561) [Proxy Voting Report 2018]' (2018) <www.scbam.com/medias/upload/pageconflict/votepolicy/vote2018.pdf> accessed 3 June 2020.
[95] Public Limited Company Act B.E.2535 (1992) s 128.
[96] ibid s 85.

350　　　　　　　　　　　　　　*Part II Jurisdictions*

investee companies. Therefore, Principle 8 of the CG Code emphasizes open engagement between a company and its shareholders.[97]

To ensure the sustainability of investee companies, shareholders play an important role. They are to be informed of any significant corporate incidents. This is in line with Principle 3 of the Thai Code, which asks institutional investors, as trustees, to actively engage in and monitor the operation and management of their investee companies. To efficiently engage in and monitor investee companies' management, signatories should regularly meet and communicate with the board members and senior management of the investee companies.[98] This provides an opportunity for an institutional investor to discuss and explain its perspective towards the investee company's business operations. In the event where serious concerns are seen, it should contact the company immediately, and seek clarification and engage with the company to resolve problems. Therefore, the stewardship policy should disclose monitoring guidelines in case of the occurrence of problems in investee companies. In fact, major asset management companies have regularly held meetings with investee companies and taken action to address potential issues.[99]

In addition, Principle 4 of the Thai Code provides that institutional investors should apply enhanced monitoring of and engagement with the investee companies if monitoring pursuant to Principle 3 is considered insufficient. Several practices are also recommended including escalation of actions, which may involve formally notifying the board of directors of any concerns.[100] An example of this can be seen in the actions taken by Kasikorn Asset Management, the largest asset management firm in Thailand with a total of 180 funds, accounting for about THB 1 trillion. In the past several years, Kasikorn has escalated three serious issues to the board of directors of its investee companies.[101] Since they were considered to be severe cases of corporate governance malpractice, Kasikorn Asset Management entered into conversations with the companies, formally informed the chairpersons of the boards, and requested that the companies adopt preventive measures to avoid such problems in the future. Another example of enhanced monitoring is the call for the inclusion of an independent director by the Thai Investors Association (TIA) in CP All Plc, which runs 7-Eleven stores in Thailand.[102] AIMC requested CP All Plc's board members to take appropriate actions.[103] Other investors, such as MFC Asset Management, decided to reduce their investment in

---

[97] CG Code (n 1) Principle 8.1: 'The board should ensure that shareholders have the opportunity to participate effectively in decision-making involving significant corporate matters.'

[98] Thai Code (n 1) 44, Principle 3.4.2.

[99] For examples, see MFC Asset Management, 'รายงานการปฏิบัติตามนโยบายธรรมาภิบาลการลงทุน (Rāyngān kār pti btai tām nyobāy thr rmāphi bāl kār lngthun) [Investment Code Compliance Report]' (2018) <www.mfcfund.com/web/Portals/0/cu/TH_Compliance_report_ICODE.pdf> accessed 3 June 2020: 'MFC has stipulated that it shall monitor the news and information disclosures related to the companies in which the funds invest, as well as meet with the directors and management of the companies' (English translation); Kasikorn Asset Management, 'Investment Governance Code 2019 Annual Review' (2019) <www.kasikornasset.com/th/about/Documents/Annual%20review%20KAsset%20I%20Code%202019%20%28Eng%29.pdf> accessed 3 June 2020: 'the equity team at KAsset held a total [of] 1,295 meetings with 451 listed companies. The meetings were held with all levels of Company's representatives as deem[ed] appropriate'; SCB Asset Management, 'Compliance Report of Investment Governance Code Policy – Annual Year 2018' (2019) (hereinafter SCB Asset Management) accessed 26 August 2019 (on file with authors): 'SCBAM has held meetings with directors and management teams as appropriate and reasonable for the matter'.

[100] Thai Code (n 1) 46, Principle 4.4.1.

[101] Kasikorn Asset Management (n 99).

[102] Jon Fernquest, 'Insider Trading at CP All: Foreign Investors Demand Action' *Bangkok Post* (21 December 2015) <www.bangkokpost.com/learning/advanced/801656/insider-trading-at-cp-all-foreign-investors-demand-action> accessed 3 June 2020.

[103] Darana Chudasri and Wichit Chantanusornsiri, 'Pressure on CP All Insider Trading Bosses' *Bangkok Post* (9 December 2015) <www.bangkokpost.com/thailand/general/788953/pressure-on-cp-all-insider-trading-bosses> accessed 3 June 2020.

CP All Plc owing to the scandal rather than undertake any monitoring activities.[104] These are real examples of an escalation according to Principle 4 of the Thai Code by Kasikorn and MFC.

Escalation is an important task for our assessment that signatories can monitor and review investee companies according to Principles 3 and 4 and whether they have taken appropriate actions. Only five out of twenty-six asset management companies indicated their application of enhanced monitoring in their stewardship reports.[105] Even though almost all the stewardship reports in 2018 show that the signatories complied with the principles, most of them did not apply enhanced monitoring of the investee companies under Principle 4. It is interesting to note that they had indicated in their stewardship reports only that there was no issue which required considering the escalation of their engagement in their investee companies. As there is insufficient evidence to prove otherwise, this would be an area for further research to identify cases where some escalated their actions, while others did not. That would help us understand why such contradictory actions occur, and such findings can be used for more effective stewardship.

16.4.1.3 Responsibility to Attend Shareholder Meetings

One of the most fundamental rights of shareholders is the right to attend and vote in shareholders' meetings.[106] Institutional investors are entitled to attend and make decisions, especially on significant corporate agendas.[107] As an asset owner and asset manager, an institutional investor has a fiduciary duty to attend and exercise voting rights for the best interest of its beneficiaries in the shareholder meetings of its investee companies.[108]

Principle 5 of the Thai Code provides that institutional investors should have a clear policy on exercising voting rights and disclosure of voting results. To comply with Principle 5, the twenty-six asset management companies, signatories to the Code, have referred to their existing proxy voting policies.[109] With the co-operation of institutional investors, AIMC developed a proxy voting guideline for investment companies to adopt to help them create their own proxy voting policies. The guideline provides the list of significant agenda items in a shareholders' meeting and the process of decision-making in the meeting. Most asset management companies publish their own proxy voting policies on their websites. Their policies are largely similar – they provide that for significant matters an institutional investor must exercise its voting rights. In addition, most of them set up criteria for decision-making on significant matters. For example, the guideline recommends that shareholders vote against the appointment of a director who attends less than 75 per cent of the company's board meetings.[110]

Based on our hand-collected data, we found that twenty-two out of twenty-five stewardship reports referred to their proxy voting reports for their implementation of Principle 5. The reports provided

---

[104] MFC Asset Management (n 99).
[105] Kasikorn Asset Management (n 99); MFC Asset Management (n 99); SCB Asset Management (n 99); BBL Asset Management, 'รายงานการปฏิบัติตามนโยบายธรรมาภิบาลการลงทุนประจำ ปี 2561 (Rāyngān kār ptibati tām nyobāy thr māphi bāl kār lng thun pra c āpī 2561) [Compliance Report of Investment Governance Code Policy – Annual Year 2018]' (2019) <www.bblam.co.th/application/files/4115/6039/3663/2561_Compliance.pdf> accessed 3 June 2020; Aberdeen Standard Asset Management (Thailand) Ltd., 'Aberdeen Standard Investment I Code Disclosures – Annual Year 2018' (2019) <www.aberdeenstandard.com/docs?documentId=TH-290419-88417-1> accessed 3 June 2020.
[106] Public Limited Company Act B.E.2535 (1992) s 102.
[107] ibid.
[108] Thai Code (n 1) 48, Principle 5.1.
[109] Thai Code (n 1) 48, Principle 5.3.
[110] ibid.

a numerical breakdown of the votes in the shareholders' meetings of their investee companies. In cases of 'abstain' and 'against' votes, the reports always provided the reasons for the vote.[111]

An institutional investor should have its own proxy voting policy for each of its investee companies and should disclose this policy.[112] It should also disclose how it voted on each resolution and the rationale for its votes, especially in the case of negative votes. While most asset management companies provide comprehensive reports with reasons for their negative votes, government funds, SSO and GPF do not disclose this information.

Even though institutional investors should exercise their voting rights in compliance with their proxy voting policies, they rarely attend shareholder meetings. Generally, asset management companies clearly state in their proxy voting policies that they may in advance nominate proxies in writing to attend the meeting on their behalf, including independent directors of investee companies. As they often use proxies, most asset management companies do not disclose the number of meetings that they attend. Only Kasikorn reported that it attended 36 shareholder meetings out of a total of 182 shareholder meetings in 2018.[113]

According to Principle 6 of the Thai Code, the role of institutional investors, as professional investors, is to participate in collective engagement, especially in general meetings, and raise questions and concerns with the board and senior management. By acting together, minority institutional investors may have sufficient bargaining power to protect minority stakes in the company. This is another important task for stewardship assessment. At present, there has not been a report on this.

16.4.2 Exercising Shareholder Rights in Investee Companies

This is the first time that the Thai Code provides a professional standard for institutional investors in Thailand, albeit only in the broadest sense. This section attempts to assess institutional investors in terms of their exercise of shareholder rights.

Based on our hand-collected data from the proxy voting reports of twenty-five asset management companies in 2018, all reported in their stewardship report that they had participated in shareholder meetings:[114] while twenty-two provided their voting history in reports that they made publicly available on their websites,[115] two of them provided the information privately to their customers,[116] and one of them did not provide any report.[117]

We collected all resolutions voted (in total 24,536 votes) and reported by the 22 asset management companies in 2018. Figure 16.7 shows how they voted: 91 % for approval, 5% for abstention, and 4% in opposition. In general, high approval votes, by themselves, do not reveal much about stewardship as the votes may be cast without proper scrutiny. Analogous to Principle 6 of the UK Code 2012, the

---

[111] This information was prepared based on publicly available information provided on asset management companies' websites which were accessed online during December 2019. Moreover, additional internet searches were done to gather information relating to their stewardship policies and annual reports. Patanaporn Kowpatanakit and Piyabutr Bunaramrueang, Annual Reports and Agendas (December 2019) (unpublished data) (on file with authors).
[112] Thai Code (n 1) 48, Principle 5.1.
[113] Kasikorn Asset Management (n 99).
[114] Kowpatanakit and Bunaramrueang (n 111).
[115] ibid.
[116] They were (1) Denali Prestige Asset Management Limited and (2) ASIA Wealth Asset Management Company Limited.
[117] At the time of writing, Phillip Asset Management Company Limited has provided its 2017 report. For government funds, SSO and GPF reported only summarily, which is insufficient for our assessment. Proxy voting reports of previous years are mostly unavailable to the public. As such, the assessment that follows is based only on the publicly available proxy voting reports of twenty-two asset management companies in 2018.

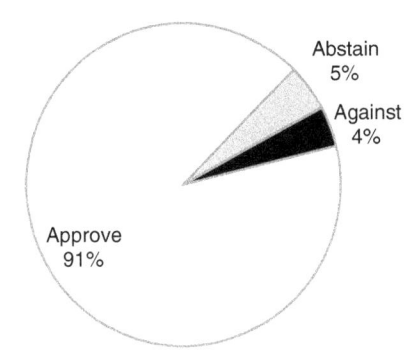

FIGURE 16.7 Vote castings of all asset management companies as reported in 2018[118]

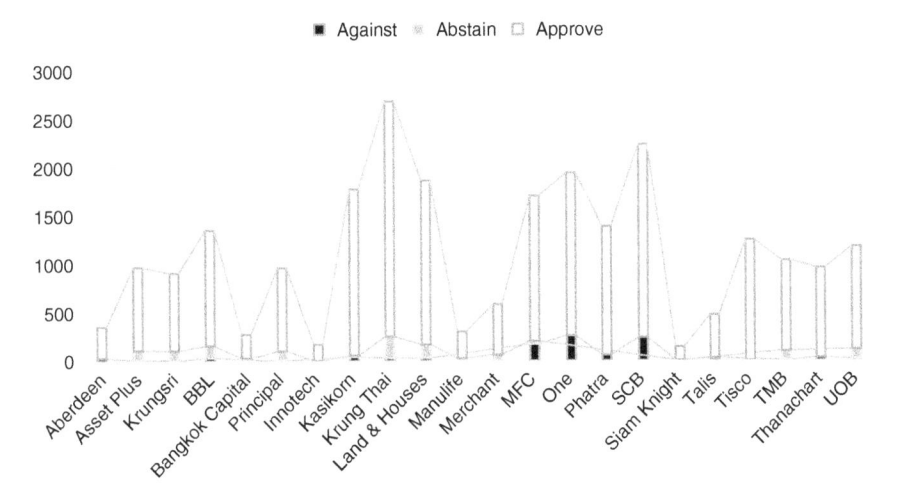

FIGURE 16.8 Vote castings of twenty-two asset management companies as reported in 2018[119]

Thai Code also emphasizes this point in its Principle 5.1: that institutional investors should not adopt a policy to indiscriminately support any and all resolutions proposed by the board of directors as it would suggest inadequate performance of their duties in the best interests of their clients.

All twenty-two asset management companies' proxy voting policies have adopted Principle 5.1, which states that they will not automatically support the board of directors of an investee company (see Figure 16.8). This is the first time that data have been collected on votes cast by institutional investors. As such, there is no basis for comparison. However, in the case of positive votes, the voting reports of asset managers did not provide the rationale for such votes. This is not contrary to the Thai Code because, similar to the UK Code, it requires only that an explanation is provided for negative votes.[120] However, this can be the baseline for a further assessment of asset manager voting data in the future.

---

[118] Kowpatanakit and Bunaramrueang (n 111).
[119] ibid.
[120] Thai Code (n 1) 48, Principle 5.2 (which is similar to UK Code 2012 (n 25) 9, Principle 6) provides:

> As set out in Principle 4, if the Investee Company does not resolve the issues identified by the Institutional Investor, the Institutional Investor should exercise its voting rights on matters related to the issues at the Annual General Meeting or Extraordinary General Meeting and provide in writing reasons for its vote against any resolution proposed by the Investee Company or its abstention to the Investee Companies.

Figure 16.9 shows that most abstentions were owing to issues at the meeting falling outside of the meeting's agenda. It appears that the institutional investors were not prepared to address these issues; therefore, they abstained according to their proxy voting policies. This is particularly interesting because many were not real agenda items that could be voted on. In practice, the final agenda item in every meeting is simply a question and answer session which is referred to herein as 'out of agenda'. We also checked the minutes of the meetings and found that the abstention votes were made with respect to these 'out of agenda' issues according to their voting policies. Therefore, the reporting of an abstention vote is meaningless and could not count as a true abstention. Again, this reflects a box-ticking exercise in stewardship reports. There are also about 22.09% of votes (252 out of 1,141 votes in abstentions total) where the issues are not identified in the reports. By not providing reasons for abstentions, they did not comply with Principle 5.4 of the Thai Code.

Now we turn to an analysis of negative votes casted by institutional investors. As shown in Figure 16.10, the top three matters that attracted negative votes were board matters

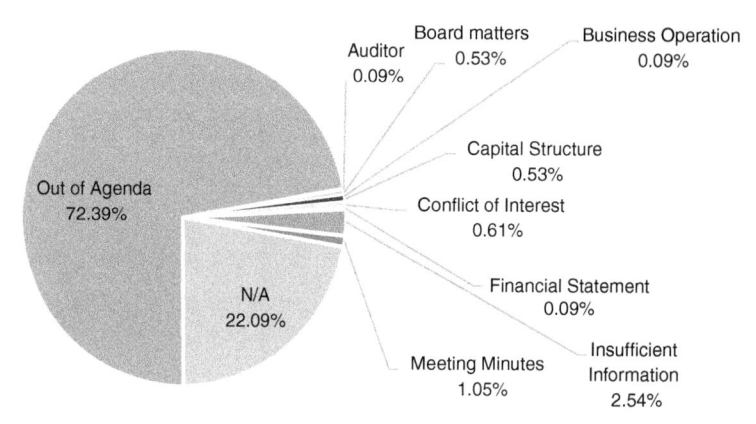

FIGURE 16.9 Institutional investors and issues they voted for abstention on as reported in 2018[121]

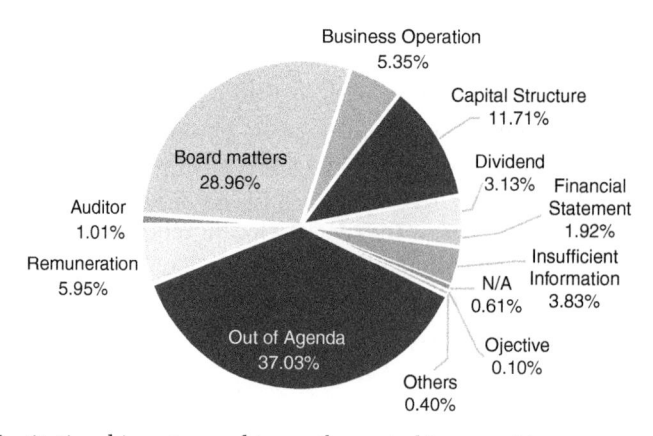

FIGURE 16.10 Institutional investors and issues they voted in opposition on as reported in 2018[122]

---

[121] ibid.
[122] ibid.

(28.96%), capital structure (11.71%) and issues that were not included on the shareholders' meeting agenda (37.03%) – totalling 991 opposition votes in 2018. For board matters, these votes mostly involved the qualification of board members and the failure to attend board meetings. Similar to abstentions, issues outside of the agenda were also a main reason for opposition, which they *had* to vote against according to their voting policies. This is box-ticking because they were not real agenda items to vote on. It is interesting to note that voting policy on any single issue may vary from one company to another. Out of agenda issues are a prime example of this variation, mostly for abstentions, while some others related to opposition votes.[123]

In order to illustrate non-compliant issues, the cases of negative votes are particularly interesting as there needs to be a clear voting policy against a common issue according to Principle 5 of the Thai Code. We find three common issues that were adopted by all asset management companies with a clear common policy to vote against, but the companies' practice, in reality, was different.

16.4.2.1 Common Voting Policy Against Untrustworthy Persons to Be Appointed as a Director

The lack of qualifications of directors and the failure of directors to attend board meetings were common issues. On this point, we will consider only the qualifications of directors because every asset management company has a clear voting policy to vote against unqualified directors.[124] As mentioned, in 2018, CP All's top executives were involved in an insider trading scandal. The executives agreed to enter into a settlement with the SEC – with the executive board chairman Korsak Chairasmisak paying a fine of THB 30,228,000 (approximately USD 1 million), which was the largest in Thailand's history.[125]

Subsequently, in 2018, Korsak Chairasmisak was scheduled to retire from CP All's board according to the law dealing with the rotation of directors.[126] At the shareholders' meeting after his scheduled retirement, he was re-nominated. About 32 per cent of shareholders voted against his reappointment – which significantly exceeded the 10 per cent disapproval received by other directors for reappointment.[127] However, only two asset management companies (Krungsri and BBL) voted against Korsak Chairasmisak's reappointment, which is surprising considering his gross misconduct.[128] According to the minutes of the shareholders' meeting, there was no discussion

---

[123] For examples, see BBL Asset Management, 'แนวนโยบายในการใช้สิทธิออกเสียงที่คณะกรรมการลงทุนได้กำหนดไว้' (Næw nyobāy nı kār chī sithṭhi xxkseīyng thī̀ khṇa krrmkār lngthun dị̂ kảh̄nd wị̂) [Proxy Voting Policy] <www.bblam.co.th/application/files/2415/2257/9216/voting_2560.pdf> accessed 3 June 2020; ONE Asset Management, 'แนวทางใช้สิทธิออกเสียงในที่ประชุมผู้ถือหุ้น (Næwthāng kār chī sithṭhi xxkseīyng nı thī̀ prachum p̄hū̂ t̄hụ̄x h̄ûn) [Proxy Voting Policy]' <www.one-asset.com/th/guideline/detail/1> accessed 3 June 2020.

[124] For examples, see Krungthai Asset Management, 'Proxy Voting Guidelines' <www.ktam.co.th/about-inside.aspx?vALuEId=12> accessed 3 June 2020; UOB Asset Management, 'นโยบายปฏิบัติเกี่ยวกับการใช้สิทธิออกเสียงในที่ประชุมผู้ถือหุ้นโดยบริษัทจัดการในนาม_กองทุน (Nyobāy pt̩ibạti keī̀y wkạb kār chī sithṭhi xxkseīyng nı thīp ra chum p̄h̄ t̄hụ̄x h̄ûn doy briṣ́ạth cạdkār nı nām ū kxngthun) [Proxy Voting Policy]' <www.uobam.co.th/files/proxyvote(th).pdf> accessed 3 June 2020.

[125] Securities and Exchange Commission, 'Settlement Committee Imposes Fines on MAKRO Insider Trading' (Bangkok, 2 December 2015) <www.sec.or.th/EN/Pages/News_Detail.aspx?SECID=6145&NewsNo=131&NewsYear=2015&Lang=EN> accessed 3 June 2020.

[126] Public Limited Company Act BE2535(1992) s 71.

[127] CP All, 'Minutes of Annual General Meeting of Shareholders for Year 2018 (Translation)' (2018) <www.cpall.co.th/wp-content/uploads/2018/06/AGMENG.pdf> accessed 3 June 2020.

[128] Given the SEC regulation at the time, he was not blacklisted by the SEC. In 2016, SEC moved to make an amendment to include those who was fined in a settlement with the SEC; see SEC Notification No Kor Jor 8/2553 Re: Determination of Untrustworthy Characteristics of Company Directors and Executives (23 April 2010) as revised on 1 August 2016, now superseded by SEC Notification No Kor Jor. 3/2560 Re: Determination of Untrustworthy

or questions raised about his misconduct. This would seem inconsistent with the stewardship reports, particularly because Korsak Chairasmisak was not qualified to be a director. While every asset management company claimed to comply with the Thai Code, only two voted against Korsak Chairasmisak's reappointment. In addition, the two asset management companies that voted against his reappointment did not provide the reasons for their negative votes, which was contrary to their obligation under the stewardship code. Such conduct demonstrates that although asset management companies claim to follow the code, they appear to be doing so in form but not in substance.

16.4.2.2 Common Voting Policy Against Capital Increases without a Clear Purpose and Justified Scheme and Price

All asset management companies have a common policy to vote against a capital increase where its purpose is not clearly identified, and where the scheme and price for the capital increase are unjustified.[129] As shown in Figure 16.10, there have been a significant number of negative votes with respect to such proposals at shareholders' meetings. More precisely, based on our hand-collected data, ten out of twenty-two asset management companies have cast negative votes in the case of such proposals.[130] At first blush, this suggests that, to some extent, asset management companies may be engaging as active stewards with respect to this issue.

However, a prominent example of a capital increase by a major listed company which had many asset management companies on its shareholder registry paints a considerably less optimistic picture. In 2018, Bangkok Mass Transit System (BTS) proposed to increase its registered capital.[131] BTS explained that it planned to utilize the additional capital to expand its businesses for itself and its subsidiaries. BTS stated that it would consider investments that would be appropriate and beneficial to its businesses, as well as providing satisfactory returns and creating long-term value for its shareholders.[132] However, it is clear from the minutes of the shareholders' meeting that BTS provided almost no details on the precise purpose of and justification for the capital increase nor any justification for the scheme and price it proposed for raising capital.

Although thirteen asset management companies[133] were significant shareholders of BTS, only two – Phatra and Krung Thai – voted against the proposal. However, in contravention of Principle 5 of the Thai Code, Krung Thai did not provide an explanation for its negative vote.[134] However, Phatra explained its negative vote by pointing out in its proxy report that BTS did not specify the clear objectives of the capital increase. In addition, Phatra noted that the

---

Characteristics of Company Directors and Executives <https://capital.sec.or.th/webapp/nrs/data/7200se.pdf> accessed 3 June 2020.

[129] For examples, see ThanachartFund Eastspring, 'นโยบายการใช้สิทธิออกเสียง (Nyobāy kār chī sīththi xxksēīyng) [Proxy Voting Policy]' <www.thanachartfundeastspring.com/TFUNDWEBV4/infoabout/id_pxvnet.aspx> accessed 3 June 2020; TMB Asset Management, 'นโยบาย การ ใช้ สิทธิ ออก เสียง (Nyobāy kār chī sīththi xxksēīyng) [Proxy Voting Policy]' <www.tmbameastspring.com/about-us/corporate-governance/> accessed 3 June 2020; Krungsri Asset Management Company Limited, 'Proxy Voting Policy' <www.krungsriasset.com/EN/About/RegulationsAndCompliance/CorporateGovernanceReform/Files/KSAM_Proxy_Voting_Policy_website_EN.aspx> accessed 3 June 2020.

[130] Asset Plus, Krungsri, Kasikorn, Krung Thai, MFC, Phatra, SCB, Siam Knight, Thanachart, and UOB.

[131] Bangkok Mass Transit System, 'Minutes of the 2018 Annual General Meeting of Shareholders (Translation)' (2018) <www.btsgroup.co.th/storage/ir/misc/ShareholderMTG/agm-2018/20180806-bts-agm-2018-minutes-en.pdf> accessed 3 June 2020.

[132] ibid.

[133] BBL, Krung Thai, Krungsri, Land & Houses, MFC, One, Phatra, Principal, Thanachart, SCB, Tisco, TMB, and UOB.

[134] Krungthai Asset Management, 'Proxy Voting Report 2018' (2018) <www.ktam.co.th/about-inside.aspx?vALuEId=13> accessed 3 June 2020.

newly issued ordinary shares would be significantly lower than the current market price. Hence, Phatra could not conclusively determine whether the capital increase was beneficial for the shareholders.[135]

Clearly, asset management companies may have legitimate differences of opinion on how they should vote their shares. However, in this case, the almost complete lack of any details from BTS about the reasons for its capital increase or any justification for the below-market pricing of its issuance of shares should have raised red flags among all the asset management companies. This suggests that asset management companies may be neglecting their responsibility to Principle 3 of the Thai Code; to act as professional investors and at least ask questions – if not register negative votes – in such instances.

16.4.2.3 Common Voting Policy Against Dividend Payments That Fail to Correspond with the Investee Companies' Dividend Policy without Reasonable Grounds

All asset management companies have articulated a common policy to vote against dividend payments that fail to correspond with the investee companies' dividend policy, unless a reasonable explanation for such a deviation is provided.[136] However, once again, there is evidence that, although such a general policy exists, asset management companies have not been complying with this policy in practice.

A clear example of this is a case involving Electricity Generating Public Company Limited (EGCO), which is Thailand's largest private electric power company. In 2018, EGCO put forward a resolution at its annual general meeting to pay dividends at 31 per cent in order to maintain its cash flow, which is lower than 40 per cent of the consolidated net profit after taxation as indicated in its dividend policy.[137] This clearly contravened EGCO's dividend policy – but EGCO provided no explanation for its deviation.

Even though eighteen asset management companies were EGCO shareholders, only one (SCB) cast a negative vote. As one would expect, SCB reported in its proxy voting report that it cast negative votes because EGCO's dividend payment contravened its dividend policy and no explanation for the deviation was provided.[138] What is surprising is that the other seventeen asset management companies voted in favour of the dividend payment. This occurred despite these asset management companies having a general policy to vote against dividend payments that fail to correspond with the investee company's dividend policy, unless a reasonable explanation for such a deviation is provided. There were discussions and questions raised about the dividend payment in the minutes of the meeting. Shareholders also pointed out that the company had a huge profit, with no investment projects. Therefore, the company could pay the dividend.[139]

---

[135] Phatra Asset Management, 'Proxy Voting Report 2018' <www.phatraasset.com/Download/qX3KyZNeNu9bA4my4DMswJ37SJ2CCXulsB3h7jkBtx193xrsVx9UAE2CBvP638yCIWbxPSHITUfHr7aGh2LzoXCyw9qoJXEsH9ChCOoJEnIzScA1OoiVoNo1OJ%2F6xZES4XUMrWSI52P7EktErZfsCl9PKdZoY%2B5bwoq4xP4pZsodCIKQFhq44necO5IStyz2FaZcyyam1QiBVgjllAa13H5Sn3WhBsAKANgflma3Ilf9v4ZCGRHYHbjlzzv%2B79XCvVSQGS8kj89cbvGsadcdCSZwd4Xct2V%2F3E9t%2BRoXlt6K%2B6ydcLfi28id7BDJFoIoWS5xPR%2BlB3E.%3D> accessed 3 June 2020.
[136] For examples, see BBL Asset Management (n 123); ONE Asset Management (n 123).
[137] Electricity Generating Public Company Limited, 'Minutes of Shareholders' 2018 Annual General Meeting of Electricity Generating Public Company Limited' (2018) <https://investor.egco.com/misc/shareholderMTG/agm2019/20190314-egco-agm2019-enc01-en.pdf> accessed 3 June 2020.
[138] SCB Asset Management (n 94).
[139] Electricity Generating Public Company Limited (n 137).

Furthermore, EGCO did not inform in its annual general meeting notice that its dividend payment would not be in accordance with the company's dividend policy. On the contrary, it said that it would be in line with the policy, although 31 per cent was clearly indicated.[140] That could be the reason why shareholders, especially asset management companies who usually rely on proxies to vote on their behalf, failed to notice. This non-compliance of asset management companies, as professional investors, seems to indicate their lack of careful consideration of all relevant information, suggesting their non-compliance with Principle 5.1 of the Thai Code.[141]

16.5 CONCLUSION

Thailand's CG Code, which was modelled on the UK's corporate governance code, has generally been seen to have been a great success. At first blush, the introduction of the Thai Code by the SEC may appear to be following in its footsteps. It has attracted numerous signatories and these signatories are producing annual stewardship reports.

However, if one drills down deeper, the situation is more complex. As the Thai Code is entirely voluntary, almost all the signatories are SEC-licensed asset management companies which have been pressured to become signatories by the SEC Disclosure Requirement. Government investment funds have also become signatories, presumably because of the government's aim to make the Thai Code a success. Although the government investment funds are large in terms of the size of the capital they control, their limited investment in listed companies reduces their ability to have an impact on corporate governance. In addition, most private mutual funds have not become signatories. This suggests that the impact of the Thai Code on corporate governance in Thailand may be limited.

The limited impact of the Thai Code is exacerbated by the fact that cumulatively institutional investors normally own small minority shareholder stakes in listed companies. In contrast, most listed companies are controlled either directly or indirectly by wealthy Thai families. In turn, the most important stewards in Thailand are family controllers, which is an issue that is entirely overlooked by the Thai Code. It may make sense to examine how stewardship develops in Singapore, which has a stewardship code focused on family-controlled companies.[142] It may also be wise for Thailand to remain cognizant of how stewardship develops in other Asian countries, with similar Asian-style family-controlled listed companies.

Further, our hand-collected data reveal that although most asset management companies have become signatories of the Thai Code, this is not as significant a development as it may first appear. Although all signatories claim to comply with all the principles in the code, only asset management companies have filed annual stewardship reports. An in-depth analysis reveals that this is currently more of a box-ticking exercise than an actual change in the stewardship behaviour of these signatories.

However, these are still early days for stewardship in Thailand. As our hand-collected data reveal, a few asset management companies appear to be playing an important stewardship role by monitoring their investee companies. The behaviour of these asset management companies, although few, may improve the long-term performance of their

---

[140] ibid.
[141] Thai Code (n 1) 48, Principle 5.1 provides: 'Institutional investors should exercise their voting rights in each Investee Company. Voting decisions should be made after careful consideration of all relevant information ....'
[142] See Puchniak and Tang, Singapore's Embrace of Shareholder Stewardship, Chapter 14, this volume.

investee companies and benefit their ultimate beneficiaries. We hope that this sort of behaviour will become more common and that stewardship will increasingly produce positive results in Thailand. We believe that this is more likely to be the case if Thailand considers expanding its concept of stewardship to include family controllers and provides more incentives for institutional investors not only to become signatories but to take stewardship more responsibly.

17

Shareholder Stewardship in India

The Desiderata

Umakanth Varottil[*]

17.1 INTRODUCTION

Stewardship codes have proliferated around the world during the last decade. It is possible to attribute the driving philosophy behind this phenomenon to the pioneering effort in the form of the UK Stewardship Code.[1] Although there is some variation in the nature and content of these 'UK-style' stewardship codes,[2] they focus on the 'stewardship'[3] role that institutional investors are to play in the governance of companies in which they have invested.[4] In some cases, the codes extend beyond shareholder interests and nudge investors to focus their attention on environmental, social and governance (ESG) matters.[5] Moreover, stewardship codes are essentially 'soft law'.[6]

In this background, the goal of this chapter is to examine whether the UK-style stewardship code, which emanated in circumstances that are specific to the UK, is capable of being transposed to other jurisdictions that experience different corporate structures as well as legal and institutional mechanisms. It does so in the context of India, which has introduced a series of stewardship codes for different types of institutional investor. This chapter advocates against the adoption of UK-style stewardship in India, owing to the specific factors that are at play in that jurisdiction, and instead calls for a *sui generis* approach to stewardship.

---

[*] I thank (i) Amit Tandon for helpful conversations regarding the subject matter of this chapter; (ii) participants at the Global Shareholder Stewardship Conference at King's College, London, 23–24 September 2019, including Chris Hodge, Guy Jubb, Dionysia Katelouzou and Dan Puchniak for comments on a previous version; and (iii) Bhavya Nahar for research assistance. Errors or omissions remain mine alone.

[1] Katelouzou and Puchniak, Global Shareholder Stewardship, Chapter 1; Davies, The UK Stewardship Code 2010–2020, Chapter 2; Lim and Puchniak, Can a Global Legal Misfit Be Fixed?, Chapter 28. The UK has recently reformed its stewardship code; see Financial Reporting Council, *The UK Stewardship Code 2020* (2019) <www.frc.org.uk/getattachment/5aae591d-d9d3-4cf4-814a-d14e156a1d87/Stewardship-Code_Dec-19-Final-Corrected.pdf> accessed 1 July 2020 [hereinafter UK Code 2020]. The dissemination of the UK-style stewardship is based on its predecessor code; see Financial Reporting Council, *The UK Stewardship Code* (September 2012) <www.frc.org.uk/getattachment/d67933f9-ca38-4233-b603-3d24b2f62c5f/UK-Stewardship-Code-(September-2012).pdf> accessed 1 July 2020 [hereinafter UK Code 2012].

[2] For empirical evidence on the uniformity or disparity across all stewardship codes, see Katelouzou and Siems, The Global Diffusion of Stewardship Codes, Chapter 30.

[3] For a detailed understanding of the term, see Katelouzou and Puchniak, Global Shareholder Stewardship, Chapter 1.

[4] Jennifer G Hill, 'Good Activist/Bad Activist: The Rise of International Stewardship Codes' (2018) 41 *Seattle University Law Review* 497, 506–507.

[5] Dionysia Katelouzou, 'Shareholder Stewardship: A Case of (Re)Embedding Institutional Investors and the Corporation?' in Beate Sjåfjell and Christopher M Bruner (eds), *Cambridge Handbook of Corporate Law, Corporate Governance and Sustainability* (CUP 2019) 581, 585.

[6] Gen Goto, 'The Logic and Limits of Stewardship Codes: The Case of Japan' (2018) 15 *Berkeley Business Law Journal* 365, 382–83. While all the codes are essentially soft law, there are some differences among the codes in terms of their levels of coerciveness. See Katelouzou and Sergakis, Shareholder Stewardship Enforcement, Chapter 27.

While the terminology of 'stewardship' is relatively new in the Indian context, the concept itself endured a longer path and has now become well entrenched among institutional investors. From the turn of the century, the Indian government began encouraging various voting methods that enabled shareholders, particularly institutional investors, to be more participative in the decision-making of companies in which they had invested. More recently, various Indian regulators have taken steps that are more concrete. The Insurance Regulatory and Development Authority of India (IRDAI) issued a set of guidelines in 2017 on a stewardship code for insurers in India (IRDAI Code);[7] the Pension Fund Regulatory and Development Authority (PFRDA) issued guidelines in 2018 on a stewardship code for pension funds (PFRDA Code);[8] and the Securities and Exchange Board of India (SEBI) issued a stewardship code in 2019 for mutual funds and alternative investment funds (AIFs) (SEBI Code).[9] These represent an important step, as several large institutional investors have either adopted or are in the process of adopting stewardship codes on terms indicated by their respective regulators.

While there has been a concerted move towards institutional shareholder stewardship in India, it has been a fragmented effort at best. Despite strident calls for a broader stewardship code from SEBI that encompasses all types of institutional shareholder, none has been forthcoming. There is a dire need for a consolidated effort among the Indian regulators in addressing investor stewardship.

As much as some may consider this situation ambiguous and unsatisfactory, it provides a suitable opportunity to engage in a pre-emptive exploration of what an optimal stewardship code might look like for India. This chapter argues that, given the different corporate structures and legal and institutional mechanisms in India, the Indian regulators would do well to deviate from UK-style stewardship in India. To that extent, this chapter echoes the concerns of commentators who note: 'For designing a "stewardship code" for India, although the UK Stewardship Code might be a useful starting point, it would be wrong to transplant the UK Code's principles and supporting guidance without adapting them to the special features of the Indian capital market.'[10] At least three reasons necessitate such a departure from the UK-style approach to stewardship.

First, while the prominence of institutional investors in the UK in the context of companies with dispersed ownership inspired the UK-style stewardship code, the roles and challenges that institutional investors experience in India are considerably different. Indian companies largely display concentrated shareholdings with the dominance of either business families or the state as controlling shareholders.[11] In such a scenario, the influence of the institutional investors, while gradually increasing, may be insufficient to bring about the level of engagement witnessed in companies with dispersed shareholding.

---

[7] Insurance Regulatory and Development Authority of India, 'Guidelines on Stewardship Code for Insurers in India' (Circular, 22 March 2017) <www.irdai.gov.in/ADMINCMS/cms/frmGuidelines_Layout.aspx?page=PageNo3096&flag=1> accessed 1 July 2020, which were revised by the Insurance Regulatory and Development Authority of India, 'Revised Guidelines on Stewardship Code for Insurers in India' (Circular, 7 February 2020) <www.lifeinscouncil.org/component/Revised%20Guidelines%20on%20Stewardship%20Code%20for%20Insurers%20in%20India.pdf> accessed 6 March 2020 [hereinafter IRDAI Code].

[8] Pension Fund Regulatory and Development Authority, 'Common Stewardship Code' (Circular, 4 May 2018) <www.pfrda.org.in/writereaddata/links/circular-%20common%20stewardship%20code%2004-05-186ec9a3b4-566b-4881-b879-c5bf0b9e448a.pdf> accessed 1 July 2020 [hereinafter PFRDA Code].

[9] Securities and Exchange Board of India, 'Stewardship Code for All Mutual Funds and All Categories of AIFs, in Relation to Their Investment in Listed Equities' (Circular, 24 December 2019) <https://ecgi.global/node/7923> accessed 1 July 2020 [hereinafter SEBI Code].

[10] Guy Jubb and Nirmal Mohanty, 'An Indian Stewardship Code: Imperatives and Challenges' (NSE Centre for Excellence in Corporate Governance, Quarterly Briefing No 19, October 2017) 3 <https://archives.nseindia.com/research/content/res_QBOctober17.pdf> accessed 1 July 2020.

[11] This compares with the position in the rest of Asia. See Gen Goto, Alan K Koh and Dan W Puchniak, 'Diversity of Shareholder Stewardship in Asia: Faux Convergence' (2020) 53 *Vanderbilt Journal of Transnational Law* 829.

Second, the goals of stewardship may depend significantly upon whether a jurisdiction's corporate law and governance systems are largely shareholder-oriented or whether they place considerable emphasis on non-shareholder constituencies as well. In the UK, stewardship is essentially a means by which institutional investors ensure sustainable long-term financial returns for their beneficiaries, which thereby broadly benefits society. Jurisdictions such as India, however, go further in imposing considerable stakeholder responsibilities on boards and managements, wherein shareholders (whether institutional or otherwise) are only one among several stakeholders. In such a scenario, an appropriate stewardship regime would help supplement the stakeholder approach of Indian corporate law.

Third, the UK-style approach to stewardship follows a code-based implementation using soft law. This has traditionally functioned in the UK context owing to the specific circumstances that exist in that jurisdiction, including its historical affinity with a code-based approach towards corporate governance and takeovers, among others. However, India has steadfastly relied on hard law in the form of the corporate statute or SEBI regulation as a method of enforcing norms in the corporate sector. The UK-style stewardship code may have crucial limitations in its applicability to the Indian circumstance. The Indian regulators may instead need to consider other approaches, including the imposition of stewardship or engagement duties on specific types of shareholder,[12] which is more in tune with India's corporate regulatory philosophy.

Given the above reasons, among others, this chapter cautions against the wholesale adoption of the UK-style stewardship code in India. Instead, the Indian regulators would do well to introduce a consolidated *sui generis* stewardship model for all institutional investors that would fit with the Indian corporate ownership structure, legal and institutional mechanisms, and corporate culture.

Section 17.2 outlines the evolution of institutional shareholder participation and activism in Indian companies, and discusses the extent of regulatory efforts to facilitate stewardship among such institutional shareholders. Section 17.3 focuses on the specific agency problems prevalent in India in the context of concentrated shareholding, and the inappropriateness of the UK-style stewardship code in that context. It argues that the stewardship concept must extend beyond institutional shareholders and encompass the actions of the controlling shareholders as well. Section 17.4 addresses the question of whether stewardship's orientation towards long-term sustainable value adequately addresses the stakeholder theory of the corporation. While ESG considerations are integral to stewardship, and indeed receive recognition as such, this chapter argues for a greater stakeholder emphasis through shareholder stewardship. Section 17.5 considers whether the soft law approach that underpins the shareholder stewardship movement around the world is apposite for jurisdictions such as India where mandatory rules-based governance has been the norm. It argues that guidelines unaccompanied by legal sanctions for breach are unlikely to have effect, and instead, a movement towards shareholder duties will be more appropriate. Section 17.6 concludes with a call for a consolidated stewardship code for all institutional investors that befits the specific Indian market circumstances.

17.2 SHAREHOLDER ACTIVISM IN INDIA: FRAGMENTED STEWARDSHIP EFFORTS

Before undertaking a critical assessment of shareholder stewardship in India, it is necessary to analyze the evolution of shareholder activism in India and the extent of its success in Indian companies. While institutional shareholders have become considerably active, their

---

[12] See Ernest Lim, *A Case for Shareholders' Fiduciary Duties in Common Law Asia* (CUP 2019); Iris H-Y Chiu and Dionysia Katelouzou, 'From Shareholder Stewardship to Shareholder Duties: Is the Time Ripe?' in Hanne S Birkmose (ed), *Shareholders' Duties* (Kluwer Law International 2017).

impact on the governance of companies continues to suffer from limitations owing to the influence of controlling shareholders. Moreover, while regulators have begun to initiate reforms towards engendering a culture of shareholder stewardship, their efforts are at best fragmented and inchoate.

17.2.1 *Evolution of Institutional Shareholder Activism*

Historically, institutional shareholders in India were rather passive.[13] Several banks, development financial institutions and mutual funds, most of whom were government-owned, held large stakes in Indian companies, but they were never perceived to be independent investors or a threat to management and controlling shareholders. They usually voted along with the controlling shareholders and management. Similarly, foreign investors who held either shares in Indian companies or depository receipts seldom exercised voting rights, except in exceptional circumstances.[14] This position ensued until about a decade ago when regulatory reforms as well as market pressures triggered shareholder activism in Indian companies.

In 2010, India's market regulator, SEBI, took an important step towards stewardship when it issued a circular to mutual funds (as they were within its regulatory purview) requiring them to 'play an active role in ensuring better corporate governance of listed companies'.[15] By imposing disclosure obligations and thereby enhancing transparency, it compelled mutual funds to take a more active and considered role while exercising their voting rights in companies. In parallel, other regulatory reforms provided investors in Indian companies with greater access to their exercise of the corporate franchise. For example, the Companies Act 2013 confirmed the ability of shareholders to engage in e-voting, and to attend shareholders' meetings virtually.[16]

Another significant development is the evolution of a home-grown proxy industry in India, which has come to exert a significant influence on corporate decision-making in Indian companies. Since 2010, three proxy advisory firms have established themselves in India,[17] and they have been extremely active in issuing recommendations regarding corporate proposals pertaining to various listed companies in India.[18] Furthermore, several global proxy advisory firms are active in issuing recommendations in relation to voting in Indian companies, and they have published proxy voting guidelines specific to India.[19] The global proxy advisory firms also hold considerable sway among institutional shareholders, particularly foreign investors.[20]

---

[13] Umakanth Varottil, 'The Advent of Shareholder Activism in India' (2012) 1 *Journal on Governance* 582.
[14] ibid.
[15] Securities and Exchange Board of India, 'Circular for Mutual Funds' (Circular, 15 March 2010) <www.sebi.gov.in/legal/circulars/mar-2010/circular-for-mutual-funds_2019.html> accessed 1 July 2020.
[16] Companies Act 2013, s 108.
[17] They are InGovern (<www.ingovern.com/> accessed 1 July 2020); Institutional Investor Advisory Services (<www.iiasadvisory.com/> accessed 1 July 2020); and Stakeholders Empowerment Services (<www.sesgovernance.com/> accessed 1 July 2020).
[18] For example, Institutional Investor Advisory Services notes on its website that, since its inception in 2010, it has covered more than 6,800 shareholders' meetings in respect of more than 780 companies and issued more than 41,000 voting recommendations (<www.iiasadvisory.com/> accessed 1 July 2020).
[19] Institutional Shareholder Services, 'India Proxy Voting Guidelines: Benchmark Policy Recommendations' (19 November 2019) <www.issgovernance.com/file/policy/active/asiapacific/India-Voting-Guidelines.pdf> accessed 1 July 2020; Glass Lewis, '2019 Proxy Paper Guidelines: An Overview of the Glass Lewis Approach to Proxy Advice – India' (2019) <www.glasslewis.com/wp-content/uploads/2016/12/Guidelines_India.pdf> accessed 1 July 2020.
[20] BQ Desk, 'Two U.S. Advisory Firms Asked Investors to Vote Against Parekh's Reappointment' *BloombergQuint* (31 July 2018) <www.bloombergquint.com/business/agm-voting-pattern-against-deepak-parekh-a-surprise-says-proxy-advisory-firm> accessed 1 July 2020.

TABLE 17.1 *Shareholding pattern of Indian companies*[21]

Shareholder type	March 2008	March 2019
Controlling shareholders (promoters)	58.7%	49.3%
Mutual funds	3.7%	7.6%
Development financial institutions	5.8%	6.3%
Foreign institutional investors	14.5%	20.7%
Total institutional shareholders	24%	34.6%
Corporate bodies	3.7%	5.5%
Individuals	8.2%	8.3%
Others	5.4%	2.3%
Total non-institutional shareholders	17.3%	16.1%

In light of the decade-long regulatory and market developments relating to shareholder activism in India, it is worth considering the growth of institutional shareholding in Indian companies during that period and the influence they exercise over corporate decision-making. Available empirical evidence set out in Table 17.1 indicates a perceptible growth in institutional shareholding and a concomitant reduction in controlling shareholders' stake.

Not only has the quantum of institutional shareholding increased but also the institutions have become more active with regard to their investments. As many as 105 resolutions put forward by company managements were defeated since 2014,[22] a phenomenon hitherto unheard of in the Indian corporate sector. The defeated resolutions include director reappointments, director remuneration, employee stock option plans, related party transactions, and raising of debt or equity.[23] In several other cases, resolutions that company managements proposed scraped through with wafer-thin margins owing to strong opposition by institutional shareholders, thereby causing considerable consternation among managers and controlling shareholders. Anecdotal evidence from certain high-profile transactions, as outlined in Table 17.2, supports the increasingly activist stance of the institutions.

Several other factors aid the efforts of institutional shareholders. First, while the shareholding in Indian companies on average continues to be concentrated, the holdings of several large listed companies have undergone dispersion. They are devoid of controlling shareholders. Well-known examples include Housing Development Finance Corporation (HDFC), ICICI Bank and Larsen & Toubro.[24] Second, as in several other jurisdictions, foreign institutional ownership is on the rise in India.[25] For example, foreign portfolio investors hold just short of 75 per cent in HDFC.[26] This allows outside shareholders to exert pressure on management. Third, even in companies with concentrated shareholding, institutional investors may, in certain cases, have the ability to determine the outcome of certain resolutions to the exclusion of the controlling shareholders. For example, the law on related party transactions, which came up for consideration in the Maruti Suzuki case, requires a 'majority of

---

[21] Institutional Investor Advisory Services, 'The Corporate Governance Landscape in India' (August 2019) 8 <https://docs.wixstatic.com/ugd/09d5d3_0e4114fb614e402c9719ecb28836e9f1.pdf> accessed 1 July 2020.
[22] ibid 5.
[23] ibid.
[24] Mahesh Vyas, 'Beyond Promoter Power' *Financial Express* (2 February 2009) <www.financialexpress.com/archive/beyond-promoter-power/417788/> accessed 1 July 2020.
[25] See the change in shareholding of foreign institutional investors in Table 17.1.
[26] *The Economic Times*, 'Shareholding Pattern – Housing Development Finance Corporation Limited' <https://economictimes.indiatimes.com/housing-development-finance-corporation-ltd/shareholding/companyid-13640.cms> accessed 1 July 2020.

TABLE 17.2 *Specific instances of institutional shareholder activism*

Maruti Suzuki Limited	2014–15	Institutional shareholders such as private sector mutual funds and insurance companies applied pressure on management to rework the terms of a related party transaction before approving it.[27]
Tata Motors Limited	2014–15	The shareholders, on the advice of proxy advisory firms, initially rejected the company's proposals to fix remuneration for top executives. It was only after the company approached the shareholders a second time, with a more detailed explanation, that they received approval.[28]
Raymond Limited	2017	Shareholders overwhelmingly (with a 97.67% vote) rejected a related party transaction involving an undervalued sale of the company's property to its controlling shareholders.[29]
Alembic Pharmaceuticals Limited	2017	In an unusual move, Unifi Capital, a shareholder holding about 3% shares in the company, mustered the support of nearly 1,000 'small shareholders' to seek board representation.[30] However, the company rejected Unifi's proposal on the ground that the small shareholders had a relationship with Unifi.[31]
HDFC	2018	The reappointment of the chairperson as a director passed with 77.36%, more than the 75% required for the purpose. A large number of institutional investors voted against the resolution on the grounds that the director was on too many boards and that the board of the company was not independent enough.[32]

the minority' voting in approving material transactions wherein the promoters are deprived of voting rights on that decision.[33] Here again, outside shareholders such as institutional investors may wield considerable influence – that, too, in controller-owned companies. Such a paradigm shift in share ownership patterns, at least in large listed companies, alters the rules of the governance game.

The available empirical and anecdotal evidence indicate a clear trend whereby institutional shareholders (domestic and foreign ones alike) are no longer passive but participate extensively in corporate decision-making. Although some of the anecdotal instances listed in Table 17.2 (such as Maruti Suzuki and Alembic Pharmaceuticals) display trends of active engagement by institutional shareholders in the management of companies, which goes beyond simple exercising of

[27] PTI, 'Maruti-Suzuki Deal: Institutional Investors Approach Sebi' *Business Today* (New Delhi, 13 March 2014) <www.businesstoday.in/sectors/auto/maruti-suzuki-deal-institutional-investors-approach-sebi/story/204263.html> accessed 1 July 2020; Amrit Raj, 'Maruti Wins Shareholder Nod for Gujarat Plant Pact' *Mint* (New Delhi, 18 December 2015) <www.livemint.com/Industry/3O9dTsO854DKXvKN1W1dbO/Marutis-shareholders-allow-Suzuki-to-own-upcoming-Gujarat-p.html> accessed 1 July 2020.
[28] Shally Seth Mohile, 'Tata Motors Shareholders Approve Remuneration Proposals' *Mint* (Mumbai, 22 January 2015) <www.livemint.com/Companies/5fEvOZQ62mL9zPciAwBAbJ/Tata-Motors-shareholders-approve-remuneration-proposals.html> accessed 1 July 2020.
[29] Moneylife Digital Team, '2017 Becomes Tipping Point of Shareholder Activism in India: Report' *Moneylife* (28 November 2017) <www.moneylife.in/article/2017-becomes-tipping-point-of-shareholder-activism-in-india-report/52297.html> accessed 1 July 2020.
[30] Sohini Das and Sudipto Dey, 'Drama in Alembic Board Room as Minority Shareholders Rise' *Business Standard* (Ahmedabad, 24 July 2017) <www.business-standard.com/article/companies/drama-in-alembic-board-room-as-minority-shareholders-rise-117072400477_1.html> accessed 1 July 2020.
[31] Reeba Zachariah, 'Board Seat: Alembic Junks Small Shareholder Plea' *The Times of India* (Mumbai, 29 July 2017) <https://timesofindia.indiatimes.com/business/india-business/board-seat-alembic-junks-small-shareholder-plea/articleshow/59815348.cms> accessed 1 July 2020.
[32] Shilpy Sinha, 'Being on Boards of Eight Other Companies Went Against Deepak Parekh at HDFC Vote' *The Economic Times* (Mumbai, 1 August 2018) <https://economictimes.indiatimes.com/industry/banking/finance/banking/being-on-boards-of-eight-other-companies-went-against-deepak-parekh-at-hdfc-vote/articleshow/65221240.cms?from=mdr> accessed 1 July 2020.
[33] Companies Act 2013, s 188(1).

voting rights, more specific empirical evidence regarding such engagement is hard to come by as it takes place behind closed doors. This chapter now turns to examine the manner and extent to which the regulatory regime surrounding shareholder stewardship has evolved in India.

17.2.2 *Stewardship Efforts in India*

Although regulatory efforts in India over the last decade catered for greater participation and activism among shareholders, the need for a specific stewardship code became evident only more recently. In 2016, the Financial Stability and Development Council (FSDC), a body that co-ordinates various regulators in the financial sector, expressed the need for such a code in India.[34] FSDC in turn formed a committee with representatives from SEBI, IRDAI and PFRDA to consider the introduction of a stewardship code in India. While reports indicate that the committee has already made its recommendations to FSDC, FSDC has yet to approve an umbrella stewardship code for Indian companies and their institutional investors.[35]

A plethora of committees and working groups have, in the meanwhile, strongly recommended that SEBI issue a uniform stewardship code for India's capital markets. The influence of the UK Stewardship Code is unmistakeable in the process. In November 2016, the India–UK Financial Partnership recommended that the Indian regulators adopt an 'Indian Stewardship Code', which 'will strengthen the ability of Indian shareholders to perform their fiduciary duties, improve the relationship between the boards of Indian companies and their shareholders and help foster shareholder loyalty'.[36] Although this effort did not recommend the text or contents of an Indian stewardship code, the UK Stewardship Code, and the experience thereunder, evidently underpin the rationale for such a code.[37]

Similarly, an influential 2017 report on corporate governance issued by a SEBI-appointed committee recommended that 'a common stewardship code be introduced in India for the entire financial sector ... by SEBI for investments by institutional investors in Indian capital markets' on the lines of codes followed in several countries such as the UK, Japan and Malaysia.[38] A more recent working group report looking into the regulation of proxy advisers noted that 'SEBI should make a Stewardship Code (like the UK Stewardship Code) mandatory for all institutional shareholders, and such code should be publicly available. This should be on a comply or explain basis.'[39] Despite repeated calls for a stewardship code that encompasses institutional investors in the Indian securities markets, a comprehensive code has not yet been forthcoming.

Curiously enough, while SEBI had been actively considering a code for institutional investors in the Indian capital markets, two other regulators that oversee significant types of institutional investor, namely insurance companies and pension funds, went ahead and released versions of stewardship codes that apply to these respective investors. While these efforts may be welcome in

---

[34] Jubb and Mohanty (n 10) 3.
[35] ibid.
[36] Guy Jubb and others, 'India-UK Financial Partnership: Responsible Shareholder Engagement an Indian Stewardship Code' (November 2016) <www.thecityuk.com/assets/2016/Reports-PDF/fffe02d39f/IUKFP-Responsible-Shareholder-2016.pdf> accessed 1 July 2020.
[37] ibid.
[38] Securities and Exchange Board of India, 'Report of the Committee on Corporate Governance' (Committee Report, 5 October 2017) <www.sebi.gov.in/reports/reports/oct-2017/report-of-the-committee-on-corporate-governance_36177.html> accessed 1 July 2020.
[39] Securities and Exchange Board of India, 'Working Group's Report on Issues Concerning Proxy Advisors' (Report, July 2019) <www.sebi.gov.in/reports/reports/jul-2019/report-of-working-group-on-issues-concerning-proxy-advisors-seeking-public-comments_43710.html> accessed 1 July 2020.

rendering express recognition of stewardship in the Indian capital markets, these efforts pushed India into a rather unintended path of utter fragmentation in stewardship efforts, which will arguably result in adverse outcomes in comparison with a unified approach among Indian regulators to the idea of shareholder stewardship.

In March 2017, IRDAI issued a set of guidelines on a stewardship code for insurance companies in India.[40] Insurers are required to adopt specific stewardship policies based on these guidelines.[41] Since then, at least twenty-five insurers have issued their stewardship policies based on the IRDAI Code.[42] Similarly, in 2018, PFRDA issued its own common stewardship code that all pension funds are required to follow.[43] In these circumstances, with the likelihood of a consolidated stewardship code for institutional investors in India beginning to look bleak, SEBI issued its own code applicable to mutual funds and AIFs, effective from 1 April 2020.[44]

At a broad level, there are similarities in the approaches adopted by IRDAI, PFRDA and SEBI. In addition, it is inevitable to note the similarities with the UK Stewardship Code, which demonstrates the strong influence of the UK-style approach among the Indian regulators.[45] Although the UK Stewardship Code has undergone reform,[46] the stewardship codes prescribed by the Indian financial regulators continue to track the previous UK Stewardship Code from 2012.[47]

As Table 17.3 indicates, the principles enshrined in the stewardship codes of PFRDA and SEBI are identical, while there are some differences in the IRDAI Code. Although the IRDAI Code originally announced in 2017 displayed differences in some substantive aspects from the PFRDA and SEBI Codes, the revised IRDAI Code issued in February 2020 minimizes those differences and brings about a convergence among the three codes.

Although all three codes appear to introduce a great deal of stringency in ensuring compliance, they lack a concrete enforcement mechanism.[48] It is yet unclear what consequences will visit upon an institutional investor who fails to comply with their stewardship codes. Arguably, the codes remain mandatory in intent, but will fail to translate that into action unless they are accompanied by detailed enforcement mechanisms. The ambiguity in the implementation of the various stewardship codes and the possible variation in the approaches that the respective regulators may adopt exacerbate the drawbacks of the fragmented stewardship approach followed in India.

Overall, the evolution of stewardship codes in India represents a rather unusual, unexpected and arguably undesirable trajectory of events. A process that was initially meant, through the efforts of the FSDC, to materialize in the form of a consolidated stewardship code that encompasses all types of institutional investor to be regulated by SEBI as the capital market regulator has wound up in a trifurcated approach.[49] Depending on the nature of the investors, they are subject to a different set of stewardship guidelines to be implemented by varied regulators, a phenomenon that is bound to result in incongruities.

---

[40] IRDAI Code (n 7), which was revised in February 2020.
[41] ibid.
[42] Information on file with the author.
[43] PFRDA Code (n 8).
[44] SEBI Code (n 9).
[45] Supporting evidence for this can also be found in Katelouzou and Siems, The Global Diffusion of Stewardship Codes, Chapter 30.
[46] UK Code 2020 (n 1).
[47] UK Code 2012 (n 1).
[48] For a more detailed discussion on matters of enforcement, see Katelouzou and Sergakis, Shareholder Stewardship Enforcement, Chapter 27.
[49] A jurisdiction that follows a bifurcated approach is Australia, which has two codes, one for asset owners and another for asset managers: Bowley and Hill, Stewardship and Collective Action, Chapter 19.

TABLE 17.3 *Comparison of the stewardship codes of the IDRAI, the PFRDA and SEBI*

	IRDAI Code	PFRDA Code & SEBI Code	UK Code 2012
Principle 1	Insurers should formulate a policy on the discharge of their stewardship responsibilities and publicly disclose it.	Institutional investors should formulate a comprehensive policy on the discharge of their stewardship responsibilities, publicly disclose it, review and update it periodically.	Institutional investors should publicly disclose their policy on how they will discharge stewardship responsibilities.
Principle 2	Insurers should have a clear policy on how they manage conflicts of interest in fulfilling their stewardship responsibilities and publicly disclose it.	Institutional investors should have a clear policy on how they manage conflicts of interests in fulfilling their stewardship responsibilities and publicly disclose it.	Institutional investors should have a robust policy on managing conflicts of interest in relation to stewardship, which should be publicly disclosed.
Principle 3	Insurers should monitor their investee companies.	Institutional investors should monitor their investee companies.	Institutional investors should monitor their investee companies.
Principle 4	Insurers should have a clear policy on intervention in their investee companies.	Institutional investors should have a clear policy on intervention in their investee companies. Institutional investors should also have a clear policy for collaboration with other institutional investors, where required, to preserve the interests of the ultimate investors, which should be disclosed [sic].[50]	Institutional investors should establish clear guidelines on when and how they will escalate their stewardship activities.
Principle 5	Insurers should have a clear policy for collaboration with other institutional investors, where required, to preserve the interests of the policyholders (ultimate investors), which should be disclosed [sic].	Institutional investors should have a clear policy on voting and disclosure of voting activity.	Institutional investors should be willing to act collectively with other investors where appropriate.
Principle 6	Insurers should have a clear policy on voting and disclosure of voting activity.	Institutional investors should report periodically on their stewardship activities.	Institutional investors should have a clear policy on voting and disclosure of voting activity.
Principle 7	Insurers should report periodically on their stewardship activities.		Institutional investors should report periodically on their stewardship and voting activities.

The remainder of this chapter adopts a critical analysis of the existing stewardship efforts and seeks to adopt a normative approach by proposing the key aspects that the Indian regulators, in particular SEBI, must consider in evolving a consolidated and uniform stewardship code that

---

[50] Note that the PFRDA Code (n 8) and the SEBI Code (n 9) have combined Principles 4 and 5 of the IRDAI Code (n 7) and the UK Code 2012 (n 1). Hence, the serial numbers of the principles thereafter do not match.

applies to all institutional investors in the Indian market. The chapter argues that the present trifurcated dispensation cannot be an end in itself, and must only be a transitory mechanism towards a consolidated approach. The regulators, under the aegis of the FSDC, must continue to formulate a code that uniformly applies to all types of institutional investor. To re-emphasize, this chapter also adopts the strong position that the Indian regulators must adapt any such stewardship code to the specifics of the Indian market and legal system, and must avoid relying excessively on a UK-style stewardship code.

17.3 SHAREHOLDING STRUCTURE: THE ROLE OF INSTITUTIONAL INVESTORS

The UK has been a supplier of voluntary codes that operate as 'soft law' in several areas affecting the governance and ownership of companies. For instance, the Cadbury Code popularized the use of corporate governance codes in a number of countries around the world.[51] While the Cadbury Code and subsequent corporate governance codes have evolved in the background of the dispersed ownership of shares in the UK and the continued influence of institutional shareholders, such a concept has found its place in other jurisdictions with considerably divergent share ownership structures. The recipient countries are generally dominated by companies with concentrated shareholding and with varying legal systems and institutional structures. While convergence advocates argue that such efforts are symptomatic of a common framework in corporate governance,[52] others counter that path-dependent tendencies would prevent a full convergence.[53]

A similar phenomenon arises in the context of stewardship codes as well. The UK-style stewardship code evolved in the backdrop of dispersed shareholding that is replete with agency problems between managers and shareholders.[54] Thus, the exertion of greater participation and engagement by institutional shareholders against managements of investee companies is altogether understandable. The dominance of institutional shareholders in the UK context is what drives the stewardship idea.[55] In such circumstances, the stewardship role that institutional investors play will likely have an impact on corporate governance in the investee companies, and thereby enable such investors to enhance the corporate returns to their beneficiaries.

The dissemination of such a UK-style stewardship code to countries that carry considerably different ownership structures (i.e., mainly concentrated shareholdings) is bound to give rise to incongruities in the implementation of such codes. One commentator has noted that 'the chances of a stewardship code increasing ownership behaviour in any particular jurisdiction will be partly dependent on the structure and legal framework of the local investment market and the power of the different market players'.[56] Similarly, another commentator has observed that 'it may very well be the case that the true intention behind adopting a stewardship code in a jurisdiction could be highly contextual and contingent upon jurisdiction-specific factors'.[57]

---

[51] Francesca Cuomo, Christine Mallin and Alessandro Zattoni, 'Corporate Governance Codes: A Review and Research Agenda' (May 2016) 24 *Corporate Governance* 222.
[52] Henry Hansmann and Reinier Kraakman, 'The End of History for Corporate Law' (2001) 89 *Georgetown Law Journal* 439.
[53] Lucian Bebchuk and Mark Roe, 'A Theory of Path Dependence in Corporate Ownership and Governance' (1999) 52 *Stanford Law Review* 127.
[54] Brian R Cheffins, 'The Stewardship Code's Achilles' Heel' (2010) 73 *Modern Law Review* 1004, 1011–13.
[55] ibid.
[56] Alice Klettner, 'The Impact of Stewardship Codes on Corporate Governance and Sustainability' (December 2017) 6 <www.researchgate.net/profile/Alice_Klettner/publication/325358712_The_Impact_of_Stewardship_Codes_on_Corporate_Governance/links/5b07850060f7e9b1ed7f1e6a2/The-Impact-of-Stewardship-Codes-on-Corporate-Governance.pdf> accessed 1 July 2020.
[57] Goto (n 6) 369. See also Goto, Koh and Puchniak (n 11).

While the UK-style stewardship code has largely emanated in the shadow of the agency problems between managers and shareholders, it is yet unclear whether, and to what extent, such a measure is suitable to address the agency problems between controller and the minority in jurisdictions such as India, where concentrated shareholding is the norm.

Despite the gradual rise in shareholder activism and institutional stewardship efforts in India, the role of institutional shareholders is likely to be substantially limited in view of the dominant role that controlling shareholders play in Indian listed companies. To that extent, the scenario that operates in India is entirely different from that in the UK. In jurisdictions such as India, shareholder activism may have a different effect on companies with controlling shareholders as opposed to those without. For example, in companies without controlling shareholders, the influence of the activist shareholders and increasing participation and engagement by institutional shareholders may have a direct bearing on the outcome of proposals made by management. On the other hand, where controlling shareholders are influential, it is unlikely that efforts on the part of regulators to enhance shareholder participation and engagement through stewardship measures will have the same beneficial effect as in companies with dispersed shareholding. The diffusion of UK-style stewardship codes across various shareholding structures overlooks this material difference.

In economies such as India, activist investors would be hard-pressed to alter the outcome of decisions made at shareholders' meetings owing to the influence of controlling shareholders. Even though the number of resolutions where institutional shareholders have made a difference is increasing gradually,[58] it still represents a miniscule proportion of all resolutions put to the vote by Indian publicly listed companies. Moreover, despite the overall growth of institutional shareholding in Indian companies and the decline in controllers' shareholding, critics have argued that the role of institutional shareholders is useful only in theory, and that efforts towards shareholder activism are unlikely to have any significant impact on corporate governance in India, primarily owing to continued concentration in shareholdings.[59] Hence, the effect of shareholder activism in Indian companies is likely to be minimal at best.

The constraints imposed on the transportability of a UK-style stewardship code to other jurisdictions such as India raise several crucial questions. Does the UK-style definition and understanding of the concept of shareholder stewardship apply equally to jurisdictions with concentrated shareholding? Does the identity or image of the 'steward' remain the same across various jurisdictions? The remainder of this section argues that the question of the identity of stewards must necessarily vary across jurisdictions, and that the conventional UK-style approach of treating predominantly institutional shareholders as stewards requires careful reconsideration. Accordingly, the concept of stewardship requires a paradigm shift, and must extend beyond institutional shareholders and to controlling shareholders as well in jurisdictions such as India, which are replete with companies that have concentrated shareholding. In such companies, undue focus on institutional shareholders will yield much less results than in companies with dispersed shareholding.

At the outset, the UK-style approach defines stewardship from a narrow perspective, encompassing only institutional shareholders. For example, the UK regulator defines stewardship as 'the responsible allocation and management of capital across the institutional investment community, to create sustainable value for beneficiaries, the economy and society'.[60] The

---

[58] See n 22 and accompanying text.
[59] George S Geis, 'Can Independent Blockholding Really Play Much of a Role in Indian Corporate Governance?' (2007) 3 *Corporate Governance Law Review* 283.
[60] Financial Conduct Authority/Financial Reporting Council, 'Building a Regulatory Framework for Effective Stewardship' (Discussion Paper, January 2019) 11 <www.fca.org.uk/publication/discussion/dp19-01.pdf> accessed 1 July 2020.

academic community, too, tends to adopt a similar definition and scope that is limited to the stewardship of institutional shareholders.[61] While such a compass is appropriate for jurisdictions with dispersed shareholding, it covers an extremely narrow domain in jurisdictions with concentrated shareholding such as India. A pure focus on institutional shareholders tends to be rather myopic. As Professor Geis notes:[62]

> Ultimately, however, Indian corporate insiders simply own too many shares to worry about activist institutional investors. Any near-term regulatory reliance on outside shareholder power as a strategy for sound governance is likely to disappoint. This does not necessarily mean that efforts to give independent shareholders a greater role in firm governance should be abandoned. But near-term priorities for regulatory reform should likely focus on protecting minority shareholders from the threat of controller opportunism – and not on strategies that rely on the flexed muscles of the outside owners.

In such a scenario, the concept of stewardship must extend not only to institutional shareholders but also to the controlling shareholders. Such a broader stewardship theory finds its place in family-owned businesses, where 'the goal orientation that is manifest in stewardship behaviours emphasizes a commitment to the continuity and longevity of the company and its stakeholders'.[63] This is somewhat consistent with the UK-style stewardship code's endeavour to address the problems of short-termism by focusing on sustainable value of the companies.[64] In such circumstances, stewardship is a collective concept embodied in the relationship between the controlling shareholders and the outside institutional shareholders. They adopt a collective responsibility not just for the sustainable growth of the company but also to act in the interests of all stakeholders.[65]

In countries such as India, controlling shareholders are either business families or the state. When it comes to business families, the concept of stewardship applies squarely to those companies given the multi-generational considerations involved.[66] Family owners' stewardship is a measure of their need for the company's continued success in the long term.[67] Some attribute the performance of family firms to the fact that 'the family understands the business and that involved family members view themselves as the stewards of the firm'.[68] In addition, such an approach 'is conducive to corporate longevity and favourable relations with stakeholders'.[69] The expansive stewardship approach that encompasses family owners is consistent with the broader outlook towards stakeholders and not limited to protecting the interests of beneficiaries of institutional investors under the narrow conception of the UK-style stewardship.

---

[61] See e.g. Iris H-Y Chiu, 'Institutional Shareholders as Stewards: Toward a New Conception of Corporate Governance' (2012) 6 *Brooklyn Journal of Corporate, Financial & Commercial Law* 387, 387; Goto (n 6) 368.

[62] George S Geis, 'Shareholder Power in India' in Jennifer G Hill and Randall S Thomas (eds), *Research Handbook on Shareholder Power* (Edward Elgar 2015) 607.

[63] Morela Hernandez, 'Toward an Understanding of the Psychology of Stewardship' (April 2012) 37 *The Academy of Management Review* 172, 176.

[64] Arad Reisberg, 'The UK Stewardship Code: On the Road to Nowhere?' (2015) 15 *Journal of Corporate Law Studies* 217, 246.

[65] The aspect of stakeholder responsibility is addressed in Section 17.4.

[66] Tarun Khanna and Yishay Yafeh, 'Business Groups and Risk Sharing around the World' (January 2005) 78 *The Journal of Business* 301, 340.

[67] Danny Miller, Isabelle Le Breton-Miller and Barry Scholnick, 'Stewardship vs. Stagnation: An Empirical Comparison of Small Family and Non-Family Business' (2008) 45 *Journal of Management Studies* 51, 51; Loraine M Uhlaner, Roberto H Floren and Jurgen R Geerlings, 'Owner Commitment and Relational Governance in the Privately-Held Firm: An Empirical Study' (2007) 29 *Small Business Economics* 275, 275.

[68] Ronald C Anderson and David M Reeb, 'Founding-Family Ownership and Firm Performance: Evidence from the S&P 500' (2003) 58 *The Journal of Finance* 1301, 1324.

[69] Miller, Le Breton-Miller and Scholnick (n 67) 73.

This idea of extending the concept of shareholder stewardship beyond institutional investors is not an obscure one confined to academic soul-searching. In fact, in Singapore, the relevant body, that is, Stewardship Asia, has already published a set of stewardship principles applicable to family businesses.[70] According to these principles, 'stewardship encapsulates the essence of responsible and meaningful value creation in a sustainable way to benefit stakeholders, as well as the larger community that they are part of. It underscores the importance of an ownership mindset, a long-term perspective and an inclusive approach.'[71] Such a stewardship approach considers the family controllers as stewards, and introduces an altogether different lens through which one can view corporate governance in family-owned firms.[72]

It is eminently feasible to extend such a broader stewardship concept to the state as a controlling shareholder in state-owned enterprises (SOEs) listed on the stock exchanges. The government may be less inclined to tunnel financial wealth from SOEs in which it has invested, but it runs the risk of managing the SOEs to gain political capital.[73] In such circumstances, the extension of the wider stewardship concept to SOEs will be beneficial.

In concluding this section, it is clear that the UK-style stewardship code, which emanated in the context of dispersed shareholding and the significant influence of institutional investors, cannot find its way into jurisdictions such as India where concentrated shareholding is the norm. Institutional investor participation and engagement is likely to have limited impact in India. However, there is considerable merit in extending the concept of stewardship beyond institutional shareholders, and to controlling shareholders such as business families and the state, which requires a paradigm shift in the stewardship discourse.

17.4 STAKEHOLDER CONSIDERATIONS

The goals of stewardship may differ across jurisdictions, depending upon the orientation of each jurisdiction's corporate law and governance along the shareholder–stakeholder spectrum, although issues of corporate sustainability and social responsibility have begun to take strong hold within the idea of stewardship around the world.[74] Given the distinctions in the goals and objectives of corporate governance, and thereby stewardship in different jurisdictions, the diffusion of the UK-style stewardship principles to jurisdictions such as India, which adopt a different orientation in the shareholder–stakeholder debate, could portend unintended consequences.

UK corporate law and governance embodies the enlightened shareholder value (ESV) principle,[75] which takes the position that the ultimate objective of company law – to generate maximum shareholder value – is also the best means of securing protection of all interests, and thereby overall prosperity and welfare.[76] The law reforms that led to this position expressly

---

[70] Stewardship Asia Centre, *Stewardship Principles for Family Businesses* (2018) <www.stewardshipasia.com.sg/sites/default/files/2020-09/SPFB-brochure-0913.pdf> accessed 19 May 2021.
[71] ibid 1.
[72] For a detailed discussion of stewardship of family businesses in Singapore, see Puchniak and Tang, Singapore's Embrace of Shareholder Stewardship, Chapter 14 and Dan W Puchniak and Samantha Tang, 'Singapore's Puzzling Embrace of Shareholder Stewardship: A Successful Secret' (2020) 53 *Vanderbilt Journal of Transnational Law* 989.
[73] Curtis J Milhaupt and Mariana Pargendler, 'Related Party Transactions in State-Owned Enterprises' in Luca Enriques and Tobias Tröger (eds), *The Law and Finance of Related Party Transactions* (CUP 2019); Mariana Pargendler, 'State Ownership and Corporate Governance' (2012) 80 *Fordham Law Review* 2917.
[74] Katelouzou (n 5).
[75] Companies Act 2006, s 172.
[76] Deryn Fisher, 'The Enlightened Shareholder – Leaving Stakeholders in the Dark: Will Section 172(1) of the Companies Act 2006 Make Directors Consider the Impact of Their Decisions on Third Parties?' (2009) 20

rejected the stakeholder theory embedded in the pluralist approach, whereby the company is to serve a wider range of stakeholder interests, without subordination to the need for achieving shareholder value. More recent reforms in the UK re-emphasize the importance of the ESV approach, and introduce greater recognition of stakeholder interests and engagement.[77] Nevertheless, even with these reforms, the underlying idea remains embedded in the ESV approach, and does not embrace the broader pluralist ideas.

Conversely, the stakeholder approach has remained the foundation of corporate law in India, and has received even greater statutory and regulatory attention in recent years. For example, Indian company law has preferred to adopt the pluralist approach, by providing recognition to both stakeholders and shareholders, without necessarily indicating a preference towards either.[78] Moreover, the Indian Parliament has gone much further to legislate the concept of corporate social responsibility (CSR),[79] thereby moving the needle considerably towards a stakeholder approach to corporate law and governance. This fundamental difference in the philosophy of corporate governance needs to find a crucial place in the discourse on stewardship.

Focusing specifically on stewardship, the concept arose in the UK on the back of the global financial crisis, which generated calls for greater shareholder engagement.[80] Stewardship was intended to address the malaise of short-termism that had afflicted the companies engulfed in the crisis. The concept therefore sought to motivate shareholders, essentially being institutional investors, to engage in a long-term focus on their investments in companies. The concept of sustainability came to be equated largely with financial sustainability, although the concomitant benefits of such an approach to the broader gamut of stakeholders and positive societal impact cannot be ignored.

As one scholar notes, in the UK, 'the goal of a stewardship code is to advance the public interest by restraining excessive risk-taking and investor short-termism'.[81] In such an approach, the focus is on the beneficiaries of the institutional investors: if institutional stewardship is able to generate optimal long-term results to the beneficiaries, the argument goes that it will lead to greater societal benefit.[82] In such a construct, institutional investors as stewards have an interest in ensuring that companies perform in a financially sustainable manner in the long term so that they are consistent with the expectations and interests of the beneficiaries of such institutional investors. Such an approach remains akin to the ESV model rather than a broader stakeholder approach.[83]

The latest round of stewardship reforms in the UK recognizes the intersection between stewardship and sustainable investing and, more specifically, ESG matters.[84] While this represents a material shift in the UK position, the recognition of ESG considerations is still entrenched in the

---

International Company and Commercial Law Review 10; Andrew Keay, 'Tackling the Issue of the Corporate Objective: An Analysis of the United Kingdom's "Enlightened Shareholder Value Approach"' (2007) 29 *Sydney Law Review* 577; Virginia Harper Ho, '"Enlightened Shareholder Value": Corporate Governance Beyond the Shareholder-Stakeholder Divide' (2010) 36 *Journal of Corporation Law* 59.

[77] Financial Reporting Council, *The UK Corporate Governance Code* (July 2018) <www.frc.org.uk/getattachment/88bd8c45-50ea-4841-95b0-d2f4f48069a2/2018-UK-Corporate-Governance-Code-FINAL.pdf> accessed 1 July 2020, applicable from 1 January 2019.
[78] Companies Act 2013, s 166(2).
[79] ibid, s 135.
[80] Cheffins (n 54) 1005.
[81] Goto (n 6) 398.
[82] Chiu (n 61) 396.
[83] ibid 398.
[84] UK Code 2020 (n 1) Principle 7 (for asset owners and asset managers).

financial impact of the investment over time.[85] It does not embrace the stakeholder theory in a pluralistic paradigm.

The transplant of such a UK-style approach that provides for the broader public interest of the beneficiaries, and one that steeps itself in the ESV model of corporate governance with its emphasis on ESG considerations in that light, is nevertheless inadequate to blend in with the pluralistic approach towards stakeholders in India. Even the reformed UK position arguably does not comport well within the Indian circumstances.

First, the three stewardship codes in India adopt the same approach as in the UK, without having any regard whatsoever to the philosophical variations in the stakeholder orientations in the two jurisdictions. For example, the IRDAI Code focuses on insurers 'as custodians of policyholders' funds', and sees stewardship as a means to 'improve the return on investments of insurers which will ultimately benefit the policyholders'.[86] Similarly, PFRDA views stewardship as being 'intended to protect the subscribers' pension wealth' and considers that corporate governance in the investee companies must give 'a greater fillip to the protection of the interests of the subscribers in such companies'.[87] Even SEBI intends for institutional investors to engage in stewardship 'to protect their clients' wealth' and 'as an important step towards improved corporate governance'.[88] Again, in these cases, the objectives of stewardship are to protect the interests of the respective beneficiaries, namely insurance policyholders, pension subscribers and mutual fund unit-holders. Although the codes allude to the need for investors to engage with companies on ESG opportunities or risks, they lack the requisite detail for meaningful implementation.

Second, the stakeholder approach in India imposes obligations on the boards of companies to 'act in good faith in order to promote the objects of the company for the benefit of its members as a whole, and in the best interests of the company, its employees, the shareholders, the community and for the protection of the environment'.[89] Similarly, the provisions relating to CSR focus on the boards of companies, requiring them to constitute a committee to examine the issues, formulate a policy and undertake CSR spending to the extent prescribed by law.[90] Furthermore, through its business responsibility reporting requirements, SEBI nudges companies to act in a sustainable manner. The combined effect of these measures is that the boards and managements of Indian companies bear stakeholder and social responsibility. On the other hand, not only are shareholders devoid of any such responsibilities but the stewardship codes emanating in India expressly seem to be driven by the need to protect the long-term interests of the beneficiaries of various types of financial investor. While it is generally the case that the long-term interests of the beneficiaries would be consistent with the sustainability interests of the company under the stakeholder theory, the current dispensation does not provide clear guidance towards the resolution of potential conflicts between these interests, were they to arise.

Third, and extending from the previous point, the introduction of the UK-style stewardship code in jurisdictions such as India undermines the pluralistic stakeholder approach. While the

---

[85] Financial Conduct Authority/Financial Reporting Council (n 60) 15. See also Alice Klettner, 'Stewardship Codes and the Pursuit of Corporate Sustainability' (January 2018) 18 <www.latrobe.edu.au/__data/assets/pdf_file/0005/855338/Klettner,-A-Stewardship-codes-and-the-pursuit-of-corporate-sustainability.pdf> accessed 1 July 2020.
[86] IRDAI Code (n 7) introductory letter.
[87] PFRDA Code (n 8) introductory letter.
[88] SEBI Code (n 9) introductory letter para 1.
[89] Companies Act 2013, s 166(2). For a comparison between this and s 172 of the UK Companies Act 2006, see Mihir Naniwadekar and Umakanth Varottil, 'The Stakeholder Approach towards Directors' Duties under Indian Company Law: A Comparative Analysis' in Mahendra Pal Singh (ed), *The Indian Yearbook of Comparative Law* 2016 (OUP 2016).
[90] Companies Act 2013, s 135.

regime expects boards to be stakeholder-focused, the stewardship codes expect institutional shareholders to be focused on the long-term interests of their beneficiaries. As Professor Chiu notes: 'It could be argued that the Stewardship Code mistakenly concentrates monitoring in the hands of shareholders, where other stakeholders may have greater incentive to monitor, thereby unnecessarily relegating the importance of other stakeholders.'[91]

Fourth, and lastly, a well-designed stewardship regime could help address some of the concerns emanating from the structure of the stakeholder approach in Indian corporate law and governance. One of the primary criticisms of the stakeholder approach towards directors' duties under Indian corporate law is that there is a lack of clarity as to whether non-shareholder constituencies can exercise any direct remedies or enforcement mechanisms in case of breaches of directors' duties to take into account stakeholder interests.[92] To that extent, despite the superficial difference between the ESV approach in the UK and the pluralist approach in India, the lack of stakeholder remedies and enforcement mechanisms makes the Indian regime similar to that of the UK. An appropriate stewardship regime that enables shareholders, who enjoy remedies such as shareholder derivative actions and shareholder class actions, could potentially use those tools to benefit broader stakeholder interests. It can thereby fill the gap in enforcement that the stakeholder regime in India presently suffers from.

In considering the shareholder–stakeholder aspects of corporate governance, as this section demonstrates, the transplant of the UK-style stewardship code into India without necessary adaptations will result in an avoidable mismatch of philosophies.

17.5 IMPLEMENTATION OF STEWARDSHIP

When it comes to implementing the concept of stewardship, the UK initially adopted the 'comply-or-explain' approach, whereby parties subject to the stewardship code could choose to either comply or disclose the reasons why they failed to comply.[93] While this was entirely understandable in the UK context, the transposition of this model to other jurisdictions that have different corporate structures, legal and institutional structures, and business culture is altogether surprising. Moreover, when there are doubts about the robustness of implementation of the code in the UK, the issues are likely to be magnified further in other jurisdictions. As noted in this section, the use of a soft law approach to stewardship in the Indian context militates against the regulatory framework in India and its legal culture. It is bound to raise significant implementation problems.[94] Also worth noting is that the UK stewardship regime itself has moved away from the traditional comply-or-explain approach to the apply-and-explain approach.[95] This is to ensure that companies not only apply the principles of the stewardship code but also adopt a proactive approach in explaining their manner of application of the code. This is expected to ensure compliance with the code in spirit, and eschew a check-the-box attitude on the part of companies and service providers.[96]

Despite the transition from a comply-or-explain approach to the apply-and-explain approach, the UK continues to rely on the use of soft law, and has not embarked on a mandatory rules-based

---

[91] Chiu (n 61) 428. See also Reisberg (n 64) 230.
[92] Naniwadekar and Varottil (n 89) 108.
[93] UK Code 2012 (n 1) 2.
[94] See also Katelouzou and Sergakis, Shareholder Stewardship Enforcement, Chapter 27.
[95] UK Code 2020 (n 1) 4, Introduction.
[96] For a discussion on the concept of 'apply and explain', see Parmi Natesan and Prieur du Plessis, 'Why King IV's "Apply and Explain" Is So Important' (20 February 2019) <www.iodsa.co.za/news/438882/Why-King-IVs-apply-and-explain-is-so-important.htm> accessed 1 July 2020.

regime.[97] One can attribute a number of reasons for this phenomenon. First, the UK has displayed a consistent pattern in the use of codes, whether it be the City Code on Takeovers and Mergers or the Corporate Governance Code.[98]

Second, it is the large and most influential group of institutional investors in the UK that have orchestrated a code-based regulatory set-up, as they have a distinct preference for soft law over mandatory governmental regulation.[99] As repeat players in the market, institutional investors are subject to reputational incentives to adhere to codes even in the absence of strict sanctions for non-compliance. The evolution of the UK stewardship code occurred in two steps wherein an initially voluntary investor-based initiative, led by the Institutional Shareholders' Committee, morphed itself into one administered by the regulator, the Financial Reporting Council.[100]

Third, such a market-oriented approach relies extensively upon a robust system of legal institutions and mechanisms with sophisticated legal and supportive institutions. These include corporate governance intermediaries such as auditors, compliance professionals, other informational intermediaries, and proxy advisory firms, who create the necessary ecosystem for shareholder participation and engagement.

This constellation of factors, being hallmarks of the UK corporate governance system, form the bedrock on which a stewardship code based initially on a comply-or-explain approach took shape in that jurisdiction. However, despite the ideal conditions for such a stewardship model to thrive, it has attracted strident criticism.[101] This is on the grounds of fragmentation of institutional investors, the increasing influence of foreign investors who stand outside the scope of the stewardship code, and the fact that a voluntary system is likely to have limited bite even in the purportedly ideal regulatory climate of the UK.

It would now be appropriate to explore the reasons why jurisdictions such as India might find it difficult to emulate the UK in implementing a code on stewardship that operates on a voluntary comply-or-explain basis or even an apply-and-explain basis. First, unlike the UK, which has extensively relied on code and soft law in the sphere of corporate law and governance, India has displayed a consistent dependence on government regulation of the corporate sector. For instance, India's basic corporate law enacted by Parliament (i.e., Companies Act 2013) set out detailed rules and regulations regarding corporate governance, such as the roles and responsibilities of independent directors and auditors, the treatment of related party transactions, and the like. In most jurisdictions, these detailed governance requirements are contained either in voluntary codes or in stock exchange listing rules. To that extent, India follows an extreme system of mandatory and prescriptive regulation on matters of corporate governance.[102] The statutory mandate is supplemented by listing regulations issued by SEBI, again representing a mandatory approach.[103] To consider the infusion of a UK-style code-based approach of stewardship in such a milieu would certainly give rise to difficulties.

---

[97] However, there are specific laws that support the UK Stewardship Code, such as the Occupational Pension Schemes (Investment and Disclosure) (Amendment) Regulations 2019, the Proxy Advisors (Shareholders' Rights) Regulations 2019 and the Senior Management Arrangements, Systems and Controls (SYSV) Sourcebook 3.4 SRD Requirements.

[98] Umakanth Varottil, 'Corporate Governance in India: The Transition from Code to Statute' in Jean J du Plessis and Chee Keong Low (eds), *Corporate Governance Codes for the 21st Century: International Perspectives and Critical Analyses* (Springer International 2017) 102–103.

[99] Bernard S Black and John C Coffee Jr, 'Hail Britannia?: Institutional Investor Behavior under Limited Regulation' (1994) 92 *Michigan Law Review* 1997.

[100] Cheffins (n 54) 1012.

[101] See Davies, The UK Stewardship Code 2010–2020, Chapter 2.

[102] This author refers to this phenomenon of including corporate governance requirements in the basic corporate statute as the 'ultra-mandatory' approach in another writing; see Varottil (n 98) 98.

[103] See Securities and Exchange Board of India (Listing Obligations and Disclosure Requirements) Regulations, 2015.

Second, the influence of the institutional investors in the UK, which has led to a code-based approach in that jurisdiction, is far more limited in India. Despite the growing incidence of shareholder participation and engagement in Indian companies, the influence of institutional shareholders in the design of the governance regimes is almost non-existent. Third, the prevalent legal institutions and mechanisms in India have not stimulated a culture of voluntary compliance. This is likely to make a soft law approach subject to large-scale deviance, and that too with minimal and unsatisfactory explanation of the reasons for such non-compliance.

For these reasons, a mandatory regime in the form of hard law is more suitable for India rather than a voluntary code-based soft law approach. Even when the Indian corporations and regulators have relied upon the comply-or-explain approach, whether for corporate governance, corporate social responsibility, or even for ESG reporting, it has been short-lived. Such a reliance on soft law has been a purely transitional mechanism before the contents of the soft law are granted the imprimatur of hard law. In that sense, the soft law approaches in the corporate sector have hardly endured in India.

While the 2017 IRDAI Code was premised explicitly on a 'comply-or-explain' basis, the PFRDA and SEBI Codes are designed to be mandatory in nature. However, the revisions to the IRDA Code in February 2020 signal a shift from the 'comply-or-explain' approach towards a mandate, thereby resulting in a convergence among all three codes. Even so, it is not clear how the regulators will address instances of non-compliance, and what the accompanying sanctions might be. Hence, unless accompanied by appropriate consequences that operate as a deterrence against breach, even the supposedly mandatory codes lack legal bite.

Indian regulators would instead do well to pay heed to developments that resulted in the pan-European initiatives that led to the EU Shareholder Rights Directive in 2017.[104] Scholars have observed that this 'introduces a duty to *demonstrate* engagement on the part of institutional investors and asset managers, and is, therefore, a tentative step towards hardening of stewardship/ engagement duties'.[105] Such a duty-based approach is likely beneficial in jurisdictions with concentrated shareholding such as India, as it will 'introduce more clarity into the expectations for shareholder conduct and intra-shareholder relations'.[106] In such a case, the statutory or legislative backing will tremendously aid in the enforcement of the requirement. The mere use of soft law for this purpose is unlikely to cut ice.

The transition from voluntary stewardship based on soft law to a shareholder participation and engagement duty embedded in hard law[107] would be more suitable for India, rather than the traditional UK-style stewardship code. Therefore, rather than heedlessly being influenced by the UK, the Indian regulators must explore elsewhere to find the appropriate regulatory tools that fit within the Indian legal, institutional and cultural contexts.

17.6 CONCLUSION

This chapter set out to examine whether the UK-style stewardship code, which emanated from and is operating under circumstances specific to that jurisdiction, is capable of being transplanted to a jurisdiction such as India, which has divergent corporate ownership structures as

---

[104] Directive (EU) 2017/828 of the European Parliament and of the Council of 17 May 2017 amending Directive 2007/36/EC as regards the encouragement of long-term shareholder engagement [2017] OJ L132/1, also referred to as SRD II.
[105] Chiu and Katelouzou (n 12) 133.
[106] ibid.
[107] The hard law could be in the form of imposing fiduciary duties on shareholders in certain specific circumstances under company law.

well as legal and institutional mechanisms. While India has sought to move towards a UK-style stewardship code, the developments have been fragmented, largely owing to the involvement of various sectoral regulators such as the insurance regulator (IRDAI), the pension regulator (PFRDA) and the securities markets regulator (SEBI). While there was an expectation that the regulators would collaborate to introduce a uniform set of guidelines that apply to all types of institutional investor, the developments thus far have been unsatisfactory. IRDAI, PFRDA and SEBI have each issued their own code, and a consolidated and uniform set of stewardship principles applicable to all institutional investors is nowhere in sight.

In such a context, this chapter sought to identify certain considerations which the regulators ought to bear in mind while introducing a uniform set of stewardship principles. The crux of this chapter is that, at least on three counts, the UK-style stewardship code is inappropriate for India, and an ill-considered introduction of its principles and implementation tools into India will not fetch the desired results. First, the shareholding structure in India is different from that in the UK, which alters the focus of stewardship. Second, the emphasis of corporate law and investor engagement in the UK is driven by the ESV principle, while in India it is founded on the pluralist stakeholder theory. Third, the soft law–based approach that has characterized UK-style stewardship as well as other codes will face considerable resistance in India, where a mandatory hard law–based approach has become the norm in the corporate sector. The regulators in India will be well advised to cast a wider net in terms of adopting principles and best practices that are suitable for implementation in India.

18

Institutional Investors in China

An Autochthonous Mechanism Unrelated to UK-cum-Global Stewardship

Dan W. Puchniak and Lin Lin[*]

18.1 INTRODUCTION

Two decades ago, the US had almost twenty times as many Fortune Global 500 companies as China.[1] Today, the number of Fortune Global 500 companies in China (124) has surpassed that in the US (121).[2] China's listed companies are leaders in many of the world's most important industries, a fact that was unthinkable at the dawn of the new millennium.[3] China now has the world's largest market for initial public offerings[4] and the world's second largest stock market, which has grown fivefold in the past decade.[5]

---

[*] This is a condensed version of an article first published as Lin Lin and Dan W Puchniak, 'Institutional Investors in China: Corporate Governance and Policy Channeling in the Market within the State' (2022) 35 *Columbia Journal of Asian Law* 74. The authors would like to thank the National University of Singapore (NUS) Faculty of Law and the NUS Centre for Asian Legal Studies (CALS) for their generous support by providing funding for this research. Section 18.5 was added to fully integrate this research into the major themes in this book.

[1] In 2000, China had 10 Fortune 500 companies as compared to the US's 179; see Scott Kennedy, 'The Biggest But Not the Strongest: China's Place in the Fortune Global 500' (Center for Strategic & International Studies, 18 August 2020) <www.csis.org/blogs/trustee-china-hand/biggest-not-strongest-chinas-place-fortune-global-500> accessed 2 June 2021.

[2] Alan Murray and David Meyer, 'The Fortune Global 500 Is Now More Chinese than American' *Fortune* (10 August 2020) <https://fortune.com/2020/08/10/fortune-global-500-china-rise-ceo-daily/> accessed 2 June 2021.

[3] See 'A Rising Star: China's Pharmaceuticals Industry Is Growing Up' *The Economist* (Beijing and Shanghai, 28 September 2019) <www.economist.com/business/2019/09/28/chinas-pharmaceuticals-industry-is-growing-up> accessed 2 June 2021 (pharmaceuticals); Yukinori Hanada, 'China's Solar Panel Markers Top Global Field But Challenges Loom' *Nikkei Asian Review* (Shanghai, 31 July 2019) <https://asia.nikkei.com/Business/Business-trends/China-s-solar-panel-makers-top-global-field-but-challenges-loom> accessed 2 June 2021 (solar panels); Wang Yue, 'China's $7.6 Trillion Online Payments Market Is No Longer Enough For Jack Ma's Ant Financial' *Forbes* (17 January 2020) <www.forbes.com/sites/ywang/2020/01/17/ant-financial-is-shifting-away-from-chinas-76-trillion-online-payments-market/?sh=37563bda45b5> accessed 2 June 2021 (online payment systems).

[4] Laure He, 'Shanghai Could Be the World's Biggest IPO Market This Year. Holding the Title Will Be Tough' (CNN Business, 1 November 2020) <https://edition.cnn.com/2020/10/31/investing/china-markets-ipo-intl-hnk/index.html> accessed 2 June 2021; Evelyn Cheng, 'Chinese Companies Are Leading the Global IPO Rush Amid a "Flight from Uncertainty"' (CNBC, 27 October 2020) <www.cnbc.com/2020/10/27/chinese-companies-are-leading-the-global-ipo-rush-amid-a-flight-from-uncertainty.html> accessed 2 June 2021; Georgina Lee, 'Shanghai Overtakes Hong Kong As World's Top IPO Destination But Mega Deals Waiting in Wings Will Shake Up Full-Year Rankings' *South China Morning Post* (31 March 2020) <www.scmp.com/business/banking-finance/article/3077611/shanghai-overtakes-hong-kong-worlds-top-ipo-destination> accessed 2 June 2021.

[5] The rise of China and the fivefold growth of its stock market over the past decade have fuelled a growing literature on this market in financial economics. See Jennifer N Carpenter and Robert F Whitelaw, 'The Development of China's Stock Market and Stakes for the Global Economy' (2017) 9 *Annual Review of Financial Economics* 233; and, more recently, Hudson Lockett, 'China's Stock Market Value Hits Record High of More Than $10tn' *Financial Times* (14 October 2020) <www.ft.com/content/7e2d1cae-8033-45b1-811c-bc7d4a413e33> accessed 2 June 2021 (confirming China as the second largest stock market).

For corporate law and governance scholars, even more surprising than China's economic miracle is the central role the Chinese government has played in achieving it. Before China's rise, the idea that a government could play the role of the most important shareholder in a twenty-first- century world-class corporation – let alone in a multitude of listed corporations at the core of the greatest economic miracle of our time – was an anathema.[6] Yet, today, the Chinese government is by far the largest controlling shareholder in the Chinese stock market.[7] Indeed, it is the largest controlling shareholder in the world.[8]

The foundation of the corporate governance system that led to the Chinese government's rise as the world's most powerful shareholder is now aptly described as 'corporatization without privatization'.[9] Starting in the 1990s, a vast array of businesses that were run as units of the government were transformed into companies under the new PRC Company Law.[10] These companies, with boards of directors and shareholders, were then listed on the Chinese stock market. Importantly, however, the government maintained – and still maintains – a controlling equity interest in its listed state-owned enterprises (SOEs).[11] This system of equity finance has become known as mixed-ownership, as SOEs' shares are split between the government as the (insider) controlling shareholder and (ostensibly, outsider) minority shareholders.[12]

There is a rich literature analyzing the government's role as China's largest controlling shareholder and the unique agency problems that flow from it.[13] This research provides valuable insights into how the Chinese Communist Party (CCP) has used the government's controlling shareholder power and other idiosyncratic governance mechanisms – such as Party Committees (*dang wei hui*) – to play a central role as a corporate governance insider in listed SOEs and even in many private-owned enterprises (POEs).[14] However, the CCP's role as the architect – and direct and indirect controller – of institutional investors in China has remained underexplored, and is often entirely ignored.[15]

---

[6]   Henry Hansmann and Reinier Kraakman, 'The End of History for Corporate Law' (2001) 89 *Georgetown Law Journal* 439, 446; Tan Cheng Han, Dan W Puchniak and Umakanth Varottil, 'State-Owned Enterprises in Singapore Model: Historical Insights into a Potential Model for Reform' (2015) 28 *Columbia Journal of Asian Law* 61, 61; Curtis J Milhaupt, 'The State as Owner – China's Experience' (2020) 36 *Oxford Review of Economic Policy* 362, 362.

[7]   Li-Wen Lin and Curtis J Milhaupt, 'We Are the (National) Champions: Understanding the Mechanisms of State Capitalism in China' (2013) 65 *Stanford Law Review* 697, 700; Curtis J Milhaupt and Wentong Zheng, 'Beyond Ownership: State Capitalism and the Chinese Firm' (2015) 103 *Georgetown Law Journal* 665, 676.

[8]   Lin and Milhaupt (n 7) 700; Milhaupt and Zheng (n 7) 676.

[9]   Nicholas Howson, 'Protecting the State from Itself? Regulatory Interventions in Corporate Governance and the Financing of China's "State Capitalism"' in Benjamin L Liebman and Curtis J Milhaupt (eds), *Regulating the Visible Hand? The Institutional Implications of Chinese State Capitalism* (OUP 2015) 51–52.

[10] Howson (n 9) 51–52; Jiangyu Wang and Tan Cheng-Han, 'Mixed Ownership Reform and Corporate Governance in China's State-Owned Enterprises' (2020) 53 *Vanderbilt Journal of Transnational Law* 1055.

[11] Enterprises in which the state holds more than 50% of the shares or listed companies of which the actual controllers disclosed in financial reports are government agencies.

[12] Howson (n 9) 51–52; Milhaupt (n 6); Wang and Tan (n 10) 1062–64.

[13] ibid; Lauren Yu-Hsin Lin, 'Institutionalizing Political Influence in Business: Party-Building and Insider Control in Chinese State-Owned Enterprises' (2021) 45 *Vermont Law Review* 437; John Zhuang Liu and Angela Huyue Zhang, 'Ownership and Political Control: Evidence from Charter Amendments' (2019) 60 *International Review of Law and Economics* 105853; Lauren Yu-Hsin Lin and Yun-chien Chang, 'Do State-Owned Enterprises Have Worse Corporate Governance? An Empirical Study of Corporate Practices in China' *European Business Organization Law Review* (forthcoming); Wang and Tan (n 10); Jiangyu Wang, 'The Political Logic of Corporate Governance in China's State-Owned Enterprises' (2014) 47 *Cornell International Law Journal* 631.

[14] Wang and Tan (n 10) 1094; Lauren Yu-Hsin Lin and Curtis J Milhaupt, 'Party Building or Noisy Signaling? The Contours of Political Conformity in Chinese Corporate Governance' (2020) ECGI Law Working Paper No 493/2020, 3 <https://ssrn.com/abstract=3510342> accessed 2 June 2021 (SOEs are now expected to expressly give the party's leadership and party committees formal legal status inside the company).

[15] This suggests a lack of awareness of the role of institutional investors in China. Wang and Tan (n 10) 1106; Tamar Groswald Ozery, 'Minority Public Shareholders in China's Concentrated Capital Markets – A New Paradigm?' (2016) 30 *Columbia Journal of Asian Law* 1, 28–30; Howson (n 9) 53–54; Milhaupt (n 6); Edward Rock, 'Institutional

This lack of focus on institutional investors in Chinese corporate governance may have made sense two decades ago. At that time, in listed Chinese companies, institutional investors' shareholdings were miniscule,[16] the CCP had an iron grip on corporate governance through the government's non-tradable controlling block shareholdings,[17] and stringent caps on foreign institutional investor shareholdings rendered them negligible.[18] All of these facts are relics of a bygone era.

The most recent statistics on China's shareholder landscape reveal that institutional investors now hold 18.7 per cent of China's A-shares market capitalization – almost double the percentage they held in 2014 and more than ten times the amount in 2003.[19] Institutional investors now account for almost half of the free float of shares in A-shares companies, more than a ninefold increase since 2007 – making institutional investors China's most important minority shareholders.[20] At the end of 2019, the assets under management by institutional investors in China reached USD 16 trillion – a tenfold increase over the past ten years, making it the world's most important market for growth in the asset management industry.[21] In 2015, the government made its controlling shareholder stakes in SOEs fully tradable and since then it has significantly decreased the size of its controlling shareholder blocks.[22] In recent years, the caps on foreign institutional investors have been progressively raised and were largely abolished in 2020.[23] This now makes any analysis of Chinese corporate governance that does not consider institutional investors incomplete.

Considering these watershed developments, it is surprising that the legal literature lacks a recent description of who China's institutional investors are, how they are regulated, and what impact they have on Chinese corporate governance.[24] This gap in the literature is especially surprising as the role of institutional investors in corporate governance is a primary

---

Investors in Corporate Governance' in Jeffrey Gordon and Wolf-Georg Ringe (eds), *The Oxford Handbook of Corporate Law and Governance* (OUP 2018).

[16] See Section 18.2.

[17] China Securities Regulatory Commission (CSRC), '上市公司股权分置改革管理办法 (Shàngshì gōngsī gǔquán fēn zhì gǎigé guǎnlǐ bànfǎ) [Measures for the Administration of the Share-Trading Reform of Listed Companies]' (No 86 [2005], 5 September 2005) art 3.

[18] See Section 18.2.

[19] A-shares are the shares of listed companies incorporated in mainland China that trade in RMBs on the two Chinese stock exchanges, the Shanghai Stock Exchange (SSE) and the Shenzhen Stock Exchange (SZSE). An "A-shares company" refers to a company listed on the SSE or the SZSE. See Section 18.2.

[20] Lockett (n 5).

[21] World Economic Forum (WEF), 'China Asset Management at an Inflection Point' (July 2020) 5 <www3.weforum.org/docs/WEF_IR_China_Asset_Management_2020.pdf> accessed 2 June 2021 [hereinafter WEF Report].

[22] Wang and Tan (n 10) 1065.

[23] State Administration of Foreign Exchange (SAFE), 'PBOC & SAFE Remove QFII/RQFII Investment Quotas and Promote Further Opening-Up of China's Financial Market' (7 May 2020) <www.safe.gov.cn/en/2020/0507/1677.html> accessed 2 June 2021. With Chinese A-shares becoming part of the MSCI EMI in 2018 and a significant increase in their weightage in the MSCI EMI in 2019, it seems likely that there will be a marked increase in shareholdings by foreign institutional investors (Zhen Wei, 'Emerging Markets since China A Shares' Inclusion' (5 December 2019) <www.msci.com/www/blog-posts/emerging-markets-since-china-a/01662775315> accessed 19 July 2021). Although recent political tensions with the US have caused some Chinese companies to be removed from the MSCI EMI owing to their alleged connection with the Chinese government, an increase in the amount of foreign institutional investment in China's stock markets still seems likely. In 2020, 2019 and 2018, CSRC approved, respectively, seventy-one, twenty and eighteen foreign institutional investors' applications for QFIIs. In 2019, CSRC approved twenty foreign institutional investors as QFIIs, indicating a more relaxed approach towards QFII. Full list of QFIIs: CSRC, '合格境外机构投资者名录 (2021年6月) (Hégé jìngwài jīgòu tóuzī zhě mínglù (2021 nián 6 yuè)) [List of Qualified Foreign Institutional Investors (June 2021)]' (9 December 2021) <www.csrc.gov.cn/csrc_en/c102049/c1606024/content.shtml> accessed 13 February 2022.

[24] The latest significant article on institutional investor activism in China in the legal literature was fifteen years ago. See Chao Xi, 'Institutional Shareholder Activism in China: Law and Practice' (2006) 17 *International Company and Commercial Law Review* 251. Robin Hui Huang has explained why institutional investors did not perform the role of lead plaintiffs in Chinese-style securities class action; see Robin Hui Huang, 'Private Enforcement of Securities Law

focus of several of the world's leading corporate law scholars.[25] This chapter aims to take the first step in addressing this conspicuous gap in the literature.

In Section 18.2, we draw on the most accurate and up-to-date Chinese sources to describe the taxonomy of institutional investors in China. The taxonomy reveals that, as the percentage of the A-shares market owned by institutional investors has grown, there has been a proliferation in the different types of institutional investor in China – what we coin the 'atomization' of the market for institutional investors. An analysis of the regulations that have driven the growth and atomization of institutional investors demonstrates that, for decades, the CCP has actively promoted the growth of institutional investors to improve corporate governance and stabilize the stock market. It also reveals that the CCP has strategically controlled the growth and influence of foreign institutional investors, making China the most domestically dominated major market for institutional investors in the world – in which the big three American institutional investors (i.e., Blackrock, State Street and Vanguard) are inconsequential. This has allowed the CCP to rapidly develop a sizable and effective market for institutional investors, while ensuring that it reinforces the China model of corporate governance in which the CCP maintains ultimate control.

In Section 18.3, we collect and analyze a growing number of empirical studies in the business school literature that provide three valuable insights into the role played by institutional investors in Chinese corporate governance. First, they provide convincing evidence that different types of institutional investor have different impacts on Chinese corporate governance – confirming the value of the taxonomy of institutional investors analyzed in Section 18.2. Second, several empirical studies find that the impact that institutional investors have on corporate governance is contingent on the extent to which the institutional investor is insulated from the CCP – highlighting the importance of distinguishing among state-owned institutional investors (SOIIs), private-owned institutional investors (POIIs) and foreign-owned institutional investors (FOIIs). Third, several empirical studies find that the impact that institutional investors have on corporate governance is contingent on whether the investee company is an SOE or a POE – reinforcing the importance of understanding the role of the CCP in China's market for institutional investors.

However, as explained in detail in Section 18.3, as insightful as these empirical studies are, they suffer from some limitations in their currency, data and analysis. They also fail to explain how institutional investors, who in almost all companies are collectively minority shareholders, produce a statistically significant impact on corporate governance. To overcome some of these blind spots in the empirical studies, we hand-collected and analyzed all publicly reported representative cases in which institutional investors, acting as minority shareholders, have been involved in activist campaigns in A-shares companies. Somewhat surprisingly, our analysis of these cases revealed that SOIIs have undertaken a significant portion of the activist campaigns

---

in China: A Ten-Year Retrospective and Empirical Assessment' (2013) 61 *The American Journal of Comparative Law* 757, 787–89. Recent articles relating to institutional investors focus more on the US and EU experience, but less on the description of China's situation; see Guo Li and Zhao Yijun, '机构投资者投票顾问的法律规制 — — 美国与欧盟的探索及借鉴 (Jīgòu tóuzī zhě tóupiào gùwèn de fǎlù guīzhì - - měiguó yǔ ōuméng de tànsuǒ jí jièjiàn) [The Regulation of Proxy Advisors: Experiments and Lessons from the US and the EU]' (2019) 1 比较法研究 *[Journal of Comparative Law]* 152.

[25] See e.g. Fisch, The Uncertain Stewardship Potential of Index Funds, Chapter 21; Lucian A Bebchuk, Alma Cohen and Scott Hirst, 'The Agency Problems of Institutional Investors' (2017) 31 *Journal of Economic Perspectives* 89, 92–93; John C Coates IV, 'The Future of Corporate Governance Part 1: The Problem of Twelve' (2018) Harvard Public Law Working Paper No 19-07, 2–5 <https://ssrn.com/abstract=3247337> accessed 2 June 2021; Ronald Gilson and Jeffrey Gordon, 'The Agency Costs of Agency Capitalism: Activist Investors and the Revaluation of Governance Rights' (2013) 113 *Columbia Law Review* 863, 874–76; Rock (n 15).

and that POIIs have succeeded in more than half of their activist campaigns targeting SOEs.[26] However, over the last decade the number of activist campaigns by POIIs, several of which have succeeded in SOEs, is on the rise.[27] Moreover, based on the searches we have conducted, FOIIs have undertaken only two activist campaigns, neither of which was in the last decade.[28] Finally, activist campaigns overall are clearly on the rise, with three times as many activist campaigns in the last decade compared to two decades ago.[29] Taken together, as explained in detail in Section 18.3, this suggests that SOIIs and POIIs are developing into an important corporate governance mechanism to mitigate private benefits of control in China – while the role of FOIIs remains limited. It also suggests that the relationship between the CCP and institutional investors is important and complex.

In Section 18.4, we aim to make sense out of this complexity by mapping and analyzing the various government bodies, regulations and tactics that the CCP has developed to control institutional investors formally and informally in China. Based on empirical, case study and interview evidence, we explain how the CCP can – and has – used various mechanisms to engage in 'policy channelling'[30] in SOIIs and POIIs, with foreign institutional investors being largely insulated from policy channelling. Equally important, however, is our evidence that the CCP uses its power to policy channel in a targeted and limited way surrounding significant stock market and political events. On a day-to-day basis, absent these extraordinary events, institutional investors in China appear to be driven mostly by free-market forces. Empirical, interview and case study evidence suggests that institutional investors often serve an important corporate governance function by acting as a check on corporate controllers in SOEs and POEs. This fits with other research on Chinese corporate governance that demonstrates that the government has created a system to mitigate private benefits of control – even when it means constraining the power of SOEs – while at the same time ensuring that the CCP maintains ultimate control.[31]

In Section 18.5, we conclude by explaining why institutional investors in China should be seen as an autochthonous corporate governance mechanism that is unrelated to the UK-cum-global stewardship movement. We demonstrate, in the context of this book, that, to accurately understand the role of institutional investors in Chinese corporate governance and how effective they are in improving corporate governance in China, these developments must be understood

---

[26] Lin Lin and Dan W Puchniak, 'Institutional Investors in China: Corporate Governance and Policy Channeling in the Market within the State' *Columbia Journal of Asian Law* (forthcoming). From 1994 to 2021, 30.2% (thirteen out of forty-three) of the activist campaigns were undertaken by SOIIs, with SOIIs and POIIs collaborating in 11.6% (five out of forty-three) of the activist campaigns. In the cases in which a POII targeted an SOE, the POII succeeded in 57.1% (four out of seven) of activist campaigns.

[27] ibid. From 1994 to 2010, 30% (three out of ten) of the activist campaigns were undertaken by POIIs, with SOIIs and POIIs collaborating in 20% (two out of ten) of the activist campaigns, whereas from 2011 to 2021, 60.6% (twenty out of thirty-three) of the activist campaigns were undertaken by POIIs, with SOIIs and POIIs collaborating in 9.1% (three out of thirty-three) of the activist campaigns and an FOII and a POII collaborating in one activist campaign.

[28] ibid. The two cases undertaken by FOIIs both occurred in 2012.

[29] ibid. From 1994 to 2010 there were ten activist campaigns, whereas from 2011 to 2021 there were thirty-three activist campaigns.

[30] The term 'policy channeling' was first coined by Milhaupt and Pargendler in their research on related party transactions in SOEs. Curtis J Milhaupt and Mariana Pargendler, 'Related Party Transactions in State-Owned Enterprises' in Luca Enriques and Tobias Tröger (eds), *The Law and Finance of Related Party Transactions* (CUP 2019) 245–46. See also Ronald J Gilson and Curtis J Milhaupt, 'Shifting Influences on Corporate Governance: Capital Market Completeness and Policy Channeling' (2021) ECGI Law Working Paper No 546/2020 <https://ssrn.com/abstract=3695309> accessed 19 July 2021. In this chapter, we extend the use of the term 'policy channeling' to institutional investors in China. In this context, 'policy channelling' refers to the CCP's instrumental use of institutional investors for economic policies or social purposes – as opposed to institutional investors focusing on maximizing the value of the funds they own/manage.

[31] Howson (n 9) 52; Wang and Tan (n 10) 1094.

384   Part II Jurisdictions

on their own terms. In this context, viewing China through an Anglo-American comparative lens will only blur, rather than sharpen, our vision.

18.2 THE RISE OF INSTITUTIONAL INVESTORS IN CHINA: A REMARKABLE, YET OVERLOOKED, HISTORY

18.2.1 *Institutional Investors in China Can No Longer Be Ignored*

The meteoric rise of institutional investors in China is difficult to overstate. As is clear in Figure 18.1, in 2003 the percentage of the A-shares market owned by institutional investors was

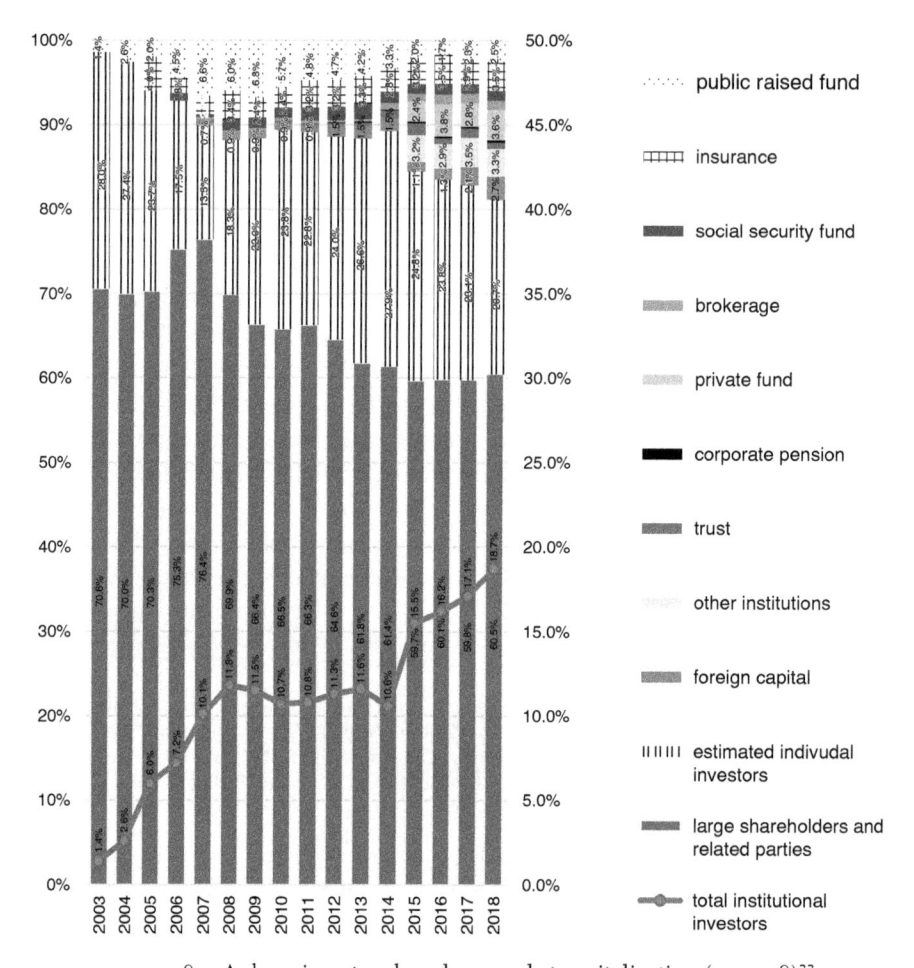

FIGURE 18.1 A-share investors based on market capitalization (2003–18)[32]

---

[32] 中金公司研究部 [CICC (China International Capital Corporation) Global Institute], '中金公司:A股"散户化"已经明显下降 (Zhōng jīn gōngsī: A gǔ "sǎnhù huà" yǐjīng míngxiǎn xiàjiàng) [CICC: The Proportion of Retail Investors in the A-shares Market Has Declined Significantly]' (2 July 2019) <https://m.21jingji.com/article/20190702/herald/b39f0f661609f2353cdfafbb8d88b974.html> accessed 19 July 2021. Other institutions include other professional institutions (其他专业机构) and products (such as asset management plans of futures firms (期货公司资产管理计划), financial companies (财务公司) and wealth management products of commercial banks (商业银行理财产品)); total institutional investors refers to investors excluding estimated individual investors, large shareholders and related parties.

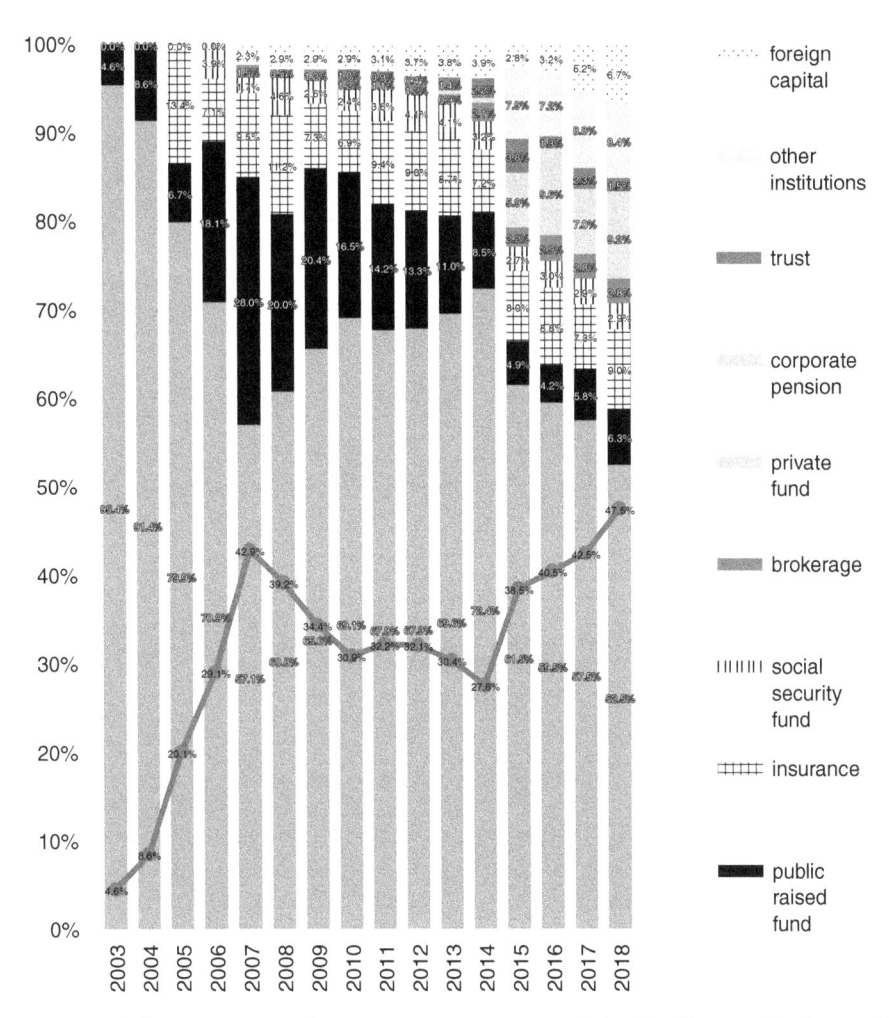

FIGURE 18.2 A-share institutional investors as a percentage of the free-float market (2003–18)[33]

a miniscule 1.4%. By 2008, the percentage of institutional investor ownership had increased more than eightfold to 11.8%. As of 2018, institutional investors held 18.7% of the market capitalization of A-shares.

The increase in control that institutional investors have over the free-float in China's A-shares market has been equally dramatic. As is evident in Figure 18.2, in 2003 institutional investors controlled merely 4.6% of the free-float of A-shares. By 2007, the portion of the free-float controlled by institutional investors had increased more than ninefold to 42.9% and in 2018 reached 47.5% – making institutional investors China's most important minority shareholders. As such, it is now clear that institutional investors are an important part of Chinese corporate governance.

The global institutional investor community has come to recognize the importance of institutional investors in China. Recent reports have identified China's asset management market as the world's most important for growth in the industry and have valued it at USD 16 trillion.[34] Yet, surprisingly, even though the role of institutional investors in corporate

---

[33] ibid.
[34] WEF Report (n 21) 5.

governance has become a core issue among Anglo-America's leading comparative corporate law scholars, the remarkable rise of Chinese institutional investors has been almost entirely overlooked in the legal literature.[35]

Before analyzing how institutional investors fit into the China model of corporate governance, it is essential to recognize that institutional investors in China are not monolithic. As illustrated in the taxonomy of institutional investors in Figure 18.3, there are a variety of institutional investors in China. It is important to understand these varieties as each of them is subject to different regulatory regimes. By mapping the regulatory developments for each variety, a clear picture emerges of how the Chinese government has used its regulatory power to facilitate and shape the growth of different types of institutional investor over the last several decades.[36]

As examined in detail in Section 18.4, the different varieties of institutional investors have distinct regulatory regimes. As a result, the manner and extent to which each variety is subject to direct and indirect government control also differs among them. However, despite these differences, our detailed analysis below reveals two features that cut across all varieties: (1) over the last several decades the Chinese government has consistently used its regulatory power to facilitate the growth of institutional investors overall; and (2) the Chinese government has designed a regulatory regime for institutional investors that reinforces the China model of corporate governance, which aims to improve the efficiency of corporate governance while ensuring that the CCP maintains ultimate control over the financial system.

18.2.2 Foreign Institutional Investors: A Small, But Growing, Piece of the Taxonomy

The first important bifurcation in the taxonomy is between domestic institutional investors and foreign institutional investors. Foreign institutional investors refers to investors who enter the A-shares market through the qualified foreign institutional investors (QFII) regime, the renminbi qualified foreign institutional investors (RQFII) regime or Mainland-Hong Kong Stock Connect (*lu gu tong*).

China is unique among most major economies with respect to how small a percentage of its stock market is owned by foreign institutional investors.[37] As can be seen in Figure 18.1, until 2007 there was no measurable foreign institutional investor ownership registered in the A-shares market. From 2007 to 2011, the level of foreign institutional ownership in the A-shares market was paltry, remaining at below 1%. Although the percentage of foreign institutional investor ownership has increased since 2016, it registered at only 2.8% of the A-shares market in 2018.

The small percentage of the A-shares market owned by foreign institutional investors makes China an outlier as foreign institutional investors have come to play a significant (and, in some countries such as the UK, even dominant) role in most of the world's other major stock markets.[38] Relatedly, the US's 'Big Three' institutional investors (BlackRock, Vanguard and

---

[35] Rock (n 15); see generally Fisch, The Uncertain Stewardship Potential of Index Funds, Chapter 21; Bebchuk, Cohen and Hirst (n 25) 92–93; Coates (n 25); Gilson and Gordon (n 25).
[36] See Lin and Puchniak (n 26) appendix 1.
[37] See Adriana De La Cruz, Alejandra Medina and Yung Tang, 'Owners of the World's Listed Companies' (OECD Capital Market Series, 17 October 2019) 38, table A.4 <www.oecd.org/corporate/owners-of-the-worlds-listed-companies.htm> accessed 2 June 2021.
[38] WEF Report (n 21).

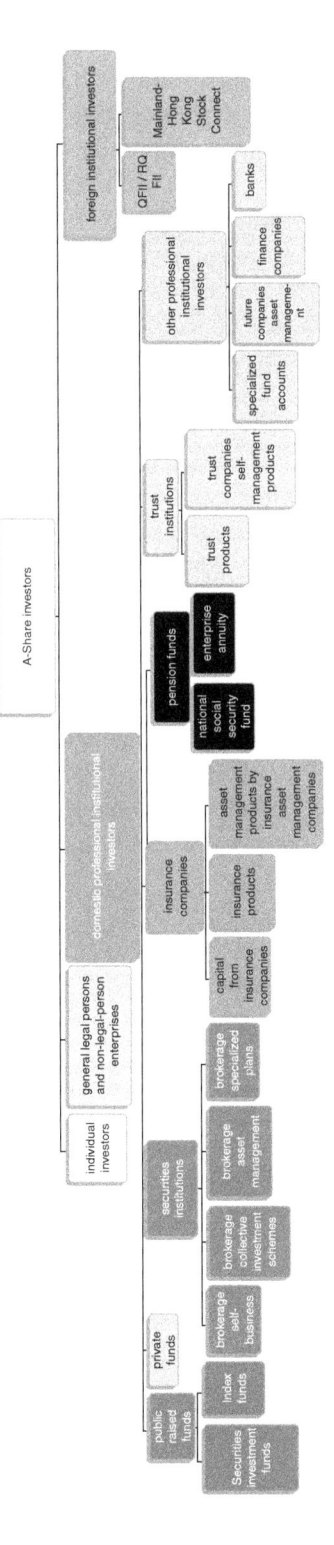

FIGURE 18.3 A taxonomy of institutional investors in China's A-shares market[39]

39 'The taxonomy is based on '起底A股投资者筹码–A股投资者结构专题2020Q2 (Qǐ dǐ A gǔ tóuzī zhě chóumǎ–A gǔ tóuzī zhě jiégòu zhuāntí 2020Q2) [Ownership Structure of the A-share Investors 2020Q2]' Sina Finance (9 September 2020) <https://finance.sina.com.cn/stock/stockzmt/2020-09-09/doc-iivhuipp3290986.shtml> accessed 2 June 2021.

State Street) – which have attracted considerable academic attention and are the largest institutional investors globally – have heretofore owned a miniscule percentage of shares in the Chinese stock market.[40]

The small percentage of foreign institutional ownership in the Chinese stock market is the result of strict regulatory caps that have historically been placed on foreign institutional investors. In 2002, the Chinese government launched the highly restrictive QFII scheme which for the first time allowed foreign institutional investors to invest in the Chinese securities market.[41] This required foreign investors to apply to the China Securities Regulatory Commission (CSRC) for its approval to invest. If approved, the foreign investor would be notified by the State Administration of Foreign Exchange (SAFE) of the limited quota that it could invest.

The approved investment amount under SAFE was subject to a one-year lock-in period during which time the investment funds had to remain in China.[42] Under no circumstances could the total combined percentage of shares held by all the QFIIs in a single listed company exceed 20 per cent of its total shares, nor could a single foreign investor own more than 10 per cent of shares in a listed company.[43] In addition, to qualify for the QFII scheme, fund management companies had to have a minimum of USD 10 billion in assets under management in their previous financial year and at least five years of operational experience, while insurance companies were required to have at least thirty years of experience and paid-in capital of at least USD 1 billion.[44] The restrictions limited QFIIs to major international investment banks who, owing to the strict quotas and restrictions, individually and collectively could own only a small percentage of shares in Chinese listed companies.

Since 2002,[45] the investment restrictions and lock-in period for QFIIs have progressively been relaxed to facilitate the inflow of more foreign institutional investments. Importantly, as part of this initiative, in 2005 the Ministry of Commerce, the CSRC, the State Administration of Taxation, the State Administration for Industry and Commerce, and SAFE jointly issued a new measure to allow strategic investments in A-shares listed companies by foreign investors. The measures took effect in 2006, and, as is clear in Figure 18.1, foreign institutional investors began to invest in the A-shares market in 2007.[46]

In 2012, the limit on total combined percentage of shares held by all the QFIIs, RQFIIs and Mainland-Hong Kong Stock Connect investors in a single listed company was increased to

---

[40] 杨佼(Yang Jiao), 'A股投资者30年变迁: 机构话语权提升, 散户持股占比降至30%(A gǔ tóuzī zhě 30 nián biànqiān: Jīgòu huàyǔ quán tíshēng, sǎnhù chí gǔ zhàn bǐ jiàng zhì 30%) [The Evolution of A-Share Investors in the Past Thirty Years: Voice of Institutional Investors Increased, the Percentage of Retail Investors Decreased to 30%]' *Yicai* (30 November 2020) <www.yicai.com/news/100858573.html> accessed 2 June 2021; See 'Shock and Tears: Behind Vanguard's Retreat from China Market' *BloombergQuint* (30 April 2021) <www.bloombergquint.com/markets/shock-and-tears-behind-vanguard-s-retreat-from-china-s-market> accessed 2 June 2021.

[41] See CSRC and PBOC, Interim Measures for the Administration of Domestic Securities Investment by Qualified Foreign Institutional Investors (24 August 2006) art 2 <www.csrc.gov.cn/pub/csrc_en/OpeningUp/RelatedPolices/QFII/201211/t20121108_216649.html> accessed 2 June 2021.

[42] Wei Huang and Tao Zhu, 'Foreign Institutional Investors and Corporate Governance in Emerging Markets: Evidence of a Split-Share Structure Reform in China' (2015) 32 *Journal of Corporate Finance* 312, 314–15.

[43] See CSRC, '关于实施《合格境外机构投资者境内证券投资管理办法》有关问题的通知 (Guānyú shíshī "hégé jìngwài jīgòu tóuzī zhě jìngnèi zhèngquàn tóuzī guǎnlǐ bànfǎ" yǒuguān wèntí de tōngzhī) [Notice on Issues Relating to the Implementation of the Measures for the Administration of Domestic Investments by Qualified Foreign Institutional Investors]' (24 August 2006) <www.csrc.gov.cn/pub/newsite/flb/flfg/bmgf/jj/hgjw/201012/t20101231_189793.html> accessed 2 June 2021.

[44] Huang and Zhu (n 42) 315.

[45] Lin and Puchniak (n 26) appendix 1.

[46] CSRC, 外国投资者对上市公司战略投资管理办法 (Wàiguó tóuzī zhě duì shàngshì gōngsī zhànlüè tóuzī guǎnlǐ bànfǎ) [Administrative Measures for Foreign Investors' Strategic Investments in Listed Companies] (31 December 2005).

30 per cent.[47] In 2018, SAFE issued new provisions[48] that abolished the lock-in period and the CSRC announced that it would further relax the qualification requirements on foreign investors.[49] In 2019, SAFE announced its decision to abolish the investment quota system under the QFII scheme and, in 2020, SAFE and the People's Bank of China (PBOC) issued a new regulation to simplify the administrative requirements on domestic investments by foreign institutional investors.[50] These policies should make it more convenient for foreign investors to invest in A-shares in the future – but the 30 per cent cap on foreign investor ownership in a single A-shares company will still limit their ability to influence corporate governance.

Although the *average* percentage of ownership by foreign institutional investors in the A-shares market has remained small (below 3 per cent), it is noteworthy that recently they have collectively acquired significant minority holdings in some high-profile listed companies.[51] For example, as of 30 April 2020, QFII, RQFII and Shenzhen Connect investors held 1.872 billion shares of Midea group, accounting for 26.74 per cent of its shares.[52] With Chinese listed companies' inclusion in the MSCI Emerging Markets Index (EMI) and the aforementioned regulatory caps recently abolished, it seems possible that foreign institutional investors will acquire significant *minority* stakes in more high-profile A-shares companies in the future.

There are two important observations that arise from our examination of the regulatory developments in the foreign component of the taxonomy of institutional investors in China. First, the remarkable rise of institutional investors in China has been driven predominantly by Chinese – not foreign – institutional investors. It appears that the lack of foreign investment has been the direct result of the Chinese government's strict regulatory caps and restrictions. Empirical evidence supports this conclusion as foreign institutional investment has increased in lockstep each time the quotas and restrictions have been eased.[53] As such, the Chinese government, through its regulatory design, has given itself a strong hand to shape and effectively control the vast majority of the market for institutional investors as they are overwhelmingly

---

[47] CSRC, '关于实施《合格境外机构投资者境内证券投资管理办法》有关问题的规定 (Guānyú shíshī 〈hégé jìngwài jīgòu tóuzī zhě jìngnèi zhèngquàn tóuzī guǎnlǐ bànfǎ〉 yǒuguān wèntí de guīdìng) [Provisions on Issues concerning the Implementation of the Administrative Measures for Securities Investment Made in China by Qualified Foreign Institutional Investors]' (27 July 2012) art 9(2).

[48] SAFE, '合格境外机构投资者境内证券投资外汇管理规定 (Hégé jìngwài jīgòu tóuzī zhě jìngnèi zhèngquàn tóuzī wàihuì guǎnlǐ guīdìng) [Provisions on the Foreign Exchange Administration of Domestic Securities Investment by Qualified Foreign Institutional Investors]' (10 June 2018).

[49] Huang and Zhu (n 42) 315.

[50] SAFE, '取消合格境外投资者 (QFII/RQFII) 投资额度限制 扩大金融市场对外开放 (Qǔxiāo hégé jìngwài tóuzī zhě (QFII/RQFII) tóuzī édù xiànzhì kuòdà jīnróng shìchǎng duìwài kāifàng) [Abolish the Limit of Investment Quota for Qualified Foreign Investors (QFII/RQFII) to Expand the Opening of the Financial Market]' (10 September 2019) <www.safe.gov.cn/safe/2019/0910/14040.html> accessed 19 July 2021; People's Bank of China (PBOC) and SAFE, '境外机构投资者境内证券期货投资资金管理规定 (Jìngwài jīgòu tóuzī zhě jìngnèi zhèngquàn qīhuò tóuzī zījīn guǎnlǐ guīdìng) [Regulations on Funds of Securities and Futures Investment by Foreign Institutional Investors, Announcement No 2 [2020] of the People's Bank of China and the State Administration of Foreign Exchange]' (7 May 2020) <www.gov.cn/zhengce/zhengceku/2020-05/07/content_5509577.htm> accessed 2 June 2021.

[51] '证监会: 超百家上市公司第一大股东是外资战略投资者 (Zhèngjiān huì: Chāo bǎi jiā shàngshì gōngsī dì yī dà gǔdōng shì wàizī zhànlüè tóuzī zhě) [CSRC: The Largest Shareholder of Over 100 Listed Companies Is a Foreign Strategic Investor]' (*Sohu*, 12 October 2020) <www.sohu.com/a/424142681_561670> accessed 19 July 2021; Gao Chang, '外资加速流入A股 3公司持股逼近上限被预警(Wàizī jiāsù liúrù A gǔ 3 gōngsī chí gǔ bījìn shàngxiàn bèi yùjǐng) [Accelerating the Inflow of Foreign Capital into A-Shares, 3 Companies Are Approaching the Upper Limit of Shareholders] *Xinhua News* (27 May 2020) <www.xinhuanet.com/fortune/2020-05/27/c_1126037849.htm> accessed 2 June 2021.

[52] ibid.

[53] Ningyue Liu, Don Bredin and Huijuan Cao, 'The Investment Behavior of Qualified Foreign Institutional Investors in China' (2020) 54 *Journal of Multinational Financial Management* 100614.

domestic – a stark contrast to most other major jurisdictions that have struggled to effectively regulate foreign institutional investors which have composed a sizable portion of their markets.[54] It has also allowed Chinese institutional investors to develop and capture market share with limited competition from foreign institutional investors.

Second, the small ownership stakes of foreign institutional investors have limited their ability to influence Chinese corporate governance – especially as most listed companies in China are dominated by powerful domestic controlling-block shareholders. As examined in detail in Section 18.3, there is some empirical evidence suggesting that foreign institutional investors have on occasion 'punched above their weight'[55] in their ability to impact corporate governance in listed companies in China, despite their small minority shareholdings. However, as explained in Section 18.4, even if foreign institutional investors increase their holdings and continue to sporadically punch above their weight, this will merely continue to assist with mitigating the extraction of wealth, reducing private benefits of control in A-shares companies but not fundamentally changing the China model of corporate governance – in which the CCP has ultimate control over SOIIs and POIIs, who dominate the market for institutional investors in China.

18.2.3 Domestic Institutional Investors: The Core of the Taxonomy

The roots of domestic institutional investors in China can be traced back to 1991 when the first batch of *securities investment funds* (SIFs, commonly referred to as mutual funds) – Wuhan Securities Investment Fund and Nanshan Venture Capital Fund – were established. In its first few years, the securities investment fund industry was fledgling and remained loosely regulated. This started to change in 1997 when the Securities Commission of the State Council (currently dissolved) issued the 'Interim Measures on the Management of Securities Investment Funds' (SIF Interim Measures), which established the first provisional framework for the industry. Within a few years, a handful of asset management companies were established, and several closed-end funds (CEFs) were launched. In addition, seventy-five CEFs, which were launched prior to the introduction of the SIF Interim Measures, continued to function.

At the dawn of the new millennium, the Chinese government made it a strategic initiative to develop SIFs as a mechanism to stabilize the market and improve Chinese corporate governance. In 1999, the CSRC began the process of liquidating and amalgamating the seventy-five CEFs launched prior to the introduction of the SIF Interim Measures. In 2000, the president of the CSRC and the vice-chairman of the Standing Committee of the National People's Congress both made the development of SIFs a priority to facilitate the development of institutional investors.[56] Their views were echoed in a CSRC policy paper published in 2000, which promoted the development of SIFs as a mechanism to stabilize the stock market and monitor the controllers of listed companies.[57]

In 2001, China's first open-ended SIF was launched, and open-ended funds quickly came to dominate the industry. In 2002, China designated institutional investors as being an

---

[54] See Brian R Cheffins, 'The Stewardship Code's Achilles' Heel' (2010) 73 *Modern Law Review* 1004.
[55] Huang and Zhu (n 42) 312–26.
[56] See '周小川指出：尽早使基金成为主要机构投资者 (Zhōu xiǎochuān zhǐchū: Jǐnzǎo shǐ jījīn chéngwéi zhǔyào jīgòu tóuzī zhě) [Zhou Xiaochuan Points Out: Make the Fund a Major Institutional Investor as Soon as Possible]' *Shanghai Securities Daily* (25 October 2000) <http://finance.sina.com.cn/2000-10-25/18600.html> accessed 2 June 2021.
[57] CSRC, '开放式证券投资基金试点办法 (Kāifàng shì zhèngquàn tóuzī jījīn shìdiǎn bànfǎ) [Experimental Rules on Open-End Securities Investment Funds]' (2000).

important feature of its corporate governance system by affirming in its inaugural Corporate Governance Code (CGC) that 'institutional investors shall play a role in the appointment of company directors, the compensation and supervision of management and major decision-making processes'.[58] On 28 October 2003, the 'PRC Securities Investment Fund Law' was promulgated, marking a major milestone as it was the first national law regulating SIFs.[59]

As illustrated in Figures 18.1 and 18.2, until 2005 SIFs were essentially the only type of institutional investor in the market. As the stock market strengthened in 2006 and boomed in 2007, the popularity, profitability and size of SIFs increased significantly – and they came to account for 6.6 per cent of capitalization and 28 per cent of the free-float of the A-shares market.[60] Since 2003, hedge funds and index funds have been gradually launched, but open-ended mutual funds continue to dominate the market.[61] In April 2018, the Guiding Opinions on Regulating the Asset Management Business of Financial Institutions[62] placed the regulation of SIFs under the unified supervision of the PBOC, the China Banking and Insurance Regulatory Commission (CBIRC) and the CSRC.[63]

As of 2019, China had a total of 6,084 public offering funds with a total value of 14.66 trillion yuan – representing a more than tenfold increase in the number of funds from a decade earlier; in 2020, there were 143 fund management companies in China.[64] Despite this rapid growth over the past decade, in absolute terms, the percentages of market capitalization and free-float of the A-shares market controlled by SIFs have declined (Figures 18.1 and 18.2) and now stand at 2.5% and 6.3% respectively. This is owing to the entry of other types of institutional investor into the market and the even more explosive growth in the capitalization of the A-shares market as a whole, which we will now describe.

The second major type of domestic institutional investor to enter the Chinese A-shares market was *insurance companies*. In 1980, China's domestic insurance business resumed and the management of insurance funds progressed substantially after the open-door and economic reform policies.[65] In 2004, the China Insurance Regulatory Commission (CIRC)

---

[58] CSRC, 'Code of Corporate Governance for Listed Companies in China' (7 January 2001) art 11 <www.csrc.gov.cn/pub/csrc_en/newsfacts/release/200708/t20070810_69223.html> accessed 2 June 2021 [hereinafter China CG Code 2002]. See Lin and Puchniak (n 26) appendix 1.

[59] 中华人民共和国证券投资基金法 (Zhōnghuá rénmín gònghéguó zhèngquàn tóuzī jījīn fǎ) [PRC Securities Investment Law] (28 August 2003).

[60] 刘雪菲 (Liu Xuefei), '2018年中国公募基金行业发展战略研究：逐鹿大资管，寻基金的危与机 (2018 Nián zhōngguó gōngmù jījīn hángyè fāzhǎn zhànlüè yánjiū: Zhúlù dà zī guǎn, xún jījīn de wēi yǔ jī) [Research on the Development Strategy of China's Public Equity Fund Industry in 2018: Competing for Big Asset Management, Looking for Crisis and Opportunities]' (*Sohu*, 10 July 2018) <www.sohu.com/a/240329974_313170> accessed 2 June 2021.

[61] The first Chinese index fund was set up in January 2003: '指数基金如何选? (Zhǐshù jījīn rúhé xuǎn?) [How to Select Index Fund]' *Economic Daily* (22 November 2019) <https://finance.sina.com.cn/roll/2019-11-22/doc-iihnzahi2509827.shtml?source=cj&dv=> accessed 2 June 2021; the first Chinese hedge fund was launched in September 2010: '国内首只对冲基金产品面世 易方达基金拨头筹 (Guónèi shǒu zhī duìchōng jījīn chǎnpǐn miànshì yìfāngdá jījīn bō tóuchóu) [First Domestic Hedge Fund Was Launched]' *Renmin Daily* (2 September 2010) <https://finance.qq.com/a/20100902/001842.htm> accessed 2 June 2021.

[62] PBOC, '关于规范金融机构资产管理业务的指导意见 (Guānyú guīfàn jīnróng jīgòu zīchǎn guǎnlǐ yèwù de zhǐdǎo yìjiàn) [The Guiding Opinions on Regulating the Asset Management Business of Financial Institutions]' (27 April 2018).

[63] Liu (n 60).

[64] Asset Management Association of China, '公募基金行业数据 (Gōngmù jījīn hángyè shùjù) [Public Fund Industry Data]' (2021) <www.amac.org.cn/researchstatistics/datastatistics/mutualfundindustrydata/> accessed 2 June 2021.

[65] 杨倩雯(Yang Qianwen), '中国保险70年: 从保险大国走向保险强国 (Zhōngguó bǎoxiǎn 70 nián: Cóng bǎoxiǎn dàguó zǒuxiàng bǎoxiǎn qiángguó) [70 Years of Insurance in China: From a Big Insurance Country to a Strong Insurance Country] *Yicai* (15 August 2019) <www.yicai.com/news/100297014.html> accessed 2 June 2021.

gave the greenlight to insurance companies to directly invest in the stock market.[66] Initially, insurance companies and their asset management subsidiaries could invest only up to 5 per cent of their total assets into the A-shares market.[67] Despite this restriction, as shown in Figures 18.1 and 18.2, in 2005, insurance companies quickly came to hold 4% of the market capitalization and 13.4% of the free-float of the A-shares market. In 2009, the revised insurance law expanded the scope of investments permitted for insurance companies, allowing them to invest indirectly in the stock market through SIFs.[68] In 2014, the CIRC raised the limit on the proportion of assets that insurance companies can invest in equities to 30 per cent.[69]

The CCP has actively encouraged insurance companies to increase their investment in the A-shares market. In 2018, as shown in Figures 18.1 and 18.2, 3.5% of the capitalization and 9.0% of the free-float of the A-shares market were owned by insurance companies. In 2019, the premiums collected by the Chinese insurance industry totalled RMB4.26 trillion, ranking third in the world in terms of their total size, after the US and Japan.[70] As less than 20 per cent of insurance funds are currently invested in equities – and the cap is 30 per cent – there is scope for future growth in the size of the investment by insurance companies in the A-shares market.[71]

The third major type of domestic institutional investor to enter the Chinese A-share market was *pension funds*. The public pension fund market is bifurcated between government pension funds – which are called *social security funds* (SSFs) – and corporate pension funds – which are called *enterprise annuities*. SSFs exist at the local and national levels, the largest of which is the National Social Security Fund (NSSF).

Established in 2000, the NSSF's operations are governed by the Ministry of Finance (MOF) and the Ministry of Labor and Social Security (MOLSS, currently dissolved); the CSRC and PBOC supervise the activities of the NSSF's investment managers and are the custodians of its funds. From 2001 to 2016, several laws were promulgated to increase the rate of return on NSSF funds.[72] One of the major initiatives has been to facilitate the NSSF in investing a portion of its

---

[66] See Xu Binglan, 'Insurance Firms Get Greenlight on Stocks' *China Daily* (25 October 2004) <www.chinadaily.com.cn/english/doc/2004-10/25/content_385567.htm> accessed 2 June 2021.

[67] China Insurance Regulatory Commission (CIRC) and CSRC, '保险机构投资者股票投资管理暂行办法 (Bǎoxiǎn jīgòu tóuzī zhě gǔpiào tóuzī guǎnlǐ zhànxíng bànfǎ) [Interim Measures for the Administration of Stock Investments of Insurance Institutional Investors]' (24 October 2004).

[68] National People's Congress (NPC), '保险法修改情况介绍 (Bǎoxiǎnfǎ xiūgǎi qíngkuàng jièshào) [Information on the Revision of Insurance Law]' (2 March 2009) <www.npc.gov.cn/zgrdw/huiyi/lfzt/bxf/2009-03/02/content_1480632.htm> accessed 2 June 2021.

[69] CIRC, '中国保险监督管理委员会关于加强和改进保险资金运用比例监管的通知 (Zhōngguó bǎoxiǎn jiāndū guǎnlǐ wěiyuánhuì guānyú jiāqiáng hé gǎijìn bǎoxiǎn zījīn yùnyòng bǐlì jiānguǎn de tōngzhī) [Notice of the China Insurance Regulatory Commission on Strengthening and Improving the Proportional Regulation of the Utilization of Insurance Funds]' (23 January 2014) art 2.

[70] China Banking and Insurance Regulatory Commission (CBIRC), '2020年全国各地区原保险保费收入情况表 (2020 Nián quánguó gè dìqū yuán bǎoxiǎn bǎofèi shōurù qíngkuàng biǎo) [Original Insurance Premium Income in Various Regions of the Country in 2020]' (28 January 2021) <www.cbirc.gov.cn/cn/view/pages/ItemDetail.html?docId=963083&itemId=954&generaltype=0> accessed 19 July 2021.

[71] See CBIRC, '2020年保险业经营情况表 (2020 Nián bǎoxiǎn yè jīngyíng qíngkuàng biǎo) [Insurance Business Operations in 2020]' (28 January 2021) <www.cbirc.gov.cn/cn/view/pages/ItemDetail.html?docId=887993&itemId=954&generaltype=0> accessed 19 July 2021.

[72] Since 2001, various regulations were issued to facilitate the development of SSF, including: MOF and MOLSS, '全国社会保障基金投资管理暂行办法 (Quánguó shèhuì bǎozhàng jījīn tóuzī guǎnlǐ zhànxíng bànfǎ) [Interim Provisions on the Administration of Investment by the National Social Security Fund]' (13 December 2001); MOF, MOLSS and PBOC, '全国社会保障基金境外投资管理暂行规定 (Quánguó shèhuì bǎozhàng jījīn jìngwài tóuzī guǎnlǐ zhàn háng guīdìng) [Interim Provisions on the Administration of Overseas Investment by the National Social Security Fund]' (27 April 2009); 全国社会保障基金条例 (Quánguó shèhuì bǎozhàng jījīn tiáolì) Regulation on the National Social Security Fund (1 May 2016).

funds in the A-shares market. Initially, the NSSF invested directly in the A-shares market. However, since 2003, the NSSF has outsourced a portion of its investments to private fund managers,[73] resulting in it being both a direct and an indirect investor in the A-shares market.[74] The portion of the NSSF's total funds that can be invested directly and indirectly in A-shares is currently capped at 40 per cent. As illustrated in Figures 18.1 and 18.2, in 2006, SSFs accounted for 0.9% of capitalization and 3.9% of the free-float of the A-shares market. Although the size of the NSSF has grown substantially over the past decade, the total capitalization of the A-shares market has increased concomitantly. As a result, over the last decade, SSFs have consistently accounted for approximately 1% to 2% of the total capitalization and 2% to 4% of the free-float of the A-shares market.

In 2011, the revised Measures for the Management of Enterprise Annuity Funds were promulgated, limiting the amount that corporate pension funds could invest in equities to 30 per cent of their financial net worth. As shown in Figures 18.1 and 18.2, corporate pension funds started investing in the A-shares market in 2012. Presently, corporate pension funds remain a small portion of the A-shares market, accounting for less than 0.5 per cent of its capitalization and free float – but they have been increasing gradually in importance since 2007 and their total cumulative value likely reached 300 billion yuan by the end of 2020.[75]

The fourth major type of domestic institutional investor to enter the Chinese A-shares market was Chinese *securities institutions*. Securities institutions (*zheng quan ji gou/quan shang*) are the Chinese version of international investment banks. They invest their own capital and the capital of their clients in a variety of investments, including the A-shares market. In 2007 and 2014, the government enacted several policies which provided greater access to, and accelerated trading in, the A-shares market. These reforms appear to have sparked the establishment of securities institutions as significant institutional investors in 2007 and propelled their growth after 2014. As shown in Figures 18.1 and 18.2, securities institutions first accounted for an extremely small percentage of the A-shares market in 2007; however, since 2016 they have consistently accounted for approximately 1 per cent of the total capitalization and 3 per cent of the free-float of the market.

The fifth major type of domestic institutional investor to enter the Chinese A-share market was *trust companies*. Prior to 2012, the CSRC had strict restrictions on the ability of trust companies to hold A-shares. In August 2012, a notice was issued to officially abolish the restrictions on trust companies investing their funds on the stock exchange.[76] As of 2018, trust companies accounted for 0.7 per cent of the total capitalization and 1.5 per cent of the free-float of the A-shares market.

---

[73] 经济观察网 (Jīngjì guānchá wǎng), '2003年 社保基金正式进入股 (2003 Nián shèbǎo jījīn zhèngshì jìnrù gǔshì) [National Social Security Fund (NSSF) Entered into an Agreement with 6 Fund Management Companies in 2003 and Entrusted Them to Make Investments in the A-Share Market]' (*Sina*, 9 April 2018) <http://finance.sina.com.cn/stock/marketresearch/2018-04-09/doc-ifyteqtq6470236.shtml> accessed 2 June 2021.

[74] Zhou Jingya, '"间接参与"股指期货融资融券 ("Jiànjiē cānyù" gǔzhǐ qīhuò róngzī róng quàn) [NSSF Indirectly Invested in Index Funds]' *CBN Daily News* (30 March 2010) <https://finance.qq.com/a/20100330/000302.htm> accessed 2 June 2021.

[75] Deng Xiongying, '3万亿年内可破! 年金规模进入爆发增长期, 权益投资占比有望上升 (3 Wàn yì niánnèi kě pò! Niánjīn guīmó jìnrù bàofā zēng cháng qí, quányì tóuzī zhàn bǐ yǒuwàng shàngshēng) [Corporate Pension Fund Growth Burst]' *Securities Daily* (5 October 2020) <https://news.stcn.com/sd/202010/t20201005_2407640.html> accessed 2 June 2021.

[76] China Securities Depository and Clearing Co., Ltd (CSDC), '中国证券登记结算有限责任公司关于信托产品开户与结算有关问题的通知 (Zhōngguó zhèngquàn dēngjì jiésuàn yǒuxiàn zérèn gōngsī guānyú xìntuō chǎnpǐn kāihù yǔ jiésuàn yǒuguān wèntí de tōngzhī) [Notice of the China Securities Depository and Clearing Corporation Limited on Issues Concerning the Account Opening and Settlement for Trust Products]' (31 August 2004) <www.chinaclear.cn/old_files/1346407535100.pdf> accessed 29 July 2021.

The sixth major type of domestic institutional investor to enter the Chinese A-share market was *private investment funds*. These are private funds that normally receive their capital from high-net-worth individuals and are managed by investment professionals who launch such funds. Private investment funds have existed since the early 2000s. However, historically, owing to legal restrictions on the establishment of private investment funds, they could invest in the stock market only indirectly by opening accounts in the name of corporations or partnerships or by purchasing products from trust companies. This restriction resulted in private investment funds incurring high operational costs. In 2014, the Securities Investment Fund Law was amended to explicitly recognize private investment funds and permit them to open trading accounts to invest directly in the A-shares market.[77] As can be seen in Figures 18.1 and 18.2, this change in the law created a significant new category of institutional investor, which by 2018 accounted for 3.6 per cent of the total capitalization and 9.2 per cent of the free-float of the A-shares market.

There are four conclusions that can be drawn from the domestic side of the China institutional investor taxonomy. First, the government has consistently promoted the growth of institutional investors in the A-shares market. Since the 1990s, the government has had an explicit policy to expand the size and scope of domestic institutional investors. It has achieved this by making the growth of institutional investors an explicit policy of the CCP and, in turn, by consistently promulgating laws relaxing investment restrictions to encourage an increasingly wide scope of financial institutions and investment managers to invest their capital in the A-shares market. This has made domestic institutional investors the primary driver of the growth of institutional investors in China and resulted in China having the world's most important growth market for assets under management.

Second, as China's market for institutional investors has grown, it has become increasingly atomized. As illuminated already, before 2005 SIFs were the only significant institutional investor in the A-shares market and until 2010 they accounted for more than 50 per cent of the market. However, today there are at least six major categories of institutional investor – none of which holds more than 4 per cent of the total capitalization of the A-shares market. This atomization of institutional investors requires a more nuanced understanding of what drives each of the varieties and provides a caution about speaking generally about 'institutional investors' in China – which may have been more justified in the early 2000s when SIFs dominated the market.

Third, as will be discussed in more detail in Section 18.4, the different varieties of domestic institutional investor have different levels of independence from the government. For example, most trust companies[78] and securities companies are SOIIs and, therefore, the CCP can more directly control their engagement and voting policies as institutional investors – which may allow the CCP to utilize them more directly for policy channelling. While some of the largest insurance companies are SOEs, there has been a proliferation of private insurance companies who act as POIIs in China. As such, as will be explained in Section 18.4, these POIIs are more independent from the CCP, but the CCP may still use its indirect control over them for policy channelling. Also, the empirical research and our hand-collected evidence from activist

---

[77] CSDC, 'Zhou Ming: Private Investment Funds Now Admitted for Account Opening and Trading' (1 April 2014) <www.chinaclear.cn/english/sdc/201404/017e5994a0f34ba680b4ced5dd8f7a18.shtml> accessed 2 June 2021.

[78] See '2021年最新68家信托公司注册资本及股东背景 (2021 Nián zuìxīn 68 jiā xìntuō gōngsī zhùcè zīběn jí gǔdōng bèijǐng) [Registered Capital and Shareholder Background of 68 Trust Companies in 2021]' *Sina Finance* (22 February 2021) <https://finance.sina.cn/fund/sm/2021-02-22/detail-ikftpnny9049345.d.html?from=wap> accessed 2 June 2021.

campaigns in Section 18.3 demonstrate the need to recognize the varieties of institutional investor in China – especially the distinction among SOIIs, POIIs and FOIIs – as these appear to affect their impact on corporate governance.

Fourth, even if all institutional investors were to speak with one voice (which is clearly not the case), collectively institutional investors will still be minority shareholders in almost every Chinese listed company. This is significant as it distinguishes China from the UK and the US where institutional shareholders collectively control a majority of shares in most listed companies – which gives them the legal right to collectively 'steward' them.[79] However, in China, similar to in most non-UK/US jurisdictions, the ability of institutional investors to collectively steward listed companies normally does not exist – which makes understanding the role that institutional investors can play as minority shareholders, in the context of companies with a dominant controlling-block shareholder, critically important. As our hand-collected evidence from activist campaigns by institutional investors who are minority shareholders in Section 18.3 demonstrates, increasingly institutional investors are engaging in shareholder activism to spur corporate governance change. As expected, these campaigns tend to be in A-shares companies with more dispersed shareholders. However, somewhat surprisingly, SOIIs have led the majority of these activist campaigns, and, in some cases, have succeeded in these campaigns against SOEs. It is to this that we now turn.

18.3 FILLING THE GAP IN THE LEGAL LITERATURE ON INSTITUTIONAL INVESTORS IN CHINA: EMPIRICAL RESEARCH AND ACTIVIST CAMPAIGNS

18.3.1 *Illuminating the Gap in the Legal Literature*

As demonstrated in Section 18.2, there has been a meteoric rise in the size, ownership stake and free-float of shares that institutional investors have in the A-shares market. However, as noted, the rise of institutional investors in China has been almost entirely overlooked in the legal literature.[80] This is somewhat surprising as the role of institutional investors in corporate governance – particularly in the US and the UK – has become a major focal point for many of the most prominent corporate law scholars.[81]

We suspect that this gap in the legal literature may have arisen for three reasons. First, comparative corporate law scholars have primarily focused on the Chinese government as China's most powerful controlling shareholder through its ownership of non-financial SOEs – which may have caused the rise in the shareholder power of institutional investors to be overlooked.[82] Second, the atomization of China's institutional investors highlighted in Section 18.2 may have made the collective rise of institutional investors in China less conspicuous and makes analyzing their impact on corporate governance more complex. Third, the rise of institutional investors in China is uniquely domestically driven, with the big three American institutional investors – which have been the focus of considerable academic attention – playing an inconsequential role.[83]

---

[79] Dan W Puchniak, 'The False Hope of Stewardship in the Context of Controlling Shareholders: Making Sense out of the Global Transplant of a Legal Misfit' *The American Journal of Comparative Law* (forthcoming).
[80] Xi (n 24).
[81] Fisch, The Uncertain Stewardship Potential of Index Funds, Chapter 21; Bebchuk, Cohen and Hirst (n 25) 92–93; Coates (n 25) 2–5; Gilson and Gordon (n 25) 865, 874–76.
[82] Lin and Milhaupt (n 7) 697; Wang (n 13) 631; Howson (n 9) 51–52; Milhaupt (n 6) 362; Wang and Tan (n 10) 1094.
[83] Jan Fichtner and Eelke M Heemskerk, 'The New Permanent Universal Owners: Index Funds, Patient Capital, and the Distinction between Feeble and Forceful Stewardship' (2020) 49 *Economy and Society* 493; Lucian Bebchuk and Scott Hirst, 'The Specter of the Giant Three' (2019) 99 *Boston University Law Review* 721; Lucian Bebchuk and Scott Hirst, 'Index Funds and the Future of Corporate Governance: Theory, Evidence, and Policy' (2019) 119 *Columbia Law Review* 2029.

However, despite the dearth in legal scholarship, over the past decade there have been a number of empirical studies in the business school literature that provide interesting insights into the role played by institutional investors in Chinese corporate governance. As these studies use different data sets, cover different time periods and focus on different issues, as would be expected, there is some variation (and even incongruency) in their findings. Also, as many of the empirical studies focus on data which extend back over a decade, the focus has tended to be on SIFs – which makes sense because, as shown in Section 18.2, SIFs were the only significant institutional investor in the A-shares market until 2005 and until 2010 they accounted for more than 50 per cent of the market.[84]

Keeping these limitations in mind, we analyze this interesting body of empirical studies. In addition, we attempt to address some of the shortcomings in the empirical studies by analyzing our hand-collected summary of the publicly reported representative activist campaigns that institutional investors have undertaken in China.[85] Ultimately, the empirical studies and activist campaigns demonstrate that the taxonomy of institutional investors analyzed in Section 18.2 matters, as different types of institutional investor appear to play different roles in Chinese corporate governance. Also, the empirical studies and activist campaigns suggest that the influence that the government has over SOIIs – and, in some instances, POIIs – may have a significant effect on their impact on corporate governance. Relatedly, there is some evidence that the impact that institutional investors have on the corporate governance of their investee companies may be contingent on whether the investee company is an SOE or a POE. Importantly, and somewhat surprisingly, our analysis also reveals that SOIIs have undertaken a majority of the activist campaigns and that SOEs have been the target of a number of successful activist campaigns.

Taken together, these results highlight the important impact that the CCP's ability to influence SOIIs, and in some cases POIIs, has on the function they play in Chinese corporate governance – and how foreign institutional investors being insulated from the CCP's influence matters. The mechanisms and tactics that the CCP uses to wield its influence, and the policy channelling reasons for wielding its influence, are the focus of Section 18.4. For now, we turn to analyzing the interesting body of empirical studies for a more granular view of the impact of institutional investors in Chinese corporate governance.

18.3.2 *An Analysis of the Existing Empirical Research*

Keeping in mind the limitations on the empirical studies highlighted earlier, there are at least three meaningful general observations that can be drawn from this body of empirical research. First, most of the empirical studies find that the impact that institutional investors have on the corporate governance of A-shares companies is contingent on the *type of institutional investor* – with statistically significant differences in several studies being found between domestic institutional investors and foreign institutional investors,[86] and between SIFs and other types of institutional investor.[87] Second, several empirical studies find a statistically significant difference

---

[84] See Section 18.2.
[85] See Lin and Puchniak (n 26) appendix 2.
[86] Yongjia Rebecca Lin and Xiaoqing Maggie Fu, 'Does Institutional Ownership Influence Firm Performance? Evidence from China' (2017) 49 *International Review of Economics & Finance* 17; Huang and Zhu (n 42) 324; Reena Aggarwal, May Hu and Jingjing Yang, 'Fraud, Market Reaction, and the Role of Institutional Investors in Chinese Listed Firms' (2015) 41 *Journal of Portfolio Management* 92, 107.
[87] Several articles generally suggest that SIFs, more so than other institutional investors, are the best at corporate governance monitoring as compared to other institutional investors: Michael Firth, Jin Gao, Jianghua Shen and Yuanyuan Zhang, 'Institutional Stock Ownership and Firms' Cash Dividend Policies: Evidence from China' (2016)

in the impact that certain institutional investors have on corporate governance based on the extent to which the institutional investor is *insulated from government pressure* – owing to their size, independence from direct government ownership, or foreign status.[88] Third, several empirical studies find that the impact that institutional investors have on the corporate governance of A-shares companies is contingent on the *type of company* in which institutional investors own shares – with statistically significant differences in several studies being found between SOEs and POEs.[89]

Collectively, these observations confirm that the taxonomy of institutional investors developed in Section 18.2 is important as there is significant empirical evidence demonstrating that the impact of institutional investors on corporate governance in China's A-shares companies differs based on the type of institutional investor. The empirical evidence confirming the importance of the extent to which institutional investors are insulated from government pressure suggests that there is also a need to understand the channels through which the government influences institutional investors and the extent to which different types of institutional investor are influenced by these policy channels – which is the focus of Section 18.4. The empirical evidence that the impact of institutional investors on corporate governance differs depending on whether the investee company is an SOE or a POE requires further analysis – which is also provided in Section 18.4.

A review of these empirical studies also suggests some more specific normative implications of the rise of institutional investors for Chinese corporate governance. Several studies suggest that SIFs – particularly domestic SIFs when compared with other types of institutional investor – improve the corporate governance of A-shares companies. Yuan, Xiao and Zou (2008) published a pioneering study that found statistically significant empirical evidence that ownership by domestic SIFs had a positive impact on the performance of A-shares companies[90] – which has been repeatedly cited in support of the Chinese government's consistent effort over the past two decades to promote SIFs as a valuable corporate governance mechanism.[91] In a later article, Aggarwal, Hu and Yang (2015) found that domestic SIFs are the only type of institutional investor to play a positive monitoring role in Chinese corporate governance – based on a positive correlation between higher domestic SIF ownership and lower fraud.[92] They also suggest that foreign institutional investors are ineffective monitors owing to their small ownership stakes and the fact that other domestic institutional investors (i.e., insurance companies, pension funds, and trusts) are compromised by their business relationships with the investee companies they are supposed to monitor.[93]

In a similar vein, Firth, Gao, Shen and Zhang (2016) conclude that SIFs improve corporate governance monitoring based on evidence of a positive correlation between SIF ownership and higher cash dividends – which is absent with respect to other institutional investors such as banks, insurance companies and securities companies.[94] Chi, Liao and Yang (2019) similarly find that SIFs significantly increase firm innovation, but this effect is not found for other types of institutional

---

65 *Journal of Banking & Finance* 91, 105; Jing Chi, Jing Liao and Jingjing Yang, 'Institutional Stock Ownership and Firm Innovation: Evidence from China' (2019) 50 *Journal of Multinational Financial Management* 44, 55; Amon Chizema, Wei Jiang, Jing-Ming Kuo and Xiaoqi Song, 'Mutual Funds, Tunneling and Firm Performance: Evidence from China' (2020) 55 *Review of Quantitative Finance and Accounting* 355, 382–83.
[88] Lin and Fu (n 86) 18.
[89] ibid.
[90] Rongli Yuan, Jason Zezhong Xiao and Hong Zou, 'Mutual Funds' Ownership and Firm Performance: Evidence from China' (2008) 32 *Journal of Banking & Finance* 1552, 1563.
[91] Lin and Fu (n 86) 18.
[92] Aggarwal, Hu and Yang (n 86) 107.
[93] ibid.
[94] Firth, Gao, Shen and Zhang (n 87) 105 (without examining the distinction between foreign and domestic SIFs).

investor, such as insurance companies, pension funds or QFIIs.[95] Chizema, Jiang, Kuo and Song (2019) also find that an increase in SIF ownership improves firm performance in A-shares companies by effectively mitigating the tunnelling behaviour of controlling shareholders.[96]

Collectively, these empirical studies suggest that SIFs – particularly domestic SIFs in comparison to other types of institutional investor – improve corporate governance in A-shares companies. However, for three reasons, this conclusion may not be as definitive as it appears. First, all these studies suffer from the risk of endogeneity as it makes sense that SIFs would invest in companies with better corporate governance, raising the spectre of reverse causality. Second, none of these studies provides a detailed explanation of how SIFs, with their minority shareholdings, produce a statistically significant impact on corporate governance.

Third, many of these studies are based on at least some data that were pre-2010, which precedes the atomization of institutional investors and was a time when SIFs dominated the institutional investors market – which raises the possibility that other types of institutional investor may now have a greater impact given their increased shareholdings. However, even considering these complicating factors, this body of empirical evidence suggests that there is reason to believe that domestic SIFs appear to improve Chinese corporate governance by acting as a monitor of corporate controllers.

In this context, it is noteworthy that one of the most cited empirical studies on the impact of institutional investors in the A-shares market provides strong empirical evidence that in certain circumstances the government can – and will – also exert political pressure on SIFs to achieve its political and economic objectives. Historically, the A-shares market was divided into tradable and non-tradable shares. In 2005, to remedy the incentive and corporate governance problems created by this unique feature of the A-shares market, the Chinese government initiated the 'split share structure reform' to convert non-tradable shares into tradable shares.[97] To compensate tradable shareholders for the dilution in their stock values that would result from the reform, the government established a requirement that in each company an amount of compensation had to be proposed by the non-tradable shareholders to the tradable shareholders, and that the proposal had to be approved by two-thirds of the tradable shareholders for the reform to be finalized.[98] If the proposal was not approved, a three-month waiting period was required before another proposal could be put forward – which would delay the reform process and, if it occurred in too many companies, would be seen as a black mark on the government officials responsible for the reform.[99] As an earlier attempt at reforming China's unique split share structure in 2001 had failed, the CSRC was determined that this new reform scheme should proceed smoothly and set the end of 2006 as the deadline for all A-shares companies to complete the reform.[100]

Firth, Lin and Zou (2010) examined the impact of state shareholders and SIFs on the amount of compensation received by tradable shareholders in the split share reform of A-shares companies. They found that there was a positive statistically significant relationship between state ownership and the compensation received by tradable shareholders.[101] Considering the earlier failed attempt to reform the split share structure, they reasoned that the government bureaucrats

---

[95] Chi, Liao and Yang (n 87) 55.
[96] Chizema, Jiang, Kuo and Song (n 87) 382–83.
[97] Huang and Zhu (n 42) 313.
[98] ibid.
[99] ibid.
[100] Robin Hui Huang, 'The New Takeover Regulation in China: Evolution and Enhancement' (2008) 42 *The International Lawyer* 153, 156–57.
[101] Michael Firth, Chen Lin and Hong Zou, 'Friend or Foe? The Role of State and Mutual Fund Ownership in the Split Share Structure Reform in China' (2010) 45 *Journal of Financial and Quantitative Analysis* 685, 697.

overseeing the non-tradable shares in SOEs had strong incentives to offer higher compensation to tradable shareholders as this would ensure that the reform proceeded as quickly as possible by setting a positive example for other A-shares companies to follow.[102] It would also advance the government's goal of listing more SOEs as it would avoid shareholder conflict and create favourable investor sentiment.[103] For the bureaucrats proposing the compensation packages on behalf of the non-tradable shares, completing the reform quickly would provide them with political credit for executing the reform successfully, which would move them up the political hierarchy.[104] Thus, the empirical evidence that bureaucrats in SOEs offered statistically significant higher compensation to tradable shareholders makes perfect sense – it allowed bureaucrats to capture political benefits of control by executing an efficient reform, while not suffering any direct consequences of providing higher compensation which came from the government. Conversely, in POEs, where private investors owned non-tradable shares, they would directly suffer the cost of providing higher compensation to tradable shareholders and would not receive any political benefits for an efficient reform – which explains why in POEs there was statistically significant lower compensation provided to tradable shareholders.

Interestingly, Firth, Lin and Zou also found a statistically significant negative relationship between SIF ownership of tradable shares and the amount of compensation provided to tradable shareholders – which is contrary to the evidence from the other empirical studies reviewed that SIFs improve corporate governance and protect (minority) shareholders' interests.[105] They also found that SIF 'ownership weakens the positive link between state ownership and compensation, suggesting that [SIFs] help state-owned firms get the reform done more quickly and at a relatively lower cost'.[106]

Importantly, Firth, Lin and Zou identified and explained a unique policy channel that was used in the context of this reform to put pressure on domestic SIFs to work with the government to ensure a quick and non-contentious reform. Specifically, for the purpose of the split share reform, the CSRC removed the authority from fund managers who normally decide how to vote shares under their management based on market forces and reallocated the decision over voting rights to the Investment Decision Committee (IDC) of the fund management companies.[107] As explained in more detail in Section 18.4, this reallocation of voting rights was critically important as the CSRC has a veto power over the appointment and removal of members of the IDCs of fund management companies,[108] who are often former government officials and CCP members. Also, to speed up the reform process, 'the CSRC put direct pressure on mutual funds to vote in the interest of expediting the reform … [by holding] regular meetings with all fund management firms and [using] these occasions to stress the need for reaching a speedy and noncontentious conclusion to the share structure reform proposals'.[109]

Firth, Lin and Zou also found a statistically significant negative relationship between ownership of voting shares by other institutional investors (e.g. insurance companies, securities

---

[102] ibid 690.
[103] ibid 689.
[104] ibid 690.
[105] ibid 697.
[106] ibid 703.
[107] ibid 693. See also Liu Ying, '股改投票权上收 基金经理翻云覆雨难 (Gǔgǎi tóupiào quán shàng shōu jījīn jīnglǐ fānyúnfùyǔ nán) [It Is Difficult for Fund Managers to Participate in Split Share Reform as the Voting Right Is Reallocated]' *China Business News* (31 August 2005) <http://futures.money.hexun.com/1303024.shtml> accessed 19 July 2021.
[108] Securities Investment Fund Law of the People's Republic of China, Standing Committee of the Eleventh National People's Congress of the People's Republic of China, adopted 28 October 2003 and revised 28 December 2012.
[109] Firth, Lin and Zou (n 101) 692.

companies and investment trusts) and compensation.[110] They concluded that this empirical finding may be owing to the relationship these other institutional investors have with the management of the investee companies – which would provide an incentive for these other institutional investors to support the compensation proposed by the management that was backed by non-tradable shareholders.[111] Importantly, they also posit that these other institutional investors 'are owned by the state [and] may also be under pressure from the CSRC to agree to the compensation terms' – suggesting that these other institutional investors were also co-opted by government pressure to ensure that the split share reform was quick and non-contentious.[112]

In another follow-up study on the split share reform, Huang and Zhu (2015) confirmed the statistically significant positive relationship between state ownership and higher compensation.[113] They also confirmed that this positive relationship decreased with the level of SIF ownership – suggesting that 'the controlling state shareholders may exert political influence on [SIF] managers and offer a lower compensation ratio for companies with [SIF] ownership'.[114] Huang and Zhu then extended Firth, Lin and Zou's research by examining the relationship between compensation and QFIIs. They found a statistically significant positive relationship between the level of QFII ownership and compensation, 'suggesting that QFIIs are less prone to political pressure'.[115] Based on several statistically significant empirical findings, they concluded that 'foreign institutional investors are less prone to political pressure than their local peers and are more likely to perform arm's length monitoring'.[116] In Section 18.4, we identify and explain the specific regulatory architecture which makes it clear why this is the case.

There are five important observations that can be derived from the empirical evidence from the split share reform. First, it demonstrates how the CCP's influence over institutional investors can be used for policy channelling – which reaffirms the importance of understanding how the policy channels for institutional investors work as they can turn the role of institutional investors on its head. Second, it demonstrates how different types of institutional investor are impacted differently by policy channelling (in this case, the difference between domestic and foreign institutional investors) and how understanding the extent to which the CCP can influence different types of institutional investor is critically important. Third, it demonstrates how the CCP may quickly rearrange the regulatory environment – in this case by reallocating the decision over voting rights from fund managers to the IDC – to enhance its ability to use certain types of institutional investor for policy channelling in particular situations. Fourth, it demonstrates how, even when the CCP wants to policy channel, free-market forces remain important – in this case, the CCP could have decided the level of compensation by fiat, but instead it chose to subject the compensation to market forces and then to use policy channelling to shape the outcome. Fifth, the ability of foreign institutional investors to have a significant impact was unique in this case. As the compensation offered by non-tradable shareholders had to be approved by two-thirds of tradable shareholders, this increased the voice of foreign institutional investors which, as highlighted in Section 18.2, normally own only a small minority of shares in A-shares companies. Also, on average, only 35 per cent of tradable shareholders chose to exercise their votes in the split share reform proposals – suggesting that a (foreign) tradable shareholder with as little as 3.5 per cent of the total shares may have been able to veto the proposal, making

[110] ibid 697.
[111] ibid.
[112] ibid 698.
[113] Huang and Zhu (n 42) 314.
[114] ibid.
[115] ibid 319.
[116] ibid 314.

the split shareholder reform atypical in terms of the ability of small minority foreign institutional investors to have formal veto power.[117]

However, even outside of the context of the split share reform, there is a body of empirical research which suggests that foreign institutional investors may have a positive impact on the corporate governance of A-shares companies – with the most consistent evidence of this effect in POEs (and sometimes contrary evidence in SOEs). Hai, Min and Barth (2018) found a statistically significant positive relationship between QFII ownership and various measures of good corporate governance, which suggests that QFIIs reduce agency costs.[118] However, this effect disappeared in SOEs, which they attributed to the negative effects of political pressure in SOEs on the ability of QFIIs to improve corporate governance.[119] Liu, Bredin and Cao (2020) found a statistically significant positive relationship between the presence of QFIIs and better operating performance in A-share companies, with this positive effect less pronounced in SOEs.[120] Li (2017) found a statistically significant negative relationship between QFII holdings and wealth tunnelling, but this effect was less pronounced in SOEs.[121] Lin and Fu (2017) found statistically significant empirical evidence demonstrating that institutional investor ownership positively affects the performance of A-shares companies – with pressure-insensitive, foreign and large institutional shareholders having greater positive effects on firm performance than pressure-sensitive, domestic and small institutional shareholders.[122] Liu, Laing, Cao and Zhang (2018) found statistically significant strong empirical evidence that QFII and SIF ownership significantly improves corporate transparency and governance.[123]

Taken together, this empirical evidence seems to suggest that foreign institutional investors have a positive impact on corporate governance in A-shares companies – especially in POEs. It also suggests that understanding the role played by the state is critically important for understanding the impact of institutional shareholders in China – as the positive corporate governance impact of foreign institutional investors seems to be negatively impacted when the state is the controlling shareholder in SOEs. However, as shown in Section 18.2 and acknowledged in several of these studies,[124] foreign institutional investors *collectively*, on average, have only accounted for between approximately 1% to 3% of A-shares market capitalization over the past two decades, which makes the consistent empirical evidence of their positive impact on corporate governance somewhat puzzling. Also, similar to our observation regarding the empirical evidence that domestic SIFs have a positive impact on corporate governance, the fact that foreign institutional investors are likely to invest in companies that have better corporate governance raises the possibility that these studies are confounded by reverse causality.

The opacity of exactly how foreign institutional investors may exercise their minority power to have a statistically significant impact on corporate governance highlights an issue that cuts across all types of institutional investor in the A-shares market. As explained in Section 18.2, although there has been a meteoric rise in the overall percentage of institutional investors in the A-shares

---

[117] Firth, Lin and Zou (n 101) 690.
[118] Jiang Hai, Huang Min and James R Barth, 'On Foreign Shareholders and Agency Costs: New Evidence from China' (2018) 54 *Emerging Markets Finance and Trade* 2815, 2831.
[119] ibid 2821.
[120] Liu, Bredin and Cao (n 53) 14.
[121] Zhen gyu Li, 'The Impact of Qualified Foreign Institutional Investors on Controlling Shareholder's Tunneling: Evidence of Listed Companies in China' (2017) 7 *American Journal of Industrial and Business Management* 522, 534.
[122] Lin and Fu (n 86) 54.
[123] Ningyue Liu, Elaine Laing, Yue Cao and Xiaofei Zhang, 'Institutional Ownership and Corporate Transparency in China' (2018) 24 *Finance Research Letters* 328, 332.
[124] Liu, Bredin and Cao (n 53) 14; Lin and Fu (n 86) 17.

market from 1.4% in 2003 to 18.7% in 2018,[125] collectively they still, on average, make up a minority of shareholders in A-shares companies – and most A-shares companies have a dominant controlling shareholder. This raises the question of exactly how institutional investors have exercised their power to impact corporate governance in A-shares companies.

To shed some light on this question, we now consider our individual hand-collected case studies that provide a window into exactly how institutional investors have had an impact on the corporate governance of A-shares companies.

18.3.3 Activist Campaigns: How Institutional Investors as Minority Shareholders Impact Corporate Governance in China

To gain a better understanding of how institutional investors may be having an impact on the corporate governance in A-shares companies, we undertook an extensive search using Chinese and English language sources to attempt to locate all the reported representative instances in which institutional investors have taken steps to intervene in the corporate governance of A-shares companies (activist campaigns). Based on our detailed review of all of the reported representative activist campaigns that we could locate,[126] they reveal six important insights about how institutional investors in China have had an impact on corporate governance.

First, institutional investors have not used activist campaigns to intervene in the corporate governance of A-shares companies very often. From 1994 to 2021 there were only 43 activist campaigns, which on average amounts to 1.54 campaigns per year.[127] By comparison, from 2018 to 2020 there were 116 activist campaigns per year in the US.[128] This stark difference between Chinese and American corporate governance is unsurprising considering that most A-shares companies have a dominant controlling shareholder and institutional investors normally are small minority shareholders – the opposite to the US where institutional shareholders hold 80 per cent of shares in listed companies and the vast majority of listed companies lack a dominant controlling shareholder.[129] The ability of institutional investors to engage in shareholder activism is significantly curtailed when they are a small minority shareholder in a company with a dominant controlling shareholder.[130] As such, it is unsurprising that our review of the forty-three activist campaigns revealed that they targeted A-share companies which were corporate governance outliers: 76.7% of companies did *not* have a dominant controlling shareholder and 62.8% of institutional investors involved in the campaigns owned more than 5% of the company's shares. Although, at the earlier stage of the development of the A-shares market, most of the listed companies were SOEs,[131] dispersedly held A-shares companies without a dominant controlling shareholder are becoming more common. This suggests that there may be more activist campaigns by institutional shareholders in A-shares companies in the future.

---

[125] See Section 18.2.
[126] See Lin and Puchniak (n 26) appendix 2.
[127] ibid.
[128] Lazard, '2018 Review of Shareholder Activism' (January 2019) <www.lazard.com/media/450805/lazards-2018-review-of-shareholder-activism.pdf> accessed 2 June 2021; Lazard, '2019 Review of Shareholder Activism' (January 2020) 3 <www.lazard.com/media/451141/lazards-2019-review-of-shareholder-activism-vf.pdf> accessed 2 June 2021; Lazard, '2020 Review of Shareholder Activism' (January 2021) 6 <www.lazard.com/perspective/lazards-annual-review-of-shareholder-activism-2020/> accessed 2 June 2021.
[129] De La Cruz, Medina and Tang (n 37) 12; Puchniak (n 79).
[130] Yu-Hsin Lin, 'When Activists Meet Controlling Shareholders in the Shadow of the Law: A Case Study of Hong Kong' (2019) 14 *Asian Journal of Comparative Law* 1, 7–8.
[131] Robin Hui Huang, 'Shareholder Derivative Litigation in China: Empirical Findings and Comparative Analysis' (2012) 27 *Banking & Finance Law Review* 619, 649.

This may explain why there were more than three times as many activist campaigns from 2011 to 2021 than there were from 2000 to 2010 – as A-shares companies have become more dispersedly held over the past decade.[132]

Second, activist campaigns by FOIIs are extremely rare. Only two out of the forty-three activist campaigns involved FOIIs and in one out of the two activist campaigns involving FOIIs, the FOII joined with a POII to undertake the campaign. We could not find in our searches even a single activist campaign involving an FOII after 2012. This is unsurprising considering that, as highlighted in Section 18.2, foreign institutional investors did not hold any meaningful percentage of A-shares companies until 2007 and since then they have held only between 1% and 3% of the shareholder capitalization of A-shares companies. In addition, although the regulations limiting foreign institutional investors have been gradually relaxed, there is still a 30 per cent cap on the percentage of shares that foreign institutional investors can own in an A-shares company – which prevents foreign institutional investors from being able to execute, or even threaten to execute, a change of control in A-shares companies.[133] It is interesting that out of the two activist campaigns involving foreign institutional investors, one targeted an SOE and the other targeted a POE, and both were successful. In the case targeting an SOE, the foreign institutional investors partnered with private domestic institutional investors to elect their directorial candidate over another candidate who was supported by a government shareholder which was the actual controller of the SOE. As explained in more detail in Section 18.4, this illustrates how foreign institutional investors in some circumstances may be able to have a positive impact on corporate governance as they are more insulated from the mechanisms that the CCP uses to carry out policy channelling in SOIIs and POIIs.

Third, thirteen out of the forty-three activist campaigns were undertaken by SOIIs, while twenty-three were undertaken by POIIs – with POIIs and SOIIs collaborating in five activist campaigns and a POII and an FOII collaborating in one activist campaign. It is noteworthy that prior to 2010 half of the activist campaigns were undertaken by SOIIs, which are owned by the government and ultimately controlled by the CCP directly or indirectly; whereas since 2010 over half of the activist campaigns were undertaken by POIIs.[134] This suggests an increasing reliance on the private market for institutional investors, in which the CCP exercises only indirect control. As discussed in Section 18.4, to varying extents, the CCP through a matrix of policy channels may also control institutional investors which it does not directly own. Taken together, this challenges the idea that the rise of institutional investors in China may threaten the CCP's ultimate control. However, as we explain in Section 18.4, merely because the CCP directly or indirectly controls SOEs does not mean that free-market forces are irrelevant. On the contrary, in normal times free-market forces govern the behaviour of SOIIs and POIIs, like institutional investors in other financial markets. However, in extraordinary times (e.g. when there is market instability, or the government wants to undertake a major reform) both SOIIs directly and POIIs indirectly may serve as agents to execute government policy. This reliance on market forces in regular times and use of policy channelling for extraordinary purposes is a phenomenon which the authors have explained and termed as the institutional shareholder 'market within the state' in a forthcoming article.[135]

---

[132] See Lin and Puchniak (n 26) appendix 2.

[133] See Section 18.2.

[134] From 1994 to 2010, 50% (five out of ten) of the activist campaigns were undertaken by SOIIs, with SOIIs and POIIs collaborating in 20% (two out of ten) of the activist campaigns, whereas from 2011 to 2021, 60.6% (twenty out of thirty-three) of the activist campaigns were undertaken by POIIs, with SOIIs and POIIs collaborating in 9.1% (three out of thirty-three) of the activist campaigns and an FOII and a POII collaborating in one activist campaign.

[135] See Lin and Puchniak (n 26). The term 'market within the state' was coined by Yongnian Zheng and Yanjie Huang in their book, Market in State: The Political Economy of Domination in China (Cambridge University Press, 2018).

Fourth, POEs were the target in eleven out of forty-three activist campaigns, and there were seven cases in which a POII targeted an SOE. It is noteworthy that in four of these cases the POII succeeded in its campaign. This illustrates how the government has allowed POIIs to serve as a check on SOEs – which further highlights the complexity and sophistication of China's market within the state. As explained in Section 18.4, although the government has promoted the emergence of POIIs to serve as a useful check on SOEs, it has also developed policy channels that ensure that the CCP maintains ultimate (indirect) control over POIIs. In addition, POEs were the target in thirty-two out of the forty-three activist campaigns, with fourteen of them involving SOIIs, which demonstrates that this may be another policy channel in which the state can influence or police POEs. It is interesting that only six of these campaigns succeeded – again illustrating how SOIIs are bound by the laws and market forces. Merely because the state is the direct owner of SOIIs does not axiomatically result in a successful activist campaign.

Fifth, the evolution of the types of institutional investor that have executed activist campaigns confirms our observation in Section 18.2 that the market for institutional investors in A-shares companies has become increasingly atomized. As illuminated in Section 18.2, prior to 2010, SIFs dominated the market. As such, it is unsurprising that, prior to 2011, eight out of ten activist campaigns were executed by SIFs. However, from 2011 to 2021, twenty out of thirty-three activist campaigns were undertaken by other types of institutional investor such as trust companies, securities companies, insurance companies and other professional institutions – illustrating how other types of institutional investor have started to participate in the corporate governance of investee companies. This reinforces the importance of the taxonomy of institutional investors described in Section 18.2 and highlights why understanding the different types of regulatory regime impacting different types of institutional investor is important – which is the focus of Section 18.4.

Sixth, 58.1 per cent (twenty-five out of forty-three) activist campaigns were successful, with successful campaigns normally resulting in institutional investors having an impact on corporate governance by preventing the company from engaging in a transaction that would harm minority shareholders or by providing minority shareholders with a voice on the board. To succeed, small minority institutional investors have had to convince other investors to support their proposals – reinforcing the observation that such campaigns normally have a chance to succeed only in dispersedly held companies without a dominant controlling shareholder. The only successful hostile takeover bid by an institutional investor was executed in 2017 by Zhemin Tianhong Investment Partnership (LP) in its successful USD 2.7 billion hostile takeover bid for Zhenxing Biopharmaceutical and Chemical Co., Ltd.[136] Arguably, the key to Zhemin's success was that Zhenxing was an outlier among A-shares companies in terms of having an extremely dispersed shareholding structure – illustrating how dispersed shareholding is a key factor in the success of activist campaigns in A-shares companies.

Finally, we would be remiss not to acknowledge what these case studies cannot tell us. Institutional investors often meet and communicate with investee companies informally – which may have an impact on corporate governance. Although most of this communication is normally unobservable, Cheng, Du, Wang and Wang (2019) examined the impact of 'site visits' (i.e., when investors visit corporate headquarters or manufacturing facilities to meet with

---

[136] Zhenxing Biopharmaceutical and Chemical Co., Ltd. has changed its name to Pacific Shuanglin Bio-pharmacy Co., Ltd. See Fu Jian Zi, '解码A股首例成功市场化敌意收购案 (Jiěmǎ A gǔ shǒu lì chénggōng shìchǎng huà díyì shōugòu àn) [Decoding the First Successful Market-Oriented Hostile Acquisition of A-shares]' (*JNJ*, 29 June 2018) <https://m.jrj.com.cn/madapter/stock/2018/06/29033024743240.shtml> accessed 2 June 2021.

managers in A-shares companies).[137] These 'site visits' are required to be disclosed in the annual reports of A-shares companies. They found a significant positive market reaction to corporate site visits and that the market reaction was stronger for visits conducted by SIF managers.[138] This suggests that some of the empirical evidence described earlier, which finds that SIFs have a positive impact on corporate governance, may result from informal activities and may not be reflected in activist campaigns. We are unaware of any similar research that has focused on foreign institutional investors, but this also raises the possibility that the empirical evidence which suggests that they have a positive impact on the corporate governance of A-shares companies may be related to their informal activities. More research will have to be done to confirm whether this is the case.

In sum, the relative infrequency of activist campaigns illustrates how A-shares companies are still dominated by controlling shareholders – with institutional shareholders remaining a small minority. However, the rise in the number of activist campaigns over the last decade appears to confirm the rising shareholder power of institutional investors highlighted in Section 18.2. The increasing variety in the types of institutional investor executing activist campaigns also confirms the atomization of institutional investors and the value of the taxonomy of institutional investors in Section 18.2. Perhaps most interesting is the extent to which SOIIs have executed campaigns against SOEs and POIIs have succeeded in campaigns against SOEs. This illustrates the complexity and sophistication of China's unique system of corporate governance, in which the CCP maintains ultimate control while promoting checks and balances within the government and a 'free market within the state'. It is to this that we now turn.

18.4 THE DUAL ROLES OF INSTITUTIONAL INVESTORS IN CHINA: CORPORATE GOVERNANCE AND POLICY CHANNELLING

18.4.1 *Illuminating the CCP's Targeted Use of Policy Channelling in an Otherwise Free Market*

The empirical research and activist campaigns in Section 18.3 suggest that there is a complex relationship between the CCP and the role that institutional investors play in Chinese corporate governance. This section aims to make sense out of this complexity by mapping the formal and informal mechanisms that the CCP utilizes to engage in policy channelling. We demonstrate that the CCP can – and has – used various mechanisms to engage in policy channelling in SOIIs and POIIs. Interestingly, for SOIIs and POIIs there are two distinct paths – composed of various government bodies, regulations and tactics – for engaging in policy channelling, with FOIIs being largely insulated from both paths.

Equally as important is our evidence that the CCP uses its power to policy channel in a targeted and limited way surrounding significant stock market and political events. On a day-to-day basis, absent these extraordinary events, institutional investors in China appear to be driven by free market-forces. Empirical, interview and case study evidence suggests that institutional investors often serve an important corporate governance function by acting as a check on corporate controllers in SOEs and POEs. This fits with other research on Chinese corporate governance that demonstrates that the government has created a system to mitigate private

---

[137] Qiang Cheng, Fei Du, Brian Yutao Wang and Xin Wang, 'Do Corporate Site Visits Impact Stock Prices?' (2019) 36 *Contemporary Accounting Research* 359, 364.
[138] ibid 381.

benefits of control – even when it means constraining the power of SOEs – while at the same time ensuring that the CCP maintains ultimate control.[139]

Ultimately, it appears that institutional investors play an important function within the unique China model of corporate governance. The CCP does not micro-manage institutional investors in a way that some conceptions of 'state capitalism' may suggest.[140] Rather, institutional investors normally function according to free-market forces and perform an important corporate governance role – with the CCP using its various mechanisms for policy channelling to execute important policies, which may benefit the market and society, while also possibly blunting the effectiveness of efficient corporate governance. This system is what we explain in our forthcoming article as 'the market within the state' for institutional investors in China.[141]

18.4.2 Illuminating, Classifying and Mapping the CCP's Mechanisms for Policy Channelling

The split share reform research provides convincing empirical evidence that the CCP can – and has – used its regulatory power to transform domestic institutional investors into a mechanism for policy channelling.[142] The CCP's use of institutional investors to achieve its political goals comports with the more recent creation of a 'National Team' of government-controlled SOIIs which were tapped to stabilize the A-shares market after its collapse in 2015.[143] Although, as explained in Section 18.2, the CCP has a long history of using its regulatory power to promote institutional investors as a market-stabilizing mechanism, the enormous scale of investment and the strategic co-ordination of a select group of SOIIs in 2015 crystallized the idea of the National Team as an important feature of the A-shares market – which investors now count on to intervene in times of market volatility.[144]

There is also empirical and anecdotal evidence that, beyond being a mechanism to facilitate regulatory reforms and stabilize the A-shares market, the CCP uses its ownership and control over SOIIs to achieve more overt political objectives. There is evidence that, prior to major CCP political events and meetings, the government uses its control over SOIIs to ensure a general

---

[139] Howson (n 9) 52; Wang and Tan (n 10) 1094.
[140] Telephone interview, 30 May 2021, investment manager, CICC (Shenzhen); telephone interview, 30 May 2021, legal counsel, DBS Securities (China); telephone interview, 30 May 2021, senior manager, CMS (Shanghai); telephone interview, 30 May 2021, legal counsel, DBS Securities (China); telephone interview, 30 May 2021, partner, Global Law Office (Beijing); telephone interview, 31 May 2021, legal officer, SAFE; Andrew Szamosszegi and Cole Kyle, *An Analysis of State-Owned Enterprises and State Capitalism in China* (US–China Economic and Security Review Commission 2011) 52.
[141] See Lin and Puchniak (n 26).
[142] Firth, Lin and Zou (n 101) 697; Huang and Zhu (n 42) 314; see Section 18.3.
[143] Moxy Ying, 'When Stocks Crash, China Turns to Its "National Team"' *The Washington Post* (9 March 2021) <www.washingtonpost.com/business/when-stocks-crash-china-turns-to-its-national-team/2021/03/09/d13c540a-80df-11eb-be22-32d331d87530_story.html> accessed 2 June 2021; Hudson Lockett and Sun Yu, 'How the Invisible Hand of the State Works in Chinese Stocks' *Financial Times* (4 February 2020) <www.ft.com/content/od41cb6e-4717-11ea-aeb3-955839e06441> accessed 2 June 2021; Evelyn Cheng, 'Goldman: Government-Directed Traders Bought Up Billions in Chinese Stocks Last Quarter' (CNBC, 11 September 2018) <www.cnbc.com/2018/09/11/goldman-government-directed-traders-bought-nearly-17-billion-in-local-stocks-last-quarter.html> accessed 2 June 2021; Shen Hong and Stella Yifan Xie, 'That Calm Chinese Stock Market? It's Engineered by the State' *The Wall Street Journal* (31 May 2018) <www.wsj.com/articles/that-calm-chinese-stock-market-its-engineered-by-the-government-1527775089?mod=e2tw> accessed 2 June 2021.
[144] ibid. Narayanan Somasundaram, 'Chinese Government-Back Funds Snap Up Stocks to Halt Plunge' *Nikkei Asian Review* (9 March 2021) <https://asia.nikkei.com/Business/Markets/Chinese-government-backed-funds-snap-up-stocks-to-halt-plunge> accessed 2 June 2021.

level of social stability by keeping the markets calm.[145] The extent to which market stability is crucial for social stability in China is evident from the fact that, with more than 100 million Chinese citizens invested in the A-shares market, shareholders form an even larger constituency than CCP members.[146]

There is also empirical and anecdotal evidence that the CCP uses its formal and informal power to pressure POIIs – a tactic that has become known as 'window guidance' – to reinforce its policy channelling through institutional investors.[147] In addition to the empirical evidence demonstrating the control over POIIs to facilitate the split share reform, anecdotal evidence suggests that window guidance is used to alter the behaviour of POIIs to bolster the CCP's ability to utilize domestic institutional investors to achieve social stability surrounding major political events.[148]

Perhaps unsurprisingly, the empirical evidence in Section 18.3 suggests that the CCP's ability to use FOIIs as a conduit for policy channelling is considerably more limited, if not non-existent. This is supported by the empirical evidence regarding the split share reform, which suggests that QFIIs acted in the interest of their beneficiaries and their investee companies' tradable shareholders in negotiating the compensation in the reform – as opposed to jettisoning their interests to make the CCP's market reform a success.[149] There appears to be no evidence that QFIIs have participated in any market stabilization efforts, including the campaign carried out by the National Team following the 2015 market collapse. The independence of QFIIs from the CCP may also help explain why several empirical studies examined in Section 18.3 found that QFIIs played a positive monitoring role in A-shares companies, despite their modest shareholdings – which, as explained in Section 18.2, have historically been limited by strict regulatory caps that have only recently been relaxed.

Taking a step back, based on the ability of the CCP to utilize institutional investors for the purpose of policy channelling, institutional investors in China can be classified into three broad categories, as depicted in Figure 18.4. The first category, *state-controlled institutional investors*, is composed of China's SOIIs. The CCP exercises two-tiers of control over SOIIs through both its shareholding network and the appointment of the 'first in command' (*yi ba shou*) of SOIIs.

First, as the controlling shareholder or actual controller who holds more than 50 per cent of the shares of SOIIs directly or indirectly, the government, through its agencies, is able to exercise legal control over SOIIs as their majority shareholder. As illustrated in Figure 18.4, the institutional architecture that has progressively been developed during the SOE reform process has created a complex network of different government agencies (e.g. the State Council, the State-owned Assets Supervision and Administration Commission of the State Council (SASAC) and

---

[145] Shen and Xie (n 143).
[146] Charlotte Yang, 'Caixin Explains: How a Stock Market Crash Created China's "National Team"' (*Caixin*, 19 October 2018) <www.caixinglobal.com/2018-10-19/caixin-explains-how-a-stock-market-crash-created-chinas-national-team-101337087.html> accessed 2 June 2021.
[147] Telephone interview, 30 May 2021, partner, Global Law Office (Beijing); telephone interview, 30 May 2021, investment manager, CMS (Shanghai); telephone interview, 30 May 2021, legal counsel, DBS Securities (China); telephone interview, 30 May 2021, investment manager, CICC (Shenzhen). See also Lockett and Yu (n 143); Cheng Pangyue, 'Drivers of Institutional Investors' Shareholder Behaviour in China's Listed Companies: A Socio-legal Research of Incentives and Challenges in the New Era' (on file with authors) 25; see CSRC, Supervision and Administration Measures for Directors, Supervisors, Senior Management and Practitioners of Securities and Fund Management Organizations (Consultation Paper) (20 November 2020) s 3(1); Tomoyuki Fukumoto, Masato Higashi, Yasunari Inamura and Takeshi Kimura, 'Effectiveness of Window Guidance and Financial Environment – In Light of Japan's Experience of Financial Liberalization and a Bubble Economy' (Bank of Japan Review, August 2010) <www.boj.or.jp/en/research/wps_rev/rev_2010/data/rev10e04.pdf> accessed 2 June 2021.
[148] Shen and Xie (n 143).
[149] Huang and Zhu (n 42) 319.

MOF and SAFE) that hold shares in SOIIs on behalf of the state.¹⁵⁰ However, it should be noted that, more recently, the government policy has been to consolidate the state-owned shares of SOIIs into MOF in order to simplify the shareholding network between government agencies and SOIIs and to strengthen the government's control over state-owned shares.¹⁵¹

As the major shareholder of SOIIs, MOF is able to exercise its shareholder rights under the PRC Company Law (e.g. participating in the appointment and dismissal of senior managers, the revision of the articles of association and other decision-making processes)¹⁵² to control the corporate governance of SOIIs. Notably, this does not mean that MOF exercises any external regulatory power over these SOIIs – which is critically important as all the domestic institutional investors, including SOIIs and POIIs, are effectively regulated by the three financial regulatory agencies (i.e., PBOC, CBIRC and CSRC; the three agencies are also known as 'one bank and two commissions', *yi hang liang hui*). Specifically, banks, insurance companies and other institutional investors such as financial asset management companies, trust companies and financing companies are subject to the regulation of CBIRC; securities companies and SIF firms are regulated by CSRC.¹⁵³ In addition, according to the Interim Measures for the Supervision and Administration of Financial Holding Companies, issued 11 September 2020, the financial holding companies are subject to regulation by PBOC.

Second, for SOIIs which are listed in the Directory of Central Financial Enterprises, the CCP is able to exercise its control through the appointment of their first in command.¹⁵⁴ According to the Interim Regulations on the Management of the Leading Personnel of Central Financial Enterprises, issued by the General Office of the CCP in 2011, the appointment of the senior managers of central financial enterprises shall be administered by the CCP (which relies on the principle referred to in Chinese as '*dang guan gan bu*', which roughly translates into English as 'the Party administers the management of cadres').¹⁵⁵ In addition, for the senior managers in SOIIs who are government officials and who are CCP members, they are bound by the Law of the People's Republic of China

---

¹⁵⁰ NPC, '中华人民共和国企业国有资产法 (Zhōnghuá rénmín gònghéguó qǐyè guóyǒu zīchǎn fǎ) [The Law of the People's Republic of China on the State-Owned Assets of Enterprises]' (28 October 2008) art 4, 11.

¹⁵¹ 中共中央、国务院关于完善国有金融资本管理的指导意见 (Zhōnggòng zhōngyāng, guówùyuàn guānyú wánshàn guóyǒu jīnróng zīběn guǎnlǐ de zhǐdǎo yìjiàn) [Guiding Opinions of the CPC Central Committee and the State Council on Improving the Management of State Financial Capital] (30 June 2018); General Office of the State Council, '国有金融资本出资人职责暂行规定 (Guóyǒu jīnróng zīběn chūzī rén zhízé zhàn háng guīdìng) [The Interim Provisions on the Duties of State-Owned Financial Capital Contributors]' (7 November 2019); MOF, '国有金融资本管理条例征求意见稿 (Guóyǒu jīnróng zīběn guǎnlǐ tiáolì zhēngqiú yìjiàn gǎo) [Regulations on the Management of State-Owned Financial Capital (Draft for Comments)]' (11 May 2020).

¹⁵² NPC, 中华人民共和国公司法 (Zhōnghuá rénmín gònghéguó gōngsī fǎ) [Company Law of the People's Republic of China (2018 Amendment)] (26 October 2018) art 37.

¹⁵³ CIRC, '保险公司管理规定 (Bǎoxiǎn gōngsī guǎnlǐ guīdìng) [Provisions on the Administration of Insurance Companies]' (19 October 2015); NPC, '中华人民共和国银行业监督管理法 (Zhōnghuá rénmín gònghéguó yínháng yè jiāndū guǎnlǐ fǎ) [Banking Supervision Law of the People's Republic of China]' (31 October 2006); NPC, '第十三届全国人民代表大会第一次会议关于国务院机构改革方案的决定 (Dì shísān jiè quánguó rénmín dàibiǎo dàhuì dì yī cì huìyì guānyú guówùyuàn jīgòu gǎigé fāng'àn de juédìng) [Decision of the First Session of the Thirteenth National People's Congress on the State Council Institutional Reform Proposal]' (17 March 2018); CSRC, '证券投资基金管理公司管理办法 (Zhèngquàn tóuzī jījīn guǎnlǐ gōngsī guǎnlǐ bànfǎ) [The Measures for the Administration of Securities Investment Fund Management Companies]' (1 November 2012).

¹⁵⁴ MOF, '中央金融企业名录 (Zhōngyāng jīnróng qǐyè mínglù) [Directory of Central Financial Enterprises]' (20 February 2021) <http://bgt.mof.gov.cn/zhuantilanmu/rdwyh/czyw/202102/t20210219_3658752.htm> accessed 19 July 2021.

¹⁵⁵ 中管金融企业领导人员管理暂行规定 (Zhōng guǎn jīnróng qǐyè lǐngdǎo rényuán guǎnlǐ zhàn háng guīdìng) [Interim Regulations on the Management of Leading Personnel of Central Financial Enterprises] (16 November 2011) art 3.

on Administrative Discipline for Public Officials and related CCP regulations.[156] These mechanisms ensure that the CCP maintains control over the governance of SOIIs and illustrates how the CCP can effectively exact its control over SOIIs for the purpose of policy channelling.

It is noteworthy that although all the members of the National Team are state-controlled institutional investors, there are many SOIIs in this category that are not part of the National Team.[157] This makes sense as the National Team merely refers to the SOIIs that were tapped to stabilize the markets in 2015 and is a loose category that appears to evolve based on market circumstances.[158] In this sense, the National Team is an illustration of how the CCP can quickly and effectively utilize SOIIs for policy channelling; it is not a fixed category of institutional investors unto itself.

The second category is *state-influenced institutional investors*, which includes domestic POIIs in China. As all state-influenced institutional investors are privately owned, unlike with state-controlled institutional investors, the CCP does not have the ability to directly control POIIs through the exercise of its shareholder rights or by directly appointing senior managers. Also, the senior managers of POIIs are generally recruited from the private sector and receive market-based salaries – unlike the public regulated salaries of the government officials who comprise most of the firsts in command in SOIIs.[159]

However, despite the initial free-market appearance of POIIs, they are categorized as state-influenced institutional investors because of the formal and informal mechanisms that the CCP may use to influence POIIs to engage in policy channelling. In terms of formal power, although the senior managers in POIIs are not directly appointed by the CCP, they are required to be approved by relevant regulatory government agencies (i.e., PBOC, CBIRC or CSRC) before their appointment. As mentioned, domestic institutional investors are regulated by PBOC, CBIRC or CSRC depending on the financial industry of which they are part. Historically, part of the regulatory power of these three government agencies is derived through their power to approve the appointment of senior managers of POIIs.[160]

---

[156] Cheng (n 147) 25. It must be noted that, strictly speaking, senior managers of SOIIs do not have formal administrative levels or ranks; see 中共中央关于国有企业改革和发展若干重大问题的决定 (Zhōnggòng zhōngyāng guānyú guóyǒu qǐyè gǎigé hé fāzhǎn ruògān zhòngdà wèntí de juédìng) [Decision on Several Major Issues Concerning the Reform and Development of State-Owned Enterprises] (22 September 1999). However, as many of those 'first in command' are appointed and removed by the Organization Department of the CCP, they have an administrative level or rank. It must be noted that not all senior managers of SOIIs are government officials and, therefore, not all of them have to follow the Law of the People's Republic of China on Administrative Discipline for Public Officials, Standing Committee of the National People's Congress (20 June 2020). Only those who were government officials before they joined SOIIs are subject to this law.

[157] Ying (n 143); see Figure 18.4.

[158] Ying (n 143); Cheng (n 143); Yang (n 146).

[159] Cheng (n 147) 22. Telephone interview with legal counsel, 30 March 2021, Ms C, DBS (Securities).

[160] CBRC, '银行业金融机构董事 (理事) 和高级管理人员任职资格管理办法 (Yínháng yè jīnróng jīgòu dǒngshì (lǐshì) hé gāojí guǎnlǐ rényuán rènzhí zīgé guǎnlǐ bànfǎ) [The Measures for the Administration of the Office-Holding Qualifications of the Directors and Senior Managers of Banking Financial Institutions]' (18 December 2013); 保险公司董事、监事和高级管理人员任职资格管理规定 (Bǎoxiǎn gōngsī dǒngshì, jiānshì hé gāojí guǎnlǐ rényuán rènzhí zīgé guǎnlǐ guīdìng) [Provisions on the Administration of the Office Qualifications for the Directors, Supervisors and Senior Executives of Insurance Companies] (23 January 2014); CIRC, '证券公司董事、监事和高级管理人员任职资格监管办法 (Zhèngquàn gōngsī dǒngshì, jiānshì hé gāojí guǎnlǐ rényuán rènzhí zīgé jiānguǎn bànfǎ) [Measures for the Supervision and Administration of the Professional Qualifications of Directors, Supervisors and Senior Managers of Securities Companies]' (19 October 2012); 证券投资基金管理公司高级管理人员任职管理办法 (Zhèngquàn tóuzī jījīn guǎnlǐ gōngsī gāojí guǎnlǐ rényuán rènzhí guǎnlǐ bànfǎ) [The Measures for the Administration of Post-Holding of Senior Officers of Securities Investment Fund Management Companies] (1 October 2004).

Taking SIF firms as an example, normally, every SIF has an IDC which is responsible for making high-level business and policy decisions in the SIF.[161] The IDC is composed of the SIF firm's senior managers,[162] which gives them an air of independence as they are private sector employees.[163] Historically, the CSRC had veto power over the appointment and removal of all IDC members which it could exercise owing to the fact that the appointment of all executives of securities companies had to be reported to the CSRC for filing.[164] Notably, following the new Securities Law, which came into force on 1 March 2020, several laws and regulations were issued to revise the *ex ante* approval requirement of the appointment of POIIs' senior managers to only *ex post* filing.[165] However, it is too early to tell whether this will make a difference in the CSRC's actual influence over POIIs. In terms of informal mechanisms, research based on anonymous interviews with senior employees in POIIs suggests that the CSRC uses window guidance to effectively control the selection of senior managers (who are also IDC members),[166] and IDCs are often composed of CCP members.[167] The CSRC's window guidance, combined with its formal veto power, suggests that IDCs provide a conduit for the CCP to pressure POIIs into engaging in policy channelling.[168]

However, it must be noted that, generally speaking, the IDC would not interfere in the day-to-day investment activities of the SIF, as it normally delegates its authority over investment decisions to the SIF's fund managers.[169] Research based on anonymous interviews with senior managers in SIFs suggests that, under normal circumstances, the IDC does not intervene in the decisions of fund managers with respect to what stock they choose to purchase or how they choose to engage in the corporate governance of investee companies.[170] The CCP's ability to directly control the day-to-day investment activities in SIFs is limited as fund managers are not within the list of senior managers whose appointments are subject to the approval of the CSRC. However, as highlighted in Section 18.3, for the purpose of the split share reform, the relevant

---

[161] Cheng (n 147) 26; telephone interview with fund manager, 18 March 2021, Mr Y, GF Securities.
[162] Which generally consists of the principals of management (including the chairman, the general manager and the chief financial officer. Telephone interview with fund manager, 18 March 2021, Mr Y, GF Securities. Telephone interview with legal counsel, 30 March 2021, CICC.
[163] Yu Jin and Hou Wei Xiang, '投资决策委员会特征与投资业绩, 投资能力–基于公墓基金的研究 (Tóuzī juécè wěiyuánhuì tèzhēng yǔ tóuzī yèjī, tóuzī nénglì-shén yú gōngmù jījīn de yánjiū) [Investment Decision-Making Committee Characteristics and Investment Performance and Ability]' (2017) 6 投资研究 [*Review of Investment Studies*] 116.
[164] CSRC, '证券公司类报备指引 (Zhèngquàn gōngsī lèi bào bèi zhǐyǐn) [Securities Company Filing Guidelines]' (14 September 2015) <www.csrc.gov.cn/zjhpublicofheb/bszn/201509/t20150914_283941.htm> accessed 2 June 2021.
[165] 中华人民共和国证券法 (Zhōnghuá rénmín gònghéguó zhèngquàn fǎ) [The Securities Law of the PRC] (1 March 2020); CSRC, '证券基金经营机构董事、监事、高级管理人员及从业人员监督管理办法 (征求意见稿) (Zhèngquàn jījīn jīngyíng jīgòu dǒngshì, jiānshì, gāojí guǎnlǐ rényuán jí cóngyè rényuán jiāndū guǎnlǐ bànfǎ (zhēngqiú yìjiàn gǎo)) [The Measures for the Supervision and Administration of Directors, Supervisors, Senior Managers and Practitioners of Securities and Fund Management Institutions (Draft for Comments)]' (20 November 2020); PBOC, '金融控股公司董事、监事、高级管理人员任职备案管理暂行规定 [The Interim Provisions on the Administration of Recordation for the Office-Holding of Directors, Supervisors, and Senior Executives of Financial Holding Companies]' (1 May 2021).
[166] Cheng (n 147) 24–25.
[167] Firth, Lin and Zou (n 101) 693.
[168] Mo Shensheng, 'Financial Restructuring and Economic Development in China from the Perspective of Institutional Arrangement' (PhD dissertation, Zhejiang University 2014).
[169] Cheng (n 147) 26; see Guiding Opinions on the Fair-Trading Rules of Securities Investment Fund Management Companies (2011 Rev) s 10.
[170] Cheng (n 147) 24–26. Telephone interview with fund manager, 26 May 2020, Mr Z, CICC; telephone interview with legal counsel, 3 March 2021, Ms X, CICC; telephone interview with fund manager, 18 March 2021, Mr Y, GF Securities; telephone interview with legal counsel, Ms C, DBS Securities (China); telephone interview with senior manager, Ms J, CMS (Shanghai).

voting decision in investee companies was reallocated from fund managers to the IDC. This illustrates how the CCP can – and has – used its regulatory power and indirect control over IDCs to engage in policy channelling. In addition, senior fund managers in SIFs are licensed by the Securities Association of China (SAC) – which is a non-profit organization under the supervision and guidance of the CSRC.[171] This provides another possible avenue through which the CCP can exert pressure on POIIs for the purpose of policy channelling, even when the IDC does not interfere in the decisions of fund managers.

The third category is *foreign-owned institutional investors*, which includes all QFIIs and the other foreign institutional investors described in Section 18.2. As mentioned earlier, there is no evidence that the CCP uses FOIIs as a mechanism for policy channelling. The senior managers of FOIIs are not required to seek the approval of the CSRC.[172] Moreover, the person in charge of the QFII's Chinese investments does not have to meet the licensing requirements of the SAC – the only requirement is for them to meet the qualifications for investment professionals in their respective home jurisdictions.[173] As such, with respect to FOIIs, the CCP lacks the direct channels of authority it has over SOIIs and the indirect channels for window guidance it has over POIIs – leaving FOIIs considerably more insulated from the primary mechanisms that the CCP uses to engage in policy channelling, which may provide one reason for the empirical evidence in Section 18.3 showing that they improve corporate governance in their investee companies.

However, based on the evidence concerning FOIIs in Section 18.2, it could be argued that by strategically capping the total amount of investment by FOIIs and their ability to purchase a controlling shareholder stake in A-shares companies, the CCP has ensured that FOIIs will not be major players in the A-shares market. Despite the recent relaxation of these restrictions, there is no evidence that the irrelevance of FOIIs in policy channelling will change in the foreseeable future. This comports with the observation made in Section 18.3 that activist campaigns by FOIIs are extremely rare.

18.4.3 Day-to-Day Corporate Governance Function of Institutional Investors in China

Equally as important as recognizing the CCP's ability to use institutional investors as a powerful mechanism for policy channelling is the observation that the CCP appears to use this power only in a selective and targeted manner. In the case of POIIs, as highlighted already, empirical and anecdotal evidence suggests that the CCP's use of policy channelling is reserved to facilitate major reforms, to stabilize the market in times of crisis or to ensure social stability surrounding major political events.[174] Based on interviews we conducted in 2020 and 2021, senior employees in POIIs uniformly were of the view that in 'normal times' POIIs worked as asset owners and/or asset managers to maximize the returns for their ultimate beneficiaries – and not for policy channelling.[175] This finding is confirmed by another research project which concluded, based

---

[171] Cheng (n 147) 26.
[172] CSRC, PBOC and SAFE, '合格境外机构投资者和人民币合格境外机构投资者境内证券期货投资管理办法 (Hégé jìngwài jīgòu tóuzī zhě hé rénmínbì hégé jìngwài jīgòu tóuzī zhě jìngnèi zhèngquàn qīhuò tóuzī guǎnlǐ bànfǎ) [The Administrative Measures for Securities and Futures Investment Made in China by QFIIs and RQFIIs]' (1 November 2020) art 6.
[173] Cheng (n 147) 26; see CSRC, Service Guide for Administrative Licensing Matters: Qualified Foreign Investor Qualification Approval (25 September 2020).
[174] Shen and Xie (n 143).
[175] Telephone interview with fund manager, 26 May 2020, Mr Z, CICC; telephone interview with legal counsel, 31 March 2021, Ms C, DBS Securities; telephone interview with senior manager, 30 March 2021, Ms J, CMS; telephone interview with fund manager, 18 March 2021, Mr Y, GF Securities.

on anonymous interviews with executives in POIIs, that on a day-to-day basis they were driven by free-market forces – and not policy channelling.[176]

We recognize that the answers provided by the employees who were interviewed in POIIs may be self-serving. However, with respect to POIIs, particularly SIFs, this comports with the empirical studies described in Section 18.3, which demonstrate the positive impact that SIFs tend to have on the performance of A-shares companies'[177] – with the notable exception of the split share reform which was an extraordinary situation where an important CCP policy objective was involved.[178] It is also supported by the evidence in Section 18.3 of the increasing number of activist campaigns by POIIs and, most importantly, that half of the activist campaigns carried out against SOEs have been successful.[179] Although the number of activist campaigns has been relatively small, this illustrates that, outside of major events and reforms, the CCP has sometimes allowed POIIs to play an active market-based role as institutional investors – even when it involves challenging the corporate governance of SOEs. This demonstrates that although the CCP can transform POIIs into state-influenced institutional investors, it appears to exercise its power in a targeted manner to achieve specific and important policy objectives – with POIIs normally being driven by free-market forces.

In terms of SOIIs, the evidence from activist campaigns in Section 18.3 also suggests that in normal times SOIIs are driven by free-market forces to improve the corporate governance of their investee companies. This is suggested by the fact that a majority of activist campaigns undertaken in the A-shares market were conducted by SOIIs.[180] Interestingly, a significant number of these campaigns targeted SOEs – suggesting that the CCP realizes the corporate governance and economic benefits of having SOIIs serve as a check on the controlling shareholder power of SOEs, which is congruent with the CCP's long-standing policy to support the development of institutional investors as a mechanism to improve corporate governance and stabilize the stock market.[181] The activist campaigns by SOIIs against POEs also demonstrate that the CCP uses SOIIs as a mechanism to serve as a check on controlling shareholder power more generally.

This comports with the government's creation of the China Securities Investor Services Centre – a non-profit organization which owns 100 shares in all A-shares companies for the purpose of facilitating lawsuits to protect minority shareholders' rights.[182] As of April 2020, the ISC had facilitated twenty-five cases by appointing attorneys for the claimant minority shareholders and had successfully filed a lawsuit in its own name to invalidate a corporate resolution in an investee company.[183] The ISC also acts as a mediator to help resolve corporate governance disputes between institutional investors and investee companies free of charge.[184] This is

---

[176] Cheng (n 147) 24. Telephone interview with fund manager, 26 May 2020, Mr Li, CICC; telephone interview with legal counsel, 31 March 2021, Ms C, DBS Securities; telephone interview with senior manager, 30 March 2021, Ms J, CMS; telephone interview with fund manager, 18 March 2021, Mr Y, GF Securities; telephone interview with partner, 30 March 2021, Ms K, Global Law Office.

[177] Chizema, Jiang, Kuo and Song (n 87) 382–83; Chi, Liao and Yang (n 87) 55; Lin and Fu (n 86) 18; Firth, Gao, Shen and Zhang (n 87) 105; Aggarwal, Hu and Yang (n 86) 107; Yuan, Xiao and Zou (n 90) 1563.

[178] Firth, Lin and Zou (n 101) 697; Huang and Zhu (n 42) 314.

[179] Lin and Puchniak (n 26) appendix 2.

[180] Firth, Lin and Zou (n 101) 697; Huang and Zhu (n 42) 314.

[181] ibid.

[182] Robin Hui Huang, 'Rethinking the Relationship between Public Regulation and Private Litigation: Evidence from Securities Class Action in China' (2018) 19 *Theoretical Inquiries in Law* 333, 359; Cheng (n 147) 20.

[183] Cheng (n 147) 24; China Securities Investor Services Center, '维权服务(Wéiquán fúwù) [Rights Protection Service]' <www.isc.com.cn/html/wqfw/> accessed 2 June 2021.

[184] Cheng (n 147) 24; CSRC, Notice by the Supreme People's Court and the China Securities Regulatory Commission of Issuing Opinions on Comprehensively Advancing Establishment of Diversified Resolution Mechanism of Securities and Futures Disputes No 305 (13 November 2018).

congruent with the amendments made to the 2020 CGC which encourage institutional investors to be actively engaged in the corporate governance of their investee companies.[185] As highlighted in Section 18.2, this is unsurprising based on the long history of the CCP promoting the development of institutional investors as a mechanism to stabilize the market and improve corporate governance. It also provides strong evidence that on a day-to-day basis – outside of extraordinary political and market events – the CCP not only allows but encourages institutional investors to be actively engaged shareholders driven primarily by free-market forces.

Finally, to be clear, we are not suggesting that the system is perfectly bifurcated between SOIIs/POIIs always serving as an effective mechanism for policy channelling in extraordinary times and always being an efficient corporate governance mechanism on a day-to-day basis. Empirical studies in Section 18.3 suggest that in some instances SOIIs may be less effective than POIIs and/or FOIIs in monitoring investee companies.[186] In other instances, empirical evidence suggests that SOEs may be more insulated against corporate governance pressure from institutional investors than POEs.[187] This suggests that sometimes, on a day-to-day basis, the lack of independence from the government may blunt the effectiveness of SOIIs and shield SOEs from effective monitoring by institutional investors. This may be more likely to occur when the circumstances in a given case elevate a corporate governance issue into an issue of political importance to the CCP. However, based on the totality of the empirical, case study and interview evidence, it is our view that this stylized picture of the CCP's formal and informal targeted use of policy channelling (or lack thereof), as depicted in Figure 18.4, largely approximates what plays out in practice.

18.5 INSTITUTIONAL INVESTORS IN CHINA: AN AUTOCHTHONOUS MECHANISM UNRELATED TO UK-CUM-GLOBAL STEWARDSHIP

Despite the relationship between institutional investors and corporate governance becoming a focal point for leading corporate law scholars, the meteoric rise of institutional investors in China has been almost entirely overlooked. The primary goal of this chapter was to fill this void in the literature and analyze the rise of institutional shareholders in China on its own terms. Given the proclivity among international organizations and many corporate law experts to view global developments in corporate governance through an Anglo-American lens,[188] we conclude this chapter by explaining why institutional investors in China should be seen as an autochthonous corporate governance mechanism that is unrelated to the UK-cum-global stewardship movement.

Unlike most of Asia's other leading economies, China has not adopted a UK-style stewardship code. However, China's CGC was amended in 2018 to include a section on 'Institutional Investors and Other Related Institutions'.[189] This section encourages all of the various

---

[185] See Section 18.2 (China CG Code 2002 (n 58) Principle 11).
[186] See Section 18.3.
[187] See Section 18.3.
[188] See generally Dan W Puchniak, 'Multiple Faces of Shareholder Power in Asia: Complexity Revealed' in Jennifer G Hill and Randall S Thomas (eds), *Research Handbook on Shareholder Power* (Edward Elgar 2015) 512–15, 521–22; Dan W Puchniak, Harald Baum and Michael Ewing-Chow (eds), *The Derivative Action in Asia: A Comparative and Functional Approach* (CUP 2012); Dan W Puchniak and Kon Sik Kim, 'Varieties of Independent Directors in Asia: A Taxonomy' in Dan W Puchniak, Harald Baum and Luke Nottage (eds), *Independent Directors in Asia: A Historical, Contextual and Comparative Approach* (CUP 2017) 112; Dan W Puchniak and Umakanth Varottil, 'Related Party Transactions in Commonwealth Asia: Complicating the Comparative Paradigm' (2020) 17 *Berkeley Business Law Journal* 1, 5–8.
[189] CSRC, 'Code of Corporate Governance for Listed Companies' (2018) 19 <www.csrc.gov.cn/zjhpublic/zjh/201809/P020180930584077967335.pdf> accessed 2 June 2021 [hereinafter China CG Code 2018].

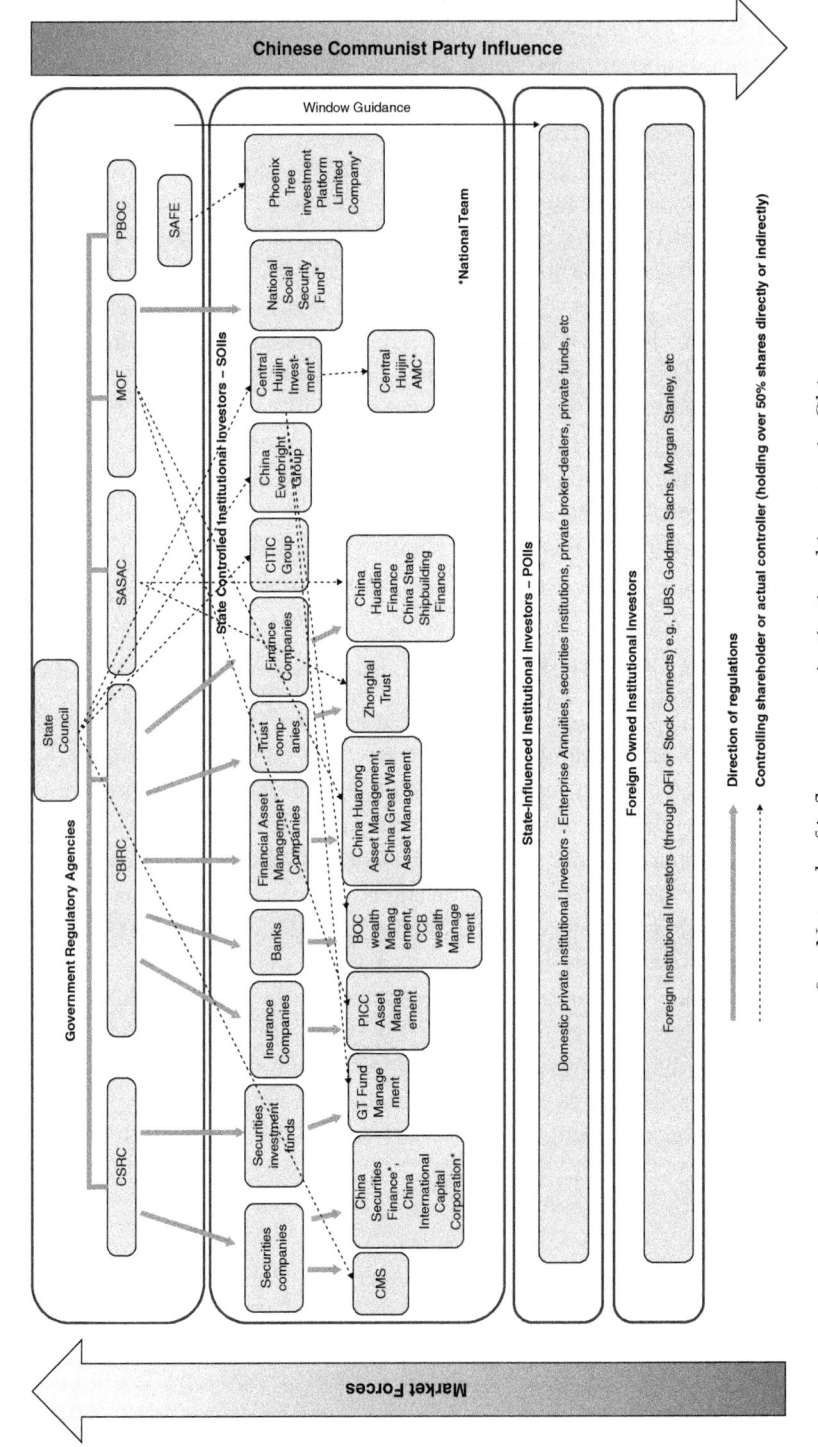

FIGURE 18.4 Network of influence over institutional investors in China

institutional investors identified in the taxonomy 'to engage in corporate governance reasonably by exercising their shareholder rights such as voting rights, inquiry rights and advisory rights in accordance with laws'.[190] It also stresses that institutional investors 'may play an active role in corporate governance by participating in decision-making on major issues, recommending candidates for directors and supervisors, and supervising the performance of directors and supervisors in accordance with laws and regulations and the company's articles of association'.[191] Finally, it 'encourages institutional investors to disclose the objectives and principles of their participation in the governance of listed companies, the strategies for exercising voting rights, and the outcome and effect of the exercise of shareholder rights'.[192] Reading these provisions on their own, an Anglo-American scholar may posit that China's idea for institutional investors to play an active role in corporate governance and disclose their stewardship policies was inspired by the UK-cum-global stewardship movement described in this book. However, for at least three reasons, this would be incorrect.

First, as we have explained in detail in this chapter, there is a long history that goes back to the 1990s of the CCP encouraging the development of institutional investors to improve the China model of corporate governance on its own terms. In fact, the 2018 Chinese CGC provisions related to institutional investors were an expansion of a provision in the inaugural 2002 Chinese CGC,[193] which encouraged institutional investors to play an active role in the corporate governance of their investee companies. As this predated the UK's inaugural 2010 stewardship code by almost a decade, the idea to use institutional investors as a mechanism to improve corporate governance was obviously not inspired by the UK Code.

Second, as highlighted in this chapter, institutional investors have consistently been promoted in China as a mechanism for improving corporate governance within the China model – not as a mechanism for changing the China model. The 2018 Chinese CGC makes it clear that the primary agency problem in China is regulating controlling shareholders.[194] In stark contrast, as explained in Chapter 28 of this book, the UK Stewardship Code was designed to transform passive institutional investors into active shareholder stewards in a dispersed shareholder environment.[195] As institutional investors collectively own a majority of shares in most UK listed companies, it is possible for them to steward most listed companies as they have the shareholder power to do so.[196] In China, where controlling shareholders predominate, this has never been seen as the role for institutional investors, who are viewed as a mechanism for monitoring corporate controllers – but not 'stewarding' listed companies.

Third, the use of institutional investors as a mechanism for the CCP's policy channelling and to reinforce the CCP's ultimate control is a unique feature of the China model without an equivalent in the UK-cum-global stewardship movement. However, this fits perfectly within the China model of corporate governance. The 2018 Chinese CGC states that 'organizations of the Communist Party of China (the Party) should be established in a listed company in accordance with the Company Law to conduct the Party's activities. Listed companies should provide necessary conditions for the activities of the Party organizations.'[197] This is entirely alien to the

---

[190] ibid art 78.
[191] ibid art 79.
[192] ibid art 80.
[193] China CG Code 2002 (n 58) art 11.
[194] China CG Code 2018 (n 189) ch 6.
[195] Lim and Puchniak, Can a Global Legal Misfit Be Fixed?, Chapter 28. See also Puchniak (n 79).
[196] Puchniak (n 79).
[197] China CG Code 2018 (n 189) art 5.

416   Part II Jurisdictions

UK-cum-global stewardship model, but it illustrates that the role of institutional investors in policy channelling in China is not an aberration but the norm.

Relatedly, it may surprise Anglo-American corporate governance experts that almost two decades ago the 2002 Chinese CGC was already encouraging listed companies to 'be concerned with the welfare, environmental protection and public interests of the community' and to 'pay attention to the company's social responsibilities'.[198] Moreover, the 2018 Chinese CGC appears to go further than the UK Code 2020 in expanding corporate purpose beyond maximizing shareholder value. It encourages listed companies to 'actively implement the concept of green development, integrate ecological and environmental protection requirements into the development strategy and corporate governance process, actively participate in the construction of ecological civilization, and play an exemplary role in pollution prevention, resource conservation, and ecological protection'.[199] Going beyond environmental concerns, it encourages listed companies to assist 'poverty-stricken counties or villages, and actively connect with and earnestly support poverty-stricken areas to develop local industries, train talents, and promote employment'.[200]

As discussed in this book, if the UK-cum-global stewardship movement has a future, it will likely be in the promotion of ESG.[201] If it moves in this direction, it will be moving in the same direction that the CCP envisaged for China's companies decades ago. However, in China, unlike in the UK, this movement does not have institutional investors at its core. The CCP is at the core of this top-down, government-centred campaign – with state-controlled companies and, more recently, institutional investors playing a role in it. This is a stark contrast to the UK Code 2020 which places institutional investors at the core of its model, which aims to transform companies into conduits for promoting ESG.

Ultimately, this chapter demonstrates that institutional investors have become an important vector in China's autochthonous corporate governance model, which can no longer be ignored. To accurately understand the role of institutional investors in Chinese corporate governance and how effective they are in improving corporate governance in China, these developments must be understood on their own terms and in the specific political economic context. The same is true for understanding how Chinese companies and institutional investors fit into the government's broad-based campaigns to address social inequality and improve the environment. To see these as part of a UK-inspired 'global shareholder stewardship' movement would make Western pundits seem like the proverbial woman who has only a hammer and sees everything as a nail.

---

[198] China CG Code 2002 (n 58) art 86.
[199] China CG Code 2018 (n 189) art 86.
[200] ibid art 87.
[201] Katelouzou and Puchniak, Global Shareholder Stewardship, Chapter 1, this volume.

19

Stewardship and Collective Action

The Australian Experience

Tim Bowley and Jennifer G. Hill[*]

19.1 INTRODUCTION

The 2008 Global Financial Crisis (GFC) gave rise to competing narratives about shareholders and their engagement in corporate governance.[1] A common view in the US depicted shareholders as instigators of the crisis, by placing pressure on corporate managers to engage in excessive risk-taking to increase profitability.[2] A similarly negative view of shareholders arguably underpins recent US developments, such as the common ownership debate[3] and the Business Roundtable's recently announced jettisoning of a shareholder-centred conception of corporate purpose, in favour of a stakeholder paradigm.[4]

A different interpretation of the GFC prevailed in a number of other jurisdictions, including the United Kingdom, where the real problem was perceived to be lack of shareholder participation in corporate governance.[5] This explanation of the GFC was based on a positive narrative concerning the corporate governance potential of shareholders. According to this narrative, greater engagement by institutional investors is a beneficial corporate governance technique,[6] which operates as a check on centralized managerial power.[7]

Shareholder stewardship codes (stewardship codes) embody this positive narrative. They reflect the growing importance of institutional investors in capital markets around the world,[8] and the

---

[*] The authors would like to acknowledge the valuable research assistance provided by Mitheran Selvendran in connection with this chapter.

[1] See Jennifer G Hill, 'Good Activist/Bad Activist: The Rise of International Stewardship Codes' (2018) 41 *Seattle University Law Review* 497.

[2] See e.g. John C Coffee Jr, 'Systemic Risk After Dodd-Frank: Contingent Capital and the Need for Regulatory Strategies Beyond Oversight' (2011) 111 *Columbia Law Review* 795, 799.

[3] See e.g. Einer Elhauge, 'Horizontal Shareholding' (2016) 129 *Harvard Law Review* 1267.

[4] See David Gelles and David Yaffe-Bellany, 'Feeling Heat, CEOs Pledge New Priorities' *The New York Times* (New York, 20 August 2019) A1 <www.nytimes.com/2019/08/19/business/business-roundtable-ceos-corporations.html> accessed 16 July 2020.

[5] According to the Walker Review, a lack of institutional investor engagement with UK banks was a key governance problem in relation to the GFC: David Walker, 'A Review of Corporate Governance in UK Banks and Other Financial Industry Entities. Final Recommendations' (26 November 2009) 72, para 5.11 <https://ecgi.global/sites/default/files/codes/documents/walker_review_261109.pdf> accessed 16 July 2020.

[6] See e.g. Financial Reporting Council, *The UK Stewardship Code 2020* (2019) 4 <www.frc.org.uk/getattachment/5aae591d-d9d3-4cf4-814a-d14e156a1d87/Stewardship-Code_Dec-19-Final-Corrected.pdf> accessed 16 July 2020 [hereinafter UK Code 2020] (referring to the potential for stewardship to 'create long-term value for clients and beneficiaries leading to sustainable benefits for the economy, the environment and society').

[7] See Walker Review (n 5) 72, paras 5.11–5.12.

[8] See e.g. Securities and Exchange Board of India, 'Report of the Committee on Corporate Governance' (Committee Report, 5 October 2017) 93 <www.sebi.gov.in/reports/reports/oct-2017/report-of-the-committee-on-corporate-governance_36177.html> accessed 16 July 2020 (noting that, as a result of this increasing importance, institutional

belief that increased engagement by institutional investors improves corporate decision-making and provides protection against excessive risk-taking.[9]

From the perspective of the positive narrative, there is considerable sense in shareholders undertaking their stewardship activities collectively. By acting collectively, shareholders can leverage their power, pool their resources and share costs, thereby making stewardship more feasible and less speculative. The Walker Review, for example, encouraged 'strengthening methods of collaboration among shareholders with similar concerns', on the basis that boards of directors were more likely to be responsive to collective, as opposed to individual, shareholder pressure.[10] The stewardship codes of many jurisdictions today refer to, and implicitly support, collective action by institutional investors.[11]

In contrast, for critics of shareholder participation in corporate governance, collective action merely exacerbates the risks posed by shareholder power.[12] Activist hedge funds engaged in co-ordinated conduct have accordingly been described as 'locusts'[13] and 'wolf packs'.[14]

This chapter examines the role of collective action as a form of stewardship, with particular reference to the Australian context. This is because Australia provides favourable conditions for institutional investor stewardship and is therefore an interesting case study concerning the potential of collective action as a stewardship tool. In particular, Australian law provides shareholders with favourable shareholder rights[15] and Australia has a capital market structure that is conducive to investor stewardship, including high levels of institutional ownership and low levels of controlling stakes held by non-institutional block-holders.[16] As a result, Australia is one of only four jurisdictions – together with the United Kingdom, the US and Canada – which the Organisation for Economic Co-operation and Development (OECD) classifies as having

---

investors are 'expected to shoulder greater responsibility towards their clients/beneficiaries by enhancing their monitoring of and engagement with their investee companies').

[9] See e.g. Andrew G Haldane, 'Who Owns a Company?' (University of Edinburgh Corporate Finance Conference, Edinburgh, 22 May 2015) 8, 11 <www.bankofengland.co.uk/-/media/boe/files/speech/2015/who-owns-a-company.pdf> accessed 16 July 2020 (stating that 'companies tend to have higher valuations when institutional shareholders are a large share of cashflow, perhaps reflecting their stewardship role in protecting the firm from excessive risk-taking').

[10] Walker Review (n 5) 85, para 5.43.

[11] See Section 19.3.

[12] See e.g. Christopher M Bruner, 'Corporate Governance Reform in a Time of Crisis' (2011) 36 *Journal of Corporation Law* 309, 309–10; Alan Dignam, 'The Future of Shareholder Democracy in the Shadow of the Financial Crisis' (2013) 36 *Seattle University Law Review* 639, 682; Leo E Strine Jr, 'Who Bleeds When the Wolves Bite? A Flesh-and-Blood Perspective on Hedge Fund Activism and Our Strange Corporate Governance System' (2017) 126 *Yale Law Journal* 1870.

[13] Mark Landler and Heather Timmons, 'Poison Ink Aimed at "Locusts"' *The New York Times* (Frankfurt, 30 March 2006) <www.nytimes.com/2006/03/31/business/media/poison-ink-aimed-at-locusts.html> accessed 16 July 2020.

[14] In the US, 'wolf pack' refers to the situation where an intervention by an activist hedge fund against a company gains momentum as a result of other activist hedge funds buying into the target company. It is claimed that this results in activist hedge funds holding, collectively, a material proportion of the target company's shares, exerting significant pressure on the target's board to acquiesce to the lead hedge fund's demands. Commentators have expressed concerns regarding the leverage that this provides hedge fund activists: .see e.g. John C Coffee Jr and Darius Palia, 'The Wolf at the Door: The Impact of Hedge Fund Activism on Corporate Governance' (2016) 41 *Journal of Corporation Law* 545.

[15] Australian corporate law, for example, provides shareholders with much stronger shareholder rights than US corporate law: Jennifer G Hill, 'Subverting Shareholder Rights: Lessons from News Corp's Migration to Delaware' (2010) 63 *Vanderbilt Law Review* 1.

[16] Ownership data reveal that institutions own significantly more than half of all publicly traded equities: see e.g. Susan Black and Joshua Kirkwood, 'Ownership of Australian Equities and Corporate Bonds' (RBA Bulletin, Reserve Bank of Australia, September 2010) 27 <https://core.ac.uk/download/pdf/6725264.pdf> accessed 16 July 2020 (noting that by early 2010 Australian institutional investors held approximately 40% of listed equities and foreign investors, which would include foreign institutional investors, approximately 40%).

a dispersed ownership structure for listed companies.[17] Yet share ownership in Australia is concentrated in the sense that relatively small groups of shareholders tend to hold a significant proportion of a company's shares. Studies covering different periods between 1990 and 2006 have found that on average the twenty largest shareholders in an Australian listed company (a significant proportion of which are institutional investors) hold between 60 per cent and 70 per cent of the company's shares.[18]

These conditions suggest that it would make considerable sense for institutional investors in Australian listed companies to undertake their stewardship activities collectively. In many companies, the collective voting power of even a handful of institutions is likely to represent a very significant proportion of a company's issued capital, giving those institutions potentially significant collective leverage.

However, the reality of collective action in Australia is more complicated. Among other things, Australia's stewardship codes address collective action briefly and in very general terms only.[19] Moreover, evidence reveals that, insofar as investors seek to exert collective influence in their stewardship activities, they typically favour indirect forms of collective action. That is, rather than wielding influence by entering into ad hoc coalitions with fellow investors, they more routinely channel collective influence through representative organizations and industry intermediaries, such as industry bodies and engagement firms.

This chapter examines these developments. It argues that the nuanced image of collective action emerging from the Australian experience highlights that collective action is by no means a simple governance phenomenon. This has implications for how stewardship codes frame their expectations regarding collective action and how securities and takeover laws apply to collective action. These insights are relevant, both in Australia and internationally, to policymakers, regulators and researchers who are interested in the role and regulation of collective action as a stewardship tool.

The chapter proceeds as follows. Section 19.2 provides an overview of the development of stewardship in Australia. Section 19.3 discusses the significance of collective action within the general stewardship framework. Section 19.4 assesses the nature and role of collective action as a stewardship tool in Australia. Sections 19.5 and 19.6 conclude and outline key insights from the analysis.

19.2 STEWARDSHIP CODES IN AUSTRALIA

19.2.1 *The Evolution of Stewardship Codes in Australia*

By international standards, Australia was a late convert to stewardship codes.[20] According to some industry representatives, the fact that Australia had emerged relatively unscathed from the GFC meant that the crisis did not initially prompt the same degree of scrutiny of investors' role in corporate governance, as it did in other countries.[21]

---

[17] OECD, 'OECD Corporate Governance Factbook 2019' (11 June 2019) 17 <www.oecd.org/daf/ca/Corporate-Governance-Factbook.pdf> accessed 16 July 2020.
[18] See e.g. Reza M Monem, 'Determinants of Board Structure: Evidence from Australia' (2013) 9 *Journal of Contemporary Accounting & Economics* 33, 38 (reporting that in 2006 the top twenty shareholders in a listed company held on average 63.68% of the company's issued shares).
[19] See Section 19.3.2.
[20] As explained later, Australian industry bodies adopted stewardship codes in 2017 and 2018. By this time, codes had already been adopted in approximately twenty other jurisdictions: Alice Klettner, 'The Impact of Stewardship Codes on Corporate Governance and Sustainability' (2017) 23 *New Zealand Business Law Quarterly* 259, 274.
[21] MSCI and Responsible Investor, 'Stewardship and ESG Integration in the Asia-Pacific Region' (2016) 14–15 <www.msci.com/documents/1296102/5003026/Responsible+Investor+and+MSCI+ESG+Research+Round+Table+Report+2016.pdf/f538f36b-03a8-455a-b0eb-072034eb1ca6> accessed 16 July 2020 (quoting industry representatives to this effect).

As stewardship codes were spreading internationally during the early years of the 2010s, Australian asset owners[22] and asset managers[23] were in fact resisting the introduction of a stewardship code in Australia. In 2012, for example, the two peak industry bodies for asset owners and asset managers, the Australian Council of Superannuation Investors (ACSI) and the Financial Services Council (FSC), made submissions to a government inquiry,[24] arguing that a stewardship code was unnecessary. The industry bodies claimed that Australia already had a strong culture of company–shareholder engagement and that a number of existing industry-promulgated guidelines covered matters commonly addressed in stewardship codes.[25] One submission noted, somewhat dismissively: 'While the UK Stewardship Code is an important international precedent ... ACSI does not believe that a similar instrument is necessary for Australian investors ... [W]e believe that if a similar code were to be introduced in Australia, it would be somewhat inconsequential and potentially send confusing signals to companies and investors.'[26]

However, the industry eventually relented. It was conscious of mounting criticism regarding the adequacy and transparency of institutions' engagement activities[27] and was also concerned that a failure to adopt a stewardship code would threaten the international standing of Australia's fund management sector.[28] The industry's two peak bodies took the initiative. The FSC issued FSC Standard 23: Principles of Internal Governance and Asset Stewardship in July 2017 (FSC Code).[29] ACSI published the Australian Asset Owner Stewardship Code in May 2018 (ACSI Code).[30]

It is not apparent from the public record why these industry bodies formulated separate codes. A likely explanation lies in the different institutional roots of the FSC and ACSI. The FSC is a representative body for asset management firms, insurance companies, financial advisers and

---

[22] e.g. pension funds (more commonly known as 'superannuation' funds in Australia).
[23] e.g. fund managers.
[24] Corporations and Markets Advisory Committee, *The AGM and Shareholder Engagement* (Discussion Paper, September 2012) <www.camac.gov.au/camac/camac.nsf/byheadline/pdfdiscussion+papers/$file/agm.pdf> accessed 16 July 2020.
[25] Australian Council of Superannuation Investors, 'ACSI Submission to the Corporations & Markets Advisory Committee – The AGM and Shareholder Engagement' (21 December 2012) 3, 6, 8 <www.camac.gov.au/camac/camac.nsf/byheadline/pdfsubmissions_6/$file/acsi_agm.pdf> accessed 16 July 2020 (claiming that industry had already adopted broadly equivalent governance guidelines such as UNPRI and rules requiring disclosure of voting practices by pension funds); Financial Services Council, 'FSC Submission – Future of the AGM' (31 December 2012) 9 <www.camac.gov.au/camac/camac.nsf/byheadline/pdfsubmissions_6/$file/fsc_agm.pdf> accessed 16 July 2020 (claiming that elements of the UK Stewardship Code had already been adopted in Australia such as the FSC's guidance regarding managing conflicts of interest and disclosing proxy voting activities).
[26] ACSI, 'ACSI Submission to the Corporations & Markets Advisory Committee' (n 25) 8.
[27] Louise Davidson, 'Asset Owner Stewardship Code Can Build Trust' (Australian Council of Superannuation Investors, May 2018) <https://web.archive.org/web/20190302030704/www.acsi.org.au/publications-1/acsi-articles/1514-asset-owner-stewardship-code-can-build-trust.html> archived 2 March 2019, accessed 16 July 2020. For an example of criticism, see Guerdon Associates, 'Pressure on Asset Managers and Proxy Advisers to Lift Their Game – But Not in Australia' (12 December 2016) <www.guerdonassociates.com/articles/pressure-on-asset-managers-and-proxy-advisers-to-lift-their-game-but-not-in-australia/> accessed 16 July 2020.
[28] Financial Services Council and Alliance Bernstein, 'Setting the Standard: Fund Managers Lift Their Game' (February 2018) 2–3 <https://web.alliancebernstein.com/APAC/investments/au/resources/pdf/Governance_in_the_AU_Asset_Management_Industry-Feb2018.pdf> accessed 16 July 2020.
[29] Financial Services Council, 'FSC Standard 23: Principles of Internal Governance and Asset Stewardship' (July 2017) <www.fsc.org.au/web-page-resources/fsc-standards/1522-23s-internal-governance-and-asset-stewardship> accessed 16 July 2020 [hereinafter FSC Code].
[30] Australian Council of Superannuation Investors, 'Australian Asset Owner Stewardship Code' (May 2018) <https://acsi.org.au/wp-content/uploads/2020/01/AAOSC_-The_Code.pdf> accessed 16 July 2020 [hereinafter ACSI Code].

other financial services firms.[31] The asset managers and asset owners that are included in its membership generally form part of commercial banks, insurance companies and other financial conglomerates.

In contrast, ACSI is the peak body for particular types of asset owner; namely, public sector superannuation funds, Australia's 'industry' superannuation funds,[32] and a handful of overseas pension funds.[33] ACSI's member funds tend not to form part of commercial financial conglomerates and the sponsors of these funds do not seek to derive profits from operating them.[34] The industry superannuation funds, which comprise the majority of ACSI's fund members, have their origins in initiatives by trade unions in the 1980s to extend occupational superannuation coverage throughout the Australian workforce.[35] The industry superannuation funds have grown significantly on the back of Australia's mandatory retirement savings scheme, making them powerful participants in the fund management sector.[36] There exists commercial tension between the memberships of the FSC and ACSI because of the significant growth of industry superannuation funds relative to the superannuation funds operated by banks and other financial conglomerates which are members of the FSC. A notable example of this tension occurred in 2018 when the industry superannuation funds commissioned the 'fox in the hen house' television advertisement. The advertisement portrayed the FSC's members as foxes whose 'for profit' business model threatened the retirement savings (i.e. hens) of Australian workers.[37] It is conceivable that these distinct institutional roots and commercial tensions explain why the FSC and ACSI adopted separate approaches to the development of stewardship codes.

When they issued their respective codes, both the FSC and ACSI were self-consciously taking a different approach to the issuers of codes in other jurisdictions. The FSC Code notes that, 'unlike other stewardship codes which focus on asset stewardship and conflicts of interest, the [FSC Code] takes a broader view and also includes the internal governance of the Asset Manager'.[38] In a media release relating to its code, ACSI acknowledged the existence of overseas codes but commented: 'However, this is the first stewardship code to focus exclusively on the activities of Australian asset owners.'[39] Both the FSC and ACSI had a relatively long tradition of policy formulation in relation to corporate governance matters – including in the area of

---

[31] Financial Services Council, 'About the FSC's Members' <www.fsc.org.au/about/membership> accessed 16 July 2020.
[32] The name 'industry' superannuation fund (hereinafter industry superannuation fund) recognizes that these funds were originally established to provide retirement savings for workers in particular industries; however, most of these funds are now open to the general public: AustralianSuper, 'Retail or Industry Super Funds, What Is the Difference?' (2020) <www.australiansuper.com/superannuation/superannuation-articles/2018/10/retail-or-industry-super-funds> accessed 16 July 2020.
[33] Australian Council of Superannuation Investors, 'Who Our Members Are' <https://acsi.org.au/members/who-our-members-are/> accessed 16 July 2020.
[34] Australian Securities and Investments Commission, 'Types of Super Funds' (*MoneySmart*, 12 February 2019) <https://moneysmart.gov.au/how-super-works/types-of-super-funds> accessed 16 July 2020.
[35] See, generally, Bernard Mees and Cathy Brigden, *Workers' Capital: Industry Funds and the Fight for Universal Superannuation in Australia* (Allen & Unwin 2017).
[36] Mees and Smith report that industry superannuation funds have tripled their market share since the mid-nineties: Bernard Mees and Sherene A Smith, 'Corporate Governance Reform in Australia: A New Institutional Approach' (2019) 30 *British Journal of Management* 75, 76–77.
[37] Joanna Mather, 'Union Funds Call a Truce' *The Australian Financial Review* (Sydney, 24 September 2018) 1.
[38] FSC Code (n 29) 7.
[39] Australian Council of Superannuation Investors, 'First State Super Endorses Stronger Stewardship' (Media Release, 1 May 2019) <https://acsi.org.au/media-releases/media-release-first-state-super-endorses-stronger-stewardship/> accessed 16 July 2020.

institutional investors' governance activities[40] – which may explain their intentionally distinctive approaches.

In summary, stewardship codes in Australia are an industry-led initiative. Instead of being imposed by an external party to encourage changes in how investors engage in corporate governance, they have been adopted by industry bodies as a response to scrutiny of investors' governance activities. Their development has also been influenced by Australia's very particular institutional and market context.

19.2.2 Overview of the Australian Codes

19.2.2.1 The FSC Code

The FSC Code is applicable to institutions which undertake asset management functions and have elected to become full members of the FSC.[41] Membership of the FSC is voluntary and financial institutions can choose their preferred level of membership.[42] Full members of the FSC currently include both Australian fund managers and a substantial number of international fund managers.[43] Klettner reports that, as of 2017, the fifty full members who were bound by the FSC Code managed a large majority of total funds under management in Australia.[44]

The FSC Code addresses not only the internal governance of asset managers[45] but also their stewardship activities.[46] In relation to stewardship, the FSC Code states that asset managers 'should' exercise effective stewardship over their investments, encourage investee companies to meet the highest standards of governance and ethical practices, and use the 'tools' available to investors to hold boards and executives accountable.[47]

The FSC Code is a designated 'FSC Standard'.[48] Compliance with FSC Standards is compulsory for full members of the FSC and non-compliance can expose full members to disciplinary action by the FSC.[49] In this sense, the FSC Code is mandatory in nature. However, the FSC Code does not in substance oblige full members to undertake any particular stewardship activities; it merely requires them to disclose their approach towards stewardship.[50] It also provides guidance regarding matters which investors' disclosures should address, although this guidance is limited to seven brief bullet points which merely identify relevant disclosure topics.[51]

---

[40] As explained by each of the organizations in their submissions to the government inquiry referred to in n 25.
[41] FSC Code (n 29) 4.
[42] Financial services organizations can apply to become full members, associate members or supporting members of the FSC; see Financial Services Council, 'Become a FSC Member' <www.fsc.org.au/about/membership/become-a-member> accessed 16 July 2020.
[43] Financial Services Council, 'FSC Full Members' <www.fsc.org.au/about/fsc-members> accessed 16 July 2020. In Australia, the distinction between 'domestic' and 'international' fund managers is complicated, however, by virtue of the fact that some large Australian fund managers have material operations in other countries.
[44] Klettner (n 20) 260.
[45] For example, the FSC Code requires asset managers to make disclosures regarding their ownership, structure, internal governance, and the experience and competencies of their key personnel: FSC Code (n 29) 8–9.
[46] ibid 7.
[47] ibid 10.
[48] Financial Services Council, 'FSC Standards Fact Sheet' (4 September 2018) <www.fsc.org.au/web-page-resources/fsc-standards/1507-fsc-standards-fact-sheet-2018> accessed 11 February 2022.
[49] ibid. This fact sheet indicates (at 2) that instances of non-compliance are overseen by the FSC's Standards, Oversight and Disciplinary Committee and may result in that committee initiating 'any appropriate response which may include disciplinary action'. The fact sheet does not indicate what form such disciplinary measures might take.
[50] The FSC Code requires asset managers to report against the code at the end of each financial year, commencing with the financial year ended 30 June 2019: FSC Code (n 29) 10.
[51] ibid.

These bullet points refer to monitoring of company performance; engagement with companies and escalation of issues which are not addressed through initial engagement efforts; use of ESG considerations in investment decision-making and engagement activities; approach to voting; collaborative engagement with other investors; approach to policy advocacy; and approach to engaging with clients regarding stewardship.[52] The FSC Code operates on a 'comply-or-explain' basis, which means that full members have the choice of providing disclosure in relation to these disclosure topics, or simply explaining why such stewardship activities are not relevant to them.[53] The FSC Code takes the view, nonetheless, that requiring investors to explain publicly their approach to stewardship will encourage them to improve their approach to stewardship.[54]

An interesting feature of the FSC Code is that environmental, social and governance (ESG) considerations are not seen as a central or defining element of stewardship.[55] Instead, as noted in the previous paragraph, ESG-focused stewardship is simply listed by the code as one of several potential stewardship activities.

19.2.2.2 The ACSI Code

The ACSI Code applies to asset owners who choose to become signatories to the code.[56] As at March 2020, there were sixteen signatories, comprising solely Australian public sector and industry superannuation funds.[57] This represents almost 40 per cent of ACSI's membership base.[58] The ACSI Code is principally focused on asset owners' stewardship in relation to their equity holdings, although it notes that 'asset owners may wish to extend the application of the Code across their portfolio'.[59]

The ACSI Code sets out six principles. Three of them state that investors 'should' undertake specific types of stewardship activity, namely: (i) engage with companies; (ii) monitor asset managers' stewardship activities; and (iii) encourage better alignment of the financial system and regulatory policy with the interests of long-term investors.[60] The other three principles provide that investors 'should' make certain disclosures regarding stewardship, namely: (i) disclose publicly how they approach their stewardship responsibilities; (ii) disclose publicly their policy for voting at company meetings and their voting activities; and (iii) report to beneficiaries regarding their stewardship activities.[61] Unlike the FSC Code, the ACSI Code does not address the internal governance of asset owners.[62]

The ACSI Code is effectively aspirational only. There is no obligation for asset owner members of ACSI to become signatories and the Code does not oblige signatories to undertake any particular form of stewardship. Instead, the ACSI Code operates on an 'if not, why not' basis, which requires signatories to explain how they apply the Code's principles or, to the extent that

---

[52] ibid.
[53] ibid 8.
[54] ibid (noting that 'good practice will develop organically' as a result of these disclosure requirements).
[55] Katelouzou and Klettner, Sustainable Finance and Stewardship, Chapter 26.
[56] ACSI Code (n 30) 5.
[57] Australian Council of Superannuation Investors, 'Current Signatories to the Code' <https://acsi.org.au/members/australian-asset-owner-stewardship-code/> accessed 15 March 2020. ACSI's website discloses that it has six international members (including CalPERS and the United Kingdom's Universities Superannuation Scheme). However, none of these international members are shown on ACSI's website as signatories to the ACSI Code.
[58] ACSI, 'Who Our Members Are' (n 33).
[59] ACSI Code (n 30) 5.
[60] ibid Principles 3, 4 and 5.
[61] ibid Principles 1, 2 and 6.
[62] A point that is specifically acknowledged by the ACSI Code: ibid 6.

they do not apply any of the principles, explain why they have not done so.[63] The Code required signatories to have published a 'stewardship statement' which contains these explanations by 30 September 2019.[64] Signatories are 'encouraged' to revise their statements every two years.[65]

Whereas the FSC Code simply references ESG-focused stewardship as one of several stewardship activities, the ACSI Code envisages that ESG considerations will play a fundamental role in shaping investors' overall approach towards stewardship. The ACSI Code states that 'ACSI members ... are committed to incorporating environmental, social and governance (ESG) considerations into their investment strategies and engaging collaboratively with companies to improve their ESG performance'.[66] It defines stewardship as 'the responsibility asset owners have to exercise their ownership rights to protect and enhance long-term investment value for their beneficiaries by promoting sustainable value creation'.[67]

19.2.2.3 Calls for a Revised Approach to Stewardship in Australia

Although they are non-prescriptive, both the ACSI Code and the FSC Code assume that they will improve stewardship practices by requiring investors to disclose their approach to stewardship.[68] However, within a year of issuing the ACSI Code, ACSI has already raised doubts regarding the efficacy of this approach and, in May 2019, published a discussion paper calling for reform of Australia's approach to stewardship.[69] The paper expresses concern about variations in investors' stewardship practices and argues for the imposition of minimum standards of stewardship, potentially as part of a regulatory, rather than industry-based, initiative.[70] Casting doubt on the existing, fragmented industry approach towards stewardship, ACSI states that one outcome of the review should be the introduction of a single stewardship code[71] that is applicable to 'all institutional investors'.[72] ACSI claims that requiring all institutions to report against the requirements of a single code would facilitate comparison and assessment of the stewardship practices of different investors.[73] To date, there have been no apparent attempts by the financial sector, the government or the regulator to initiate the review called for by ACSI.

---

[63] ibid.
[64] ibid 5–6. The ACSI Code does not indicate what consequences, if any, it might impose if a signatory fails to publish a stewardship statement. However, failure to publish a statement would potentially become a matter of public record, since ACSI's website contains a list of signatories together with hyperlinks to their stewardship statements: see ACSI, 'Current Signatories to the Code' (n 57). As at the time of writing, this list indicates that all signatories have published stewardship statements.
[65] ACSI Code (n 30) 5.
[66] ibid 4.
[67] ibid 5.
[68] See FSC Code (n 29) 8. The ACSI Code states that transparency 'will lead to increased accountability for asset owners to beneficiaries and other stakeholders': ACSI Code (n 30) 5.
[69] Australian Council of Superannuation Investors, 'Towards Stronger Investment Stewardship' (May 2019) <https://acsi.org.au/wp-content/uploads/2020/02/ACSI-Towards-Stronger-Investment-Stewardship-May-2019.pdf> accessed 16 July 2020.
[70] Specifically, ACSI argues that the review should focus on 'what effective stewardship entails, what the minimum expectations should be, and how to strike the right balance between regulation and voluntary codes': ibid 5.
[71] A similar discussion about the need to introduce a single stewardship code has taken place in India: see Varottil, Shareholder Stewardship in India, Chapter 17.
[72] ACSI, 'Towards Stronger Investment Stewardship' (n 69). ACSI's discussion paper does not explain what the phrase 'all institutional investors' contemplates. It is therefore not clear, for example, whether the phrase is intended to refer to all institutional investors operating in Australia, irrespective of whether they are domestic or international.
[73] ibid.

19.3 COLLECTIVE ACTION AND STEWARDSHIP

19.3.1 *The Potential of Collective Action as a Stewardship Tool*

A shareholder who wishes to participate in a company's governance faces a potentially challenging cost–benefit analysis.[74] This cost–benefit analysis can be particularly challenging for institutional investors, given the large number of investments in their diversified portfolios, free-riding concerns, the pressure to seek economies in their governance activities owing to industry competition, and conflicts of interest.[75] As a result of these considerations, some commentators have queried whether institutions actually have sufficient incentives to act as stewards.[76]

Collective action, however, has the potential to make stewardship more feasible. By acting collectively, shareholders can pool their resources, share the costs of their stewardship activities, and leverage their influence.[77] Consequently, stewardship may be significantly less speculative and more cost-effective if undertaken collectively rather than individually.

The potential governance benefits of collective action mean that collective action is generally recognized by stewardship codes as a desirable stewardship tool. However, the codes can differ in terms of the emphasis they place on collective action.[78] In the US, stewardship principles were adopted in 2017 by the Investor Stewardship Group.[79] Although the principles contemplate collaboration between institutional investors, this appears to be directed at adopting and implementing corporate governance and/or stewardship principles, rather than as an activity undertaken to facilitate engagement with companies.[80] The UK Code 2020 is far more direct and specific about collective action than its US counterpart. For example, Principle 10 of the UK Code states that institutional investors should, 'where necessary, participate in collaborative engagement to influence issuers'.[81] Principle 10 requires signatories to disclose the collaborative engagement they undertake and the reasons why.[82]

19.3.2 *The Australian Codes and Collective Action*

Neither of the Australian Codes obliges, or even explicitly encourages, investors to undertake any form of collective action. This is consistent with their non-prescriptive approach towards stewardship.[83]

---

[74] See e.g. Edward B Rock, 'The Logic and (Uncertain) Significance of Institutional Shareholder Activism' (1991) 79 *Georgetown Law Journal* 445.

[75] ibid. More recently, see Lucian A Bebchuk, Alma Cohen and Scott Hirst, 'The Agency Problems of Institutional Investors' (2017) 31 *Journal of Economic Perspectives* 89. In the Australian context, see Geofrey P Stapledon, 'Disincentives to Activism by Institutional Investors in Listed Australian Companies' (1996) 18 *Sydney Law Review* 152.

[76] See e.g. Ronald J Gilson and Jeffrey N Gordon, 'The Agency Costs of Agency Capitalism: Activist Investors and the Revaluation of Governance Rights' (2013) 113 *Columbia Law Review* 863, 868–69. See also Fisch, The Uncertain Stewardship Potential of Index Funds, Chapter 21, which argues that index funds have particularly limited incentives to engage in stewardship.

[77] See e.g. Gaia Balp and Giovanni Strampelli, 'Institutional Investor Collective Engagements: Non-activist Cooperation vs Activist Wolf Packs' (2020) 14 *Ohio State Business Law Journal* 135.

[78] See further, Katelouzou and Siems, The Global Diffusion of Stewardship Codes, Chapter 30.

[79] Investor Stewardship Group, 'The Principles' <https://isgframework.org/stewardship-principles/> accessed 16 July 2020. See Fisch, The Uncertain Stewardship Potential of Index Funds, Chapter 21 for further details regarding stewardship in the US.

[80] ibid Principle F.

[81] UK Code 2020 (n 6) 19. See Davies, The UK Stewardship Code 2010–2020, Chapter 2 for further details regarding stewardship in the United Kingdom.

[82] ibid.

[83] See Section 19.2.2.

The FSC Code addresses collective action in only brief terms. It states that asset managers should disclose in their stewardship statement, 'where relevant', their approach to 'collaborative engagement with other investors including involvement with industry groups and associations'.[84] Besides the reference to 'industry groups and associations', the FSC Code does not elaborate on the forms of collective action which investors could undertake.

The ACSI Code goes somewhat further. Principle 3 of the ACSI Code is headed 'Asset Owners Should Engage with Companies (Either Directly, Indirectly or Both)'.[85] Under this principle, the code acknowledges that investors can undertake engagement 'in collaboration with other investors'.[86] It also observes that collective action may be helpful where investors wish to escalate issues of concern. It notes how, in these circumstances, investors could raise their concerns collectively with asset managers or other asset owners, or hold discussions with 'other equity, bondholders or stakeholders'.[87]

An interesting feature of the ACSI Code is that it highlights a distinction between direct and indirect forms of collective action. Specifically, it notes that collective action can be undertaken 'with other individual asset owners' or 'through a third-party service provider'.[88] As this chapter will show, the latter form of collective influence-wielding is prominent in the Australian market.

19.4 HOW INSTITUTIONAL INVESTORS USE COLLECTIVE ACTION AS A STEWARDSHIP TOOL IN AUSTRALIA

19.4.1 *Overtly Aggressive Interventions*

Overtly aggressive activist interventions, such as board spills and other high-profile public campaigns, are not common in Australia.[89] Industry research reports an average of approximately seventy-five activist campaigns a year in the period 2013–17.[90] This is in the context of a market comprising more than 2,000 listed entities.[91] These campaigns predominantly targeted small-capitalization companies.[92]

Overseas hedge funds, domestic activist investors and institutional investors did not play a prominent role in these campaigns.[93] Evidence suggests, instead, that overtly aggressive

---

[84] FSC Code (n 29) 10.
[85] ACSI Code (n 30) 10.
[86] ibid 8, 10.
[87] ibid 10–11.
[88] ibid 11.
[89] This section draws heavily on research in Tim Bowley, 'The Importance of Context: The Nature of Australian Shareholder Activism and Its Regulatory Implications' (PhD thesis, University of Sydney 2019).
[90] JP Morgan, 'Shareholder Activism in Australia: Navigating the Evolving Landscape' (April 2017) <www.jpmorgan.com/pdfdoc/Shareholder-Activism-in-Australia.pdf> accessed 16 July 2020; FTI Consulting, *Australia* (31 December 2017) <https://ftiactivism.com/map/countries/australia/> accessed 16 July 2020.
[91] ASX, 'Historical Market Statistics' <www.asx.com.au/about/historical-market-statistics.htm#No%20of%20Companies> accessed 16 July 2020 (reporting 2,242 listed entities as at October 2019).
[92] JP Morgan (n 90) 6 (reporting that 77% of campaigns targeted companies with a market capitalization of less than AUD 100 million). A 2018 report by Activist Insight and Schulte Roth & Zabel reports that nearly two-thirds of Australian companies targeted in 2018 had a market capitalization of less than USD 50 million, which they describe as a 'historical pattern': Activist Insight and Schulte Roth & Zabel, 'The Activist Investing Annual Review 2019' (2019) 6, 23 <www.srz.com/images/content/1/6/v14/162469/TheActivistInvestingAnnualReview-2019-compressed.pdf> accessed 16 July 2020.
[93] JP Morgan (n 90) 8 (reporting that dedicated activist funds accounted for only 24% of campaigns in 2016, up from 12% in 2014); Activist Insight and Arnold Bloch Leibler, 'Shareholder Activism in Australia: A Review of Trends in Activist Investing' (2016) 5 <https://abl.sfo2.cdn.digitaloceanspaces.com/public/Expertise/ABL-Shareholder-Activism-Report.pdf> accessed 16 July 2020 (reporting that the capital available for domestic activist funds is 'scarce'). As to the limited involvement of institutional investors in such campaigns, see JP Morgan (n 90) 9; Activist Insight and

campaigns are largely undertaken by non-institutional block-holders[94] such as company founders, trading companies, private investment vehicles and entrepreneurs.[95]

The low levels of hedge fund activism mean that, to date, Australia has not witnessed the type of 'wolf pack' collective action seen in other jurisdictions,[96] or the interaction between activist investors and institutional investors highlighted in the US by Gilson and Gordon.[97]

However, in recent years, environmental and social activists have begun to play a role that is somewhat analogous to the role of hedge funds described by Gilson and Gordon. At several annual shareholder meetings of large capitalization companies in 2018, environmental and social activists tabled voting proposals addressing ESG-related concerns, such as requesting more comprehensive disclosure from companies regarding climate change risks.[98] These proposals appear to have provided an opportunity for institutional investors to escalate their ESG-related concerns.[99] A number of them received significant levels of shareholder support, including from institutional investors.[100] Although these interventions have been high-profile, in absolute terms they are, however, relatively infrequent.[101]

19.4.2 Co-ordinated Share Voting

Institutional investors do not appear to routinely seek to co-ordinate their share voting. Although Australia's takeover laws constrain such behaviour,[102] this, of itself, does not appear to explain institutions' infrequent attempts to form voting blocks. This is because a safe-harbour existed for nearly twenty years, which permitted institutional investors to co-ordinate their share voting at shareholder meetings in precisely this way.[103] In 2015, the Australian Securities and Investments Commission (ASIC) reported that it was aware of only one instance of institutions relying on the safe-harbour during that period.[104] Based on market feedback, ASIC concluded that institutions'

Arnold Bloch Leibler (n 93) 5–6; Myriam Robin, 'Shareholder Activism Not in "Mentality" of Australian Fund Managers' *The Sydney Morning Herald* (Sydney, 12 May 2017) 26 <afr.com/markets/live/shareholder-activism-not-in-mentality-of-australian-fund-managers-20170511-gw2hma> accessed 16 July 2020 (noting anecdotal evidence regarding the disinclination of institutional investors to undertake aggressive activist interventions).

[94] JP Morgan (n 90) 8 (reporting that the 'bulk' of campaigns identified by its research were undertaken by 'usually existing investors' in small-capitalization companies who are 'often one-time activists'). The unpublished doctoral research by one of this chapter's authors reports similar findings: see Bowley (n 89).

[95] Bowley (n 89).

[96] See Coffee and Palia (n 14).

[97] Gilson and Gordon (n 76).

[98] Noted in Australian Securities and Investments Commission, 'Report 609 Annual General Meeting Season 2018' (January 2019) 8–10 <https://download.asic.gov.au/media/4997407/rep609-published-31-january-2019.pdf> accessed 16 July 2020.

[99] Each of the companies targeted was in the S&P/ASX 200 index, which comprises substantial listed entities. Proxy votes in favour of the ESG resolutions represented on average 18.6% of all proxy votes; in two cases, proxy votes in favour of the resolutions exceeded 40%: ibid. As these proposals targeted large companies, in which institutional investors tend to concentrate their investments, these voting data suggest that these proposals attracted material levels of voting support from institutions.

[100] ibid.

[101] ibid 9 (noting that in 2018, in relation to the 200 largest entities included in the S&P/ASX 200 index, there were 7 such interventions, involving 4 companies).

[102] See Section 19.5.4.

[103] The safe-harbour was contained in Australian Securities and Investments Commission, 'Class Order 00/455 Collective Action by Institutional Investors' (4 October 2013) <www.legislation.gov.au/Details/F2013C00876> accessed 16 July 2020.

[104] Australian Securities and Investments Commission, 'Consultation Paper 228 Collective Action by Investors: Update to RG 128' (February 2015) 7 <http://download.asic.gov.au/media/2962782/cp228-published-17-february-2015.pdf> accessed 16 July 2020.

reluctance to use the safe-harbour was owing to the fact that institutional investors primarily sought to engage with companies in behind-the-scenes interactions rather than at shareholder meetings.[105] Another possible explanation, not explored by ASIC, is whether the emergence of proxy advisers may have contributed to a degree of standardization in institutions' voting practices, negating the need for institutions to co-ordinate their voting directly.[106]

In light of the apparent lack of demand from investors for a safe-harbour to permit them to co-ordinate their share voting, ASIC declined to renew the safe-harbour.[107]

19.4.3 Behind-the-Scenes Engagement with Companies

Consistent with ASIC's observation, evidence indicates that there is indeed a significant amount of private interaction (or 'engagement') between institutional investors and their investee companies in Australia.[108] However, it is unclear to what extent institutions seek to leverage their influence by undertaking their engagement activities collectively. Investors' stewardship disclosures made in accordance with the Australian codes frequently contain only generic statements regarding investors' approach to collective engagement with companies. Examples include non-specific statements such as 'engagement can be undertaken ... in collaboration with other investors'[109] and '[w]here appropriate, we will hold joint engagement meetings with other investors who share our concerns'.[110]

A number of stewardship disclosures suggest that institutions resort to joint engagement only as an escalation mechanism in relation to major governance concerns. The stewardship statement of the superannuation fund, AustralianSuper, notes that collective action may be reserved for more difficult engagements in order to 'amplify our voice and influence'.[111] Fund manager JP Morgan notes that, as part of its escalation approach, it 'will hold joint engagement meetings with other investors who share our concerns'.[112] The fund manager Colonial states that '[t]he vast majority of our engagement is conducted by each team directly with companies',[113] although it acknowledges that, as part of its escalation approach, 'we might collaborate on further engagement with other like-minded investors'.[114]

---

[105] ibid 10.
[106] See Section 19.4.4 for discussion of the role of proxy advisers in Australia.
[107] Australian Securities and Investments Commission, 'Consultation Paper 228' (n 104) 12.
[108] See e.g. Productivity Commission, *Executive Remuneration in Australia* (Inquiry Report No 49, 19 December 2009) 303 <www.pc.gov.au/inquiries/completed/executive-remuneration/report/executive-remuneration-report.pdf> accessed 16 July 2020 (noting a submission from the representative body for company directors that 'there has been a considerable increase in active engagement by large institutional investors').
[109] Cbus, 'Cbus Stewardship Statement – For the Period Ended 30 September 2019' (2020) 2 <www.cbussuper.com.au/content/dam/cbus/files/governance/reporting/Stewardship-Statement.pdf> accessed 16 July 2020.
[110] JP Morgan Asset Management, 'Principles of Internal Governance and Asset Stewardship' (2019) <https://am.jpmorgan.com/content/dam/jpm-am-aem/asiapacific/au/en/policies/principles-internal-governance-asset-stewardship.pdf> accessed 16 July 2020. See also Christian Super, Stewardship Statement: 1 July 2017 to 30 June 2018 (2018) 3 <www.christiansuper.com.au/files/Christian-Super-Stewardship-Statement_2018.pdf> accessed 16 July 2020 (referring to their preparedness to '[work] with likeminded investors').
[111] AustralianSuper, 'Stewardship Statement: 1 July 2018 to 30 June 2019' (2019) 2 <www.australiansuper.com/investments/how-we-invest/esg-management> accessed 16 July 2020.
[112] JP Morgan Asset Management (n 110) paras 3.2, 3.5.
[113] Colonial First State Global Asset Management, 'Principles of Internal Governance and Asset Stewardship 2018' (June 2018) 16 <www.firststateinvestments.com/content/dam/cfsgam/about-us-files/responsible-investment/ri-policies/principles-of-internal-governance-and-asset-stewardship-2018.pdf> accessed 16 July 2020.
[114] ibid 14. See also Cbus, 'Escalation Process' <www.cbussuper.com.au/about-us/sustainability/escalation-process> accessed 16 July 2020 (noting that escalation may include '[e]xpressing concerns ... collectively with asset managers or other asset owners' and '[h]olding discussions with other equity, bondholders or stakeholders').

In recent years, instances have come to light in the financial press of institutional investors collectively pushing for changes in the affairs of prominent listed companies.[115] However, it is not possible to establish how common this form of collective action is in practice based on this anecdotal evidence.

19.4.4 Collective Influence-Wielding through Intermediary Organizations

An interesting feature of the Australian landscape is the significant role played by intermediary organizations in facilitating institutional investors' collective influence in the governance of listed companies.

Industry bodies, in particular, are a long-established feature of the Australian governance landscape[116] and play an important role in advocating for the interests of institutional investors in Australia. As noted earlier, the two principal industry bodies are the FSC and ACSI. The FSC can trace its origins to the Australian Investment Managers Group (AIMG), which was established in 1990.[117] The AIMG's purposes included assisting investors to take action against companies where warranted.[118] ACSI was established in 2001 by industry superannuation funds to advocate for the funds' interests in matters of corporate governance.[119] Today, both ACSI and the FSC advocate for law reform, publish policies outlining investors' expectations regarding the governance practices of publicly traded companies, and are members of the Australian Securities Exchange (ASX) Corporate Governance Council, the body which issues the 'comply or explain' corporate governance code applicable to ASX-listed entities.[120] They also occasionally engage in high-profile company-specific governance interventions.[121]

In their stewardship disclosures, investors often cite their involvement in industry bodies as a form of collective action.[122] Stewardship disclosures also refer to investors' participation in

---

[115] See e.g. Mercedes Ruehl and Robert Harley, 'How the Wild, Wild Westfield Restructure Deal Was Eventually Won' *The Australian Financial Review* (29 December 2014) 38 <www.afr.com/property/commercial/how-the-wild-wild-westfield-restructure-deal-was-eventually-won-20141227-12euzy> accessed 16 July 2020 (reporting how a 'cabal of institutions' opposed a restructuring transaction involving Westfield Retail and Westfield Group); Elizabeth Knight, 'Angry Shareholders Ignored Westpac's Bluff and Raised the Stakes' *The Sydney Morning Herald* (Sydney, 26 November 2019) 22 <www.watoday.com.au/business/banking-and-finance/angry-shareholders-ignored-westpac-s-bluff-and-raised-the-stakes-20191126-p53ea9.html?ref=rss&utm_medium=rss&utm_source=rss_feed> accessed 16 July 2020 (noting how a 'wall of shareholders' demanded board change at the bank, Westpac, in light of its alleged serious breaches of money-laundering laws).

[116] See, generally Jennifer G Hill, 'Institutional Investors and Corporate Governance in Australia' in Theodor Baums, Richard M Buxbaum and Klaus J Hopt (eds), *Institutional Investors and Corporate Governance* (Walter de Gruyter 1993).

[117] ibid 600.

[118] ibid.

[119] For an overview of the history and activities of ACSI, see Mees and Smith (n 36).

[120] ASX Corporate Governance Council, 'Corporate Governance Principles and Recommendations' (4th edn, February 2019) <www.asx.com.au/documents/regulation/cgc-principles-and-recommendations-fourth-edn.pdf> accessed 16 July 2020.

[121] See e.g. Nassim Khadem, 'Investors Willing to Flex Muscle Against Companies in the Wake of AMP' *The Sydney Morning Herald* (Sydney, 9 May 2018) 21 <www.smh.com.au/business/banking-and-finance/investors-willing-to-flex-muscle-against-companies-in-the-wake-of-amp-20180508-p4ze31.html> accessed 16 July 2020 (noting how ACSI demanded board change at financial services group AMP and observing that 'this is not the first time ACSI … has moved to influence companies'); James Eyers and Jemima Whyte, 'UniSuper, ACSI Split Over Bloodletting' *The Australian Financial Review* (Sydney, 28 November 2019) 4 (reporting ACSI's call for board change at the bank, Westpac, in light of its alleged breaches of money-laundering laws).

[122] Colonial First State Global Asset Management (n 113) 16 ('[o]ccasionally we engage with companies alongside other investors as part of an industry group'); JP Morgan Asset Management (n 110) para 3.5 (disclosing that collective engagement activities include 'indirect engagement through industry bodies').

organizations which represent the collective interests of investors on specific ESG-related issues. Examples include the Investor Group on Climate Change,[123] the Climate Action 100+ Australasian Engagement Group,[124] the Carbon Disclosure Project,[125] the Workforce Disclosure Initiative[126] and the Responsible Investment Association Australasia.[127]

Institutional investors also rely on engagement providers to facilitate their private interactions with investee companies.[128] These organizations undertake behind-the-scenes engagement assignments with companies on behalf of multiple investor clients. The principal organizations are Regnan and ACSI,[129] both of which report material levels of activity. For example, in 2018–19, ACSI held 267 meetings with 192 companies in the S&P/ASX 300 index.[130] In 2018, Regnan undertook eighty-six engagements with fifty-five companies in the S&P/ASX 200 index, covering issues such as climate change, human capital management, ethical business conduct, board composition and independence, and ESG disclosures.[131] Hermes EOS also reports some activity in Australia.[132]

Institutions' stewardship disclosures indicate that investors use engagement firms in order to leverage their influence and achieve economies in their engagement activities. The pension fund, AustralianSuper, states that using ACSI's engagement services enables AustralianSuper to 'expand the breadth of our engagement coverage and strengthen our voice and influence'.[133] Research by the Australian Institute of Company Directors into institutional investor share voting and engagement practices concludes that, through their ongoing interaction with

---

[123] Colonial First State Global Asset Management (n 113) 16; AustralianSuper, 'ESG Management and Responsible Investing' <www.australiansuper.com/investments/how-we-invest/esg-management> accessed 16 July 2020; UniSuper, 'Responsible Investing at UniSuper' <www.unisuper.com.au/investments/how-we-invest/responsible-and-sustainable-investing> accessed 16 July 2020.

[124] AustralianSuper, '2017–18 Annual Report' (2018) 23 <www.australiansuper.com/-/media/australian-super/files/about-us/annual-reports/2018-annual-report.pdf> accessed 16 July 2020; Cbus, 'Sustainability' <www.cbussuper.com.au/about-us/sustainability> accessed 11 February 2022.

[125] See e.g. AustralianSuper, 'ESG Management and Responsible Investing' (n 123); UniSuper (n 123).

[126] Cbus (n 124).

[127] Perpetual Corporate Trust, 'Principles of Internal Governance and Asset Stewardship' (2018) 5 <www.perpetual.com.au/~/media/perpetual/pdf/corporate-trusts/pct-principles-of-internal-governance-and-asset-stewardship.ashx?la=en> accessed 16 July 2020.

[128] Investors note their use of engagement firms in their stewardship disclosures: see e.g. Pendal Group, 'Principles of Internal Governance and Asset Stewardship' (July 2018) 9 <www.pendalgroup.com/wp-content/uploads/2018/09/Principles-of-Internal-Governance-and-Asset-Stewardship.pdf> accessed 16 July 2020; Christian Super (n 110) 3 (disclosing its use of ACSI); Cbus (n 124) (disclosing that it uses ACSI for ASX 300 holdings and Hermes EOS for global shareholdings).

[129] In addition to its role as industry advocate, ACSI also provides company engagement and proxy advisory services to those of its members who subscribe for these services: Australian Council of Superannuation Investors, '2019 Annual Report' (2019) 12–14 <https://acsi.org.au/wp-content/uploads/2020/02/19-ACSI-Annual-Report.pdf> accessed 16 July 2020.

[130] ibid 12.

[131] Pendal Group, 'Corporate Sustainability and Responsibility 2018' (2018) 2 <www.pendalgroup.com/wp-content/uploads/2018/11/2018-Corporate-Sustainability-Report-.pdf> accessed 16 July 2020.

[132] Hermes EOS, 'Public Engagement Report Q3 2018' (2018) 2 (reporting engagement with two companies in relation to environmental concerns) <www.hermes-investment.com/us/insight/stewardship/public-engagement-report-q3-2018/> accessed 16 July 2020. In March 2019, ACSI and Hermes EOS announced that they had entered into an agreement to pool their engagement services, giving investors access to ACSI's services in the Australian market and Hermes' services in overseas markets: Australian Council of Superannuation Investors, 'ACSI and Hermes EOS to Share Company Engagement Expertise' (12 March 2019) <https://acsi.org.au/media-releases/media-release-acsi-and-hermes-eos-to-share-company-engagement-expertise/> accessed 16 July 2020.

[133] AustralianSuper, 'Stewardship Statement' (n 111) 3. Similarly, the university sector pension fund notes that using ACSI for engagement services 'provides a strong unified voice on issues and widens the extent of our own direct engagement': UniSuper, 'UniSuper Stewardship Statement' (2018) 2 <www.unisuper.com.au/-/media/files/investments/responsible-investing/unisuper-stewardship-statement.pdf?la=en&rev=1bb631bd83a04735b91b15ff1aa833fb&hash=6716D49343AB9D8DE864D61595A55D66#:~:text=Statement%20(2018),of%20its%20members'%20retirement%20savings> accessed 11 February 2022.

investors, engagement firms can be 'highly influential' in developing the views of institutional investors into consensus positions on corporate governance issues.[134]

Proxy advisers also play a role in facilitating institutions' collective influence.[135] By analyzing and providing recommendations regarding voting proposals, proxy firms make it feasible for institutional investors to exercise their voting power in relation to the significant number of voting proposals put before them each year.[136] Proxy advisers' policies and guidelines also augment institutional investor 'voice' by making clear to companies the expectations of institutional investors and the intermediaries that advise them.[137]

19.5 LESSONS FROM AUSTRALIA

19.5.1 Collective Action Is Not a Simple Governance Phenomenon

In theory, market conditions in Australia suggest that it would be both feasible and beneficial for institutions to undertake their stewardship activities collectively.[138] Nonetheless, direct forms of collective action – such as investors jointly undertaking proxy contests, co-ordinating their share voting or jointly engaging behind-the-scenes with corporate managers – are not common in practice. Institutional investors' stewardship statements suggest that they reserve direct forms of collective action for serious governance concerns only.

Evidence indicates instead that investors more typically wield collective influence through intermediary organizations such as industry bodies and engagement firms. In this regard, the Australian experience is not unique. Overseas commentators have also noted the role of intermediaries in leveraging institutional investor influence in corporate governance.[139]

It can make considerable sense for institutions to undertake their stewardship activities collectively through intermediary organizations, as opposed to forming ad hoc coalitions and directly engaging with companies. By acting through an intermediary, an investor does not need to assume the role (and directly bear the cost) of initiating and co-ordinating an intervention.[140]

---

[134] Australian Institute of Company Directors, *Institutional Share Voting and Engagement: Exploring the Links between Directors, Institutional Shareholders and Proxy Advisers* (September 2011) 45 <www.companydirectors.com.au/~/media/875F338434474CCC80CA71B22DE7BBAE.ashx> accessed 16 July 2020.

[135] Relevantly, some institutions' stewardship disclosures note the use of proxy firms as a form of collective action. Under the heading 'Indirect Company Engagement', AustralianSuper discloses its use of the proxy advice service provided by ACSI: AustralianSuper, 'Stewardship Statement' (n 111) 3. See also UniSuper, 'Responsible Investment Report – 1 July 2018–31 December 2018' (2019) 2 <www.unisuper.com.au/-/media/files/investments/responsible-investing/responsible-investing-reports/responsible-investment-report-july-december-2018.pdf?la=en&rev=d449ce500ddc4417b9c9958840f3b25b&hash=C6D8805DD35D12E515A066BB1E465147> accessed 11 February 2022. Tuch has noted how proxy firms act as a form of representative body for institutional investors in the US and the UK: Andrew F Tuch, 'Proxy Adviser Influence in a Comparative Light' (2019) 99 Boston University Law Review 1459, 1480, 1488 (Tuch suggests that proxy advisers may be 'functional substitutes' for investors' representative bodies).

[136] Australian Institute of Company Directors (n 134) 71 (noting that institutional investors can receive voting proposals from up to 300 companies each year, the majority of which need to be addressed within a 2-month 'peak AGM season' which occurs in October and November).

[137] Ben Power, 'Proxy Music' *Company Director* (March 2018) 45 <https://aicd.companydirectors.com.au/membership/company-director-magazine/2018-back-editions/march/proxy-music> accessed 16 July 2020 (quoting a Commissioner of the Australian corporate regulator who observes that proxy advisers 'play an important role ... promoting a focus on corporate governance issues relevant to shareholders').

[138] See Section 19.1.

[139] See e.g. Balp and Strampelli (n 77); Tuch (n 135). See Strampelli, Institutional Investor Stewardship in Italian Corporate Governance, Chapter 6, which notes the role of the investor organization, Assogestioni, in facilitating shareholder influence-wielding in Italian corporate governance.

[140] Co-ordinating a coalition of investors may be a difficult exercise given the potential divergence in interests and objectives of investors: Elroy Dimson, Oğuzhan Karakaş and Xi Li, 'Coordinated Engagements' (29 October 2019) 4 <https://ssrn.com/abstract=3209072> accessed 16 July 2020.

Moreover, free-riding concerns are mitigated where an intermediary organization has a significant membership or client base.[141] Intermediaries specialize in representing the interests of institutional investors and, as a result of this focus, may accumulate knowledge and expertise that enables them to achieve economies unavailable to ad hoc coalitions of investors. Because they are 'repeat players', intermediaries may also be able to adopt a strategic approach towards their governance activities. In the Australian context, Mees and Smith claim that ACSI has adopted a 'gradualist, due process approach ... with their biannually updated corporate governance guides consistently more progressive and demanding than those issued by other key institutions'.[142]

The foregoing considerations are likely to be significant ones for institutional investors given their limited incentives to engage in corporate governance activities.[143]

There are potentially two additional explanations for the significant role played by intermediary organizations in Australia. First, the activities of intermediaries will generally fall outside of the reach of Australia's restrictive acting-in-concert takeover laws. In summary, these complex laws can expose investors who co-ordinate their governance activities to significant regulatory consequences, including public filing obligations, restrictions on acquiring shares in the target company, and the risk of criminal or civil sanctions for breaching Australia's 20 per cent takeovers 'threshold'.[144] However, the law contains an exemption which applies to service providers such as engagement and proxy firms.[145] In addition, stewardship activities undertaken by an industry body will generally fall outside the reach of takeover laws provided that the activities are based on the body's independent assessment of where its members' interests lie and do not involve an agreement or understanding with its investor-members regarding an intervention against a particular company.[146]

Second, by acting through intermediaries, individual investors are able to avoid direct confrontation with companies. Commentators have claimed that owing to the small, concentrated and interconnected nature of the Australian market, investors can be reluctant to engage in confrontational behaviour with investee companies.[147] This would suggest that investors may see an advantage in allowing intermediaries to take the lead in engaging with companies and advocating for the interests of investors.[148]

19.5.2 Exploring the Governance Significance of Intermediary-Led Stewardship

The Australian experience highlights the governance potential of intermediary-led stewardship. Whereas Professors Gilson and Gordon emphasize the role of activist hedge funds in leveraging

---

[141] Balp and Strampelli (n 77).
[142] Mees and Smith (n 36) 86.
[143] See nn 74–75 and accompanying text.
[144] For an overview, see Australian Securities and Investments Commission, 'Regulatory Guide 128 Collective Action by Investors' (June 2015) <https://download.asic.gov.au/media/3273670/rg128-published-23-june-2015.pdf> accessed 16 July 2020.
[145] Corporations Act 2001 (Cth) s 16(1)(a).
[146] See also Hill (n 116) 606–7 (concluding that takeover laws should not present a barrier to the activities of industry bodies).
[147] See e.g. Paul Garvey, 'Change of Name Not Enough to Spare Sandalwood Group Quintis' *The Australian Business Review* (Sydney, 24 March 2017) 23 <www.theaustralian.com.au/business/companies/change-of-name-not-enough-to-spare-sandalwood-group-quintis/news-story/ae9dab3ab5ce2b48269ab3c1c3833e44> accessed 16 July 2020 (quoting an Australian activist investor who claims that '[t]he number of people who operate in this market, be it at fund management level, broker level, management level, is very small ... Most people here would know each other within two or three degrees of separation in the corporate world, and I think that means people here are probably more reluctant to genuinely confront [corporate] underperformance').
[148] This consideration has also been noted outside of the Australian context: see Dimson, Karakaş and Li (n 140) 11.

the governance influence of rationally reticent institutional investors,[149] experience in Australia suggests that intermediary organizations can play a similar role. It is important that both policymakers and researchers appreciate this potential governance significance of intermediaries.

That said, there is some divergence of views regarding the effectiveness of intermediary-led stewardship. Balp and Strampelli go so far as to suggest that intermediaries are a 'promising lever by which to foster a more convincing and viable corporate governance role for non-activist institutional investors' and, in particular, may 'activate passively managed funds with particularly weak financial incentives for being active'.[150] Others suggest that there are limits to intermediary-led stewardship. In a 2011 report, the UK Financial Reporting Council criticized investors' apparent preference for undertaking collective action through governance intermediaries and claimed that direct collective action is preferable for addressing significant corporate governance concerns: '[M]any statements around the principle of collective engagement focused on membership of collective bodies. While this is welcome, it skirts round the main reason for [encouraging investors to engage in collective action], which is the need for investors to be able to join forces at critical moments to ensure that boards acknowledge and respond to their concerns.'[151]

Doidge, Dyck, Mahmudi and Virani note that intermediary-led stewardship may be less well suited for addressing company-specific issues, such as issues of commercial strategy.[152] They claim that there is likely to exist a greater variation in the views of individual investors regarding such company-specific issues, making it more costly for intermediaries to establish a common viewpoint on which to base an intervention.[153] If this is indeed correct, intermediary-led activism may not serve as a functional substitute for the role of hedge funds highlighted by Gilson and Gordon.

Jurisdiction-specific considerations are likely to be relevant to this debate. For example, the Australian investment community is relatively small,[154] has an established tradition of using industry bodies to advocate for its interests,[155] and is serviced by relatively few industry bodies and engagement firms.[156] In jurisdictions without such features, it may be unrealistic to expect intermediaries to play a significant role in mobilizing investors' stewardship activities.[157] Any

---

[149] Gilson and Gordon (n 76).
[150] Balp and Strampelli (n 77).
[151] Financial Reporting Council, 'Developments in Corporate Governance 2011: The Impact and Implementation of the UK Corporate Governance and Stewardship Codes' (December 2011) 22 <www.frc.org.uk/document-library/frc/2011/developments-in-corporate-governance-2011-the-imp> accessed 16 July 2020.
[152] Craig Doidge, Alexander Dyck, Hamed Mahmudi and Aazam Virani, 'Collective Action and Governance Activism' (2019) 23 Review of Finance 893, 895.
[153] According to Doidge, Dyck, Mahmudi and Virani (n 152), it generally makes more sense for intermediaries to pursue 'process proposals' in relation to mainstream issues of corporate governance practice. This is because such proposals can be put forward in respect of multiple companies (enabling economies of scale) and because such proposals are likely to be easier to formulate since investors' views on 'process' issues are likely to be more closely aligned than in respect of highly company-specific issues. Highlighting this point, the Australian press recently reported a divergence in views between ACSI and one of its members, the superannuation fund UniSuper, over the company-specific issue of which directors should be removed from the board of the bank, Westpac, in light of serious allegations of compliance failure at that bank: Eyers and Whyte (n 121).
[154] See Garvey (n 147) and accompanying text.
[155] See Section 19.4.4.
[156] ibid.
[157] Tuch suggests that industry bodies have played a significant role in the UK because of (i) the geographical proximity of institutional investors in that country; (ii) shareholders in English companies enjoying favourable legal rights; and (iii) policy settings that have encouraged investors to participate in corporate governance. Tuch notes that, in contrast, industry organizations are less prominent in the US and suggests that this may be owing to the geographical dispersion of significant investors in the US, weaker shareholder rights and a more management-centred approach to corporate governance. See Tuch (n 135) 1488–89.

434   Part II Jurisdictions

analysis of the governance significance of intermediaries may therefore need to pay close regard to market conditions in particular jurisdictions.

19.5.3 Recognizing the Varieties of Collective Action When Developing Stewardship Norms

The Australian codes do not prescribe in detail what is expected of investors in terms of collective action. As explained earlier, ACSI has expressed concern regarding this approach, arguing that it may be necessary to introduce a single code containing minimum standards, in order to promote greater consistency in investors' stewardship activities.[158] Given that the Australian codes currently refer to collective action in very general terms, any such overhaul of the Australian approach to stewardship would need to consider, among other things, the extent to which collective action should be addressed in more prescriptive terms.

This chapter's analysis indicates that formulating more prescriptive requirements regarding collective action would not necessarily be straightforward. In view of the varieties of collective action highlighted by this chapter, a key challenge would involve determining what forms of collective action should be prescribed. This would require consideration of the issues noted in Section 19.5.2 regarding the feasibility, and relative effectiveness, of different forms of collective action.

This chapter's analysis also suggests that it is necessary for investors' stewardship statements to provide more detailed disclosure concerning collective action. The generic disclosures commonly found in Australian investors' stewardship statements – such as claims that investors are prepared to act 'with other like-minded investors'[159] or utilize the services of an intermediary organization[160] – provide little insight into what this chapter has revealed to be a governance practice which can be quite varied in nature. In order for outsiders to fully appreciate the nature, extent and impact of investors' stewardship activities, it would seem necessary for investors to report, in more particular terms, on the forms of collective action they undertake, the circumstances in which different forms of collective action are used, and the extent to which they are used.

The recently revised UK Code illustrates a potential approach. Principle 10 of the UK Code requires signatories, where necessary, to participate in collaborative engagement to influence companies. The UK Code requires signatories to disclose what forms of collaborative engagement they have participated in and why, 'including those undertaken directly or by others on their behalf'.[161] The last phrase would appear to acknowledge that collective action can be undertaken directly or through intermediaries. Consistent with the new code's approach of requiring investors' stewardship disclosures to focus on activities and outcomes,[162] Principle 10 requires investors to disclose the issues addressed by their collective action, the method of collective action used, their own role and contribution in relation to the collective action, and the outcomes of the collective action.[163] Assuming that, in practice, investors give effect to the UK Code's desire for disclosures to be 'as specific and as transparent as possible',[164] Principle 10's disclosure requirements should prompt disclosures which are more granular than the current non-specific disclosures observed, for example, in the stewardship statements of Australian

[158] See nn 69–73 and accompanying text.
[159] See nn 109–10, 114 and accompanying text.
[160] See Section 19.4.4.
[161] UK Code 2020 (n 6) 19.
[162] ibid 6.
[163] ibid 19.
[164] ibid 6.

investors. Such particularized disclosures should enable observers to understand better the role played by collective action and its significance as a mechanism for facilitating investors' stewardship activities.

19.5.4 Collective Stewardship and Acting-in-Concert Rules

Acting-in-concert rules ensure that persons who accumulate voting power through co-operative stake-building or the co-ordinated exercise of shareholder influence are subject to takeover regulation.[165] These rules can apply to shareholders who act collectively in relation to the governance of their companies[166] and are often regarded as a constraint on collective action.[167] The Australian experience suggests, however, that a more subtle analysis is required when considering the precise impact of acting-in-concert rules on investors' attempts to wield collective influence in corporate governance.

This point can be highlighted by reference to the attempt by the Australian regulator ASIC to accommodate collective action under Australia's acting-in-concert rules. In *Regulatory Guide 128: Collective Action by Investors* (RG 128), issued in 2015,[168] ASIC outlined the scope which it believes exists for shareholders to engage in collective action without attracting the operation of Australian takeover law. According to RG 128, acting-in-concert rules do not apply where shareholders exchange information or views with one another, exhort each other to address issues of concern, or jointly raise 'general issues' of concern with corporate managers.[169] ASIC also indicates that it is unlikely to take enforcement action in respect of temporary collective action which seeks to promote 'the improvement of a company's corporate governance'[170] – which it defines as collective action directed at mainstream corporate governance concerns, such as better disclosure practices and more comprehensive board performance evaluation processes.[171]

However, RG 128 provides little comfort for investors who wish to use collective action to escalate their governance concerns. RG 128 cautions that 'if . . . conduct extends to the formulation of joint proposals to be pursued together or there is an understanding that the investors will act or vote in a particular way, then concerns may arise'.[172] It states that if shareholders threaten to pursue their objectives by co-ordinating their voting or collectively seeking to change the composition of a company's board, such conduct is likely to trigger the application of the acting-in-concert rules.[173]

RG 128's accommodation of low-intensity forms of collective action should provide comfort to investors who seek to engage in lower-intensity forms of stewardship – such as information

---

[165] Reinier Kraakman and others (eds), *The Anatomy of Corporate Law: A Comparative and Functional Approach* (2nd edn, OUP 2009) 255; Martin Winner, 'Active Shareholders and European Takeover Regulation' (2014) 11 *European Company and Financial Law Review* 364, 367.
[166] The Walker Review, for example, recognized that collective shareholder action could sometimes collide with, and contravene, these rules: Walker Review (n 5) para 5.44.
[167] The extent to which collective action should be accommodated by acting-in-concert rules has been explored by regulators in several jurisdictions: see e.g. Ana Taleska, 'Shareholder Proponents as Control Acquirers: A British, German and Italian Perspective on the Regulation of Collective Shareholder Activism via Takeover Rules' (2018) 19 *European Business Organization Law Review* 797.
[168] Australian Securities and Investments Commission, 'Regulatory Guide 128' (n 144).
[169] ibid table 1.
[170] ibid para 128.49.
[171] ibid para 128.50.
[172] ibid table 1.
[173] ibid tables 1, 2 and 3.

sharing and non-confrontational engagement with investee companies. However, it is questionable whether RG 128 will significantly enhance the overall levels of this type of collective stewardship by investors. This is because, as this chapter shows, these types of lower intensity collective action are already facilitated to a significant extent by intermediary organizations, including industry bodies and engagement firms, whose activities are not generally caught by acting-in-concert rules.[174]

The more significant aspect of RG 128 is arguably its hostile stance towards higher-intensity forms of collection action, such as investors jointly making demands or threatening to exercise their collective voting power against the re-election of directors. As this chapter shows, it appears that investors are more likely to engage in direct forms of collective action in order to assist them in undertaking these more difficult forms of intervention.[175] It is therefore possible that RG 128 fails to provide regulatory latitude for collective stewardship in situations where such latitude is most needed.

The Australian experience highlights, therefore, the need for any attempt to accommodate collective stewardship under acting-in-concert laws to be guided by a thorough understanding of the actual role and nature of collective action in any given jurisdiction.

19.6 CONCLUSION

Australia provides an interesting case study concerning the role of collective action as a form of stewardship. It reveals collective action to be a nuanced governance practice. In particular, it highlights the significance of intermediary-led collective action and argues that this form of collective action warrants further research, as well as more detailed consideration when developing stewardship norms. The Australian experience also highlights the potential regulatory challenge of accommodating collective action under acting-in-concert rules, yielding insights which are relevant to regulators and researchers in other jurisdictions who are examining the intersection of collective action and takeover law.

---

[174] See nn 144–46 and accompanying text.
[175] See Section 19.4.3.

20

Stewardship Principles in Canada

Cynthia A. Williams

20.1 INTRODUCTION

The Stewardship Principles for institutional investors in Canada have been developed by investors themselves through the auspices of the Canadian Coalition for Good Governance (CCGG), an organization of institutional investors that by 2020 represents CAD 4.5 trillion under management. First published in 2005, entitled 'Statement of Principles Regarding Member Activism' (CCGG Principles 2005), this Canadian policy document preceded the UK's first government-promulgated stewardship code in 2010, which is generally understood to be the first official stewardship code, although the CCGG Principles 2005 followed various unofficial stewardship initiatives and Codes of Good Governance from the UK.[1] More will be said about the CCGG Principles 2005 later in the chapter.

That Canada would be an early adopter of the stewardship trend is somewhat surprising. Canada has often borrowed from both the UK and the US in its approaches to securities regulation and corporate governance,[2] but often after observing for some years how new initiatives have worked out in the originating country. This dynamic was at work here, in fact, since in the UK institutional investors comprising the Institutional Shareholders Committee had been articulating their responsibilities as engaged investors since 1991, and the government in the Myners Review in 2001 first suggested an official Stewardship Code.[3]

Yet, it isn't immediately obvious why Canada would have needed stewardship principles. It is a country that has long had a predominance of public companies with controlling shareholders who are by definition exercising stewardship.[4] Half of Canada's largest publicly held companies had a shareholder owning 20 per cent or more shares in 2012, at about the time that the CCGG Principles 2005 were being revised and republished (2010).[5] Moreover, as will be described,

---

[1] The CCGG Principles 2005 (on file with the author). For a discussion of the early stewardship initiatives and the diffusion of stewardship codes generally, see Katelouzou and Siems, The Global Diffusion of Stewardship Codes, Chapter 30.

[2] See Andrew MacDougall, Robert Yalden and John Valley, 'Canada' in Willem JL Calkoen (ed), *The Corporate Governance Review* (8th edn, Law Business Research 2018).

[3] See Davies, The UK Stewardship Code 2010–2020, Chapter 2, Section 2.1. The Institutional Shareholders' Committee in the UK had emphasized shareholders' responsibilities regarding the environmental and social risks of investee companies since its 2002 statement. See Cynthia A Williams and John M Conley, 'An Emerging Third Way? The Erosion of the Anglo-American Shareholder Value Construct' (2005) 38 *Cornell International Law Journal* 493. This language about environmental and social risks was weakly borrowed in Canada by CCGG in its 2005 Principles.

[4] See MacDougall, Yalden and Valley (n 2) 65. For a specific discussion of stewardship principles as exercised in jurisdictions with controlling shareholders, see Katelouzou and Puchniak, Global Shareholder Stewardship, Chapter 1 and Lim and Puchniak, Can a Global Legal Misfit Be Fixed?, Chapter 28. See also Dan W Puchniak, 'The False Hope of Stewardship in the Context of Controlling Shareholders: Making Sense Out of the Global Transplant of a Legal Misfit' *The American Journal of Comparative Law* (forthcoming)

[5] See Brian R Cheffins, 'Hedge Fund Activism Canadian Style' (2014) 47 *University of British Columbia Law Review* 1.

Canadian shareholders have extensive rights to exercise influence pursuant to the Canada Business Corporations Act (CBCA), the federal statute under which the largest publicly traded companies are typically incorporated. Canadian shareholders are still somewhat cautious about using some of those rights, including a right under the CBCA to nominate individuals for the board and include that nominee in the company's proxy circular,[6] a right denied to US shareholders (among others). Perhaps it was thought useful to encourage investors to use concentrated but private mechanisms of influence other than proxy contests and public criticisms of under-performing companies, since those techniques were not often being used in the Canadian 'culture of passivity'.[7]

In other respects, Canada's policy leadership regarding principles of investor stewardship is not surprising. As regards policies protecting shareholders and shareholders' rights, Canada is a country that 'punches above its weight' internationally through the International Organization of Securities Commissioners (IOSCO). Provincial securities commissioners from Canada established IOSCO, holding the first meeting in Quebec in 1983, and establishing the organization as a non-profit in Montreal in 1987. Canada is one of only two countries with two representatives on the board of IOSCO today, who are from the Quebec and Ontario Securities Commissions; the other country with two representatives is the US.[8] Securities policy development at both federal and provincial levels in Canada proceeds with serious deliberation and consultation, informed by norms of collaboration and respectful communication. Moreover, Toronto, where one-third of the country's population lives, has a rich array of policy organizations informing many contiguous disciplines, such as accounting, auditing, valuation, insurance and disclosure, as well as organizations of directors, of chief executive officers (CEOs), of economists, of risk officers and so forth. Thus, new policy ideas are both generated in Toronto and communicated across disciplines, even as Toronto policymakers participate globally across a range of disciplines.[9] Similar dynamics, and thoughtful policy development across a range of issues, including regarding shareholders and shareholders' rights and responsibilities, exist in other provinces, including Quebec.

In any case, at the time of this chapter's writing, 2020, Canada's voluntary stewardship principles have been revised twice: in 2010 and 2017. The 2017 version was 'reviewed again in 2020 following the release of the newly updated U.K. Stewardship Code, with an eye to ensuring they continue to reflect and are compatible with the highest standards of stewardship'.[10] The principles posted on CCGG's website have a 2020 date, but are substantially the same as the 2017 version. This text will refer to them as the CCGG Principles 2017/2020. While the CCGG Principles 2017/2020 contain seven principles versus the five of the CCGG Principles 2010, the fundamentals have not changed: investors are expected to monitor investee companies, exercise voting rights, engage on governance matters when problems occur, monitor and engage with regulators and policymakers on matters affecting shareholders' rights, and provide transparency on their voting and engagement activities.[11] The two additional principles added to the 2010

---

[6] See Canada Business Corporations Act (CBCA), RSC 1985, c C44, s 137.
[7] Cheffins (n 5).
[8] International Organization of Securities Commissions (IOSCO), 'IOSCO Board' <www.iosco.org/about/?subsection=display_committee&cmtid=11> accessed 14 August 2020. The two board members from the US are the Chair of the Securities and Exchange Commission (SEC) and the Chair of the Commodities Futures Trading Commission (CFTC).
[9] This author is an American who has been living in and around Toronto for the past seven years, and so has had the opportunity to observe the policy development and communications processes from a comparative perspective, both as an academic observer and as a participant.
[10] Catherine McCall (Executive Director of the Canadian Coalition for Good Governance), email communication with the author (2 June 2020) (on file with the author).
[11] See Canadian Coalition for Good Governance (CCGG), 'Principles for Governance Monitoring, Voting and Shareholder Engagement' (December 2010) <https://ccgg.ca/wp-content/uploads/2019/03/Principles_for_Governance_

framework in 2017 are that investors will develop a policy approach to stewardship and communicate it to their members and that they will focus on long-term sustainable value.[12]

The purpose of these principles, as articulated in 2005, 2010 and 2017, as with stewardship codes generally, is to improve the effectiveness of companies' boards by encouraging large institutional investors to pay attention to the quality of boards' monitoring of management. This purpose is well articulated in the CCGG Principles 2017/2020: '[I]n the modern publicly traded corporation, corporate governance is a shared responsibility. While the board of directors oversees management, shareholders have a significant role in corporate governance in overseeing that the board fulfills its responsibilities and holding directors to account when this is not the case.'[13]

The stewardship model thus builds upon the triangular relationship among management, the board and shareholders, which is how corporate governance is understood in common-law jurisdictions without co-determination.[14] While we expect the board to provide oversight, develop strategy and monitor management's exercise of its powers, shareholder stewardship is expected to oversee the board's exercise of its powers, and engage with boards where shareholders perceive weaknesses. This type of shareholder stewardship and engagement is not intended to promote changes in strategies, as would shareholder activists; rather, it is intended to identify problems, perhaps provide ideas, but ultimately to expect that boards will solve those problems. If boards do not solve identified problems after shareholders have engaged with the board, there is always the potential for an escalation of investors' engagement, such as by bringing criticisms publicly, putting shareholder proposals on the agenda of the AGM, or even engaging in a proxy contest or takeover attempt. Through stewardship, shareholders promote their collective views more directly to companies, communicating (in Canada through CCGG) regularly with the independent directors of between thirty-five and fifty companies, initiating discussions of governance issues, strategy issues and concerns with environmental and social risk.

This chapter will provide some of the regulatory context in which shareholder rights have developed in Canada, and then provide some further detail about Canada's current stewardship principles. It will then explore questions about shareholder stewardship in general, and in Canada. First, is the focus on stewardship as a way of mitigating risk properly calibrated in Canada? Second, how, if at all, have the stewardship principles motivated institutional investors to take on climate change risk, which is understood by the federal government in Canada and the Bank of Canada to pose serious, systemic risk to the Canadian economy? And third, if a coalition of investors that has assets under management comparable to the size of the entire capital markets in Canada does not take on this systemic risk, collectively, can it be said that by fulfilling their individualized stewardship responsibilities, company by company, they will be promoting 'the long-term sustainable creation of value, so companies and their investors can prosper and, in the process, benefit the market and society as a whole', as the stewardship principles suggest? This author recognizes that this standard by which to evaluate the

---

Monitoring_Voting_and_Shareholder_Engagement-Formatted__2_-1-1.pdf> accessed 14 August 2020 [hereinafter CCGG Principles 2010].

[12] See CCGG, 'Stewardship Principles' (May 2020) <https://ccgg.ca/wp-content/uploads/2020/05/2020-Stewardship-Principles-CCGG-new-branding.pdf> accessed 14 August 2020 [hereinafter CCGG Principles 2017/2020].

[13] ibid 1.

[14] Of course, it is also true that by articulating the expectations that asset managers and other institutional investors monitor, vote and engage as needed with investee companies, stewardship norms may have an effect within those institutions as well as a potential effect on investee companies. On the 'investment side' of stewardship, see Dionysia Katelouzou, *The Path to Enlightened Shareholder Stewardship* (CUP) (forthcoming).

440   *Part II Jurisdictions*

stewardship principles may seem to depart from the purpose of the principles, but will suggest in this chapter that using the power of their collective financial power as the authoring body of the principles to focus only outward, at what investee companies are doing, risks falling short of what their collective ambition could, and should, be in light of climate change.

20.2 THE REGULATORY CONTEXT

Canada is the second-largest country in the world by land mass, after Russia, but with a population of only 37.59 million as of 2019.[15] It has well-regulated, efficient capital markets, with a value of USD 2.55 trillion of equities being traded, and USD 2.0 trillion of debt.[16] Further data about the stock exchanges in Canada are provided in Section 20.2.2.

20.2.1 *Canadian Securities Regulation*

Securities regulation in Canada is divided among the thirteen provinces and territories, each with their own respective securities laws and regulator.[17] In general, all provincial and territorial securities laws serve the purpose of creating fair and efficient capital markets. Despite this unity in purpose, each province and territory operates as a 'closed system', with their respective regulators qualifying distributions of securities according to their statutes.[18] For example, if an issuer wishes to distribute its securities in the province of Ontario, it must comply with the Ontario Securities Act. As a result, when an issuer is registered in one province and seeks to distribute its securities in another province, it is faced with the regulatory burden of having to comply with another set of laws.

The regulators ('Commissions') have attempted to alleviate this burden by establishing an organization, the Canadian Securities Administrators (CSA), to co-ordinate among most of the provinces and to harmonize regulations across the Canadian capital markets.[19] In 2008, the CSA created a 'passport system' allowing market participants in all provinces, except Ontario, to participate 'in all passport jurisdictions by dealing only with its principal regulator and complying with one set of harmonized laws'.[20] On 8 September 2014, after efforts to directly establish a national regulator were frustrated,[21] British Columbia, Ontario, Saskatchewan, New Brunswick, Prince Edward Island and the Yukon (participating jurisdictions) signed the first

---

[15] Statistics Canada, 'Population Estimates, Quarterly' (2019) <www150.statcan.gc.ca/t1/tbl1/en/tv.action?pid=1710000901> accessed 14 August 2020.
[16] Securities Industry and Fund Managers Association (SIFMA), '2019 Outlook: Trends in the Capital Markets' (17 December 2018) 6 <www.sifma.org/wp-content/uploads/2018/12/2019-Outlook-FINAL.pdf> accessed 14 August 2020.
[17] The statutory provisions applicable to a number of important provincial markets include the Ontario Securities Act (OSA), RSO 1990, c S5; the Alberta Securities Act (ASA), SA 2000, c S4; the British Columbia Securities Act (BCSA), RSBC 1996, c 418; and the Nova Scotia Securities Act (NSSA), RSNS 1989, c 418.
[18] Mary G Condon, Anita Anand, Janis Pearl Sarra and Sarah Bradley, *Securities Law in Canada: Cases and Commentary* (3rd edn, Emond Montgomery 2017) 176.
[19] Canadian Securities Administrators, 'Who We Are' (2009) <www.securities-administrators.ca/aboutcsa.aspx?id=77> accessed 14 August 2020.
[20] See Multilateral Instrument 11-102 – Passport System.
[21] The prospect of establishing a national regulator has been difficult, given judicial interpretations of the Constitution Act, 1867, 30 and 31 Vict, c-3 and the Charter of Rights and Freedoms [part I of the *Constitution Act, 1982*] (Charter). The provinces' power to regulate *property and civil rights* has consistently been interpreted to be in conflict with the federal government's power to regulate *trade and commerce*. See *Reference re Securities Act* [2011] SCC 66, [2011] 3 SCR 837, holding that the previously proposed federal Securities Act, which would have established a federal securities regulator, was outside of Parliament's power and an infringement of the provinces' power to regulate property.

draft of the 'Memorandum of Agreement Regarding the Cooperative Capital Markets Regulatory System'. The signatories of this memorandum have made a 'strong commitment . . . to implement a cooperative capital markets regulatory system', particularly through the creation of a 'single operationally independent *capital markets regulatory authority* (the "CMRA")'.[22] According to the participating jurisdictions, the CMRA would foster more globally competitive Canadian capital markets, encourage market innovation, bolster investor protection by creating consistent regulatory standards, better co-ordinate enforcement activities and enhance Canada's ability to manage systemic risks.[23] This co-operative approach was recently upheld as Constitutional, in legal challenges brought on the basis that the federal government's role in regulating capital markets independent of the co-operating provinces and territory is limited to the detection, prevention and management of systemic risks to the stability of the Canadian economy.[24]

That securities regulation is provincial, albeit with increasing federal co-operation, has had positive implications for the kinds of collaborative regulatory involvement that the investor coalition of CCGG promotes. Thus, investors in any given province are close to the locus of securities regulation, have long-standing relationships with regulators and other policy advocates, and can work co-operatively with regulators to promote their policy initiatives. This author's observation is that regulatory processes of consultation and deliberation in Canada are generally careful and thoughtful, and so may not be fast, but they do generally proceed with a fair amount of co-operation and consensus-building. Acting in collaboration with other policy organizations, CCGG has been able to convince federal and/or provincial authorities to promulgate a number of important corporate governance regulations, such as majority voting requirements (federal, through the CBCA), gender diversity disclosure on the board (Ontario Securities Commission initially and, as of 2020, federal through the CBCA) and annual, voluntary say-on-pay (federal, through the CBCA).

20.2.2 *The Exchanges*

Of the provinces and territories, Ontario has the largest securities exchange in Canada, the Toronto Stock Exchange (TSX), owned by the TMX Group, which also owns the TSX Venture Exchange (TSXV), headquartered in Calgary, Alberta. A report published by the Market Intelligence Group in June 2020 showed the TSX and TSXV total collective market cap to be CAD 2.98 trillion, with 44 per cent of their listed companies headquartered in Ontario.[25] Ontario is also the home of the largest securities regulator in Canada, the Ontario Securities Commission (OSC), with more than 560 employees as of 2020.[26]

The majority of TSXV issuers have resource-dependent businesses, as do a significant minority of TSX issuers. As of June 2020, the Market Intelligence Group reported that mining was the dominant industrial sector on these exchanges, comprising 56 per cent of all TSXV and 13 per cent of TSX listed issuers (second only to exchange traded funds, which account for

---

[22] Cooperative Capital Markets Regulatory System, 'Memorandum of Agreement Regarding the Cooperative Capital Markets Regulatory System' (2015) 1–3 <http://ccmr-ocrmc.ca/wp-content/uploads/moa-04162015-en.pdf> accessed 14 August 2020 (emphasis added).
[23] See Condon, Anand, Sarra and Bradley (n 18) 1.
[24] See *Reference re Pan-Canadian Securities Regulation* [2018] SCC 48 [81], [132].
[25] See TSX, 'The MiG Report: Toronto Stock Exchange and TSX Venture Exchange' (June 2020) <www.tsx.com/resource/en/2355> accessed 14 August 2020.
[26] See Ontario Securities Commission, 'Our Structure' (2020) <www.osc.gov.on.ca/en/About_our-structure_index.htm> accessed 14 August 2020.

48 per cent of TSX listed issuers).[27] It is also worth noting that oil and gas is Alberta's most dominant sector (41 per cent by market capitalization, comprising 19 per cent oil and gas and 22 per cent utilities and pipelines), and Alberta is Canada's second largest capital market.[28]

The dominance of the natural resource sectors in Canadian capital markets, and in its economy, underscores the challenges facing Canada in the transition to a low-carbon economy. The importance of these sectors also underscores the need for clear, comparable disclosure of how companies are managing the strategic risks of that transition. CCGG has been advocating for the OSC to take up the issue of standardized environmental, social and governance (ESG) factors disclosure, which may ultimately include climate risk disclosure.[29]

20.2.3 *Canadian Business Corporations Act*

The CBCA is a federal statute under which about half of large, publicly listed companies in Canada are incorporated. Its provisions are closely mirrored by most of the provinces' corporate statutes for smaller companies incorporated provincially. As stated already, the CBCA gives shareholders extensive rights, well beyond the shareholder rights seen in the US, for instance, but more in line with the kinds of shareholder rights found in other civil law and common law jurisdictions.[30]

Many of these statutory rights give shareholders the power to go beyond stewardship to engage in shareholder activism or launch proxy contests using the company's own money, by virtue of being permitted to nominate specific candidates for board positions and having those candidates included in management's proxy circular. Thus, the backdrop of institutional investor stewardship in Canada is this statutory power to go active. Yet, until recently, institutional investors were reluctant to even publicly criticize underperforming companies, let alone engage in a proxy contest or put a proposal on the agenda.[31] Canada's stewardship principles were developed, in part, to address that reluctance.

20.3 CANADA'S STEWARDSHIP PRINCIPLES

CCGG was established in 2003 by three asset managers – Claude Lamoureaux, CEO of Ontario Teachers' Pension Plan; Mike Wilson, former federal finance minister and then-chair of Barclays Canada; and Stephen Jarislowsky of the asset management firm bearing his name, Jarislowsky Fraser.[32] The impetus was the burgeoning corporate governance trend, including the

---

[27] See TSX (n 25). The second most prominent sector listed on the TSXV is Oil and Gas at 9% and the fifth most prominent sector on the TSX at 5% (subordinate only to the financial sectors and the broad sector referred to as Diversified Industries).

[28] Alberta Securities Commission, '2020 Annual Report: Adapting to New Market Realities and Fostering Resilience' (2020) 10, 13 <www.albertasecurities.com/-/media/ASC-Documents-part-1/Publications/ASC_Annual_Report_2020_Final_website.ashx> accessed 14 August 2020.

[29] See CCGG, 'Letter to Ontario Securities Commission ("OSC") Draft 2019-2020 Statement of Priorities' (23 May 2019) <https://ccgg.ca/wp-content/uploads/2019/05/FINAL-CCGG-Submission-to-OSC-re-2019-20-SOP-Chair-signed-1-1.pdf> accessed 14 August 2020.

[30] See MacDougall, Yalden and Valley (n 2) 74; Reinier Kraakman and others (eds), *The Anatomy of Corporate Law: A Comparative and Functional Approach* (3rd edn, OUP 2017); Gen Goto, 'Legally "Strong" Shareholders of Japan' (2014) 3 *Michigan Journal of Private Equity & Venture Capital Law* 125.

[31] Proxy contests are still predominantly being initiated by shareholder activists from outside of Canada, although Canadian institutional investors are now more likely to publicly support those contests. See text accompanying nn 49–51.

[32] Email communication from David R Beatty (first managing director of CCGG) dated 24 July 2020 (on file with the author).

founders' observations of the development of corporate governance principles in the UK with the Cadbury Code in 1992, and then the Canadian development of fourteen voluntary guidelines for corporate governance best practices by the 1994 Dey Committee Report.[33] Although voluntary, to be listed on the TSX, companies needed to report on their implementation, or not, of the principles, that is, to 'comply or explain'.[34] In 2003, Peter Dey, the author of the 1994 Dey Committee Report, and former chair of the OSC, suggested that compliance with the corporate governance principles be made mandatory, which suggestion was not taken up by regulators or the TSX.[35] In reaction, CCGG's founders established it in order to concentrate asset managers' and asset owners' potential corporate governance influence over Canadian companies. By 2005, CCGG promulgated the first version of the Canadian stewardship principles. Then, as now, there was no requirement of public acknowledgement by any particular asset manager or owner of 'compliance' with the principles, but asset managers are asked about their compliance when bidding for business from different asset owners.

20.3.1 The Expanding Purpose of Canada's Stewardship Principles

One of the developments that can be seen by comparing the CCGG Principles 2005 to the current version is a change in the ambition of the principles. Thus, the 2005 Principles stated:[36]

> A Member who decides it is in the best interests of their beneficiaries to take on actions in respect of a Company should devote appropriate resources to these activities, but these should be commensurate with the benefits for beneficiaries. The primary duty of a Member, in all matters including dealings with a Company, is to their beneficiaries and not to the wider public. It is understood that a Member may have mutually-exclusive groups of beneficiaries whose interests may differ.

When discussing the reason for investors to closely monitor their investments, the CCGG Principles 2005 state that it is to '[satisfy] themselves, to the extent possible, that the Company's board and management have appropriate strategies, structures, and controls in place to maximize shareholder value'.

Articulating the corporate purpose as maximizing shareholder value would have been standard fare in any 'shareholder-oriented' jurisdiction such as Canada in 2005. Yet, three months before the CCGG Principles 2005 were published, the Supreme Court of Canada rejected the idea that companies exist to maximize shareholder value, embracing a stakeholder construct for company directors' fiduciary duties.[37] The Supreme Court of Canada reiterated and elaborated upon that stakeholder construct for directors' fiduciary duties again in 2008,[38] landing Canada squarely in the 'stakeholder capitalism' camp. This shift, amid broader trends in institutional investor social and environmental activism globally,[39] had an impact on the 2010 revisions of the Canadian stewardship principles. In the CCGG Principles 2010, the goal of shareholder stewardship was still shareholder value, but incorporating a broader perspective:[40]

---

[33] ibid.
[34] Michael Barrier, 'A New Dey in Canada: Peter Dey, the Principal Author of Landmark Voluntary Guidelines for Corporate Governance Now Wants to Require Companies to Follow Them' (2003) 60 *Internal Auditor* 40.
[35] ibid.
[36] CCGG Principles 2005 (Appendix A).
[37] *Peoples Department Stores Inc (Trustee of) v Wise* [2004] SCC 68, [2004] 3 SCR 461.
[38] *BCE Inc v 1976 Debentureholders* [2008] SCC 69, [2008] 3 SCR 560.
[39] See generally Cynthia A Williams, 'Corporate Social Responsibility and Corporate Governance' in Jeffrey Gordon and Wolf-Georg Ringe (eds), *The Oxford Handbook of Corporate Law and Governance* (OUP 2018).
[40] CCGG Principles 2010 (n 11) 1.

CCGG believes that companies that follow well-accepted principles of "good governance" have less risk and generate greater long term value for their shareholders than comparable companies with less robust governance practices. "Governance" includes how the board is structured and how it operates, the board's approach to executive compensation and shareholder engagement and the board's oversight of the company's risk management policies, including its environmental and social risks.

By 2017, the goal of shareholder stewardship, while still directed to company success, included promoting social welfare, still through the mechanism of improving companies' governance. This broadening of the goals for shareholder stewardship is consistent with what we have seen in other countries' stewardship codes, notably in the UK.[41] As the CCGG Principles 2017/2020 stated: 'Stewardship for institutional investors means fulfilling their responsibilities as fiduciaries in meeting their obligations to their beneficiaries or clients. Stewardship is intended to enhance the long-term sustainable creation of value, so companies and their investors can prosper and, in the process, benefit the market and society as a whole.'[42]

Some implications of this progressively broadened concept of the goal of shareholder stewardship, from ensuring that companies are properly structured to maximize shareholder wealth to the enhancement of long-term sustainable value creation for the benefit of shareholders, the market and society, will be discussed later in the chapter.

20.3.2 *The Content of the Principles Today*

The most recent version of CCGG's Stewardship Principles, adopted in 2017, sets out seven principles for active share ownership. Quoting each principle, we see a framework that suggests:[43]

1. Institutional investors should develop, implement and disclose their approach to stewardship and how they meet their stewardship responsibilities.
2. Institutional investors should monitor the companies in which they invest.
3. Institutional investors should adopt and publicly disclose their proxy voting guidelines and how they exercise voting rights.
4. Institutional investors should engage with portfolio companies.
5. Institutional investors should collaborate with other institutional investors where appropriate.
6. Institutional investors should engage with regulators and other policy makers where appropriate.
7. Institutional investors should focus on promoting the creation of long-term sustainable value.

Other than Principles 1 and 7, these are essentially the same as those published in 2010, although some of the explanatory material is expanded.

The commentary to Principle 1 is unique in that it is the only principle that includes inward-facing aspects that seek reflection on and oversight of institutional investors' own governance. Thus, the commentary states:[44]

---

[41] See Davies, The UK Stewardship Code 2010–2020, Chapter 2.
[42] See CCGG Principles 2017/2020 (n 12) 1. For discussion of the broad societal goals of the UK Code 2020, see Davies, The UK Stewardship Code 2010–2020, Chapter 2. For a discussion of the potential for stewardship codes generally to promote the societal goal of 'sustainable finance', see Katelouzou and Klettner, Sustainable Finance and Stewardship, Chapter 26.
[43] CCGG Principles 2017/2020 (n 12).
[44] ibid 4.

Institutional investors should implement mechanisms to deal with conflicts of interest within their investment activities, including how conflicts of interests are identified and managed with the objective of putting the interests of beneficiaries or clients first. The mechanisms should address situations where the interests of beneficiaries or clients diverge from each other.

Institutional investors should have structures and processes in place to seek to ensure that their compensation programs are properly aligned with the goal of enhancing the long-term sustainable value of the institutional investors' assets for the benefit of their beneficiaries or clients. Compensation programs should incorporate appropriate benchmarks, if relevant, and risk mitigation features.

As with prior versions of the principles, there is a continuum of investor activities that starts with monitoring investee company activities and voting proxies, and shifts to more active engagement upon perceiving problems with investee companies. Examples of the kinds of issue in 2017 on which investors' monitoring and voting aspects of stewardship should shift to engagement, which the principles suggest is a shift indicative of perceived problems with investee companies and more intensive active ownership, are: disclosure that is inadequate, problems with shareholders' rights or executive compensation, problems with board composition or independence, board oversight of strategy, or board oversight of risk, including 'material sustainability factors relating to matters such as environmental, social and governance risks'.[45]

The most interesting addition to the principles in 2017, in this author's view, is Principle 7, which states that 'Institutional investors should focus on promoting the creation of long-term sustainable value'. The explanatory material in its entirety states:[46]

Institutional investors should focus on a company's long-term success and sustainable value creation in preference to short-term considerations (understanding that beneficiaries or clients may have specific objectives and investment horizons). This focus should include understanding the company's strategy.

Institutional investors should make sure they understand the risks and opportunities associated with material sustainability factors, including environmental, social and governance issues, and integrate them into their investment and stewardship activities. Institutional investors also should be aware of systemic risks that can affect the companies in which they invest.

These two paragraphs seem to be focusing on two separate issues, both of which are worth acknowledging. The first engages with the corporate governance debate of long-term versus short-term investment horizons. This issue has emerged in particular after the global financial crisis as hedge-fund shareholder activists became more assertive in trying to shape companies' strategies. In Canada, shareholder activism became a focus of governance attention in 2012 when Bill Ackman's Pershing Capital launched a successful proxy contest to run Canadian Pacific (CP) Railroad,[47] although there were activists from the US, predominantly, engaging in Canada previously. In the US, hedge fund activism has raised concerns about 'short-termism' and the demonstrated reductions in research and development at even successful firms targeted by activists.[48] In Canada, the discussions are quite different, since under-performing companies

---

[45] CCGG Principles 2017/2020 (n 12) 6.
[46] ibid 7.
[47] See Cheffins (n 5) 1.
[48] See John C Coffee Jr and Darius Palia, 'The Wolf at the Door: The Impact of Hedge Fund Activism on Corporate Governance' (2016) 41 *Journal of Corporation Law* 545; Leo E Strine Jr, 'Who Bleeds When the Wolves Bite? A Flesh-and-Blood Perspective on Hedge Fund Activism and Our Strange Corporate Governance System' (2017) 126 *The Yale Law Journal* 1870.

had not typically been subject to as rigorous market discipline as in the US until activists arrived. One law firm's analysis (the Davies Corporate Governance Report) notes Canadian institutional investors' growing willingness by 2020 to express dissatisfaction with under-performing companies publicly, and to support activists in proxy contests, and dates the shift to the creation of CCGG, which has allowed an institutional investor voice for improvements in governance.[49] In the CP contest, that analysis suggests, institutional investors were quietly supportive, and gave their votes to Ackman, but, subsequently, and given the experience of 'voice' through CCGG on governance matters generally, institutional investors have become more publicly assertive in favour of changes in the boards of under-performing companies.[50] This more public voice is not through CCGG itself expressing views on the governance aspects of specific transactions; in fact, CCGG has a policy against public statements on specific transactions. Rather, individual Canadian institutional investors have become more willing to make such statements, and to publicly express their support for activists in individual proxy contests, according to that law firm's analysis.[51]

The second paragraph carries forward, and expands upon, an aspect of the stewardship principles that was in evidence in the CCGG Principles 2010 as well: that institutional investors should understand the material environmental and social risks that their investments entail, including any systemic risks. Indeed, even the CCGG Principles 2005 suggested that one reason why institutional investors might intervene in portfolio companies would be 'significant concerns with social responsibility'.[52] While neither the 2010 nor the 2017 Principles and guidance provide further elaboration on material environmental and social (E&S) risks, CCGG has issued quite specific guidance to boards in 2018 regarding its expectations about how 'relevant E&S risks and opportunities are captured in corporate strategy and risk management practices'.[53] These matters are also included where relevant in engagement meetings with independent directors. Including material environmental and social risks in both the Principles and the guidance stands in significant contrast to stewardship and corporate governance principles issued for the first time in 2018 in the US by the Investor Stewardship Group (ISG), which contain nothing about environmental or social risks.[54]

The guidance quoted earlier from the CCGG Principles 2017/2020 also states that institutional investors should 'be aware of systemic risks that can affect the companies in which they invest', which is a concept that is now incorporated into the UK Code 2020.[55] As will be

---

[49] See Davies Ward Phillips & Vineberg, 'Governance Insights 2019' (2019) 38 <www.dwpv.com/en/Insights/Publications/2019/Davies-Governance-Insights-2019> accessed 14 August 2020.
[50] ibid.
[51] ibid.
[52] See CCGG Principles 2005 (Appendix A) (stating that the reasons for 'intervening when necessary' would be where there were 'significant concerns about a Company's strategy; • operational performance; • apparent failure of directors in holding management accountable; • apparent failure of internal controls; • succession planning; • evidence of failure to comply with the requirements of corporate and/or securities legislation and or/regulation; • remuneration levels, incentive packages, perquisites, or severance packages, which are not consistent with the relevant environment; and • approach to corporate social responsibility').
[53] CCGG (E&S Committee), 'The Directors' E&S Guidebook' (*Harvard Law School Forum on Corporate Governance*, 1 July 2018) <https://corpgov.law.harvard.edu/2018/07/01/the-directors-es-guidebook/> accessed 14 August 2020. For the guidebook itself, see CCGG, 'The Directors' E&S Guidebook' (2018) <https://ccgg.ca/wp-content/uploads/2019/01/The-Directors-ES-Guidebook-2018.pdf> accessed 14 August 2020.
[54] See Investor Stewardship Group, 'The Principles' <https://isgframework.org/stewardship-principles/> accessed 14 August 2020.
[55] CCGG Principles 2017/2020 (n 12) 7. See Principle 4 of the UK Code 2020: 'Signatories identify and respond to market-wide and systemic risks to promote a well-functioning financial system' (Financial Reporting Council, *The UK Stewardship Code 2020* (2019) 11 <www.frc.org.uk/getattachment/5aae591d-d9d3-4cf4-814a-d14e156a1d87/Stewardship-Code_Dec-19-Final-Corrected.pdf> accessed 14 August 2020).

discussed, the transition to a low-carbon economy is a major systemic risk for the Canadian economy, and for its financial institutions and institutional investors. As engaged owners, these institutions and investors face difficult choices, where the limits of stewardship principles, and possibly even engaged ownership, may be evident. This topic will be taken up in Section 20.4.

20.4 ANALYSIS

20.4.1 *What the Implications of the CCGG Stewardship Principles Have Been*

As part of the research for this chapter, this author asked a number of leading lawyers, asset managers and asset owners in Toronto for their views on the effects of the CCGG Principles. The responses are well represented by the following quote: 'CCGG has a useful role to play in achieving currency for its norms and in addressing specific situations that arise by convening [its] membership.' When pressed about the importance of the principles per se, aside from CCGG's role, one asset manager responded as follows about the importance of stewardship codes with regulatory oversight versus voluntary principles:

> In my experience, the UK Stewardship Code and the Japanese Stewardship Code stand out and investors care far more about them than any other because they are overseen by the relevant regulator. In early days, most large global investors only cared about signing on to those ones and filing updates under them for that reason. When the UK FCA ... decided to start asking for more robust 'statements of compliance' to the UK Stewardship Code and started 'tiering' signatories (and this was under the earlier version of the Code), it really got investors to pay way more attention and care more ....
>
> Perhaps because of that regulatory oversight (formal or informal) signing the Japanese and UK Code seemed much more important to getting business in those markets than any other Code. I don't recall any institutional client ever asking about any other Code, but [our firm] would be asked if it was a signatory to those and if not, we would be asked to explain why ....
>
> ... [V]oluntary codes like the CCGG code, the ICGN code or the other national codes with no regulatory oversight ... can certainly act as a useful guide for investors who are trying to improve their stewardship practices. But I think to have an impact, it needs to be overseen, at least informally, by a regulator at least on a 'comply or explain' basis. That being said, given that it represents the view of most of Canada's largest investors, I think the CCGG code would be a great model/basis for a national Code for Canada. I suppose additional impact could result from asset owners requiring their asset managers to explain how managers comply with it (like UN PRI has effectively done).

Certainly, the comments of a small number of non-randomly selected market professionals cannot be taken as definitive. These comments do suggest two things worthy of note, though. First, it seems to be the actions of CCGG as a convening entity that are making a difference in corporate governance in Canada (as also concluded by the Davies Corporate Governance Report (see Section 20.3.2) and a recent empirical study),[56] not the Principles per se. Since the Principles would not exist without CCGG having convened the institutional investors who comprise it, both asset managers and asset owners, and since the Principles do represent a developing normative consensus by CCGG's members, how sharp a distinction can be

---

[56] See text accompanying n 49; Craig Doidge, Alexander Dyck, Hamed Mahmudi and Aazam Virani, 'Collective Action and Governance Activism' (2019) 23 *Review of Finance* 893, finding that companies that CCGG engaged were 58% more likely to adopt corporate governance reforms such as majority voting, say-on-pay and changes to executive compensation to increase the incentive component of the CEO's pay versus companies not engaged by CCGG.

drawn between the Principles and CCGG's actions is unclear. Second, if Canada goes in the direction of a mandatory 'comply or explain' stewardship code, the CCGG Principles would be a logical place to start the regulatory process. One question worth further thought for the engaged ownership community, and academics studying these codes, is whether it is necessary for there to be regulatory oversight in order for principles or codes to have a demonstrable effect, or whether essentially soft-law initiatives generated by the investment community itself can have an effect, and, if so, what effect, and under what conditions.

20.4.2 Reducing Risk through Active Ownership May Not Be the Canadian Challenge

When Canada's stewardship principles were revised in 2010, the goal was to encourage 'active ownership' by Canadian institutional investors in order to promote best corporate governance practices. Throughout the document, one theme that emerges is that governance improvements will lower risks at investee companies and promote long-term value. It is likely that the emphasis on lowering risk was affected by observing the 2007–08 global financial crisis, which was the impetus for the UK Code 2010, even though Canada's banks and other financial institutions came out of it relatively unscathed. Of note, that outcome was generally understood to be the result of decision-makers at the Office of the Superintendent of Financial Institutions (OSFI) refusing to let its supervised banks and insurance companies join the debt-fuelled binging on mortgage-backed securities and credit default swaps that so unravelled the global financial markets in 2007–08. In other words, it was a combination of good regulation and smart regulators that reduced risks for Canada's banks and insurance companies, not shareholder stewardship (keeping in mind that Canada has had shareholder stewardship principles promulgated since 2005).

But there may be a deeper problem with this concern with reducing risk: in Canada, many industry and government reports about Canada's business community bemoan Canada's 'long-standing culture of conservatism and risk aversion'.[57] A report in 2012 by Deloitte concluded that Canadian business owners' aversion to risk transcends all industries and grows along with company size.[58] An OpEd in the *Toronto Star*, when discussing policy efforts by Jim Flaherty, the sixth Canadian finance minister in as many administrations to try to increase Canadian productivity, described the problem as follows:[59]

> We don't use our brainpower to create new wealth. We have a highly educated population, generous tax incentives for research and development and lower corporate tax rates than any leading economic power. Yet our businesses remain reluctant to invest in new products and technologies ... They don't even capitalize on the exciting discoveries made in our universities and government laboratories.

When Canada was shocked in 2012 by the arrival of hedge-fund shareholder activist Bill Ackman from the US, one commentator wrote a column in an important Canadian newspaper,

---

[57] Dan Ovsey, 'Are "Fat and Happy" Canadians Too Chicken to Invest in Growth and Innovation?' *Financial Post* (1 October 2012) <https://business.financialpost.com/executive/are-fat-and-happy-canadians-too-chicken-to-invest-in-growth-and-innovation> accessed 14 August 2020 (reporting on a study by Deloitte Global identifying Canada as a 'productivity laggard', particularly in manufacturing, and connecting that study to a contemporaneous Industry Canada study on Canadian business leaders' risk aversion).
[58] ibid (citing Deloitte Report co-author Bill Currie, Deloitte Canada Vice Chair and Americas Managing Director).
[59] Carol Goar, 'Jim Flaherty the Latest to Leap into "Innovation Gap"' *The Toronto Star* (10 March 2010) <www.thestar.com/opinion/2010/03/10/goar_jim_flaherty_the_latest_to_leap_into_innovation_gap.html> accessed 14 August 2020.

The Globe and Mail, entitled 'Dear Bill Ackman: Save Us from Ourselves'.[60] In it, that author, Derek DeCloet, stated: 'Our business community is rather different from America's .... It's a small, polite group of people for a small, polite country .... No one wants to be the attack dog.'[61] Canada's venture capital community is beset with the same problem of risk aversion, and so has developed slowly, funding smaller projects than in the US and focusing on known industries.[62]

Certainly, mitigating unwarranted risks which have no possibility of potential upside, such as those related to compensation, environmental harm or social instability, is an important role for any company's board, and properly subject to shareholder engagement and oversight. But, in many instances, a productive role for investors in Canada may be to encourage companies to take on more risk, that is, to invest in growth, take on debt for a new product or expand production, or invest in more research and development. It may well be that discussions of this type occur as part of CCGG's private engagements with companies, but there is no language in any of the principles indicating that, in some instances, encouraging companies to take greater risk is merited.

20.4.3 *Reducing Climate Risk through Active Ownership (among Other Mechanisms) Is the Canadian Challenge*

It is clear that climate change presents material societal and political challenges throughout the world, as well as presenting material economic risks and opportunities to companies and investors.[63] Climate change awareness is motivating governments to agree to accelerate a transition to a low-carbon economy, seen most specifically in the global agreement by close to 200 countries in Paris in December 2015, to limit the warming of the Earth to 'well under' 2 degrees Celsius compared to the pre-industrial era, and 'pursuing efforts' to limit to 1.5 degrees Celsius.[64]

In Canada, government policy to meet Canada's obligations under the Paris Agreement is set out in the Pan-Canadian Framework on Clean Growth and Climate Change, which was agreed to by the federal government and all of the provinces and territories with the exception of Saskatchewan in December 2016.[65] That commitment is to reduce Canada's greenhouse gas emissions by 30 per cent below 2005 levels by 2030.[66]

---

[60] Derek DeCloet, 'Dear Bill Ackman: Save Us from Ourselves' *The Globe and Mail* (13 June 2012) <www.theglobeandmail.com/report-on-business/rob-magazine/top-1000/dear-bill-ackman-save-us-from-ourselves/article4256142/> accessed 14 August 2020 (cited in Cheffins (n 5) 1 fn 7).

[61] ibid.

[62] Business Development Canada (BDC) Capital, 'Canada's Venture Capital Landscape: Challenges and Opportunities' (June 2017) <www.bdc.ca/EN/Documents/analysis_research/venture-capital-landscape-paper-en.pdf> accessed 14 August 2020.

[63] See World Economic Forum, 'The Global Risks Report 2020' (12 January 2020) <www3.weforum.org/docs/WEF_Global_Risk_Report_2020.pdf> accessed 14 August 2020.

[64] Paris Agreement, art 2(1)(a) (United Nations Framework Convention on Climate Change, 'Paris Agreement' (2015) <https://unfccc.int/files/essential_background/convention/application/pdf/english_paris_agreement.pdf> accessed 14 August 2020): 'Holding the increase in the global average temperature to well below 2°C above pre-industrial levels and pursuing efforts to limit the temperature increase to 1.5°C above pre-industrial levels, recognizing that this would significantly reduce the risks and impacts of climate change.' The Paris Agreement entered into force as of 4 November 2016, when countries representing 55% of global GHG emissions had ratified the Agreement. To date, 193 countries have ratified the Agreement (United Nations Framework Convention on Climate Change, 'Paris Agreement: Status of Ratification' (2020) <https://unfccc.int/process/the-paris-agreement/status-of-ratification> accessed 14 August 2020).

[65] Environment and Climate Change Canada, *Pan-Canadian Framework on Clean Growth and Climate Change* (2016) <http://publications.gc.ca/collections/collection_2017/eccc/En4-294-2016-eng.pdf> accessed 14 August 2020.

[66] ibid.

Moreover, policy recommendations specific to finance have been developed by the Expert Panel on Sustainable Finance (Expert Panel), which was tasked in 2018 by the Minister of Environment and Climate Change and the Minister of Finance to 'identify (1) global trends in sustainable finance, including climate-related risk disclosure; (2) roles and responsibilities for sustainable finance in Canada; [and] (3) opportunities and challenges relating to sustainable finance and climate-related risk disclosure in Canada; and [to] (4) provide recommendations of potential next steps the Government of Canada may wish to consider within its area of jurisdiction'.[67] Recognizing that there is no universal definition of sustainable finance, the Expert Panel defined it as 'capital flows (as reflected in lending and investment), risk management (such as insurance and risk assessment) and financial processes (including disclosure, valuation, and oversight) that assimilate environmental and social factors as a means of promoting sustainable economic growth and the long-term stability of the financial system'.[68] As the Expert Panel stated in its final report, '[f]inance is not going to solve climate change, but it has a critical role to play in supporting the real economy through the transition. ... [C]limate change opportunity and risk management need to become business-as-usual in financial services, and embedded in everyday business decisions, products and services.'[69]

The final report of the Expert Panel set out fifteen recommendations to the government in three categories: ways in which it could create investment opportunities by mapping a clear transition plan; ways in which it could create the necessary foundations for public and private actors to develop the sustainable finance market at scale; and ways it could support the development of products and markets for sustainable growth.[70] Of particular relevance to this analysis, Recommendation 6 suggests to the Finance Ministry that it '[c]larify the scope of fiduciary duty in the context of climate change'.[71] Given that there can be legacy misperceptions of whether investment trustees may consider environmental and social factors in their portfolio constructions and voting, in contrast to the rapidly evolving understanding of the financial materiality of climate change, the Expert Panel recommended that Finance Canada clarify that 'consideration of climate factors is firmly within the remit of fiduciary duty'.[72] It also suggested that federally regulated pension funds be asked to discuss in their Statements of Investment Principles whether *and how* climate is considered, and any rationale for non-consideration.[73]

In addition to this policy encouragement for investors to take climate change risks into account in their own portfolio construction and voting, in a thorough-going manner, in 2019 the Bank of Canada for the first time in its Annual Financial System Review discussed climate change as a vulnerability to both Canada's economy and its financial system.[74] The Financial System Review stated:

> The move to a low-carbon economy involves complex structural adjustments, creating new opportunities as well as transition risk. Investor and consumer preferences are shifting toward

---

[67] Environment and Climate Change Canada, 'Expert Panel on Sustainable Finance: Terms of Reference' <www.canada.ca/en/environment-climate-change/services/climate-change/expert-panel-sustainable-finance.html> accessed 14 August 2020.

[68] Environment and Climate Change Canada, *Expert Panel on Sustainable Finance Interim Report* (2018) <http://publications.gc.ca/collections/collection_2018/eccc/En4-350-2018-eng.pdf> accessed 14 August 2020.

[69] Environment and Climate Change Canada, *Final Report of the Expert Panel on Sustainable Finance: Mobilizing Finance for Sustainable Growth* (2019) 2 <http://publications.gc.ca/collections/collection_2019/eccc/En4-350-2-2019-eng.pdf> accessed 14 August 2020.

[70] ibid 2–3.

[71] ibid 3.

[72] ibid 20, Recommendation 6.1.

[73] ibid 21, Recommendation 6.1 (emphasis added).

[74] Bank of Canada, 'Financial System Review – 2019' (2019) 28, Vulnerability 5: Climate Change <www.bankofcanada.ca/2019/05/financial-system-review-2019/#Vulnerability-5-Climate-change> accessed 14 August 2020.

lower-carbon sources and production processes, suggesting that the move to a low-carbon economy is underway. Transition costs will be felt most in carbon-intensive sectors, such as the oil and gas sector. If some fossil fuel reserves remain unexploited, assets in this sector may become stranded, losing much of their value. At the same time, other sectors such as green technology and alternative energy will likely benefit.

Both physical and transition risks are likely to have broad impacts on the economy. Moving labour and capital toward less carbon-intensive sectors is costly and takes time. Global trade patterns may also shift as production costs and the value of resources change. The necessary adjustments are complex and pervasive and might lead to increased risk for the financial system. In addition to insurance companies, many other parts of the financial system are exposed to risks from climate change. Banks have loans to carbon-intensive sectors as well as to connected sectors – for example, those upstream or downstream in supply chains. Asset managers hold carbon-intensive assets in and outside Canada.

The problem of climate change and the transition to a low-carbon economy is difficult everywhere but is particularly acute in Canada. It is a large, cold country, with people primarily clustered along its southern border but also living at great distances to the north. These geographic aspects require extensive systems of transportation, and intensive amounts of energy for heating, including the use of carbon-intensive and polluting diesel generators in the north. Moreover, 17 per cent of the Canadian economy is tied directly and indirectly to the extraction, refining, transport and sale of oil, gas, coal and minerals.[75] Transitioning away from these GHG-intensive sources of energy and economic inputs to the Canadian economy over the next decades will have effects on both producers and consumers; and could disproportionately affect particular provinces in Canada, notably Alberta, and particular people, such as those who work in the oil, gas and coal industries.

This, then, is a central risk to the Canadian economy, and presents systemic and material financial risk for Canadian asset managers and institutional investors in Canada. As one might expect of a coalition, where consensus requires general statements and common positions, there is little public evidence of how CCGG's Principles encouraging awareness of systemic issues and material environmental and social risks are affecting investors' actions in this regard. CCGG is on record supporting the OSC's review of whether there should be more required ESG disclosure, including climate change disclosure.[76] Climate change is also an issue that both CCGG as a coalition and some institutional shareholders individually are presumably raising with companies as part of their engagement activities.[77] Again, as one might expect, there is no public disclosure about the content of those discussions or their results, which makes sense, since confidentiality allows such discussions to occur, year after year, with the independent directors of Canadian companies. But it does raise questions about how effective shareholder stewardship is, at least on this systemic issue.[78]

---

[75] Natural Resources Canada, 'Ten Key Facts on Canada's Natural Resources' (2019) <www.nrcan.gc.ca/sites/www.nrcan.gc.ca/files/emmc/pdf/2019/2019-KFF-EN.pdf> accessed 14 August 2020.
[76] CCGG, 'CCGG Submission to OSC re 2020–21 Statement of Priorities' (29 May 2020) <https://ccgg.ca/wp-content/uploads/2020/05/CCGG-Submission-to-OSC-re-2020-21-Statement-of-Priorities.pdf> accessed 14 August 2020.
[77] CCGG, '2019 Annual Report' (2020) <https://ccgg.ca/wp-content/uploads/2020/05/CCGG-2019-Annual-Report_LinkedPDF-FINAL.pdf> accessed 14 August 2020 (stating that there had been board engagements with the independent directors of thirty-five Canadian companies, which as a general matter include discussions of strategy concerns, corporate governance matters, environmental and social risks).
[78] See Doidge, Dyck, Mahmudi and Virani (n 56) (firms with which CCGG engages are 58% more likely to adopt the suggested governance changes versus a matched set of firms not so engaged).

But again, there is a deeper problem here. Engaged investors may well be raising issues of inadequate disclosure of transition risks with their investee companies, to try to encourage those companies to do things differently or be more transparent about their actions. Voting records on climate-related shareholder proposals in Canada would seem to indicate that at least some institutional investors are voting for more climate-related disclosure.[79] The public statements of many of the large public pension funds in Canada indicate that they are aware of climate change risks, are engaging companies in discussions of them and are often promoting better climate disclosure from investee companies.[80]

A significant, and unresolved, question, though, is about the investors' own actions, that is, what they are investing in and what transition trajectories they are – or are not – supporting with their investments. Shareholder stewardship does not answer that question because it is not asking that question. It is almost exclusively outward-facing, seeking to encourage investors to be engaged owners of companies and to monitor companies' actions, vote thoughtfully and engage in further discussions and actions when companies' actions are problematic, including those producing social or environmental risks. Shareholder stewardship is not directed towards reflection or examination of the institutional investors' own actions, except as regards investors' conflicts of interests or compensation arrangements. There are no public reporting requirements of individual asset managers' or asset owners' efforts to meet the standards of the CCGG Principles, although CCGG is currently engaged in encouraging individual participants to reflect their membership in CCGG and adherence to the Principles on their websites. It may be that participating in a process to develop the norms of engagement, including on 'material environmental and social risks' and other systemic risks, has helped to shape the institutional investors' own actions in those regards. Might the investors participating in CCGG, for instance, show more awareness of environmental and social risks, including climate change as a systemic risk, than investors who are not participating? To this author's knowledge, that comparative study has not been done, and it would be difficult to do since most of the country's largest asset managers and investors are part of CCGG, so one would be comparing investors with very different capacities to do the underlying analyses. Yet, even without that study, it is worth noting, and concluding, that the power of CCGG could well be directed towards further normative development of an understanding among Canada's largest investors that they have responsibilities to be shifting capital away from industries that present systemic risk, and to be supporting emergent companies, technologies and transition pathways.

20.5 CONCLUSION

Institutional investors in Canada are in a different position from their colleagues and common-law 'cousins' in the US, where institutional investors collectively own large proportions of the outstanding stock of many S&P 500 companies.[81] In Canada, investors are embedded in an economy that is affected with a resource curse today, in that 17 per cent of the country's GDP is dependent on carbon-intensive fossil fuels and mining. Being part of a relatively small capital market (CAD 4.55 trillion), they must – and do – globally diversify their holdings. And many

---

[79] See Davies Ward Phillips & Vineberg (n 49) 103 (climate change disclosure was one of the most frequent topics within the sixty shareholder proposals brought to the AGM in 2019; voting totals for all proposals averaged 13%).

[80] See Canada Pension Plan Investment Board, 'CPPIB's Approach to Climate Change' <www.cppinvestments.com/public-media/headlines/2017/cppibs-approach-climate-change> accessed 14 August 2020 (discussing their engagement).

[81] See John C Coates IV, 'The Future of Corporate Governance Part 1: The Problem of Twelve' (2018) Harvard Public Law Working Paper No 19-07 <https://ssrn.com/abstract=3247337> accessed 14 August 2020.

companies in Canada still have majority owners. So even if institutional investors concentrate their ownership positions within any one company, there are many Canadian companies where they would still be in a minority shareholding position.

CCGG, by representing CAD 4.5 trillion of invested capital, and essentially the entirety of the large asset manager and institutional investor community in Canada, effectively solves the minority shareholder problem, as well as the polite community norms 'problem', if it is one (observing events in the US on a regular basis, this author is not certain that polite community norms are, in fact, problematic). CCGG can communicate on behalf of investors – its logo is 'CCGG: The Voice of the Investor' – and put pressure on companies towards better corporate governance. But CCGG is also doing more than advocating for best practices in corporate governance. By articulating, as of 2018, its expectations of companies concerning environmental and social risks through its publication 'The Directors' E&S Guidebook',[82] and by engaging on behalf of the investor community on those issues with individual companies as well, CCGG would seem to have an important role to play in encouraging Canada to address its fossil-fuel dependence.

That said, and as also stated in Section 20.4.1, it is CCGG that is important in the Canadian context, and not the stewardship principles per se. By collating investors' views, and articulating them in a Canadian context, it is possible that the Principles have started to have an influence within asset managers' and asset owners' thinking about their own organizations. If so, that is a second way in which CCGG is having an influence. It is a testament to the foresight of the founders of CCGG, and to the foresight of its early management, that close to two decades later its initiative has developed into an institution that is well-positioned to address a problem critical to the future of the Canadian economy, and thus to Canada – its need to transition to a low-carbon economy.

---

[82] CCGG, 'The Directors' E&S Guidebook' (n 53).

21

The Uncertain Stewardship Potential of Index Funds

Jill Fisch

21.1 INTRODUCTION

Policymakers around the world are demanding that large institutional investors act as responsible stewards of their portfolio companies.[1] The principal rationale behind the stewardship movement is that engaged institutional investors offer the potential to reduce managerial agency costs.[2] Some commentators have also argued that institutional investors should go further and address broader societal concerns such as the interests of non-shareholder stakeholders and environmental, social and governance (ESG) considerations through their voting power, a perspective that has been formalized in the 2020 version of the UK Stewardship Code.[3]

The challenge for the stewardship movement is that it treats institutional investors – primarily large asset managers – as shareholders rather than intermediaries. Both the structure and the business model of mutual funds limit their potential stewardship role in ways that stewardship advocates do not seem to appreciate fully. Because of this, although the increasingly concentrated institutional ownership of public corporations has substantially mitigated the agency problems identified by Berle and Means,[4] institutional intermediaries cannot replicate the actions and incentives of true block-holders.[5] As a result, commentators' expectations about the potential value of investor stewardship may be unrealistic.

As this chapter explains, the asset management industry, which dominates institutional share ownership in the US, faces two critical constraints. First, its business model – and, in particular, the increasing flow of assets into low-cost passively managed investment vehicles such as index funds and exchange traded funds (ETFs) (collectively 'index funds') – is not consistent with the kind of analysis necessary to provide substantial firm-specific oversight of corporate officers and directors of their portfolio companies on a cost-effective basis. Second, as the scope of the

---

[1] See e.g. Jennifer G Hill, 'Good Activist/Bad Activist: The Rise of International Stewardship Codes' (2018) 41 *Seattle University Law Review* 497, 506–13 (describing global attention to stewardship following the UK's creation of the world's first stewardship code).

[2] See e.g. Bowley and Hill, Stewardship and Collective Action, Chapter 19 (observing that UK Stewardship Code was adopted to address lack of shareholder participation in corporate governance and based on the view that greater engagement would operate 'as a check on centralized managerial power').

[3] See Financial Reporting Council, *The UK Stewardship Code 2020* (2019) 8 <www.frc.org.uk/getattachment/5aae591d-d9d3-4cf4-814a-d14e156a1d87/Stewardship-Code_Final2.pdf> accessed 18 May 2020 [hereinafter UK Code 2020] (advocating 'stewardship that creates long-term value for clients and beneficiaries leading to sustainable benefits for the economy, the environment and society').

[4] See Adolf A Berle and Gardiner C Means, *The Modern Corporation and Private Property* (Macmillan 1932).

[5] See Alex Edmans and Clifford G Holderness, 'Blockholders: A Survey of Theory and Evidence' in Benjamin E Hermalin and Michael S Weisbach (eds), *The Handbook of the Economics of Corporate Governance* (Elsevier 2017) (identifying challenges in defining what level of ownership characterizes a block-holder and presenting data on large-block ownership in the US).

stewardship movement becomes more capacious, it calls for investors to make operational and governance choices, but the relationship between asset managers and fund beneficiaries provides a tenuous basis for making those choices.

Although commentators have called for mutual funds to devote greater resources to stewardship through more frequent engagement as well as the increased use of shareholder proposals and even litigation,[6] they have not reflected on the tension between the costs of that stewardship and the benefits that today's mutual funds offer their beneficiaries by providing diversified investment vehicles at unprecedently low fees.[7] Nor do they explain why it would be cost-effective for those who offer a low-cost financial product that does not require firm-specific investment analysis to invest resources to develop operational or governance expertise. Indeed, even with respect to the broad-based governance initiatives in which institutions have been actively engaged, there are questions about the extent to which the policies they advocate are consistent with enhancing firm value.

To address the concern that institutional investors may be poorly positioned to incorporate the economic and non-economic preferences of their beneficiaries into their stewardship, or lack the authority to make those choices on behalf of those beneficiaries, several recent proposals have called for asset managers to determine those preferences by consulting with their beneficiaries.[8] For asset managers such as mutual funds, where direct consultation may be impractical, some commentators have called for pass-through voting.[9] The limitations of these proposals highlight the difficulty inherent in developing a workable stewardship policy for an institutional intermediary, particularly a policy that incorporates non-economic considerations.

The chapter proceeds as follows. Section 21.2 describes US developments in response to the global stewardship movement and, in particular, efforts to encourage institutional investors to engage with their portfolio companies as 'good corporate stewards'. Section 21.3 focuses on the specific case of the index fund, offering a brief explanation of its structure and business model. Section 21.4 explains why this business model is inconsistent with aggressive firm-specific stewardship – specifically, a stewardship model that entails firm-specific monitoring of operational decisions. Section 21.5 considers the challenge presented by demands that index funds incorporate ESG and sustainability considerations into their stewardship efforts. Finally, Section 21.6 explores the distinctive nature of index fund beneficiaries – the individuals who invest in index funds – and the implications for proposals to empower those beneficiaries; Section 21.7 concludes.

A cautionary note is in order. This chapter focuses on the specific role of index funds, and does not consider the extent to which the limitations identified herein are applicable to other types of institutional investors such as actively managed mutual funds, hedge funds, banks, public pension funds and sovereign wealth funds. Notably, the observations in this chapter are decidedly US-centric and have more limited applicability to jurisdictions in which other types of institutional investors dominate. The core observation of this chapter, however, is that institutional context matters. Thus, in considering the potential value of investor stewardship,

---

[6] See e.g. Lucian Bebchuk and Scott Hirst, 'Index Funds and the Future of Corporate Governance: Theory, Evidence, and Policy' (2019) 119 *Columbia Law Review* 2029; Sean Griffith and Dorothy Lund, 'A Mission Statement for Mutual Funds in Shareholder Litigation' (2020) 87 *University of Chicago Law Review* 1149.

[7] Research demonstrates that 'the growth of explicitly indexed funds worldwide enhances competition in the asset management industry'; Martijn Cremers, Miguel A Ferreria, Pedro Matos and Laura Starks, 'Indexing and Active Fund Management: International Evidence' (2016) 120 *Journal of Financial Economics* 539.

[8] See EU High-Level Group on Sustainable Finance, 'Financing a Sustainable European Economy' (2018) 74 <https://ec.europa.eu/info/sites/info/files/180131-sustainable-finance-final-report_en.pdf> accessed 18 May 2020 ('Pension funds should consult beneficiaries on their sustainability preferences and build those into their investment strategy.').

[9] Caleb N Griffin, 'We Three Kings: Disintermediating Voting at the Index Fund Giants' (2020) 79 *Maryland Law Review* 954.

policymakers would do well to reflect on the business model and structural details of the institutions that they seek to engage.

21.2 INVESTOR STEWARDSHIP: THE US PERSPECTIVE

As reflected in the 2010 version of the UK Stewardship Code, investor stewardship was initially intended to encourage institutional investors to respond to managerial agency problems – primarily excessive risk-taking and short-termism.[10] In the US, stewardship reflected the potential ability of the re-concentration of ownership to address the classic Berle and Means problem of unchecked managerial power in the US publicly traded corporation.[11] Berle and Means wrote at a time when the stock of US public companies was held primarily by dispersed retail investors who lacked the incentive and expertise to monitor management and limit agency costs. The rise of the institutional investor offered the possibility of reducing these agency costs.

Today, institutional investors own approximately 70 per cent of the stock of large US public companies, and these holdings are concentrated in a handful of the largest institutions.[12] In the US, the largest institutional investors are asset management firms such as BlackRock, Vanguard, State Street, Charles Schwab, and Fidelity, each of which manages trillions of dollars in assets. Collectively, BlackRock, Vanguard and State Street (commonly known as the 'Big Three')[13] are the largest owner in 88 per cent of the S&P 500 and the largest shareholder in 40 per cent of listed firms in the US.[14]

Despite the growing size of their holdings, for many years institutional investors in the US were not actively engaged in corporate governance – they often did not vote their shares, they ignored the governance of their portfolio companies[15] and they did not even seek to collect the damages available to them through shareholder litigation.[16] Over the past thirty years, however, that situation has changed substantially. Institutional investors have become increasingly active through a range of public and private engagement efforts, and corporations have responded to these efforts with governance structures that provide greater transparency and accountability.[17]

---

[10] Financial Reporting Council, *The UK Stewardship Code* (2010) <www.frc.org.uk/getattachment/e223e152-5515-4cdc-a951-da33e093eb28/UK-Stewardship-Code-July-2010.pdf> accessed 18 May 2020. See Davies, The UK Stewardship Code 2010–2020, Chapter 2 (describing the objectives of the first version of the UK Code).

[11] See e.g. Mariana Pargendler, 'The Corporate Governance Obsession' (2016) 42 *Journal of Corporation Law* 359, 370–71 (describing Berle and Means' identification of corporate governance problems as based, in part, on 'unchecked managerial power').

[12] Ben W Heineman Jr and Stephen Davis, 'Are Institutional Investors Part of the Problem or Part of the Solution? Key Descriptive and Prescriptive Questions About Shareholders' Role in U.S. Public Equity Markets' (October 2011) 4 <https://millstein.law.columbia.edu/sites/default/files/content/docs/80235_CED_WEB.pdf> accessed 18 May 2020.

[13] See e.g. Jan Fichtner, Eelke M Heemskerk and Javier Garcia-Bernardo, 'Hidden Power of the Big Three? Passive Index Funds, Re-concentration of Corporate Ownership, and New Financial Risk' (June 2017) 19 *Business and Politics* 298, 298,304 (explaining that BlackRock, Vanguard and State Street dominate the passive fund industry and terming them the 'big three').

[14] Bob Eccles, 'Concentration in the Asset Management Industry: Implications for Corporate Engagement' *Forbes* (17 April 2019) <www.forbes.com/sites/bobeccles/2019/04/17/concentration-in-the-asset-management-industry-implications-for-corporate-engagement/#4573da24402f> accessed 18 May 2020.

[15] See e.g. Paul Rose, 'The Corporate Governance Industry' (2007) 32 *Journal of Corporation Law* 887, 897 ('Unless an institutional investor believes that it can conduct research for less, or that more expensive but discerning research will enable it to obtain better returns (after subtracting its own research costs), the investor may be better off outsourcing its corporate governance research.').

[16] James Cox and Randall Thomas, 'Leaving Money on the Table: Do Institutional Investors Fail to File Claims in Securities Class Actions?' (2002) 80 *Washington University Law Quarterly* 855.

[17] See e.g. Jill E Fisch, Assaf Hamdani and Steven D Solomon, 'The New Titans of Wall Street: A Theoretical Framework for Passive Investors' (2020) 168 *University of Pennsylvania Law Review* 17 (detailing growth of engagement by institutional investors in corporate governance).

Even with the increasing involvement of institutional investors in corporate governance, the 2008 global financial crisis (GFC) caused a number of commentators to believe that investors were falling short.[18] In the UK, this led the UK Financial Reporting Council (FRC) to adopt the 2010 UK Stewardship Code, which is often described as 'the world's first stewardship code'.[19] The UK Stewardship Code, which has subsequently been refined,[20] is the model for stewardship codes around the world.[21] Commentators and regulators in many jurisdictions have embraced the idea that institutional investors have an obligation to engage in active stewardship of their portfolio companies and have identified a variety of potential benefits from stewardship.[22] In April 2017, the European Union (EU) imposed a requirement, as part of its revised Shareholder Rights Directive, that institutional investors publicly disclose how they integrate shareholder engagement into their investment strategies or explain why they do not do so.[23]

US regulators have not adopted a formal requirement of investor stewardship. Certain components of what might be deemed a stewardship function are implicit, however, in other legal requirements that apply to institutional investors. For example, both the courts and Congress have recognized that investment advisers owe fiduciary duties to the mutual funds they manage.[24] The Securities and Exchange Commission (SEC) in 2003 adopted rules requiring mutual funds to develop voting policies and procedures as well as to disclose how they voted their proxies at their portfolio companies.[25] At the same time, the SEC adopted rules under the Investment Advisers Act requiring investment advisers to adopt policies to ensure that funds' voting power is exercised in the 'best interest' of the fund.[26]

In 2017, a group of leading institutional investors in the US went further, forming the Investor Stewardship Group (ISG), to establish 'the Framework for US Stewardship and Governance'.[27] According to its website, the ISG consists of forty-five signatories and

---

[18] Arad Reisberg, 'The UK Stewardship Code: On the Road to Nowhere?' (2015) 15 *Journal of Corporate Law Studies* 217, 219.

[19] Lee Roach, 'The UK Stewardship Code' (2011) 11 *Journal of Corporate Law Studies* 463. For a timeline of the stewardship codes around the world, see Katelouzou and Siems, The Global Diffusion of Stewardship Codes, Chapter 30.

[20] Financial Reporting Council, *The UK Stewardship Code* (September 2012) <www.frc.org.uk/getattachment/d67933f9-ca38-4233-b603-3d24b2f62c5f/UK-Stewardship-Code-(September-2012).pdf> accessed 18 May 2020; Katelouzou and Siems, The Global Diffusion of Stewardship Codes, Chapter 30; UK Code 2020 (n 3).

[21] See Simon Wong, 'Is Institutional Investor Stewardship Still Elusive?' (*Harvard Law School Forum on Corporate Governance*, 2015) <https://corpgov.law.harvard.edu/2015/09/24/is-institutional-investor-stewardship-still-elusive-2/> accessed 18 May 2020 ('Five years after the launch of the landmark UK Stewardship Code, counterparts can be found on four continents'); see also Katelouzou and Siems, The Global Diffusion of Stewardship Codes, Chapter 30 (providing evidence about the diffusion of the UK code).

[22] See Yutaro Shiraishi, Naoshi Ikeda, Yasuhiro Arikawa and Kotaro Inoue, 'Stewardship Code, Institutional Investors, and Firm Value: International Evidence', (2022), 4, <https://papers.ssrn.com/sol3/papers.cfm?abstract_id=3462453> accessed 8 February 2022 (reporting findings "consistent with the view that stewardship codes encourage institutional investors, who typically hold a widely diversified portfolio, to monitor their portfolio firms.").

[23] European Commission, 'Shareholders' Rights Directive Q&A' (14 March 2017) <https://ec.europa.eu/commission/presscorner/detail/en/MEMO_17_592> accessed 18 May 2020. See Katelouzou and Sergakis, Shareholder Stewardship Enforcement, Chapter 27, Section 27.3.2 (describing the Shareholder Rights Directive as imposing 'semi-hard law duties' on institutional investors).

[24] Howard Schiffman, 'The Relationship between the Investment Advisor and the Mutual Fund: Too Close for Comfort' (1976) 45 *Fordham Law Review* 183, 183–84.

[25] Disclosure of Proxy Voting Policies and Proxy Voting Records by Registered Management Investment Companies, 17 CFR §§239-249-270-274 (2003).

[26] Proxy Voting by Investment Advisers, 17 CFR § 275 (2003).

[27] Investor Stewardship Group, 'About the Investor Stewardship Group and the Framework for U.S. Stewardship and Governance' <https://isgframework.org/> accessed 18 May 2020.

twenty-four additional 'endorsers'.[28] The group includes some of the world's largest asset managers and pension funds such as BlackRock, the California Public Employees' Retirement System, Goldman Sachs Asset Management, Hermes and the Union Bank of Switzerland.[29]

The ISG framework, a framework that Jennifer Hill calls an 'investor-led' stewardship code,[30] sets out both 'common expectations' regarding the corporate governance practices of portfolio companies and 'a set of fundamental stewardship responsibilities for institutional investors'.[31] In celebrating the one year anniversary of its release of the framework, the ISG touted its 'remarkable success'.[32] Yet, whether the ISG framework will stimulate a meaningful change in the stewardship function of asset managers in the US remains to be seen. Notably, to date, the number of signatories is limited, although it includes several major asset managers. A substantial component of the framework focuses on the governance of portfolio companies as opposed to the stewardship activities of asset managers, and the governance principles endorsed by the ISG do not appear to extend significantly beyond existing legal requirements or minimum standards.[33] The stewardship principles are similarly limited.[34] Although the ISG adopted the framework in the wake of criticisms by commentators that some US institutional investors (in particular, three of the ISG signatories – BlackRock, Vanguard and State Street) are devoting insufficient effort to governance and stewardship,[35] the principles are not binding on either issuers or signatories.[36] Indeed, the ISG website explicitly notes that signatories retain the discretion to 'implement the stewardship principles in a manner they deem appropriate'.[37]

An additional concern about the ISG framework is its failure to define the objectives of investor stewardship explicitly or to designate the extent to which institutional investors can or should incorporate objectives other than wealth maximization into the stewardship function.[38] Although a growing number of investors and policymakers are arguing that investor stewardship should include attention to non-shareholder stakeholders and social policy goals as well as economic value, and stewardship codes increasingly reference these goals, they provide little

---

[28] Investor Stewardship Group, 'Signatories' <https://isgframework.org/signatories-and-endorsers/> accessed 18 May 2020.
[29] ibid.
[30] Hill (n 1) 510–11.
[31] Investor Stewardship Group (n 27); the ISG's stewardship principles can be found at Investor Stewardship Group, 'The Principles' <https://isgframework.org/stewardship-principles/> accessed 18 May 2020 [hereinafter ISG Stewardship Principles].
[32] Andrew Healy, 'Investor Stewardship Group Achieves Remarkable Success in Its First Year' *Businesswire* (New York, 18 December 2018) <www.businesswire.com/news/home/20181218005480/en/Investor-Stewardship-Group-Achieves-Remarkable-Success-Year> accessed 18 May 2020.
[33] Investor Stewardship Group, 'Corporate Governance Principles for US Listed Companies' (1 January 2018) <https://isgframework.org/corporate-governance-principles/> accessed 18 May 2020. For example, Principle 1 states that 'Boards are accountable to shareholders', a principle that is reflected in existing statutory and common law principles, such as fiduciary duties and the power of shareholder to elect and remove directors.
[34] Principle A of the ISG Stewardship Principles (n 31), for example, states that 'Institutional investors are accountable to those whose money they invest', a principle that is inherent in the legal status of asset managers and other institutional investors as fiduciaries.
[35] See e.g. Bebchuk and Hirst (n 6) 2043 (identifying 'the shortcomings of current stewardship decisions' by index funds); Dorothy Lund, 'The Case Against Passive Shareholder Voting' (2018) 43 *Journal of Corporation Law* 493, 497 ('passive funds have failed to act as seriously engaged owners').
[36] In describing the ISG, Hill observes: 'The Walker Review's clear message was that regulator/quasi-regulator-sanctioned codes have more clout than investor-led codes' (Hill (n 1) 510).
[37] Investor Stewardship Group (n 27).
[38] See Bernard S Sharfman, 'The First Critique of the "Framework for U.S. Stewardship and Governance"' (*Oxford Law*, 29 November 2017) <www.law.ox.ac.uk/business-law-blog/blog/2017/11/first-critique-framework-us-stewardship-and-governance> accessed 18 May 2020 (arguing that 'as stewards, the objective of such management must be wealth maximization').

guidance as to how a responsible steward is supposed to strike a balance between competing economic and non-economic objectives or between shareholders and other stakeholders.[39]

These issues are highlighted in the case of passive investment vehicles such as index funds. Although these investment vehicles hold title and exercise voting rights with respect to an increasing percentage of global equities and are particularly important for their growing ownership of the US equity markets, their distinctive structure and business model provide practical limitations on their potential effectiveness as corporate stewards. The risk of imposing extensive stewardship obligations on index funds is that it may have the consequence of reducing the viability of index funds as an investment tool for unsophisticated retail investors, creating demands for managerial decisions that constrain efficient corporate decision-making, or introducing additional agency costs. As a result, this chapter suggests caution in the effort to expand institutional investor stewardship obligations.

21.3 THE BUSINESS MODEL OF INDEX FUNDS

This chapter focuses on a particular segment of the institutional investor market – index funds. Index funds are a type of mutual fund, an investment vehicle that consists of a pool of assets managed by an investment adviser pursuant to an advisory agreement. In the case of an index fund, the advisory services provided are minimal because the fund's investment strategy is simply to track the return of a designated index such as the Dow Jones Industrial Average (DJIA) or the S&P 500.[40] There are thousands of potential indexes, but the majority of assets are invested in funds that track the most popular indexes.[41] Thus, for example, the DIA ETF, which is offered by State Street asset management, seeks to provide investment returns that track those of the DJIA, and as of 2019 consisted of approximately USD 22 billion in assets under management.[42]

Estimates vary as to the precise percentage of equity held by index funds; one estimate from 2017 indicated that index funds hold approximately 18 per cent of the global stock market.[43] That number continues to grow. Within the mutual fund industry, funds that passively track an index will, if current trends continue, top 50 per cent of US stock funds in 2019.[44] Moreover, with the growth of passive investing, the mutual fund industry has experienced substantial concentration such that most mutual fund assets are invested by the top three or four mutual fund companies. In turn, BlackRock, Vanguard, State Street and Fidelity collectively own as much as 15 per cent or 20 per cent of the large public companies.[45]

---

[39] See e.g. Business Roundtable, 'Business Roundtable Redefines the Purpose of a Corporation to Promote "An Economy That Serves All Americans"' (Washington, 19 August 2019) <www.businessroundtable.org/business-roundtable-redefines-the-purpose-of-a-corporation-to-promote-an-economy-that-serves-all-americans> accessed 18 May 2020.

[40] For a more complete discussion of the structure of index funds, see Fisch (n 17).

[41] For a comprehensive explanation of the creation and structure of indexes and index funds, see Adriana Z Robertson, 'Passive in Name Only: Delegated Management and "Index" Investing' (2019) 36 Yale Journal on Regulation 795.

[42] State Street Global Advisors, 'SPDR® Dow Jones® Industrial Average ETF Trust' <https://us.spdrs.com/en/etf/spdr-dow-jones-industrial-average-etf-trust-DIA> accessed 25 November 2019.

[43] Trevor Hunnicutt, 'Less Than 18 Percent of Global Stocks Owned by Index Investors: BlackRock' Reuters (New York, 4 October 2017) <www.reuters.com/article/us-funds-blackrock-passive/less-than-18-percent-of-global-stocks-owned-by-index-investors-blackrock-idUSKCN1C82TE> accessed 18 May 2020.

[44] Charles Stein, 'Shift from Active to Passive Approaches Tipping Point in 2019' Bloomberg (31 December 2018) <www.bloomberg.com/news/articles/2018-12-31/shift-from-active-to-passive-approaches-tipping-point-in-2019> accessed 18 May 2020.

[45] Fichtner, Heemskerk and Garcia-Bernardo (n 13) 298, 304 (presenting data on the size and holdings of the largest US asset managers and showing that BlackRock, Vanguard, State Street and Fidelity were the four largest as of June 2016).

Two aspects of the index fund model are particularly relevant in evaluating index funds' potential to engage in effective stewardship. The first is that, because the investment model of index funds is to track an index passively, the advisers of the fund have no reason to engage in firm-specific research and analysis to inform their investment decisions. In contrast to active managers, hedge funds and other stock pickers, index funds do not, indeed they cannot, trade on the basis of information. Rather than the potential opportunity to beat some designated benchmark, index funds offer their investors a market rate of return. Because they are designed to replicate the returns of what is typically a broad-based index, these funds also offer their investors substantial diversification.

The second aspect of the index fund model that is relevant to its potential for effective stewardship is its fee structure. Because they do not rely on costly firm-specific research, index funds incur lower management costs, and they pass these reduced costs on to mutual fund investors in the form of very low fees. Because funds that track the same index will, if properly designed, produce near-identical returns, a fund sponsor cannot distinguish itself in terms of the skill of its advisers. Nor can a sponsor charge a premium for adviser quality. The result is that the fees charged by index funds to investors are very low and substantially lower than those of actively managed funds. Indeed, Fidelity introduced four no-fee index funds in 2018.[46] The combination of low cost and diversification makes index funds a popular tool for retirement accounts, and a substantial proportion of the assets under management in index funds are retirement savings, a subject to which this chapter will return in Section 21.6.

21.4 PASSIVE INVESTORS AND FIRM OVERSIGHT

As the preceding discussion explains, neither index funds nor the investment advisers who manage them necessarily acquire any firm-specific information about their portfolio companies in connection with the decision to invest in those companies. Unlike the prototypical rational investor that evaluates the information available in the market in order to make an informed investment decision, index fund advisers mechanically cause the fund to invest in the securities necessary to match the return of the designated index. While the fund buys and sells securities on a regular basis – to meet purchase and redemption requests, to rebalance as necessary and to adjust to changes in the underlying index – those transactions are mechanical and non-discretionary.

The irrelevance of information to index fund trading makes index funds an anomaly with respect to federal securities regulation which creates a disclosure regime designed to enable investors to make informed trading decisions. Indeed, the threshold criterion for determining securities disclosure obligations is the concept of materiality, which is defined as information that there is a 'substantial likelihood that a reasonable shareholder would consider ... important in making an investment decision'.[47] From the perspective of an index fund, the disclosures made by its portfolio companies are arguably irrelevant, at least with respect to the fund's investment decisions.

Index fund sponsors would, of course, challenge the claim that they do not use or benefit from corporate disclosures. They use disclosures to make informed voting decisions and, increasingly, they engage with their portfolio companies in an effort to improve their corporate governance,

---

[46] Eric Rosenbaum, 'Who Won the Zero-Fee ETF War? It Looks Like No One' (*CNBC*, 11 October 2019) <www.cnbc.com/2019/10/10/who-won-the-zero-fee-etf-war-it-looks-like-no-one.html> accessed 18 May 2020 (reporting that Fidelity 'launched four core index mutual funds at no fee').

[47] *Basic Inc. v Levinson*, 485 US 224, 231 (1988) (quoting *TSC Indus., Inc. v Northway, Inc.*, 426 US 438, 449 (1976)).

risk management and economic success.[48] Although commentators disagree as to whether passive funds exert sufficient effort with respect to these initiatives and whether their efforts lead to improved firm performance, there is little question that index fund sponsors and advisers are devoting increasing resources to stewardship. Indeed, the call for stewardship – from both academics and policymakers – is premised on the expectation that those efforts should be increased.

Some academics question whether those demands are cost effective.[49] Specifically, for stewardship to have a meaningful impact on a firm-specific basis – by reducing managerial agency costs, improving operational decision-making or modifying firm structure – investors require firm-specific information to identify existing deficiencies and to evaluate, within the context of the firm's operations, appropriate changes to address those deficiencies. In addition to acquiring information, investors must develop the necessary expertise to evaluate that information such that their challenges are reliable.[50] As Ron Gilson explained, 'for investors, distinguishing between short-sighted and well-disciplined managements – and between far-sighted companies and those for whom the payoff will never materialize – is often impossible'.[51]

Firm-specific engagement aimed at disciplining management or identifying value-enhancing structural or operational changes exists in today's markets; indeed, it is precisely the business model of the activist hedge fund. Hedge funds invest in portfolio companies with the plan of evaluating firm-specific information and proposing structural or operational changes designed to improve firm performance. Although commentators debate the extent to which hedge fund activism contributes to sustainable economic value as opposed to relying on short-term strategies that conflict with the interests of long-term holders,[52] hedge funds may be considered high-powered investor stewards.[53] Although one can debate whether hedge fund activism is fairly categorized as stewardship, at least when stewardship is focused on maximizing economic value and reducing agency costs, the debate is largely semantic.[54]

What makes it feasible for hedge funds to engage in effective stewardship? Three factors are key. First, hedge funds invest in a limited number of portfolio companies and take a substantial economic position in each. As a result, a hedge fund has the potential to receive a substantial

---

[48] Voting levels have increased. Index funds are likely to be at least as effective as many other types of shareholder such as retail investors and algorithmic traders at rationally voting their shares. In most cases, the level of firm-specific information necessary to make an informed voting decision is relatively limited.

[49] See e.g. Dorothy S Lund, 'Nonvoting Shares and Efficient Corporate Governance' (2019) 71 *Stanford Law Review* 687, 696 (arguing that index funds should not vote in corporate elections because it is not cost-effective for them to incur expenditures to monitor their portfolio companies).

[50] Some actively managed firms are going on the offensive. Schroders published a report in September 2018 saying that passively managed funds lacked the resources for reliable research on whether companies live up to ESG standards. The report said that these lower-cost funds lack the 'specialist knowledge' needed to lobby the boards of portfolio companies for ESG changes. Ovidiu Patrascu, 'ESG in Passive: Let the Buyer Beware' (*Schroders*, 3 September 2018) <www.schroders.com/en/insights/economics/esg-in-passive-let-the-buyer-beware/> accessed 18 May 2020 ('There doesn't appear to be a cheap way to get real sustainability', said Jessica Ground, the global head of stewardship at Schroders); ibid.

[51] Ronald Gilson, 'Legal and Political Challenges to Corporate Purpose' (2019) 31 *Journal of Applied Corporate Finance* 18, 20.

[52] See e.g. Dionysia Katelouzou, 'The Rhetoric of Activist Shareholder Stewards' (2022) (working paper) (citing the empirical debate over the effect of hedge fund activism on the long-term value of portfolio companies).

[53] See e.g. ibid (evaluating activism by UK activist hedge funds within stewardship framework); Jill E Fisch and Simone M Sepe, 'Shareholder Collaboration' (2020) 98 *Texas Law Review* 863 (describing the collaborative role of hedge funds).

[54] This chapter considers the question of whether stewardship should encompass non-economic or non-shareholder objectives later on.

benefit from its engagement, both in absolute terms and as a proportion of the overall value of the fund. For example, hedge fund Trian Partners invested USD 3.5 billion of its USD 12.7 billion fund in Proctor & Gamble.[55] The hedge fund's lack of diversification also minimizes the free rider effect – although other shareholders in the target company may benefit from the activism, they will not benefit to the same degree as the hedge fund.[56] Second, hedge funds can devote substantial resources to gathering the type of firm-specific information necessary to engage in effective stewardship.[57] The standard hedge fund fee structure pays the fund advisers 2 per cent of assets under management and 20 per cent of profits, making it cost-effective for substantial activism-based expenditures.[58] Third, hedge funds have specialized knowledge. They hire managers and employees that can offer firm and industry expertise.[59]

All three of these features are absent from the index fund business model. Index funds offer broad diversification; the very point of an index fund is to provide its investors with broad market exposure rather than a selected small group of stocks. Index funds offer their investors very low fees; in fact, the market appeal of the index fund is its potential to charge less than actively managed funds. Finally, given that index funds do not engage in information-based investment decisions, they derive limited value from paying to develop firm or industry expertise. As a result, there is a substantial risk that index funds will impose what Zohar Goshen and Richard Squire term 'principal competence costs' – 'mistakes due to a lack of expertise, information, or talent'.[60]

Concededly, index funds can, and increasingly do, engage in some level of stewardship that is cost-effective within their existing business model.[61] They can develop expertise with respect to corporate governance issues that affect a substantial proportion of companies in their portfolios. They can identify and evaluate market-wide trends and risks such as climate change and cybersecurity and can call upon those companies that lag behind to adopt the best practices of industry leaders.[62]

Notably, even this level of engagement may present challenges.[63] For example, although it seems uncontroversial to call for index funds to demand better governance from their portfolio companies, experts often disagree both on what constitutes good governance and on the

---

[55] Berkeley Lovelace Jr, 'Billionaire Nelson Peltz: P&G Is Making My Board Battle the "Dumbest Thing I've Ever Been Involved In"' (*CNBC*, 6 October 2017) <www.cnbc.com/2017/10/06/billionaire-activist-peltz-my-proxy-fight-with-procter-gamble-will-be-close.html> accessed 18 May 2020.

[56] This distinguishes hedge funds from mutual funds. See e.g. Lund, 'Nonvoting Shares and Efficient Corporate Governance' (n 49) (identifying the free rider concern as a limit on index fund engagement).

[57] See e.g. Zsolt Katona, Marcus Painter, Panos N Patatoukas and Jean Zeng, 'On the Capital Market Consequences of Alternative Data: Evidence from Outer Space' (9th Behavioural Finance Conference, Miami, 30 July 2018) <https://ssrn.com/abstract=3222741> accessed 18 May 2020 (describing persistent above-market returns that hedge funds can obtain through their purchase and use of costly satellite data of store parking lots).

[58] For example, Trian spent an estimated USD 25 million in its proxy fight with Proctor & Gamble. Barrett J Brunsman, 'P&G Expects Proxy Battle to Cost $35 Million' *Cincinnati Business Courier* (15 August 2017) <www.bizjournals.com/cincinnati/news/2017/08/02/p-g-expects-proxy-battle-to-cost-35-million.html> accessed 18 May 2020.

[59] See CNV Krishnan, Frank Partnoy and Randall S Thomas, 'The Second Wave of Hedge Fund Activism: The Importance of Reputation, Clout, and Expertise' (October 2016) 40 *Journal of Corporate Finance* 296 (providing empirical evidence that successful activists bring expertise to their engagements).

[60] Zohar Goshen and Richard Squire, 'Principal Costs: A New Theory for Corporate Law and Governance' (2017) 117 *Columbia Law Review* 767, 770.

[61] It is beyond the scope of this chapter to address the potential that index funds, or mutual funds generally, will limit their stewardship out of a desire to further other business relationships with their portfolio companies such as the opportunity to manage their 401(k) plans. See e.g. Gerald F Davis and E Han Kim, 'Business Ties and Proxy Voting by Mutual Funds' (2007) 85 *Journal of Financial Economics* 552, 553 (noting the argument that mutual funds that manage corporate pension plans may be more 'acquiescent to existing governance practices').

[62] See Fisch (n 17) (describing engagement efforts by the large index fund providers).

[63] See Alicia Davis, 'The Institutional Appetite for "Quack Corporate Governance"' (2015) *Columbia Business Law Review* 1, 11–12 (finding that institutional investors mistakenly believe high-quality internal governance devices to be value-enhancing).

relationship of specific governance features to firm economic value.[64] Thus, while index funds have championed director independence, and institutional investor pressure has led issuers to boards that are almost entirely independent of management, empirical evidence has failed to establish a connection between board independence and firm economic value.[65] Similarly, index funds were among the investors who, through the Harvard shareholder rights project, sought to persuade their portfolio companies to eliminate their staggered boards.[66] Yet the empirical evidence on the impact of staggered boards is mixed, and research suggests that staggered boards can be value-enhancing in some cases.[67] It is well known that institutional investors were a leading force in the shift to making executive pay structures more performance-based, but stock options, a popular feature of early performance-based structures, turned out to create problematic incentives for executives to take excessive risk.[68] Most recently, index funds have been vocal opponents of dual class stock structures, and the Council of Institutional Investors has urged exchanges and regulators to ban or limit companies with a dual class stock structure.[69] Again, however, the empirical data fail to support the claim that dual class stock reduces firm value.[70]

One problem with broad-based governance initiatives is the possibility that the effect of governance is firm-specific and that, as a result, determining whether a governance reform will enhance value at a particular company requires firm-specific knowledge.[71] This in turn, increases the cost of effective stewardship. To the extent that one cannot reliably ascertain the economic impact of particular governance models or structures, either in general or with respect to individual firms, it may be rational for index funds to adopt a diversified market-wide approach to governance.

Assuredly, index funds could devote greater resources to stewardship to address these concerns. Index funds could sponsor shareholder proposals, serve as lead plaintiffs in shareholder litigation and meet with officers and directors at a greater percentage of their portfolio companies. Index funds could hire investment advisers with firm and industry expertise and pay those advisers to devote more hours to acquiring and evaluating firm-specific information. But these

---

[64] See e.g. Sean J Griffith, 'Opt-In Stewardship: Toward an Optimal Delegation of Mutual Fund Voting Authority' (2020) 98 *Texas Law Review* 983 (observing that 'the connection between governance and performance remains elusive' and arguing that, as a result, 'mutual funds should stop voting on governance issues').

[65] Sanjai Bhagat and Bernard Black, 'The Uncertain Relationship between Board Composition and Firm Performance' (1999) 54 *The Business Lawyer* 921, 924, 933.

[66] Daniel Gallagher and Joseph Grundfest, 'Did Harvard Violate Federal Securities Law? The Campaign Against Classified Boards of Directors' (2014) Rock Center for Corporate Governance at Stanford University Working Paper No 199 <https://ssrn.com/abstract=2536586> accessed 18 May 2020.

[67] ibid; KJ Martijn Cremers and Simone M Sepe, 'The Shareholder Value of Empowered Boards' (2016) 68 *Stanford Law Review* 67, 71–72.

[68] See e.g. Zhiyong Dong, Cong Wang and Fei Xie, 'Do Executive Stock Options Induce Excessive Risk Taking?' (2010) 34 *Journal of Banking & Finance* 2518, 2527 (finding evidence 'that managers indeed take on too much risk in response to the convex payoff structure of stock options').

[69] See e.g. Council of Institutional Investors, 'CII Welcomes S&P Dow Jones' Decision to Ban New Multi-class Companies from Key Stock Indexes' (1 August 2017) <www.cii.org/spdjmulticlassban> accessed 18 May 2020 (explaining that '[t]he Council of Institutional Investors (CII) welcomes S&P Dow Jones' decision to ban new multi-class companies from its key US stock indexes').

[70] See George D Banks and Bernard Sharfman, 'Standing Up for the Retail Investor' (*Harvard Law School Forum on Corporate Governance*, 10 June 2018) <https://corpgov.law.harvard.edu/2018/06/10/standing-up-for-the-retail-investor/> accessed 18 May 2020 (criticizing institutions for advocating the elimination of dual class stock despite the economic success of companies like Google, Facebook and Berkshire Hathaway).

[71] See e.g. Matthew D Cain, Jill E Fisch, Sean J Griffith and Steven D Solomon, 'How Corporate Governance Is Made: The Case of the Golden Leash' (2016) 164 *University of Pennsylvania Law Review* 649, 697 (providing empirical evidence supporting 'the proposition that corporate governance should be decided on a firm-by-firm basis').

efforts are costly. While index fund providers could potentially distinguish themselves on the basis of their stewardship activities and thereby justify charging higher fees, it is unclear at present whether investors will be willing to pay a premium to invest in funds that engage in greater stewardship. Even if they are, it is unclear whether index funds are the most efficient providers of firm-specific monitoring.

21.5 INDEX FUNDS AND STEWARDSHIP OBJECTIVES

Determining the appropriate objectives of investor stewardship adds an additional complication. The original UK Stewardship Code did not define stewardship or its objectives.[72] That omission has been remedied, and today, in both the UK and the EU, most calls for institutional investor stewardship do not restrict themselves to encouraging investors to seek to enhance the economic value of their portfolio companies but instead urge a broader focus on non-shareholder stakeholders or the public interest.[73] This broader focus is reflected in the UK Code 2020, which adopts a definition of 'stewardship that creates long term value for clients and beneficiaries leading to sustainable benefits for the economy, the environment and society'.[74]

This mandate complicates the decision-making framework for funds and their advisers as well as placing additional demands on fund expertise. How are funds and their managers to determine which societal values warrant attention? How are fund decision-makers to weigh the potentially competing interests of the customers, suppliers, employees and communities affected by the operations of their portfolio companies and to balance those interests against shareholder economic value?[75] Although increasing the sustainability of a firm's operations may enhance firm economic value, there are reasons to question the consistent alignment of societal objectives with profit maximization.[76]

Stewardship addressed to a broader range of objectives also exacerbates the agency problem faced by index funds and their advisers as intermediaries for investors in the funds. The problem posed is similar to the one debated eighty years ago between Adolph Berle and Merrick Dodd. Dodd argued broadly that corporate managers had a responsibility to operate their businesses in the interests of the general public.[77] Berle responded, though not out of opposition to the general idea that corporations should have a public responsibility, with a broad concern about unconstrained managerial discretion.[78] Investor stewardship raises similar concerns. If advisers use

---

[72] Reisberg (n 18).
[73] See Dionysia Katelouzou, 'Shareholder Stewardship: A Case of (Re)Embedding Institutional Investors and the Corporation?' in Beate Sjåfjell and Christopher M Bruner (eds), *Cambridge Handbook of Corporate Law, Corporate Governance and Sustainability* (CUP 2019) 581 ('Outside the United States, the currently prevailing narrative, especially in policy circles, views shareholder engagement as a desirable corporate governance attribute able not only to improve corporate governance and performance, but also to ensure long-term stability and social responsibility.').
[74] UK Code 2020 (n 3) 8 (Principle 1), 15 (Principle 7). The Code goes on to explain: 'Signatories systematically integrate stewardship and investment, including material environmental, social and governance issues, and climate change, to fulfil their responsibilities.'
[75] See Stephen M Bainbridge, 'In Defense of the Shareholder Wealth Maximization Norm: A Reply to Professor Green' (1993) 50 *Washington and Lee Law Review* 1423, 1436 (explaining that this role is analogous to the untenable competing duties imposed on a 'lawyer for the situation').
[76] See Leo E Strine Jr, 'Our Continuing Struggle with the Idea That For-Profit Corporations Seek Profit' (2012) 47 *Wake Forest Law Review* 135 ('the cost, simplistic, and single-minded, short-term focus of stockholders on stock price may result in outcomes that, from a broader societal perspective, are deeply uncomfortable').
[77] E Merrick Dodd Jr, 'For Whom Are Corporate Managers Trustees?' (May 1932) 45 *Harvard Law Review* 1145, 1148 (arguing that corporations that corporations have a 'social service [responsibility] as well as a profit-making function').
[78] See e.g. William W Bratton and Michael L Wachter, 'Shareholder Primacy's Corporatist Origins: Adolf Berle and the Modern Corporation' (2008) 34 *Journal of Corporation Law* 99, 129 (explaining: 'To make managers trustees for

fund engagement to maximize the fund's economic value, investors in that fund have metrics to evaluate whether that engagement is successful and cost-justified. At the present, however, the metrics for evaluating the social responsibility of a portfolio company or a socially responsible investment fund are problematic – as many commentators have observed, sustainability disclosures are limited, incomplete and largely unreliable.[79]

Obligating investment managers to incorporate broad-based stewardship objectives also increases the risk of self-dealing.[80] As with corporate managers,[81] the heads of institutional intermediaries may 'use other people's money to advance their own view of the good'.[82] There is little reason to think that fund managers have particular expertise in identifying the most appropriate social goals, and there is a realistic possibility that the goals they advocate may instead be controversial or unique.[83] At the same time, the substantial voting power exercised by the large mutual fund companies gives leaders like Larry Fink at BlackRock a 'bully pulpit'[84] to take public positions that cause some to acclaim him as a 'visionary'[85] despite the fact that, if the principles he advocates sacrifice economic value, it is the customers in BlackRock's funds who will bear the cost.

Asset managers also face competing incentives. Advocating social responsibility may help asset management firms resist regulatory interventions motivated by fears of their growing power. A firm that is publicly associated with social responsibility may be more attractive to an employer as the administrator of a company 401(k) plan. A mutual fund company may favour social polices that sacrifice returns at their portfolio companies to attract discretionary investments by some investors even if other investors prefer decisions motivated exclusively by economics. A critical component of the trade-off among investors is that mutual funds manage a substantial quantity of retirement investments, many of which are owned by unsophisticated employees who are defaulted into their employer's choice of 401(k) investment option and face the real prospect of having inadequate retirement savings if the economic returns of their investments are not maximized.

In addition, there are reasons to believe that even well-intentioned and unconflicted asset managers may be imperfect proxies for the interests of their beneficiaries. Scholars have identified significant differences between the voting preferences of retail and institutional

---

the community would free them of any meaningful constraint because almost all corporate activity could be justified in the interests of one group or another.').

[79] See e.g. Jill E. Fisch, 'Making Sustainability Disclosure Sustainable' (2019) 107 *Georgetown Law Journal* 923, 926 (critically observing that sustainability disclosures are neither standardized nor audited and that issuers vary substantially in the information they provide); Jon Sindreu and Sarah Kent, 'Why It's So Hard to Be an "Ethical" Investor' *The Wall Street Journal* (1 September 2018) <www.wsj.com/articles/why-its-so-hard-to-be-an-ethical-investor-1535799601> accessed 18 May 2020 (observing: 'A Journal analysis of four leading ESG ratings providers found that they come to completely different conclusions about what makes a company a "sustainable" investment.').

[80] As Leo Strine observes, although Henry Ford defended his decision not to pay corporate dividends as improving social welfare, 'Ford's desire to deny [the Dodge Brothers] dividends that could be used to fund their own eponymous car manufacturing operations might have also contributed to Henry Ford's high-mindedness' (Strine (n 76) 32).

[81] As Stephen Bainbridge observes: 'The real object and purpose of a corporation for profit is to make a profit and to make dividends for the stockholders, and a person who holds the stock of a company has a right to have the business of the company conducted, as far as practicable at least, so that it will make profits and pay dividends.' Steven Bainbridge, 'A Predecessor to Dodge v. Ford Motor Co.' (March 2019) <www.professorbainbridge.com/professorbainbridgecom/2019/07/a-predecssor-to-dodge-v-ford-motor-co.html> accessed 18 May 2020, citing *Arbuckle v Woolson Spice Co.* 1901 WL 708, at *2 (Ohio Cir. Ct. Jan. 12, 1901).

[82] Strine (n 76).

[83] ibid.

[84] Peter Georgescu, 'Fink Swims Against the Sharks' *Forbes* (30 May 2019) <www.forbes.com/sites/petergeorgescu/2019/05/30/fink-swims-against-the-sharks/#51da2d865dde> accessed 18 May 2020.

[85] ibid.

investors on a variety of issues from election of directors and executive compensation to support for shareholder proposals.[86] Particularly worrisome in this regard is the fact that one of the largest gaps is with respect to sustainability and ESG issues. As one study reported, environmental and social proposals were supported by 29 per cent of institutional investors but only 16 per cent of retail investors.[87]

Although retail voting patterns suggest that mutual fund voting currently favours ESG issues more than the voting of retail investors,[88] some commentators assert that investors will sacrifice returns in favour of principles.[89] Recent asset flows support this, finding increasing investor demand for ESG-conscious index funds even though the cost of such funds is significantly higher than other index funds. To the extent that fund beneficiaries are willing to pay for fund stewardship, the prospect of more effective index fund stewardship increases dramatically. On the other hand, studies also suggest that retail investors do not support their asset managers sacrificing returns in favour of social policy initiatives.[90] One possibility is to retain the low costs of an index-based investment strategy while committing the fund to a more ESG-oriented voting policy.[91] Indeed, Institutional Shareholder Services (ISS) offers a specialty set of socially responsible investment voting guidelines.[92] Although such a fund's voting approach must be relatively inflexible to limit costs,[93] the approach offers mutual fund customers a cost-effective way of increasing the social orientation of their investments. Notably, however, it does so by

---

[86] Ning Chiu, 'How Do Retail Shareholders Vote?' (Davis Polk, 16 October 2018) <www.davispolk.com/insights/client-update/how-do-retail-shareholders-vote> accessed 7 February 2022 (finding substantial greater support by institutional investors for social and environmental proposals than by retail investors); Gretchen Morgenson, 'Small Investors Support the Boards. But Few of Them Vote.' The New York Times (6 October 2017) <www.nytimes.com/2017/10/06/business/small-investors.html> accessed 18 May 2020 (reporting on an analysis of shareholder voting that found 'a striking contrast between the views of institutional investors and those of individuals').

[87] Michael S Fischer, 'Shareholder Support for ESG Proposals Rose This Proxy Season' (ThinkAdvisor, 2 October 2018) <www.thinkadvisor.com/2018/10/02/shareholder-support-for-esg-proposals-rose-this-pr/> accessed 22 May 2020.

[88] Some reports nonetheless criticize mutual funds, particularly ESG funds, for voting records that do not show greater support for ESG proposals. See e.g. Lewis Braham, 'Sustainability Ratings Tell Half the Story' Barron's (7 October 2017) <www.barrons.com/articles/sustainability-ratings-tell-half-the-story-1507350027/> accessed 18 May 2020 (unfortunately, because most analyses of fund voting evaluate proposals by category rather than by the substance of the proposal, they risk presenting a misleading picture of fund voting policies); see e.g. Morningstar, 'Investing in a Sustainable Future' <www.morningstar.com/company/esg-investing> accessed 18 May 2020. Thus, for example, Morningstar's presentation of voting data on ESG proposals seems to assume that an ESG-oriented fund would properly support 100 per cent of shareholder proposals on those topics irrespective of their content. See Jackie Cook and Jon Hale '2019 ESG Proxy Voting Trends? More Support for ESG Issues, but the Largest Firms Lag' (Morningstar, 13 February 2020) 13–14 (explaining the methodology of classifying shareholder proposals).

[89] See Gilson (n 51) 21 (predicting they will).

[90] See Jeff Patch, 'CalPERS Must Set Aside Politics and Remember Its Fiduciary Responsibility' (Morning Consult, 10 January 2018) <https://morningconsult.com/opinions/calpers-must-set-aside-politics-and-remember-its-fiduciary-responsibility/> accessed 22 May 2020 (in an analogous survey of CalPERs pension fund beneficiaries, 86 per cent of participants indicated that their pension fund should be focused on generating returns and 'shouldn't make investment decisions on the basis of politics, even if [they] support the idea or cause'); Spectrum Group, 'Tensions with Pensions: An Analysis of Public Pension Fund Members' Knowledge and Sentiment About How Their Money Is Being Invested' (2018) <https://spectrem.com/Content_Whitepaper/Tensions-with-pensions.aspx> accessed 18 May 2020.

[91] Gina Rao has made such a proposal. Gita R Rao, 'Give Mutual Fund Investors a Voice in Shareholder Proxy Voting' MarketWatch (12 December 2017) <www.marketwatch.com/story/give-mutual-fund-investors-a-voice-in-shareholder-proxy-voting-2017-12-12> accessed 18 May 2020 (advocating an index fund that commits in its prospectus to follow an ESG voting policy).

[92] Institutional Shareholder Services, 'United States SRI Proxy Voting Guidelines 2020 Policy Recommendations' (31 December 2019) <www.issgovernance.com/file/policy/active/specialty/SRI-US-Voting-Guidelines.pdf> accessed 18 May 2020.

[93] See Andrey Malenko and Nadya Malenko, 'Proxy Advisory Firms: The Economics of Selling Information to Voters' (October 2019) 74 The Journal of Finance 2441 (noting the 'one-size fits all' criticism of proxy adviser recommendations).

transferring the task of determining appropriate social policy from asset managers to ISS, a delegation that has been criticized in other contexts.[94]

21.6 THE ROLE OF FUND BENEFICIARIES

One possible solution to the agency problem is empowering mutual fund beneficiaries to determine or oversee the stewardship objectives of their asset managers. This could be done at the entity level through shareholder voting or approval of fund stewardship policies or at the beneficiary level through the implementation of pass-through voting. This section questions the efficacy of the two approaches.

As early as the 1970s, the SEC expressed concern about the growing institutionalization of the public equity markets and the effect of that institutionalization on proxy voting.[95] Among its concerns was the fact that institutional voting might not reflect the views of those with true economic interest in the shares. The SEC in 1978 explicitly considered the desirability of obtaining these views 'by means of a polling or pass-through voting requirement'.[96] At that time, the SEC reported that 'substantially all of the commentators who addressed the issue ... were opposed to such a requirement', citing suggestions that the undertaking would be costly and difficult and that fund shareholders were unlikely to have an interest in or desire to vote on the issues affecting their portfolio companies.[97]

Subsequent technological developments have reduced the cost and difficulty of pass-through voting, leading to renewed calls for pass-through voting.[98] For example, Jennifer Taub has argued that pass-through voting would enable fund beneficiaries to overcome the passivity of fund advisers.[99] Dorothy Lund argues that pass-through voting would reduce the 'incidence of uninformed voting'.[100] Caleb Griffin suggests that mutual funds could use standard voting instructions to democratize index fund voting either by enabling fund beneficiaries to complete an issue-based survey that would form the basis for the beneficiary's proxy voting guidelines or by stipulating in advance that their votes should mirror those of a proxy adviser or another institutional investor.[101]

---

[94] See e.g. David Larcker, Allan McCall and Gaizka Ormazabal, 'Outsourcing Shareholder Voting to Proxy Advisory Firms' (2015) 58 *The Journal of Law & Economics* 173, 203 ('The outsourcing of voting to proxy advisory firms appears to have the unintended economic consequence that boards of directors are induced to make choices that decrease shareholder value.').

[95] Shareholder Communications, Shareholder Participation in the Corporate Electoral Process and Corporate Governance Generally, 17 CFR §240.10 (1978) (noting that 'major institutions held, as at the end of 1977, more than 33% of the total stock outstanding in the United States'. Ironically, the number today is closer to 70 per cent).

[96] ibid 33–34.

[97] ibid.

[98] See e.g. John C Coffee Jr, 'Brave New World? The Impact(s) of the Internet on Modern Securities Regulation' (1997) 52 *The Business Lawyer* 1195, 1210–1 3 (observing that 'on the longer-term horizon, there is even the visionary possibility that the Internet can be used to pass through voting rights in securities held by pension and mutual funds to the fund's own owners or beneficiaries'); John C Wilcox, Electronic Communication and Proxy Voting: The Governance Implications of Shareholders in Cyberspace' (1997) 11 *Insights* 8, 11 (discussing company communications with investors through new electronic media and wondering whether 'pass-through voting' for investors in pension funds and mutual funds will develop). Indeed, there has been some development of pass-through voting in pension plans; James A Fanto, 'Investor Education, Securities Disclosure, and the Creation and Enforcement of Corporate Governance and Firm Norms' (1999) 48 *Catholic University Law Review* 15, 35 fn 79 (observing that 'pass-through voting has developed within both defined contribution and defined benefit pension plans').

[99] Jennifer S Taub, 'Able but Not Willing: The Failure of Mutual Fund Advisers to Advocate for Shareholders' Rights' (2009) 34 *Journal of Corporation Law* 843, 888–89.

[100] Lund, 'The Case Against Passive Shareholder Voting' (n 35) 530.

[101] Griffin (n 9).

These commentators accurately highlight the potential for pass-through voting to reduce agency costs, and technological advances such as internet voting make pass-through substantially less difficult to implement than it was in the 1970s. The fact remains, however, that mutual fund investors are poorly positioned to direct the proxy voting of their proportionate interest in the fund's portfolio companies. Addressing the complex questions necessary to formulate an effective stewardship policy is even harder.

In understanding this point, it is important to keep the characteristics of retail mutual fund investors in mind. Individual investors held 89 per cent of mutual fund assets in 2018. Mutual fund investors differ from other retail investors. They select their mutual funds, in the best-case scenario on the basis of investment style and cost and in the worst case on the basis of less rational criteria such as the name of the fund. Typically, they do not engage in firm-specific research into the portfolio companies held by the mutual funds in which they invest; indeed, in most cases they are unlikely to know the portfolio companies in which the mutual fund is invested. Their very purpose in choosing a mutual fund is to delegate investment discretion to the fund manager.

Further, retail investors hold a substantial percentage of their mutual fund investments in retirement accounts that have distinctive characteristics. In 2019, 95 per cent of mutual fund investors held their funds inside employer-sponsored retirement plans, individual retirement accounts and variable annuities.[102] Of mutual-fund owning households, 35 per cent held funds exclusively through employer-sponsored retirement plans, and, in many cases, assets held outside such plans were the result of 401(k) rollovers.[103] The purchase of a mutual fund in a 401(k) is different from a market-based investment decision. Although plan participants choose the specific funds in which they invest, that choice is limited by the menu of investment options selected by the employer. In addition, an increasing number of employers enrol their employees in their retirement plans automatically.[104] The money of those employees is invested in a default option designated by the employer unless the employee chooses an alternative. Default options are commonly index funds or target date funds that include one or more index funds.

In addition, employee-investors are distinctive. Recent empirical research suggests that people who invest exclusively through 401(k) plans have very low levels of financial literacy – lower, in fact, than other investors.[105] One study reports that 'only slightly more than one third (37 percent) of workplace-only investors have some basic financial knowledge as measured by the Big Three, and only 35 percent can answer the question about compound interest correctly'.[106]

Concededly, setting priorities with respect to stewardship and ESG involves different skill sets than financial literacy. Even if investors do not understand compound interest, they can identify and express their preferences with respect to policy issues like corporate political spending, executive compensation and climate change. The problem is that, even if investors' general

---

[102] Investment Company Institute, *2020 Investment Company Fact Book* (60th edn, 2020) 146.
[103] ibid.
[104] See e.g. Bob Pisani, 'America's Retirement Accounts Are Growing, but Not Fast Enough' (*CNBC*, 12 June 2019) <www.cnbc.com/2019/06/12/americas-retirement-accounts-are-growing-but-not-fast-enough.html>accessed 18 May 2020 (reporting that '[a]t year-end 2018, 48% of Vanguard plans had adopted automatic enrolment and 66% of new plan entrants were signed up that way').
[105] See Jill Fisch, Annamaria Lusardi and Andrea Hasler, 'Defined Contribution Plans and the Challenge of Financial Illiteracy' (2020) 105 *Cornell Law Review* 741 (reporting that levels of financial literacy among workplace-only investors were 'strikingly low').
[106] ibid.

policy positions are clear, understanding the business ramifications of those positions with respect to a particular portfolio company is quite complex.[107]

Moreover, extrapolating from investors' general policy positions into a workable set of voting guidelines is more difficult than it initially appears. Media reports highlight this challenge when they criticize mutual funds for their voting records.[108] For example, corporations face an increasing number and range of ESG-related shareholder proposals, particularly proposals seeking reporting or the adoption of formal board policies with respect to various social policy concerns,[109] but there are reasons why a shareholder who supports diversity may not support a particular diversity proposal.[110] Similarly, a shareholder who opposes food waste or is concerned about climate change might nonetheless decide that requiring an issuer to report publicly on such issues is not cost-justified. If it is difficult even to figure out what a rational shareholder would prefer, it is hard to see how the average mutual fund investor could develop meaningful policy positions, especially when the impact of his or her preferences on the policies of the underlying portfolio companies is likely to be quite small.

A more practical concern with pass-through voting is voter turnout.[111] Ordinary retail investors typically vote fewer than 30 per cent of their shares in corporate elections. Voting participation by retail stockholders in mutual funds is even lower, and mutual funds have consistently experienced difficulty in obtaining a quorum in their shareholder meetings, even though a quorum may require as few as one-third of the outstanding shares of the fund.[112] Low voter turnout is more common among shareholders in passive funds, who tend to 'set it and forget it'.[113] Moreover, because any given mutual fund generally holds hundreds of portfolio companies or more, the number of occasions on which mutual fund shareholders will be called upon to vote is substantially greater than for ordinary retail investors.

---

[107] A recent *Wall Street Journal* article highlights the impact of the 'stakeholder model' on PG&E. Allysia Finley, "'Stakeholder' Capitalism in Action' *The Wall Street Journal* (21 October 2019) <www.wsj.com/articles/stakeholder-capitalism-in-action-11571696787> accessed 18 May 2020.

[108] See e.g. Braham (n 88).

[109] Shareholders at Amazon's 2019 annual meeting, for example, introduced resolutions asking the company to disclose 'the environmental and social impacts of food waste generated from the company's operations' and to 'report on its efforts to address hate speech and the sale of offensive products throughout its businesses'. Amazon.com Inc. Schedule 14A (11 April 2019) 15, 23–24 <www.sec.gov/Archives/edgar/data/1018724/000119312519102995/d667736ddef14a.htm> accessed 21 May 2020. Shareholders were asked to vote on eleven proposals sponsored by fellow shareholders; ibid.

[110] Consider, for example, the Amazon shareholder proposal on 'board diversity' (calling on the board to implement a 'Rooney Rule', with the 'true diversity' proposal introduced by some conservative groups calling for greater ideological diversity on corporate boards): Kevin Mooney, 'Conservative Shareholders Push Facebook to Achieve "True Diversity"' *The Daily Signal* (29 May 2019) <www.dailysignal.com/2019/05/29/conservative-shareholders-push-facebook-to-achieve-true-diversity/> accessed 18 May 2020.

[111] Paul Schott Stevens, 'SEC Should Reject Complex, Costly "Pass-Through" Proxy Voting' (*Investment Company Institute*, 2 October 2018) <www.ici.org/viewpoints/view_18_passthrough_voting> accessed 18 May 2020. Notably, although some commentators such as Lund argue that low turnout is unproblematic if it reduces the instances of uninformed voting, if particular groups of shareholders are systematically underrepresented, it is problematic to view voting results as indicative of shareholder preferences; Lund, 'The Case Against Passive Shareholder Voting' (n 35) 530.

[112] Ross Kerber, 'Vanguard Asks Passive Investors to Pay Attention for Proxy Vote' *Reuters* (Boston, 20 September 2017) <www.reuters.com/article/us-vanguard-investors/vanguard-asks-passive-investors-to-pay-attention-for-proxy-vote-idUSKCN1BU2G9> accessed 18 May 2020; Paul Schott Stevens, 'U.S. Securities and Exchange Commission Proxy Voting Roundtable "Broker Proxy Voting"' (24 May 2007) <www.sec.gov/comments/4-537/4537-32.pdf> accessed 18 May 2020 (observing that, in a sample of mutual fund annual meetings involving a non-routine matter, half required a re-solicitation because of the failure to obtain quorum).

[113] ibid.

Of course, limited participation need not prevent a mutual fund from following the preferences of those beneficiaries who participate actively. Because participation is likely to be higher by wealthier investors, however, this approach cuts against the democratic claims of some pass-through voting advocates. There are also reasons to question whether the preferences of wealthy retail shareholders with respect to particular policy issues or more generally regarding the trade-off between corporate profit and non-economic values mirror those of less sophisticated workplace-only investors.

Perhaps the most problematic concern about pass-through voting, however, is that to the extent that a mutual fund adviser votes in accordance with the preferences of its beneficiaries, it loses its power to negotiate with issuers for change.[114] A key rationale for increased investor stewardship is the prospect that, because of their size and voting power, institutional investors have the ability to influence the behaviour of their portfolio companies. Indeed, this influence can be observed not merely through voting outcomes but by noting the number of shareholder resolutions that result in negotiated withdrawals following management's acquiescence or commitment to voluntary action.[115] An institutional investor that relinquishes control over its voting decisions sacrifices a powerful component of its ability to engage successfully.

21.7 CONCLUSION

Investor stewardship is a potentially powerful tool for influencing corporate behaviour. As a result, it should be handled with care. Because index funds own an increasing percentage of global equity, they face growing scrutiny about their stewardship role, and a number of commentators have demanded that they do more to influence the decisions made at their portfolio companies. This chapter argues for caution in making such demands. Index funds offer their investors broad diversification at low cost, a model that is in tension with demands for high-quality, firm-specific engagement. Further, to the extent that stewardship encompasses the pursuit of broad societal goals or balancing economic and non-economic objectives, index funds lack the tools to do so in a way that is faithful to the interests of their beneficiaries. Although these concerns could be addressed by giving index fund shareholders a greater voice, it is not clear that such reforms would be efficient or cost-effective.

---

[114] See Marcel Kahan and Edward Rock, 'Index Funds and Corporate Governance: Let Shareholders Be Shareholders' (2020) 100 *Boston University Law Review* 1771 (ascribing the ability of asset managers to influence portfolio company behaviour to the heft associated with their voting power).

[115] See e.g., Paul Rissman and Diana Kearney, 'Rise of the Shadow ESG Regulators: Investment Advisers, Sustainability Accounting, and Their Effects on Corporate Social Responsibility' (2019) 49 *The Environmental Law Reporter* 10155, 10171 (reporting that 45% of shareholder proposals requesting a sustainability report 'were withdrawn by the filer following an engagement with management that produced a commitment to publish, and therefore never came to a vote').

22

Encouraging Sustainable Investment in South Africa

CRISA and Beyond

Natania Locke

22.1 INTRODUCTION

The role of shareholder stewardship in South Africa, and the manner in which it has been expressed in soft and hard law, can be understood only by explaining the unique South African context. The year 2019 celebrated the twenty-fifth anniversary of free and democratic elections in South Africa. Apartheid left behind an extensive legacy of inequality, evidenced in part in the dichotomy of a well-developed financial system and a mature securities market – while most of the population can never hope to be part of either.

There can be no true freedom or equality without addressing the repression of poverty.[1] Sustainability in South Africa is very much focused on improving the lives of ordinary people in the long-run. The last twenty-five years have not seen a rapid improvement in the living conditions of the poorest people in the country. Unemployment stands at 29 per cent and the majority of persons affected are younger than thirty-five years old.[2] Poor public basic education exacerbates the unemployment problem.[3]

Urbanization has led to the rise of massive informal settlements.[4] Crime and poverty are rampant in these settlements and living conditions are poor. The lack of basic services in the townships has led to extensive civil unrest in recent years. Work, good education and basic services are scarce in rural areas. Women and girls are hardest hit by these realities as they are often tasked with manually fetching water across great distances, meaning that they cannot attend school or work. Infrastructure is poorly located, inadequate and under-maintained,[5] and the economy is unsustainably resource intensive.[6]

Crime thrives in unequal societies and South Africa is no exception.[7] However, corruption is the crime most central to the discussion that follows. Two judicial commissions of inquiry are currently underway in South Africa. The first relates to the so-called state capture, that is, systemic

---

[1] 'While poverty persists, there is no true freedom' (Nelson Mandela (Make Poverty History rally, London, Trafalgar Square, 2005)).
[2] Statistics South Africa, 'Quarterly Labour Force Survey Quarter 2: 2019' (30 July 2019) 1 <www.statssa.gov.za/publications/P0211/P02112ndQuarter2019.pdf> accessed 3 July 2020.
[3] National Planning Commission, 'Diagnostic Overview' (2011) 13–15, 17 <www.gov.za/sites/default/files/gcis_document/201409/npcdiagnosticoverview1.pdf> accessed 3 July 2020. This led to: National Planning Commission, *National Development Plan 2030: Our Future – Make It Work* (2012) <www.gov.za/sites/default/files/gcis_document/201409/ndp-2030-our-future-make-it-workr.pdf> accessed 3 July 2020.
[4] National Planning Commission, 'Diagnostic Overview' (n 3) 19–20.
[5] ibid 16–17.
[6] ibid 17–19.
[7] See South African Police Service, 'Crime Statistics 2018/2019' <www.saps.gov.za/services/crimestats.php> accessed 3 July 2020.

large-scale corruption at the highest level of government.[8] The second investigates allegations of impropriety regarding investment decisions, conflicts of interests that led to personal gain by directors and employees, and corrupt activities at the Public Investment Corporation (PIC), South Africa's state-owned asset manager that has sole investment control over the funds of government-linked pension funds.[9] Corruption has also proved a barrier to the success of black economic empowerment.[10]

This chapter starts with an exposition of the context of shareholder stewardship in South Africa and the institutional investor landscape (Section 22.2). This is followed by a discussion of the two main soft-law initiatives that support shareholder stewardship in South Africa, namely the Code for Responsible Investing in South Africa (CRISA)[11] in Section 22.3 and the King IV Report on Governance for South Africa (King IV) in Section 22.4.[12] Hard-law provisions that support the soft-law measures, especially for retirement funds and their service providers, are discussed in Section 22.5. Section 22.6 concludes with some recommendations for improvement of the current system.

22.2 STEWARDSHIP IN SOUTH AFRICA

South Africa was only the second country after the United Kingdom to adopt a stewardship code.[13] However, from the outset it was clear that CRISA was more informed by the UN Principles of Responsible Investment (PRI)[14] than an attempt to emulate the UK Code 2010.[15] The decision to draft a separate code for responsible investing was a direct result of comments by the South African PRI Network suggesting that institutional investors needed additional guidance.[16] At the time of CRISA's publication, thirty South African institutions were already signatories of the PRI.[17] The South African Government Employees Pension Fund (GEPF) was one of the founding signatories of the PRI. The PIC is also a signatory of the PRI.[18]

---

[8] Judicial Commission of Inquiry to Inquire into Allegations of State Capture, Corruption and Fraud in the Public Sector Including Organs of State (Proclamation 3 of 2018, Government Gazette No 41403, 25 January 2018); see also Commission of Inquiry into State Capture website <www.sastatecapture.org.za> accessed 3 July 2020.

[9] Commission of Inquiry into Allegations of Impropriety Regarding Public Investment Corporation (Proclamation 30 of 2018, Government Gazette No 41979, 17 October 2018) <www.gov.za/sites/default/files/gcis_document/201906/42549gon954.pdf> accessed 9 February 2022. The allegations include political interference to pressure the Public Investment Corporation (PIC) to make investments.

[10] Adri du Plessis and Jan Pretorius, 'Substantive Equality and the Beneficiaries of Broad-Based Black Economic Empowerment' (2017) 80 *Journal of Contemporary Roman-Dutch Law* 390 fn 9 (where some of the allegations are set out). Black economic empowerment is a comprehensive government programme to increase the economic participation of black people, backed by the Broad-Based Black Economic Empowerment Act 53 of 2003. See in general Department of Trade and Industry, 'Economic Empowerment' <http://www.thedtic.gov.za/economic-empowerment/> accessed 9 February 2022.

[11] Institute of Directors in Southern Africa, 'Code for Responsible Investing in South Africa 2011' (2011) <www.iodsa.co.za/page/crisaresourcecentr> accessed 3 July 2020 [hereinafter CRISA].

[12] Institute of Directors in Southern Africa, 'King IV Report on Governance for South Africa 2016' (2016) [hereinafter *King IV*] <https://cdn.ymaws.com/www.iodsa.co.za/resource/collection/684B68A7-B768-465C-8214-E3A007F15A5A/IoDSA_King_IV_Report_-_WebVersion.pdf> accessed 3 July 2020.

[13] CRISA was released in 2011 with the first effective date for reporting on 1 February 2012.

[14] PRI, 'What Are the Principles for Responsible Investment?' <www.unpri.org/about-us/what-are-the-principles-for-responsible-investment> accessed 9 February 2022 [hereinafter PRI]. See also PRI, 'About the PRI' <www.unpri.org/pri/about-the-pri> accessed 3 July 2020.

[15] CRISA (n 11) 4, 6.

[16] ibid 6.

[17] ibid 4.

[18] Sixty-five South African institutions are signatories of the PRI – nine asset owners, seven service providers (investment consultants) and forty-nine investment managers. See <www.unpri.org/signatories/signatory-resources/signatory-directory> accessed 9 February 2022.

The GEPF dwarfs all other retirement funds and is by far the greatest investor in the South African equity market. It is considered one of the world's mega-retirement funds. By the end of 2016, it held about 40 per cent of all assets held by retirement funds in South Africa.[19] As the name suggests, its assets consist of the retirement funds of public sector workers and, as such, are guaranteed by state funds. GEPF makes exclusive use of one asset manager, the PIC. Together, these two entities held 11 per cent of the top twenty-five companies on the Johannesburg Stock Exchange (JSE) by market capitalization at the end of 2016.[20]

The South African institutional investor landscape is dominated by retirement funds, which held 24.4 per cent of the JSE by the end of 2016.[21] Long-term insurance companies and collective investment schemes[22] combined held 34 per cent of the market capitalization of JSE-listed shares.[23]

The main purpose of CRISA is to provide guidance to institutional investors on how they should execute investment analysis and investment activities, and exercise rights so as to promote sound governance by investee companies.[24] However, 'governance' is used as an expression of behaviour that supports sustainable development.[25] Stewardship in the South African context takes on a broader meaning than protection of the assets of ultimate beneficiaries against the potential abuses identified by agency theory.[26] Instead, the use of shareholder ownership and rights to influence companies to create long-term value is described as having a societal benefit over and above economic results for beneficiaries.[27] This sprouts from King IV, where sustainable development is an underpinning philosophy,[28] and a stakeholder-inclusive model of governance is expressly advanced.[29]

The public role of companies also receives recognition in the Companies Act 71 of 2008, albeit less expressly.[30] One of the purposes of the Act is set out to be the development of the South African economy 'by encouraging transparency and high standards of corporate governance as

---

[19] Lynne Thomas, 'Ownership of JSE-Listed Companies' (Research Report for National Treasury, September 2017) 13 <www.gov.za/sites/default/files/gcis_document/201710/ownership-monitor-sept-2017.pdf> accessed 3 July 2020.

[20] ibid 16.

[21] ibid 10–15. This report used data from the South African Reserve Bank to determine the originating institution and to avoid 'double counting', which can occur when assets are managed by an investment manager. Note that the data could not distinguish between voting and non-voting holdings and therefore also include holdings in preference shares, which usually do not carry voting rights.

[22] A collective investment scheme is one in which members of the public are invited to invest money or other assets in a portfolio, for which they receive participatory interests in the portfolio in return. Investors share in the risk of failure of the portfolio in proportion to their participatory interest (Collective Investment Schemes Control Act 45 of 2002, s 1). Collective investment schemes will not be considered in depth here.

[23] Thomas (n 19) 12.

[24] CRISA (n 11) 3, 7.

[25] ibid 7.

[26] Katelouzou and Puchniak, Global Shareholder Stewardship, Chapter 1. See in general Dionysia Katelouzou, 'Shareholder Stewardship: A Case of (Re)Embedding Institutional Investors and the Corporation?' in Beate Sjåfjell and Christopher M Bruner (eds), *Cambridge Handbook of Corporate Law, Corporate Governance and Sustainability* (CUP 2019) 581, 589–99 and the sources cited there.

[27] CRISA (n 11) 6, 7.

[28] King IV (n 12) 23, 26 and the discussion in Section 22.4 of this chapter. 'Sustainable development' in both CRISA and King IV is defined broadly with reference to the well-known statement from the Brundtland Report as 'development that meets the needs of the present without compromising the ability of future generations to meet their needs.' See United Nations, *Our Common Future*, Report of the World Commission on Environment and Development (OUP 1987) ch 1 para 49.

[29] King IV (n 12) 4, 17.

[30] Government Gazette No 32121 of 9 April 2009.

appropriate, given the significant role of enterprises within the social and economic life of the nation'.[31] Another purpose of the Act is to 'reaffirm the concept of the company as a means of achieving economic and social benefits'.[32] This is supported by extending standing for the statutory derivative action, to protect the legal interests of the company, to any person who has been granted leave by the court to do so.[33] The court may grant such leave when it is satisfied that it is necessary and expedient to protect the legal rights of the applicant.

'Stewardship' in South Africa is therefore directly concerned with the promotion of sustainable investment practices. All stewardship activities, such as engagement and voting policy, are directly concerned with this overall objective.[34]

The definition of 'stewardship' in the new UK Code 2020, as 'the responsible allocation, management and oversight of capital to create long-term value for clients and beneficiaries leading to sustainable benefits for the economy, the environment and society',[35] seems to stop slightly short of ascribing equal or even greater importance to societal benefit compared to the benefit of clients and beneficiaries. The definition suggests that returns to clients and beneficiaries remain the primary concern of stewardship and that greater economic, environmental and societal benefits are secondary. This has not changed materially from the definition used in the revised UK Code 2012.[36] CRISA contains no formal definition of 'stewardship', even though it covers much of the same types of conduct that are encouraged in the UK Codes.[37] Instead, the focus is on responsible investing, and the public good is put at least on equal footing with returns to clients and beneficiaries.

That being said, it has to be acknowledged that the broader view of governance favoured by CRISA suits institutional asset owners that take a long-term view by their very nature better than, say, collective investment schemes. Although there is no differentiation in the way that the soft-law provisions are set out,[38] the fact that hard law has focused on retirement funds in particular may be an acknowledgement that they are different.[39] The election by the legislator to focus on retirement funds for hard-law regulation may also be a manifestation of the public function that retirement funds play, in that they serve a social security role.[40] As such, they play an immediately apparent public function, perhaps in contradistinction to other investment vehicles.

---

[31] s 7(b)(iii).

[32] s 7(d).

[33] s 165(2)(d).

[34] See the discussion in Section 22.3.

[35] Financial Reporting Council, *The UK Stewardship Code 2020* (2019) 4 <www.frc.org.uk/getattachment/5aae591d-d9d3-4cf4-814a-d14e156a1d87/Stewardship-Code_Dec-19-Final-Corrected.pdf> accessed 3 July 2020 [hereinafter UK Code 2020].

[36] Financial Reporting Council, *The UK Stewardship Code* (September 2012) 1, Principle 1 and Principle 7 <www.frc.org.uk/getattachment/d67933f9-ca38-4233-b603-3d24b2f62c5f/UK-Stewardship-Code-(September-2012).pdf> accessed 3 July 2020. The absence of a definition for 'stewardship' was mentioned as one of the flaws of the UK Code by Arad Reisberg, 'The UK Stewardship Code: On the Road to Nowhere?' (2015) 15 *Journal of Corporate Law Studies* 217, 228. The inclusion of express concern for sustainability and ESG factors is more prevalent in recently adopted codes. See also Van der Elst and Lafarre, Shareholder Stewardship in the Netherlands, Chapter 4; Goto, The Japanese Stewardship Code, Chapter 10; Tan, Institutional Investor Stewardship in Malaysia, Chapter 15; Kowpatanakit and Bunaramrueang, The Thai Institutional Investors Stewardship Code and Its Implementation, Chapter 16; Bowley and Hill, Stewardship and Collective Action, Chapter 19; Ouko, The Stewardship Code in Kenya, Chapter 23; Becker, Andrade and Prado, The Brazilian Stewardship Framework, Chapter 24. Further on stewardship and sustainability, see Katelouzou and Klettner, Sustainable Finance and Stewardship, Chapter 26.

[37] See the discussion in Section 22.3.

[38] See Sections 22.3 and 22.4.

[39] See Section 22.5.

[40] Katelouzou, 'Shareholder Stewardship' (n 26) 582–87 (on the public function of stewardship). See also Rosemary Hunter, 'Which Decisions, If Any, by the Board of a Retirement Fund Are Subject to Review in Terms of the Promotion of Administrative Justice Act or Common Law? And Why Does It Matter?' (Annual Conference of

South African listed entities often have at least one block-holder of shares.[41] Block-holding is set at 5 per cent of the beneficial holding of each class of share, as this is the threshold at which holdings must be reported to the company to signal possible changes in control.[42] This notification obligation applies also to asset managers who have authority to exercise rights of disposal or voting rights with respect to the relevant securities.[43] When the block-holdings of the top twenty-five companies by market capitalization are considered, it emerges that institutional shareholders dominate, especially the GEPF and the PIC.[44] Other South African companies, private individuals and the South African government together make up only 7 per cent of the shareholdings of the top twenty-five at the end of 2016.

Foreign institutional shareholders held 1 per cent of shares of the top twenty-five companies per market capitalization listed on the JSE at the end of 2016.[45] CRISA is meant to apply to these institutional shareholders to the extent that they invest in South African companies.[46] However, as will be seen from the following discussion, there is currently no mechanism in place to monitor the extent to which such investors incorporate CRISA into their investment activities and decisions.

22.3 CODE FOR RESPONSIBLE INVESTING IN SOUTH AFRICA

CRISA was the product of the Committee on Responsible Investing in South Africa, which was convened by the Institute of Directors in Southern Africa (IoDSA), a private industry body. IoDSA is also the convenor of the South African codes of corporate governance.[47] The largest asset owners and service providers all participated in the CRISA committee's work, either through direct representation or via industry associations such as the Association for Saving and Investment South Africa (ASISA) and the Principal Officers Association (now BATSETA).[48] Basic industry acceptance of the stewardship code was therefore pretty much a given.

CRISA provides guidance to institutional investors. 'Institutional investor' is defined with reference to the definition in section 1 of the Financial Services Board Act 97 of 1990: 'to the extent that these legal persons or institutions own and invest *in the equity* of a company and have obligations in respect of investment analysis, activities and returns to ultimate beneficiaries'.[49] This means that

---

Pension Lawyers Association Paper, 5 March 2019) for a discussion of the public nature of retirement funds (on file with the author).

[41] Thomas (n 19) 15.

[42] Companies Act 71 of 2008, s 122(1)(a). Notification must be made for every 5 per cent of holdings acquired or disposed of in regulated companies. 'Regulated companies' are profit companies that are public companies or state-owned companies (ss 118(1)(a) and (b)). Transactions in private companies need be notified only if more than 10 per cent of the securities of the company has been transferred in the previous twenty-four months (s 118(1)(c)). The company must notify the Takeover Regulation Panel of the change in block holding, as well as the other holders of the relevant class of shares, unless the transaction was a disposition of less than 1 per cent of the shares (s 122(3)). It is clear from a reading of the Companies Regulations 2011 (Government Notice No R351, Government Gazette No 34239, 26 April 2011) ch 5 (Takeover Regulations) that the notification obligation is triggered only when voting securities as acquired or disposed. Reg 81 defines 'acquisition' for purposes of the relevant parts of the Act, including s 122, as 'any act or transaction as a result of which a person acquires or has an increased voting power in a company, irrespective of whether that person acquired any securities of the company in or as a result of that act or transaction'.

[43] Companies Regulations 2011 (Government Notice No R351, Government Gazette No 34239, 26 April 2011) ch 5 reg 82.

[44] Thomas (n 19) 16.

[45] Thomas (n 19) 26.

[46] CRISA (n 11) 8.

[47] See Section 22.4.

[48] See CRISA (n 11) 5 for a full list of committee members,

[49] CRISA (n 11) 9 (emphasis added). The Financial Services Board Act has since been repealed and replaced by the Financial Sector Regulation Act 9 of 2017, Sch 4. The definition of 'financial institution' in s 1 of the Financial Sector

only equity investments bring institutional investors under the scope of CRISA. This approach may require reconsideration in view of the extension to other asset classes in the hard law applicable to most pension funds,[50] as well as the inclusion of other asset classes in the new UK Code 2020.[51]

CRISA sets out five principles, which are elaborated on in seventeen recommendations for practical implementation. The recommendations are replete with references to sustainability, including environmental, social and governance (ESG) factors. The principles and recommendations operate on an 'apply or explain' basis.[52] The completely voluntary nature of CRISA mirrors the approach that applied for the King III report,[53] which was the operative corporate governance code at the time of CRISA's release. There is no official sign-on system in place and no central register where record is kept of the signatories to CRISA.

Principle 1 expects the inclusion of sustainability considerations, including ESG, into the investment decisions and activities of institutional investors.[54] This approach is in aid of 'superior risk-adjusted returns' to ultimate beneficiaries. Recommendations 1 and 2 focus on the development, implementation and monitoring of an investor policy, which includes sustainability considerations, including ESG. Recommendation 14 asks for public disclosure of these policies. Legislation that affects a majority of the institutional investors in South Africa supports the substance of these recommendations.[55]

Principle 2 provides that an institutional investor's investment arrangements and activities should demonstrate that it accepts its ownership responsibilities.[56] Recommendation 3 encourages the development of a responsible ownership policy, including guidelines for the identification of sustainability concerns, including ESG, at an investee company. The responsible ownership policy should further set out the intervention and engagement with a company after such sustainability concerns have been identified, and how concerns will be escalated, if not resolved.[57] Controls must be put in place to prevent receiving price-sensitive information when engaging with investee companies.[58] Voting policies must be set out, as must the criteria that the investor will use to reach voting decisions, and the policy must provide for public disclosure of full voting records. Active voting policies are encouraged even when passive investment strategies are followed.[59]

The duty to implement the responsible ownership policy is that of the institutional investor, who must monitor compliance both internally and when services are provided by third parties.[60] Mandates with service providers must deal with sustainability concerns, including ESG, and compliance with these mandates must be monitored.[61] CRISA subsequently published an adaptation of the International Corporate Governance Network's Model Mandate for use in

---

Regulation Act must be considered in the future, as well as the definitions of 'financial service' and 'financial product' in ss 2 and 3, respectively. However, the ultimate effect of these provisions should remain unchanged.

[50] See Section 22.5.
[51] UK Code 2020 (n 35) 4.
[52] On enforcement in general, see Katelouzou and Sergakis, Shareholder Stewardship Enforcement, Chapter 27.
[53] See the discussion in Section 22.4.
[54] CRISA (n 11) 10. This is similar to PRI (n 14) Principle 1. The gist of this principle is also found in the UK Code 2020 (n 35) Principle 7 for asset owners and asset managers.
[55] See Section 22.5.
[56] CRISA (n 11) 10. This is similar to PRI (n 14) Principle 2.
[57] This type of engagement is encouraged in the UK Code 2020 (n 35) Principle 9 for asset owners and asset managers. Escalation receives separate attention in the UK Code 2020 (n 35) Principle 11.
[58] CRISA (n 11) 10, recommendation 7.
[59] ibid recommendation 4. Voting policy and disclosure of voting are set out in the UK Code 2020 (n 35) Principle 12 for asset owners and asset managers.
[60] CRISA (n 11) recommendation 5. This is provided for separately in the UK Code 2020 (n 35) Principle 8 for asset owners and asset managers.
[61] CRISA (n 11) recommendation 6.

the South African context.[62] This expressly phrases, as part of the asset manager's fiduciary responsibility towards the client, that it manages the portfolio in accordance with the client's responsible ownership policy.[63] The Model Mandate stipulates that asset managers must allow asset owners access to its staff and systems to enable monitoring.[64] CRISA further recommends publication of the processes to ensure compliance by service providers of both CRISA and the investment policies of the institutional investor.[65]

Principle 3 advocates a collaborative approach among institutional shareholders, other shareholders, service providers, regulators, investee companies and ultimate beneficiaries to promote responsible investing and sound governance.[66] This collaboration must be mindful of the consequences of 'acting in concert'.[67] The South African Takeover Regulation Panel has engaged with the PRI South Africa Network to publish a guideline of the type of engagement that will not be considered 'acting in concert' for purposes of change in control.[68] The crux of this guideline is that the Takeover Regulation Panel will not consider engagement to be 'acting in concert' if it merely entails a discussion of mutually important matters or a sharing of concerns about specific investee companies.[69] There must be a more formal plan of co-operation for parties to become concert parties. Mandatory offer provisions are triggered at 35 per cent combined holdings of voting securities,[70] which means that even if a finding of concert parties is reached in a particular case, they will not be bound to make a mandatory offer as long as their combined holdings remain lower than this threshold.[71] They will also be bound to make a mandatory offer only if they have acquired additional securities at the time of acting in concert.[72]

Principle 4 holds that an institutional investor must recognize situations that hold the potential for conflicts of interest and should actively manage conflicts when they occur.[73] The development of a formal policy on preventing and managing conflicts of interests is recommended, as well as processes to monitor compliance.[74]

Principle 5 provides that the various policies and their implementation must be transparent, as must how CRISA will be implemented by the institutional investor.[75] This should enable the

---

[62] Institute of Directors in Southern Africa, 'Adaptation of the ICGN Model Mandate Initiative for South Africa' (July 2014) <https://cdn.ymaws.com/www.iodsa.co.za/resource/collection/2BB91484-C408-4372-A045-FAF4E98560F5/Position_Paper__Model_Mandate.pdf> accessed 3 July 2020.
[63] CRISA (n 11) 3.
[64] Institute of Directors in Southern Africa (n 62) 6.
[65] CRISA (n 11) 11, recommendation 17. This is similar to PRI (n 14) Principle 4.
[66] ibid 11, Principle 3 and recommendation 8. This reflects PRI (n 14) Principles 2 and 5. It may also be found in the UK Code 2020 (n 35) Principle 10 for asset owners and asset managers.
[67] 'Act in concert' is defined as 'any action pursuant to an agreement between or among two or more persons, in terms of which any of them co-operate for the purpose of entering into or proposing an affected transaction or offer' (Companies Act 71 of 2008, s 117(1)(b)). All public companies and state-owned companies are subject to the Takeover Regulations, as well as some private companies in restricted circumstances (s 118 (1)). See further the Companies Regulations 2011 (n 43) reg 84.
[68] PRI South Africa Network Engagement Working Group, 'Collaborative Engagement: Takeover Regulation Panel' (1 March 2012) <https://cdn.ymaws.com/www.iodsa.co.za/resource/collection/58CA7BC8-8C67-4CF7-A644-0EDB06165C8B/2013.05.14_PRI_Collaborative_Engagement_Guidance.pdf> accessed 3 July 2020.
[69] ibid 2.
[70] Companies Act 71 of 2008, s 123 read with reg 86.
[71] PRI South Africa Network Engagement Working Group (n 68) 7.
[72] ibid 8 with reference to reg 84(7).
[73] CRISA (n 11) 11. This is similar to the UK Code 2020 (n 35) Principle 3 for asset owners and asset managers.
[74] CRISA (n 11) 11, recommendations 9 and 10.
[75] ibid 11, which is similar to PRI (n 14) Principle 6. The three relevant policies are the investment policy incorporating sustainability and ESG, the responsible ownership policy, and the policy on detection and management of conflicts of interest (recommendation 14). See further the UK Code 2020 (n 35) Principle 5 for asset owners and asset managers.

stakeholders of the institutional investor to make informed decisions.[76] It emerges from the recommendations that follow on the principle that investee companies and the ultimate beneficiaries of institutional investors are seen as their main stakeholders. Engagement to discover information requirements is encouraged.[77] There is some similarity between this principle and the UK Code 2020 Principle 6 for asset owners and managers. However, the latter makes it clearer that the needs and preferences of ultimate beneficiaries should be considered by institutional investors when they draft their policies. There is a difference in focus – CRISA phrases this principle as giving *information to* stakeholders to enable their decision-making, whereas the UK Code 2020 phrases it as the collection of *information from* stakeholders to enable institutional investor decision-making. While both are important, the latter is absent from CRISA and should be considered in future revisions. The UK Code 2020 includes *information to* stakeholders under the reporting expectations of Principle 7.

Disclosure should be made at least annually and publicly about the extent to which the institutional investor applies CRISA. If an institutional investor does not apply some of the principles or recommendations of CRISA, it should disclose this fact, as well as the reasons and any alternative measures put in place.[78] All of these disclosures should be made public.[79] To encourage engagement by investee companies with institutional investors, full disclosure of voting records by institutional investors and their service providers is recommended.[80]

A CRISA Practice Note elaborates on the disclosures required.[81] Among other things, the Practice Note provides that voting and the nature and extent of shareholder engagements should be reported on by asset managers rather than asset owners, so as to avoid double counting.[82] This is in line with the approach adopted by the PRI.[83] The extent to which disclosure has been delegated to an asset manager must be disclosed, as should the mandate and how it monitors compliance by the asset manager with its investment policy. Disclosures may be made on the investor's website, or as part of its annual integrated report, or in its responsible investment report.[84] The Practice Note acknowledges that the various policies may be included in responsible investment policies that include the requirements of both CRISA and the PRI. The 'apply or explain' disclosure on the principles and recommendations of CRISA may similarly be done as part of the integrated annual report or the responsible investment report of the institutional investor or its service provider.[85]

Despite the clarity of these provisions and the reported acceptance of the principles of CRISA in the institutional investor community, disclosure on an 'apply or explain' basis has been virtually absent. On the asset owner side, the GEPF has a publicly available responsible investing policy[86] and basic disclosures regarding its support for the PRI.[87] There they indicate

---

[76] *CRISA* (n 11) 11.
[77] ibid recommendation 11.
[78] *CRISA* (n 11) recommendation 12.
[79] ibid recommendation 13.
[80] ibid recommendation 15.
[81] Institute of Directors in Southern Africa, 'Guidance on Disclosure of the Application of CRISA' (CRISA Practice Note, 2013) <www.iodsa.co.za/page/CRISAPN> accessed 3 July 2020.
[82] ibid 3–4.
[83] ibid.
[84] ibid 4.
[85] ibid 6–7.
[86] Government Employees Pension Fund, 'GEPF Responsible Investment Policy' (2017) <www.gepf.co.za/wp-content/uploads/2019/08/Responsible_Investing_Policy_20170921.pdf> accessed 3 July 2020.
[87] See Government Employees Pension Fund, 'Responsible Investment' <www.gepf.gov.za/responsible-investment/> accessed 3 July 2020.

that engagement with investee companies occurs via its asset manager, the PIC. No reference is made on its website of reporting in terms of CRISA, even though the GEPF was represented on the CRISA committee. Other asset owners that are PRI signatories have followed a similar pattern.[88]

While many asset managers publish their reports on responsible investment and stewardship, ownership responsibilities, and conflict of interest management on their websites,[89] the 'apply or explain' disclosure in terms of CRISA is mostly absent from these reports. A survey of the transparency reports of South African signatories of the PRI also shows that many asset managers opt to keep their responsible investing policy and coverage private.[90] Similarly, the annual integrated reports seem not to include much in the way of 'apply or explain' disclosures of CRISA as set out in the Practice Note.[91]

It seems that both asset owners and asset managers, certainly the largest ones, have opted to become direct signatories of the PRI and to report annually in terms of that commitment, instead of actively engaging with CRISA.[92] The fact that some of the largest pension funds in South Africa will engage only asset managers that are signatories of the PRI may play a role in this.[93]

---

[88] The Consolidated Retirement Fund for Local Government does not make its responsible investing policy public; the LA Retirement Fund indicates on its website that it is 'supportive of' *CRISA*, but no disclosures are made on an 'apply or explain' basis (LA Retirement Fund, 'Principles for Responsible Investment' <https://laretirementfund.co.za/investments/principles-for-responsible-investment/> accessed 3 July 2020). The LA Retirement Fund has local government employees as members. The focus is on PRI and disclosure is made directly to PRI (see PRI, 'LA Retirement Fund' (PRI Reporting Framework 2019) <https://reporting.unpri.org/surveys/PRI-reporting-framework-2019/F330F7EC-7BFB-4EA1-AB91-11E3BAE573F0/bf735de92be04caa8c32fcbc25cbdd2c/html/2/?lang=en&a=1> accessed 3 July 2020); Sanlam Ltd makes extensive disclosures on sustainability policy on its website, but *CRISA* is not mentioned once (See Sanlam, 'Sustainability 2018' <www.sanlam.com/investorrelations/sustainability/sustainability2018/Pages/default.aspx> accessed 3 July 2020); SASRIA (SOC) Ltd makes no mention of *CRISA* in its website. In its PRI transparency disclosure, it indicated that all of its asset managers must be PRI signatories. No mention is made of *CRISA* (see PRI, 'SASRIA (SOC) Limited' (PRI Reporting Framework 2019) <https://reporting.unpri.org/surveys/PRI-reporting-framework-2019/8F81574D-5839-4AD9-AD0C-F659932C74BF/57749b1a39a14fe6942aabb90698b3c1/html/2/?lang=en&a=1> accessed 3 July 2020); likewise, the Eskom Pension and Provident Fund requires all of its asset managers to be signatories to the PRI (see PRI, 'Eskom Pension and Provident Fund' (PRI Reporting Framework 2019) <https://reporting.unpri.org/surveys/PRI-reporting-framework-2019/15385B1C-903C-454E-B23A-5D459ADCBF37/57749b1a39a14fe6942aabb90698b3c1/html/2/?lang=en&a=1> accessed 11 February 2022). Eskom is the state-owned energy supplier.

[89] See, for instance, Allan Gray, 'Responsible Investing' <www.allangray.co.za/responsible-investing/> accessed 3 July 2020; Aeon Investment Management, 'CRISA Disclosure' <www.aeonim.co.za/crisa-disclosure/> accessed 3 July 2020; Old Mutual Investment Group, '2019 Responsible Investment Report' (21 June 2019) <www.oldmutualinvest.com/institutional/knowledge-room/2019-responsible-investing-report> accessed 9 February 2022; Public Investment Corporation, 'Environmental, Social and Governance' <www.pic.gov.za/investment-philosophy-and-approach/environmental-social-governance> accessed 3 July 2020; Sanlam Investments, 'Transformation and Corporate Governance' <www.sanlaminvestments.com/about/governance/Pages/default.aspx> accessed 3 July 2020 (also one of the few that includes a specific *CRISA* disclosure in its responsible investment report); Alexander Forbes Investments, 'Responsible Investing' <www.alexanderforbesinvestments.co.za/about-us/who-we-are/responsible-investing> accessed 3 July 2020; STANLIB, 'Responsible Investing' <www.stanlib.com/our-story-institutional/#about> accessed 3 July 2020; Coronation Fund Managers, 'Stewardship' <www.coronation.com/en/institutional/stewardship/> accessed 9 February 2022.

[90] See n 18.

[91] Public Investment Corporation, *Integrated Annual Report 2018* (2018) 63, 114 <www.pic.gov.za/DocAnnualReports1/Public-Investment-Corporation-Integrated-Annual-Report-2018.pdf> accessed 3 July 2020. The *Integrated Annual Report* mentions CRISA only in passing, citing broad approval of its principles.

[92] See n 18 for a full list of South African signatories to the PRI.

[93] See also the comments in Stephanie Giamporcaro and Suzette Viviers, 'SRI in South Africa: A Melting Pot of Local and Global Influences' in Céline Louche and Tessa Hebb (eds), *Socially Responsible Investment in the 21st Century: Does It Make a Difference for Society?* (Emerald 2014) 222–23 where the authors claim that investment managers sign up to the PRI not with the motive of truly applying the principles but rather to open up new business channels.

Missing from CRISA is a principle referring specifically to the internal governance of institutional investors,[94] as is the case in Principle 2 for asset owners and asset managers of the UK Code 2020. This is understandable in light of the scope of King IV.

22.4 KING IV: IMPORTANCE AND INTERACTION

The early adoption of a stewardship code was a direct consequence of the progressive nature of South Africa's non-mandatory code of corporate governance, which assumes the acceptance of non-financial reporting. CRISA followed short on the heels of King III.[95] King II already recommended sustainability reporting by companies,[96] but King III went further and devoted a whole chapter solely to integrated reporting, and financial and sustainability disclosure.[97]

King IV, which revised King III, applies to all entities that are directed by a governing body.[98] This means that it applies also to institutional investors, if adopted, regardless of whether they are organized in the form of a company. This makes it superfluous for CRISA to have a separate principle devoted to internal governance because institutional investors will report on governance in terms of King IV. However, it would have been best if CRISA had expressly required adoption of the governance code.

King IV is phrased in an 'apply and explain' way, meaning that it is assumed that all principles of the code are adhered to, and that it is left to individual entities to report on the manner in which they adhere to the principles and recommendations.[99] While compliance with the individual recommendations of the code therefore remains voluntary, entities that have adopted King IV must show that they have complied with the basic principles of the code. These principles were reduced in number from seventy-five in King III to only sixteen in King IV.[100] However, without compliance with these principles, entities will not be able to claim that they are practising sound corporate governance. It further means that while CRISA is meant to be complementary to King IV,[101] it has perhaps fallen behind in terms of current thinking.

King IV assumes that all entities have adopted non-financial reporting. This assumption underlies all the principles of the code. Reporting in the annual directors' report on compliance with King IV is mandatory in terms of the listing requirements of the JSE.[102] A direct consequence of this approach is that all listed entities adopt non-financial reporting as a matter of course, not because it is mandated by legislation or even by the listing requirements but because they would be unable to report on their compliance with the code of corporate governance without simultaneously having adopted non-financial reporting. Most of the large asset managers, as well as asset owners such as long-term insurers, therefore adopt integrated reporting as a matter of course owing

---

[94] See International Corporate Governance Network, *ICGN Global Governance Principles* (2016) 11–13, Principle 1 <https://ecgi.global/code/icgn-global-governance-principles-2016?field_categories_tid[0]=9376&field_categories_tid[1]=9463> accessed 11 February 2022.

[95] Institute of Directors in Southern Africa, 'King Report on Governance for South Africa 2009' (2009) [hereinafter *King III*].

[96] Institute of Directors in Southern Africa, 'King Report on Corporate Governance for South Africa 2002' (2002).

[97] *King III* (n 95) 108–11. The chairman of the King Committee on Corporate Governance for South Africa, which produced the King Reports, is also an emeritus chair of both the International Integrated Reporting Council and the Global Reporting Initiative. See Global Reporting Initiative, 'About GRI' <www.globalreporting.org/information/about-gri/Pages/default.aspx> accessed 3 July 2020.

[98] *King IV* (n 12) 35.

[99] *King IV* (n 12) 7.

[100] Principle 17 applies only to institutional investors.

[101] CRISA (n 11) 6. See also Dionysia Katelouzou, *The Path to Enlightened Shareholder Stewardship* (CUP) (forthcoming) for the similar approach that is followed in the UK.

[102] JSE, 'JSE Limited Listing Requirements' (Service Issue 27) par 8.63(a).

to their listing obligations.[103] However, even if an entity is not listed, reporting on compliance with King IV is impossible without adopting a non-financial reporting framework.

Entities not listed on an exchange are encouraged to adopt King IV voluntarily. However, it must be noted that even the GEPF only moved to the voluntary adoption of King IV in 2018.[104] This may partly be because retirement funds previously received separate guidance on their governance arrangements in the form of a Circular issued by the Financial Services Board.[105] At the time the Circular was issued, the focus of the King II code was still narrowly on the governance of companies. King IV is the first to expressly extend to all governed entities or to adopt specific guidance for institutional investors. However, the Circular is still active and has not been replaced with King IV or even updated with an appropriate reference to King IV. Best practice in governance has moved on considerably since 2007 and it begs the question why adoption of King IV by retirement funds is not actively encouraged by the Financial Sector Conduct Authority (FSCA). In fact, the FSCA should encourage all of its supervised entities to adhere to King IV.

Part 6.4 of King IV provides sector-specific guidance to retirement funds.[106] 'Retirement funds' are defined for the purposes of the supplement as including pension funds, provident funds, preservation funds and retirement annuity funds.[107] The sector supplement rephrases each of the principles of King IV to fit the retirement fund sector. In some cases, the principle is merely restated with the appropriate adjustments for the sector. In other cases, the supplement provides greater explanation of the particular principle immediately following the restatement. For instance, Principle 3 is restated as: 'The board should ensure that the fund is and is seen to be a responsible corporate citizen.'[108] Then follows an explanation – in the context of retirement funds, Principle 3 conveys the same message as regulation 28 of the Pension Funds Act,[109] and is given effect by ensuring that its investment analyses and practices, as well as those of its service providers, adhere to ESG considerations as provided for in Principle 1 of CRISA. Principle 4, which sees sustainability as one of several factors that are important for value creation, is emphasized for retirement funds in that a long-term view of financial performance is encouraged.[110] Principle 5, which sets out disclosure as a sound basis of governance, cross-refers to Principle 5 of CRISA, which requires accountability on investment decisions and activities.[111] The supplement pays additional attention to delegation of responsibility. Further explanation under restated Principle 10 emphasizes that the board retains responsibility for the decisions of service providers. Principle 17 expressly recommends that the principles and practices of CRISA be implemented by retirement funds as a matter of good corporate governance.

Sector-specific guidance is further meant to give guidance to those entities that do not fall exactly within a sector but are mostly closely aligned with their organization structure.[112] Other

---

[103] See, for instance, Alexander Forbes Group Holding Ltd; Coronation Fund Managers Ltd; Discovery Ltd; Investec Ltd; Liberty Holdings Ltd; Momentum Metropolitan Holdings Ltd; Old Mutual Ltd; Peregrine Holdings Ltd; PSG Konsult Ltd; RMB Holdings Ltd (holding company of Ashburton Investments); Sanlam Ltd; Sasfin Holdings Ltd. Issuer details are available at JSE, 'Find an Equity Issuer' <https://clientportal.jse.co.za/companies-and-financial-instruments> accessed 9 February 2022.
[104] Government Employees Pension Fund, *2018 Annual Report* (November 2018) 14 <www.gepf.gov.za/wp-content/uploads/2019/08/AR_2018_20181128_Final_Submitted-min.pdf> accessed 3 July 2020.
[105] Financial Services Board, 'Circular PF No. 130 Good Governance of Retirement Funds' (11 June 2007).
[106] *King IV* (n 12) 95.
[107] ibid.
[108] ibid 97.
[109] See the discussion in Section 22.5.
[110] *King IV* (n 12) 97.
[111] ibid.
[112] *King IV* (n 12) 75.

institutional investors could therefore use part 6.4 as guidance, even though they are not retirement funds.

Outside of the sector-specific guidance, King IV provides that the governing body of an entity that is an institutional investor[113] must ensure that responsible investment is practised to promote good governance and value creation by the investee company.[114] The governing body of the institutional investor carries the final responsibility to ensure responsible investing,[115] which should be guided by a formal responsible investing policy.[116] Outsourced investment decisions and activities must be overseen by the governing body to ensure that the responsible investing policy is implemented.[117] Service providers must be held to account for compliance with the formal mandate.[118] The responsible investing policy and how it is applied should be disclosed.[119] These recommended practices overlap with CRISA and do not really offer anything new apart from clarifying that the final responsibility for implementing responsible investing lies with the board.

22.5 LEGAL REQUIREMENTS TO CONSIDER ESG ISSUES

CRISA applies to all institutional investors that hold equity in companies and that have voluntarily adopted CRISA. King IV applies to all institutional investors that are governed by a governing body and that have adopted King IV. However, both represent soft-law measures that are not actively enforced by a regulator.[120] Additionally, some hard-law measures support responsible investing in South Africa. Two types of institutional investor are particularly subject to statutory provisions, namely pension funds that are regulated by the Pension Funds Act 24 of 1956, and intermediary services, to which asset managers and other service providers are bound. Common law fiduciary duties and the duty of care and diligence apply to both asset owners and service providers, regardless of their form of incorporation. In some instances, statutory statements of the fiduciary duties of institutional investors remove any doubt.

22.5.1 *Pension Funds*

The provisions below apply to pension funds registered in terms of section 4 of the Pension Funds Act 24 of 1956.[121] 'Pension fund' is defined very broadly for purposes of the Act and includes provident funds, retirement annuity funds, beneficiary funds and unclaimed benefit

---

[113] 'Institutional investor' is defined as

> any juristic person or institution referred to in the definition of financial institution in section 1 of the Financial Services Board Act, No 97 of 1990, to the extent that these juristic persons or institutions are the holders of beneficial interests in the securities of a company. It includes retirement funds and insurance companies as well as the custodians, nominees and service providers who act under mandate in respect of any investment decisions and investment activities exercised in relation to these securities. (ibid 13)

This definition was adapted from the one in CRISA, which includes an express reference to fiduciary obligations (CRISA (n 11) 9). See also n 49 earlier in this chapter.

[114] *King IV* (n 12) 73, Principle 17.
[115] ibid recommended practice 20.
[116] ibid recommended practice 21.
[117] ibid recommended practice 22 and 23.
[118] ibid recommended practice 24.
[119] ibid recommended practice 25.
[120] For a discussion about the increasingly fluid nature of corporate governance, where the 'hard law' / 'soft law' dichotomy may be more apparent than real, see Dionysia Katelouzou and Peer Zumbansen, 'The New Geographies of Corporate Governance' (2020) 42 *University of Pennsylvania Journal of International Law* 51.
[121] s 2(1).

funds.[122] All of these funds were also included under the ambit of 'retirement funds' as described for the purposes of King IV.

All pension funds regulated by the Pension Funds Act must have an investment policy statement, which must be annually reviewed.[123] Regulation 28, issued in terms of section 36 of the Act, provides greater guidance as to the content of these investment policies. It provides the following in its preamble:[124]

> A fund has a fiduciary duty to act in the best interest of its members whose benefits depend on the responsible management of fund assets. This duty supports the adoption of a responsible investment approach to deploying capital into markets that will earn adequate risk adjusted returns suitable for the fund's specific member profile, liquidity needs and liabilities. Prudent investing should give appropriate consideration to any factor which may materially affect the sustainable long-term performance of a fund's assets, *including factors of an environmental, social and governance character*. This concept applies *across all assets and categories of assets* and should promote the interests of a fund in a stable and transparent environment.

Two immediate observations follow. First, the preamble expressly includes material ESG factors as part of the considerations of a prudent investor. This is bolstered in regulation 28(2)(c), which provides: 'A fund and its board must at all times apply the following principles – ... (ix) before making an investment in and while invested in an asset consider any factor which may materially affect the sustainable long-term performance of the asset including, but not limited to, those of an environmental, social or governance character.'[125] The fact that ESG factors are expressly mentioned as risk factors that should be considered as potentially impactful to the performance of pension fund assets means that these issues may not be ignored; if they are, this would amount to a breach of the Pension Funds Act.

The second observation is that the investment policy of the pension fund must apply this approach across all assets and categories of asset, not only to its investments in equity. It therefore goes further than CRISA.

Pension funds cannot circumvent their duties by delegating activities to third-party service providers, as regulation 28(2)(d) provides: 'With the appointment of third parties to perform functions which are required to be performed in order to comply with the principles in (c) above, the fund retains the responsibility for compliance with such principles.'

The FSCA issued a Guidance Notice in June 2019 on how ESG aspects must be integrated into the investment policies of pension funds regulated in terms of the Pension Funds Act.[126] It

---

[122] s 1. A full list of the registered funds in terms of the Pension Funds Act is available at Financial Sector Conduct Authority, 'Retirement Fund' <www.fsca.co.za/Regulated%20Entities/Pages/Retirement-Fund-Verifications.aspx> accessed 3 July 2020.

[123] reg 28(2)(b).

[124] Government Notice No R98 in Government Gazette No 162 of 26 January 1962 (emphasis added). Similar legislation is in place in the UK. See the Pensions Act 1995, s 35 read with the Occupational Pension Schemes (Investment) Regulations 2005 as amended by the Occupational Pension Schemes (Investment and Disclosure) (Amendment and Modification) Regulations 2018 (2018/988). See further Katelouzou, *Institutional Shareholders and Corporate Governance* (n 101) for a discussion of the comparable legislation in the UK.

[125] 'Material' or 'materiality' is not defined in the regulation or in the Pension Funds Act. However, it is submitted that the definition favoured by the International Integrated Reporting Council, *The International <IR> Framework* (13 December 2013) 5 <https://integratedreporting.org/wp-content/uploads/2015/03/13-12-08-THE-INTERNATIONAL-IR-FRAMEWORK-2-1.pdf> accessed 3 July 2020, and which is adopted by King IV (n 12) 14, would also be appropriate in this context, namely matters that 'could substantively affect the organization's ability to create value over the short, medium and long term'.

[126] Financial Sector Conduct Authority, 'FSCA Communication 1 of 2019 (PFA)' (Guidance Notice 1, 14 June 2019) [hereinafter FSCA Guidance Notice 1].

further sets out the FSCA's expectations on disclosure and reporting of sustainability issues. It remains to be seen whether the industry pays attention to the Guidance Notice, which is not binding law. The communication that accompanied the issuance of the Guidance Notice indicates that the FSCA will especially apply the requirements of paragraph 4 in assessing and enforcing compliance with regulation 28.[127]

Paragraph 4.1 of the Guidance Notice requires that the investment policy statement reflect how its general investment philosophy and objectives seek to ensure the sustainability of its assets. No closed list of content is recommended, but certain information must be included in the investment policy statement. Apart from the date on which the policy was approved, and by whom, the policy must indicate how often it will be reviewed. The policy must indicate how the ongoing sustainability of current and future assets will be monitored and evaluated, including the extent to which ESG factors are considered, and their potential impact on the assets.

The investment policy must include the active ownership policy of the fund. 'Active ownership' is defined to mean 'the prudent fulfilment of responsibilities relating to the ownership of, and an interest in, an asset'.[128] These responsibilities include:

(a) guidelines to be applied for the identification of sustainability concerns in that asset;
(b) mechanisms of intervention and engagement with the responsible persons in respect of the asset when concerns have been identified and the means of escalation of activities as a holder or owner of that asset if these concerns cannot be resolved; and
(c) voting at meetings of shareholder owners or holders of an asset, including the criteria that are used to reach voting decisions and the methodology for recording voting.

The investment mandates with service providers must reflect these policies.[129]

If the fund holds assets that limit the application of ESG factors, sustainability criteria or the full application of the active ownership policy, the fund must explain why it is to the benefit of the fund and its membership.[130] If the benefit cannot be explained, the fund must show how it is planning to take remedial action or explain its failure to take remedial action.

The Guidance Notice recommends disclosure of the investment policy of the fund not only to members but also to be made available on the fund's website.[131] It further recommends transparent disclosure of all sustainability matters to stakeholders.[132] As was noted earlier,[133] funds do not currently follow consistent disclosure practices, and the vagueness of the Guidance Notice will probably not remedy this situation.

The reporting recommendations of the Guidance Notice require that the director's report forming part of the annual financial statements of the fund must include a note on how the fund's investment policy adheres to the recommendations of the Guidance Notice and indicate any changes in the investment policy, particularly in dealing with sustainability issues.[134] The question is whether these disclosures will be monitored by the FSCA and if there will be enforcement consequences for inadequate disclosure. The fact that the FSCA

---

[127] ibid para 3.3.
[128] FSCA Guidance Notice 1 (n 126) para 2.
[129] ibid para 4.3.
[130] ibid para 4.2.
[131] ibid para 5.1.
[132] ibid para 5.2.
[133] See Section 22.3.
[134] FSCA Guidance Notice 1 (n 126) paras 6.2–6.3.

opted for a Guidance Notice instead of a Directive,[135] as was previously planned, signals the opposite.

Pension funds not regulated by the Pension Funds Act are not mandated to make their investment policy statement public.[136] Moreover, pension funds created by separate statute are not regulated by the FSCA, and their members do not have recourse to the Pension Funds Adjudicator to resolve disputes.[137] This means that oversight is dampened and recourse made harder, a situation which is made worse by the fact that these pension funds represent a large section of working people in South Africa.[138] These significant pension funds are not regulated by the FSCA, causing a fissure in the regulatory structure of financial institutions that ought to be reconsidered, as there is no central regulator that supervises sustainability inclusion in these funds' investment policy and actions. The government-backed nature of these funds and the fact that trustees are appointed by ministerial approval ought to make no difference in the manner in which oversight is exercised over the fulfilment of their duties.[139]

22.5.2 *Asset Managers and Other Service Providers*

Some statutory provisions also apply to asset managers and other service providers directly, regardless of whether they act for pension funds or for other types of asset owner. Asset managers are regulated by the Financial Advisory and Intermediary Services Act 37 of 2002. Section 15 provides for industry codes of conduct, which are compiled by the registrar in consultation with the relevant financial services industry bodies. Section 16 provides the minimum content of such codes of conduct, which includes that the service provider and its representatives will 'act honestly and fairly, and with due care, skill and diligence, in the interests of clients and the integrity of the financial services industry'.[140] The General Code of Conduct for Authorised Financial Services Providers and Representatives provides that when a provider renders a financial service, 'the service must be rendered in accordance with the contractual relationship and reasonable requests or instructions of the client, which must be executed as soon as reasonably possible and with due regard to the interests of the client which must be accorded appropriate priority over any interests of the provider'. [141]

---

[135] See Financial Services Board, 'Sustainability Reporting and Disclosure Requirements' (Draft Directive, March 2018).

[136] The GEPF did so voluntarily (see Government Employees Pension Fund, 'Investment Policy Statement' (August 2019) <www.gepf.gov.za/wp-content/uploads/2019/08/GEPF_Investment_Policy_Statement.pdf> accessed 3 July 2020). The Transnet Retirement Fund publishes an outline of its policy (see Transnet Retirement Fund, 'Member Investment Options' <https://mra.momentum.co.za/TRFund/member-investment-options/> accessed 3 July 2020).

[137] See Financial Services Board, 'FSB's Statement to Clarify Which Authority Has the Relevant Oversight over the Transnet Employee's Pension Fund' (Press Release, 12 October 2017) <www.fsca.co.za/News%20Documents/2017-10-12.pdf> accessed 3 July 2020. The Pension Funds Adjudicator is an alternative dispute resolution mechanism for disputes between pension funds and members. Its appeal body is the Financial Services Tribunal, created by the Financial Sector Regulation Act 9 of 2017, s 219.

[138] Latest figures published by Statistics South Africa reveal that of the 11,172,000 people employed in the formal sector in South Africa, 3,130,000 are employed in 'community and social services' (see Statistics South Africa (n 2) 56). National and provincial state departments and those employed in local government are included in this figure. See also South African Market Insights, 'South Africa's Formal Business Sector' (26 June 2019) <www.southafricanmi.com/south-africas-formal-business-sector.html> accessed 3 July 2020.

[139] The PIC is a registered financial service provider for purposes of the Financial Advisory and Intermediary Services Act 7 of 2002 (see Section 22.5.2). This brings it directly under supervision of the FSCA, regardless of its public nature.

[140] s 16(1)(a). On a similar provision in the UK, see Katelouzou and Zumbansen (n 120) 52–53.

[141] General Code of Conduct for Authorised Financial Services Providers and Representatives (Board Notice 80 of 2003, Government Gazette No 25299, 8 August 2003) cl 3(1)(d).

The General Code of Conduct must be read with the Codes of Conduct for Administrative and Discretionary FSPs.[142] This provides that the mandate of a discretionary FSP, such as an investment manager, must be approved by the FSCA.[143] The initially approved mandate is referred to as a 'specimen mandate'. The FSCA may subsequently insist that specific amendments or additions be included in the specimen mandate in the interests of the client. The discretionary FSP is not allowed to unilaterally make substantial amendments to the mandate without the FSCA's approval.[144] A likely consequence of the Guidance Notice discussed earlier will be that the FSCA will require specific inclusion of the investment policies of pension funds, including ESG and active ownership policies, in the specimen mandates. It is further advisable to have specific provisions in the mandate to facilitate the monitoring activities of asset owners, such as the disclosure of information about the ESG enquiries made in connection with particular assets or investments. However, this type of practical guidance is already provided in the CRISA Model Mandate, which supports regulation 28 and the provisions of the Financial Advisory and Intermediary Services Act.[145]

22.5.3 *Fiduciary Duties and the Duty of Care and Diligence*

The boards of pension funds regulated by the Pension Funds Act owe statutory duties to:

(a) take all reasonable steps to ensure that the interests of members in terms of the rules of the fund and the provisions of this Act are protected at all times . . .;

(b) act with due care, diligence and good faith;

. . .

(f) have a fiduciary duty to members and beneficiaries in respect of accrued benefits or any amount accrued to provide a benefit, as well as a fiduciary duty to the fund, to ensure that the fund is financially sound and is responsibly managed and governed in accordance with the rules and this Act; and

(g) comply with any other prescribed requirements. [146]

Adherence to the principles of responsible investing and, per implication, the principles of CRISA can arguably resort under each of the quoted provisions. Sustainability and ESG factors are factors to consider in risk governance. Sound risk governance is aimed at protecting the interests of the members. A failure to exercise sound risk governance could be seen as both a breach of the duty to act in the best interests of the fund and a breach of the duty to act with care and diligence.

Furthermore, in the terms of the Financial Institutions (Protection of Funds) Act 28 of 2001, a financial institution, and its agent, who invests the funds of the financial institution must observe the utmost good faith and exercise proper care and diligence with regard to such funds.[147] Pension funds, and asset managers who act for them, fall under the ambit of this provision, as do long-term insurance companies and collective investment schemes.[148]

---

[142] Codes of Conduct for Administrative and Discretionary FSPs (Board Notice 79 of 2003, Government Gazette No 25299, 8 August 2003) ch II.
[143] cl 5.2. See also the Financial Sector Regulation Act 9 of 2017, s 290.
[144] cl 5.3.
[145] Institute of Directors in Southern Africa (n 62) 11–12, 25–28 where detailed guidance is provided for the type of information needed for the quarterly reports that need to be submitted to the FSCA on non-compliance with reg 28.
[146] s 7C(2).
[147] s 2(a).
[148] The definition of 'financial institution' in the Financial Sector Regulations Act 9 of 2017 applies for purposes of the Financial Institutions (Protection of Funds) Act. A financial institution includes 'a person licensed or required to be

These statutory provisions are not in substitution of common law fiduciary duties[149] and the duty of care and diligence.[150] Most pension funds and long-term insurers delegate their investment decisions and activities wholly or in part to asset managers. While delegation in this manner is not only legal but the norm, the boards of these asset owners remain responsible in the final instance for monitoring and evaluating the adherence of the asset manager to the mandate.

Asset managers will exercise discretion in their investment decisions. The asset owner relies on the asset manager to exercise such discretion with care and diligence and in its best interests. This will include taking care to include ESG factors in its risk determinations, and to consider sustainability of investments in the long run. A disregard of these duties to increase short-term profits, and by implication increase remuneration, would constitute a breach of fiduciary duty to the fund. This is because the asset manager would be putting its own interests ahead of those of the fund.[151]

The legislation setting up pension funds outside of the Pension Funds Act typically includes similar provisions to section 7C(2) of the Pension Funds Act, which confirms the fiduciary responsibility of the board of the pension fund.[152] Furthermore, the boards of these pension funds owe common law fiduciary duties to their funds. This includes acting in the best interest of the fund in the long term. Investment decisions and activities that take only a short-term view, or that disregard material risk issues, such as relevant ESG factors, will be in breach of this duty. Arguably, a decision by a board to support an asset manager that takes such an approach will similarly be in breach of this duty.

Furthermore, all pension fund boards owe a duty of care and diligence to the pension fund. Disregard of material risks, including ESG issues, will be in breach of this duty as well, as will the failure to monitor service providers for their careful management of the risks that the fund's assets are exposed to.

The boards of insurance companies owe their fiduciary duties to the company.[153] However, owing to the importance of sustainability and ESG factors to risks in the insurance industry,

---

licensed in terms of financial sector law' (s 1). Financial sector laws are set out in Schedule 1 and include the Long-Term Insurance Act 52 of 1998 and the Collective Investment Schemes Control Act 45 of 2002.

[149] The presence or absence of a common law fiduciary obligation was described in *Volvo (Southern Africa) (Pty) Ltd v Yssel* [2009] ZASCA 82, [2009] 4 All SA 497 (SCA) [17] as follows: 'What is called for is an assessment, upon a consideration of all the facts, of whether reliance by one party upon the other was justified in the circumstances.' See also *Phillips v Fieldstone Africa (Pty) Ltd* [2003] ZASCA 137, [2004] 1 All SA 150 (SCA) [31]. See *Commentary on the Companies Act*, ch 8 30–42-1 (RS 9 of 2012); *Henochsberg on the Companies Act 71 of 2008*, 298(10)–298(20) (SI 19 of 2019) and the sources cited there. For fiduciary duties of pension fund trustees see *TEK Corporation Provident Fund v Lorentz* [1999] ZASCA 54, 4 All SA 297 (SCA) [15]; *PPWAWU National Provident Fund v Chemical, Energy, Paper, Printing, Wood and Allied Workers' Union* [2007] ZAGPHC 146, (2008) (2) SA 351 (W) [20]–[30]; Muthundinne Sigwadi, 'The Personal Liability of Pension Fund Trustees for Breach of Fiduciary Duties' (2008) 20 S Afr Mercantile LJ 331.

[150] *Fisheries Development Corp of SA Ltd v Jorgensen; Fisheries Development Corporation of SA Ltd v A W J C Investments (Pty) Ltd* (1980) (4) SA 156 (W) 165F–166E as confirmed in *Philotex (Pty) Ltd v Snyman; Braitex (Pty) Ltd v Snyman* [1997] ZASCA 92, (1998) (2) SA 138 (SCA) 144B–145G; *Commentary on the Companies Act* (n 149) ch 8 190–204; *Henochsberg on the Companies Act 71 of 2008* (n 149) 298(9) and the sources cited there.

[151] See also Rosemary Hunter, 'Pension Funds and Climate Risk: Why Pension Funds Must Invest Responsibly for Climate Resilience' (Fasken, Legal Opinion for ClientEarth and JustShare NPC, 4 April 2019) para 71 <https://justshare.org.za/wp-content/uploads/2019/04/2019_Pension-fund-legal-opinion-by-Fasken.pdf> accessed 3 July 2020.

[152] For instance, Rules of the Government Employees Pension Fund, Government Employees Pension Law 1996, r 4.1.19; Transnet Pension Fund Act 62 of 1990, Sch 1 and r 5(5).

[153] The FSCA will grant a new license to operate an insurance business in South Africa only to a public company incorporated in South Africa, but there are some existing insurance companies operating as mutual funds incorporated by separate legislation. See, for instance, the AVBOB Mutual Assurance Society Incorporation (Private) Act 7 of 1951. However, even in the latter case, fiduciary duties are owed to the fund and not to members directly.

much the same reasoning advanced in the context of pension funds may be advanced in favour of the inclusion of these considerations in the prudent fulfilment of the fiduciary responsibility of the board of insurance companies.[154]

22.6 CONCLUSIONS AND RECOMMENDATIONS

The exposition in this chapter shows that South African shareholder stewardship, along with corporate governance generally, is intimately connected to sustainability concerns. While active ownership does receive attention in CRISA, the focus of stewardship is on responsible investing decisions. In certain sectors, this approach is supported by hard law.

South Africa has a fragmented retirement fund industry.[155] More than 3,000 funds had less than ZAR 1 billion of assets under management in 2017, leading to governance and capacity constraints. This leads to an over-reliance on investment consultants and investment managers,[156] which is why mostly investment managers are signatories of the PRI, with so few asset owners. Capacity constraints make it more important that clear guidance on practices must be offered by the FSCA and industry associations such as ASISA and BATSETA.[157] Board members elected to South African pension funds often do not have the relevant knowledge or experience to fulfil their duties.[158]

The value of the recent FSCA Guidance Notice lies mostly in the signal that the regulator will take a more proactive role in supervising disclosures. A prescribed common framework for disclosures to the FSCA that would be publicly available, so that different pension funds would be comparable, was previously recommended by the PRI South Africa Network.[159] This has not yet been put in place. The problem is that beneficiaries of South African pension funds are generally passive and often ill-informed.[160] The chance that they will keep board members in check is therefore slim. Moreover, their only recourse on non-compliance with requests for changes in investment approach is to appoint other board members, but even here their power is often limited. For instance, half of the trustees of umbrella funds must typically be independent industry professionals.[161] Membership of pension funds is mostly linked to place of employment and so beneficiaries have little or no choice as to which pension fund they belong to. They have no option to switch funds if they are dissatisfied with the board members' investment policy or lack of monitoring of service providers. The value of monitoring by beneficiaries is therefore questionable, which means that appropriate supervision by the regulator becomes more important. The South Africa Roadmap implied that the FSCA was not able to effectively monitor

---

[154] See in general Benjamin J Richardson, *Fiduciary Law and Responsible Investing: In Nature's Trust* (Routledge 2013) 200–205.
[155] Brian Tomlinson, Adrian Bertrand and Will Martindale, 'Fiduciary Duty in the 21st Century: South Africa Roadmap' (2017) 4 <www.unpri.org/fiduciary-duty/fiduciary-duty-in-the-21st-century-south-africa-roadmap/263.article> accessed 3 July 2020. This document sets out the South African response to the PRI, UNEP FI and the Generation Foundation's implementation project to implement the recommendations of Rory Sullivan and others, 'Fiduciary Duty in the 21st Century' (2015) <www.unpri.org/fiduciary-duty/fiduciary-duty-in-the-21st-century/244.article> accessed 3 July 2020.
[156] Tomlinson, Bertrand and Martindale (n 155) 11.
[157] ibid.
[158] See, for instance, Financial Sector Conduct Authority, 'Statement Supporting the Draft Conduct Standard – Minimum Skills and Training Requirements for Board Members of Pension Funds' (22 May 2019) 3 <www.fsca.co.za/Regulatory%20Frameworks/Pages/Retirement-Funds.aspx> accessed 3 July 2020.
[159] Tomlinson, Bertrand and Martindale (n 155) 9.
[160] On beneficiaries as stakeholders, see Sullivan and others (n 155) 17–18.
[161] Kobus Hanekom, *Manual on Retirement Funds and Other Employee Benefits* (LexisNexis South Africa 2000) paras 2.3.3. and 9.4.6. The Pension Fund Rules typically determine the rights of members to elect trustees.

investment practice against regulation 28.[162] Considered against the extensive framework already in place since 2011, this is surprising and troubling. The failure, it seems, lies not in adequate regulation but rather in appropriate and well-resourced supervision.

The CRISA committee has moved to ASISA for permanent secretarial support.[163] CRISA remains important despite the extensive regulatory environment that it supports, as the guidance issued by the committee can be updated more quickly to respond to global best practice. Extensive guidance is essential in the South African context, as not all pension funds have the financial resources to appoint expert independent advisers to assist in monitoring their service providers. CRISA also remains important for institutional investors not subject to extensive hard-law regulation in this area, such as insurance companies and collective investment schemes. However, perhaps CRISA should have been moved to the FSCA.

The efficiency of the stewardship framework would be enhanced if the framework were overseen by the FSCA in a unified manner, including oversight of those pension funds that fall outside the regulatory ambit of the Pension Funds Act.[164] Despite some concerns over capacity, the FSCA is already the regulator of most pension funds, the insurance industry, collective investment schemes, as well as investment managers and other financial advisory services. This might provide an opportunity to prescribe greater uniformity of disclosure practices to enable users to draw meaningful conclusions about the extent to which institutional investors adhere to the principles of CRISA. Signatories should be public and annual public disclosures should be enforced. Publication of examples of best-practice disclosure would also assist in the improvement of disclosures.[165] At the same time, adherence to King IV should be actively encouraged by the FSCA, if not mandated.

CRISA needs an update.[166] King IV now deals with the governance expectations of institutional investors expressly, and devotes sector-specific guidelines to retirement funds. It even begs the question of whether a separate responsible investing code is still necessary. King IV considers sustainability as central to its entire governance framework. Moreover, it applies on an 'apply and explain' basis, whereas CRISA is still at the less binding 'apply or explain' basis of enforcement. Comparison with the UK Code 2020, the most recently updated stewardship code, shows that CRISA has fallen behind in extending responsible investing decisions to asset classes other than equity. The UK Code 2020 has also moved to an 'apply and explain' basis of enforcement.

Also, it is vitally important to get the sustainability component of shareholder stewardship right, from a social perspective. Retirement funds present the only vehicle by which most ordinary South Africans could hope to participate in the investment market. They are important not only as social security but also as a long-term mechanism to lead to greater economic equality. There is global awareness that sustainability and ESG factors are inseparable from the financial considerations that inform responsible investing. The stakes, however, are especially high in South Africa.

---

[162] Tomlinson, Bertrand and Martindale (n 155) 70.
[163] See the recommendation in Tomlinson, Bertrand and Martindale (n 155) 12.
[164] A switch was made in 2012 in the UK from an investor-led stewardship code to a regulator sanctioned code. See Jennifer G Hill, 'Good Activist/Bad Activist: The Rise of International Stewardship Codes' (2018) 41 *Seattle University Law Review* 497, 510. Disclosures are made public and rated on a tiering system, which makes clear who performs best against the principles of the code. See also Davies, The UK Stewardship Code 2010–2020, Chapter 2 and Katelouzou and Micheler, The Market for Stewardship and the Role of the Government, Chapter 3.
[165] ibid. See Bowley and Hill, Stewardship and Collective Action, Chapter 19.
[166] Since the finalization of this chapter, a draft revision of CRISA was published for public comment. See Institute of Directors in Southern Africa, 'Draft CRISA Code for Public Comment' (2020) <www.iodsa.co.za/page/crisaresourcecentr> accessed 25 May 2021.

23

Stewardship in Kenya

Just a Code or Something More?

Austin Ouko

23.1 INTRODUCTION

In 2017, the Kenya Capital Markets Authority (CMA) promulgated the Stewardship Code for Institutional Investors 2017 (Kenya Code).[1] Preceding this, in 2015, the CMA had published the Code of Corporate Governance Practices for Issuers of Securities to the Public 2015 (Corporate Governance Code). The two codes were informed by the need to respond to the changing business environment, coupled with the desire to align Kenyan local standards to global best practices to strengthen the institutional environment for listed companies.[2]

The Kenya Code is influenced by the 2010 UK Stewardship Code, given the UK's relatively long-standing code and a shared legal tradition.[3] It is notable that, as a former British colony, Kenya largely inherited its corporate law and regulatory framework from the UK. The Kenyan Companies Act 1962 (which was recently repealed) was almost entirely based on the 1948 UK Companies Act. Similarly, the 2015 Companies Act is based on the 2006 UK Companies Act.[4] The Kenya Code also borrowed from the International Corporate Governance Network (ICGN)

---

[1] Stewardship Code for Institutional Investors 2017 (9 May 2017), enacted by the Capital Markets Authority vide Kenya Gazette Notice No 6016 dated 23 June 2017 [hereinafter Kenya Code].

[2] Capital Markets Authority, *Code of Corporate Governance Practices for Issuers of Securities to the Public 2015* (Kenya Gazette Notice No 1420 of 2015) <www.cma.or.ke/index.php?option=com_phocadownload&view=category&download=360:code-of-corporate-governance-practices-for-issuers-of-securities-to-the-public-2015-code-8&id=92:corporate-governance-for-issuers&Itemid=285> accessed 5 June 2020 [hereinafter Corporate Governance Code]; Capital Markets Authority, 'New Corporate Governance Code for Listed Companies and Guidelines on Prevention of Money Laundering and Terrorism Financing in Capital Markets Gazetted' (9 March 2016) <www.cma.or.ke/index.php?option=com_content&view=article&id=178:new-corporate-governance-code-for-listed-companies-and-guidelines-on-prevention-of-money-laundering-and-terrorism-financing-in-capital-markets-gazetted&catid=12&Itemid=207> accessed 5 June 2020, speech by Paul Muthaura, CEO of Capital Markets Authority [hereinafter CMA]. The CMA under its powers in s 11(3)(v) and 12A of the Capital Markets Authority Act, Chapter 485A of the Laws of Kenya published the Capital Markets (Securities) (Public Offers, Listing and Disclosures) (Amendment) Regulations on 4 March 2016 vide Kenya Gazette Notice No 1420. It replaced the previous Guidelines on Corporate Governance Practices by Public Listed Companies (2002). The new code came into operation on 4 March 2017 after a transition period of one year from the date of gazettement.

[3] Financial Reporting Council, *The UK Stewardship Code* (September 2012) <www.frc.org.uk/getattachment/d67933f9-ca38-4233-b603-3d24b2f62c5f/UK-Stewardship-Code-(September-2012).pdf> accessed 5 June 2020. See also Owen Walker, 'New UK Stewardship Code to Look at Adoption of ESG Criteria' *Financial Times* (London, 29 January 2019) <www.ft.com/content/86b44c2c-dd32-36bc-aada-4338c60c5b7f> accessed 5 June 2020.

[4] Kiarie Mwaura, 'Regulation of Directors in Kenya: An Empirical Study' (2002) 13 *International Company and Commercial Law Review* 465, 465.

framework for investor stewardship.[5] It also has some components of the South African and Malaysian stewardship codes, as they are emerging economies sharing a common law heritage.[6]

The development and liberalization of international financial markets have allowed capital, predominantly from the US and the UK, to seek out profitable destinations for their investments in other countries. As a result, US and UK investment institutions have become commonplace in global shareholder markets, including in developing and African countries such as Kenya. As they expand beyond their shores, they bring with them their primary goal of maximizing shareholder value.[7] In turn, this might imply that a stewardship code and shareholder engagement designed to exploit US and UK corporate governance practices should prove equally effective elsewhere. It is in this context that this chapter seeks to examine the Stewardship Code in Kenya, as a developing country with a highly concentrated shareholder landscape.[8]

Also, this chapter will examine a startling fact that distinguishes Kenya from every other jurisdiction that has adopted a stewardship code. Three years after the issuance of the Kenya Code, *none* of the twenty-five licensed fund managers, institutional investors or asset owners have signed up to it. This raises two important questions: why has there been no support from the institutional investors for the Kenya Code; and what should be done to increase the level of engagement that institutional investors have with the Kenya Code?

This chapter will analyze the theoretical and contextual issues relating to the Stewardship Code in Kenya, and the impact it has had on institutional investors' engagement with publicly listed companies since it was issued. The chapter is divided as follows: Section 23.2 will discuss Kenya's capital markets landscape, its corporate law and regulatory framework in regard to how shareholders are to exercise their powers. Section 23.3 will explore the impact that the Kenya Code has had since it was issued. Section 23.4 concludes by finding that the requisite statutory and regulatory ingredients for shareholders' engagement and, more so, institutional investors' engagement are present in Kenya, but their engagement with companies is virtually non-existent.

23.2 THE KENYAN CAPITAL MARKET STRUCTURE, CORPORATE LAW AND REGULATORY FRAMEWORK

23.2.1 *Capital Markets and Institutional Investors within the Shareholder Landscape*

The Kenyan capital market is relatively small, with only sixty-four companies currently listed in the Nairobi Securities Exchange (NSE), which is the country's only securities exchange.[9] The top five companies account for 60 per cent to 70 per cent of market capitalization, while the top twenty dominate more than 95 per cent of market capitalization. It may be worth noting that, in contrast to the UK and US markets, the Kenyan capital market has no history of widely dispersed shareholding, and institutional shareholders have dominated the market since its inception. Many of the leading

---

[5] World Bank Group, 'Kenya: Strengthening and Deepening of Capital Markets, Stewardship Code: Issues Paper' (19 February 2015) (on file with author).
[6] ibid.
[7] John C Coffee Jr, 'Convergence and Its Critics: What Are the Preconditions to the Separation of Ownership and Control?' in Joseph McCahery, Piet Moerland, Luc Renneboog and Theo Raaijmakers (eds), *Corporate Governance Regimes: Convergence and Diversity* (OUP 2002) as cited in Timothy Broadhurst, 'Does Shareholder Activism Help or Hinder Shareholder Value Enhancement? Empirical Evidence from the UK' (DPhil thesis, Cranfield University 2009).
[8] World Bank Group (n 5).
[9] Nairobi Securities Exchange, 'Listed Companies' <www.nse.co.ke/listed-companies/list.html> accessed 5 June 2020.

companies have controlling positions held by overseas investors, including many multinational corporations. For the companies without significant overseas investors, Kenyan institutional investors tend to hold significant stakes, often in excess of 50 per cent in aggregate. Institutional investors include pension funds and insurance companies as asset owners.[10] Further, out of the sixty-four companies, the government of Kenya has controlling shareholdings in six companies.[11] The government also owns significant minority shareholdings in four other listed companies.[12]

The market is regulated by the CMA. The Capital Markets Act which established the CMA was enacted in 1989.[13] As per the Act, the regulatory functions of the CMA are to license and supervise all capital market intermediaries. It defines capital market intermediaries to include stockbrokers, derivatives brokers, REIT managers, trustees, dealers, investment advisers, fund managers, investment banks, central depositories, authorized securities dealers, authorized depositories, online forex brokers, commodity dealers, commodity brokers, businesses engaged in securities exchange, commodities exchange or derivatives exchange, registered venture capital companies, collective investment schemes and credit rating agencies.[14] The CMA regulates public offers of securities such as equities and bonds, and the issuance of other capital market products such as collective investment schemes. It is mandated with the responsibility of reviewing the legal framework to respond to market dynamics and promotion of investor education, public awareness and protection of investors' interest.[15]

Although the capital market is relatively small, and in some ways nascent, this has not been a hindrance to embedding good corporate governance best practices through a stewardship code. The basic regulatory ingredients of stewardship are in place – as will be discussed in this section. There is a critical mass of issuers and investors, and a supportive regulatory framework. The relatively small number of issuers can allow for a more manageable approach to investor stewardship when compared with larger markets found in developed countries.[16] Table 23.1 shows Kenya's capital market shareholding structure over the last decade.

Local investors and individual investors accounted for 79.09% of shares held in the equity market with 20.91% being held by foreign investors (see Table 23.1).[17] The Capital Markets (Foreign Investors) Regulations 2002 define a 'local investor' as being an individual who is a natural person who is a citizen of an East African Community Partner State.[18]

The main institutional investors are sixteen licensed investment banks, twenty-five registered fund managers, pension funds/retirement benefits schemes, insurance companies, mutual funds

---

[10] World Bank Group (n 5).
[11] East African Portland Cement Limited, National Bank of Kenya, Uchumi Limited, Kenya Re-insurance Corporation, Kenya Power and Lighting Limited, and Kenya Electricity Generating Company Limited.
[12] See Corporate Governance Code (n 2), which defines a 'substantial or significant shareholder' as a 'person who is the beneficial owner of, or is in a position to exert control over, not less than fifteen percent of the shares of a company'.
[13] Chapter 485A of the Laws of the Kenya.
[14] Capital Markets Act, ss 2, 23.
[15] See Capital Markets Authority, 'Who We Are' <www.cma.or.ke/index.php/about-us/who-we-are> accessed 11 February 2022.
[16] World Bank Group (n 5).
[17] Capital Markets Authority, 'Quarterly Statistical Bulletin Quarter 2' (Issue 39/2019, 22 July 2019) 31 <www.cma.or.ke/index.php/about-us/action-plans/strategic-plan/category/41-2019?download=360:capital-markets-authority-cma-quarterly-statistical-bulletin-quarter-2-2019> accessed 22 February 2022; see Retirement Benefits Authority, 'Registered Fund Managers' <www.rba.go.ke/registered-fund-managers/> accessed 5 June 2020.
[18] Capital Markets (Foreign Investors) Regulations 2002 (amended by Legal Notice No 113 of 2015). It goes ahead to define a local investor as a body corporate established or incorporated under the Companies Act or under the provisions of any written law of an East African Community (EAC) (the EAC is a regional intergovernmental organization of six partner states, comprising Burundi, Kenya, Rwanda, South Sudan, Tanzania and Uganda) partner state in which the citizens or the government of an EAC partner state have beneficial interests in 100% of its ordinary shares.

TABLE 23.1 *Trends in investor holdings at the NSE (2009–19)*

Type of investor	2009	2010	2011	2012	2013	2014	2015	2016	2017	2018	2019
East African institutions (%)	74.2	73.6	68.33	66.70	64.58	64.16	65.68	66.38	68.36	68.50	67.51
East African individual investors (%)	15.7	13.8	12.23	12.01	12.89	14.58	12.84	12.49	11.47	11.54	11.59
Foreign investors (%)	10.3	12.6	19.44	21.29	22.53	21.26	21.48	21.13	20.17	19.97	20.91

(unit trusts) and savings and credit societies.[19] Private equity firms are present but with minimal activity when compared to the other groups, though they are rapidly gaining ground.[20] As at 31 December 2018, the retirement benefits sector had 942 registered schemes and controlled assets worth USD 11.67 billion; accounting for more than 10 per cent of the country's gross domestic product (GDP). Fund managers and approved issuers held the majority of the assets amounting to USD 9.80 billion.[21] Every retirement benefit scheme board of trustees must appoint one or more licensed professional fund managers to undertake the scheme's investment management activities.[22] Retirement benefits schemes holdings of shares quoted at the NSE account for 8 per cent of the market capitalization, which is among the largest holdings by a group of institutional investors. Given that the total market float is about 40 per cent, retirement benefits schemes control about 20 per cent of the float, which is significant.[23]

23.2.2 *Companies Act*

In 2015, Kenya enacted a new Companies Act (Companies Act 2015), which draws heavily on the 2006 UK Companies Act, as stated in Section 23.1.[24] The Companies Act 2015 contains rules governing the creation and financing of companies, shareholders' rights, directors' duties and other issues concerning the management of companies. Importantly for this chapter, the Act introduced a number of rules to ensure greater opportunity for shareholders' engagement in a company's business. It removes the old requirements for the use of hard-copy documents, and allows companies to use electronic communication with shareholders as the default position.[25]

Shareholders holding at least 10 per cent of the paid-up capital with voting rights are statutorily allowed to request that the directors call for a general meeting.[26] The request to convene a meeting is effective if it states the general nature of the business to be dealt with at the meeting.

---

[19] Capital Markets Authority, 'List of Licensees' <www.cma.or.ke/index.php?option=com_phocadownload&view=category&id=49&Itemid=254> 5 June 2020.

[20] Rogers Kinoti M'ariba, 'Investment Management Structures: An Exploratory Review of Institutional Investors in Kenya' (2018) 2 *International Journal of Economics, Business and Management Research* 57.

[21] Retirement Benefits Authority, 'Retirement Benefits Industry Report for December 2018' (December 2018) 8 <www.rba.go.ke/download/retirement-benefits-industry-report-for-december-2018/> accessed 5 June 2020.

[22] Kinoti (n 20).

[23] Kinoti (n 20).

[24] Austin Ouko, 'Directors' Duty of Care and Skill: Implications from Kenya's Recent Law Reform' (2016) 9 *International Company and Commercial Law Review* 306, 315. The Companies Act No 17 of 2015 [hereinafter Companies Act 2015] received Presidential Assent on 11 September 2015, § 1 of the Act came into force on 15 September 2015. The operationalization of the remaining sections of the Act has been split into two major phases. Parts 1 to 14, Part 23, Part 31, Part 32, Part 38, Part 40, Part 42 and the First Second and Sixth Schedules came into operation on 6 November 2015 through Legal Notice No 232 of 13 November 2015. The remaining parts of the Act will be commenced by notice in the *Kenya Gazette* in accordance with s 1(3) of the Act.

[25] See Companies Act 2015, ss 266, 267, 277, 282, 289, 339.

[26] Companies Act 2015, s 277.

The directors are required to do so within twenty-one days from the date on which the request was made, and must hold the meeting on a date not more than twenty-eight days after the date of the notice convening the meeting.[27]

Further, section 312 of the Companies Act 2015 allows shareholders of a public company representing at least 5 per cent of the total voting rights, or shareholders who are at least 100 in number and whose shares are paid up by an amount averaging at least 10,000 Kenya shillings (USD 100) per member, to require a resolution to be proposed at an annual general meeting (AGM). The request for a resolution to be proposed must identify the resolution, and be received by the company at least six weeks before the AGM date. Thereafter, the company is required to send a copy of the resolution to each member of the company entitled to receive notice of the AGM.[28] It is noteworthy that shareholder activism in the US got a foothold in 1942, when the US Securities and Exchange Commission (SEC) passed a rule (the predecessor to the current Rule 14a-8) which enjoined companies to include shareholders' proposals in proxy statements, and to put such proposals to a vote in the company's general meetings.[29]

At the core of any discussion about shareholder engagement is the role of voting and, more so, of proxy voting.[30] In its simplest form, it is arguably the main method by which a company's shareholders can affect its governance and signal their views to management. The Companies Act 2015 provides that the voting process starts when shareholders receive a notice of the meeting by mail, or other electronic forms, from the company.[31] The notice must state the time, date and place of the meeting.[32] It must contain information regarding the general nature of the business to be dealt with at the meeting, subject to any contrary provision in the company's by-laws.[33] Shareholders should be given fourteen to twenty-one days to consider how to vote on matters proposed in the meeting. To cast their votes, a shareholder can attend the meeting in person, or appoint one or more proxies to vote shares on their behalf.[34] The voting process ends when a shareholder's vote is recorded.

Shareholders are empowered to bring legal action against a director on behalf of the company in the form of a derivative suit. The Companies Act 2015 allows shareholders to bring a derivative action for breach of duty, including the duty to exercise reasonable care, skill and diligence, or the duty to promote the success of the company. A member who intends to bring a derivative claim must apply to the Court for permission to do so.[35] Prior to the Companies Act 2015, the common law guided derivative actions in Kenya. Under common law, one ordinarily had to fall

---

[27] Companies Act 2015, s 278.
[28] Companies Act 2015, s 313.
[29] Under Rule 14a-8 of the US Securities Exchange Act of 1934, any shareholder continuously holding shares worth $2,000 (or 1% of the market value of equity) for at least one year is allowed to include 1 (and only 1) proposal with a 500-word supporting statement in the proxy distributed by the company for its annual meeting. These proposals request a vote in favour of or against a particular issue from all shareholders, and must be submitted at least 120 days before the proxy is mailed to the shareholders. The company may ask the SEC to exclude a proposal if it violates certain conditions. Alternatively, the company may persuade the proponent to withdraw the proposal by agreeing to it (or to other concessions). Proposals that are neither excluded nor withdrawn are included in the proxy – together with a statement by the board explaining its opposition – and voted on at the annual meeting by all shareholders of record as of a given date indicated in the proxy materials.
[30] Brian R Cheffins, *Company Law: Theory, Structure and Operation* (Clarendon Press 1997) 17–18; Eilís Ferran, *Company Law and Corporate Finance* (OUP 1999) 118–22 as cited in Bo Gong, 'Understanding and Augmenting Institutional Shareholder Activism: A Comparative Study of the UK and China' (DPhil thesis, Durham University 2011).
[31] Companies Act 2015, s 282.
[32] ibid, s 285.
[33] ibid.
[34] ibid, ss 297, 298.
[35] ibid, s 238.

under the exceptions to the rule in the famous English case of *Foss v Harbottle*[36] that 'a company is a separate legal personality and the company alone is the proper Plaintiff to sue on a wrong suffered by it'. The exceptions to the rule in *Foss v Harbottle* were mainly where there was fraud on the minority caused by the majority shareholder(s). The action to be commenced also had to be in the best interest of the company, and without any ulterior motive.[37] Pursuant to the Act's provision, derivative actions by shareholders are beginning to be reported.[38]

The Companies Act 2015 requires the boards of public companies to prepare annual financial statements and publish them on their websites for easy access by shareholders.[39] Among other issues, they are also required to disclose details of their remuneration and other benefits, and obtain shareholders' approval.[40] This approach is almost similar to the say-on-pay provisions within the US Dodd Frank Act 2010.[41] Section 770 of the Companies Act 2015 requires companies to set out their corporate governance principles, policies and strategies, and annually assess the extent to which the company has observed those policies and strategies.

The Companies Act 2015 gives a mandatory list of decisions that shareholders should be permitted and encouraged to make regarding the management of the company including: appointment of directors,[42] approving director's pay,[43] approving director's long-term service contracts,[44] and appointment and removal of auditors.[45] In these cases, it is thought that the involvement of the shareholders is likely to improve the quality of corporate decisions. The debate, then, is whether, beyond this limited, mandatory list of decisions, shareholders should be permitted and encouraged to insert themselves into the management of a company and whether such engagement is likely to be fruitful.[46]

23.2.3 *The Code for Corporate Governance Practices 2015*

The Corporate Governance Code sets out the principles and specific recommendations on structures and processes which publicly listed companies should adopt in making good corporate governance an integral part of their business dealings and culture.[47] The Code advocates for the adoption of standards that go beyond the minimum prescribed by legislation. It adopts an 'apply or explain' approach which is principle-based rather than rule-based.[48] This approach requires boards to fully disclose and explain any non-compliance to their shareholders and the CMA in their annual reports and AGMs.[49] The reasoning behind this approach is to allow

---

[36] (1843) 2 Hare 461.
[37] See *Nurcombe v Nurcombe* [1985] 1 All ER 65.
[38] See *Isaiah Waweru Ngumi & 2 Others v Muturi Ndungu* [2016] eKLR; *Ghelani Metals Limited & 3 others v Elesh Ghelani Natwarlal & another* [2017] eKLR.
[39] Companies Act 2015, ss 635, 650.
[40] ibid, ss 281, 650, 659.
[41] Dodd-Frank Wall Street Reform and Consumer Protection Act, Pub L No 111-203, 124 Stat 1376 (2010) § 951. One of the provisions of the Act mandates that publicly traded firms must let shareholders have an up-or-down non-binding vote on executive pay, known as a 'say on pay' vote, at least once every three years (the SEC has the authority to exempt firms based on size or other criteria). At their first meeting, firms must let shareholders vote on whether to hold the say-on-pay vote every one, two or three years. The Act also requires institutional investors to disclose how they voted their shares on say-on-pay.
[42] Companies Act 2015, s 132.
[43] ibid, s 682.
[44] ibid, s 157.
[45] ibid, ss 721(5) 739.
[46] See Davies, The UK Stewardship Code 2010–2020, Chapter 2.
[47] Corporate Governance Code (n 2); CMA (n 2), speech by Paul Muthaura.
[48] ibid.
[49] ibid.

shareholders to enforce governance standards on the belief that they have incentives to maximize their investment, and that they want companies they invest in to be successful.[50]

The Corporate Governance Code prescribes principles for board operations and control relating to the appointment, composition, size, qualifications and remuneration of board members. It includes the rights of shareholders, stakeholder relations, ethics and social responsibility, accountability, risk management and internal control, and transparency and disclosure.[51] In recognition of the fact that the single most important institution in corporate governance is the board, shareholders are urged to ensure that only credible people who can add value to the company's business are elected to boards during general meetings.[52] The Corporate Governance Code requires boards to establish and implement a system that provides necessary information to shareholders, and to take into consideration the interests of shareholders in decision-making.[53]

The board is required to disclose its remuneration policies and procedures in the annual report. Interestingly, the Corporate Governance Code prescribes that executive directors' remuneration packages should include an element that is linked to corporate performance, including share option schemes, to ensure the maximization of the shareholders' value. The remuneration package should also be appropriately disclosed.[54] At first blush, review of the public disclosures of the executives' remuneration packages reveals that actual reality seems to deviate from the Code's prescription. The disclosures reveal how dismally performing companies are paying their executives excessive packages, notwithstanding poor returns. Some have been paying their executives sums equivalent to more than half their net earnings.[55] As one would expect, these disclosures are raising eyebrows and spurring debate among the companies' shareholders and asset owners, who have begun asking questions and demanding a change in governance.[56]

On shareholders' rights, in compliance with the Companies Act 2015, the Corporate Governance Code prescribes that the board has to recognize, respect and protect the rights of shareholders and facilitate the effective exercise of those rights.[57] Shareholders should receive relevant information on the company's performance through distribution of annual reports and accounts, and half-yearly results as a matter of best practice. The reports are to be available across

---

[50] Iain MacNeil and Xiao Li, '"Comply or Explain": Market Discipline and Non-compliance with the Combined Code' (2006) 14 *Corporate Governance: An International Review* 486.
[51] Corporate Governance Code (n 2) s 2.1.
[52] ibid.
[53] ibid, s 2.3.2.
[54] ibid, s 2.9.
[55] See Victor Juma, 'Revealed: Kenya's List of Most Expensive CEOs' *Business Daily Africa* (Nairobi, 2 July 2018) <www.businessdailyafrica.com/corporate/companies/Kenya-s-list-of-most-expensive-CEOs/4003102-4642004-355ywb/index.html> accessed 5 June 2020, which pointed out that the CEO of the publicly listed company Sameer Africa, Allan Walmsley, was paid Sh 25.9 million or nearly twice the tyre distributor's net earnings of Sh 13 million in the year ending in December 2017. Sanlam's former chief executive Mugo Kibati pocketed Sh 53.6 million, a figure that was marginally higher than the insurer's net profit of Sh 53 million in the same period. BOC Kenya's former CEO Millicent Onyonyi was paid Sh 28.9 million, which was 73% of the gas manufacturer's net profit of Sh 39.3 million. See also Charles Mwaniki, 'Collymore's Sh196m Pay Shines a Light on Co-op, KCB' *Business Daily Africa* (Nairobi, 8 August 2018) <www.businessdailyafrica.com/corporate/companies/Collymore-s-Sh196m-pay-shines-a-light-on-Co-op–KCB/4003102-4703060-vtwj1fz/index.html> accessed 5 June 2020; Macharia Kamau, 'Report: Safaricom Paid CEO Eye-Watering Sh16m Monthly' *The Standard* (Nairobi, 8 August 2018) <www.standardmedia.co.ke/business/article/2001291076/safaricom-paid-ceo-eye-watering-sh16m-monthly> accessed 5 June 2020.
[56] Constant Munda, '15 NSE Firms Issue Alerts as Profits Plunge Sh14bn' *Business Daily Africa* (Nairobi, 1 April 2019) 1 <www.businessdailyafrica.com/news/15-NSE-firms-issue-alerts-as-profits/539546-5050954-5srqoq/index.html> accessed 5 June 2020.
[57] Corporate Governance Code (n 2) s 3.1.

multiple communication channels suitable to shareholders' different media consumption habits. These include websites, postal mail and newspapers.[58] Every shareholder has a right to participate and vote at the general shareholders' meetings, including the elections of directors.[59]

The board is required to ensure that the right of shareholders to full participation at AGMs is protected by giving them sufficient information on each subject to be discussed at the AGM. Information must also be provided on the voting rules or procedures and proxy models with different voting options. Shareholders should be given an opportunity to question the management. They must also be given an opportunity to place items on the agenda, the opportunity to vote in absentia, and sufficient information to enable them to consider the costs and benefits of their votes.[60]

The Corporate Governance Code encourages companies, as a matter of best practice, to organize regular investor briefings, particularly when the half-yearly and annual results are declared, or as may be necessary to explain their performance, and promote interaction with investors.[61] Investor briefings have been a key feature of most publicly listed companies. The boards of listed companies are to encourage establishment and use of the company's website by shareholders, so as to speed up communication and interaction among shareholders and the company.[62] This should make it easier for shareholders to find information about the listed companies, and share that information with other investors. The board is required to ensure that minority shareholders are protected from any adverse actions by the controlling shareholders, and that they have an effective means of redress.[63]

The Corporate Governance Code requires institutional investors under the jurisdiction of the CMA to have transparent, honest and fair practices in their dealings with the companies in which they invest. The Code goes ahead to recommend that institutional investors should take up the role of stewardship as the representatives of their clients or investors in listed companies and other approved products through their organizations. Particularly, it encourages institutional investors to make direct contact with the company's management and board, to discuss performance and corporate governance matters, as well as to vote during the AGMs.[64] In order to facilitate the implementation of these recommendations, the CMA developed the Kenya Code, to ensure that institutional investors deliberately engage the boards and management of listed companies.[65]

The information provided here shows that the basic statutory and regulatory ingredients of shareholders' engagement are in place. There is a relative critical mass of issuers and investors. Further, in some ways, the relatively small number of issuers may allow for a more manageable approach to institutional investor engagement with companies they invest in, when compared with larger markets with a large number of investee companies.[66]

23.2.4 Stewardship Code for Institutional Investors 2017

As already stated, in 2017 the CMA issued the Stewardship Code for Institutional Investors. The Kenya Code was developed by a special committee appointed by the CMA board in February 2015, known as the Capital Markets Stewardship Code Committee (Committee).

---

[58] ibid.
[59] ibid, s 3.1.1 (e) and (f).
[60] ibid.
[61] ibid, s 3.1.1 (m).
[62] ibid, s 3.1.1 (n).
[63] ibid, s 3.2.
[64] ibid, s 3.3.
[65] CMA (n 24), speech by Paul Muthaura.
[66] World Bank Group (n 5).

The Committee comprised eight members representing various institutional and capital markets players, namely: listed companies, the National Treasury, the Association of Retirement Benefit Schemes, the Fund Managers Association, the Association of Kenya Insurers, the Insurance Regulatory Authority, the Actuarial Society of Kenya and the National Social Security Fund. The Committee was facilitated by consultants from the World Bank Group.[67]

The main aim of the Kenya Code is to encourage the institutional investment community to take action to serve as responsible stewards for their beneficiaries.[68] This should help in promoting good corporate governance and the sustainable success of listed companies in the capital markets. The Kenya Code seeks to reinforce the implementation of the Corporate Governance Code, to ensure that listed companies adhere to the corporate governance requirements.[69]

The Kenya Code plays a critical role in providing a market-based system for institutional investors to hold issuers to account for their corporate governance practices. It applies to asset owners and asset managers investing in the debt and equity companies listed in the securities exchange.[70] The asset owners and managers are required to either apply the principles of the Kenya Code in their investment practices or explain why specific aspects of the provisions may not have been adhered to. This statement is to be displayed publicly on the institutional investors' own websites, and the CMA's. Its primary focus is on domestic investors domiciled in Kenya. However, overseas institutional investors are also encouraged to become signatories to the Kenya Code.[71]

The Kenya Code defines stewardship as being responsible management and oversight of assets for the benefit of the institutional investors' ultimate beneficiaries or clients.[72] The Kenya Code defines institutional investors as asset owners and asset managers with equity and debt holdings in public listed companies. It defines asset owners as collective investment vehicles which collect funds on behalf of their beneficiaries or clients and manage them internally or externally. They include pension funds, private pension scheme providers, insurance companies, takaful operators and investment trusts.[73] The Capital Markets Regulations on collective investment schemes govern the operations of the schemes.[74] Asset managers are defined as agents of asset owners who provide fund management and other investment services to asset owners on a commercial basis. This is pursuant to an investment management agreement or the governing documents of individual investment funds, and they often act as stewards and nominees of asset owners.[75] There are currently twenty-five fund managers, sixteen investment banks and fourteen investment advisers licensed to operate by the CMA.[76]

---

[67] Capital Markets Authority, 'Stewardship Code for Institutional Investors Exposed' (6 August 2015) <www.cma.or.ke/index.php/news-publications/press-center/353-stewardship-code-for-institutional-investors-exposed> accessed 11 February 2022. The Capital Markets (Foreign Investors) Regulations, Legal Notice No 28 of 2008 defines an 'institutional investor' as a body corporate including a financial institution, collective investment scheme, fund manager, dealer or other body corporate whose ordinary business includes the management or investment of funds whether as principal or on behalf of clients.

[68] Kenya Code (n 1) 3.

[69] ibid.

[70] ibid.

[71] ibid.

[72] Kenya Code (n 1) 2.

[73] ibid 2.

[74] The Capital Markets (Collective Investment Schemes) Regulations 2001, which was enacted on 28 December 2001 (Capital Markets Authority, 'Regulations' <www.cma.or.ke/index.php/regulatory-frame-work/regulations> accessed 11 February 2022).

[75] Kenya Code (n 1) 2.

[76] Capital Markets Authority, 'List of Licensees' (n 19).

The Kenya Code applies to institutional investors on an 'apply or explain' basis. It defines 'apply or explain' to mean that the principles and best practices in the Kenya Code shall be applied by institutional investors, and an explanation must be given for any departure or non-adherence.[77]

The author emailed the CMA's Directorate of Market Operations to inquire as to why the Kenya Code is anchored and grounded on the principle of 'apply or explain' rather than the rule-based 'comply or explain', which is basically a continuous improvement approach. The approach assumes that entities will apply the Kenya Code's principles and requires them to explain how they achieve this. The intention here is to move beyond the 'tick-the-box' comply or explain approach, and to describe how the implemented practices achieve the intent of the principles and to demonstrate the outcomes.[78] The author was also informed that the rationale behind the approach is for the provisions to allow for a great deal of flexibility, including demonstrating the application of the spirit of the Kenya Code.[79] There is a mix of mandatory and voluntary provisions, as well as incentives given to institutional investors who do not fully comply, to encourage them to commit and move towards the full application of the Kenya Code. For example, it is mandatory for institutional investors to develop and disclose their policies on stewardship and responsible investments, and the Code also makes it mandatory for them to develop voting guidelines. 'Apply or explain' requires the institutional investor to apply all the provisions of the Kenya Code, to explain their basis for indicating that they have applied the same and to explain any non-application by providing satisfactory reasons for it, as well as timelines to the full application of the Kenya Code.[80]

The Kenya Code is premised on seven core principles, which involve: stewardship or responsible investment policies; monitoring of companies held in investment portfolios; active and informed voting practices; engagement, escalation and collaboration with other institutional investors; conflicts of interest; focus on sustainability issues, including environmental, social and ethical factors; and public disclosures and client reporting.[81] These principles are substantially similar to those in the 2010 and 2012 UK Stewardship Codes.

Principle 1, on stewardship or responsible investment policies, requires an institutional investor to develop and disclose publicly a policy on how they approach stewardship or responsible investment.[82] The stewardship policies should include their approach to stewardship in investment analysis, including the integration of environmental, social and governance (ESG) factors, voting at shareholders' meetings, engagement with listed companies, managing conflicts of interest, and client or beneficiary reporting.[83] The core conflict of interest arises when institutional investors are unwilling to actively engage and hold the board and management of investee companies accountable because they fear losing corporate business. For example, the investee company can retaliate by withholding business when investment managers vote against management's proposals. This may be enough to make investment houses hesitant about embracing stewardship.[84]

---

[77] Kenya Code (n 1) definitions section.
[78] Ng Siew Quan, 'Comply or Explain 2.0: What's the Difference?' *The Business Times* (10 August 2018) <www.businesstimes.com.sg/hub/boardroom-matters/comply-or-explain-20-what%E2%80%99s-the-difference> accessed 5 June 2020.
[79] See World Bank Group (n 5).
[80] CMA (n 2), speech by Paul Muthaura.
[81] Kenya Code (n 1) 3–4.
[82] ibid, s 1.2.
[83] ibid.
[84] Simon Wong, 'How Conflicts of Interest Thwart Institutional Investor Stewardship' (September 2011) *Butterworths Journal of International Banking and Financial Law* 481 <https://ssrn.com/abstract=1925485> accessed 5 June 2020.

Principle 2 concerns the monitoring of companies held in investment portfolios.[85] Institutional investors are required to actively monitor the strategy, risk, performance, governance and other factors that influence sustainable long-term success of the firms they invest in. In monitoring companies held in their portfolios, institutional investors are to hold regular meetings with the companies' management and directors, to discuss financial, strategic and governance matters. They are to develop an understanding of companies' governance practices, and the extent to which they support minority investor interests. This means that they need to monitor the firms' compliance with governance codes and to assess the quality of explanations for non-compliance.[86]

Principle 3 is on active and informed voting guidelines and practices.[87] It requires institutional investors to develop responsible voting guidelines to allow them to vote their equity positions diligently, and in a way that supports good corporate governance practices. These guidelines provide guidance to institutional investors for identifying the types of governance practices that may justify voting for or against a management resolution. The specific guidelines may reflect how negative voting activity could be triggered in shareholder meeting resolutions relating to director elections, appointing the company auditor, approval of financial statements, approval of director remuneration, or other corporate actions. Institutional investors should be prepared to vote against management resolutions, or abstain when such resolutions conflict with the guidelines or good corporate governance practices. The reasoning behind any resolutions they do not support should also be communicated to the company. Public disclosure of the institutional investor's voting record should be a standard feature of reporting to clients.[88]

Principle 4 of the Kenya Code requires institutional investors to engage with companies to build dialogue and understanding.[89] They are to express concerns or exert influence in areas that give rise to a concern, which may include collaboration with other institutional investors as well as an escalation of engagement if concerns regarding the company persist. This engagement may take many forms, such as face-to-face meetings, letters, emails or telephone conversations with the firm. Institutional investors can collaborate when it is the most effective or efficient way to engage with firms. Institutional investors can make use of institutional investor associations to facilitate collective engagement. In collective meetings with management outside of the annual general meeting, institutional investors should not seek information that gives them an advantage over other investors.[90]

Principle 5 directs institutional investors to avoid or minimize conflicts of interest.[91] They are to have an effective process in place for identifying and managing conflicts that might interfere with their obligations to act in the interest of clients or beneficiaries. Particular care should be taken in voting and engagement activity where the institutional investor is an interested party, such as investment holdings in related companies held in clients' portfolios (such as corporate pension fund clients).[92]

Principle 6 requires institutional investors to act responsibly in promoting sustainable markets and societies, and to put into consideration environmental, social and ethical issues in their

---

[85] Kenya Code (n 1) ss 2.2, 2.4.
[86] ibid.
[87] ibid, 5.
[88] ibid, ss 3.1, 3.2, 3.5, 3.6.
[89] ibid, 7.
[90] ibid, ss 4.1, 4.2, 4.8, 4.9.
[91] ibid, s 5.5.
[92] ibid.

investment process.[93] Institutional investors need to call for ethical and responsible conduct by listed firms as a component of their engagement activity.[94]

Principle 7 requires institutional investors annually to publicly disclose their policies and activities relating to stewardship on their website and on the CMA's website.[95]

The Kenya Code urges asset owners to publicly support it by becoming signatories. Asset owners are to establish compliance with the Kenya Code as a component of asset management mandates. Further, they are urged to call for asset managers to consider sustainability, environmental, social and ethical issues, both as an aspect of risk assessment and as part of responsible investment. In doing so, they are required to show diligence in overseeing that asset managers take on these tasks, and call for disclosures and reporting from asset managers regarding stewardship performance, and not just financial performance reports.[96]

The Kenya Code requires listed companies to provide an opportunity for institutional investors to engage with both company executive management and board members when relevant to governance concerns.[97] They shall engage with institutional investors who may oppose or challenge corporate actions or resolutions at shareholder meetings; establish an investor relations function; and provide sufficient disclosure about governance and sustainability performance to provide hooks for institutional investor dialogue. Additionally, listed companies shall encourage corporate pension funds to consider stewardship responsibilities as asset owners.[98]

Promulgation of the Kenya Code is a step in the right direction because institutional investors at times have more bargaining power and expertise to step in and monitor managerial behaviour when compared to the asset owners and ultimate beneficiaries. As explained earlier in this chapter, the size of the holdings of institutional investors in Kenya can imply that they occupy a position which grants them the luxury of considerable power in terms of voting strength. They are in a position to wield a great deal of influence over the board of directors by conveying their displeasure over certain activities to the board. Further, it is arguable that the allure of exercising the 'exit' option with larger shareholdings is considerably diminished, unless they voluntarily opt to sell their shares at prices lower than those that are prevalent in the market.[99] In such a scenario, engagement becomes a less costly option than 'exit'.[100] Once the option of easy liquidity is unavailable, the long-term interests of the company automatically synchronize with the interests of the institutional shareholder.[101]

However, it is also arguable that although the potential flight of institutional investors acts as an incentive for the board to behave well, the role of institutions as shareholders does not reconcile with their role as stewards. As investors, institutional investors have the role of seeking maximum return for their asset owners, and therefore need to move around in search of the best opportunities with the highest returns. The expectation that institutional investors will hang around a company long enough to act as a control mechanism on the company's management is open to question.[102]

---

[93] ibid, 8.
[94] ibid.
[95] ibid, 9.
[96] ibid, 10, see Responsibilities of Assets Owners.
[97] ibid, 11, see Responsibilities of Listed Companies.
[98] ibid.
[99] Iragavarapu Sridhar, 'Corporate Governance and Shareholder Activism in India – Theoretical Perspective' (2016) 6 *Theoretical Economics Letters* 731–41.
[100] John Hendry and others, 'Responsible Ownership, Shareholder Value and the New Shareholder Activism' (2007) 11 *Competition & Change* 223, 232.
[101] Sridhar (n 99).
[102] Lois Musikali, 'The Law Affecting Corporate Governance in Kenya: A Need for Review' (2008) 19 *International Company and Commercial Law Review* 213, 217.

23.3 IMPACT OF THE KENYAN STEWARDSHIP CODE

Three years after the issuance of the Kenya Code, none of the twenty-five licensed fund managers, institutional investors or asset owners have signed up to it. This raises the question of why there has not been any support from the institutional investors, and what should be done to increase their buy-in.

Further, not much institutional investor engagement with investee companies has been reported.[103] It has been observed that even in companies with significant individual shareholders, the shareholders are not that sophisticated in terms of appreciating the need to attend AGMs and exercise their rights as shareholders of the company.[104] Classically, how AGMs in Kenya and the larger East African region are conducted has aptly been described thus:[105]

> ... 10 minutes to the start, the board is whisked in and head straight to the stage. The meeting commences with the formal proceedings and voting followed by brief remarks from the chief executive and chairperson. After 4 minutes of shareholder feedback and questions, the meeting ends. Five minutes for handshakes. Exit CEO and chairperson. Lunch is served. See you next year. At face value this would pass as a well-run AGM. The board is happy with the level of engagement. On the other side, the minority shareholders, who seem to be the only investors with time to attend these meetings, are satisfied with the dividend announcement and free merchandise; and if either were unsatisfactory, well, there's always next year.

After three Kenyan banks went into receivership, the governor of the Central Bank of Kenya stated that the collapse of the banks could have been averted had the banks' shareholders interrogated and had serious discussion about the numbers presented in their annual reports, instead of only demanding small gifts such as umbrellas, baseball caps and, lately, power banks, during AGMs.[106]

Among the reasons for lack of shareholder engagement and activism is the perception that shareholders' efforts will not bring about any change or compliance with corporate governance principles.[107] Institutional investors are mostly uninterested in engaging in time-consuming and lengthy discussions with investee companies; they prefer to just alternate their portfolio investments.[108] The growing trend towards diversification of portfolios in order to mitigate market risk is a counter-indicator of the proximity that should exist between investors and companies, since it becomes an issue for either the institutional investors or their fund managers

---

[103] Jacob Gakeri, 'Enhancing Kenya's Securities Markets through Corporate Governance: Challenges and Opportunities' (March 2013) 3 *International Journal of Humanities and Social Science* 94, 114. Gakeri argues that shareholder engagement or activism is virtually non-existent in Kenya and East Africa in general.

[104] Musikali (n 102).

[105] Nuru Mugambi, 'Why Firms Should Encourage Investor Activism at AGMs' *Business Daily Africa* (Nairobi, 27 September 2015) <www.businessdailyafrica.com/analysis/539548-2887600-h0vf3z/index.html> accessed 5 June 2020.

[106] Kimathi Njoka, 'Dawning of the Age of Shareholder Activism' *The East African* (Nairobi, 20 December 2004) <https://allafrica.com/stories/200412210673.html> accessed 5 June 2020; Moses Michira, 'Central Bank of Kenya Governor Mocks Investors' Appetite for Caps and Power-Banks' *The Standard* (Nairobi, 18 April 2016) <www.standardmedia.co.ke/business/article/2000198627/central-bank-of-kenya-governor-mocks-investors-appetite-for-caps-and-power-banks> accessed 5 June 2020. The late Abdulmalek Janmohamed, a former director of Imperial Bank of Kenya, which is under receivership by the Kenya Deposit Insurance Corporation, is alleged to have run a USD 34 million embezzlement scheme at the bank for more than thirteen years – which led to the bank's ultimate collapse.

[107] Irene-marie Esser and Michele Havenga, 'Shareholder Participation in Corporate Governance' (2008) *Speculum Juris* 74.

[108] Konstantinos Sergakis, 'The UK Stewardship Code: Bridging the Gap between Companies and Institutional Investors' (15 June 2013) 47 *Revue juridique Thémis de l'Université de Montreal* 109.

to maintain beneficial contact with every single investee company, especially when many others might be included in the same portfolio.[109]

Monitoring the strategies and activities of investee companies, as well as engaging in a dialogue in order to draw managers' attention to crucial governance and performance issues, thus becomes quite onerous or even unrealistic in current investment strategies. Shareholders are not very interested in engaging in such activities since they know that the 'exit' possibility is a quicker and – in their perception – safer method of managing their portfolios. However, concentrating on a reduced number of holdings would be preferable since it would allow asset owners and managers to better engage investee companies.[110]

In Kenya, generally when performance or company behaviour does not align with shareholders' interests, shareholders (including institutional investors) have tended to stay loyal and passive.[111] Shareholders are normally indifferent and do not see a company's under-performance as being their problem to complain about, as investing in stocks is seen as a gamble. A lack of good returns from investment is seen as a 'bad investment' in the wrong company, as opposed to poor firm performance the emphasis being on the shareholder for not being lucky as opposed to managerial ineffectiveness.[112] This view might be informed by the fact that the concept of shareholder engagement and activism in Kenya is not as popular as it is in the US and other developed economies.[113] Or it may be that much of the engagement happens behind the scenes through direct discussions with the management of investee companies, and is thus not reported.

The passiveness can also be attributed to the common free rider problem that stems from the fact that, by monitoring companies, institutional investors provide a public good at a private cost.[114] Monitoring by institutional shareholders typically involves identifying companies whose actions are in conflict with shareholders' interests, and attempting to bring about change through negotiation with management, proxy fights, and involvement in the selection of board members.[115] If institutional investors do expend their resources in monitoring their portfolio companies and ensuring good corporate governance, the cost of doing so would have to be incurred by the activist institution, while the benefits will accrue to other shareholders, including competitors of the activist, who have not shouldered any of the burden.[116]

Additionally, short-term relative metrics, which are the norm in the investment management industry, also discourage the development of a long-term stewardship view.[117] Some commentators have argued that short-termism goes along with investor apathy since, in the presence of immediate targets, investors tend to pay less attention to the general corporate strategy for the future, the company's management philosophy, and the exercise of their voting rights. As they concentrate on short-term profits, they exercise a form of trading activeness, which is the exact opposite of shareholder engagement, which would entail a greater involvement in corporate

---

[109] ibid.
[110] ibid.
[111] See Njoka (n 106); Rufus Mwanyasi, 'Activism Now Needed to Shake Up Sleeping Boards of NSE Firms' *Business Daily Africa* (Nairobi, 5 April 2016) <www.businessdailyafrica.com/analysis/shake-up-sleeping-boards-of-NSE-firms/539548-3147194-5197vqz/index.html> accessed 5 June 2020.
[112] Musikali (n 102).
[113] Esser and Havenga (n 107).
[114] Anat R Admati, Paul Pfleiderer and Josef Zechner, 'Large Shareholder Activism, Risk Sharing, and Financial Market Equilibrium' (December 1994) 102 *Journal of Political Economy* 1097.
[115] ibid.
[116] Sridhar (n 99).
[117] See John Kay, 'The Kay Review of UK Equity Markets and Long-Term Decision Making' (Department for Business, Innovation and Skills, July 2012) <https://assets.publishing.service.gov.uk/government/uploads/system/uploads/attachment_data/file/253454/bis-12-917-kay-review-of-equity-markets-final-report.pdf> accessed 5 June 2020.

affairs, since they ignore the priority of the change in the corporate strategy, and exclusively favour the meeting of a specific set of targets.[118]

This could result in damage suffered by investee companies; as evidenced by an empirical study conducted by Admati, Pfleiderer and Zechner in 2014.[119] The study revealed that nearly two-thirds of companies (65%) agree or strongly agree that a company whose shareholder base is dominated by short-term investors cannot focus on strategic decisions because of a focus on short-term results. Just over half (51%) believe that short-term investors lead a company to focus on cost-cutting, while the majority of companies (57%) agree or strongly agree that a company whose shareholder base is dominated by short-term investors will have reduced market value and/or reduced long-term growth. The empirical study shows that investor horizons matter for engagement. Long-term investors intervene more intensively than short-term investors, and engagements are primarily triggered by concerns about a firm's corporate governance or strategy, rather than about short-term issues.[120]

However, although improved investor practices, particularly as regards to voting and engagement activity, have been demonstrated in many of the markets that have adopted a stewardship code, there is no long track record, and thus there is limited evidence to suggest a clear linkage between stewardship codes and financial outcomes. Thus, while progress is being made, the stewardship idea remains relatively untested in terms of measurable effects.[121]

It is noteworthy that many of the stewardship codes that now operate around the world, including the Kenya Code, are based on the 2010 and 2012 UK Stewardship Code, and it may be that the well-articulated challenges of legal transplants might have played a factor in its implementation and impact owing to the intriguing differences in jurisdictions.[122] In particular, it can be seen that the frequent company law reforms in developing countries tend to add new forms of shareholder protection to existing ones. However, law reform and institutional change often do not lead to 'replacement' (or 'displacement') but to the 'layering' of rules from various backgrounds.[123] It has been suggested that 'law-in-books' and 'law-in-action' diverge, sometimes considerably.[124] A likely explanation for this gap between law-in-books and law-in-action is that copying legal rules is easier than implementing them in the absence of an effective judiciary, trustworthy legal and administrative infrastructure, and efficient political and economic institutions. Another explanation may be derived from the 'law matters' hypothesis.[125] From this standpoint, the Kenya Code might be applied and embraced fully in developed countries like the UK, Denmark and the Netherlands because their advanced legal system better promotes financial sector development as compared to in a country like Kenya, whose judiciary is still not effective and whose political and economic institutions are not efficient.[126] This finding is

---

[118] Sergakis (n 108).
[119] Admati, Pfleiderer and Zechner (n 114).
[120] ibid; Petrina Tan, 'Institutional Investor Stewardship in the UK and Malaysia: Functionally Similar, Contextually Different' (18 December 2018) NUS Law Working Paper No 2018/032 <https://ssrn.com/abstract=3302969> accessed 5 June 2020; Joseph McCahery, Zacharias Sautner and Laura Starks, 'Behind the Scenes: The Corporate Governance Preferences of Institutional Investors' (2016) 71 *Journal of Finance* 2905, 2929.
[121] Dionysia Katelouzou and Mathias Siems, 'Disappearing Paradigms in Shareholder Protection: Leximetric Evidence for 30 Countries, 1990–2013' (2015) 15 *Journal of Corporate Law Studies* 127.
[122] Jennifer G Hill, 'Good Activist/Bad Activist: The Rise of International Stewardship Codes' (2018) 41 *Seattle University Law Review* 497.
[123] Katelouzou and Siems (n 121).
[124] ibid.
[125] ibid.
[126] ibid. See David Maraga, 'Statement by Chief Justice David Maraga on Judiciary Budget Cuts' (4 November 2019) <www.judiciary.go.ke/statement-by-chief-justice-david-maraga-on-judiciary-budget-cuts/> accessed 5 June 2020; David Maraga, 'Chief Justice: There Are Deliberate Attempts to Undermine Judiciary' *The Standard*

consistent with the claim that for corporate law to play a facilitative function, it must be combined with other legal, market and cultural control mechanisms which are often absent in developing countries.[127]

In the most simplistic scenario, identical legal rules should ideally lead to largely similar outcomes. However, even when law is transplanted, the law cannot necessarily precede the development of a country's enterprise or financial sector.[128] Structural differences in the ownership concentration of firms, the quality of the banking sector, the existence or absence of stock markets, and the extent to which the state controls the financial sector, either directly as an owner or indirectly through regulation and case-by-case interventions, can create conditions that put developing countries like Kenya and a developed country like the UK on different development paths; this is not easily altered by changing the laws on the books.[129] Further, as Bebchuk and Roe posit, social forces and structures such as a jurisdiction's history, politics and ownership structures play a key role in whether a transplanted legal rule will be effective.[130]

In response to the author's email enquiry to the CMA as to why none of the institutional investors or asset owners had signed up to the Kenya Code, the author was informed that the CMA has been sensitizing them on the Code and their responsibilities through public forums such as conferences and meetings. Despite none of them signing up, during a meeting between the CMA and institutional investors and asset owners, the CMA noted their interest in implementing the Kenya Code and taking up their responsibilities. As a mechanism for enhancing awareness of the code, the CMA is planning to officially relaunch the Kenya Code within this financial year – despite the Kenya Code having been operational since 23 June 2017. The efficacy of this is thus debatable, and may simply end up being another event without actual impact. The CMA intends to develop proposals to encourage potential signatories to sign up, and develop appropriate guidelines to enable institutional investors to implement and report on their level of application. Further, the author was informed that the CMA does not have a targeted assessment of the impact of the Kenya Code. After the (re)launch of the Kenya Code, the CMA will be conducting periodic assessments on its impact in the market.

23.4 CONCLUSION

As this chapter has shown, the requisite statutory and regulatory ingredients for shareholders' engagement and, more so, institutional investors' engagement are present in Kenya just like in the UK. Even if it were clear that institutional shareholders have capacity to engage beyond reactive voting, there is a further question about the strength of their financial incentives to engage. The financial incentives relate to the immediate value of the fund and the remuneration of asset managers. Further, even in the absence of immediate financial benefit, institutional investors might have a reputational incentive to engage with the companies.[131]

(6 November 2019) <www.standardmedia.co.ke/article/2001348235/chief-justice-there-are-deliberate-attempts-to-undermine-judiciary> accessed 5 June 2020; International Commission of Jurists, 'ICJ Kenya Condemns Attempts to Undermine the Judiciary' (2017) <https://icj-kenya.org/news/icj-kenya-condemns-attempts-to-undermine-the-independence-of-the-judiciary/> accessed 11 February 2022.

[127] Katelouzou and Siems (n 121).
[128] ibid.
[129] Katharina Pistor, 'Patterns of Legal Change: Shareholder and Creditor Rights in Transition Economies' (2000) 1 *European Business Organization Law Review* 59.
[130] Lucian Bebchuk and Mark Roe, 'A Theory of Path Dependence in Corporate Ownership and Governance' (1999) 52 *Stanford Law Review* 127.
[131] See Davies, The UK Stewardship Code 2010–2020, Chapter 2.

But institutional investor engagement is virtually non-existent in Kenya. It is the role of institutional investors to offer oversight of management of companies, although not to the extent of micro-managing or 'second guessing' said management. The corporate law concept of separation of ownership and control relies on the appointment and performance of high-quality directors who enjoy substantial autonomy in discharging their obligations without need for detailed oversight by owners of the company, at any rate in 'normal' situations.[132]

Further, as this chapter has demonstrated, for investor stewardship to succeed, it requires willingness and good faith on the part of listed companies, asset owners and institutional investors. This is relatively easy to prescribe, but much more difficult to achieve, particularly to the extent that it may introduce new requirements and costs. The greatest challenge is that, while processes and disclosures can be required by regulation, it is impossible to regulate 'willingness'.[133]

Therefore, although it is still too early to make a call on the impact of the Kenya Code, more needs to be done to ensure that the existing level of shareholder apathy and passiveness is eliminated. The UK Financial Reporting Council, in its January 2015 report on the UK Code, noted that a culture of stewardship 'may take time', and acknowledged the need for a more robust evidence base as to its impact.[134]

---

[132] David Walker, 'A Review of Corporate Governance in UK Banks and Other Financial Industry Entities: Final Recommendations' (26 November 2009) para 5.30 <https://ecgi.global/sites/default/files/codes/documents/walker_review_261109.pdf> accessed 7 May 2020. See also the marvellously incomplete statement in UK Code 2012 (n 3) at p 1: 'In publicly listed companies responsibility for stewardship is shared. The primary responsibility rests with the board of the company, which oversees the actions of its management. Investors in the company also play an important role in holding the board to account for the fulfilment of its responsibilities.'

[133] World Bank Group (n 5).

[134] Financial Reporting Council, 'Developments in Corporate Governance and Stewardship 2014' (January 2015) <www.frc.org.uk/getattachment/6f0a7c78-abd2-4480-bf6f-188e02b06a9c/Developments-in-Corporate-Governance-and-Stewardship-2014.pdf> accessed 5 June 2020.

24

The Brazilian Stewardship Framework

Bruno Bastos Becker, Rafael Andrade and Viviane Muller Prado

24.1 INTRODUCTION

Investment funds and pension funds are the most important types of domestic institutional investor in Brazil.[1] The Brazilian investment funds industry experienced accelerated growth in size and relevance in the recent decades: the number of funds increased by more than 400 per cent in the last twenty years,[2] and in June 2019 the total amount of assets under the management of the investment funds industry represented approximately 74 per cent of Brazil's gross domestic product (GDP) in 2018.[3] Brazil is also currently the country with the most regulated investment funds in the world.[4] Further, domestic public and private pension funds managed assets accounting for 13.4 per cent of Brazil's GDP in 2018,[5] covering almost 7.5 million people[6] – 3 per cent of the Brazilian population.[7]

At first glance, these figures suggest the importance of institutional investors in Brazil's economy. However, the role played by these investors in the Brazilian capital markets is still limited. On one hand, domestic investment and pension funds have historically invested in fixed-income assets – the majority of which are public bonds – with only a small share in variable-income assets, like equities. In June 2019, public bonds amounted to 48 per cent of investment funds' portfolios and 74 per cent of pension funds' portfolios.[8] At the same time,

---

[1] The same applies to other Latin American countries. See OECD/International Financial Corporation, *Strengthening Latin American Corporate Governance: The Role of Institutional Investors* (2011) 35 <www.oecd-ilibrary.org/governance/strengthening-latin-american-corporate-governance_9789264116054-en> accessed 18 July 2020.

[2] The number of investment funds increased from 4,500 in December 2002 to more than 18,800 in November 2019. See the Brazilian Financial and Capital Markets Association (ANBIMA), 'Consolidado Histórico de Fundos de Investimento [Consolidated History of Investment Funds]' (November 2019) <www.anbima.com.br/data/files/71/72/5A/EA/2643F6102CEA02F6192BA2A8/Consolidado%20Historico%20de%20Fundos%20de%20Investimento_201911_valor.zip> accessed 18 July 2020.

[3] See ANBIMA, 'Indústria de fundos alcança R$ 5 trilhões de patrimônio líquido [Fund Industry Reaches R$ 5 Trillion in Net Worth]' (ANBIMA News, 18 June 2019) <www.anbima.com.br/pt_br/noticias/industria-de-fundos-alcanca-r-5-trilhoes-de-patrimonio-liquido.htm> accessed 18 July 2020.

[4] Brazil had 18,388 funds at the end of the third quarter of 2019, including funds of funds. See the International Investment Funds Association (IIFA), 'Worldwide Regulated Open-End Fund Assets and Flows – Third Quarter 2020' (2020) 13 <https://cdn.ymaws.com/iifa.ca/resource/collection/8956AA40-A06F-4064-AF88-2CF48B82744E/IIFA_-_Worldwide_Open-End_Fund_Report_-_Q4_2020.pdf> accessed 4 February 2022.

[5] See the Brazilian National Association of Pension Funds (ABRAPP), 'Consolidado Estatístico [Consolidated Statistics]' (June 2019) 2 <https://www.abrapp.org.br/wp-content/uploads/2020/09/Consolidado-Estat%C3%ADstico_06_2019.pdf> accessed 4 February 2022.

[6] ibid 7; among active participants, retirees and beneficiaries.

[7] Estimates from the Brazilian Institute of Geography and Statistics (*Instituto Brasileiro de Geografia e Estatística* – IBGE) as of July 2019. See IBGE, 'Estimativas da população com referência a 1° de julho de 2019 [Population Estimates with Reference to 1 July 2019]' 1 <https://agenciadenoticias.ibge.gov.br/agencia-detalhe-de-midia.html?view=mediaibge&catid=2103&id=3097> accessed 18 July 2020.

[8] For figures for investment funds, see ANBIMA (n 3); for figures for pension funds, see ABRAPP (n 5).

investment and pension funds' shareholdings accounted for 11% and 18.2% of their portfolios, respectively.[9]

On the other hand, Brazilian companies have historically concentrated ownership among a few companies with managerial control.[10] According to the Organisation for Economic Co-operation and Development (OECD), the weighted average market value of publicly traded companies ownership is primarily held by private corporations (34%), followed by institutional investors (25%), free-float investors (20%), investors from the public sector (13%) and strategic individuals (8%).[11] As a result, institutional investors are usually minority shareholders, with a limited influence on the investee companies' corporate governance.

According to the OECD, the role of institutional investors as 'stewards' in concentrated ownership environments is mainly to 'provide an informed counterbalance to controlling shareholders, and prevent the board and management from working against the interests of the company and its shareholders as a whole'.[12] Yet, the common domestic and international perception is that the managers of investment and pension funds are not fulfilling such roles in many Latin American countries.[13]

In Brazil, the passivity of institutional investors can be seen from the almost non-existent cases of aggrieved investors trying to recover losses from publicly traded companies.[14] Furthermore, a recently published OECD report noted that 'most of the managers of Brazilian funds are far from [possessing] an activist or engaged attitude, even with regards to simple issues such as voting in general meetings'.[15] In fact, Brazilian institutional investors choose to 'vote with their feet', exiting from investments that do not fulfil their expectations.

Following an international trend and seeking to change the above-described environment by promoting a 'stewardship culture' among institutional investors,[16] Brazil had its first stewardship code launched in 2016[17] by the Brazilian Association of Capital Markets Investors (*Associação de Investidores no Mercado de Capitais* – AMEC), consisting of a set of principles detailing the fiduciary duties of institutional investors (AMEC Code). The AMEC Code was the first of its kind not only in Brazil but also in Latin America.[18]

---

[9] See ANBIMA (n 3) and ABRAPP (n 5).

[10] See Adriana De La Cruz, Alejandra Medina and Yung Tang, 'Owners of the World's Listed Companies' (OECD Capital Market Series, 17 October 2019) 12, 18, 19, 37 <www.oecd.org/corporate/owners-of-the-worlds-listed-companies.htm> accessed 18 July 2020.

[11] ibid 37; in the US and in the UK, institutional investors respectively hold 72% and 63% of the publicly traded companies weighted average market value.

[12] OECD/International Financial Corporation (n 1) 41.

[13] ibid.

[14] See Viviane M Prado, 'Não Custa Nada Mentir: Desafios para o Ressarcimento de Investidores [It Costs Nothing to Lie: Challenges for Investor Compensation]' (September 2016) <http://dx.doi.org/10.13140/RG.2.2.19418.34240> accessed 4 February 2022.

[15] See Maria H Santana, Luciana Dias and Rafael Andrade, 'Equity Market Development in Latin America: Brazil' (OECD 2019) 25 <www.oecd.org/corporate/ca/Brazil-Latin-America-Equity-Markets.pdf> accessed 18 July 2020.

[16] For details see Katelouzou and Puchniak, Global Shareholder Stewardship, Chapter 1.

[17] See Associação de Investidores no Mercado de Capitais (AMEC), 'Código AMEC de Princípios e Deveres dos Investidores Institucionais: Stewardship [AMEC Code of Principles and Duties of Institutional Investors: Stewardship]' (27 October 2016) <https://www.amecbrasil.org.br/wp-content/uploads/2016/06/CODIGOAMEC STEWARDSHIPMinutaparaConsultaPublica.pdf> accessed 4 February 2022 [hereinafter AMEC Code].

[18] The creation of the AMEC Code was justified as follows:

> The role of institutional investors cannot be separated from the fiduciary duties they assume when they become responsible for managing funds on behalf of a group of people. They are the stewards of third parties' funds. This means that they "take care" of the securities, the assets that are addressed in this AMEC Code. The

Therefore, the AMEC Code seeks to promote a more active role of institutional investors in Brazilian capital markets through a principle-based mechanism. However, a comparison between the Code's structure with the already established regulation for both investment and pension funds (which are the main targets of the Code) shows that some of the AMEC Code's principles were already previously reflected in regulatory and self-regulatory rules applicable to these institutions. The main purposes of this chapter are therefore: (i) to describe the background and rules of the AMEC Code; and (ii) to map and organize the broader 'stewardship framework' regarding such institutional investors by assessing both the public and the private rules applicable to investment and pension funds in Brazil.

The chapter proceeds as follows. Section 24.2 describes the AMEC Code's context, drafting process, content and implementation process. Section 24.3 describes Brazil's previous (and current) rules applicable to investment funds and pension funds, both issued by public authorities (i.e. regulation) and private bodies (i.e. self-regulation by associations). Section 24.4 concludes the chapter by suggesting that although the AMEC Code and other public and private rules provide stewardship-related duties for institutional investors in Brazil, there is no clear endeavour from the regulators to align their efforts to enforce these duties.

24.2 THE AMEC CODE

Founded in 2006, AMEC claims to be a forum for corporate governance debate among institutional investors in Brazil. AMEC's mission is 'to defend the rights of minority shareholders in Brazilian publicly-held companies by promoting good corporate governance practices and creating value to the companies'.[19]

AMEC's members profile reflects its focus on institutional investors' activities in publicly traded companies: there are currently sixty-one members, managing approximately USD 160 billion of capital in the Brazilian stock market.[20] Among its members are domestic (e.g. XP, Leblon Equities, and 3G Radar) and foreign (e.g. BlackRock, Franklin Templeton, Hermes, Robeco, and Aberdeen) asset managers, domestic and foreign investment branches of big retail banks (e.g. Itaú, Bradesco and Banco do Brasil, UBS, Deutsche Bank, and Santander), domestic pension funds of public and private companies (e.g. Petros and Funcesp) and even BNDES Participações S.A. (BNDESPAR), the private equity arm of the state-owned Brazilian Development Bank (*Banco Nacional de Desenvolvimento Econômico e Social* – BNDES).[21]

24.2.1 Background and Drafting Process

There is no public information on the motivation for AMEC and its members to propose a stewardship code in Brazil. Even before the launch of such a code, some stewardship-related rules were already in force through public or private regulation for both investment and pension

---

AMEC Code, comprising a set of principles and guidelines on the best ways to fulfil fiduciary duties, is necessary because of the crucial role played by the institutional investors. (see AMEC Code (n 17) 5)

[19] See AMEC, 'Profile' <https://amecbrasil.org.br/amec/profile/?lang=en> accessed 4 February 2022. In 2018, the AMEC received the 'Excellence in Corporate Governance Award' by the International Corporate Governance Network (ICGN) 'for serving as a critical voice for domestic and foreign institutional investors in the Brazilian capital markets': see ICGN, '2018 Award' (26 June 2018) <www.icgn.org/2018-award> accessed 18 July 2020.

[20] ibid.

[21] The list of AMEC's members is available at AMEC, 'Members' <https://amecbrasil.org.br/members/?lang=en> accessed 4 February 2022.

funds. Despite the presence of such rules, two scandals involving publicly listed companies in the first half of the 2010s illustrated the lack of monitoring by institutional investors in investee companies in Brazil. This is possibly one of the reasons that led AMEC to believe that a stewardship code was necessary in the Brazilian corporate landscape.

The first scandal, which saw the decline of a new group of enterprises called the 'X Group', took place between 2012 and 2013. The 'X Group' comprised six public companies.[22] In less than two years, the companies lost more than 90 per cent of their market value.[23] The second scandal, the Car Wash Operation (*Operação Lava Jato*), unveiled a major corruption scheme of the state-owned enterprise Petroleo Brasileiro S.A. (Petrobras), the largest and most traded company on the Brazilian Stock Exchange (*B3 – Brasil, Bolsa, Balcão*).[24] Petrobras suffered enormously after the beginning of the Car Wash Operation: its share price dropped, lawsuits were initiated, and the company went through a complete internal review.[25] The developments of the Car Wash Operation also implicated major domestic pension funds in the corruption scheme.[26] Both scandals affected the companies' and their investors' activities (and profits).

There was an ongoing process of consolidating corporate governance rules (previously dispersed across several documents)[27] during the same period. However, this did not focus on regulating the roles and duties of institutional investors. Therefore, there was a loophole to be filled.

At the beginning of 2015, AMEC started discussions for the creation of a stewardship code in Brazil targeting institutional investors, in particular pension funds and asset managers.[28] The drafting process had several phases and was led by a working group established in November 2015. The group first mapped and studied stewardship codes from other jurisdictions.[29] Then, these

[22] OGX (oil and gas), MPX (energy), MMX (mining), LLX (logistics), OSX (oil and gas) and CCX (mining).

[23] See 'How a Brazilian Billionaire Lost $25 Billion in 18 Months' (*CNBC*, 30 August 2013) <www.cnbc.com/id/100999661> accessed 18 July 2020.

[24] The Car Wash Operation is considered the biggest corruption scandal ever uncovered in Brazil and possibly the world. As revealed by investigators, major Brazilian contractors and Petrobras officers colluded to overbill and share among themselves Petrobras's construction projects. The profits of this scheme were split among the companies and Petrobras executives, and were also used to bribe Brazilian politicians, who used their political influence to assure the maintenance of the officers in their positions within Petrobras.

[25] For example, the company recognized an asset write-off of USD 2.1 billion directly related to the overbilling uncovered by the investigations. See Paul Kiernan, 'Brazil's Petrobras Reports Nearly $17 Billion in Asset and Corruption Charges' *The Wall Street Journal* (22 April 2015) <www.wsj.com/articles/brazils-petrobras-reports-nearly-17-billion-impairment-on-assets-corruption-1429744336> accessed 18 July 2020.

[26] See Julia Leite and Gerson Freitas Jr, 'Brazil's Biggest Pension Funds Targeted in New Fraud Probe' *Bloomberg* (6 September 2016) <www.bloomberg.com/news/articles/2016-09-05/police-target-brazil-s-four-biggest-pension-funds-in-fraud-probe> accessed 18 July 2020.

[27] There were two main corporate governance codes: (i) the Brazilian Institute of Corporate Governance (IBGC) Code of Best Practices of Corporate Governance; and (ii) the Brazilian Association of Public Companies (ABRASCA) Self-Regulatory Code of Best Practices of Corporate Governance. At the end of 2013, the main Brazilian capital market entities (e.g. ANBIMA, ABRAPP and AMEC) gathered in a work group to study and propose an agenda for corporate governance in the country. The outcome of this effort was the Brazilian Corporate Governance Code, launched in November 2016. This document is composed of principles and recommended practices for publicly listed companies in Brazil. An English version of the Brazilian Corporate Governance Code is available; see Brazilian Investor Relations Institute (IBRI), 'Brazilian Corporate Governance Code – Listed Companies' (November 2016) at <https://www.google.com/url?sa=t&rct=j&q=&esrc=s&source=web&cd=&ved=2ahUKEwinj9qZjufiAhX1FLkGHU8FBkcQFnoECAkQAQ&url=https%3A%2F%2Fecgi.global%2Fdownload%2Ffile%2Ffid%2F17257&usg=AOvVaw12qNCWf_xvagvwXFoluhuj> accessed 4 February 2022.

[28] AMEC Code (n 17) 6.

[29] The AMEC Code was mainly inspired by the UK Code 2012. However, the codes from South Africa, the Netherlands, Canada, Switzerland, Japan, Malaysia, Italy, Taiwan and Hong Kong were also considered for the drafting of the AMEC Code. See AMEC, 'Apresentação sobre o Código AMEC de Princípios e Deveres dos Investidores Institucionais – Stewardship [Presentation on AMEC Code of Principles and Duties of Institutional Investors – Stewardship]' (October 2016) <www.amecbrasil.org.br/wp-content/uploads/2016/10/amec-apresentacao-Codigo-Stewardship.pdf> accessed 18 July 2020.

foreign codes were evaluated vis-à-vis the Brazilian capital markets. After the Brazilian code was drafted and reviewed, the draft was submitted for a public hearing, generating the final version which was then presented to market players and the Brazilian Securities and Exchange Commission (*Comissão de Valores Mobiliários* – CVM) in a roadshow.[30] The AMEC Code was officially launched on October 2016.[31]

24.2.2 Objectives and Content

One of the main goals of the AMEC Code is to foster the culture of institutional investors (particularly pension funds and asset managers) as intermediaries of third parties' assets – therefore, institutional investors are to act on behalf (and in the interest) of their ultimate beneficiaries.[32] According to AMEC, the performance of institutional investors as stewards leads to the adoption of good corporate governance practices, thus adding value to the companies and their beneficiaries.[33]

The majority of institutional investors in Brazil have no power to individually influence the activities of their investee companies owing to the concentrated ownership environment. Therefore, the AMEC Code focuses on their proactive roles as minority shareholders, as described in its introduction:[34]

> Brazilian institutional investors do not accept the idea of being labeled activists because of the perception that the term refers to investors who seek to dominate the management of investees in the US market. That would make no sense in the local context, where the shareholding structure with defined control prevails. However, not being an activist does not justify being passive when it comes to fulfilling one's fiduciary duties and responsibilities towards its clients. The responsible engagement in the activities of the issuers of securities is part of the institutional investors' fiduciary duty. Not activists, but active players.

Following international practice, the AMEC Code is a principle-based document.[35] This means that it 'prioritizes substance over form' and 'works like a compass, not a prescription'.[36] The Code itself and other main documents issued by AMEC are also available in English, demonstrating the focus on not only domestic players but also foreign institutional investors. However, the annual 'comply or explain' reports that must be filed by signatories do not need to be written in English or any other specific language, such as Portuguese.

A relevant characteristic of the AMEC Code is the focus on the fiduciary duties of institutional investors owed to their final beneficiaries.[37] This is why AMEC recommends that institutional investors follow the Code's principles 'to fulfil their fiduciary duty towards the end beneficiaries'.[38] These duties are also constantly mentioned in the document to justify several recommendations provided by the Code. It is worth noting that the fiduciary duties of investment and pension funds have historically been the focus of state and private regulation, and therefore have already been addressed previously.[39]

---

[30] ibid.
[31] To date, the AMEC Code (n 17) has not been amended in any way.
[32] AMEC Code (n 17) 5.
[33] ibid 7.
[34] ibid 6.
[35] For details see Katelouzou and Siems, The Global Diffusion of Stewardship Codes, Chapter 30.
[36] AMEC Code (n 17) 7.
[37] See Katelouzou and Klettner, Sustainable Finance and Stewardship, Chapter 26.
[38] AMEC Code (n 17) 9.
[39] See further Section 24.3.

The AMEC Code comprises seven principles, each with defined guidance on how it is to be applied.[40] Principle 1 recommends institutional investors to '[i]mplement and disclose a stewardship program'.[41] With this principle, AMEC intends to highlight the need for institutional investors to understand stewardship as a long-term process that must be planned with concrete parameters, such as when and how their activities are going to evolve. The main concern is therefore to ensure that the signatories do not consider the Code as merely aspirational. In fact, in order to help the signatories put the principles established into practice, AMEC even released an Implementation Handbook in 2017 covering the recommended practices to be followed.[42]

Principle 2 states that signatories must 'implement and disclose mechanisms to manage conflicts of interest'.[43] Alternatives to deal with conflicts of interest represent a key issue for institutional investors and, therefore, AMEC gives examples of situations where such conflicts may take place (i.e. 'between the institutional investors and their end beneficiaries, between several business segments of institutional investors, between the institutional investors and the invested assets and between the end beneficiaries themselves'). It is worth noting that Principle 2 is also linked to specific rules set in the Brazilian legislation. According to article 115, paragraph 1 of the Brazilian Corporate Law,[44] shareholders cannot exercise their voting rights in a general meeting of an investee company if they have a conflict of interest.

Principle 3 is the only principle that does not correspond directly with the UK Code 2012,[45] the principal source of inspiration for the AMEC Code (however, Principle 3 is a principle in the UK Code 2020, concerning asset owners and asset managers).[46] Principle 3 urges institutional investors to 'take environmental, social and governance (ESG) factors into account during their investment processes and stewardship activities', because such factors are considered to be 'crucial aspects when it comes to the fulfilment of their fiduciary duty'.[47] Despite this strong statement, the Code recognizes that ESG factors might not always be the 'final drivers for an investment decision'.[48]

---

[40] The seven principles of the AMEC Code are: (1) 'Implement and disclose a stewardship program'; (2) 'Implement and disclose mechanisms to manage conflicts of interest'; (3) 'Take ESG factors into account in investment processes and stewardship activities'; (4) 'Monitor the issuers of invested securities'; (5) 'Be active and diligent in the exercise of voting rights'; (6) 'Establish collective engagement criteria'; and (7) 'Be transparent as to stewardship activities'. See AMEC Code (n 17) 9.

[41] AMEC Code (n 17) 11.

[42] AMEC, 'Cartilha de Implementação do Código AMEC de Princípios e Deveres dos Investidores Institucionais Stewardship [The AMEC Code Implementation Handbook]' (2017) <www.amecbrasil.org.br/stewardship/cartilha-de-implementacao/> accessed 18 July 2020.

[43] AMEC Code (n 17) 11.

[44] Corporation Act, Law no 6.404/76, art 115.

[45] Principle 1 of the AMEC Code corresponds to Principle 1 of the UK Code 2012; Principle 2 of the AMEC Code corresponds to Principle 2 of the UK Code 2012; Principle 4 of the AMEC Code corresponds to Principle 3 of the UK Code 2012; Principle 5 of the AMEC Code corresponds to Principle 6 of the UK Code 2012; Principle 6 of the AMEC Code corresponds to Principle 5 of the UK Code 2012; and Principle 7 of the AMEC Code corresponds to Principle 7 of the UK Code 2012 (Financial Reporting Council, *The UK Stewardship Code* (September 2012) <www.frc.org.uk/getattachment/d67933f9-ca38-4233-b603-3d24b2f62c5f/UK-Stewardship-Code-(September-2012).pdf> accessed 18 July 2020). ESG principles have been included in the recently revised UK Code 2020. See Davies, The UK Stewardship Code 2010–2020, Chapter 2.

[46] AMEC Code (n 17) 12.

[47] ibid.

[48] ibid. The guidance of the AMEC Code on Principle 3 reads:

> The ESG factors impact on the issuers of securities and significantly affect their sustainability. The analysis and monitoring of ESG factors is part of the evaluation of the risks and opportunities associated with the investments, although they are not the final drivers for an investment decision. By carefully managing the assets of their end beneficiaries, institutional investors should consider relevant ESG factors as crucial aspects when it comes to the fulfilment of their fiduciary duty, being duly transparent about the way these factors will

A possible explanation for such affirmative is AMEC's intentions to clarify that all investment decisions must consider ESG factors even if the institutional investor understands that other aspects are more relevant for a given investment decision. However, as there is no guidance from the Code with respect to the extent that these ESG factors can be sacrificed to make way for other interests, this possibly creates an endless escape for institutional investors to place priority on other aspects.

Principles 4 and 5 relate to the signatories' engagement with investee companies. More precisely, the former requires them to monitor the issuers of securities,[49] while the latter compels signatories to be active and diligent in the exercise of voting rights.[50] Therefore, these principles are not limited to dealing with equity, instead covering any type of security[51] that is in an institutional investor's portfolio. As most of the resources of domestic investment and pension funds are allocated to assets that are not in equity but instead are fixed income (mainly public bonds but also private bonds), the broad reach of the AMEC Code seems to be a correct and perhaps fundamental adjustment to the Brazilian landscape.[52]

The AMEC Code also recommends the signatories to communicate with other institutional investors and with each other whenever appropriate (Principle 6).[53] The last principle, Principle 7, in a certain way resembles the first: it states that signatories must 'be transparent with respect to their stewardship activities'.[54]

24.2.3 Implementation Process

AMEC members (currently sixty-one) are not obliged to adhere to the AMEC Code. Further, there is no need to be an AMEC member in order to become a signatory to the Code.[55] As of December 2019, nineteen institutional investors are signatories to the AMEC Code: among them are three major pension funds (including Petros, Petrobras's employee pension fund); the largest global investment management company (BlackRock); and BNDESPAR, the private equity arm of the state-owned Brazilian Development Bank, as listed in Table 24.1.[56]

According to the internal rules of the AMEC Code,[57] two of the obligations of the signatories are: (i) observing the AMEC Code principles; and (ii) publishing reports on an annual basis (no later than ninety days after the end of each year), proving the full adherence of the signatory's activities to the principles and duties established in the Code or explaining the reasons why it

---

be considered. Investors should evaluate the view of the issuers of securities about relevant ESG topics. (AMEC Code (n 17) 12)

[49] ibid.
[50] ibid 13.
[51] While explaining the definition of securities in Brazil, Mattos Filho indicated that there are three ways countries may define securities: (i) countries' legislation may list, in a more specific or open manner, securities that are under supervision, (ii) countries may define a list of closed types of 'securities', or (iii) countries may start with a list of securities, and aggregate new types over time, which is the Brazilian case. See Ary Oswaldo Mattos Filho, *Direito dos Valores Mobiliários*, Tomo 1 [*Securities Law*, Vol 1] (Fundação Getúlio Vargas 2017) 53.
[52] Neither the AMEC Code (n 17) nor its related documents have further explanation as to why AMEC used the term 'securities' instead of 'equity' as usually done by the stewardship codes of other jurisdictions (with the exception of the UK Code 2020: see Davies, The UK Stewardship Code 2010–2020, Chapter 2).
[53] AMEC Code (n 17) 13.
[54] ibid 14.
[55] While there is no written rule on this, it can be inferred from the fact that Funcef is not an AMEC member but is still a signatory of the Code.
[56] See AMEC, 'Signatories' <https://amecbrasil.org.br/stewardship/signatories/?lang=en> accessed 4 February 2022.
[57] See AMEC, 'Internal Rules and Enforcement – AMEC Stewardship Code' (2018) <https://en.amecbrasil.org.br/wp-content/uploads/2018/05/Stewardship-Code-Internal-Rules.pdf> accessed 18 July 2020.

TABLE 24.1 *Reporting by signatories of the AMEC Code*[58]

S/N	Entity	Type	Origin	Reports 2017	Reports 2018
1	Aberdeen Standard	Asset manager	Foreigner	Yes	Yes
2	Argucia	Asset manager	Domestic	Yes	Yes
3	Banco do Brasil	Asset manager	Domestic	Yes	Yes
4	BlackRock	Asset manager	Foreigner	No	Yes
5	BNDESPAR	Development bank	Domestic	No	Yes
6	Bridge Trust	Asset manager	Domestic	Yes	No
7	Cartica	Asset manager	Foreigner	Yes	Yes
8	Claritas (Principal Financial Group)	Asset manager	Foreigner	Yes	Yes
9	Funcef	Pension Fund	Domestic	Yes	No
10	Funcesp	Pension Fund	Domestic	No	Yes
11	Hermes	Asset manager	Foreigner	Yes	Yes
12	Itaú	Asset manager	Domestic	Yes	Yes
13	JGP	Asset manager	Domestic	No	No
14	Leblon	Asset manager	Domestic	Yes	No
15	Petros	Pension Fund	Domestic	No	No
16	Robeco	Asset manager	Foreigner	Yes	Yes
17	Santander	Asset manager	Foreigner	Yes	Yes
18	Teorema	Asset manager	Domestic	Yes	Yes
19	Victoire	Asset manager	Domestic	No	No

failed to comply with them.[59] In other words, AMEC adopted a 'comply or explain' system, even though the AMEC Code does not explicitly mention this.

Further, AMEC established a phased implementation process for its Code. Therefore, there was no monitoring (or review) of reports issued by signatories for the 2017 activities disclosed in the 2018 report. For reports covering activities taking place in 2018 and 2019, AMEC monitored the signatories directly and provided feedback privately for the purpose of education. Only from the 2020 report (to be released in 2021) onwards will AMEC monitor and enforce the Code. Non-compliance may lead to warnings or even exclusion of the entity from the list of signatories.[60]

As shown in Table 24.1, thirteen of the nineteen signatories issued reports for 2017 and 2018 activities, although they varied substantially in terms of content and purpose. For international asset managers in particular, the majority of the reports were globally focused. In fact, as Table 24.2 shows, while all seven foreign asset manager signatories filed reports regarding their activities in 2018, not all of them mentioned activities specific to Brazil or to the Code itself. This means that the reports were not drafted and issued solely or mainly for AMEC purposes but, rather, had a more general intent to inform their investors of their global activities.

The AMEC Code's internal rules provide for the creation of a committee to assess the reports and decide on the imposition of penalties where applicable.[61] The committee will consist of six to eight members, with up to four being AMEC representatives, along with one representative from each of the following capital market entities: (i) the Brazilian Financial and Capital Markets Association (ANBIMA); (ii) the Brazilian National Association of Pension Funds (ABRAPP); (iii) the Brazilian

---

[58] Based on the authors' own elaboration with reference to AMEC's website; ibid.
[59] See ibid 2, art 3.
[60] ibid.
[61] See AMEC, 'Internal Rules and Enforcement' (n 58) 1, art 2.

TABLE 24.2 *Reporting by foreign signatories of the AMEC Code*[62]

Foreign asset manager	Mentions AMEC Code?	Mentions investment or stewardship activity in Brazil?
Aberdeen Standard	No	Yes. Investment in John Deere and relationship with deforestation in the country.
BlackRock	No. Mentions only AMEC's monthly calls to discuss regulatory issues.	No
Cartica	Yes	Yes
Claritas (Principal Financial Group)	Yes	Yes. Broad comments on stewardship activities, but no specific investment.
Hermes	Yes	No. Mentions only the collapse of two iron ore tailings dams in Brazil as part of the risk management.
Robeco	No	Yes
Santander	Yes	Yes

Association of Capital Markets Analysts and Investment Professionals (APIMEC); and (iv) the Brazilian Institute of Corporate Governance (IBGC).[63] The committee should have been formed by December 2019.[64] However, there is no news regarding its formation to this date.[65]

The committee's assessment of the reports will be private. Hence, only the specific signatory will have access to its own. However, from the 2020 report (to be released in 2021) on, AMEC plans to award to the best three to five reports. The rationale is that such awards can be used for commercial benefit, allowing and incentivizing institutional investors to see value in assuming a stewardship role with respect to investee companies.[66] Despite this goal, neither the AMEC Code nor its related documentation establishes any criteria for assessing the quality of the reports.

24.3 STEWARDSHIP DUTIES IN THE PUBLIC AND PRIVATE REGULATION

During the process of the launching of the Code, AMEC recognized that other regulatory bodies were stewardship-related.[67] In fact, there are several public and private entities responsible for supervising, monitoring and sanctioning Brazilian capital market players. Even before the AMEC Code, many of them had already defined stewardship-related duties in their regulatory and self-regulatory norms, which we will now discuss.

24.3.1 *Asset Managers*

24.3.1.1 Institutional Regulatory Framework

The CVM is the agency responsible for regulation of the issuance and trade of securities.[68] According to Brazilian law, shares of publicly traded investment funds are considered

---

[62] Based on the authors' own elaboration with reference to AMEC's website, see n 56.
[63] ibid.
[64] See AMEC, 'Internal Rules and Enforcement' (n 58) 4, art 12.
[65] As of 30 March 2020.
[66] On social enforcement in the context of stewardship, see Katelouzou and Sergakis, Shareholder Stewardship Enforcement, Chapter 27.
[67] AMEC Code (n 17) 6.
[68] Securities Act, Law no 6.385/76, art 8.

securities;[69] therefore, CVM regulates not only public companies but all kinds of investment fund as well: both traditional (i.e. retail, mutual) and alternative (i.e. private equity and venture capital), and public and private.[70] CVM also regulates fund managers (or asset managers).[71]

Until very recently, there was no statutory framework for investment funds.[72] This meant that during the recent and steady growth of investment funds, most of the applicable rules were established by an administrative body (i.e. the CVM), not going through an ordinary legislative process. Recently, however, Federal Law no. 13.784/19 changed this landscape by adding to the Brazilian Civil Code (Federal Law no. 10.406/02) specific rules applicable to investment funds on the limitation of liability of service providers (e.g. asset managers) and the CVM's jurisdiction to rule on issues relating to investment funds in Brazil. It is, however, worth noting that none of these amendments creates specific stewardship duties with respect to the asset managers of investment funds.

Another important player in the investment funds industry is ANBIMA, a self-regulatory entity established in 2009 as a result of the merger of two former associations.[73] In theory, membership of ANBIMA is voluntary; however, the main service providers of the Brazilian capital market are part of it and therefore subject to its rules. A possible reason for entering into this voluntary membership is to benefit from the influential role that ANBIMA plays: it has co-operation agreements with domestic regulatory bodies, including the CVM,[74] and is a member of the International Investment Funds Association (IIFA) and the International Organization of Securities Commissions (IOSCO).[75] At the end of 2019, ANBIMA had 265 members, including asset managers, investment banks and brokerage firms.[76]

Therefore, both the CVM and ANBIMA are main sources for stewardship rules for asset managers of investment funds.

24.3.1.2 Public Regulation

There are currently twenty-seven 'types' of investment fund in Brazil, monitored by at least fourteen different administrative regulations issued by the CVM.[77] Among these regulations,

---

[69] ibid, art 2.
[70] See Bruno Becker, 'Fundos de Investimento no Brasil: anatomia funcional e análise crítica regulatória [Investment Funds in Brazil: Functional Anatomy and Regulatory Review]' (PhD thesis, São Paulo University Law School 2019).
[71] Securities Act (n 68) art 23.
[72] Except for (i) specific mentions in broader statutes, e.g. arts 49 and 50 of Federal Law no 4.728/65, and (ii) regulation of specific funds, e.g. real estate investment funds are regulated by Federal Law no 8.668/93, and infrastructure and research, development and innovation funds are regulated by Federal Law no 11.478/07.
[73] Namely, the Brazilian Investment Banks Association (ANBID) and the Brazilian Association for Financial Market Entities (ANDIMA).
[74] The main co-operation agreement signed between CVM and ANBIMA in July 2018 defines the adoption, by CVM, of ANBIMA's oversight activities with respect to the qualification of portfolio managers; pricing of financial assets; and distribution of investment fund shares. In sum, the agreement established that the CVM may use the supervision activities carried out by ANBIMA, avoiding overlaps in regulatory and self-regulatory activities. See CVM and ANBIMA, 'Convenio para Aproveitamento de Autorregulação na Industria de Fundos de Investimento Brasileira, Celebrado entre a Comissão de Valores Mobiliários – CVM e ANBIMA – Associação Brasileira das Entidades dos Mercados Financeiro e de Capitais [Agreement for the Use of Self-Regulation in the Brazilian Investment Funds Industry, Celebrated between the Securities and Exchange Commission – CVM and ANBIMA – Brazilian Association of Entities in the Financial and Capital Markets]' (18 July 2018) <www.cvm.gov.br/export/sites/cvm/convenios/anexos/ANBIMA_FIs.pdf> accessed 18 July 2020.
[75] For more information regarding ANBIMA domestic and international activities, see ANBIMA, 'Institutional Relations' <www.anbima.com.br/en_us/institucional/estrategia-internacional.htm> accessed 18 July 2020.
[76] See ANBIMA, 'Duas instituições se tornaram nossas associadas em dezembro [Two Institutions Became Our Associates in December]' (10 December 2019) <www.anbima.com.br/pt_br/noticias/duas-instituicoes-se-tornaram-nossas-associadas-em-dezembro-8A2AB2B96EFBF226016EFFDD97096995.htm> accessed 18 July 2020.
[77] This number considers funds active in Brazil as of December 2018, notwithstanding the fact that some regulations may have changed or been extinguished.

two play an important role in the stewardship duties of asset managers. ICVM 555[78] is the foundational regulation for the investment funds industry, applying to all investment funds registered with the CVM and their asset managers. ICVM 558,[79] on the other hand, sets out the rules for asset managers of both investment funds and managed portfolios. Both regulations were enacted with the aim of modernizing the investment funds regulatory framework in Brazil, paying heed to asset manager duties and the disclosure of information.

Both CVM regulations set out the fiduciary duties of asset managers. More specifically, they state that asset managers owe a duty of care and loyalty in protecting the asset owners of the managed funds.[80] The regulations also impose on the asset managers two concrete (and less principle-based) duties regarding the duty of care, which directly relate to the stewardship-related obligations.[81] First, ICVM 555 stipulates that an asset manager must exercise all rights related to the assets owned by the investment fund in accordance with the voting policy defined in its by-laws.[82] Second, ICVM 558 states that asset managers must be diligent and adopt all action (even through litigation) necessary to protect the rights of the asset owners.[83]

Nevertheless, these two specific regulations have not been the focus of the CVM's oversight and enforcement in the last decades.[84] While the CVM has stressed the 'important role of activist investors for the good functioning of their investee companies' corporate governance',[85] there is no enforcement action penalizing asset managers for their failure to participate in the investee companies' shareholders' meetings or to exercise their voting rights even when such an obligation is stated in the fund's by-laws. Furthermore, there is no public information available on cases where the CVM investigated asset managers for not using the proper legal tools to protect the rights of asset owners (e.g. for not filing lawsuits for the compensation of damages against the managers of investee companies).

Finally, the CVM regulations also impose duties on information disclosure. According to ICVM 555, where the investment fund by-laws stipulate the exercise of voting rights in investee companies, the asset manager must disclose, on a monthly basis, information on its vote, including the reasons for such vote (or non-vote).[86] However, to this date, there were no enforcement action targeting asset managers for not fulfilling this duty.

---

[78] CVM Rule 555/14 (ICVM 555), in force since 1 October 2015.
[79] CVM Rule 558/15 (ICVM 558), in force since 4 January 2016.
[80] ibid, art 92(I) and ICVM 555 (n 78) art 16(I).
[81] It is worth mentioning that the CVM rules previously in force had already established identical duties. See CVM Rule 306/99, art 14(II) and CVM Rule 409/04, arts 65-A(II) and (III).
[82] ICVM 555 (n 78) art 78, para 3(II).
[83] ICVM 558 (n 79) art 92(III).
[84] CVM oversight activities are performed on a risk-based system. This means that the CVM focuses its activities on topics deemed to be the most critical in terms of probability of occurrence and potential damage to the market. Therefore, the CVM discloses a biannual plan with the risk events that will be proactively monitored. Since this oversight model was implemented, six Biannual Risk-Based Plans have been released by the CVM – each of them with a chapter dedicated to investment funds and asset managers. None of the six plans, however, prioritized asset managers' stewardship-related duties. See CVM, 'Supervisão Baseada em Risco [Risk Based Supervision]' <www.cvm.gov.br/menu/acesso_informacao/planos/sbr/sbr.html> accessed 18 July 2020.
[85] In the original wording, '[O] importante papel dos investidores ativistas para o bom funcionamento da governança corporativa das companhias'; see CVM, 'Pedido de Interrupção do Prazo de Convocação de Assembleia Geral Extraordinária – Fibria Celulose S.a. – Procs. Sei 19957.007756/2018-46 e 19957.007885/2018-34 [Request for Interruption of the Call Period for the Extraordinary General Meeting – Fibria Celulose S.a. – Proceedings no 19957.007756/2018-46 and 19957.007885/2018-34]' (4 September 2018) <www.cvm.gov.br/decisoes/2018/20180904_R1.html> accessed 18 July 2020.
[86] ICVM 555 (n 78) art 59, para 2.

24.3.1.3 Private Regulation

The leading self-regulatory body for asset managers in Brazil is ANBIMA. In 2015, the association issued the 'ANBIMA Code of Best Practices for Investment Funds'.[87] In 2019, ANBIMA substituted the above 2015 Code with the Code of Regulation and Best Practices for Asset Management (ANBIMA Code), a 146-page document with very specific rules regarding the investment management industry.[88] While stewardship-related duties are not the main focus of the ANBIMA Code, they are nonetheless a subject that has been covered by the document.

The ANBIMA Code is basically a repetition of the CVM regulations that deal with stewardship duties. It states that asset managers must develop activities in accordance with good faith, transparency, diligence and loyalty regarding asset owners, while fulfilling all its regulatory and self-regulatory duties.[89] The ANBIMA Code also states that asset managers must exercise voting rights diligently in investee companies.[90]

Recently, ANBIMA also issued the 'ANBIMA Rules and Procedures on the Code of Regulation and Best Practices for Asset Management' (ANBIMA Rules and Procedures), which address the duty of asset managers to exercise voting rights in portfolio companies.[91] It requires asset managers to draft and disclose a minimum set of obligatory information on the exercise of voting rights (Voting Policy).[92] For instance, the Voting Policy must describe general principles that guide asset managers in situations of mandatory voting.[93] The Voting Policy must also address the measures to be adopted where conflicts of interest arise.[94]

Asset managers are responsible for exercising voting rights at the general shareholders' meetings of investee companies. For this, the ANBIMA Rules and Procedures divide the exercise of voting rights: (i) into mandatory or optional; and (ii) by type of asset (e.g. shares or real estate). For example, voting is mandatory in: (i) the election of minority shareholders' representatives at the Board of Directors; (ii) the approval of stock option plans for company directors and managers; (iii) mergers, acquisitions and any changes in the company's structure that could impact the value of the asset owned by the fund; and (iv) matters involving

---

[87] There are two ways in which an asset manager may be subject to the ANBIMA Code of Regulation and Best Practices of Investment Funds: (i) if the asset manager is an ANBIMA member, it must comply with the rules; (ii) even if the asset manager is not an ANBIMA member, it may still voluntarily adhere to the Code. ANBIMA has dedicated areas to monitor members' compliance with the Code's provisions. In the event of non-compliance with any rule, ANBIMA may impose penalties ranging from a warning, the imposition of a fine, and even the exclusion of the membership (in the case of members) or the revocation of the term of adhesion to the Code (in the case of non-members). See ANBIMA, 'ANBIMA Code of Regulation and Best Practices of Investment Funds' (2015) 33, art 61 <www.anbima.com.br/data/files/74/46/3F/49/A4C085100B51AF7568A80AC2/Code-of-Regulation_1_.pdf> accessed 18 July 2020.

[88] See ANBIMA, 'Código ANBIMA de Regulação e Melhores Práticas para Administração de Recursos de Terceiros [ANBIMA Code of Regulation and Best Practices for Asset Management]' (23 May 2019) <www.anbima.com.br/pt_br/autorregular/codigos/administracao-de-recursos-de-terceiros.htm> accessed 18 July 2020 [hereinafter ANBIMA Code 2019]. An updated version of the ANBIMA Code will enter into force as of 20 July 2020 (ANBIMA, 'Código ANBIMA de Regulação e Melhores Práticas para Administração de Recursos de Terceiros [ANBIMA Code of Regulation and Best Practices for Asset Management]' (22 January 2020) <www.anbima.com.br/data/files/09/31/22/21/DFDCF6106CCA02F69B2BA2A8/codigo_Administracao_Recursos_Terceiros_20_07_20.pdf> accessed 18 July 2020.

[89] ANBIMA Code 2019 (n 88) Title II, Chapter IV, art 6°(I) and (II).

[90] ANBIMA Code 2019 (n 88) Title III, Chapter XI, art 53.

[91] See ANBIMA, 'Regras e Procedimentos ANBIMA do Código de Administração de Recursos de Terceiros [ANBIMA Rules and Procedures on the Code of Regulation and Best Practices for Asset Management]' (23 May 2019) 28–33 <https://www.anbima.com.br/data/files/0A/C6/4C/FA/31B797109C2486976B2BA2A8/2.%20Regras_procedimentos_Codigo_ART_vigente%20a%20partir%20de%2017.05.21.pdf> accessed 4 February 2022.

[92] ibid 32–33, art 7.

[93] ibid 32–33, art 7, sole para.

[94] ibid 32–33, art 7, sole para(III).

differential treatment.[95] Among other circumstances, voting is optional: (i) where voting is too costly; (ii) where the investment is not material for the fund's portfolio; or (iii) where the portfolio company does not provide enough information on the shareholders' meeting agenda.[96]

Disclosure is also addressed by the ANBIMA Rules and Procedures, which stipulate that asset managers must inform asset owners of how they voted in investee companies' meetings. This duty to disclose does not apply for: (i) matters protected by a confidentiality agreement or if confidentiality is determined by applicable regulations; (ii) decisions which, at the discretion of the asset manager, are considered to be strategic; or (iii) matters where the exercise of voting rights by the asset manager are considered optional by the ANBIMA Rules and Procedures.[97]

Only one enforcement action relating to the stewardship duties of asset managers was found in the ANBIMA Codes and Rules and Procedures.[98]

Finally, it is worth mentioning that the ANBIMA Code does not require asset managers to consider ESG factors in their investment decision-making, but ANBIMA has been taking some initiatives regarding such matters. First, in 2015, ANBIMA established a Technical Group to study and promote sustainable development practices among its members.[99] Second, since 2016, ANBIMA surveys the level of adoption of sustainability practices by asset managers (with two editions to date).[100] And third, in January 2020, ANBIMA released a guide to help its members incorporate ESG factors into their investment analysis process.[101]

24.3.2 Pension Funds

24.3.2.1 Institutional Regulatory Framework

There are two main players regulating pension funds in Brazil. In the governmental sphere, pension funds are regulated[102] and overseen by the National Pension Funds Authority (*Superintendência Nacional de Previdência Complementar* – PREVIC).[103] PREVIC also monitors the related rules issued by the National Monetary Council (*Conselho Monetário Nacional* – CMN), the highest institution of the Brazilian financial system. In the private sphere, Pension Funds Brazilian Association (*Associação Brasileira das Entidades Fechadas de Previdência*

---

[95] ibid 29–31, art 5.
[96] ibid 31–32, art 6, para 1(I).
[97] ibid 29, art 4.
[98] The research covered the public information available for the year 2019. The only identified case that dealt with non-compliance with stewardship-related duties (i.e. Proceeding no ART006/2019 decided on 29 November 2019) involved the exclusion of an asset manager from ANBIMA's board of affiliates because of several irregularities, including the failure to implement the voting policy in situations of conflict of interest. The ANBIMA summary hearing regarding the case is available in Portuguese at ANBIMA, 'Processo n° ART006/2019' (29 November 2019) <www.anbima.com.br/data/files/31/B1/A3/2B/21DDE6106C984BF69B2BA2A8/Julgamento_GWI_ART006.pdf> accessed 18 July 2020.
[99] Information regarding ANBIMA's Consultative Group on Sustainability is available at ANBIMA, 'Sustentabilidade [Sustainability]' <www.anbima.com.br/pt_br/representar/grupos-consultivos-para-temas-emergentes/sustentabilidade/sustentabilidade.htm> accessed 18 July 2020.
[100] See ANBIMA, '2ª Pesquisa de Sustentabilidade [Sustainability Survey Second Edition]' (2018) <www.anbima.com.br/data/files/4C/92/36/CF/D6C17610167AA07678A80AC2/Relatorio-Sustentabilidade-2018.pdf> accessed 18 July 2020.
[101] See ANBIMA, 'Guia ASG: Incorporação dos aspectos ASG nas análises de investimento [ESG Guide: Incorporation of ESG Factors into Investment Analysis]' (January 2020) <www.anbima.com.br/data/files/1A/50/EE/31/BFDEF610CA9C4DF69B2BA2A8/ANBIMA-Guia-ASG-2019.pdf> accessed 18 July 2020.
[102] Regulations issued by PREVIC must follow the guidance of the Council of Complementary Private Pension Funds (*Conselho de Gestão de Previdência Complementar* – CGPC).
[103] Law no 12.154/09, art 1.

Complementar – ABRAPP) represents the interest of pension funds, while working as a self-regulatory body. At the end of 2018, ABRAPP had 258 members,[104] representing 98 per cent of Brazilian pension funds.[105] Therefore, to assess the stewardship rules specifically applicable to pension funds (beyond AMEC's Code), an understanding of rules issued by PREVIC (and CMN) and ABRAPP is required.

Historically, regulation of pension funds has been more lenient (or less active) than for its counterparts in the bank and investment funds sectors. Even with rules in place concerning the internal organization of pension funds,[106] there has been less oversight than is performed by CVM and ANBIMA.[107] Furthermore, PREVIC has been deemed a watchdog with weaker powers as compared to the Brazilian Central Bank and CVM.

A possible consequence of this ineffective monitoring is the outbreak of scandals in the pension funds sector, ranging from deficit and low returns to corruption. In fact, pension funds were involved in almost all, if not all, corruption scandals revealed over the last decade (e.g. the 'Mensalão Scandal'[108] and the 'Greenfield Operation' (part of the Car Wash Operation)), which saw the investigation of all major pension funds in Brazil.[109] Governance-related issues involving pension funds were so severe that, in 2017, PREVIC had to intervene and investigate Brazil's biggest fund in terms of beneficiaries, the pension fund for post office workers at the state-owned company Correios (Postalis), for huge losses, tax fraud and corruption.[110]

This background explains why the recent initiatives involving the regulation of public and private pension funds are focused on the internal governance and oversight of these entities. Stewardship initiatives have therefore been a secondary concern, even though occasionally addressed (almost exclusively related to ESG concerns in the pension fund's investments).

24.3.2.2 Public Regulation

The main administrative regulations for pension funds in Brazil are the CMN Resolution 4.661/2018[111] and the PREVIC Instruction no. 6/2018.[112] These regulations are considered to be an important milestone for the industry, since they substantially changed the guidelines for the application of resources, in addition to introducing stricter rules on risk management, internal controls and clear division of roles in the sector's regulation.

Both regulations prescribe stewardship-related duties for pension funds, some being principle-based while others command mandatory compliance. CMN Resolution 4.661/2018 imposes

---

[104] ABRAPP, 'Relatório de Atividades e Iniciativas 2018 [Activities and Initiatives Report 2018]' (2019) 5 <www.abrapp.org.br/Documentos%20Pblicos/RelatorioAtividades2018.pdf?ID=291> accessed 18 July 2020.
[105] ABRAPP, 'Consolidado Estatístico [Statistics Consolidated]' (December 2018) 2 <https://www.abrapp.org.br/wp-content/uploads/2020/09/Consolidado-Estat%C3%ADstico_12.2018.pdf> accessed 4 February 2022.
[106] In particular the CGPC Resolution no 13/2004.
[107] As recognized by PREVIC representatives. See 'PREVIC Chief Studies Changes to Pension Funds Governance Rules' *Valor Econômico* (9 February 2018) <www.valor.com.br/international/news/5315943/previc-chief-studies-changes-pension-funds-governance-rules> accessed 18 July 2020.
[108] 'What Is Brazil's "mensalão"' *The Economist* (São Paulo, 18 November 2013) <www.economist.com/the-economist-explains/2013/11/18/what-is-brazils-mensalao> accessed 18 July 2020.
[109] Leite and Freitas (n 26).
[110] Anthony Boadle, 'Brazil Intervenes in Fraud-Hit Postalis Pension Fund' *Reuters* (4 October 2017) <www.reuters.com/article/brazil-postalis/update-3-brazil-intervenes-in-fraud-hit-postalis-pension-fund-idUSL2N1MF0JN> accessed 18 July 2020. See also: Juliana Schincariol, 'Postalis intervention follows years of warnings' *Valor Econômico* (Rio de Janeiro, 11 October 2017) <www.valor.com.br/international/news/5152230/postalis-intervention-follows-years-warnings> accessed 18 July 2020.
[111] CMN Resolution no 4.661/2018.
[112] PREVIC Rule no 6/2018.

a duty of care and loyalty on the funds and requires them to adopt practices that ensure compliance with the fiduciary duties owed to their ultimate beneficiaries.[113] These duties must be followed by all individuals who directly or indirectly participate in the analysis, advice and decision-making on investments of pension funds.[114] The regulation also requires the pension funds to assess the technical capacity and potential conflicts of interest of their service providers and those involved in the decision-making process for their investments.[115] Finally, the internal control of the pension fund must mitigate any potential conflicts of interest.[116]

Furthermore, Resolution CMN 4.661/2018, for the first time in the history of pension funds regulation, mentions ESG concerns.[117] It mandates that the analysis of assets must consider, whenever possible, aspects related to the economic, environmental, social and governance sustainability of investments.[118] The previous regulation stated only that pension funds should disclose whether or not they observed principles of environmental responsibility in their investments, and there was no regulatory duty for such principles to be effectively applied.[119] Thus, a study published in 2016 found that only 25 per cent of the fifty largest Brazilian pension funds integrated ESG factors into their investment policies.[120]

Finally, it is worth noting that CMN has been trying to foster corporate governance of investee companies as a factor to be considered by pension funds in their investment decision-making. This aligns with Principle 3 of the AMEC Code. In 2000, the Brazilian Stock Exchange created special listing segments (Level 1, Level 2 and New Market) that required improvements in the corporate governance of listed companies, including rules of one-share-one-vote, minimum free float and independent board members.[121] The CMN increased the investment limits that pension funds could deploy in companies listed on the New Market and Level 2, as well as determining that pension funds could invest only in the IPO of companies listed in these segments.[122] These efforts helped institutionalize the existence of the special listing segments; however, the regulatory incentive had no practical effect as pension funds historically have always had – and still have – low exposure to equity assets.[123]

---

[113] CMN Resolution no 4.661/2018 (n 111) arts 4(II) and (IV).
[114] ibid, art 4, paras 1° and 2°.
[115] ibid, arts 4 and 13.
[116] ibid, art 11, para 1.
[117] A recent example of compliance with the rules in CMN Resolution no 4.661/2018 is a PREVIC initiative in launching an update of its 'Guidelines for Investment Best Practices' in 2019. The new version of this guide innovated by adding a chapter on ESG-related duties, with guidelines on how pension funds could integrate ESG factors into their internal processes. According to PREVIC, the incorporation of these factors into the pension funds' decision-making process improves their risk management and generates long-term sustainable returns. See PREVIC, 'Guia de Melhores Práticas de Investimentos [Guide to Best Investment Practices]' (2019) <https://www.fachesf.com.br/pdf/guia_previc/novo-guia-previc-melhores-praticas-de-investimentos.pdf> accessed 4 February 2022.
[118] CMN Resolution no 4.661/2018 (n 111) art 10, para 4.
[119] CMN Resolution no 3.792/2009, art 16, para 3 (VIII).
[120] See SITAWI 'Responsible Investment in Brazil 2016 – ESG Incorporation by Pension Funds' (June 2016) 20 <http://info.sitawi.net/ribrazil2016> accessed 18 July 2020.
[121] For more specific information regarding the special listing segments for differentiated corporate governance levels created by B3, see B3, 'Listing' <www.b3.com.br/en_us/regulation/regulatory-framework/regulations-and-manuals/listing.htm> accessed 18 July 2020. See also Ronald J Gilson, Henry Hansmann and Mariana Pargendler, 'Regulatory Dualism as a Development Strategy: Corporate Reform in Brazil, the United States, and the European Union' (2011) 63 *Stanford Law Review* 475.
[122] CMN Resolution no 2.829/2001.
[123] See Maria Helena Santana and others, 'Novo Mercado and Its Followers: Case Studies in Corporate Governance Reform' (International Financial Corporation and Global Corporate Governance Forum – Focus 5, 2008) 20 <https://www.ifc.org/wps/wcm/connect/45b36361-1d58-4c1b-98f1-999c15dd76bd/Novo%2BMercado%2Btext%2Bscreen%2B4-21-08.pdf?MOD=AJPERES&CVID=jtCwuvl> accessed 4 February 2022.

24.3.2.3 Private Regulation

For more than twenty years, ABRAPP has been guiding its associates (i.e. pension funds) to follow ESG principles in their investment policies,[124] and to adopt good corporate governance standards to avoid corrupt practices.[125]

In 2016, the association launched the 'Self-Regulation Code of Investment Governance' (ABRAPP Investment Code),[126] as a response to the corruption scandals revealed by the Car Wash Operation beginning in 2014. Furthermore, in 2019, it launched the 'ABRAPP Self-Regulation Code of Corporate Governance' (ABRAPP Corporate Governance Code).[127] These two Codes are voluntary, which means that no ABRAPP member is required to adhere to them. To date, out of approximately 250 associates, 58 pension funds are signatories to the ABRAPP Investment Code[128] and 7 pension funds are signatories to the ABRAPP Corporate Governance Code.[129]

Both Codes assign stewardship duties to the signatories. For example, the ABRAPP Investment Code provides that the investment management practices of pension funds should 'strengthen the fiduciary relationship' between the beneficiaries of the pension funds and other stakeholders, including civil society.[130] The ABRAPP Corporate Governance Code requires the adoption of socially responsible practices in the pension funds investments.[131]

The Codes do not require the signatories to report that they comply with the rules and principles set forth therein. Although it is provided that ABRAPP will supervise the signatories, there is no public information on the sanctioning for non-compliance with the Code's obligations.

24.3.3 *The AMEC Code and Other Public and Private Regulatory Bodies*

In February 2017, the Principles for Responsible Investment (PRI) released the report 'Fiduciary Duty in the 21st Century: Brazil Roadmap'.[132] Among other topics, it recommended Brazilian regulators (e.g. CVM and PREVIC) to adopt the AMEC Code, making the Code mandatory for pension funds and asset managers. The main motivation seems to be the adoption of ESG

---

[124] See ABRAPP, 'Princípios Básicos de Responsabilidade Social [Basic Principles of Social Responsibility]' <https://www.abrapp.org.br/wp-content/uploads/2021/01/Responsabilidade_Social.pdf> accessed 4 February 2022.

[125] See ABRAPP, 'Guia de Boas Práticas Anticorrupção para EFPC sob a ótica da Lei No 12.846/13 [Guide to Good Anticorruption Practices for EFPC from the Perspective of Law No 12.846/13]' (2014) <https://www.abrapp.org.br/produto/guia-de-boas-praticas-anticorrupcao-para-efpc-sob-a-otica-da-lei-no-12-846-13/> accessed 4 February 2022.

[126] See ABRAPP, 'Self-Regulation Code of Investment Governance' (2016) <https://www.abrapp.org.br/autorregulacao/governanca-de-investimentos/> accessed 4 February 2022 [hereinafter ABRAPP Investment Code].

[127] See ABRAPP, 'Código De Autorregulação Em Governança Corporativa [Self-Regulation Code of Governance Corporate]' (2019) <https://www.abrapp.org.br/wp-content/uploads/2021/01/codigo_corporativa.pdf> accessed 4 February 2022 [hereinafter ABRAPP Corporate Governance Code].

[128] For the list of the ABRAPP Investment Code signatories, see ABRAPP, 'Código De Autorregulação Em Governança de Investimentos – Quem Aderiu [Self-Regulation Code of Investment Governance – Signatories]' <https://www.abrapp.org.br/autorregulacao/governanca-de-investimentos/> accessed 4 February 2022.

[129] For the list of the ABRAPP Corporate Governance Code signatories, see ABRAPP, 'Código De Autorregulação Em Governança Corporativa – Quem Aderiu [Self-Regulation Code of Governance Corporate – Signatories]' <https://www.abrapp.org.br/autorregulacao/governanca-corporativa/> accessed 4 February 2022.

[130] ABRAPP Investment Code (n 126) art 2(V).

[131] ABRAPP Corporate Governance Code (n 127) part B, principle 8.

[132] Brian Tomlinson and others, 'Fiduciary Duty in the 21st Century: Brazil Roadmap' (2017) <www.unpri.org/download?ac=1386> accessed 18 July 2020.

principles in the AMEC Code.[133] According to PRI, 'international examples suggest that codes are only effective where they have market-wide adoption'.[134]

The PRI report also recommended the regulators to monitor institutional investors' compliance with the Code. However, the regulators did not adopt the recommendation. In fact, publicly available information shows that Brazilian regulators and self-regulators, though urged by AMEC, have not expressly included the principles of the AMEC Code into their practices.[135]

In 2018, PREVIC conducted a public consultation to reform its practice of hiring asset managers outsourced by pension funds.[136] AMEC suggested to PREVIC that one of the attributes that pension funds should consider when selecting managers is the existence of stewardship behaviour towards investee companies.[137] Yet, the final version of PREVIC's rules does not contain such a rule.[138]

The same occurred with ABRAPP. Representatives of ABRAPP had already stated that 'the entity has always advocated in favour of the [AMEC Stewardship] Code and, as a result of that, its members have been adhering to it or studying the possibility of doing so in the near future'.[139] However, the ABRAPP Self-Regulatory Codes have yet to expressly contemplate the AMEC Code.[140]

Finally, AMEC also urged ANBIMA to include the AMEC Code in its self-regulation standards. During the public hearing for the launch of the 2019 ANBIMA Code, AMEC issued a letter suggesting that ANBIMA systematize the AMEC Code into the new rules, stating that 'the edition of the ANBIMA Code is the main opportunity so far to give life to these words'.[141] However, ANBIMA did not substantially change its proposal and kept a long, detailed rule-based code,[142] without any reference to the AMEC Code or its principles.

24.4 CONCLUSION

Analysis of the public and private regulations regarding the stewardship duties applicable to Brazilian institutional investors, particularly pension funds and asset managers, allows us to make three observations.

---

[133] ibid 11. According to the report, '[w]e welcome AMEC's code setting a framework for investors to strategically engage with their investee companies on ESG issues. Our stakeholders noted that AMEC's Code and Resolution 3.792 complemented each other.'

[134] ibid.

[135] There is no information on similar AMEC proposals implemented by CVM.

[136] PREVIC, 'Consulta Pública N° 4/2018 [Public Hearing No 4/2018]' (2018) <www.previc.gov.br/acesso-a-informacao/participacao-social-2/consultas-publicas-encerradas/consulta-publica-no-4-2018> accessed 18 July 2020.

[137] See AMEC, 'Carta/AMEC/Presi n° 18/2018 [AMEC President Letter no 18/2018]' (23 November 2018) <www.amecbrasil.org.br/cartaamecpresi-n-182018/> accessed 18 July 2020.

[138] The rule, however, encourages pension funds to assess whether the asset manager is a signatory of self-regulation codes that promote best practices, transparency and ethical standards in portfolio management. See PREVIC Revised Instruction 12/19, art 2(VIII).

[139] AMEC, 'Relatório da Administração 2018 – Annual Report [Management Report 2018 – Annual Report]' (2018) 31 <www.amecbrasil.org.br/wp-content/uploads/2013/04/RA2018_amec_site-dupla.pdf> accessed 18 July 2020.

[140] However, some guides released by ABRAPP recommend adoption of the AMEC Code (n 17). See ABRAPP, 'Guia para elaboração de Relatório Anual e de Sustentabilidade – Melhores Práticas de Transparência em Informações ASG [Guide for Preparing the Annual and Sustainability Report – Best Practices for Transparency in ESG Information]' (2019) 10, 12 <https://www.abrapp.org.br/produto/guia-para-elaboracao-de-relatorio-anual-de-sustentabilidade-melhores-praticas-de-transparencia-em-informacoes-asg/> accessed 4 February 2022.

[141] See AMEC, 'President Letter No 4/2018' (2018) <https://amecbrasil.org.br/cartaamecpresi-n-042018/> accessed 4 February 2022.

[142] See Section 24.3.1.3.

First, there are several regulations and codes in Brazil that already have stewardship-related rules and principles. Many of them cover the key concerns addressed by stewardship codes around the world, with engagement in investee companies and consideration of ESG factors by institutional investors in their investment decisions.

Second, despite the existence of various stewardship initiatives, there is no sound effort by public and private regulators to monitor or enforce these rules and principles. Therefore, the enforcement of stewardship-related duties does not seem to be a priority for such entities.

Third, there is no clear endeavour from the public and private regulators to align their norms in relation to stewardship-related duties. In fact, each of the entities responsible for the oversight of asset managers (CVM and ANBIMA) and pension funds (PREVIC and ABRAPP) has launched rules or self-regulation codes that somehow deal with the issue of stewardship, but without co-ordination. In many cases, the stewardship duties often overlap with other rules. The lack of co-ordination among regulators certainly hampers the promotion and enforcement of stewardship initiatives in the Brazilian corporate landscape. Despite so many widespread duties and principles, the common perception remains that Brazilian institutional investors do not act as if they were the real owners of the money they manage. However, recent events in the Brazilian capital market suggest that this passivity may change.

As previously mentioned, the largest Brazilian company (Petrobras) was involved in a corruption scandal of unprecedented proportions after the start of the Car Wash Operation. Affected shareholders tried to recover damages, alleging that the company had released false information regarding its business, the effectiveness of internal controls, and compliance with anti-corruption laws. Consequently, several civil actions were initiated in the US against the company, one of which settled with investors for USD 2.95 billion.[143]

This would probably mark the end of affected shareholders trying to recover losses from a publicly traded company in Brazil.[144] But in this Petrobras scandal, the story was different. Institutional investors – among them the three main domestic pension funds and 320 other investment funds – engaged in a collective arbitration procedure against Petrobras.[145] News in the media claims that the institutional investors engaged in the arbitral proceeding for two main reasons: (i) the strong calls from beneficiaries harmed by the scheme; and (ii) the fiduciary duties that the fund managers owed to the asset owners.[146]

The Petrobras scandal marks the first, but not the last, case. In the middle of 2019, the tragic collapse of a dam owned by a mining company (Vale S.A.) occurred, which saw share prices plummet after the disastrous environmental effects. At least twenty-five asset managers and pension funds initiated a collective arbitral proceeding against the company, alleging that it had

---

[143] Brendan Pierson, 'Petrobras to Pay $2.95 Billion to Settle U.S. Corruption Lawsuit' *Reuters* (New York, 3 January 2018) <www.reuters.com/article/us-petrobras-classaction/petrobras-to-pay-2-95-billion-to-settle-u-s-class-action-over-corruption-idUSKBN1ES0L2> accessed 18 July 2020.

[144] Unlike other jurisdictions such as the US, there were very few cases in the Brazilian capital market where investors applied legal tools to recover their losses. See Viviane M Prado (n 14).

[145] Camila Maia, 'Leading Brazilian Pension Funds Join Arbitration Against Petrobras' *Valor Econômico* (São Paulo, 14 November 2017) <www.valor.com.br/international/news/5192457/leading-brazil-pension-funds-join-arbitration-against-petrobras> accessed 18 July 2020.

[146] According to Valor Econômico, a major Brazilian economic newspaper: 'Investors hope that with the participation of Brazil's biggest funds in the arbitration process, this will have a snowball effect and all major shareholders will eventually join. With the pressure put on the company [Petrobras] by shareholders and pensioners, fund managers will likely be convinced that it is their fiduciary duty to demand payment for incurred losses.' ibid.

not revealed the risks regarding such a dam, information that the investors say would be important in obtaining the correct valuation of Vale's shares.[147]

Both arbitration proceedings await a final outcome. There is no certainty in the reasons that led large Brazilian institutional investor shareholders to seek compensation from listed companies, especially if their so-called fiduciary duties did in fact have some influence on the decision to engage in the arbitration proceedings. Another reason to consider would be the mere fear of institutional investors missing out on the opportunity of obtaining the same outcomes that foreign investors have received in similar situations abroad.[148]

Regardless of the incentive that motivated institutional investors to act in these specific cases, this (apparent) change in conduct seems to be a good indication that domestic institutional investors are beginning to understand their duty to monitor investee companies and are beginning to adopt stewardship principles. This includes handling the available legal instruments, if necessary, to defend the interests of their ultimate beneficiaries. Whether this will become entrenched practice and whether stewardship codes and rules remain relevant, however, is yet to be seen.

---

[147] Graziella Valenti, 'Investors Begin Arbitration Proceedings Against Vale' *Valor Econômico* (São Paulo, 17 July 2019) <www.valor.com.br/international/news/6352741/investors-begin-arbitration-proceedings-against-vale> accessed 18 July 2020.

[148] As with the Petrobras case, the arbitration proceeding against Vale was filed after the beginning of a class action against the company in the US regarding the same set of facts. See Perry Cooper, 'Vale SA Faces Investor Class Action After Dam Collapse' (*Bloomberg Law*, 29 January 2019) <https://news.bloomberglaw.com/class-action/vale-sa-faces-investor-class-action-after-dam-collapse> accessed 18 July 2020.

PART III

Comparisons

25

Investment Management, Stewardship and Corporate Governance Roles

Roger M. Barker and Iris H.-Y. Chiu

25.1 INTRODUCTION

When the Stewardship Code was introduced in the UK in 2010 (UK Code),[1] it was ambiguous as to what 'stewardship' meant, in the context of institutional investors' legal duties to their clients and beneficiaries, while engaging in the corporate governance roles specified in the UK Code.[2] Are there two types of 'stewardship', that is, investors' 'soft' responsibilities as corporate governance actors in the companies they invest in, and investors' 'hard' responsibilities to their clients and beneficiaries? Or, does the UK Code's focus on corporate governance roles, which it assumes to be 'good stewardship', mean that playing an active role in investee companies is equivalent to discharging investors' 'hard' responsibilities to clients and beneficiaries?

The first interpretation may cause problems for the fabric of company law in the UK. Investors do not owe duties, especially fiduciary duties, to the companies they invest in. The second may also cause problems as it is uncertain on what basis one can assume that institutional investors' engagement with corporate governance roles necessarily results in either good investment management performance or the fulfilment of legal responsibilities. Indeed, empirical research presents mixed evidence as to the impact of investor engagement with corporate performance,[3] and it is not necessarily the case that being an engaged shareholder is part and parcel of fulfilling institutional investors' fiduciary or contractual duties to their clients and beneficiaries.[4] However, it is arguable that the revised European Shareholders' Rights Directive 2017 (SRD II) now makes the assumption

---

[1] Financial Reporting Council, *The UK Stewardship Code* (July 2010) <www.frc.org.uk/getattachment/e223e152-5515-4cdc-a951-da33e093eb28/UK-Stewardship-Code-July-2010.pdf> accessed 28 May 2020 [hereinafter UK Code 2010].

[2] Iris H-Y Chiu, 'Turning Institutional Investors into "Stewards": Exploring the Meaning and Objectives of "Stewardship"' (2013) 66 *Current Legal Problems* 443.

[3] Mariassunta Gianetti and Xiaoyun Yu, 'The Corporate Finance Benefits of Short Horizon Investors' (ECGI Working Paper 2016) on positive short- and long-term performance post shareholder engagement, while, on the contrary, see Bonnie G Buchanan, Jeffrey M Netter, Annette B Poulsen and Tina Yang, 'Shareholder Proposal Rules and Practice: Evidence from a Comparison of the United States and United Kingdom' (2012) 49 *American Business Law Journal* 739.

[4] Pension trustees, for example, are subject to a duty of care in the exercise of trustee powers, subject to the experience and knowledge of the trustee concerned. Specific aspects of such a duty of care include a duty to consider the suitability of any investment, a duty to review suitability, a duty to ensure diversification of assets and a duty to obtain and consider proper advice. The duty of care operates at the standard of an 'ordinary prudent man', and there is no special provision for a higher standard of care in view of professional knowledge or expertise. The Pensions Act 1995 requires pension trustees to obtain written advice on their investments before establishing a Statement of Principles, and trustees may rely on the obtainment of advice as a proxy for discharge of duty. Trustees Act 2000, ss 1–6; Pensions Act 1995, s 35.

explicit that institutional investors' roles as engaged shareholders are best practice for their investment management.[5]

The UK Code 2020 now clarifies that 'stewardship' refers to the quality of investment management for clients and beneficiaries.[6] Consistent with SRD II, engagement with investee companies is now part of good stewardship. This applies to both 'asset owners' (i.e. fund vehicles that collect or pool investors' capital together) and 'asset managers' (i.e. the delegates to whom funds entrust the management of portfolios of capital).

We have argued elsewhere[7] that the regulatory and legal frameworks for investment management do not necessarily cohere with engaged corporate governance roles, and that this policy preference for funds and asset managers to engage in such roles is owing to policymakers' need to build 'self-regulatory' credibility in the corporate sector. UK policymakers have, since the 1990s, looked to the private sector to develop self-healing techniques to address one corporate scandal or collapse after another.[8] This is to minimize the need for regulatory intrusion and also to galvanize proximate and resourceful actors such as shareholders. The reliance on shareholders to 'do the right thing' in monitoring the corporate economy for the common good is, however, a lofty ambition, and one that institutional investors have not quite lived up to, and may not be well placed to fulfil.[9]

Section 25.2 discusses the development of soft and hard law in compelling institutional investors to monitor their investee companies. This discussion is focused on the UK and the EU, as the UK has developed the pioneer version of soft law – in the UK Code – to govern institutions' shareholder conduct, and the UK and the EU are the markets where institutional investors have extensively participated for the purposes of managing their investment mandates. Some reference may be made to US markets, where relevant, as institutions participate as minority shareholders in the US markets much like in the UK and the EU. Section 25.3 discusses the main challenges to institutions' shareholder engagement role, drawing from the limitations of investment management roles and their legal and regulatory frameworks in the UK and the EU. We argue that, within the investment chain, value concerns in investment management and the governance of funds continue to pose challenges for engaged corporate governance roles for institutional investors. These concerns also persist, and are to an extent augmented, in relation to new expectations regarding 'environmental, social and governance' (ESG) engagement, discussed in Section 25.4. Section 25.5 provides a brief conclusion.

25.2 THE DEVELOPMENT OF EXPECTATIONS FOR INSTITUTIONAL INVESTORS' ENGAGEMENT IN CORPORATE GOVERNANCE ROLES

In the wake of corporate scandals in the early 1990s, UK policymakers urged the industry to find a robust solution for addressing corporate sector weaknesses, such as poor and misleading financial reporting. Sir Adrian Cadbury led a committee that contextualized corporate sector

---

[5] Iris H–Y Chiu and Dionysia Katelouzou, 'Making a Case for Regulating Institutional Shareholders' Corporate Governance Roles' (2018) *Journal of Business Law* 67; Directive (EU) 2017/828 of the European Parliament and of the Council of 17 May 2017 amending Directive 2007/36/EC as regards the encouragement of long-term shareholder engagement [2017] OJ L132/1 (SRD II).

[6] Financial Reporting Council, *UK Stewardship Code 2020* (2019) 4 <www.frc.org.uk/getattachment/5aae591d-d9d3-4cf4-814a-d14e156a1d87/Stewardship-Code_Dec-19-Final-Corrected.pdf> accessed 28 May 2020 [hereinafter UK Code 2020].

[7] Roger M Barker and Iris H-Y Chiu, *Corporate Governance and Investment Management: The Promises and Limitations of the New Financial Economy* (Edward Elgar 2017).

[8] See Section 25.2.

[9] Barker and Chiu (n 7).

malaises such as poor financial reporting and transparency within the governance health of companies, and recommended that listed companies reform their governance, such as their board composition. The first and iconic Corporate Governance Code was, however, expressed to be an effective self-regulatory measure as institutional investors would be the main constituents that would hold publicly listed companies to account for their governance practices.[10]

In 2001, although the Myners Review[11] found that institutional investors were largely disengaged and voting levels were not healthy, continued reliance was placed on the role of institutional investors, and efforts were made to galvanize them and not to replace their roles with regulatory intrusion. Voting records, according to the annual surveys by the Investment Association, have improved significantly over the years.[12] Although institutions' voting levels have been reported to increase, this could be owing to the perception that they would be forced to engage in voting by regulation were no improvement to be perceived by policymakers. Further, the rise of the proxy advisory industry has helped with discharging voting responsibilities, although it remains questionable to what extent institutions are indeed 'engaged'.[13]

Mainstream institutional investors continued to show chequered patterns of corporate engagement through the 1990s, although the wind of 'defensive shareholder activism' inspired by the American pensions giant CalPERS started to influence fund and asset managers' behaviour. Defensive shareholder activism is defined as 'a defensive safeguarding of invested capital, which is exposed at hazardous moments in the company's existence because of increasing costs of exit'.[14] This type of shareholder behaviour may be activated in the face of performance failures in an investee company and/or management failures observed to threaten the viability of the investment, in particular governance failures.[15] In the UK, for example, the furore over executive pay arose in the mid-1990s after media reports of it skyrocketing at privatized utilities companies generated extremely negative opinion. The Greenbury Committee, which was tasked to look into the issue, took a 'corporate governance' approach by recommending more disclosure to shareholders of the relation between executive remuneration and corporate performance, the more robust involvement of the remuneration committee of the board in designing appropriate

---

[10] e.g. Adrian Cadbury, *Report of the Committee on the Financial Aspects of Corporate Governance* (Financial Reporting Council, Gee Publishing 1992) para 6.6 <https://ecgi.global/code/cadbury-report-financial-aspects-corporate-governance> accessed 28 May 2020. UK policymakers' convictions about institutions' corporate governance roles is extensively discussed in ch 2 of Iris H-Y Chiu, *The Foundations and Anatomy of Shareholder Activism* (Hart 2010).

[11] Paul Myners, 'Institutional Investment in the United Kingdom: A Review' (HM Treasury 2001) <https://uksif.org/wp-content/uploads/2012/12/MYNERS-P.-2001.-Institutional-Investment-in-the-United-Kingdom-A-Review.pdf> accessed 28 May 2020.

[12] See The Investment Association (IA), 'Adherence to the FRC's Stewardship Code Survey at 31 September 2014' (June 2015) 7 <www.theia.org/sites/default/files/press-releases/document/20150526-fullstewardshipcode.pdf> accessed 28 May 2020 (recording that voting levels were at about 84%, increasing from 78% the year before). According to the IA, levels of voting have been hovering about the 80% mark for several years.

[13] David Larcker and Allan McCall, 'Researchers: The Power of Proxy Advisory Firms' (*Stanford Business*, 13 January 2014); Michael C Schouten, 'Do Institutional Investors Follow Proxy Advice Blindly?' (2012) <http://ssrn.com/abstract=1978343> accessed 28 May 2020; Stephen J Choi, Jill E Fisch and Marcel Kahan, 'The Power of Proxy Advisors: Myth or Reality?' (2010) 59 *Emory Law Journal* 869; Paul Rose, 'The Corporate Governance Industry' (2007) 32 *Journal of Corporation Law* 887.

[14] Andreas Jansson, 'No Exit! The Logic of Defensive Shareholder Activism' (2014) 10 *Corporate Board: Roles, Duties & Composition* 16.

[15] This seems to be characteristic of UK pension and mutual funds; see Peter Cziraki, Luc Renneboog and Peter Szilagyi, 'Shareholder Activism through Proxy Proposals: The European Perspective' (2010) 16 *European Financial Management* 738; Najah Attig, Sadok El Ghoul and Omrane Guedhami, 'Institutional Investment Horizon and Firm Credit Ratings' in Narjess Boubakri and Jean-Claude Cosset (eds), *Institutional Investors in Global Capital Market* (International Finance Review Vol 12, Emerald 2015); also see Chiu, *The Foundations and Anatomy of Shareholder Activism* (n 10) general discussion in chs 1–2.

executive remuneration, and the presentation of the committee report before shareholders in the annual report.[16]

After the Greenbury recommendations were introduced, the quality and comparability of corporate disclosure on executive remuneration made to shareholders was unsatisfactory and generally low.[17] The government took further action to improve disclosure and to introduce an advisory shareholder vote on pay ('say on pay') in order to compel shareholders to engage with the issue, via the Directors' Remuneration Report Regulations 2002 (DRRR). There is mixed evidence in the UK itself regarding the success of the DRRR prior to the 2008 global financial crisis (GFC).[18]

Through the 1990s, we also saw the beginnings of the development of hedge fund activism. This is referred to as 'offensive activism', which Armour and Cheffins define as taking an equity stake in order to facilitate corporate governance interventions.[19] Offensive activism has become an important investment management strategy for some funds.[20] Private equity funds take large concentrated stakes in order to assume management or governance powers over private companies,[21] while hedge funds take minority stakes in public companies.

Hedge fund activists are seen as being able to exert pressure by forging alliances with other investors and their proxy advisers, and by running high-profile campaigns in the media. Some view their activism as a much-needed form of monitoring for investee companies,[22] so as to ensure that the management of these companies focuses on value creation. There seems to be a significant body of consistent[23] empirical evidence on positive operating performance for companies subject to activist campaigns five to ten years after the campaign has concluded and the hedge fund has exited.[24] Moreover, hedge fund activism could produce a wider effect on

---

[16] Richard Greenbury, *Directors' Remuneration* (17 July 1995).

[17] Lee Roach, 'The Directors' Remuneration Report Regulations 2002 and the Disclosure of Executive Remuneration' (2004) 25 *The Company Lawyer* 141.

[18] Fabrizio Ferri and David A Maber, 'Say on Pay Votes and CEO Compensation: Evidence from the UK' (2013) 17 *Review of Finance* 527 on relative success but see Martin Conyon and Graham Sadler, 'Shareholder Voting and Directors' Remuneration Report Legislation: Say on Pay in the UK' (2010) 18 *Corporate Governance: An International Review* 296.

[19] John Armour and Brian Cheffins, 'The Rise and Fall (?) of Shareholder Activism by Hedge Funds' (2012) 14 *Journal of Alternative Investments* 17.

[20] Such as Third Point, Pershing Square.

[21] This model is discussed generally in Mike Wright and Ken Robbie (eds), *Management Buy-Outs and Venture Capital: Into the Next Millennium* (Edward Elgar 1999).

[22] Nicole M Boyson and Robert M Mooradian, 'Corporate Governance and Hedge Fund Activism' (2011) 14 *Review of Derivatives Research* 169; Thomas W Briggs, 'Corporate Governance and the New Hedge Fund Activism: An Empirical Analysis' (2007) 32 *Journal of Corporation Law* 681; Shane Goodwin, 'Corporate Governance and Hedge Fund Activism' (DPhil Thesis, Oklahoma State University 2015); Paul Rose and Bernard Sharfman, 'Shareholder Activism as a Corrective Mechanism in Corporate Governance' (2015) 2014 *Brigham Young University Law Review* 1015. Further, there is empirical research that shows actual governance improvements such as better financial reporting; see CS Agnes Cheng, Henry He Huang and Yinghua Li, 'Hedge Fund Intervention and Accounting Conservatism' (2015) 32 *Contemporary Accounting Research* 392; and, on reduction in managerial rent-seeking, Heqing Zhu, 'The Preventive Effect of Hedge Fund Activism' (2013) <https://ssrn.com/abstract=2369533> accessed 28 May 2020.

[23] But see evidence to the contrary, John C Coffee and Darius Palia, 'The Impact of Hedge Fund Activism: Evidence and Implications' (2014) ECGI Law Working Paper No 266/2014 <http://ssrn.com/abstract=2496518> accessed 28 May 2020; Frank Partnoy, 'U.S. Hedge Fund Activism' in Jennifer G Hill and Randall S Thomas (eds), *Research Handbook on Shareholder Power* (Edward Elgar 2015).

[24] Lucian Bebchuk, Alon Brav and Wei Jiang, 'The Long-Term Effects of Hedge Fund Activism' (2015) 115 *Columbia Law Review* 1085; Marco Becht, Julian Franks, Jeremy Grant and Hannes Wagner, 'Returns to Hedge Fund Activism: An International Study' (2017) 30 *The Review of Financial Studies* 2933; Alon Brav, Wei Jiang and Hyunseob Kim, 'The Real Effects of Hedge Fund Activism: Productivity, Asset Allocation, and Labor Outcomes' (2015) 28 *The Review of Financial Studies* 2723. On medium-term value creation, see Nick WA Stokman, 'Influences of Hedge Fund Activism on the Medium Term Target Value' (2007) <https://ssrn.com/abstract=1019968> accessed 28 May 2020.

corporate culture.[25] Some commentators find qualitative changes in terms of better corporate governance and management accountability after an episode of hedge fund activism.[26]

However, other commentators[27] are of the view that hedge fund activism brings only disruption to the management role and makes it more likely that boards will be captured by short-termist shareholder demands, to the detriment of other stakeholders such as employees. Empirical research[28] shows that only the most disruptive forms of shareholder activism, such as agitating for the merger, sale or part-sale of a company, achieve significant share price reactions. Such disruptive behaviour could be deleterious to wider stakeholder interests and the longer-term prospects for the enterprise.[29] Partnoy and Thomas[30] refer to hedge fund activism as a form of 'financial innovation' in investment strategy that is mediated through its corporate governance role. Hedge funds have shown special interest in merger arbitrage, capital issues such as buy-backs and dividends, and the exploitation of short-term information asymmetries, all for the purposes of exploiting for financial gain. Such exploitation could be seen as an application of their quasi-proprietary rights, such as in asking for share buy-backs in order to extract value from return of capital,[31] or in engagement, voting or litigation pursuant to their profit-extraction agenda.[32] Hence, a number of commentators have argued that the substance of hedge fund activism is short-termist[33] and disruptive in nature.

It was against this context of uneven levels of incentive-based shareholder activism that the GFC imploded. Although the crisis was owing to risk mismanagement on the part of many mainstream banks in relation to financial innovation,[34] the UK government took

---

[25] Dionysia Katelouzou, 'Myths and Realities of Hedge Fund Activism: Some Empirical Evidence' (2013) 7 *Virginia Law & Business Review* 459.

[26] Shane Goodwin, Akshay Singh, Walter Slipetz and Ramesh Rao, 'Myopic Investor Myth Debunked: The Long-Term Efficacy of Shareholder Advocacy in the Boardroom' (2014) <https://ssrn.com/abstract=2555701> accessed 28 May 2020.

[27] David J Berger and Kenneth M Murray, 'As the Market Turns: Corporate Governance Litigation in an Age of Stockholder Activism' (2009) 5 *New York University Journal of Law & Business* 207; Dan Bernhardt and Ed Nosal, 'Gambling for Dollars: Strategic Hedge Fund Manager Investment' (2013) Federal Reserve Bank of Chicago Working Paper No 2013-23 <http://ssrn.com/abstract=2367475> accessed 28 May 2020; William W Bratton, 'Hedge Funds and Governance Targets' (2007) 95 *Georgetown Law Journal* 1375. But see Katelouzou (n 25).

[28] Sarah Gordon, 'Activist Hedge Funds Not So Good for Shareholders' *Financial Times* (20 May 2015) <www.ft.com/content/ddbabe64-fee1-11e4-84b2-00144feabdc0> accessed 28 May 2020; Becht and others (n 24).

[29] Robby Houben and Gert Straetmans, 'Shareholder Rights and Responsibilities in the Context of Corporate Social Responsibility' (2016) 27 *European Business Law Review* 615 argue that some forms of offensive activism raise the risk profile of the company, having implications for their cost of raising capital and their longer-term prospects.

[30] Frank Partnoy and Randall S Thomas, 'Gap Filling, Hedge Funds, and Financial Innovation' (2006) Vanderbilt Law and Economics Research Paper No 06-21 <http://ssrn.com/abstract=931254> accessed 28 May 2020.

[31] The self-interests of the activist would be predominant as share repurchases bring about increase in share price and a windfall from the capital return; see Balasingham Balachandran, Keryn Chalmers and Janto Haman, 'On-Market Share Buybacks, Exercisable Share Options and Earnings Management' (2008) 48 *Accounting & Finance* 25; Harrison Liu and Edward P Swanson, 'Is Price Support for Overvalued Equity a Motive for Increasing Share Repurchases?' (2016) 38 *Journal of Corporate Finance* 77; José-Miguel Gaspar and others, 'Can Buybacks Be a Product of Shorter Shareholder Horizons?' (2005) AFA 2005 Philadelphia Meetings Paper <https://ssrn.com/abstract=649482> accessed 28 May 2020. Also aligns with managerial incentives; see Jesse M Fried, 'Open Market Repurchases: Signaling or Managerial Opportunism?' (2001) 2 *Theoretical Inquiries in Law* 865 also again in Jesse M Fried, 'Informed Trading and False Signaling with Open Market Repurchases' (2005) 93 *California Law Review* 1323.

[32] Partnoy and Thomas (n 30).

[33] Véronique Bessière, Michael Kaestner and Anne-Laurence Lafont, 'Hedge Fund Activism: Insights from a French Clinical Study' (2011) 21 *Applied Financial Economics* 1225 on governance being used as an excuse to engage for instrumental returns.

[34] Markus Brunnermeier and others, *The Fundamental Principles of Financial Regulation* (Geneva Reports on the World Economy, Centre for Economic Policy Research 2009).

a 'root-and-branch' approach to uncovering deficits in bank management and commissioned a corporate governance review of banks. Although institutional shareholder apathy is not regarded as the key cause of the UK banking crisis, the Walker Review on corporate governance in banks and financial institutions took the view that shortcomings in institutional shareholder oversight provided a tolerant or indeed encouraging context for misjudgements of risk made at the board level of the failed UK banks.[35] In response, the Institutional Shareholders' Committee, the trade association representing institutions, developed a broadly framed code to encourage institutions to be more active and engaged.[36] As this code has received bottom-up acceptance among institutions, the Financial Reporting Council (FRC) in the UK adopted this formally as a 'Stewardship Code' in 2010,[37] to reflect the expectations for institutions that to engage with their investee companies is a matter of 'stewardship' – a term which had previously been more associated with the benevolent role that corporate directors should adopt in the fulfilment of their legal duties to their companies, but which was now appropriated by the investment industry to describe the governance role of institutional shareholders.

The UK Stewardship Code originally was subject to a comply-or-explain regime, and applied only to voluntary signatories.[38] The first UK Code focused on institutions' relationships with their investee companies. This development cemented expectations of institutions' corporate governance behaviour,[39] and a slew of legal reforms in relation to corporate disclosure followed, as means to moderate and change corporate behaviour in various areas, but crucially reliant on shareholders to monitor and call companies to account.

For example, faith continues to be placed in institutions' role in say on pay and to provide the essential monitoring governance expected of 'good corporate equity owners'. Hence, law reform supports this policy direction by first providing institutions with information and then empowering them with 'say' in the general meeting.[40] The UK introduced a binding shareholder vote on forward-looking pay policy, to take place at least every three years.[41] Further, an annual shareholder advisory vote will be taken in a backward-looking manner to signal shareholder approval, or otherwise, on the previous year's implementation of pay packages.[42] The EU has now introduced this in SRD II, which provides for a binding say on pay every four years.[43]

---

[35] David Walker, 'A Review of Corporate Governance in UK Banks and Other Financial Industry Entities. Final Recommendations' (26 November 2009) <https://ecgi.global/sites/default/files/codes/documents/walker_review_261109.pdf> accessed 28 May 2020.

[36] Institutional Shareholders' Committee, 'Code on the Responsibilities of Institutional Shareholders' (November 2009) <www.plsa.co.uk/portals/0/documents/0039_isc_statement_of_principles_2007_0607.pdf> accessed 11 February 2022; Howard Davies, *The Financial Crisis: Who Is to Blame?* (Polity Press 2010).

[37] UK Code 2010 (n 1).

[38] On the relative ineffectiveness of comply-and-explain, see John Parkinson and Gavin Kelly, 'The Combined Code on Corporate Governance' (1999) 70 *The Political Quarterly* 101. Disclosure is often sub-optimal and the FRC has, in the recent UK Code 2020, enforced a system of disclosure vetting before listing an institution as a 'signatory'.

[39] More detail on the development of the UK Stewardship Code is discussed elsewhere in this book: see Davies, The UK Stewardship Code 2010–2020, Chapter 2 and Katelouzou and Micheler, The Market for Stewardship and the Role of the Government, Chapter 3.

[40] The US led in this reform; see Securities Exchange Act of 1934 rr 14a–21(a). On say on pay reforms, see global survey in Randall S Thomas and Christoph Van der Elst, 'Say on Pay Around the World' (2015) 92 *Washington University Law Review* 653.

[41] s 439A of the Companies Act, inserted via the Enterprise and Regulatory Reform Act 2013.

[42] Companies Act 2006, s 439.

[43] SRD II (n 5) Art 9a.

Other disclosure requirements imposed on companies include narrative statements regarding prospects and risks, under the reformed Strategic Report;[44] the directors' narrative management report to the markets; the EU's non-financial disclosure statement regarding the company's performance in non-financial matters such as environmental impact, human rights impact and anti-corruption matters;[45] the directors' duty statement (also known as the section 172 report) that explicates how directors have taken into account stakeholders' interests including employees', creditors', suppliers', customers' and their community's interests in managing the company;[46] and non–corporate law mandatory disclosures in relation to supply chain diligence,[47] pay ratio,[48] gender pay gap reporting,[49] corporate tax transparency[50] and conflict mineral sourcing assurance.[51] Many of these disclosure statements are 'enforceable' only via market discipline, in relation to shareholders' response to their disclosure, whether in voice or exit. Hence it can be argued that although mainstream institutional investors have shown a chequered track record in terms of their involvement in investee companies, there is no let-up in relation to the public and policy expectation that they fulfil a monitoring role in the corporate sector.

Indeed, the near-legalization of funds' and asset managers' roles in engaging with their investee companies was undertaken in SRD II. Under the Directive, member states shall require institutional investors and asset managers to develop an engagement policy on (or otherwise explain) how institutional investors and asset managers intend to integrate shareholder engagement in their investment strategy, monitor their investee companies' performance,[52] exercise their voting rights, use proxy advisers' services, and co-operate with other shareholders. This has now been implemented for the investment management sector in the UK by the Financial Conduct Authority (FCA).[53]

The relentless reliance placed by policymakers upon the roles of institutional shareholders persists, in spite of findings that many institutions that signed up to the UK Code do not engage in purposeful and meaningful dialogue with investee companies.[54] The FRC even implemented a tiering system to classify institutional shareholders according to their quality of stewardship in

---

[44] Companies Act 2006, s 414A; discussed in Iris H-Y Chiu, 'Institutional Shareholders as Stewards: Towards a New Conception of Corporate Governance?' (2012) 6 *Brooklyn Journal of Financial, Corporate and Commercial Law* 387.
[45] Companies Act 2006, s 414CA; see Iris H-Y Chiu, 'Unpacking the Reforms in Europe and UK Relating to Mandatory Disclosure in Corporate Social Responsibility: Instituting a Hybrid Governance Model to Change Corporate Behaviour?' (2017) 14 *European Company Law* 193.
[46] Companies Act 2006, s 414CZA, implementing disclosure requirements into the director's duty under s 172 of the Act.
[47] Modern Slavery Act 2015, s 54, discussed in Iris H-Y Chiu, 'Disclosure Regulation and Sustainability: Legalisation and New Governance Implications' in Beate Sjåfjell and Christopher M Bruner (eds), *Cambridge Handbook of Corporate Law, Corporate Governance and Sustainability* (CUP 2019).
[48] Companies Act 2006, paras 19B and C of Sch 8, to report pay ratios among highest, median and lowest paid employees.
[49] Equality Act 2010, s 78.
[50] Finance Act 2015, ss 122(1), (4), (5) and (6), requiring country-by-country reporting of tax paid by multinational enterprises in order to discern tax arbitrage.
[51] EU Conflict Minerals Regulation 2017, art 7, to be in force from 2021, discussed in Chiu, 'Disclosure Regulation and Sustainability' (n 47).
[52] SRD II (n 5) art 3g.
[53] Applying to all institutions involved in portfolio management, whether UCITs, alternative investment funds, insurers; see Financial Conduct Authority (FCA) Handbook, SYSC 3.4.4-10.
[54] Julia Mundy, Lisa Jack and Sandra Einig, 'Is the Stewardship Code Fit for Purpose?' (CIMA Global Academic Research Programme, March 2019) <www.cimaglobal.com/Documents/Thought_leadership_docs/Academic-research/4841-stewardship-code-research-report.pdf> accessed 28 May 2020. The report finds that engagement can be highly instrumental for a fund's private information advantages and is seldom collective or escalated. Funds and asset managers seldom integrate stewardship into core strategy and remain deferential to management.

order to incentivize optimal behaviour.[55] With the legalization of duties for the investment management sector, the FRC has now introduced soft law to govern asset owners' (funds), asset managers' and their service providers' investment management behaviour more generally, incorporating engagement with investee companies.[56] This soft law complements the legalization of SRD II's duties and edges us closer to a more comprehensive regime for regulating investment management behaviour. Although this regime still firmly entrenches the notion that engaged corporate governance roles is expected behaviour, it has become part of the wider strategic governance of the investment management industry in the UK and the EU.

25.3 ASPECTS OF CHALLENGE FOR CORPORATE GOVERNANCE 'STEWARDSHIP' IN THE INVESTMENT MANAGEMENT SECTOR

Although the legal framework and soft law in the UK and the EU increasingly compel the investment management industry to engage in corporate governance roles as part of good stewardship, their effectiveness would be challenged by the business models of investment management, the structures of investment management and the governance of funds.

25.3.1 Investment Management Business Models

Leaving aside dedicated activist hedge funds whose engagement strategy is instrumental to their value generation strategy, we consider how mainstream investment management could be strategically integrated with expected corporate governance roles. In the UK and the EU, institutional investment management has grown owing to the need to serve the long-term savings goals of working populations, and certain established business models have developed. These factors also apply to markets such as the US. The two main investment management mandates that funds may be offered by their asset managers would be active or passive mandates, and strategies that mix features along the spectrum from passive to active. Active management refers to strategies employed in order to generate 'alpha' by informed and researched stock-picking and turnover of portfolio, so as to beat the average market returns embodied in particular stock market indices. Passive management refers to investment management strategies that adhere closely to a particular stock market index. These are generally low cost as there is less need for research and judgement-based effort on the part of asset managers.

Active management mandates are riddled with agency problems that permeate investment management practice, crucially affecting asset managers' corporate governance roles. Asset managers are optimally positioned in the investment chain to generate rents for themselves and other participants in the chain. For example, asset managers are reported to practise 'churning' (i.e. excessive trading of securities in order to generate transactions fees and charges).[57] In this sense they are more likely motivated by exit than by exercising voice in engaging with investee companies.[58] Other examples of rent-seeking for the investment chain as

---

[55] Financial Reporting Council, 'Tiering of signatories to the Stewardship Code' <www.frc.org.uk/news/november-2016/tiering-of-signatories-to-the-stewardship-code> accessed 22 February 2022.
[56] UK Code 2020 (n 6) Principles 9–11.
[57] See e.g. Norma Cohen, 'How Fund Managers Spend Your Money' *Financial Times* (7 June 2014) <www.ft.com/content/5dfc402a-ebdd-11e3-8cef-00144feabdc0> accessed 28 May 2020. The FCA has also found that asset managers do not optimally keep transaction costs under control; see Financial Conduct Authority, 'Asset Management Market Study Final Report' (Market Study 15/2.3, June 2017) para 7.2 <www.fca.org.uk/publication/market-studies/ms15-2-3.pdf> accessed 28 May 2020.
[58] Mundy, Jack and Einig (n 54).

a whole include arrangements made with brokers or trading venues for routing orders and receiving commissions or kickbacks and third-party payments such as research payments bundled in dealing commissions to brokers and analysts.[59] These can consume much of the returns generated in active management, flatlining returns to investors. Indeed, in the current low-yield and competitive environment, Fama and French[60] have found that active fund management fees and charges inevitably reduce or nullify the returns for investors. In this context, active asset managers are increasingly struggling to deliver comfortably excess returns in their investment management, and regulators have also intruded into fee charging practices, to reduce conflicts of interest deleterious to investors. Legislation has been introduced to make fees and charges more controlled,[61] transparent and justifiable.[62] Active managers hardly have any more incentive to engage intensively with investee companies as such efforts are costly in terms of research and time.[63]

Funds have also become disillusioned with the high cost and lacklustre returns in active management and many now prefer passively managed investment products that track an index or replicate an index composition, and charge lower fees.[64] In particular, after the mandatory charge cap of 0.75 per cent of fund assets was introduced by the UK government[65] for defined contribution pension schemes, many asset managers of these schemes would invariably prefer to offer passively managed products such as those that track an established benchmark such as a stock market index or can be in the form of exchange-traded products (ETFs) that track an index or synthetic ETFs that aim to correlate with an index.

Passive investing creates another type of agency problem (i.e. that of 'neglect' and ultimate disengagement from the real economy). Funds are tied into a mechanistic approach to stock selection, and it is such a constrained approach that it makes investment management cost-effective. Further, as passive investing is engaged with a benchmark and not with the underlying corporate assets as such, the sense of disengagement could be augmented between asset managers and investee companies. On the other hand, passive funds may feel tied to certain companies in the index – in which they are, more or less, permanently invested – and are thus incentivized to revisit their 'ownership' role in investee companies. There seems to be some evidence that passive and large investors such as BlackRock do take shareholder engagement seriously as part of their investment management practice.[66] However, as passive funds are low cost in nature, the demands of shareholder engagement seem contrary to their cost-conscious

---

[59] Some of these practices are discussed in Graham Busby, 'Conflicts of Interest and Inducements under MiFID' (2008) *Journal of International Banking Law and Regulation* 1.

[60] Eugene F Fama and Kenneth R French, 'Luck Versus Skill in the Cross-Section of Mutual Fund Returns' (2010) 65 *The Journal of Finance* 1915.

[61] For example, MiFID 2014, art 24(8) and Commission delegated legislation specifying that bundled dealing commissions cannot continue to be passed on to investors. Research charges need to be specifically costed up front and passed on to investors with their consent.

[62] e.g. Financial Conduct Authority, 'Asset Management Market Study: Interim Report' (Market Study 15/2.2, November 2016) <www.fca.org.uk/publication/market-studies/ms15-2-2-interim-report.pdf> accessed 28 May 2020; and Financial Conduct Authority (n 57).

[63] Mundy, Jack and Einig (n 54).

[64] Lodewjik van Setten, *The Law of Institutional Investment Management* (OUP 2009) paras 4.48ff, 4.86ff; see also Fisch, The Uncertain Stewardship Potential of Index Funds, Chapter 21.

[65] See discussion in Andrew Wood, Louise Amantani, Duncan McDougall and Niall Baker, *Landscape and Charges Survey 2013: Charges and Quality in Defined Contribution Pension Schemes* (Department for Work and Pensions, February 2014) 51ff, ch 4 <https://assets.publishing.service.gov.uk/government/uploads/system/uploads/attachment_data/file/281128/rr859-defined-contribution-pension-schemes.pdf> accessed 28 May 2020.

[66] John Authors, 'Passive Investors Are Good Corporate Stewards' *Financial Times* (19 January 2016) <www.ft.com/content/c4e7a4f6-be8a-11e5-846f-79b0e3d20eaf> accessed 28 May 2020; Ian R Appel, Todd R Gormley and Donald B Keim, 'Passive Investors, Not Passive Owners' (2016) 121 *Journal of Financial Economics* 111 <www.stern.nyu.edu/sites/default/

approach.[67] Further empirical evidence finds that passive indexed asset managers often vote with management[68] and thus provide little in the way of a monitoring role.

In sum, the development of professional asset management has produced two rather extreme and perverse effects. One is substantial agency cost in the exercise of significant amounts of discretion in investment management, while the other is completely market-led and marked by a lack of discretionary intervention. In either case it is highly questionable whether meaningful investment intermediation through good corporate ownership is achieved to connect the long-term expectations of savers with the long-term wealth creation by the corporate economy.

It may be argued that long-term investors such as pension funds should be incentivized to exercise voice in investee companies and to persuade their asset managers to do so, too. There are two barriers. One is that funds may be invested in pooled mandates (that may be active or passive) and not tailor-made mandates, hence making it difficult to instruct asset managers to take certain corporate governance positions. This is the issue of the investment chain canvassed shortly. The second is that pension funds that are defined benefit in nature have maturing liabilities, just like insurers managing annuities, and liability-driven strategies may be cost-conscious and not necessarily long-termist.[69]

Where defined contribution schemes are concerned, scheme trustees or the internal governance committee of the employer that monitors contract-based providers need to regularly assess investment performance and review objectives.[70] Empirical research shows that such reviews take place regularly, frequently on a quarterly basis,[71] and these performance reviews can drive short-termism in defined contribution scheme management, which can encourage exit over voice and the avoidance of costly efforts in engaged corporate governance roles.

For retail, collective investment schemes such as Undertakings for Collective Investment in Transferable Securities (UCITS; see Directive 2009/65/EC), as well as non-UCITS open-ended (NURS) and closed-ended schemes, are subject to regular periodic accountability.[72] Alternative investment fund managers, under EU legislation, are subject to harmonized reporting obligations to investors on a yearly basis.[73] However, in addition to the mandatory annual report, funds and investors could enter into agreements to have additional reporting frequency such as on a quarterly basis.[74] The regulatory regime for regular reporting has played no small part in encouraging funds and their asset managers to pursue short-termist investment performance.[75]

---

files/assets/documents/1%20Gormley%20Passive%20Investors%20Not%20Passive%20Owners.pdf> accessed 28 May 2020.

[67] John Plender, 'Pay-Offs and Perils of Passive Investing' *Financial Times* (27 October 2013) <www.ft.com/content/cf04a1e2-3b1e-11e3-87fa-00144feab7de> accessed 28 May 2020.

[68] Tom Eckett, 'Index Funds Rarely Challenge Management in Shareholder Votes' (*ETF Stream*, 10 October 2019) <www.etfstream.com/news/9398_index-funds-rarely-challenge-management-in-shareholder-votes/> accessed 28 May 2020. See also: Lucian Bebchuk and Scott Hirst, 'Index Funds and the Future of Corporate Governance: Theory, Evidence, and Policy' (December 2019) 119 *Columbia Law Review* 2029; Fisch, The Uncertain Stewardship Potential of Index Funds, Chapter 21.

[69] Discussed in Barker and Chiu (n 7) ch 4.

[70] Pensions Act 2004, s 244.

[71] Wood and others (n 65) 107–8, para 10.2.3.

[72] Undertakings in Collective Investments in Transferable Securities Directive 2009, art 68.

[73] Alternative Investment Fund Managers Directive 2011, art 22.

[74] Where investors use online platforms, hedge funds may even in due course aim to provide weekly or daily accounting transparency. See BNY Mellon, 'Risk Roadmap: Hedge Funds and Investors' Evolving Approach to Risk' (August 2012) <http://web.archive.org/web/20180312002312/www.thehedgefundjournal.com/sites/default/files/riskroadmap.pdf> archived 12 March 2018, accessed 28 May 2020.

[75] Some empirical research disagrees, although most empirical research shows that investment management is short-termist in nature. See Brian J Bushee, 'Do Institutional Investors Prefer Near-Term Earnings Over Long-Run Value?'

Guyatt argues that investor myopia is entrenched as it is seen as a defensible practice in light of regulatory requirements.[76]

Furthermore, as Vayanos and Woolley have argued, asset owners and trustees tend to be uncertain as to the competence and diligence of the asset managers to whom they outsource fund management responsibilities.[77] It is increasingly recognized that most active asset managers find it extremely difficult to sustain portfolio outperformance relative to benchmarks over an extended period of time.[78] Consequently, if a fund develops negative deviation from the performance of a benchmark – even over a relatively short period – it becomes increasingly difficult for asset owners or trustees to simply ignore this development or seek to justify a continuation of the investment management mandate.[79]

Funds and asset owners, therefore, are reluctant to move away from the norm and adopt 'outlier' modes of investment thinking that do not strictly conform to the dominant practice of short-termist evaluation.[80]

Further, for retail collective investment schemes or alternative funds, investors' redemptions are generally unquestioned rights, albeit governed by terms of the fund and by regulation.[81] Regulation has played a key part in securing investors' rights in redemption as a means of investor protection, hence funds' requirement to meet liquidity needs may be contrary to integrating engaged corporate governance roles in their investment management. The provision of liquidity for investors means that a price for exit has to be regularly, if not constantly, available.[82] This reinforces the marketized model of investment management which commoditizes corporations as narrowly represented in securities assets that are regularly bought and sold, and reinforces the model of investment gains as derived from trading gains instead of real productivity and operational performance. A number of empirical researchers are of the view that a liquid market for securities may be essential for capital formation but adverse to corporate governance (i.e.

(2001) 18 *Contemporary Accounting Research* 207; Alberto Manconi, Massimo Massa and Ayako Yasuda, 'The Role of Institutional Investors in Propagating the Crisis of 2007–2008' (2012) 104 *Journal of Financial Economics* 491; Michael Porter, *Capital Choices: Changing the Way America Invests in Industry* (Harvard Business School Press 1994); Xuemin Yan and Zhe Zhang, 'Institutional Investors and Equity Returns: Are Short-Term Institutions Better Informed?' (2009) 22 *The Review of Financial Studies* 893. On the contrary, see Jeffrey L Callen and Xiaohua Fang, 'Institutional Investor Stability and Crash Risk: Monitoring versus Short-Termism?' (2013) 37 *Journal of Banking & Finance* 3047 (arguing that companies with institutional investors that are long-termist in nature do not 'hoard' bad news until the very last minute causing share price crashes and volatility, and that empirical research reveals that most companies are not subject to such share price crashes and short-termist pressures from investors); Mark J Roe, 'Corporate Short-Termism: In the Boardroom and in the Courtroom' (2013) 68 *The Business Lawyer* 977 (arguing that short-termist traders are only part of the landscape, the most short-termist being high-frequency traders, and there are plenty of long-termist institutions whose holding periods have not changed much over the years, e.g. Vanguard and Fidelity).

[76] Danyelle Guyatt, 'Meeting Objectives and Resisting Conventions: A Focus on Institutional Investors and Long-Term Responsible Investing' (2005) 5 *Corporate Governance: The International Journal of Effective Board Performance* 139

[77] Dimitri Vayanos and Paul Woolley, 'Curse of the Benchmarks' (March 2016) Financial Markets Group Discussion Paper No 747 <www.lse.ac.uk/fmg/assets/documents/paul-woolley-centre/articles-of-general-interest/DP747CurseoftheBenchmarks.pdf> accessed 28 May 2020.

[78] Hendrik Bessembinder, 'Do Stocks Outperform Treasury Bills?' (2018) 129 *Journal of Financial Economics* 440.

[79] Vayanos and Woolley (n 77).

[80] Guyatt (n 76). On herding and group conformance, David Marginson and Laurie McAulay, 'Exploring the Debate on Short-Termism: A Theoretical and Empirical Analysis' (2008) 29 *Strategic Management Journal* 273.

[81] The right to request redemption for UCITs investors must be met, UCITS Directive, art 84; AIFMD, arts 16, 18.

[82] For example, the *Financial Times* describes the 2019 implosion of Neil Woodford's investment business (owing to its inability to fulfil redemption requests relating to its Equity Income Fund) and M&G's decision to bar withdrawals from its UK property fund for the second time in three years as 'ignominious failures that have cast a shadow across the entire sector' (Chris Flood, 'UK Fund Industry Has Had a Year to Forget – Especially the Regulator' *Financial Times* (16 December 2019) <www.ft.com/content/daa6d154-c81f-4969-bc8c-85981b44b728> accessed 28 May 2020).

investors are not encouraged to be actively engaged with their investments over the long-term). Under relative conditions of less liquidity, shareholders are more likely to be engaged.[83]

25.3.2 Investment Chain

As Morley points out, investment management is structured as a 'separation of funds from managers',[84] in a complex chain structure crucially involving funds delegating to asset managers who further use a web of service providers in investment management.[85] This phenomenon means that investors' capital is being placed under the ownership of an entity, the fund, which is a separate legal entity from the fund manager, an investment management company (which is often the one that has constituted the fund). The investor's relationship is with the fund, which may be structured as a trust, a company or under contract. The fund entity appoints the management company to invest and manage the fund assets, usually by contract. In this way, investors in a fund do not have a direct legal relationship with the fund manager, who is crucial to making strategic and operational decisions in relation to the investment management of the fund's assets. Such a structure of 'separation of funds from management' can be observed in pension funds, which outsource investment management to various portfolio managers,[86] retail collective investment funds such as the popular UCITS,[87] as well as hedge and private equity funds.[88]

As the responsibility for investment management is disaggregated and reposed in a separate entity from the fund, the scope of legal responsibility owed by the fund manager (and other investment entities contracting with the fund) to the ultimate investor is limited. The fund may take action against fund managers for sub-optimal investment management, but investors do not have direct recourse to such an action, having to rely on instructing the fund as such.[89] In the same vein, the investment management strategy and practice adopted by the management company are usually not susceptible to the fund investor's input or influence.[90]

The separation of funds from management is a structure that is arguably accepted if not endorsed in much of financial regulation. In the EU, UCITS, the fund entity, is referred to as the 'investment company' and is distinct from the 'management company'.[91] The 'investment company' and the 'management company' are subject to different authorization and regulatory

---

[83] Kerry Back, Tao Li and Alexander Ljungqvist, 'Liquidity and Governance' (2013) ECGI – Finance Working Paper No 388 <http://ssrn.com/abstract=2350362> accessed 28 May 2020.
[84] John Morley, 'The Separation of Funds and Managers: A Theory of Investment Fund Structure and Regulation' (2014) 123 *Yale Law Journal* 1228.
[85] John Kay, 'The Kay Review of UK Equity Markets and Long-Term Decision Making' (Department for Business, Innovation and Skills July 2012) paras 3.9, 3.10, 4.10, 4.12 <https://assets.publishing.service.gov.uk/government/uploads/system/uploads/attachment_data/file/253454/bis-12-917-kay-review-of-equity-markets-final-report.pdf> accessed 28 May 2020 [hereinafter Kay Review].
[86] Whether in relation to defined benefit or contribution schemes, employers' fund entities often appoint outside investment managers for portfolios.
[87] Discussed in Barker and Chiu (n 7) ch 5.
[88] Discussed in Barker and Chiu (n 7) chs 6, 7.
[89] But enforcement by fund against fund manager may not be a realistic prospect if the fund manager and the fund are related; see discussion shortly.
[90] Although Ewan McGaughey ('Does Corporate Governance Exclude the Ultimate Investor?' (2016) 16 *Journal of Corporate Law Studies* 221) refers to old case law to support his argument that ultimate investors are owed fiduciary duties and can instruct funds, and are therefore not excluded from corporate governance, the lack of a direct relationship with the fund manager makes investors less incentivized or concerned to do so. Moreover, in a collective investment vehicle, it is hard to see how particular investors' preferences can percolate to the fund management level as the fund mediates investors' preferences as a whole.
[91] UCITs Directive 2009, arts 5, 6.

regimes. The separation structure allows funds to be incorporated in low tax jurisdictions within the EU, such as Luxembourg and Ireland, and still enjoy rights of passporting to other EU member states for marketing and distribution.[92] Management companies can be located in other EU member states and are separately authorized. The Alternative Investment Fund Managers Directive (AIFMD) also recognizes that fund entities ('alternative investment funds' or AIFs) are separate from the fund manager, which is the subject of the Directive.[93] AIFs are expressly not regulated under the Directive, and this allows AIFs to incorporate in low tax jurisdictions chosen by the relevant funds and their investors.

One important implication of the separation structure is that investors are able to have relatively stronger exit rights from each distinct fund, and investors may see much less need for control or voice.[94] Hence, the important right of redemption already discussed may pose a compliance necessity that undercuts funds' incentives to encourage asset managers to undertake engaged and costly corporate governance roles. The implications of the investment chain for corporate governance as observed are voting apathy and general lack of engagement by asset managers and funds in their investee companies.[95] Further, if funds are invested in asset managers' pooled products, so that the fund does not enjoy a tailor-made investment management mandate, the funds would not be able to identify particular interests in investee companies in their portfolio in order to influence asset managers' strategies towards them.[96]

That said, it may be argued that ultimate fund beneficiaries have interests in the long-term well-being of investee companies, and it is perverse that the interposition of structures within the investment chain could result in the muteness or non-conveyance of such preferences. It is argued that there is potential for distributed ledger technology (DLT) to change the state of institutional shareholder stranglehold on corporate governance, if the use of DLT is able to penetrate the layers of the investment chain to identify share ownership and allocate shareholder rights to beneficiaries. Where the individual beneficial owner is obscured by the financial institution custodian that holds the legal rights to shares, DLT can be used to record levels of intermediated securities ownership, ultimately identifying and empowering beneficial share owners to exercise corporate governance rights.[97] It is less clear that the DLT can be used to identify and allocate shareholder rights to beneficiaries in funds that invest in corporate equities, as these beneficiaries' rights, usually contractual in nature, can be based only on units in funds. They do not have proprietary rights in particular shares.[98] Nevertheless, commentators take the

---

[92] Barker and Chiu (n 7) ch 5.
[93] Indeed, funds can be incorporated offshore, such as in Bermuda, while the fund manager is regulated under the Directive.
[94] Morley (n 84).
[95] Myners (n 11); Walker (n 35). The apathy of shareholders was especially critiqued in the wake of the 2007–09 Global Financial Crisis; see Jennifer Hughes, 'FSA Chief Lambasts Uncritical Investors' *Financial Times* (12 March 2009) <www.ft.com/content/9edc7548-0e8d-11de-b099-0000779fd2ac> accessed 28 May 2020; and Kate Burgess, 'Myners Lashes Out at Landlord Shareholders' *Financial Times* (London, 22 April 2009) <www.ft.com/content/c0217c20-2eaf-11de-b7d3-00144feabdc0> accessed 28 May 2020.
[96] Nick Fitzpatrick, 'FUNDS vs MANDATES: Would You Invest in a Pooled Fund?' *Funds Europe* (March 2009) <www.funds-europe.com/funds-vs-mandates-would-you-invest-in-a-pooled-fund> accessed 28 May 2020, on funds' increasingly likely use of pooled investment structures rather than tailor-made mandates.
[97] Christoph Van der Elst and Anne LaFarre, 'Blockchain and Smart Contracting for the Shareholder Community' (2019) 20 *European Business Organization Law Review* 111; David Yermack, 'Corporate Governance and Blockchains' (2017) 21 *Review of Finance* 7; Vedat Akgiray, 'The Potential for Blockchain Technology in Corporate Governance' (OECD 2019) OECD Corporate Governance Working Papers No 21 <www.oecd-ilibrary.org/docserver/ef4eba4c-en.pdf?expires=1590824852&id=id&accname=guest&checksum=1E5028A5C21F72F02DCCE09A18AE2627> accessed 28 May 2020.
[98] This is the investment practice of pooled mandates; see Fitzpatrick (n 96).

view that a new cadre of beneficial owners can be brought into the corporate governance landscape, and corporate governance can become relevant to those outside the institutional sector.[99] This may in part be assisted by hard law as in the UCITS Directive and soft law as in the UK Code 2020.

In 2010, the European Commission introduced an initiative to improve investor protection by imposing conduct of business obligations on the management companies of UCITS funds.[100] The Directive imposes certain duties on management companies in order to secure the best interests of unit-holders in funds, such as due diligence in monitoring their portfolios and ensuring that the portfolios are managed within the investment limits and risk appetite.[101] Further, as part of regulating the investment management practices of fund managers, the Directive also imposes a duty on management companies to develop policies on how their voting rights in investee companies should be exercised for the benefit of the funds.[102] The beauty of such regulatory duties is that they 'cut across' the investment chain structures to construct a compliance requirement for asset managers that is ultimate investor–facing. Although it is questionable if ultimate investors can enforce against such duties under a breach of statutory action,[103] regulators can take enforcement action.

It can also be argued that SRD II introduces reform that cuts across the structures of the investment chain as it requires asset owners and managers to publicly disclose their engagement policies (or a sufficient alternative), the former's equity investment strategy, and the latter's adherence to asset owners' objectives and needs.[104] Disclosure may, however, rightly be criticized, as the Kingman Review in the UK has done, in relation to the obscurity of achieved outcomes.[105] The UK Code 2020, in setting out best practices for asset owners and asset managers in stewardship, further 'cuts across' the investment chain structures to encourage consistent and robust investment management practices from funds to their asset managers and service providers. Asset owners and managers should mirror best practices in terms of communicating their investment beliefs, strategy, governance processes and culture for achieving good stewardship,[106] and this allows beneficiaries to discern consistency between funds' mandates and asset management strategies.

Further, Principle 6 of the UK Code 2020 requires asset owners and managers to seek beneficiaries' needs and preferences in order to shape their investment management strategies, including stewardship activities.[107] The Principle also envisages that asset owners and managers will report on, and make adequate disclosure of, their stewardship activities and outcomes. This Principle is perhaps the most revolutionary innovation in the revised UK Code, as it overcomes investment chain structures, and compels asset owners and managers to be accountable directly to beneficiaries.[108] The possibility of using DLT technology to facilitate ease of engaging with

---

[99] van der Elst and LaFarre (n 97).
[100] Commission Directive 2010/43/EU of 1 July 2010 implementing Directive 2009/65/EC of the European Parliament and of the Council as regards organisational requirements, conflicts of interest, conduct of business, risk management and content of the agreement between a depositary and a management company.
[101] Commission Directive 2010, art 23.
[102] Commission Directive 2010, art 24.
[103] Financial Services Markets Act 2000, s 138D.
[104] SRD II (n 5) arts 3g, 3h.
[105] John Kingman, 'Independent Review of the Financial Reporting Council' (Department for Business, Energy and Industrial Strategy December 2018) Para 2.86 <https://assets.publishing.service.gov.uk/government/uploads/system/uploads/attachment_data/file/767387/frc-independent-review-final-report.pdf> accessed 28 May 2020.
[106] UK Code 2020 (n 6) Principles 1, 2, 5–8.
[107] UK Code 2020 (n 6) 13–14.
[108] See other discussions in this book, notably Katelouzou and Micheler, The Market for Stewardship and the Role of the Government, Chapter 3.

ultimate beneficiaries may also make adherence to this Principle difficult to avoid. It remains to be seen if Principle 6 will fundamentally change the disincentives and barriers to becoming engaged shareholders in investee companies. This is because taking into account beneficiary preferences and needs for accountability does not mean that beneficiaries will be galvanized into promoting corporate governance engagement as stewardship. Beneficiaries may not be experts who are able to constructively comment on what investment preferences work for the investment performance of the fund, and there may be disparate preferences which may not, on aggregate, become influential for the fund as a whole.[109] The implementation of this practice is likely to yield interesting observations in due course.

The difficulties inherent in achieving effective stewardship by institutional investors were highlighted by the UK government–sponsored review of UK equity markets following the banking crisis (the Kay Review).[110] This Review noted how the fragmentation of functions throughout the equity investment chain reduced the incentives for collective investor engagement with listed companies. It recommended that a new industry-led body – The Investor Forum – be established as a means of facilitating a greater magnitude of stewardship activities of asset managers and asset owners. Given the growing pressure on institutional investors to deliver more of a stewardship orientation, the investment industry acquiesced in this initiative – although there is no obligation for any individual fund manager to work with the Forum. Between 2014 and 2018, the Forum claims to have co-ordinated investor engagement with twenty-three UK companies at board level. However, given its modest resources and the fact that engagement activities occur behind closed doors, its likely impact on the overall UK investor stewardship landscape is uncertain.[111]

25.3.3 Fund Governance

It may be viewed as somewhat ironic that asset owners and managers should be seen as the champions of good corporate governance in the wider corporate sector when their own corporate governance has not been regarded as being particularly optimal.

First, there is the issue of expertise on the part of funds in being able to monitor their asset managers. Specifically, does the governance structure of funds permit them to overcome their core agency problem? – namely, that their investments are not being directly managed by their beneficiaries, or even by the fund entity itself, but by externally located fund managers, who therefore require careful monitoring.

Commentators[112] have pointed out that many employment defined contribution schemes are administered in companies as part of general human resources. The dedication of resources to

---

[109] A strong line on this issue has been taken by Robert Shillman, Chairman of the US industrial sensor company Cognex. He argues that asset managers are wrong to use their proxy voting power to 'pressure "their" companies to include ESG factors when making business decisions'. Writing in his company's 2018 annual report, he reflects:

> If they asked [the fund investors], 'Do you want the board of directors and the managers of your companies to spend time and energy on environmental, social and governance issues or do you want them to spend all of their time and energy on increasing the value of your shares?', I'm rather sure that an overwhelming number of them would choose the latter.

Quoted in Robert Armstrong, 'Warren Buffett on Why Companies Cannot Be Moral Arbiters' *Financial Times* (29 December 2019) <www.ft.com/content/ebbc9b46-1754-11ea-9ee4-11f260415385> accessed 28 May 2020.
[110] See Kay Review (n 85).
[111] The Investor Forum, 'Review 2018' (January 2019) 3 <www.investorforum.org.uk/wp-content/uploads/2019/01/Annual_Review_2018.pdf> accessed 28 May 2020.
[112] Gordon L Clark and Roger Urwin, 'DC Pension Fund Best-Practice Design and Governance' (2010) <http://ssrn.com/abstract=1652680> accessed 28 May 2020; Dietrich Hauptmeier and Graham Mannion, 'Effective Investment

help employees choose a suitable fund, or monitor the funds they have participated in, is extremely thin and limited. In the UK, the Department for Work and Pensions[113] has introduced reforms to mandate the establishment of 'Independent Governance Committees' in employers to oversee the DC schemes and provide governance over mandates. For trust-based schemes, a committee of trustees subject to similar duties has to be appointed.[114] There is some critique regarding how effective these committees are and, in particular, whether they are sufficiently accountable.[115] However, the FCA believes that they are working, although it has imposed more explicit duties upon them, to consider the value for money of their investment mandates and to consider ESG matters in relation to investment stewardship.[116]

Next, funds have been subject to less advanced prescriptions and practices for their own governance compared to the listed companies they invest in, and it may be queried whether funds have therefore the moral authority to challenge investee companies' governance.[117] Funds are usually set up by asset managers themselves, and many funds, though separate from their asset managers as legal persons, are managed by representatives of asset managers, and invariably delegate fund management back to the asset managers. In this sense, fund trustees or directors of funds that are structured as companies could be excessively deferential to their relevant asset managers. The connections with asset managers present conflicts of interest in being able to steward the interests of the beneficiaries in the fund.[118] There has been fund litigation in the hedge funds realm by investors against asset managers directly where funds have underperformed and the fund entity, managed by directors related to asset managers, has refused to sue.[119] The FCA has only very recently introduced reforms to intervene in board composition at funds so that independent directors are appointed to apply critical challenge and monitoring on fund boards.[120] Now, 25 per cent of fund boards are required to be independent formally, as well as in character and judgement. It is envisaged that these directors will also have sufficient expertise to discharge their monitoring roles.

We may query whether such reforms will improve governance at funds in the interests of the ultimate investor. Directors are subject to duties to the corporate entity that is the fund as

---

Governance in Defined Contribution Schemes' in Paul Thornton and Donald Fleming (eds), *Good Governance for Pension Schemes* (CUP 2011) 267.

[113] Department for Work and Pensions, *Better Workplace Pensions: Further Measures for Savers* (Cm 8840, March 2014) <https://assets.publishing.service.gov.uk/government/uploads/system/uploads/attachment_data/file/298436/better-workplace-pensions-march-2014.pdf> accessed 28 May 2020.

[114] The Pensions Regulator, *Governance and Administration of Occupational Trust-Based Schemes Providing Money Purchase Benefits* (Code of Practice No 13, July 2016) <www.thepensionsregulator.gov.uk/-/media/thepensionsregulator/files/import/pdf/code-13.ashx> accessed 28 May 2020.

[115] Josie Cox, 'Governance Bodies Set Up to Protect 12 Million Pensioners Are Not Doing Their Job, Charity Claims' *The Independent* (17 February 2018) <www.independent.co.uk/news/business/news/pension-savings-governance-bodies-fail-protect-money-igc-aviva-blackrock-fca-a8214296.html> accessed 28 May 2020.

[116] FCA Handbook COBS 19.5.1B; 19.5.5.

[117] Amy Whyte, 'Asset Managers Among the Worst-Governed Public Firms, Study Finds' (*Institutional Investor*, 22 June 2018) <www.institutionalinvestor.com/article/b18r4btg8ydfdc/asset-managers-among-the-worst-governed-public-firms,-study-finds> accessed 28 May 2020.

[118] A rare example of where a fund's board of directors appears to have meaningfully challenged management occurred in the case of Invesco Perpetual Enhanced Income Ltd, a Jersey-registered investment trust. In April 2018, a dispute between the trust board and its management company over management fees led to the temporary resignation of Invesco Perpetual as fund manager. Kate Beioley, 'Investors Pull Money from IPE Amid Invesco Row' *Financial Times* (5 July 2018) <www.ft.com/content/33003312-7e9c-11e8-8e67-1e1a0846c475> accessed 28 May 2020.

[119] *Certain Limited Partners in Henderson PFI Secondary Fund II LLP v Henderson PFI Secondary Fund II LP & Ors* [2012] EWHC 3259, [2013] 3 All ER 887.

[120] FCA Handbook COLL 6.6.25.

a whole, and, depending on the fund structure, investors may not even be shareholders in the fund entity. However, with the imposition by the FCA of regulatory duties on authorized fund entities in relation to investor protection, such as pre- and post-sale communications,[121] proper valuation,[122] monitoring duties for outsourcing,[123] and the duty to ensure that outsourcing and delegation achieve 'value for money',[124] it is arguable that independent directors should at least be alert to compliance concerns, therefore contributing towards investor protection.

25.4 STEPS AHEAD AND ENGAGEMENT WITH ESG

Although we raise questions as to whether fund structures, practices and, indeed, their regulatory framework are always compatible with the expectations that they should act as engaged investors, raising the standards of corporate governance in the companies they invest in, the policy trajectory is towards increasing the investment management sector's roles in shaping corporate behaviour and governance. We suggest that what is important is that we recognize the limitations of the investment management sector in bearing upon the corporate sector, although we accept that institutions as investors are proximate and well placed to do so. For instance, policy trajectory is now relentless on institutions playing their part in influencing investee companies in their ESG performance, in particular in environmental sustainability.[125] Although companies should respond to the increasing hazards of climate change and their social footprint, such behavioural change is not merely a relational matter between companies and shareholders, and should also not be seen as a panacea for wider social issues.[126]

Owing to policy and social pressure, pension funds in particular have become more conscious of integrating ESG factors into investment management,[127] although shorter-term fund vehicles such as retail collective investment schemes are less engaged.[128] However, pension funds are not entirely convinced that ESG factors can be integrated into investment management, as they are concerned that integrating ESG factors into investment management is inconsistent with the fulfilment of their own fiduciary duties.

First, the fiduciary duty of loyalty does not permit pension fund trustees to integrate their own values, morals or preferences into investment management, and hence the objective pursuit of financial returns has historically been seen as key, although not necessarily paramount.[129] Second, the regulatory duty imposed on trustees to act as 'prudent investors' usually means the practice of portfolio diversification. However, it is uncertain whether pursuing ESG integration into conventional investment management would unduly preclude investing in many companies, making the portfolio less diversified and more risky.[130]

---

[121] FCA Handbook COLL 4.1, 4.2.
[122] ibid 6.3.
[123] ibid 6.6.
[124] ibid 4.5.7, 6.6.20–22, 8.3.5A, 8.5.16–19.
[125] See Katelouzou and Klettner, Sustainable Finance and Stewardship, Chapter 26.
[126] Jonathan Ford, 'Don't Expect the Earth from Fund Managers on Climate Change' *Financial Times* (19 January 2020) <www.ft.com/content/a865ff18-394b-11ea-a6d3-9a26f8c3cba4> accessed 28 May 2020.
[127] Riikka Sievänen, Hannu Rita and Bert Scholtens, 'The Drivers of Responsible Investment: The Case of European Pension Funds' (2012) 117 *Journal of Business Ethics* 137. Also see the influence of social culture in Scandinavia, Elias Bengtsson, 'A History of Scandinavian Socially Responsible Investing' (2008) 82 *Journal of Business Ethics* 969.
[128] Paul Cox, Stephen Brammer and Andrew Millington, 'An Empirical Examination of Institutional Investor Preferences for Corporate Social Performance' (2004) 52 *Journal of Business Ethics* 27.
[129] *Cowan v Scargill* [1985] 1 Ch 270.
[130] Rosy Thornton, 'Ethical Investments: A Case of Disjointed Thinking' (2008) 67 *The Cambridge Law Journal* 396. Question also asked in Benjamin Richardson, 'Do the Fiduciary Duties of Pension Funds Hinder Socially Responsible Investment?' (2007) 22 *Banking and Finance Law Review* 145.

Woods[131] also suggests that the 'prudent investor' rule for investment trustees has been interpreted narrowly by courts to mean the adoption of prevailing conventional investment management practices, and hence investment trustees are slow to take leadership in embracing 'new-fangled' investment criteria that may be more controversial.

The UNEPFI report, otherwise known as the Freshfields Report,[132] has produced a definitive analysis on the compatibility of fiduciary duties with ESG considerations.[133] It recommends that pension funds could take into account ESG considerations where investments already satisfy the 'business case'; where similarly competing investments are presented, the choice of the one with better ESG performance is not incompatible with fiduciary duties. Further, ESG factors may be imperative where the objective of the fund is for such purpose or where the consent of beneficiaries may be found. Richardson[134] argues that the report supports not only the proposition that ESG factors are not incompatible with the legal and regulatory duties imposed on funds but also that they may indeed be important for the fulfilment of those duties. Empirical research also provides support, finding that investment management integrating ESG concerns is better managed in terms of downside volatility.[135]

The uncertainty about fiduciary duties has become less of a barrier with the ramping up of policy rhetoric on the importance of non-financial considerations for investment management performance.[136] However, in order to dispel ambiguities, the UK has taken the step of introducing regulatory duties for funds and asset managers in relation to the taking into account of ESG factors in mainstream investment management, and not just in the niche sectors of sustainable finance. The FCA has now introduced duties for all investment firms to consider ESG factors material to financial performance of funds that they oversee and manage, as well as to consider non-financial considerations that present financial risk or are important to beneficiaries.[137] These should be part of the firm's investment strategy for their relevant investment horizons. Although the FCA acknowledged that the meaning of 'ESG' is not entirely settled in the industry and the FCA is not providing a definition, the area of practice will evolve organically while firms are not allowed to ignore it.[138] In this manner, although the duties to consider and also to account to beneficiaries how such consideration has been made will place ESG matters within the legitimate remit of investment management, there is considerable discretion in how funds relate to ESG and what developments of ESG in industry practice they take account of. Funds are able to determine what aspects of ESG are financially material and to what extent, and there is much ambiguity as to how to ascertain the importance of non-financial considerations. It may be argued that Principle 6 of the UK Code 2020 takes this up by requiring engagement with beneficiaries to ascertain

---

[131] Claire Woods, 'Funding Climate Change: How Pension Fund Fiduciary Duty Masks Trustee Inertia and Short-Termism' in James Hawley, Shyam Kamath and Andrew Williams (eds), *Corporate Governance Failures: The Role of Institutional Investors in the Global Financial Crisis* (University of Pennsylvania Press 2011) 242, ch 11.

[132] UNEP Finance Initiative, 'Fiduciary Responsibility: Legal and Practical Aspects of Integrating Environmental, Social and Governance Issues into Institutional Investment' (July 2009) <www.unepfi.org/fileadmin/documents/fiduciaryII.pdf> accessed 28 May 2020.

[133] See Katelouzou and Klettner, Sustainable Finance and Stewardship, Chapter 26.

[134] Richardson (n 130).

[135] Andreas GF Hoepner, Michael Rezec and Sebastian Siegl, 'Does Pension Funds' Fiduciary Duty Prohibit the Integration of Environmental Responsibility Criteria in Investment Processes?' (2011) <http://ssrn.com/abstract=1930189> accessed 28 May 2020.

[136] UNEP FI (n 132) has since clarified that ESG issues can be material to investment performance and it is not beyond the scope of fiduciary duties to take them into account.

[137] FCA Handbook SYSC 3.2.23 for investment firms, 4.1.15 for pension schemes.

[138] Financial Conduct Authority, 'Independent Governance Committees: Extension of Remit' (Policy Statement, 17 December 2019) <www.fca.org.uk/publication/policy/ps19-30.pdf> accessed 28 May 2020.

their preferences.[139] However, where beneficiary preferences are mixed, it will be queried as to how that helps funds to determine the importance of non-financial ESG as such.

As to what ESG means, although the FCA has decided not to impose any definitions in case of incompatibility with industry developments and obsolescence, it can be argued that there is plenty of industry and multi-stakeholder development in this space that can provide guidance to funds: from stock exchange indices, to recognized and voluntary frameworks for evaluating performance in business and human rights,[140] environmental sustainability,[141] anti-corruption footprint,[142] supply chain labour standards[143] and many other ESG matters.[144]

It may be argued that the EU is developing greater clarity in the area of environmental sustainability as a taxonomy of sustainable investments has been introduced based on certain outcomes, such as the achievement of a circular economy, the reduction of emissions, the protection of biodiversity and so on.[145] Companies or funds targeting these outcomes could qualify as sustainable investments, thus providing greater clarity as to what sustainable finance means for the investment management sector's grappling with its new ESG duties. That said, the European initiative extends only to the 'E' aspect of ESG, and there remains work to be done in defining outcomes that are socially oriented in nature, such as in line with the UN's Sustainable Development Goals[146] that include no poverty, reducing inequalities, zero hunger, and peace and justice.

Although we are of the view that the investment management sector will likely tread slowly into this area of ESG oversight, it is aware of the policy pressures upon it, and it is likely that we are looking forward to the co-evolution of practice and law/regulation in the area of ESG performance in the mainstream investment as well as niche sectors. Unfortunately, however, there is still a way to go before the law and the practice of investment management place the achievement of ESG outcomes on a similar level to that of the generation of financial returns.

25.5 CONCLUSION

In this chapter we discuss the UK's and the EU's policy approaches to 'stewardship' on the part of the institutional investment sector, which is one of persistent nudging towards compulsion, to engage with their investee companies in order to monitor and change corporate behaviour, often for the purposes of wider social good. Institutions are seen as proximate to their investee companies and well placed to exercise shareholder powers, especially in jurisdictions such as the UK where dispersed ownership and significant shareholder powers in the legal framework are favourable conditions for stewardship. However, owing to limitations in the business models,

---

[139] UK Code 2020 (n 6) 13–14.
[140] The Shift-Mazars framework for reporting on corporate impact on human rights is found at Shift/Mazars, 'UN Guiding Principles Reporting Framework' (2015) <www.ungpreporting.org/wp-content/uploads/UNGPReportingFramework_withguidance2017.pdf> accessed 28 May 2020.
[141] Such as the ISO40001 standard for assurance.
[142] Such as Transparency International's work on measuring corruption at Transparency International, 'Measuring Corruption' <www.transparency.org.uk/corruption/measuring-corruption/> accessed 28 May 2020.
[143] Such as the SA8000 provided by Social Accountability International, at Social Accountability International, 'SA8000 ® Standard' <https://sa-intl.org/programs/sa8000/> accessed 28 May 2020.
[144] Such as the comprehensive reporting standards developed by the Global Reporting Institute for all corporate social responsibility matters; see Global Reporting Initiative, 'GRI Standards' <www.globalreporting.org/standards> accessed 28 May 2020.
[145] Regulation (EU) 2020/852 of the European Parliament and of the Council of 18 June 2020 on the establishment of a framework to facilitate sustainable investment, and amending Regulation (EU) 2019/2088
[146] See UN Sustainable Development Goals, 'Sustainable Development Goals' <https://sustainabledevelopment.un.org/?menu=1300> accessed 28 May 2020.

structures and governance of the investment management industry, and such phenomena prevailing in the UK, as well as the EU and the US, we are sceptical that institutions will become key drivers of corporate behavioural change for wider good. There is also the misplaced perception that corporate behavioural change is a private matter for the corporate governance relationship, especially since greater causes such as sustainability are increasingly at stake.

At a less ambitious level, perhaps 'stewardship' can be a starting point for cultural adjustment on the part of the investment management industry as it considers how its structures, incentives, business models and governance affect the ultimate saver. There are numerous issues with the investment management industry that UK and EU regulators are only beginning to grapple with,[147] and the UK Code 2020 has rightly turned back to focusing on how funds and the investment chain serve their ultimate beneficiaries. How funds and asset managers use their corporate governance rights is not unimportant, but this should be crucially contextualized in their relationship with ultimate savers, and not be treated either as a panacea for corporate governance problems or as the ultimate market-based solution for social good.

---

[147] As discussed in Section 25.3.2.

26

Sustainable Finance and Stewardship

Unlocking Stewardship's Sustainability Potential

Dionysia Katelouzou and Alice Klettner

26.1 INTRODUCTION

Across the world, policymakers are grappling with how to improve the sustainability of financial markets. Challenges include addressing the root causes of short-termism; correcting the failure of corporations and investors to manage the financial risks associated with climate change, social inequality and economic degradation; and mobilizing business to support sustainable development. The Covid-19 pandemic has added to these challenges, yet also provides an opportunity to reassess the purpose of financial markets and their role in social and economic recovery.[1] With some of the largest corporations and investment managers, such as BlackRock, already taking an increased focus on sustainability and driving change on environmental issues, human rights, stakeholder engagement and transparency, 'a fundamental reshaping of finance'[2] is taking place. At the same time, the responsibilities of the business corporation and its obligations towards civil society are at the centre of policy fights and heated public debates, prompting a paradigmatic shift in the way we understand corporate governance today.[3] The era of shareholder-oriented corporate governance with corporate purpose confined to profit maximization is at an end, while shifting perceptions regarding the role and obligations of the business corporation and its key actors in different social contexts are reflections of changes in a wider-ranging debate over the governance of economic markets.[4]

It is within this context that corporate governance and company law debates are fusing with increasing claims of sustainability, the latter being defined as the deployment of business and

---

[1] See e.g. Andrew Hill, 'The Business of Saving the World' *Financial Times* (28 April 2020) <www.ft.com/content/9364e16a-7f0f-11ea-82f6-150830b3b99a> accessed 25 May 2020; CB Bhattacharya, 'How the Great COVID-19 Reset Can Help Firms Build a Sustainable Future' (*World Economic Forum*, 15 May 2020) <www.weforum.org/agenda/2020/05/the-covid-19-reset-sustainability/> accessed 25 May 2020.

[2] Larry Fink, 'A Fundamental Reshaping of Finance' (2020) <www.blackrock.com/sg/en/larry-fink-ceo-letter> accessed 25 May 2020.

[3] See e.g. Martin Lipton, 'Corporate Governance: The New Paradigm' (*Harvard Law School Forum on Corporate Governance*, 11 January 2017) <https://corpgov.law.harvard.edu/2017/01/11/corporate-governance-the-new-paradigm/> accessed 25 May 2020; Colin Mayer, 'The Future of the Corporation: Towards Humane Business' (British Academy Project, 11 October 2018) <www.wlrk.com/docs/TheFutureoftheCorporationTowardsHumaneBusiness.pdf> accessed 25 May 2020; Dionysia Katelouzou, 'Reflections on the Nature of the Public Corporation in an Era of Shareholder Activism and Stewardship' in Barnali Choudhury and Martin Petrin (eds), *Understanding the Company: Corporate Governance and Theory* (CUP 2017) 117–44; Dionysia Katelouzou and Peer C Zumbansen, 'Transnational Corporate Governance: The State of the Art and Twenty-First Century Challenges' in Peer Zumbansen (ed.), The Oxford Handbook of Transnational Law (OUP, 2021), 615.

[4] Paddy Ireland, 'Financialization and Corporate Governance' (2009) 60 *Northern Ireland Legal Quarterly* 1; Paddy Ireland, 'Efficiency or Power? The Rise of the Shareholder-Oriented Joint Stock Corporation' (2018) 25 *Indiana Journal of Global Legal Studies* 291. See also the contributions to Jean-Philippe Robé, Antoine Lyon-Caen and Stéphane Vernac, *Multinationals and the Constitutionalization of the World Power System* (Routledge 2016).

finance in a manner that protects the stability and resilience of the environment, facilitates social justice and promotes long-term economic prosperity securing the 'social foundation' of humanity without further degradation of the 'planetary boundaries'.[5] This chapter explores the role of an emerging, but important aspect of contemporary corporate governance, that of investor stewardship, within this integrated framework of sustainability. It assesses the potential for stewardship codes to support and encourage investment behaviour that promotes the long-term viability of environmental, social and economic welfare, thereby contributing towards the sustainability of the financial system as a whole.

If we view investor stewardship as long-term, responsible ownership of shares and more recently of other assets,[6] there is certainly potential for investors to steer investee companies towards a more sustainable path. However, investors sit within a financial system that presents many different market incentives that can interfere with this common-sense mission.[7] Institutional investors, such as large pension funds, often act as intermediaries between fund beneficiaries and asset managers, meaning that their role as shareholders is less direct than might be imagined. They operate within a legal framework of fiduciary duties, reporting requirements and contractual mandates that sets the boundaries for their approach towards sustainability. In this chapter we argue that the recent development of stewardship codes across the world, as one aspect of a broader emerging socially oriented regulatory framework aimed at promoting the incorporation of environmental, social and governance (ESG) factors into business decision-making, has the potential to influence investors' choices and effect changes that enable the transition to sustainable finance. We explore both the potential of and the challenges for stewardship codes as a tool for improving the sustainability of finance and we argue that these codes are a valuable element of an emerging international network of regulatory measures that provides a powerful pathway for change. Although much of this network is based on voluntary initiatives, it taps into hard legal rules (across contract, trust, corporate and tort law)[8] which often provide confusing or even contradicting messages about the extent to which sustainability concerns can be integrated into investment decision-making. Stewardship codes, we argue, can untangle this complex nexus and unlock sustainable finance in at least two ways. First, by supporting a progressive interpretation of the legal duties of pension fund trustees and company directors, stewardship codes can help harness the financial clout of large investors in order to steer business towards a more sustainable future.[9] Second, stewardship codes have the potential to infiltrate the complex modern investment chain to reach service providers and financial intermediaries that have so far been hidden from view, extending the influence of those who think to the long term. Not all stewardship codes currently grasp this full potential, but, as they

---

[5] Beate Sjåfjell and Christopher M Bruner, 'Corporations and Sustainability' in Beate Sjåfjell and Christopher M Bruner (eds), *Cambridge Handbook of Corporate Law, Corporate Governance and Sustainability* (CUP 2019) 3, 7–10.

[6] For this extension, see Financial Reporting Council, *UK Stewardship Code 2020* (2019) <www.frc.org.uk/getattachment/5aae591d-d9d3-4cf4-814a-d14e156a1d87/Stewardship-Code_Dec-19-Final-Corrected.pdf> accessed 25 May 2020 [hereinafter UK Code 2020].

[7] See e.g. Dirk Schoenmaker and Willem Schramade, 'Investing for Long-Term Value Creation' (2019) 9 *Journal of Sustainable Finance & Investment* 356.

[8] On the private law governing investment intermediaries in the UK, see e.g. Iris H–Y Chiu and Dionysia Katelouzou, 'Making a Case for Regulating Institutional Shareholders' Corporate Governance Roles' (2018) *Journal of Business Law* 67.

[9] They do this both directly, through encouraging fund trustees to consider ESG factors as part of their fiduciary duties to beneficiaries, but also indirectly, by encouraging investors to enter into dialogue with companies which then encourages those company directors to consider ESG factors in their decision-making.

are revised, updated and strengthened in the future, we hope that their potential will be further unlocked.

The chapter proceeds as follows. Section 26.2 sets the context by explaining what we mean by sustainable finance and why a transition is deemed necessary. It provides an update on some of the key international initiatives and national policies designed to encourage and promote a more sustainable global finance system. Section 26.3 focuses on the role of institutional investors within sustainable finance with a view to promoting stewardship and the incorporation of ESG factors into investment and risk management processes. We look at what sustainable finance means for institutional investors in both a practical and a legal sense and we examine whether and how twenty-five stewardship codes around the world incorporate ESG considerations into their principles. We show that ESG investing is increasingly becoming a core component of stewardship codes, but it is not always expressly connected to hard-law fiduciary or other investment management duties and transparency obligations around ESG. In Section 26.4 we take a critical stance on stewardship codes and explore the possibilities for enhancing their impact in the specific area of sustainable finance. We argue that, to unlock greater potential, stewardship codes should maximize their scope and influence to encompass as much of the investment chain as possible, and, where possible, extend the purpose of ESG integration beyond private financial benefit to encompass a much broader public benefit test. In Section 26.5 we conclude that stewardship codes have an important role to play as one of many mutually reinforcing regulatory instruments pursuing the common goal of sustainable development.

26.2 SUSTAINABLE FINANCE AND REGULATORY INITIATIVES TO SUPPORT IT

26.2.1 *Definitions and Objectives of Sustainable Finance*

Sustainable finance is part of a broader universe of sustainability efforts aimed at achieving sustainable development – a concept first defined in the Brundtland Report in 1987 as 'development that meets the needs of the present without compromising the ability of future generations to meet their own needs'.[10] Today this concept forms the basis of the United Nations (UN) 2030 Agenda for Sustainable Development and its seventeen Sustainable Development Goals (SDGs) which aim to eradicate poverty, protect the planet, and promote peace and prosperity for all.[11] Calls for sustainable development have been generally associated with the corporate social responsibility (CSR) movement.[12] In most jurisdictions today, company directors are expected to take account of environmental and social issues in their decision-making, to the extent that this is in the best interests of the company, and to prepare relevant reports on either a voluntary or a mandatory basis.[13] Yet, it has become obvious in more recent years that the support of the finance sector is also essential in achieving sustainable development, both to

---

[10] United Nations, *Our Common Future*, Report of the World Commission on Environment and Development (OUP 1987) <https://sustainabledevelopment.un.org/content/documents/5987our-common-future.pdf> accessed 25 May 2020.
[11] Transforming Our World: The 2030 Agenda for Sustainable Development, United Nations General Assembly Res 70/1 (25 September 2015) UN Doc A/RES/70/1.
[12] For earlier literature on CSR, see e.g. Amiram Gill, 'Corporate Governance as Social Responsibility: A Research Agenda' (2008) 26 *Berkeley Journal of International Law* 452. For more recent attempts to widen the CSR scope to address structural gender inequality and colonial dependency in global supply chains, see Banu Ozkazanc-Pan 'CSR as Gendered Neocoloniality in the Global South' (2019) 160 *Journal of Business Ethics* 851.
[13] See e.g. Andrew Keay, 'Moving towards Stakeholderism? Constituency Statutes, Enlightened Shareholder Value, and More: Much Ado about Little?' (2011) 22 *European Business Law Review* 1; Afra Afsharipour 'Redefining Corporate Purpose: An International Perspective' (2016) 40 *Seattle University Law Review* 466; Florian Möslein

facilitate CSR and longer-term value creation as well as to direct finance towards greener and more socially inclusive economic activities.[14]

Definitions of sustainable finance range from very broad ideas around creating a stable and resilient finance system to narrower definitions of financial decision-making that integrate ESG factors.[15] The common theme is that financial markets should address the existential challenge of transitioning towards sustainability by looking to the long term and integrating social and environmental risks and opportunities. If the economy prioritizes human well-being, social equity and protection of the environment, we can be more confident of long-term health and prosperity for a wider proportion of the population. The EU's High-Level Expert Group on Sustainable Finance explains:[16]

> For the financial system, sustainability has a dual imperative. The first is to ensure that environmental, social and governance (ESG) factors are at the heart of financial decision-making. The second is to mobilise capital to help solve society's key challenges that require long-term finance: creating jobs, especially for young people, improving education and retirement finance, tackling inequality, and accelerating the shift to a decarbonised and resource-efficient economy.

Sustainable finance can be seen as a response to ongoing economic crises, social disparities, environmental problems and the growing discontentment with the functioning of financial agents.[17] The 2008 global financial crisis (GFC) revealed the failure of financial systems to account for systemic risk and the consequent costs for both business and society, which brought home the importance of good governance and risk management as well as the ability to look to the long term. For instance, the Kay Review in the UK stressed that the purpose of the equity markets is to support the real economy: to sustain high-performing companies and earn good returns for savers without undue risk.[18] In this context, short-termism and the financialization of business are seen as having contributed to a decline in the long-term success of many companies.[19]

These economic concerns have coincided with environmental concerns over climate change to create the conditions necessary for co-ordinated change. The Paris Agreement on Climate Change[20] is one of the major triggers of policy attention in this area as countries contemplate exactly how they will meet agreed targets for reducing carbon emissions and how they will align financial flows with a pathway towards climate-resilient development.[21] The European

---

and Karsten Sørensen, 'Nudging for Corporate Long-Termism and Sustainability? Regulatory Instruments from a Comparative and Functional Perspective' (2018) 24 *Columbia Journal of European Law* 391.

[14] Dirk Schoenmaker and Willem Schramade, *Principles of Sustainable Finance* (OUP 2018).

[15] See EU High-Level Expert Group on Sustainable Finance, *Financing a Sustainable European Economy* (Interim Report, July 2017) 11 <https://ec.europa.eu/info/sites/info/files/170713-sustainable-finance-report_en.pdf> accessed 25 May 2020; Schoenmaker and Schramade, *Principles of Sustainable Finance* (n 14); Ali M Fatemi and Iraj J Fooladi, 'Sustainable Finance: A New Paradigm' (2013) 24 *Global Finance Journal* 101.

[16] *Financing a Sustainable European Economy* (n 15) 8.

[17] Joakim Sandberg, 'Toward a Theory of Sustainable Finance' in Thomas Walker, Stéfanie D Kibsey and Rohan Crichton (eds), *Designing a Sustainable Financial System* (Palgrave Macmillan 2018).

[18] John Kay, 'The Kay Review of UK Equity Markets and Long-Term Decision Making' (Department for Business, Innovation and Skills July 2012) 14 <https://assets.publishing.service.gov.uk/government/uploads/system/uploads/attachment_data/file/253454/bis-12-917-kay-review-of-equity-markets-final-report.pdf> accessed 25 May 2020.

[19] ibid 18–19.

[20] United Nations Paris Agreement (adopted 13 December 2015): UNFCCC, Report of the Conference of the Parties on Its Twenty-First Session (29 January 2016) UN Doc FCCC/CP/2015/10/Add. 1, 21.

[21] For a review of the sustainable development provisions of the Paris Agreement, see Marie-Claire C Segger, 'Advancing the Paris Agreement on Climate Change for Sustainable Development' (2016) 5 *Cambridge International Law Journal* 202. For the implementation risks under the Trump Administration, see Rafael Leal-

Commission's Action Plan for Financing Sustainable Growth explains that 'Europe has to close a yearly investment gap of almost EUR 180 billion to achieve EU climate and energy targets by 2030'.[22] A 2019 report supported by the Principles for Responsible Investing (PRI) predicts a USD 1.6 trillion repricing in sectors ranging from energy to agriculture.[23] As we make the switch to renewable energy, greener construction, sustainable farming methods and more efficient transport, there will be massive changes in the value of certain assets and industries.[24] It is becoming increasingly obvious that ESG factors can no longer be seen as 'non-financial', but have significant financial implications, and companies can 'do well by doing good'.[25] But from the perspective of return on investments, the empirical evidence is more contradictory. While an exhaustive account of the empirical literature on the link between ESG and performance remains out of the scope of this chapter, it is safe to say that embedded efforts to improve the sustainability of finance can have a positive impact on business performance as well as wider benefit for civil society.[26]

As the SDGs have moved away from the Brundtland approach of 'do no harm', to invoke a proactive need for joint action among corporate actors (including investors) and civil society, there are now significant challenges for companies and investors in actively investing for the SDGs.[27] One issue is the fact that sustainability has tended to be discussed in a 'weak' form associated with the business case for CSR, which limits CSR to activities that improve long-term financial performance.[28] These weak CSR initiatives, often confusing sustainability with stakeholder responsiveness,[29] have failed to address society's bigger problems and the case is now increasingly made for a stronger form of corporate sustainability that accepts a slowing of overall financial growth and promotes cleaner, more equitable growth in both developed and developing nations.[30]

Arcas and Antonio Morelli, 'The Resilience of the Paris Agreement: Negotiating and Implementing the Climate Regime' (2018) 31 *Georgetown Environmental Law Review* 1.

[22] European Commission, 'Action Plan: Financing Sustainable Growth' COM (2018) 97 <https://ec.europa.eu/transparency/regdoc/rep/1/2018/EN/COM-2018-97-F1-EN-MAIN-PART-1.PDF> accessed 25 May 2020.

[23] PRI, 'UN-Supported Investor Group Finds Large Gap between Stock-Market Winners and Losers from "Inevitable Policy Response" to Climate Change' (10 December 2019) <www.unpri.org/news-and-press/un-supported-investor-group-finds-large-gap-between-stock-market-winners-and-losers-from-inevitable-policy-response-to-climate-change/5212.article> accessed 25 May 2020.

[24] International Monetary Fund, *Global Financial Stability Report: Lower for Longer* (October 2019) 81ff (ch 6: Sustainable Finance) <www.imf.org/en/Publications/GFSR/Issues/2019/10/01/global-financial-stability-report-october-2019> accessed 25 May 2020; Sonia Labatt and Rodney R White, *Carbon Finance: The Financial Implications of Climate Change* (Wiley 2007).

[25] See e.g. Fatemi and Fooladi (n 15).

[26] For the mixed evidence on the link between sustainability and investors' performance, see Katelouzou and Micheler, The Market for Stewardship and the Role of the Government, Chapter 3.

[27] See e.g. Willem Schramade, 'Investing in the UN Sustainable Development Goals: Opportunities for Companies and Investors' (2017) 29 *Journal of Applied Corporate Finance* 87; Jose M Diaz-Sarachaga, Daniel Jato-Espino and Daniel Castro-Fresno, 'Is the Sustainable Development Goals (SDGs) Index an Adequate Framework to Measure the Progress of the 2030 Agenda?' (2018) 26 *Sustainable Development* 663.

[28] Archie B Caroll and Kareem M Shabana, 'The Business Case for Corporate Social responsibility: A Review of Concepts, Research and Practice' (2010) 12 *International Journal of Management Reviews* 85, 86–87. For a recent critique, see Michael L Barnett 'The Business Case for Corporate Social Responsibility: A Critique and an Indirect Path' (2019) 58 *Business & Society* 167.

[29] Barnett (n 28).

[30] For the 'stronger' notion of sustainability, see the contributions to Beate Sjåfjell and Christopher M Bruner (eds), *Cambridge Handbook of Corporate Law, Corporate Governance and Sustainability* (CUP 2019), and especially for developing countries, see 331–44 (Alvaro Pereira, 'The Pacific Alliance: An Opportunity for a Sustainable System of Corporate Law and Governance in Latin America' (analyzing the Pacifil Alliance, an economic bloc formed by Chile, Colombia, Mexico and Peru)); 431–45 (Chao Xi, 'Shareholder Voting and Corporate Sustainability in China: an Empirical Study'); 460–74 (Harpeet Kaur, 'Achieving Sustainable Development Goals in India'); 475–89

Thus, the overall aims and objectives of sustainable finance include: (i) provision of finance for improving sustainability; (ii) enhancing the overall resilience and stability of the finance system; (iii) improving transparency and information flow to enable better decision-making based on incorporation of ESG issues; and (iv) delivering a financial system that meets community and consumer expectations for sustainability. This includes finding and directing the dollars needed to deliver on the UN SDGs and Paris Agreement targets to facilitate the transition to a low-carbon, resource-efficient, socially inclusive economy. The key question, of course, is how to establish sustainable finance and whether law (defined in a broad way to include both national and international instruments, both binding and non-binding) can contribute to foster it.

26.2.2 A Snapshot of the Institutional Framework of Sustainable Finance

The governance of sustainable finance is largely fragmented. There are many international, supranational and national initiatives and policies promoting and supporting aspects of sustainable finance. Although they have emerged in a rather unco-ordinated fashion, they provide a strong basis for a common understanding around different aspects of sustainable finance, and are increasingly being joined together through mutual recognition to form a regulatory network of mostly voluntary standards.[31] The formal creation of the United Nations Environment Programme Finance Initiative (UNEP FI) in 2003 was a significant milestone in recognizing the need for co-ordinated policy development, and UNEP's 2014 'Inquiry: Design of a Sustainable Finance System' marked increased efforts towards finding concrete policy options.[32]

Voluntary international initiatives have been leading best practice in the area through a process of private, industry-led governance which Thistlethwaite thoroughly distinguishes from public law.[33] He explains how these initiatives support technical consensus-building as well as reflexive learning processes to generate authority and legitimacy around emerging practices. Regulatory scholars have long pointed out this ability of soft law to create learning systems for both the regulator and the regulatee.[34] Perhaps the most well-established international initiative for institutional investors is the PRI, a voluntary and aspirational set of six investment principles aimed at incorporating ESG issues into investment practice.[35] They were developed by the investment industry with support from the UNEP FI and launched in April 2006. Since then, the number of signatories has grown from 100 to more than 2,300 representing more than USD 83 trillion of assets across 50 markets.[36] Although the PRI are very broad in their nature, research has found that they can facilitate the emergence of collective

---

(Benedict Sheehy and Cacik Rut Damayati, 'Sustainability and Legislated Corporate Social Responsibility in Indonesia').

[31] On the role of transnational private regulation in general, see Kenneth W Abbott and Duncan Snidal, 'Strengthening International Regulation through Transnational New Governance: Overcoming the Orchestration Deficit' (2009) 42 *Vanderbilt Journal of Transnational Law* 501.

[32] The inquiry has resulted in many reports examining different aspects of sustainable finance (UN Environment Programme, 'Publications' <https://www.unep.org/publications-data> accessed 7 February 2022). For a general review, see UNEP/World Bank Group, 'Roadmap for a Sustainable Financial System' (November 2017) <https://wedocs.unep.org/bitstream/handle/20.500.11822/20715/Roadmap_for_a_Sustainable_Financial_System_Summary.pdf?sequence=1&amp%3BisAllowed=> accessed 7 February 2022.

[33] Specifically, on the use of 'private environmental governance', see Jason Thistlethwaite, 'Private Governance and Sustainable Finance' (2014) 4 *Journal of Sustainable Finance & Investment* 61.

[34] See e.g. Sharon Gilad, 'It Runs in the Family: Meta-regulation and Its Siblings' (2010) 4 *Regulation & Governance* 485; Christine Parker, *The Open Corporation: Effective Self-Regulation and Democracy* (CUP 2002).

[35] UN Global Compact, 'Who Cares Wins: Connecting Financial Markets to a Changing World' (December 2004) <www.unepfi.org/fileadmin/events/2004/stocks/who_cares_wins_global_compact_2004.pdf> accessed 25 May 2020.

[36] More information is available: PRI, 'About the PRI' <www.unpri.org/pri/about-the-pri> accessed 25 May 2020.

action among investors by providing a mobilizing structure and normalizing the responsible investment ideology.[37]

On the other hand, the PRI have been criticized for their lack of accountability and enforcement, which enables them to act as a 'shroud of legitimacy' for traditional non-responsible investment practices.[38] To address these shortcomings, the PRI is making efforts to strengthen its accountability by increasing disclosure requirements for signatories based on privately developed standards such as the Task Force on Climate-Related Financial Disclosures (TCFD), set up by the G20's Financial Stability Board.[39] The TCFD has developed recommendations for voluntary, consistent climate-related financial risk disclosures for use by companies in providing information to investors, lenders, insurers and other stakeholders.[40] In February 2019, the PRI announced that reporting against TCFD based indicators would become mandatory for its signatories in 2020.[41] A further investor-focused initiative, Climate Action 100+, also supports the TCFD in the context of its mission of pressing for the world's largest corporate greenhouse gas emitters to take necessary action on climate change.[42] In September 2019, this initiative had 370 signatories representing more than USD 35 trillion in assets under management.[43] This mutual recognition of international initiatives has important implications for the building of a regulatory network of private standard-setting and governance on sustainable governance.[44]

As well as these international initiatives, individual nations and regions are taking action on sustainable finance through policy agendas that span a wide range of traditionally separate areas of law and regulation. They target banks, pension funds, insurance companies, credit rating agencies, regulators, peak bodies and listed companies. For institutional investors, stewardship codes now form part of the framework for sustainable finance in many countries across Europe, Asia, the Americas, Africa and Australasia.[45] We discuss their role as national soft-law instruments in Sections 26.3 and 26.4. However, in some countries, hard-law developments are also emerging, altering the institutional framework for finance in an attempt to improve sustainability.[46]

The European Union has been at the forefront of these developments and EU legislative efforts are now setting a precedent internationally. In late 2016 the High-Level Expert Group on Sustainable Finance (HLEG), comprising twenty senior experts from civil society, the finance sector and academia, was set up to provide advice to the European Commission on how to steer

[37] Jean-Pascal Gond and Valeria Piani, 'Enabling Institutional Investors' Collective Action: The Role of the Principles for Responsible Investment Initiative' (2013) 52 *Business & Society* 64.
[38] Taylor Gray, 'Investing for the Environment? The Limits of the UN Principles of Responsible Investment' (2009) <https://ssrn.com/abstract=1416123> accessed 25 May 2020.
[39] See Task Force on Climate-Related Financial Disclosures, 'Recommendations of the Task Force on Climate-Related Financial Disclosures' (14 December 2016) <www.fsb.org/wp-content/uploads/Recommendations-of-the-Task-Force-on-Climate-related-Financial-Disclosures.pdf> accessed 25 May 2020.
[40] ibid.
[41] See Edward Baker and Senita Galijatovic, 'FAQ on Mandatory Climate Reporting for PRI signatories' (*UNPRI*, 2020) <www.unpri.org/reporting-for-signatories/faq-on-mandatory-climate-reporting-for-pri-signatories/5356.article> accessed 25 May 2020.
[42] See Climate Action 100+ <www.climateaction100.org/> accessed 25 May 2020.
[43] Climate Action 100+, '2019 Progress Report' (September 2019) <https://climateaction100.files.wordpress.com/2019/10/progressreport2019.pdf> accessed 25 May 2020.
[44] Further on transnational private regulation, see e.g. Fabrizio Cafaggi, 'Transnational Governance by Contract: Private Regulation and Contractual Networks in Food Safety' in Axel Marx, Miet Maertens, Johan Swinnen and Jan Wouters (eds), *Private Standards and Global Governance: Economic, Legal and Political Perspectives* (Edward Elgar 2012).
[45] See further Katelouzou and Puchniak, Global Shareholder Stewardship, Chapter 1.
[46] For the hard-law aspects of stewardship in the UK, see Dionysia Katelouzou, *The Path to Enlightened Shareholder Stewardship* (CUP) (forthcoming).

the flow of finance towards sustainable investment and protect the stability of the financial system.[47] Based on the HLEG's recommendations, on 8 March 2018, the European Commission issued its Action Plan on Financing Sustainable Growth, setting out an ambitious agenda of ten action points.[48] The EU Action Plan recognizes that in order for capital to flow towards sustainable activities, there has to be a shared understanding of what sustainable means. On 24 May 2018, the Commission issued a proposal for a regulation on the establishment of a framework to facilitate sustainable investment, which aims to provide technical definitions of sustainable economic activities (taxonomy regulation).[49] This ground-breaking legislation is likely to influence global standards on sustainability and provide opportunities for businesses involved in climate change mitigation and adaptation; protection of natural resources; waste recycling and pollution prevention. Also of interest in the context of stewardship are the Action Plan's points that relate to the duties of institutional investors (Action 7) and efforts to improve disclosure (Action 9).[50] These build on earlier legislative efforts to increase the role of institutional investors in corporate governance, particularly the Shareholder Rights Directive II (SRD II) which aims to encourage long-term shareholder engagement in listed companies, and improve transparency on shareholder engagement.[51]

National initiatives are underfoot in many countries, although most are still at a relatively early stage of policymaking. For instance, the UK government published its Green Finance Strategy in July 2019.[52] In Canada, an expert panel was set up by the government in April 2018 to engage with business experts around investments that benefit the environment.[53] In contrast, the US and Australia both lack a centralized government-led plan for sustainable finance, but state and industry-led action is afoot. In the US, California has set a target of 50 per cent renewable energy by 2030, and New York has set up the NY Green Bank to increase investment into clean energy markets.[54] In Australia, leaders across banking, finance, peak bodies and academia are collaborating as part of the Australian Sustainable Finance Initiative to prepare a sustainable finance roadmap to be launched in 2020.[55] China has a more top-down approach set out in its 2016 'Guidelines for Establishing the Green Financial System', which aims to incentivize more private capital to be directed towards green sectors and away from polluting sectors.[56]

[47] COM (2016) 0601.
[48] COM (2018) 97.
[49] COM (2018) 0353.
[50] See further Section 26.3.
[51] Directive (EU) 2017/828 of the European Parliament and of the Council of 17 May 2017 amending Directive 2007/36/EC as regards the encouragement of long-term shareholder engagement [2017] OJ L132/1 (SRD II). For an analysis of the stewardship related provisions of the SRD II, see Iris H–Y Chiu and Dionysia Katelouzou, 'From Shareholder Stewardship to Shareholder Duties: Is the Time Ripe?' in Hanne S Birkmose (ed), *Shareholders' Duties* (Kluwer Law International 2017) 131–52.
[52] See Department for Business, Energy & Industrial Strategy, 'Transition to a Green Financial System and Mobilising Investment in Clean and Resilient Growth' (2 July 2019) <www.gov.uk/guidance/green-finance> accessed 25 May 2020.
[53] The Panel's final report was published in June 2019; see Environment and Climate Change Canada, *Final Report of the Expert Panel on Sustainable Finance: Mobilizing Finance for Sustainable Growth* (2019) <www.canada.ca/en/environment-climate-change/services/climate-change/expert-panel-sustainable-finance.html> accessed 25 May 2020.
[54] Cary Krosinsky and Gabriel Thoumi, 'The State of Sustainable Finance in the United States' (UNEP February 2016) <https://wedocs.unep.org/bitstream/handle/20.500.11822/9828/-The_state_of_sustainable_finance_in_the_United_States-2016The_State_of_Sustainable_Finance_in_the_US.pdf.pdf?sequence=3&amp%3BisAllowed=> accessed 7 February 2022.
[55] See Australian Sustainable Finance Initiative, 'What Is ASFI?' <www.sustainablefinance.org.au/> accessed 25 May 2020.
[56] See People's Bank of China, 'The People's Bank of China and Six Other Agencies Jointly Issue "Guidelines for Establishing the Green Financial System"' (1 September 2016) <www.pbc.gov.cn/english/130721/3131759/index.html> accessed 25 May 2020.

This brief examination of selected international, regional and national initiatives reveals the emerging (albeit fragmented) regulatory network of sustainable finance that is changing prevailing industry norms and expectations. While this list is by no means exhaustive,[57] each of the initiatives just outlined has individual impacts relating to a specific aspect of sustainable finance, as well as a cumulative overall effect on the behaviour of organizations within the finance system. This reflects the global nature of finance, particularly for large investors, and the fact that foreign direct investment makes up a large proportion of investment on most stock exchanges.[58] In terms of policy-making, a trend that is likely to continue, especially in Western nations, is the high involvement of and consultation with the private sector as a form of 'global governance', with or without state intervention.[59] Sustainable finance strategies hope to mobilize the private sector to support sustainable development, while at the same time encouraging the mainstreaming of incorporation of ESG into financial decision-making. It is this second aim that brings us to consider in more detail the role of institutional investors and stewardship in sustainable finance.

26.3 INSTITUTIONAL INVESTORS, SUSTAINABILITY AND STEWARDSHIP

As introduced earlier, institutional investors and the investment industry are a key focus of sustainable finance policy. In this section we examine the practicalities of sustainable finance for institutional investors. We introduce the key strategies for sustainable investing and how they currently interact with both: (i) hard law, primarily investors' legal duties and reporting requirements; and (ii) soft law in the form of stewardship codes.

26.3.1 *Strategies for Sustainable Investing*

Sustainable investment, also called responsible investment or socially responsible investment (SRI), is not a new phenomenon.[60] It emerged in the 1960s alongside growing opposition to apartheid in South Africa and against the background of the Vietnam War. Religious or socially oriented organizations increasingly stipulated that their investment portfolios must exclude, for example, gambling outfits, weapons manufacturers or South African business interests.[61] Thus, the early SRI movement was focused primarily on actively removing or choosing investments based on specific ethical guidelines.[62] It has since matured and expanded into mainstream investment practice, but under different labels and different strategies.[63] Since around 2005 (after the UN Global Compact published its report 'Who Cares Wins'),[64] the term SRI has been somewhat overtaken by the term ESG, which encompasses a wider range of strategies that aim to

---

[57] See, for instance, the list on International Capital Market Association, 'Sustainable Finance Initiatives' <www.icmagroup.org/green-social-and-sustainability-bonds/sustainable-finance-initiatives/> accessed 25 May 2020.

[58] For example the UK's Office for National Statistics reports a record high of 54.9% of all UK shares held by foreign investors at the end of 2018; see Office for National Statistics, 'Ownership of UK Quoted Shares: 2018' (14 January 2020) <www.ons.gov.uk/economy/investmentspensionsandtrusts/bulletins/ownershipofukquotedshares/2018> accessed 25 May 2020.

[59] See e.g. Virginia Haufler, *A Public Role for the Private Sector: Industry Self-Regulation in a Global Economy* (Carnegie Endowment for International Peace 2001).

[60] See e.g. Lloyd Kurtz, 'Socially Responsible Investment and Shareholder Activism' in Andrew Crane and others (eds), *The Oxford Handbook of Corporate Social Responsibility* (OUP 2008).

[61] Russell Sparkes and Christopher J Cowton, 'The Maturing of Socially Responsible Investment: A Review of the Developing Link with Corporate Social Responsibility' (2004) 52 *Journal of Business Ethics* 45.

[62] ibid.

[63] ibid; Joakim Sandberg, Camen Juravle, Ted M Hedesström and Ian Hamilton, 'The Heterogeneity of Socially Responsible Investment' (2009) 87 *Journal of Business Ethics* 519.

[64] UN Global Compact (n 35).

integrate environmental, social and governance issues into securities valuation and investment decision-making.[65] Research conducted in 2019 found that ESG was almost universally top-of-mind for senior executives across forty-three global institutional investment firms.[66]

From the point of view of an institutional investor, sustainable finance involves integrating ESG factors when making investment decisions, including portfolio selection and management. This is not as simple as it sounds; the Global Sustainable Investment Alliance (GSIA) counts seven distinct strategies for sustainable investing, each of which defines sustainability in a slightly different way.[67] The simplest and most popular strategy (stemming from SRI) is 'negative screening', whereby unsavoury investments, commonly tobacco, gambling, weapons trading, etc., are excluded from the portfolio. The GSIA estimates USD 19.8 trillion funds globally are invested this way and it is the most dominant strategy in Europe.[68] Integration of ESG factors into investment decision-making is the next most popular strategy, at USD 17.5 trillion globally, although the way in which this is done varies greatly.[69] The third most used strategy globally, at USD 9.8 trillion, is the use of 'corporate engagement and shareholder action' to influence corporate behaviour, which is particularly popular in Japan.[70] ESG is also increasingly embraced by activist hedge funds, such as Jana Partners and Trian Partners, as the fulcrum of their activist campaigns.[71] Promoting ESG through shareholder engagement (and sometimes more aggressive forms of shareholder activism) corresponds most closely with the investment behaviour promoted by stewardship codes as it involves monitoring, information gathering, active voting and engagement in dialogue with investee companies.[72]

In general, this diversity of investment approaches demonstrates the flexible yet nebulous nature of the concept of sustainability.[73] But despite some definitional uncertainty, it is very clear that sustainable investing as a whole is on the increase worldwide. In Europe, total assets committed to sustainable strategies grew by 11 per cent from 2016 to 2018, and in the US by 38 per cent.[74] In Australia and New Zealand, a responsible approach to investing was used in relation to 63 per cent of assets managed professionally in 2018, and in Japan, sustainable investing quadrupled between 2016 and 2018, growing from just 3 per cent of totally professionally managed assets in the country to 18 per cent.[75] Interesting in the context of stewardship is the

---

[65] Emiel van Duuren, Auke Plantinga and Bert Scholtens, 'ESG Integration and the Investment Management Process: Fundamental Investing Reinvented' (2016) 138 *Journal of Business Ethics* 525; Lauren Caplan, John S Griswold and William F Jarvis, 'From SRI to ESG: The Changing World of Responsible Investing' (Commonfund Institute, September 2013) <https://files.eric.ed.gov/fulltext/ED559300.pdf> accessed 25 May 2020; Neil S Eccles and Suzette Viviers, 'The Origins and Meanings of Names Describing Investment Practices That Integrate a Consideration of ESG Issues in the Academic Literature' (2011) 104 *Journal of Business Ethics* 389.

[66] Robert G Eccles and Svetlana Klimenko, 'The Investor Revolution' *Harvard Business Review* (May–June 2019) <https://hbr.org/2019/05/the-investor-revolution> accessed 25 May 2020.

[67] Global Sustainable Investment Alliance (GSIA), '2018 Global Sustainable Investment Review' (2019) <www.gsi-alliance.org/wp-content/uploads/2019/06/GSIR_Review2018F.pdf> accessed 25 May 2020.

[68] ibid.

[69] ibid.

[70] ibid 10, 15.

[71] Charles M Nathan, 'On Governance: ESG Investing Takes on New Meaning for Activist Hedge Funds and Corporate Boards' (*The Conference Board*, 29 January 2018) <www.conference-board.org/blog/environmental-social-governance/ESG-Investing-Hedge-Funds-Corporate-Boards> accessed 25 May 2020. Generally, on hedge fund activism, see Dionysia Katelouzou, 'Myths and Realities of Hedge Fund Activism: Some Empirical Evidence' (2013) 7 *Virginia Law & Business Review* 459.

[72] See further Katelouzou, *The Path to Enlightened Shareholder Stewardship* (n 46).

[73] Claire Woods and Roger Urwin, 'Putting Sustainable Investing into Practice: A Governance Framework for Pension Funds' (2010) 92 *Journal of Business Ethics* 1, 2.

[74] GSIA (n 67).

[75] ibid 4.

fact that the strategy of 'corporate engagement and shareholder action' is increasing in popularity.[76]

26.3.2 Hard-Law Duties, Reporting Requirements and ESG

As the practice of sustainable investing has become more mainstream, the question of its compatibility with the duties that institutional investors owe to their clients and beneficiaries has come under increased scrutiny by academics and policymakers alike.[77] In most countries, large institutional investors, particularly pension and investment trustees, are under a legal duty (often fiduciary in nature) to act in the best interests of their beneficiaries and clients.[78] There has been much debate over the extent to which this requires investors to maximize investment returns.[79] In its earlier days, SRI was seen as an investment approach that involved the potential sacrifice of financial returns in order to make the world a better place. Hence, investors were unclear over whether this kind of investing could breach their legal duties.[80]

In order to clarify the situation, in 2005 UNEP FI published a report by law firm Freshfields Bruckhaus Deringer which analyzed investors' legal duties in ten jurisdictions around the world.[81] The report, in what was seen as a radical decision at the time, concluded that 'integrating ESG considerations into an investment analysis so as to more reliably predict financial performance is *clearly permissible* and is arguably required in *all* jurisdictions'.[82] A decade later in 2015, UNEP FI launched a collaborative project, 'Fiduciary Duty in the 21st Century' which followed up on the 2005 report, stressing that, far from being a barrier, investors' legal duties place a *positive obligation* on investors to integrate ESG issues.[83] Country roadmaps, based on industry and expert interviews, were produced for sixteen markets across the world. The project concluded with a Final Report released in 2019.[84] It notes that while there was little change in the law between 2005 and 2015, there was significant change between 2015 and 2019:[85]

---

[76] ibid.
[77] See e.g. Benjamin J Richardson, 'Keeping Ethical Investment Ethical: Regulatory Issues for Investing for Sustainability' (2009) 87 *Journal of Business Ethics* 555; UNEP Finance Initiative, '2009 Overview' (2009) <www.unepfi.org/fileadmin/documents/unepfi_overview_2009.pdf> accessed 25 May 2020; Joakim Sandberg, 'Socially Responsible Investment and Fiduciary Duty: Putting the Freshfields Report into Perspective' (2011) 101 *Journal of Business Ethics* 143; Law Commission, *Fiduciary Duties of Investment Intermediaries* (Law Com No 350, 2014) <www.lawcom.gov.uk/app/uploads/2015/03/lc350_fiduciary_duties.pdf> accessed 25 May 2020.
[78] For a recent account of the fiduciary duties of pension funds trustees in English law, see Anna Tilba and Arad Reisberg, 'Fiduciary Duty under the Microscope: Stewardship and the Spectrum of Pension Fund Engagement' (2019) 82 *Modern Law Review* 456, 466–80. On the fiduciary duties that investment managers owe to clients, see Arthur B Laby, 'The Fiduciary Structure of Investment Management Regulation' in John D Morley and William A Birdthistle (eds), *Research Handbook on Mutual Funds* (Edward Elgar 2018).
[79] See e.g. Joakim Sandberg, '(Re-)Interpreting Fiduciary Duty to Justify Socially Responsible Investment for Pension Funds' (2013) 21 *Corporate Governance: An International Review* 436.
[80] ibid; Carmen Juravle and Alan Lewis, 'Identifying Impediments to SRI in Europe: a Review of the Practitioner and Academic Literature' (2008) 17 *Business Ethics: A European Review* 285.
[81] Freshfields Bruckhaus Deringer, 'A Legal Framework for the Integration of Environmental, Social and Governance Issues into Institutional Investment' (*UNEP Finance Initiative*, October 2005) <www.unepfi.org/fileadmin/documents/freshfields_legal_resp_20051123.pdf> accessed 25 May 2020.
[82] ibid 13 (emphasis added).
[83] Rory Sullivan, Will Martindale, Elodie Feller and Anna Bordon, 'Fiduciary Duty in the 21st Century' (*UNPRI*, 2015) 9 <www.unpri.org/download?ac=1378> accessed 25 May 2020.
[84] Rory Sullivan and others, 'Fiduciary Duty in the 21st Century: Final Report' (*UNEP Finance Initiative*, 2019) <www.unepfi.org/wordpress/wp-content/uploads/2019/10/Fiduciary-duty-21st-century-final-report.pdf> accessed 25 May 2020.
[85] ibid 8.

Globally, there are over 730 hard and soft-law policy revisions, across some 500 policy instruments, that support, encourage or require investors to consider long-term value drivers, including ESG issues. Policy change has clarified that ESG incorporation and active ownership are part of investors' fiduciary duties to their clients and beneficiaries.

The report divides these policy instruments into three broad categories: (i) pension fund regulations; (ii) stewardship codes; and (iii) corporate disclosures.[86] It recognizes that these legal changes are often part of wider sustainable finance policy agendas. Before we move to explore how the current stewardship codes promote sustainability, we must briefly mention recent changes in reporting requirements around sustainable investing.

The mainstreaming of CSR means that most of the largest corporations in the US produce sustainability reports on a voluntary basis, and many countries in Europe and Asia (such as, China, India and Singapore) mandate that corporations disclose (material) ESG information.[87] By contrast, the governance, transparency and accountability requirements placed on institutional investors (operating as specialized funds or trusts rather than listed corporations) have received sparse attention. This is now changing in the EU with the SRD II and the EU Action Plan introducing legislation to improve the disclosures of institutional investors around ESG.[88] With a concerted aim to limit possible 'greenwashing',[89] the EU proposed regulation will require investors to go further than just stating *whether* they incorporate ESG, by delving into exactly *how* they incorporate ESG risks into investment strategy.[90] Coming into force in March 2021, the EU legislation will improve coherence and consistency across member states by bringing all professional investors under its scope – not only pension funds but hedge funds, investment managers, advisory services and insurance companies.[91]

The EU proposed regulation also asks investors to publish on their websites how their remuneration policy integrates ESG risks.[92] This is an important development in integrating sustainability into the internal governance systems of investors that aims to improve accountability as well as transparency. Indeed, the incorporation of ESG into investment decision-making has a close parallel in the incorporation of CSR into corporate decision-making. To be effective, both require true integration into existing governance and remuneration systems rather than being treated as an optional add-on.[93] As Woods and Urwin suggest, this may involve

---

[86] ibid 13.
[87] The literature here is voluminous, but see, among others, Afra Afsharipour and Shruti Rana, 'The Emergence of New Corporate Social Responsibility Regimes in China and India' (2014) 14 *UC Davis Business Law Journal* 175; Jerry KC Koh and Victoria Leong, 'The Rise of the Sustainability Reporting Megatrend: A Corporate Governance Perspective' (2017) 18 *Business Law International* 233; Constance Z Wagner, 'Evolving Norms of Corporate Social Responsibility: Lessons Learned from the European Union Directive on Non-financial Reporting' (2018) 19 *Transactions: The Tennessee Journal of Business Law* 619; Jill E Fisch, 'Making Sustainability Disclosure Sustainable' (2019) 107 *Georgetown Law Journal* 923. For a list of ESG mandatory disclosure requirements across twenty-three countries, see Initiative for Responsible Investment, 'Corporate Social Responsibility Disclosure Efforts by National Governments and Stock Exchanges' (2015) <https://iri.hks.harvard.edu/files/iri/files/corporate_social_responsibility_disclosure_3-27-15.pdf> accessed 25 May 2020.
[88] See also Section 26.2.
[89] On greenwashing, see e.g. William S Laufer, 'Social Accountability and Corporate Greenwashing' (2003) 43 *Journal of Business Ethics* 253.
[90] European Commission, 'Proposal for a Regulation of the European Parliament and of the Council on Disclosures Relating to Sustainable Investments and Sustainability Risks and Amending Directive (EU) 2016/2341' COM (2018) 354.
[91] ibid art 2.
[92] ibid art 4.
[93] See e.g. Alice Klettner, Thomas Clarke and Martijn Boersma, 'The Governance of Corporate Sustainability: Empirical Insights into the Development, Leadership and Implementation of Responsible Business Strategy' (2014) 122 *Journal of Business Ethics* 145.

amending the fund's overall mission and investment beliefs as well as clear leadership from fund trustees.[94] In a practical sense institutional investors will need to retrain their managers and implement clear risk parameters and investment timelines.[95] Just as corporate governance systems and the duties of company directors have been slowly reinterpreted to incorporate CSR,[96] the governance of institutional investors and duties of fund trustees are coming under increasing scrutiny in relation to ESG.[97]

Thus, hard law on institutional investing and ESG, in countries where it exists, provides boundaries in relation to two issues: (i) the scope of investors' legal duties in terms of incorporation of ESG; and (ii) the need for transparency and reporting around inclusion of ESG in investment decision-making. We see these two issues as mirroring the core objectives of current stewardship codes which aim to: (i) promote responsible asset ownership as a way to fulfil investors' duties to their clients and beneficiaries; and, (ii) encourage transparency around responsible asset ownership through stewardship policy statements and other disclosures.[98] However, the key question is the extent to which the stewardship codes integrate ESG and sustainability into their dual aims of responsible investment and transparency.

26.3.3 Integration of ESG into Stewardship Codes

Research analyzing the content of stewardship codes shows that, although they all promote responsible investing and long-termism, the extent to and the context within which they expressly refer to ESG are very variable.[99] Table 26.1 – based on data collected by Katelouzou and Siems – confirms these earlier findings.[100] From the twenty-five codes considered here, the overwhelming majority (84 per cent) refers at least once to ESG factors. Indeed, only four codes do not mention ESG factors at all (i.e. Denmark 2016,[101] Korea 2016,[102] Switzerland 2013 and US 2017). Several stewardship codes mention ESG only briefly in a list of many topics that investors may wish to monitor in their investee companies,[103] while at the other end of the spectrum are codes that emphasize ESG integration and sustainability as a core concern for investment

---

[94] Woods and Urwin (n 73).
[95] Ibid.
[96] Keay (n 13).
[97] See e.g. Sarah Barker, Mark Baker-Jones, Emilie Barton and Emma Fagan, 'Climate Change and the Fiduciary Duties of Pension Fund Trustees – Lessons from the Australian Law' (2016) 6 *Journal of Sustainable Finance & Investment* 211; Magnus Jansson, Joakim Sandberg, Anders Biel and Tommy Gärling, 'Should Pension Funds' Fiduciary Duty Be Extended to Include Social, Ethical and Environmental Concerns? A Study of Beneficiaries' Preferences' (2014) 4 *Journal of Sustainable Finance & Investment* 213.
[98] Alice Klettner 'The Impact of Stewardship Codes on Corporate Governance and Sustainability' (2017) 23 *New Zealand Business Law Quarterly* 259. See also Katelouzou and Puchniak, Global Shareholder Stewardship, Chapter 1.
[99] Dionysia Katelouzou, 'Shareholder Stewardship: A Case of (Re)Embedding Institutional Investors and the Corporation?' in Beate Sjåfjell and Christopher M Bruner (eds), *Cambridge Handbook of Corporate Law, Corporate Governance and Sustainability* (CUP 2019) 581–95; Klettner (n 98).
[100] Table 26.1 reports the relative frequencies of the words 'environmental, social and governance' or 'ESG' or 'environment and social' among twenty-five stewardship codes around the world. Unlike Katelouzou and Siems, we consider only current codes, with the exception of the UK where we consider both the 2012 and the 2020 versions. Focusing on relative frequencies is important because of the unequal sizes of the codes. For more on these twenty-five codes and the methodology applied (e.g. text formatting), see Katelouzou and Siems, The Global Diffusion of Stewardship Codes, Chapter 30.
[101] But the Danish code does refer to CSR twice.
[102] But the Korean code refers to 'non-financial' factors three times.
[103] See e.g. UK 2012, Australia (FSC) 2017, Italy 2016, Japan 2017, Taiwan 2016 and Singapore 2016.

TABLE 26.1 *ESG consideration in stewardship codes around the world*

Stewardship code	ESG considerations (relative frequencies)	Stewardship code	ESG considerations (relative frequencies)
South Africa 2011	0.62%	India (IRDAI) 2017	0.10%
Australia (ACSI) 2018	0.44%	Netherlands 2018	0.08%
Brazil 2016	0.32%	Japan 2017	0.06%
EFAMA 2018	0.31%	Singapore 2016	0.05%
Kenya 2017	0.29%	Taiwan 2016	0.05%
India (SEBI) 2019	0.29%	Italy 2016	0.04%
Thailand 2017	0.29%	Australia (FSC) 2017	0.04%
ICGN 2016	0.28%	UK 2012	0.03%
UK 2020	0.23%	Denmark 2016	0.00%
India (PRDA) 2018	0.21%	Korea 2016	0.00%
Canada 2017	0.20%	Switzerland 2013	0.00%
Malaysia 2014	0.13%	US 2017	0.00%
Hong Kong 2016	0.13%		

analysis and activity. Among them, the Code for Responsible Investing in South Africa (CRISA), published in 2011, takes the strongest stance in prioritizing ESG factors, building explicitly on the PRI.[104] This is but another example of the continuously evolving assemblage of norms and cross-references between different standard-setters in the area of corporate governance and sustainable finance.[105]

As Table 26.1 shows, CRISA makes the most frequent reference to ESG factors, followed by the Australia 2018 Code. Australia has two industry-based stewardship codes addressed to investors, one directed to asset owners (ACSI 2018) and one directed to asset managers (FSC 2017). The stark difference in the consideration of ESG-focused activities by the two Australian stewardship codes may perhaps be surprising. The Australia (FSC) 2017 Code makes very little reference to ESG-related activities as one of the several aspects of stewardship, while the Australia (ACSI) 2018 Code has sustainability as a key part of the definition of stewardship, stating, for instance: 'One way that asset owners can help protect and enhance their investments for the long term is by considering ESG matters through their stewardship practices.'[106] This difference may be attributed to the institutional nature and priorities of the two issuing bodies.[107] The Australia (ACSI) 2018 Code, for instance, specifically states that '[t]he Australian Council of Superannuation Investors (ACSI) exists to provide a strong, collective voice on ESG issues on behalf of our members'.[108]

Seven other codes include ESG considerations as one of the stewardship principles, though with varying emphasis.[109] For instance, both Principle 6 of the Canadian Code and Principle 3 of the Japanese Code refer to ESG issues in the context of risk management, while Principle 2 of

---

[104] See also Locke, Encouraging Sustainable Investment in South Africa, Chapter 22.
[105] See Section 26.2.
[106] Australian Council of Superannuation Investors, 'Australian Asset Owner Stewardship Code' (May 2018) 5 <https://acsi.org.au/wp-content/uploads/2020/01/AAOSC_-The_Code.pdf> accessed 25 May 2020 [hereinafter Australia (ACSI) 2018 Code].
[107] For the differences between the two codes, see Bowley and Hill, Stewardship and Collective Action, Chapter 19.
[108] Australia (ACSI) 2018 Code (n 106) 4.
[109] These are the following codes: Brazil 2016, Canada 2017, the Netherlands 2018, Hong Kong 2016, Kenya 2017, Malaysia 2014 and Thailand 2017.

the Hong Kong Code encourages investors to take into account ESG issues in the context of their potential to impact on goodwill, reputation and performance. While we consider only current codes, for the UK we take into account both the 2012 and the 2020 versions of the UK Code.[110] As evidenced by the relative frequencies reported in Table 26.1, the 2020 revisions to the UK Code strengthened its focus on ESG. The UK Code 2020 states: 'Environmental, particularly climate change, and social factors, in addition to governance, have become material issues for investors to consider when making investment decisions and undertaking stewardship.'[111] In addition, the new Principle 7 of the UK Code 2020 requires asset managers and asset owners to integrate and report material ESG factors in their investment and engagement activities and explain how their decisions best serve the views and needs of their clients/beneficiaries.[112] But not only national stewardship codes integrate ESG as a key parameter of stewardship; regional (EFAMA 2018) and international (ICGN 2016) codes follow this trend too.[113]

Overall, there is a clear trend around the world towards galvanizing ESG-investing through stewardship codes.[114] But differences in emphasis still remain, which might be explained by economic, political, cultural or legal differences.[115] For example, South Africa's strong focus on sustainability began in the apartheid years, whereas Thailand and Kenya emphasize ESG in an attempt to actively attract foreign investors.[116] Elsewhere, where a stakeholder-focused corporate governance model is entrenched, and hard law on ESG is relatively strong, such as in the Netherlands and Denmark, stewardship codes may have less of a need to emphasize ESG. Of course, cross-country differences in the detail of investors' fiduciary or other duties may also have a role to play.

From the twenty-five current stewardship codes considered in this chapter, only six do not mention at all the terms 'fiduciary' or 'duties'.[117] But even these codes do not entirely disregard the responsibilities of investors to their ultimate beneficiaries. In some cases, this omission can be attributed to legal traits, as is the case in Denmark where investors' duties are of contractual rather than of fiduciary nature.[118] Other times, a different terminology is being used. For instance, the US Code, despite not specifically mentioning the words 'fiduciary' or 'duties', states in Principle A:[119] 'Institutional investors are accountable to those whose money they invest. A.1 Asset managers are responsible to their clients, whose money they manage. Asset owners are

---

[110] On the previous stewardship codes, see Katelouzou and Siems, The Global Diffusion of Stewardship Codes, Chapter 30.
[111] UK Code 2020 (n 6) 4.
[112] ibid.
[113] European Fund and Asset Management Association, 'EFAMA Stewardship Code: Principles for Asset Managers' Monitoring of, Voting in, Engagement with Investee Companies' (2018) <www.efama.org/sites/default/files/files/EFAMA%20Stewardship%20Code_FINAL.pdf> accessed 7 February 2022; International Corporate Governance Network, ICGN Global Governance Principles (2016) <www.icgn.org/sites/default/files/ICGNGlobalStewardship Principles.pdf> accessed 25 May 2020 [hereinafter ICGN Code].
[114] See also Katelouzou, 'Shareholder Stewardship' (n 99).
[115] On how such differences explain cross-country diversity in corporate governance, see Ruth V Aguilera and Gregory Jackson, 'Comparative and International Corporate Governance' (2010) 4 The Academy of Management Annals 485.
[116] See Alice Klettner, 'Stewardship Codes and the Role of Institutional Investors in Corporate Governance: An International Comparison and Typology' (2021) 32 British Journal of Management 988.
[117] These are the following codes: Denmark 2016, India (IRDAI) 2017, India (PRDA) 2018, India (SEBI) 2019, UK 2020 and US 2017.
[118] See Birkmose and Madsen, The Danish Stewardship Code, Chapter 7 (explaining the contractual rather than fiduciary nature of the relevant investor duties in Denmark).
[119] Investor Stewardship Group, 'The Principles' <https://isgframework.org/stewardship-principles/> accessed 25 May 2020.

responsible to their beneficiaries. A.2 Institutional investors should ensure that they or their managers, as the case may be, oversee client and/or beneficiary assets in a responsible manner.'

The highest number of references to fiduciary duties are made in the Brazilian stewardship code, followed by the Canadian Code, the ICGN and the Kenyan Code. For instance, the Brazilian Code states: 'The role of institutional investors cannot be separated from the fiduciary duties they assume when they become responsible for managing funds on behalf of a group of people. They are the stewards of third parties' funds.'[120] These references to fiduciary or other types of investment management duties and the broader contours of accountability along the investment chain confirm the strong investment management aspect embedded in these largely voluntary codes and suggest a 'regulatory complementarity' between hard-law duties and soft-law stewardship codes.[121] But from the nineteen codes that explicitly link stewardship practices to the fulfilment of investors' legal duties, only four codes (i.e. Brazil 2016, ICGN 2016, Kenya 2017 and Thailand 2017) clearly regard the consideration of ESG factors as part of institutional investors' fiduciary responsibility. The guidance to Principle 3 of the Brazilian code states:[122]

> The analysis and monitoring of ESG factors is part of the evaluation of the risks and opportunities associated with the investments, although they are not the final drivers for an investment decision. By carefully managing the assets of their end beneficiaries, institutional investors should consider relevant ESG factors as crucial aspects when it comes to the fulfillment of their fiduciary duties, being duly transparent about the way these factors will be considered.

Also, both the ICGN Global Principles and the Kenyan Code consider ESG factors to be core components of investors' fiduciary or other legal obligations,[123] while the Thai Code makes a clear connection between 'investment duties' and 'monitoring the investments, business and ESG performance of investee companies'.[124] Principle 7 of the UK Code 2020, with its emphasis on the integration of 'stewardship and investment, including *material* environmental, social and governance issues, and climate change',[125] to fulfil investors' responsibilities to clients and beneficiaries, may provide an influential blueprint for other codes to unlock sustainable finance.

These findings lead to the conclusion that even though ESG investing is increasingly becoming a core component of stewardship codes, it is not always expressly connected to fiduciary or other investment management duties. This may be attributed to legal or cultural traits and the contractual arrangements that incorporate duties of responsible investment. A more cynical explanation behind this lacking link may be the abovementioned tension

---

[120] Associação de Investidores no Mercado de Capitais (AMEC), 'Código AMEC de Princípios e Deveres dos Investidores Institucionais: Stewardship [AMEC Code of Principles and Duties of Institutional Investors: Stewardship]' (27 October 2016) 1 <www.amecbrasil.org.br/wp-content/uploads/2016/06/CODIGOAMECSTEWARDSHIPMinutaparaConsultaPublica.pdf> accessed 7 February 2022.

[121] On this symbiosis of different stewardship-related rules, see Katelouzou, *The Path to Enlightened Shareholder Stewardship* (n 46). For earlier work on the rights and responsibilities/accountability of institutional investors, see Katelouzou, 'Reflections on the Nature of the Public Corporation in an Era of Shareholder Activism and Shareholder Stewardship' (n 3).

[122] AMEC (n 120) 12.

[123] See e.g. the ICGN code: 'This includes the consideration of wider ethical, environmental and social factors as core components of fiduciary duty' (ICGN Code (n 113) 5) and the Kenyan code: 'In the investment context, the main focus of institutional investors is on those aspects of social, environmental and ethical practice by issuers that may pose a material commercial risk or opportunity. Attention to these sustainability issues in the investment process shall be regarded as part of an institutional investor's fiduciary responsibility to the ultimate beneficiaries' (Stewardship Code for Institutional Investors 2017 (9 May 2017), enacted by the Capital Markets Authority vide Kenya Gazette Notice No 6016 dated 23 June 2017).

[124] Securities and Exchange Commission, 'Investment Governance Code for Institutional Investors' (2017) 37 <www.sec.or.th/cgthailand/EN/Documents/ICode/ICodeBookEN.pdf> accessed 25 May 2020.

[125] UK Code 2020 (n 6) 4 (emphasis added).

between soft-law ESG-related stewardship and hard-law duties. Here, the extent to which financially disadvantageous ESG decisions can be undertaken by asset managers and asset owners under the aegis of stewardship activities is very much an open question, discussed further in Section 26.4.[126]

Before concluding this section, it is worth considering the role of stewardship codes in improving transparency around investment decision-making. Disclosure of stewardship policies and reporting to clients and beneficiaries feature prominently in the principles of most stewardship codes around the world. Katelouzou and Siems show that all of the twenty-five codes considered here refer to the development of a disclosure policy on stewardship.[127] Also, all but three codes (i.e. Australia (FSC) 2017, Singapore 2015 and US 2017) refer to reporting obligations on stewardship and voting activities.[128] These can support hard-law reporting requirements such as those introduced by SRD II and other efforts to improve transparency including the various voluntary initiatives referred to in Section 26.2. Transparency relates to the investment management aspects of stewardship, and aims to increase accountability across the investment chain.[129] By engaging with investee companies through formal and informal means and asking questions,[130] investors facilitate information flow within and out of companies – on all matters, but increasingly on sustainability. However, while improving transparency around stewardship is one of the key aims of stewardship codes globally, transparency is not often expressly linked to ESG factors. Here some inspiration can be taken from CRISA, which requires investors to disclose publicly a 'policy on incorporation of sustainability considerations, including ESG, into investment analysis and investment activities' as well as ensuring that this policy is implemented.[131]

26.4 UNLOCKING THE SUSTAINABLE FINANCE POTENTIAL OF STEWARDSHIP CODES

Stewardship codes are but a small part of a broader network of interlocking regulatory initiatives that can directly or indirectly contribute to the promotion of sustainable finance. Despite their own set of limitations, stewardship codes, through their flexible and largely voluntary nature, can play an important role in interpreting and extending the scope of hard law.[132] As discussed in Section 26.3, the two areas of hard law that interact most strongly with stewardship codes are investors' fiduciary duties and reporting requirements. Evidently, sustainability is not yet entirely integrated into these areas by current stewardship codes. But we are optimistic that stewardship codes have the potential to place sustainability at the core of these dual requirements. In countries where hard law on sustainability is strong, such as in Europe, stewardship codes can act as implementation guidelines. In countries where hard law is weak, owing to either a strong profit maximization culture (US) or less developed financial markets (emerging markets of Africa and Asia), stewardship codes can help to spread best practice and have an educative effect, preparing investors for potential strengthening of hard-law provisions.[133] To unlock their full

---

[126] On this, see Davies, The UK Stewardship Code 2010–2020, Chapter 2.
[127] Katelouzou and Siems, The Global Diffusion of Stewardship Codes, Chapter 30.
[128] ibid.
[129] For instance, the Denmark code states that '[t]he stewardship code should result in increased transparency as to how the individual investor chooses to exercise stewardship activities'. On the investment management parameters of stewardship, see further Katelouzou, *The Path to Enlightened Shareholder Stewardship* (n 46).
[130] On the various facets of shareholder engagement, see ibid.
[131] Institute of Directors in Southern Africa, 'Code for Responsible Investing in South Africa 2011' (2011) 11 (Principle 5 on transparency) 10 (Principle 1 on implementation) <www.iodsa.co.za/page/crisaresourcecentr> accessed 25 May 2020.
[132] On the interplays between hard and soft law in the area of stewardship, see Katelouzou, *The Path to Enlightened Shareholder Stewardship* (n 46).
[133] On the need to harden stewardship obligations, see Chiu and Katelouzou (n 51).

sustainability potential, stewardship codes first need to place ESG considerations at the centre of investment practice as fundamental tenets rather than optional extras, using investors' fiduciary and other duties as a persuasive influence. They also need to encourage transparency around this integration of ESG so that information can flow to interested stakeholders. To unlock additional potential, stewardship codes should try to: (i) maximize their scope and influence to encompass as much of the investment chain as possible; and (ii) where possible extend the purpose of ESG integration beyond private financial benefit to encompass a much broader public benefit test.

26.4.1 *Maximizing the Scope and Influence of Stewardship Codes*

The financial clout of pension funds, one of the key targeted audiences of stewardship codes, across the world is huge and, if channelled in an appropriate way, could make a real difference to sustainable development. As the UK Parliamentary committee report on Greening Finance commented:[134]

> There are many hundreds of billions of pounds in UK pension schemes and these 'asset owners' sit at the top of the investment chain. The UK Sustainable Investment and Finance Association (UKSIF) argued that these 'sleeping giants' often 'do not realise the financial power they wield'. Ensuring that these funds manage environmental risks effectively could assist in the transition to a low carbon economy and reduce the UK's overall exposure to climate risk. However, only 5% of 1,241 European Pensions schemes have considered the investment risk posed by climate change, according to the consultancy firm Mercer's 2017 European Asset Allocation Report.

The investment industry is highly concentrated, with the top ten asset managers holding 34 per cent of externally managed assets.[135] Indeed, some of these huge funds now view themselves in accordance with the theory of 'universal ownership', meaning that their holdings are so large that they are vulnerable to the fortunes of the economy as a whole rather than individual companies.[136] They cannot simply sell certain shares to reduce risk and thus will be more likely to monitor and engage, in other words, exercise voice rather than exit.[137] This concentration of shares in the hands of institutional investors reduces the well-known managerial agency costs and arguably creates conditions more suited to stewardship behaviour.[138] However, the outsourcing of asset management and other investment functions to specialist service providers can create new agency problems.[139]

---

[134] House of Commons Environmental Audit Committee, 'Greening Finance: Embedding Sustainability In Financial Decision Making' (HC 1063 2018) <https://publications.parliament.uk/pa/cm201719/cmselect/cmenvaud/1063/106305.htm> accessed 25 May 2020.

[135] Eccles and Klimenko (n 66).

[136] James Hawley and Andrew Williams, 'The Emergence of Universal Owners: Some Implications of Institutional Equity Ownership' (2000) 43 *Challenge* 43; Matthew J Kiernan, 'Universal Owners and ESG: Leaving Money on the Table?' (2007) 15 *Corporate Governance: An International Review* 478; Steven Lydenberg, 'Universal Investors and Socially Responsible Investors: A Tale Of Emerging Affinities' (2007) 15 *Corporate Governance: An International Review* 467.

[137] Albert O Hirschman, *Exit, Voice, and Loyalty: Responses to Decline in Firms, Organizations, and States* (Harvard University Press 1970).

[138] Lucian A Bebchuk, Alma Cohen and Scott Hirst, 'The Agency Problems of Institutional Investors' (2017) 31 *Journal of Economic Perspectives* 89.

[139] ibid; Ronald Gilson and Jeffrey Gordon, 'The Agency Costs of Agency Capitalism: Activist Investors and the Revaluation of Governance Rights' (2013) 113 *Columbia Law Review* 863 (arguing that the reconcentration of ownership in the hands of institutional investors gives rise to a new type of agency costs, which they call 'the agency costs of agency capitalism').

This is where we find the sustainable finance potential of stewardship codes. They have the ability to educate and persuade these dominant players to change norms of practice and to increase transparency and awareness of how monies are invested. This is supported by the reputational benefits associated with following good stewardship practices.[140] By harnessing the power of the funds at the top of the investment chain, stewardship codes can also change practices deeper in the investment chain by influencing the nature of contractual mandates.[141]

Of course the first step is to persuade the powerful to take action and here the great weakness of stewardship codes is their voluntary nature.[142] Most apply to investors on a 'comply-or-explain' basis and, for many, signing up is entirely voluntary.[143] This varies depending on whether the code is issued by an industry association or government regulator, but codes generally cannot force investors to engage in stewardship behaviour. We argue that this does not matter. Codes do not stand alone as a solitary lever for change; rather, they form an important part of a much wider framework for investor behaviour. They can, and already are, steadily changing norms and expectations within the industry to harness the power of these huge funds.[144]

Nevertheless, some codes have definitely been more successful than others in gaining the attention of large investors. The UK Code had 178 asset managers, 103 asset owners and 12 service providers as signatories as of September 2021.[145] At the end of 2019, the Japanese Code, issued by a government agency, had 273 signatories.[146] In contrast, the Australia (ACSI) 2018 Code has sixteen signatories (out of its thirty-nine members),[147] the Brazilian Code issued by an industry association (AMEC) in 2016 has nineteen signatories,[148] and the Kenyan Code issued by the Kenya Capital Markets Authority none.[149] Although these numbers are not directly comparable owing to variation in market size, they provide support for research that suggests that the identity of the issuer of a code is an important factor in its effectiveness.[150] As discussed in the country-specific chapters of this book, national differences in culture, governance, share ownership patterns, and the interaction between stewardship codes and wider legal and regulatory

---

[140] See e.g. Davies, The UK Stewardship Code 2010–2020, Chapter 2.
[141] Klettner (n 98); Bebchuk, Cohen and Hirst (n 138).
[142] Arad Reisberg, 'The UK Stewardship Code: On the Road to Nowhere?' (2015) 15 *Journal of Corporate Law Studies* 217; Iris H-Y Chiu, 'Reviving Shareholder Stewardship: Critically Examining the Impact of Corporate Transparency Reforms in the UK' (2014) 38 *Delaware Journal of Corporate Law* 983; Lee Roach, 'The UK Stewardship Code' (2011) 11 *Journal of Corporate Law Studies* 463; Brian R Cheffins, 'The Stewardship Code's Achilles' Heel' (2010) 73 *Modern Law Review* 1004.
[143] Further on the enforcement of stewardship codes, see Katelouzou and Sergakis, Shareholder Stewardship Enforcement, Chapter 27.
[144] See e.g. the views of the CEO of Hermes Investment Management, Saker Nusseibeh, 'Stewardship: The 2020 Vision' (*Harvard Law School Forum on Corporate Governance*, 1 November 2019) <https://corpgov.law.harvard.edu/2019/11/01/stewardship-the-2020-vision/> accessed 25 May 2020.
[145] The last list of signatories to the 2012 version of the UK Code is available: <https://www.frc.org.uk/document-library/corporate-governance/stewardship-statements/stewardship-code-2012-signatory-list> accessed 7 February 2022. The current list of signatories to the UK Code 2020 is available: <www.frc.org.uk/investors/uk-stewardship-code/uk-stewardship-code-signatories> accessed 4 February 2022.
[146] The breakdown across trust banks, investment managers, insurance companies and pension funds is available at Financial Services Agency, 'Stewardship Code : 281 Institutional Investors Have Signed Up to the Principles for Responsible Institutional Investors as of April 30, 2020' (2020) <www.fsa.go.jp/en/refer/councils/stewardship/20160315.html> accessed 25 May 2020.
[147] ACSI, 'Current Signatories to the Code' <https://acsi.org.au/members/australian-asset-owner-stewardship-code/> accessed 25 May 2020.
[148] AMEC, 'Signatories' <https://en.amecbrasil.org.br/stewardship/signatories/> accessed 25 May 2020.
[149] See Ouko, Stewardship Code in Kenya, Chapter 23.
[150] Ruth Aguilera, Chris Florackis and Hicheon Kim, 'Advancing the Corporate Governance Research Agenda' (2016) 24 *Corporate Governance: An International Review* 172; James E Cicon, Stephen P Ferris, Armin J Kammel and Gregory Noronha, 'European Corporate Governance: A Thematic Analysis of National Codes of Governance' (2012) 18 *European Financial Management* 620. But cf Katelouzou and Siems, The Global Diffusion of Stewardship Codes, Chapter 30 (finding no evidence that the identity of the issuer matters).

frameworks will also impact on code effectiveness.[151] In some countries, such as Germany and China, a path towards stewardship and sustainability is being followed without any perceived need for a stewardship code.[152]

Certainly, the influence of a stewardship code can be improved by strengthening the regulatory and contractual framework around it. The UK Code is the best example of a code with a level of regulatory supervision. The FRC assesses the quality of disclosure of all UK Code signatories, and places them in tiers based on whether they report well or need to improve.[153] The fact that tiering information is publicly available acts as a reputational incentive for signatories to improve. The UK Code is also a good example of how codes can gain increased influence over time: it began as an industry-based code which was then adopted by the FRC.[154] In Australia, the Financial Services Council (the leading peak body for fund managers) has created a stewardship code in the form of mandatory standards for its members.[155] This improves its influence through contractual rather than supervisory methods. Lastly, the code issued by the European industry association European Fund and Asset Management Association (EFAMA) has been amended in line with the revised SRD II with the aim of positioning itself as a guide on how to comply with the new laws.[156] There are many ways that soft law can be combined within a layered meta-regulatory regime to enhance and maximize its influence.[157] Here, we limit ourselves to the above examples which are merely intended to illustrate the various ways (such as through supervision and enforcement, contractual obligations, etc.) to improve the sustainability potential of stewardship codes.

In terms of their scope, stewardship codes recognize the realities of the modern investment industry: heterogeneous shareholders; variation in investment strategies; and the fact that asset owners often outsource fund management, creating complex contractual investment chains between beneficiaries and investee companies.[158] By recognizing these practicalities of modern investment, stewardship codes have the potential to reach *all financial intermediaries*, including those who may otherwise be seen simply as service providers rather than regulated financial institutions. These intermediaries, such as broker dealers, may not be subject to legal fiduciary-style duties, yet similar duties can be placed upon them indirectly through their contractual mandates with asset owners.[159]

---

[151] See e.g. Locke, Encouraging Sustainable Investment in South Africa, Chapter 22 and Becker, Andrade and Prado, The Brazilian Stewardship Framework, Chapter 24. See also Katelouzou and Puchniak, Global Shareholder Stewardship, Chapter 1 and Koh, Puchniak and Goto, Shareholder Stewardship in Asia, Chapter 29.

[152] See Ringe, Stewardship and Shareholder Engagement in Germany, Chapter 9 and Puchniak and Lin, Institutional Investors in China, Chapter 18, respectively.

[153] Further on the tiering exercise, see Financial Reporting Council, 'Tiering of Signatories to the Stewardship Code' (14 November 2016) <www.frc.org.uk/news/november-2016/tiering-of-signatories-to-the-stewardship-code> accessed 25 May 2020.

[154] See the detailed history of the UK code, see Katelouzou, *The Path to Enlightened Shareholder Stewardship* (n 46). For a snapshot, see Katelouzou and Micheler, The Market for Stewardship and the Role of the Government, Chapter 3.

[155] FSC Standard 23: Principles of Internal Governance and Asset Stewardship, July 2017.

[156] Susanna Rust, 'EFAMA Adopts Stewardship Code to Align with EU Laws' (*IPE*, 31 May 2018) <www.ipe.com/efama-adopts-stewardship-code-to-align-with-eu-laws/10024971.article> accessed 25 May 2020.

[157] Gilad (n 34); Christine Parker, 'Meta-regulation: Legal Accountability for Corporate Social Responsibility' in Doreen McBarnet, Aurora Voiculescu and Tom Campbell (eds), *The New Corporate Accountability: Corporate Social Responsibility and the Law* (CUP 2009); Parker (n 34); Julia Black, 'Paradoxes and Failures: "New Governance" Techniques and the Financial Crisis' (2012) 75 *Modern Law Review* 1037; Cristie Ford, 'New Governance in the Teeth of Human Frailty: Lessons from Financial Regulation' (2010) 2010 *Wisconsin Law Review* 441; Julia Black and Robert Baldwin, 'Really Responsive Risk-Based Regulation' (2010) 32 *Law & Policy* 181.

[158] See e.g. Terry McNulty and Donald Nordberg, 'Ownership, Activism and Engagement: Institutional Investors as Active Owners' (2016) 24 *Corporate Governance: An International Review* 346.

[159] For a proposal to expand fiduciary duties on all financial intermediaries, including broker dealers, in the US, see Tamar Frankel, 'Fiduciary Duties of Brokers-Advisers-Financial Planners and Money Managers' (2009) Boston

Stewardship codes can play a significant role in co-opting such important players and extending fiduciary duties and transparency (albeit in soft law) along the investment chain, thereby dealing with the agency costs of outsourcing.[160]

Many codes deal with improving transparency and accountability along the investment chain either through recommending disclosure of the use of service providers (such as proxy advisers)[161] or by emphasizing that signatories must not 'blindly delegate' their stewardship responsibilities.[162] For instance, the Korean Code states:[163]

> Institutional investors take on ultimate stewardship responsibilities even when they entrust all or part of their stewardship activities to external investors or other (advisory) service providers. Institutional investors should monitor and supervise to ensure that outsourced activities are executed in accordance with their own stewardship policy. Hence the Principles apply to proxy advisors, investment advisors etc. that provide (advisory) services related to the detailed contents of the Principles.

Indeed, as powerful actors sitting at the top of a long set of relationships, institutional investors, through stewardship, have the potential to draw information upwards when it might otherwise stay hidden. Business outsourcing has become a complex problem for accountability, particularly acute in long global supply chains.[164] However, suppliers increasingly have to account to listed companies, who must report to investors, who can then make better informed decisions and explain their investment strategies to beneficiaries. The incorporation of ESG information into this flow of data has great potential for improving sustainability across the economy. Indeed, in 2019 UNEP FI announced a new collaboration with the PRI and law firm Freshfields Bruckhaus Deringer to explore the wider legal framework around investing for sustainability impact.[165] It is likely that rules around providing financial advice as well as variation in the fiduciary duties of different categories of investor and intermediary will come under more scrutiny in future in terms of their incorporation of sustainability considerations.

University School of Law Working Paper No 09-36 <https://ssrn.com/abstract=1446750> accessed 25 May 2020. But for a critical view on the imposition of fiduciary duties on proxy advisers, see Donna Musolli, 'A Distraction in Disguise: How a Focus on Regulating the Proxy-Advisory Industry Fails to Address the Unnecessary Creation of an Extra Layer of Conflict' (2017) <www.law.msu.edu/king/2016-2017/Musolli.pdf> accessed 7 February 2022.

[160] On business outsourcing, see generally George S Geis, 'Business Outsourcing and the Agency Cost Problem' (2007) 82 *Notre Dame Law Review* 955.

[161] See e.g. the Malaysian Code (Securities Commission Malaysia and Minority Shareholders Watch Group, *Malaysian Code for Institutional Investors* (27 June 2014) 16, Guidance 6.6 <www.sc.com.my/api/documentms/download.ashx?id=9f4e32d3-cb97-4ff5-852a-6cb168a9f936> accessed 25 May 2020), the Thailand Code (Securities and Exchange Commission (n 124) 49, Principle 5.5) and the UK Code 2020 (n 6) 13–14, Principle 6.

[162] Klettner (n 98) 265. See e.g. Securities and Futures Commission, 'Principles of Responsible Ownership' (7 March 2016) 1 <www.sfc.hk/web/EN/rules-and-standards/principles-of-responsible-ownership.html> accessed 25 May 2020. See also the Council of Experts on the Stewardship Code, 'Principles for Responsible Institutional Investors «Japan's Stewardship Code» – To Promote Sustainable Growth of Companies through Investment and Dialogue' (29 May 2017) 15 <www.fsa.go.jp/en/refer/councils/stewardship/20170529/01.pdf> accessed 25 May 2020 (stating that '[w]hen institutional investors use the service of proxy advisors, *they should not mechanically depend on the advisors' recommendations* but should exercise their voting rights at their own responsibility and judgment and based on the results of the monitoring of the investee companies and dialogue with them' (own emphasis)).

[163] Korea Stewardship Code Council, 'Principles on the Stewardship Responsibilities of Institutional Investors' (16 December 2016) 2, para 2 <http://sc.cgs.or.kr/eng/about/sc.jsp> accessed 25 May 2020.

[164] See e.g. Kishanthi Parella, 'Outsourcing Corporate Accountability' (2014) 89 *Washington Law Review* 747.

[165] See UNEP Finance Initiative, 'Groundbreaking Work to Assess Real-World Sustainability Impact for Investors: A Legal Framework for Impact' (27 November 2019) <www.unepfi.org/news/industries/investment/groundbreaking-work-to-assess-real-world-sustainability-impact-for-investors/> accessed 25 May 2020.

26.4.2 Moving ESG Away from a Pure Financial Business Case

Normalizing the integration of ESG into investors' legal duties to clients and beneficiaries may pave the way for extending those duties beyond the immediate business case.[166] At present, most jurisdictions still place an overriding financial priority on 'the best interests of beneficiaries'.[167] Until now, the mainstream approach has been that ESG factors can and should be incorporated, but the purpose of this is to promote long-term financial gains and mitigate long-term risks. In other words, ESG factors cannot be considered solely for reasons of ethics or justice.

The situation changes if end-beneficiaries give express permission to their pension fund to invest based on ethics. However, this may be seen as a risky move unless precise boundaries are drawn. This is not impossible and it is why the EU is focusing on financial advisers and the advice and information that institutional investors, including asset managers, insurance companies and investment or insurance advisers, give to clients and fund beneficiaries.[168] The only person who can really decide what is in their long-term best interests is the fund beneficiary him/herself. Many people might be focused on maximal financial returns, but many will not, especially if accurately informed of the potential social and environmental harm this could cause. Research based in Sweden has found that beneficiaries on average prefer their pension funds to go beyond financial concerns and engage in SRI.[169] In the UK, there is also evidence of changing consumer preferences:[170]

> There is evidence that demand for sustainable investment is growing, with young people driving this trend. In 2017 40% of those surveyed in an annual YouGov poll for 'Good Money Week' wanted a 'fossil fuel free' pension option, up from 35% in 2016 and 32% in 2015. In the 2017 poll, over half of 18 to 34-years-olds (54%) said they would like to be offered fossil free investments as standard, compared to the national average of 40%, and only 34% of those over 55. Overall, 57% of the UK public with a pension believe investment managers have a responsibility to ensure holdings are managed in a way that is positive for society and the environment, according to the survey.

Investors cannot be given free rein to use pension monies to subjectively 'do good' in the world and thus we need to find a way to define and account for social and environmental benefit and/or harm. Richardson refers to social accounting and sustainability indicators as potential tools for this.[171] The EU taxonomy is likely to provide a good start in terms of technical standards for defining sustainable economic activities.[172] This could ultimately be supported by changes to investors' legal duties to their clients and beneficiaries that incorporate an underlying public interest or sustainable development test.[173] Lydenberg explains that investors are pulled in opposite directions by two powerful streams of intellectual thought, the legal and the economic.[174] He argues that modern finance has permitted economic 'rationality' (efficient, private value-maximization) to downplay the importance of legal 'reasonableness' (wisdom,

---

[166] See Section 26.3.2.
[167] For example, Australian legislation requires trustees to maintain pension funds solely for the provision of retirement benefits; in Germany, best interests are defined in a financial sense while taking into account risks; and in the UK the primary concern of trustees must be to generate appropriate risk-adjusted returns – see Sullivan, Martindale, Feller and Bordon (n 83).
[168] The Commission has solicited feedback on amendments to delegated acts under the Markets in Financial Instruments Directive (MiFID II) and the Insurance Distribution Directive.
[169] Jansson, Sandberg, Biel and Gärling (n 97).
[170] Greening Finance (n 134) 17, para 37 <https://publications.parliament.uk/pa/cm201719/cmselect/cmenvaud/1063/106305.htm#_idTextAnchor025> accessed 25 May 2020.
[171] Richardson (n 77).
[172] See Section 26.2.2.
[173] Richardson (n 77) 566; Schoenmaker and Schramade (n 7).
[174] Steve Lydenberg, 'Reason, Rationality and Fiduciary Duty' (2014) 119 *Journal of Business Ethics* 365.

discretion and consideration of one's impact on the world). The potential of stewardship codes is in providing the foundations for increased consumer awareness of how funds are being invested. This has yet to be generally achieved. The UK Code 2020, for instance, has been less ambitious compared to its 2019 draft;[175] instead of talking about 'sustainable value', it refers to the creation of 'long-term value for clients and beneficiaries leading to sustainable benefits for the economy, the environment, and society'.[176]

26.5 CONCLUSION

Stewardship codes must be viewed as an influential part of the overall legal framework that applies to institutional investors. Their role is not to single-handedly change investment behaviour but to act as one of many mutually reinforcing regulatory instruments pursuing common 'good' goals. These regulatory instruments include some of the international initiatives referred to in this chapter as well as binding and non-binding national laws that impact on investor behaviour.

While we are not blind to the limitations that the investment management business models pose for stewardship,[177] and we recognize the responsibility of the board to address sustainability,[178] we are optimistic that, as well as encouraging active, long-term ownership, stewardship codes have the potential to place ESG and sustainability firmly within the scope of investors' fiduciary and other duties, helping to cement modern interpretation of long-standing legal obligations.[179] To fully unlock their potential when it comes to sustainability, it is important that stewardship codes take a strong stance on the incorporation of ESG factors as a central element of investment practice. Many codes have already done this, but others need to be much clearer about the way in which investors' legal duties and ESG support each other.[180] When hard law leaves actors with a level of discretion, soft law has an important influencing role around the way in which actors exercise that discretion.[181] Within the wider framework of increased reporting requirements and heightened awareness of environmental and social threats, stewardship codes have the potential to strengthen the links between civil society and business.[182] With the support of the interlocking regulatory framework emerging to govern sustainable finance, stewardship codes can bring the public, 'reasonable man'[183] viewpoint back into financial decision-making. This will be particularly important as we assess the social and financial impacts of the Covid-19 pandemic and navigate a path to recovery.

---

[175] Financial Reporting Council, 'Consulting on a Revised UK Stewardship Code' (30 January 2019) <www.frc.org.uk/consultation-list/2019/consulting-on-a-revised-uk-stewardship-code> accessed 25 May 2020.
[176] See also Davies, The UK Stewardship Code 2010–2020, Chapter 2.
[177] See Barker and Chiu, Investment Management, Stewardship and Corporate Governance Roles, Chapter 25 as well as Davies, The UK Stewardship Code 2010–2020, Chapter 2.
[178] See Mähönen, Sjåfjell and Mee, Stewardship Norwegian-Style, Chapter 8.
[179] James P Hawley, Keith L Johnson and Edward J Waitzer, 'Reclaiming Fiduciary Duty Balance' (2011) 4 Rotman International Journal of Pension Management 4.
[180] Klettner (n 98).
[181] Cary Coglianese and Evan Mendelson, 'Meta-regulation and Self-Regulation' in Robert Baldwin, Martin Cave and Martin Lodge (eds), The Oxford Handbook on Regulation (OUP 2010).
[182] Jonathan D Raelin and Krista Bondy, 'Putting the Good Back in Good Corporate Governance: The Presence and Problems of Double-Layered Agency Theory' (2013) 21 Corporate Governance: An International Review 420.
[183] Lydenberg (n 174).

27

Shareholder Stewardship Enforcement

Dionysia Katelouzou and Konstantinos Sergakis

27.1 INTRODUCTION

'Shareholder stewardship', in the sense of institutional shareholders' monitoring and engaging with companies in such a way that both companies and the ultimate providers of capital prosper,[1] has gained importance across the globe as the new normative means of ensuring sound *modus operandi* of institutional investors and asset managers in listed equity and more recently in other assets.[2] Shareholder stewardship on the part of institutional shareholders, being strongly associated with both good corporate governance and socially approved responsible investing,[3] has been mainly promoted in recent years through voluntary, soft and flexible stewardship *norms* (stewardship codes and best practice principles) which are most of the times self-regulatory in nature.[4] In some contexts, these soft-law norms attempted to formalize what previously consisted of entirely 'social norms'[5] and expectations about shareholder engagement[6] and socially approved responsible investing.[7] Other times, the creation of soft stewardship norms was an attempt to prevent top-down regulation of investment practices,[8] or simply a form of 'halo signalling' demonstrating commitment to good corporate governance standards.[9]

---

[1] This term is borrowed from Dionysia Katelouzou, *The Path to Enlightened Shareholder Stewardship* (CUP) (forthcoming), which provides a comprehensive analysis of the broader concept of stewardship, and its corporate governance as well as investment management aspects.

[2] Note, however, that in recent years a new trend has appeared which expands stewardship to other assets, such as infrastructure and fixed income. See e.g. Financial Reporting Council, *UK Stewardship Code 2020* (2019) <www.frc.org.uk/getattachment/5aae591d-d9d3-4cf4-814a-d14e156a1d87/Stewardship-Code_Dec-19-Final-Corrected.pdf> accessed 10 May 2020. For such activities, the term 'stewardship' (rather than 'shareholder stewardship') is more accurate. See Katelouzou and Puchniak, Global Shareholder Stewardship, Chapter 1; Katelouzou, *The Path to Enlightened Shareholder Stewardship* (n 1).

[3] For an overview of the growing public interest in stewardship codes, see Dionysia Katelouzou, 'Shareholder Stewardship: A Case of (Re)Embedding Institutional Investors and the Corporation?' in Beate Sjåfjell and Christopher M Bruner (eds), *Cambridge Handbook of Corporate Law, Corporate Governance and Sustainability* (CUP 2019) 581–95.

[4] In this study we use the term 'norm' in the sense of *legal* norms, either soft or hard in nature, and we do not refer to non-legal norms. But see Martha Finnemore, 'Are Legal Norms Distinctive?' (2000) 32 *New York University Journal of International Law & Politics* 699, questioning the distinction between legal and non-legal norms.

[5] The literature on social norms is voluminous. See e.g. Amir N Licht, 'Social Norms and the Law: Why Peoples Obey the Law' (2008) 4 *Review of Law & Economics* 715, 717 (defining social norms as 'behaviours that are seen as desirable or legitimate in the shaped view of societal members and whose violation elicits at least informal disapproval').

[6] See Davies, The UK Stewardship Code 2010–2020, Chapter 2.

[7] See Locke, Encouraging Sustainable Investment in South Africa, Chapter 22.

[8] This is the case in the UK. See Katelouzou, *The Path to Enlightened Shareholder Stewardship* (n 1).

[9] See Puchniak and Tang, Singapore's Embrace of Shareholder Stewardship, Chapter 14.

Against this mainstream approach of designing and enforcing shareholder stewardship via soft-law norms, the revised EU Shareholder Rights Directive (SRD II)[10] elevates the operability framework of shareholder stewardship to higher standards of transparency and promotes long-term shareholder engagement on the part of institutional investors and asset managers through the imposition of semi-hard rules.[11] At the same time, hard law, in the form of disclosure obligations or expansive fiduciary duties, is being increasingly introduced to address certain aspects of the broader stewardship role (related to both corporate governance and investment management aspects) of specific market actors.[12] This coexistence of soft-law, semi-hard and hard law across the globe raises important questions about the future of stewardship frameworks[13] and their enforcement. The twofold function of stewardship, as a corporate governance monitoring mechanism for the benefit of investee companies, shareholders and wider stakeholders and as an internal investment management tool on behalf of ultimate investors,[14] may not be equally evidenced across the different stewardship codes,[15] but has important ramifications for legal and regulatory frameworks attempting either to encourage or less often to impose day-to-day stewardship practice at the national and international levels.

One of the central problems of shareholder stewardship around the world is rendering institutional investors good monitors of their investee companies, and improving their accountability to both companies and their own beneficiaries and clients.[16] In this chapter we investigate this problem focusing on the availability (or not) of strategies to enforce shareholder stewardship around the world. We adopt a *broad* approach to enforcement mechanisms in the area of shareholder stewardship and set out a simple conceptual taxonomy based on three dimensions. Our taxonomy takes into account the *nature of the norm-enforcer* and distinguishes between self-enforcement and third-party enforcement. In the latter we consider public, quasi-public, private, market and social norm-enforcers. These actors may or may not be the standard-setters of the relevant soft or hard rules. We then distinguish between formal and informal enforcement *mechanisms* so as to highlight the wide variety of enforcement options that all these actors have at their disposal. Finally, we take into account the *temporal* dimension of enforcement and distinguish between *ex ante* (monitoring and deterrence) and *ex post* (compliance).[17]

---

[10] Directive (EU) 2017/828 of the European Parliament and of the Council of 17 May 2017 amending Directive 2007/36/EC as regards the encouragement of long-term shareholder engagement [2017] OJ L132/1 (SRD II).

[11] On the hardening of stewardship through the SRD II, see Iris H–Y Chiu and Dionysia Katelouzou, 'From Shareholder Stewardship to Shareholder Duties: Is the Time Ripe?' in Hanne S Birkmose (ed), *Shareholders' Duties* (Kluwer Law International 2017) 131–52.

[12] In the UK, see e.g. the Pension Protection Fund (Pensionable Service) and Occupational Pension Schemes (Investment and Disclosure) (Amendment and Modification) Regulations 2018, SI 2018/988 and the Occupational Pension Schemes (Investment and Disclosure) (Amendment) Regulations 2019, SI 2019/982 requiring trustees to set out and disclose stewardship of scheme investments. For more on the coexistence of these multiple regulatory layers of stewardship, see Katelouzou, *The Path to Enlightened Shareholder Stewardship* (n 1).

[13] On the symbiosis of soft law and semi-hard law stewardship norms in the EU, see Dionysia Katelouzou and Konstantinos Sergakis, 'When Harmonization Is Not Enough: Shareholder Stewardship in the European Union' (2021) 22 *European Business Organization Law Review* 203.

[14] Dionysia Katelouzou, 'Reflections on the Nature of the Public Corporation in an Era of Shareholder Activism and Stewardship' in Barnali Choudhury and Martin Petrin (eds), *Understanding the Company: Corporate Governance and Theory* (CUP 2017) 117–44; Katelouzou, *The Path to Enlightened Shareholder Stewardship* (n 1).

[15] An aspect of investment management often incorporated in stewardship codes is the management of conflicts of interests and the supply of relevant disclosures. See Katelouzou, *The Path to Enlightened Shareholder Stewardship* (n 1). For differences across forty-one stewardship codes in incorporating this principle, see Katelouzou and Siems, The Global Diffusion of Stewardship Codes, Chapter 30, this volume.

[16] See also Katelouzou and Puchniak, Global Shareholder Stewardship, Chapter 1.

[17] But see John C Coffee Jr, 'Law and the Market: The Impact of Enforcement' (2007) 156 *University of Pennsylvania Law Review* 229, 254 (distinguishing between 'regulation' that is *ex ante* enforcement and enforcement which always operates *ex post*).

We then turn to an in-depth analysis of the current enforcement mode in the context of shareholder stewardship. We find that the overwhelming majority of stewardship norms are incorporated in soft stewardship 'codes'[18] which, unlike corporate governance codes, are completely voluntary in nature, relying solely on market and social enforcement mechanisms. An exception to this trend has been the implementation of article 14b of the SRD II in the EU by some member states in a rather formalistic fashion and the introduction of administrative sanctions and measures for the breach of the semi-hard engagement rules of the SRD II. However, the EU example coexists within a wider international framework that largely opts for enforcement by market actors in reflection of the largely soft-law nature of the underpinning shareholder stewardship norms.[19]

Looking forward, we outline the broad contours of an enforcement framework in the context of shareholder stewardship employing our proposed enforcement taxonomy. Our starting point is that, for market actors (specifically institutional investors and asset managers)[20] to be able to absorb bottom-up or, most importantly, top-down regulation, flexibility in adapting to best shareholder stewardship practices is needed. We therefore caution against formal public enforcement when shareholder stewardship norms are hard-law in nature,[21] and illustrate, as a way of example, the defects of administrative penalties imposed by National Competent Authorities (NCAs) in the EU. Nevertheless, we are not agnostic about the enforcement abilities of public or quasi-public actors. We therefore see a facilitating role for such actors in two distinct ways. First, where ultimate beneficiaries have suffered damages from deficient disclosure of engagement policies (where hard-law stewardship norms have been established), we support the introduction of a facilitating system of civil claims initiated by public or quasi-public authorities that can serve both restorative-compensatory objectives and public interests. Second, and irrespective of the hard- or soft-law nature of the underpinning stewardship norm(s), public and quasi-public actors can support shareholder stewardship enforcement via informal mechanisms (such as public information diffusion, reputational mechanisms such as 'name and shame', ongoing dialogue and private meetings). We also advance the importance of promoting and refining (formal and informal) enforcement by market and social actors, especially through voluntary networks.

Our proposed enforcement taxonomy is multi-actor and multi-modal along a time continuum, and essentially pertains to a single key point: to enforce shareholder stewardship effectively, various actors, mechanisms and timing in enforcement need to work together. But there is no global 'one-size-fits-all' approach to shareholder stewardship enforcement. Rather, the specifics will depend on the soft-/hard-law nature of the stewardship norm that is to be enforced and on the country's quality of institutions, economic history and culture.

[18] We define stewardship codes broadly as including stewardship 'preliminary initiatives'. See Katelouzou and Siems, The Global Diffusion of Stewardship Codes, Chapter 30.

[19] There are, however, cases where hard law (disclosure) duties are imposed on institutional investors via investment management law. This is, for instance, the case in the US, where in 2003 the Securities and Exchange Commission (SEC) imposed an obligation on investment management companies (the managers of mutual funds) and their advisers to disclose proxy voting policies and proxy votes. For a thorough analysis of the voting disclosure obligations of mutual funds in the US, see Edward Rock, 'Institutional Investors in Corporate Governance' in Jeffrey Gordon and Wolf-Georg Ringe (eds), *The Oxford Handbook of Corporate Law and Governance* (OUP 2018) 376. Such mandatory disclosures, however, deal with a specific aspect of stewardship, that of voting, which is not the only form that stewardship engagement can take. For a comprehensive analysis of the stewardship ecosystem and the coexistence of soft- and hard-law rules relating to both the corporate governance and the investment management aspects of stewardship in the UK, see Katelouzou, *The Path to Enlightened Shareholder Stewardship* (n 1).

[20] In this chapter, we do not examine stewardship aspects and duties applicable to service providers. Nevertheless, we argue that the enforcement rationales, challenges and perspectives analyzed hereinafter apply to a considerable extent *mutatis mutandis* to service providers.

[21] Even though we are not aware of any completely mandatory shareholder stewardship regime around the world, there are academics that support the introduction of such regimes under certain circumstances. See Varottil, Shareholder Stewardship in India, Chapter 17.

The remainder of the chapter proceeds as follows. Section 27.2 lays the groundwork for a general understanding of the existing enforcement rationales and methods in the area of corporate governance and stewardship, and presents a new taxonomy as a way to understand the complex system of enforcement. Section 27.3 turns its focus on the current enforcement mechanisms of shareholder stewardship norms, and points out their weaknesses and dissonance. Section 27.4 builds on the proposed enforcement taxonomy and advances a multi-actor enforcement system consisting of a continuum of largely complementary formal and informal mechanisms which include all involved actors – public, quasi-public, private, market and social. While we generally caution against formal public enforcement (namely administrative penalties) in an area mainly comprising soft-law norms, we support a refinement of informal enforcement mechanisms by public, quasi-public and market actors and a mobilization of voluntary networks and social actors. Finally, where hard-law stewardship norms exist, we see a potential for formal enforcement mechanisms initiated by public or quasi-public actors to facilitate civil claims, especially when public interests are at stake. Section 27.5 concludes.

27.2 ENFORCEMENT MECHANISMS IN CORPORATE GOVERNANCE: A BROAD APPROACH

The implementation and enforcement of corporate governance norms, especially those found in corporate governance codes or guidelines, has always received considerable – but frequently contradictory – attention.[22] In general, enforcement mechanisms have traditionally served the laudable objectives of accountability of regulatees[23] and of inculcation of a sound compliance culture.[24] The seminal work of Armour in 2010 on corporate law enforcement distinguished between 'public' and 'private' enforcement and between 'formal' and 'informal' enforcement, on the basis of two criteria: the nature of the enforcer and the nature of the proceedings (court or non-judicial proceedings) respectively.[25] This four-way categorization of corporate law enforcement has served as a good starting point for understanding the enforcement strategies in the area of corporate law, but it has certain limitations. First, non-public (private) enforcement cannot be confined anymore to 'parties who contract with firms – their investors, customers, and suppliers', as Armour contends.[26] Other norm-enforcers such as market and social actors are equally important. Second, in the specific area of corporate governance, which mainly comprises soft (non-binding) law,[27] 'formal' enforcement confined to judicial control and administrative sanctions is only one of the available enforcement mechanisms, and not always the most important one. Rather, in an area that mainly comprises soft-law norms, which are increasingly promoted through 'stewardship networks' formed by quasi-public or market actors, 'formal' enforcement can take place within such networks in the form of 'membership sanctions' (including the suspension or expulsion of a member) and 'adherence procedures' that target a single member (such as rating the network member's quality of adherence to a set of norms).[28]

---

[22] See e.g. Eddy Wymeersch, 'The Enforcement of Corporate Governance Codes' (2006) 6 *Journal of Corporate Law Studies* 113.
[23] Iain MacNeil, 'Enforcement and Sanctioning' in Eilís Ferran, Niamh Moloney and Jennifer Payne (eds), *The Oxford Handbook of Financial Regulation* (OUP 2015) 280.
[24] Dan Awrey, William Blair and David Kershaw, 'Between Law and Markets: Is There a Role for Culture and Ethics in Financial Regulation?' (2013) 38 *Delaware Journal of Corporate Law* 191.
[25] John Armour, 'Enforcement Strategies in UK Corporate Governance: A Roadmap and Empirical Assessment' (2008) ECGI Law Working Paper No 106/2008 <https://ssrn.com/abstract=1133542> accessed 10 May 2020.
[26] ibid 5.
[27] For the varying coerciveness of corporate governance norms, see Dionysia Katelouzou and Peer Zumbansen, 'The New Geographies of Corporate Governance' (2020) 42 *University of Pennsylvania Journal of International Law* 51.
[28] For a detailed analysis of the formation of voluntary networks that promote stewardship standards and their enforcement parameters, see Katelouzou, *The Path to Enlightened Shareholder Stewardship* (n 1).

In addition, self-enforcement[29] and 'informal' enforcement of corporate governance and stewardship norms play an equally important role. To better understand shareholder stewardship enforcement, we take a *broad* approach and start with a simple conceptual taxonomy based on three dimensions (Table 27.1).

The first dimension we take into account is the nature of the *norm-enforcer*.[30] We consider a broad range of enforcers and distinguish between *self-enforcement* and *third-party enforcement*. Self-enforcement has been defined as norm adherence 'even if no one else can observe or punish a violation'.[31] In the area of corporate governance (and shareholder stewardship, as we will see later), however, this element of 'invisibility of adherence'[32] is lacking and self-enforcement is usually associated with *unilateral* enforcement through reputation (e.g. a company unilaterally improves its corporate governance and through costly advertising is rewarded by the stock market).[33] It is also important to note that in the case of self-enforcement, the norm-enforcer is the same as the norm-follower (i.e. the board of directors in the case of a corporate governance code or an institutional investor in the case of a stewardship code). But self-enforcement of corporate governance and stewardship norms is not a 'genuine' one as the compliance with the relevant norms is assisted by the 'comply-or-explain'[34] principle, a cornerstone of corporate governance, whereby the concerned parties can either comply with a set of best practices or explain the reasons for deviating. However, the obvious problem with self-enforcement is that it relies on both the self-interest and the morality of the

TABLE 27.1 *A broad enforcement taxonomy*

	Enforcement Mechanisms		
		Formal	Informal
Norm enforcer	Self		Ex ante
	Public	Ex post	Ex ante / Ex post
	Quasi-public	Ex post	Ex ante / Ex post
	Private	Ex post	Ex ante / Ex post
	Market	Ex post	Ex ante / Ex post
	Social	Ex post	Ex ante / Ex post

---

[29] For an early study on the potential of self-enforcement in the area of corporate law, see Bernard Black and Reinier Kraakman, 'A Self-Enforcing Model of Corporate Law' (1996) 109 *Harvard Law Review* 1911.

[30] It should be borne in mind that not all norm-enforcers are *standard-setters* of the soft- or hard-law norms subject to enforcement mechanisms.

[31] On the costs and benefits of self-enforcement, see Amitai Aviram, 'Path Dependence in the Development of Private Ordering' (2014) *Michigan State Law Review* 29.

[32] For an analysis of self-enforcement in the area of corporate governance and stewardship, see Katelouzou, *The Path to Enlightened Shareholder Stewardship* (n 1).

[33] See also Eirk Berglöf and Stijn Claessens, 'Enforcement and Corporate Governance' (2004) World Bank Policy Research Working Paper No 3409 <https://ssrn.com/abstract=625286> accessed 10 May 2020.

[34] On the comply-or-explain principle, see Andrew Keay, 'Comply or Explain: In Need of Greater Regulatory Oversight?' (2014) 34 *Legal Studies* 279; Iain MacNeil and Xiao Li, '"Comply or Explain": Market Discipline and Non-compliance with the Combined Code' (2006) 14 *Corporate Governance: An International Review* 486; Konstantinos Sergakis, 'Deconstruction and Reconstruction of the "Comply or Explain" Principle in EU Capital Markets' (2015) 5 *Accounting, Economics and Law: A Convivium* 233.

norm-follower (boards in the context of corporate governance codes and institutional shareholders in the context of shareholder stewardship), which may not always track socially efficient standards.[35] This is why third-party enforcement has relative advantages, especially when the norms subject to enforcement are adversarial.

Our broad approach to norm-enforcers includes third-party enforcement public, quasi-public, private (contractual), market and social actors (Table 27.1). Starting with public actors, traditionally public enforcers have played only a minimal role in the context of corporate governance,[36] but their role is complemented by quasi-public bodies that pursue a monitoring or facilitating function in providing information about the quality of compliance with corporate governance codes and alerting the market of non-compliance.[37] Similarly, private actors, in other words parties who contract with the norm-followers (that is, companies in the case of corporate governance norms and investors in the case of stewardship norms), have not generally occupied a key role in enforcing corporate governance norms.[38] For instance, even though a deficient (incomplete or misleading) corporate governance statement, included in periodic accounts, could give rise to civil claims for damages,[39] apathy, collective action problems and procedural hurdles (especially outside the US) make it very difficult for shareholders to bring litigation.[40] Rather, shareholders and other market actors (not contractually related with the norm-follower) can – and do – engage in informal enforcement. In the UK, for instance, all the corporate governance codes since the Cadbury Report specifically call upon investors (especially institutional ones) to play a decisive role in monitoring the companies' corporate governance statements through shareholder engagement and dialogue.[41] But empirical evidence suggests that investors do not generally sufficiently monitor the provided explanations unless there is poor performance.[42]

Finally, social actors, such as the media and various civil society groups (workforce,[43] consumers,[44] public-interest groups and non-governmental organizations (NGOs)), are a key device for promoting good corporate governance norms, especially in the context of

---

[35] See Aviram (n 31) and Katelouzou, *The Path to Enlightened Shareholder Stewardship* (n 1).

[36] See also Armour (n 25) 213.

[37] For instance, in the Netherlands, the Dutch Corporate Governance Code Monitoring Committee (see <www.mccg.nl/english> accessed 10 May 2020).

[38] For the lack of formal private enforcement in the UK, see Armour (n 25).

[39] Konstantinos Sergakis, *The Law of Capital Markets in the EU: Disclosure and Enforcement* (Bloomsbury Publishing 2018) 86, 97; for a similar argument in the area of deficient disclosure of notification of major shareholdings and ensuing civil claims by shareholders, see Michel Germain and Véronique Magnier, *Les Sociétés Commerciales* (22nd edn, LGDJ 2017) 992–93.

[40] See generally Bernard S Black, 'Shareholder Passivity Reexamined' (1990) 89 *Michigan Law Review* 520, 584–91; Christopher Gulinello, 'The Retail-Investor Vote: Mobilizing Rationally Apathetic Shareholders to Preserve or Challenge the Board's Presumption of Authority' (2010) *Utah Law Review* 547, 573–74; Sergakis, *The Law of Capital Markets in the EU* (n 39) 43–45. On Asia, see Dan W Puchniak, 'The Derivative Action in Asia: A Complex Reality' (2013) 9 *Berkeley Business Law Journal* 1.

[41] See e.g. Financial Reporting Council, *The UK Corporate Governance Code* (July 2018) 2 <www.frc.org.uk/getattachment/88bd8c45-50ea-4841-95b0-d2f4f48069a2/2018-UK-Corporate-Governance-Code-FINAL.pdf> accessed 10 May 2020: 'The ability of investors to evaluate the approach to governance is important ... In line with their responsibilities under the UK Stewardship Code, investors should engage constructively and discuss with the company any departures from recommended practice.'

[42] Sridhar R Arcot, Valentina G Bruno and Antoine Faure-Grimaud, 'Corporate Governance in the UK: Is the Comply or Explain Approach Working?' (2010) 30 *International Review of Law & Economics* 193.

[43] See e.g. the high-profile shaming campaign launched by Amazon employees in relation to climate change: Dave Lee, 'Hundreds of Amazon Employees Publicly Attack Its Climate Record' *Financial Times* (San Francisco, 28 January 2020) <www.ft.com/content/33dce38e-4128-11ea-bdb5-169ba7be433d> accessed 10 May 2020.

[44] Consumers start showing increased levels of awareness and demonstrate their preference for companies that respond to climate and social change: Salesforce Research, 'Ethical Leadership and Business' (2019) <https://c1.sfdcstatic.com/content/dam/web/en_us/www/documents/research/salesforce-research-ethical-leadership-and-business.pdf> accessed 10 May 2020.

sustainability.[45] International NGOs have been successful in pushing companies to respect human rights and the environment, organizing demonstrations to protest against perceived unsustainable behaviour as well as advocating frameworks and standards to promote sustainability.[46] Other NGOs have been active as a response to corporate greed[47] or to the protection of shareholders.[48] Being part of corporate 'meta-regulation',[49] enforcement conducted by social actors is often more efficient than legal enforcement, especially when the norms are self-regulatory in nature, as is mostly the case in the context of corporate governance.[50]

The second dimension we take into account is related to enforcement *mechanisms*; we distinguish between *formal* and *informal* enforcement mechanisms.

Formal enforcement includes the obvious (judicial or quasi-judicial) mechanisms, such as state-emanated administrative or criminal proceedings[51] and civil litigation,[52] traditionally coined as

---

[45] On corporate shaming see generally David A Skeel Jr, 'Shaming in Corporate Law' (2001) 149 *University of Pennsylvania Law Review* 1811.

[46] See e.g. the No Dirty Gold campaign: Earthworks, 'No Dirty Gold' <https://earthworks.org/campaigns/no-dirty-gold/> accessed 10 May 2020; the pressures by Rainforest Action Network on major financial institutions including Citicorp: Rainforest Action Network, 'Press Releases' <www.ran.org/press-releases/> accessed 10 May 2020.

[47] For example, the Occupy Wall Street protests in Japan and Korea: Na-Young Kim and Timothy W Martin, 'Snapshot of a South Korean Boycott: "This Mart Doesn't Sell Japanese Products!"' *The Wall Street Journal* (Seoul, 18 July 2019) <www.wsj.com/articles/boycott-of-everything-japanese-mushrooms-across-south-korea-11563461208> accessed 10 May 2020.

[48] For example, in South Korea the NGO Solidarity for Economic Reform brings derivative actions on behalf of shareholders via minority shareholder campaigns and shareholder activism: Hyeok-Joon Rho and Kon-Sik Kim, 'Invigorating Shareholder Derivative Actions in South Korea' in Dan W Puchniak, Harald Baum and Michael Ewing-Chow (eds), *The Derivative Action in Asia: A Comparative and Functional Approach* (CUP 2012) 194. Another South Korean NGO named People's Solidarity for Participatory Democracy has filed a number of lawsuits in partnership with minority shareholders. In Japan, the non-orofit organization (NPO) *Kabunushi Onbuzuman* (Shareholders Ombudsman) initiates derivative actions on behalf of shareholders with a very high success rate. On such initiatives, see Dan W Puchniak and Masafumi Nakahigashi, 'Japan's Love for Derivative Actions: Irrational Behavior and Non-economic Motives as Rational Explanations for Shareholder Litigation' (2012) 45 *Vanderbilt Journal of Transnational Law* 1, 46.

[49] On the role of meta-regulation in enforcing corporate social responsibility (CSR), see Amiram Gill, 'Corporate Governance as Social Responsibility: A Research Agenda' (2008) 26 *Berkeley Journal of International Law* 452.

[50] But for the increasing legalization of corporate governance norms following the Global Financial Crisis, see Marc T Moore, *Corporate Governance in the Shadow of the State* (Hart 2013).

[51] In the area of corporate law, such measures have mainly dominated the area of securities regulation. Administrative measures include the issuance of a public statement indicating the nature of the infringement and the identity of the (legal or natural) person concerned, as well as the publication of an order requiring the concerned persons to cease the conduct constituting an infringement and to avoid repetition of similar activities. They may also refer to the withdrawal or suspension of the authorization of an institution (e.g. an investment firm, market operator or regulated market) and the temporary or permanent ban of investment firms or any member of their management body. See e.g. Market Abuse Regulation, art 30 (Regulation (EU) No 596/2014 of the European Parliament and of the Council of 16 April 2014 on market abuse (market abuse regulation) and repealing Directive 2003/6/EC of the European Parliament and of the Council and Commission Directives 2003/124/EC, 2003/125/EC and 2004/72/EC [2014] OJ L173/1); Transparency Directive, art 28 (Directive 2013/50/EU of the European Parliament and of the Council of 22 October 2013 amending Directive 2004/109/EC of the European Parliament and of the Council on the harmonisation of transparency requirements in relation to information about issuers whose securities are admitted to trading on a regulated market, Directive 2003/71/EC of the European Parliament and of the Council on the prospectus to be published when securities are offered to the public or admitted to trading and Commission Directive 2007/14/EC laying down detailed rules for the implementation of certain provisions of Directive 2004/109/EC [2013] OJ L294/13); Prospectus Regulation, art 38 (Regulation (EU) 2017/1129 of the European Parliament and of the Council of 14 June 2017 on the prospectus to be published when securities are offered to the public or admitted to trading on a regulated market, and repealing Directive 2003/71/EC [2017] OJ L168/12). Criminal sanctions have been largely marginalized owing to the high standard of proof and the lack of harmonization across the EU. At the international level, they are also relatively scarce except in Australia where they have been particularly prominent in securities regulation violations. On this, see Michelle Welsh and Vince Morabito, 'Public vs Private Enforcement of Securities Laws: An Australian Empirical Study' (2014) 14 *Journal of Corporate Law Studies* 39.

[52] On the difficulties of civil litigation in the area of corporate governance owing to collective action problems, see Alfred F Conard, 'Beyond Managerialism: Investor Capitalism?' (1988) 22 *University of Michigan Journal of Law Reform* 117, 152–63; Black (n 40). But US-style actions have allowed private enforcement to gain considerable prominence in Asia, Australia and Canada, but not in Europe. See e.g. Coffee (n 17); Puchniak (n 40) 9.

formal public and formal private enforcement, respectively. Academic literature has been divided between formal public and formal private enforcement systems, some arguing in favour of the incentives that private parties have to bring a civil claim against a non-compliant behaviour,[53] others sustaining the idea that formal public enforcement is better suited to protect public interests.[54] But in our taxonomy, formal enforcement mechanisms also include *membership sanctions* and *adherence procedures* that target an individual norm-follower which is a member of a network. Such a network may be more or less institutionalized, and membership may or may not be completely voluntary.[55] This broadening of what can be perceived as formal enforcement in the corporate governance context is owing to the expansive reach of soft-law norms which often operate within networks with enforcement capacities.

Informal enforcement is also a highly valuable element in securing compliance with both hard- and soft-law norms.[56] There is no other way to define informal enforcement than negatively, as enforcement mechanisms that cannot be considered formal ones. Informal enforcement mechanisms consist of information diffusion mechanisms such as annual reports and guidelines, reputational mechanisms such as public shaming and public warning, and measures taking place in private such as dialogue and private meetings. Such informal mechanisms can accentuate compliance via reputational mechanisms and continuous dialogue with the relevant parties, and serve educational purposes through information diffusion for the improvement of the compliance culture and mindset. An example of such informal enforcement is the case of the Dutch Corporate Governance Code Monitoring Committee,[57] a quasi-public actor which reports annually on the compliance of Dutch listed companies with the Dutch Corporate Governance Code to the Minister of Economic Affairs, the Minister of Security and Justice, and the Minister of Finance. Even though these annual reports take place within a network consisting of companies following a corporate governance code and are adherence-related procedures, they do not qualify as formal enforcement mechanisms in our taxonomy since they do not target individual companies in a *sanctioning* way; instead, they analyze and provide information about general compliance trends in relation to a set of norms.

The third dimension we take into account is a *temporal* one: we distinguish between *ex ante* enforcement aiming to nudge the norm-followers to comply with a set of soft- or hard-law norms (monitoring and deterrence) and *ex post* enforcement taking place after an action has (not) taken place (compliance).[58] All the mechanisms falling under the formal category of our taxonomy take place *ex post*, since they come into play once the norm-follower has declared its stance towards a set of norms. Informal mechanisms take place before but also after such declaration has been made. *Ex ante* informal enforcement mechanisms can vary from advertising adherence (in the case of self-enforcement) to private meetings and from behind-the-scenes dialogue to public reputational campaigns. All the *ex ante* informal mechanisms initiated by third parties

---

[53] Rafael La Porta, Florencio Lopez-de-Silanes and Andrei Shleifer, 'What Works in Securities Laws?' (2006) 61 *The Journal of Finance* 1.
[54] Bernard S Black, 'The Legal and Institutional Preconditions for Strong Securities Markets' (2001) 48 *UCLA Law Review* 781. On the coexistence and the distinctive features of private and public enforcement, see Guido Ferrarini and Paolo Giudici, 'Financial Scandals and the Role of Private Enforcement: The Parmalat Case' (2005) ECGI Law Working Paper No 40/2005, 42 <https://ssrn.com/abstract=730403> accessed 10 May 2020; Howell E Jackson and Mark J Roe, 'Public and Private Enforcement of Securities Laws: Resourced-based Evidence' (2009) 93 *Journal of Financial Economics* 207.
[55] See further Katelouzou, *The Path to Enlightened Shareholder Stewardship* (n 1).
[56] For the role of social enforcement in promoting social and economic development, see Joseph E Stiglitz, 'Participation and Development: Perspectives from the Comprehensive Development Paradigm' (2002) 6 *Review of Development Economics* 163, 173.
[57] See n 37.
[58] This is consistent with the previous literature: La Porta, Lopez-de-Silanes and Shleifer (n 53); Coffee (n 17); Armour (n 25).

can also take place *ex post*. In addition, *ex post* informal enforcement can be undertaken by standard-setters through information diffusion (such as annual reports).[59]

We believe that the three dimensions we take into account – nature of enforcers, type of enforcement mechanisms and temporal application of enforcement – in this new taxonomy are clearer than other commonly used distinctions in this field, and have the advantage of allowing a distinction between various norm-enforcers and mechanisms which often take place in overlapping and complementary ways.[60] Let us now turn our attention to the enforcement of shareholder stewardship around the world.

27.3 SHAREHOLDER STEWARDSHIP ENFORCEMENT AROUND THE WORLD

27.3.1 *Charting the Mainstream*

Stewardship codes and principles around the world are generally non-binding, either completely voluntary in nature or sometimes with some coercive elements, such as an expectation that the comply-or-explain or apply-and-explain approach will be followed on either a voluntary or a mandatory basis.[61] Table 27.2 shows that from the twenty-five stewardship codes studied, twenty are voluntary in nature.[62] From these, thirteen include an expectation that a defined group of investors will adopt the code based on a comply-or-explain system, but this is on a voluntary basis. This means that both the adoption of the stewardship principles and the expectation to disclose and explain any non-adoption are voluntary, and enforcement relies on the part of either the institutional investors themselves (self-enforcement) or the market. This is completely different from their corporate governance codes counterparts, almost all of which are mandatory for public listed companies, but on a comply-or-explain basis.[63] This distinction between corporate governance codes and stewardship codes on the basis of enforcement parameters is extremely important as it reflects the lighter touch of stewardship codes and a hesitancy (at least for now)[64] to place hard-law rules on institutional investors in their role as minority shareholders. This is not the case with boards of directors, management or companies in their corporate governance obligations – which have a longer history of hard-law obligations, still at their core. It is worth noting, however, that corporate governance codes themselves started as self-regulatory measures, completely voluntary in nature, and it was only after a decade or so from the first corporate governance initiative (the Cadbury Code 1992) that the coerciveness of corporate governance codes started to pick up. Nothing, therefore, excludes the possibility that stewardship codes will become more coercive in the future following the enforcement trends of their corporate governance codes counterparts.[65]

---

[59] On the ongoing continuum running from *ex ante* to *ex post* enforcement and back to *ex post*, see Section 27.4.1.
[60] Earlier literature has already underscored some overlaps between public and private enforcement mechanisms; see e.g. Simeon Djankov, Rafael La Porta, Florencio Lopez-de-Silanes and Andrei Shleifer, 'Courts' (2003) 118 *Quarterly Journal of Economics* 453; Berglöf and Claessens (n 33).
[61] On the varying coercive elements of soft legal norms, see Katelouzou and Zumbansen (n 27).
[62] These are data based on Katelouzou and Siems, The Global Diffusion of Stewardship Codes, Chapter 30. Here we only take into account codes that are in force at the time of writing this chapter, with the exception of the UK, where we consider both the 2012 and the 2020 versions.
[63] See e.g. FCA Handbook, Listing Rules, 9.8.6R(5) (06/08/2007) and 9.8.6R(6) (06/08/2007); in Canada the British Columbia Securities Commission, National Instrument 58-101 Disclosure of Corporate Governance Practices (2016) <www.bcsc.bc.ca/58-101_[NI]_12312016/> accessed 10 May 2020.
[64] For the likely hardening of stewardship obligations, see Chiu and Katelouzou, 'From Shareholder Stewardship to Shareholder Duties' (n 11).
[65] For a detailed analysis of the likely enforcement trends in the area of stewardship, see Katelouzou, *The Path to Enlightened Shareholder Stewardship* (n 1).

Indeed, Table 27.2 shows that five stewardship codes have a mandatory element in ensuring enforcement. The Australian Code 2017 for asset managers (FSC) is mandatory for its members on a comply-or-explain basis.[66] Similarly, the two Indian codes (PFRDA and SEBI) are mandatory for their members, even though a concrete enforcement mechanism is still lacking.[67] Finally, the UK Code 2012 and the UK Code 2020 adopt the comply-or-explain and the apply-and-explain principle respectively, which is mandatory for FCA-authorized asset managers.[68] From the five codes with a mandatory element, all but the Australian FSC code have been introduced by public (including quasi-public) actors.[69] But Table 27.2 reveals that most of the codes introduced by a (quasi-)public standard setter have no enforcement coerciveness.

Notwithstanding the variety of approaches in setting and enforcing shareholder stewardship codes across the world, which depict different cultural, market or political features and

TABLE 27.2 *Setting and enforcing shareholder stewardship codes around the world*

Code	Standard setter	Enforcement *modus operandi*
Australia (ACSI) 2018	Market[70]	Voluntary
Australia (FSC) 2017	Market	Mandatory element
Brazil 2016	Market	Voluntary
Canada 2017	Market	Voluntary
Denmark 2016	Public	Voluntary comply or explain
EFAMA 2018	Market	Voluntary comply or explain
Hong Kong 2016	Public	Voluntary comply or explain
ICGN 2016	Market	Voluntary
India (IRDAI) 2017	Public	Voluntary comply or explain
India (PFRDA) 2018	Public	Mandatory element
India (SEBI) 2019	Public	Mandatory element
Italy 2016	Market	Voluntary comply or explain
Japan 2017	Public	Voluntary comply or explain
Kenya 2017	Public	Voluntary comply or explain
Korea 2016	Market	Voluntary comply or explain
Malaysia 2014	Public	Voluntary
Netherlands 2018	Market	Voluntary comply or explain
Singapore 2016	Quasi-Public	Voluntary
South Africa 2011	Market	Voluntary comply or explain
Switzerland 2013	Market	Voluntary comply or explain
Taiwan 2016	Public	Voluntary comply or explain
Thailand 2017	Public	Voluntary comply or explain
UK 2012	Public	Mandatory element
UK 2020	Public	Mandatory element
US 2017	Market	Voluntary

[66] See Bowley and Hill, Stewardship and Collective Action, Chapter 19.
[67] For a critical analysis, see Varottil, Shareholder Stewardship in India, Chapter 17.
[68] FCA Handbook, Conduct of Business Sourcebook, 2.2.3R (06/12/2010). For a detailed analysis of the enforcement parameters of the UK stewardship codes and their transformation from completely voluntary codes to more coercive ones, see Katelouzou, *The Path to Enlightened Shareholder Stewardship* (n 1).
[69] On the nature of the stewardship codes' issuers, see Katelouzou and Siems, The Global Diffusion of Stewardship Codes, Chapter 30 defining a public issuer as an issuer 'entirely composed of persons representing the state, including state-owned entities'. In other words, a public issuer (standard setter) can include both public and quasi-public actors.
[70] We use the term 'market' standard-setter to include all but the 'public' standard-setter. Note that Katelouzou and Siems in Chapter 30 use the term 'private' for exactly the same category. But given the terminology we adopt in this chapter for the norm-enforcers, market rather than private has a better denotation.

incentives,[71] Katelouzou explains that 'private ordering' in the sense of self-enforcement or third-party enforcement by market actors (at times standard setters), interested in either completely voluntary compliance or comply-or-explain disclosures, has been the main vehicle for the shaping and implementation of shareholder stewardship norms, at least until recently.[72] While the effectiveness of voluntary mechanisms in ensuring compliance with shareholder stewardship codes, instilling stewardship awareness and promoting shareholder stewardship practices is controversial,[73] Table 27.2 confirms this worldwide trend of enforcing shareholder stewardship through the market.

27.3.2 *The Revised Shareholder Rights Directive: An Exception That Proves the Rule*

Notwithstanding the predominance of private ordering in the context of stewardship, the SRD II, aiming, among other things, at encouraging effective and sustainable shareholder engagement and improving transparency along the investment chain, could be seen as a tentative step towards top-down stewardship 'rules' which can be potentially enforced in morett formal ways by public actors. Under the SRD II, institutional investors and asset managers are expected to develop an engagement policy which would describe, among other things, how the financial and non-financial performances of investee companies are monitored, how dialogue is conducted, how voting rights are exercised, how other shareholders or stakeholders have been engaged with, and how actual and potential conflicts of interests are managed.[74] This engagement policy, along with its implementation, needs to be annually disclosed on a comply-or-explain basis.[75] Be that as it may, the degree of flexibility offered by the comply-or-explain principle is considerable and not uncommon in EU company law and corporate governance.[76]

However, the SRD II is not far off imposing a 'duty to demonstrate engagement'[77] on grounds of public interests relating to sustainable, long-term shareholder behaviour.[78] Additionally, institutional investors and asset managers are expected to disclose their investment strategies annually (including how their investment strategy contributes to the medium to long-term performance of their assets) and their arrangements with each

---

[71] See Katelouzou and Puchniak, Global Shareholder Stewardship, Chapter 1.
[72] For a comprehensive analysis of private ordering in stewardship, see Katelouzou, *The Path to Enlightened Shareholder Stewardship* (n 1).
[73] For the UK Code, see e.g. Arad Reisberg, 'The UK Stewardship Code: On the Road to Nowhere?' (2015) 15 *Journal of Corporate Law Studies* 217. In countries dominated by block-holders, voluntary compliance and market enforcement is even weaker. See e.g. Puchniak and Tang, Singapore's Embrace of Shareholder Stewardship, Chapter 14 and Tan, Institutional Investor Stewardship in Malaysia, Chapter 15. See also Lim and Puchniak, Can a Global Legal Misfit Be Fixed?, Chapter 28.
[74] SRD II (n 10) art 3g(1)(a).
[75] SRD II (n 10) art 3g(1)(b).
[76] See e.g. art 46a of the fourth company law Directive 2006/46/EC of the European Parliament and of the Council of 14 June 2006 amending Council Directives 78/660/EEC on the annual accounts of certain types of companies, 83/349/EEC on consolidated accounts, 86/635/EEC on the annual accounts and consolidated accounts of banks and other financial institutions and 91/674/EEC on the annual accounts and consolidated accounts of insurance undertakings [2006] OJ L224/1; art 20(1) of Directive 2013/34/EU of the European Parliament and the Council of 26 June 2013 on the annual financial statements, consolidated financial statements and related reports of certain types of undertakings, amending Directive 2006/43/EC of the European Parliament and of the Council and repealing Council Directives 78/660/EEC and 83/349/EEC [2013] OJ L182/19. Both Directives adopt the comply-or-explain principle for corporate governance statements of listed companies, allowing for different company law frameworks and governance systems to coexist harmoniously while allowing for information to be disclosed across the EU.
[77] Chiu and Katelouzou, 'From Shareholder Stewardship to Shareholder Duties' (n 11).
[78] See further Katelouzou, 'Shareholder Stewardship' (n 3).

other.[79] These provisions are indicative of a gradual shift from a purely private company law agenda (with enabling rules between shareholders and companies) to a top-down capital markets law agenda (with stricter, and based on increased disclosure, obligations for all market actors in the investment chain) and the development of semi-hard stewardship duties.[80]

These semi-hard-law rules do not operate in a normative *vacuum* in the EU, however, since four (then) member states, namely the UK,[81] the Netherlands,[82] Italy[83] and Denmark,[84] had introduced measures to increase the level and quality of institutional shareholders' engagement with investee companies and facilitate a stewardship orientation among institutional investors before the introduction of SRD II. The importance of such normative competition between pre-SRD II soft-law norms and SRD II semi-hard rules[85] becomes apparent when enforcement of the latter is at stake. While article 3g of the SRD II operates on a comply-or-explain basis and is therefore mostly faithful to the tradition of most stewardship codes,[86] article 14b, which deals with enforcement, enables – but not obliges – member states to provide for effective, proportionate and dissuasive measures and penalties for violations of the SRD II transposed provisions into national law. The transposed engagement and transparency disclosure obligations applicable to institutional investors and asset managers are therefore potentially subject to formal enforcement by public authorities.

Perhaps surprisingly, the transposition of article 14b across the member states reveals two different trends. On the one hand, there are member states that have not imposed any public enforcement mechanisms in relation to investors' engagement policies. These include member states with pre-existing stewardship norms, such as the UK where, upon transposition of the SRD II stewardship-related rules, the Financial Conduct Authority (FCA) did not specify any enforcement action, acknowledging the fact that these actors will need to gradually adapt to the new rules.[87] This *reticent enforcement approach* matches the self-regulatory character of pre-existing stewardship norms in the UK and serves the preservation of a national stewardship space. The same reticent approach is also noticeable in member states with no pre-existing stewardship norms, where a certain level of reticence to impose *ex post*, formal, public

---

[79] SRD II (n 10) art 3h–3i.
[80] Chiu and Katelouzou, 'From Shareholder Stewardship to Shareholder Duties' (n 11).
[81] Davies, The UK Stewardship Code 2010–2020, Chapter 2. The UK left the EU on 31 January 2020. A transition period is in place until 31 December 2020. EU law continues to apply to the UK until the end of the transition period.
[82] In the Netherlands, a stewardship code was introduced in 2018 by Eumedion (Eumedion, 'Dutch Stewardship Code' (2018) <www.eumedion.nl/en/public/knowledgenetwork/best-practices/2018-07-dutch-stewardship-code-final-version.pdf> accessed 10 May 2020), an institutional investors' forum, to replace the 2011 Eumedion 10 Best Principles for Engaged Share-Ownership (Eumedion, 'Best Practices for Engaged Share-Ownership' (2011) <www.eumedion.nl/en/public/knowledgenetwork/best-practices/best_practices-engaged-share-ownership.pdf> accessed 10 May 2020). See Van der Elst and Lafarre, Shareholder Stewardship in the Netherlands, Chapter 4, this volume.
[83] In Italy, Assogestioni, an association of asset managers, adopted stewardship principles in 2013 and revised them in 2015 and 2016 (Assogestioni, 'Italian Stewardship Principles' (2016) <www.assogestioni.it/sites/default/files/docs/prin cipi_ita_stewardship072019.pdf> accessed 10 May 2020). See Strampelli, Institutional Investor Stewardship in Italian Corporate Governance, Chapter 6, this volume.
[84] See Birkmose and Madsen, The Danish Stewardship Code, Chapter 7.
[85] For an in-depth analysis of such normative competition, see Katelouzou and Sergakis (n 13).
[86] SRD II (n 10) art 3g imposes requirements on institutional investors and asset managers to develop and publish an engagement policy. See Chiu and Katelouzou, 'From Shareholder Stewardship to Shareholder Duties' (n 11) on the coerciveness of art 3g.
[87] Financial Conduct Authority, 'Proposals to Promote Shareholder Engagement: Feedback to CP 19/7 and Final Rules' (Policy Statement, May 2019) <www.fca.org.uk/publication/policy/ps19-13.pdf> accessed 10 May 2020.

enforcement mechanisms (administrative sanctions) may be owing to the novel and emerging character of shareholder stewardship rules.[88] For instance, Belgium does not specify the enforcement mechanism but merely mentions that NCAs, namely the Financial Services and Markets Authority (FSMA) in Belgium, will be in charge of ensuring the good implementation ('*bonne application*') of the transposed SRD II rules, thus opting for enforcement by a public body.[89] Sweden has also opted for a public enforcement approach by mentioning that the Swedish Financial Supervisory Authority (Finansinspektionen) will be in charge of ensuring compliance with the transposed provisions.[90] Luxembourg[91] and Spain[92] do not provide for any formal public enforcement mechanism in the area of stewardship rules, although they do provide for formal public sanctions in relation to other SRD II rule violations.

On the other hand, there are member states that have taken a strict, *formalistic enforcement approach* by opting for *ex post*, formal public enforcement through the imposition of highly dissuasive administrative sanctions. For example, Italy provides for administrative penalties that can go from €2,500 to €150,000 for the breach of disclosure obligations in relation to the engagement policies of institutional investors and asset managers.[93] This is even though market actors in Italy have already expressed serious concerns about the inability of the 'extraordinarily draconian and disproportionate' sanctions to promote the SRD II's goal of improving relationships between companies and investors and their likely negative impact

---

[88] On the different transposition trends of the other stewardship-related articles of SRD II (n 10), see further Katelouzou and Sergakis (n 13).

[89] *Proposition de loi portant transposition de la directive (UE) 2017/828 du Parlement européen et du Conseil du 17 mai 2017 modifiant la directive 2007/36/CE en vue de promouvoir l'engagement à long terme des actionnaires, et portant des dispositions en matière de société et d'association* [Law Proposal for transposition of Directive (EU) 2017/828 of the European Parliament and of the Council of 17 May 2017 amending Directive 2007/36/EC as regards the encouragement of long-term shareholder engagement] DOC 55 0553/01 (4 October 2019).

[90] Proposition 2018/19:56, s 6.4 (Regeringskansliet, 'Nya EU-regler om aktieägares rättigheter [New EU Rules on Shareholders' Rights]' (7 March 2019) 61–62 <www.regeringen.se/4942f2/contentassets/f2bdee003b8343a38a0e79de75573c21/prop-201819-56.pdf> accessed 10 May 2020). Nevertheless, the administrative penalties that can potentially be imposed by the Swedish NCA are considerably high (€5m maximum), alongside remarks, public warning and issuance of administrative order: Investment Funds Act (SFS 2004:46) ch 12, ss 8–9. Sweden does not further specify which formal or informal mechanisms should be used in this framework.

[91] The law that transposed the SRD II rules provides for joint and several liability of directors in the case of damages resulting from violation of the obligations resulting from these rules: *Loi du 1er août 2019 modifiant la loi modifiée du 24 mai 2011 concernant l'exercice de certains droits des actionnaires aux assemblées générales de sociétés cotées aux fins de transposer la directive (UE) 2017/828 du Parlement européen et du Conseil du 17 mai 2017 modifiant la directive 2007/36/CE en vue de promouvoir l'engagement à long terme des actionnaires* [Law of 1 August 2019 amending the amended law of 24 May 2011 on the exercise of certain rights of shareholders at general meetings of listed companies for the purpose of transposing Directive (EU) 2017/828 of the European Parliament and of the Council of 17 May 2017 amending Directive 2007/36/EC as regards the encouragement of long-term shareholder engagement] Memorial A No 562 of 2019 (24 August 2019) art 7.

[92] For example, Spain provides that the NCA (*Comisión Nacional del Mercado de Valores*) will be competent to impose any sanctions in light of violations of the transposed SRD II (n 10) rules in relation, among others, to the identification of shareholders (art 3a), the transmission of information (art 3b), the facilitation of the exercise of shareholder rights (art 3c) and the information to be provided and voted on the remuneration report (art 9b): *Anteproyecto de Ley por la que se modifica el texto refundido de la Ley de Sociedades de Capital, aprobado por el Real Decreto Legislativo 1/2010, de 2 de julio, y otras normas financieras, para adaptarlas a laDirectiva (UE) 2017/828 del Parlamento Europeo y del Consejo, de 17 de mayo de 2017, por la que se modifica la Directiva 2007/36/CE en lo que respecta al fomento de la implicación a largo plazo de los accionistas* [Draft Bill amending the consolidated text of the Capital Companies Law, approved by the Royal Legislative Decree 1/2010, of July 2, and other financial regulations, to adapt them to the Directive (EU) 2017/828 of the European Parliament and of the Council of 17 May 2017 amending Directive 2007/36/EC as regards the encouragement of long-term shareholder engagement] (24 May 2019) art 19.

[93] *Articolo 193-bis.1 del decreto legislativo 24 febbraio 1998, n. 58* (*Decreto Legislativo 10 maggio 2019, n. 49*).

upon small-sized investors.[94] A similar range of fines is also found in violations of other SRD II transposed rules in Italy,[95] denoting a general preference for high fines across the board. Greece has taken an even stricter stance by providing for maximum administrative penalties up to €5m for all types of violation of the SRD II transposed rules.[96] Surprisingly, however, the draft bill provides for reprimand as an alternative to the administrative penalty, giving the NCA considerable freedom in the choice between informal and formal enforcement mechanisms.[97] The Netherlands also provides for administrative sanctions, but, unlike Italy and Greece, it has chosen a much lower maximum for the same types of violation, namely €20,000.[98] France, on the other hand, has opted for an injunction request to the president of the tribunal with a potentially applicable fine that seeks to force the concerned parties to respect the SRD II transposed rules.[99] The French focus on the role of courts in enforcing the stewardship-related obligations of the SRD II denotes a rather different perception of the severity of shareholder stewardship violations and does not put emphasis on the punitive character of enforcement mechanisms for not having respected such obligations. The French transposition remains nonetheless attached to formal *ex post* public enforcement mechanisms in the area of shareholder stewardship.

These two diametrically opposed approaches – namely the introduction or lack of formal enforcement mechanisms by public actors – to securing compliance with the stewardship-related provisions of the SRD II depict different national legal traditions in enforcing corporate governance norms. Most importantly, they indicate in some cases a lack of

---

[94] See Minerva Analytics Ltd's response to the Italian consultation of the transposition of SRD II: Minerva Analytics, 'Consultazione pubblica concernente lo schema di Decreto legislativo per l'attuazione della direttiva (UE) 2017/828 del Parlamento europeo e del Consiglio, del 17 maggio 2017' <www.dt.mef.gov.it//export/sites/sitodt/modules/documenti_it/regolamentazione_bancaria_finanziaria/regolamentazione_bancaria_finanziaria/consultazione_828/MINERVA_ANALYTICS.pdf> accessed 10 May 2020.

[95] For example, among many examples, the *Decreto Legislativo* 10 *maggio* 2019, n. 49 provides for administrative sanctions that range from €10,000 to €150,000 for the breach of disclosure obligations in relation to the remuneration policy (*articolo* 192-bis *del decreto legislativo* 24 *febbraio* 1998, n. 58) and to obligations with regard to related-party transactions (RPTs) (*articolo* 193-bis.1 *del decreto legislativo* 24 *febbraio* 1998, n. 58) applicable to natural and legal persons. A new *Decreto Legislativo* was proposed on 29 January 2020, increasing the maximum administrative sanctions from €150,000 to €10m for listed companies and for natural persons to €2m for the breach of disclosure obligations in relation to the remuneration policy and to €1.5m with regard to RPT breaches. Even though there is no similar proposal for the stewardship-related provisions of SRD II (n 10), we find such measures raising the same concerns as expressed in this chapter about accentuating public enforcement mechanisms in stewardship and corporate governance more generally. Indeed, the lack of clarity on the criteria of applicability of the proposed sanctions not only increases the NCA's discretionary space but does so in an area that is dependent upon malleable and qualitative governance criteria (such as remuneration policy objectives and the evaluation methods of RPTs). This can only create further unpredictability and legal uncertainty. See: *Schema di decreto legislativo recante attuazione dell'articolo 7 della legge 4 ottobre 2019, n. 117, per quanto riguarda l'incoraggiamento dell'impegno a lungo termine degli azionisti e la disciplina del sistema di governo societario* [Legislative decree scheme implementing article 7 of law 4 October 2019, n. 117, as regards the encouragement of the long-term shareholder engagement and the regulation of the corporate governance system] (31 January 2020) <www.senato.it/service/PDF/PDFServer/BGT/1142682.pdf> accessed 10 May 2020.

[96] Σχέδιο νόμου για την εταιρική διακυβέρνηση ανωνύμων εταιρειών, σύγχρονη αγορά κεφαλαίου και ενσωμάτωση της οδηγίας (ΕΕ) 2017/828 του Ευρωπαϊκού Κοινοβουλίου και του Συμβουλίου [Corporate governance of Sociétés Anonymes, modern capital market and transposition of Directive (EU) 2017/828 of the European Parliament and of the Council], art 36 (under public consultation).

[97] It is noteworthy that the enforcement option of a reprimand is newly introduced and may imply a tacit recognition of the efficiency of the use of informal enforcement mechanisms by public actors as an alternative to the disproportionately high (compared to other jurisdictions) administrative penalties.

[98] *Wet giraal effectenverkeer* [Dutch Giro Securities Transaction Act], art IV, referring to art 1, s 2 of the *Wet op de economische delicten* [Economic Offences Act]: <www.rijksoverheid.nl/onderwerpen/straffen-en-maatregelen/vraag-en-antwoord/hoe-hoog-zijn-de-boetes-in-nederland> accessed 10 May 2020.

[99] Code monétaire et financier [Monetary and Financial Code], art L533-22.

familiarity with and understanding of the complexities of stewardship responsibilities and of the inherent difficulty in addressing stewardship deficiencies with strict, formal public enforcement.[100] We therefore argue in Section 27.4 that the future of stewardship enforcement cannot be confined to *ex post*, formal enforcement imposed by public actors (in the form of administrative penalties), currently promoted at the EU level; rather, it needs to remain in the sphere of a multilayered interaction among all (public, quasi-public, private, market and social) actors who are interested in or affected by shareholder stewardship activities (including the norm-followers) and make use of both formal and informal means in both an *ex ante* and an *ex post* dimension.

27.4 THE FUTURE OF STEWARDSHIP ENFORCEMENT

27.4.1 *The Enforcement Taxonomy as a Roadmap for the Future*

As we have seen, our enforcement taxonomy is three-dimensional.[101] It takes into account: (i) the nature of the norm-enforcer (self, public, quasi-public, private, market and social); (ii) the nature of the enforcement mechanisms (formal and informal); and (iii) the temporal dimension of enforcement actions. In the context of shareholder stewardship, (non-)compliance can refer to either a hard-law norm, as is the case with the SRD II rules that have been transposed into national law, or a soft-law norm, such as those incorporated in a stewardship code.

In terms of norm-enforcers, starting with self-enforcement, asset owners or asset managers can build a good reputation advertising their voluntary (unilateral) adherence to sound shareholder stewardship standards. A characteristic example is BlackRock, the world's *largest asset manager*, whose CEO Larry Fink has addressed several letters to company CEOs announcing BlackRock's drastic change in shareholder stewardship practices.[102] Of course, one can see BlackRock's unilateral advertising as part of informal market enforcement taking place within the voluntary normative framework set up by the Investor Stewardship Group (ISG),[103] of which BlackRock is a key member. But BlackRock's professed principles seem to go beyond the ISG stewardship principles in an effort to build a strong stewardship reputation unilaterally. Self-enforcement in the area of shareholder stewardship can be an efficient and cost-effective way to publicize a new shareholder stewardship mantra, but serious concerns have been raised as to whether the reputational incentives to portray stewardship in a favourable way can overcome the index fund manager's incentives to under-invest in stewardship.[104] As for third-party enforcement, we distinguish in Table 27.3 among public actors, such as NCAs in the EU; quasi-public actors, such as non-profit organizations, companies or other entities created with the involvement of public actors; private actors, that is, parties that are contractually related with the norm-followers, such as investors' clients and beneficiaries; market actors, including national, EU or

---

[100] See also Katelouzou and Sergakis (n 13).
[101] See Section 27.2.
[102] For the most recent one in January 2020, related to BlackRock's commitment, inter alia, to divest from companies engaged in coal production, see Larry Fink, 'A Fundamental Reshaping of Finance' (2020) <www.blackrock.com/sg/en/larry-fink-ceo-letter> accessed 10 May 2020.
[103] Investor Stewardship Group, 'About the Investor Stewardship Group and the Framework for U.S. Stewardship and Governance' <https://isgframework.org/> accessed 10 May 2020.
[104] See Lucian Bebchuk and Scott Hirst, 'Index Funds and the Future of Corporate Governance: Theory, Evidence, and Policy' (December 2019) 119 *Columbia Law Review* 2029, 2119 (reporting that each of the Big Three index funds 'allocates to stewardship less than 0.2% of their estimated fees and devotes, on average only a few thousand dollars in stewardship costs to large positions').

international investor associations and any other market actor interested in shareholder stewardship activities; and social actors, including consumers, investee companies' employees, media, NGOs, ultimate beneficiaries when not contractually related to the norm-followers, etc.

Table 27.3 also distinguishes between formal and informal enforcement mechanisms. In our taxonomy, formal mechanisms are not confined to judicial control and administrative sanctions; they also include membership sanctions and adherence procedures (directed at individual norm-followers) within stewardship networks. The last enforcement dimension of our taxonomy refers to temporal traits. *Ex ante* mechanisms aim to nudge parties to comply with a set of soft- or hard-law norms, while *ex post* mechanisms intervene after an action has (not) taken place.

What is not articulated in Table 27.3, but will become clearer as the analysis evolves, is that the various formal and informal mechanisms are part of an enforcement continuum. *Ex ante* informal enforcement by social and market actors can be seen as the one end of the enforcement continuum (deterrence) while public formal enforcement is at the opposite pole (compliance). But between these two polar extremes, various enforcement strategies take place, often in a symbiotic way.

Let us now examine in more detail this multi-actor, multi-modal shareholder enforcement framework based on our taxonomy.

TABLE 27.3 *The enforcement taxonomy applied to shareholder stewardship*

		Mechanisms	
		Formal	Informal
Actors	Self-enforcement		Advertising
			Development of joint initiatives (to promote self-adherence)
	Public (NCAs)	Administrative sanctions (penalties) and measures (injunctions etc.)	Public information diffusion (annual reports, guidelines, etc.)
		Restitution orders	Public reputational procedures (public warning, name and shame, name and fame, etc.)
			Private measures (warning notice, meetings and dialogue)
	Quasi-public	Membership sanctions and adherence procedures (within networks)	Public information diffusion (annual reports, guidelines, etc.)
		Restitution orders	Public reputational procedures (public warning, name and shame, name and fame, etc.)
			Private measures (warning notice, meetings and dialogue)
	Private	Civil claims	Public reputational procedures (name and shame, name and fame, etc.)
			Private measures (meetings and dialogue)
	Market	Membership sanctions and adherence procedures (within networks)	Public information diffusion (annual reports, guidelines, etc.)
			Public reputational procedures (public warning, name and shame, name and fame, benchmarking/ratings, etc.)
			Private measures (warning notice, meetings and dialogue)
	Social		Public reputational procedures (public campaigns, name and shame, name and fame, etc.)
			Private measures (meetings and dialogue)

27.4.2 *The Challenges and Opportunities of Formal Enforcement*

27.4.2.1 The Limits of Public Enforcement

Shareholder stewardship occupies a multilayered, decentred regulatory space[105] where 'authority over enforcement' is fragmented among public, quasi-public, private, market and social actors (see also Table 27.3). In this context, formal public enforcement is only marginally important – being applicable only in the context of (semi-)hard-law norms in the EU – and could even be seen as 'pathological', an indicator that self-regulation and compliance are problematic.[106] This may explain why in the EU only four member states (Italy, Greece, the Netherlands and France) have opted for formal public enforcement in the form of administrative sanctions when transposing the SRD II's stewardship-related rules. Fortunately, formal public enforcement in the area of shareholder stewardship still remains the exception rather than the rule, but its occurrence demands continuing caution for various reasons.

First, formal public enforcement is likely to transform the whole shareholder stewardship agenda into merely a liability concern. Stewardship norm-followers, that is, asset owners and asset managers, will perceive public formal enforcement mechanisms as a general operational hurdle and the far-reaching effects of sanctions will render shareholder stewardship practices unattractive and perhaps unorthodox.[107] In turn, as the norm-followers will be more focused on the liability aspects of the disclosure statements, rather than on promoting good shareholder stewardship practices across the investment chain, the educational benefits that are expected to occur through shareholder stewardship disclosures will be inevitably weakened.[108] Moreover, formal public enforcement may have a general distorting effect both *ex ante* (monitoring and deterrence) and *ex post* (compliance). For instance, private, market and social actors, or other relevant stakeholders, may mechanistically rely on NCAs to safeguard them from poor or non-compliance risks and might not be motivated to initiate third-party informal or formal enforcement themselves.[109]

The second series of concerns relates to the challenges around the applicability of formal public enforcement mechanisms in an area mainly regulated through disclosure of stewardship statements based on the comply-or-explain principle.[110] Compliance with principles-based regulation is not an objective matter and its assessment becomes even more difficult when compliance with a comply-or-explain regime is mandatory, as is the case with article 3g (SRD II). For instance, an investor who believes that it complies with the prescribed engagement policy, but in reality does not, will not provide any non-compliance explanations, and therefore the public actors (and consequently the market and social actors) cannot discover non-compliance as it occurs. Moreover, NCAs will be faced with significant challenges in exercising their formal enforcement mechanisms owing to the inherent difficulty of deciphering the extent to which

---

[105] Further on the fragmentation of corporate governance regulatory spaces, see Dionysia Katelouzou and Peer Zumbansen, 'Transnational Corporate Governance: The State of the Art and Twenty-First Century Challenges' in Peer Zumbansen (ed), The Oxford Handbook of Transnational Law (OUP 2021) 615.

[106] See generally William Richard Scott, *Institutions and Organizations: Ideas, Interests and Identities* (4th edn, SAGE 2014).

[107] Konstantinos Sergakis, 'Legal vs Social Enforcement of Shareholder Duties' in Hanne S Birkmose and Konstantinos Sergakis (eds), *Enforcing Shareholders' Duties* (Edward Elgar 2019) 143.

[108] Mark Fenwick and Erik PM Vermeulen, 'Institutional Investor Engagement: How to Create a "Stewardship Culture"' (2018) TILEC Discussion Paper No 2018-006, 14-18, 43 <https://ssrn.com/abstract=3098235> accessed 10 May 2020.

[109] Sergakis, 'Legal vs Social Enforcement of Shareholder Duties' (n 107) 143.

[110] SRD II (n 10) art 3g.

parts or the entirety of the engagement disclosure statement(s) are non-compliant, and whether adequate explanation is given. Further monitoring and interpretation hurdles may arise from the fact that the regulated investors may produce and divulge more than one disclosure statement to comply with different stewardship obligations.[111] The multiplication of such statements will inevitably produce a plethora of information that may be arduous to evaluate and decipher before taking further enforcement action.

This becomes more difficult to cope with because commonality of shareholder stewardship expectations between investors (norm-followers) and regulators (norm-enforcers) as well as among different investors (such as active or passive asset managers, pension funds, index funds, etc.)[112] in the same or different jurisdictions is still lacking. In a regulatory area where expectations are not crystallized, a formal public enforcement regime is arguably unattainable for both the public enforcers and the norm-followers.

27.4.2.2 Facilitating Private Claims via Public and Quasi-public Actors

While we caution against formal public enforcement, we see some space for facilitating an *ex post*, formal role of public (or quasi-public) enforcers when the objective is restorative or compensatory, that is, to remedy damages caused by shareholder stewardship-related violations. Here, we have to go back a step and consider the practicalities of *ex post* formal enforcement role by private parties who are contractually related to the followers of stewardship norms, that is, asset managers and asset owners. The potential of formal enforcement by private (contractual) actors becomes apparent if one considers the investment management aspect of stewardship, namely, the relationships among asset managers, institutional investors and ultimate investors.[113] Here the ultimate investors (beneficiaries and clients) are becoming increasingly aware of the ramifications of their investment and can influence institutional investors towards sound shareholder stewardship. Indeed, many institutional investors have attracted in recent years a considerable clientele by responding to environmental, social and governance (ESG) concerns.[114] Yet, the incentives of ultimate investors to initiate (formal) litigation are in general weak.[115] In the specific context of shareholder stewardship, additional difficulties relate to incomplete or inaccurate shareholder stewardship statements.[116] For example, proving the violation of a shareholder engagement duty or how it caused damage to a contractual party may not be a straightforward task for potential claimants.[117]

---

[111] For example, following the SRD II transposed rules, regulatees may well choose to issue a public policy statement on their engagement policy (SRD II (n 10) art 3g) and another one on their investment strategy (SRD II (n 10) arts 3h or 3i). This is the case of Credit Suisse Asset Management (Schweiz) AG who explains in two different statements how it complies with articles 3g and 3i, respectively. It is also noteworthy that in its engagement policy statement Credit Suisse also specifically mentions its adherence to the EFAMA Stewardship Code, thereby confirming the symbiosis of different stewardship rules. See Credit Suisse, 'Shareholder Engagement' (2020) <www.credit-suisse.com/ch/en/asset-management/regulatory/shareholder-engagement.html> accessed 10 May 2020.

[112] See e.g. Fisch, The Uncertain Stewardship Potential of Index Funds, Chapter 21 on how index funds perceive stewardship.

[113] On the investment side of stewardship, see Katelouzou, *The Path to Enlightened Shareholder Stewardship* (n 1) and Barker and Chiu, Investment Management, Stewardship and Corporate Governance Roles, Chapter 25.

[114] See e.g. Ron Lieber, '3 Steps to a Socially Conscious Portfolio' *The New York Times* (14 February 2020) <www.nytimes.com/2020/02/14/your-money/how-to-build-an-esg-funds-portfolio.html> accessed 10 May 2020; Suzette Viviers and Johan Steyn, 'Asset Managers Can Stand Out by Being Truly Responsible Investors' *Business Day* (8 August 2019).

[115] See text accompanying nn 39–41.

[116] Christoph Van der Elst, 'Shareholder Engagement Duties: The European Move Beyond Stewardship' in Hanne S Birkmose and Konstantinos Sergakis (eds), *Enforcing Shareholders' Duties* (Edward Elgar 2019) 79–80.

[117] Despite the procedural hurdles, some inspiration in this context can be taken by the introduction of a civil liability regime on Credit Rating Agencies under article 35s of the CRA EU regulation. See Regulation (EU) No 462/2013 of

Even though there are some academic voices claiming that beneficiaries of pension funds, mutual fund clients and life insurance policyholders can control UK asset managers over shareholder voting rights,[118] besides their obvious contractual rights, expanding such arguments in non-voting aspects of shareholder stewardship, such as engaging in dialogue with companies and monitoring, is difficult.[119] Reservations in relation to the efficiency of such initiatives can be formulated in light of the absence of a common engagement denominator that could facilitate the classification of claims and achieve legal certainty in the design of formal private enforcement mechanisms. Additional problems arise out of the disempowerment and disaggregation of ultimate investors within a collective investment vehicle that prevents them from developing initiatives to hold other market actors accountable.[120]

Despite the obvious hurdles of a formal enforcement regime initiated by private actors, there is undoubtedly a political impetus to protect the legitimate interests of ultimate investors as well as wider public interests.[121] We, therefore, provide a first exploratory approach on how civil claims for disclosure-related violations of shareholder stewardship requirements, as the ones imposed via the transposed SRD II rules in relation to the development and disclosure of an engagement policy, can be facilitated by public or quasi-public enforcers.[122]

Unblocking collective action problems[123] in the area of civil claims could be the crucial thrust for the introduction of a dissuasive *ex post* formal enforcement mechanism that can cut across the boundaries of private and (quasi-)public enforcers.[124] In general, we contend that public and quasi-public enforcers have a facilitating role to play in protecting ultimate beneficiaries from damages from deficient shareholder stewardship statements issued by institutional investors who are in charge of their assets.[125] Public enforcers, such as NCAs, should be given the power to ask civil courts to order the violator to pay a sum to the NCA, which will then distribute it among the ultimate beneficiaries. Such restitution schemes are not unknown. For example, in the UK the FCA has power to apply to the court for a restitution order, under section 382 of the Financial Services and Markets Act 2000 (which provides the regulatory framework of financial services), against any person contravening relevant requirements of this Act, related to both misconduct and general prohibitions. The FCA needs to consider on a case-by-case basis if this is the best

---

the European Parliament and of the Council of 21 May 2013 amending Regulation (EC) No 1060/2009 on credit rating agencies [2013] OJ L146/1.

[118] See e.g. Ewan McGaughey, 'Does Corporate Governance Exclude the Ultimate Investor?' (2016) 16 *Journal Corporate Law Studies* 221.

[119] For a comprehensive analysis in the UK context, see Katelouzou, *The Path to Enlightened Shareholder Stewardship* (n 1).

[120] Iris H-Y Chiu and Dionysia Katelouzou, 'Making a Case for Regulating Institutional Shareholders' Corporate Governance Roles' (2018) *Journal of Business Law* 67, 79.

[121] Katelouzou, 'Shareholder Stewardship' (n 3).

[122] We do not consider a generalized formal private enforcement framework or address legal traits that govern the contractual relationships between ultimate investors and their institutional investors, deriving from trust law, or contractual arrangements between institutional investors and asset managers.

[123] On this notion, see Chiu and Katelouzou, 'Making a Case for Regulating Institutional Shareholders' Corporate Governance Roles' (n 120) 79; John Armour, Dan Awrey, Paul Davies, Luca Enriques, Jeffrey N Gordon, Colin Mayer and Jennifer Payne, *Principles of Financial Regulation* (OUP 2016) 218. For an early analysis, see Hanne S Birkmose, 'The Transformation of Passive Institutional Investors to Active Owners: "Mission Impossible"?' in Hanne Birkmose, Mette Neville and Karsten E Sørensen (eds), *The European Financial Market in Transition* (Kluwer Law International 2011) 107; Stefan Krasa and Anne P Villamil, 'Monitoring the Monitor: An Incentive Structure for a Financial Intermediary' (1992) 57 *Journal of Economic Theory* 197.

[124] See also Iris H-Y Chiu, 'Private vs Public Enforcement of Shareholder Duties' in Hanne S Birkmose and Konstantinos Sergakis (eds), *Enforcing Shareholders' Duties* (Edward Elgar 2019) 126 (arguing in favour of granting enforcement power to regulatory bodies).

[125] Of course, the issuing of stewardship statements is only a small part of investment management stewardship. See Katelouzou, *The Path to Enlightened Shareholder Stewardship* (n 1).

course of action, taking into account a series of factors, such as the identifiable character of losses, the number of harmed investors, the availability of other redress mechanisms, and whether or not harmed investors can bring their own proceedings.[126]

Outside Europe, innovative models have arisen so as to allow quasi-public actors, such as government-founded, non-profit organizations, to facilitate civil claims on behalf of harmed investors. For example, in Taiwan, the Securities and Futures Investors Protection Centre (SFIPC) has the power to bring such compensation claims, and has already achieved an impressive record in filing civil cases. Over the years, the SFIPC has been given additional powers to instigate class actions for securities fraud cases related to breaches of trust or breaches of the duty of care and/or loyalty.[127] The SFIPC's status and successful activity denote the non-negligible role that quasi-public actors can perform, in an *ex post* formal enforcement spectrum, in facilitating civil claims and can inspire the introduction of restitution orders for losses caused by the violation of hard-law shareholder stewardship norms.

Granting such restitution order powers to public or quasi-public actors (see also Table 27.3) can overcome the collective action problem and the complexities of financial intermediation that have dissociated ultimate investors from institutional investors. While it is not our intention to provide here all the details of such (quasi-)public-driven schemes that aim to facilitate civil claims, it is important to debate the rationales of introducing such schemes in the presence of losses that are owing to violations of hard-law shareholder stewardship norms. Furthermore, our proposal of attributing to public or quasi-public actors a facilitating role in providing redress for harmed parties is easily justified when other enforcement means by ultimate beneficiaries are impracticable.

27.4.2.3 Strengthening Formal Enforcement within Stewardship Networks

Our taxonomy extends the definition of formal enforcement to membership sanctions and adherence procedures that target a single member within stewardship networks. Such networks are usually developed by stewardship standard setters, as is the case with the Financial Reporting Council (FRC)'s signatory list to the UK stewardship code.[128] Yet not all enforcement measures taking place within such a network are considered formal enforcement mechanisms in our taxonomy. For instance, information diffusion measures such as publishing a list of signatories to a stewardship code or an annual report do not qualify as formal enforcement mechanisms in our taxonomy because they lack a sanctioning character directed at a specific member of the network.

A characteristic example of such a membership and adherence sanction relates to the UK stewardship code, which is subject to a tiering exercise. The FRC introduced a three-tier system in 2016, arranging the signatories' statements into three categories (Tier 1, Tier 2 and Tier 3) depending on their overall quality and engagement with the UK stewardship code's principles.[129]

---

[126] Financial Conduct Authority, 'The Enforcement Guide' (2014) s 11.3 <www.handbook.fca.org.uk/handbook/document/EG_Full_20140401.pdf> accessed 10 May 2020.

[127] Wang R Tseng and Wallace WY Wang, 'Derivative Actions in Taiwan: Legal and Cultural Hurdles with a Glimmer of Hope for the Future' in Dan W Puchniak, Harald Baum and Michael Ewing-Chow (eds), *The Derivative Action in Asia: A Comparative and Functional Approach* (CUP 2012) 215, 240–41.

[128] On a comprehensive analysis of the role of such networks and investors' associations in the UK, see Katelouzou, *The Path to Enlightened Shareholder Stewardship* (n 1).

[129] See further Financial Reporting Council, 'Tiering of Signatories to the Stewardship Code' (14 November 2016) <www.frc.org.uk/news/november-2016/tiering-of-signatories-to-the-stewardship-code> accessed 10 May 2020.

The FRC gave to Tier 3 asset managers a period to improve their statements to Tier 1 or Tier 2 standard or be removed from the list of signatories to the code.[130] In August 2017, Tier 3 was removed and about twenty asset managers were completely removed from the list of signatories.[131] This is a characteristic example of a membership sanction targeting specific norm-followers within an organizational and cognitive stewardship network. Removal from a signatory list has a clear impact on the targeted norm-followers with reputational effects and loss of legitimacy.

While the FRC's tiering exercise is currently the only example of a formal (but not judicial) enforcement mechanism,[132] similar membership sanctions and adherence procedures can be developed in the future by other stewardship standard setters within established stewardship networks, such as the Italian Assogestioni or the Dutch Eumedion, or even public actors, such as the Financial Service Agency in Japan, or take place within newly developed stewardship networks.[133] Such a network is the Association of Responsible Investors (Assodire) in Italy formed by three institutional investors (Inarcassa, Cassa Forense and Enpam) with the aim, inter alia, of defining a best practice policy for their members and issuing an *ex post* judgment so as to align shareholder stewardship activities with such policy.[134] While Assodire has yet to propose the introduction of membership or adherence sanctions, it is clear that investors' networks have a key role to play in promoting shareholder stewardship. Within the polycentric and multi-actor regulatory space of stewardship, and provided that an active market for stewardship exists,[135] it is expected that such networks will seek to establish interconnections with other (public, quasi-public, private, market and social) enforcers and gain visibility, prominence and legitimacy by portraying themselves as good stewards through the lens of market discipline and peer pressure at the national, regional and international levels.[136] This is also supported by the applications of network theory in corporate governance, and specifically in the role of institutional shareholders.[137] Enriques and

---

[130] It is noteworthy that the FRC has clarified that Tier 1 is not synonymous with perfection; it only signals the provision of a good overview of stewardship practices: see Financial Reporting Council, 'Developments in Corporate Governance and Stewardship 2016' (January 2017) 26 <www.frc.org.uk/getattachment/ca1d9909-7e32-4894-b2a7-b971b4406130/Developments-in-Corporate-Governance-and-Stewardship-2016.pdf> accessed 10 May 2020. To maintain and promote the reporting quality, we suggest a further refinement of tiering mechanisms in the form of additional sub-tiers within Tier 1 to enable clients and other interested parties to better understand the quality of stewardship statements. A possible way forward in this respect can be the creation of a 'standard Tier 1' and a 'premium Tier 1', the latter offering an additional layer of competitive and reputational advantage compared to the standard Tier 1 signatories.

[131] Financial Reporting Council, 'FRC Removes Tier 3 Categorisation for Stewardship Code Signatories' (3 August 2017) <www.frc.org.uk/news/august-2017/frc-removes-tier-3-categorisation-for-stewardship> accessed 10 May 2020.

[132] The transition of the quasi-public body, the Financial Reporting Council, to the Audit, Reporting and Governance Authority (ARGA) in 2020 is likely to have implications for this tiering exercise. See, further, Katelouzou, *The Path to Enlightened Shareholder Stewardship* (n 1).

[133] A comparable mechanism has been introduced in 2020 within the organizational framework of the Principles for Responsible Investment (PRI). PRI announced that it will delist parties who do not engage with the principles and make the necessary changes in their statements. Such delisting options were introduced in 2018 as a potential option for deviant parties but with a discretionary period until 2020. Once a signatory party is delisted, it will not be allowed to rejoin the PRI for a year. See further Elina Rolfe, 'Moving the Needle on PRI Membership' (UNPRI, 27 February 2020) <www.unpri.org/pri-blog/moving-the-needle-on-pri-membership/5494.article> accessed 10 May 2020.

[134] WeWelfare, '*Assodire: L'unione delle Casse a difesa degli investitori* [Assodire: the union of the Banks in defense of investors]' *Il Messaggero* (11 February 2020) <www.ilmessaggero.it/economia/welfare/assodire_lunione_delle_casse_a_difesa_degli_investitori-5044197.html> accessed 10 May 2020.

[135] On the problems, however, on the demand side of this market, see Katelouzou and Micheler, The Market for Stewardship and the Role of the Government, Chapter 3.

[136] See Katelouzou, *The Path to Enlightened Shareholder Stewardship* (n 1).

[137] Luca Enriques and Alessandro Romano, 'Institutional Investor Voting Behavior: A Network Theory Perspective' (2019) *University of Illinois Law Review* 223.

Romano have argued that network-level competition might increase the incentives of institutional investors to collect information and co-operate within a formal network, a geographic area or a clique.[138] Public disclosure of shareholder stewardship policies and outcomes, membership of a network or inclusion on a signatory list can further advance such co-operative behavioural patterns.

Of course, we are not agnostic of individualistic or opportunistic motives when aiming to enter and remain a member in such a network. Indeed, institutional investors or asset managers may sign up to stewardship codes or principles in a purely formalistic fashion so as to extract reputational benefits by publicizing their supposed avant-garde or sustainable stewardship strategies and to attract more clients or attempt to conceal dubious practices. Even if such actors do attempt to instrumentalize shareholder stewardship norms for their own benefit, membership or adherence sanctions, such as exclusion from a signatory list or relinquishing of a membership, can eliminate such abuses.

27.4.3 The Importance of Informal Enforcement

A significant aspect of shareholder stewardship enforcement consists of informal mechanisms, defined in the negative as not including any (quasi-)judicial proceedings or membership sanctions and adherence procedures directed at an individual norm-follower within stewardship networks. Informal enforcement can take place both *ex ante* and *ex post* (see also Table 27.1).

Starting with self-enforcement, here informal mechanisms rely on the advertising of voluntary adherence to shareholder stewardship norms.[139] Additionally, a group of institutional investors may proceed to the formation of a group so as to signal the self-adherence to high standards of shareholder stewardship (see also Table 27.3). For example, in 2020 various Italian institutional investors announced the formation of a group so as to better exercise their shareholder stewardship activities and to aspire to their own high standards via the increase of awareness, research studies, training courses, and the assistance of institutional investors in their activities.[140]

Turning to third-party enforcement, a wide range of informal mechanisms is available to public, quasi-public, private, market and social enforcers.

Public enforcers can diffuse public information publicly through the publication of annual reports, guidelines, etc.[141] Such measures (often taking place within a stewardship network) do not target any individual party but provide an overarching view of the enforcer's activity during a specific period.[142] Such measures are highly informative since they provide insights into compliance trends, into any action that the enforcer has taken or intends to take and into further guidelines for improving statements in the future. These measures can also provide concrete

---

[138] ibid 266.
[139] See e.g. BlackRock's letters to CEOs: Larry Fink (n 102) and accompanying text.
[140] See e.g. the 'Centro di tutela dei diritti degli Azionisti Istituzionali' created by Associazione Italiana per la Previdenza Complementare (Assoprevidenza) in collaboration with the Consiglio Nazionale dei Dottori Commercialisti e degli Esperti Contabili (CNDCEC) (Assoprevidenza, 'Nasce il Centro di tutela dei diritti degli Azionisti Istituzionali per far contare di più gli investitori previdenziali e assistenziali [The Center for the Protection of Institutional Shareholder Rights was created to make social security and welfare investors count more]' (19 February 2020) <https://assoprevidenza.it/comunicati-stampa/5427/> accessed 10 May 2020).
[141] See e.g. Corporate Governance Code Monitoring Committee, 'Final Document Van Manen Committee 2018' (Monitoring Report, 2018) <www.mccg.nl/?page=5787> accessed 10 May 2020. For an example of guidelines, see Financial Reporting Council, 'What Constitutes an Explanation under "Comply or Explain": Report of the Discussions between Companies and Investors' (February 2012) <www.frc.org.uk/getattachment/a39aa822-ae3c-4ddf-b869-db8f2ffe1b61/what-constitutes-an-explanation-under-comply-or-exlpain.pdf> accessed 10 May 2020.
[142] See further Katelouzou, *The Path to Enlightened Shareholder Stewardship* (n 1).

examples of good or bad shareholder stewardship practices, and enable norm-followers to better align their practices with the enforcer's expectations. Public enforcers can also use public reputational mechanisms (such as public warnings, 'name and shame', etc.) or engage in private dialogue. Such informal mechanisms can operate on either an *ex ante* or an *ex post* basis, depending on the release of shareholder stewardship statements and any consequent action (discrepancy of a practice from the statement) that can raise compliance concerns.

Private enforcers are also expected to adopt informal enforcement mechanisms (independently from any civil claims) such as public reputational mechanisms (public warnings, 'name and shame' and 'name and fame', etc.) or measures taking place in private (private meetings and dialogue) so as to exert pressure or reward institutional investors.

Informal enforcement can be also exercised by market actors with some variations. Starting with investors' associations, a characteristic example of an informal enforcement mechanism is the ICGN's Global Stewardship Awards,[143] which operate as a public reputational mechanism via 'name and fame' (see Table 27.3). For instance, the ICGN category of Stewardship Disclosure Awards aims 'to recognise those investors who provide genuine insight into their shareholder stewardship policies and how they are implemented and whose approach to disclosure provides a model that others might follow'.[144] We consider such public reputational mechanisms to be very valuable in incentivizing norm-followers to further enhance their shareholder stewardship profile and benefit from positive reputational effects (see also Table 27.3).

An additional reputational mechanism taken by market actors publicly can be third-party ratings. Such ratings can perform a monitoring function by classifying investors based not only on their general adherence to shareholder stewardship norms (e.g. the issuance or not of a stewardship statement) but on the information provided in a stewardship statement, thereby enabling the issuance of a rating that values specific components of stewardship, such as active engagement or ESG-focused engagement.[145] Such ratings can provide additional reputational advantages for market actors who are particularly interested in the topics covered by the ratings. Norm-followers would therefore be incentivized to adopt a more transparent disclosure stance for competition and overall reputational benefits. Of course, such third-party ratings are not without their own set of problems. For instance, one-size-fits-all stewardship checklists may have harmful effects by pressuring investors to adopt a homogenized set of stewardship practices.[146]

Going beyond the use of rating systems, it is worthwhile to note that followers of stewardship norms will eventually need to reach a broadly common consensus about the different features of 'good' and 'bad' shareholder stewardship policies, and, most importantly, engagement outcomes, so as to use the full spectrum of informal enforcement mechanisms at their disposal.[147]

---

[143] International Corporate Governance Network, 'ICGN 2019 Global Stewardship Awards' (2019) <www.icgn.org/events/icgn-2019-global-stewardship-awards#:~:text=A%20cornerstone%20of%20ICGN's%20policy,London%20on%2026%20November%202019> accessed 7 February 2022.

[144] International Corporate Governance Network, 'Stewardship Disclosure Awards' <www.icgn.org/events/global-stewardship-awards-2019/stewardship-disclosure-awards> accessed 10 May 2020.

[145] In the context of Italy, see Simone Alvaro, Marco Maugeri and Giovanni Strampelli, 'Investitori istituzionali, governo societario e codici di stewardship' (2019) 19 *Quaderni Giuridici Consob* 59.

[146] In the broader area of corporate governance, see Paul Rose, 'The Corporate Governance Industry' (2007) 32 *Journal of Corporation Law* 887.

[147] John Kingman, 'Independent Review of the Financial Reporting Council' (Department for Business, Energy and Industrial Strategy, December 2018) <https://assets.publishing.service.gov.uk/government/uploads/system/uploads/attachment_data/file/767387/frc-independent-review-final-report.pdf> accessed 10 May 2020. It should also be noted that the characterization of the quality of policies and of their outcomes will also differ greatly between the two worlds of corporate governance and investment management stewardship. See further Katelouzou, *The Path to Enlightened Shareholder Stewardship* (n 1).

Without delving into the specificities and varieties of shareholder stewardship strategies that can be legitimately developed by different types of investor,[148] we argue that public, quasi-public, private and market enforcers need to maintain an ongoing dialogue on general shareholder stewardship expectations and provide more details to the concerned parties regarding the expectations of best practice shareholder stewardship.

Informal enforcement by social actors can also play a beneficial role in enforcing shareholder stewardship. Various stakeholders (such as NGOs, employees of investee companies, consumers and others) may wish to understand what kind of informational exposure is matched with a 'certified', awarded or sanctioned shareholder stewardship disclosure statement so as to mount pressure for change. Social actors can engage in informal enforcement mechanisms by exerting pressure on norm-followers via public reputational procedures (public campaigns, 'name and shame', 'name and fame', etc.) or private measures (meetings and dialogue) with parties with whom they are related (e.g. ultimate beneficiaries of a fund managed by another asset owner) or whose activities have an impact on their activities (e.g. employees of investee companies or NGOs).

Signs of such informal enforcement trends by social actors are already visible through shaming campaigns against investors avoiding the integration of ESG factors[149] or purporting to serve ESG agendas but doing so in an ambiguous way.[150] Indeed, NGOs are increasingly interested in holding not only companies but also investors to account as they legitimately consider the latter as the enablers, in their 'capital provider' capacity, of unsustainable corporate strategies that contribute to climate change. The same trends may be manifested by issuers themselves or even their employees who have been seen as credible social enforcers against income inequality, in light of their capacity to contribute to corporate governance and aim to redistribute wealth maximization within corporations.[151] Buoyed by the increasing potential of such stakeholders in monitoring stewardship statements and ensuing practices, we argue that formal and informal enforcement by social actors can complement more established enforcement mechanisms by public, quasi-public, private and market actors, and act as a social 'safety valve' in the presence of deviant stewardship practices.

27.4.4 Mobilizing a Multi-actor and Multi-modal Enforcement System

Leaving aside the juridification of stewardship via the transposition of the SRD II, it remains a reality that shareholder stewardship around the world still consists of largely soft-law norms that maintain the merits of flexibility and adaptability to market actors' profiles and needs. Our taxonomy recognizes this reality and offers a multi-actor and multi-modal perspective designed

---

[148] For instance, on how activist hedge funds approach stewardship, see Dionysia Katelouzou 'The Rhetoric of Activist Shareholder Stewards' (2020) (Working paper).

[149] See e.g. Greenpeace's latest intervention during the 2020 World Economic Forum held in Davos, accusing pension funds of contributing to climate change by investing in fossil fuels: Climate Action Network, 'Press Release' (23 January 2020) <https://climatenetwork.org/2020/01/23/press-release-immediately-shift-investments-from-fossil-fuels-into-renewables-and-nature-protection-and-restoration-civil-society-said-to-the-world-economic-forum-wef-participants/> accessed 7 February 2022.

[150] For example, climate activists (such as Sierra Club campaign and Sunrise Project) have expressed serious doubts as to BlackRock's commitment in January 2020 to divest from companies engaged in coal production, launch funds that ban fossil-fuel shares, and vote against managers who fail to make progress on climate change: Emma Newburger, 'Activists Respond to BlackRock's Climate Change Investment Strategy: "There Are Questions Left Unanswered"' CNBC (16 January 2020) <www.cnbc.com/2020/01/16/activists-respond-to-blackrocks-plan-to-tackle-climate-change.html> accessed 10 May 2020.

[151] Andreas Kokkinis and Konstantinos Sergakis, 'A Flexible Model for Efficient Employee Participation in UK Companies' (2020) 20 *Journal of Corporate Law Studies* 453.

to deal with the complexity of shareholder stewardship along a continuum of *ex ante* and *ex post* enforcement mechanisms (see also Table 27.3).

We are of the view that any future regulatory design of enforcement mechanisms shall not merely depict the regulatory objectives of transparency across the investment chain in a 'top-down' fashion, which, if excessive, can also harm engagement,[152] but shall be reflective of the dynamic and decentralized enforcement stewardship processes by multiple actors from (quasi-)public ones (such as the FRC in the UK) to national, regional and international market actors (such as the Italian Assogestioni or EFAMA) and from private (contractual) actors to social actors (such as the South Korean NGO 'People's Solidarity for Participatory Democracy').[153]

As far as enforcement mechanisms are concerned, we lay out several formal (i.e. the ordinary enforcement channels that aim to enforce a compliance stance, such as administrative penalties and measures, restitution orders, civil claims as well as membership sanctions and adherence procedures within stewardship networks) and informal (i.e. other mechanisms relating to information diffusion, public reputational procedures and private means) mechanisms (see also Table 27.3). But the preferred enforcement mechanism essentially depends on the nature of shareholder stewardship norms in a jurisdiction and the nature of standard-setters. When stewardship norms are soft in nature, informal enforcement mechanisms have a key role to play, but their efficiency also depends on formal membership sanctions taking place within stewardship networks. When soft-law stewardship norms coexist with hard-law ones, as is the case in the EU, the role of public enforcers cannot be disregarded. In such cases of symbiotic norms, a shareholder stewardship enforcement can take some aspiration from the approach that the FCA adopts in the area of proxy advisers, that is, a gradual escalation of enforcement mechanisms from informal (warning notice, public statement) to formal (administrative penalty) mechanisms, depending on the reaction of the regulatee following the initial warning notice.[154] The adoption of such a gradual escalation of public enforcement from informal to formal mechanisms can provide a beneficial alternative to member states that have shown a monolithic preference for formal enforcement in relation to article 3g (SRD II) and leave space for enforcement by market actors.[155]

Finally, the temporal aspect of our taxonomy (*ex ante* and *ex post* mechanisms) highlights a continuum of actions by enforcers of norms (from private guidance and advice to sanctioning a breach) that all aim to attain good stewardship standards. But this distinction, based on the time of the intervention, is a thin one. An *ex post* enforcement mechanism that takes place after an action has (not) been taken such as a formal sanction or an informal 'name and shame' campaign can trigger future *ex ante* enforcement: parties subject to *ex post* enforcement will have to reflect upon the consequences of their past actions and potentially alter their compliance stance for the next (annual) engagement and disclosure exercise. For instance, while a tiering exercise taking place within a stewardship network operates *ex post*, taking place after the disclosure of shareholder stewardship statements, it also has an *ex ante* function in deterring deviant parties from repeating their non-compliant stance in the future (see also Table 27.1). In turn, *ex ante* and *ex post* enforcement – despite functioning in parallel temporal dimensions – are not completely autonomous (see also Table 27.1).

[152] On the risks of over-regulation and its impact upon engagement, see Rock (n 19) 371, 373.
[153] See Kim and Martin (n 47) and accompanying text.
[154] The Proxy Advisors (Shareholders' Rights) Regulations 2019, SI 2019/926, ss 11–15 (available at <www.legislation.gov.uk/uksi/2019/926/made/data.pdf> accessed 10 May 2020).
[155] The FCA itself recognizes the role of market enforcement. See F paras 7.11 and 7.12 of the Explanatory Memorandum to the Proxy Advisors (Shareholders' Rights) Regulations 2019 (available at <www.legislation.gov.uk/uksi/2019/926/pdfs/uksiem_20190926_en.pdf> accessed 10 May 2020).

Our temporal, multi-actor and multi-modal enforcement taxonomy essentially pertains to a single key point: to enforce shareholder stewardship effectively, various actors, mechanisms and timing in enforcement need to work together. But it needs to be borne in mind that all these monitoring, deterrence and compliance trends are still developed with variable levels of success and sophistication around the world. This is owing to the various national specificities that may facilitate or impede the valuable contribution of public, quasi-public, private, market and social actors in enforcing shareholders stewardship. While we do not envisage including in Table 27.3 all the hypothetical constructs, the exact continuum of mechanisms, from behind-the-scenes meetings and dialogue to administrative sanctions, depends on the nature of the norm subject to enforcement (soft versus hard law), on whether the enforcer is also the standard-setter and on national, legal, market and cultural specificities. We do not thus expect countries to apply our enforcement taxonomy in a uniform fashion; this is owing to the 'one size does not fit all' mantra in corporate governance and shareholder stewardship. For instance, the efficiency of formal and informal enforcement actions by social actors may be disproportionately variable across the globe since it is mostly dependent on civil society traits. Thus, our humble aim is to advance a multi-actor and multi-modal enforcement system that offers flexibility and variety in enforcement actions and can be adjusted to any national or supranational framework.

27.5 CONCLUSION

In this chapter we have attempted to decipher the enforcement of shareholder stewardship around the world. We adopt a *broad* approach to enforcement mechanisms in the area of shareholder stewardship and set out a simple conceptual taxonomy based on three pillars: (i) the nature of the enforcer (self, public, quasi-public, private, market and social); (ii) the nature of the enforcement mechanisms (formal and informal); and (iii) the *ex ante* or *ex post* timeliness and responsiveness of enforcement mechanisms to (in)actions. We support more partnership between formal and informal enforcement mechanisms in light of the emerging symbiosis of semi-hard- and soft-law (national and supranational) shareholder stewardship norms. Overall, we view enforcement as having *blurred boundaries*, often comprising both rules- and principles-based regulation,[156] enforced by different public, quasi-public, private, market and social actors at different times. This echoes Park's comparative advantage theory of enforcement in the context of securities laws, whereby '[d]ifferent enforcers have different advantages, and a decentralized system allows for specialization in enforcement approaches'.[157]

Using the recent EU efforts as a case study, we underscore the weaknesses of introducing formal public enforcement in an area traditionally enforced informally through market actors. But, while we caution against public enforcement, we support a role for public (or quasi-public) enforcers in facilitating civil claims and the ensuing award of damages to the ultimate investors. We recognize, however, that the latter may seem a premature initiative for further legal reform, given the soft-law nature of most stewardship duties around the world.

Owing to the nature of shareholder stewardship norms and their overlap with the corporate governance aspects of the shareholder role of institutional investors, we support formal

---

[156] For a regulatory proposal to introduce stewardship duties under investment management law and mix them with stewardship principles under soft law, see Chiu and Katelouzou, 'Making a Case for Regulating Institutional Shareholders' Corporate Governance Roles' (n 120) 98. In such a scenario, the rules-based regulation would be enforced by public regulators, the principles-based regulation by market ones.

[157] James J Park, 'Rules, Principles, and the Competition to Enforce the Securities Law' (2012) 100 *California Law Review* 115, 181.

membership sanctions and adherence procedures taking place within stewardship networks as well as informal mechanisms by public, quasi-public, private, market and social enforcers through public information diffusion, public reputational procedures and private measures. We acknowledge, however, that some refinement is necessary through tiering, ratings and benchmarking, ongoing guidance and dialogue. It is further important to highlight that informal enforcement should not be exclusively seen as a facilitative measure for the maintenance of flexibility and adaptation to best stewardship standards; it is also a revived form of enabling the 'crank in the window'[158] through which market and social discipline will allow the continuous representation of a series of private and public interests, including those of the ultimate investors.

While there is no global 'one-size-fits-all' approach to shareholder stewardship enforcement, we are optimistic that market and social discipline, provided that an active market for stewardship exists, can have additional layers of influence on stewards, promoting continuous interaction among public, quasi-public, market and social actors. Informal enforcement is thus needed as a 'safety valve' – though not the only one – for achieving high shareholder stewardship standards.

---

[158] Chiu has used this metaphor to denote the potential of the ideological transformation of stewardship as an enabling spectrum for the visibility and promotion of 'stakeholder interests and communitarian values': Iris H–Y Chiu, 'Institutional Shareholders as Stewards: Toward a New Conception of Corporate Governance' (2012) 6 *Brooklyn Journal of Corporate, Financial & Commercial Law* 387, 431.

28

Can a Global Legal Misfit Be Fixed?

Shareholder Stewardship in a Controlling Shareholder and ESG World

Ernest Lim and Dan W. Puchniak[*]

28.1 REMOVING THE ANGLO-AMERICAN-CENTRIC BLINDERS TO EXAMINE THE FUTURE OF STEWARDSHIP

Prior to this book project, the primary metric used by leading academics and pundits to evaluate whether a stewardship code was a success or failure appeared to be clear: did the code transform rationally passive institutional shareholders into actively engaged shareholder stewards? Since the UK issued the world's first stewardship code in 2010 (UK Code 2010),[1] a vigorous debate has raged, and a thoughtful academic literature has developed, attempting to answer this question.[2] In December 2018, the UK government–commissioned Kingman Review definitively provided an answer by pointedly concluding that the UK Code was 'not effective in practice'.[3] In short, the UK Code had failed to transform rationally passive institutional shareholders into actively engaged shareholder stewards.[4]

In response, the UK's Financial Reporting Council (FRC) issued its third edition of the UK Stewardship Code (the UK Code 2020), which makes environmental, social and governance (ESG) considerations its primary focus.[5] The FRC's hope is that this may finally achieve the UK Code's elusive goal of transforming rationally passive institutional investors into actively engaged shareholder stewards.[6] Predictably, there has been a debate about whether this hope will become a reality, which has caused the academic literature – the latest of which is contained in this book – to continue to grow.[7]

---

[*] The authors would like to acknowledge the generous research funding from the NUS Law Centre for Asian Legal Studies. The authors would also like to thank Jordan Ng Qi Le for his exceptional research assistance. As always, any errors remain our own.

[1] Financial Reporting Council, *The UK Stewardship Code* (July 2010) <www.frc.org.uk/getattachment/e223e152-5515-4cdc-a951-da33e093eb28/UK-Stewardship-Code-July-2010.pdf> accessed 19 May 2021 [hereinafter UK Code 2010].

[2] Dan W Puchniak, 'The False Hope of Stewardship in the Context of Controlling Shareholders: Making Sense Out of the Global Transplant of a Legal Misfit' *The American Journal of Comparative Law* (forthcoming); Gen Goto, Alan K Koh and Dan W Puchniak, 'Diversity of Shareholder Stewardship in Asia: Faux Convergence' (2020) 53 *Vanderbilt Journal of Transnational Law* 829; Koh, Puchniak and Goto, Shareholder Stewardship in Asia, Chapter 29.

[3] John Kingman, 'Independent Review of the Financial Reporting Council' (Department for Business, Energy and Industrial Strategy, December 2018) 8 <https://assets.publishing.service.gov.uk/government/uploads/system/uploads/attachment_data/file/767387/frc-independent-review-final-report.pdf> accessed 19 May 2021 [hereinafter Kingman Review].

[4] Puchniak (n 2).

[5] Financial Reporting Council, *The UK Stewardship Code 2020* (2019) <www.frc.org.uk/getattachment/5aae591d-d9d3-4cf4-814a-d14e156a1d87/Stewardship-Code_Dec-19-Final-Corrected.pdf> accessed 19 May 2021 [hereinafter UK Code 2020]; Puchniak (n 2).

[6] Puchniak (n 2).

[7] Davies, The UK Stewardship Code 2010–2020, Chapter 2.

While this debate has raged on in the UK, as detailed in this book, stewardship codes have been issued in many of the world's leading economies and now exist in twenty jurisdictions on six continents, with more jurisdictions considering adopting them. Virtually all these non-UK codes, except for the Singapore Family Code, focus on the goal that has been at the core of the UK Code since its inception: transforming rationally passive institutional investors into actively engaged shareholder stewards. Based on the UK-centric debate and academic literature prior to this book project, the metric of success for these non-UK codes was assumed to be the same as in the UK.[8]

However, as explained by one of us in detail elsewhere, pundits and academics have overlooked a critical fact: outside of the UK/US, it may not matter nearly as much if stewardship 'succeeds' in changing the behaviour of institutional investors.[9] This is because, with the notable exception of the UK/US, institutional investors are collectively minority shareholders in most listed companies in almost every jurisdiction in the world.[10] Moreover, in most jurisdictions, with the notable exception of the UK/US, most listed companies already have a rationally active – non-institutional – controlling shareholder as their 'steward'.[11]

The impact of this observation on the 'success' of UK-style codes globally is difficult to overstate. It is uncontroversial that *if* a stewardship code in the UK/US succeeds in incentivizing institutional investors to become actively engaged shareholders, institutional investors will axiomatically steward the vast majority of UK/US listed companies.[12] This is an indisputable fact because institutional shareholders collectively control the vast majority of shares in UK/US listed companies.[13] As such, if a stewardship code succeeds in the UK/US, it would solve the 'ownerless corporations' problem that stewardship in the UK was designed to solve.[14] Stewardship would also have a significant impact on the systemic corporate governance problems that drove its adoption because institutional investors would steward a large enough swath of UK/US listed companies for their actions to have systemic consequences.[15] In short, the design of the UK code 'fits' the shareholder structure in the UK/US because *if* it succeeds, it will produce its intended result.

However, in non-UK/US jurisdictions, the situation is entirely different: *if* a stewardship code succeeds in incentivizing institutional investors to become actively engaged shareholders, institutional investors *will not* steward the vast majority of listed companies. In turn, institutional investors will not have the ability to effectively act as a mechanism to address the type of systemic corporate governance problems that the UK Code was designed to solve.[16] Perhaps, more importantly, most listed companies in most non-UK/US jurisdictions have a controlling shareholder, who has the economic incentive and shareholder power to steward the company it controls.[17] However, nothing in the UK Code's history or text suggest that it was ever intended to apply to controlling shareholders; that said, the (overlooked) reality is that controlling

---

[8] Puchniak (n 2); Goto, Koh and Puchniak (n 2); Koh, Puchniak and Goto, Shareholder Stewardship in Asia, Chapter 29.
[9] Puchniak (n 2).
[10] ibid.
[11] ibid.
[12] ibid.
[13] ibid.
[14] ibid.
[15] ibid. For a novel perspective on how stewardship can play a role in addressing systemic risk, see Jeffrey Gordon, 'Systemic Stewardship' (2021) ECGI Law Working Paper No 566/2021 <https://ssrn.com/abstract=3782814> accessed 19 May 2021.
[16] Puchniak (n 2).
[17] ibid.

shareholders are the 'natural stewards' of most listed companies outside of the UK/US.[18] In short, the design of the UK Code is a 'global legal misfit' because, even if it 'succeeds' by changing the behaviour of institutional investors in non-UK/US jurisdictions, this will not produce its intended result.[19]

An obvious question that arises is: why would jurisdictions around the world adopt UK-style stewardship codes if they are global legal misfits? A detailed answer to this question, which is based on fresh empirical evidence and the jurisdiction-specific case studies in this book, is provided in a forthcoming article by one of us.[20] To summarize its conclusion, governments and institutional investors around the world have issued stewardship codes to serve their own purposes.[21] The result has been that stewardship codes have served diverse functions globally – acting as a mechanism that governments can use to engage in 'halo signalling',[22] as a tool for governments to advance their own diverse political agendas, or as a mechanism for institutional investors to stave off being regulated by the government.[23] This development, which is likely to continue, is something that the original drafters of the UK Code would never have anticipated and which, prior to this book project, had been overlooked in the literature.[24]

This chapter addresses another question that naturally flows from the fact that UK-style stewardship codes are global legal misfits: what *ought* to be the role of shareholder stewardship in a world dominated by controlling shareholders? There are three important factors that define the context in which we answer this question. First, as this chapter is forward-looking, we answer this question based on a prediction that was made and explained in the introductory chapter of this book: that if stewardship has a future, its future will most likely be as a mechanism to advance the ESG movement. As such, this chapter will focus on the role that shareholder stewardship ought to play in helping to advance ESG in a world dominated by controlling shareholders. This makes sense as the UK Code 2020 has reoriented stewardship to focus on ESG and, therefore, this focus will provide a window into how stewardship ought to work globally in light of the new UK Code 2020 and the global rise of ESG.

Second, in evaluating the role of stewardship codes in jurisdictions where controlling shareholders predominate, we will consider viable alternatives to shareholder stewardship for advancing ESG. This is important as there are several corporate governance tools that may serve to advance ESG. An accurate understanding of the role that stewardship should (or should not) play in controlled jurisdictions cannot be evaluated in a vacuum. The utility of stewardship must therefore be juxtaposed against these functional substitutes to determine the value of shareholder stewardship in practice, as it is only one tool in the toolbox for improving corporate governance in controlled jurisdictions with a focus on ESG.

Third, the Singapore Family Code is the only stewardship code that does not see institutional investors as the primary target of shareholder stewardship.[25] Moreover, it is the only stewardship code in the world that focuses on a type of controlling shareholder.[26] As such, we will evaluate

---

[18] ibid.
[19] ibid.
[20] ibid.
[21] ibid; Ernest Lim, 'Concentrated Ownership, State-Owned Enterprises and Corporate Governance' (2021) 41 *Oxford Journal of Legal Studies* 663.
[22] Puchniak (n 2). 'Halo signalling' refers to the strategic adoption of regulation to attract foreign investment notwithstanding the apparent practical irrelevance of such regulation to the jurisdiction's corporate environment. See Puchniak and Tang, Singapore's Embrace of Shareholder Stewardship, Chapter 14.
[23] Puchniak (n 2).
[24] ibid.
[25] ibid; Puchniak and Tang, Singapore's Embrace of Shareholder Stewardship, Chapter 14.
[26] ibid.

the strengths and weaknesses of the Singapore Family Code as it provides the only window into a stewardship code that attempts to 'fix' the UK Stewardship Code model by creating a code that 'fits' the shareholding structure of a jurisdiction dominated by controlling shareholders (and where institutional investors collectively own only a small minority of shares in listed companies).[27]

At the risk of ruining the suspense, ultimately, we conclude that it will be difficult to 'fix' this global legal misfit to effectively address the core corporate governance problems in controlled jurisdictions, with a view towards advancing the ESG movement globally. Although a reoriented approach to shareholder stewardship may play a role in nudging controlling shareholders towards ESG, hard law will likely be necessary to bring about real change. Unfortunately, this suggests that shareholder stewardship may be used as a 'smoke screen' by controlling shareholders and governments to send a formal signal that they are addressing ESG in controlled jurisdictions when, in reality, functional change will be limited in practice. If this occurs, the history of shareholder stewardship in controlled jurisdictions may not be a repeat of the UK experience, but it will likely rhyme.

28.2 POSSIBLE APPROACHES TO STEWARDSHIP CODES IN A CONTROLLING SHAREHOLDER AND ESG WORLD

What ought to be the role of shareholder stewardship in a controlling shareholder and ESG world? As a starting point, consider the definition of stewardship in the UK Code 2020: 'Stewardship is the responsible allocation, management and oversight of capital to create long-term value for clients and beneficiaries leading to sustainable benefits for the economy, the environment and society.'[28] This definition applies to asset owners and asset managers – but not to controlling shareholders. Under UK law, unlike asset managers who owe fiduciary duties to their clients, and asset owners to their beneficiaries, controlling shareholders are generally not subject to fiduciary duties[29] – illustrating how issues involving controlling shareholders are distinct from those involving asset owners and asset managers, which are the focal points of the UK Code.[30]

In a similar vein, shareholder passivity, short-termism and complex investment chains associated with institutional investors are not the key issues facing concentrated ownership jurisdictions. Rather, a central and persistent issue is controlling shareholders extracting private benefits of control by diverting resources from the company to the controller at the expense of the company and minority shareholders.[31]

---

[27] ibid.
[28] UK Code 2020 (n 5) 4.
[29] But controlling shareholders of Premium-listed companies on the London Stock Exchange are subject to certain governance arrangements with their companies in order to prevent disproportionate exercises of power that adversely affect minority shareholders: FCA Listing Rule 6.5.4. This is not a fiduciary duty on the part of the company or the controlling shareholder but merely a restriction imposed by the listing rules. One of us has also argued that controlling shareholders in the common law Asian jurisdictions should be subject to fiduciary duties: Ernest Lim, *A Case for Shareholders' Fiduciary Duties in Common Law Asia* (CUP 2019) 205–72.
[30] Law Commission, *Fiduciary Duties of Investment Intermediaries* (Law Com No 350, 2014) 106 paras 5.95–5.97 <www.lawcom.gov.uk/app/uploads/2015/03/lc350_fiduciary_duties.pdf> accessed 19 May 2021; but note that, under US law, controlling shareholders owe fiduciary duties to minority shareholders (but usually in the context of freeze-outs and closely held companies); see *Jones v HF Ahmanson & Co.*, 460 P2d 464 (Cal 1969); Andreas Cahn, 'The Shareholders' Fiduciary Duty in German Company Law' in Hanne S Birkmose (ed), *Shareholders' Duties* (Kluwer Law International 2017) (under German law, shareholders are subject to fiduciary duties).
[31] For an overview of how private benefits of control work in different jurisdictions and types of company, see Dan W Puchniak, 'Multiple Faces of Shareholder Power in Asia: Complexity Revealed' in Jennifer G Hill and Randall

But this does not mean that controlling shareholders play no role, or should play no role, in creating long-term sustainable benefits. On the contrary, the question is whether, in the exercise of their formal powers (voting rights) and their informal powers (influence over the board and managers), controllers should act responsibly, given that the exercise of such powers will impact not only the minority shareholders and companies (of which they are the controllers) but also the broader economy, environment and society. It would be highly anomalous if institutional shareholders are expected to be stewards but not controllers because the latter wield more powers and play a more important role than the former in concentrated ownership jurisdictions. This is especially the case in today's world as ESG and a focus on 'corporate purpose' have become the zeitgeist of corporate law and governance, representing one of the more recent rationales cited as driving the adoption of stewardship codes.[32]

But what then should be expected of controllers? There are three main approaches. The first is to stick to soft law, that is, either to amend the existing stewardship codes to include controlling shareholders or to draft a new code for controllers or concentrated ownership companies. The second is not to use the stewardship code as a mechanism but to amend the rules regulating the extractions of private benefits of control by controllers – specifically the stock exchange rules on related party transactions (RPTs) – such that the bodies responsible for considering and approving the RPTs have to take into account ESG considerations. The third and final approach is to resort to directors' duties: to argue that directors are legally required to consider sustainability considerations as part of their duties of care and loyalty.

28.2.1 First Approach: Reforming the Stewardship Codes

Singapore is the only jurisdiction in the world to have created a separate stewardship code for non-institutional shareholders: the Singapore Family Code.[33] But, as is evident in the title of the code, it is directed only at a specific type of company, namely family controlled ones, not state-owned enterprises (SOEs), which are the other dominant type of company in Singapore and in many other concentrated ownership jurisdictions.[34] It is curious that stewardship principles apply only to family businesses, but not to SOEs, which play a more crucial role in the Singapore economy and society. After all, SOEs control and manage the key infrastructure, energy and public utilities systems as well as the provision of vital financial and technological services.[35] In emerging economies especially, SOEs play a key role in preventing redundancy, redistributing income and reducing prices of goods and services below market rate.[36] In addition, SOEs in China, which is now an economic superpower, are at the core of its economy and have become some of the most powerful companies in the world.[37]

S Thomas (eds), *Research Handbook on Shareholder Power* (Edward Elgar 2015). See also Lim, *A Case for Shareholders' Fiduciary Duties in Common Law Asia* (n 29).

[32] Ernest Lim, *Sustainability and Corporate Mechanisms in Asia* (CUP 2020) ch 5; Katelouzou and Klettner, Sustainable Finance and Stewardship, Chapter 26, Section 26.3.2.

[33] Stewardship Asia Centre, *Stewardship Principles for Family Businesses* (2018) <www.stewardshipasia.com.sg/sites/default/files/2020-09/SPFB-brochure-0913.pdf> accessed 19 May 2021 [hereinafter Singapore Family Code].

[34] For an excellent overview of the unique corporate governance issues involving SOEs, see Curtis J Milhaupt and Mariana Pargendler, 'Governance Challenges of Listed State-Owned Enterprises Around the World: National Experiences and a Framework for Reform' (2017) 50 *Cornell International Law Journal* 473; see also Lim, *Sustainability and Corporate Mechanisms in Asia* (n 32).

[35] Michael A Witt and Gordon Redding (eds), *The Oxford Handbook of Asian Business Systems* (OUP 2014).

[36] ibid.

[37] Tan Cheng Han, Dan W Puchniak and Umakanth Varottil, 'State-Owned Enterprises in Singapore Model: Historical Insights into a Potential Model for Reform' (2015) 28 *Columbia Journal of Asian Law* 61, 62; Li-Wen

There are three possible explanations as to why SOEs are not subject to stewardship principles in Singapore. First, and most likely, given that the SOEs in Singapore are generally known for their efficiency and for taking a long-term approach to value creation,[38] it is unnecessary for the SOEs, at least in Singapore, to adhere to stewardship principles. Second, it may seem unlikely for the state as the controlling shareholder of SOEs to willingly propose and issue a set of rules that will constrain its powers. However, as Puchniak and Lan explain, in the context of Singapore, the state, somewhat counter-intuitively, has created an institutional architecture to constrain its own controlling shareholder power[39] – which might make Temasek justified in referring to itself as a 'good steward'.[40] Finally, given that the body that issued the Singapore Family Code – Stewardship Asia – is a non-government organization that is affiliated with and supported by Temasek Holdings, which is the controlling shareholder of the SOEs in Singapore, it would seem to present a direct conflict of interest if Stewardship Asia drafted rules for controlling shareholders. However, as highlighted in the introductory chapter in this book, somewhat curiously in the context of institutional investors, this has been done in many jurisdictions (i.e., Australia, Brazil, Canada, Italy, the Netherlands, Norway, South Africa, Switzerland and the US)[41] where institutional investors have drafted stewardship codes regulating institutional investors (i.e., themselves).[42]

Similar to Singapore's other stewardship code that applies only to institutional shareholders (the Singapore Stewardship Principles for Responsible Investors), the Singapore Family Code is purely voluntary and non-binding; no companies are required to sign up to it and, for signatories, no sanctions or disincentives are imposed. The Singapore Family Code makes it clear that it is not intended to be prescriptive. Rather, it is merely a set of guidelines or 'signposts'.[43] The soft-law nature of the Singapore Family Code is not necessarily problematic because soft law may perform a critical function in shaping, transmitting and normalizing best practices and norms.[44] Further, precisely because the Singapore Family Code is merely a set of non-binding guidelines, it may be more acceptable to family businesses and arguably gain more traction.

The Singapore Family Code states in the preamble that 'stewardship encapsulates the essence of responsible and meaningful value creation in a sustainable way to benefit stakeholders, as well as the larger community that they are a part of'.[45] This is consistent with the 'central question'[46] that the Singapore Family Code seeks to address: 'How does Family Business thrive and sustain growth while enhancing the wealth of its stakeholders and the well-being of the societies in

---

Lin and Curtis J Milhaupt, 'We Are the (National) Champions: Understanding the Mechanisms of State Capitalism in China' (2013) 65 *Stanford Law Review* 697, 699.

[38] James S Ang and David K Ding, 'Government Ownership and the Performance of Government-Linked Companies: The Case of Singapore' (2006) 16 *Journal of Multinational Financial Management* 64, 85–86; Carlos D Ramírez and Ling Hui Tan, *Singapore, Inc. Versus the Private Sector: Are Government-Linked Companies Different?* (IMF Working Paper 03/156, 2003) <www.imf.org/external/pubs/ft/wp/2003/wp03156.pdf> accessed 19 May 2021.

[39] Dan W Puchniak and Luh Luh Lan, 'Independent Directors in Singapore: Puzzling Compliance Requiring Explanation' (2017) 65 *The American Journal of Comparative Law* 265, 306–10.

[40] Dan W Puchniak and Samantha Tang, 'Singapore's Puzzling Embrace of Shareholder Stewardship: A Successful Secret' (2020) 53 *Vanderbilt Journal of Transnational Law* 989, 1009–10.

[41] Katelouzou and Puchniak, Global Shareholder Stewardship, Chapter 1; Puchniak (n 2).

[42] Bowley and Hill, Stewardship and Collective Action, Chapter 19, Section 19.2.1; Williams, Stewardship Principles in Canada, Chapter 20, Section 20.1; Fisch, The Uncertain Stewardship Potential of Index Funds, Chapter 21, Section 21.2.

[43] Singapore Family Code (n 33) 2.

[44] Katelouzou and Klettner, Sustainable Finance and Stewardship, Chapter 26, Section 26.4.

[45] Singapore Family Code (n 33) 1.

[46] ibid 8.

which it operates over the long term?'.[47] Thus, stewardship is to promote the long-term viability of the company and the goal is to benefit stakeholders (the term of which is undefined) and the society. For example, practice note (e) to Principle 2 states: 'Embrace the responsibility for creating long-term social and economic value to a wider group of stakeholders, and not just myopically focusing on family wealth to foster ownership mentality amongst all those who play a role in the success of the business.'[48] This is in accordance with the increasing global focus on 'corporate purpose' going beyond mere shareholder value and the desire for companies to address broader issues related to ESG.[49]

However, one glaring omission in the Singapore Family Code is that it does not explicitly state who is responsible for taking action under the principles: is it the shareholders, the directors, the managers or the employees? It would seem logical that the controlling family shareholders should be made explicitly responsible under the Code to ensure compliance with it, as they – by definition – have the legal power through their voting rights to control the corporate governance in family companies. This appears to have been the design intention and impetus for creating the Code in the first place, as it reorients the core concept of shareholder stewardship to focus on controlling shareholders in family businesses and has nothing to do with institutional investors.[50] However, this is left ambiguous in the Code and, more importantly, if the family controllers are the intended target – which we assume is the case[51] – the Code should make their obligations as stewards under the Code clear. Without this being clarified, it is impossible to hold the family controlling shareholders, or any other constituency within family companies, accountable – a problem in the Code which must be rectified.

By contrast, there is no dispute that all versions of the UK Code – and indeed every other stewardship code in the world – are directed at institutional investors and the obligations of institutional investors are made clear in the UK Code.[52] Moreover, at least under the UK model, for domestic UK qualified institutional investors, compliance with the Code is mandatory and, under the UK Code 2020, all institutional investors bound by the Code must 'apply and explain' its principles – a harder obligation than the UK's original voluntary 'comply or explain' approach.[53] For signatories who fail to furnish adequate disclosure, regulators can consider adopting a tiering mechanism, like the one deployed in the UK by the FRC, to put pressure on institutional investors to provide high-quality disclosure.[54]

Another problem is that the subjects of the Singapore Family Code – family companies – are not required to produce any disclosure or to take any follow-up action as to how they have implemented the principles. Nor has the issuer of the Code, Stewardship Asia, put in place

---

[47] ibid.
[48] ibid 4.
[49] Edward Rock, 'For Whom Is the Corporation Managed in 2020? The Debate over Corporate Purpose' (2020) ECGI Law Working Paper No 515/2020 <https://ssrn.com/abstract=3589951> accessed 11 May 2021; Colin Mayer, *Prosperity: Better Business Makes the Greater Good* (OUP 2019).
[50] Puchniak and Tang, Singapore's Embrace of Shareholder Stewardship, Chapter 14; Puchniak (n 2). See Lim, *Sustainability and Corporate Mechanisms in Asia* (n 32) 188–95.
[51] Given its ambition of making Singapore the standard-bearer for a new Asian model of corporate governance.
[52] Puchniak (n 2).
[53] Changes driven by the criticisms of the Kingman Review (n 3) 8, 46. See Katelouzou and Puchniak, Global Shareholder Stewardship, Chapter 1 and Davies, The UK Stewardship Code 2010–2020, Chapter 2.
[54] Financial Reporting Council, 'Tiering of signatories to the Stewardship Code' <www.frc.org.uk/news/november-2016/tiering-of-signatories-to-the-stewardship-code> accessed 22 February 2022. See Puchniak and Katelouzou, Global Shareholder Stewardship, Chapter 1.

a mechanism to identify and monitor who has signed up to the Singapore Family Code. As a result, there are no mechanisms to monitor its effectiveness.[55]

Considering the problems with the Singapore Family Code, it is suggested that should other concentrated ownership jurisdictions adopt stewardship codes for controlling shareholders, they should consider ensuring that the following actions are taken. First, the code needs to clarify that all controlling shareholders (regardless of whether they are the controllers of SOEs, family companies or other types of companies) are subject to the code – expected to act as stewards – and they are the ones who are expected to take actions to promote stewardship.

Second, the code should make clear what stewardship means. It is suggested that stewardship in concentrated ownership companies is the responsible exercise of formal and informal powers by controlling shareholders[56] to create long-term value for the company leading to sustainable benefits for the society, environment and economy. Thus, controllers are expected to consider and give effect to ESG considerations. The beneficiaries of stewardship include not only the shareholders as a whole but also the stakeholders and society in general.

Third, the code should specify the actions that are expected of controlling shareholders. It is suggested that controlling shareholders should be expected to provide clear and informative disclosure of: (a) the values, strategies and goals underlying their investments and how these are aligned with stewardship; (b) how they have promoted stewardship in their exercise of all their voting rights; (c) how they have engaged with the directors, managers and minority shareholders for the purpose of promoting stewardship; and (d) actual or potential conflicts of interests related to stewardship and how they have managed these conflicts. Finally, mechanisms should be put in place to monitor who has signed up to the code and to assess the quality of disclosure of the controlling shareholders.[57]

However, it could be argued that to characterize controlling shareholders as stewards and to expect controllers to make the above disclosures is not only onerous but highly problematic. This is because it would make sense for institutional shareholders to take into account ESG considerations in their investment strategies and decisions insofar as these impact on the economic interests of their clients/beneficiaries to whom they owe fiduciary duties – a point which dovetails with ESG being the future of stewardship, which was highlighted in the introductory chapter of this book.[58] But controlling shareholders generally owe no fiduciary duties upwards (for they are usually the ultimate beneficiaries). Nor, at least in concentrated ownership commonwealth jurisdictions, do controllers owe such duties downwards (for they owe no duties to the company, unlike directors).[59] Further, to expect controlling shareholders to be stewards will subject their exercise of voting powers to constraints, but this is contrary to the principle in

---

[55] This can be contrasted with the more robust reporting expectations of the UK Code 2020: Davies, The UK Stewardship Code 2010–2020, Chapter 2, Section 2.3. See also Katelouzou and Sergakis, Shareholder Stewardship Enforcement, Chapter 27.

[56] The definition of a controlling shareholder can be adopted from the listing rules. For example, the Singapore Exchange defines a 'controlling shareholder' as one who holds 15 per cent or more of the issued shares or who in fact exercises control over the company: Singapore Exchange, 'SGX Rulebook: Definitions and Interpretation' <http://rulebook.sgx.com/rulebook/definitions-and-interpretation-0> accessed 19 May 2021.

[57] For empirical evidence that non-binding stewardship codes are likely to be ineffective, see Lucian A Bebchuk, Alma Cohen and Scott Hirst, 'The Agency Problems of Institutional Investors' (2017) 31 *Journal of Economic Perspectives* 89, 90, 108. In the context of corporate governance, see Lucian Bebchuk and Roberto Tallarita, 'The Illusory Promise of Stakeholder Governance' (2020) 106 *Cornell Law Review* 91.

[58] Katelouzou and Puchniak, Global Shareholder Stewardship, Chapter 1. Max M Schanzenbach and Robert H Sitkoff, 'Reconciling Fiduciary Duty and Social Conscience: The Law and Economics of ESG Investing by a Trustee' (2020) 72 *Stanford Law Review* 381, 399–400.

[59] Cf Ernest Lim, 'Controlling Shareholders and Fiduciary Duties in Asia' (2018) 18 *Journal of Corporate Law Studies* 113, 115.

commonwealth jurisdictions that votes are property rights and shareholders can generally exercise them as they please[60] (subject to minimal restrictions, the most important of which is that shareholders must act bona fide for the company's benefit as a whole).[61] Finally, it is unlikely for the government, as the controlling shareholder of SOEs, to voluntarily come up with a stewardship code for itself unless there is an external impetus or pressure for doing so – but normally there appears to be none.

There are, however, several counter-arguments that may suggest that it would make sense to characterize controlling shareholders as stewards. First, it is morally and socially unacceptable that while the conduct of controlling shareholders, especially in concentrated ownership jurisdictions, has significant impact on companies, societies and the environment, controllers are not expected to do anything – unlike institutional investors who are relatively less powerful and yet are expected to be stewards.[62] Second, expecting controlling shareholders to act as stewards pursuant to a stewardship code poses no effective constraint on their behaviour because the codes are generally voluntary and non-binding and no sanctions are attached for non-compliance.[63] Third, one cannot rule out the possibility that to promote its international standing and to enhance its legitimacy, the government as the controller may agree to have a code.[64] This will not only augment its reputation but could also attract more investment from minority shareholders.[65] Finally, the actions of shareholders, especially controlling shareholders, are already subject to significant restrictions, the three most important of which are: (1) minority shareholders remedies (e.g. minorities can often sue the company and its controllers for unfair treatment through direct or derivative actions);[66] (2) restrictions on RPTs (i.e., transactions between controllers (or their affiliates) and the company), which are often regulated by company law and/or the listing rules;[67] and (3) fiduciary duties of controlling shareholders in the US and equivalent duties in other jurisdictions,[68] with the notable exception of

---

[60] See e.g. *North-West Transportation Co Ltd v Beatty* [1887] UKPC 39, (1887) 12 App.Cas. 589; *Burland v Earle* [1902] AC 83 (PC), 94 (Lord Davey); *Northern Counties Securities Ltd v Jackson & Steeple Ltd* [1974] 1 WLR 1133; *Multinational Gas and Petrochemical Co v Multinational Gas and Petrochemical Services Ltd* [1983] Ch 258.

[61] *Allen v Gold Reefs of West Africa Ltd* [1900] 1 Ch 656.

[62] The adoption of stewardship codes for institutional investors even in jurisdictions dominated by controlling shareholders may be driven by the goal of achieving jurisdiction-specific ESG goals, but is of dubious efficacy as minority institutional investors are generally passive: Puchniak (n 2) part IV(e).

[63] Katelouzou and Puchniak, Global Shareholder Stewardship, Chapter 1. It could be argued that the UK Code has become more mandatory – at least since domestic institutional investors became subject to it. Financial Reporting Council, *The UK Stewardship Code* (September 2012) <www.frc.org.uk/getattachment/d67933f9-ca38-4233-b603 -3d24b2f62c5f/UK-Stewardship-Code-(September-2012).pdf> accessed 11 May 2021 [hereinafter UK Code 2012] (under the UK Code 2012 they were required to 'comply or explain' – they could not opt out – which is unique to the UK Code); see also UK Code 2020 (n 5) 4 (the UK Code 2020 now employs the 'apply and explain' principle).

[64] Puchniak and Tang, Singapore's Embrace of Shareholder Stewardship, Chapter 14; Puchniak (n 2).

[65] Conversely, this may be ineffective where the motivation behind adopting stewardship is solely 'halo signalling', seeking to attract foreign investment by bolstering an image as a jurisdiction which embraces cutting-edge global norms of 'good' corporate governance without effecting any actual changes to the corporate governance mechanism: Puchniak and Lan (n 39) 272; Puchniak and Tang (n 40) 1004–1005; Goto, Koh and Puchniak (n 2) 874–80; Puchniak (n 2) part IV(c). See generally Jeffrey Gordon, 'Convergence and Persistence in Corporate Law and Governance' in Jeffrey Gordon and Wolf-Georg Ringe (eds), *The Oxford Handbook of Corporate Law and Governance* (OUP 2018) 28–30.

[66] Harald Baum and Dan W Puchniak, 'The Derivative Action: An Economic, Historical and Practice Oriented Approach' in Dan W Puchniak, Harald Baum and Michael Ewing-Chow (eds), *The Derivative Action in Asia: A Comparative and Functional Approach* (CUP 2012); Arad Reisberg, *Derivative Actions and Corporate Governance* (OUP 2007).

[67] Dan W Puchniak and Umakanth Varottil, 'Related Party Transactions in Commonwealth Asia: Complicating the Comparative Paradigm' (2020) 17 Berkeley Business Law Journal 1, 20–28. See more generally Luca Enriques and Tobias Tröger (eds), *The Law and Finance of Related Party Transactions* (CUP 2019).

[68] Lim, A Case for Shareholders' Fiduciary Duties in Common Law Asia (n 29) 318–28.

commonwealth jurisdictions which do not have such duties. However, it may be argued that these restrictions are not intended to promote stewardship; rather, they are intended to protect minority investors from oppressive behaviour or to minimize private benefits of control. Thus, it is worth considering whether instead of developing a brand-new stewardship code for controlling shareholders, the listing rules can be tweaked such that the approval of RPTs requires ESG factors to be considered.

28.2.2 Second Approach: Reforming the Listing Rules on Related Party Transactions

RPTs are arguably the most pervasive means through which controlling shareholders extract private benefits of control. RPTs are commonly subject to three controlling techniques: opinions from the audit committee and independent financial adviser as well as approval from disinterested shareholders. The requirements of the contents of both sets of opinions vary slightly among jurisdictions.[69] But, essentially, both opinions have to state whether the transaction is fair and reasonable and whether it is in the best interests of the issuer and the shareholders as a whole.[70] However, the listing rules do not provide any guidance as to what amounts to 'fair and reasonable' and what amounts to 'best interests'.

It is suggested that the stock exchange can provide clarification by requiring the opinions to state, in determining whether the transaction is in the issuer's interests, how ESG considerations have been taken into account. After all, it is well established that ESG considerations have a material bearing on corporate interest.[71] In doing so, an important effect of stewardship, which is to produce long-term benefits for the environment, economy and society, can be met.

Modifying the listing rules in this way would have several advantages. First, this modification should be acceptable to the controllers and issuers because the stock exchange would not be imposing any additional duties or restrictions on the ability of controllers to engage in RPTs; nor would the exchange be constraining the behaviour of controllers. The stock exchange would merely be clarifying the requirements of the existing rules regulating RPTs. Second, requiring the opinion to state how ESG factors have been considered is consistent with existing practices and norms. This is because boards of listed companies should incorporate (or are already incorporating) ESG considerations in their decision-making processes (insofar as they impact on corporate interests) and companies are already required to furnish ESG/sustainability reports.[72] Thus, no significant cost would be imposed on the company (through its audit committee) if it were required to consider ESG factors in assessing whether RPTs are in its interests.

Finally, incorporating ESG considerations into the assessment of RPTs should bring about an increase in good RPTs (i.e., those that are consistent with the long-term value of the company leading to sustainable benefits for the environment, the economy and society). In doing so, the stock exchanges in concentrated ownership jurisdictions would be sending a strong signal to minority investors that they are serious about integrating ESG considerations into their listing rules, not only pertaining to the reporting obligations by companies but also in key transactions involving companies and their controllers. However, it must be remembered that an RPT

[69] Puchniak and Varottil (n 67) 22–24; Enriques and Tröger (n 67) 12–14; Lim, *A Case for Shareholders' Fiduciary Duties in Common Law Asia* (n 29) 218.
[70] In other jurisdictions, the listing rules require the opinions from the audit committee and the independent financial adviser to state that the transaction is not detrimental to the interests of the issuer and those of the minority shareholders.
[71] Lim, *Sustainability and Corporate Mechanisms in Asia* (n 32) 7–9.
[72] ibid ch 2.

regulatory regime is not simply about the black-letter law; rather, it is about the manner and context in which the law is enforced. This suggests that for such an approach to work, rule of law and attention to how the rules should be applied in the local context must be carefully considered.[73]

28.2.3 *Third Approach: Directors' Duties*

The last approach – to require directors to consider, and where appropriate give effect to, ESG factors as part of their duty of loyalty and care insofar as ESG considerations are relevant to corporate interest – is an indirect mechanism to attain the goals of stewardship in concentrated ownership jurisdictions.[74] These directors could be the controlling shareholders themselves or the affiliates of the controllers. So, instead of targeting the controllers directly, this mechanism would impose requirements on the controllers, but in their capacities as directors, not as controlling shareholders. It is not uncommon in family-owned companies for the controlling shareholder to also be a director and manager, or for the controller's family members to be directors and/or managers. In SOEs, the controlling shareholder, which is the state, is not itself the director; rather, the controller's current or former affiliates or employees are likely to be the directors. These directors are often current or former politicians or those who currently or previously work(ed) with the controlling shareholder.[75]

However, there are two key problems with this approach. First, because controlling shareholders normally[76] wield the power to appoint and dismiss directors, insofar as the directors are not the controllers themselves, the directors are unlikely to defy the controllers if the latter's interests conflict with ESG considerations.[77] For example, there could be situations where the reduction of carbon emissions or the switch to environmentally sustainable products would be costly insofar as it would have a clear negative impact on the company's short-term profitability, although there is tentative evidence that such actions will result in a long-term increase in share price. In this situation, it could be argued that the controllers' interests (at least in the short-term) will conflict with giving effect to climate change considerations; trade-offs may be required.[78] There is a risk that directors may prioritize the controller's interests at the expense of the long-term interests of the company and the environment.

Second, because the voting powers wielded by controlling shareholders are different from the functions and responsibilities of directors, there are important areas in which the controllers operate that will not be covered by the requirement to incorporate ESG considerations. In the context of most common law and civil law concentrated ownership jurisdictions, for example,

---

[73] Puchniak and Varottil (n 67).
[74] But it remains more effective in achieving ESG goals than relying on the duties of institutional investors: Puchniak (n 2).
[75] For an example of this in Singapore, see Puchniak and Lan (n 39) 313–17.
[76] In certain jurisdictions, minority shareholders are given the right to appoint directors. Cumulative voting which benefits minority shareholders may allow them to successfully elect directors. But it remains uncommon for corporate law to grant minority board representation. See Luca Enriques, Henry Hansmann, Reinier Kraakman and Mariana Pargendler, 'The Basic Governance Structure: Minority Shareholders and Non-shareholder Constituencies' in Reinier Kraakman and others (eds), *The Anatomy of Corporate Law: A Comparative and Functional Approach* (3rd edn, OUP 2017) 80–81; see also Dan W Puchniak and Kon Sik Kim, 'Varieties of Independent Directors in Asia: A Taxonomy' in Dan W Puchniak, Harald Baum and Luke Nottage (eds), *Independent Directors in Asia: A Historical, Contextual and Comparative Approach* (CUP 2017).
[77] Lim, 'Concentrated Ownership, State-Owned Enterprises and Corporate Governance' (n 21).
[78] Alan Schwartz and Reuben Finighan, 'Impact Investing Won't Save Capitalism' *Harvard Business Review* (17 July 2020) <https://hbr.org/2020/07/impact-investing-wont-save-capitalism> accessed 19 May 2021.

the powers wielded and exercised by shareholders include but are not limited to the following: to appoint and dismiss directors without cause; to alter the corporate constitution; to dictate to or overrule the directors by altering the constitution; to exercise management power if provided for in the constitution; to authorize transactions between the company and its directors by ordinary resolution that would otherwise amount to a breach of directors' duties; to ratify breaches of directors' duties; to approve mergers and acquisitions; and to approve significant transactions.[79] Of course, it is not always appropriate or relevant for controlling shareholders to incorporate ESG considerations whenever controllers exercise these powers. But the point remains that directors' duties are insufficient in themselves for the purpose of achieving the goals of stewardship in concentrated ownership jurisdictions.

28.2.4 Implementation: Stewardship as One Tool in the Toolbox to Control Controllers

None of these three approaches are mutually exclusive. It is desirable to have all three, but we must consider how likely it is that these approaches will be implemented. The stewardship codes for institutional shareholders in jurisdictions with the highest concentration of shareholder ownership, which are mostly in Asia, have been drafted and issued by governmental bodies or entities that are affiliated with the state.[80] A stewardship code for controlling shareholders is likely to be issued by the same body. Thus, it is likely for now that the code for controllers (should there be one) in most jurisdictions will take the form of soft law (given that hard law will be opposed by the state in those jurisdictions where the state is a major controlling shareholder – which is common outside of the US/UK, particularly in Asia).[81] However, this does not mean that soft law is ineffectual provided that: (1) soft law includes provisions that controlling shareholders should disclose how they have promoted stewardship; (2) a tracking mechanism is put in place to ascertain which controllers have signed up to the code and which have not and appropriate pressure is applied to the latter group to sign up; and (3) an independent and expert regulatory body or a non-government organization implements a system to assess whether and how the signatories have implemented the code.

In jurisdictions which have codes drafted by institutional investors themselves – which comprise most of the codes outside of Asia[82] – it is yet to be seen whether controlling shareholders may take a similar approach. In the past, this development may have seemed far-fetched. However, if controlling shareholders observe stewardship codes for controllers emerging in other jurisdictions, they may see drafting a code to regulate themselves (insofar as they are not controllers in SOEs) as a strategy to pre-empt a government-issued code from emerging in their own jurisdiction.[83] In addition, with the increasing pressure on companies to commit to ESG and demonstrate a purpose beyond maximizing shareholder value, controlling shareholders may see drafting a stewardship code as a cost-effective way to signal their commitment to this agenda – without requiring any real action. Most importantly, if controlling shareholders

---

[79] Lim, *A Case for Shareholders' Fiduciary Duties in Common Law Asia* (n 29) 11–12; Enriques, Hansmann, Kraakman and Pargendler (n 76) 80–81; Luca Enriques, Gerard Hertig, Hideki Kanda and Mariana Pargendler, 'Related-Party Transactions' in Reinier Kraakman and others (eds), *The Anatomy of Corporate Law: A Comparative and Functional Approach* (3rd edn, OUP 2017); Gen Goto, 'Legally "Strong" Shareholders of Japan' (2014) 3 *Michigan Journal of Private Equity & Venture Capital Law* 125; See Paul Davies and Klaus J Hopt, 'Corporate Boards in Europe – Accountability and Convergence' (2013) 61 *The American Journal of Comparative Law* 301.
[80] See Puchniak (n 2).
[81] ibid.
[82] Katelouzou and Puchniak, Global Shareholder Stewardship, Chapter 1; Puchniak (n 2).
[83] Katelouzou and Puchniak, Global Shareholder Stewardship, Chapter 1; Davies, The UK Stewardship Code 2010–2020, Chapter 2, Section 2.1.

draft codes for themselves, it is unlikely that such codes will have much of an impact on their actual behaviour – it will merely be another iteration of 'halo signalling'.

28.3 THE FUTURE OF STEWARDSHIP IN A CONTROLLING SHAREHOLDER AND ESG WORLD

The future of stewardship will be in jurisdictions in which institutional shareholders are collectively minority shareholders and listed companies are dominated by controlling shareholders.[84] This is clear because it describes the shareholder landscapes in almost every jurisdiction in the world, with the notable exceptions of the UK/US.[85] Given this reality, if the past is any predictor of the future, stewardship will not play the role intended by the UK Code in any non-UK/US jurisdiction – which debunks current conventional wisdom.[86]

This raises the question addressed in this chapter: what ought to be the role of shareholder stewardship in a controlling shareholder and ESG world? With the increasing focus on corporate purpose and the related rise of ESG – both of which will likely increase post-Covid 19 – the need for governments and institutional investors to be *seen* to be acting in the interests of society as a whole, and especially the environment, is likely to intensify. As the UK Code 2020 has been reframed as a signal for societal and ESG interests, it will likely serve as an appealing mechanism for governments and institutional investors that already have UK-style codes to reform towards as a signalling device. As such, even though UK-style codes are 'global legal misfits', jurisdictions that already have them may amend them towards the UK Code 2020, citing their commitment to society, ESG and corporate purpose. In Asia, some jurisdictions may decide to follow the Singapore Family Code model and claim that they are tailoring their approach to a new form of Asian corporate governance – with family owners as the natural stewards of a significant portion of listed companies.[87] Other non-UK/US jurisdictions outside of Asia may see the Singapore model as a better 'fit' given their relative dearth of institutional investors and predominance of controlling shareholders.

However, if this occurs, based on our analysis in this chapter, most likely these developments will merely be about *signalling* a shift in focus towards a more inclusive society, the environment and corporate purpose using the bright lights of stewardship. This may shift attention away from the hard-law regulations and reforms outlined in this chapter that may advance ESG more effectively than stewardship. For example, it would appear to be more efficient and effective to tweak listing rules so that ESG considerations become part of the RPT approval process than to create a controlling shareholder stewardship code from scratch which, based on Singapore's experience, is unlikely to have much real bite. Also, as one of us has explained in detail elsewhere, it may be worth considering whether imposing fiduciary duties on controlling shareholders in concentrated ownership jurisdictions that presently do not have them (e.g. in common law Asian countries) may be more worthwhile than attempting to nudge controlling shareholders towards ESG through shareholder stewardship.[88] As emphasized earlier, shareholder stewardship could work together with these hard-law solutions as they are not mutually

---

[84] Puchniak (n 2).
[85] ibid.
[86] ibid; Goto, Koh and Puchniak (n 2); Koh, Puchniak and Goto, Shareholder Stewardship in Asia, Chapter 29.
[87] For an analysis of the Singapore Family Code and how it aims to create a model for Asia, see Puchniak and Tang (n 40). Kowpatanakit and Bunaramrueang, The Thai Institutional Investors Stewardship Code and Its Implementation, Chapter 16, Section 16.5 (suggesting that it may make sense for Thailand to follow the Singapore model of stewardship, given Thailand's similar shareholder structure).
[88] Lim, *A Case for Shareholders' Fiduciary Duties in Common Law Asia* (n 29).

exclusive. However, the risk is that shareholder stewardship serves as a 'smoke screen' for controlling shareholders and governments to signal a movement towards ESG to ultimately avoid the tough choices required to change the hard law governing controlling shareholders.

In sum, although reorienting stewardship codes in controlled jurisdictions to focus on controlling shareholders may provide a nudge towards ESG, it appears that hard law will likely be necessary to bring about real change. For this to occur in controlled jurisdictions, the entrenched interests of controlling shareholders will have to be challenged – something which powerful corporations, families and governments, who themselves are the dominant controlling shareholders around the world, will likely be able to avoid.[89] As such, it is likely that shareholder stewardship in controlled jurisdictions will be built on either misfitted UK-style codes or new codes fitted to controlled jurisdictions with little bite. Hopefully, for the future of ESG – which must succeed in controlled jurisdictions to have a global impact – we are wrong.

---

[89] Puchniak (n 2); Lim, *Sustainability and Corporate Mechanisms in Asia* (n 32).

29

Shareholder Stewardship in Asia

Functional Diversity within Superficial Formal Convergence

Alan K. Koh, Dan W. Puchniak and Gen Goto[*]

29.1 INTRODUCTION

In 2010, when the UK enacted the world's first stewardship code (UK Code[1]), the impetus behind it was clear. By that time, institutional investors had come to hold a substantial majority of the shares in UK listed companies.[2] However, as most institutional investors lacked incentives to use their shareholder power to monitor management,[3] they were branded as 'rationally passive' shareholders.[4] According to the received wisdom of the time, left unmonitored by institutional investors who collectively controlled the UK's shareholder float, managers of UK listed companies engaged in excessive risk-taking and short-termism, which were identified as significant contributors to the 2008 global financial crisis (GFC).[5] The UK Code was therefore intended to perform the function of motivating institutional investors to become socially responsible and

---

[*] This chapter draws and expands upon material from an article first published as Gen Goto, Alan K Koh and Dan W Puchniak, 'Diversity of Shareholder Stewardship in Asia: Faux Convergence' (2020) 53 *Vanderbilt Journal of Transnational Law* 829. We are grateful to the *Vanderbilt Journal of Transnational Law* for its exceptional editorial work on the article and for allowing us to reuse material from it.
  We are grateful to Dionysia Katelouzou, Curtis Milhaupt and Roger Barker for discussions on some of the ideas presented in this chapter; to Kyung-Hoon Chun, Martin Gelter, Jennifer Hill, Kenneth Khoo, Lin Lin, Ron Masulis, Morgan Ricks, Tan Cheng Han, Samantha S Tang, Randall Thomas, Umakanth Varottil, Wang Jiangyu and Yesha Yadav for feedback on an earlier draft presented at the 'Comparative Corporate Law & Governance: Asian and Global Perspectives' Conference organized by NUS Law and Vanderbilt Law School held at NUS Law on 25–26 July 2019; to the organizers of the Global Shareholder Stewardship Conference held at King's College London on 23–24 September 2019 for hosting Puchniak and Koh and to the participants at this event for their feedback on a draft version of the article first published in the *Vanderbilt Journal of Transnational Law*; and to Lim Jiawen and Chong Shou Yu for their excellent research assistance. Any errors remain our own. Financial support from the NUS Law Centre for Asian Legal Studies (CALS) at NUS Law, the Nomura Foundation, King's College London, the British Academy, and the Nanyang Technological University Start-Up Grant 04INS000773C300 is gratefully acknowledged.

[1] Unless otherwise indicated, by this we mean what Davies calls the 'First Version' of the UK Code, that is, the 2010 and 2012 versions collectively. See generally Davies, The UK Stewardship Code 2010–2020, Chapter 2. In contradistinction, UK Code 2.0 refers to the 2020 version.

[2] See Office for National Statistics, 'Ownership of UK Quoted Shares: 2018' (14 January 2020) tables 1 and 3 <www.ons.gov.uk/economy/investmentspensionsandtrusts/bulletins/ownershipofukquotedshares/2018> accessed 1 December 2020.

[3] See Lucian A Bebchuk, Alma Cohen and Scott Hirst, 'The Agency Problems of Institutional Investors' (2017) 31 *Journal of Economic Perspectives* 89, 96–100.

[4] Ronald Gilson and Jeffrey Gordon, 'The Agency Costs of Agency Capitalism: Activist Investors and the Revaluation of Governance Rights' (2013) 113 *Columbia Law Review* 863, 895; Gerald F Davis, 'A New Finance Capitalism? Mutual Funds and Ownership Re-concentration in the United States' (2008) 5 *European Management Review* 11, 19–20.

[5] See e.g. Iris H–Y Chiu and Dionysia Katelouzou, 'From Shareholder Stewardship to Shareholder Duties: Is the Time Ripe?' in Hanne S Birkmose (ed), *Shareholders' Duties* (Kluwer Law International 2017) 131; Paul Davies, 'Shareholders in the United Kingdom' in Jennifer G Hill and Randall S Thomas (eds), *Research Handbook on Shareholder Power* (Edward Elgar 2015) 373; Brian R Cheffins, 'The Stewardship Code's Achilles' Heel' (2010) 73 *Modern Law Review* 1004, 1005–1006.

engaged shareholders.[6] It would do so by incentivizing institutional investors, through the use of soft law, to act as 'good stewards' by exercising their control over listed companies through their collective voting rights, the goal of exercising such control being to mitigate the excessive risk-taking and short-termism by corporate management to avoid another financial crisis.[7]

Since the UK Code was adopted in 2010, stewardship codes and related initiatives have proliferated throughout Asia. Among those adopting stewardship codes are Asia's largest developed economy (Japan), the four tiger economies (Hong Kong, Singapore, South Korea and Taiwan) and two of Asia's most important high-growth economies (Malaysia and Thailand).[8] Asia's third largest economy (India) has recently adopted three different stewardship codes, each of which targets different segments of the financial industry.[9] Asia's largest economy (People's Republic of China (PRC)) recently inserted more detailed provisions into its revised corporate governance code to promote what may, when viewed through a UK lens, appear to be 'shareholder stewardship' among institutional investors.[10] In addition, several of Asia's most important developing economies (including Kazakhstan and the Philippines) have placed the creation of a stewardship code on their corporate governance reform agendas.[11]

This chapter explores reasons for the popularity of stewardship codes in Asia and the implications of this development for comparative corporate law and governance. For reasons we touch on in this chapter and which are explored in greater detail elsewhere, Asian jurisdictions bear little resemblance to shareholder stewardship's intellectual birthplace.[12] It would therefore be hasty to attribute the popularity of stewardship codes in Asia to the same reasons that drove the UK Code's adoption in 2010. As we show in this chapter, the popularity of stewardship codes in Asia can be at least partly explained by the fact that they are convenient vehicles for local actors (whether governments, interest groups or market players) to further their own particular interests. A stewardship code has value as a policy tool because it is an inexpensive, non-binding and malleable vehicle, and one which a jurisdiction can formally adopt to send a signal of 'good' corporate governance to the world.

---

[6] Cheffins (n 5) 1014–15.
[7] Jennifer G Hill, 'Good Activist/Bad Activist: The Rise of International Stewardship Codes' (2018) 41 *Seattle University Law Review* 497, 506; Chiu and Katelouzou (n 5) 135; Cheffins (n 5) 1004–1006.
[8] ISS Corporate Solutions, 'Prepping for the Trend: Stewardship Code Coming to Asia' (2019) <www.isscorporatesolutions.com/prepping-for-the-trend-stewardship-code-coming-to-asia/> accessed 1 December 2020.
[9] In India, stewardship codes have been issued by the insurance regulator for insurance companies, by the pension fund regulator for pensions and, most recently, by the securities regulator for mutual funds and alternative investment funds. For a detailed analysis of these codes and stewardship in India, see Varottil, Shareholder Stewardship in India, Chapter 17.
[10] The PRC has a long history of promoting institutional investors as a corporate governance mechanism to stabilize the stock market and mitigate private benefits of control in its controlling shareholder–dominated listed companies. The expanded provisions in the revised Chinese Corporate Governance Code 2018 continued to promote this agenda and separately promoted environmental, social and governance (ESG) considerations in listed companies generally. Through a UK lens, these initiatives may be (mis)described as 'shareholder stewardship'. However, as Lin and Puchniak explain, to accurately understand these developments, they should be understood on their own terms in the context of the PRC's unique corporate governance model. See Puchniak and Lin, Institutional Investors in China, Chapter 18; Lin Lin and Dan W Puchniak, 'Institutional Investors in China: Corporate Governance and Policy Channeling in the Market within the State' *Columbia Journal of Asian Law* (forthcoming).
[11] TheCityUK/Astana International Financial Center (AIFC), 'Responsible Shareholder Engagement – A Kazakh Stewardship Code' (7 March 2017) <www.thecityuk.com/research/responsible-shareholder-engagement-a-kazakh-stewardship-code/> accessed 1 December 2020; Securities and Exchange Commission, 'Philippines Corporate Governance Blueprint 2015' (29 October 2015) 20–21 <https://web.archive.org/web/20200317052640/www.sec.gov.ph/wp-content/uploads/2015/01/SEC_Corporate_Governance_Blueprint_Oct_29_2015.pdf> archived 17 March 2020, accessed 1 December 2020.
[12] See discussion at Section 29.3.1; see further Dan W Puchniak, 'The False Hope of Stewardship in the Context of Controlling Shareholders: Making Sense Out of the Global Transplant of a Legal Misfit' *The American Journal of Comparative Law* (forthcoming)

While this helps us understand why stewardship codes came to be widely adopted in Asia, drawing positive or normative conclusions from stewardship's proliferation in Asia becomes more difficult. This observation is important. As we address in this chapter and explain in greater detail elsewhere,[13] leading corporate governance scholars, prominent international organizations and market participants have drawn positive and normative conclusions acting on the erroneous assumption that stewardship codes generally fulfil similar functions across jurisdictions.[14] This risk of error is not limited to stewardship codes. Other examples in corporate governance in Asia (and elsewhere) exist whereby jurisdictions adopt globally recognized mechanisms of 'good' corporate governance at a superficial formal level and then alter their function to serve local purposes;[15] stewardship is but the latest example of this. Such a trend would suggest that while corporate governance may seem to exhibit convergence at a superficial (i.e. formal) level, it remains local, path dependent and divergent in practice.[16]

The experience of stewardship in Asia contributes to our understanding of comparative corporate governance in two major ways. First, it enriches our understanding of corporate governance convergence. The difference between 'formal' and 'functional' convergence in corporate governance as popularized by Ronald Gilson is well known.[17] According to Gilson, functional convergence is likely to occur before formal convergence owing to the latter's greater cost.[18] The experience of Asian jurisdictions, which on one hand adopted stewardship codes quickly and cheaply in a seeming convergence on form, while on the other hand exhibiting little to no convergence in function, appears to belie this received wisdom in an apparent demonstration of what has been oxymoronically termed 'divergence within convergence' by Jeffrey Gordon.[19] The contradiction, however, disappears when we distinguish between formal convergence as 'true' convergence (i.e. convergence in both function and substance of the law or institutions)[20] and formal convergence as merely *superficial* convergence in form. As we show in this chapter, superficial convergence as exhibited by Asian stewardship codes[21] is not only consistent with their divergent functions within their respective jurisdiction-specific contexts,[22] but the two components – superficial convergence in form with functional divergence – together comprise a distinct and important form of convergence that we dub 'faux convergence'.[23]

---

[13] See generally Gen Goto, Alan K Koh and Dan W Puchniak, 'Diversity of Shareholder Stewardship in Asia: Faux Convergence' (2020) 53 *Vanderbilt Journal of Transnational Law* 829; Puchniak (n 12).

[14] See discussion in Section 29.2.

[15] See e.g. Dan W Puchniak and Kon Sik Kim, 'Varieties of Independent Directors in Asia: A Taxonomy' in Dan W Puchniak, Harald Baum and Luke Nottage (eds), *Independent Directors in Asia: A Historical, Contextual and Comparative Approach* (CUP 2017) 131–32 (observing that, under some idiosyncratic and domestic conditions, some Asian jurisdictions adapted and distorted the role of independent directors to achieve goals other than good corporate governance).

[16] ibid. See also, Dan W Puchniak, 'The Derivative Action in Asia: A Complex Reality' (2012) 9 Berkeley Business Law Journal 1.

[17] Foundationally, Ronald J Gilson, 'Globalizing Corporate Governance: Convergence of Form or Function' (2001) 49 *The American Journal of Comparative Law* 329, 356.

[18] ibid 338.

[19] Jeffrey Gordon, 'Convergence and Persistence in Corporate Law and Governance' in Jeffrey Gordon and Wolf-Georg Ringe (eds), *The Oxford Handbook of Corporate Law and Governance* (OUP 2018) 28–32, 41 (citing Puchniak and Kim (n 15)). Evidence of both forms of divergence is found in OECD, 'Corporate Governance Factbook 2017' (2017) 43–44 <www.oecd.org/daf/ca/OECD-Corporate-Governance-Factbook-2017.pdf> accessed 1 December 2020.

[20] Which is what we infer Gilson probably meant, although his seminal paper did not state so expressly; see Goto, Koh and Puchniak (n 13) 878–79.

[21] See Section 29.3.1.

[22] See Sections 29.3.2–29.3.3.

[23] See Section 29.4.

The second contribution of stewardship in Asia as a demonstration of faux convergence is in posing a formidable challenge to the 'global governance' agenda[24] of actors such as the World Bank, the International Monetary Fund (IMF) and the Organisation for Economic Cooperation and Development (OECD), as well as comparative corporate governance research as a field. The notion that there are global or universal mechanisms representing or advancing 'good' corporate governance has been a staple of international actors and leading research.[25] In turn, substantial energy and resources have been devoted by international actors to proselytizing global standards of 'good' corporate governance, and by non-leading Western jurisdictions to signalling their agreement (superficial or otherwise) to such standards. The faux convergence that we have observed simultaneously seems to satisfy both groups of actors, but not without cost. At best, it complicates efforts in ascertaining the extent to which jurisdictions really commit to 'good' corporate governance practices and often sidelines local experts, as local elites are normally in charge of creating the superficial law that serves a purely signalling function. Worse, it risks misleading institutions and scholars alike into concluding erroneously that 'true' convergence has occurred.[26] In turn, the advance of faux convergence risks rendering moot the global governance project of forcing or encouraging *substantive* reforms to actually 'improve' or 'change' corporate governance.

This chapter will proceed as follows. Section 29.2 illuminates the widespread assumption that UK-style stewardship has been transplanted around the world. Section 29.3 draws on in-depth jurisdiction-specific case studies in this book to reveal that, despite Asian jurisdictions generally adopting UK-style stewardship codes in form, stewardship has come to serve diverse jurisdiction-specific functions in Asia – some of which run counter to the UK model. Section 29.4 discusses the implications of this significant gap between the form and the function of stewardship in Asia on the comparative corporate governance convergence debate. It also emphasizes how the analysis of stewardship in Asia demonstrates that *local* knowledge, context and expertise are critical for an accurate understanding of comparative corporate law.

29.2 THE WIDESPREAD ASSUMPTION THAT UK-STYLE STEWARDSHIP HAS GONE GLOBAL

It is well known and widely accepted that for more than four decades institutional shareholders in the UK have collectively owned a majority of shares in UK listed companies.[27] Currently, 68 per cent of the shares of UK listed companies are owned by institutional investors. In turn, the foundational idea of the UK Code 2010 – that incentivizing institutional investors to act collectively as engaged stewards could solve the UK's most important systemic corporate governance problems – makes sense.[28] This rationale is also the impetus for the UK Code 2020, which seeks to incentivize institutional investors to act as engaged stewards to solve the

---

[24] On the 'global governance' movement, see Gordon (n 19) 44–49.
[25] For a critique of one of the most prominent examples of this approach, see Dan W Puchniak and Umakanth Varottil, 'Related Party Transactions in Commonwealth Asia: Complicating the Comparative Paradigm' (2020) 17 *Berkeley Business Law Journal* 1.
[26] See examples in Section 29.2. While this risk is heightened by those (especially institutions) who would take a superficial, check-the-box approach to comparative corporate law and governance, even otherwise seasoned comparative scholars risk falling into this trap if they were to work without true jurisdictional experts.
[27] Puchniak (n 12). See also, Katelouzou and Puchniak, Global Shareholder Stewardship, Chapter 1.
[28] ibid.

UK's corporate governance problems *and* guide listed companies towards embracing environmental, social and governance (ESG) considerations.[29]

Following the enactment of the UK Code 2010, despite many sceptics, the UK's idea of creating a soft law code to incentivize institutional investors to solve the most important systemic corporate governance problems quickly took on a life of its own. As Jennifer Hill observed, the UK Code's bold claims that '[s]tewardship aims to promote the long term success of companies ... [and] [e]ffective stewardship benefits companies, investors and the economy as a whole'[30] 'proved alluring from a comparativist standpoint, providing clear incentives for transplantation'.[31] At least formally, it appears that the UK Code sparked a global stewardship movement, with broadly similar codes and other initiatives now existing in at least twenty jurisdictions over five continents – with many other jurisdictions also placing shareholder stewardship on their corporate governance reform agendas.[32]

What is conspicuously absent is any serious attempt to identify the precise actors in each national corporate governance context and define the subject(s) and goal(s) of stewardship in each. Put simply, the question that has not yet been fully explored is: what is the intended and actual function(s) of stewardship in Asian jurisdictions, and does this depart from the original UK stewardship model? Instead, what largely prevails is an implicit assumption that the intended and actual functions of 'stewardship' in Asia have been (and are) similar to the UK.

For example, two leading UK-based scholars have previously assumed that stewardship globally is the same as stewardship in the UK, and is driven by the same factors:[33]

> However, the [UK] Code has since taken its place in the transnational governance space and inspired international developments in the institution of Stewardship Codes in many other countries, including the Netherlands, Switzerland, Japan and Malaysia ... the gradual internationalisation of soft law governance obligations of stewardship on the basis of the UK Stewardship Code is likely to be driven by the common concerns shared by many jurisdictions with listed markets in relation to the increasing presence of institutional investors (especially foreign ones) in their markets and the potentially active role they can play.

US scholars have also been content to proceed based on a monolithic view of stewardship premised on the UK model. Jeffrey Gordon has identified a global shift away from 'efficiency' and towards political and social 'stability' as the end goal of corporate governance.[34] Among those interested in stability are large institutional investors owing to their diversified portfolios and long-term horizons, as well as 'global governance'[35] institutions.[36] Together with resistance against short-termist hedge funds, Gordon points to the global stewardship movement as a manifestation of the increasing concern with stability.[37] Gordon's vision of stewardship – as promoting long-term

---

[29] ibid.
[30] Financial Reporting Council, *The UK Stewardship Code* (September 2012) <www.frc.org.uk/getattachment/d67933f9-ca38-4233-b603-3d24b2f62c5f/UK-Stewardship-Code-(September-2012).pdf> accessed 1 December 2020.
[31] Hill (n 7) 506–507.
[32] Katelouzou and Puchniak, Global Shareholder Stewardship, Chapter 1; Puchniak (n 12).
[33] Chiu and Katelouzou (n 5) 135. See also Iris H–Y Chiu, 'Learning from the UK in the Proposed Shareholders' Rights Directive 2014? European Corporate Governance Regulation from a UK Perspective' (2015) 114 *Zeitschrift Für Vergleichende Rechtswissenschaft (ZVgIRWiss)* 121, 150–51.
[34] Gordon (n 19) 54: 'This is demonstrated by the growing global governance movement for "Stewardship Codes" and the concerted campaign against the purported "short-termism" of hedge funds.' Interestingly, Gordon also suggests that 'family shareholding groups', especially those planning for future generations, value stability.
[35] Such as the IMF, the World Bank and the OECD. See Gordon (n 19) 45.
[36] ibid 54.
[37] ibid.

shareholder value and as a bulwark against short-term hedge fund activism – exemplifies the conventional understanding of global stewardship based on the UK model.[38]

Reports in the popular press almost uniformly assume that stewardship movements across the world follow the UK model closely.[39] What is more troubling is the fact that the OECD, a key actor in global governance, has done largely the same.[40] In the *G20/OECD Principles of Corporate Governance*, institutional shareholders are called on to 'disclose their policies with respect to corporate governance', and the adoption of voluntary stewardship codes was cited in connection.[41] By the time the *OECD Survey of Corporate Governance Frameworks in Asia* was released in 2017, stewardship had become yet another box to tick, nestled under '[e]xercising voting rights' as a subset of '[g]overnance-related responsibilities of institutional investors'.[42] Despite the observation in an earlier section of this OECD document that thirteen out of the fourteen Asian jurisdictions surveyed had concentrated shareholding structures,[43] nowhere in the document was the importance (or lack thereof) of 'institutional investors' explained or 'stewardship' defined or its function explained with respect to each jurisdiction's context. The irresistible inference is that the authors had, consciously or not, implicitly assumed that all these stewardship-implementing jurisdictions understood stewardship in the same way because their stewardship codes were all seemingly modelled on the UK Code.

Even sophisticated governance and legal professionals are not immune to the uniform stewardship assumption.[44] A recent example is Ernst & Young's (EY) *Q&A on Stewardship Codes*.[45] EY cannot be faulted for clarity, as it states clearly its view of what stewardship codes are[46] and how they are applied, following the orthodoxy set by the UK Code.[47] Yet there is nothing in the document to suggest that the existence of shareholders other than institutional investors – or the role of institutional investors in corporate governance – is contemplated.

---

[38] See also Gilson and Gordon (n 4) (premising its argument on 'rationally reticent' institutional shareholder behaviour, the solution to which is arbitrage by a class of actors specializing in activism).

[39] See e.g. Fiona Reynolds, 'Stewardship Codes Guide Best Practice' *Investment Magazine* (6 September 2017) <www.investmentmagazine.com.au/2017/09/stewardship-codes-guide-best-practice/> accessed 1 December 2020; Schroders, 'Schroders Sees Wide Adoption of Stewardship Codes in Asia' (*AsianInvestor*, 16 July 2018) <www.asianinvestor.net/article/schroders-sees-wide-adoption-of-stewardship-codes-in-asia/445470> accessed 1 December 2020; Amanda White, 'Top US Funds Embrace Stewardship Code' (*top1000funds*, 17 February 2017) <www.top1000funds.com/2017/02/top-us-funds-embrace-stewardship-code/> accessed 1 December 2020; Masayuki Yuda, 'Shareholders Find Their Voice at Japan's Annual Meetings' *Nikkei Asian Review* (Tokyo, 12 July 2018) <https://asia.nikkei.com/Business/Business-trends/Shareholders-find-their-voice-at-Japan-s-annual-meetings> accessed 1 December 2020; Owen Walker, 'Beacon of British Stewardship Needs a Brighter Flame' *Financial Times* (27 January 2019) <www.ft.com/content/1a3a57be-5c15-3e03-bae0-10bd5804bf20> accessed 1 December 2020.

[40] OECD, *G20/OECD Principles of Corporate Governance* (2015) 29–30 <www.oecd.org/daf/ca/Corporate-Governance-Principles-ENG.pdf> accessed 1 December 2020.

[41] ibid.

[42] OECD, 'OECD Survey of Corporate Governance Frameworks in Asia' (2017) 27 <www.oecd.org/daf/ca/OECD-Survey-Corporate-Governance-Frameworks-Asia.pdf> accessed 1 December 2020.

[43] ibid 5–6. The exception was Mongolia, on which nothing was said about shareholding structure other than that a majority of listed companies may be considered non-state-owned. Of the thirteen concentrated shareholding jurisdictions, only China was identified as having substantial institutional investor ownership (at 19.86%).

[44] See e.g. Ruth Sullivan, 'UK Seen As Model for Stewardship Guidelines' *Financial Times* (1 August 2010) <www.ft.com/content/0e0bbc50-9c02-11df-a7a4-00144feab49a> accessed 1 December 2020 (Kerrie Waring was then COO at the International Corporate Governance Network).

[45] EY, 'Q&A on Stewardship Codes' (August 2017) <www.ey.com/Publication/vwLUAssets/ey-stewardship-codes-august-2017/$FILE/ey-stewardship-codes-august-2017.pdf> accessed 1 December 2020.

[46] ibid 2.

[47] ibid.

Another telling example comes from Institutional Shareholder Services,[48] the world's leading proxy advisory firm:[49]

> Following the formal release of Stewardship Codes ("the Code") in Japan, Malaysia, Hong Kong, and Taiwan, three other countries including Singapore, South Korea, and Thailand are following suit as a way of promoting sustainable growth as well as corporate and shareholder value by means of active voting and constructive engagement. The UK Code is modeled after by other codes, with nuanced differences.

There are exceptions to the overall tendency to characterize stewardship in other jurisdictions as essentially the same as in the UK, of which Hill's 2018 article is a notable example. While noting that '[s]tewardship codes reflect the view that engagement by institutional investors is an integral part of any corporate governance system'[50] and that many Asian and other jurisdictions have 'jumped on the stewardship bandwagon',[51] Hill proceeds to classify stewardship codes into three major categories by their source[52] and discusses key differences between the UK and Japanese codes.[53] Although Hill correctly identifies the difference in policy objectives between the two codes,[54] she does not go so far as to consider the alternative possibility that stewardship itself means different things in these two jurisdictions. In a subsequent article, Hill summarized recent developments in Asia as follows: 'Japan adopted its own Stewardship Code, based on the U.K. model, in 2014, and many other Asian jurisdictions have now followed suit.'[55]

Similarly, while there is clear awareness in the *ICGN Global Stewardship Principles* that 'there are different models of corporate finance and ownership of listed companies around the world' and that '[family or state owned corporate models] can differ in very basic principles such as shareholder primacy versus stakeholder primacy, and may require deeper consideration in terms of how stewardship can be effectively applied',[56] there is no further consideration of whether stewardship itself can stand as a more-or-less singular concept when applied to clearly different jurisdictional contexts.

29.3 MULTIPLE FACES OF STEWARDSHIP IN ASIA: FUNCTIONAL DIVERSITY MASKED BY FORMAL UNIFORMITY

29.3.1 *The Mask of Formal Uniformity in Asia Creates Confusion and a Puzzle*

It is understandable why so many leading organizations, academics and pundits have mistakenly assumed that stewardship functions the same way in Asia (and around the world) as in the UK. As Puchniak demonstrates elsewhere, based purely on an analysis of the content of the stewardship codes, the extent to which stewardship codes around the world, and particularly in Asia, mirror the UK Code is striking.[57] It is clear from reading the Asian Codes[58] that they are based on the same core

---

[48] ISS Corporate Solutions (n 8).
[49] ibid.
[50] Hill (n 7) 506.
[51] ibid.
[52] ibid. (regulatory- or quasi-regulator-issued), 508 (private industry actors), 509 (investors).
[53] ibid. (comparing and contrasting the features of the stewardship codes in Japan and the UK).
[54] ibid.
[55] Jennifer G Hill, 'The Trajectory of American Corporate Governance: Shareholder Empowerment and Private Ordering Combat' [2019] *University of Illinois Law Review* 507, 516.
[56] International Corporate Governance Network, *ICGN Global Stewardship Principles* (2016) 23 <www.icgn.org/sites/default/files/ICGNGlobalStewardshipPrinciples.pdf> accessed 1 December 2020.
[57] Puchniak (n 12). See also, Katelouzou and Puchniak, Global Shareholder Stewardship, Chapter 1; Puchniak (n 12).
[58] Save Singapore's Family Code, which is excluded from this analysis.

TABLE 29.1 *Percentages of the latest version of jurisdiction-specific codes containing each of the seven principles in the UK Code 2010/12*[59]

Principles	1 Public Disclosure	2 Conflict of interest	3 Monitoring investee	4 Escalation	5 Collective action	6 Voting Policy	7 Periodic reporting
Global[60]	95.45	100.00	100.00	81.82	90.91	100.00	100.00
Asia[61]	100.00	100.00	100.00	80.00	90.00	100.00	100.00

concept as the UK Code: to use a soft law instrument to change the behaviour of institutional investors from rationally passive shareholders to actively engaged shareholders to solve a systemic corporate governance problem.[62]

In addition, examination of all Asian codes focusing on institutional investors (i.e. every code except the Singapore Family Stewardship Code) reveals that they – with few exceptions – contain the same seven principles comprising the primary content of the UK Code.[63] As Table 29.1 shows, Asian codes demonstrate comparable or higher levels of content uniformity (i.e. adoption of the seven principles) than codes globally. Based purely on this metric, it would not be unreasonable to conclude that the UK model of stewardship has been transplanted to Asia.

As reflected in Table 29.1, the level of similarity between the UK Code and the Asian codes is consistent with the fact that in all Asian jurisdictions local experts, academics and/ or the code itself in each jurisdiction cite the UK Code as a model.[64] The only Asian stewardship code not modelled on the UK Code is the Singapore Family Stewardship Code. This code, which is the only stewardship code that is not directed at institutional investors,[65] is so different from the UK Code that it was the only stewardship code explicitly excluded from an extensive empirical analysis comparing the text of stewardship codes globally.[66]

---

[59] Puchniak (n 12); Katelouzou and Puchniak, Global Shareholder Stewardship, Chapter 1.
[60] Following the adoption of the UK Code 2010, nineteen jurisdictions adopted twenty-two codes. India (three) and Australia (two) implemented different inaugural codes directed towards different types of institutional investor, while all other jurisdictions adopted a single inaugural code directed towards all institutional investors. Subsequently, several jurisdictions released amended version(s) of their code(s). The preamble, principles and guidance for the *latest version* of each code in each jurisdiction as of July 2020 were reviewed to determine whether each of the seven core principles contained in the UK Code had an equivalent provision in the latest version(s) of each code(s) in every jurisdiction that has adopted a stewardship code for institutional investors. The figures here represent the percentage of the latest version of each code in each jurisdiction as of July 2020 that contained each of the seven principles from the UK Code 2010. For details of the coding for each principle in each jurisdiction, see Katelouzou and Puchniak, Global Shareholder Stewardship, Chapter 1, Appendix.
[61] Asia includes a total of ten codes from eight jurisdictions.
[62] Katelouzou and Puchniak, Global Shareholder Stewardship, Chapter 1 and Lim and Puchniak, Can a Global Legal Misfit Be Fixed?, Chapter 28; Puchniak (n 12).
[63] ibid.
[64] Katelouzou and Puchniak, Global Shareholder Stewardship, Chapter 1 and Lim and Puchniak, Can a Global Legal Misfit Be Fixed?, Chapter 28; Puchniak (n 12).
[65] Puchniak and Tang, Singapore's Embrace of Shareholder Stewardship, Chapter 14, Section 14.4.
[66] See Katelouzou and Siems, The Global Diffusion of Stewardship Codes, Chapter 30, Section 30.2.1 ('Note that for Singapore we do not include in our analysis the Stewardship Principles for Family Businesses ... as our focus is on the ownership responsibilities of institutional investors.').

This high degree of similarity, at this level of abstraction, does not mean that the codes were straightforward examples of 'copy-paste jobs' of the entire UK Code *in toto*[67] (or, for the purpose of building a comparative corporate governance lexicon, what we shall call 'identical formal legal transplants') featuring codes being copied word-for-word without meaningful changes. As Katelouzou and Siems demonstrate using content analysis, the specific language used in the codes analyzed differs in wording and some codes are more alike than others.[68] The fact that the same core seven principles are used and the basic structure is largely maintained may be attributable to the UK Code's strong influence, but the fact that the text of each code's respective English versions differs across jurisdictions cannot. If the negative reaction to a recent attempt by a jurisdiction to copy-paste an entire statute of another jurisdiction[69] is any guide, it may be that extreme forms of formal legal transplant by copy-paste are no longer considered legitimate practice, regardless of how much the implementing jurisdiction wishes to follow the source jurisdiction's example.

One explanation for the textual differences between each Asian code and the UK Code – even where the 'same' principles are adopted – may lie in the different processes by which each code came into being. Another explanation is the relative sophistication of the codes' drafters. Even if imitation is the highest form of flattery and anti-plagiarism standards imposed on students and scholars do not technically apply to legislators and other rule-makers, drafters may be balancing the desire to emulate the UK Code (or some other code) against the recognition that they should express at least some content in their own words. Accordingly, it would not be meaningful to set the test for convergence in form so high that only a plagiarism check-triggering copy-paste job would pass the test. Rather, the relatively minor differences between each of the Asian codes and the UK Code serve to ensure each Asian code's legitimacy without detracting from the conclusion that substantial formal convergence on at least a superficial level has occurred.

The Malaysian Code bears special mention as it is the only Asian code to place part of the substantive content – two out of seven UK Code principle-equivalents, to be precise – outside the main text (i.e. not under a numbered principle) of the Code. A conscious decision was taken to place the collective action principle in the Introduction instead of the main text owing to market manipulation and competition law concerns.[70] Periodic reporting is also located in the Introduction,[71] although it is unclear precisely why this was done. The technique of placing substantive content in the Preamble reveals the intent of the Malaysian Code's creators to do their best to implement the UK Code's basic features even where the domestic legal system seemingly poses obstacles.

Accordingly, any deviations from the seven-principle basic structure should, in the absence of specific evidence to the contrary, be presumed to be deliberate choices. Deviations are observed with respect to only two out of seven principles: escalation and collective action. For escalation, the outliers are Japan and South Korea. In Japan, the original 2014 Code contained no reference

---

[67] More extreme examples of copy-pasting are not unheard of in lawmaking more generally. A recent example is Nigeria's Control of Infectious Disease Bill, 2020, which has been characterized as a 'plagiarised' copy of the 1977 version of Singapore's Infectious Diseases Act. See e.g. Ruth Olurounbi, 'Coronavirus: Nigeria's Proposed COVID-19 Law Tears the Country Apart' *The Africa Report* (15 May 2020) <www.theafricareport.com/27969/coronavirus-nigerias-proposed-covid-19-law-tears-the-country-apart/> accessed 1 December 2020.

[68] See generally Katelouzou and Siems, The Global Diffusion of Stewardship Codes, Chapter 30.

[69] See n 67.

[70] Tan, Institutional Investor Stewardship in Malaysia, Chapter 15, Section 15.3.

[71] Minority Shareholder Watchdog Group (MSWG) and Securities Commission Malaysia (SC), 'Malaysian Code for Institutional Investors' (June 2014) 5 <www.iicm.org.my/wp-content/uploads/2018/05/MALAYSIAN-CODE-FOR-INSTITUTIONAL-INVESTORS-MCII.pdf> accessed 1 December 2020.

to escalation; rather, the Japan Code expects institutional investors to 'arrive at a common understanding with investee companies, and to work with them in solving problems'.[72] The effect is that of a code that is 'much friendlier to investee companies as compared to the UK [Code]'.[73] Despite two subsequent revisions in 2017 and 2020, Japan remains an outlier in this respect.[74]

In South Korea, the picture is more complex. The Korean Code itself does not mention escalation[75] and is accordingly coded as negative in Puchniak's forthcoming article ,[76] but this is not the full picture. The Korea Corporate Governance Service, which led the committee that drafted the Korean Code,[77] has released a Guidebook that 'explains and supplements the Korean Code'.[78] As this Guidebook contains a list of 'additional activities' that 'generally correspond to the "escalated stewardship activities" under the UK Code',[79] Korea may be interpreted as a jurisdiction that has implemented the escalation principle, albeit on an even softer level than the stewardship code proper. Korea is also the only jurisdiction as of 2020 that has not implemented the collective action principle. This is attributed to both interest group opposition from the business community and the legal obstacle posed by a statutory filing requirement for acting-in-concert that may possibly be applicable to collective action.[80] Previously, Japan's 2014 Code did not contain the collective action principle,[81] but this was addressed in the 2017 revision.[82]

---

[72] Goto, Japanese Stewardship Code, Chapter 10, Section 10.4.1.1 ('Second, while Principles 4 and 5 of the UK Code 2012 refer to the possibility of escalating stewardship activities when necessary, and recommend that institutional investors act collectively with other investors, no such reference can be found in the Japanese principles. Instead, Principle 4 of the Japanese Code 2014 expects that institutional investors shall arrive at a common understanding with investee companies, and to work with them in solving problems. This might have an effect of giving Japanese companies room to argue that institutional investors requesting certain actions, such as an increase in payouts, are not making sufficient efforts to reach a common understanding. In a similar vein, Principle 7 calls on institutional investors to have in-depth knowledge of investee companies and their business environment, as well as develop skills and resources necessary for appropriate engagement.').

[73] Goto, Japanese Stewardship Code, Chapter 10, Section 10.4.1.1. Such language surely only further perpetuates stereotypes about the Japanese aversion to confrontation and desperation for harmony – *quaere* if the Japan Code's creators were aware of this.

[74] See Goto, Japanese Stewardship Code, Chapter 10, Section 10.4.1.2 (no mention of any changes).

[75] Kang and Chun, Korea's Stewardship Code and the Rise of Shareholder Activism, Chapter 11, Section 11.3.1.3 ('while the UK Code's fourth principle refers to "escalation" of stewardship activities, the Korean Code is silent on that issue').

[76] Puchniak (n 12) See also, Katelouzou and Puchniak, Global Shareholder Stewardship, Chapter 1.

[77] See Kang and Chun, Korea's Stewardship Code and the Rise of Shareholder Activism, Chapter 11, Section 11.2.3 ('The KCGS is a private non-profit organization founded in 2002 whose major founding members/sponsors were: the Korea Exchange; the Korea Financial Investment Association (KOFIA); the KLCA; and the KOSDAQA. Eleven members of the second committee were composed of: three from the KCGS; three from the finance industry; two from academia; one from the Korea Financial Investment Association (KOFIA); one from the Korea Capital Market Institute (KCMI); and one from a foreign institutional investor.').

[78] Kang and Chun, Korea's Stewardship Code and the Rise of Shareholder Activism, Chapter 11, Section 11.3.1.1 (defining the KCGS Guidebook as 'a publication by the KCGS that explains and supplements the Korean Code').

[79] Kang and Chun, Korea's Stewardship Code and the Rise of Shareholder Activism, Chapter 11, Section 11.3.2.

[80] Kang and Chun, Korea's Stewardship Code and the Rise of Shareholder Activism, Chapter 11, Section 11.3.1.3.

[81] There appears to have also been concern over whether acting-in-concert rules would have applied to collective action, but the Financial Services Agency attempted to address this by issuing an interpretation to resolve this concern: see Gen Goto, 'The Logic and Limits of Stewardship Codes: The Case of Japan' (2018) 15 *Berkeley Business Law Journal* 365, 385 fn 86.

[82] Goto, Japanese Stewardship Code, Chapter 10, Section 10.4.1.2 ('... the 2017 revision added a paragraph on collective engagement, to which no reference was made in the original 2014 text, in the guidance section to Principle 4, stating that "it would be beneficial for" institutional investors "to engage with investee companies in collaboration with other institutional investors (collective engagement) as necessary"').

It is also noteworthy, as observed by Puchniak, that Asia stands out globally in following the UK's approach of having a government-linked institution issue its stewardship codes. In Asia, all the stewardship codes (i.e. eleven codes in eight jurisdictions) are issued by either government or quasi-government agencies.[83] Conversely, all the non-Asian codes (i.e. twelve codes in ten jurisdictions) are private institutional investor–issued codes, with the exceptions of Denmark and Kenya.[84] This further illustrates that, on a formal level, Asia appears to have firmly embraced the UK stewardship model – and provides another possible reason why so many experts have assumed that the UK model has been transplanted to Asia.

The fact that government-linked institutions have issued all the codes in Asia creates a puzzle. One would expect that a government-linked institution would tailor its jurisdiction-specific code to fit that particular jurisdiction's shareholder landscape. As explained in Puchniak's forthcoming article, there is no jurisdiction in Asia in which institutional investors collectively own a majority of shares in listed companies. In fact, in almost all Asian jurisdictions with a code, with the notable exceptions of Japan and Korea, a majority of listed companies are dominated by controlling-block shareholders.[85] Moreover, stable-shareholders in Japan and controlling-minority shareholders in Korea create blocs of non-institutional shareholders possessing both the economic incentives and the voting rights to exercise a significant influence over the corporate governance of most listed companies in their respective jurisdictions.[86]

As such, there is no jurisdiction in Asia, with the possible exception of Japan in the foreseeable future,[87] where institutional investors have the potential power under corporate law to steward most listed companies – and this holds true even if their UK-style codes were to achieve the desired effect of incentivizing institutional investors to act collectively. This suggests two conflicting possibilities. First, government-linked institutions in Asia had no idea that the shareholder structures in their jurisdictions were incongruent with a UK-style code. Second, Asian government-linked institutions adopted UK-style codes with the intention that they would function much differently in their jurisdictions than in the UK. Based on several in-depth jurisdiction-specific case studies in this book, the evidence clearly supports the latter.

As will be explained, it appears that a variety of jurisdiction-specific factors – including market signalling, politics, and ESG considerations – drove governments in Asia to adopt UK-style stewardship codes. As a result, the intended and actual functions of UK-style stewardship codes in Asia have significantly departed from – and in some cases run counter to – the intended and actual functions of the UK Code.

---

[83] Puchniak (n 12).
[84] ibid.
[85] ibid.
[86] ibid.
[87] The growing influence of institutional investors has been observed, for example, in a 2019 proxy fight at LIXIL, a leading housing equipment manufacturer in Japan. See Akihiro Ota, 'Shareholders Prevail in Lixil Showdown, Restoring Ousted CEO' *Nikkei Asian Review* (Tokyo, 26 June 2019) <https://asia.nikkei.com/Business/Companies/Shareholders-prevail-in-Lixil-showdown-restoring-ousted-CEO> accessed 1 December 2020. The openness of Shimachu's management in switching from its negotiated deal to another non-solicited bidder offering a higher price could also arguably be explained by pressure from institutional investors. See 'Japan's Shimachu Backs Nitori's ¥214 Billion Takeover Bid' *Japan Times* (14 November 2020) <www.japantimes.co.jp/news/2020/11/14/business/corporate-business/japan-shimachu-nitori-takeover/> accessed 1 December 2020. See also Leo Lewis, 'Japan Rethinks Its Opposition to Hostile Takeovers' *Financial Times* (1 November 2020) <www.ft.com/content/45178018-82af-45b8-b6a0-76fdcec0a9ea> accessed 1 December 2020.

29.3.2 UK-Style Codes as an Effective and Malleable Vehicle for Political Agendas

It is difficult to find almost any criticism of a government adopting a UK-style stewardship code. Rather, adoption of a UK-style code is almost certain to have the jurisdiction listed alongside many of the world's most important economies for joining a club that is seen as an indicium of being on the cutting-edge of the latest global trend in 'good' corporate governance.[88] Building stewardship codes largely around obligations in soft law makes it easy for governments to issue them and limits their actual bite.[89] The UK Code has in this sense offered an inexpensive and quick-to-implement model of stewardship code that is convenient for other jurisdictions to follow. Perhaps most importantly, the concept of 'stewardship' is ambiguous and virtually free of doctrinal baggage and undertones, which makes it a malleable vehicle compatible with a myriad of political agendas.

The Japanese Code stands out as a political tool of expedience deployed by its then-incumbent political administration under former Prime Minister Abe Shinzō to promote economic growth. Specifically, the expectation seems to have been that Japanese domestic institutional investors would pressure management to boost corporate earnings and productivity by using Japanese companies' massive cash reserves more effectively.[90] This in turn appears to promote, or at least incentivize, a more arguably short-termist orientation among institutional investors that emphasizes shareholders' interests.[91] Accordingly, the Japanese Code's image of a profit-seeking institutional shareholder may thus be sharply contrasted with the UK Code's vision of the enlightened shareholder with a long-term orientation.[92]

But why did the Abe administration choose to implement its desired corporate governance changes via the medium of a 'stewardship code'? The answer may lie with the mutable nature of 'stewardship' as a concept, which enabled Japan to have its proverbial cake and eat it too: introduce the idea that institutional investors should be loyal to the interests of beneficiaries, but without triggering technical discussions on the precise elements of fiduciary duties and the legal consequences of their breach. Further, the idea of a soft law 'code' may also have been appealing to Japanese policymakers, as creation and implementation of soft law codes do not require undergoing the full legislative process applicable to 'hard' law.[93]

Similarly, the Korean government may have used stewardship to exert its political agenda and power on private industry. The Korean Code was the product of efforts by financial regulators[94] who sought to strengthen capital market regulation and address problems created by chaebols – the often besmirched individual- or family-controlled *chaebol* conglomerates.[95] Since the Korean Code's

---

[88] Ringe, Stewardship and Shareholder Engagement in Germany, Chapter 9, Section 9.5 (describing how Germany is 'swimming upstream by refusing to follow the international trend towards [issuing a stewardship code]').

[89] On enforcement of stewardship generally, see Katelouzou and Sergakis, Shareholder Stewardship Enforcement, Chapter 27.

[90] Goto, Koh and Puchniak (n 13) 853, 861.

[91] ibid 856, 863.

[92] On the connection between the UK Code and enlightened shareholder value, see Iris H–Y Chiu, 'Institutional Shareholders as Stewards: Toward a New Conception of Corporate Governance' (2012) 6 *Brooklyn Journal of Corporate, Financial & Commercial Law* 387, 398.

[93] Goto, Koh and Puchniak (n 13) 863.

[94] Albeit acting somewhat indirectly. On the process and actors involved in creation of the Korean Code, see Kang and Chun, Korea's Stewardship Code and the Rise of Shareholder Activism, Chapter 11, Section 11.2.2.

[95] Kang and Chun, Korea's Stewardship Code and the Rise of Shareholder Activism, Chapter 11, Section 11.2.1 ('In Korea, the motivation was different. Unlike its UK counterpart on which it was modelled, the usual targets of the Korean Code were corporations that had strong controlling (family) shareholders. At the risk of oversimplifying, one

introduction, there has been a visible increase in activism by previously passive institutional investors[96] as well as by the previously-not-entirely-passive national pension fund, the country's largest institutional investor.[97] In this sense, the Korean Code may be at least associated with – if not credited with – observable changes in institutional investor behaviour.[98] A recent study suggests that the influence of the Korean National Pension Service (NPS) – the national public pension fund – over dividend yield in investee companies has increased since the advent of the Korean Code.[99] Even if the Korean Code were to function as per form (i.e. motivating institutional investors to act), it remains to be seen if its impact would be significant or lasting in a landscape dominated by controlling shareholders, and where institutional investors (including the NPS) may, according to critics, have been co-opted as part of a broader political agenda.[100]

Malaysia's embrace of a UK-style stewardship code may have also been motivated by political concerns. While the Malaysian Code may be outwardly attributed to 'industry',[101] Malaysia is a state where 'industry' is 'inextricably linked to the state by means of its ownership and control' of government-linked companies (GLCs) and government-linked investment companies (GLICs).[102] Malaysia's core corporate governance problem – extraction of private benefits of control by the state as controlling shareholder from GLCs and GLICs[103] – is unaddressed by the Malaysian Code.[104] Given that the Malaysian state is the real actor behind stewardship efforts,[105] and that state or state-linked entities and bodies feature prominently among the signatories to the Malaysian Code[106] and are

may say that the Korean Code intended to address problems of strong but less-than-majority owners while the UK Code intended to address problems of ownerless corporations.').

[96] Kang and Chun, Korea's Stewardship Code and the Rise of Shareholder Activism, Chapter 11, Section 11.4.1.2.
[97] On the activism of Korea's National Pension Service, see Kang and Chun, Korea's Stewardship Code and the Rise of Shareholder Activism, Chapter 11, Sections 11.4.2–11.4.3.
[98] Bearing in mind the fallacy of *post hoc ergo propter hoc*.
[99] Yun Kyung Kim and Yunsung Koh 'Effects of Public Pension Funds and Stewardship Code on Dividends and Firm Value: Evidence from National Pension Service of Korea' (2020) 26 *Asia Pacific Business Review* 453. The authors of this study note the possibility that the NPS may act in alignment with the interests of the government but not the ultimate beneficiaries. However, the authors do not expressly recommend constraining government intervention despite mentioning it as 'one of the central principles of pension fund's [*sic*] governance with responsibility, transparency and accountability'.
[100] Kang and Chun, Korea's Stewardship Code and the Rise of Shareholder Activism, Chapter 11, Section 11.4.4.1 ('The government expects other institutional investors to join the Korean Code actively. Also, there is a political and social atmosphere that makes it difficult for institutional investors (large ones in particular) to turn down participation in shareholder stewardship. Under these circumstances, it can be argued that pension-fund socialism will be further strengthened such that politics may significantly hamper corporations' economic activities. In this light, it is possible that the political decision-making behaviour of the NPS – which, in the past, had been exercised relatively intermittently – will be exercised in a more systematic manner.').
[101] On this process see Tan, Institutional Investor Stewardship in Malaysia, Chapter 15, Section 15.2.
[102] Tan, Institutional Investor Stewardship in Malaysia, Chapter 15, Section 15.5 ('The emergence of the Malaysian Code can be traced back to industry sponsored guidelines … Indeed, the Malaysian Code's origins and its subsequent development was consciously tagged to industry and intended to be driven by the institutional investors themselves rather than by external regulators. Further, it must be noted that in the case of Malaysia, what constitutes industry is inextricably linked to the state by means of its ownership and control of these GLICs and GLCs.'). GLCs and GLICs are entities over which the federal government has substantial influence, even control. On the roles of these state-linked companies and the ways in which they are subject to government control, see ibid.
[103] Tan, Institutional Investor Stewardship in Malaysia, Chapter 15, Section 15.6 ('… oversight of the GLICs and GLCs by the Malaysian Ministry of Finance via the Minister of Finance Incorporated allows controlling shareholders to secure political and business benefits from the GLICs and GLCs …').
[104] Tan, Institutional Investor Stewardship in Malaysia, Chapter 15, Section 15.5.
[105] Tan, Institutional Investor Stewardship in Malaysia, Chapter 15, Section 15.5 ('the primacy of GLICs in the corporate governance of its investee companies indicates that they are a key driving force in the development of stewardship in Malaysia').
[106] Tan, Institutional Investor Stewardship in Malaysia, Chapter 15, Section 15.4 ('… four out of five of the asset owner signatories to the Malaysian Code are GLICs. The remaining asset owner signatory, SOCSO, is not a GLIC, although it is a government body mandated with enforcing social security laws … The prominence of GLICs and

heavily represented on the Code's oversight body,[107] this should not surprise. As Tan explains, there is a real risk that Malaysia's government is using stewardship to achieve its political agenda, such that it is unclear 'whether the interests of the state are aligned with those of the asset owners, the asset managers and more importantly, those of the ultimate beneficiaries or clients which are at the end of the investment chain'.[108] This is an acute concern considering the government's position as the predominant controlling shareholder of Malaysia's institutional investors and listed companies, combined with its history of corruption – most recently highlighted by the 1MDB scandal.[109]

29.3.3 Halo Signalling as a Key Driver for Adopting UK-Style Misfits

The concept of 'halo signalling' has been defined as 'the strategic adoption of regulation to attract foreign investment notwithstanding the apparent practical irrelevance of such regulation to the jurisdiction's corporate environment'.[110] As halo signalling does not involve the corporate governance mechanism effecting actual change, importance is placed on the jurisdiction's formal adoption of a mechanism that is considered to be the global gold standard of 'good' corporate governance. Where stewardship is concerned, the gold standard is the UK Code. The fact that the UK Code is a poor fit is irrelevant, as the impetus for adopting a code is to signal formal compliance with the gold standard, and not to effect actual change.

Asia's stewardship codes provide rich examples of signalling in action. The two jurisdictions where 'signalling' has been a key driver are Hong Kong and Singapore, which share at least three features that illuminate their governments' embrace of halo signalling. First, institutional investors are a small minority in Hong Kong (12%) and Singapore (6%). Rather, controlling shareholders hold the majority of shares in listed companies.[111] Yet, both jurisdictions adopted codes that mirrored the UK Code – which focuses on institutional investors, not controlling shareholders.[112]

The second feature is the conspicuous involvement of government-linked bodies and their agendas for issuing stewardship codes. In both Hong Kong and Singapore, the government-linked bodies involved in the issuance of stewardship codes expressly provided rationales for adoption that mirrored the original rationale of the UK Code. However – and tellingly – the rationales provided are entirely incongruent with the actual, and well-known, corporate governance context in each jurisdiction.

In Singapore, the Preamble of its Institutional Investor Code makes the following observations: 'Many countries are seeing a trend towards fragmented ownership, especially in listed companies, with many shareholders each holding a small proportion of shares. Coupled with increasingly shorter shareholding tenure, the ownership mentality is arguably being eroded and

---

entities associated with GLICs in the list of signatories amounts to 50 per cent of the total number of signatories, bringing into sharp relief the absence of signatories which are not aligned or linked to the state').

[107] Tan, Institutional Investor Stewardship in Malaysia, Chapter 15, Section 15.3 ('Oversight of the effective adoption of the Malaysian Code is carried out through the II Council ... [which] comprises representatives from statutory bodies, GLICs, the MSWG, government-linked fund managers and a private fund manager').

[108] ibid.

[109] ibid.

[110] Puchniak and Tang, Singapore's Embrace of Shareholder Stewardship, Chapter 14, Section 14.2.3. For a description of the situation in which the term 'halo signalling' was first coined, see Dan W Puchniak and Luh Luh Lan, 'Independent Directors in Singapore: Puzzling Compliance Requiring Explanation' (2017) 65 *The American Journal of Comparative Law* 265, 277.

[111] See Puchniak (n 12). Research has found that more than 90 per cent of Singapore's public listed companies have block shareholders who exercise controlling power. Luh Luh Lan and Umakanth Varottil, 'Shareholder Empowerment in Controlled Companies: The Case of Singapore' in Jennifer G Hill and Randall S Thomas (eds), *Research Handbook on Shareholder Power* (Edward Elgar 2015) 579.

[112] Puchniak (n 12).

replaced by a prevalent short-term view of investment and portfolio management. Hence, the emphasis on stewardship is relevant and timely.'[113]

Similarly, the Hong Kong Securities and Futures Commission issued the following statement to justify its introduction of a stewardship code: 'In the last couple of decades there has been a notable increase in institutional ownership of publicly listed companies, with these institutions increasingly demanding a voice in corporate governance. In many instances, institutional investors exert rights traditionally held by individuals, families or bloc alliances.'[114]

To the uninitiated, these statements seem to suggest that institutional investors are on the rise in Hong Kong and Singapore. Yet, as this book shows, there is ample evidence that institutional investors remain a minority in listed companies for both jurisdictions.[115] The dissonance between the advertised rationale for adopting a UK-style code and the actual corporate governance reality is compelling evidence that such statements were made for the purpose of halo signalling.

Second, shareholder 'short-termism', where shareholders focus on short-term gains rather than long-term corporate growth, is not a serious corporate governance problem in Hong Kong and Singapore. As Hong Kong and Singapore have emerged as two of the world's wealthiest jurisdictions, concentrated shareholding in listed companies has *increased*,[116] while institutional investors have played less significant roles in corporate governance in both jurisdictions.[117] In such an environment, shareholder short-termism is rarely a problem because controlling shareholders generally take a long-term perspective on corporate growth. As David Donald observes, 'the typical Asian holding structure might already reunite "ownership and control" in the hands of investors with a long-term outlook for the company's operational success'.[118] As such, the main corporate governance problem in jurisdictions with concentrated shareholding is controlling shareholder opportunism and abuse, and not the form of shareholder short-termism addressed by the UK Code.

Third, Hong Kong and Singapore are International Financial Centres (IFCs). IFCs have a strong incentive to engage in halo signalling because such jurisdictions 'sell their services – regulatory framework among them – to internationally active financial institutions based in the US or UK' who set the global norms for 'good' corporate governance.[119] Hong Kong and Singapore are thus heavily reliant on attracting foreign capital, creating a level of pressure to engage in halo signalling that is not experienced to the same extent by jurisdictions with larger domestic markets.[120]

In fact, Singapore may have taken the concept of signalling one step further. By developing the concept of 'family stewardship', Singapore has also sought to position itself as a stewardship

---

[113] Stewardship Asia Centre, *Singapore Stewardship Principles for Responsible Investors* (November 2016) 3 <www.stewardshipasia.com.sg/sites/default/files/2020-09/Section%202%20-%20SSP%20%28Full%20Document%29.pdf> accessed 1 December 2020.

[114] Donald, Stewardship in the Hong Kong International Financial Centre, Chapter 13, Section 13.3.

[115] Puchniak (n 12).

[116] Tan Cheng Han, Dan W Puchniak and Umakanth Varottil, 'State-Owned Enterprises in Singapore Model: Historical Insights into a Potential Model for Reform' (2015) 28 *Columbia Journal of Asian Law* 61, 66; Donald, Stewardship in the Hong Kong International Financial Centre, Chapter 13, Section 13.3.

[117] Dan W Puchniak and Samantha Tang, 'Singapore's Puzzling Embrace of Shareholder Stewardship: A Successful Secret' (2020) 53 *Vanderbilt Journal of Transnational Law* 989, 1003; Donald, Stewardship in the Hong Kong International Financial Centre, Chapter 13, Section 13.1. However, hedge funds have played an increasingly important (but not necessarily positive) role in Hong Kong: Ernest Lim, *A Case for Shareholders' Fiduciary Duties in Common Law Asia* (CUP 2019) 70–77.

[118] Donald, Stewardship in the Hong Kong International Financial Centre, Chapter 13, Section 13.1.

[119] ibid.

[120] See also Katelouzou and Siems, The Global Diffusion of Stewardship Codes, Chapter 30, Section 30.3.3 (finding a textual similarity between the Hong Kong and Singapore codes, on the one hand, and the UK Code, on the other).

leader in a way that resonates with a seminal corporate governance problem in Asia, which may allow it to become a leader in an emerging movement of Asian corporate governance.[121] The Singapore Family Stewardship Code may further claim two distinctions. First, it seems to be one of the rare stewardship codes in Asia to be based on a premise that is clearly correct for its context,[122] namely that controlling shareholders are the key corporate governance problem in Singapore.[123] Second, it also appears to be the only stewardship code in Asia to respond to the controlling shareholder problem directly by targeting a subset of them: controlling family shareholders without restriction as to company size or scale.[124] Stewardship Asia has also taken pains to promote the Family Stewardship Code in other jurisdictions in the region.[125] As such, the Family Stewardship Code goes beyond mere *signalling*; it is a corporate governance model made at least partly for *export*.

But that is not to say that signalling is a uniquely Asian phenomenon. In a quirky twist, the UK has itself embarked on what appears to be a signalling offensive. When compared with the original UK Code – which failed to achieve its original objectives[126] – UK Code 2.0 with its pivot to ESG manifests a transformed and much expanded vision of the original stewardship concept.[127] One face-value explanation is that the UK state – as the Financial Reporting Council – has through the UK Code 2.0 co-opted corporate managers and those with influence over them into supporting the UK state's attempt at complying with its climate change treaty obligations.[128] However, a more cynical view may be that those invested in the UK stewardship movement and/or its position as a global corporate governance leader placed ESG at the core of the UK Code 2.0 to ensure the UK's position as the leader in the global corporate governance movement – as ESG has become an issue of global importance. In this light, the UK Code 2.0 may be seen less as a serious commitment to change than just another attempt at signalling compliance with yet another global corporate governance norm – ESG.[129]

29.3.4 'Faux Convergence': Expanding the Comparative Taxonomy

It is a historical fact that the first stewardship code was created in the UK in 2010. Since then, as this chapter has shown, a litany of jurisdictions across Asia have claimed to have adopted UK-inspired stewardship codes. At first blush, these codes appear to be about institutional investor stewardship and nominally contain (with few exceptions) the same seven principles as the UK Code. Thus, it makes perfect sense that corporate governance scholars, experts and pundits would assume that the UK stewardship model (version 1.0) has been transplanted to Asia.

However, as our Asian case studies reveal, there is more to it than meets the eye – at least for the external, presumably occidental, observer. Stewardship codes in Asia resemble the UK's substantially in form – but not in motivations and functions. Asian jurisdictions appear to have seized upon the malleable concept of stewardship to signal – implicitly or explicitly to the occident – that they 'understand' and are committed to the UK notion of good corporate

---

[121] Puchniak and Tang, Singapore's Embrace of Shareholder Stewardship, Chapter 14.
[122] Section 29.3.1.
[123] Puchniak and Tang, Singapore's Embrace of Shareholder Stewardship, Chapter 14, Section 14.4.1.
[124] Puchniak and Tang, Singapore's Embrace of Shareholder Stewardship, Chapter 14, Section 14.4.1; Lim and Puchniak, Can a Global Legal Misfit Be Fixed?, Chapter 28; Puchniak (n 12).
[125] Puchniak and Tang, Singapore's Embrace of Shareholder Stewardship, Chapter 14, Section 14.4.2.
[126] On how and why the UK Code failed, see Davies, The UK Stewardship Code 2010–2020, Chapter 2, Section 2.3.
[127] See Davies, The UK Stewardship Code 2010–2020, Chapter 2.
[128] ibid Section 2.4.2.2.
[129] This would mean that the UK has converged towards Asian jurisdictions – poetic justice?

governance through the act of adopting a stewardship code. Simultaneously, Asian jurisdictions have, albeit to varying extents, mostly capitalized on stewardship codes and the attending debate as a cost-effective way to achieve their own local goals.

What seems at first glance to be formal convergence upon stewardship and stewardship codes is really the more complex phenomenon of what we have coined 'faux convergence'. It is 'faux' because what you see is not quite what you get: apparent convergence in form through adoption of a tool of good corporate governance reveals itself, upon closer examination, to be the adoption of a different tool with different functions. The result is divergence *in function* notwithstanding superficial convergence *in form*. Although beyond the scope of this chapter, we posit that the theory of faux convergence also explains other developments and phenomena old and new in comparative corporate law and governance, including independent directors, and codes of corporate governance.[130]

The emergence of faux convergence has several practical and theoretical implications for comparative corporate governance. The first practical implication is that deleterious consequences can flow from the increasing pressure on jurisdictions to 'formally' converge – at least on a superficial level via faux convergence – on established norms of good corporate governance. Efforts by the IMF, OECD, World Bank and others to promote a common 'toolbox' of mechanisms for good corporate governance may cause governments to waste valuable resources on the superficial adoption of tools for good corporate governance, rather than allocating them to address the real jurisdiction-specific corporate governance problems head on.[131] Investors (perhaps surprisingly) appear to rely on evidence of the adoption of certified tools of 'good corporate governance' as an important metric in their allocation of capital. Not having independent directors, a code of corporate governance or a stewardship code in name may perversely make a jurisdiction a less attractive place to invest in because it is seen as not being part of the 'good corporate governance' club. Hence, the march of faux convergence risks greater misallocation of capital, turning attempts by global institutions to proselytize 'good' corporate governance on its head.

The second practical implication is that faux convergence's existence may lead comparative corporate law researchers astray. Specifically, scholars may erroneously assume or conclude that the widespread adoption of common tools of 'good corporate governance' suggests a global trend in how corporate governance functions – when in fact it does not. This can happen to even the most seasoned experts who would otherwise be aware of the pitfalls of such assumptions. An example of this is an otherwise insightful chapter on convergence and persistence in which the author, one of the world's comparative corporate governance giants, appears to assume that the jurisdictions adopting stewardship codes aim to enhance the voice of long-term, stable, institutional investors – congruent with the aim of the UK Code.[132] As this chapter has demonstrated, this assumption is unsupported by the evidence. We can only speculate as to the full extent to which otherwise seasoned researchers have been misled into seeing 'true' (formal and functional) convergence when deeper analysis would have revealed faux convergence in action, whether in stewardship or other fields in comparative law and governance.

From a theoretical perspective, faux convergence challenges widely accepted ideas about convergence theory. To take one example: the standard assumption has been that 'national elites', who are rent-extractors, 'may defend [their] domestic corporate governance regime' against formal convergence pressures.[133] Faux convergence turns this assumption on its head.

---

[130] Goto, Koh and Puchniak (n 13).
[131] See Puchniak and Varottil (n 25).
[132] See n 19 and accompanying text.
[133] Gordon (n 19) 29.

As the Asian jurisdiction case studies canvassed in this chapter have demonstrated, mechanisms originally intended as tools of 'good' corporate governance can be subverted by elites for their own ends. A superficially adopted corporate governance tool can be simultaneously wielded to maintain or reinforce a jurisdiction's existing corporate governance system, to further the jurisdictional elites' own agendas and to signal to the world – notwithstanding little to no commitment to real change – that the jurisdiction's elites have adopted 'good corporate governance'. This is arguably the case for Hong Kong and Singapore where the signalling motivation is more clearly dominant, but also potentially applicable to jurisdictions that appear to have adopted stewardship codes to advance other concurrent political agendas, including Japan, Malaysia and South Korea.[134]

Whatever the results of future detailed investigations may be, we caution that faux convergence, if found, makes it impossible to draw any normative conclusions based on Anglo-American values about a country's corporate governance from a mere yes/no observation as to whether some corporate governance idea in vogue has been adopted. There is no substitute for the sort of local knowledge, context and expertise that has been brought to bear by the contributors to this book. Insofar as stewardship – specifically, the vision which emanated from the UK Code – is concerned, it is hardly 'economic perfection of transcendental value toward which other jurisdictions can only aspire to converge'.[135] It is but a pot,[136] and a pot which at least several Asian jurisdictions have put to any number of uses, just not what the British initially envisioned.[137]

Finally, faux convergence in stewardship codes may well be just the tip of the comparative corporate governance iceberg. Only future research will reveal the true extent to which non-Western states and their elites have thwarted the grandest ambitions of those who would seek global compliance around a narrow, Western-defined standard of the 'good'. As in other things in life, it is worth reminding ourselves that in corporate governance, nothing is really what it seems, and to assume otherwise is hubris.

---

[134] It is also noteworthy that Gordon assumes that national elites are monolithic. In Japan and South Korea, a more nuanced view is that there are at least two rival groups of national elites – one that hopes to preserve the existing corporate governance system and one that hopes to change it. This adds another layer of complexity to the analysis.
[135] C.f. Donald, Stewardship in the Hong Kong International Financial Centre, Chapter 13, Section 13.3.
[136] C.f. John Fowles, *The French Lieutenant's Woman* (1969) ch 48 ('Duty is but a pot. It holds whatever is put in it, from the greatest evil to the greatest good.').
[137] *Quaere*: what is the *tertium comparationis* in this book?

30

The Global Diffusion of Stewardship Codes

Dionysia Katelouzou and Mathias Siems[*]

30.1 INTRODUCTION

In a world of increasing economic, technological and legal globalization, transfer of laws and regulations between different legal systems is commonplace. Contemporary comparative law refers to these as 'legal transplants' and discusses that there is often a one-way transfer ('diffusion') from one country to another.[1] Corporate law and corporate governance have travelled extensively around the world through imitation, institutional investors' lobbying, economic pressure or otherwise.[2] The UK has historically been a leading exporter of legal norms and principles, especially to former British colonial common-law countries.[3] More recently, the 1992 Cadbury Report and its successors have had significant influence on the development of corporate governance codes even in countries with no colonial ties.[4] At the same time, the US has also been influential in the corporate law field, especially in investor-related provisions,[5] while the EU has been an exporter of harmonized/standardized corporate law models even outside the EU, such as in Turkey and Ukraine.[6]

The worldwide spread of stewardship codes in recent years presents a promising, but yet untested, terrain in which to explore and fine-tune the diffusion of stewardship norms. There is a widespread belief among investors and the public that many regulators and investor groups around the world have adopted a stewardship code ostensibly modelled after the UK Stewardship Code, mainly the 2012 version.[7] This diffusion hypothesis stems, in part, from the

---

[*] Winner of the 2021 Cleary Gottlieb Steen & Hamilton Law Prize (Best paper in the ECGI Law Working Paper series). We thank for their helpful comments the participants of presentations of earlier versions of this chapter at the 1st Global Shareholder Stewardship Conference at KCL, and seminars at the LSE, the EUI and the University of Frankfurt.

[1] See references in Section 30.2.3.

[2] The literature here is voluminous. See, among others, Jeffrey Gordon, 'Convergence and Persistence in Corporate Law and Governance' in Jeffrey Gordon and Wolf-Georg Ringe (eds), *The Oxford Handbook of Corporate Law and Governance* (OUP 2018); Abdul A Rasheed and Toru Yoshikawa (eds), *The Convergence of Corporate Governance: Promise and Prospects* (Palgrave MacMillan 2012); Mathias Siems, *Convergence in Shareholder Law* (CUP 2008).

[3] Brian R Cheffins, 'Corporate Governance Reform: Britain as an Exporter' in Thomas Clarke (ed), *Corporate Governance: Critical Perspectives on Business and Management*, vol 1 (Routledge 2004).

[4] See e.g. Cally Jordan, 'Cadbury Twenty Years On' (2013) 58 *Villanova Law Review* 1; Ruth Aguilera and Alvaro Cuervo-Caruzza, 'Codes of Good Governance Worldwide: What Is the Trigger?' (2004) 25 *Organization Studies* 415.

[5] See the landmark article: Henry Hansmann and Reinier Kraakman, 'The End of History for Corporate Law' (2001) 89 *Georgetown Law Journal* 439.

[6] Michael Kort, 'Standardization of Company Law in Germany, Other EU Member States and Turkey by Corporate Governance Rules' (2008) 5 *European Company & Financial Law Review* 379; Rilka Dragneva and Antoaneta Dimitrova, 'The Politics of Demand for Law: The Case of Ukraine's Company Law Reform' (2010) 12 *European Journal of Law Reform* 297.

[7] Mark Cobley, 'UK Exports Shareholder Stewardship to the World: From Milan to Tokyo to Kuala Lumpur, the UK's Stewardship Code is Catching On Worldwide' *Financial News* (15 April 2014) <www.fnlondon.com/articles/stewardship-climbs-the-agenda-for-fund-managers-20140415> accessed 24 January 2022.

chronology of the development of stewardship codes and,[8] in part, from the capacity of the UK as a rule-generator and standard-setter in the area of corporate governance.[9] Both will be considered in this chapter by employing the method of 'content analysis'.

In this chapter, we collect information from forty-one stewardship codes (including some earlier principles) published between 1991 and 2019,[10] and systematically examine, with computational tools, whether formal diffusion of stewardship codes took place. While we find support for the diffusion story of the UK as a stewardship norm exporter, especially in former British colonies in Asia, we also find evidence of diffusion from transnational initiatives, such as the European Fund and Asset Management Association (EFAMA) and the International Corporate Governance Network (ICGN) codes, and we report some regional clusters, such as Korea–Japan. To unpack the norm diffusion dynamics, we also examine how successfully the seven principles of the UK Code 2012 have travelled around the world, and we find that the principles on escalating engagement activities and shareholder collective action travelled the least. Our findings therefore raise doubt as to the one-way view of norm diffusion by the UK as well as the one-way view of norm-reception by policy and market actors of other countries or regional and international organizations.

These findings add to the existing academic literature in the field of comparative corporate law and corporate governance, albeit by adopting a novel methodology. Our findings also have implications for future shareholder stewardship policy and for future research on applying content analysis in the field of comparative corporate governance. For example, the analysis of these codes can contribute to the wider debate about the legitimacy and effectiveness of soft law in today's global economy. From a normative perspective, it may also show how far, despite the lack of a global regulator, it is possible to direct the behaviour of institutional investors in a uniform way.

The chapter proceeds as follows. Section 30.2 will set out the scope and method of our analysis. Section 30.3 will consider precise textual patterns of diffusion, while Section 30.4 will focus on the diffusion of the seven UK stewardship principles and provide some reasons to account for this phenomenon. Section 30.5 ends with a brief summary of the main findings and an outlook on future work in this area and the challenges that remain.

30.2 SCOPE AND METHOD OF ANALYSIS

30.2.1 *Scope: Stewardship Codes across Countries*

We evaluate the text of forty-one documents that can be considered 'stewardship codes' as displayed in Table 30.1. For the purposes of this study, a stewardship code is defined as a non-binding set of principles, standards or best practices that is accompanied by recommendations and suggestions directed to institutional investors (mainly asset owners and asset managers) and in some cases to service providers or lawmakers,[11] issued by public or private bodies, and relating to the oversight role of institutional investors to create long-term value for clients and beneficiaries and promote corporate sustainability, including engagement and monitoring of investee

---

[8] The UK was the first country to introduce a stewardship code in 2010, the origins of which date back to 1991. See further Section 30.3.1.

[9] Cheffins (n 3).

[10] This chapter includes the UK Stewardship Code 2020 (see Table 30.1) as it was published on 24 October 2019 [hereinafter UK Code 2020], but not the revised Japanese Code published on 24 May 2020 or the revised Indian (IRDAI) Code published on 7 February 2020. For the last, see Varottil, Shareholder Stewardship in India, Chapter 17.

[11] This concerns the UK Code 2020 and the ICGN Global Shareholder Stewardship Principles 2016 respectively: see Table 30.1.

TABLE 30.1 *Stewardship codes around the world*

Country and year(s)	Full name of code	Drafted by
Australia (ACSI) 2018	Australian Asset Owner Stewardship Code	Australian Council of Superannuation Investors
Australia (FSC) 2017	Principles of Internal Governance and Asset Stewardship	Financial Services Council
Brazil 2016	AMEC Stewardship Code	Associação de Investidores no Mercado de Capitais
Canada 2005	Statement of Principles Regarding Member Activism	Canada Coalition for Good Corporate Governance
Canada 2010	Principles for Governance, Monitoring, Voting and Shareholder Engagement	Canada Coalition for Good Corporate Governance
Canada 2017	CCGC Stewardship Principles	Canada Coalition for Good Corporate Governance
Denmark 2016	Stewardship Code	Committee on Corporate Governance of the Danish Business Authority
EFAMA 2011	EFAMA Code for External Governance: Principles for the Exercise of Ownership Rights in Investee Companies	European Fund and Asset Management Association
EFAMA 2018	EFAMA Stewardship Code: Principles for Asset Managers' Monitoring of, Voting in, Engagement with Investee Companies	European Fund and Asset Management Association
Hong Kong 2016	Principles of Responsible Ownership	Securities and Futures Commission
ICGN 2003	ICGN Statement on Institutional Shareholder Responsibilities	International Corporate Governance Network
ICGN 2007, 2013	ICGN Statement of Principles on Institutional Shareholder Responsibilities	International Corporate Governance Network
ICGN 2016	ICGN Global Stewardship Principles	International Corporate Governance Network
India (IRDAI) 2017	Guidelines on Stewardship Code for Insurers	Insurance Regulatory and Development Authority of India (IRDAI)
India (PFRDA) 2018	Common Stewardship Code	Pension Fund Regulatory and Development Authority (PFRDA)
India (SEBI) 2019	Stewardship Code	Securities and Exchange Board of India (SEBI)
Italy 2013, 2015, 2016	Italian Stewardship Principles for the Exercise of Administrative and Voting Rights in Listed Companies	Assogestioni
Japan 2014, 2017	Principles for Responsible Institutional Investors	Council of Experts on the Stewardship Code, Financial Services Agency
Kenya 2017	Stewardship Code for Institutional Investors	Capital Markets Authority
Korea 2016	Principles on the Stewardship Responsibilities of Institutional Investors	Korea Corporate Governance Service
Malaysia 2014	Malaysian Code for Institutional Investors	Minority Shareholder Watchdog Group
Netherlands 2011	Best Practices for Engaged Share-Ownership	Eumedion
Netherlands 2018	Dutch Stewardship Code	Eumedion

TABLE 30.1 (continued)

Country and year(s)	Full name of code	Drafted by
Singapore 2016[12]	Stewardship Principles for Responsible Investors	Stewardship Asia Centre
South Africa 2011	Code for Responsible Investing in South Africa	Committee on Responsible Investing by Institutional Investors in South Africa
Switzerland 2013	Guidelines for Institutional Investors Governing the Exercising of Participation Rights in Public Limited Companies	Swiss Association of Pension Fund Providers, together with other associations
Taiwan 2016	Stewardship Principles for Institutional Investors	Taiwan Stock Exchange
Thailand 2017	Thai Securities and Exchange Commission Investment Governance Code	Securities and Exchange Commission, Thailand
UK 1991	The Responsibilities of Institutional Shareholders	Institutional Shareholders' Committee
UK 2002, 2005, 2007	The Responsibilities of Institutional Shareholders and Agents – Statement of Principles	Institutional Shareholders' Committee
UK 2009	Code on the Responsibilities of Institutional Investors	Institutional Shareholders' Committee
UK 2010, 2012, 2020	The UK Stewardship Code	Financial Reporting Council of the United Kingdom
US 2017	Stewardship Framework for Institutional Investors	Investor Stewardship Group

companies (corporate governance aspects) as well as their responsibilities towards their clients and end-beneficiaries, avoiding conflicts of interests and reporting duties (investment management aspects).[13]

Some of these documents are explicitly called 'stewardship codes', while others use substantive terms such as 'responsible ownership' or 'institutional investors' rather than 'stewardship', and/or refer to the document not as a 'code' but as 'principles' or 'guidelines'. To some extent, these differences indicate an evolutionary process from 'pure' self-regulation in terms of the degree of government/state involvement to more mandated forms of full or partial self-regulation, notably in the UK where, over time, the principles for the responsibilities of institutional investors, initially developed by the (now dissolved) Institutional Shareholders' Committee (ISC) in 1991, became more formalized as a 'stewardship code' introduced in 2010 under the auspices of the Financial Reporting Council (FRC), and further revised in 2012 and

---

[12] Note that for Singapore we do not include in our analysis the Stewardship Principles for Family Businesses (Stewardship Asia Centre, *Stewardship Principles for Family Businesses* (2018) <www.stewardshipasia.com.sg/sites/default/files/2020-09/SPFB-brochure-0913.pdf> accessed 24 January 2022) as our focus is on the ownership responsibilities of institutional investors. On those principles, see Dan W Puchniak and Samantha Tang, 'Singapore's Puzzling Embrace of Shareholder Stewardship: A Successful Secret' (2020) 53 *Vanderbilt Journal of Transnational Law* 989; and Lim and Puchniak, Can a Global Legal Misfit Be Fixed?, Chapter 28, this volume.

[13] Note, however, that the recent UK Code 2020 defines stewardship in a much broader way as 'the responsible allocation, management and oversight of capital to create long-term value for clients and beneficiaries leading to sustainable benefits for the economy, the environment and society'. On the meaning of stewardship, see Dionysia Katelouzou, *The Path to Enlightened Shareholder Stewardship* (CUP) (forthcoming).

2019.[14] Another example of this evolution can be found in the Netherlands, where the Eumedion Best Practices for Engaged Share-Ownership of 2011 turned into a Dutch Stewardship Code in 2018.[15] Here, the issuer of both documents is the same, but the change in the terminology reflects the incorporation of new stewardship obligations stemming from the revised Shareholder Rights Directive which was transposed in the Netherlands in June 2019.[16] Yet, in other instances, differences in the titles are merely of a terminological nature since some codes with different titles are, in fact, very similar in substantive terms and they all use a principles-based approach.[17] In the remainder of the chapter, we will use the term stewardship code to refer to all these documents.

Table 30.1 also contains information about the issuers of these codes. It can be seen that they range from regulatory bodies, stock exchanges and committees organized by them, to national, supranational or international investor associations, and other investor-related groups.[18] Most of these codes relate to specific countries, but we also include six transnational codes, two drafted by the EFAMA and four by the ICGN.[19] Two investor associations in Australia and three public authorities in India have published stewardship codes meant to apply to specific sectors; yet, in substance, these codes address general issues of stewardship; thus, we included them in our analysis as separate observations.

The list of countries and codes in Table 30.1 is similar to (though more comprehensive than) websites and other publications that have listed and compared stewardship codes.[20] By contrast, a table in the Corporate Governance Factbook of the Organisation for Economic Co-operation and Development (OECD) on the 'roles and responsibilities of investors' covers more countries than Table 30.1.[21] However, for some of these countries, this refers to binding laws, which do not fall under the scope of this chapter. Some of the non-binding instruments mentioned by the OECD are predominantly about the investment management relationship between institutional investors and their clients – not their stewardship position as shareholders of companies. Finally, we exclude countries for which a stewardship code is not available in English,[22] given that our method – to be explained in the following – relies on textual measures of similarity.

---

[14] See further Financial Reporting Council, 'UK Stewardship Code' <www.frc.org.uk/investors/uk-stewardship-code> accessed 24 January 2022.

[15] See Van der Elst and Lafarre, Shareholder Stewardship in the Netherlands, Chapter 4 for details.

[16] Eumedion, 'Institutional Investors Establish the First Edition of a Dutch Stewardship Code' (18 September 2017) <https://en.eumedion.nl/clientdata/217/media/clientimages/2017-09-press-notice-draft-stewardship-code.pdf> accessed 24 January 2022.

[17] For instance, the UK 2012 Code and the Malaysian 2014 Code are very similar, even though only the former uses the phrase 'stewardship' in its title. Also, the EFAMA and the Italian codes (of any year) are similar, but only the former uses the term 'code'. For the similarity measures, see Section 30.3.2.

[18] See further Section 30.4.2, suggesting categories of 'private' and 'public' issuers.

[19] The UN Principles for Responsible Investment (PRI) <www.unpri.org> accessed 24 January 2022, also relate to some of the issues addressed in stewardship codes. However, as those principles have a narrower focus, we exclude them in this chapter (also having established that they overlap less than 1% with any of the forty-one codes, applying the method described in Section 30.3.2).

[20] European Corporate Governance Institute (ECGI), 'Stewardship Codes' <https://ecgi.global/content/codes-stewardship> accessed 24 January 2022; FCLTGlobal, 'Interactive Portal to Global Stewardship Codes' <www.fcltglobal.org/interactive-portal-to-global-stewardship-codes/> accessed 24 January 2022; Alice Klettner, 'The Impact of Stewardship Codes on Corporate Governance and Sustainability' (2017) 23 *New Zealand Business Law Quarterly* 259.

[21] OECD, 'Corporate Governance Factbook 2021' (2021) 124–33 <www.oecd.org/corporate/Corporate-Governance-Factbook.pdf> accessed 24 January 2022.

[22] Notably this applies to the Norwegian Recommendation 2019: Verdipapirfondenes Forening, 'Bransjeanbefaling for medlemmene i Verdipapirfondenes forening: Utøvelse av eierskap [Industry Recommendations for the Members of the Norwegian Fund and Asset Management Association: Exercise of Ownership Rights]' (1 January 2020) <https://vff.no/storage/Bransjeanbefaling-ut%C3%B8velse-av-eierskap-januar-2020.pdf> accessed 24 January 2022.

30.2.2 Method: Content Analysis in Social Sciences and Law

The method of 'content analysis' is frequently used across the social sciences. In a nutshell, it refers to the analysis of the 'informational contents of textual data' employing tools that are 'objective, systematic, and quantitative'.[23] The tools range from simple ones, such as counting the number of words, to complex forms of readability and sentiment analysis via computational methods. The main advantage of content analysis is that it can provide quantitative measures of comparisons for qualitative information. For example, in political science a frequent example of content analysis provides measurements of the substantive orientation of documents in terms of left–right-wing orientation.[24]

As legal rules are typically based on a particular text (legislation, case law, contracts, etc.), it is possible to use content analysis also in legal scholarship.[25] Yet, examples are rare: there is some research that employs content analysis for court decisions – notably in the US, for example, to map the political orientation of the opinions of the justices of the US Supreme Court.[26] Following a growing trend of quantitative research in comparative constitutional law, there are also some examples of research on constitutional texts using content analysis.[27]

In the present case, the raw material of our analysis is the forty-one stewardship codes of Table 30.1. In this regard, some limitations of the application of content analysis need to be acknowledged. First, as this analysis can consider only existing codes, it is not possible to answer the question of why some large economies, such as Germany and China, do not have such a code (yet).[28] Second, a textual analysis of stewardship codes does not consider the application of the codes in practice; thus, for example, our findings can analyze whether and how the Kenyan code is similar to other codes, but not why Kenyan institutional investors have not subscribed to the

---

On this, see Mähönen, Sjåfjell and Mee, Stewardship Norwegian-Style, Chapter 8. For codes included in this chapter that are also available in other languages, see Section 30.4.2.

[23] Philipp Mayring, 'Qualitative Content Analysis' (2000) 1 *Forum: Qualitative Social Research* <www.qualitative-research.net/index.php/fqs/article/view/1089/2385> accessed 24 January 2022; Stanley Baran, *Introduction to Mass Communication* (2nd edn, McGraw-Hill 2002) 410.

[24] For an example, see The Manifesto Project, 'Project Description' <https://manifesto-project.wzb.eu/> accessed 24 January 2022. See also Justin Grimmer and Brandon M Stewart, 'Text as Data: The Promise and Pitfalls of Automatic Content Analysis Methods for Political Texts' (2013) 21 *Political Analysis* 267.

[25] For general discussion, see Mark A Hall and Ronald F Wright, 'Systematic Content Analysis of Judicial Opinions' (2008) 96 *California Law Review* 63; Maryam Salehijam, 'The Value of Systematic Content Analysis in Legal Research' (2018) 23 *Tilburg Law Review* 34; Wolfgang Alschner, Joost Pauwelyn and Sergio Puig, 'The Data-Driven Future of International Economic Law' (2017) 20 *Journal of International Economic Law* 217.

[26] See e.g. Martin-Quinn Scores, 'Project Description' <https://mqscores.lsa.umich.edu> accessed 24 January 2022; Keith Carlson, Michael A Livermore and Daniel Rockmore, 'A Quantitative Analysis of Writing Style on the U.S. Supreme Court' (2016) 93 *Washington University Law Review* 1461. For two European examples, see Jens Frankenreiter, 'Writing Style and Legal Traditions' in Michael A Livermore and Daniel N Rockmore (eds), *Law as Data: Computation, Text, and the Future of Legal Analysis* (Santa Fe Institute Press 2019); Kody Moodley, Pedro V Hernandez Serrano, Gijs van Dijck and Michel Dumontier, 'Similarity and Relevance of Court Decisions: A Computational Study on CJEU Cases' in Michał Araszkiewicz and Víctor Rodríguez-Doncel (eds), *Legal Knowledge and Information Systems*, vol 322 (IOS Press 2019).

[27] See e.g. David S Law, 'Constitutional Archetypes' (2016) 95 *Texas Law Review* 153; David S Law, 'Constitutional Dialects: The Language of Transnational Legal Orders' in Gregory Shaffer, Tom Ginsburg and Terence C Halliday (eds), *Constitution-Making and Transnational Legal Order* (CUP 2019); Tom Ginsburg, 'Constitutional Specificity, Unwritten Understandings and Constitutional Agreement' in András Sajó and Renáta Uitz (eds), *Constitutional Topography: Values and Constitutions* (Eleven International 2010); András Jakab, Arthur Dyevre and Giulio Itzcovich, 'Conclusion' in András Jakab, Arthur Dyevre and Giulio Itzcovich (eds), *Comparative Constitutional Reasoning* (CUP 2017).

[28] For possible reasons, see Ringe, Stewardship and Shareholder Engagement in Germany, Chapter 9 and Puchniak and Lin, Institutional Investors in China, Chapter 18. Yet, in some countries elements of stewardship have been included in the corporate governance principles. See also Katelouzou and Puchniak, Global Shareholder Stewardship, Chapter 1 (elaborating the complementarity between stewardship codes and corporate governance codes).

code.[29] Third, the use of content analysis is unable to consider subtle nuances of the text (also noting that we rely on the English text for all codes, even for non-English-speaking countries). Thus, given these limitations, we do not claim that this method is superior to more conventional tools of legal analysis; however, as we show in the following, it can be a useful tool to uncover textual patterns in a systematic way.

30.2.3 Concepts: Legal Transplants and Diffusion

The analysis provided in this chapter is inspired by and contributes to core concepts of comparative law, in particular 'legal transplants' and 'diffusion', as well as the broader theme of 'legal families' and other taxonomies of legal systems.[30] The traditional focus of the literature on legal transplants is that norms of a particular piece of legislation are deliberately copied with minor modifications.[31] However, recent discussions have broadened the scope of discussion as far as both the object of the transplant and the procedure for the transfer are concerned: thus, transplants may concern not only the positive law but, for example, also case law or – as in the present case – non-binding codes.[32] It is also said that the process leading to a transplant may be by means not of simply copying the rules but of a general legal and cultural influence.[33]

This latter notion of a broader foreign influence often uses other terms than 'legal transplant', for example referring to 'legal circulation', 'cross-fertilization', 'migration' or 'diffusion'.[34] Beyond comparative law, social scientists often also use the notion of diffusion, for example in the innovation literature and in the fields of political science, public administration and organizational studies.[35] It has been suggested that legal research should follow this terminology.[36] Findings from these other disciplines can also be relevant for law; for example, research by political scientists and sociologists examines whether policy diffusion is a result of 'social construction, coercion, competition, or learning'.[37] A recent article on corporate governance codes also phrases their evolution as the 'diffusion of regulatory innovations', finding, for example, that certain models diffuse because standard-setters aim to signal that they conform to international benchmarks, but possibly also because they are motivated by efficiency considerations.[38]

This chapter therefore uses the term diffusion as the main conceptual framework. As regards the types of 'diffusion', it focuses only on 'formal' diffusion and considers how far textual characteristics have diffused between stewardship codes. Thus, our systematic analysis does

---

[29] See Ouko, Stewardship Code in Kenya, Chapter 23.
[30] For these categories, see further Section 30.4.2.
[31] For such cases, see e.g. Helen Xanthaki, 'Legal Transplants in Legislation: Defusing the Trap' (2008) 57 *International & Comparative Law Quarterly* 659. For the history of legal transplants, see John W Cairns, 'Watson, Walton, and the History of Legal Transplants' (2013) 41 *Georgia Journal of International & Comparative Law* 637.
[32] Though some stewardship codes include 'comply or explain' or other more coercive requirements; see Section 30.4.2.
[33] See Mathias Siems, *Comparative Law* (3rd edn, CUP 2022) 288–9.
[34] For the different terms, see e.g. Vlad F Perju, 'Constitutional Transplants, Borrowing, and Migrations' in Michel Rosenfeld and András Sajó (eds), *The Oxford Handbook of Comparative Constitutional Law* (OUP 2012).
[35] For example, Everett M Rogers, *Diffusion of Innovations* (5th edn, Free Press 2003); Erin R Graham, Charles R Shipan and Craig Volden, 'The Diffusion of Policy Diffusion Research in Political Science' (2013) 43 *British Journal of Political Science* 673.
[36] William Twining, 'Social Science and Diffusion of Law' (2005) 32 *Journal of Law and Society* 203; William Twining, 'Diffusion of Law: A Global Perspective' (2004) 36 *Journal of Legal Pluralism and Unofficial Law* 1.
[37] Frank Dobbin, Beth Simmons and Geoffrey Garrett, 'The Global Diffusion of Public Policies: Social Construction, Coercion, Competition, or Learning?' (2007) 33 *Annual Review of Sociology* 449.
[38] Carsten Gerner-Beuerle, 'Diffusion of Regulatory Innovations: The Case of Corporate Governance Codes' (2017) 13 *Journal of Institutional Economics* 271.

not imply that any such rules operate in a functionally identical way. Indeed, some codes that are formally similar function differently in practice, which is the phenomenon that has been coined 'faux convergence', and observed in the case of stewardship codes.[39]

30.3 EVIDENCE OF STEWARDSHIP DIFFUSION

30.3.1 *The Shareholder Stewardship Movement and Citation Patterns*

The term 'stewardship' to refer to the corporate governance role of institutional shareholders was used for the first time by the UK's Institutional Shareholders' Committee Code of 2009.[40] In the academic literature, however, the same term can be found much earlier in the context of the stewardship theory of management, an alternative of the agency theory, which defines situations in which managers act as stewards in alignment with the objectives of their shareholder-principals.[41] Inherent in the term stewardship is the notion of accountability: accountability of managers in the context of the managerial stewardship theory, and accountability of institutional shareholders in the context of shareholder stewardship.[42]

Shareholder stewardship was formalized in the UK Stewardship Code introduced by the FRC in 2010. However, stewardship traces can be found much earlier in the UK in the early 1990s, albeit using different nomenclature. In 1991 (one year before the landmark Cadbury Report), the ISC, a private body comprising four major institutional shareholder associations (insurance companies, pension funds, trusts and asset managers) published a statement of best practices on the responsibilities of institutional shareholders.[43] Although this ISC statement (along with its 2002, 2005 and 2007 versions) cannot be considered as thorough as subsequent stewardship codes, it is nonetheless important in the evolution of stewardship as it was the first document to define the responsibilities of institutional shareholders to use their influence as owners to ensure that the companies in which they have invested adopt good corporate governance standards. Historically, therefore, the UK was clearly the forerunner in the development of stewardship responsibilities for institutional shareholders.

To further understand the evolution of stewardship codes, Figure 30.1 distinguishes between preliminary stewardship initiatives and stewardship codes (in a narrow sense). A preliminary initiative is defined as a set of principles, standards or best practices relating to the stewardship role of institutional investors, but which is limited in its scope (for instance, it applies to a specific group of institutional investors), in its content (for instance, it refers only to voting rights) or in its drafting style (for instance, it is drafted as a policy statement or has no guidance even though it adopts a principles-based approach). This distinction is important for countries with more than one document referring to institutional shareholders' responsibilities, such as the UK, Canada and the Netherlands. All three countries adopted a stewardship code after implementing what can be termed as first-generation principles. But some countries such as India, Switzerland and

---

[39] Gen Goto, Alan K Koh and Dan W Puchniak, 'Diversity of Shareholder Stewardship in Asia: Faux Convergence' (2020) 53 *Vanderbilt Journal of Transnational Law* 829. See also Katelouzou and Puchniak, Global Shareholder Stewardship, Chapter 1. Likewise, there may be cases where formally different rules have a functionally similar effect; for such a distinction in the 'convergence' literature, see e.g. Siems (n 33) 289–90.

[40] UK 2009 (see Table 30.1).

[41] For the managerial stewardship theory, see James H Davis, F David Schoorman and Lex Donaldson 'Toward a Stewardship Theory of Management' (1997) 22 *Academy of Management Review* 20.

[42] For this distinction, see Katelouzou (n 12).

[43] For the origins of stewardship, see ibid.

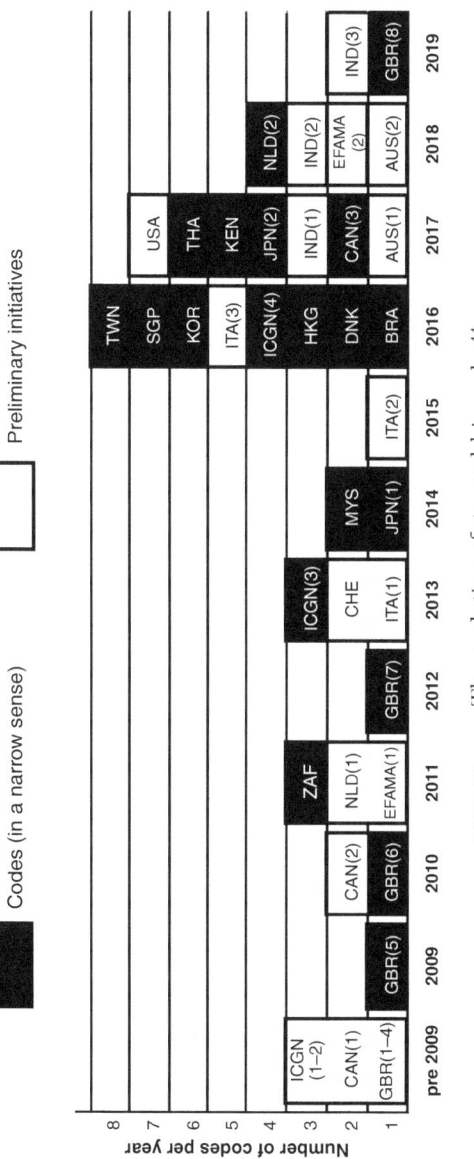

FIGURE 30.1 'The evolution of stewardship codes[44]

[44] Abbreviations based on UN standard. John Moen, 'Complete List of Country & Dialing Codes' (*WorldAtlas*, 2018) <www.worldatlas.com/aatlas/ctycodes.htm> accessed 24 January 2022.

the US have still to adopt what can be characterized as a comprehensive stewardship code. In the following, we treat all forty-one documents as stewardship codes (in a wider sense).

From the timeline, shown in Figure 30.1, it is evident that the development and adoption of stewardship norms is a recent phenomenon. Only a few counties[45] as well the ICGN adopted codes up to 2009. Then, between 2010 and 2015, eight countries addressed shareholder stewardship through the adoption of stewardship codes or preliminary initiatives. Over the same period the UK revised its code, while EFAMA adopted a code 'on external governance' to provide principles and best practice for asset managers in engaging with their investee companies. The period between 2016 and 2017 marked a spike in the evolution of stewardship codes with eleven more countries adopting stewardship codes or similar initiatives (whereas in 2018 and 2019 we see only new codes in countries that already had such codes previously[46]).

There may be various interrelated reasons explaining these developments. In the UK, for instance, the 2010 Code was adopted as a reaction to the financial crisis of 2007–08,[47] while in other countries different claims have been put forward. In Japan, shareholder stewardship was part of a broader government programme of economic liberalization and sound corporate governance.[48] In Kenya, the stewardship code, together with the preceding corporate governance code, was part of efforts to attract local and foreign investments and promote the country as the premier financial centre in central/east Africa.[49] The Indian codes are partly linked to the fragmented efforts to promote shareholder activism in India,[50] while other countries, such as Singapore, adopted stewardship codes to legitimize themselves as good standard promoters.[51] The presence of foreign institutional investors, the need to prevent the loss of investment incurred by ultimate beneficiaries, and the increasing calls for sustainability were also among the factors driving the adoption of stewardship codes.[52] Thus, using some of the terminology of the prior diffusion literature,[53] the diffusion of stewardship codes is owing to some 'shared social constructs' but also forms of 'coercion' and 'competition' as far as issuers follow the 'leader' of the stewardship movement (i.e. the UK) or one of the international codes.

It is also possible to examine the citation patterns of the forty-one stewardship codes vis-à-vis one another in order to identify traces of formal diffusion. Ten codes make specific references to foreign codes in their preambles, but in only two of them is there an explicit, visible influence by another code. All the Italian codes explicitly mention the EFAMA code as a point of reference,[54] while the Thai Code acknowledges that it 'derives from the principles set out in the UK Stewardship Code'.[55] The UK Code is also cited as a point of reference by the Danish

---

[45] Apart from those indicated in Figure 30.1, Norway had its first preliminary stewardship initiative ('Recommendation') issued in 2003 (see text in n 22).
[46] Here too, apart from the countries indicated in Figure 30.1, it concerns Norway with the revised Norwegian Recommendation 2019 (see also n 22).
[47] See e.g. Davies, The UK Stewardship Code 2010–2020, Chapter 2.
[48] See Gen Goto, 'The Logic and Limits of Stewardship Codes: The Case of Japan' (2018) 15 *Berkeley Business Law Journal* 365; and Goto, Japanese Stewardship Code, Chapter 10, this volume.
[49] See Ouko, Stewardship Code in Kenya, Chapter 23.
[50] See Varottil, Shareholder Stewardship in India, Chapter 17.
[51] See Puchniak and Tang, Singapore's Embrace of Shareholder Stewardship, Chapter 14.
[52] See e.g. Iris H-Y Chiu and Dionysia Katelouzou, 'From Shareholder Stewardship to Shareholder Duties: Is the Time Ripe?' in Hanne S Birkmose (ed), *Shareholders' Duties* (Kluwer Law International 2017) 131; and Katelouzou and Klettner, Sustainable Finance and Stewardship, Chapter 26, this volume.
[53] See Section 30.2.3.
[54] For example, Italy 2016 (see Table 30.1) 11: 'The adopted Principles are inspired by those contained in the EFAMA Code for External Governance.' See also Strampelli, Institutional Investor Stewardship in Italian Corporate Governance, Chapter 6, this volume.
[55] Thailand 2017 (see Table 30.1) 32.

Code,[56] the 2013 ICGN Code[57] and the Dutch 2011 Code which also refers to transnational developments, including the EFAMA and ICGN codes.[58] Generic references to other codes (but with no evidence of a direct influence) are also found in the Swiss[59] and Brazilian[60] codes as well as the Australian 2017 Code developed by the Financial Services Council (FSC).[61]

Thus, explicit comparative citation is, as expected, limited in the stewardship codes. But the absence of citation of foreign codes does not necessarily reflect the extent of foreign stewardship codes' influence, which may be unacknowledged in the final codes or to which reference may be made at other preparatory stages of the drafting process.[62] To better assess the formal diffusion of stewardship, we now examine the language similarities among the codes.

30.3.2 Measurement of Identical Strings of Words

In a recent article, Allee and Elsig asked whether 'the contents of international treaties [are] copied and pasted'. Specifically, they analyze preferential trade agreements, finding similarities of more than 90%.[63] In the present case, we pose a similar question for the contents of stewardship codes; yet, we also consider how far similar word patterns may be owing to deliberate copying or at least a sign of a more indirect influence.

In order to get a realistic picture of how far the language of stewardship codes overlaps, the texts of these codes have to be edited and formatted in a way that makes them comparable. Yet, this should not interfere with the substance of the texts, nor should it distort the writing style of the codes. Therefore, in this part of the analysis, we did not 'stem' words,[64] or replace abbreviations or other idiosyncrasies of the codes.[65]

---

[56] Denmark 2016 (see Table 30.1) 3: '... the Committee has sought to ensure that the Code is in line with leading foreign stewardship principles, notably including The UK Stewardship Code'.

[57] ICGN 2013 (see Table 30.1) 21 (endorsing the definition of 'stewardship' of the UK Code). The prior 2007 Code included an Annex with practical examples from national and international markets referring to the Canadian and UK codes.

[58] Netherlands 2011 (see Table 30.1) 2: 'The best practices are also in line to the greatest possible extent with international guidelines on the behaviour required of institutional investors, such as the UK Stewardship Code, the Statement of Principles on Institutional Shareholder Responsibilities from the International Corporate Governance Network (ICGN), the United Nations Principles for Responsible Investment (UNPRI) and the Code for External Governance of the European Fund and Asset Management Association (EFAMA).' Both the EFAMA and the UK codes are also mentioned in the Norwegian Recommendation 2019 (see n 22).

[59] Switzerland 2013 (see Table 30.1) 12: 'In England, a document entitled "UK Stewardship Code" was published in July 2010 which formulates a specific code of conduct for institutional investors in the form of seven principles. Similar codes are currently in preparation in various other countries.'

[60] Brazil 2016 (see Table 30.1) 2: 'As in corporate governance codes that have proliferated all over the world after the 2001 crisis (more than 100 codes), at least 11 countries already have "stewardship / responsible investment" codes ... The UK Stewardship Code, issued by the FRC – Financial Reporting Council, was launched in September 2012 and is the most advanced document in promotion and adherence terms.'

[61] Australia (FSC) 2017 (see Table 30.1) 7: 'Stewardship codes exist in other jurisdictions including the Netherlands, Switzerland, South Africa, Singapore, Japan and across Europe as articulated in the EFAMA Code for External Governance.'

[62] For the purposes of this study, we limit ourselves to the text of the final codes and we did not consider any preparatory materials from the drafting bodies (which usually may not be publicly available).

[63] Todd Allee and Manfred Elsig, 'Are the Contents of International Treaties Copied and Pasted? Evidence from Preferential Trade Agreements' (2019) 63 *International Studies Quarterly* 603. For a similar example, see Joshua M Jansa, Eric R Hansen and Virginia H Gray, 'Copy and Paste Lawmaking: Legislative Professionalism and Policy Reinvention in the States' (2018) 47 *American Politics Research* 739.

[64] In contrast to the analysis in Section 30.4.

[65] There is only one exception: EFAMA 2011 and the Italian codes use the abbreviation 'IMCs' for 'investment management companies'; yet, as EFAMA 2018 uses the full term, we also replaced IMCs by the full term in EFAMA 2011 and the Italian codes for reasons of consistency.

However, in order to make the texts comparable, we implemented the following adjustments. First, some of the codes are published in documents which contain further information that is not specifically related to shareholder stewardship, such as general information about the drafting body. We removed such text. Second, while the core elements of the stewardship codes are typically a number of principles together with specific explanations for each of these principles,[66] some of the codes also contain preliminary or supplementary remarks. As those additional remarks also contain meaningful information, for example, referring to the purpose of the code and providing definitions, they were generally included;[67] however, we excluded forewords by the panel chair in the codes,[68] listings of the participants of the drafting panel, and bibliographies or other lists of references. Third, given this decision, we also removed footnotes which provided mere references; we retained footnotes with substantive explanations, notably in cases where a particular statement (e.g. a definition) could have also been included in the main text of a code. Fourth, some but not all of the codes include a table of contents, and some but not all of them list the principles at the beginning and then restate them with explanations later in the text. We removed such duplicates.[69] Fifth, minor formatting was applied in order to reduce the risk of 'false negatives'; for example, all spelling was changed to American English and all capital letters were replaced by small letters.[70]

Our comparison tool is the plagiarism detection software program 'WCopyfind',[71] which has been used before in empirical legal studies, notably in order to detect overlaps between court opinions in the US.[72] This program allows for pairwise comparison of documents to locate similarities in the language used. The forty-one texts of the codes were uploaded in this program with the aim of identifying identical strings. Following Allee and Elsig, we set the required length of the strings at different thresholds in order to check the robustness of the results. For the main analysis that followed, we searched for strings of four or more words. This is a slightly stricter threshold than the one used for the purposes of identifying plagiarism;[73] yet, while it is clear that students need to be given the benefit of doubt, a similar line of reasoning does not apply here. Moreover, using a lower threshold had the advantage that it was possible to compare similarities between pairs of codes where a higher threshold would merely exhibit identical 'nil results'.[74]

Using this method, for example, the codes of UK 2012 and Malaysia 2014 show an overlap of 501 words. Some of them well exceed the four- or six-word thresholds. For instance, the phrase 'signatories are encouraged to review their policy statements annually, and update them where necessary to reflect changes in actual practice. It should include contact details of an individual who can be contacted for further' is found in both codes, with the likely explanation being that

---

[66] See also Table 30.8 of the Annex on the differentiated word count of the codes.
[67] In contrast to the analysis in Section 30.4, which excludes everything not related to the principles.
[68] Namely, for Malaysia 2014 and South Africa 2011.
[69] For Australia (FSC) 2017 we also excluded a summary table found in the preliminary remarks.
[70] We also removed all bullet points while retaining numbers and punctuation marks.
[71] Available at The Plagiarism Resource Site, 'WCopyfind' <https://plagiarism.bloomfieldmedia.com/software/wcopyfind/> accessed 24 January 2022.
[72] See e.g. Paul M Collins Jr, Pamela C Corley and Jesse Hamner, 'The Influence of Amicus Curiae Briefs on US Supreme Court Opinion Content' (2015) 49 *Law & Society Review* 917; Adam Feldman, 'Counting on Quality: The Effects of Merits Brief Quality on Supreme Court Decisions' (2016) 94 *Denver University Law Review* 43. For another example, see Rachael K Hinkle, 'Into the Words: Using Statutory Text to Explore the Impact of Federal Courts on State Policy Diffusion' (2015) 59 *American Journal of Political Science* 1002.
[73] Some discuss that a 'five-word rule' may be the strictest standard; see StackExchange, 'What Exactly Is the "Five (Consecutive) Word" Plagiarism Rule?' <https://writing.stackexchange.com/questions/7546/what-exactly-is-the-five-consecutive-word-plagiarism-rule/7563> accessed 24 January 2022.
[74] As a result, we identified 776 of such pairs (i.e. 50% of the total of 40*39= 1,560 pairs of codes), while a threshold of 6 words, as used by Collins, Corley and Hamner (n 72) and Feldman (n 72), would identify only 442 pairs (i.e. 28% of the total). Allee and Elsig (n 63) and Hinkle (n 72) also use four-word strings as one their specifications.

TABLE 30.2 *Most similar pairs of codes by common strings*

Rank	Older code	Newer code	Common strings (in words)	All words of older code	All words of newer code	Overlap in older code	Overlap in newer code
1	UK 2009	EFAMA 2011	561	1392	1809	40.30%	31.01%
2	UK 2012	Malaysia 2014	501	2954	2967	16.96%	16.89%
3	ICGN 2013	Malaysia 2014	411	7228	2967	5.69%	13.85%
4	EFAMA 2011	Italy 2016	473	1809	2615	26.15%	18.09%
5	UK 2002	Canada 2005	382	1474	1136	25.92%	33.63%
6	UK 2012	Hong Kong 2016	372	2954	2232	12.59%	16.67%
7	ICGN 2016	Kenya 2017	323	5062	3735	6.38%	8.65%
8	Malaysia 2014	Thailand 2017	298	2967	3819	10.04%	7.80%
9	UK 2012	India (IRDAI) 2017	284	2954	964	9.61%	29.46%
10	Korea 2016	Japan 2017	261	3231	4637	8.08%	5.63%

Malaysia copied this phrase from the earlier UK code. Other identical strings of words are more ambiguous: for example, both have phrases such as 'should reflect the institutional' and 'how they will discharge'. A sceptic may regard such a match of words as accidental and thus possibly a 'false positive'. Yet, there could also be cases of 'false negatives', for example, where a particular phrase is used in passive voice in one code and active voice in another, thus not showing a match. Overall, the measurement of common strings of words should, therefore, be seen as a parsimonious proxy for a measurement of similarity among the codes, which also needs to be carefully interpreted.[75]

In the overall results, it is no surprise that the pairs of codes that overlap most are the ones from the same issuer: for example, Italy 2016 contains more than 90% of the text of Italy 2015; the same is the case for Japan 2017 and 2014, and for UK 2002, 2005 and 2007, the overlap is even above 98%. We also treat the Indian codes as deriving from the same issuer since SEBI, PFRDA and IRDAI are all regulatory bodies established by the Government of India; indeed, India (SEBI) 2019 and India (PFRDA) 2018 are very similar as the former includes 84% of the latter code.[76] Table 30.2 excludes these same-issuer 'top' pairs of similarities and displays only the highest ranked pair of codes of the same two issuers.[77]

The most prominent result of Table 30.2 is that, in this top-ten list, the UK is in five instances the country of the code that has influenced a code from another issuer, with three referring to the 2012 Code and one each to the 2002 and 2009 codes, respectively. In four instances a UK code impacted the stewardship codes of common-law countries (Malaysia, Canada, Hong Kong, India), but we also see diffusion to the EFAMA 2011. It is also noteworthy that the UK Code 2012 also had an influence on the Japanese Code 2017 (UK 2012–Japan 2017 follows at rank 11 of the most similar pairs[78]).

---

[75] For instance, WCopyfind can capture similarity only of language (not of ideas or arguments) and wholly different words can have the same meaning.
[76] India (IRDAI) 2017 is more distinct, overlapping not more than 22% with the other two Indian codes, yet the revised version of the IRDAI code (see n 10) will shift it closer to the other codes.
[77] For example, as the pair of UK 2009–EFAMA 2011 is ranked first, the table excluded the pairs of UK 2012–EFAMA 2011, UK 2009–EFAMA 2011, etc.
[78] Overlap of strings: 255 words; as regards UK 2012–Japan 2014 the overlap is 219 words.

As regards the overlap between other codes, our data confirm the impact of the EFAMA on the Italian codes, which has been mentioned explicitly in the latter.[79] The impact of the ICGN Code on Malaysia and Kenya is also not surprising as developing countries often pay close attention to recommendations by international bodies.[80] Table 30.2 also reveals two other highly overlapping pairs, namely Malaysia and Thailand, and Korea and Japan. This may be regarded as plausible as they refer to neighbouring countries; yet, they require some further explanations. With regard to the Thai code, our findings seem to confirm the impact of the UK Code (as stated in the Thai Code itself), given that the Malaysian Code was itself impacted by the UK Code.[81] With regard to Korea–Japan, the direction of causality may actually be the reverse (from Japan to Korea) as there has also been a considerable impact from Japan 2014 to Korea 2016.[82]

As a robustness check, we also ran WCopyfind with a higher threshold of requiring strings of six or more words. Here, the relationships among the pairs of the UK codes and EFAMA, Malaysia, Canada, Hong Kong and India retain a high number of common strings, as does the EFAMA and Italy pair.[83] For ICGN and Malaysia–Kenya, the numbers drop by a bit more than half.[84] The largest reduction in the number of overlapping strings shows for the pairs of Malaysia–Kenya and Korea–Japan,[85] thus confirming the cautious interpretation of the previous paragraph.

The codes examined here have different sizes,[86] which is bound to affect the extent of overlaps between pairs of code. Thus, Table 30.2 includes information about the percentage of common words as regards each of the two codes of each of the pairs. As expected, smaller codes have a larger overlap in terms of percentages compared to the overlap of larger codes (see e.g. the UK–India pair). Both percentages, however, need to be considered in interpreting the data. While it is clear that any influence will go in the direction of the older to the newer code, the overlap in the older code is also relevant: for example, assume that a newer code fully copied an older code while also adding further provisions, making this newer code ten times larger than the older code. Here, the overlap in the newer code is 10% – and thus apparently quite low; yet, by adding the information that the overlap in the older code is 100%, it is possible to recognize this complete copying of the older code.

30.3.3 Network and Cluster Analysis Based on Common Strings of Words

The full information about the common strings of words forms a matrix displaying the overlap of each of the forty-one codes with the other codes. Such a matrix can be visualized as a network and can be used for cluster analysis.[87] In this section we focus on the percentages of common

---

[79] See Section 30.3.1.
[80] On the impact of other international codes, such as the OECD Principles of Corporate Governance, on developing countries, see e.g. Mathias Siems and Oscar Alvarez-Macotela, 'The G20/OECD Principles of Corporate Governance 2015: A Critical Assessment of Their Operation and Impact' (2015) *Journal of Business Law* 310.
[81] The UK 2012–Thailand 2017 overlap is also fairly high (176 words); this difference between Thailand–Malaysia and Thailand–UK 2012 is mainly owing to the fact that the Thai and Malay codes more frequently use the phrase 'institutional investors should ...' (38 and 31 times) than the UK code (21 times).
[82] Overlap of strings: 229 words.
[83] Overlap of strings: 512, 343, 309, 271, 249 and 259 words.
[84] Overlap of strings: 199 and 125 words.
[85] Overlap of strings: 102 and 36 words.
[86] For the size of all codes, see Table 30.8 of the Annex.
[87] This section uses the social network analysis program UCINET, available at <https://sites.google.com/site/ucinetsoftware/home> accessed 24 January 2022.

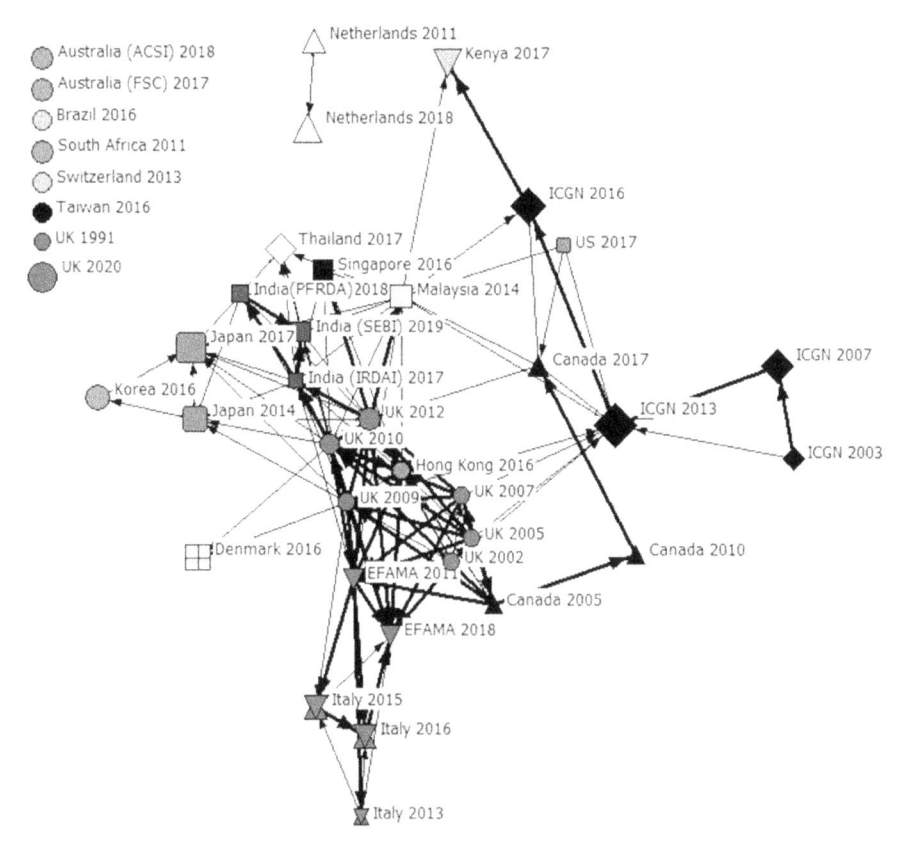

FIGURE 30.2 Network showing all >6 per cent overlaps of pairs of codes

strings per code as a measure of similarity; thus, in Figure 30.2 the codes are the 'nodes' of the network and the percentage similarities are the 'ties' between these nodes.

Figure 30.2 displays all country pairs where, at least in one direction, there is an overlap of more than 6% between the codes (see Table 30.2, applying a four-word threshold). A bold tie is used for pairs in which the 6% threshold is exceeded as regards both codes. The arrows of the ties indicate the possible diffusion from the older to the newer code. The size of each node reflects the different sizes of the codes;[88] the variations in the shapes and colours of the nodes identify all codes of the same country; and the layout of the network reflects the similarities between pairs of nodes (i.e. the position of the codes is determined by their linguistic closeness to each other).

Figure 30.2 shows that eight codes are not connected to any other code; in addition, the two Dutch codes are connected only to each other. Different reasons account for these isolates. To start with, it is no surprise that UK 1991, being a very preliminary initiative,[89] is unconnected to the other codes. It is not only its drafting style with the lack of explicit principles and guidance but also its content, with its sole focus on the corporate governance of investee companies identifying matters, such as the composition of the board, that should be a matter of concern to institutional shareholders, which isolates the early UK Code 1991 from subsequent codes. At the other extreme, the UK Code 2020, representing a significant departure from the UK Code 2012, is also an isolate. Being thirty-two pages long, the UK Code 2020 shifts the idea of stewardship in

---

[88] See Table 30.8 of the Annex.
[89] See also Section 30.3.1.

new directions not yet reflected in the other codes. For example, the UK Code 2020, with its extended focus comprising twelve principles aimed at asset managers and asset owners, and six principles aimed at service providers, broadens stewardship across all assets other than listed equity, and puts emphasis on reporting specific stewardship activities and outcomes rather than just stewardship policies.[90]

South Africa 2011 also differs in substance from most of the other codes given its strong focus on the integration of issues of environmental, social and corporate governance (ESG) into investment management,[91] a trend, however, which has become more commonplace now.[92] As for the two Australian codes, which also differ from most of the other codes, their idiosyncratic language reflects the very particular institutional and market context in which the two codes were developed and the fact that both drafting bodies (the ASCI and the FSC) already had a well-established local tradition of policy-making and governance activism to draw on.[93] Also, in issuing their codes, both the FSC and the ACSI believed that they were taking different approaches from other stewardship codes, as reflected in the language of both codes.[94]

As regards the remaining isolated countries, Brazil, the Netherlands and Taiwan have in common that their codes may have originally been written in a language other than English. Thus, it could be owing to variations of the translations into English (or possibly backward translations if some of their text was indeed translated from English) that they use a less 'mainstream' language. This finding is confirmed by the observation that two further non-English-speaking countries, Denmark and Korea, are only loosely connected with the main network. Exceptions are then the codes of Italy, Thailand and Japan which, even though they were presumably originally written in a language other than English, form part of the network of Figure 30.2. For the three Italian codes and the Thai one, this may be attributed to the fact that they all explicitly refer to foreign models in their codes.[95] As for the similarity between the Japanese codes and the UK ones, this should not be surprising given that Japan has a long tradition of copying business-law rules from common-law countries.[96] The high similarity between the two countries' codes is also explained by the fact that the first version of the Japanese Code was created by way of directly translating the UK Code 2012 into Japanese for consideration by the Council of Experts.[97]

The main part of the network displays the UK Code 2012 at the centre, surrounded by other English-speaking (or common-law) countries, in particular from Asia (i.e. Malaysia, Hong Kong, Singapore and India, which all enacted codes in the subsequent years). The US 2017, Kenya 2017 and Canada 2010 and 2017 codes are, however, less closely connected with this

---

[90] See Katelouzou and Micheler, The Market for Stewardship and the Role of the Government, Chapter 3.
[91] See further Locke, Encouraging Sustainable Investment in South Africa, Chapter 22, elaborating that CRISA was more informed by the UN PRI, mainly owing to the impact of the South African PRI Network. While the textual similarity between UN PRI and CRISA is less than 1% (see also n 19), an analysis of marker terms for 'responsible ownership', to be published in a companion paper, finds that these terms are indeed frequently used in the South African code.
[92] See Katelouzou and Klettner, Sustainable Finance and Stewardship, Chapter 26.
[93] See Bowley and Hill, Stewardship and Collective Action, Chapter 19.
[94] According to Australia (ASCI) 2018 (see Table 30.1) 4: 'Stewardship codes exist in numerous markets in the world, including a fund manager stewardship code in Australia. However, this is the first code to focus on the stewardship activities of Australian asset owners.' Also, Australia (FSC) 2017 (see Table 30.1) 7 states: 'unlike other stewardship codes which focus on asset stewardship and conflicts of interest, the FSC standard takes a broader view and also includes the internal governance of the asset manager.'
[95] See Section 30.3.1.
[96] For the similarity, see n 78 and the corresponding text. For transplants in Japanese business law, see e.g. Hideki Kanda and Curtis J Milhaupt, 'Re-examining Legal Transplants: The Director's Fiduciary Duty in Japanese Corporate Law' (2003) 51 The American Journal of Comparative Law 887.
[97] See Goto, Japanese Stewardship Code, Chapter 10, Section 10.1.

core.[98] Thus, it seems that within the group of English-speaking countries, trends for stewardship diffusion are particularly strong in Asia, but less so in other parts of the world (also noting again the outlier positions of Australia and South Africa).

Network analysis provides various tools to identify community structures.[99] Some of them rely on binary data, but for a valued network it is preferable to use tools that consider the full information of the dataset. Using such a method also has the advantage that it does not rely on a particular cut-off point (such as 6% in the network of Figure 30.1). The method applied here calculates 'hierarchical clusters'. This refers to a procedure that divides data into subgroups 'by successively increasing the tolerated level of within-cluster dissimilarity – (s)tarting with the lowest level of aggregation, where only identical observations are clustered together, observations and clusters are merged until the sample is allocated into two groups that constitute the top of the hierarchy'.[100]

Specifically, Figure 30.3 uses hierarchical clustering of the current versions of the stewardship codes enacted by different issuers and in force in December 2019.[101] The previous versions of the codes were excluded since they are often very similar to current versions by the same issuer (and

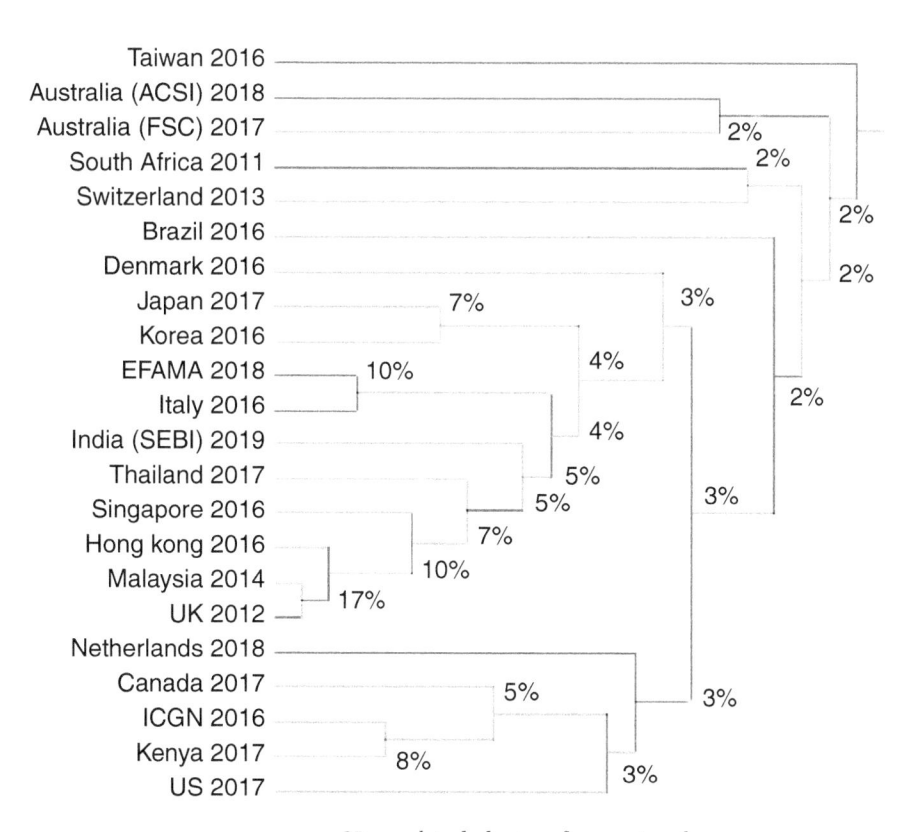

FIGURE 30.3 Hierarchical cluster of current codes

---

[98] The Canada 2005 code, however, is still fairly close to the UK 2002 code. See also Table 30.2.
[99] See e.g. Anuška Ferligoj, Patrick Doreian and Vladimir Batagelj, 'Positions and Roles' in John Scott and Peter J Carrington (eds), *The SAGE Handbook of Social Network Analysis* (SAGE 2011); David Knoke and Song Yang, *Social Network Analysis* (2nd edn, SAGE 2008).
[100] Michael Graff, 'Law and Finance: Common-Law and Civil Law Countries Compared – An Empirical Critique' (2008) 75 *Economica* 60, 72.
[101] Thus, for the UK, we use UK 2012, not UK 2020. For India, we use the most recent code, India (SEBI) 2019. See also the text accompanying n 77.

therefore would dominate the cluster analysis and make all other possible clusters disappear). Thus, a limitation of this figure, compared to the network, is that it does not include information about the older codes that had been more similar to the other codes: for example, in Figure 30.2 (as well as Table 30.2), it can be seen that EFAMA 2011 and India (IRDAI) 2017 had been closer to the UK codes than the more recent EFAMA and India codes; thus, here we observe a divergence over time from the UK 2012 model.

As with the network, the cluster analysis uses the percentages of common strings (in order not to reward or penalize according to the size of the codes). Yet, hierarchical clustering requires a symmetric matrix: for this reason, the data have been symmetrized averaging both sides of the matrix. These numbers showing the degree of similarity have then also been added to Figure 30.3: for example, it can be seen that Malaysia 2014 and UK 2012 are 17% similar, this being the average of the percentage numbers reported in Table 30.2.

In substance, the clusters based on low similarities of 3% or less should best be disregarded. Considering the codes only connected through such low-ranked scores, this includes all the isolated nodes of the network of Figure 30.2. Figure 30.3 shows that the main clusters are the ones of the UK and the Asian common-law countries (Malaysia, Hong Kong and Singapore), thus here too confirming the network of Figure 30.2. This is then followed by Thailand 2017, and then subsequently India (SEBI) 2019, EFAMA 2018 and Italy 2016 (which also form a cluster), and then Japan 2017 and Korea 2016 (also a separate cluster).

A further way of analyzing the position of codes within the network is to examine the 'coreness' of each node,[102] using the same information about current codes as in the cluster analysis performed already. Here, the UK 2012 has the highest value of coreness, followed by Malaysia 2014, Hong Kong 2016, EFAMA 2018 and Thailand 2017. At the other end, or at the periphery of the network, are South Africa 2011, Brazil 2016, Switzerland 2013, Taiwan 2016 and Australia (FSC) 2017.[103]

Overall, both the cluster analysis and the coreness of each node point again at the central position of the UK Code 2012 in the stewardship network, at the same time as they show that stewardship diffusion took place among common-law Asian countries. In addition, it confirms the similarities between Italy and EFAMA and between Korea and Japan. To further understand the diffusion processes of stewardship, we now turn to analyze the substantive orientation of the principles of the codes.

30.4 DIFFUSION OF UK-STYLE STEWARDSHIP PRINCIPLES

30.4.1 *The Principles of the UK 2012 Code across the World*

One of the key findings of our content analysis so far has been the coreness of the UK Code 2012 in the stewardship network and the language similarities between the UK Code 2012 and the codes of Asian common-law countries. To further test the impact of the UK Code 2012 on the text of other codes, we used a set of words that are good 'markers' for each of the seven principles of this code (see Table 30.3) and then counted how often these words are mentioned in each of the forty-one codes. The choice to focus on the seven principles of the UK Code 2012 is reflective of

---

[102] For the precise technical definition, see Analytictech, 'Network > Core/Periphery > Continuous' <www.analytictech.com/ucinet/help/1g11dj.htm> accessed 24 January 2022.

[103] The precise numbers for the 'coreness' of these countries are UK 2012: 0.454; Malaysia 2014: 0.397; Hong Kong 2016: 0.272; EFAMA 2018: 0.249; Thailand 2017: 0.246; and then South Africa 2011: 0.112; Brazil 2016: 0.110; Switzerland 2013: 0.106; Taiwan 2016: 0.082; Australia (FSC) 2017: 0.076.

TABLE 30.3 *'Marker' words for the principles of the UK Code 2012*

Principle	Word
1 Institutional investors should publicly disclose their policy on how they will discharge their stewardship responsibilities.	*disclos*
2 Institutional investors should have a robust policy on managing conflicts of interest in relation to stewardship which should be publicly disclosed.	*conflict*
3 Institutional investors should monitor their investee companies.	*monitor*
4 Institutional investor should establish clear guidelines on when and how they will escalate their stewardship activities.	*escal*
5 Institutional investors should be willing to act collectively with other investors where appropriate.	*collect*
6 Institutional investors should have a clear policy on voting and disclosure of voting activity.	*vote*
7 Institutional investors should report periodically on their stewardship and voting activities.	*report*

the UK-inspired principles-based approach to corporate governance and stewardship that motivated many to talk about the 'the seven magic stewardship principles'.[104]

To calculate the frequencies, we first removed all stop-words and decomposed all the words in the corpus into their roots,[105] by applying Porter's stemming method.[106] The analysis presented in Section 30.3 included the recitals and some other preliminary information; by contrast, the present analysis focuses only on the principles-related text of the codes, that is, the core principles of each code and the accompanying text (guidance, recommendations or related commentary).[107]

The most common marker word in the UK Code 2012 is *discl* (14 times), followed by *vote* (11 times), while the least common one is *escal* (2 times). Looking at all the codes, *vote* is the most common word marker (679 times) followed by *discl* (369 times), while *escal* is the least common (61 times). To some extent, such differences may reflect that some of the marker words (such as *vote*) are of a more general nature while others are more specific. Yet, we suggest that they reflect differences in substance. Voting is considered an essential aspect of stewardship activities and the exercise of voting rights is a key expression of shareholders' rights and recognition of shareholders' responsibilities. On the other hand, while Principle 4 of the UK Code 2012 asks that the investors establish clear processes on escalating their stewardship activities, especially when there are concerns about risks to long-term value, escalating engagement (for instance, through voting against managerial resolutions, requesting a general meeting, or proposing changes to board membership) is not advocated by seventeen other codes which adopt a more consensus-style language.

Figure 30.4 presents the results in detail in chronological order. A common feature of all stewardship codes is that investors are expected to disclose information about their stewardship policy along with other policies (including conflicts of interests and voting). Out of the forty-one codes examined, India (SEBI) 2019, Australia (ACSI) 2018 and UK 2012 are the three codes that refer most frequently to disclosure obligations, while the Malaysian, Taiwanese and the first two Indian (IRDAI 2017 and PFRDA 2018) codes also have very close frequencies to the UK Code 2012, adding more evidence to the earlier Asian common-law cluster.[108] Interestingly, earlier stewardship initiatives,

---

[104] Dionysia Katelouzou and Henning Jacobsen, 'Global Shareholder Stewardship Conference' (Conference Report, September 2019) <www.kcl.ac.uk/law/assets/docs/global-shareholder-stewardship-conference-final-report.pdf> accessed 24 January 2022.
[105] For instance, 'disclosure' and 'disclose' are collapsed to the same word 'disclos' for frequency counting.
[106] Martin F Porter, 'An Algorithm for Suffix Stripping' (1980) 14 *Program: Electronic Library and Information Systems* 130.
[107] See also Table 30.8 of the Annex on the word count of the codes according to this measure.
[108] See Section 30.3.3.

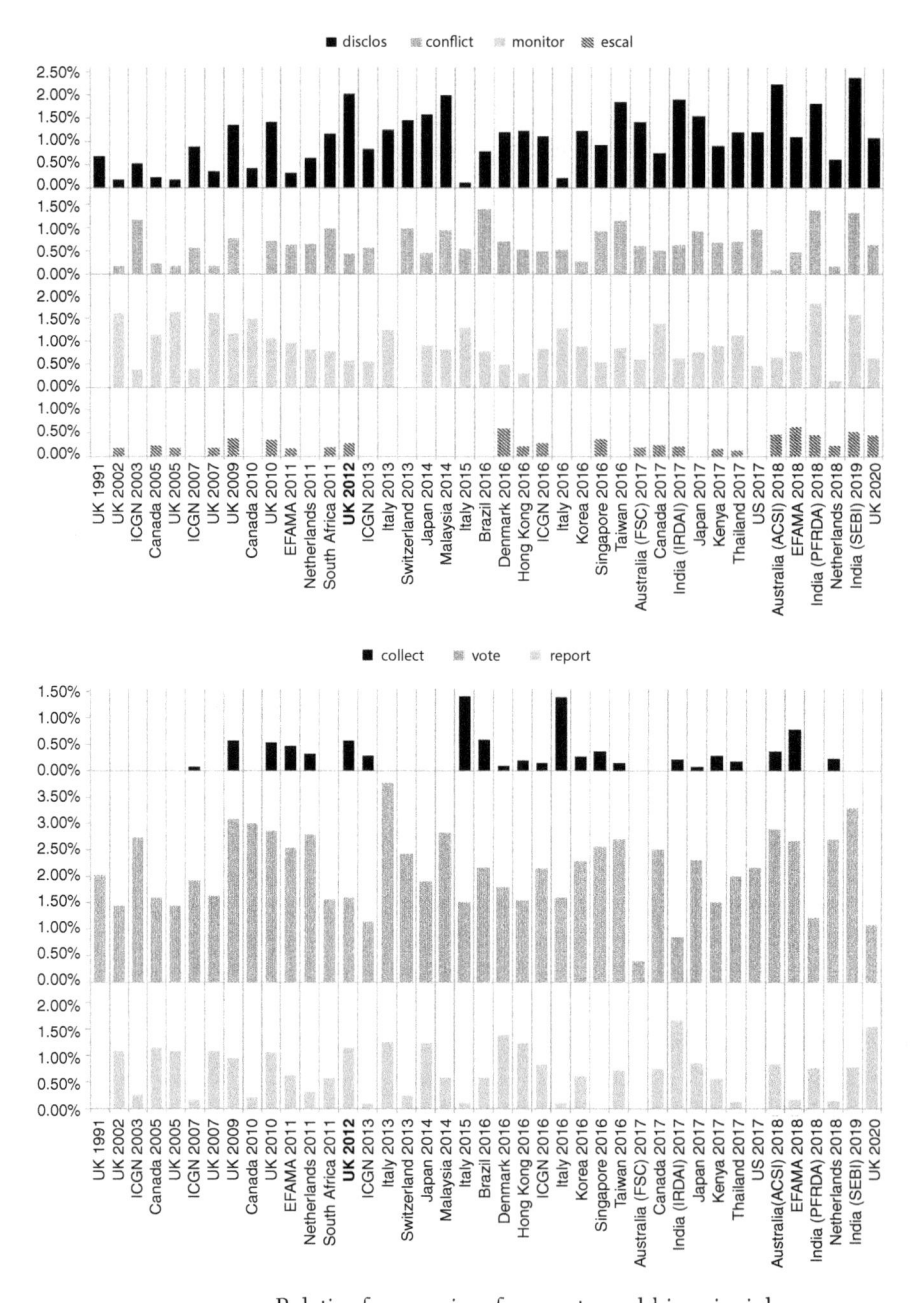

FIGURE 30.4 Relative frequencies of seven stewardship principles

including the first four versions of the UK Code, the two first Canadian codes, EFAMA 2011 and the first two Italian codes, make less reference to disclosure. Stewardship codes, similar to corporate governance codes, are disclosure-based regulatory mechanisms which rely on transparency to encourage good stewardship practices. One would therefore expect that codes that emphasize disclosure would also emphasize reporting requirements (i.e. *report*). Indeed, India (IRDAI) 2017, which is the code with the most frequent reference to reporting requirements, also makes frequent references to disclosure. The UK Code 2012 itself also frequently refers to both disclosure and reporting obligations. However, earlier codes, such as UK 2002, 2005 and 2007 as well as Canada 2005, seem to emphasize reporting rather than disclosure. An exception here is the UK Code 2020 which, despite being the most recent code, makes more frequent reference to reporting rather than disclosure obligations, perhaps because of its unique emphasis on the investment side of stewardship and the duties of institutional investors to their clients and beneficiaries.[109] But, overall, Figure 30.4 shows that *disclos* became more frequent only much later in 2012 or so and this may indicate a stronger emphasis on public disclosure.[110]

All but three codes (UK 1991, Canada 2010 and Italy 2013) include a principle relating to how institutional investors manage conflicts of interests that may affect their stewardship activities. In general, *conflict* appears less frequently in most codes,[111] perhaps owing to its nature of acting as support for the overarching stewardship policy.

Monitoring of investee companies is recognized as an essential part of shareholder stewardship and all codes (except the very first UK Code and the Swiss one) mention the word *monitor* at least once. Monitoring includes both informal and formal activities, ranging from dialogue to attending annual general meetings. Despite the widely accepted merits of shareholder monitoring, the UK Code 2012 mentions *monitor* less frequently compared to all the earlier versions of the code (except the 1991 one). This suggests a gradual shift from a monolithic, corporate governance-inspired view of stewardship as a corporate governance tool of shareholder discipline to a more holistic approach to the responsibilities of equity-owning institutional investors,[112] and is associated with a movement away (at least in the UK) from stewardship as solely focusing on shareholder engagement.[113] But this untangling of stewardship from shareholder monitoring and engagement is not taking place outside the UK. Rather, the two more recent Indian codes (i.e. India (PRFDA) 2018 and India (SEBI) 2019) make more frequent reference to *monitor* compared to the earlier India (IRDAI) 2017 Code.

Associated with this trend is the fact that *escal* (the word marker for escal-ation, escal-ate) is the least frequent word across all the codes. This refers to a set of best practices for when and how investors might take action when their monitoring or engagement reveals concerns about a company that are not appropriately addressed by its management. The UK Code 2012 ranks tenth, while EFAMA 2018 makes the most frequent reference to this principle, followed by Denmark and India (SEBI) 2019. Seventeen codes, including the earlier EFAMA Code, all the Italian codes, the two Japanese codes and the Korean and Malaysian codes, make no reference to the word *escal*. This is owing to the way in which escalation of shareholder engagement and more aggressive forms of shareholder activism are perceived by different local markets. The Japanese codes, for instance, adopt a gentler language emphasizing 'constructive engagement' and dialogue, reflecting perhaps the 'internalist', 'firm-centric' focus of the alternative Japanese conception of the company as an organization or 'community'.[114]

---

[109] On the investment side of stewardship, see Katelouzou (n 12).

[110] We do not claim that this increase of *disclos* over time is only and necessarily attributed to the impact of the UK 2012 code. There has been a great emphasis on disclosure over the last decades, partly because of the spread of corporate governance codes, so it is likely that these general trends also explain the more frequent use of the word 'disclose' over time.

[111] An exception here is the Brazil 2016 Code which mentions *conflict* seven times and links the policy on conflicts of interest with other hard-law requirements that protect the interests of the end beneficiaries. Other codes that mention conflict frequently are the India (PRFDA) 2018 and India (SEBI) 2019 codes.

[112] See further Dionysia Katelouzou, 'Shareholder Stewardship: A Case of (Re)Embedding Institutional Investors and the Corporation?' in Beate Sjåfjell and Christopher M Bruner (eds), *Cambridge Handbook of Corporate Law, Corporate Governance and Sustainability* (CUP 2019).

[113] See also Davies, The UK Stewardship Code 2010–2020, Chapter 2.

[114] On the limits of hedge fund activism in Japan, see John Buchanan, Dominic Heesang Chai and Simon Deakin, *Hedge Fund Activism in Japan: The Limits of Shareholder Primacy* (CUP 2012).

Collect, the word marker for Principle 5 of the UK Code 2012, is also not well-perceived across the various codes. Eighteen codes, including all the Canadian codes, the four earlier versions of the UK Code, the 2014 version of the Japanese Code, the two latest India codes and the UK Code 2020, do not make any reference to shareholder collective action.[115] Similar to escalating activity, many codes prefer not to endorse collective engagement by institutional investors (there are eight codes that do not include either of these two word markers). However, it is interesting to note that, unlike the relatively low frequencies of *escal* across all codes, the most recent Italian codes mention *collect* thirteen times each. This emphasis on shareholder collective action in the Italian context is not surprising if one considers the strategic role of *Assogestioni*, the issuer of the Italian stewardship principles, in facilitating collective engagement by institutional shareholders especially in relation to the appointment of a minority of the members of the management and the statutory auditors' boards.[116] Outpaced only by Italy 2015 and Italy 2016, EFAMA 2018 also refers to *collect* very often, which adds further support to the cluster identified above.[117]

Finally, all forty-one codes, following Principle 5 of the UK Code 2012, require institutional investors to develop a policy for voting. Among the codes that mention *vote* most frequently are Italy 2013, India (SEBI) 2019, UK 2009, Canada 2010 and Australia (ACSI) 2018. While *vote* is the most frequent word marker in the UK Code 2012 itself, *vote* is mentioned more frequently in some of the previous versions of the code (that is, the 2009, 2010, 1991 and 2007 versions), and the UK Code 2012 ranks thirtieth in the frequency of this word marker. Interestingly, even though the importance attributed to the exercise of voting rights by institutional investors is such that there is no single code that does not mention the word *vote* at least once, it seems that more recent stewardship codes, such as the UK Code 2020, place less emphasis on voting perhaps because of their expansive scope. But on the antipode is the India (SEBI) 2019 Code, which makes the second most frequent reference to *vote* after the Italian 2013 Code. This may be striking as the other two Indian codes (i.e. India (PRFDA) 2018 and India (IRDAI) 2017) rank thirty-seventh and forty-first in the frequency of the word marker *vote*, although this may be explained by the detailed guidance provided by the latest Indian code in relation to Principle 5 on voting policy and disclosure.[118]

30.4.2 Understanding the Diffusion Patterns

Our findings so far have revealed different diffusion patterns for the seven key principles of the UK Code 2012. To understand these patterns, we now take into account a select number of possible explanatory categories related to both the characteristics of the codes and the country of the code (thus, for the latter we excluded the ICGN and EFAMA codes). Table 30.4 contains an overview of the categories; the precise coding is available in Table 30.9 in the Annex.[119]

---

[115] But note that some codes, including the UK 2020, the India (SEBI) 2019 and the India (PFRDA) 2018, make references to collaborative rather than collective engagement. For the rationale behind this changing terminology in the UK, see Katelouzou (n 12).

[116] On this co-ordination role performed by Assogestioni, see Strampelli, Institutional Investor Stewardship in Italian Corporate Governance, Chapter 6.

[117] See Section 30.3.3.

[118] The Guidance to Principle 5 includes twenty-two references to the word marker *vote*. In total, the India (SEBI) Code refers to *vote* twenty-eight times.

[119] Table 30.9 of the Annex.

TABLE 30.4 *Possible explanatory categories*

Category	Explanation	Source
Type of issuer	Private (1) or public (0) issuer. 'Public' is assumed if the issuer was composed entirely of persons representing the state (including state-owned entities)	Own coding
Other languages	Codes that have also been published in another language (1); otherwise (0)	Own coding
Nature of code	Code (1) or preliminary initiative (0), see Section 30.3.1 for details	Own coding
Enforcement mode	Categorical variable with (0) for codes of an entirely voluntary nature, (1) for codes following a 'comply or explain' approach and (2) for codes that have a mandatory element for a specific group of investors	Own coding
Legal family	Common law (1) or civil law (0), as defined in the comparative private law	Own coding
Global financial centre	Countries with cities that feature in the top 20 global financial centres (1); otherwise (0)	Long finance[120]

First, stewardship codes around the world emanate from different issuers, and this can influence the content and innovation of a code. Even though the codes' issuers can be classified into alternative categories,[121] we divide the stewardship codes into two groups based on the type of issuer: public ones where the code's issuer is entirely composed of regulators or quasi-regulators and committees acting on behalf of the state, including state-owned entities;[122] and private ones which are initiated by entirely private industry participants, investor-related groups or associations and international organizations. The UK is the only country where the type of issuer has shifted over time, but in other countries many issuers coexist at the same time.[123]

Next, we take into account whether the code has also been published in a language other than English. Owing to our focus on linguistic diffusion, it is possible that such codes may use different words than the ones only written and published in English. A similar way of presenting this criterion may be whether English is the original or the translated language of a code. Yet, it cannot be excluded that in some of the non-Anglophone countries, the two language versions of the code were co-drafted,[124] given that international (and Anglophone) investors are often the main audience of these codes. Thus, while it is possible that this criterion plays a role, it may also be the case that the unknown drafting history, as well as unknown differences in the mode of any translation,[125] influence any linguistic differences between these two groups of codes.

We also hypothesize that the nature and the enforcement mode of the codes are, in most instances, decided before the drafting of substantive details (reflected in the word patterns).

[120] Mark Yeandle, 'The Global Financial Centres Index 20' (*Financial Centre Futures*, September 2016) <www.longfinance.net/media/documents/GFCI20_26Sep2016.pdf> accessed 24 January 2022.
[121] See e.g. Jennifer G Hill, 'Good Activist/Bad Activist: The Rise of International Stewardship Codes' (2018) 41 *Seattle University Law Review* 497 (grouping the stewardship codes into three categories depending on the issuer).
[122] This includes Malaysia and Singapore given that various public bodies (Malaysia) and the country's sovereign wealth fund (Singapore) were the entities behind the issuer of these codes. See also Puchniak and Tang, Singapore's Embrace of Shareholder Stewardship, Chapter 14 and Tan, Institutional Investor Stewardship in Malaysia, Chapter 15.
[123] See Table 30.9 of the Annex for details.
[124] As done in some multilingual jurisdictions, see e.g. Silva Ferreri, 'Law, Language and Translation in Multilingual Contexts' (2014) 25 *King's Law Journal* 271.
[125] In particular, whether the translation follows a functional or more literal mode. For references to the literature, see Siems (n 33) 157.

Thus, we distinguish between preliminary initiatives and codes based on the three previously mentioned criteria (drafting style, content and scope), as explained earlier.[126] With respect to the enforcement mode,[127] even though stewardship codes, similar to corporate governance codes, are in general non-binding and fall into the category of soft rather than hard law, they vary in terms of their coerciveness.[128] Some codes, such as Brazil 2016 or Canada 2017, are completely voluntary, while others, such as Taiwan 2016 and Japan 2017, adopt the 'comply-or-explain' approach and have more coercive implications than traditional regulatory theories suggest. Other codes have different elements of coerciveness but equally cannot be flouted without consequences: for instance, India (SEBI) 2019 is mandatory for its members; the comply-or-explain approach of UK 2012 is mandatory for FCA-authorized asset managers; while UK 2020 adopts an 'apply and explain' approach, also on a mandatory basis for FCA-authorized asset managers.[129]

For the country-specific codes, we also divide them into civil-law and common-law countries, given that legal families can be a possible source of policy diffusion.[130] We use the mainstream classification of the comparative private law scholarship;[131] thus, for example, Japan has been classified as a civil-law country, despite having also been influenced by US law in some fields. This criterion largely matches the previous one given that all codes that have also been published in a language other than English are the codes of civil-law countries. Yet, it excludes the non-country-specific codes (i.e. the ICGN and EFAMA codes). Finally, for the country-specific codes, we classify countries as having one or more cities that feature in the top twenty global financial centres, given that pressure by institutional investors may have shaped the language and substantive orientation of these codes.

Next, we aim to determine whether there is a significant difference between the means of any two groups by calculating t-test statistics for the six explanatory categories (Table 30.5).[132] The observations are for the codes enacted after the UK Code 2012; if the same issuer has enacted more than one code, we use the most recent code (relevant for Italy, Japan and ICGN), given that codes by the same issuer would not be independent of each other;[133] thus, the overall number of observations is twenty-one. Given this low number of observations (as well as the possible endogenous nature of some of the variables), we cannot claim that the subsequent findings are of a causal nature; yet, they do show some interesting patterns.

Table 30.5 shows that none of the six explanatory categories can explain the differences across the codes in the use of the words *collect* and *vote*. The type of the issuer has an impact on the frequency of the words *disclos*, *conflict* and *report*: we find that codes issued by public bodies focus more on stewardship-related disclosure, conflicts of interests, and reporting requirements.

---

[126] See Section 30.3.1.
[127] See also Katelouzou and Sergakis, Shareholder Stewardship Enforcement, Chapter 27.
[128] On the coercive elements of soft legal norms, see Dionysia Katelouzou and Peer Zumbansen, 'The New Geographies of Corporate Governance' (2020) 42 *University of Pennsylvania Journal of International Law* 51.
[129] However, while in theory the FCA could disqualify the FCA-authorized asset managers that do not comply with the UK stewardship code, no action has been taken so far and it is unlikely that public enforcement will gain any importance in the context of stewardship. See further, Katelouzou and Sergakis, Shareholder Stewardship Enforcement, Chapter 27.
[130] Cf. Holger Spamann, 'Contemporary Legal Transplants: Legal Families and the Diffusion of (Corporate) Law' (2009) *Brigham Young University Law Review* 1813.
[131] For an overview, see Siems (n 33) 86–90; for criticism see 92–108.
[132] For the categorical enforcement variable, we test each of the categories to see whether it is different from the other two categories.
[133] Therefore, we also exclude the UK 2020 code. As India (PRDFA) 2018 and India (SEBI) 2019 are very similar (see Section 30.3.2), we consider only India (SEBI) 2019, together with India (IRDAI) 2017.

TABLE 30.5 *Tests of group differences between post-2012 codes*

Keywords	Group category	Difference and means	p-value and significance level[134]
Disclos	Type of issuer	Public > private (0.0151 vs. 0.0110)	0.0853*
Conflict	Type of issuer	Public > private (0.0085 vs. 0.0058)	0.0844*
Monitor	Enforcement	Mandatory > others (0.0110 vs. 0.0070)	0.0840*
Escal	Other language	No > Yes (0.0028 vs. 0.0010)	0.0660*
Collect	[none]		
Vote	[none]		
Report	Type of issuer	Public > private (0.0080 vs. 0.0039)	0.0490**

For the disclosure and reporting requirements, this may be owing to the fact that public issuers, part of whose role is to improve the business environment and encourage good stewardship activities, are paying increasing attention to disclosure and transparency and may consider such codes within their enforcement activities even if they do not have the means to effectively enforce any disregard of the disclosure and reporting obligations.[135] For *conflict*, it is less clear why this variable is significant; possibly, it may be owing to the fact that public authorities have a particularly strong interest in preventing conflict of interests. More generally, it can be noted that the type of the issuer is the variable with the most impact, probably because public issuers are more likely to copy the already established UK Code 2012 (also having been developed by a public issuer).

The word *monitor* is more often used in codes that have a mandatory element. This may be owing to the emphasis of such codes on engagement activities, but it is also likely that this is owing to the diffusion of the monitoring norm from the UK coercive code to other similarly coercive codes, prominently in India and Australia. Finally, escalation is found more often in codes only available in English, possibly since 'escalate' is an English term less commonly used than the other words, and, thus, non-native speakers (or translators) may tend to avoid it.

It is also noteworthy that the categories about the nature of the code, legal families and the global financial centre are insignificant for any of the marker words: thus, to phrase it in a positive way, it cannot be said that the diffusion of stewardship principles is obstructed by the diverse nature of a code, the civil-/common-law divide or the diversity of financial centrality.

30.4.3 Is the UK a Stewardship Exporter?

Section 30.4.2 observed that the UK principles relating to escalation activities and collection action seem to have travelled less successfully compared to the other principles of the UK Code 2012. It is the aim of this section to explore in more detail whether, based on the seven marker words, the UK can be considered a stewardship exporter.

Table 30.6 sheds light on this question by presenting the differences in coverage of the seven marker words between the UK Code 2012 and its twenty-two subsequent counterpart codes.[136] It divides the frequencies (see Figure 30.4) into three categories that provide a comparison to the UK Code 2012. The highest category (>90%) refers to instances where there is strong evidence of

---

[134] * = 10%, ** = 5% significance level.
[135] Consider e.g. Stewardship Asia, the issuer of the Singapore 2016 Code, which, even though it has been categorized as a public issuer for the purposes of this study, does not have any enforcement powers. See further Puchniak and Tang (n 17).
[136] As in Section 30.4.2, we take into account only one code per issuer, which is the most recent one, with the exception of the UK. As we are interested in the impact of UK 2012 on other countries, we exclude UK 2020.

TABLE 30.6 Coverage of principles at a level equivalent to the UK Code 2012

disclos	conflict	monitor	escal	collect	vote	report
Brazil 2016	Australia (ACSI) 2018	Netherlands 2018	Brazil 2016	Australia (FSC) 2017	Australia (FSC) 2017	Australia (FSC) 2017
Canada 2017	Netherlands 2018	Switzerland 2013	Italy 2016	Canada 2017	India (IRDAI) 2017	EFAMA 2018
Italy 2016	Korea2016	Denmark 2016	Japan 2017	Denmark 2016	India (PFRDA) 2018	Italy 2016
Kenya 2017	Australia (FSC) 2017	Hong Kong 2016	Korea2016	Hong Kong 2016	US 2017	Kenya 2017
Netherlands 2018	Brazil 2016	US 2017	Malaysia 2014	ICGN 2016	Australia (ACSI) 2018	Netherlands 2018
Singapore 2016	Canada 2017	Australia (ACSI) 2018	Switzerland 2013	India (IRDAI) 2017	Brazil 2016	Singapore 2016
Australia (FSC) 2017	Denmark 2016	Australia (FSC) 2017	Taiwan 2016	India (PFRDA) 2018	Canada 2017	Switzerland 2013
Denmark 2016	EFAMA 2018	Brazil 2016	Australia (FSC) 2017	India (SEBI) 2019	Denmark 2016	Thailand 2017
EFAMA 2018	Hong Kong 2016	Canada 2017	Denmark 2016	Japan 2017	EFAMA 2018	Australia (ACSI) 2018
Hong Kong 2016	ICGN 2016	EFAMA 2018	EFAMA 2018	Kenya 2017	Hong Kong 2016	Brazil 2016
ICGN 2016	India (IRDAI) 2017	ICGN 2016	ICGN 2016	Korea2016	India (SEBI) 2019	Canada 2017
Japan 2017	India (PFRDA) 2018	India (IRDAI) 2017	India (PFRDA) 2018	Malaysia 2014	ICGN 2016	ICGN 2016
Korea 2016	India (SEBI) 2019	India (PFRDA) 2018	India (SEBI) 2019	Netherlands 2018	Italy 2016	India (PFRDA) 2018
Switzerland 2013	Italy 2016	India (SEBI) 2019	Singapore 2016	Switzerland 2013	Japan 2017	India (SEBI) 2019
Taiwan 2016	Japan 2017	Italy 2016	US 2017	Taiwan 2016	Kenya 2017	Japan 2017
Thailand 2017	Kenya 2017	Japan 2017	Australia (ACSI) 2018	Thailand 2017	Korea2016	Korea2016
US 2017	Malaysia 2014	Kenya 2017	Denmark 2016	US 2017	Malaysia 2014	Malaysia 2014
Australia (ACSI) 2018	Singapore 2016	Korea2016	EFAMA 2018	Australia (ACSI) 2018	Netherlands 2018	Taiwan 2016
India (IRDAI) 2017	Switzerland 2013	Malaysia 2014	ICGN 2016	Singapore 2016	Singapore 2016	Denmark 2016
India (PFRDA) 2018	Taiwan 2016	Singapore 2016	India (PFRDA) 2018	Brazil 2016	Switzerland 2013	Hong Kong 2016
India (SEBI) 2019	Thailand 2017	Taiwan 2016	India (SEBI) 2019	EFAMA 2018	Taiwan 2016	India (IRDAI) 2017
Malaysia 2014	US 2017	Thailand 2017	US 2017	Italy 2016	Thailand 2017	US 2017

Shadings refer to: >90% | 50–90% | <50%

UK influence; the intermediate category (50–90%) refers to instances where some influence may be assumed; while the final category (<50%) shows cases of little influence.

It can be seen that *conflict*, *monitor* and *vote* are the categories where the UK influence has been pronounced for all but a few codes. For *disclos*, *escal* and *report*, the evidence of UK influence is mixed,[137] while least influence is noticeable for *collect*. This suggests that, while facilitating collective engagement by institutional investors has been championed by UK policymakers, expanding the opportunities for collective action has not been promoted by other stewardship codes, especially those developed in countries where public companies are dominated by family or state ownership, such as Hong Kong and Malaysia, or by 'silent' shareholders with distaste for confrontation and criticism, such as potentially in Japan.[138][139]

Next, we calculate the overall similarity of the twenty-one (subsequent) codes to the UK Code 2012. The ranking of Table 30.7 is based on the difference between the UK Code 2012 and the other codes in each of the categories. For the purposes of the ranking, a code that is more than 100% similar to the UK one (because it refers to a particular principle more often) is capped at this number (i.e. it is not rewarded or penalized). For purposes of comparison, Table 30.7 also

TABLE 30.7 *Ranked similarity to the UK Code 2012 (with 'over-compliance' disregarded)*

Rank	Average similarity for keywords		Comparison: similarity to UK Code based on similarity of strings[139]
1	India (SEBI) 2019	81.17%	7.38% (rank 6)
2	EFAMA 2018	81.11%	9.20% (rank 4)
3	Denmark 2016	80.39%	5.93% (rank 10)
4	Australia (ACSI) 2018	79.74%	5.10% (rank 11)
5	India (IRDAI) 2017	79.51%	19.46% (rank 1)
6	ICGN 2016	78.09%	3.65% (rank 14)
7	India (PFRDA) 2018	76.15%	7.01% (rank 7)
8	Hong Kong 2016	74.16%	14.43% (rank 3)
9	Singapore 2016	72.02%	8.34% (rank 5)
10	Kenya 2017	70.70%	3.77% (rank 13)
11	Brazil 2016	70.03%	2.99% (rank 17)
12	Canada 2017	69.91%	6.32% (rank 9)
12	Taiwan 2016	68.22%	1.74% (rank 21)
14	Japan 2017	66.08%	6.93% (rank 8)
15	Malaysia 2014	64.22%	16.77% (rank 2)
16	Thailand 2017	63.77%	5.30% (rank 11)
17	Korea 2016	60.15%	3.32% (rank 15)
18	Italy 2016	59.96%	2.20% (rank 20)
19	Australia (FSC) 2017	52.48%	1.15% (rank 22)
20	US 2017	48.91%	2.78% (rank 18)
21	Netherlands 2018	46.54%	3.05% (rank 15)
22	Switzerland 2013	41.80%	2.67% (rank 18)

[137] Note that, in Section 30.4.1, the influence of *escal* appeared even less pronounced since this section also included the pre-2012 codes as well as multiple codes per issuer.

[138] On the antagonism of the Japanese code to collective action, see Ken Hokugo and Alicia Ogawa, 'The Unfinished Business of Japan's Stewardship Code' (Columbia Business School Center on Japanese Economy and Business, Working Paper Series July 2017) <https://academiccommons.columbia.edu/doi/10.7916/D8D79PTM> accessed 24 January 2022. Yet, the position of such cultural difference of Japan is contentious; see the overview of the debate in Siems (n 33) 188–90.

[139] Based on the average as used for the clusters; see Section 30.3.3.

includes the ranking of the similarity to the UK Code 2012 based on the similarity of strings. Both rankings are moderately correlated.[140]

Both EFAMA 2018 and ICGN 2016 rank highly, perhaps because transnational codes tend to provide an overarching model for best corporate governance practices. From the country-specific codes, the India (SEBI) 2019 Code appears to be the most similar to the UK Code 2012, followed by EFAMA 2018 and the Danish Code. The two other Indian codes, the Singapore and the Hong Kong codes also rank highly, confirming the earlier findings about the similarities in the content between these codes and the UK Code.[141] From the top-ranked codes, the similarity between the Danish and the UK 2012 codes may surprise the reader, especially since the language used by the Danish Code (based on the similarity of strings) is not so similar to that of the UK Code 2012.[142] But this textual disparity may be attributed to the translation process, and the similarity of the Danish principles to those in the UK Code 2012 aligns with the fact that the Danish Code explicitly cites the UK Code.[143] A further key disparity concerns the Malaysian Code, which, even though it is drafted in a way similar to the UK Code 2012, ranks only fifteenth when it comes to the specific principles, mainly because the principles of escalating activity and shareholder collective action have not been adopted. The US, Dutch and Swiss codes are the codes that were influenced the least by the UK stewardship principles. The Dutch Code, for instance, has eleven principles, among which are principles on communicating with relevant stakeholders and not borrowing shares, both of which are absent from the UK Code 2012.

Finally, we calculate the t-test statistics for all the six explanatory categories of Table 30.5 with the aim of determining whether the ranking of Table 30.7 exhibits significant group differences.[144] We find that only the nature of the issuer and the availability in a language other than English are significant at the 10% level (p = 0.0690 and 0.0820). Public issuers have a higher mean similarity (72.02%) than private issuers (62.61%). This may be owing to the fact that public issuers around the world are more likely to draft codes on the basis of pre-existing public codes, while private codes may be more irregular as they are shaped by diverse types of issuer. Codes not available in another language (in other words, the codes of the Anglophone countries and the ICGN and EFAMA codes) have a higher mean of similarity (71.00%) compared to the other codes (61.88%), plausibly because some of the translated codes may use linguistically different terms. All the other categories cannot explain the diffusion patterns. This is in line with our previous findings and confirms that neither the divide between legal families (i.e. between common and civil law jurisdictions) nor the divide between financial centres and periphery can be said to have promoted or obstructed the diffusion of stewardship principles.

30.5 CONCLUSION

We confirm in this chapter a conclusion made many times in this handbook: within a mere decade of the introduction of the first UK stewardship code, shareholder stewardship has rapidly become a popular concept among policymakers, private standard-setters, companies and investors around the globe. Employing the method of content analysis and using information from

---

[140] The Spearman rank correlation is 0.6279.
[141] See Section 30.3.3.
[142] ibid.
[143] See Section 30.3.1.
[144] As in Section 30.3.2, this is based on twenty-one observations; see also n 133.

forty-one stewardship codes,[145] this chapter has shown that there is in reality both uniformity and diversity among these codes.[146]

Three of our main findings are as follows: first, while some overall formal (textual) diffusion can be observed especially among former British colonies in Asia, stewardship has travelled in non-linear ways and has often been vernacularized or adapted to local contexts.[147] For instance, Japan has adopted a 'milder and more nuanced' version of the UK Code 2012. While the English version of the Japanese Code uses the same word 'monitor', the original Japanese version requests investors to 'properly grasp the circumstances of investee companies'.[148]

Second, even though diffusion processes are too varied and complex to be reduced to a direct one-way transfer,[149] among the seven key stewardship principles of the UK Code, most of them have diffused widely, while the principles on escalating engagement activities and collective action are the least travelled. Our findings also support the claims about the way in which UK-originated norms have been renegotiated at the local context, with the possibility of 'faux convergence'.[150] In other words, even when codes are drafted in a similar way to the 'good' UK stewardship standards, as is the case of the Malaysian and Singapore codes, it is done on a superficial level, often omitting key UK stewardship principles.

Third, there is no strong legal family effect on the diffusion patterns. While we find support for the diffusion of the UK stewardship model to common-law countries in Asia, we also find (i) evidence of diffusion from the UK to a number of civil-law countries (notably Japan and Denmark); (ii) impact of the transnational EFAMA and ICGN codes on a number of codes (notably Italy, Malaysia and Kenya); (iii) a regional cluster in Asia across the legal family divide (namely with Thailand, Japan and Korea showing some similarity to the common-law countries); as well as (iv) some idiosyncratic results (e.g. the US and one of the Australian codes being very different from the UK model). Thus, as in other fields of business law,[151] conventional paradigms such as the legal family divide seem to be weakening.

Following on from these findings, future research could further enhance our understanding of diffusion in the area of stewardship norms. From a technical perspective, the text of the codes could be analyzed with further tools,[152] and it may also be possible to consider the non-English-language versions of the codes.[153] From a broader perspective, future research could follow the insight that stewardship may mean something different for different types of company and investor. For example, the practice of stewardship at the firm level may be analyzed to see how differences in shareholder ownership structure impact the application of the stewardship codes.[154] As Singapore has enacted a separate stewardship code for family

---

[145] It is noteworthy, however, that compared to the widespread adoption of corporate governance codes, only a minority of countries have adopted what we defined at the beginning of this chapter as stewardship codes, either preliminary stewardship initiatives or codes in the narrow sense. See Section 30.3.1.

[146] Further on diversity and complexity of shareholder stewardship, see Katelouzou and Puchniak, Global Shareholder Stewardship, Chapter 1.

[147] See generally Amitav Acharya, 'How Ideas Spread: Whose Norms Matter? Norm Localization and Institutional Change in Asian Regionalism' (2004) 58 *International Organization* 239.

[148] Goto (n 48) 385.

[149] Twinning (n 36).

[150] See Goto, Koh and Puchniak (n 39).

[151] See Dionysia Katelouzou and Mathias Siems, 'Disappearing Paradigms in Shareholder Protection: Leximetric Evidence for 30 Countries, 1990–2013' (2015) 15 *Journal of Corporate Law Studies* 127.

[152] For example measures of cosine similarity between texts and applying forms of topic modelling, as used in some studies of content analysis, e.g. Jansa, Hansen and Gray (n 63).

[153] See Table 30.9 of the Annex.

[154] For such research questions, see also Ruth V Aguilera, Vicente J Bermejo, Javier Capapé and Vicente Cuñat, 'Firms' Reaction to Changes in the Governance Preferences of Active Institutional Owners' (2019) ECGI Finance Working Paper No 625/2019 <https://ssrn.com/abstract=3411566> accessed 24 January 2022; Florencio Lopez-de-Silanes,

businesses,[155] and as there is also soft law for sovereign wealth funds,[156] it may also be suggested that a 'one-size-fits-all' model of stewardship may not be the right way forward.

Finally, the dominant current models may also be subject to change and thus a topic of future research. The transposition of the EU's Shareholder Rights Directive (SRD) II is likely to have an impact on the operability of national stewardship codes in Europe.[157] Furthermore, as the UK Code 2020 has come into force, it is conceivable that future research may want to track a possible second round of exportation of the revised UK model into the transnational arena.[158] Hence, we expect that, while the future of stewardship norms and practices is not perfectly predictable and diffusion involves various actors, local contexts and complex pathways, stewardship norms and practices will continue to travel globally.

30.6 ANNEX

TABLE 30.8 *Length of stewardship codes*

Abbreviated name of code[159]	Full text (in words)[160]	Principles and specific guidance only (in words)[161]	As previous column but excluding stopwords[162]
Australia (ACSI) 2018	2964	1721	1074
Australia (FSC) 2017	2640	836	488
Brazil 2016	2184	924	506
Canada 2005	1136	762	436
Canada 2010	1176	778	466
Canada 2017	1984	1348	795
Denmark 2016	3044	1776	1001
EFAMA 2011	1809	1104	629
EFAMA 2018	2254	1110	637
Hong Kong 2016	2232	1810	968
ICGN 2003	1942	1424	769
ICGN 2007	4665	2348	1244
ICGN 2013	7228	3969	2167
ICGN 2016	5062	2452	1441
India (IRDAI) 2017	964	906	473
India (PFRDA) 2018	1413	1129	655
India (SEBI) 2019	1696	1371	760

Joseph McCahery and Paul Pudschedl, 'ESG Performance and Disclosure: A Cross-Country Analysis' (2019) ECGI Law Working Paper No 481/2019 <https://ssrn.com/abstract=3506084> accessed 22 January 2022.

[155] See Puchniak and Tang (n 17).
[156] Notably, the 'Santiago Principles' of the International Forum of Sovereign Wealth Funds (International Forum of Sovereign Wealth Funds, 'Santiago Principles' <www.ifswf.org/santiago-principles> accessed 24 January 2022).
[157] See e.g. Dionysia Katelouzou and Konstantinos Sergakis, 'When Harmonization Is Not Enough: Shareholder Stewardship in the European Union' (2021) 22 *European Business Organization Law Review* 203 (advancing a symbiotic relationship between the SRD II transposed rules and the national stewardship codes).
[158] For instance, the 2020 revision of the Japanese code seems to follow the UK Code 2020 in its emphasis on ESG. See Financial Services Agency, 'Publication of the Draft of the "Principles for Responsible Institutional Investors" «Japan's Stewardship Code» – To Promote Sustainable Growth of Companies through Investment and Dialogue – (Draft)' (20 December 2019) <www.fsa.go.jp/en/news/2019/20191220.html> accessed 24 January 2022.
[159] See Table 30.1 in Section 30.2.1.
[160] Following the formatting and editing as explained in Section 30.3.2.
[161] As explained in Section 30.4.1.
[162] ibid.

30 *The Global Diffusion of Stewardship Codes* 661

TABLE 30.8 *(continued)*

Abbreviated name of code	Full text (in words)	Principles and specific guidance only (in words)	As previous column but excluding stopwords
Italy 2013	984	121	80
Italy 2015	2596	1583	924
Italy 2016	2615	1615	937
Japan 2014	3362	1590	888
Japan 2017	4637	2285	1298
Kenya 2017	3735	2926	1780
Korea 2016	3231	1921	1133
Malaysia 2014	2967	1498	850
Netherlands 2011	2583	1079	611
Netherlands 2018	3709	2220	1297
Singapore 2016	1828	952	544
South Africa 2011	2406	982	512
Switzerland 2013	1943	733	413
Taiwan 2016	2146	1220	702
Thailand 2017	3819	2666	1585
UK 1991	1474	261	148
UK 2002	1462	1001	558
UK 2005	1465	985	552
UK 2007	1392	989	554
UK 2009	1504	962	518
UK 2010	1908	1041	560
UK 2012	2954	1264	691
UK 2020	4331	3016	1755
US 2017	714	704	416

TABLE 30.9 *Coding of explanatory categories for diffusion*[163]

Abbreviated name of code[164]	Type of issuer	Nature of code	Enforcement mode	Other languages	Legal family	Global financial centre
Australia (ACSI) 2018	1	0	0	0	1	1
Australia (FSC) 2017	1	0	2	0	1	1
Brazil 2016	1	1	0	1	0	0
Canada 2005	1	0	0	0	1	1
Canada 2010	1	0	0	0	1	1
Canada 2017	1	1	0	0	1	1
Denmark 2016	0	1	1	1	0	0
EFAMA 2011	1	0	0	0	n.a.	n.a.
EFAMA 2018	1	0	1	0	n.a.	n.a.
Hong Kong 2016	0	1	1	0	1	1
ICGN 2003	1	0	0	0	n.a.	n.a.
ICGN 2007	1	0	0	0	n.a.	n.a.
ICGN 2013	1	1	0	0	n.a.	n.a.

[163] For the definition of the categories, see Section 30.4.2.
[164] See Table 30.1 in Section 30.2.1.

TABLE 30.9 *(continued)*

Abbreviated name of code	Type of issuer	Nature of code	Enforcement mode	Other languages	Legal family	Global financial centre
ICGN 2016	1	1	0	0	n.a.	n.a.
India (IRDAI) 2017	0	0	1	0	1	0
India (PFRDA) 2018	0	0	2	0	1	0
India (SEBI) 2019	0	0	2	0	1	0
Italy 2013	1	0	0	1	0	0
Italy 2015	1	0	1	1	0	0
Italy 2016	1	0	1	1	0	0
Japan 2014	0	1	1	1	0	1
Japan 2017	0	1	1	1	0	1
Kenya 2017	0	1	1	0	1	1
Korea 2016	1	1	1	1	0	0
Malaysia 2014	0	1	0	0	1	0
Netherlands 2011	1	0	1	1	0	0
Netherlands 2018	1	1	1	1	0	0
Singapore 2016	0	1	0	0	1	1
South Africa 2011	1	1	1	0	1	0
Switzerland 2013	1	0	1	1	0	1
Taiwan 2016	0	1	1	1	0	0
Thailand 2017	0	1	2	1	0	0
UK 1991	1	0	0	0	1	1
UK 2002	1	0	0	0	1	1
UK 2005	1	0	0	0	1	1
UK 2007	1	0	0	0	1	1
UK 2009	1	1	1	0	1	1
UK 2010	0	1	1	0	1	1
UK 2012	0	1	2	0	1	1
UK 2020	0	1	2	0	1	1
US 2017	1	0	0	0	1	1

Index

Abe, Shinzo, 226, 227, 624
Aberdeen Standard Investments, 327, 509
Acadian Asset Management LLC, 104
Accenting legal standards, stewardship codes as, 31, 34
Ackman, Bill, 445–46, 448–49
Active investment management
  generally, 536, 538
  agency problems and, 536–37
  high cost of, 537
  short-term focus of, 539
Activist Insight, 426
Admati, Anat R., 504
Affin Hwang Asset Management Berhad, 327
'Agency capitalism', 174, 284–85
Agency problems
  active management and, 536–37
  ESG and, 8
  in index funds, 464–65
  mutual funds and, 467
  passive management and, 537–38
Aggarwal, Reena, 397
Aguilar, Javier Capapé, 183
Aguilera, Ruth V., 183
Ahold NV, 109
AIIAN Asset Management Sdn Bhd, 327
AkzoNobel, 94
Alembic Pharmaceuticals Limited, 364, 365–66
Allee, Todd, 641, 642
Allianz Global Investors GmbH, 66, 105, 202, 208–10
Allianz SE, 208–10
Alternative Investment Funds (AIFs), 541
Altruism, 76
Alvaro, Simone, 147
Amazon, 310, 469
Amundi Asset Management SA, 210
Ariyoshi, Naoya, 233
Armour, John, 532, 575–76
ASEAN Corporate Governance Scorecard, 337
Asian Financial Crisis (1997)
  Taiwan and, 276
  Thailand and, 335, 336, 346
Asset managers. *See also specific company or country*
  asset owners distinguished, 50, 71
  concentration of, 566
  ESG and, 199

  Exchange Traded Funds (ETFs) and, 454
  fund beneficiaries and, 454–55
  stewardship and, 199
  UN Principles of Responsible Investment (UNPRI) and, 212, 217
Asset owners, asset managers distinguished, 50, 71. *See also specific country*
Australia
  generally, 419
  acting-in-concert rules
    collective action and, 435–36
    intermediary organizations and, 432
  Australian Council of Superannuation Investors (ACSI) Code
    applicability of, 423
    aspirational nature of, 423–24
    asset owners and, 421
    collective action, 426
    deviation from UK Code 2010/2012, 16
    ESG in, 424, 562
    FSC Code compared, 421–22
    global diffusion and, 635
    historical background, 420
    as industry-led initiative, 422
    issuance of, 420
    network analysis and, 646
    policy disclosure, 649
    principles, 423
    regulatory framework and, 568
    revised approach, calls for, 424
    Seven Core Principles in, 620
    signatories, 567
    stewardship statements, 424
    types of firm represented by, 421
    voting policies, 652
  Australian Institute of Company Directors, 430–31
  Australian Investment Managers Group (AIMG), 429
  Australian Securities Exchange (ASX) Corporate Governance Council, 429, 430
  AustralianSuper, 428, 430
  best interests of beneficiaries in, 570
  Carbon Disclosure Project, 430
  Climate Action 100+ Australasian Engagement Group, 430
  collective action in

Australia (cont.)
    generally, 418–19, 436
    ACSI Code, 426
    acting-in-concert rules and, 435–36
    advantages of, 419
    co-ordinated share voting, 427–28
    engagement, 428–29
    ESG and, 427
    FSC Code, 426
    indirect forms of, 419
    intermediary organizations and, 429–32
    not simply governance issue, 419, 431–32
    overtly aggressive interventions, 426–27
    potential as stewardship tool, 425
    proxy votes, 427
    varieties of, 434–35
conflicts of interest in, 604
dispersed shareholders in, 418–19
Family Business Campaign (FB77) and, 313–14
Financial Services Council (FSC) Code
    ACSI Code compared, 421–22
    additional principles in, 19
    applicability of, 422
    asset managers and, 420–21
    citation patterns, 640–41
    collective action, 426
    'comply or explain', 423, 581
    coreness and, 648
    deviation from UK Code 2010/2012, 14–15, 16
    disclosure requirements, 422
    enforcement of, 422–23
    ESG in, 423, 562, 565
    foreign institutional investors and, 23
    global diffusion and, 635
    historical background, 420
    as industry-led initiative, 422
    influence of UK Code 2010/2012, 22–23
    issuance of, 420
    network analysis and, 646
    reporting requirements, 422
    revised approach, calls for, 424
    Seven Core Principles in, 620
    stewardship, 422
    types of firm represented by, 420–21
    voluntary nature of, 20
industry superannuation funds, 421
institutional investor control in, 27
intermediary organizations
    ACSI as, 429, 430, 432
    acting-in-concert rules and, 432
    avoiding confrontation by using, 432
    collective action and, 429–32
    ESG and, 429–30
    FSC as, 429
    proxy adviseors, 431
    stewardship and, 432–34
Investor Group on Climate Change, 430
Malaysia compared, 318
proxy advisors in, 431
Regnan, 430

Regulatory Guide 128: Collective Action by Investors (RG 128), 435–36
Responsible Investment Association Australasia, 430
Securities and Investments Commission (ASIC), 427–28, 435–36
self-regulation in, 604
sustainable finance in, 556, 558
Sustainable Finance Initiative, 556
Workforce Disclosure Initiative, 430

Bainbridge, Stephen, 465
Balp, Gaia, 148, 433
Banco do Brasil, 509
Bank of Canada, 450–51
Bank of East Asia (BEA), 291–92, 294
Bank Vontobel, 121
Barbarism, 286
Barclays Canada, 442
Barnier, Michel, 194
Barth, James R., 401
Bayer AG, 201, 202
Bebchuk, Lucian A., 331, 505
Becht, Marco, 133
Belgium
    climate-related financial disclosure in, 189
    Denmark compared, 172
    Financial Services and Markets Authority (FSMA), 584
Berle, Adolf A., 117–18, 284, 287, 289, 301, 454, 456, 464–65
Bermejo, Vicente J., 183
Bezos, Jeff, 310
Birkmose, Hanne S., 187, 191
BlackRock
    generally, 310
    in Brazil, 509, 513
    Carillion and, 59
    China compared, 382, 386–88
    climate change and, 595
    concentration of asset managers, 84, 456, 459
    engagement and, 537
    ESG and, 66
    in Germany, 210
    index funds and, 64
    in Investor Stewardship Group (ISG), 458
    mutual funds and, 465
    statistics, 122
    stewardship and, 199–200, 458, 586
    sustainability and, 549
BOC Kenya, 496
Bradesco, 509
Brandes Investment Partners, 233–34
Bratton, William W., 465
Brazil
    generally, 509
    asset managers in
        institutional regulatory framework, 515–16
        private regulation of, 518–19
        public regulation of, 516–17
    Association of Capital Markets Investors (AMEC)

Index

members, 509
objectives of, 509
Association of Capital Markets Investors (AMEC) Code
  ABRAPP and, 523, 524
  ANBIMA and, 523, 524
  citation patterns, 640–41
  communication, 513
  'comply or explain', 511
  conflicts of interest and, 512, 651
  coreness and, 648
  CVM and, 524
  deviation from UK Code 2010/2012, 16, 512–13
  drafting process, 510–11
  enforcement of, 524
  engagement, 513
  ESG in, 35, 512–13, 564
  fiduciary duties in, 511
  historical background, 509–11
  implementation of, 514
  legal standards, as complementing, 33
  need for, 524
  network analysis and, 646
  objectives of, 508–9
  pension funds and, 521
  policy disclosure, 512
  PREVIC and, 523, 524
  principles, 512–13
  promulgation of, 508
  regulatory agencies and, 524
  reporting requirements, 514–15
  signatories, 513–14, 567
  transparency, 513
  UN Principles of Responsible Investment (UNPRI) and, 522–23
  voluntary nature of, 654
Banco Nacional de Desenvolvimento Econômico e Social (BNDES), 509, 513
BNDES Participações S.A. (BNDESPAR), 509, 513
Brazilian Association for Financial Market Entities (ANDIMA), 516
Brazilian Association of Capital Markets Analysts and Investment Professionals (APIMEC), 514–15
Brazilian Association of Public Companies (ABRASCA) Self-Regulatory Code of Best Practices of Corporate Governance, 510
Brazilian Financial and Capital Markets Association (ANBIMA)
  generally, 514–15
  AMEC Code and, 523, 524
  asset managers and, 516, 518–19
  pension funds and, 520
Brazilian Institute of Corporate Governance (IBGC) Code of Best Practices of Corporate Governance, 510, 514–15
Brazilian Investment Banks Association (ANBID), 516
Brazilian National Association of Pension Funds (ABRAPP)
  AMEC Code and, 523, 524
  pension funds and, 514–15, 519–20, 522
Brazilian Stock Exchange, 521

'Car Wash Operation', 510, 520, 524
Civil Code, 516
conflicts of interest in, 604
Conselho Monetário Nacional (CMN), 520–21
corporate law, 512
Correios, 520
Funcesp, 509
'Greenfield Operation', 520
institutional investors in
  limited role of, 507–8
  as minority shareholders, 511
  passivity of, 508
  statistics, 507–8
  stewardship and, 525
investment funds in, 507
Mensalão Scandal, 520
National Pension Funds Authority (PREVIC)
  AMEC Code and, 523, 524
  pension funds and, 519–20, 521
OECD on, 508
pension funds in
  AMEC Code and, 521
  ESG and, 522
  institutional regulatory framework, 519–20
  private regulation of, 522
  public regulation of, 520–21
Petrolero Brasiliero S.A. (Petrobras), 510, 524
Petros, 509, 513
Principles of Responsible Investment (UNPRI) and, 522–23
Securities and Exchange Commission (CVM)
  AMEC Code and, 524
  asset managers and, 515–17, 518
  pension funds and, 520
self-regulation in, 604
US compared, 524
'X Group' scandal, 510
Bredin, Don, 401
Brundtland Report, 473, 551

Cadbury, Adrian, 530–31
Canada
  generally, 439–40
  Business Corporations Act (CBCA), 437–38, 441, 442
  Canadian Coalition for Good Governance (CCGG) Principles
    additional principles in, 19, 438–39
    climate change and, 449–52, 453
    collective action, 652
    compensation and, 445
    'comply or explain', 448
    conflicts of interest and, 445, 651
    corporate relations triangle and, 439
    deviation from UK Code 2010/2012, 15
    Directors' E&S Guidebook, 453
    enumeration of principles, 444
    ESG in, 562–63, 564
    expansion of purpose of, 443–44
    'hardening' and, 22
    identical word strings, measurement of, 643, 644

Canada (cont.)
    impact of, 453
    implications of, 447–48
    influence of UK Code 2020, 438
    long-term sustainability, 445–46
    minority shareholders and, 453
    monitoring, 445
    network analysis and, 646–47
    policy disclosure, 649–50, 651
    promulgation of, 437, 443
    purpose of, 439
    revisions of, 438
    risk reduction and, 448–49
    securities regulation and, 441
    Statement of Principles Regarding Member Activism, 437
    text of, 14
    voluntary nature of, 654
    voting policies, 652
    voting proxies, 445
Canadian Pacific (CP) Railroad, 445
Canadian Securities Administrators (CSA), 440
capital market in, 440
Capital Markets Regulatory Authority (CMRA), 440–41
Charter of Rights and Freedoms, 440
climate-related financial disclosure in, 189
Coalition for Good Governance, 10
conflicts of interest in, 604
Constitution Act 1867, 440
controlling-block shareholders in, 437
controlling shareholders concept in, 6–7
corporate governance in, 437
Davies Corporate Governance Report, 446, 447–48
Dey Committee Report, 442–43
dispersed shareholders in, 418–19
Expert Panel on Sustainable Finance, 450
extractive industry in, 451
Finance Canada, 450
Global Financial Crisis (2008) in, 448
institutional investor control in, 27
Ministry of Environment and Climate Change, 450
Ministry of Finance, 450
multiple stewardship codes in, 638
Office of Superintendent of Financial Institutions (OSFI), 448
Ontario Securities Act, 440
Ontario Securities Commission (OSC), 438, 441, 451
Ontario Teachers' Pension Plan, 442
Pan-Canadian Framework on Clean Growth and Climate Change, 449
Paris Agreement on Climate Change and, 449
provincial nature of law in, 440–41
proxy contests in, 442
Quebec Securities Commission, 438
securities regulation in, 437, 440–41
self-regulation in, 604
shareholder rights in, 438
sustainable finance in, 556
Toronto Stock Exchange (TSX), 441–43
TSX Venture Exchange (TSXV), 441–42

    UK compared, 437, 444
    US compared, 437, 452
Cao, Huijuan, 401
Cao, Yue, 401
Capital One, 210
Carillion plc, 59
Cassa Forense, 592
Charitable organizations, 80
Charles Schwab, 456
Cheffins, Brian R., 288, 289, 532
Cheil Industries, 255–56
Cheng, Qiang, 404–5
Chi, Jing, 397–98
China
    activist campaigns in
        generally, 382–83
        CCP and, 403–4, 405
        foreign-owned institutional investors (FOIIs), 382–83, 403
        infrequency of, 402–3, 405
        private-owned enterprises (POEs), 403, 404
        private-owned institutional investors (POIIs), 382–83, 403–4, 405
        securities investment funds (SIFs), 404
        'site visits', 404–5
        state-owned enterprises (SOEs), 403, 404, 405
        state-owned institutional investors (SOIIs), 382–83, 403, 405
    A-shares market, 381
    Banking and Insurance Regulatory Commission (CBIRC), 391, 408, 409
    'China model', 382, 386, 390, 406, 415–16
    Chinese Communist Party (CCP)
        activist campaigns and, 403–4, 405
        corporate governance, role in, 380
        institutional investors and, 382, 386, 390, 394–95, 413, 415–16
        insurance companies and, 392
        policy channeling and, 400–1
        private-owned enterprises (POEs) and, 380
        state-owned enterprises (SOEs) and, 380
    company law, 380
    controlling shareholders concept in, 7, 37
    Corporate Governance Code, 390–91, 412–16, 614
    'corporatization without privatization', 380
    Directory of Central Financial Enterprises, 408
    economic growth of, 379
    empirical research on
        generally, 382, 396
        compensation, 398–400
        conclusions from, 400–1
        foreign-owned institutional investors (FOIIs), 401–2
        insulation from government pressure, based on, 396–97
        policy channeling, 399
        private-owned enterprises (POEs), 399
        qualified foreign institutional investors (QFIIs), 400, 401
        securities investment funds (SIFs), 397–98
        state-owned enterprises (SOEs), 398–99

type of company, based on, 397
type of institutional investor, based on, 396, 397
ESG in, 416
Family Business Campaign (FB77) and, 313–14
foreign-owned institutional investors (FOIIs)
   generally, 382
   activist campaigns, 382–83, 403
   empirical research, 401–2
   limited influence of, 390
   minority holdings, 389
   policy channeling, 407, 411
   regulation of, 388–90
   statistics, 386–88
Guiding Opinions on Regulating the Asset Management Business of Financial Institutions, 391
Hong Kong, relationship with, 291, 293
institutional investors in
   generally, 614
   'atomization' of, 382, 394
   as autochthonous mechanism of corporate governance, 383–84, 413–16
   CCP and, 382, 386, 390, 394–95, 413, 415–16
   concentrated shareholding, 618
   corporate governance function of, 405–6, 411
   diversity of, 385–86
   government, role of, 380, 394
   importance of, 385–86
   independence of, 394–95
   insurance companies, 391–92
   lack of academic focus on, 381–82, 395
   limited influence of, 395
   pension funds, 392–93
   private investment funds, 394
   securities institutions, 393
   state-controlled institutional investors, 407–9
   statistics, 381, 384–85
   trust companies, 393
insurance companies in, 391–92
Insurance Regulatory Commission (CIRC), 391–92
Interim Measures for the Supervision and Administration of Financial Holding Companies, 408
Interim Measures on the Management of Securities Investment Funds (SIF Interim Measures), 390
interim Regulations on the Management of the Leading Personnel of Central Financial Enterprises, 408
Investment Decision Committees (IDCs), 399, 400, 410–11
Law on Administrative Discipline for Public Officials, 408–9
Mainland–Hong Kong Stock Connect, 386, 388–89
Measures for the Management of Enterprise Annuity Funds, 393
Ministry of Commerce, 388
Ministry of Finance (MOF), 392, 407–8
Ministry of Labor and Social Security (MOLSS), 392
Nansham Venture Capital Fund, 390
National Social Security Fund (NSSF), 392–93
pension funds in, 392–93

People's Bank of China (PBOC), 389, 391, 392, 408, 409
policy channeling in
   generally, 383
   CCP and, 400–1
   empirical research, 399
   foreign-owned institutional investors (FOIIs), 407, 411
   mapping of mechanism for, 406–11
   political objectives of, 406–7
   private-owned institutional investors (POIIs) and, 405, 407, 411–12
   qualified foreign institutional investors (QFIIs), 407, 411
   securities investment funds (SIFs), 410–11, 412
   state-controlled institutional investors, 407–9
   state-owned institutional investors (SOIIs) and, 405, 406–9, 412
   targeted use of, 405–6
   'window guidance', 407
private investment funds in, 394
private-owned enterprises (POEs)
   activist campaigns, 403, 404
   CCP and, 380
   empirical research, 399
private-owned institutional investors (POIIs)
   generally, 382, 394–95
   activist campaigns, 382–83, 403–4, 405
   policy channeling and, 405, 407, 411–12
   state-owned institutional investors (SOIIs) versus, 413
qualified foreign institutional investors (QFIIs)
   generally, 386
   compensation and, 400
   empirical research, 400, 401
   policy channeling, 407, 411
   regulation of, 388–89
renminbi qualified foreign institutional investors (RQFIIs), 386, 388–89
Securities Association of China (SAC), 411
securities institutions in, 393
Securities Investment Fund Law, 391, 394
securities investment funds (SIFs)
   generally, 390–91
   activist campaigns, 404
   empirical research, 396, 397–98
   policy channeling, 410–11, 412
Securities Investor Services Centre (ISC), 412
securities law, 410
Securities Regulatory Commission (CSRC)
   compensation and, 398, 400
   foreign-owned institutional investors (FOIIs) and, 388
   National Social Security Fund (NSSF) and, 392
   policy channeling and, 399, 408, 409, 410–11
   qualified foreign institutional investors (QFII) and, 388–89
   securities investment funds (SIFs) and, 390, 391
   trust companies and, 393
Shanghai Stock Exchange (SSE), 381
Shenzhen Connect, 389
Shenzhen Stock Exchange (SZSE), 381
Singapore compared, 302

China (cont.)
  social security funds (SSFs), 392–93
  State Administration for Industry and Commerce, 388
  State Administration of Foreign Exchange (SAFE), 388–89, 407–8
  State Administration of Taxation, 388
  state-controlled institutional investors, 407–9
  State Council, 407–8
  State-owned Assets Supervision and Administration Commission (SASAC), 407–8
  state-owned enterprises (SOEs)
    generally, 603
    activist campaigns, 403, 404, 405
    CCP and, 380
    empirical research, 398–99
    government, role of, 380
  state-owned institutional investors (SOIIs)
    generally, 382, 394–95
    activist campaigns, 382–83, 403, 405
    National Team, 406, 409
    policy channeling and, 405, 406–9, 412
    private-owned institutional investors (POIIs) versus, 413
  sustainable finance in, 556
  trust companies in, 393
  UK compared, 383–84, 395, 413–16
  US compared, 379, 395, 402
  Wuhan Securities Investment Fund, 390
  Zhemin Tianhong Investment Partnership, 404
  Zhenxing Biopharmaceutical and Chemical Co., Ltd., 404
Chiu, Iris H.-Y., 598, 375
Chizema, Amon, 398
Cho, Yang-Ho, 255
Chun, Kyung-Hoon, 625
CK Hutchinson Holdings, 313
Climate Action 100+, 555
Climate change
  Canadian Coalition for Good Governance (CCGG) Principles and, 449–52, 453
  Paris Agreement on Climate Change, 449, 552, 554
  pension funds and, 81
  stewardship codes and, 188–89
  sustainable finance and, 552–53
  UK Code 2010/2012 and, 47–48, 62–64
  UK Code 2020 and, 66
Cluster analysis, 647–48
Coffee, John C. Jr., 143, 467
Cohen, Alma, 331
Collective action. See specific country
'Collective action problem', 249–50
Collective investment schemes, 473, 538–40
Colonial, 428
Comparison of stewardship codes
  generally, 38–43
  enforcement, 22
Complementing legal standards, stewardship codes as, 31, 32–34
Complexity of stewardship, 5
Concentration of ownership, 176

Conceptions of stewardship
  generally, 5
  controlling actors concept, 7–8
  controlling shareholders concept, 6–7
  corporate governance concept, 5–6, 12
  ESG concept, 8
  future evolution of, 37
  investment management concept, 8–9
Conflicts of interest. See specific country
Controlling actors concept of stewardship, 7–8
Controlling-block shareholders. See also specific country
  in Asia, 623
  characterizing as stewards, 606–8
  comparison, 27
  controlling shareholders concept of stewardship, 6–7
  director duties and, 603, 609–10
  effectiveness of stewardship codes and, 25
  ESG and, 601, 602
  extension of stewardship concept to, 371, 372
  fiduciary duties of, 606
  halo signalling and, 611–12
  institutional investors versus, 302, 603
  intermediary organizations versus, 454
  outside UK and US, 6, 27–28, 600–1, 611
  problems with, 602
  reform of stewardship codes and
    generally, 603
    applicability, clarification of, 606
    controlling-block shareholders, defining, 606
    duties of shareholders, clarification of, 606
    limitations of, 612
    responsible persons, clarification of, 606
    stewardship, defining, 606
  related party transaction (RPT) rules and
    ESG and, 608–9
    reform of, 603, 608–9
  role of stewardship, 601, 602, 611
  stewardship codes and, 610–11
Co-operatives, 113
Coop (Swiss company), 113
Coreness, 648
Corporate governance. See also specific country
  generally, 530, 547–48
  in Asia
    corporate governance convergence and, 615, 616, 628–30
    'faux convergence', 628–30
  corporate governance concept of stewardship, 5–6, 12
  distributed ledger technology (DLT) and, 541–42
  'divergence within convergence', 615
  engagement and, 616
  ESG and, 545–47
  'faux convergence', 615–16, 628–30
  formal convergence, 615
  functional convergence, 615
  fund governance, 543–45
  'global governance' agenda, 616
  halo signalling and, 29–30, 572
  investment chain and, 540–43

investment management and, 530 (*See also* Investment management)
OECD on, 629
'separation of funds from managers', 540–41
superficial convergence, 615
sustainable corporate governance
    institutional investors and, 177
    in Norway, 186–89
Corporate social responsibility (CSR)
    ESG compared, 196
    in India, 373
    in Norway, 185–86
    return on investment, effect on, 74
    socially responsible investment (SRI) and, 560–61
    sustainable finance and, 551–52, 553
    in Taiwan, 261–62, 265–66, 275–77, 280
Council of Institutional Investors, 463
Covid-19 pandemic, 549, 571, 611
CP All plc, 350–51, 355–56
Credit Suisse Asset Management (Schweiz) AG, 121, 122, 589
Criteria Caixa S.A., 291
CSR. *See* Corporate social responsibility (CSR)
Cumulative voting, 609
Cuñat, Vicente, 183

Dalton Investments, 233–34
DeCloet, Derek, 448–49
Defined contribution schemes, 538, 543–44
DekaBank, 208–10
Deka Investment GmbH, 208–10
Deloitte, 448
Denmark
    Alternative Investment Fund Managers Act, 167, 168
    asset managers, dialogue with directors, 172, 173
    Belgium compared, 172
    Business Authority, 154–55
    Capital Markets Act, 167–68
    Committee on Corporate Governance
        generally, 32, 150, 173
        collaboration with board and, 162
        compliance reports, 170
        'comply or explain' and, 162–63
        corporate governance concept and, 171–72
        engagement and, 159–60
        escalation of activities and, 161
        institutional investors and, 172
        monitoring and dialogue and, 160–61
        on phasing out of Stewardship Code, 171
        proportionality principle and, 157–59
        reporting requirements and, 160
        Stewardship Code and, 154–55, 157, 172–73
        voting policies and, 161
    Companies Act, 151, 152, 167–68
    concept of stewardship in, 176
    Corporate Governance Code, 190
    Danish Shareholders' Association, 167
    directors, dialogue with institutional investors and asset managers, 172, 173
    Financial Business Act, 162, 167, 168, 169
    financial institutions in, 152–53
    Financial Statements Act, 160–61, 163
    Financial Supervisory Authority, 156, 169
    future of stewardship in, 171
    Global Financial Crisis (2008) in, 150
    increase in engagement, empirical evidence of, 166–67
    institutional investors in
        Committee on Corporate Governance and, 172
        dialogue with directors, 172, 173
        under SRD II, 168, 169
        statistics, 176–77
    Kenya compared, 504
    legal framework for stewardship in, 151, 152–53
    Malaysia compared, 323
    Nasdaq OMX Copenhagen, 153
    Netherlands compared, 172
    Norway compared, 175–76, 187
    Recommendations on Corporate Governance
        generally, 151
        'comply or explain' and, 163
        corporate governance concept and, 171–72
        Stewardship Code compared, 150, 151, 154–55, 156, 172–73
    regulatory framework for stewardship in, 151
    shareholders in
        meetings, 152
        registration, 152
        shareholder democracy, 152, 153
        statistics, 153–54
    SRD II and
        generally, 34, 150, 151
        asset managers under, 169
        as complementing Stewardship Code, 187
        'comply or explain', 169
        effect of, 173
        engagement, disclosure requirements, 168–69
        impact on stewardship, 170–71
        institutional investors under, 168, 169
        overlap with Stewardship Code, 169–71
        ownership, disclosure requirements, 168
        transposing of, 167–68
    Stewardship Code
        generally, 151
        citation patterns, 640–41
        collaboration with board, 162
        Committee on Corporate Governance and, 154–55, 157, 172–73
        'comply or explain', 156, 162–63
        conflicts of interest and, 162
        consultations leading to, 156–57
        contractual nature of duties under, 155–56
        corporate governance concept and, 156, 171–72
        deviation from UK Code 2010/2012, 150, 151, 155–56, 158
        engagement, 159–60, 583
        escalation of activities, 161, 651
        ESG in, 35, 561, 563, 565
        goals of, 150, 154–55, 191
        as governmental stewardship code, 623

Denmark (cont.)
    increase in engagement, empirical evidence of, 166–67
    legal family effect, lack of, 659
    legal standards, as complementing, 32
    monitoring and dialogue, 160–61
    network analysis and, 646
    overlap with SRD II, 169–71
    phasing out of, 171
    principles, 155
    proportionality principle, 157–59
    Recommendations on Corporate Governance compared, 150, 151, 154–55, 156, 172–73
    reporting requirements, 160, 164–66
    as 'semi-hard law', 163
    Seven Core Principles in, 658
    as 'soft' law, 156, 162–63
    SRD II as complementing, 187
    as substituting legal standards, 34
    target of, 155
    voting policies, 161–62
  UK compared, 172
Deutsche Bank, 208–10, 509
Dey, Peter, 442–43
DIA (ETF), 459
Diffusion of stewardship codes. *See* Global diffusion of stewardship codes
Director duties, 603, 609–10
Direct registration system, 293–94
Dispersed shareholders, 284, 286–87, 292, 369, 418–19, 491
Distributed ledger technology (DLT), 541–42
Dobbin, Frank, 293
Dodd, Merrick, 117–18, 464–65
Doidge, Craig, 433, 447
Donald, David C., 627
Doosan, 241
Dow Jones Industrial Average (DJIA), 459
Du, Fei, 404–5
DuPont de Nemours, 294
DWS Investment GmbH, 208–10
Dyck, Alexander, 433, 447

East African Community (EAC), 492
Economic crises, stewardship codes and, 29, 30
EFAMA. *See* European Fund and Asset Management Association (EFAMA)
Effissimo Capital Management, 233–34
Eisenberg, Melvin, 287
Elliott Advisors, 148, 249
Elliott Capital, 291–92, 294
Elliott Management Corp., 94
Elsig, Manfred, 641, 642
Endowment funds, 79
Enforcement of stewardship codes. *See also specific country*
  generally, 575
  'apply and explain', 581
  broad approach to, 573, 597
  burring of boundaries, 597
  civil claims, 574, 589–91
  comparison, 22
  'comply or explain', 580, 581–82, 588–89
  continuum of, 587
  ex ante enforcement, 579–80, 593, 596, 597
  ex post enforcement, 579–80, 593, 596, 597
  formal enforcement
    generally, 578–79, 597
    adherence procedures, 579, 597–98
    civil claims, 574, 589–91
    'comply or explain' and, 588–89
    informal enforcement versus, 575–76, 587, 596
    liability issues, 588
    limits of public enforcement, 588–89, 597
    membership sanctions, 579, 584–85, 597–98
    in stewardship networks, 591–93
  informal enforcement
    generally, 574, 579, 597
    ex ante enforcement, 593
    ex post enforcement, 593
    formal enforcement versus, 575–76, 587, 596
    investor associations, 594
    NGOs, 595
    private actors, 594
    public actors, 593–94
    self-enforcement, 593
    social actors, 595
    third-party enforcement, 593–95
    third-party ratings, 594
  lax enforcement as challenge, 24, 36
  mandatory enforcement, 582
  mechanisms of, 573
  multi-actor and multi-modal system of, 574, 595–97, 598
  'name and shame', 574, 594, 595, 596
  norm-enforcers
    generally, 573, 597
    investor associations, 594
    NGOs, 577–78, 595
    private actors, 575–76, 577, 594
    public actors, 575–76, 577, 593–94
    self-enforcement, 576–77, 586, 593
    social actors, 577–78, 595
    third-party enforcement, 577–78, 586–87, 593–95
    unilateral enforcement, 576–77
  reasons for deviation from UK Code 2010/2012, 24
  refinement, necessity of, 598
  reticent enforcement approach, 583–84
  'soft' law as predominant paradigm, 572, 574
  taxonomy of, 598
    generally, 576
    table, 587
    three-dimensional nature of, 586
  temporal dimension of, 573, 579–80, 596, 597
  UK as outlier, 20–24
  voluntary enforcement, 580, 581–82
Engagement. *See also specific country*
  generally, 197
  corporate governance and, 616
  disclosure requirements, 196
  ESG and, 91, 558
  Global Financial Crisis (2008) and, 193, 613–14

hedge fund activism and, 56–57, 142, 201, 461–62
index funds and, 198–99
institutional investors and, 529
SRD II and, 46–47, 377, 529–30, 535, 582
sustainable finance and, 558
Enlightened shareholder value (ESV) principle, 372–73, 374
'Enlightened stewardship', 72–73
Enpam, 592
Enriques, Luca, 592–93
Enron, 118
Environmental, social, and governance (ESG). *See also specific country*
   agency problems, 8
   asset managers and, 199
   controlling-block shareholders and, 601, 602
   corporate governance and, 545–47
   CSR compared, 196
   director duties and, 603, 609–10
   economic impact of, 206
   engagement and, 91, 558
   ESG concept of stewardship, 8
   EU and, 547
   halo signalling and, 611–12
   index funds and, 466–67
   institutional investors and, 606
   moving beyond mere business case, 570–71
   mutual funds and, 468–69
   OECD and, 339
   pension funds and, 77, 545–47
   related party transaction (RPT) rules and, 608–9
   return on investment, effect on, 73–76
   rise of, 34–35, 36, 37
   socially responsible investment (SRI) and, 196, 557–58, 559–61
   SRD II and, 560, 565
   in stewardship codes, 561–65
   as strengthening stewardship, 36, 37, 197
   sustainable finance and, 558
   UN Principles of Responsible Investment (UNPRI) and, 196
Ernst & Young, 618
Escalation of activities. *See specific country*
ESG. *See* Environmental, social, and governance (ESG)
Ethnocentrism, 292
Ethos, 123
European Commission
   Action Plan for Financing Sustainable Growth, 552–53, 556, 560
   on escalation of activities, 161
   Green Paper (2010), 194–95
   Green Paper (2011), 195
   on monitoring and dialogue, 160–61
   Reflection Group, 195
   on stewardship, 157–58
   Sustainable Finance Action Plan, 189, 195
   Sustainable Finance Initiative, 188–89, 190, 191
European Fund and Asset Management Association (EFAMA)

Stewardship Code
   generally, 4, 11, 196
   adoption of, 640
   cluster analysis and, 648
   coreness and, 648
   deviation from UK Code 2010/2012, 16
   enforcement of, 596
   escalation of activities, 651
   ESG in, 563
   global diffusion and, 632, 635
   identical word strings, measurement of, 643, 644
   influence of UK Code 2010/2012, 13–14, 136
   Italy Stewardship Principles compared, 136, 137–38, 146, 635
   legal family effect, lack of, 659
   Norway Recommendation, influence on, 180–82
   policy disclosure, 649–50
   regulatory framework and, 568
   Seven Core Principles in, 658
Stewardship Principles, influence of, 180–81
European Green Deal, 188
European Securities and Markets Authority (ESMA), 144
European Union. *See also specific country*
   Alternative Investment Fund Managers Directive (AIFMD), 167–68, 214, 541
   CSR Directive, 216
   Disclosure Regulation, 189, 191
   ESG and, 547
   as exporter of legal norms and principles, 631
   High-Level Expert Group on Sustainable Finance (HLEG), 552, 555–56
   legal transplants from, 631
   Market in Financial Instruments Directive (MiFID), 214, 216
   National Competent Authorities (NCAs), 574
   Non-financial Reporting Directive (NFRD), 128
   shareholder empowerment in, 174–75
   Shareholder Rights Directive I (SRD I)
      adoption of, 195
      Italy and, 133, 135
      Netherlands and, 93
      shareholder control and, 92
   Shareholder Rights Directive II (SRD II) (*See also specific country*)
      adoption of, 195
      enforcement of, 582–86
      engagement, 46–47, 377, 529–30, 535, 582
      ESG and, 560, 565
      impact on stewardship codes, 660
      investment chain and, 542
      perception of institutional investors in, 178
      policy disclosure, 457, 582–83
      regulatory framework and, 568
      'say-on-pay' in, 534
      'semi-hard' law in, 573, 574, 582–86
      shareholder empowerment and, 175
      socially responsible investing (SRI) and, 560
      'soft' law and, 536
      sustainable finance and, 556

European Union (cont.)
  transparency and, 217
  UK Code 2010/2012, influence of, 33–34, 192
  Takeover Bids Directive, 161
  Taxonomy Regulation, 191
  Undertakings for Collective Investment in Transferable Securities (UCITS), 167–68, 214, 216
  Undertakings for Collective Investment in Transferable Securities Directive (UCITS), 538, 540, 542
Excessive risk-taking
  stewardship and, 196, 417–18
  in US, 417
Excessive risk-taking as cause
  as cause of Global Financial Crisis (2008), 69, 192, 298, 301, 417, 613–14
  UK Code 2010/2012, restraining as goal of, 223, 238, 298, 301, 373, 456, 613–14
Exchange traded funds (ETFs), 454, 537
Exit rights, 541

Facebook, 310
Fama, Eugene F., 537
Family-controlled business enterprises. *See specific country*
Far East Organization, 313
FEMSA (Mexican company), 105
Fidelity International, 66, 310, 456, 459
Fiduciary duties
  in Brazil, 511
  of controlling-block shareholders, 606
  of pension funds, 545–47
  in South Africa, 487
  in Taiwan, 267
  in UK, 529
Fiduciary managers, 83–85
Filho, Mattos, 513
Fink, Larry, 465, 586
Finland
  concept of stewardship in, 176
  institutional investors in, 176–77
  lack of stewardship code in, 176
Firth, Michael, 397, 398–400
Fisch, Jill E., 465
Flaherty, Jim, 448
Ford, Henry, 465
Formal design and content of stewardship, 5
401(k) plans, 468
France
  administrative penalties in, 585, 588
  climate-related financial disclosure in, 189
  enforcement in, 585, 588
  Germany compared, 218
  Hong Kong compared, 293
  Italy compared, 131
Franklin Templeton, 509
Franks, Julian, 133
Free-rider problem, 198, 503
French, Kenneth R., 537
Freshfields Bruckhaus Deringer, 559, 569
Freshfields Report, 546, 559, 569

Friedman, Milton, 91, 117–18
Fu, Xiaoqing Maggie, 401
Function of stewardship, 5

Gao, Jin, 397
Garrett, Geoffrey, 293
Geis, George S., 371
Germany
  generally, 193
  ARUG II, 214
  asset managers in, 207–11, 218–20
  BaFin, 210–11
  Basic Law, 288
  benefits of potential stewardship code in, 217–21
  best interests of beneficiaries in, 570
  Capital Investment Act (Kapitalanlagegesetzbuch), 201
  controlling shareholders concept in, 37, 204–5
  Corporate Governance Code (CGC), 204, 211
  Corporate Governance Commission, 211
  DAX, 200, 208, 212
  economic arguments against stewardship code, 205–7
  engagement in, 200–2
  foreign investors in, 208–10
  France compared, 218
  functional arguments against stewardship code, 204–5
  German Association of Investment Professionals (DVFA) Code, 214, 216
  German Investment Funds Association (BVI) Rules of Conduct, 213–14, 216
  hedge fund activism in, 201
  Hong Kong compared, 293
  institutional investors in, 207–11
  Italy compared, 131, 133
  legal objections to stewardship code, 202–4
    checks and balances, as disrupting, 202–3
    dialogue between board and investors and, 204
    passive investments and, 203–4
    private benefits and, 203
  legitimacy of institutional investors in, 215
  Netherlands compared, 218
  Norway compared, 186–87
  pension funds in, 218
  political arguments against stewardship code, 207–11, 221
  private initiatives in, 213–15, 216
  regulation as alternative to stewardship code, 211–12
  reluctance to adopt stewardship code, 192–93, 202, 221
  self-regulation in, 215
  shareholder involvement in, 50
  SRD II and, 34, 211, 214, 216, 221
  Stock Corporation Act (Aktiengesetz), 201, 203, 211
  substitutes for stewardship code in, 215–17
  Switzerland compared, 112, 114–15, 116
  UK compared, 218, 288
  voluntary compliance in, 212, 215
  voting rights in, 201
Gilson, Ronald J., 174, 284, 427, 432–33, 461, 615
Glass Lewis, 123, 247
Global Compact, 179–80, 183, 186, 557–58

Global diffusion of stewardship codes
  generally, 3-4, 11
  in Asia
    generally, 614, 616
    corporate governance convergence and, 615, 616, 628-30
    differences from UK Codes, 621-23
    difficulty in drawing conclusions from, 615
    'faux convergence', 628-30
    'global governance' agenda, as challenge to, 616
    governmental stewardship codes, 623
    policy tools, stewardship codes as, 614
    Seven Core Principles, 620
    'soft' law, 619-20
    UK Codes versus, 614
  Australia and, 635
  constraints on, 370
  core concept
    generally, 12-13
    deviation from UK Code 2010/2012, 14-15
  'cut and paste', 621
  difficulties in transplanting law, 504-5
  diffusion defined, 637-38
  diversity in, 601, 659
  EFAMA Stewardship Code and, 632, 635
  empirical research
    generally, 632
    citation patterns, 640-41
    cluster analysis, 647-48
    coreness, 648
    data collection, 632
    explanations of diffusion patterns, 652-55, 661-62
    future research, 659-60
    hierarchical clusters, 647-48
    historical evolution of stewardship codes, 638-40
    identical word strings, measurement of, 641-44
    implications of, 632
    length of stewardship codes, 660-61
    methodology of study, 636-37
    network analysis, 644-47
    ranked similarity with UK Code 2010/2012, 657-58
    scope of study, 632-35
    Seven Core Principles, 648-52
    UK as exporter of stewardship, 655-58
  explanations of diffusion patterns
    civil law versus common law countries, 654
    coding, 661-62
    enforcement method and, 653-54
    language and, 653
    nature of code and, 653-54
    table, 653
    t-test statistics, 654-55, 658
    type of issuer and, 653
  future research, 659-60
  ICGN Stewardship Code and, 632, 635
  incongruities in, 369-70
  India and, 635
  Japan-Korea regional cluster of global diffusion, 632, 644, 648
  legal family effect, lack of, 659
  legal transplants (*See* Legal transplants)
  Malaysia-Thailand regional cluster of global diffusion, 644
  primary content
    generally, 13
    deviation from UK Code 2010/2012, 15-16
  questions raised by, 370
  regional clusters, 632, 644, 648
  terminology, 637-38
  text
    generally, 13-14
    deviation from UK Code 2010/2012, 16
  titles, 14
  UK Code 2010/2012,
    generally, 11-14, 616
    assumptions regarding, 616-19, 631-32
    controlling-block shareholders and, 28-29
    empirical evidence, 632
    institutional investor control and, 28-29
    level of, 17
    monolithic view of, 617-18
    OECD on, 618
    ranked similarity, 657-58
    Seven Core Principles, 11-14, 17, 620, 648-52, 655, 659
    UK as exporter of stewardship, 655-58
Global Financial Centres Index, 293
Global Financial Crisis (2008)
  in Canada, 448
  in Denmark, 150
  engagement and, 193, 613-14
  excessive risk-taking as cause of, 69, 192, 298, 301, 417, 613-14
  hedge fund activism and, 445
  short-term focus as cause of, 298, 301, 613-14
  stewardship and, 112, 175, 239
  sustainable finance and, 552
  in Thailand, 336
  in UK, 417, 533-34
  UK Code 2010/2012 and, 3, 44, 228, 261, 457, 640
  US attitudes towards, 417
Global Forum on Transparency and Exchange of Information, 186
Global Reporting Initiative (GRI) Sustainability Reporting Guidelines, 261-62, 277, 280, 322
Global Sustainable Investment Alliance (GSIA), 558
Goldman Sachs Asset Management, 458
Gordon, Jeffrey N., 174, 284, 427, 432-33, 615, 617-18, 630
Goshen, Zohar, 462
Goto, Gen, 260, 292, 622
'Governance nexus', 9
Governmental stewardship codes
  generally, 17-18, 244
  in Asia, 623
  geographic divide with private stewardship codes, 19-20
  motives for creating, 18
  UK Code 2010/2012 and, 19
Grant, Jeremy, 133

Greece
  administrative penalties in, 585, 588
  enforcement in, 585, 588
Griffin, Caleb, 467
Griffith, Sean J., 463
GS (Korean company), 241
G20
  Financial Stability Board, 188–89, 555
  Principles of Corporate Governance (*See* OECD/G20 Principles of Corporate Governance)
  Task Force on Climate-Related Financial Disclosures (TCFD), 188–89, 555
Guiding Principles on Business and Human Rights (UNGP), 179–80, 183, 186
Guoco Management Company, 291
Guyatt, Danyelle, 539

Hai, Jiang, 401
Halo signalling
  generally, 610–11
  in Asia, 29–30, 285
  to attract foreign investment, 607
  controlling-block shareholders and, 611–12
  corporate governance and, 29–30, 572
  defined, 601
  ESG and, 611–12
  in Hong Kong, 30, 626–28
  political motivations for, 601
  in Singapore, 189–90, 626–28
  in Taiwan, 30
  in Thailand, 30
  in UK Code 2010/2012, 29–30
  in UK Code 2020, 628
Hanjin Group, 241, 255
Hanjin Kal, 255
Hanwha, 241
Hart, Oliver, 91
Hedge fund activism. *See also specific country*
  alliances and, 532–33
  disruptive role of, 533
  engagement and, 56–57, 142, 201, 461–62
  as financial innovation, 533
  Global Financial Crisis (2008) and, 445
  institutional investors and, 142–43
  'offensive' activism, 532
  shareholder functional capacities and, 51
  short-term focus of, 533
Heineken, 104–5
Heritage Foundation, 293
Hermes Equity Ownership Services, 325–26, 430, 458, 509
Hierarchical clusters, 647–48
Hill, Jennifer G., 4, 458, 617, 619
Hirst, Scott, 331
Historical evolution of stewardship codes, 638–40
Hoepner, Andreas, 206, 212, 215
Holding companies, 293
Hong Kong
  generally, 286
  China, relationship with, 291, 293
  controlling-block holdings in, 291
  entrepreneurial shareholders in, 291, 293, 296
  family-controlled business enterprises in, 291, 293, 295, 296, 313
  France compared, 293
  Germany compared, 293
  halo signalling in, 30, 626–28
  Hang Seng Index, 291
  holding companies in, 293
  institutional investors, minor role of, 291–92
  as International Financial Centre (IFC), 285–86, 293–95, 296, 627
  in Korea, 260
  Principles of Responsible Ownership
    generally, 296, 614
    adoption of, 289–90
    cluster analysis and, 648
    coreness and, 648
    deviation from UK Code 2010/2012, 289, 290
    entrepreneurial shareholders and, 296
    ESG in, 562–63
    halo signalling and, 30
    identical word strings, measurement of, 643, 644
    network analysis and, 646–47
    unintended consequences of, 294
  Registrar of Companies, 290
  Securities and Futures Commission (SFC), 7, 289–90, 627
  Singapore compared, 295
  state-owned Assets Supervision and Administration Commission of the State Council (SASAC) and, 291, 296
  state owned enterprises (SOEs) in, 291
  Stock Exchange of Hong Kong (SEHK), 290, 291
  UK compared, 293
  US compared, 293–94
Hong Leong Company, 291
HSBC Hong Kong, 291
HSBC plc, 291
Hu, May, 397
Huang, Wei, 400
Hyundai Heavy Industry, 241
Hyundai Motors, 241

Iceland
  concept of stewardship in, 176
  institutional investors in, 176–77
  lack of stewardship code in, 176
ICGN. *See* International Corporate Governance Network (ICGN)
ICICI Bank, 364
Imperial Bank of Kenya, 502
Inarcassa, 592
Independent governance committees, 80–83
Index funds. *See also* Mutual funds
  generally, 455, 470
  activist hedge funds compared, 461–62
  agency problems in, 464–65
  business model, 459
  competing incentives in, 465
  cost–benefit analysis, 199–200

disclosure and, 460–61
engagement and, 198–99
ESG and, 466–67
fee structure, 460
as imperfect proxies, 465–66
passive investment, 460
principal competence costs, 462
reputational incentives and, 64
self-dealing and, 465
shareholder functional capacities and, 52
statistics, 459
stewardship and, 198–200, 461, 462–67
in US, 459
Index tracking
financial incentives and, 53–54, 55
reputational incentives and, 64
shareholder functional capacities and, 51–52
India
generally, 362
Companies Act 2013, 363, 376
controlling-block shareholders in, 370
CSR in, 373
family-controlled business enterprises in, 361, 371
Financial Stability and Development Council (FSDC), 366, 367–69
government, role of, 361
Housing Development Finance Corporation (HDFC), 364
India–UK Financial Partnership, 366
institutional investors, minor role of, 361, 377
Insurance Regulatory and Development Authority of India (IRDAI) Code (2017)
generally, 361, 378, 614
cluster analysis and, 648
comparison of Codes, 367
'comply or explain', 22–23, 377
global diffusion and, 635
historical background, 366
identical word strings, measurement of, 643, 644
issuance of, 367
monitoring, 651
network analysis and, 646–47
policy disclosure, 649, 650
rationale for adoption, 640
stakeholders, adoption of UK approach, 374
voting policies, 652
Insurance Regulatory and Development Authority of India (IRDAI) Code (2020)
generally, 378
collective action, 652
comparison of Codes, 367
global diffusion and, 635
historical background, 366
identical word strings, measurement of, 643, 644
mandatory nature of, 377
monitoring, 23
network analysis and, 646–47
rationale for adoption, 640
Seven Core Principles in, 620
stakeholders, adoption of UK approach, 374
voluntary nature of, 23
lack of comprehensive stewardship code in, 638–40
mutual funds in, 363
patterns of shareholding in, 364
Pension Fund Regulatory and Development Authority (PFRDA) Code
generally, 361, 378, 614
collective action, 652
comparison of Codes, 367
global diffusion and, 635
historical background, 366
identical word strings, measurement of, 643, 644
issuance of, 367
mandatory nature of, 377, 581
monitoring, 23, 651
network analysis and, 646–47
policy disclosure, 649
rationale for adoption, 640
Seven Core Principles in, 620
stakeholders, adoption of UK approach, 374
voluntary nature of, 23
voting policies, 652
proxy advisers in, 363
regulation in, 362, 376
Securities and Exchange Board of India (SEBI) Code
generally, 361, 378, 614
cluster analysis and, 648
collective action, 652
comparison of Codes, 367
escalation of activities, 651
global diffusion and, 635
historical background, 361, 366
identical word strings, measurement of, 643, 644
issuance of, 366–67
mandatory nature of, 377, 581, 654
monitoring, 23, 651
mutual funds and, 363
network analysis and, 646–47
policy disclosure, 649
rationale for adoption, 640
recommendations regarding, 367–69
Seven Core Principles in, 620, 658
stakeholders, adoption of UK approach, 374
voluntary nature of, 23
voting policies, 652
shareholder activism in
evolution of, 363–66
limited impact of, 370
shareholder proposals in, 364
stakeholder approach
generally, 362
adoption of UK approach, 374
non-shareholders and, 375
obligations on boards, 374
pluralistic nature of, 374–75
stewardship in
deviation from UK approach recommended, 360, 361–62, 372, 375, 376–78

India (cont.)
   'hard law' approach recommended, 377
   historical background, 361, 366–69
   influence of UK Code 2010/2012, 366
   lack of formal code, 361
   monitoring and, 23
   sui generis approach recommended, 360, 362
   voluntary nature of, 20, 23
   UK compared, 370, 375
Indonesia, Family Business Campaign (FB77) and, 313–14
Industrial cross-holdings, 284
ING Investments NV, 105–6
Institutional investor control
   in Australia, 27
   in Canada, 27
   as challenge, 36–37
   comparison, 27
   effectiveness of stewardship codes and, 25
   private stewardship codes and, 28
   rise of, 174
   in UK, 25–26, 27, 600
   UK Code 2010/2012, global diffusion of, 28–29
   in US, 25–26, 456, 600
Institutional investors. *See also specific country*
   controlling-block shareholders versus, 302, 603
   cost–benefit analysis, 199–200
   defined, 482
   engagement and, 529
   ESG and, 606
   expending stewardship concept beyond, 372
   hedge fund activism and, 142–43
   as minority shareholders, 600
   negative perception of, 177, 178
   OECD on, 508
   as passive shareholders, 613
   positive perception of, 177–78, 417–18
   rise of, 287–89, 290–91
   socially responsible investment (SRI) and, 550, 551 (*See also* Socially responsible investment (SRI))
   stewardship and, 175, 194
   sustainability and (*See* Socially responsible investment (SRI))
   sustainable corporate governance and, 177
   UN Principles of Responsible Investment (UNPRI) and, 217
Institutional Shareholder Services Inc. (ISS), 287, 466–67, 619
Intermediary organizations
   in Australia (*See* Australia)
   controlling-block shareholders versus, 454
   sustainable finance and, 568–69
International Corporate Governance Network (ICGN)
   Excellence in Corporate Governance Award, 509, 594
   Global Stewardship Forum, 280
   Global Stewardship Principles, 197, 217
   Model Mandate, 476–77, 486
   Statement of Principles on Institutional Shareholder Responsibilities, 318

Stewardship Code
   generally, 4, 10–11, 195
   adoption of, 640
   citation patterns, 640–41
   controlling shareholders concept in, 7
   core concept of, 14–15
   diversity of stewardship models, recognition of, 619
   ESG in, 563, 564
   global diffusion and, 632, 635
   identical word strings, measurement of, 644
   influence of UK Code 2010/2012, 13–14
   Kenya Stewardship Code, influence on, 490–91
   legal family effect, lack of, 659
   Seven Core Principles in, 658
International Financial Centres (IFCs), 285–86, 293–95, 296, 627
International Forum of Sovereign Wealth Funds, 190
International Investment Funds Association (IIFA), 516
International Labour Organization (ILO), 186
International Monetary Fund (IMF), 616, 629
International Organization of Securities Commissioners (IOSCO), 438, 516
International organizations, 4
Invesco Perpetual Enhanced Income Ltd., 544
Investee companies, stewardship and, 194
Investment consultants, 83–85
Investment management
   generally, 536, 548
   active management
      generally, 536, 538
      agency problems and, 536–37
      high cost of, 537
      short-term focus of, 539
   corporate governance and, 530
   distributed ledger technology (DLT) and, 541–42
   fund governance, 543–45
   investment chain and, 540–43
   investment management concept of stewardship, 8–9
   passive management
      generally, 536, 538
      agency problems and, 537–38
   'separation of funds from managers', 540–41
ISS, 123
Italy
   generally, 131
   administrative penalties in, 584–85, 588
   asset managers in, 133–34
   Association of Responsible Investors (Assodire), 592
   Assogestioni Corporate Governance Committee, 141
   bi-engagement in, 146
   blocking requirement in, 134–35
   conflicts of interest in, 604
   Consolidated Law on Finance
      asset managers and, 133–34
      disclosure requirements, 147–48
      lists of candidates, 139, 144
      'say-on-pay' and, 134
      shareholder meetings, 135

slate voting system and, 134, 139
voting rights, 137
Corporate Governance Code, 135
de facto controlled companies in, 143–44
enforcement in, 584–85, 588, 596
engagement in
bi-engagement, 146
collective engagement, 130, 140–44
disclosure requirements, 147
institutional investors and, 132, 135
Stewardship Principles and, 138–39
Financial Markets Supervisory Authority (CONSOB), 131, 139, 144
France compared, 131
Germany compared, 131, 133
institutional investors in
generally, 130
changes in, 132–33
engagement and, 132, 138–39
interactions with minority-appointed directors, 144–47
legal framework for, 133–35
monitoring of, 140–41
statistics, 131–32
voting participation by, 132
Investment Managers' Committee, 141, 144
Italian Stock Exchange, 131
meetings, minority shareholders calling, 134
minority-appointed directors in
generally, 134
collective engagement and, 130, 140–44
conflicts of interest and, 141
de facto controlled companies and, 143–44
hedge fund activism and, 142–43
independence of, 141
interactions with institutional investors, 144–47
selection of candidates, 141
slate voting system and, 139–40
statistics, 140
Stewardship Principles and, 139–40, 143–44, 145–46
record date system in, 130, 135
'say-on-pay' in, 134
self-regulation in, 604
slate voting system in, 130, 134, 139–40, 142
Spain compared, 131
SRD I and, 133, 135
SRD II and, 33–34, 130
stewardship networks in, 592
Stewardship Principles
generally, 131, 136, 148
as accenting legal standards, 34
citation patterns, 640–41
cluster analysis and, 648
collective action, 652
'comply or explain', 147
conflicts of interest and, 651
deviation from UK Code 2010/2012, 15
EFAMA Stewardship Code compared, 136, 137–38, 146, 635
enforcement of, 22, 147–48

engagement, 138–39, 583
enumeration of principles, 136
escalation of activities, 651
as governmental stewardship code, 28
'hardening' and, 22
identical word strings, measurement of, 643–44
legal family effect, lack of, 659
legal standards, as complementing, 33–34
minority-appointed directors and, 139–40, 143–44, 145–46
network analysis and, 646
policy disclosure, 649–50
publication of, 130, 136
relevance of, 148
review of, 148–49
voting policies, 137–38, 652
UK compared, 133
US compared, 133, 146
Itaú, 509

Jana Partners, 558
Janmohamed, Abdulmalek, 502
Japan
generally, 223
Abenomics, 30
bank financing in, 225
as civil law country, 654
Companies Act, 227
'corporate community' in, 224
Corporate Governance Code, 226–27
corporate governance in, 630
Council of Experts Concerning the Japanese Version of the Stewardship Code, 222–23, 234, 237
Defined-Benefit Corporate Pension Act, 233
directors in, 225
Family Business Campaign (FB77) and, 313–14
family-controlled business enterprises in, 313
Financial Services Agency (FSA), 222, 232, 233, 234, 592
Government Pension Investment Fund (GPIF), 232
growth-oriented governance in, 226–27
Kabunushi Onbuzuman (NGO), 578
Korea, regional cluster of global diffusion with, 632, 644, 648
Korea compared, 13–14, 243, 247
lifetime employment system in, 224–25
Malaysia compared, 327
Ministry of Health, Labor and Welfare, 233
reforms in corporate governance system, 225–27
shareholder activism in, 20
shareholders in
generally, 623
changes in share-ownership system, 225
cross-shareholding, 225, 226–27
meetings, 224
'stable shareholders', 224
Stewardship Code
generally, 614
adoption of, 222, 227
cluster analysis and, 648
collective action, 652

678   Index

Japan (cont.)
   collective engagement, 231
   'comply or explain', 654
   conflicts of interest and, 231
   context of adoption, goals derived from, 227
   deviation from UK Code 2010/2012, 15, 16, 223, 228–31, 232, 238, 621–22, 659
   disclosure requirements, 231, 234
   economic crises and, 30
   effects of, 235
   escalation of activities, 229, 621–22, 651
   ESG in, 236–37, 562–63
   expansion of scope of assets, 237
   foreign investors and, 233–34
   as governmental stewardship code, 28, 189
   identical word strings, measurement of, 643–44
   influence of UK Code 2010/2012, 222–23, 238
   investee companies and, 228, 229–30
   legal family effect, lack of, 659
   legal standards, as complementing, 32
   list of signatories, 232–34
   monitoring, 230–31
   network analysis and, 646
   passive investors and, 231–32
   pension funds and, 231–32, 233
   political motivations of, 624
   principles, 222, 229–31
   rationale for adoption, 640
   revision of, 660
   service providers to institutional investors, 237–38
   signatories, 567
   strengthening institutional investors as goal of, 223, 227, 238
   text, goals derived from, 228
   tiering system, lack of, 234
   2017 revision, 231–32
   2020 revision, 231–32, 236–38
   ultimate beneficiaries of, 228
  stewardship networks in, 592
  sustainable finance in, 558
  traditional corporate governance system, 224–25
  UK compared, 223, 619
  US compared, 223
Jarislowsky, Stephen, 442
Jarislowsky Fraser, 442
Jiang, Wei, 398
JP Morgan, 428

Kahan, Marcel, 52
Kang, Sang Yop, 242, 625
Kasikorn Asset Management, 350, 352
Katelouzou, Dionysia, 72–73, 190, 289, 464, 565, 582, 621
Kazakhstan, stewardship in, 614
KB Asset Management, 250–51
Kenya
  generally, 491, 505–6
  Actuarial Society of Kenya, 497–98
  'apply or explain' in, 495–96
  Association of Kenya Insurers, 497–98
  Association of Retirement Benefit Schemes, 497–98
  capital market in, 491–93
  Capital Markets Act 1989, 492
  Capital Markets Authority (CMA), 490, 497–98, 505
  Capital Markets (Collective Investment Schemes) Regulations 2001, 498
  Capital Markets (Foreign Investors) Regulations 2002, 492
  Capital Markets (Foreign Investors) Regulations 2008, 498
  Capital Markets Stewardship Code Committee, 497–98
  Central Bank of Kenya, 502
  Code of Corporate Governance Practices for Issuers of Securities to the Public 2015 (Corporate Governance Code), 495–97
  Companies Act 1962, 490
  Companies Act 2015, 490–95, 496
  controlling shareholders concept in, 6–7
  Denmark compared, 504
  Deposit Insurance Corporation, 502
  derivative actions in, 494–95
  engagement, lack of, 502–3, 506
  executive compensation, disclosure of, 496
  financial statements in, 495
  foreign investors in, 491
  free-rider problem in, 503
  Fund Managers Association, 497–98
  institutional investors in, 492–93
  Insurance Regulatory Authority, 497–98
  investor briefings in, 497
  local investors in, 492
  Malaysia compared, 491
  Nairobi Securities Exchange (NSE), 491, 493
  National Social Security Fund, 497–98
  National Treasury, 497–98
  Netherlands compared, 504
  passive nature of shareholders in, 503
  proxy voting in, 494
  'say-on-pay' in, 495
  shareholder meetings in, 493–94
  shareholder resolutions in, 494
  shareholder rights in, 496–97
  short-term focus in, 503–4
  South Africa compared, 491
  Stewardship Code for Institutional Investors, 2017,
   'apply or explain' in, 498, 499
   conflicts of interest and, 500
   definitions, 498
   difficulties in transplanting law, 504–5
   engagement, 500, 501
   ESG in, 35, 500–1, 564
   goals of, 498
   as governmental stewardship code, 623
   ICGN Stewardship Code, influence of, 490–91
   identical word strings, measurement of, 644
   influence of UK Code 2010/2012, 490, 504
   lack of signatories, 491, 502, 505, 567
   legal family effect, lack of, 659
   legal standards, as complementing, 32
   monitoring, 500
   network analysis and, 646–47

policy disclosure, 499, 501
positive aspects of, 501
potential problems with, 501
principles, 499–501
promulgation of, 490
rationale for adoption, 640
voluntary nature of, 21
voting guidelines and practices, 500
transparency in, 497
UK compared, 504, 491, 494–95
US compared, 491, 495
Khazanah, 326
Kibati, Mugo, 496
Kim, Yun Kyung, 625
Klettner, Alice, 422
Koh, Alan K., 260, 292
Koh, Yunsung, 625
Kohlberg Kravis Roberts & Co., 233–34
Korea
generally, 239, 240
chaebols, 241–43, 249, 259, 624
'collective action problem' and, 249–50
Commercial Code, 242, 248
conservative nature of business community, 249
controlling-block shareholders in, 239, 241–43, 259, 623
corporate governance in, 241–43, 630
derivative actions in, 242
enforcement in, 596
Fair Trade Commission, 242
family-controlled business enterprises in, 241–43, 259, 313, 624–25
Federation of Korean Industries (FKI), 243
Federation of Middle Market Enterprises of Korea, 243
Financial Services Commission (FSC), 243
Financial Supervisory Services (FSS), 243
institutional investors in, 249
Japan, regional cluster of global diffusion with, 632, 644, 648
Japan compared, 13–14, 243, 247
KEPCO University, 259
Korea Capital Market Institute (KCMI), 244, 622
Korea Corporate Governance Service (KCGS), 244, 247, 622
Korea Development Bank (KDB), 258
'Korea discount', 242–43
Korea Electric Power Corporation (KEPCO), 258–59
Korea Exchange, 244
Korea Federation of SMEs, 243
Korea Financial Investment Association (KOFIA), 622
Korea Listed Companies Association (KLCA), 243, 244, 622
KOSDAQ Listed Companies Association (KOSDAQA), 243, 244, 622
Ministry of Health and Welfare, 252, 253–54
National Finance Act, 252–53
National Pension Act, 253–54
National Pension Service (NPS)
generally, 30–31
in capital market, 252
corporate governance of, 260
engagement and, 253
ESG and, 253–54, 257–58
investee companies and, 256–57
lack of consistency in, 258–59
'pension-fund socialism' and, 257
political influence of, 625
role of government, 240
shareholder activism and, 239–40, 252–55, 257
Stewardship Code and, 253
voting rights and, 252–53
'pension-fund socialism' and, 257
People's Solidarity for Participatory Democracy (NGO), 578, 596
shareholder activism in
incentives for, 250–51
lack of consistency in, 258–59
NPS and, 239–40, 252–55, 257
under Stewardship Code, 250–51, 259
shareholders
meetings, 248
pre-Code weakness of, 248–50
proposals, 248
removal of directors by, 248
Solidarity for Economic Reform (NGO), 578
Stewardship Code
generally, 614
adoption of, 239, 243–44
applicability of, 245
cluster analysis and, 648
collective action, 247
'comply or explain', 247
deviation from UK Code 2010/2012, 239, 246–47, 622
disclosure requirements, 247
enforcement of, 247–48
engagement, 248
escalation of activities, 247, 622, 651
ESG in, 35, 561
Guidebook, 247
halo signalling and, 260
influence of UK Code 2010/2012, 243
legal family effect, lack of, 659
list of participants, 247
motivations for, 241
network analysis and, 646
NPS and, 253
opposition to, 243–44
parts, 244–45
policy channeling and, 30–31
political motivations of, 624–25
principles, 246–47
proxy advisors and, 569
removal of directors, 248
shareholder activism under, 250–51, 259
shareholder meetings, 248
shareholder proposals, 248
stewardship defined, 245
terminology, 245
voting policies, 248

Korea (cont.)
  Trust Act of Korea, 245
  tunnelling in, 241–43, 259
Korean Air, 255, 258
Korsak Chairasmisak, 355–56
Krung Thai, 356–57
Kumpulan Wang Persaraan (Diperbadankan), 326
Kuo, Jing-Ming, 398
Kwangju Shinsegae, 250–51

Lafarre, Anne, 187
Laing, Elaine, 401
Lamoureaux, Claude, 442
Lan, Luh Luh, 303, 604
Large portfolio end-investors as market participants, 79–80
Larsen & Toubro, 364
Leblon Equities, 509
Lee, Jae-Yong, 256
Lee, Kun-Hee, 256
Legal & General Investment Management, 327
Legal transplants. *See also* Global diffusion of stewardship codes
  'cut and paste', 621
  defined, 637
  from EU, 631
  identical legal transplants, 621
  terminology, 637
  from UK, 631
  from US, 631
LG (Korean company), 241
Liao, Jing, 397–98
Lim, Ernest, 622, 623
Lin, Chen, 398–400
Lin, Lin, 7
Lin, Zhen Gyu, 401
Linaburg–Maduell Transparency Index, 303
Listed companies, 284
Liu, Ningyue, 401
LIXIL, 623
Lotte, 241
Lund, Dorothy, 467, 469
Luxembourg, enforcement in, 584

Madsen, Marina B., 187, 191
Mahmudi, Hamed, 433, 447
Majoch, Arleta, 212, 215
Malaysia
  generally, 317
  Australia compared, 318
  Barisan Nasional Coalition, 333
  Bumiputera ('sons of the soil'), 328
  Bursa Malaysia
    generally, 320, 325
    Listing Requirements, 316, 318, 321
    Sustainability Reporting Guide, 322
  Capital Market Masterplan, 317, 329
  Code for Institutional Investors
    generally, 614
    adoption of, 316, 319
    'apply and explain', 324
    asset managers and, 319–20, 327
    asset owners and, 326
    cluster analysis and, 648
    collective action, 323, 621
    compliance statements, 326
    conflicts of interest and, 321–22
    coreness and, 648
    deviation from UK Code 2010/2012, 322, 621, 659
    effectiveness of, 316
    engagement, 321
    escalation of activities, 651
    ESG in, 322
    evaluation of, 325–27
    historical background, 317–19
    identical word strings, measurement of, 642–43, 644
    industry-driven nature of, 329–30, 333
    influence of UK Code 2010/2012, 316–17, 318, 319, 635
    investee companies and, 320–21
    legal family effect, lack of, 659
    monitoring, 320–21
    network analysis and, 646–47
    policy channeling and, 31
    policy disclosure, 320, 649
    political motivations of, 625–26
    proportionality principle, 323
    Seven Core Principles in, 658
    signatories, 325–26
    as 'soft law', 323
    stewardship defined, 319
    text of, 14
    ultimate beneficiaries, 324–25
    voluntary nature of, 323
    voting policies, 322–23
  Companies Act 2016, 316, 321
  Constitution, 328
  Corporate Governance Blueprint, 318, 319
  Corporate Governance Code
    'apply and explain' and, 324
    Code for Institutional Investors and, 316, 317, 318
    long-term goals and, 319–20
    monitoring and, 320–21
  corporate governance in, 630
  Denmark compared, 323
  Employees Provident Fund, 317, 326, 328, 332
  Employees Provident Fund Act 1991, 328
  government, role in stewardship, 327–30
  Government Linked Companies (GLCs), role in stewardship, 317, 328–30, 332, 625–26
  Government Linked Investment Companies (GLICs), role in stewardship, 317, 324, 325–26, 327–30, 332, 625–26
  The Green Book: Enhancing Board Effectiveness, 317
  Guide of Best Practices for Institutional Investors, 317
  heterogeneity of institutional investors in, 331
  Institutional Investors Council Malaysia (II Council), 316, 324–25, 326, 327, 333
  Japan compared, 327
  Kenya compared, 491
  Kuala Lumpur Stock Exchange, 318

lack of incentives for stewardship, 331–32
Lembaga Tabung Haji, 332
limited effectiveness of stewardship, 330–31
Ministry of Finance, 328, 332
Minority Shareholder Watchdog Group (MSWG), 317, 318, 322, 323, 324
non-governmental institutional investors, minor role of, 328, 329, 332–33
1MDB scandal, 332, 333
Securities Commission, 318, 322, 323
shareholder activism in, 329
South Africa compared, 322
Steering Committee, 318
structural issues regarding stewardship, 333–34
Thailand, regional cluster of global diffusion with, 644
Tun Razak Exchange, 332
UK compared, 323, 324–25, 326, 327, 642–43
UN Principles of Responsible Investment (UNPRI) and, 322
Market for stewardship
  generally, 67, 88
  demand factors
    generally, 67
    altruism, 76
    economic benefits, 75
    investors, financial return for, 73–75
    issuers, financial return for, 75
  evolution of stewardship as market-driven concept, 68–71
  government, role of
    generally, 68, 85
    as facilitator of market, 85–86
    as financial adviser, 87–88
    pension funds and, 67
    regulator versus financial contributor, 68
    as supervisor of market, 85–86
  market participants
    generally, 67–68
    charitable organizations, 80
    fiduciary managers, 83–85
    independent governance committees, 80–83
    investment consultants, 83–85
    large portfolio end-investors, 79–80
    pension beneficiaries, 76–78
    pension trustees, 80–83
    small portfolio end-investors, 78–79
  pension funds and
    beneficiaries as market participants, 76–78
    government, role of, 67
    recommendations, 88
  UK Code 2020, role of, 71–73
Market Post Observation System, 264–65
Maruti Suzuki Limited, 364–66
Materiality, 460
Maugeri, Marco, 147
Means, Gardiner C., 284, 287, 301, 454, 456
Mees, Bernard, 432
MFC Asset Management, 349, 350–51
Migros, 113
Milhaupt, Curtis J., 383

Min, Huang, 401
Mitsubishi Motors, 235
Mitsubishi UFJ Trust Bank, 235
Mizhuo Financial Group, 235
Mizhuo Trust Bank, 235
Mongolia, shareholder structure in, 618
Monitoring. *See specific country*
Monks, Robert A.G., 287–88
Monsanto, 202
Montagnon, Peter, 65
Morley, John, 540
Morningstar, 466
MSCI Emerging Markets Index, 381, 389
MSCI Europe Index, 129
Muddy Waters, 304
Mutual funds
  agency problems and, 467
  characteristics of investors, 468
  ESG and, 468–69
  fund beneficiaries, asset managers and, 454–55
  index funds (*See* Index funds)
  in India, 363
  negotiating power of, 470
  pass-through voting, 455, 467–70
  stewardship, costs and benefits of, 455
  in Thailand, 343–44
  in US, 206, 457
  voter participation levels, 469–70
  voting guidelines, 469
Myners, Paul, 193, 240, 288

Namyang Dairy Products, 254
Negative screening, 558
Nestlé S.A., 119
Netherlands
  administrative penalties in, 585, 588
  Civil Code (DCC), 92, 93
  conflicts of interest in, 604
  Corporate Governance Code (DCGC)
    'comply or explain', 95–96
    engagement, 91
    information, shareholder right to, 93
    institutional approach, 92
    institutional investors and, 94–95
    long-term value creation and, 92, 96, 109
    Monitoring Committee, 579
    reasonableness and fairness, 94
    shareholder rights and duties, 93–95
    shareholders and, 96
    Stewardship Code and, 96, 97
  corporate governance concept in, 109
  Denmark compared, 172
  empirical findings on stewardship
    approval rates, 101–3
    institutional voting behavior, 103–7
    methodology, 99–100
    overall statistical analysis, 107
    ownership concentration, 107–9
    participation, 100–1
    withdrawn resolutions, 109

Netherlands (cont.)
  enforcement in, 585, 588
  Germany compared, 218
  institutional investors in, 94–95, 109–10
  Kenya compared, 504
  Ministry of Economic Affairs, 579
  Ministry of Finance, 579
  Ministry of Security and Justice, 579
  Monitoring Committee, 96
  multiple stewardship codes in, 638
  National Civil Pension Fund, 210
  Norway compared, 187
  Pension Act, 95
  self-regulation in, 604
  SRD I and, 93
  SRD II and
    generally, 33, 96–97
    implementation of, 92, 109
    Stewardship Code and, 187, 635
    voting, 98
  Stewardship Code
    generally, 93
    additional principles in, 19
    Best Practices, 97
    citation patterns, 640–41
    communication, 97–98
    cooperation, 97–98
    corporate governance concept and, 109
    DCGC and, 96, 97
    dialogue, 97–98
    engagement, 97, 583
    ESG in, 563
    Implementation Progress Report, 98–99
    institutional investors and, 110
    legal standards, as complementing, 32, 33
    network analysis and, 645, 646
    Seven Core Principles in, 658
    'soft' law requirements, 95–99
    SRD II and, 187, 635
    voting policies, 98
  stewardship networks in, 592
Network analysis, 644–47
New Zealand, sustainable finance in, 558
Nigeria Control of Infectious Disease Bill, 621
Nomura Asset Management, 327
Nomura Islamic Asset Management, 327
Norway
  generally, 175–76
  activist shareholders in, 186–87
  Act on Financial Institutions and Financial Groups, 187
  Act on Securities Trading, 187
  Act Relating to the Management of Alternative Investment Funds, 187
  Alfred Berg Kapitalforvaltning, 182
  Argentum Fondsinvesteringer AS, 179
  concept of stewardship in, 176
  conflicts of interest in, 604
  Corporate Governance Board (NCGB) Code of Practice for Corporate Governance, 179–80
  Corporate Governance Code, 181, 182–83, 184
  creditor protection in, 190
  CSR in, 185–86
  Denmark compared, 175–76, 187
  directors in, 190
  DNB Kapitalforvaltning, 182
  engagement in, 186
  Equinor Kapitalforvaltning, 179, 182
  ESG in, 180
  Folketrygdfondet, 179, 182, 185, 190
  fragmented regulatory framework for stewardship in, 178–80
  Fund and Asset Manager Association (VFF), 176, 180–81
  Germany compared, 186–87
  government, role of
    CSR in and, 185–86
    Diverse and Value-Creating Ownership (State Guidelines), 185–86
    as dominant actor, 176, 179, 185
    lack of focus on stewardship, 186
  Government Pension Fund Global
    generally, 79, 178, 210
    International Forum of Sovereign Wealth Funds and, 190
    lack of need for stewardship code and, 190
    management principles, 183–85
    Recommendation on Use of Ownership and, 182
    role of in stewardship, 179
  Holberg Fondsforvaltning, 182
  Institutional Investor Forum, 182
  institutional investors in, 176–77, 178–79
  KLP Kapitalforvaltning AS, 182
  Kommunal Landspensjonskasse Gjensidig Forsikringsselskap (KLP), 179
  lack of need for stewardship code in, 182–83, 187, 190–91
  Ministry of Trade, Industry and Fisheries, 182
  minority shareholder protection in, 190
  Netherlands compared, 187
  Nordea Fondene, 182
  Norges Bank Investment Management (NBIM), 178, 183–85, 188
  Odin Forvaltning, 182
  Oslo Pensjonsforsikring, 182
  preliminary stewardship initiative in, 4
  Recommendation on Use of Ownership
    generally, 176
    additional principles in, 19
    deviation from UK Code 2010/2012, 14–15, 181
    domestic law and, 181
    EFAMA Stewardship Code, influence of, 180–82
    EFAMA Stewardship Principles, influence of, 180–81
    flexibility of, 188
    investment versus corporate governance, 182–83
    narrow scope of, 182
    not considered stewardship code, 178
    Securities Funds Act and, 181
    voting rights, 182
  Securities Funds Act, 180–81, 187–88
  shareholder primacy versus sustainable corporate governance, 186–89

Singapore compared, 179
SRD II and, 186, 187–88
Storebrand ASA, 179, 182
sustainable corporate governance in, 186–89
Telenor, 179
UN Principles of Responsible Investment (UNPRI) and, 179–80

Oasis Management Company, 233–34
OECD/G20 Principles of Corporate Governance,
  generally, 275–76
  assumptions regarding UK Codes in, 618
  engagement and, 195–96
  Norway and, 179–80, 183, 184
  positive perception of institutional investors in, 178
  Thailand and, 336, 337–38
Oikonomou, Ioannis, 206
Olam International, 304
Onyonyi, Millicent, 496
Organization for Economic Co-operation and Development (OECD)
  Asia, stewardship codes in as challenge to, 616
  on Brazil, 508
  on corporate governance, 629
  Corporate Governance Committee, 184
  Corporate Governance Factbook, 635
  ESG and, 339
  on global diffusion of UK Code 2010/2012, 618
  on Government Linked Investment Companies (GLICs), 328
  Guidelines for Multinational Enterprises, 183, 186, 188
  on institutional investors, 508
  Principles of Corporate Governance (See OECD/G20 Principles of Corporate Governance)
  Survey of Corporate Governance Frameworks in Asia, 618
Orientalism, 292
'Ownerless companies', 6

Pargendler, Mariana, 4, 383, 456
Paris Agreement on Climate Change, 449, 552, 554
Paris Climate Accord, 62–63
Park, Geun-Hye, 242, 256
Park, James J., 597
Parmalat, 118, 134
Partnoy, Frank, 533
Passive investment management
  generally, 536, 538
  agency problems and, 537–38
Pass-through voting, 455, 467–70
Pension funds. See also specific country
  assets under management by, 218
  beneficiaries as market participants, 76–78
  climate change and, 81
  defined, 482–83
  defined contribution schemes, 538, 543–44
  disincentives to stewardship, 538
  ESG and, 77, 545–47
  fiduciary duties of, 545–47
  government, role of, 67

  market for stewardship and
    beneficiaries as market participants, 76–78
    government, role of, 67
  NEST, 73
  'prudent investor' rule, 545–46
  purpose of, 77
  SRI, effect of, 77
  sustainable finance and, 566
  trustees as market participants, 80–83
Permodalan Nasional Berhad, 326
Pershing Capital, 445
Pfleiderer, Paul, 504
PGGM Investments, 105–6
Phatra, 356–57
Philippines
  Family Business Campaign (FB77) and, 313–14
  stewardship in, 614
Phillip Asset Management Company Limited, 352
Policy channeling
  in China (See China)
  defined, 383
  in Korea, 30–31
  in Malaysia, 31
  stewardship codes and, 29, 30–31
Policy disclosure. See specific country
Porter, Martin F., 649
PPG Industries, 94
Prayut Chan-o-cha, 30
Preliminary stewardship initiatives, 4, 638–40
Principal competence costs, 462
Principles of Responsible Investment (UNPRI)
  generally, 635
  asset managers and, 212, 217
  Brazil and, 522–23
  ESG and, 196
  institutional investors and, 217
  Malaysia and, 322
  Norway and, 179–80
  South Africa and, 35, 472, 479, 646
  stewardship networks and, 592
  sustainable finance and, 553, 554–55, 569
Private ordering, 582
Private stewardship codes
  generally, 17–18
  additional principles in, 19
  geographic divide with governmental stewardship codes, 19–20
  institutional investor control and, 28
  investors initiating, 244
  market participants initiating, 244
  motives for creating, 18
  Seven Core Principles in, 18–19
  UK Code 2010/2012 and, 18–19
Procter & Gamble, 462
Proxy advisers
  in Australia, 431
  in India, 363
  in Korea, 569
  sustainable finance and, 569
  in Switzerland, 123

Proxy advisers (cont.)
  in Taiwan, 268
  in UK, 531
Proxy Insight, 99–100, 102, 103–4, 105, 109
'Prudent investor' rule, 545–46
Puchniak, Dan W., 7, 260, 292, 295, 303, 344, 604, 622, 623

Raymond Limited, 364
Razak, Datuk Seri, 332
Reform of stewardship codes
  generally, 603
  applicability, clarification of, 606
  controlling-block shareholders, defining, 606
  duties of shareholders, clarification of, 606
  limitations of, 612
  responsible persons, clarification of, 606
  stewardship, defining, 606
Regional clusters, 632, 644, 648
Related party transaction (RPT) rules
  ESG and, 608–9
  reform of, 603, 608–9
Reporting requirements. See specific country
Retirement funds. See specific country
Richardson, Benjamin, 546
Risk-taking. See Excessive risk-taking
Robeco, 509
Roche, 119
Rock, Edward, 52, 206
Roe, Mark, 505
Romano, Alessandro, 592–93
Roosevelt, Franklin Delano, 287
Rose, Paul, 456

Sameer Africa, 496
Samsung C&T, 255–56
Samsung Group, 241, 249, 256, 313
Sanlam, 496
Santander, 509
Santiago Principles, 190
SAP (German company), 201–2
Satyam, 118
Sautner, Zacharias, 206
SBM Offshore, 107
SCB Asset Management, 349
Schluep, Walter, 118
Schroders, 79, 280, 461
Schulte Roth & Zabel, 426
Schweizerische Mobiliar, 113
Securities regulation, 578
Self-dealing, 465
'Separation of ownership and control', 284, 287
Seven Core Principles. See also specific country
  enumeration of, 10
  global diffusion of, 13, 17
  private stewardship codes and, 18–19
Shareholder activism. See also specific country
  'defensive' activism, 531–32
  hedge funds (See Hedge fund activism)
  'offensive' activism, 532
Shareholder-Director Exchange (SDX), 146

Shareholder empowerment, 174–75, 197
Shareholders. See specific topic
Sharfman, Bernard S., 458
Shen, Jianghua, 397
Shillman, Robert, 543
Shinsegae, 241
Short-term focus
  of active investment management, 539
  as cause of Global Financial Crisis (2008), 298, 301, 613–14
  of hedge fund activism, 533
  in Kenya, 503–4
  UK Code 2010/2012, restraining as goal of, 238, 298, 301, 373, 456, 613–14
Siems, Mathias, 190, 289, 565, 621
Sierra Club, 595
Signalling. See Halo signalling
Sika, 120
Simmons, Beth, 293
Singapore
  Accounting and Corporate Regulatory Authority, 308
  Central Provident Fund (CPF), 304–5
  China compared, 302
  Companies Act, 303
  controlling actors concept in, 7–8
  controlling-block shareholders in, 302, 305
  controlling shareholders concept in, 37
  Family Business Campaign (FB77), 313–14
  family-controlled business enterprises in, 298, 302–3, 304, 313–14
  halo signalling in, 189–90, 626–28
  Hong Kong compared, 295
  institutional investors, minor role of, 298, 299–300, 302, 304–5
  as International Financial Centre (IFC), 627
  Monetary Authority of Singapore, 308
  Norway compared, 179
  'pre-emptive corporate governance' in, 300
  Singapore Exchange (SGX), 14, 606
  state-owned enterprises (SOEs), Stewardship Principles for Family Businesses inapplicable to, 603, 604
Stewardship Asia
  generally, 14, 372
  conflicts of interest and, 604
  lack of enforcement authority, 299, 308, 655
  monitoring and, 605–6
  Stewardship Principles for Family Businesses and, 299, 300–1, 310
  Stewardship Principles for Responsible Investors and, 297, 300
  supporters versus signatories, 298, 307
  Temasek, relationship with, 308–10
Stewardship Principles for Family Businesses
  generally, 190, 372
  adoption of, 310
  ambiguity regarding responsible persons, 605
  Asian perspective, 313–14
  change and, 312
  cluster analysis and, 648
  communication, 311

Index

cultural perspective, 313–14
deviation from UK Code 2010/2012, 14, 299, 301, 313, 314, 601–2, 620
disclosure requirements, lack of, 605–6
enforcement of, 20
ESG in, 312
goals of, 604–5
inclusiveness, 312
influence of, 611
institutional investors not primary focus of, 12, 14, 601–2, 620
integration of short-term and long-term perspectives, 311–12
monitoring, 605–6
ownership mentality and, 311
principles, 311–12
rationale for adoption, 640
rationale for separate stewardship code, 299, 300–1
as 'soft' law, 604
state-owned enterprises (SOEs), inapplicable to, 603, 604
succession and, 312
success of, 314–15
unique nature of, 310–11, 627–28
voluntary nature of, 20, 604
Stewardship Principles for Responsible Investors
adoption of, 297
'comply or explain', 307
deviation from UK Code 2010/2012, 306–8, 659
disruption versus signalling, 308–9
enforcement of, 22
ESG in, 565
halo signalling and, 30, 189–90, 305–6, 308–9, 626–27
influence of UK Code 2010/2012, 297
institutional investors as focus of, 12
lack of regulatory agency, 299, 307–8
lack of single stewardship model, 306–7
network analysis and, 646–47
Preamble, 626–27
as preserving status quo, 300
rationale for adoption, 298, 299–300, 640
supporters versus signatories, 298, 307
'toothless' nature of, 298–99, 300, 306–8
voluntary nature of, 22, 307
Switzerland compared, 112
Temasek
generally, 298
conflicts of interest and, 604
disclosures by, 303
engagement and, 304, 309–10
role in capital market, 303–4
state control of, 303–4
stewardship and, 604
Stewardship Asia, relationship with, 308–10
Stewardship Principles for Responsible Investors and, 300
SK Group, 241, 249
Small portfolio end-investors as market participants, 78–79
Smith, Sherene A., 432
Socially responsible investment (SRI)

CSR and, 560–61
duties of institutional investors, 559–61
engagement and, 558
ESG and, 196, 557–58, 559–61
'hard law', 561
institutional investors and, 550, 551
investment strategies, 557–59
negative screening, 558
pension funds, effect on, 77
reporting requirements, 560–61
return on investment, effect on, 73, 74, 76
South Africa and, 557
statistics, 558
strategies for, 557–59
SOEs. *See* State-owned enterprises (SOEs)
'Soft' law. *See also specific topic*
in Asia, 619–20
in Denmark, 156, 162–63
'hard' law versus, 529, 573
in Malaysia, 323
in Netherlands, 95–99
as predominant paradigm of enforcement, 572, 574
rise of, 3
'semi-hard' law versus, 573
in Singapore, 604
SRD II and, 536
in UK, 3, 369, 375–76, 535–36
Song, Xiaoqi, 398
SOSCO, 325–26
South Africa
generally, 472
apartheid, legacy of, 471
asset managers in
generally, 482
ESG and, 485–86, 487
fiduciary duties of, 487
Association for Saving and Investment South Africa (ASISA), 475, 488, 489
BATSETA, 475, 488
black economic empowerment, 472
Code for Responsible Investing in South Africa (CRISA)
'acting in concert' and, 477
'apply or explain', 476, 478–79
conflicts of interest and, 322, 477
coreness and, 648
deviation from UK Code 2010/2012, 15, 16, 478, 480
deviation from UK Code 2020, 489
disclosure requirements, 477–78
engagement, 477
ESG in, 15, 35, 476, 562, 565, 646
ICGN Model Mandate and, 476–77, 486
institutional investors and, 475–76
King IV Report compared, 481, 482
legal standards, as complementing, 32, 33
network analysis and, 646
pension funds and, 483
principles, 476–78
purpose of, 473
recommendations, 489

South Africa (cont.)
  responsible ownership policies, 476–77
  retirement funds and, 474
  sustainability, 476
  transparency, 477–78
  UN Principles of Responsible Investment (UNPRI) and, 35, 472, 479, 646
  voting policies, 476
 Codes of Conduct for Administrative and Discretionary FSPs, 486
 collective investment schemes in, 473
 Committee on Responsible Investing in South Africa, 475
 Companies Act 71 of 2008, 473–74, 475
 conflicts of interest in, 604
 controlling-block shareholders in, 475
 corruption in, 471–72
 fiduciary duties in, 482, 486–88
 Financial Advisory and Intermediary Services Act 37 of 2002, 485
 financial institutions, fiduciary duties of, 486–87
 Financial Institutions (Protection of Funds) Act 28 of 2001, 486–87
 Financial Sector Conduct Authority (FSCA), 481, 483–85, 486, 488–89
 Financial Sector Regulation Act 9 of 2017, 475–76
 Financial Services Board, 481
 Financial Services Board Act 97 of 1990, 475–76
 foreign institutional investors in, 475
 General Code of Conduct for Authorised Financial Services Providers and Representatives, 485
 Government Employees Pension Fund (GEPF), 472–73, 475, 479, 481
 Institute of Directors in Southern Africa (IoDSA), 475, 486
 insurance companies, fiduciary duties of, 487–88
 Johannesburg Stock Exchange (JSE), 473, 475, 480
 Kenya compared, 491
 King II Report, 480
 King III Report, 476, 480
 King IV Report on Governance for South Africa
  generally, 473
  applicability of, 480
  'apply and explain', 480, 489
  CRISA compared, 481, 482
  reporting requirements, 480–81
  responsible investment, 482
  retirement funds and, 481
  sector specific guidance, 481–82
  sustainability, 489
  voluntary nature of, 481
 Malaysia compared, 322
 Pension Funds Act 24 of 1956, 482–83, 485, 486, 487, 489
 Pension Funds Adjudicator, 485
 pension funds in
  generally, 482
  active ownership policies, 484
  CRISA and, 483
  delegation of activities, 483
  disclosure requirements, 484–85
  ESG and, 483–84, 487
  fiduciary duties of, 487
  pension fund defined, 482–83
  recommendations, 488–89
  reporting requirements, 484–85
  unregulated funds, 485
 poverty in, 471
 Principal Officers Association, 475
 PRI South Africa Network, 472, 477, 488
 Public Investment Corporation (PIC), 472–73, 475, 479
 retirement funds in
  CRISA and, 474
  fragmentation of industry, 488
  King IV Report and, 481
  recommendations, 489
  statistics, 473
  sustainability and, 489
 Roadmap, 488–89
 self-regulation in, 604
 socially responsible investment (SRI) and, 557
 sound risk governance in, 486
 sustainability in, 473, 474
 Takeover Regulation Panel, 477
South Korea. *See* Korea
Sovereign Asset Management, 249
Sovereign wealth funds (SWFs), 79
Spain
 enforcement in, 584
 Italy compared, 131
'Spiritual values of ownership', 287
Squire, Richard, 462
SRI. *See* Socially responsible investment (SRI)
Standard Life Aberdeen, 54–55
Starks, Laura T., 206
State owned enterprises (SOEs)
 in Asia, 284
 in China (*See* China)
 disincentives for stewardship, 607
 in Hong Kong, 291
 stewardship and, 372
State Street Asset Management, 459
State Street Global Investors
 generally, 310
 China compared, 382, 386–88
 concentration of asset managers and, 84, 456
 statistics, 122
 stewardship and, 199–200, 458
Stewardship. *See specific topic*
'Stewardship ecology', 31
Stock picking
 financial incentives and, 54, 55
 reputational incentives and, 64
 shareholder functional capacities and, 52–53
Strampelli, Giovanni, 147, 433
Strine, Leo E. Jr., 464, 465
Substituting legal standards, stewardship codes as, 31, 34
Sumimoto Mitsui Banking Corporation, 291
Sunrise Project, 595
Suntory Holdings, 313
Sustainability. *See also specific country*

Index

defined, 549–50
ESG (*See* Environmental, social, and governance (ESG))
institutional investors and (*See* Socially responsible investment (SRI))
socially responsible investment (SRI) (*See* Socially responsible investment (SRI))
stewardship codes, role of
   generally, 550–51, 565–66, 571
   'comply or explain', 567
   intermediary organizations and, 568–69
   maximizing scope and influence of, 566–69
   pension funds and, 566
   proxy advisers and, 569
   regulatory framework and, 568
   voluntary nature of, 567
sustainable corporate governance
   institutional investors and, 177
   in Norway, 186–89
sustainable finance
   generally, 551, 571
   climate change and, 552–53
   CSR and, 551–52, 553
   defined, 551, 552
   engagement and, 558
   ESG and, 558
   institutional framework, 554–57
   objectives of, 554
   pension funds and, 566
   UN Principles of Responsible Investment (UNPRI) and, 553, 554–55, 569
Sustainable Development Goals (SDGs), 188, 547, 551, 553, 554
Sweden
   climate-related financial disclosure in, 189
   concept of stewardship in, 176
   Financial Supervisory Authority, 584
   Fourth Swedish National Pension Fund, 234
   institutional investors in, 176–77
   lack of stewardship code in, 176
Swissair, 121
Swiss Life, 113
Switzerland
   generally, 112, 129
   activist investors in, 124–25
   additional principles in, 19
   'anchor' shareholders in, 120
   boards of directors in, 114–15
   citation patterns, 640–41
   Code of Best Practice (SCBP), 116–17, 125–26
   codification of corporation law in, 114
   conflicts of interest in, 604
   Constitution, 113, 128
   cooperatives in, 113
   coreness and, 648
   costs and benefits of control in, 120–21
   deviation from UK Code 2010/2012, 14–15, 16, 126
   direct democracy in, 113–14
   drivers of stewardship in, 123–24
   dual-class common stock in, 120

   ESG in, 35, 111, 561
   family-controlled business enterprises in, 111–12, 119
   Germany compared, 112, 114–15, 116
   GINI coefficient in, 113
   as grassroots society, 111, 112
   group responsibility initiative, 128–29
   Guidelines for Institutional Investors Governing the Exercising of Participation Rights in Public Limited Companies, 125, 126
   institutional investors in, 112, 122, 124–25
   lack of comprehensive stewardship code in, 638–40
   long-term shareholders, role of, 119–20
   majority control in, 116–17
   minority shareholder protection in, 116–17
   monitoring in, 651
   proxy advisers in, 123
   proxy materials in, 117
   reserved powers in, 115
   Revolution of 1848 and, 113
   'say-on-pay' initiative, 127–28
   self-regulation in, 604
   Seven Core Principles in, 658
   shareholder rights in, 115–16
   Singapore compared, 112
   SIX Swiss Exchange, 125, 126
   SRD II and, 126
   stakeholders versus shareholders, 111, 117–19, 129
   statutory reform in, 127–29
   US compared, 113, 115, 116, 117, 122
   Valais (Canton), 112
   voluntary nature of stewardship in, 112, 126
   voting participation in, 122–23
   voting rights in, 116
   weighted voting rights (WVRs) in, 120

Taiwan
   generally, 263
   Asian Financial Crisis (1997) and, 276
   civil claims in, 591
   Company Act
      generally, 278
      conflicts of interest and, 270
      derivative actions and, 273
      fiduciary duties under, 267
      removal of directors and, 273
      shareholder proposals under, 262, 267
   Corporate Governance Code (CG Code), 265–66, 276, 277, 278
   Corporate Governance Evaluation System, 278
   corporate governance in, 276
   Corporate Social Responsibility Best Practice Principles for TWSE/GTSM Listed Companies (CSR Code), 261–62, 276
   Corporation Rules Governing the Preparation and Filing of Corporate Social Responsibility Reports by TWSE Listed Companies (CSR Rules), 265–66, 277
   Ethical Corporate Management Best Practice Principles for TWSE/TPEx Listed Companies (Business Integrity Code), 276–77

Taiwan (cont.)
  fiduciary duties in, 267
  Financial Supervisory Commission (FSC), 265–66, 269
  Insurance Act, 278
  R.O.C. Securities Investment Trust & Consulting Association (SITCA), 263, 278
  Securities and Exchange Act Amendment (TSEA), 262, 269, 274, 278
  Securities Investment Trust and Consulting Act, 267
  Securities Investor and Futures Trader Protection Act (SFIPA), 263, 272, 274, 275
  Securities Investor and Futures Trader Protection Center (SFIPC)
    generally, 263, 272, 283
    civil claims, 591
    class actions, 272–73
    derivative actions, 273
    disgorgement of profits, 273–74
    investor education programmes, 275
    litigation, 274
    mediation, 272
    removal of directors, 273
    shareholder meetings, attending, 275
  shareholder activism in, 267–68
  shareholder proposals in, 267–68
  shareholder structure in
    generally, 262, 263–64
    statistics, 264
    table, 262
    TPEx listed companies, 265
    TWSE listed companies, 264–65
  Stewardship Code
    generally, 614
    achievability of goals, 277–78
    adoption of, 261
    applicability of, 268
    asset owners versus asset managers, 266–67
    Chapters, 266
    Code Q&A, 269
    'comply or explain', 266, 654
    conflicting objectives of, 282
    conflicts of interest and, 270
    coreness and, 648
    CSR in, 261–62, 277, 280
    deviation from UK Code 2010/2012, 16, 267, 268, 271, 274
    disclosure requirements, 269–70
    duties of institutional investors under, 266–68
    effects of, 279
    engagement, 271
    escalation of activities, 269, 271
    ESG in, 261–62, 277, 280
    goals of, 282
    halo signalling and, 30
    'long-term interests' of clients under, 267
    monitoring, 270, 278–80, 282
    motivations for, 261
    network analysis and, 646
    opt-in nature of, 268–69, 282
    policy disclosure, 270, 649
    Principles, 263, 270–71
    progress reports, 271
    proxy advisers and, 268
    Recommendations on Disclosure of Stewardship Information, 269, 279
    reporting requirements, 269–70
    responsible investing and, 275–77
    sustainability and, 275–77, 280–81
    tiering system and, 281, 282–83
    2020 revision, 283
    voluntary nature of, 268–69, 282
    voting policies, 271, 281–82
  Taipei Exchange (TPEx)
    Business Integrity Code and, 276–77
    CG Code and, 276, 278
    disgorgement of profits and, 274
    listed companies, 264
    shareholder structure in TPEx listed companies, 265
    Stewardship Code and, 279
  Taiwan Depository & Clearing Corporation, 263, 264
  Taiwan Financial Services Roundtable, 263
  Taiwan Stock Exchange (TWSE)
    Business Integrity Code and, 276–77
    CG Code and, 276, 278
    corporate governance and, 262–63
    Corporate Governance Center, 278
    CSR Rules and, 277
    disgorgement of profits and, 274
    Enhancing Institutional Investor Stewardship and Listed Companies Investors Relation Forum, 263–64
    Global Trend of Responsible Investment and Corporate Governance Forum Taipei, 280
    listed companies, 264
    monitoring and, 282
    notification of, 268–69
    Recommendations on Disclosure of Stewardship Information, 269–70, 279
    shareholder structure in TWSE listed companies, 264–65
    Stewardship Code and, 279
    tiering system and, 281
    2020 revision to Stewardship Code and, 283
  UK compared, 278–79
Taiwan Semiconductor Corporation (TSMC), 262, 264–65
Taiyo Pacific Partners, 233–34
Tan, Petrina, 625–26
Tang, Samantha S., 295, 344
Tata Motors Limited, 364
Taub, Jennifer, 467
Telecom Italia, 148
Terminology, 9
Thailand
  generally, 335
  Asian Financial Crisis (1997) and, 335, 336, 346
  Association of Investment Management Companies (AIMC), 339, 346–47, 349
  Association of Provident Funds, 339
  Bangkok Mass Transit System (BTS), 356–57

Bank of Thailand, 336–37
Corporate Governance Code (CG Code)
  engagement, 350
  Investment Governance Code for Institutional Investors as complementing, 335
  Investment Governance Code for Institutional Investors compared, 339–40
  SEC and, 335–37
  success of, 336–38, 358
corporate governance in, 337–38
Electricity Generating Public Company Limited (EGCO), 357–58
Family Business Campaign (FB77) and, 313–14
family-controlled business enterprises in, 344–46
Federation of Thai Capital Market Organizations, 339
15 Principles of Good Corporate Governance, 337
foreign investors in, 339–40
Global Financial Crisis (2008) in, 336
Government Pension Fund (GPF), 339, 340, 343, 346–47, 352
institutional investors in, 342–44
Investment Governance Code for Institutional Investors
  generally, 614
  abstentions, 354
  adoption of policies, 347–48
  asset managers and, 341, 342, 358–59
  capital increases, voting against, 356–57
  CG Code, as complementing, 335
  CG Code compared, 339–40
  citation patterns, 640–41
  cluster analysis and, 648
  'comply or explain', 337, 340
  conflicts of interest and, 348–49
  coreness and, 648
  deviation from UK Code 2010/2012, 348
  disclosure requirements, 340
  dividends, voting against, 357–58
  empirical analysis of voting under, 352–55
  engagement, 339, 349–51
  escalation of activities, 350–51
  ESG in, 35, 339, 345–46, 564
  exercise of shareholder rights, 352–55
  halo signalling and, 30
  influence of UK Code 2010/2012, 338, 340, 346
  insurance companies and, 341
  introduction of, 335
  legal family effect, lack of, 659
  legal standards, as complementing, 32
  letters of intent, 347
  limited impact of, 358
  monitoring, 350
  network analysis and, 646
  policy disclosure, 339–40
  Principles, 338
  provident funds, 341
  proxy voting policies, 351–52
  reporting requirements, 348
  SEC and, 335, 338–39, 340
  securities companies, 342
  self-assessments, 340
  shareholder meetings, attending, 351–52
  signatories, 340–42
  steering committee, 338–39
  untrustworthy directors, voting against, 355–56
  voluntary nature of, 340
Malaysia, regional cluster of global diffusion with, 644
mutual funds in, 343–44
National Corporate Governance Committee, 336–37
Office of Insurance Commission, 339, 341
Private Sector Collective Action Coalition Against Corruption (CAC), 347
provident funds in, 341, 343
Public Limited Company Act, 337, 349
Securities and Exchange Commission Act, 335–36, 337, 348–49
Securities and Exchange Commission (SEC)
  asset managers and, 358
  Association of Investment Management Companies (AIMC) and, 346
  CG Code and, 335–37
  Investment Governance Code for Institutional Investors and, 335, 338–39, 340
  membership, 335–36
  Private Sector Collective Action Coalition Against Corruption (CAC) and, 347
  signatories to Code and, 340–42
Social Security Fund (SSF), 343
Social Security Office (SSO), 339, 340, 346–47, 352
Stock Exchange of Thailand (SET), 336–37, 342–43, 344–46
Thai General Insurance Association, 339
Thai Institute of Directors Association (IOD), 337–38
Thai Investors Association (TIA), 350–51
Thistlethwaite, Jason, 554
Thomas, Randall S., 533
Thomson Reuters Eikon, 99, 107
3 G Radar, 509
TMX Group, 441
Transparency, 217
Trian Partners, 462, 558
Tuch, Andrew F., 433
Tunnelling, 6, 241–43, 259
Turkey, legal transplants in, 631
2030 Agenda for Sustainable Development, 551

UBS, 122, 509
Ukraine, legal transplants in, 631
UNCTAD Principles on Promoting Responsible Sovereign Lending and Borrowing, 183
Unilever, 106–7
Union Bank of Switzerland, 458
United Kingdom
  Association of Member Nominated Trustees (AMNT), 84
  best interests of beneficiaries in, 570
  Cadbury Code, 68, 369, 442–43
  Cadbury Report, 45, 68–69, 70, 288, 631
  Canada compared, 437, 444
  changing consumer preferences in, 570
  charitable organizations in, 80

United Kingdom (cont.)
  China compared, 383–84, 395, 413–16
  Church of England, 80
  Church of England Pension Board, 63–64
  City Code on Takeovers, 375–76
  civil claims in, 590–91
  climate-related financial disclosure in, 189
  collective action in, 425
  Companies Act 1948, 490
  Companies Act 2006, 60, 490
  Competition and Markets Authority (CMA)
    fiduciary managers and, 83
    investment consultants and, 74
    pension funds and, 67, 87
    pension trustees and, 82, 83
  controlling-block shareholders in, 27–28
  Corporate Governance Code (CGC)
    generally, 44, 278–79, 375–76
    Code 2010/2012 compared, 45
    engagement and, 49
    market for stewardship and, 69, 72
    as self-regulatory mechanism, 531
    women on boards and, 62
  corporate governance concept in, 6
  Denmark compared, 172
  Department for Business, Energy & Industrial Strategy (BEIS), 85, 86
  Department for Business, Innovation & Skills (BIS), 78
  Department for Work and Pensions (DWP), 60–61, 63, 85, 86, 544
  derivative actions in, 494–95
  Directors' Remuneration Report Regulations 2002 (DRRR), 532
  disclosure requirements in, 535
  dispersed shareholders in, 369, 418–19, 491
  Duchy of Cornwall, 80
  economic arguments against stewardship code, 205–6
  enlightened shareholder value (ESV) principle in, 372–73, 374
  ESG in, 15
  executive compensation in, 531–32
  as exporter of legal norms and principles, 631
  Financial Conduct Authority (FCA)
    asset managers and, 55
    climate change and, 62, 63
    'comply or explain' and, 279
    enforcement and, 20, 21, 654
    engagement and, 535
    ESG and, 545–47
    foreign investors and, 210
    fund governance and, 544–45
    market for stewardship and, 75, 76, 80, 84, 85–86
    regulatory authority of, 307–8
    reputational incentives and, 62
    reticent enforcement approach, 583–84
    voluntary compliance and, 213
  Financial Reporting Council (FRC)
    generally, 192, 376
    climate change and, 63, 64
    Code 2010/2012 and, 10, 193–94, 457, 534, 634–35
    Code 2020 and, 261, 599
    Corporate Governance Code (CGC) and, 278–79
    on culture of stewardship, 506
    enforcement powers, 596
    failure of Code 2010/2012 and, 48–49
    halo signalling and, 628
    hedge fund activism and, 57
    historical evolution of stewardship codes and, 638
    on intermediary organizations, 433
    ISC Code on the Responsibilities of Institutional Investors and, 228–29
    list of signatories, 591
    market for stewardship and, 69, 71, 75, 85–86, 643
    regulatory authority of, 307–8, 568
    Report on Developments in Corporate Governance and Stewardship, 325
    reputational incentives and, 62
    'soft' law and, 535–36
    statements of commitment and, 307
  Financial Services and Markets Act 2000, 590–91
  Financial Services Authority, 194
  foreign investors in, 210
  Germany compared, 218, 288
  Global Financial Crisis (2008) in, 417, 533–34
  Greenbury Committee, 531–32
  Green Finance Strategy, 556
  Greening Finance, 566
  Hong Kong compared, 293
  India compared, 370, 375
  India–UK Financial Partnership, 366
  institutional investor control in, 25–26, 27, 600
  institutional investors in
    fiduciary duties of, 529
    responsible ownership and, 288–89
    'soft law' and, 376
  Institutional Shareholders' Committee (ISC)
    generally, 324–25, 376, 437
    Code 2010/2012 and, 634–35
    Code on the Responsibilities of Institutional Investors, 69, 228–29, 534
    historical evolution of stewardship codes and, 638
    membership, 228–29
    'Responsibilities of Institutional Shareholders in the UK', 9–10, 288
  Investment Association, 531
  investment management concept in, 8–9
  Investor Forum, 56, 62, 63, 84, 543
  Italy compared, 133
  Japan compared, 223, 619
  Kay Review
    generally, 543
    engagement and, 55–56, 84
    institutional investors and, 193
    market for stewardship and, 70–71
    short-term focus, restraining, 228
    sustainable finance and, 552
  Kenya, investments in, 491
  Kenya compared, 491, 494–95, 504
  Kingman Review
    Code 2010/2012 and, 44–45, 599

economic arguments, 205–6
engagement and, 57–58
failure of Code 2010/2012 and, 48–49, 55, 65
investment chain and, 542
market for stewardship and, 70
Labour Party, 288
Law Commission
climate change and, 63
financial performance and, 60–61
market for stewardship and, 76, 77
legal institutions in, 376
legal transplants from, 631
London Stock Exchange, 210, 602
Malaysia compared, 323, 324–25, 326, 327, 642–43
market for stewardship in (See Market for stewardship)
multiple stewardship codes in, 638
Myners Review, 44, 49, 437, 531
non-executive directors (NEDs), 45–46
pension funds
Competition and Markets Authority (CMA) and, 67, 87
fiduciary duties of, 529
Pensions Act 1995, 529
Pensions Regulator (tPR), 85, 86
proxy advisers in, 531
Proxy Advisors (Shareholders' Rights) Regulation 2019, 86
'say-on-pay' in, 534
Seven Core Principles (See also specific country)
enumeration of, 10
global diffusion of, 13, 17
private stewardship codes and, 18–19
shareholder activism in, 531–32
Shareholders Association (UKSA), 78
Shareholders Society (ShareSoc), 78
shareholder voting levels in, 531
'soft law' in, 3, 369, 375–76, 535–36
SRD II and, 46–47, 86
sustainability in, 373
sustainable finance in, 556
Sustainable Investment and Finance Association (UKSIF), 81–82
Taiwan compared, 278–79
tiering system in
adherence procedures and, 591–92
disclosure and, 234, 605
engagement and, 55
membership sanctions and, 591–92
quality of stewardship and, 535–36
reporting and, 281, 282–83, 326, 592
Treasury, 85, 86
Universities Superannuation Scheme, 423
US compared, 425
voluntary compliance in, 213
Walker Review
Code 2010/2012 and, 44
corporate governance and, 534
engagement and, 48, 57
failure of Code 2010/2012 and, 48–49, 50
Global Financial Crisis (2008) and, 193

hedge fund activism and, 57
investee companies and, 240–41
market for stewardship and, 69
non-executive directors (NEDs) and, 46
on shareholder collaboration, 418
shareholder functional capacities and, 50, 52
women on boards in, 62
United Kingdom Code 2010/2012 (first version)
generally, 45
adoption of, 3, 44–45, 192, 261
applicability of, 268
asset managers and, 220
asset owners versus asset managers, 320
climate change and, 47–48, 62–64
cluster analysis and, 648
collective action, 652
collectivization of engagement and, 55–56
core concept of, 12–13
coreness and, 648
criticism of, 376
deviation from (See specific country)
disclosure requirements, 194
'early intervention' and, 58
EFAMA Stewardship Code, influence on, 13–14, 136
enforcement of
'comply or explain', 21, 279, 375, 534, 581, 605, 654
components of, 21
foreign institutional investors, 23
lax enforcement as challenge, 36
obligations, 21
tiering system, 21, 23, 282–83
UK as outlier, 20–24
engagement
generally, 583
corporate governance and, 616
failure of Code and, 48–50, 65
global diffusion and, 600
Global Financial Crisis (2008) and, 613–14
procedures, 46–47
shareholder functional capacities and, 51
escalation of activities, 651
ESG in, 8, 35, 47–48
excessive risk-taking, restraining as goal of, 223, 238, 298, 301, 373, 456, 613–14
failure of, 48–50, 65
financial incentives of asset owners and managers and, 53–55
focus on institutional investors, 301–2, 605
foreign investors and, 210
global diffusion of (See Global diffusion of stewardship codes)
Global Financial Crisis (2008) and, 3, 44, 228, 261, 457, 640
goals of, 228
governmental stewardship codes and, 19
halo signalling and, 29–30
hedge fund activism and, 56–57
identical word strings, measurement of, 642–44
incentives for institutional investors, 298, 301
lack of 'ownership' in, 289

United Kingdom Code 2010/2012 (first version) (cont.)
  legal standards, as complementing, 32
  as 'misfit', 601, 611
  as model, 457
  monitoring, 651
  network analysis and, 646–47
  'ownership mindset,' encouraging, 240–41
  perception of institutional investors in, 178
  policy disclosure, 649, 650–51
  primary content of, 13
  private stewardship codes and, 18–19
  rationale for adoption, 640
  regulatory framework of, 568
  reputational incentives of asset owners and managers and, 55
  shareholder functional capacities and, 50–53
  short-term focus, restraining as goal of, 238, 298, 301, 373, 456, 613–14
  signatories, 567
  SRD II, influence on, 33–34, 192
  statements of commitment, 307
  stewardship defined, 288, 370
  text of, 13–14
  title, 14
  transparency and, 217
  voluntary nature of, 213
  voting policies, 652
  as world's first stewardship code, 10
United Kingdom Code 2020 (second version)
  generally, 45
  adoption of, 261, 640
  'apply and explain', 21, 23, 72, 289, 375, 581, 605, 654
  collective action, 425, 652
  consideration of beneficiaries' needs and preferences, 542–43
  criticism of, 376
  disclosure requirements, 434–35
  engagement, 47, 57–59, 616–17
  'enlightened stewardship' and, 72–73
  escalation of activities, 58
  ESG in
    generally, 59–61, 197, 454
    beneficiary preferences and, 546–47
    climate change and, 66
    financial performance and, 59–61
    halo signalling and, 628
    incentives and, 62–65
    institutional investors and, 616–17
    as model, 611
    as primary focus of Code, 599, 601
    revision of Code to include, 563
    stewardship and, 373–74, 564
  evolution of, 65
  expansion of goals in, 47, 288
  financial performance and, 59–61
  focus on institutional investors, 605
  future research and, 660
  global diffusion of (See Global diffusion of stewardship codes)
  halo signalling and, 628
  investment chain and, 542
  lack of 'ownership' in, 289
  legitimacy of institutional investors, importance for, 66
  market for stewardship, role in, 71–73 (See also Market for stewardship)
  market integrity and, 47
  market risk, addressing, 59
  as 'misfit', 601, 611
  NEST, 73
  network analysis and, 645–46
  policy disclosure, 651
  prospects for success, 65–66
  reporting requirements, 58, 71, 72
  reputational incentives of asset owners and managers and, 62–65, 66
  stewardship defined, 464, 474, 530, 602, 634
  sustainability, 72, 571
  voluntary nature of, 213
  voting policies, 652
United Nations
  Brundtland Report, 473, 551
  Environmental Programme Finance Initiative (UNEP FI), 546, 554, 559–60, 569
  Freshfields Report, 546, 559–60, 569
  Global Compact, 179–80, 183, 186, 557–58
  Guiding Principles on Business and Human Rights (UNGP), 179–80, 183, 186
  Principles of Responsible Investment (UNPRI) (See Principles of Responsible Investment (UNPRI))
  Sustainable Development Goals (SDG), 188, 547, 551, 553, 554
  2030 Agenda for Sustainable Development, 551
  UNCTAD Principles on Promoting Responsible Sovereign Lending and Borrowing, 183
United States
  generally, 455
  'Avon Letter', 287–88
  Brazil compared, 524
  Business Roundtable, 417
  California Public Employees' Retirement System (CalPERS), 234, 423, 458, 466, 531
  Canada compared, 437, 452
  charitable organizations in, 80
  China compared, 379, 395, 402
  collective action in, 425
  conflicts of interest in, 604
  controlling-block shareholders in, 27–28
  corporate governance concept in, 6
  Department of Labor (DOL), 287–88
  direct registration system in, 293–94
  dispersed shareholders in, 292, 418–19, 491
  Dodd–Frank Wall Street Reform and Consumer Protection Act, 178, 495
  economic arguments against stewardship code, 206
  Employee Retirement Income Security Act (ERISA), 287–88
  ESG in, 35, 561, 563–64, 565
  excessive risk-taking in, 417
  as exporter of legal norms and principles, 631

fiduciary managers in, 84
401(k) plans, 468
Global Financial Crisis (2008), attitudes towards, 417
Hong Kong compared, 293–94
index funds in, 459 (*See also* Index funds)
institutional investor control in, 25–26, 456, 600
institutional investors in
   level of activity, 456
   responsible ownership and, 287–88
   shareholder activism and, 427
   statistics, 122, 174
Investment Advisers Act, 457
Investor Stewardship Group (ISG), 425, 446, 457–59, 586
Italy compared, 133, 146
Japan compared, 223
Kenya, investments in, 491
Kenya compared, 491, 495
lack of comprehensive stewardship code in, 638–40
legal transplants from, 631
managerial power in, 456
mutual funds in, 206, 457 (*See also* Mutual funds)
network analysis and, 646–47
New York Green Bank, 556
Rule 14a-8, 494
'say-on-pay' in, 495
Securities and Exchange Commission (SEC), 206, 457, 467, 494, 574
self-regulation in, 604
Seven Core Principles in, 658
shareholder activism in, 427, 494
shareholder involvement in, 50
shareholder protection in, 276
sustainable finance in, 556, 558
Switzerland compared, 113, 115, 116, 117, 122
UK compared, 425
University of California, 234
'wolf pack' in, 418
UNPRI. *See* Principles of Responsible Investment (UNPRI)
Urwin, Roger, 560–61

Vale S.A., 524–25
Van der Elst, Christoph, 187
Vanguard
   China compared, 382, 386–88
   concentration of asset managers, 84, 456, 459
   in Germany, 210
   proxy voting and, 137
   statistics, 122
   stewardship and, 199–200, 458
Vayanos, Dimitri, 539
Vietnam War, 557
Virani, Aazam, 433, 447
Vivendi, 148
Voting policies. *See specific country*

Wachter, Michael L., 465
Wagner, Hannes, 133
Walker, David, 193, 288
Walmsley, Allan, 496
Wang, Brian Yutao, 404–5
Wang, Xin, 404–5
Wilson, Mike, 442
'Wolf pack', 418, 427
Wolters Kluwer, 99
Wong, Simon, 457
Woodford, Ned, 539
Woods, Claire, 546, 560–61
Woolley, Paul, 539
World Bank, 17, 293, 337, 616, 629
World Bank Group, 498
WorldCom, 118
World Economic Forum, 293

Xiao, Jason Zezhong, 397
XP (Brazilian asset manager), 509

Yang, Jingjing, 397–98
Yuan, Rongli, 397

Zechner, Josef, 504
Zhang, Xiaofei, 401
Zhang, Yuanyuan, 397
Zho, Xiaoyan, 206, 212, 215
Zhu, Tao, 400
Zingales, Luigi, 91
Zou, Hong, 397, 398–400
Zuckerberg, Mark, 310
Z/Yen (commercial institution), 293

Lightning Source UK Ltd.
Milton Keynes UK
UKHW051631010722
405226UK00010B/42